OXFORD COMMENTARIES ON INTERNATIONAL LAW

General Editors: *Professor Philip Alston*, Professor of International Law at New York University, and *Vaughan Lowe QC*, Essex Court Chambers, London and Emeritus Fellow of All Souls College, Oxford

# The Rio Declaration on Environment and Development

# The Rio Declaration on Environment and Development

*A Commentary*

Edited by

JORGE E. VIÑUALES

Harold Samuel Professor of Law and Environmental Policy
University of Cambridge

OXFORD
UNIVERSITY PRESS

**OXFORD**
UNIVERSITY PRESS

Great Clarendon Street, Oxford, OX2 6DP,
United Kingdom

Oxford University Press is a department of the University of Oxford.
It furthers the University's objective of excellence in research, scholarship,
and education by publishing worldwide. Oxford is a registered trade mark of
Oxford University Press in the UK and in certain other countries



First Edition published in 2015



Published in the United States of America by Oxford University Press
198 Madison Avenue, New York, NY 10016, United States of America

British Library Cataloguing in Publication Data
Data available

Library of Congress Control Number: 2014951282

ISBN 978–0–19–968677–3

Printed and bound by
CPI Group (UK) Ltd, Croydon, CR0 4YY

# *Acknowledgment*

The editor gratefully acknowledges the financial support of the Swiss National Science Foundation, which greatly facilitated the work leading to this commentary. The editors of Oxford University Press also supported the publication process with great commitment and professionalism. Last but not least, I would like to acknowledge the excellent work done by my former assistants Martina Kunz and Leslie-Anne Duvic-Paoli in gathering the source materials circulated among the contributors as well as in the organization of a workshop held in Geneva in October 2013.

# *Table of Contents*

# *Table of Cases*

## INTERNATIONAL COURTS AND TRIBUNALS

### African Commission on Human and Peoples' Rights



### African Court of Human and Peoples' Rights



### Court of Justice of the European Union (formerly European Court of Justice)



### European Committee of Social Rights

### European Court of Human Rights



### Inter-American Commission on Human Rights



### Inter-American Court of Human Rights

**International Court of Justice and Permanent Court of International Justice**



**Inter-State Arbitration Awards**

**WTO and GATT Disputes**

## NATIONAL COURTS

### Australia



### Bangladesh



### Canada



### France



### India



### Netherlands



### Philippines



### Singapore

# *Table of Treaties and Instruments*

## TREATIES AND ILC DRAFTS

## UNITED NATIONS RESOLUTIONS

### General Assembly

**Human Rights Council**



**Security Council**

## EUROPEAN UNION LAW

### Directives



### Regulations



## NATIONAL LAW

### Australia



### Germany



### Ghana



### New Zealand



### Peoples' Republic of China

# *List of Abbreviations*

| | |
|---|---|
| 10YFP | 10-Year Framework of Programmes |
| AB | Appellate Body (of the WTO) |
| ABS | Access and Benefit Sharing |
| ACCC | Aarhus Convention Compliance Committee |
| ACHR | American Convention on Human Rights |
| AD | anno domini |
| ADR | Alternative Dispute Resolution |
| African Commission | African Commission of Human and Peoples' Rights |
| AIESEC | International Association of Students in Economic and Commercial Sciences |
| AJIL | American Journal of International Law |
| AmDRDM | 1948 American Declaration of the Rights and Duties of Man |
| art | Article(s) |
| ASEAN | Association of Southeast Nations |
| ASR | Articles on State Responsibility |
| BioCF | Bio Carbon Fund |
| BioCF T3 | The Bio Carbon Fund Tranche |
| BYIL | British Yearbook of International Law |
| CAFE | Corporate average fuel economy |
| CARICOM | Caribbean Community |
| CARU | Administrative Commission on the Uruguay River |
| CBD | Convention on Biological Diversity |
| CBDR | common but differentiated responsibilities |
| CCS | carbon capture and storage |
| CDFC | Community Development Carbon Fund |
| CDM | Clean Development Mechanism |
| CEDAW | Convention on the Elimination of Discrimination against Women |
| CERCLA | Comprehensive Environmental Response, Compensation and Liability Act |
| CERD | Committee on the Elimination of Racial Discrimination |
| CERES | Coalition for Environmentally Responsible Economies |
| CESCR | Committee on Economic Social and Cultural Rights |
| CFC | Chlorofluorocarbon |
| CGIAR | Consultative Committee on Agricultural Research |
| Ci-Dev | Carbon Initiative for Development |
| CIF | Climate investment funds |
| CISDL | Centre for International Sustainable Development Law |
| CITES | Convention on International Trade in Endangered Species of Wild Fauna and Flora |
| CJEU | Court of Justice of the European Union |
| CLC | Convention on Civil Liability for Oil Pollution Damage |

| | |
|---|---|
| CMP | Conference of the Parties (of the UNFCCC) acting as the Meeting of the Parties to the Kyoto Protocol |
| CMS | Convention on the Conservation of Migratory Species of Wild Animals |
| CNRS | Centre national de la recherche scientifique |
| COP | Conference of the Parties |
| CP | Clean Production |
| CPF | Carbon Partnership Facility |
| CRAMRA | Convention on the Regulation of Antarctic Mineral Resource Activities |
| CSD | Commission on Sustainable Development |
| CSO | civil society organizations |
| CSR | corporate social responsibility |
| CTE | Committee on Trade and Environment (WTO) |
| CWA | Clean Water Act (US) |
| DESA | Department of Economic and Social Affairs/UN Secretariat |
| DESD | UN Decade of Education for Sustainable Development |
| Doc | Document |
| DSD | Division for Sustainable Development/DESA |
| EC | European Community |
| ECA | (UN) Economic Commission for Africa |
| ECE | (UN) Economic Commission for Europe |
| ECHR | European Convention on Human Rights |
| ECI | environmental cost-spreading investment |
| ECLAC | (UN) Economic Commission for Latin America and the Caribbean |
| ECOSOC | UN Economic and Social Council |
| ECSR | European Committee of Social Rights |
| ECtHR | European Court of Human Rights |
| ed | Editor |
| EEZ | Exclusive economic zone |
| EGS | environmental goods and services |
| EIA | Environmental Impact Assessment |
| EJIL | European Journal of International Law |
| ENMOD | Convention on the Prohibition of military or any other hostile use of environmental modification techniques |
| EPA | Environmental Protection Agency |
| EPL | Environmental Policy and Law |
| EPR | Extended Producer Responsibility |
| ERC | emissions reduction credits |
| ERs | Emission Reductions |
| ESCAP | (UN) Economic and Social Commission for Asia and the Pacific |
| ESCWA | (UN) Economic and Social Commission for Western Asia |
| ESC(R) | Economic, Social and Cultural (rights) |
| EU ETS | EU Emissions Trading System |
| FAO | Food and Agriculture Organization of the UN |
| FCPF | Forest Carbon Partnership Facility |

| | |
|---|---|
| ff | Following pages/paragraphs |
| G77 | Group of 77 |
| GA (or UNGA) | United Nations General Assembly |
| GAOR | UN General Assembly Official Records |
| GATT | General Agreement on Tariffs and Trade |
| GCS | Government crediting system |
| GEA | green economy agenda |
| GEF | Global Environment Facility |
| GEO | Global Environment Outlook |
| GIELR | Georgetown International Environmental Law Review |
| GMO | Genetically modified organism |
| GNP | Gross national product |
| GUPES | Global Universities Partnership on Environment and Sustainability |
| GYBN | Global Youth Biodiversity Network |
| HELR | Harvard Environmental Law Review |
| HFA | Hyogo Framework for Action |
| HILJ | Harvard International Law Journal |
| HIPC | highly indebted poor countries |
| HLPF | High Level Political Forum on Sustainable Development |
| HRC | UN Human Rights Committee |
| IACtHR | Inter-American Court of Human Rights |
| IAEA | International Atomic Energy Agency |
| IANYD | (UN) Inter-Agency Network on Youth Development |
| IB-ETS | Installation-based emission trading system |
| ICAO | International Civil Aviation Organization |
| ICCPR | International Covenant on Civil and Political Rights |
| ICESCR | International Covenant on Economic, Social and Cultural Rights |
| ICJ | International Court of Justice |
| ICLQ | International & Comparative Law Quarterly |
| ICommHR | Inter-American Commission on Human Rights |
| ICPD | International Conference on Population and Development |
| ICRC | International Committee of the Red Cross |
| ICRW | International Convention for the Regulation of Whaling |
| ICSID | International Centre for Settlement of Investment Disputes |
| ICtHR | Inter-American Court of Human Rights |
| IDI | Institut de Droit International |
| IDLO | International Development Law Organization |
| IEA | international environmental agreements |
| IFC | International Finance Corporation |
| IFIs | international financial institutions |
| IFRC | International Federation of Red Cross and Red Crescent Societies |
| IHL | International humanitarian law |
| IISD | International Institute for Sustainable Development |
| ILA | International Law Association |
| ILC | International Law Commission |

| | |
|---|---|
| ILM | International Legal Materials |
| ILO | International Labour Organisation |
| IMO | International Maritime Organisation |
| INFOTERRA | Global Environmental Information Exchange Network (UNEP) |
| INTOSAI | International Organization of Supreme Audit Institutions |
| IOPC Fund | International Oil Pollution Compensation Fund |
| IPBES | Intergovernmental Platform on Biodiversity & Ecosystem Services |
| IPCC | Intergovernmental Panel on Climate Change |
| IPRs | Intellectual Property Rights |
| IRRC | International Regulatory Review Commission |
| ISBA | International Seabed Authority |
| ISDR | International Strategy for Disaster Reduction |
| ITLOS | International Tribunal for the Law of the Sea |
| ITPGR | International Treaty on Plant Genetic Resources for Food and Agriculture |
| IUCN | International Union for Conservation of Nature |
| JEL | Journal of Environmental Law |
| JI | joint implementation mechanism |
| JPOI | Johannesburg Plan of Implementation |
| LDCs | least developed countries |
| LMO | Living Modified Organism |
| LRTAP | Long-Range Transboundary Air Pollution |
| LULUCF | Land Use, Land-use Change, and Forestry |
| MARPOL | International Convention for the Prevention of Pollution from Ships |
| MDG | Millennium Development Goal |
| MEA | multilateral environmental agreement |
| MEPL | Marine Environmental Protection Law (CN) |
| MERCOSUR | Mercado Común del Sur (Southern Common Market) |
| MGYC | Major Group for Children and Youth |
| MNC | Multinational corporations |
| MOP | Meeting of the Parties |
| MRV | Monitoring, Reporting, and Verification |
| NAAEC | North American Agreement on Environmental Cooperation |
| NAFTA | North American Free Trade Agreement |
| NCP | National Oil and Hazardous Substances Pollution Contingency Plan (US) |
| NEPA | National Environmental Policy Act (US) |
| NGLS | UN Non-Governmental Liaison Service |
| NGO | non-governmental organization |
| NIEO | New international economic order |
| NMM | new market mechanisms |
| NSWLEC | New South Wales Land and Environment Court |
| OAS | Organization of American States |
| OAU | Organization of African Unity |
| ODA | Official Development Assistance |

| | |
|---|---|
| ODS | ozone-depleting substances |
| OECD | Organisation for Economic Co-operation and Development |
| OHCHR | Office of the High Commissioner for Human Rights |
| OPA | Oil Pollution Act (US) |
| ORPC | Convention on Oil Pollution Preparedness, Response and Cooperation |
| OSPAR Convention | Convention for the Protection of the Marine Environment of the North-East Atlantic |
| p. (pp.) | Page or pages |
| para | Paragraph(s) |
| PCA | Permanent Court of Arbitration |
| PCF | Prototype Carbon Fund |
| PCIJ | Permanent Court of International Justice |
| PIC Convention | Rotterdam Convention on the Prior Informed Consent Procedure for Certain Hazardous Chemicals and Pesticides in International Trade |
| PMR | Partnership for Market Readiness |
| PNUE | Programme des Nations Unies pour l'environment |
| POPs Convention | Convention on Persistent Organic Pollutants |
| PPMs | processes and production methods |
| PPP | Polluter-pays principle |
| PrepCom | Preparatory Committee |
| PRTR | pollutant release and transfer register |
| PTD | public trust doctrine |
| RCADI | Recueil des cours de l'Académie de droit international |
| RECIEL | Review of Community and International Environmental Law |
| REDD | Reducing Emissions from Deforestation and Forest Degradation in Developing Countries |
| REDD+ | Reducing emissions from deforestation and forest degradation, and enhancement of forest carbon stocks |
| REDI | Revista Española de Derecho Internacional |
| REFiT | Renewable energy feed in tariffs |
| REIPPPP | Renewable Energy Independent Power Producer Procurement Programme |
| RES | renewable electricity/energy standards |
| RGDIP | Revue générale de droit international public |
| RIAA | Reports of International Arbitral Awards |
| SADC | Southern African Development Community |
| SC (or UNSC) | United Nations Security Council |
| SCM Agreement | Agreement on Subsidies and Countervailing Measures |
| SCMM | sectoral carbon market mechanisms |
| SCP | Sustainable Consumption and Production |
| SDG | Sustainable Development Goal |
| SDR | Special Drawing Rights |
| SEA | strategic environmental assessments |
| SEM | submissions on enforcement matters |
| SOLAS | Convention for the Safety of Life at Sea |
| SPS Agreement | Agreement on Sanitary and Phytosanitary Measures |

| | |
|---|---|
| SRFC | Sub-Regional Fisheries Commission |
| SRI | Socially Responsible Investment |
| STOPIA | Small Tankers Oil Pollution Indemnification Agreement |
| TBT Agreement | Technical Barriers to Trade Agreement |
| TFEU | Treaty on the Functioning of the EU |
| TIS | Tradable Intensity Standard |
| TOPIA | Tanker Oil Pollution Indemnification Agreement |
| TPP | Trans-Pacific Partnership |
| TRIMS | Agreement on Trade Related Investment Measures |
| TRIPS | Trade Related Aspects of Intellectual Property Rights |
| TLL | Tort Liability Law (CN) |
| UCF | Umbrella Carbon Facility |
| UDHR | UN Declaration of Human Rights |
| UN | United Nations |
| UNCC | United Nations Compensation Commission |
| UNCCD | UN Convention to Combat Desertification |
| UNCED | UN Conference on Environment and Development |
| UNCHE | UN Conference on the Human Environment |
| UNCITRAL | UN Commission on International Trade Law |
| UNCLOS | UN Convention on the Law of the Sea |
| UNCTAD | UN Conference on Trade and Development |
| UNDESA | UN Department of Economic and Social Affairs |
| UNDP | UN Development Programme |
| UNDRIP | UN Declaration on the Rights of Indigenous Peoples |
| UNECE | UN Economic Commission for Europe |
| UNEP | UN Environment Programme |
| UNESCO | UN Educational, Scientific and Cultural Organization |
| UNFCCC | UN Framework Convention on Climate Change |
| UNGA | UN General Assembly |
| UNHCR | United Nations High Commissioner for Refugees |
| UNISDR | UN Office for Disaster Risk Reduction |
| UNITAR | UN Institute for Training and Research |
| UNPRI | UN Principles for Responsible Investment |
| UNSG | United Nations Secretary General |
| UNTS | United Nations Treaty Series |
| UNSC | UN Security Council |
| UPOV | International Union for the Protection of New Varieties of Plants |
| US | United States of America |
| VCLT | Vienna Convention on the Law of Treaties |
| WCED | World Commission on Environment and Development |
| WIPO | World Intellectual Property Organization |
| WPAY | World Programme of Action for Youth |
| WRI | World Resources Institute |
| WSSD | World Summit on Sustainable Development |
| WTO | World Trade Organization |
| YbIEL | Yearbook of International Environmental Law |
| YbILC | Yearbook of the International Law Commission |
| YOUNGO | Youth Non-Governmental Organizations (within the framework of UNFCCC) |

# *List of Contributors*

**Virginie Barral**: Senior Lecturer at the School of Law of the University of Hertfordshire. Dr Barral holds a PhD from the European University Institute. She has worked for the French Ministry for the Environment, and at Eversheds LLP. Dr Barral has recently completed a monograph based on sustainable development in international law and has several publications in the field. She was also a year in review contributor for the *Yearbook of International Environmental Law* between 2006 and 2014. Her research interests are in the field of general international law, including its environmental aspects, the role of judges, and the relationship between courts at the international level.

**Annyssa Bellal**: Legal Advisor at Geneva Call, PhD in public international law from the Graduate Institute of International and Development Studies, Switzerland. Dr Bellal is an international lawyer, specializing in international humanitarian, human rights, and criminal law. She has been a lecturer in international law at the National University of Ireland and at the University of Geneva, as well as a Hauser Global Law School Visiting Scholar at New York University, and an O'Brien Fellow in Residence at the University of McGill Centre for Human Rights and Legal Pluralism. Dr Bellal has also acted as a legal adviser for the United Nations Office of the High Commissioner for Human Rights, the International Committee of the Red Cross, and the Swiss Federal Department of Foreign Affairs.

**Laurence Boisson de Chazournes**: Professor of International Law and International Organization at the Faculty of Law, University of Geneva, Switzerland. She has gained a wide-ranging reputation in academic circles for her contribution to international law, in such fields as the law of international organizations, international economic law, and international environmental law, while at the same time being recognized for her practical work as Senior Counsel to the World Bank and as advisor to many international organizations. Professor Boisson de Chazournes has served as chairperson of WTO arbitration panels and as an arbitrator. She has also pleaded before the ICJ and other dispute settlement fora.

**Antônio Augusto Cançado Trindade**: Judge at the International Court of Justice. Former President of the Inter-American Court of Human Rights. Emeritus Professor of International Law of the University of Brasilia, Brazil. Member of the *Curatorium* of the Hague Academy of International Law. Member of the *Institut de Droit international*. Judge Cançado Trindade is the author of numerous books, articles, studies, and courses in international law at large. In 2005, he gave the general course of public international law at the Hague Academy. He is Doctor Honoris Causa at the University Panteion of Athens, Greece, and at seven other Universities in seven distinct Latin American countries.

**Neil Craik**: Associate Professor, University of Waterloo, Canada. Professor Craik's teaching and research interests are broadly in the areas of public and regulatory law, with a focus on international environmental law, domestic and comparative environmental law, natural resources law, and municipal and planning law. His current research examines bi-lateral and tri-lateral environmental governance structures in North America, with a particular focus on the impact of federalism on transnational regulatory activities and the regulatory role of private transboundary environmental litigation.

**Philippe Cullet**: LLM (London), JSM, JSD (Stanford), Professor of International and Environmental Law at SOAS, University of London. Professor Cullet is the Convenor of the International Environmental Law Research Centre (IELRC) and a Senior Visiting Fellow at the Centre for Policy Research (CPR), New Delhi. He has published widely in environmental law, natural resources law, water law and policy, human rights, and the socio-economic aspects of intellectual property. His monographs include *Water Law, Poverty and Development—Water Law Reforms in India* (Oxford University Press 2009), *Intellectual Property and Sustainable Development* (Butterworths 2005) and *Differential Treatment in International Environmental Law* (Ashgate 2003). Professor Cullet engages regularly with policymakers at the national and international levels. He was the Convenor of the Sub-group on groundwater law of the Planning Commission of India that prepared the Model Bill for the Conservation, Protection and Regulation of Groundwater, 2011.

**Pierre-Marie Dupuy**: Emeritus Professor of International Law at the University of Paris II (Panthéon-Assas) and at The Graduate Institute, Geneva. Previously Professor Dupuy held teaching positions at the University of Strasbourg, Paris Val-de-Marne University, the University of Paris II (Panthéon-Assas), and the European University Institute, Florence. He has also given the General Course at The Hague Academy of International Law. In addition, he has published many leading texts and articles on various aspects of public international law. Professor Dupuy is also a distinguished practitioner, having represented numerous sovereign clients before the International Court of Justice and acted as an arbitrator in many well-known international arbitral proceedings, including at the International Centre for the Settlement of Investment Disputes (ICSID) and Permanent Court of Arbitration (PCA). His interests and areas of expertise include international dispute settlement, international environmental law, public international law, and international organizations.

**Leslie-Anne Duvic-Paoli**: PhD candidate in international law at the Graduate Institute of International and Development Studies, Geneva. Her doctoral research, under the supervision of Professor Viñuales, focuses on the prevention principle in international environmental law. She is also a teaching assistant for the Graduate Institute's LLM programme in international law and an editorial assistant for the *Transnational Environmental Law* journal. Prior to her doctoral studies, Ms Duvic-Paoli worked on maritime and security issues in various think tanks and research centres, including the Royal United Services Institute for Defence and Security Studies in London. She holds a Master's degree in international relations/political science from Sciences Po Paris, and another in public law from the University of Paris I (Panthéon-Sorbonne).

**Jonas Ebbesson**: Professor of Environmental Law and Dean of the Faculty of Law Stockholm University, Sweden. He is also the Chairman of the Aarhus Convention Compliance Committee. His research and writings cover various international, EU, and transnational dimensions of environmental law, including legal aspects of public interest, public participation, and access to justice in environmental law; transnational corporate responsibility; justice in environmental law; and the impact of law for social-ecological resilience. Among his books are (as editor) *Access to justice in environmental matters in the EU—Accès à la justice en matière d'environnement dans l'UE* (Kluwer 2002), and (as co-editor) *Environmental law and justice in context* (Cambridge University Press 2009).

Previously, Professor Ebbesson has acted as consultant and adviser for various governmental, non-governmental, and intergovernmental bodies, including the United Nations Environment Programme (UNEP) and United Nations Economic Commission for Europe (UNECE), the Organisation for Security and Co-operation in Europe (OSCE), the European Environmental Bureau (EEB), and the Nordic Council.

**Malgosia Fitzmaurice:** Chair of public international law at the University of London, Queen Mary, United Kingdom. Professor Fitzmaurice specializes in international environmental law and the law of treaties, and has published widely on both subjects. In July 2001, she was invited to deliver keynote lectures on 'International Protection of the Environment' at the Hague Academy of International Law. She has lectured widely in the United Kingdom and abroad at various universities, such as Utrecht and Brussels, and at the World Bank in 2001. She has also participated in many international conferences. Until 2001, she was a member of the Board of Editors and one of the Editors of the Netherlands Yearbook of International Law. She is the Editor in Chief of the International Community Law Review and a Co-Rapporteur of the International Law Association Committee on Non-State Actors. She has taught extensively in various law schools, including in the United States. Professor Fitzmaurice's previous teaching positions include Readership in international law at the Department of Law, University of Amsterdam. She has also worked at the Iran-United States Claims Tribunal in The Hague. Professor Fitzmaurice is an Editor in Chief of the series Queen Mary Studies in International Law published by Martinus Nijhoff.

**Francesco Francioni:** Professor of International Law and Human Rights, European University Institute, and Law Faculty of the University of Siena, Italy. Doctor of Laws (Florence), LLM (Harvard). He is also General Editor of the *Italian Yearbook of International Law*, member of the Board of Editors of the *European Journal of International Law*, member of the American Law Institute, and of the Executive Board of the European Society of International Law, and a member of the Italian delegation at many diplomatic conferences and international negotiations, especially in the field of environmental law and cultural heritage. Professor Francioni has taught courses at the Hague Academy of International Law (1995), Cornell Law School (1983–1986), Texas Law School (1988–2007), and Oxford University (1999–2003).

**Gilles Giacca:** Legal Adviser within the Arms Unit of the ICRC's Legal Division. His main research interests lie in the field of public international law, collective security, international humanitarian law, human rights law, refugee law, as well as weapons law. He previously worked as a research fellow at the Faculty of Law of the University of Oxford and co-ordinated the Human Rights for Future Generations programme.

**Christophe Golay:** Research Fellow and Coordinator of the Project on Economic, Social and Cultural Rights at the Geneva Academy of International Humanitarian Law and Human Rights. Dr Golay is also a Lecturer at the Geneva Centre for Education and Research in Humanitarian Action. He was Legal Adviser to the first United Nations Special Rapporteur on the Right to Food (2001–2008). He recently published *The Fight for the Right to Food. Lessons Learned*, with J. Ziegler, C. Mahon. and S-A. Way (Palgrave Macmillan 2011) and *Droit à l'alimentation et accès à la justice* (Bruylant 2011). He is the author of numerous articles on the right to food, economic, social, and cultural rights, human rights, and development, and the co-editor of *Economic, Social and Cultural Rights in International Law: Contemporary Issues and Challenges* (Oxford University Press 2014).

**Mamadou Hébié**: Dr Mamadou Hébié is a lecturer at the Graduate Institute, Geneva, with a focus on interstate dispute settlement mechanisms. He holds a PhD *summa cum laude*, with the examining board's utmost praise, and a Diploma in Advanced Studies-specialization international law, from the Graduate Institute, Geneva. Dr Hébié also graduated from Harvard Law School and the Geneva Academy of International Humanitarian Law and Human Rights, and is a recipient of Diplomas in International Law from the Hague Academy of International Law and the International Institute of Human Rights. He acted as adviser of the Argentine Republic in the ARA Libertad case before the International Tribunal for the Law of the Sea.

**Takhmina Karimova**: Human Rights Officer at the Office of the High Commissioner for Human Rights. Dr Karimova holds a diploma of jurist from the Tajik State National University, an LLM from the University of Essex, and a PhD in International Law from the University of Geneva and IHEID. She was a Research Fellow at the Faculty of Law, University of Geneva from 2012 to 2014, and Co-ordinator of professional training on Economic, Social, and Cultural Rights at the Geneva Academy of International Humanitarian Law and Human Rights in 2013. Her most recent publications include the Geneva Academy Briefing No. 6, '*What amounts to 'a serious violation of international human rights law'? An analysis of practice and expert opinion for the purpose of the 2013 Arms Trade Treaty*', Geneva, August 2014, 'The Nature and Meaning of 'International Assistance and Cooperation' under the International Covenant on Economic, Social and Cultural Rights' (in E. Riedel et al (ed), *Contemporary Issues in the Realization of Economic, Social and Cultural Rights*, (Oxford University Press 2014)).

**Martina Kunz**: PhD Candidate at the University of Cambridge, United Kingdom, and previously Teaching and Research Assistant at the Graduate Institute, Geneva. She studied international law at the Graduate Institute (LLM), Tsinghua University (China Scholarship Council Visiting Scholar), and the University of Geneva (LLB). She is fluent in German, English, Chinese, French, and Spanish. Ms Kunz has worked on a number of international and comparative law research projects for universities, NGOs, and international organizations, mainly in the fields of environmental law, economic law, and public law at large.

**Magnus Jesko Langer**: Associate, Levy-Kaufmann-Kohler, Attorneys-at-law, PhD Candidate in International Law. Mr Langer holds degrees in international relations (licence HEI) and in law (LLB, Geneva, LLM, HEID). He has served as legal assistant in a number of cases before the International Court of Justice, including the Case concerning Pulp Mills in the River Uruguay (*Argentina v. Uruguay*).

**Claire Mahon**: International human rights lawyer based in Geneva, Switzerland. She is a dual national of Australia and New Zealand. She has practised as a lawyer both at the national and international level. She was a Research Fellow at the Geneva Academy of International Humanitarian Law and Human Rights, an Adjunct Clinical Professor of Law at the University of Michigan Law School, and a guest lecturer at The Graduate Institute, Geneva. She also regularly teaches as a guest lecturer in various university courses on the topics of international human rights law, international organizations, and public international law. From 2009–2010 Ms Mahon was the Special Advisor to Mrs Mary Robinson (former UN High Commissioner for Human Rights and former President of Ireland) in her role as Chair of the GAVI Alliance. From 2007–2008 she was legal advisor to Mr Jean Ziegler, then UN Special Rapporteur on the Right to Food (see further the former Research Unit on the Right to Food). She has previously worked for Amnesty International, the International Commission of Jurists, the International Service for Human Rights, the Centre on Housing Rights and Evictions, and the UN Office of the High Commissioner for Human Rights. Her work has focused on monitoring economic, social, and cultural rights, including in the field. Ms Mahon has experience in designing and providing training on international human rights law and practice to diplomats, advocates, field officers, UN staff, and students in over 20 countries.

**Sandrine Maljean-Dubois:** Director of Research for the C.N.R.S. and Director of the Centre d'études et de recherches internationales et communautaires (CERIC), Aix-en-Provence, France. She has edited several books in international and European environmental law. She has published numerous articles in this field, especially relating to the protection of biodiversity and biosecurity, the articulation between international environmental law and WTO law or international law and climate change. She was the Director of the French section of the Center for Studies and Research in International Law and International Relations in the Hague Academy of International Law in 2008 on the topic of the implementation of international environmental law.

**Makane M. Mbengue:** Associate Professor of International Law, University of Geneva, Switzerland, and Visiting Professor, Sciences Po Paris, France. A native of Senegal, Dr Mbengue received his LLB from the University Gaston Berger of Saint-Louis (Senegal) in Public Law. In 1998, he received a Masters degree (Maitrise in the French system) in Public Law from the University of Saint-Louis. In 1999, he received an LLM in Business and Economic Law from the same University. In 2001, he obtained the Certificate of the Center for Studies and Research in International Law and International Relations. Dr Mbengue completed his PhD in international law, *summa cum laude*, from the University of Geneva in June 2007. Dr Mbengue is also the author of a number of articles in widely respected and cited scientific journals and books on trade and environment, international dispute-settlement, the law of treaties, the law of international watercourses, and WTO law. From 2001 to 2005, he worked as a researcher for the Swiss National Science Foundation on a project entitled 'Trade, the Environment and the International Regulation of Biotechnology'. From September 2004 to June 2005, he was a law clerk at the International Court of Justice (The Hague, Netherlands). He has been a consultant for the World Bank, the World Health Organization, the Nile Basin Initiative, and the Swiss Federal Office of Public Health.

**Claire Molinari:** Analyst at investment manager Sarasin & Partners, specializing in evaluating environmental, social, and governance issues in investment decision-making. Dr Molinari's research interests include intergenerational equity, fiduciary duty in investment, and environmental risk for long-term investors. She holds a DPhil and MSc from the University of Oxford, where she was a Clarendon Scholar, a Maîtrise in international law from Université de Paris II (Panthéon-Assas), and a BA/LLB (Hons) from the University of Melbourne. Dr Molinari is admitted as an Australian lawyer.

**Phoebe Okowa**: Professor of Public International Law at Queen Mary, University of London. Professor Okowa read law at the Universities of Nairobi and Oxford. She previously taught at the University of Bristol. In 2011, Professor Okowa was a Hauser Global Visiting Professor at New York University School of Law. She is the joint editor (with Professor Malcom Evans) of *Foundations of Public International Law* (Oxford University Press) and (with Professor Malgosia Fitzmaurice) of *Queen Mary Studies in International Law* (Brill). She has published extensively in the field of public international law broadly construed, including *State Responsibility for Transboundary Air Pollution* (Oxford University Press 2000) and *Environmental Justice in Law and Context* (Cambridge University Press 2009) with Professor Jonas Ebbesson.

**Jacqueline Peel**: Professor at the Melbourne Law School. Professor Peel holds the degrees of Bachelor of Science and Bachelor of Laws (Hon I) from the University of Queensland, a Master of Laws from New York University where she was a Fulbright scholar, and a PhD from the University of Melbourne. In 2003–2004, she returned to NYU Law School as a Hauser Research Scholar and Emile Noël Fellow. Prior to her appointment at Melbourne, she completed an internship at the United Nations International Law Commission, working with Professor James Crawford on the ILC's State responsibility articles. From 1997 to 1999 she practised environmental and planning law at the national law firm of Allens Arthur Robinson. Professor Peel's research interests are in the areas of environmental law (domestic and international), risk regulation, and the role of science and climate change law. She has published numerous articles and several books on these topics, including (with A. Zahar and L. Godden) *Australian Climate Law in a Global Context* (Cambridge University Press 2013); (with P. Sands) *Principles of International Environmental Law* (3rd edn, Cambridge University Press 2012); *Environmental Law:* (with L. Godden) *Scientific, Policy, and Regulatory Dimensions* (Oxford University Press 2010; *Science and Risk Regulation in International Law* (Cambridge University Press 2010); and *The Precautionary Principle in Practice* (Federation Press 2005).

**Peter H. Sand**: Lecturer in International Environmental Law at the University of Munich, Germany. Peter Sand was formerly a legal adviser for the United Nations Environment Programme and the World Bank. His publications include *Lessons Learned in Global Environmental Governance* (1990), *Transnational Environmental Law* (1999), and over a hundred articles in international legal journals and collections. He has been visiting professor at Duke Law School and at the universities of Paris, Geneva, Addis Ababa and Helsinki, and he served on the UN Security Council's Compensation Commission for environmental claims arising from the 1991 Gulf War.

**Komlan Sangbana**: PhD candidate and teaching assistant at the Department of public international law of the Faculty of Law of the University of Geneva. His doctoral work focuses on the legal regime applicable to the pollution of international watercourses, under the supervision of Professor Boisson de Chazournes. Mr Sangbana holds a Diplôme d'études approfondies (DEA) in Public Law from the University of Lomé (Togo). He is a member of the Platform for international freshwater law (University of Geneva).

**Priscilla Schwartz**: Senior Lecturer in Law at the School of Law and Social Sciences, University of East London. Dr Schwartz obtained her PhD in Law, LLM, LLB (Hons), and BA from the University of London and the University of Sierra Leone. She researches on growth promotion in Africa through international economic law (IEL), and the sustainability of economic activities. She is the Deputy Chair of the African IEL Network, and the book review editor of the MJIEL. Dr Schwartz is a Barrister and Solicitor with over 18 years PQE advising governments and companies operating in the energy and natural resource sectors.

**Dinah Shelton**: Manatt/Ahn Professor of International Law Emeritus, George Washington University, United States. Previously she was Professor of International Law and director of the doctoral programme in international human rights law at the University of Notre Dame Law School from 1996–2004. Professor Shelton previously taught at Santa Clara University and was a visiting lecturer at the University of California, Davis, Stanford University, the University of California, Berkeley, the University of Paris, and the University of Strasbourg, France. From 1987 to 1989, she was the director of the Office of Staff Attorneys at the U.S. Court of Appeals for the Ninth Circuit. Professor Shelton is the author or editor of three prize-winning books: *Protecting Human Rights in the Americas* (winner of the 1982 Inter-American Bar Association Book Prize and co-authored with Thomas Buergenthal); *Remedies in International Human Rights Law* (awarded the 2000 Certificate of Merit, American Society of International Law); and the three volume *Encyclopedia of Genocide and Crimes against Humanity* (awarded a 'Best Research' book award by the New York Public Library). She also has authored many articles and books on international law, human rights law, and international environmental law. She is a member of the board of editors of the American Journal of International Law. Professor Shelton serves on the boards of many human rights and environmental organizations. In 2006, she was awarded the prestigious Elizabeth Haub Prize in Environmental Law, and has served as a legal consultant to the United Nations Environment Programme, UNITAR, World Health Organization, European Union, Council of Europe, and Organization of American States. In 2009, she became the first woman nominated by the United States to become a member of the Inter-American Human Rights Commission, established by the Organization of American States to promote and protect human rights in the Western Hemisphere. She was elected to a four-year term in June, 2009.

**Tim Stephens**: Associate Professor, Associate Dean and Australian Research Council Future Fellow at the Faculty of Law, University of Sydney. Dr Stephens teaches and researches in public international law, with his published work focusing on the international law of the sea, international environmental law and international dispute settlement. Major career works include *The International Law of the Sea* (Hart 2010) with Donald R. Rothwell, and *International Courts and Environmental Protection* (Cambridge University Press 2009). In 2010 Dr Stephens was awarded the International Union for the Conservation of Nature (IUCN) Academy of Environmental Law Junior Scholarship Prize for 'outstanding scholarship and contributions in the field of international environmental law'. He has been a consultant for several non-governmental organisations, including a long association of work for the International Fund for Animal Welfare in relation to cetacean conservation. In 2014, Dr Stephens was appointed, on the nomination of the Australian Government, to the List of Experts for the South Pacific Regional Fisheries Management Organisation. Between 2010 and 2013 Dr Stephens was Co-Director of the Sydney Centre for International Law. Dr Stephens has a PhD in law from the University of Sydney, an MPhil in geography from the University of Cambridge, and a BA and LLB (both with Honours) from the University of Sydney.

**Mara Tignino**: Senior Researcher and Coordinator of the Platform for International Water Law at the Faculty of Law of the University of Geneva, Switzerland. She also serves as legal expert for UNITAR. Dr Tignino holds a PhD in International Law from the Graduate Institute of International and Development Studies in Geneva *summa cum laude*. Before joining the University, she worked as an external consultant at the Secretariat of the Basel convention on the Control of Transboundary Movements of Hazardous Wastes and their Disposal. In 2000, she received a bachelor in Political Science from the University LUISS in Rome *cum laude*; in 1998, Dr Tignino obtained the Certificate in European Political Studies at the Institut d'études politiques in Strasbourg. She has been a Visiting Scholar at George Washington University Law School in Washington DC and a Visiting Professor at the Faculty of Law of the University LUISS in Rome and the Université Catholique in Lille. Her recent publications include the books *L'eau et la guerre: éléments pour un régime juridique* (Bruylant 2011) and *International Law and Freshwater: the Multiple Challenges* (Edward Elgar 2013) (co-edited with L. Boisson de Chazournes and C. Leb).

**Marie-Louise Tougas**: Legal adviser at the International Committee of the Red Cross. She was in charge of the file protection of the environment in armed conflict. She is a member of the Québec Bar as well as the holder of an LLD in International Law from Laval University and an LLM from Queens University. Before joining the ICRC, she worked for defence teams of the International Criminal Tribunal for Rwanda. She also collaborated with LICADHO, in Cambodia.

**Jorge E. Viñuales**: Harold Samuel Professor of Law and Environmental Policy at the University of Cambridge. Previously, Professor Viñuales held the Pictet Chair in International Environmental Law at the Graduate Institute of International and Development Studies in Geneva, where he remains a visiting professor. He has published widely in his specialty areas, most recently his books *International Environmental Law* (Cambridge University Press 2015) (co-authored with P.-M. Dupuy), *The Foundations of International Investment Law* (Oxford University Press 2014) (co-edited with J. Pauwelyn and Z. Douglas), *Foreign Investment and the Environment in International Law* (Cambridge University Press 2012), *Harnessing Foreign Investment to Promote Environmental Protection: Incentives and Safeguards* (Cambridge University Press 2013) (co-edited with P.-M. Dupuy), and *Diplomatic and Judicial Means of Dispute Settlement* (Martinus Nijhoff 2012) (co-edited with L. Boisson de Chazournes and M. G. Kohen). Professor Viñuales has wide experience as a practitioner. He has worked on many arbitration disputes under ICSID, UNCITRAL, ICC, or LCIA rules, including several high profile inter-state, investor-state, and commercial disputes, and he regularly advises companies, governments, international organizations, and major NGOs on different matters of environmental law, investment law, human rights, and public international law at large. Professor Viñuales was educated in France (Doctorat—Sciences Po, Paris), the United States (LLM—Harvard Law School), Switzerland (Licence and Diplôme d'études approfondies in international relations—HEI; liz jur—Universität Freiburg; Licence and Diplôme d'études approfondies in political science—Université de Genève), and Argentina (Abogado—UNICEN). His native language is Spanish and he is fluent in English, French, and Italian.

**Christina Voigt**: Dr juris Christina Voigt is Professor at the Department of Public and International law, University of Oslo, Norway. She is the author of *Sustainable Development as a Principle of International Law* (M. Nijhoff 2009) and edited volumes, such as *Sustainable Development in International and National Law* (with H.C. Bugge, Europa Law Publishing 2008), *Rule of Law for Nature* (Cambridge University Press 2013) and *The Common Interest in International Law* (with W. Benedek, K. De Feyter and M. Kettemann, Intersentia 2014). Her teaching and research is in international environmental law and public international law. She works in particular on legal issues of climate change, sustainability and the interface between environmental and trade law. In 2009, Dr Voigt was awarded the International Union for the Conservation of Nature (IUCN) Academy of Environmental Law Junior Scholarship Prize for her academic writing. In 2009 and 2010, Dr Voigt worked for the Norwegian government as lead negotiator on REDD+ (Reducing emissions from deforestation and forest degradation in developing countries) in the UN climate negotiations. In 2013, Dr Voigt was co-chair for the UNFCCC work program on results-based financing for REDD+, which successfully achieved a decision on this matter by COP 19 in Warsaw, November 2013. She works as legal consultant for the Norwegian Ministry of the Environment and several governmental and non-governmental organisations. Dr Voigt received her legal education at the Universität Passau (Germany), holds an LLM in Environmental Law from the University of Auckland, New Zealand, and received a doctorate in law from the University of Oslo. She has taught/is teaching guest courses in international environmental law and in climate change law at the University of Lund, Sweden (2003–2007), the University of Dar es Salaam, Tanzania (2011–12) and the University of Auckland, New Zealand (2014).

**Margaret A. Young**: Associate Professor at Melbourne Law School, University of Melbourne, Australia. Dr Young is the author of *Trading Fish, Saving Fish: The Interaction between Regimes in International Law* (Cambridge University Press 2011), which was awarded the International Union for Conservation of Nature (IUCN) Academy of Environmental Law Junior Scholar Prize in 2012. Her edited collection *Regime Interaction in International Law: Facing Fragmentation* (Cambridge University Press 2012) includes contributions from leading international, comparative and constitutional law scholars and is based on the conference she convened at the University of Cambridge in 2009 on Regime Interaction in International Law: Theoretical and Practical Challenges. Dr Young joined the Faculty at Melbourne Law School in 2009. She was previously the William Charnley Research Fellow in Public International Law at Pembroke College and the Lauterpacht Centre for International Law, University of Cambridge, where she also lectured in Cambridge's LLM course on WTO law. Dr Young has worked at the World Trade Organization (Appellate Body Secretariat) and the United Nations International Law Commission, is a former associate to the Chief Justice of the Federal Court of Australia, and has practised as a solicitor at a major Australian national law firm. She holds a PhD and an LLM from the University of Cambridge and a BA/LLB (Hons) from the University of Melbourne and has been a Visiting Scholar at Columbia Law School.

# 1. The Rio Declaration on Environment and Development

## *Preliminary Study*

Jorge E. Viñuales*



* Harold Samuel Professor of Law and Environmental Policy, University of Cambridge, United Kingdom.

# I) Introduction

It came as a surprise to the editor, but also to several contributors and even to the publisher and the reviewers of this volume, that a commentary of the Rio Declaration on Environment and Development had not been produced in the more than twenty years since the 1992 Earth Summit. The Declaration has indeed become the canonical formulation of the legal concept of sustainable development as well as of the main principles of international environmental law underpinning treaties, treaty negotiations, domestic legislation, and a now substantial body of domestic and international jurisprudence. Yet, aside from some studies specifically commissioned by United Nations bodies,[1] no such commentary had been attempted until now.

It would be misplaced for me to provide an explanation of this lacuna, which may be due to anything from mere inadvertence, indifference, carefully reflected disinterest, or rejection of its usefulness. It is rather the need for it that deserves to be highlighted. There is little in common among the hundreds of treaties that we traditionally organize under the heading 'international environmental law', or the increasing references to environmental considerations in other 'branches' of international law, other than the principles and policies gathered in the Rio Declaration. In my view, and I understand that this view is largely shared by the distinguished contributors who have accepted to participate in this project, the Rio Declaration is perhaps the most representative instrument of the entire body of norms, treaties, domestic laws, and decisions governing our relation with the environment.

The Rio Declaration does not cover all questions,[2] nor is it for all principles the first or the foremost legal expression. It is a consensual statement, laboriously reached during the last days of the last preparatory meeting ('PrepCom IV')[3] before the 1992 Earth Summit, bringing together the main principles and policies that underpin our approach to the environment, with its many trade-offs and ambiguities.

These principles and policies have been fleshed out legally in many forms, sometimes in great detail, in norms or treaties or laws relating, aside from environmental protection,

[1] Commission on Sustainable Development, Report of the Expert Group Meeting on Identification of Principles of International Law for Sustainable Development, Geneva, Switzerland, 26–8 September 1995 ('Report-principles'); United Nations Secretary-General, *Rio Declaration on Environment and Development. Report of the Secretary-General*, 10 February 1997, UN Doc E/CN.17/1997/8 ('UNSG Report'); United Nations Department of Social and Economic Affairs, Division for Sustainable Development, *Review of implementation of Agenda 21 and the Rio Principles*, December 2011 ('UNDESA Report').

[2] See section III.3 of this chapter.

[3] For the account of the chairman of the Preparatory Committee, who also chaired, at the very end of PrepCom IV, the meeting of the informal contact group that drafted the final version of the Declaration, see Koh, T. T.-B., 'UNCED Leadership: A Personal Perspective', in Sjösted, G. et al (eds), *Negotiating International Regimes: Lessons Learned from the United Nations Conference on Environment and Development* (Graham & Trotman 1994), 165–9.

to questions as diverse as trade, investment, human rights, the law of the sea, or the law of armed conflict. In this regard, the Rio Declaration is best approached as a 'moment' in the emergence and refinement of the norms governing our relations with the environment. Such principles and policies do not 'belong' exclusively or, in some cases, even primarily to the Rio Declaration. But the Declaration is unique in that it brings them all together at once to lay the normative foundations of how 'development' was to be understood in the aftermath of the Cold War, and not unrestrained development, but development under demanding and yet inevitable environmental constraints.

The Rio Declaration cannot be understood in isolation from the historical context where it emerged, with its many attempts at defining policies guiding our relationship to the environment but, also, the struggle of developing and newly independent countries to reach higher levels of economic and social development. In this preliminary study, I would like to start by situating the Rio Declaration in this broad historical context before examining the details of its negotiation (I). I will then briefly present and analyse different readings of the overall structure of the Declaration (II). As I shall endeavour to show, the Declaration clearly conveys the double nature of environmental protection as both a 'branch' and a 'perspective' influencing all areas of international law. The third section focuses on the contents and impact of the Declaration (III). After identifying the main functions that can be performed by the 'statements' included in the Declaration, I use such functions as an analytical chart to assess the normative and jurisprudential impact of each principle. The fourth and final section examines the current position of the Rio Declaration in the global efforts towards achieving prosperity (economic and social development and growth) within the bounds set to it by the increasingly pressing environmental concerns (IV).

## II) The Rio Declaration in Historical Perspective

### 1. Two storylines

Situating the Rio Declaration in its historical context requires selecting an appropriate level of detail and a narrative. Most often, a chronological narrative is offered placing the Rio Declaration as a major result of the 1992 United Nations Conference on Environment and Development ('UNCED', also known as the 'Earth Summit') that met in Rio de Janeiro, Brazil,[4] itself a continuation of the United Nations Conference on the Human Environment that had met in Stockholm twenty years earlier ('Stockholm Conference').[5] The Rio Declaration is thus mentioned as a step in a storyline that runs from Stockholm to Rio 1992, to the 2002 World Summit on Sustainable Development ('WSSD') held in

[4] Report of the United Nations Conference on Environment and Development. Rio de Janeiro 3–14 June 1992, vol 2, Proceedings of the Conference, UN Doc A/CONF.151/26/Rev.1. On the UNCED see generally Johnson, S., *The Earth Summit. The United Nations Conference on Environment and Development (UNCED)* (Graham & Trotman/Martinus Nijhoff 1993).

[5] On the Stockholm Conference see Kiss, A. and Sicault, D., 'La Conférence des Nations Unies sur l'environnement (Stockholm, 5–16 June 1972)' (1972) 18 *Annuaire français de droit international* 603; Kennet, K., 'The Stockholm Conference on the Human Environment' (1972) 48 *International Affairs* 33; Sohn, L. B., 'The Stockholm Declaration on the Human Environment' (1973) 14 *HILJ* 423.

Johannesburg, South Africa,[6] and until the more recent 2012 United Nations Conference on Sustainable Development ('2012 Rio Summit') and its aftermath.[7]

The perspective adopted in this preliminary study differs somewhat from the traditional approach. It situates the Rio Declaration within two storylines, one focusing on the broad historical context of the Rio Principles and the other on the specific steps that led to their formulation.

The first storyline places less emphasis on the chronological line, without deviating too much from it, and centres the narrative on the core goals advanced over half a century of international negotiations. This storyline is intended to highlight why the Rio Declaration deserves to stand out among the numerous instruments addressing environmental considerations as the most emblematic set of principles guiding our relationship with the environment.

The second storyline is more specific. It focuses on the steps followed between the late 1980s and the early 1990s to reach the statement of principles and policies eventually entitled, after much negotiation, the Rio Declaration on Environment and Development. It thus covers the procedural dimensions of the *travaux préparatoires*, but also the broader policy context in which such steps were taken.

## 2. The broader context of the Rio Declaration

The broader context of the Rio Declaration precedes by at least a decade the 1972 Stockholm Conference.[8] What in the run-up to Stockholm was to be increasingly understood as the 'human environment',[9] was previously envisioned as either 'nature' conservation or 'natural resource' exploitation. The decolonization process, which accelerated in the late 1950s and the beginning of the 1960s, brought within the United Nations General Assembly ('UNGA') a growing number of newly independent States which, together with existing developing States, justifiably sought to reshape different international agendas to meet their needs.[10]

One major result of this political fact was the adoption by the UNGA of Resolution 1803 (XVII) on 'Permanent Sovereignty over Natural Resources' in 1962.[11] This resolution is often neglected in historical overviews of international environmental law and, yet, it epitomizes one of the two poles of the environment-development equation underpinning all sustainable development conferences until today. Through the lenses of this resolution, the environment is understood as a 'natural resource' to be appropriated and exploited to foster development.

[6] Report of the World Summit on Sustainable Development, Johannesburg, South Africa, 26 August–4 September 2002 (UN Doc A/CONF.199/20), in particular Resolution 2 ('Plan of Implementation of the World Summit on Sustainable Development').

[7] *The Future We Want*, 11 September 2012, UN Doc A/RES/66/288.

[8] This section draws upon Viñuales, J. E., 'The Rise and Fall of Sustainable Development' (2013) 22 *RECIEL* 3.

[9] The stream of work of the Stockholm Preparatory Committee which led to the drafting and adoption of the Stockholm Declaration was prompted by a recommendation made in a 1970 Report from the UN Secretary-General calling for a statement of 'rights and obligations of citizens and Governments with regard to the preservation and improvement of the human environment', UN Doc A/CONF.48/PC/2, para 16, cited in Sohn, 'The Stockholm Declaration on the Human Environment', 426.

[10] See Virally, M., 'Droit international et décolonisation devant les Nations Unies' (1963) 9 *Annuaire français de droit international* 509.

[11] 'Permanent Sovereignty over Natural Resources', 14 December 1962, UN Doc A/RES/1803/XVII. References to the entitlements of States over their natural resources appeared already in earlier resolutions, such as UNGA Resolution 523 (VI) (12 January 1952), UNGA Resolution 626 (VII) (21 December 1952), and UNGA Resolution 1314 (XIII) (12 December 1958). See Gess, K., 'Permanent Sovereignty over Natural Resources' (1964) 13 *ICLQ* 398.

At the other end of the spectrum, many see, with the benefit of hindsight, the 1972 Stockholm Conference as the high-water mark of environmental protection achieved in a global conference.[12] Despite its clear anthropocentric focus (which can be contrasted with the more conservationist World Charter for Nature adopted ten years later)[13] and the significant room it devoted to development considerations,[14] the Stockholm Declaration has remained the benchmark of environmental protection efforts at the international level. As is well known, the Stockholm Conference also adopted a Plan of Action[15] including, among others, a recommendation that led to the establishment of the United Nations Environment Programme ('UNEP').[16]

Ten years later, it was the Governing Council of this organization that, based on a discouraging assessment of progress made on environmental protection,[17] triggered the process that eventually led to the UNCED and the Rio Declaration. Despite efforts deployed since the Stockholm Conference to place the environment on the agenda of policy makers, all major environmental indicators had continued to deteriorate. At the roots of this failure was the environment-development equation and, more specifically, the inability of the environmental message to spread beyond environment ministries, particularly to those circles of government that handled economic and social policies. As noted by Gro Harlem Brundtland, the president of the World Commission on Environment and Development ('WCED', also known as the 'Brundtland Commission'), in an interview given in 2004, a key reason why previous efforts had been ineffective was the failure to garner support from government economists.[18]

When the WCED was established in 1983, a key dimension was therefore to reach out to this sceptical or simply unfamiliar audience. The message was therefore adjusted. The concept of 'sustainable development' came into play to align economic and environmental considerations. The elaboration of the concept of sustainable development by the WCED in its report *Our Common Future*[19] amounted to nothing short of a breakthrough. Born in the 1980s as a conservation concept,[20] 'sustainable development' was one among different competing terms seeking to reconcile economic development and environmental protection. Other

[12] See eg the accounts of Pallemaerts, M., 'International Environmental Law from Stockholm to Rio: Back to the Future?' (1992) 1 *RECIEL* 254; Mann, H., 'The Rio Declaration' (1992) 86 *Proceedings of the American Society of International Law* 405; Wirth, D. A., 'The Rio Declaration on Environment and Development: Two Steps Forward and One Back, or Vice Versa' (1995) 29 *Georgia Law Review* 599.

[13] World Charter for Nature, 28 October 1982, UN Doc A/RES/37/7 ('World Charter for Nature').

[14] Development considerations were very present in the run-up to Stockholm. Two indications, among others, of the strength of the development debate can be found in the UNGA Resolution 'Development and Environment', 20 December 1971, UN Doc 2849 (XXVI) and the Founex Report on Development and Environment (1971), available at: <http://www.stakeholderforum.org> (accessed on 20 April 2014).

[15] 'Action Plan for the Human Environment', 16 June 1972, UN Doc A/CONF 48/14, 10–62.

[16] 'Institutional and financial arrangements for international environmental cooperation', 15 December 1972, UN Doc A/RES/2997/XXVII ('Resolution 2997').

[17] See Caldwell, L., *International Environmental Policy* (Duke University Press 1996), 95–7.

[18] Interview Gro Harlem Brundtland, March 2004, referred to in Selin, H. and Linner, B.-O., 'The Quest for Global Sustainability: International Efforts on Linking Environment and Development', CID Graduate Student and Postdoctoral Fellow Working Paper no 5 (January 2005), 47, available at: <http://www.hks.harvard.edu> (accessed on 20 April 2014).

[19] Report of the World Commission on Environment and Development, Our Common Future, 10 March 1987 ('Our common future' or 'Brundtland Report').

[20] International Union for the Conservation of Nature and Natural Resources (IUCN), United Nations Environment Programme (UNEP) and World Wildlife Fund (WWF), *World Conservation Strategy: Living Resource Conservation for Sustainable Development* (IUCN, UNEP, and WWF, 1980) available at: <http://data.iucn.org/dbtw-wpd/edocs/WCS-004.pdf> (accessed on 20 April 2014).

concepts had been proposed over time, including the concept of 'eco-development'[21] or that of a 'green economy',[22] but they were unsuccessful in garnering consensus among different stakeholders. 'Sustainable development' proved to be superior in accommodating the developmental concerns expressed by countries such as Algeria, Brazil, and India since the run-up to the Stockholm Conference while remaining sufficiently colourless for industrialized countries not to object.

It is in this context that the process leading to the UNCED was launched and that the UNGA adopted Resolution 44/228 of 22 December 1989 convening the UNCED.[23] The detail of the process that resulted in the adoption of the Rio Declaration will be discussed in the next section. For present purposes, my focus will be rather on the overall place of the UNCED within the broad storyline starting in the 1960s. The concept of sustainable development mainstreamed by the Brundtland Commission and crowned at the UNCED breathed new life into global environmental governance and triggered a decade of considerable normative developments. Important indications of this renewed activity are provided not only by the conclusion of several major environmental treaties over the 1990s, including the UN Framework Convention on Climate Change ('UNFCCC')[24] and its Kyoto Protocol,[25] the Convention on Biological Diversity ('CBD')[26] and its Biosafety Protocol,[27] the UN Convention to Combat Desertification ('UNCCD'),[28] the Fish Stocks Agreement[29] or the Rotterdam Convention on Prior Informed Consent ('PIC Convention'),[30] but also by the increase in the number of ratifications of major existing conventions.[31]

Despite these developments, actual implementation remained elusive. Its normative pull notwithstanding, the concept of sustainable development could still not provide an answer to the very real conflicts opposing the two terms of the environment-development

[21] The concept of 'eco-development' was advanced as part of the preparation of the so-called 'Founex II' conference, held in 1974. The project paper by Ignacy Sachs can be found in the collection of papers of Maurice Strong (IV. UN Conference on the Human Environment/UN Environment Programme years: 1970–1975, Series III. UNEP file: 1968 Jan-1975 Dec, Subseries B), donated by Strong himself to the Environmental Science and Public Policy Archives, Harvard University. A further elaboration of this concept can be found in Glaeser, B. (ed), *Ecodevelopment: Concepts, Projects, Strategies* (Pergamon Press 1984), which includes a preface by Sachs.

[22] The concept of 'green economy' is of more recent vintage. Its origins are usually traced back to Pearce, D. W., Markandya, A., and Barbier, E. B., *Blueprint for a Green Economy* (London: Earthscan 1989). The 'blueprints' offered by the authors are, however, embedded within the concept of sustainable development and can be seen as an interpretation of it. A modernized version of the green economy concept appears in Barbier, E., *A Global Green New Deal: Rethinking the Economic Recovery* (Cambridge University Press 2010) as well as in UNEP, *The Green Economy Report—A Synthesis for Policy Makers* (UNEP 2011).

[23] 'United Nations Conference on Environment and Development', 22 December 1989, UN Doc A/44/228 ('Enabling resolution').

[24] United Nations Framework Convention on Climate Change, 9 May 1992, 31 ILM 849 ('UNFCCC').

[25] Kyoto Protocol to the United Nations Framework Convention on Climate Change, Kyoto, 11 December 1997, 2303 UNTS 148 ('Kyoto Protocol').

[26] Convention on Biological Diversity, 5 June 1992, 1760 UNTS 79 ('CBD').

[27] Cartagena Protocol on Biosafety to the Convention on Biological Diversity, (2000), 29 January 2000, 39 ILM 1027 ('Biosafety Protocol').

[28] United Nations Convention to Combat Desertification in those Countries Experiencing Serious Drought and/or Desertification, Particularly in Africa, UN Doc A/AC.241/15/Rev. 7 (1994), 17 June 1994, 33 ILM 1328 ('UNCCD').

[29] Agreement for the Implementation of the Provisions of the United Nations Conventions on the Law of the Sea of 10 December 1982 Relating to the Conservation and Management of Straddling Fish Stocks and Highly Migratory Fish Stocks, 4 August 1995, 2167 UNTS 88 ('Fish Stocks Agreement').

[30] Rotterdam Convention on the Prior Informed Consent Procedure for Certain Hazardous Chemicals and Pesticides in International Trade, 10 September 1998, 2244 UNTS 337 ('PIC Convention' or 'Rotterdam Convention').

[31] UNEP, *Global Environmental Outlook 5: Environment for the Future We Want* (UNEP 2012), 464, Figure 17.1.

equation. Whereas, from a conceptual standpoint, sustainable development amounted to an aspiration, almost a belief in the synergies between development and environmental protection, in practice, such synergies proved to be far from obvious. The risk of clashes became clearer in the late 1990s, as the attention focused on implementation. A first indication was provided at the follow-up meeting of the UNGA in 1997. As noted in the 'Programme for the Further Implementation of Agenda 21', adopted on that occasion:

> [f]ive years after the United Nations Conference on Environment and Development, the state of the global environment has continued to deteriorate [...] Some progress has been made in terms of institutional development, international consensus-building, public participation and private sector actions and, as a result, a number of countries have succeeded in curbing pollution and slowing the rate of resource degradation. Overall, however, trends are worsening.[32]

The shift from normative development to a specific focus on implementation was even clearer at the 2002 WSSD,[33] which focused on multi-stakeholder partnerships largely as an attempt to integrate the private sector and, perhaps, also to compensate for the lack of political will to take bolder steps.[34] In addition, the WSSD marked a noticeable change on the overall goals pursued. Within the broader context of the UN Millennium Declaration and the Millennium Development Goals,[35] the WSSD's agenda emphasized the social and economic development components over the environmental pillar of sustainable development. The so-called 'WEHAB Agenda', which stands for water and sanitation, energy, health, agricultural productivity, and biodiversity and ecosystem management, moved the focus of the negotiations one step further in the direction of development.

The trend was subsequently confirmed by other global conferences, most recently the 2012 Rio Summit.[36] It is still early to evaluate the impact of the outcome document on global environmental governance. Aside from the strengthening of the UNEP, particularly through the extension of its Governing Council to all the members of the UN General Assembly and the commitment to a larger budget,[37] the main contribution of this document lies in the efforts towards measuring progress. Measurement is, indeed, at the heart of three significant achievements of the Summit: (i) a call for the development of 'sustainable development goals' ('SDGs') for the period starting after 2015;[38] (ii) these goals are to be regularly assessed by a 'High-Level Political Forum';[39] and (iii) a

[32] UNGA Resolution S/19-2, 28 June 1997, Annex, 'Programme for the Further Implementation of Agenda 21'.

[33] See Report of World Summit on Sustainable Development in Johannesburg (South Africa), 26 August to 4 September 2002. UN Doc A/CONF.199/20, 1, 2002, Resolution 1: 'Political Declaration' and 6, Resolution 2: 'Plan of Implementation of the World Summit on Sustainable Development'.

[34] See Andonova, L. and Levy, M., 'Franchising Governance: Making Sense of the Johannesburg Type II Partnerships', in Schram Stokke, O. and Thommessen, Ø.B. (eds), *Yearbook of International Co-operation on Environment and Development* (Earthscan 2004), 19.

[35] 'Millennium Declaration', 13 September 2000, UN Doc A/RES/55/2.

[36] *The Future We Want*, 11 September 2012, UN Doc A/RES/66/288.

[37] *The Future We Want*, para 88.

[38] *The Future We Want*, paras 245–51. At the time of writing, the work of the 'Open Working Group on Sustainable Development Goals' established to define these goals was still in progress. The document is expected to be elaborated before the end of July 2014. See <http://sustainabledevelopment.un.org/owg.html> (accessed on 1 May 2014).

[39] *The Future We Want*, para 85(e). The 'High-Level Forum for Sustainable Development' held its first session in September 2013 and will meet annually. The next session is scheduled for June–July 2014. Sessions include a ministerial segment meeting for two days at the end of each session. See <http://sustainabledevelopment.un.org/index.php?menu=1556> (accessed on 1 May 2014).

call for the development of 'broader measures of progress to "complement" gross domestic product'.[40] Despite the environmental significance of these and other elements, the 2012 Rio Summit moved further away from the balance between the two terms of the environment-development equation laboriously found at the 1992 Earth Summit. Social and economic development is no longer seen as 'one' overarching objective of sustainable development,[41] but as 'the' main challenge. As noted in the Outcome document, 'poverty eradication is the *greatest global challenge facing the world today* and an indispensable requirement for sustainable development'.[42] The shift towards development considerations cannot be stated more clearly. The urgent need to fight poverty is, of course, not in question. It is the hierarchy introduced between the components of sustainable development that must be highlighted. We may recall, in this context, the wording of resolution 2849 (XXVI) of 1971, one of the early expressions of developing country distrust towards environmental considerations. The last paragraph of this resolution reiterated, indeed, 'the primacy of independent economic and social development as *the main and paramount objective of international co-operation*, in the interests of the welfare of mankind and of peace and world security.'[43]

The understanding presented so far is summarized graphically in Figure 1.1:

**Figure 1.1.** The first storyline

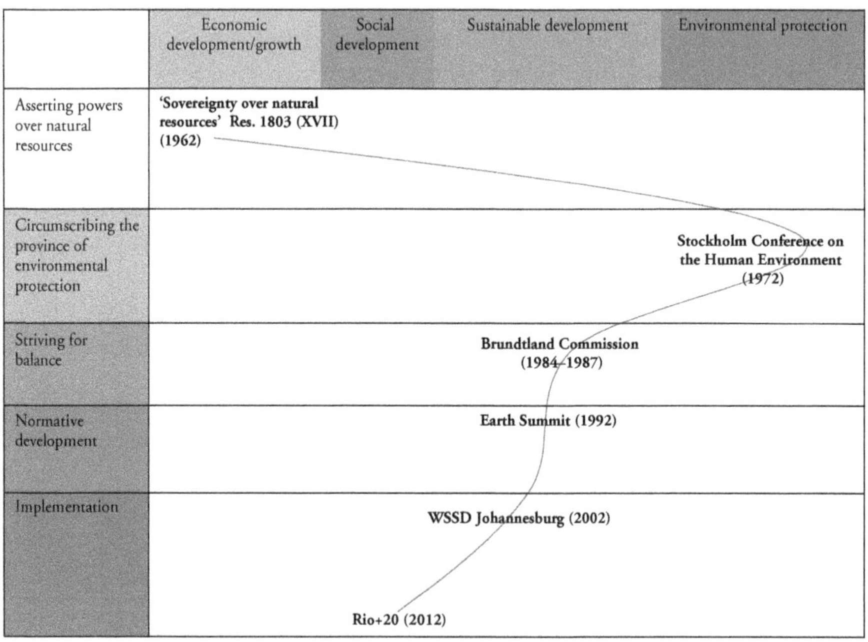


[40] *The Future We Want*, para 38. The United Nations Statistical Commission is in charge of this portfolio. So far, a number of reports have been elaborated, including a report by three distinguished academics, a note by the UN Secretary-General as well as, more recently, a background document surveying existing practices. See <http://unstats.un.org/unsd/broaderprogress/progress.html> (accessed on 1 May 2014).

[41] See eg Report of World Summit on Sustainable Development in Johannesburg, 'Political Declaration', para 11.

[42] *The Future We Want*, para 2 (italics added).

[43] 'Development and Environment', para 11 (italics added).

The storyline summarized in Figure 1.1 places the UNCED and, as discussed next, the Rio Declaration, in the broader context of half a century of environment-related negotiations. The trajectory described by the grey line represents the evolution of such efforts from two perspectives, their situation within the environment-development equation but also their main concern, which has evolved over time from the recognition of environmental problems as a question of global cooperation, to the search of an appropriate programme, to normative development and, more recently, to implementation.

Within this broad picture, the UNCED is situated as a transitional moment, where a balance between environment and development considerations was struck, which allowed for a remarkable normative development at the international and domestic levels. The Rio Declaration captures this moment. Although at the time it was perceived by developed countries as an instrument skewed towards development considerations, in hindsight, it embodies a nuanced balance with a strong environmental component, particularly through the assertion of the main principles of international environmental law (both old—derived from Stockholm—and new—such as the precautionary approach). In the next section, I will zoom in on the historical process that led to the adoption of this document in order to show how the environment-development equation influenced the detail of the negotiations.

## 3. The birth of the Rio Declaration

In its report *Our Common Future* the WCED made the following recommendation:

> Building on the 1972 Stockholm Declaration, the 1982 Nairobi Declaration, and many existing international conventions and General Assembly resolutions, there is now a need to consolidate and extend relevant legal principles in a new charter to guide state behaviour in the transition to sustainable development. It would provide the basis for, and be subsequently expanded into, a Convention, setting out the sovereign rights and reciprocal responsibilities of all states on environmental protection and sustainable development.[44]

The report appended as Annex I a statement of principles prepared by a group of international legal experts to the attention of the UNGA. The Commission noted, however, that such principles were 'submitted to assist the General Assembly in its deliberations and [had] not been approved or considered in detail by the Commission'.[45]

This recommendation was followed by the UNGA, which included in the abovementioned Resolution 44/228 convening the UNCED a specific paragraph identifying the following objective:

> To promote the further development of international environmental law, taking into account the Declaration of the United Nations Conference on the Human Environment, as well as the special needs and concerns of the developing countries, and to examine in this context the feasibility of elaborating general rights and obligations of States, as appropriate, in the field of the environment, and taking into account relevant existing international legal instruments[46]

[44] 'Our common future', ch 12, s 5.2. para 85. For a detailed procedural history of the Rio Declaration see Handl, G., 'Rio Declaration on Environment and Development', *United Nations Audiovisual Library of International Law* (2012), available at: <http://legal.un.org/avl/ha/dunche/dunche.html> (accessed on 1 May 2012).

[45] 'Our common future', ch 12, s 5.2, para 86. For further detail see Munro, R. D. (Chairman) and Lammers, J.G. (Rapporteur), *Environmental Protection and Sustainable Development. Legal Principles and Recommendations Adopted by the Experts Group on Environmental Law of the World Commission on Environment and Development* (Graham & Trotman/Martinus Nijhoff 1987).

[46] 'Enabling resolution', para 15(d).

In the meantime, in November 1989, the International Union for the Conservation of Nature ('IUCN') had undertaken work on a 'Draft Covenant', which was later introduced into the work of the UNCED Preparatory Committee ('PrepCom') by the delegation of Iceland.[47] However, as noted by a distinguished commentator 'it was felt that the time was not yet ripe to discuss such a project in intergovernmental meetings'.[48]

The work of the PrepCom, under the general chairmanship of Ambassador Tommy Thong-Bee Koh from Singapore, unfolded between 1991 and early 1992 in one organizational session in New York and four substantive sessions in Nairobi, Geneva (twice) and New York.[49] The negotiations took place, formally, in three working groups and a plenary, although, informally, several 'contact groups' were set up to reach basic agreements and hammer out the details of the different texts. The drafting of the instrument/charter/statement/declaration of general principles and obligations was entrusted to Working Group III ('WG III'), established at the second substantive session, under the chairmanship of Dr Bedrich Moldan from Czechoslovakia. The terms of reference of WG III broadened the substantive scope of the instrument to be drafted, as compared with paragraph 15(d) of Resolution 44/228, by referring to:

> general rights and obligations of States and regional economic integration organizations, as appropriate, *in the field of environment and development* [...] taking due account of the conclusions of all the regional preparatory conferences.[50]

The regional preparatory conferences referred to in this paragraph took place in Bergen, in May 1990 (for Europe and North America), Bangkok, in October 1990 (for Asia and the Pacific), Tlatelolco, in March 1991 (for Latin America and the Caribbean), and Cairo, both in July (for Africa) and September 1991 (for the Near East and West Africa).[51] Although several proposals were submitted at the third substantive session of the PrepCom and subsequently compiled in a document ('L.8'),[52] the negotiation of what became the Rio Declaration was not undertaken until the fourth and final session, PrepCom IV, held at the UN Headquarters in New York from 2 March to 3 April 1992.

The conceptions of what the instrument should be were radically different, particularly as a result of the divergent views of developed and developing countries as to the proper

[47] See UN Doc A/CONF.151/PC/WG.III/4. The IUCN has pursued work on a 'Draft Covenant', which now has several editions. See IUCN, *Draft International Covenant on Environment and Development* (4th edn, IUCN 2010).

[48] Kiss, A., 'The Rio Declaration on Environment and Development', in Campiglio, L. et al (eds), *The Environment after Rio: International Law and Economics* (Graham & Trotman 1994) 55, at 55.

[49] See the account by Koh, 'UNCED Leadership: A Personal Perspective'. For a structured account of developments in each setting see Chasek, P., 'The Story of the UNCED Process', in Sjösted, G. et al (eds), *Negotiating International Regimes: Lessons Learned from the United Nations Conference on Environment and Development* (Graham & Trotman 1994) 45 (as part of the team of the Earth Summit Bulletin, Chasek reported in real time the developments both in the formal and the informal meetings over the PrepCom).

[50] UN Doc A/46/48, sub-paragraph (ii) (italics added). This point is highlighted by Sand, P., 'International Law on the Agenda of the 1992 "Earth Summit"' (1992) 3 *Colorado Journal of International Environmental Law and Policy* 343, 347.

[51] Sand, 'International Law on the Agenda of the 1992 "Earth Summit"', 347.

[52] Chairman's consolidated draft entitled 'Earth Charter[:][/] The Rio de Janeiro Declaration on Environment and Development', UN Doc A/CONF.151/PC/WG.III/L.8/Rev.1 and Add. 1 and 2 ('L.8').

balance between environmental and developmental considerations. The atmosphere is captured by an anecdote reported by one commentator:

During the negotiations, one delegate from the developed countries stated thus: 'The Earth Charter should be framed and put in the room of every child of the world'. A delegate from the developing countries immediately retorted: 'Not every child has a room, maybe not even a bed!'[53]

This divergence underpinned virtually all aspects of the negotiations, starting with the very title and location of the instrument to be adopted. Maurice Strong, the Secretary-General of the UNCED (and previously of the 1972 Stockholm Conference) favoured the adoption of an 'Earth Charter', with a strong environmental focus. Conversely, the G77 and China advocated for a title that would reflect the importance of development considerations and proposed a 'Rio de Janeiro Declaration on Environment and Development'. Although most non-governmental organizations and industrialized countries favoured an 'Earth Charter', the United States was itself sceptical with respect to Strong's idea and noted, by reference to the 1982 World Charter for Nature, that it was important not to raise unrealistic expectations.[54] Discussions on this question started at PrepCom III and continued at PrepCom IV. At the latter meeting, it became clear that the G77's position would prevail. In this context, Strong introduced an 'Earth Pledge' which was displayed at the UNCED in a giant poster that was signed by hundreds of delegates as well as by presidents Bush (United States), Mitterrand (France), and Collor de Mello (Brazil).[55]

There was also disagreement as to whether the Declaration would be a stand-alone instrument, a position favoured by the G77, or a mere prologue to the ambitious and far-reaching Agenda 21, as suggested by the United States.[56] This disagreement explains why the G77 opposed the attempts of developed countries at negotiating the preamble first, in order to avoid that this point take too much time and eventually lead to a preamble instead of a full declaration.[57]

As to the content of the instrument, it largely reflects the convoluted negotiation process that eventually led to the formulation of the different principles. The bulk of the negotiation of WG III at PrepCom IV was indeed devoted to the statement of principles. The chairman, Dr Moldan, presented his reference document, which had been circulated in the intersessional period,[58] incorporating the proposals compiled in L.8. The G77, represented by Pakistan and China, opposed this document and stated that they would submit a new document that could serve as the basis for the negotiations and that, in the meantime, the discussions should focus on L.8. This inauspicious beginning was emblematic of what would follow. After the G77 submitted its new draft ('L.20'),[59] several other

[53] Foo Kim Boon, 'The Rio Declaration and its influence on international environmental law' (1992) *Singapore Journal of Legal Studies* 347, 348.

[54] Kovar, J., 'A Short Guide to the Rio Declaration' (1993) 4 *Colorado Journal of International Environmental Law and Policy* 119, 123 (Kovar worked for the Office of the Legal Adviser of the US State Department).

[55] Kovar, 'A Short Guide to the Rio Declaration', 122–3.

[56] UN Doc A/CONF.151/PC/WG.III/L.21 ('L.21'), suggesting that the declaration should be a 'prologue to Agenda 21'.

[57] See the chapter on the preamble by Francioni in this commentary. See also Ling, C.Y., *The Rio Declaration on Environment and Development: An assessment* (Third World Network 2012), 24–8; Kovar, 'A Short Guide to the Rio Declaration', 122–4.

[58] This document, containing 13 principles, is summarized in Earth Summit Bulletin, vol 1, no 1.

[59] 'Rio de Janeiro Charter/Declaration on Environment and Development', UN Doc A/CONF.151/PC/WG.III/L.20/Rev.1 ('L.20').

new drafts were submitted *inter alia* by the United States ('L.21'), Japan ('L.22'), Canada ('L.23'), Australia ('L.24'), the EC countries ('L.25') the Nordic countries ('L.27'), and the UK and Denmark ('L.28').[60]

A deadlock concerning the question of which draft would be used as the basis for negotiations was overcome by an intervention of Tommy Koh and the creation of a 'contact group' under the alternate chairmanship of Mr Mukul Sanwal, of India,[61] and Mr Ole Holthe, of Norway. After a cluster approach, separating 'easy principles' from most contentious ones, was agreed and subsequently reversed by the G77, negotiations were conducted on a principle-by-principle basis. Yet, after a few days some principles that were deemed to be ripe for consensus (eg those relating to women, capacity-building or the 'Stockholm' principle, ie prevention) were delegated to smaller drafting groups. The contact group produced a bracketed text, which was forwarded to WG III for finalization.

Yet, the negotiations faced another deadlock and on 31 March, Tommy Koh was asked to step in. He asked the co-chairs of the contact group to produce a negotiating text by the 1st April at 6:30 pm and convened another small contact group consisting of eight industrialized countries (the US; Portugal, the Netherlands and Germany, on behalf of the EC; Australia, on behalf of CANZ—Canada, Australia, and New Zealand; Norway, alternating with Sweden; Japan; Russia) and eight developing countries (Pakistan, India, Iran, Brazil, Mexico, Nigeria, Tanzania, and China). This group met on the evening of the 1st April under the chairmanship of Mr Koh and produced by 6:15 of the following day an unbracketed text with a preamble and 27 principles.[62] This text was presented by Koh to the PrepCom IV plenary as his own draft and adopted for referral to the UNCED.[63]

In Rio, the negotiations were formally conducted in two main settings, namely the Plenary, chaired by the Brazilian President Fernando Collor de Mello, which included a ministerial and a summit segment (from 12–14 June), and the Main Committee, chaired by Tommy Koh, where the political negotiations actually took place. The Main Committee approved the draft 'Rio Declaration on Environment and Development' adopted at PrepCom IV 'by acclamation' without making any changes.[64] The text was

[60] See also the draft presented by: the United States, UN Doc A/CONF.151/PC/WG.III/L.21 ('L.21'); Japan, 'Rights and Obligations', UN Doc A/CONF.151/PC/WG.III/L.22 ('L.22'); Canada, UN Doc A/CONF.151/PC/WG.III/L.23 ('L.23'); Australia, UN Doc A/CONF.151/PC/WG.III/L.24 ('L.24'); EC countries, 'Elements for the Earth Charter', UN Doc A/CONF.151/PC/WG.III/L.25 ('L.25'); Nordic countries, 'Earth Charter. Elements for Consideration', UN Doc A/CONF.151/PC/WG.III/L.27 ('L.27'); 'Proposal submitted by Denmark and the United Kingdom of Great Britain and Northern Ireland on the basis of the work of several non-governmental organizations from around the world', UN Doc A/CONF.151/PC/WG.III/L.28 ('L.28').

[61] Sanwal subsequently published an illuminating article on the conceptual structure of the Rio Declaration, which I will discuss later in this chapter. See Sanwal, M., 'Sustainable Development, the Rio Declaration and Multilateral Cooperation' (1993) 4 *Colorado Journal of International Environmental Law and Policy* 45.

[62] Koh, 'UNCED Leadership', 168; Kovar, 'A Short Guide to the Rio Declaration', 122; Ling, *The Rio Declaration*, 10.

[63] 'Principles on general rights and obligations. Draft principles proposed by the Chairman. Rio Declaration on Environment and Development', 2 April 1992, UN Doc A/CONF.151/PC/WG.III/L.33/Rev.1 ('L.33').

[64] Report of the United Nations Conference on Environment and Development. Rio de Janeiro 3–14 June 1992, vol 2, Proceedings of the Conference, UN Doc A/CONF.151/26/Rev.1 (vol 2) ('UNCED vol 2'), ch III, section A, para 10.

forwarded to the Plenary, which adopted it. However, at this point, the United States and France added a number of interpretive statements concerning some principles and the Palestinian delegation also made a statement.[65]

The perception of the Rio Declaration in the immediate aftermath of the UNCED was contrasted. As noted at the time by Alexandre Kiss:

> The Rio Conference can be considered in different ways, like a bottle which is seen half full or half empty, according to the optimism or the pessimism of the person who contemplates it. The Declaration itself has disappointed some, who hold that it does not constitute real progress when compared to the Stockholm Declaration and the 1982 World Charter for Nature.
>
> However, this instrument, which is often supported by other texts adopted by the Rio Conference, confirms several international environmental law rules and reinforces emerging ones, some of which are particularly important...[66]

Observers from industrialized countries were discouraged by the strong development dimension of the instrument, which they viewed as a step backwards as compared to the Stockholm Declaration.[67] Observers from developing countries saw instead such dimension as a positive adjustment to the environmental focus of Stockholm.[68] As noted in the previous section, with the benefit of hindsight, the balance struck by the Rio Declaration is more sensitive to environmental considerations than the trend subsequently followed, particularly since the late 1990s. Such sensitivity is conveyed by the re-affirmation, but also the introduction, of the main cardinal principles of international environmental law.

## III) The Architecture(s) of the Rio Declaration

### 1. Structure and scope

The analysis of the structure of the Rio Declaration is a necessary step in any attempt at understanding its normative scope. The discussion of the *travaux préparatoires* suggests that there is no uniform or carefully reflected structure pursued by the delegations in drafting this instrument.

However, one of the co-chairs of the contact group that drafted the main basis for negotiation, Mr Mukul Sanwal, subsequently published an article identifying different clusters of principles explicitly relating to certain issues.[69] Sanwal's 1993 article is valuable not only because of his role in the drafting process, but also because it spells out the policy programmes within the overall programme of the declaration. Another interesting contribution, perhaps more representative of pro-environment and legally-oriented views,

[65] The United States made interpretive statements to Principles 3, 7, 12 and 23, whereas France did so for Principle 22. See UNCED vol 2, ch III, section B, paras 16, 21, and 22.

[66] Kiss, *The Rio Declaration*, 63–4. For a survey of views by different political figures see Panjabi, R. K. L., 'From Stockholm to Rio: A Comparison of the Declaratory Principles of International Environmental Law' (1992–1993) 21 *Denver Journal of International Law and Policy* 215, 273–6.

[67] See eg Mann, 'The Rio Declaration', 409; Pallemaerts, 'Back to the Future?', 256; Wirth, 'Two Steps Forward and One Back', 648.

[68] See eg Pathak, R. S. and Jaitly, A., 'Rio Declaration—Economic Issues for Developing Countries' (1992) 1 *RECIEL* 267, at 267; Porras, I., 'The Rio Declaration: A New Basis for International Co-operation' (1992) 1 *RECIEL* 245, 252; Sanwal, 'Sustainable Development', 48–9.

[69] Sanwal, 'Sustainable Development'.

is that provided by Alexander Kiss in a brief chapter published in 1994.[70] Kiss focuses on the contribution of the declaration to international environmental law as well as on what he sees as the foundations of a law of sustainable development.

These two 'models' of the structure of the Rio Declaration are useful to distil the core values underpinning this instrument as well as its broader implications for our understanding of the law governing our relations with the environment.

## 2. Models

Sanwal sees the Rio Declaration as a clarification as well as a further development of the concept of sustainable development.[71] Although he does not use these terms, his model can be understood as a set of programmes within the overall programme of sustainable development. More specifically, one gathers the impression that the principles of the Rio Declaration are taken as modular components that can be combined into programmes addressing different questions.

He refers to four main programmes concerning:[72] (1) the balancing between substantive requirements of development and procedural requirements (broadly understood) for implementing environmental protection; (2) the adoption by States of certain procedures (again, broadly understood) to integrate environmental protection in decision-making processes; (3) international cooperation on socio-economic issues; and (4) the development of a global partnership to conserve, protect, and restore the integrity and health of the Earth's ecosystems. The ways in which different principles (or modules) are combined into these four programmes is summarized in Figure 1.2:

**Figure 1.2.** Sanwal's model

| Balance | Integration | Cooperation | Partnership |
|---|---|---|---|
| 1. Human beings at the centre of concerns (Principle 1)<br>2. A right to development (Principles 2 and 3)<br>3. Environmental protection as an integral part of development (Principle 4)<br>4. Eradicating poverty as an indispensable requirement for sustainable development (Principle 5) | 1. Effective environmental legislation (Principle 11)<br>2. Public participation in environmental matters (Principle 10)<br>3. Application of the precautionary approach (Principle 15)<br>4. Promotion of the polluter-pays principle (Principle 16)<br>5. Adoption of environmental impact assessment (Principle 17)<br>6. Notification in case of risk or emergencies (Principles 18 and 19) | 1. Decrease disparities in the standard of living (Principle 5)<br>2. Strengthen endogenous capacity (Principle 9)<br>3. Promote a supportive and open international economic system (Principle 12)<br>4. Prevent the transfer of harmful activities and substances (Principle 14)<br>5. Develop a legal liability regime as a transboundary regulatory instrument (Principle 13) | 1. Reducing and eliminating unsustainable patterns of production and consumption (Principle 8)<br>2. Promoting appropriate demographic policies (Principle 8)<br>3. Exchanging scientific and technical knowledge (Principle 9)<br>4. Enhancing the development, adaptation, diffusion, and transfer of new and innovative technologies (Principle 9)<br>5. Promoting a supportive and open international economic system (Principle 12) |

[70] Kiss, 'The Rio Declaration'. The view expressed by Kiss is a summary of the position followed in a broader article co-authored with S. Doumbe-Bille: Kiss, A. and Doumbe-Bille, S., 'La Conférence des Nations Unies sur l'environnement et le développement (Rio de Janeiro-juin 1992)' (1992) 38 *Annuaire français de droit international* 823.

[71] Sanwal, 'Sustainable Development', 48.

[72] Sanwal, 'Sustainable Development', 49–51.

Although there is some overlap among the programmes identified by this model of the Rio Declaration and despite the fact that some of the key principles (eg differentiation in Principles 6 and 7) are not clearly brought to bear, Sanwal's account provides much texture to an otherwise dry statement of principles. Specifically, it suggests that there are different possible readings of the text and that principles may be relevant for more than one programme.

The model outlined by Kiss in his chapter pursues a different objective, namely to capture the contribution of the Rio Declaration to the development of international law. The topographic accidents that this account seeks to highlight are therefore different from the outset. He distinguishes between 'legal principles' and 'policy guidelines'. Within the first category, he further distinguishes between rules that had already been stated in the Stockholm Declaration (confirmed) and those that the Stockholm Declaration did not mention (newly stated). As for 'policy guidelines', the Declaration identifies three clusters of provisions relating, respectively, to 'development', the 'World Economic Order' and 'participation'. The overall model can be summarized graphically as follows:

**Figure 1.3.** Kiss' model

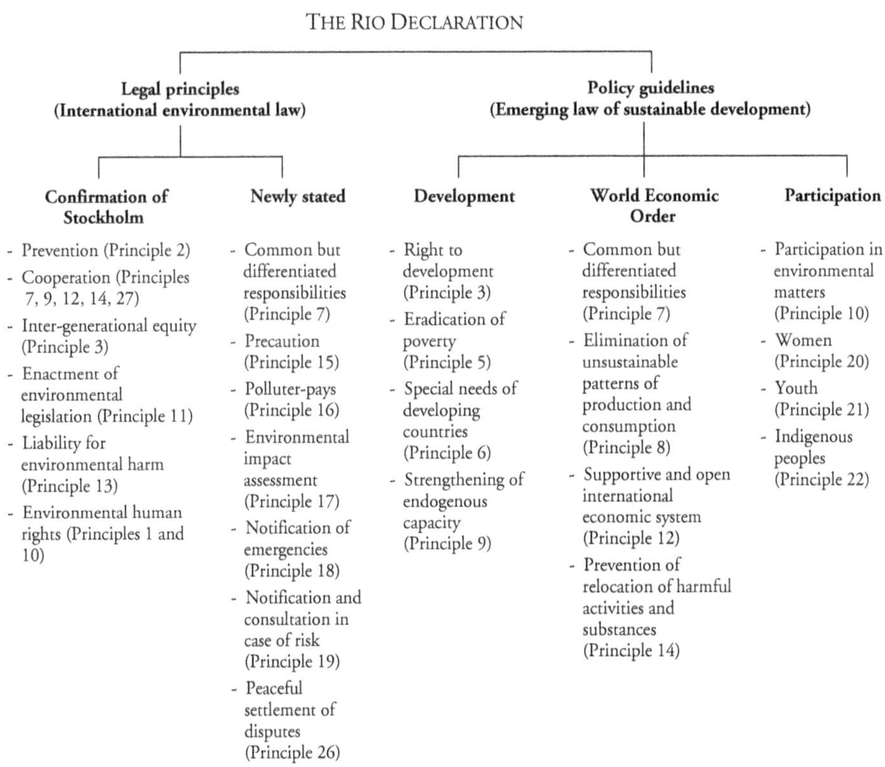


The model advanced by Kiss has advantages and disadvantages. One problem is that a statement of a rule in the Stockholm Declaration is not a reliable indication of whether the rule existed or not prior to its general statement in Rio. In fact, there are cases where a principle characterized as newly stated was grounded in customary international law before 1992 (eg Principle 18, which Kiss explicitly mentions) as well as other cases where the customary status of a principle is still subject to some controversy (eg Principle 15). The model is, however, interesting because it confirms that the principles of the Rio Declaration can indeed be organized in clusters (in Kiss' account 'development', 'World Economic Order', and 'participation'). Perhaps most importantly, Kiss' model introduces a relatively clear distinction between the principles relating to international environmental law and those concerning more broadly sustainable development, and it links the latter with the broader body of development law, including the New International Economic Order elaborated in the 1970s.[73]

The most salient features of the preceding models can be incorporated into a third model specifically intended to single out the main provinces of the declaration. This third model operates within a broad framework defined by the need to maintain and contribute to peace (Principle 25) through global cooperation (Principle 27) and dispute settlement (Principle 26). Within such broad bounds, the backbone of the Declaration is defined by five main principles stating that human beings are at the centre of sustainable development (Principle 1), that the right to development must be exercised in a manner that is respectful across time (Principle 3) and space (Principle 2), by integrating environmental considerations in all policies (Principle 4) and pursuing the eradication of poverty as a priority (Principle 5). Three other sets of principles further specify the programme defined in the backbone: a 'development set' elaborating on the economic and social development agenda attached to Principle 3 (Principles 8, 9, 12, 14, 20, 21, 22, and 23); an 'environment set' elaborating on prevention and environmental integration (Principles 8, 10, 11, 13, 15, 16, 17, 18, 19, and 24); and a 'differentiation set' distributing the benefit/burden entailed by these two programmes (Principles 6, 7, and 9). Figure 1.4 summarizes this model graphically:

**Figure 1.4.** The architecture of the Rio Declaration

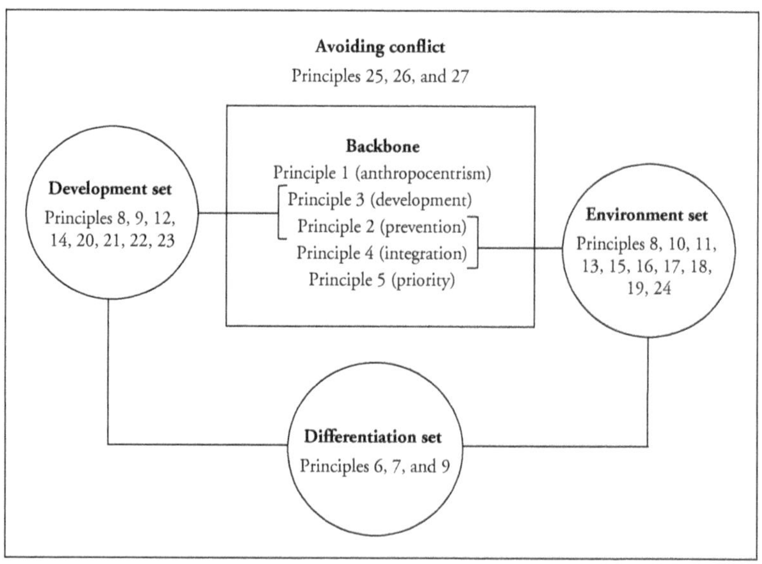


[73] UNGA Resolution 3201 (S-VI), 'Declaration on the Establishment of a New International Economic Order', 1 May 1974, UN Doc A/RES/S-6/3201. On the principles of the NIEO see 'Progressive Development of the Principles and Norms of International Law relating to the New International Economic Order', Report of the Secretary-General, 23 October 1984, UN Doc A/39/504/Add.1.

This architecture of the Rio Declaration has, as the other models, advantages and disadvantages. It does not provide sufficient detail either to clearly disentangle legal principles from policies or to identify more specific programmes (eg participation or human rights) within the declaration. The distinction between sets also obscures to some extent the close connections among principles and, more generally, among what we nowadays call the three pillars of sustainable development. However, this architecture is useful for present purposes because (i) it clarifies the province of environmental principles within the declaration, (ii) it sets apart several principles relating primarily to economic and social development, which are also the connectors with the international law of development elaborated in the 1970s and 1980s and with other branches of international law (international economic law, human rights, and humanitarian law), (iii) it shows the key role of differentiation principles in connecting the development and the environment sets, and (iv) it singles out the role of the prevention principle within the backbone of the declaration as the connector between the right to development and the integration requirement. It would be more accurate to place the second component of Principle 3 (intergenerational equity) together with the second and third components of Principle 2 (prevention in a transboundary and global context) and, conversely, to locate the first component of Principle 2 (sovereignty over natural resources) together with the right to development stated in Principle 3. But such a conceptual cartography would break the different principles of the declaration into smaller pieces and thereby blur, rather than clarify, the overall picture. In the next section, the implications of the four features or 'accidents' of the Rio Declaration's topography are analysed in more detail.

## 3. The significance of the Rio Declaration

The Rio Declaration is in many ways a crossroads, where different historical trends met and found expression. Its significance can only be understood if the relation between such trends and their condensed legal expression is explained.

The first trend, which emerged in the 1960s, is the growing environmental awareness. In a remarkable effort, Jacques Grinevald has brought together and commented the main scientific contributions that catalysed the environmental movement.[74] In addition to those books and writings that captured the attention of public opinion,[75] several major contributions were made in the fields of ecology,[76] economics,[77] philosophy,[78] and law,[79] to name but some of them. I have drawn the policy storyline in section I) 2 above. This trend found expression in the run-up to the Stockholm

[74] For a review of the main scientific contributions that catalysed the environmental movement see Grinevald, J., *La Biosphère de l'Anthropocène. Climat et pétrole, la double menace. Repères transdiciplinaires (1824–2007)* (Georg 2007), 115ff.

[75] See eg Carson, R., *Silent Spring* (Houghton Mifflin 1962); Boulding, K. E., 'The Economics of the Coming Spaceship Earth', in Jarrett, H. (ed), *Environmental Quality in a Growing Economy* (John Hopkins University Press 1966), 3–14; Nicholson, M., *The Environmental Revolution: A Guide for the New Masters of the World* (Hodder & Stoughton 1969); Commoner, B., *The Closing Circle: Nature, Man, and Technology* (Alfred Knopf 1971); Meadows, D. H. et al, *The Limits to Growth* (Universe Books 1972).

[76] See eg Odum, E. P., *Fundamentals of Ecology* (3rd edn, Sounders 1971).

[77] See eg Georgescu-Roegen, N., *The Entropy Law and the Economic Process* (Harvard University Press 1971).

[78] See eg White, L., 'The historical roots of our ecological crisis' (1967) 155 *Science* 1203; Lovelock, J., *GAIA: A New Look at Life on Earth* (Oxford University Press 1979).

[79] See eg Falk, R., *This Endangered Planet: Prospect and Proposals for Human Survival* (Random House 1971).

Conference and, even more, in the process that led to the UNCED. Some empirical studies show that around 1992, several indicators of environmental awareness, such as the ratification of environmental treaties, financial contributions to the environment fund created in 1972 to finance the UNEP[80] or the creation of domestic environmental institutions,[81] experienced peaks or significant rises. The Rio Declaration conveys this trend through the formulation of several environmental principles, the 'environment set', some of which go beyond the programme outlined in the Stockholm Declaration.[82] As I noted earlier, these principles are themselves more specific expressions of the overarching principles of prevention (Principle 2) and integration of prevention within other policies (Principle 4). In some cases, these expressions can be seen as autonomous norms operating at the international level. As will be discussed in this commentary, the prevention principle is widely understood to be expressed by the duties of cooperation (Principles 18 and 19), the requirement to conduct an environmental impact assessment (Principle 17), increasingly involving the public (Principle 10), and the duty or at least the entitlement to follow a precautionary approach when scientific information is not sufficient to understand the risks of certain activities (Principle 15). In other cases, such expression is more accurately seen as an exhortation to adopt measures on questions such as unsustainable patterns of production and consumption or demographic policies (Principle 8), liability for environmental harm (Principle 13), prevention of environmental harm in armed conflict (Principle 24), or, more generally, legislating on other environmental problems (Principle 11), or as parameters guiding the adoption of such policies, such as the cost-internalization required by the polluter-pays principle (Principle 16). Importantly, although some of these principles and policies explicitly allow for differentiation (Principles 11, 15, and to a lesser extent 2), most of them set a general environmental standard applicable to all States. Of course, as will be discussed in the relevant chapters, differential and developmental considerations are often implicit in the wording of some environmental principles, but the clear focus on environmental protection and the scope of the environment set highlight the significance of the Rio Declaration for international environmental law.

The second trend originated in the 1960s with the decolonization process and the struggle of developing and newly independent countries to reshape the international legal order to reflect their own needs. As noted by Michel Virally, one of the pioneers of what came to be known as the international law of development:

> [i]t is only when, through decolonisation, a multitude of new actors breaks into the international sphere, all coming from the poorest and less economically advanced regions, that a new disequilibrium will become significant. It will now be a disequilibrium between the industrialised or developed world (capitalist or socialist), and those who will be called the Third World.[83]

The article from which this paragraph is excerpted is illuminating because it anticipates with remarkable accuracy the areas of international law that will be most affected by

[80] UNEP, *Global Environment Outlook 5. Environment for the Future We Want* (2012), ch 17, 464 and 466.
[81] Selin and Linner, 'The Quest for Global Sustainability', 35–6.
[82] See the discussion of A. Kiss' model in section II) 2 of this chapter.
[83] Virally, M., 'Où en est le droit international du développement?' (1975) *Revue juridique et politique: Indépendance et coopération* 279, 282 (translation).

the growing developmental concerns. Interestingly, Virally saw the international law of development not as a separate 'branch' of international law but as a 'perspective' that concerned all States (not only developing States) and would necessarily influence most, if not all, branches of international law.[84] This observation is particularly important for present purposes. In the preceding paragraph I referred to a number of environmental principles that, together, provide some 'branch' identity to the array of norms, treaties, and legally-linked treaties that we call international environmental law. As with any other branch, international environmental law could hardly remain indifferent to the development perspective. It is therefore unsurprising to find references to development in some environmental principles or, perhaps more tellingly, to find such references in addition to both a 'differentiation' and a more clearly 'development' set of principles. But there is more. Much in the same way as the law of development, the law of environmental protection operates both as a 'branch' and as a 'perspective', penetrating all areas of international law, from human rights, to humanitarian law, to international trade or investment law, to name a few. Thus, behind the term 'sustainable development law', there is in fact a highly complex array of norms, treaties, and legally-linked treaties that share very little in common except for the fact that they are influenced by both the developmental and environmental 'perspectives'. To understand the significance of the Rio Declaration with respect to this complex question, it is therefore important to use conceptual categories capable of capturing this linguistic and legal sedimentation.

What I called the 'development set' consists of principles and policies intended to (i) preserve and renew the law of economic and social development as a 'branch' (Principles 3, 8, 9, and 12), (ii) adjust or influence international environmental law and other branches of international law, either directly or through its combination with environmental law (Principles 1, 2, 14, 20, 21, 22, and 23). The influence of development law as a perspective on international environmental law as a branch is mediated by an important set of principles, which I have called the 'differentiation set'. This set has, in fact, a wider scope, as it may drive also the influence of both development and environmental law as 'perspectives' on branches such as trade law, investment law, the law of the sea, and others. However, in the context of the Rio Declaration, Principles 6, 7, and 9 are intended to highlight the special situation of development countries (Principle 6), and thereafter distribute the burden (Principle 7) of environmental protection measures and the related means to accomplish it (Principle 9). The significance of the Rio Declaration lies in the statement of these general differentiation principles, particularly of Principle 7. The main shortcoming of the differentiation set is the lack of a stand-alone reference (a principle) to the provision of financial resources, despite the critical importance of this issue for differentiation purposes.

The two trends identified and their articulation through differentiation are expressed, in a condensed but legally meaningful manner, by the prevention principle formulated in Principle 2. In its contemporary understanding, the prevention principle highlights both the use of a State's own natural resources and the prevention of environmental harm per se. It articulates the two building blocks of the development and environment sets, namely right to development (Principle 3) and the need

[84] Virally, 'Où en est le droit international du développement?', 279–80.

to integrate environmental—ie prevention—considerations in development policies (Principle 4). The differentiation dimension was introduced in Principle 2 through the addition 'and developmental policies' to the wording of the original Stockholm Principle 21. The co-chair of the contact group that negotiated this wording wrote in this regard that '[t]he addition reflects the recognition that development must not be constrained by the generalized rules of international law for the environment'.[85] All in all, the so-called 'Stockholm Principle' and perhaps even more the Rio formulation can be seen as the legal cornerstone of international environmental law as adjusted by development considerations.

## IV) The Principles and their Impact

### 1. Methodology

Any attempt at assessing the impact of the Rio Declaration must clarify what is being assessed and how the assessment is carried out. The chapters of this commentary assess the 'normative impact' and, when applicable, the 'jurisprudential relevance' of each principle brought under the umbrella of the Rio Declaration.

'Normative impact' is understood as the influence of a principle in the drafting of subsequent instruments, mostly treaties but also soft-law instruments, including codification works conducted by bodies such as the International Law Commission ('ILC'),[86] the Institut de Droit International ('IDI')[87] or the International Law Association ('ILA').[88] This is the approach that has been followed in some previous efforts at assessing the impact of the Rio Declaration, whether by the Commission on Sustainable Development ('CSD'),[89] the UN Secretary-General[90] or the UN Division for Economic and Social Affairs.[91] However, two important caveats must be added. First, one must not always identify a 'principle' with a given formulation either in the Rio Declaration or in another instrument. Principles such as no-harm, prevention, notification in case of emergency, cooperation on shared resources, or peaceful settlement of disputes, to name but a few, existed prior to the Rio Declaration itself and found expression in a variety of instruments, sometimes explicitly (eg in a treaty provision) and other times implicitly (eg when the architecture of the entire treaty or of an identifiable part of it is based on the principle). In these cases, the assessment concerns

[85] Sanwal, 'Sustainable Development', 49.

[86] International Law Commission, Draft articles on the prevention of transboundary harm from hazardous activities (2001), *GAOR A/56/10* ('ILC Prevention Articles').

[87] Institut de Droit International, Resolution on 'Environment' (Rapporteur L. Ferrari Bravo) ('IDI—Environment'), Resolution on 'Responsibility and Liability under International Law for Environmental Damage' (Rapporteur F. Orrego Vicuña) ('IDI—Responsibility'), Resolution on 'Procedures for the Adoption and Implementation of Rules in the Field of Environment' (Rapporteur F. Paolillo) ('IDI—Procedures'), all adopted at the Strasbourg Session (1997).

[88] International Law Association, 'New Delhi Declaration of Principles of International Law Relating to Sustainable Development', 2 April 2002 ('New Delhi Declaration'). This declaration was followed by an instrument adopted by the ILA Committee on International Law on Sustainable Development, Resolution no 7/2012, Annex: '2012 Sofia Guiding Statements on the Judicial Elaboration of the 2002 New Delhi Declaration of Principles of International Law Relating to Sustainable Development'.

[89] Report-principles, 26–28 September 1995 (this report must be seen as an attempt at codification but it also surveys, when appropriate, the impact of the Rio Principles in the three years following its adoption).

[90] UNSG Report, 10 February 1997, UN Doc E/CN.17/1997/8.

[91] UNDESA Report, *Review of implementation of Agenda 21 and the Rio Principles*, December 2011.

the impact of an existing principle and may concern instruments adopted before the Rio Declaration or which express the principle without taking up the specific formulation of the Declaration. They are nevertheless integrated in the assessment because, as noted earlier in this chapter, the Rio Declaration is viewed as a synthesis of principles, including some that pre-existed its adoption. The second caveat concerns the theoretical foundation of assessing the 'normative impact' of the principles expressed by the Rio Declaration. From the perspective of the 'functions' that a principle may perform, a very important one lies in its ability to shape a norm, a treaty (or an identifiable part of it), or a legally linked set of treaties. In this regard, assessing the 'normative impact' of a principle amounts to assessing the extent to which it has performed an architectural function in international law.

The large majority of chapters also assess the 'jurisprudential relevance' of the principles gathered in the Rio Declaration. The caveats above also apply *mutatis mutandis* to this assessment. There are indeed cases that do not refer explicitly to the Rio Declaration, and yet, they concern a variation (typically derived from treaty law) of a principle included in the Rio Declaration. The assessment of jurisprudential 'relevance' must therefore not be equated with one of 'impact' of the Rio Declaration as an instrument but rather as an attempt at understanding how the many principles brought under the umbrella of the declaration may operate in a jurisprudential context. From a theoretical standpoint, two main functions of these principles are being assessed in this context, namely an 'interpretive' and a 'decision-making' function. The interpretive function of a principle may aim to clarify a norm,[92] or to update its content[93] or to conciliate competing norms or the values underpinning them.[94] The decision-making function refers to the operation of a norm as a primary rule of obligation defining a conduct, which can be used to decide a case.[95]

In the following section, I briefly discuss each principle identifying its substantive centre of gravity as well as some concrete legal manifestations from the perspective of 'architectural', 'interpretive', or 'decision-making' functions. Much more detailed analysis is of course provided in the chapters of this volume. My main goal here is simply to summarize the main findings of the substantial research effort conducted by the contributors to this commentary and thereby to highlight the approach that we have all followed, namely to bring the principles gathered in the Rio Declaration down to earth by clarifying their strictly legal manifestations. Although, analytically, it would have been more elegant to organize the discussion following the five clusters of the model identified in the previous section ('backbone', 'environment set', 'development set', 'differentiation

[92] See eg *Responsibilities and Obligations of States sponsoring Persons and Entities with respect to Activities in the Area*, Case no 17, ITLOS (Seabed Dispute Chamber), Advisory Opinion of 1 February 2011 ('Advisory Opinion on the Area'), paras 110–16.

[93] *Award in the Arbitration regarding the Iron Rhine ('Ijzeren Rijn') Railway between the Kingdom of Belgium and the Kingdom of the Netherlands*, 27 RIAA (2005) 35, paras 58–9; *Shrimp-turtle*, Appellate body, paras 129–31, 152–3; Indus Waters Kishenganga (partial award), para 452.

[94] See eg *S.D. Myers Inc. v. Canada, NAFTA Arbitration* (UNCITRAL Rules), Partial Award (13 November 2000), para 247.

[95] *Trail Smelter*, RIAA III 1905–1982 ('Trail Smelter'), 1965. *Corfu Channel* case, Judgment of 9 April 1949, ICJ Reports 1949, 22 ('*Corfu Channel* case'), 22. (although this case does not concern environmental matters, the ICJ has equated the prevention principle applied in it with the modern prevention principle, see *Pulp Mills on the River Uruguay (Argentina v. Uruguay)*, Judgment, ICJ Reports 2010, 14 ('*Pulp Mills*'), para 101).

set', 'avoiding conflict'), I preferred to follow a more reader-friendly approach in this part of the presentation, discussing each principle according to the order of appearance in the text of the Rio Declaration. This choice responds to the spirit of this commentary, which is not only to highlight the historical importance of the Rio Declaration as an umbrella bringing together a set of key principles but also to give the latter greater purchase in everyday legal practice.

## 2. The principles enshrined in the Rio Declaration

### *2.1. Principle 1: Human beings and the environment*

Principle 1 of the Rio Declaration takes a clearly anthropocentric stance structuring efforts towards sustainable development around human beings:

> [h]uman beings are at the centre of concerns for sustainable development. They are entitled to a healthy and productive life in harmony with nature.

The core element of this principle concerns therefore the relations between environmental protection and human welfare. As noted in the chapter by F. Francioni in this commentary, when compared to the more decidedly human rights-oriented Principle 1 of the Stockholm Declaration,[96] the formulation of Principle 1 of the Rio Declaration appears as a regression. Out of the possible legal expressions of this principle, it is true that the recognition of a human right to an environment of a certain quality is still controversial at the international level. Aside from two regional treaties, the African Charter of Human and Peoples' Rights[97] and the San Salvador Protocol to the American Convention on Human Rights,[98] and the more recent ASEAN Declaration on Human Rights,[99] this right has not been expressly formulated or recognized in major human rights instruments.

However, the environmental components of general human rights have been increasingly recognized since the 1990s both at the regional[100] and the global[101] levels, both from

[96] 'Declaration of the United Nations Conference on the Human Environment', Stockholm, 16 June 1972, UN Doc A/CONF 48/14/Rev.1, 2ff. Principle 1 stated: 'Man has the fundamental right to freedom, equality and adequate conditions of life, in an environment of a quality that permits a life of dignity and well-being, and he bears a solemn responsibility to protect and improve the environment for present and future generations. In this respect, policies promoting or perpetuating apartheid, racial segregation, discrimination, colonial and other forms of oppression and foreign domination stand condemned and must be eliminated.'

[97] African Charter on Human and Peoples' Rights, 27 June 1981, (1982) 21 ILM 58, art 24. This provision was discussed in *Social and Economic Rights Action Center (SERAC) and others v. Nigeria*, African Commission Application no 155/96 (2001–2002) ('*Ogoni* case'), para 52.

[98] Additional Protocol to the American Convention on Human Rights in the Area of Economic, Social and Cultural Rights, 16 November 1988, OAS Treaty Series no 69, art 11(1). This provision, which is considered not to be directly justiciable, has been used for interpretation purposes. See *Kawas-Fernandez v. Honduras*, ICtHR Series C no 196, Judgment (merits, reparation and costs) (3 April 2009), para 148.

[99] ASEAN Human Rights Declaration, 19 November 2012, art 28(f), available at: <http://www.asean.org>.

[100] In the European context, the leading case was *Lopez Ostra v. Spain*, ECtHR Application no 16798/90, Judgment (9 December 1994), and a good retrospective of the case law appears in *Tatar v. Romania*, ECtHR Application no 67021/01, Judgment (6 July 2009), paras 85–8 (in French). In the Inter-American context the leading case was *Mayagna (Sumo) Awas Tingni Community v. Nicaragua*, ICtHR Series C no 79, Judgment (31 August 2001) ('*Awas Tingi* case') and a good retrospective of the case law is provided in *Indigenous People Kichwa of Sarayaku v. Ecuador*, ICtHR Series C no 245, Judgment (merits and compensation) (27 June 2012), paras 145–7 and 159–68 ('*Sarayaku* case').

[101] See eg *Kitok v. Sweden*, HRC Complaint 197/1985 (27 July 1988); *Bernard Ominayak and the Lubicon Lake Band v. Canada*, HRC Complaint no 167/1984 (26 March 1990); *Ilmari Länsman et al v. Finland*,

a substantive and procedural perspective (see Principle 10). Moreover, at the domestic level, a growing number of constitutions refer to a human right to an environment of a certain quality.[102] Although, as noted by Francioni, human rights approaches to environmental protection are inherently limited by the need to establish a link between environmental degradation and an impairment of a human right, Principle 1 highlights the important relationship between environmental protection and the respect for human rights and, in this regard, it brings into the Rio Declaration these important legal developments.

## *2.2. Principle 2: Prevention*

As mentioned earlier in this introduction, the prevention principle is in many ways the foundational principle of the Rio Declaration. It not only affirms, by its very wording, the continuity with the Stockholm Declaration (Principle 21 was almost identically phrased) but it also connects, within the backbone of the Rio Declaration, the development and environment sets. This is clear from the wording of Principle 2, according to which:

> States have, in accordance with the Charter of the United Nations and the principles of international law, the sovereign right to exploit their own resources pursuant to their own environmental and developmental policies, and the responsibility to ensure that activities within their jurisdiction or control do not cause damage to the environment of other States or of areas beyond the limits of national jurisdiction.

Thus stated, the prevention principle has three main components, which are analysed in detail in the chapter by L.-A. Duvic-Paoli and myself, namely (i) sovereignty over natural resources, (ii) prevention of transboundary environmental harm, and (iii) prevention of environmental harm beyond national jurisdiction. The 'sovereignty' dimension links the principle to the right to development stated in Principle 3 of the Rio Declaration, as well as to what I have called the 'development set', whereas the 'prevention' dimension brings together the intergenerational equity aspect of Principle 3 and the integration principle stated in Principle 4 and, thereby, what I have called the 'environment set'. The prevention dimension is increasingly understood as a duty of due diligence with respect to the environment, irrespective of its location, including purely domestic activities.

The prevention principle has had wide influence on the architecture of environmental treaties, whether it is expressly referred to[103] or not,[104] as well as on codification efforts undertaken

HRC Complaint no 511/1992 (8 November 1995); *Jouni E. Länsman et al v. Finland*, HRC Complaint no 671/1995 (30 October 1996); *Apirana Mahuika et al v. New Zealand*, HRC Complaint no 547/93 (27 October 2000); *Diergaardt v. Namibie*, HRC Complaint no 760/1997 (6 September 2000); *Brun v. France*, HRC Complaint no 1453/2006 (18 October 2006); *Poma Poma v. Pérou*, HRC Complaint no 1457/2006 (27 March 2009).

[102] See Shelton, D., 'Substantive Rights', in Fitzmaurice, M., Ong, D., and Merkouris, P. (eds), *Research Handbook on International Environmental Law* (Edward Elgar 2010), 265, 267 (most constitutions adopted after 1992 provide for a right to an environment of a certain quality).

[103] See eg Convention on Long-Range Transboundary Air Pollution, 13 November 1979, 1302 UNTS 217 ('LRTAP Convention'), preamble; United Nations Convention on the Law of the Sea, 10 December 1982, 1833 UNTS 397 ('UNCLOS'), art 194(2); UNFCCC, preamble, para 8; CBD, art 3; UNCCD, preamble, para 15; Stockholm Convention on Persistent Organic Pollutants, 22 May 2001, (2001) 40 ILM 532 ('POP Convention'), preamble, para 10.

[104] Prevention provides the architectural basis of many instruments, including International Convention for the Prevention of Pollution from Ships, 17 February 1973, as modified by the Protocol of 1978 relating thereto, UNTS 1340 I-22484 ('MARPOL 73/78'); Convention on International Trade in Endangered Species of Wild Fauna and Flora, 3 March 1973, 983 UNTS 243 ('CITES'); Convention on Environmental Impact Assessment in a Transboundary Context, 25 February 1991, 1989 UNTS 310 ('Espoo Convention').

by the CSD,[105] the IDI,[106] the ILC[107] and the ILA.[108] It has also played a significant interpretive and decision-making function in international jurisprudence, particularly in cases such as the *Trail Smelter* Arbitration,[109] the ICJ's Advisory Opinion on the *Legality of Nuclear Weapons*[110] or its judgments in the cases relating to the *Gabčíkovo-Nagymaros Projet*[111] and the *Pulp Mills over the River Uruguay*,[112] or the Advisory Opinion of the ITLOS' Seabed Chamber on the *Responsibilities and Obligations of States sponsoring Persons and Entities with respect to Activities in the Area*.[113]

## 2.3. *Principle 3: From a right to development to intergenerational equity*

At the heart of Principle 3 of the Rio Declaration lies a tension between the right to development and the needs of future generations. Principle 3 combines these two components by stating that:

> [t]he right to development must be fulfilled so as to equitably meet developmental and environmental needs of present and future generations.

As noted in the chapter by C. Molinari, over time the gravity centre has shifted from the first to the second component. At the time of the adoption of the Rio Declaration, the wording of Principle 3 was perceived as a success of developing countries in having their right to development expressly recognized. Developed countries managed however to introduce a reference to the rights of future generations in order to stress that the right to development was not without limitations.

In retrospective, the second component has received a clearer legal expression than the first, from the perspective of both its architectural function as well as its interpretive and to some extent decision-making functions. Indeed, aside from the significant number of treaties referring to the need to take into account future generations,[114] at the 2012 Rio Summit renewed impetus was given to the idea of institutionalizing intergenerational equity in some form, as analysed in a report by the UN Secretary-General discussing different options.[115] From a judicial standpoint, intergenerational equity has been taken into account as one aspect in the assessment of the international legality of nuclear weapons[116] as well as in domestic procedures for the granting of permits.[117] Significantly, in one case it served as the basis for extending the scope of *jus standi* to future generations.[118]

[105] See Report-principles, 26–28 September 1995, paras 51–69.
[106] See IDI—Environment, art 6; IDI—Responsibility, art 3.
[107] See ILC Prevention Articles, (2001), *GAOR A/56/10*.
[108] See New Delhi Declaration, art 1(1).
[109] See *Trail Smelter*, 1965.
[110] *Legality of the Threat or Use of Nuclear Weapons*, ICJ Reports 1996, 226, para 29.
[111] *Gabčíkovo-Nagymaros Project (Hungary/Slovakia)*, ICJ Reports 1997, 7, para 140.
[112] *Pulp Mills*, paras 101 and 185.
[113] Advisory Opinion on the Area, paras 115–20.
[114] See eg International Convention for the Regulation of Whaling, 2 December 1946, 161 UNTS 361 ('Whaling Convention'), Preamble, first recital; Convention Concerning the Protection of the World Cultural and Natural Heritage, 16 November 1972, 1037 UNTS 151 ('WHC'), art 4; UNFCCC, art 3(1).
[115] See UN Secretary-General, *Intergenerational Solidarity and the Needs of Future Generations. Report of the Secretary-General*, 15 August 2013, UN Doc A/68/322 ('UNSG Report').
[116] *Legality of the Threat or Use of Nuclear Weapons*, para 36.
[117] *State of Himachal Pradesh and others v. Ganesh Wood Products and others*, 1995 (6) SCC 363, cited in Ramlogan, R., *Sustainable Development: Towards a Judicial Interpretation* (Martinus Nijhoff 2011) 226.
[118] *Minors Oposa v. Secretary of the Department of Environment and Natural Resources* (DENR) (1994) 33 ILM 173 (30 July 1993) ('*Minors Oposa* case'), 185. See however *E.H.P. v. Canada*, HRC Complaint no.

Despite this noticeable shift, which reflects the increasing influence of international environmental law on legal categories, the policy process is moving into the direction of giving more and more importance to development considerations under the malleable banner of sustainable development.[119]

## 2.4. *Principle 4: Sustainable development through integration*

Principle 4 formulates the main expression of the concept of sustainable development in the Rio Declaration, namely the requirement of integration:

> In order to achieve sustainable development, environmental protection shall constitute an integral part of the development process and cannot be considered in isolation from it.

Because of its plasticity, sustainable development pervades the Rio Declaration, often taking more developmental than sustainable forms. However, Principle 4 states a strongly environmental dimension of development policies. It is, indeed, possible to assess whether a policy has taken into account environmental protection or not, although it is much more difficult to define what would be the proper degree of integration.

The principle of integration has been very influential on treaty practice. In their chapter in this commentary, V. Barral and P.-M. Dupuy trace this impact at two levels. First, numerous treaties dealing with areas and questions apparently unrelated to the environment have integrated environmental considerations. Major examples of integration *avant la lettre* (prompted by the Stockholm Conference) or post Rio include articles 35(3) and 55 of the 1977 Protocol I to the 1949 Geneva Conventions,[120] Part XII of the UNCLOS,[121] and a variety of references to the environment in treaties concerning trade and investment, including the preamble of the Marrakesh Agreement on the World Trade Organization.[122] One can view such integration as a legal expression of environmental law as a 'perspective' influencing international law as a whole and not merely a 'branch' of it. Second, integration has been explicitly referred to in a number of environmental treaties, particularly in connection with the use of the relevant resources. Examples include the UNFCCC,[123] the CBD[124] or the UNCCD.[125]

The principle of integration has also been influential in judicial practice, mostly performing an interpretive function to take into account environmental considerations in treaties that did not explicitly referred to them. Major illustrations include the ICJ's decision in the cases concerning the *Gabčíkovo-Nagymaros Project*[126] or the *Pulp Mills over the River Uruguay*,[127] the decision of the WTO Appellate Body in the *Shrimp-Turtle* case,[128]

67/1980 (27 October 1982), para 8(a), where the reference to future generations was seen as a mere 'expression of concern'.

[119] See section I) 2 of this chapter.

[120] Protocol Additional to the Geneva Conventions of 12 August 1949, and Relating to the Protection of Victims of International Armed Conflicts, 6 August 1977, 1125 UNTS 3 ('Protocol I').

[121] UNCLOS, art 194(2).

[122] Agreement establishing the World Trade Organization, 15 April 1994, 1867 UNTS 154. See also Gordon, K. and Pohl, J., 'Environmental Concerns in International Investment Agreements: a survey' (2011) *OECD Working Papers on International Investment* no 2011/1.

[123] UNFCCC, art 3(4) (displaying a sort of reverse integration of development considerations).

[124] CBD, art 6(b). [125] UNCCD, art 4(2)(a).

[126] *Gabčíkovo-Nagymaros Project*, paras 140–1. [127] *Pulp Mills*, paras 76–7.

[128] *United States—Import Prohibition of certain Shrimp and Shrimp Products*, WT/DS58/AB/R, 1998 ('*Shrimp-Turtle*'), paras 129–31, 152–3.

or the awards of the tribunals constituted to hear the *Iron-Rhine* case[129] and the *Indus Waters Kishenganga* case.[130]

## 2.5. Principle 5: Poverty eradication

At the 1972 Stockholm Conference, Indira Gandhi, then Prime Minister of India, famously noted that 'poverty is the worst form of pollution'.[131] Principle 5 of the Rio Declaration stated this priority in clear terms:

> All States and all people shall cooperate in the essential task of eradicating poverty as an indispensable requirement for sustainable development, in order to decrease the disparities in standards of living and better meet the needs of the majority of the people of the world.

The chapter by C. Golay and T. Karimova in this volume addresses this eminently developmental principle, which confirms the anthropocentric approach stated at the beginning of the declaration's 'backbone' in Principle 2. Principle 5 places the eradication of poverty as a step in the process of reducing the disparities in the standards of living. These goals or, more precisely, the priority of poverty eradication within the overall goal of reducing disparities is to be achieved through cooperation at all levels. Cooperation appears in several principles of the Rio Declaration in more (Principles 18 and 19) or less (Principles 5, 7, and 27) specific forms.

Despite the broad formulation of Principle 5, as noted by Golay and Karimova, the goal pursued is deeply rooted in human rights law.[132] Of particular relevance in this regard is the International Covenant on Economic, Social and Cultural Rights ('ICESCR'),[133] which in several provisions, particularly article 11, gives legal grounding to the goal pursued by Principle 5, through the recognition of the rights to food,[134] housing,[135] and water/sanitation.[136] Such grounding provides some room for future judicial or quasi-judicial practice, particularly after the entry into force of the Optional Protocol to the ICESCR in May 2013.[137]

The focus on poverty eradication expressed by Principle 5 has been very influential in the policy processes after Rio. Three major reaffirmations of this priority are found in the 2000 MDGs, particularly in MDG 1 aimed at halving extreme poverty and hunger by 2015, the 'Political

[129] *Iron-Rhine*, paras 58–9, 220–34.

[130] *Kishenganga Arbitration*, para 452.

[131] This is referred to by M. Strong, cited in UNEP, Global Environment Outlook 3 (2002), chapter 1, available at: <http://www.unep.org/geo/geo3/english/038.htm> (accessed 1 May 2014).

[132] They refer in this regard to the Statement on Poverty and the International Covenant on Economic, Social and Cultural Rights, UN Doc E/2002/22 -E/C.12/2001/17, 10 May 2001; See also for example, UNGA Resolution 55/106 of 4 December 2000 on Human Rights and Extreme Poverty and Commission on Human Rights resolution 2001/31 of 23 April 2001 on the same subject matter.

[133] International Covenant on Economic, Social and Cultural Rights, 16 December 1966, 993 UNTS 3 ('ICESCR').

[134] Committee on Economic, Social and Cultural Rights (Committee), *General Comment 12: The right to adequate food (Art 11)*, UN Doc E/C.12/1999/5, 12 May 1999.

[135] Committee, *General Comment 4: The right to adequate housing (Art. 11 (1) of the Covenant), (Sixth session, 1991)*, UN Doc E/1992/23, 13 December 1991.

[136] Committee, *General Comment N° 15 (2002): The right to water (arts 11 and 12 of the International Covenant on Economic, Social and Cultural Rights)*, UN Doc E/C.12/2002/11, 20 January 2003. Committee, *Statement on the right to sanitation*, UN Doc E/C.12/2010/1 18 March 2011.

[137] The Optional Protocol was adopted as a UNGA Resolution A/RES/63/117, 10 December 2008, entered into force 5 May 2013.

Declaration' issued after the 2002 WSSD,[138] and, more recently, the Outcome document of the 2012 Rio Summit. According to the latter 'poverty eradication is the greatest global challenge facing the world today and an indispensable requirement for sustainable development'.[139] Poverty eradication is expected to be a major priority of the SDGs that are currently being discussed and which will complement the MDGs as part of the post 2015 agenda.

## 2.6. *Principle 6: Special situation of developing countries*

Principle 6 states the general need for differentiation and, within it, the specific needs of developing countries:

> The special situation and needs of developing countries, particularly the least developed and those most environmentally vulnerable, shall be given special priority. International actions in the field of environment and development should also address the interests and needs of all countries.

The negotiation of this principle only raised controversy on the question of whether countries in a transition to a market economy were to be expressly mentioned or not.

This discussion concerned the first core element of Principle 6, namely the parameters of differentiation. Indeed, there was consensus (i) on the need to recognize the special needs of developing countries, and (ii) on the particular situation of 'less developed' and 'environmentally vulnerable' countries. As noted by M. Hébié in his chapter in this volume, the need to prioritize (the first sentence of Principle 6) is formulated in mandatory terms ('shall') requiring some degree of differentiation to take into account the special needs of developing countries. General differentiation has had significant normative impact, influencing the architecture of treaties as important as the UNCLOS,[140] the Montreal Protocol,[141] the CBD and its Biosafety Protocol,[142] the UNFCCC and its Kyoto Protocol,[143] or the Stockholm Convention on Persistent Organic Pollutants ('POP Convention').[144] General differentiation has also been reasserted in soft-law instruments, including the Programme of Action for the Sustainable Development of Small Island Developing States ('Barbados Programme of Action'),[145] the Mauritius Strategy for the Further Implementation of the Barbados Programme[146] or the Programme of Action for the Least Developed Countries 2011–2020 ('Istanbul Programme of Action'),[147] to name but a few.

The second core element of Principle 6 is less specific. It also responds to the key controversy, namely the place of countries in transition within the general differentiation framework. The reference to 'the interests and needs of all countries' was a compromise achieved through the intervention of PrepCom chairman, Tommy Koh,

[138] 'Political Declaration', paras 3, 7, and 11.

[139] *The Future We Want*, para 2.

[140] UNCLOS; see particularly Part IX.

[141] Montreal Protocol on Substances that Deplete the Ozone Layer, 16 September 1987, 1522 UNTS 29 ('Montreal Protocol'), see particularly art 5.

[142] Biosafety Protocol, preamble, para 8.

[143] Kyoto Protocol, arts 3 and 10.

[144] POP Convention, art 4(7).

[145] 'Programme of Action for the Sustainable Development of Small Island Developing States', UN Doc A/CONF.167/9, October 1994.

[146] 'Mauritius Strategy for the Further Implementation of the Programme of Action for the Sustainable Development of Small Island Developing States', UN Doc A/60/401, 3 October 2005.

[147] 'Programme of Action for the Least Developed Countries 2011–2020', UN Doc A/CONF.219/7, 13 May 2011.

to overcome the opposition of developing countries and countries in transition. The latter were not expressly mentioned but their needs are clearly encompassed by the wording used.

In both cases, Principle 6 seeks to allocate 'actions in the field of environment and development'. The wording is vague, although it is clearly distributional in nature. There are different objects of distribution according to this broad key, including the priorities of different States (some may focus on development whereas others on environmental protection) but also, and more concretely, the allocation of financial and technical assistance. Financial assistance is only implicitly referred to in the Rio Declaration, whereas technical assistance is addressed in Principle 9. Yet, aside from a differentiation in the nature and extent of obligations, the special situation of developing and other categories of countries has been taken into account through assistance systems, framed as sections of an environmental treaty or more generally called for in the form of official development assistance (eg chapter 33, paragraph 13, of Agenda 21).

## *2.7. Principle 7: Common but differentiated responsibilities*

Principle 7 can be seen, conceptually, as a more specific application of the general principle of differentiation enshrined in Principle 6 and, earlier, in Principle 12 of the Stockholm Declaration. According to Principle 7:

> States shall cooperate in a spirit of global partnership to conserve, protect and restore the health and integrity of the Earth's ecosystem. In view of the different contributions to global environmental degradation, States have common but differentiated responsibilities. The developed countries acknowledge the responsibility that they bear in the international pursuit of sustainable development in view of the pressures their societies place on the global environment and of the technologies and financial resources they command.

There has been a tendency in the literature to overstate the presence of this Principle in international law, blurring the difference between common but differentiated responsibility ('CBDR') and general differentiation. Conceptually, however, CBDR has some specific features which do not overlap entirely with general differentiation, namely (i) it concerns the distribution of the burden of environmental protection, (ii) it focuses on global environmental problems, (iii) the distribution is operated among States, (iv) it focuses on the basis not only of the special needs of developing countries, but also of the different contributions to the problem and the different technological and financial resources available to developed countries.

In this recognizable form, the principle of CBDR has performed an important architectural function in at least four systems of legally linked treaties, namely the Vienna Convention on the Protection of the Ozone Layer and its Montreal Protocol,[148] the UNFCCC and its Kyoto Protocol,[149] the CBD,[150] and the UNCCD.[151] These treaty regimes, particularly those concerning ozone and climate change, are fundamentally shaped by CBDR in their distribution of commitments and assistance. The system established by the Montreal Protocol is more nuanced than the one of the Kyoto Protocol in that, unlike the latter, the former imposes similar substantive obligations

[148] Vienna Convention for the Protection of the Ozone Layer, 22 March 1985, 1513 UNTS 293; Montreal Protocol, art 5.

[149] UNFCCC, arts 3(1) and 4; Kyoto Protocol, arts 3 and 10, and Annex B.

[150] CBD, art 20, particularly para 4.

[151] UNCCD, arts 3(d) and 6.

to both developed and developing (countries operating under article 5) with variations only in the modalities (timeframe) and availability of technical and financial assistance (particularly through the Multilateral Fund created by an amendment to the Protocol). Other more recent treaties, including the POP Convention[152] and the Minamata Convention on Mercury,[153] also refer to the principle of CBDR. These and other examples illustrate what P. Cullet suggests in his chapter in this volume, namely that CBDR has become so pervasive in post-Rio multilateral environmental agreements that one cannot understand contemporary international environmental law without reference to it. At the same time, the rigid expression of CBDR in the Kyoto Protocol and, to a lesser extent, in the UNFCCC is perhaps the major obstacle to the development of an effective international climate change regime. It is noteworthy in this regard that the decision of the Conference of the Parties launching the current negotiation process, the Durban Platform on Enhanced Action,[154] did not refer explicitly to CBDR, although the latter has been reintroduced in the current discussions through a reference to article 3(1) of the UNFCCC.

Regarding the jurisprudential relevance of Principle 7, it can be assessed by reference to a proxy, namely the operation of the general differentiation clauses in treaties such as the UNCLOS or the GATT. Cullet refers, in this regard, to some early disputes before the WTO dispute settlement body concerning 'Governmental Assistance to Economic Development' (article XVIII, particularly section B)[155] or the *Advisory Opinion on the ITLOS Seabed Chamber on the Activities in the Area*.[156] In the latter case, several provisions recognizing the special needs of developing countries in connection with the exploitation of the resources of the Area were examined. Although the Chamber concluded that, as a matter of principle, there is no difference in the rules governing the responsibility of developed and developing States that sponsor such activities (*inter alia* to prevent the development of 'sponsors of convenience'), it acknowledged that some specific regulations may introduce different levels of diligence, particularly with respect to the requirements of the precautionary approach.[157] Thus, differentiation was analysed in a specifically environmental context, in connection with a global resource, and in the light of different capabilities of developed and developing countries. This is a clear application of the 'differentiation set' (Principles 6 and 7) to qualify the operation of the 'environment set' (Principle 15) to take into account developmental concerns. The jurisprudential relevance of CBDR has also been discussed, albeit hypothetically, in connection with the extension of the Emissions Trading Directive to aviation, including to companies from developing countries.[158]

[152] POP Convention, preamble, para 13.

[153] Minamata Convention on Mercury, 10 October 2013, available at: <http://www.mercuryconvention.org> (accessed on 20 April 2014) ('Minamata Convention'), preamble, para 8 and arts 13–14.

[154] 'Establishment of an Ad Hoc Working Group on the Durban Platform for Enhanced Action', Decision 1/CP.17, 15 March 2012, Doc FCCC/CP/2011/9/Add. 1, 2.

[155] *India—Quantitative Restrictions on Imports of Agricultural, Textile and Industrial Products*, Report of the Panel, WTO Doc WT/DS90/R, para 5.155; *European Communities—Conditions for the Granting of Tariff Preferences to Developing Countries*, Report of the Appellate Body, WTO Doc WT/DS246/AB/R (2004), para 175.

[156] *Advisory Opinion on the Area*, paras 110–16.

[157] *Advisory Opinion on the Area*, paras 151–63.

[158] *Air Transport Association of America and Others v. Secretary of State for Energy and Climate Change*, CJEU Case C-366/10 (21 December 2011). On the impact of CBDR on the extension of the ETS scheme to aviation see Scott, J. and Rajamani, L., 'EU Climate Change Unilateralism' (2012) 23 *EJIL* 469.

## 2.8. Principle 8: Sustainable patterns of production and consumption and demographic policies

Perhaps the broadest expression of sustainable development in the Rio Declaration is the call embodied in Principle 8:

> [t]o achieve sustainable development and a higher quality of life for all people, States should reduce and eliminate unsustainable patterns of production and consumption and promote appropriate demographic policies.

This principle has two distinct components, each formulating the concern, respectively, of developing and developed countries.

Developing countries strongly advocated for identifying unsustainable patterns of production and consumption as underlying processes defeating 'sustainable' development. This reference is broader—and less clear—than the principle of integration enshrined in Principle 4. Indeed, the integration of the environmental dimension in developmental policies as an expression of sustainable development is limited in two respects. First, it refers to developmental policies rather than, more broadly, to growth and development or socio-economic prosperity policies, which encompass the policies of developed countries as well. Second, it focuses on adjusting the policies and not, directly, on the processes generating pollution as such. In this context, the first sentence of Principle 8 is much more encompassing. At the same time, it places the 'quality of life' of different peoples as a zero-sum game or, in other words, as a trade-off, implying that the peoples of developing countries cannot attain proper standards of living if the quality of life sustained by the production and consumption patterns in developed countries is not reduced. Not surprisingly, the normative impact of this component of Principle 8 has been selective. As discussed by C. Voigt in her chapter in this commentary, the judgmental aspect of this component has been stripped from the now prevailing concept of sustainable consumption and production ('SCP'), which is itself aimed at decoupling prosperity from environmental degradation.[159] The Plan of Implementation adopted at the 2002 WSSD called for the elaboration of a 10-Year Framework of Programmes ('10YFP').[160] The 10YFP was subsequently developed under the aegis of the so-called 'Marrakech Process' launched in 2003[161] and eventually adopted at the Rio 2012 Summit.[162]

The second component of Principle 8 relates to what developed countries saw as a major area of unsustainability in developing countries, namely population growth. A key

[159] UNEP, *ABC of SCP—Clarifying Concepts on Sustainable Consumption and Production*, 2010, available at: <http://www.uneptie.org/scp/marrakech/pdf/ABC%20of%20SCP%20%20Clarifying%20Concepts%20on%20SCP.pdf>.

[160] 'Plan of Implementation of the World Summit on Sustainable Development', para 14.

[161] See the general presentation of the Marrakech process on the website of the UNEP's Sustainable Production and Consumption Branch: <http://www.unep.fr/scp/marrakech/about.htm#MP> (accessed on 1 May 2014).

[162] The 10 YPF was circulated on the initiative of Brazil for consideration under item 10 of the Agenda of the Rio 2012 Summit. See *Annex to the letter dated 18 June 2012 from the Permanent Representative of Brazil to the United Nations addressed to the Secretary-General of the United Nations Conference on Sustainable Development. A 10-year framework of programmes on sustainable consumption and production patterns*, UN Doc A/CONF.216/5. The 10 YPF was adopted at Rio. See *The Future We Want*, para 226. A Secretariat has been set up to administrate the 10 YPF under the aegis of the UNEP. For an overview of the SCP policies, see UNEP, *Global Outlook on SCP Policies. Taking action together* (2012).

consideration in designing demographic policies is the respect and promotion of human rights, particularly of women's rights. As a follow-up to the UNCED, an International Conference on Population and Development ('ICPD') was held at Cairo, Egypt, in September 1994. The ICPD adopted a Programme of Action.[163] The statement of principles in this programme is formulated using human rights language. Principle 4 of this statement strongly affirms the link between the human rights of women and population policies. Principle 6 restates the contents of Principle 8 of the Rio Declaration. A report published in 2014 reviewed progress with the 1994 Programme finding that, overall, 'achievements over the ensuing 20 years [had] been remarkable'.[164] This report has, again, a very strong human rights focus and calls for the development of stronger accountability mechanisms.[165]

## *2.9. Principle 9: Science and technology*

Principle 9 of the Rio Declaration must be seen as an application of the broader principle of cooperation to matters of science and technology. As noted by S. Maljean-Dubois, this principle is stated in less demanding terms (eg 'should' instead of 'must') than its predecessor in the Stockholm Declaration (Principle 20). According to Principle 9:

> States should cooperate to strengthen endogenous capacity-building for sustainable development by improving scientific understanding through exchanges of scientific and technological knowledge, and by enhancing the development, adaptation, diffusion and transfer of technologies, including new and innovative technologies.

This principle has two main components, both aimed at the same goal, namely to strengthen endogenous capacity-building for sustainable development. The first component relates to scientific cooperation, whereas the second concerns the development and transfer of technologies.

Scientific information is a pre-condition for environmental management and, more generally, for any attempt at integrating environmental considerations into developmental policies. Gathering the relevant data, summarizing it and converting it into information that can be used for policy-making is a complex and costly undertaking. In several cases, such cooperation has taken the form of international bodies or networks that specialize in the information relevant for a specific environmental problem. The most visible example is the Intergovernmental Panel for Climate Change ('IPCC') established in 1988, which has so far elaborated five assessment reports on climate change and several specialized reports on more specific related topics.[166] Another, more recent, example is the creation in 2012 of the Intergovernmental Platform on Biodiversity and Ecosystem Services ('IPBES').[167] But there are many other institutions embodying international

[163] Report of the International Conference on Population and Development, UN Doc A/CONF.171/13/Rev.1, Resolution 1, Annex.

[164] *Framework of actions for the follow-up of the Programme of Action of the International Conference on Population and Development beyond 2014, Report of the Secretary-General*, 12 February 2014, UN Doc a/69/62, Summary.

[165] *Framework of actions for the follow-up of the Programme of Action*, paras 32–46 (placing the issues addressed in the report in a human rights perspective and referring to the chapter on 'Governance' with respect to accountability mechanisms).

[166] The reports are available on the website of the IPCC: <http://www.ipcc.ch> (accessed on 20 April 2014).

[167] See <http://www.ipbes.net> (accessed on 20 April 2014).

cooperation in scientific matters, such as the EMEP which provided the backbone of the LRTAP Convention,[168] the Scientific Council of the Convention on Migratory Species,[169] the Ozone monitoring by the WHO's Global Atmospheric Watch[170] or, more generally, the UNEP-led inter-agency network that prepares the Global Environment Outlook.[171]

The second component focuses on a major distributional question; namely, the development and the transfer of technology. This component emphasizes the differentiation dimension of Principle 9, which recognizes the need for technology sharing in order to enhance the sustainability of the development process of different countries. Although environmental agreements often contain provisions concerning technology transfer,[172] their actual implementation has remained limited so far. One major legal obstacle to technology transfer is the protection afforded to innovation by intellectual property rights ('IPRs'). IPRs are both a major driver of innovation and a significant obstacle to their diffusion. Respect for IPRs, embodied at the international level in treaties such as the TRIPs,[173] the Paris Convention[174] and, increasingly, investment agreements, raises also potential frictions with technology transfer considerations, which, in turn, may lead to international disputes. As noted by Maljean-Dubois, Brazil and India started consultations under the aegis of WTO dispute settlement procedures in connection with the seizure in The Netherlands of generic drugs in transit.[175]

## *2.10. Principle 10: Public participation*

The three pillars of 'environmental democracy' identified in Principle 10 have significantly influenced the interpretation of human rights provisions as well as, more generally, domestic and international legislative practice. Principle 10 focuses on procedural environmental rights:

> Environmental issues are best handled with the participation of all concerned citizens, at the relevant level. At the national level, each individual shall have appropriate access to information concerning the environment that is held by public authorities, including information on hazardous materials and activities in their communities, and the opportunity to participate in decision-making processes. States shall facilitate and encourage public awareness and participation by making information widely available. Effective access to judicial and administrative proceedings, including redress and remedy, shall be provided.

The wording is somewhat convoluted and, except for the explicit assertion that 'each individual shall have appropriate access to information concerning the environment' (access

[168] See LRTAP Convention, art 9.

[169] Convention on the Conservation of Migratory Species of Wild Animals, 23 June 1979, 1651 UNTS 356 ('CMS'), art 8. See <http:www.cms.int/meetings/scientific-council> (accessed on 20 April 2014).

[170] See <http://www.wmo.int/pages/prog/arep/gaw/ozone/> (accessed on 20 April 2014).

[171] See <http://www.unep.org/geo/> (accessed on 20 April 2014).

[172] Montreal Protocol, art 10A; Basel Convention on the Control of Transboundary Movements of Hazardous Wastes and their Disposal, 22 March 1989, 1673 UNTS 57 ('Basel Convention'), art 10; CBD, art 16; UNFCCC, art 4; Kyoto Protocol, art 10.

[173] Agreement on Trade-Related Aspects of Intellectual Property Rights, 15 April 1994, 1869 UNTS 299 ('TRIPs Agreement').

[174] Paris Convention on the Protection of Industrial Property, 18 March 1883 (subsequently amended several times), 828 UNTS 305.

[175] *European Union and a Member State—Seizure of Generic Drugs in Transit*, DS/408 (Complainant: India), DS/409 (Complainant: Brazil).

to environmental information), the other two pillars, namely participation in environmental decision-making and access to justice are not clearly formulated in human rights terms. However, the three components have been well established as human rights in both treaty practice and jurisprudence.

With respect to the architectural function of Principle 10, among the many treaties and soft law instruments discussed in J. Ebbesson's contribution to the present commentary, the clearest and most important expression of the three pillars of environmental democracy is the 1998 Aarhus Convention on Access to Information, Public Participation in Decision-making and Access to Justice in Environmental Matters ('Aarhus Convention').[176] Although this treaty is a regional instrument, concluded under the aegis of the United Nations Economic Commission for Europe, it is open to the ratification of countries from outside this regional group (eg Tajikistan or Turkmenistan)[177] as well as of some regional economic integration organizations (eg the then European Community).[178] Public participation has also been integrated to varying degrees in other post-Rio treaties, including the UNFCCC,[179] the CBD,[180] UNCCD,[181] the PIC Convention,[182] the POP Convention[183] and, more recently, the Minamata Convention.[184] In addition, in 2010 the UNEP adopted *Guidelines for the Development of National Legislation on Access to Information, Public Participation and Access to Justice in Environmental Matters* ('Bali Guidelines').[185]

From the standpoint of its interpretive and decision-making functions, Principle 10 and its subsequent expression in treaty law has had significant jurisprudential relevance. The Compliance Committee established by the Aarhus Convention has already received some 100 complaints for violation of the Convention,[186] the overwhelming majority of which has been brought by civil society organizations. Indeed, unlike most other non-compliance procedures ('NCPs'), the NCP established by the Aarhus Convention can be triggered by the public. Principle 10 has also been expressly referred to in the jurisprudence of human rights courts. The European Court of Human Rights ('ECtHR') has made reference to it in a number of cases[187] in order to interpret the right to private and family life enshrined in article 8 of the European Convention on Human Rights ('ECHR').[188] The Inter-American Court of Human Rights ('ICtHR') has also recognized a procedural dimension to the right to property enshrined in article 21 of the American Convention on Human Rights ('ACHR'),[189] which the Court has interpreted in an environmental light to protect the relation between indigenous and tribal peoples and their traditional lands.[190] The African Commission has also considered that some

[176] Aarhus Convention on Access to Information, Public Participation in Decision-making and Access to Justice in Environmental Matters, 25 June 1998, 2161 UNTS 447 ('Aarhus Convention').
[177] Aarhus Convention, art 19(3). [178] Aarhus Convention, arts 17 and 19(1).
[179] UNFCCC, art 6. [180] CBD, art 14(a). [181] UNCCD, arts 5(d), 16, and 19.
[182] PIC Convention, art 15. [183] POP Convention, art 10.
[184] Minamata Convention, art 18.
[185] UNEP Guidelines for the Development of National Legislation on Access to Information, Public Participation and Access to Justice in Environmental Matters, adopted by the UNEP Governing Council in decision SS.XI/5, 26 February 2010.
[186] The complaints are available at: <http://www.unece.org/env/pp/pubcom.html> (accessed on 20 April 2014).
[187] See eg ECtHR, *Okyay et al v. Turkey*, 36220/97 of 12 July 2005; ECtHR, *Taskin et al v. Turkey*, 46117/99 of 10 November 2004; and ECtHR, *Tătar v. Romania*, 67021/01 of 27 January 2009.
[188] Convention for the Protection of Human Rights and Fundamental Freedoms, 4 November 1950, 213 UNTS 221 ('ECHR').
[189] American Convention on Human Rights, 22 November 1969, 1144 UNTS 123 ('ACHR').
[190] See *Sarayaku* case, paras 145–7 and 159–68 (summarizing the case law since the *Awas Tingni* case).

provisions of the African Charter on Human and Peoples' Rights ('African Charter'),[191] particularly articles 16 (individual right to health) and 24 (collective right to a generally satisfactory environment) have a procedural dimension requiring States to provide sufficient information and participation.[192] These are but some representative illustrations of the major jurisprudential relevance of the participatory components formulated in Principle 10.

## *2.11. Principle 11: Environmental legislation*

The core components constituting Principle 11 are very important for the 'environment set' of principles. They provide, as noted by M. Kunz in her chapter in this commentary, a 'connecting node', ie a sort of crossroads where many other principles intersect. If the principles of the 'environment set' can be seen as condensed environmental policies that are subsequently spelled out in detail in treaty regimes, a logical extension is for such treaties to be effectively implemented at the domestic level. Principle 11 simply recalls such a need and qualifies it by reference to the specific 'context' where environmental legislation intervenes:

> States shall enact effective environmental legislation. Environmental standards, management objectives and priorities should reflect the environmental and developmental context to which they apply. Standards applied by some countries may be inappropriate and of unwarranted economic and social cost to other countries, in particular developing countries.

The two components, the requirement to enact effective environmental legislation, and the contextual qualification, are as pervasive as they are difficult to trace in specific legal instruments.

Regarding the first, one could see the normative impact of the components of Principle 11 in most environmental treaties to the extent that the latter often set parameters and require States to take measures to come or stay within those parameters. The Montreal Protocol, the UNFCCC and its Kyoto Protocol, or the CBD are all based on the idea that States will adopt the policies they see fit to stay within the parameters set by the treaty. Even the more specific requirements imposed by treaties such as the Convention on International Trade in Endangered Species ('CITES')[193] (the system of permits), Basel Convention[194] (the shipment-based prior informed consent procedure) or the PIC Convention (the substance-based prior informed consent procedure)[195] leave significant room for manoeuvre for States to select the domestic legal expressions that appear most appropriate to their context. Broadly speaking, States follow one of three options: (i) adopting a new and specific piece of legislation to implement a treaty; (ii) amending an existing general environmental act or further specifying such instrument through the adoption of regulations; or (iii) not taking any action, on the assumption that the requirements of the treaty are already addressed in existing domestic instruments.

Regarding the jurisprudential relevance of the two components of Principle 11 and, particularly, their ability to perform an interpretive or decision-making function, again, one must distinguish the statement from its content and look at the latter. From this

[191] African Charter on Human and Peoples' Rights, 27 June 1981, (1982) 21 ILM 58 ('African Charter').
[192] See *Ogoni* case, para 53. [193] CITES, arts III–V. [194] Basel Convention, art 6.
[195] PIC Convention, arts 5–6.

perspective, it is possible to see the requirement for 'effective' environmental legislation in the practice of human rights courts in the European, American, and African contexts, which have interpreted provisions such as article 8 of the ECHR (right to private and family life), article 21 of the ACHR (right to property) or articles 16 and 24 of the African Charter (individual right to health and collective right to a generally satisfactory environment) as entailing a positive duty to regulate the activities of third parties that may cause, through their environmental impact, impairments of human rights.[196] At the same time, States enjoy a significant margin of manoeuvre in adjusting their policies to their specific context, which, as noted by Kunz, international law recognizes through concepts such as the 'margin of appreciation doctrine',[197] 'the police powers doctrine',[198] and some general exceptions in trade treaties (eg article XX(a), (b) or (g) of the GATT).[199]

### *2.12. Principle 12: The environment and trade*

Principle 12 states a key concern of developing countries dating back to the Stockholm Conference and brought to the forefront, on the eve of the UNCED, by the trade dispute between Mexico and the United States regarding the incidental killing of dolphins in tuna harvesting by Mexican fishing vessels.[200] 'Green protectionism' (restrictions to imports) or even 'green colonialism' (*de facto* extraterritorial extension of environmental policies) were indeed perceived as 'threats' by developing countries, who saw environmental protection as a potential barrier to the export of their products to developed country markets. Both threats are reflected in the wording of Principle 12:

> States should cooperate to promote a supportive and open international economic system that would lead to economic growth and sustainable development in all countries, to better address the problems of environmental degradation. Trade policy measures for environmental purposes should not constitute a means of arbitrary or unjustifiable discrimination or a disguised restriction on international trade. Unilateral actions to deal with environmental challenges outside the jurisdiction of the importing country should be avoided. Environmental measures addressing transboundary or global environmental problems should, as far as possible, be based on an international consensus.

The first two sentences of Principle 12 target fears of protectionism, whereas the two latter are primarily concerned with extraterritorial environmental regulation. Openness (access), non-discrimination (by reference to the chapeau of article XX of the GATT), and multilateralism (or even more, an international consensus) are re-affirmed as the policies that should shape the interaction between trade and environmental law.

196 See eg *Tatar v. Romania*, paras 85–8; *Sarayaku* case, paras 145–7; *Ogoni* case, paras 52–3.

197 See eg *Turgut v. Turkey*, ECtHR Application no 1411/03, Judgment—Merits (8 July 2008), para 90.

198 See eg *Chemtura Corporation (formerly Crompton Corporation) v. Government of Canada*, UNCITRAL, Award (2 August 2010), para 266.

199 See eg *Shrimp-Turtle* case. To understand the relevance of this case (which rejected the US argument that its measure was justified by art XX), one must recall that the reason why the requirements of the chapeau of art XX were not met concerned the attempt by the US to impose its own environmental policies on third countries. A similar argument has been made in connection with the extension of the ETS Directive to aviation. See Scott and Rajamani, 'EU Climate Change Unilateralism'. According to Scott and Rajamani, such extension does not take sufficiently into account the specific context of developing countries and, therefore, is inconsistent with the principle of CBDR (Principle 7 of the Rio Declaration and art 3 of the UNFCCC).

200 Panel Report, *United States—Restrictions on Imports of Tuna*, DS21/R-39S/155 (3 September 1991), ('*Tuna-Dolphin I*').

The normative impact of Principle 12 has been significant. The approach pursued since 1992 has consisted in playing down the potential for tensions and highlighting the synergies between trade and the environment. The Marrakech Agreement establishing the WTO set the tone for this synergistic view, often called 'mutual supportiveness',[201] by incorporating a reference to sustainable development in its preamble.[202] As noted in the chapter by M. Young in this commentary, another major development influenced by Principle 12 has been the creation of the WTO Committee on Trade and Environment. The Ministerial Declaration setting the CTE's terms of reference explicitly mentions Principle 12 as one of the parameters defining the Committee's mandate.[203] In addition, efforts to keep trade-restrictive environmental policies within strict bounds also found expression in the adoption of the Agreements on Sanitary and Phytosanitary Measures,[204] Technical Obstacles to Trade,[205] and Subsidies and Countervailing Measures.[206] References to the need to conciliate environmental measures and trade also appear in a number of instruments adopted under the aegis of the Rio process or its aftermath, including Agenda 21,[207] the Forest Principles,[208] the UNFCCC,[209] or the Biosafety[210] and ABS Protocols[211] to the CBD.

Regarding the jurisprudential relevance of Principle 12, although it has seldom been referred to explicitly in the case law,[212] its components have featured prominently in disputes concerning trade and the environment. Of particular relevance are the decisions of WTO Panels and the Appellate Body on article XX of the GATT. This body of decisions addresses at the same time questions of protectionism (through the assessment of consistency with the 'chapeau' of article XX) and questions of extraterritoriality (through the assessment of the availability of letters (g), (b), and, more recently, (a) of article XX). As noted by Young in her chapter, unilateral environmental measures have been considered to be consistent with trade disciplines in their design (falling under the exceptions in letters (a), (b) and (g) of article XX) but not in their application (which has been found to breach the requirements of the chapeau[213]). These cases suggest that the 'shoulds' provided for in

[201] See Pavoni, R., 'Mutual Supportiveness as a Principle of Interpretation and Law-Making: A Watershed for the "WTO-and-Competing-Regimes" Debate?' (2010) 21 *EJIL* 649.

[202] Agreement establishing the World Trade Organization, 15 April 1994, 1867 UNTS 154, preamble, para 1.

[203] WTO Ministerial Declaration on Trade and Environment, adopted in Marrakesh on 15 April 1994, see: <http://www.wto.org/english/tratop_e/envir_e/issu5_e.htm> (accessed on 20 April 2014).

[204] Agreement on Sanitary and Phytosanitary Measures, 15 April 1994, 1867 UNTS 493.

[205] Agreement on Technical Barriers to Trade, 15 April 1994, 1868 UNTS 120.

[206] Agreement on Subsidies and Countervailing Measures, 15 April 1994, 1869 UNTS 14.

[207] Report of the United Nations Conference on Environment and Development, A/CONF.151/26/Rev.l (vol l), Resolution 1, Annex 2: Agenda 21 ('Agenda 21'), para 17.118.

[208] Non-Legally Binding Authoritative Statement of Principles for a Global Consensus on the Management, Conservation and Sustainable Development of All Types of Forests (1992) A/CONF.151/26 (vol III) ('Forest Principles'), para 13–14.

[209] UNFCCC, art 3(5).

[210] Biosafety Protocol, preamble.

[211] Nagoya Protocol on access to genetic resources and the fair and equitable sharing of the benefits arising from their utilization to the Convention on Biological Diversity, 29 October 2010, art 4, available at: <http://www.cbd.int/abs/doc/protocol/nagoya-protocol-en.pdf> (accessed on 20 April 2014).

[212] Young notes that Principle 12 has only been explicitly referred to in the Shrimp-Turtle disputes: *Shrimp-Turtle* case, para 168.

[213] See *Shrimp-Turtle* case, especially para 163, 177; *Brazil—Measures Affecting Imports of Retreaded Tyres*, 3 December 2007, AB-2007-4 ('*Brazil-Tyres*'), paras 246, 252; *European Communities—Measures Prohibiting the Importation and Marketing of Seal Products*, 22 May 2014, AB-2014-1/AB-2014-2—Reports of the Appellate Body ('*EC-Seals*'), para 5.316–5.339.

the first and second sentences of Principle 12 may have greater purchase in litigation than those appearing in its third and fourth sentences.

## 2.13. *Principle 13: Liability and compensation*

As other principles of the Rio Declaration, Principle 13 can be seen as a crossroads where several considerations intersect. Its origins can be traced back to Principle 22 of the Stockholm Declaration, dealing with international liability regimes, which was an extension of the prevention principle stated in Principle 21. Principle 13 is also an extension of prevention (Principle 2) but, acknowledging the challenges involved in the development of liability regimes at the international level, it has both domestic and international legal dimensions. As such, it can also be seen as an extension of Principle 11 on environmental legislation and as a preface to Principle 14 concerning the relocation of dangerous activities, a question very present in the minds of delegates, after the Bhopal disaster in India. All these elements find expression in the wording of Principle 13:

> States shall develop national law regarding liability and compensation for the victims of pollution and other environmental damage. States shall also cooperate in an expeditious and more determined manner to develop further international law regarding liability and compensation for adverse effects of environmental damage caused by activities within their jurisdiction or control to areas beyond their jurisdiction.

From a conceptual standpoint, the most meaningful distinction is between domestic and international liability regimes. In both cases, the call in Principle 13 was followed by some normative developments.

Regarding the domestic law component, it can be seen as a pragmatic acknowledgment of the main avenue (either tort or civil liability laws) through which transboundary damage is likely to be compensated. In her chapter in this commentary, M. Fitzmaurice refers to several instruments adopted at the domestic level and focusing on environmental liability, including the 2004 Environmental Liability Directive,[214] the 1980 Comprehensive Environmental Response, Compensation and Liability Act ('CERCLA')[215] or the 1990 Oil Pollution Act ('OPA').[216] None of these pieces of legislation were developed as a result of the renewed call for environmental liability legislation, but they do illustrate the importance attached to this question in domestic law beyond the more general systems of torts and nuisance.

Conversely, the call made in Principle 13 did have some influence on international efforts. Indeed, starting in the 1990s, a number of liability-focused instruments, such as the 1993 Lugano Convention on Environmental Liability,[217] the 1999 Liability Protocol to the Basel Convention,[218] the 2003 Liability Protocol to both the Helsinki Convention and the Industrial Accidents Convention,[219] the 2006 ILC Principles on the allocation of

[214] Directive 2004/35/CE of the European Parliament and of the Council of 21 April 2004 on Environmental Liability with Regard to the Prevention and Remedying of Environmental Damage, L 143/56 EN *Official Journal of the European Union* 30.4.2004.

[215] Comprehensive Environmental Response, Compensation, and Liability Act, 42 U.S.C. §9601 et seq. (1980) ('CERCLA').

[216] Oil Pollution Act of 1990, 33 U.S.C. 2701 note ('OPA').

[217] Convention on Civil Liability for Damage Resulting from Activities Dangerous to the Environment, 21 June 1993, (1993) 32 ILM 1228 (not in force).

[218] Protocol on Liability and Compensation for Damage Resulting from Transboundary Movements of Hazardous Wastes and Their Disposal, 10 December 1999, UN Doc UNEP/CHW.1/WG/1/9/2.

[219] Protocol on Civil Liability and Compensation for Damage Caused by the Transboundary Effects of Industrial Accidents on Transboundary Waters, 21 May 2003, available at: <http://www.unece.org/env/civil-liability/welcome.html> (accessed on 20 April 2014).

loss,[220] and, more recently, the 2010 Nagoya-Kuala Lumpur Supplementary Protocol to the Biosafety Protocol[221] have brought back the question of liability to a field dominated by prevention. Yet, at the time of writing, none of these instruments had entered into force. The failure of these treaties suggests that liability for environmental damage will remain limited to very specific areas, such as oil pollution or nuclear accidents, or, as noted previously, will be channelled through domestic legislation.

## *2.14. Principle 14: Dangerous substances and activities*

The introduction of Principle 14 in the Rio Declaration was influenced by two previous instruments, namely the 1989 Basel Convention and the 1991 Bamako Convention,[222] which responded to cases of relocation of dangerous substances to developing countries for their cheap disposal. This acute North-South problem intervened within the broader context of calls for 'environmental justice' in developed countries and disasters such as the Bhopal tragedy in India. Of course, the debate did not have only an ethical basis. Important economic and health considerations were also involved. Increasingly demanding environmental regulation in developed countries provided indeed an incentive for some dangerous activities to be relocated to less regulated (*de jure* or *de facto*) contexts. In addition, developed countries were concerned about the 'circle of poison' problem, which refers to the presence of chemicals and substances that have been banned in developed countries in food imported from developing countries. The formulation of Principle 14 had to accommodate these different considerations, and it did so in a statement, which is more exhortatory than mandatory:

> States should effectively cooperate to discourage or prevent the relocation and transfer to other States of any activities and substances that cause severe environmental degradation or are found to be harmful to human health.

However, as noted by M. Mbengue in his chapter in this volume, Principle 14 remains the most general statement regarding cooperation with respect to the relocation of dangerous substances and activities. The policy that finds expression in this principle has had significant normative impact as well as some influence in international jurisprudence.

Regarding its normative impact, although the reference to effective cooperation is quite open, in treaty practice such cooperation has taken the form of 'prior informed consent' procedures following the 'shipment-by-shipment' model of the Basel Convention, taken up in article 27 of the 1997 Joint Convention on Radioactive Waste[223] or articles 7–10, 12 of the 2000 Biosafety Protocol, or a 'substance-by-substance' one, based on previous

[220] Draft principles on the allocation of loss in case of transboundary harm from hazardous activities, Text adopted by the International Law Commission at its fifty-eighth session (2006), *Yearbook of the International Law Commission, 2006*, vol II (2). The first preambular clause of the ILC Principles expressly refer to Principles 13 and 16 of the Rio Declaration.

[221] Nagoya-Kuala Lumpur Supplementary Protocol Liability and Redress to the Cartagena Protocol on Biosafety, 15 October 2010, available at: <http://bch.cbd.int/protocol/NKL_text.shtml> (accessed on 20 April 2014).

[222] Bamako Convention on the ban on the Import into Africa and the Control of Transboundary Movement and Management of Hazardous Wastes within Africa, 30 January 1991, 30 ILM 773 ('Bamako Convention').

[223] Joint Convention on the Safety of Spent Fuel Management and on the Safety of Radioactive Waste Management, 29 September 1997, available at: <http://www-ns.iaea.org/conventions/waste-jointconvention.asp> (accessed on 20 April 2014).

soft-law instruments,[224] and which will find expression in the PIC Convention and in article 11 of the Biosafety Protocol. Mbengue also notes that the full expression of Principle 14, which could only be achieved so far in the 'ban' imposed by the Bamako Convention, also underpins the attempted 1995 amendment of the Basel Convention, banning exports of hazardous waste from OECD to non-OECD countries.[225] This amendment has not yet entered into force but it remains an apposite example of how the policy expressed in Principle 14 has found normative expression.

Regarding the jurisprudential relevance of Principle 14, its underlying policy was referred to in a statement of CARICOM Heads of Government opposing the shipments of MOX fuel from the United Kingdom to Japan, through the Caribbean. This statement was referred to by Ireland in its request for provisional measures in the well-known *MOX Plant* case before the ITLOS.[226] Mbengue also refers to other illustrations of the potential relevance of the policy of Principle 14, particularly one paragraph, rather neglected so far by commentators, of the ICJ's Order on Provisional Measures in the *Construction of a Road in Costa Rica Along the San Juan River* (*Nicaragua v. Costa Rica*) where the Court links the prevention principle to the 'plausible' right not to be harmed by the activities of other States.[227] This statement can be extended to Principle 14, which can be seen for this purpose as a manifestation of the prevention principle.

## *2.15. Principle 15: Precaution*

Principle 15 is a major example of how the Rio Declaration contributed to the development of international law. Precaution had already been formulated in previous instruments, particularly in the Bergen Declaration adopted in one of the regional preparatory conferences of the UNCED.[228] The wording of Principle 15 had to be adjusted to take into account different concerns, such as the preference of the United States for the term 'approach' over that of 'principle' and the differential dimension advocated for by developing countries. The less precise wording eventually agreed upon left significant room for interpretation or, less optimistically, for uncertainty over its specific content:

> In order to protect the environment, the precautionary approach shall be widely applied by States according to their capabilities. Where there are threats of serious or irreversible damage, lack of full scientific certainty shall not be used as a reason for postponing cost-effective measures to prevent environmental degradation.

This formulation does not clarify whether States are required to regulate in the absence of full scientific certainty or only authorized to do so. In addition, the trigger ('threats of serious or irreversible damage') remains subject to divergent interpretations. The precautionary approach has also been referred to as a procedural rule shifting the burden of proof from the regulator (who would have to establish an actual risk) to the claimant (who would have to establish the absence of any risk). Despite the uncertainties surrounding

[224] See the 'International Code of Conduct on the Distribution and Use of Pesticides' (1985) and the 'London Guidelines for the Exchange of Information on Chemicals in International Trade' (1987).

[225] Decision III/1, 'Amendment to the Convention', 28 November 1995, UNEP/CHW.3/35.

[226] Ireland's Request for Provisional Measures in the *MOX Plant* case *(Ireland v. United Kingdom),* ITLOS Case no 10, paras 33–43.

[227] *Construction of a Road in Costa Rica Along the San Juan River (Nicaragua v. Costa Rica),* Order on Request presented by Nicaragua for the indication of provisional measures, 13 December 2013, para 19.

[228] Report of the Economic Commission for Europe on the Bergen Conference (8–16 May 1990), A/CONF.151/PC/10, annex I, para 7.

precaution as a legal norm, its normative impact and jurisprudential relevance must not be underestimated.

The normative impact of precaution can be assessed by reference to three main categories of instruments. The first category concerns subsequent resolutions or declarations of principles where precaution has been expressly referred to, including paragraphs 70–4 of the 1995 Report of the CSD's Expert Group,[229] the preamble of the IDI 1997 Resolution on 'Environment' and Principle 13 of its Resolution on 'Responsibility and Liability',[230] article 7 of the ILC 2001 Prevention Articles,[231] or Principle 4 of the ILA 2002 New Delhi Declaration.[232] The second category encompasses a variety of treaties relating to different substantive areas of international law, from freshwater resources,[233] to climate change,[234] to biodiversity,[235] to chemical regulation,[236] which make reference to the precautionary approach. Precaution has played a particular role in the protection of the marine environment, a role sufficiently important to consider it as a third category of instruments. Indeed, several treaties concluded after 1992 have taken precaution as their foundational basis, organizing a detailed regime to protect the marine environment or portions of it on the basis of precaution. These include the London Dumping Convention as restructured by the 1996 London Protocol,[237] the 1992 OSPAR Convention[238] and, to some extent, the 1995 UN Agreement on Straddling Fish Stocks.[239]

Precaution, in its different facets, has also played a significant role in international jurisprudence, although its acceptance has varied from one jurisdiction to another. The precautionary principle has been invoked a number of times before the ICJ. Yet, the only reference to precaution in a majority decision was made in the *Pulp Mills* case, where the Court stated that the precautionary approach may be relevant for interpretive purposes.[240] A similarly restrictive approach has been followed in the case law of WTO panels and of the Appellate Body. Whereas in the *EC-Hormones* case the Appellate Body considered that the precautionary approach had been incorporated in article 5.7 of the SPS Agreement without further pursuing the inquiry,[241] a subsequent panel constituted to hear the *EC-Biotech* case expressly stated that precaution had no customary basis.[242] On the other hand, precaution has been given more room in the opinions of certain ICJ judges, including A. A. Cançado Trindade,[243] the author of the chapter on precaution in the present commentary, as well as by the ITLOS and the ECtHR.[244] In its *Advisory*

[229] Report-principles. [230] Adopted at the Strasbourg Session (1997).

[231] Read in the light of its commentary, para 4. [232] See n 89 in this chapter.

[233] See eg Convention on the Protection and Use of Transboundary Watercourses and International Lakes, 18 March 1992, 1936 UNTS 269 ('Helsinki Convention'), art 2(5)(a).

[234] See eg Montreal Protocol, preamble, para 6; UNFCCC, art 3(3).

[235] See eg CBD, preamble, para 9. [236] See eg POP Convention, preamble, para 8.

[237] Protocol to the Convention on the Prevention of Marine Pollution by Dumping of Wastes and Other Matter, London, 7 November 1996, (1997) 36 ILM 1.

[238] Convention for the Protection of the Marine Environment of the North-East Atlantic, 22 September 1992, 2354 UNTS 67 ('OSPAR Convention')

[239] Fish Stocks Agreement, arts 5(c) and 6. [240] *Pulp Mills*, para 164.

[241] *European Communities—Measures Concerning Meat and Meat Products (Hormones)—Arbitration under Article 21.3(c) of the Dispute Settlement Understanding, Appellate Body* (29 May 1998) DSR 1998:V, WT/DS26/15 and WT/DS26/15,1833 ('*EC– Hormones*'), paras 123–5.

[242] *European Communities—Measures Affecting the Approval and Marketing of Biotech Products*, Panel Report (29 September 2006), WT/DS291/R, WT/DS292/R, WT/DS293/R ('EC—Biotech products'), para 7.88. In taking this view, the panel followed the Appellate Body in *EC—Hormones*, para 124.

[243] *Pulp Mills*, Separate Opinion of Judge Cançado Trindade. [244] *Tatar v. Romania*, para 120.

*Opinion on the Activities in the Area*, the ITLOS Seabed Chamber referred specifically to Principle 15 from the perspective of its interpretive function:

> the precautionary approach has been incorporated into a growing number of international treaties and other instruments, many of which reflect the formulation of Principle 15 of the Rio Declaration. In the view of the Chamber, this has initiated a trend towards making this approach part of customary international law.[245]

Significantly, the Chamber also recognized the differentiated operation of precaution depending on the context of the country applying the approach.[246] Despite the increasing recognition of precaution, so far it has not operated as a governing primary rule of obligation at the international level. For examples of such a function, one must turn to the case law of the Court of Justice of the European Union (formerly European Court of Justice), which has applied the precautionary principle enshrined in the foundational treaties of the EU[247] in several cases.[248]

## 2.16. *Principle 16: The polluter-pays principle*

The polluter-pays principle as enshrined in Principle 16 of the Rio Declaration is envisioned as a parameter that should guide domestic legislation in the apportionment of the costs of pollution. The concerns of developing countries regarding the use of the polluter-pays principle as a constraint on development efforts led to its confinement to the domestic level as well as to a softer ('should endeavour') formulation:

> National authorities should endeavour to promote the internalization of environmental costs and the use of economic instruments, taking into account the approach that the polluter should, in principle, bear the cost of pollution, with due regard to the public interest and without distorting international trade and investment.

The principle has four main components, namely: (i) the internalization of cost as the main target; (ii) the identification of the cost-bearer; (iii) the methods of internalization; and (iv) the overall bounds within which such internalization has to take place.

Although the 'internalization of costs' is intended to prevent pollution and stimulate resource-efficiency, strictly speaking this principle 'allocates' the cost rather than specifically calling for its prevention. The 'cost' to be internalized can be characterized by reference to the economic concept of negative externality. Significantly, unlike other principles such as prevention or precaution, which may be considered to operate only with respect to externalities of a certain degree (significant, serious, irreversible harm), the 'costs' to be internalized under the polluter-pays principle are not qualified by any specific threshold. The second component concerns the identification of the polluter. Depending on the circumstances, it may be difficult to determine whether the producer or the consumer is the appropriate polluter. This has, in turn, implications for the method of internalization. The reference to the use of economic instruments, such as taxes or negotiable permits, confirms the aforementioned emphasis on 'allocation' rather than on 'prevention' of the damage, which could entail banning an activity altogether. Normally, the higher costs entailed

[245] *Tatar v. Romania*, para 135. [246] *Tatar v. Romania*, paras 151–63.

[247] *Tatar v. Romania*, para 120 (unofficial translation from the French original).

[248] See eg *Pfizer Animal Health SA v. Council*, CJEC n° T-13/99, paras 114–15; *Gowan Comércio Internacional e Serviços L*[da] *v. Ministero della Salute*, CJEU Case C-77/09, Judgment (22 December 2010), para 75.

by the tax or the requirement to hold a certain amount of permits will be transferred from the producer to the end consumer, which may cause distributional inequities in the same form as an indirect (rather than a direct) tax, which affects all equally irrespective of their income. Finally, and somewhat controversially, international trade and investment must not be 'distorted' whereas merely paying 'due regard' to the public interest seems to be sufficient.

Thus characterized, the polluter-pays principle has had significant normative influence not only at the domestic level but also as the architectural foundation of some treaty regimes (which must, in turn, be implemented domestically). The chapter by P. Schwartz surveys a variety of regulatory tools that have been used to internalize costs in the particularly important and wide-ranging area of decarbonization. She refers *inter alia* to five internalization techniques, namely emission standards, emission charges, emissions trading schemes, subsidies, and liability systems. Such techniques can be purely domestic or internationally-induced. By way of illustration, several Protocols to the LRTAP Convention provide for emission standards.[249] The Montreal Protocol and the Kyoto Protocol provide for some form of allowance trading.[250] There are two major regimes providing for the internalization of costs through liability arising from oil pollution[251] or nuclear accidents.[252] Importantly, the chapter by Schwartz addresses a dimension of cost internalization that was not—and is still not[253]—fully grasped in international environmental negotiations, namely the relations between cost internalization and international

[249] See eg Protocol to the 1979 Convention on Long-Range Transboundary Air Pollution on the Reduction of Sulphur Emissions, 14 June 1994, 2030 UNTS 122 ('Sulphur Protocol II'), art 2(4)-(5); Protocol to the 1979 Convention on Long-Range Transboundary Air Pollution Concerning the Control of Nitrogen Oxides or their Transboundary Fluxes, 31 October 1988, 28 I.L.M. 212, 216 ('$NO_x$ Protocol'), art 2(2); Protocol to the 1979 Convention on Long-Range Transboundary Air Pollution on the Reduction of Acidification, Eutrophication and Ground-Level Ozone, 30 November 1999, Document of the Economic and Social Council EB.AIR/1999/1 ('Gothenburg Protocol'), introducing a more sophisticated system, including standards based on best available technology or limit values but also specific measures (see Annex IX).

[250] Montreal Protocol, art 2(5); Kyoto Protocol, arts 6, 12, and 17.

[251] The current system is based on instruments adopted in 1992: Protocol amending the International Convention on Civil Liability for Oil Pollution Damage, 27 November 1992, available at: <htttp://www.ecolex.org> (TRE-001 177) ('CLC/92'): Protocol to Amend the International Convention on the Establishment of an International Fund for Compensation for Oil Pollution Damage, 27 November 1992, available at: <http://www.ecolex.org> (TRE-001 176) ('FUND/92'). This system has been completed by a 2003 Protocol to the International Convention on the Establishment of an International Fund for Compensation for Oil Pollution by oil, 16 May 2003, available at: <http://www.ecolex.org> (TRE-001 401) ('FUND/2003').

[252] Regarding nuclear accidents, there are two systems. First, there is one based on the Convention on Third Party Liability in the Field of Nuclear Energy, 29 July 1960, 956 UNTS 251 ('Paris Convention'). The regime established by the Paris Convention has been supplemented by another treaty, the Convention Supplementary to the Paris Convention of 29 July 1960 on Third Party Liability in the Field of Nuclear Energy, 31 January 1963, 1041 UNTS 358 ('Brussels Supplementary Convention'). The 'Paris/Brussels' system was amended in 1964, 1982 and 2004. The latter amendment, which is the result of a process of reflection initiated following the Chernobyl accident is a major overhaul of the original, but it is not yet in force. See Montjoie, M., 'Nuclear Energy' in Crawford, J., Pellet, A., and Olleson, S. (eds), *The Law of International Responsibility* (Oxford University Press 2010), 915. Second, there is a system based on the Convention on Civil Liability for Nuclear Damage, 21 May 1963, 1063 UNTS 265 ('Vienna Convention'). This treaty was amended by a Protocol to amend the Vienna Convention on Civil Liability for Nuclear Damage, 12 September 1997, 2241 UNTS 302, which leaves in place the two systems (initial system and amended system). The 1997 revision also resulted in the adoption of a Convention on Supplementary Compensation for Nuclear Damage, 12 September 1997, IAEA INFCIRC/567 ('Complementary Vienna Convention', not yet in force). The two systems have been linked through a Joint Protocol Relating to the Application of the Vienna Convention and the Paris Convention, September 27, 1988, 1672 UNTS 293.

[253] See Viñuales, J. E., 'Green Investment after Rio 2012' (2014) 16 *International Community Law Review* 153–76.

investment law. This is the area where an increasing number of international disputes have arisen in the last several years[254] and where reference to the polluter-pays principle is undoubtedly relevant.

## 2.17. *Principle 17: Environmental impact assessment*

Principle 17 addresses a technique that, after its introduction in the domestic law (namely the National Environmental Policy Act or 'NEPA') of the United States in 1970,[255] has progressively gained ground not only in domestic law but also in regional and international law. As noted by N. Craik in his chapter in this volume, the negotiation process of Principle 17 was influenced by the adoption of the EIA Directive in 1985[256] as well as, in 1991, of both a regional instrument (the Espoo Convention[257]) and an instrument governing the Antarctic.[258] Principle 17 envisages EIAs as a 'national instrument':

> Environmental impact assessment, as a national instrument, shall be undertaken for proposed activities that are likely to have a significant adverse impact on the environment and are subject to a decision of a competent national authority.

Significantly, the wording of Principle 17 does not limit its scope to a transboundary context. EIAs must be undertaken whenever an activity is 'likely to have a significant adverse impact on the environment' as such, including in a purely domestic context. The reference to 'proposed activities... that... are subject to a decision of a competent national authority' is intended to exclude policies, plans or programmes, which may nevertheless be subject to a 'strategic environmental assessment' ('SEA') under some legal frameworks.[259] The identification of such activities typically follows two approaches, namely: a list identifying types of activities that are deemed by their very nature to require an EIA;[260] or the conduct of a sort of preliminary assessment to determine whether an EIA is required.[261]

Since its introduction in the NEPA, the requirement to conduct an EIA has become one of the main environmental protection techniques (together with the creation of special areas). A number of treaties have established EIA requirements for activities likely to have a transboundary impact or to affect areas beyond national jurisdiction. Although both the Espoo Convention and the Madrid Protocol were concluded prior to the adoption of Principle 17 of the Rio Declaration, there is a clear connection between the formulation of the latter (based on the EC and Nordic drafts) and these two instruments. The requirement to conduct an EIA has also been introduced in article 14 of the CBD, further specified by a decision of the Conference of the Parties.[262] EIAs have also been incorporated

[254] See Viñuales, J. E., *Foreign Investment and the Environment in International Law* (Cambridge University Press 2012), ch 1.

[255] National Environmental Policy Act, 42 *U.S.C.* §4321 et seq (1969).

[256] Council Directive of 27 June 1985 on the assessment of the effects of certain public and private projects on the environment, (85/337/EEC), Official Journal no L 175, 05/07/1985 P. 0040–0048 ('EIA Directive').

[257] Espoo Convention.

[258] Protocol on Environmental Protection to the Antarctic Treaty, 4 October 1991, (1991) 30 ILM 1455 ('Madrid Protocol').

[259] UNECE Protocol on Strategic Environmental Assessment to the Convention on Environmental Impact Assessment in a Transboundary Context, 21 May 2003, available at: <http://www.unece.org/env/eia/sea_protocol.html> (accessed on 20 April 2014).

[260] See eg Espoo Convention, art 2(2) and Appendix I.

[261] Madrid Protocol, art 8 and Annex I.

[262] 'Guidelines for Incorporating Biodiversity-Related Issues into Environmental Impact Assessment Legislation and/or Processes and in Strategic Environmental Assessment', Report of the 6th Meeting of the Conference of the Parties to the Convention on Biological Diversity, UN Doc UNEP/CBD/COP/6/7, Annex.

into some soft law guidelines, such as those adopted by the Arctic Council in 1997,[263] or in codification efforts. Examples of the latter include article 5 of the 1997 IDI Resolution on 'Environment', devoted to EIA,[264] or section 4(2)(c) of the ILA New Delhi Declaration, which refers to the conduct of EIAs as an expression of the precautionary principle.[265]

Regarding the jurisprudential relevance of the EIA requirement, in the *Pulp Mills* case, the ICJ recognized it as part of general international law,[266] although it added some qualifications to its scope and contents. The Court considered EIAs as an extension of the prevention principle, stated in Principle 2, but limited its spatial scope to a transboundary context. However, in its *Advisory Opinion on Activities in the Area*, the ITLOS Seabed Chamber has considered instead that EIAs must also be conducted for activities in the global commons.[267] Although the reasoning of the Chamber intervenes within the context of a treaty regime (the UNCLOS), the connection between prevention and EIA suggests that the latter should apply also beyond national jurisdiction, as does the former. The other qualification introduced by the ICJ in the *Pulp Mills* case concerns the specific content of the EIA. The Court reasoned that the specific content of the international norm requiring the conduct of an EIA is to be defined by domestic law.[268] The treaties and soft-law instruments mentioned in the previous paragraph often specify the content of the EIA obligation. Whether the formal source of the international norm is custom or general principles of law, in both cases a body of practice is required for the norm to emerge (international practice or domestic practice transposable to the international plane). The conclusion of the ICJ is therefore debatable, and it should not be interpreted as stating that the norm has almost no content but that some aspects of a procedural nature (deadlines, format of the application, etc) are defined at the domestic level.

## 2.18. *Principle 18: Notification and assistance in case of emergency*

Principle 18 states a norm that, in its core content, namely the duty to notify disasters and other emergencies, has customary grounding both as part of the prevention principle and, even before, as part of basic duties of good neighbourliness.[269] But Principle 18 goes beyond this basic duty and adds a reference to assistance:

> States shall immediately notify other States of any natural disasters or other emergencies that are likely to produce sudden harmful effects on the environment of those States. Every effort shall be made by the international community to help States so afflicted.

[263] 'Guidelines for Incorporating Biodiversity-Related Issues into Environmental Impact Assessment Legislation and/or Processes and in Strategic Environmental Assessment', Report of the 6th Meeting of the Conference of the Parties to the Convention on Biological Diversity, UN Doc UNEP/CBD/COP/6/7, Annex; and 1997 Guidelines for EIA in the Arctic, adopted by the Arctic Council in the 1997 Alta Declaration on the Protection of the Arctic Environmental Protection Strategy online <http://arctic-council.org/filearchive/The%20Alta%20Declaration.pdf>.

[264] Adopted at the Strasbourg Session (1997).

[265] New Delhi Declaration, 4(2)(c).

[266] *Pulp Mills*, para 204.

[267] *Advisory opinion on the Area*, paras 145, 148.

[268] In the *Pulp Mills* case, the Court held that: 'it is for each State to determine in its domestic legislation or in the authorization process for the project, the specific content of the environmental impact assessment required in each case, having regard to the nature and magnitude of the proposed development and its likely adverse impact on the environment as well as to the need to exercise due diligence in conducting such an assessment. The Court also considers that an environmental impact assessment must be conducted prior to the implementation of a project. Moreover, once operations have started and, where necessary, throughout the life of the project, continuous monitoring of its effects on the environment shall be undertaken', *Pulp Mills*, para 205.

[269] *Corfu Channel* case, 22–3; *Military and Paramilitary Activities in and Against Nicaragua (Nicaragua v. United States of America)*, Merits, Judgment, ICJ Reports 1986, 14 ('*Nicaragua* case'), para 215; Tokyo Economic Summit Conference Statement on the Soviet Nuclear Reactor Accident at Chernobyl, 5 May 1986, para 2; ILC Prevention Articles, art 17.

Thus, Principle 18 has two main components, notification in case of emergency and a duty of assistance. As noted by P. Okowa in her chapter in this commentary, the legal nature of each component is not the same. Whereas the first is solidly grounded in treaty and customary law, the second is merely exhortative in nature and is devolved to the 'international community'. As for third States, Okowa refers to the survey of practice conducted within the framework of the ILC's codification work on protection of persons in the event of disaster to conclude that, subject to what may be provided in treaty law, no such duty of assistance exists in the current state of customary international law.[270] In both cases, however, what distinguishes Principle 18 from Principle 19 (to which it was linked in the preparatory work) is the nature of the trigger event, namely a 'natural disaster or other emergencies'. This event is characterized in Principle 18 as events 'likely to produce sudden harmful effects on the environment of those States'. The scope of the principle is therefore transboundary.

Regarding the normative impact of Principle 18, one must again make a distinction between the two components. The duty to notify in the event of emergency has significantly influenced treaty practice as well as codification efforts. The 1986 Early Notification Convention[271] concluded shortly after the Chernobyl disaster is perhaps the most emblematic instrument, but there are several other global and regional treaties fleshing out this duty, including the 1992 UNECE Convention on Industrial Accidents,[272] the Tampere Convention on the Provision of Telecommunication Resources for Disaster Mitigation and Relief Operations[273] or the 2005 ASEAN Agreement on Disaster Management,[274] to name but a few examples. In addition, this duty has been elaborated upon in some codification efforts undertaken under the aegis of the ILC. Here, the question has been addressed in connection with the duty of prevention of environmental harm[275] and, more recently, as part of its work on the protection of persons in the event of disaster.[276]

In addition to the duty to notify, a broader approach, focusing on the reduction of vulnerability and the organization of response, has developed in the context of the Hyogo Framework for Action adopted in 2005.[277] This framework emphasizes questions of assistance. The type of financial and technical assistance envisaged in the Hyogo Framework is primarily intended to build resilience before disaster occurs. Thus, to this extent, it differs from the assistance contemplated in the second component of Principle 18. Aside from the Hyogo Framework, reference to assistance in case of disaster can be found in

[270] ILC, Preliminary Report on the Protection of Persons in the Event of Disasters, by Eduardo Valencia-Ospina, Special Rapporteur, 5 May 2008, UN Doc A/CN.4/598, para 35.

[271] Convention on Early Notification of a Nuclear Accident, 18 November 1986, INFCIRC/335.

[272] Convention on the Transboundary Effects of Industrial accidents, 17 March 1992, 2105 UNTS 457 ('Convention on Industrial Accidents').

[273] Tampere Convention on the Provision of Telecommunication Resources for Disaster Mitigation and Relief Operations, 18 June 1998, 2296 UNTS 5.

[274] ASEAN Agreement on Disaster Management and Emergency Response, 25 July 2005 ('ASEAN Agreement').

[275] ILC Prevention Articles, art 8; 2006 ILC Principles, Principle 5(a).

[276] Protection of persons in the event of disasters, 15 May 2014, UN Doc A/CN.4/L.831, art 13 (duty to seek external assistance, which presupposes notification).

[277] Hyogo Framework for Action 2005–2015: Building the Resilience of Nations and Communities to Disasters, United Nations World Conference on Disaster Reduction, Kobe, Japan, 18–22 January 2005, A/CONF.206/6.

several other treaties, including the 1992 Convention on Industrial Accidents[278] or 1992 UNECE Convention on Watercourses.[279] Again, perhaps the most emblematic treaty in this regard was also a response to the Chernobyl disaster, namely the 1986 Convention on Assistance in Case of Nuclear Accident.[280] Even when a duty of assistance is envisaged, its formulation remains generally flexible limiting its legal enforceability. This said, one must not overlook that developed States have as a rule provided significant assistance in case of emergency, as illustrated by the international response to the Indian Ocean Tsunami in 2004, the earthquake in Haiti in 2010 or the more recent earthquake in the Philippines in 2013.[281]

## *2.19. Principle 19: Notification and consultation on activities with transboundary impact*

Principle 19 was initially the first component of a principle proposed by EC countries at PrepCom IV which encompassed also Principle 18.[282] Notification is not only required in the event of an emergency but, logically, it must also intervene in cases where a State plans to conduct certain activities that may pose significant risks of transboundary harm:

> States shall provide prior and timely notification and relevant information to potentially affected States on activities that may have a significant adverse transboundary environmental effect and shall consult with those States at an early stage and in good faith.

Thus, unlike the notification contemplated in Principle 18, the one in Principle 19 must take place prior to the conduct of the relevant activities (and not after an emergency has occurred) and such notification aims at prompting consultations sufficiently in advance. Thus characterized, the duty to notify and consult is clearly an application of the obligation of cooperation, which, in turn, is an extension of the prevention principle. As noted by L. Boisson de Chazournes and K. Sangbana, it is as such firmly grounded in general international law,[283] with particular relevance, historically, for the management of shared watercourses.[284] Although the two components of Principle 19 (notification and consultation) each have their specific features, their impact on treaties and judicial decisions can be analysed together.

Many treaties can be mentioned as expressions of the duty to notify and consult. A major area of normative development is, of course, the law of international watercourses and, specifically, those treaties and provisions concerning the non-navigational uses of international watercourses. After years of codification work under the aegis of

[278] Convention on Industrial Accidents, art 12(1).

[279] Convention on the Protection and Use of transboundary Watercourses and International Lakes, Helsinki 17th March 1992, <http://www.unece.org/fileadm/DAM/en/water/pdf/watercon.pdf>.

[280] Convention on Assistance in the Case of a Nuclear Accident or Radiological Emergency, 18th November 1986, INFCIRC/336.

[281] Phillipines Typhoon, *Disasters Emergency Committee*, <http//www.dec.org.uk/facts-and-figures> (accessed on 20 April 2014).

[282] See L.25, Principle 9 (italics added).

[283] *Corfu Channel* case, 22–3; ILC Prevention Articles, commentary and art 8, para 3; Munro and Lammers, *Environmental Protection and Sustainable Development*, 99 and 104.

[284] Farrajota, M. M., 'Notification and Consultation in the law applicable to international Watercourses' in Boisson de Chazournes, L. and Salman, S.M.A. (eds), *Water Resources and International Law* (Martinus Nijhoff Publishers 2005), 281–339.

the ILC (and previously of the ILA), a UN Convention on the Non-Navigational Uses of International Watercourses was concluded in 1997 and entered into force in 2014.[285] Article 12 requires notification of 'planned measures which may have a significant adverse effect upon other watercourse States'. The duty is complemented by a duty not to authorize or pursue the relevant activity pending consultations.[286] This treaty is emblematic of a large number of treaties concerning specific watercourses with similar or more sophisticated notification and consultation arrangements.[287] Beyond the regulation of watercourses, other instruments give also expression to the duty to notify and consult, including the ILC Prevention Articles[288] or the 1991 Espoo Convention discussed in connection with Principle 17.[289]

Regarding the jurisprudential relevance of the duties stated in Principle 18, it is possible to point to several cases, both old and new. In the 1957 *Lake Lanoux* arbitration between France and Spain concerning the diversion by the former of the waters of the River Carol, the tribunal noted that France could not be the sole judge of whether the works had an impact on Spain or not.[290] In a similar vein, the ICJ noted in the *Pulp Mills* case that the duty to cooperate in good faith entailed that:

> as long as the procedural mechanism for co-operation between the parties to prevent significant damage to one of them is taking its course, the State initiating the planned activity is obliged not to authorize such work and, *a fortiori*, not to carry it out.[291]

In some other cases, the content of the duty to cooperate has been specified by international tribunals. Examples include the affirmation of a duty to exchange information,[292] jointly evaluate the environmental impact of the relevant activity[293] or even consult with the secretariat of an applicable environmental treaty.[294]

## 2.20. *Principle 20: The role of women*

Principle 20 opens a series of three principles recognizing the role of specific groups within the overall framework of sustainable development:

> Women have a vital role in environmental management and development. Their full participation is therefore essential to achieve sustainable development.

Although it is possible to see Principle 20 (as well as Principles 21 and 22) as extensions of Principle 10 (public participation), it would be more accurate to view it as a broad

[285] United Nations Convention on the Law of the Non-Navigational Uses of International Watercourses, 21 May 1997, 36 ILM 700 ('1997 New York Convention').

[286] 1997 New York Convention, art 17(3).

[287] In their chapter, L. Boisson de Chazournes and K. Sangbana refer among others to art 24 of the 2002 Water Charter of the Senegal River; art 20 of the 2008 Water Charter of the River Niger Basin; arts 7–13 of the 1975 Statute of the River Uruguay; art 11 of the 1994 Danube River Protection Convention; arts 5 and 26 of the 1995 Agreement on the cooperation for the sustainable development of the Mekong River Basin; art 8 of the 2010 Agreement on the Nile River Basin Cooperative Framework.

[288] ILC Prevention Articles, arts 8 and 9.

[289] Espoo Convention.

[290] *Lake Lanoux* case *(Spain v. France)*, Award of 16 November 1957, RIAA vol XII, 281ff ('*Lake Lanoux* case'), para 21.

[291] *Pulp Mills*, para 144.

[292] *MOX Plant* case, para 89(a).

[293] *See Fisheries Jurisdiction* case *(UK v. Iceland)*, Decision on Jurisdiction, ICJ Reports 1974, 3 ('*Fisheries Jurisdiction*'), para 72; *Pulp Mills*, para 281; *MOX Plant* case, para 89(b).

[294] *Certain Activities Carries Out by Nicaragua in the Border Area (Costa Rica v. Nicaragua), Request for the Indication of Provisional Measures, Order* (8 March 2011) ('*Costa Rica v. Nicaragua*'), paras 80 and 86(2).

statement aimed at highlighting the position and the role of women in environmental management and development, one corollary (among others) of which is the need to ensure their 'full participation' in decision-making. As noted by C. Mahon, a focus on women was deemed necessary because in many societies, as a result of socioeconomic and cultural constraints, women perform domestic tasks such as food production, water collection, and gathering of wood for fire that brings them closer to the environment. They thus develop a particular knowledge of their environment and they are, at the same time, more exposed to environmental hazards. This position also calls for attention from a developmental perspective because the tasks performed by women tend to prevent them from accessing education and fully participating in decision-making. By addressing the role of women, Principle 20 captures their position and role in 'environmental management' and 'development' and call for both the integration of women and an improvement of their situation in decision-making.

The recognition of the role of women in Principle 20 had significant normative impact in subsequent international instruments. The wording of Principle 20 (the 'vital role' of women) features in the preamble of the CBD[295] and a close variant ('important role') appears in the preamble of the UNCCD.[296] Principle 20 is also one of the sources of the 2003 Protocol to the African Charter on Human and People's Rights on the Rights of Women (2003),[297] which refers in its preamble—somewhat inaccurately—to the 'United Nations Plans of Action on the Environment and Development in 1992'. The link between Principle 20 and the Protocol can also be established through the influence of the former on several policy developments that also influenced the latter, including the outcome document of the aforementioned 1994 ICPD[298] and the Platform for Action of the Fourth World Conference on Women held in Beijing in 1995.[299] The role of women was also specifically recognized in the UN Millennium Declaration[300] and, more recently, in the outcome document of the Rio 2012 Summit.[301]

Regarding its jurisprudential relevance, the close links of Principle 20 with the Convention on the Elimination of Discrimination against Women ('CEDAW')[302] and, more broadly, with international human rights law suggests that it may be relevant for interpretive purposes. The Committee on the Elimination of Discrimination against Women has so far heard some twenty specific complaints.[303] Although, to my knowledge, the Committee has not dealt with environment-related cases so far, the prohibition of discrimination against women remains potentially relevant from an environmental perspective given precisely the greater exposure of women to environmental hazards, particularly in developing countries.

295 CBD, preamble, para 13.

296 UNCCD, prologue, para 20.

297 Protocol to the African Charter on Human and Peoples' Rights on the Rights of Women in Africa, adopted by the 2nd Ordinary Session of the Assembly of the Union, Maputo, CAB/LEG/66.6 (13 September 2000).

298 'Programme of Action', Report of the International Conference on Population and Development, New York, 1994, 'Programme of Action', UN Doc A/CONF.171/13.

299 Report of the Fourth World Conference on Women, New York, 1995, UN Doc A/CONF.177/20.

300 'Millennium Declaration', paras 20 and 25.

301 *The Future We Want*, paras 236–44.

302 Convention on the Elimination of All Forms of Discrimination Against Women, 18 December 1979, 1249 UNTS 455 ('CEDAW').

303 See: <http://tbinternet.ohchr.org/_layouts/treatybodyexternal/TBSearch.aspx?Lang=en&TreatyID=3&DocTypeID=17> (accessed on 20 April 2014).

## 2.21. Principle 21: The role of the youth

Much as Principle 20, Principle 21 recognizes the role of another specific group, the youth, in sustainable development:

> The creativity, ideals and courage of the youth of the world should be mobilized to forge a global partnership in order to achieve sustainable development and ensure a better future for all.

Whereas Principle 21 could be seen as an application of Principle 10 (public participation), again, this view would only capture part of it. Indeed, Principle 21 can also be seen as an extension of intergenerational equity, as contemplated by Principle 3, in that the youth is the most direct representative of future generations. As noted by M. J. Langer, in practical terms, Principle 21 aims at (i) fostering environmental education and awareness (a cultural change) and (ii) increasing participation of the youth in institutional processes as an expression of intergenerational equity. Pinned down to these two components, the exhortation enshrined in Principle 21 has indeed had some normative impact and jurisprudential relevance.

Regarding its normative impact, Langer refers to several treaties adopted in 1992 or after, including the UNFCCC,[304] the CBD,[305] and UNCCD,[306] but also the Aarhus Convention,[307] the Protocol on Water and Health to the Helsinki Convention,[308] or the POP Convention,[309] which all contain provisions on environmental education, awareness-raising, and participation. Of particular note are the processes launched within the context of the UNFCCC—the 'United Nations Joint Framework Initiative on Children, Youth, and Climate Change',[310] and the CBD—the Global Youth Biodiversity Network ('GYBN'),[311] which both seek to institutionalize the input of youth organizations in the work of the conventions.

Moving to the Principle's jurisprudential relevance, as with other principles, it is necessary to dissociate Principle 21 of the Rio Declaration as a source from its content. Although the Principle as such has not featured in the case law, it is possible to identify cases involving both the intergenerational equity and environmental education components mentioned above. Concerning the first, the cases referred to in the context of Principle 3 are also relevant in this context, particularly the decision of the Supreme Court of the Philippines in *Minors Oposa* granting *jus standi* to future generations represented by the present generation of children.[312] Less well-known are the cases referred to by Langer in connection with environmental education,[313] particularly the decision of the European Committee on Social Rights in *Marangopoulos v. Greece*[314] where the State was found to

[304] UNFCCC, arts 4(1)(i) and 6. [305] CBD, art 13; Biosafety Protocol, art 23(1).

[306] UNCCD, art 19. [307] Aarhus Convention, art 3(3).

[308] Protocol on Water and Health to the 1992 Convention on the Protection and Use of Transboundary Watercourses and International Lakes, 17 June 1999, 2331 UNTS 202, art 9(1).

[309] POP Convention, 10(1)(c).

[310] See UNFCCC note on *United Nations Joint Framework Initiative on Children, Youth and Climate Change*, <http://unfccc.int/cc_inet/cc_inet/youth_portal/items/6519.php> (accessed on 20 April 2014).

[311] See 'The long road to the establishment of GYBN', available at: <http://www.gybn.net/HistoryofGYBN.aspx> (accessed on 20 April 2014).

[312] *Minors Oposa* case.

[313] See also ICtHR, *Case of the 'Juvenile Reeducation Institute' v. Paraguay*, Preliminary Objections, Merits, Reparations and Costs, Judgment of 2 September 2004, para 172.

[314] *Marangopoulos Foundation for Human Rights (MFHR) v. Greece*, European Committee of Social Rights, Complaint no 30/2005, Decision on the Merits, 6 December 2006.

be in breach of the European Social Charter because of its failure to provide sufficient environmental health education to persons living close to a lignite mine.

## 2.22. *Principle 22: Indigenous people and sustainable development*

Principle 22 concerns the role of another specific group, indigenous people, which has received increasing attention in international human rights law, particularly after the conclusion of the 1989 ILO Convention no 169[315] and, more recently, the 2007 UN Declaration on the Rights of Indigenous Peoples ('UNDRIP').[316] Principle 22 provides that:

> Indigenous people and their communities and other local communities have a vital role in environmental management and development because of their knowledge and traditional practices. States should recognize and duly support their identity, culture and interests and enable their effective participation in the achievement of sustainable development.

As noted by D. Shelton in her chapter in this commentary, indigenous peoples are highly integrated in the environment that they inhabit and, as a result, they have both developed a deep understanding of it while, at the same time, their way of life is particularly vulnerable to environmental change. The approach taken in Principle 22 is similar to that in Principle 20, highlighting their 'vital role' in both 'environmental management' and 'development' and calling for 'effective' (rather than 'full') participation in sustainable development. Shelton observes that in this statement the need for the recognition of indigenous peoples' 'rights' (as opposed to their 'identity, culture and interests') remains elusive, particularly in connection with their entitlement to self-determination and their ancestral lands. The principle is therefore not clearly rights-based. Yet, subsequent developments have changed this situation and the rights of indigenous and tribal peoples are nowadays well established in treaties, policy instruments, and international jurisprudence.

Regarding first the normative impact of the Principle, a distinction must be made between the more progressive approach represented by the ILO Convention no 169, which eventually prevailed in practice, and the reluctant formulation of Principle 22 in its initial understanding, echoed by chapter 26 of Agenda 21, which laboriously avoids recognizing specific rights to land and self-determination. The CBD and the 2010 Nagoya Protocol on Access and Benefit Sharing were also influenced by Principle 22 in that they require the participation of indigenous people (their 'approval and involvement' and, in the Nagoya Protocol, their 'prior informed consent') in processes leading to the wider use of traditional knowledge.[317] Yet, these instruments do not clearly articulate the recognition of indigenous peoples in terms of 'rights'. For a rights-based approach one must look at the developments in international human rights law, particularly the UNDRIP, which largely supersedes the more reluctant approach embodied in the formulation of Principle 22, and the case law of the ICtHR and the African Commission, to which I now turn.[318]

[315] Convention (No. 169) concerning Indigenous and Tribal Peoples in Independent Countries, 27 June 1989, (1989) 28 ILM 1382.

[316] 'United Nations Declaration on the Rights of Indigenous Peoples', UNGA Resolution 61/295, 13 September 2007, Annex, UN Doc A/RES/61/295 ('UNDRIP').

[317] CBD, art 8(j); Nagoya Protocol, art 7.

[318] The case law of the ECtHR on this point is more restrictive. See Koivurova, T., 'Jurisprudence of the European Court of Human Rights Regarding Indigenous Peoples: Retrospect and Prospects' (2011) 18 *International Journal on Minority and Group Rights* 1.

In a stream of cases that goes from the 2001 *Awas Tingni* decision to the more recent 2012 *Sarayaku* case, the ICtHR has expanded the interpretation of Article 21 of the ACHR on the right to property to give specific protection to the relation between indigenous and tribal peoples and their traditional lands. Shelton notes by reference to the *Saramaka* case[319] that this body of decisions recognizes not only the right of such peoples over their ancestral lands but also some participatory rights, including a share of the benefits of activities conducted in their lands. The African Commission has also affirmed the need to protect the rights of indigenous and tribal peoples. In the *Endorois* case, the Commission found that Kenya had violated the African Charter as a result of the measures adopted to remove the Endorois people from their ancestral land for environmental purposes.[320] This case is also interesting as an illustration of potential conflicts between human rights and environmental measures (Kenya grounded its action on nature conservation considerations).

## *2.23. Principle 23: The environment of oppressed peoples*

Principle 23 can be seen as an extension of several principles of the Rio Declaration, particularly Principles 22 and 2. The term 'peoples' in Principle 23 encompasses that of 'indigenous people' in Principle 22 but goes well beyond it covering all peoples under oppression, domination or occupation:

> The environment and natural resources of people under oppression, domination and occupation shall be protected.

The environment of these peoples is envisaged both as a resource and as their surroundings. The protection afforded is therefore not only to preserve the natural resources of these peoples from exploitation by the oppressing, dominating, or occupying power but also to protect the peoples from threats arising from the deterioration of their environment. As noted by M. Tignino, such protection is therefore similar to that offered to States under Principle 2 with the difference that, in the context of Principle 23, there is technically no transboundary element as the harm to the environment affects the oppressed, dominated, or occupied territory.

Regarding the normative impact of Principle 23, as with other principles of the Rio Declaration, Principle 23 only places in an environmental light a principle that had long been recognized in international practice, in instruments such as article 47 of the 1907 Hague Regulations,[321] article 33 of the 1949 Geneva Convention IV,[322] UNGA Resolution 1803(XVII) on 'Permanent Sovereignty over Natural Resources', common article 1 to the 1966 International Human Rights Covenants[323] and, later, article 21 of the African Charter on Human and Peoples' Rights. With respect to the latter, Tignino

[319] *Case of the Saramaka People v. Suriname*, Preliminary Objections, Merits, Reparations, and Costs, Judgment, 28 November 2007, ICtHR Ser. C no 172.

[320] See *Centre for Minority Rights Development (Kenya) and Minority Rights Group International on behalf of Endorois Welfare Council v. Kenya*, African Commission Application no 276/2003 ('*Endorois* case'). For a similar factual configuration see *African Commission on Human and Peoples' Rights v. Kenya*, Order on provisional measures, 15 March 2013, African Court, Application no 006/2012.

[321] Convention on the Laws and Customs of War on Land (Hague IV), 18 October 1907, Annex, art 47.

[322] Geneva Convention (IV) Relative to the Protection of Civilian Persons in Time of War, 12 August 1949, 75 UNTS 287.

[323] ICESCR; International Covenant on Civil and Political Rights, 16 December 1966, 999 UNTS 171 ('ICCPR').

refers to a resolution of the African Commission interpreting article 21 in the light of the Rio Declaration:

> in accordance with the Rio Declaration and African Charter principle of State sovereignty over natural resources, the State has the main responsibility for ensuring natural resources stewardship with, and for the interest of, the population and must fulfil its mission in conformity with international human rights law and standards[324]

Article 21 of the African Charter has been interpreted in a spirit similar to that of the right to property of indigenous and tribal peoples as understood by the ICtHR. Indeed, in the *Ogoni* case, the African Commission found that Nigeria had violated the rights afforded to individuals and peoples under the African Charter, including articles 16 (individual right to health), 21 (collective right to natural resources), and 24 (collective right to a generally satisfactory environment) as a result of the oil exploitation operations it had allowed and conducted in the land where the Ogoni lived.[325] This case illustrates both the resource preservation and environmental protection dimensions contemplated in Principle 23. Aside from the decisions of human rights courts, environmental and resource depletion has arisen in a number of decisions both domestic and international. Tignino provides several examples, including the decision of a Singapore Court of Appeal in the 1956 *De Bataafsche Petroleum v. War Damage Commission* case, condemning the seizure and use by Japanese forces of Malaysian oil resources[326] and three cases before the ICJ.[327] Of the latter, only one (*DRC v. Uganda*) proceeded to the merits and the ICJ had the opportunity to confirm the customary grounding of the principle of permanent sovereignty over natural resources, although it considered that it did not apply to the specific facts of that case.[328] Thus, there is sufficient evidence to conclude that the principle incorporated in Principle 23 is relevant from a jurisprudential perspective.

## *2.24. Principle 24: The environment in armed conflict*

Principle 24 is a broad statement of some basic principles of international humanitarian law formulated mainly in articles 35(3) and 55 of the 1977 Protocol I to the 1949 Geneva Convention,[329] article 1 of the 1976 ENMOD Convention[330] as well as in customary international law:[331]

> Warfare is inherently destructive of sustainable development. States shall therefore respect international law providing protection for the environment in times of armed conflict and cooperate in its further development, as necessary.

[324] Resolution on a Human Rights' Based Approach to Natural Resources Governance, 51st Ordinary Session of the African Commission on Human and Peoples' Rights, 18 April–2 May 2002.

[325] *Ogoni* case, paras 55–8.

[326] *De Bataafsche Petroleum v. War Damage Commission*, 22 Malayan Law Journal 155 (1956), reproduced in Marco Sassoli and Antoine Bouvier, *How Does Law Protect in War? Cases, Documents and Teaching Materials on Contemporary Practice in International Humanitarian Law*, ICRC, 2003, vol II, 1072.

[327] *Certain Phosphates Lands in Nauru (Nauru v. Australia)*, Preliminary Objections, Judgment, ICJ Reports 1992, 240; *East Timor* case, Dissenting opinion, Judge Weeramantry, ICJ Reports 1995, 197–9; Dissenting opinion, Judge Skubizewski, ICJ Reports 1995, 276; *Armed Activities on the Territory of Congo (Democratic Republic of Congo v. Uganda)*, Judgment, ICJ Reports 2005, 168 ('*DRC v. Uganda*').

[328] *DRC v. Uganda*, para 244.

[329] Protocol I, 6 August 1977, 1125 UNTS 3.

[330] Convention for the Prohibition of Military or other Hostile Use of Environmental Modification Techniques, 10 December 1976, 1108 UNTS 151 ('ENMOD Convention').

[331] See Henckaerts, J.-M. and Doswald-Beck, L., *Customary International Humanitarian Law* (Cambridge University Press 2009), rules 43–5.

The first sentence hides a vivid debate during the preparatory committee concerning the opportunity to condemn the use of weapons of mass destruction, particularly nuclear weapons. The final formulation reflects the position of the United States and other industrialized States, which places the centre of gravity on sustainable development and avoids matters of disarmament. The second sentence contains two noticeable components. First, it refers to 'international law' therefore going beyond the law of armed conflict, which provides very limited explicit protection to the natural environment, and including international environmental law, human rights law, among others. Second, it calls for cooperation in the further development of international law on this question.

The latter component paved the way for some subsequent initiatives taken by the UNGA and by the ILC. As noted by M.-L. Tougas in her chapter in this commentary, in 1994 a codification initiative was conducted under the aegis of the International Committee of the Red Cross ('ICRC'). This initiative led to the adoption of *Guidelines for military manuals on the protection of the environment in times of armed conflict*,[332] which were subsequently endorsed by the UNGA. The ILC has also undertaken codification efforts on the effect of armed conflict on treaties and, more recently, on the protection of the environment 'in relation to' armed conflict. The first process led to the adoption in 2011 of *Draft articles on the effects of armed conflicts on treaties*, which set the presumption of continued application of environmental treaties despite the outburst of armed conflict.[333] The second process is only starting and the ILC Rapporteur, Mrs Marie Jacobsson from Sweden, has framed it in a way so as to encompass not only the armed conflict phase but also the phases preceding and following armed conflict, potentially including the entire life-cycle of certain weapons of mass destruction.[334]

Unlike some other principles of the Rio Declaration, Principle 24 has been referred to in international jurisprudence not only in its substance but as such. In its *Advisory Opinion on the Legality of Nuclear Weapons*, the ICJ explicitly referred to Principle 24 to assert that:

> Respect for the environment is one of the elements that go to assessing whether an action is in conformity with the principles of necessity and proportionality. This approach is supported, indeed, by the terms of Principle 24 of the Rio Declaration.[335]

Other bodies have referred to the substance of Principle 24, without mentioning the principle as such. Examples are rare because, except for its intersections with international criminal law or human rights law, international humanitarian law—like international environmental law—has no specialized courts. Tougas refers in this connection to a decision of the Eritrea-Ethiopia Claims Commission which, in fact, dismissed the claim as not reaching the gravity threshold established in article 35(3) of the 1977 Protocol I.[336] One could also refer, in this regard, to a 2000 report prepared by a Special Committee to advise the Prosecutor of the International Criminal Tribunal for the Former-Yugoslavia

[332] ICRC, *Guidelines for military manuals and instructions on the protection of the environment in times of armed conflict*, 1993, online: <http://www.icrc.org/eng/resources/documents/misc/57jn38.htm>.

[333] *Draft articles on the effects of armed conflicts on treaties*, UN Doc A/CN.4/L.777, 11 May 2011, arts 6, 7, and Annex.

[334] See ILC, 'Report on the work of its sixty-fifth session', UN Doc A/68/10, at ch IX.

[335] *Legality of the Threat or Use of Nuclear Weapons*, para 30.

[336] Central Front Ethiopia's Claim 2, Ethiopia/Eritrea Claims Commission, Partial Award, 28 April 2004, para 100.

on whether to prosecute the NATO bombing campaign in Yugoslavia.[337] The Committee noted that the demanding threshold of article 35(3) was unlikely to provide an adequate basis for prosecution.[338] Principle 24 could also be relevant in the context of the application submitted by the Marshall Islands against India, Pakistan and the United Kingdom in connection with obligation to pursue in good faith and conclude negotiations leading to nuclear disarmament,[339] which is in some respects an extension of the questions analysed by the ICJ in its 1996 advisory opinion.

## 2.25. *Principle 25: Peace, development and environmental protection*

Principle 25 goes a step further than Principle 24 and, rather than seeking to protect the environment in armed conflict, it boldly states that development and environmental protection are interdependent with peace:

> Peace, development and environmental protection are interdependent and indivisible.

Peace is thus seen as a fourth pillar of sustainable development or, more specifically, as a necessary basis for it. However, the relationship is one of interdependence as both environmental degradation and social and economic underdevelopment, particularly poverty, may be drivers of conflict. Principle 25 is clearly a policy statement. As such, it may be said to have no more (but no less) legal content than the concept of sustainable development. As noted by A. Bellal and G. Giacca in their chapter in this commentary, the main normative expressions of Principle 25 are to be found in the notion of environmental security as applied to the action of the United Nations Security Council and in efforts towards disarmament.

Regarding the first, the Security Council has a discretionary power under article 39 of the Charter to characterize an environment-driven event as a threat to international peace and security. Bellal and Giacca refer in this connection to the 2004 Report of the High Level Panel on Threats, Challenges and Change according to which '[t]he Security Council is fully empowered under Chapter VII of the Charter of the United Nations to address the full range of security threats with which States are concerned'.[340] Yet, this power has not been explicitly exercised in an environmental context yet, although the Security Council has already addressed under Chapter VII the flow of refugees from conflict as a threat to peace,[341] which could be extended to flows arising from environmental threats.

As for disarmament, environmental and development considerations could serve as additional reasons to pursue disarmament efforts from the broader perspective discussed in the context of Principle 24, namely environmental protection 'in relation to' armed

[337] Final Report to the Prosecutor by the Committee Established to Review the NATO Bombing Campaign against the Federal Republic of Yugoslavia, 13 June 2000.

[338] Final Report to the Prosecutor by the Committee Established to Review the NATO Bombing Campaign, para 15.

[339] The Marshall Islands submitted three separate applications on 24 April 2014 against, respectively, India, Pakistan, and the UK. See <http://www.icj-cij.org> (accessed on 1 May 2014).

[340] See UNGA 'Report of the High Level Panel on Threats, Challenges and Change' (2 December 2004) UN Doc A/59/565. See also 'Security Council holds first-ever debate in impact of climate change on peace, security, hearing over 50 speakers', UN Press release, <http://www.un.org/News/Press/docs/2007/sc9000.doc.htm> (accessed on 20 April 2014). See Penny, C., 'Greening the Security Council: Climate Change as an Emerging "Threat to International Peace and Security"' (2007) 7 *International Environmental Agreements: Politics, Law, Economics* 35.

[341] Wilson, G., *An Introduction to International Refugee Law* (Brill 2013), 267–89.

conflict, including questions as to production, storage, stationing, transportation, and decommissioning, instead of the sole use through detonation. Disarmament is more broadly relevant to free resources that can be allocated to social and economic development.[342] As noted in the previous section, the 2014 application of the Marshall Islands instituting proceedings before the ICJ against India, Pakistan, and the UK for breach of the obligation to pursue disarmament is also relevant for Principle 25, as it could bring its contents to bear in the context of an international dispute.

## *2.26. Principle 26: International environmental dispute settlement*

Principle 26 is a restatement of a customary principle of international law requiring States to settle their disputes peacefully:

> States shall resolve all their environmental disputes peacefully and by appropriate means in accordance with the Charter of the United Nations.

As noted by T. Stephens in his chapter in this commentary, the application of this general principle to environmental disputes entails some nuances. First, it is difficult to define precisely what is an 'environmental dispute' as disputes which apparently do not relate to the application of an environmental treaty or norm may nevertheless have environmental components because of their significance for natural resources, such as raw materials or watercourses. Second, environmental disputes call for their peaceful settlement not only as a matter of State interest but also to protect the environment per se. Indeed, whereas States are not required to reach a settlement and can leave their dispute unresolved as long as they remain within the bounds of peaceful means, the prevention of environmental harm calls for a more proactive obligation not to harm the environment per se irrespective of States' interests. In line with Principles 2 and 25 of the Rio Declaration, the settlement of disputes in this context is not only a matter of 'peace' but also one of 'environmental protection'. Third, the latter point is also important for the selection of the 'appropriate means', which may include mechanisms specifically tailored to the needs of environmental protection such as the so-called non-compliance procedures or NCPs. These three nuances must be kept in mind in analysing the normative impact and jurisprudential relevance of the restatement made in Principle 26.

The aftermath of the Rio Declaration saw significant developments in environmental dispute settlement. From a judicial perspective, developments such as the creation in 1993, within the ICJ, of a Special Chamber on Environmental Matters (which was never used),[343] the establishment in of a similar Chamber within the ITLOS or the adoption by the PCA of a set of arbitration rules specifically targeting environmental and natural resource disputes,[344] can all be seen as attempts to provide a proper forum to environmental disputes. From a non-judicial perspective, the 'appropriate means' envisioned in

[342] See 'Declaration on the Right to Development', 4 December 1986, UN Doc A/RES/41/128, art 7.

[343] A 'Chamber for Environmental Matters' was created in 1993 pursuant to art 26(1) of the Statute of the International Court of Justice (Press Release 93/20, Constitution of a Chamber of the Court for the Environmental Matters, 19 July 1993). This Chamber was never put to use and, eventually, in 2006, the Court decided not to reconstitute it. Another example is the 'Chamber for Marine Environmental Disputes' established by the ITLOS in 1997 pursuant to art 15(1) of its Statute (Press Release ITLOS/Press 5, 3 March 1997).

[344] Permanent Court of Arbitration (PCA), Optional Rules for Arbitration of Disputes relating to the Environment and/or Natural Resources ('PCA Optional Rules').

Principle 26 were shaped by the institutional innovations introduced by the 1987 Montreal Protocol in connection with the management of non-compliance,[345] which later spilled over to many other multilateral environmental agreements.[346] The non-adversarial nature of NCPs, which can be triggered by the non-complying State in an attempt to either seek assistance or justify its situation, highlights the preventive and mitigating objectives pursued by these mechanisms.

Concerning the jurisprudential relevance of Principle 26, as noted by Stephens, the principle does not seem to have been explicitly referred to in international litigation. This said, the obligation to settle environmental disputes peacefully lies at the roots of a growing body of environmental jurisprudence that spans virtually all areas of international law, from human rights and humanitarian law to the law of the sea, to international economic law concerning both trade and investment transactions. Several studies have been devoted to this body of decisions.[347] For present purposes it will suffice to note that the specificities of environmental matters sometimes call for procedural adjustments, including a relaxation of the requirements on *jus standi*, adjustments to the burden and/or standard of proof, certain modalities for the provision of expert evidence and increased transparency in the proceedings.

## *2.27. Principle 27: Cooperation in a spirit of global partnership*

Principle 27 introduces an important, albeit broad, component into the Declaration namely a call for cooperation 'in a spirit of global partnership' among States and people to implement the principles of the Rio Declaration:

> States and people shall cooperate in good faith and in a spirit of partnership in the fulfilment of the principles embodied in this Declaration and in the further development of international law in the field of sustainable development.

In essence, this principle has three components. First, it calls for a broader form of cooperation than the one envisioned in Principles 14, 18, and 19. Such cooperation must take place between States and people. As noted by P. Sand in his chapter in this commentary, the drafters consciously avoided speaking of 'peoples', which may have raised controversial questions (much as for Principle 22) as to the type of cooperation envisaged. The term 'people' clearly refers to civil society at large and such is the way in which it will be subsequently understood. Second, such cooperation must aim at implementing the

345 See Koskenniemi, M., 'Breach of Treaty or Non-Compliance? Reflections on the Enforcement of the Montreal Protocol' (1992) 3 *YbIEL* 123.

346 See Treves, T. et al (eds), *Non-Compliance Procedures and Mechanisms and the Effectiveness of International Environmental Agreements* (TMC Asser Press 2009); Urbinati, S., *Les mécanismes de contrôle et de suivi des conventions internationales de protection de l'environnement* (Giuffrè 2009).

347 See eg Boyle, A., 'Between Process and Substance: Sustainable Development in the Jurisprudence of International Courts and Tribunals', in Bugge, H. and Voigt. C. (eds), *Sustainable Development in International and National Law* (Europa Law Publishing 2008), 201–19; French, D., 'Environmental Dispute Settlement: The First (Hesitant) Signs of Spring?' (2007) 19 *Hague Yearbook of International Law* 3; Jennings, R., 'The Role of the International Court of Justice in the Development of International Environment Protection Law' (1992) 1 *RECIEL* 240; Lecucq, O. and Maljean-Dubois, S. (eds), *Le rôle du juge dans le développement du droit de l'environnement* (Bruylant 2008); Romano, C., *The peaceful settlement of international environmental disputes: a pragmatic approach* (Kluwer 2000); Stephens, T., *International Courts and Environmental Protection* (Cambridge University Press 2009); Viñuales, J. E., 'The Contribution of the International Court of Justice to the Development of International Environmental Law' (2008) 32 *Fordham International Law Journal* 232.

principles stated in the Declaration. Third, cooperation is also needed to 'further' develop 'international law in the field of sustainable development'. As noted by Sand, this apparently innocuous wording hides the profound division between developed and developing countries, the former favouring the reference made in UNGA Resolution 44/228 to 'international environmental law' and the latter calling for the reference to 'international law in the field of sustainable development', which eventually prevailed. The nuance is therefore important and signals the position of the Rio Declaration as an instrument at a crossroads between environmental protection and development considerations.

Regarding the legal manifestations of Principle 27, Sand identifies two main concepts. The first are the so-called public-private partnerships or 'PPPs' for sustainable development, which developed over the 1990s and particularly in the 2000s, after the 2002 Johannesburg Summit gave them renewed impetus.[348] The second is the concept of environmental trusteeship applied to the powers of States over nature and natural resources. This idea, which Sand traces back to the initiatives of Maurice Strong already at the time of preparatory work of the Stockholm Declaration, was explored by the UN on the impulsion of Secretary-General Kofi Annan[349] and eventually abandoned.[350] However, the idea has found fertile ground in some domestic legal systems through the 'public trust doctrine',[351] and it also underpins the concept of 'world heritage' shaping the WHC, that of 'common heritage of mankind' shaping Part XI of the UNCLOS or the pool of plant genetic resources managed under the 2001 International Treaty on Plant Genetic Resources.[352]

As for the jurisprudential relevance of Principle 27, although it has not as such been referred to in judicial practice, the concept of a public trust has received some attention in cases both old (eg the 1893 *Pacific Fur Seal Arbitration* invoking the trust idea to assert the extended jurisdiction of the US over fur seals[353]) and new (eg the decision of the Supreme Court of Pennsylvania in *Robinson Township v. Commonwealth* using the concept of a public trust to invalidate a law facilitating hydraulic fracturing as a gas extraction method[354]).

## 3. The lacunae of the Rio Declaration

The principles briefly discussed in the foregoing section cover vast ground, particularly when understood in the light of previous and subsequent normative developments. Yet, the Rio Declaration failed to address several matters or, at least, to address them explicitly.

[348] 'Report of the World Summit on Sustainable Development', UN Doc A/CONF.199/20 (2002). See Sand, P. H., 'Environmental Summitry and International Law' (2002) 13 *YbIEL* 21, 27–8; Witte, J. M., Streck, C., and Benner, T. (eds), *Progress or Peril? Partnerships and Networks in Global Environmental Governance: The Post-Johannesburg Agenda* (Global Public Policy Institute 2003); Beisheim, M., Campe, S., and Schäferhoff, M., 'Global Governance through Public-Private Partnerships', in Enderlein H., Wälti, S., and Zürn, M. (eds), *Handbook on Multi-Level Governance* (Edward Elgar 2010), 370–82.

[349] 'Renewing the United Nations: A Programme for Reform', UN Doc A/51/950 (14 July 1997), para 85.

[350] Estrada Oyuela, E. (ed), *Expert Consultations on International Environmental Governance: Chairman's Summary*, UNEP IEG Working Document (29 May 2001), 1.

[351] Sand, P. H., *The Rise of Public Trusteeship in International Environmental Law*, GlobalTrust Working Paper Series 03/2013 (Tel Aviv University: Buchmann Faculty of Law 2013).

[352] International Treaty on Plant Genetic Resources for Food and Agriculture, 3 November 2001, 2400 UNTS 379.

[353] 'Bering Sea Fur Seals Fisheries Arbitration' (Great Britain/United States, 15 August 1893); Moore, J. B. (ed), *History and Digest of the International Arbitrations to which the United States has been a Party* (US Government Printing Office 1898), vol 1, 755, at 814.

[354] *Robinson Township, et al v. Commonwealth* (19 December 2013) 63 MAP 2012.

Before a more general assessment of the Rio Declaration can be attempted in the last section of this preliminary study, it is useful to mention three main questions that were not sufficiently covered by the declaration.

A lacuna of the declaration that came under criticism from contemporary observers is the avoidance of any clear and explicit reference to individual rights.[355] Although several principles, including Principles 1, 10, and 22, implicitly refer to human rights, the wording carefully avoids recognizing explicitly a human right to an environment of a certain quality or a human right to environmental participation or the rights of indigenous peoples. Despite its importance, this lacuna has been significantly covered by subsequent developments in international human rights practice. As discussed in the relevant chapters of this commentary, human rights courts and treaty bodies have recognized some environmental content (both substantive and procedural) as part of general human rights. Moreover, in 1998 a specific treaty on environmental participation (the aforementioned Aarhus Convention) was concluded under the aegis of the UNECE and, in 2007, the UN General Assembly adopted an important resolution on the rights of indigenous peoples, the UNDRIP. In this regard, the wording of the declaration has been clearly overtaken by subsequent practice and the declaration as such must be seen merely as a step or a moment in the crystallization of the now extremely important connection between human rights and environmental protection.

Another lacuna concerns the key issue of finance. The importance of the topic and the tortuous negotiation process of the chapter on finance of Agenda 21[356] make the absence of a clear reference (let alone a principle) to finance in the declaration all the more conspicuous. Although financial matters are mentioned in Principle 7 (CBDR) and they are arguably implicit in Principle 9 (technology transfer), it is difficult to explain the absence of a specific principle on a matter as important as finance other than by the political divide on this matter between developed and developing countries. Of course, a principle on finance may not have performed any particular function or, at least, not an effective one in practice. Negotiations on financial issues are a major subject of debate in all international conferences, whether environmental or other. However, a restatement of the basic position of international law in this matter would have been welcome and useful to address questions as controversial as 'conditionality' in financial assistance,[357] 'loss and damage' in the context of climate change negotiations,[358] the role of the private sector[359] or, more generally, the relations between general official development aid and specifically environmental financial assistance.

The third lacuna concerns most environmental instruments so far, including the Outcome document of the Rio 2012 Summit, namely the absence of any reference to investment law.[360] Although Principle 16 specifically states that cost internalization

[355] See the discussion in Shelton, D., 'What happened in Rio to human rights?' (1992) 3 *YbIEL* 75.

[356] On the difficult negotiation of the finance chapter of Agenda 21 see Ricupero, R., 'Chronicle of a Negotiation: The Financial Chapter of Agenda 21 at the Earth Summit' (1993) 4 *Colorado Journal of International Environmental Law and Policy* 81.

[357] On this question see Fairman, D. and Ross, M., 'International Aid for the Environment: Lessons from Economic Development Assistance', *CSIA Discussion Paper 94-03*, Kennedy School of Government, Harvard University, April 1994.

[358] A 'mechanism' has been recently set up under the aegis of the UNFCCC to address this issue. See 'Warsaw international mechanism for loss and damage associated with climate change' (Decision -/CP.19).

[359] On this question see Dupuy, P.-M. and Viñuales, J. E. (eds), *Harnessing Foreign Investment to Promote Environmental Protection: Incentives and Safeguards* (Cambridge University Press 2013).

[360] See Viñuales, 'Green Investment after Rio 2012'.

measures must not distort trade and investment, the declaration does not contain a principle similar to Principle 12 (concerning trade law and environmental measures) for investment law. However, both environmental and development policies, which entail regulatory change (either regulation or deregulation) are being increasingly challenged before investment arbitration tribunals on the grounds that they are in breach of bilateral investment treaties ('BITs') or investment chapters in bilateral or multilateral trade agreements.[361] This important question is only now starting to attract the attention it deserves from policy-makers,[362] particularly thanks to the work of organizations such as the UNCTAD,[363] the OECD[364] or the International Institute for Sustainable Development.[365] Yet, other organizations, including the UNEP, have not yet fully grasped the importance of investment 'law' in the move to a green economy they actively advocate for. Even for those organizations focusing on trade, it would be important to integrate the idea that the very same environmental measure can come across both trade and investment disciplines[366] and consistency with one does not necessarily entail consistency with the other.[367]

In addition to the three areas identified, one could also refer to other lacunae in the Rio Declaration, such as the absence of references to the status of certain resources such as common areas, common heritage of mankind, common concern of mankind, or shared natural resources, which are important distributional or 'balancing' concepts in international environmental law. But despite these and other potential lacunae, one must not underestimate the importance and reach of the Rio Declaration as the expression of environmental protection in the form of both a 'branch' and a 'perspective' influencing, much like development law, all areas of international regulation. At this point in this preliminary inquiry, one may ask whether the Rio Declaration could, to an extent to be determined, operate as a constitutional instrument.

361 See Viñuales, *Foreign Investment and the Environment in International Law*.

362 See Gordon, K. and Pohl, J., 'Environmental Concerns in International Investment Agreements: a survey' (2011) *OECD Working Papers on International Investment* no 2011/1 ('OECD Report').

363 UNCTAD, *World Investment Report. Towards a New Generation of Investment Policies* (2012), chapter IV (Investment Policy Framework for Sustainable Development).

364 OECD, *Harnessing Freedom of Investment for Green Growth*, Freedom of Investment Roundtable, 14 April 2011.

365 See Mann, H. et al, *IISD Model International Agreement on Investment for Sustainable Development. A Negotiator's Handbook* (IISD, 2006).

366 Several claims were brought under trade and investment agreements as a result of the same feed-in-tariff scheme adopted by Ontario, Canada. See *Canada—Certain Measures Affecting the Renewable Energy Generation Sector*, Panel Report (19 December 2012), WT/DS412/R and WT/DS426/R, Appellate Body Report (6 May 2013), WT/DS412/AB/R and *Canada—Measures Relating to the Feed in Tariff Program*, WT/DS426/AB/R ('Canada—Renewables'); *Mesa Power Group LL.C. v. Government of Canada*, NAFTA (UNCITRAL) Arbitration, Notice of Arbitration (4 October 2011); *Windstream Energy LL.C. v. Government of Canada*, NAFTA (UNCITRAL), Notice of Arbitration (28 January 2013).

367 Examples of differences between trade and investment include the understanding of 'likeness' in a non-discrimination context (see eg *Parkerings-Compagniet AS v. Republic of Lithuania*, ICSID Case no ARB/05/8, Award (11 September 2007), which uses a definition of likeness that would encompass production processes and methods) or the operation of countermeasures (see eg *Corn Products International Inc. v. United Mexican States*, ICSID Case no ARB(AF)/04/1, Decision on Responsibility (15 January 2008), paras 161, 176). See generally DiMascio, N. and Pauwelyn, J., 'Nondiscrimination in Trade and Investment Treaties: Worlds Apart of Two Sides of the Same Coin?' (2008) 102 *AJIL* 48; Kurtz, J., 'The use and abuse of WTO law in investor–state arbitration: Competition and its discontents' (2009) 20 *EJIL* 749.

## V) Concluding Remarks: the Unlikely Constitution

The Rio Declaration cannot be considered as a 'constitutional' instrument in the ordinary meaning of this term. It is neither a foundational norm (*Grundnorm*), understood as a norm giving validity to subsequent norms, nor a 'higher law', from the perspective of legal hierarchy. Moreover, it has no 'organic' dimension, as it does not lay the foundations of institutions capable of organizing international activity regarding sustainable development. Yet, if article 2 of the United Nations Charter and, more specifically, the elaboration of its principles in UNGA Resolution 2625 (XXV)[368] can to some extent be seen as having a constitutional dimension,[369] a similar argument can be made for the Rio Declaration.

As noted earlier in this preliminary study, the Rio Declaration is the only international instrument adopted by consensus that brings together, around a common backbone, most foundational principles of international environmental law (the 'environment set') placing them in a developmental perspective (the 'development set'), in an attempt to conciliate them with socio-economic development. Importantly, the environment and the development sets are conciliated through a set of principles (the 'differentiation set') in a manner that, although it seemed skewed to many observers at the time of the UNCED, represents a fair balance in hindsight. Such balance is placed within the broader context of peace and conflict resolution as understood in the Charter of the United Nations.

Thus, the term 'constitutional instrument' can only be used for the Rio Declaration if it is intended to highlight its emblematic or representative character of the main principles and policies organizing our relations to the environment. No other international instrument of the same standing and adopted by consensus brings these principles and policies together at once; and no other instrument provides a sufficient basis to understand such principles and policies not only as the foundations of a 'branch' but also as the expression of a 'perspective', increasingly noticeable and important in all areas of international regulation. The chapters in this commentary spell out these two dimensions in great detail by referring to the legal expression of each principle of the Rio Declaration, whether in environmental instruments or beyond.

## VI) Select Bibliography

### *Books*

Campiglio, L., Pineschi, L., Siniscalco, D., and Treves, T., *The Environment after Rio: International Law and Economics* (London/Leiden: Graham & Trotman/Martinus Nijhoff 1994).

Chasek, P. and Wagner, L. M., *The Roads from Rio: Lessons Learned from Twenty Years of Multilateral Environmental Negotiations* (London: Routledge 2012).

[368] UNGA Resolution 2625 (XXV), 'Declaration on Principles of International Law concerning Friendly Relations and Co-operation among States in accordance with the Charter of the United Nations', 24 October 1970, UN Doc A/RES/25/2625.

[369] See Abi-Saab, G., 'La reformulation des principes de la charte et la transformation des structures juridiques de la communauté internationale' in *Le droit international au service de la paix, de la justice et du développement: mélanges Michel Virally* (Pedone 1991), 1–8; Dupuy, P.-M., 'L'unité de l'ordre juridique international: cours général de droit international public (2000)', in *RCADI*, vol 297 (2002), 9–489 (discussing art 2 of the United Nations Charter as the foundation of the substantive unity of international law).

Dodds, F., Strauss M., and Strong, M. F., *Only One Earth: The Long Road via Rio to Sustainable Development* (London: Routledge 2012).
Grubb, M., *The 'Earth Summit' Agreements: An Analysis of the Rio '92 UN Conference on Environment and Development* (London: Earthscan 1993).
Halpern, S. L., *United Nations Conference on Environment and Development: Process and documentation*. Academic Council for the United Nations System (ACUNS) reports and papers, no 2, 1993, available on <http://www.ciesin.org/docs/008-585/unced-home.html> (accessed on 20 April 2014).
Holmberg, J., Thomson, K., and Timberlake, L., *Facing the Future: Beyond the Earth Summit* (London: Earthscan 1993).
Johnson, S., *The Earth Summit: the United Nations Conference on Environment and Development (UNCED)* (London/Leiden: Graham & Trotman/Martinus Nijhoff 1992).
Lafferty, W. M. and Eckerberg K., (eds), *From the Earth Summit to Local Agenda 21: Working Towards Sustainable Development* (London: Earthscan 1998).
Schrijver, N., *The Evolution of Sustainable Development in International Law: Inception, Meaning and Status* (Leiden: Martinus Nijhoff 2008).
Singhvi, L.M., *A Tale of Three Cities: The 1993 Rede Lecture and Related Summit Declarations* (Cambridge University Press 1996).
Sjöstedt, G., Spector, B. I., and Zartman, I. W., *Negotiating International Regimes: Lessons Learned from the United Nations Conference on Environment and Development (UNCED)* (London/Leiden: Graham & Trotman/Martinus Nijhoff 1994).
Thomas, C. (ed), *Rio: Unravelling the Consequences* (London: Routledge 1994).

## *Articles and chapters*

Adede, A. O., 'The Treaty System from Stockholm (1972) to Rio De Janeiro (1992)' (1995/1996) 13 *Pace Environmental Law Review* 33.
Adede, A. O., 'The Road to Rio', in Campiglio et al (eds) *The Environment After Rio: International Law and Economics* (London/Leiden: Graham & Trotman/Martinus Nijhoff 1994) 3.
Baker, B., 'Environmental Controversies and Compromises at the Rio Conference' (1992/1993) 2(2) *Currents: International Trade Law Journal* 45.
Batt, J. and Short, D. C., 'The Jurisprudence of the 1992 Rio Declaration on Environment and Development: A Law, Science, and Policy Explication of Certain Aspects of the United Nations Conference on Environment and Development' (1992/1993) 8 *Journal of Natural Resources & Environmental Law* 229.
Bekhechi, M.A., 'Le droit international à l'épreuve du développement durable: Quelques réflexions à propos de la Déclaration de Rio sur l'environnement et le développement' (1993) 59 *Hague Yearbook of International Law* 59.
Beyerlin, U., 'Rio-Konferenz 1992: Beginn einer neuen globalen Umweltrechtsordnung?' (1994) 54 *Zeitschrift für ausländisches öffentliches Recht und Völkerrecht* 124.
Boon, Foo Kim, 'The Rio Declaration and Its Influence on International Environmental Law' (1992) *Singapore Journal of Legal Studies* 347.
Cropper, A., 'Unsaid '92' (1992) 1 *Review of European Community & International Environmental Law* 314.
Doumbe-Bille, S. and Kiss, A.-Ch., 'Conférence des Nations Unies sur l'Environnement et le Développement (Rio De Janeiro-juin 1992)' (1992) 38 *Annuaire français de droit international* 823.
Esty, D. C., 'Beyond Rio: Trade and the Environment' (1993) 23 *Environmental Law* 387.
Freestone, D., 'The Road from Rio: International Environmental Law After the Earth Summit' (1994) 6 *JEL* 193.
Getches, D. H., 'The Challenge of Rio' (1993) 4 *Colorado Journal of International Environmental Law and Policy* 1.

Handl, G., 'Controlling Implementation of and Compliance with International Environmental Commitments: The Rocky Road from Rio' (1994) 5 *Colorado Journal of International Environmental Law and Policy* 305.

Housman, R. F. and Pershkow, B., 'Fear and Loathing in Rio' (1992) 3 *Touro Journal of Transnational Law* 167.

Jennings, R., 'The Role of the International Court of Justice in the Development of International Environment Protection Law' (1992) 1 *Review of European Community & International Environmental Law* 240.

Johnson, P. M., 'La Conférence des Nations Unies sur l'environnement et le développement ou le Sommet de la Planète Terre, Rio de Janeiro' (1991/1992) 7 *Revue québécoise de droit international* 244.

Khor, M., 'The North-South battles that dominate Earth Summit' (1992) *Earth Summit Briefings* no 1. Third World Network.

Kimball, L. A. and Boyd, W. C., 'International Institutional Arrangements for Environment and Development: A Post-Rio Assessment' (1992) 1 *Review of European Community & International Environmental Law* 295.

Kindall, M. P. A., 'UNCED and the Evolution of Principles of International Environmental Law' (1991/1992) 25 *John Marshall Law Review* 19.

Kiss, A., 'Environnement et développement ou environnement et survie?' (1991) 118 *Journal du droit international (Clunet)* 263.

Kiss, A., 'The Rio Declaration on Environment and Development', in Campiglio et al (eds) *The Environment After Rio: International Law and Economics* (London/Leiden: Graham & Trotman/ Martinus Nijhoff 1994), 55–64.

Koh, T. T-B., 'UNCED Leadership: A Personal Perspective', in Sjöstedt et al, *Negotiating International Regimes: Lessons Learned from the United Nations Conference on Environment and Development (UNCED)* (London/Leiden: Graham & Trotman/Martinus Nijhoff 1994), 165.

Kohona, P. T. B., 'UNCED—The Transfer of Financial Resources to Developing Countries' (1992) 1 *Review of European Community & International Environmental Law* 307.

Kovar, J. D., 'A Short Guide to the Rio Declaration' (1993) 4 *Colorado Journal of International Environmental Law and Policy* 119.

Mann, H., 'The Rio Declaration' (1992) 86 *American Society of International Law Proceedings* 405.

Marchisio, S., 'Gli atti di Rio nel diritto internazionale' (1992) 75 *Rivista di diritto internazionale* 581.

McConnell, M., 'Reflections on the United Nations Conference on Environment and Development' (1992/1993) 8 *Journal of Natural Resources & Environmental Law* 347.

Miles, G., 'UNCED: A Pacific Regional Perspective' (1992) 1 *Review of European Community & International Environmental Law* 317.

von Moltke, K., 'The Last Round: The General Agreement on Tariffs and Trade in Light of the Earth Summit' (1993) 23 *Environmental Law* 519.

Mouthaan, S., 'International Environmental Law and the 1992 Rio Earth Summit: A Brave New World' (1995/1996) 17 *Holdsworth Law Review* 119.

Pallemaerts, M., 'International Environmental Law from Stockholm to Rio: Back to the Future?' (1992) 1 *Review of European Community & International Environmental Law* 254.

Pallemaerts, M., 'International Environmental Law in the Age of Sustainable Development: A Critical Assessment of the UNCED Process' (1995/1996) 15 *Journal of Law and Commerce* 623.

Palmer, G., 'Earth Summit: What Went Wrong at Rio' (1992) 70 *Washington University Law Quarterly* 1005.

Panjabi, R. K. L., 'Idealism and Self-Interest in International Environmental Law: The Rio Dilemma' (1992/1993) 23 *California Western International Law Journal* 177.

Panjabi, R. K. L., 'The South and the Earth Summit: The Development/Environment Dichotomy' (1992/1993) 11 *Dickinson Journal of International Law* 77.

Panjabi, R. K. L., 'From Stockholm to Rio: A Comparison of the Declaratory Principles of International Environmental Law' (1992/1993) 21 *Denver Journal of International Law and Policy* 215.

Parson, E. A., 'Assessing UNCED and the State of Sustainable Development' (1993) 87 *American Society of International Law Proceedings* 508.

Pathak, R. S. and Jaitly, A., 'Rio Declaration—Economic Issues for Developing Countries' (1992) 1 *Review of European Community & International Environmental Law* 267.

Porras, I. M., 'The Rio Declaration: A New Basis for International Co-operation' (1992) 1 *Review of European Community & International Environmental Law* 245.

Ricupero, R., 'Chronicle of a Negotiation: The Financial Chapter of Agenda 21 at the Earth Summit' (1993) 4 *Colorado Journal of International Environmental Law and Policy* 81.

Robinson, N. A., 'Colloquium: The Rio Environmental Law Treaties IUCN's Proposed Covenant on Environment and Development' (1995/1996) 13 *Pace Environmental Law Review* 133.

Rose, G. and Jackson, S., 'Industry's Response to UNCED: Environmental Management Post-Rio' (1992) 1 *Review of European Community & International Environmental Law* 320.

Rosencranz, A., Campbell, R., and O'Neil, D. A., 'Rio Plus Five: Environmental Protection and Free Trade in Latin America' (1996/1997) 9 *GIELR* 527.

Sand, P. H., 'International Law on the Agenda of the United Nations Conference on Environment and Development: Towards Global Environmental Security' (1991) 60 *Nordic Journal of International Law* 5.

Sand, P. H., 'International Law on the Agenda of the 1992 Earth Summit' (1992) 3 *Colorado Journal of International Environmental Law and Policy* 343.

Sand, P. H., 'UNCED and the Development of International Environmental Law' (1992/1993) 8 *Journal of Natural Resources & Environmental Law* 209.

Sand, P. H., 'International Environmental Law After Rio' (1993) 4 *EJIL* 377.

Sanwal, M., 'Sustainable Development, the Rio Declaration an Multilateral Cooperation' 4 *Colorado Journal of International Environmental Law and Policy* 45.

Shelton, D., 'What Happened in Rio to Human Rights?' (1992) 3 *YbIEL* 75.

Shelton, D., 'Stockholm Declaration (1972) and Rio Declaration (1992)', *Max Planck Encyclopedia of Public International Law*, Oxford University Press, 2008, online edition, <http://www.mpepil.com>.

Shibata, A., 'International Law-Making Process in the United Nations: Comparative Analysis of UNCED and UNCLOS III' (1993/1994) 24 *California Western International Law Journal* 17.

Strong, M. F., 'Very Important Prospect: United Nations Conference on Environment and Development, to Be Held in the Riocentro Conference Centre, Rio De Janeiro, Brazil, During 1–12 June 1992' (1991) 18 *Environmental Conservation* 102.

Strong, M. F., 'Beyond Rio: Prospects and Portents' (1993) 4 *Colorado Journal of International Environmental Law and Policy* 21.

Thomas, L. M., 'The Business Charter for Sustainable Development: Action Beyond UNCED' (1992) 1 *Review of European Community & International Environmental Law* 325.

Tromans, S., 'International Law and UNCED: Effects on International Business' (1992) 4 *JEL* 189.

Villarino Marzo, C., 'La Cumbre de la Tierra: Entre el Derecho del Medio Ambiente y el Derecho del Desarrollo' (1992) 44 *Revista Española de Derecho Internacional* 708.

Villarino Marzo, C., 'The Story of the UNCED Process', in Sjöstedt et al, *Negotiating International Regimes: Lessons Learned from the United Nations Conference on Environment and Development (UNCED)* (London/Leiden: Graham & Trotman/Martinus Nijhoff 1994), 45.

Willetts, P., 'From Stockholm to Rio and Beyond: The Impact of the Environmental Movement on the United Nations Consultative Arrangements for NGOs' (1996) 22 *Review of International Studies* 57.

Wirth, D. A., 'The Rio Declaration on Environment and Development: Two Steps Forward and One Back, or Vice Versa?' (1994/1995) 29 *Georgia Law Review* 599.

Wirth, T. E., 'The Road from Rio—Defining a New World Order' (1993) 4 *Colorado Journal of International Environmental Law and Policy* 37.

# 2. The Philosophy of the Rio Declaration

Pierre-Marie Dupuy*



## I) Introduction

The Rio Declaration on Environment and Development was adopted on 13 June 1992. And yet, we feel the need to write its commentary, article by article, more than twenty years later, while, in the meantime, two other conferences have already been convened, on the tenth and twentieth anniversary of the Rio Conference. It thereby demonstrates that the agreed text has since then remained, if not without a future, at least without an equivalent. The Rio Declaration is both a text of reference and the result of an exceptional event. Contrary to what happened during the Stockholm Conference, devoted twenty years earlier to the same topic, the United Nations managed in 1992 to bring together the entirety of member State delegations, from the East as well as from the West, from the South and from the North, to reaffirm that 'we have only one Earth' and that our actions put it into danger.

The Stockholm Declaration had already constituted an act, political as well as legal, of a singular importance; but it had never been adopted by all member States and was the illustration of fundamentally different approaches between developed and developing States regarding the challenges of environmental protection. As for the Rio Conference, it is the first and undoubtedly remains until now the only conference that can be called, as it was, the 'Earth Summit'. As in Stockholm, the declaration that was adopted at the end of the conference amounts to a wake-up call as much as it is a catalogue of collective commitments. Its primary objective, as corroborated by its title, is to reconcile the visions of affluent countries to that of populations concerned with their own development. It is however regrettable that the key concept of 'sustainable development' was not given a proper definition in the Rio Declaration, hence echoing the persistent divergences between the poor and the rich. These differences of opinion are undoubtedly one of the reasons why the text adopted in 1992 failed to affirm the promotion of a healthy environment as a

* Emeritus professor of international law at the University Panthéon-Assas (Paris 2) and at the Graduate Institute of International and Development Studies, Geneva.

fundamental human right, despite the fact that the key elements of the principle had already been provided for in Principle 1 of the Stockholm Declaration.[1]

The underlying philosophy of the Rio Declaration is, nevertheless, hindered by antagonistic trends. As with other texts negotiated globally, it would be relatively artificial to look for a complete and coherent unity in the inspiration underlying the document. Yet, there is little doubt that the projects elaborated within the framework of the United Nations keep the trace of the ideas debated at the time about the comparatively new need to unite to ensure that the planet, threatened by the anarchy of human actions, remains inhabitable. Nevertheless, the text is the result of negotiations and compromises between national delegations: the cult of national sovereignty and the common adherence to the imperative of economic growth contradict in part the cult of collective enterprise found in the global cooperation framework needed to save an endangered Earth. And yet, this imperfect text exemplifies how perceptions have evolved on an Earth that we find ourselves constrained to share and whose degradation incites us to introduce a collective duty of solidarity.

## II) A Fresh Look at the Earth

The Rio Declaration is animated by a tension between the concern to re-establish the ecological balance and the desire to avoid compromising economic development. It could be simplistic to summarize this tension as a divergence of opinions on the basis of a North/South divide. There are, admittedly, differences between their approaches to environmental issues: the alarm regarding the need to protect the environment is considerably stronger in industrialized countries, which have long been confronted by environmental degradation, given their comparatively early industrial revolution. Nevertheless, none of the States attending the Rio Conference was ready to sacrifice, even partially, economic growth to ecological restoration. In any case, the Earth, recognized as wounded, is identified by the Declaration as 'the Earth, our home'; but this tender solicitude does not diminish the conviction that man remains the measure of all things, to quote the famous expression of the antique sophist Protagoras: the protection of Nature remains subordinated to the usage that humanity will make of its resources.

### 1. 'The Earth, our home'

In Hymn XII of the Atharva-Veda, the sacred text of Hinduism and jewel of the Vedic culture, invocations such as this one are found:

> Thy snowy mountain heights, and thy forests, O earth, shall be kind to us!... Upon the firm, broad earth, the all-begetting mother of the plants, that is supported by (divine) law, upon her, propitious and kind, may we ever pass-our lives![2]

Admittedly, there is no equivalent to this chant of the Earth in the declaration adopted at Rio, whereas numerous similar invocations can be found in other cultures. The lyricism of the Stockholm Preamble and its prophetic resonance has actually disappeared. In the Rio Declaration man is only 'both creature and moulder of his environment'. There is

[1] 'Man has the fundamental right to freedom, equality and adequate conditions of life, in an environment of a quality that permits a life of dignity and well-being.'

[2] See Ralph Griffith, *The Hymns of the Atharvaveda*, 1895–6, full text on the Internet. <http://www.sacred-texts.com/hin/av.htm>.

no emphasis on the key and formidable powers he has on the future of the Planet either. Yet, one should not forget that the Rio Preamble, 'seeking to build upon' the Stockholm Preamble, refers back to it from its very first words.

In this respect, the reference, in the last paragraph of the Preamble, to the fact that the Earth is 'our home' is a welcome and encouraging statement. The expression is rich in meaning. Strikingly, the text prefers the term of 'home' to the notion, at the time already almost traditional and associated with the concept of humanity, of 'common heritage'. But such a change does not impoverish the overall philosophy of the Declaration. Shared by all, the 'home' is indeed understood as a heritage shared by all generations, past, present, and future, of the community of human beings. In addition, the term 'home' has a connotation that is less legal than that of 'heritage', and is also more intimist, family-oriented, and community-based. All members of the universal brotherhood are hosted, albeit more and more cramped given the galloping demographic growth, on the same earth. This implies a constant reorganization of the restricted space, a place of residence and a reservoir of resources for mankind, condemned to a concerted management of its organized survival. If we consider, as we should, that the *evolutive* interpretation of the Declaration and its Preamble is necessary for its permanent adaptation to the inspiration of collective action, the wealth of the expression 'our home' is then to be underlined.

But also, and most importantly, the word 'home' introduces an affective dimension; it refers, yet in a manner more implicit than in 1972, to what can be considered as an inversion of the relationship between humanity and its womb. In the ancestral text of Antharva-Veda mentioned above, the Vedic tradition impressed by its serene attachment to the permanence of the mother Earth. A similar feeling could also be found in the homeric hymn written as early as the sixth century BC that celebrates the 'well-founded Earth, mother of all, eldest of all beings (who) feeds all creatures that are in the world'.[3] Traditionally, and since the dawn of time, the cultures of the world have perceived the nourishing earth as a source of inexhaustible wealth and fertility. On the opposite, in the latter third of the twentieth century and at the beginning of the following millennium, men sense, at least occasionally, that their mother has truly aged; the advanced age of the Earth mother weighs upon it even more so that its resources, too long thought inexhaustible, have been exploited in an unrestrained manner.

From then on a new fear of global scarcity appears, with the disappearance of fish in the seas, gold in mines, oil in deposits that are being avidly sucked up, breathable air above sprawling cities, and also of the entire biodiversity as exemplified by the adoption of the convention concerned with its protection at the same place and time (1992) as the Declaration. Man starts to be spasmodically aware, beyond the apocalyptic revelation of the annihilating power of the military atom, that unrestrained freedom can lead to the sterilization of his own living space. Beyond their prudent 'instructions', governmental delegations themselves, at least during the brief euphoria of a conference to which they were all invited, realized at Rio that their disorganized actions were threatening to definitely silence the Spring.[4]

Reading the addition, after all relatively inspired, to the Preamble of the Declaration, we would almost hope that by designating the Earth as 'our home', the diplomats gathered

[3] Homer, Hymn XXX, 'To Earth the Mother of All', translation by H.G. Evelyn-White, in the Loeb Classical Library (New York, 1914), 456.

[4] Carson, R., *Silent Spring* (Houghton Mifflin Harcourt 1962).

at Rio wanted to revive the sacralization of the Earth, at least from a rhetorical perspective. It is this same sacralization that had swamped ancient civilizations, before the disenchantment of the world with technical culture and a thirst for progress. Had a number of philosophers, such as those part of the 'Deep Ecology' movement,[5] or Michel Serres in France, not already called, well before the adoption of the Rio Declaration, for a renewed sacralization of the now dependent Earth mother?

Reading Principle 7, one might almost think that its call to the international community derives from such an inspiration. Inter-State cooperation is worded as an obligation to 'conserve, protect and restore the health and integrity of the Earth's ecosystem'. The reference to health is an encouraging perspective to consider not only Nature as a person, but also, more largely and following an intentionally holistic vision (as it speaks of 'restoring its integrity'), Earth itself, envisaged within the framework of the ecosystem made of its interdependent elements. It would however be wrong to think that the Declaration goes that far.

## 2. The enduring relevance of Protagoras

It would be vain to look in the text adopted at Rio for an invitation to the conclusion of the 'natural contract' called for by Michel Serres,[6] Arne Naess,[7] or Klaus Meyer-Abich,[8] who wanted to elevate Nature or its elements (such as trees for instance) to the level of true subjects of law, including by giving them legal standing.

On the contrary, the deliberate anthropocentric inspiration of the Declaration and the retained subordination of Nature to man is present from the very first principle. It opens the normative section of the Declaration by providing that 'human beings are at the centre of concerns for sustainable development'. Such an assertion undoubtedly only makes space for a conceptualization of the respect for Nature within a narrow instrumental framework turned towards the pre-eminence of the human being over nature—and this despite the fact that Darwin's evolutionism had revealed, since the publication of *The Origin of Species* in 1859, that man is only an element of a natural environment of which he is an integral part.

No Copernican revolution here. Man remains at the centre of the system. He remains the master; he remains conceptualized almost irrespective of the dependent state in which he is nevertheless put towards his own environment. Reading Principle 1 of the Declaration, we tend to think that ecological imbalances remain limited, without questioning the famous assertion of Protagoras, four centuries BC, according to which 'Man is the measure of all things'. Admittedly, the three monotheisms have not fundamentally questioned the pertinence of the expression, which is today contested, but at least not by the Rio Declaration. Indeed, according to the text, there is no environmental protection without development, as understood by human beings.

The upholding of the primacy of the duality between man and Nature is for that matter illustrated in the notion of 'sustainable development'. Even if the concept is not defined

[5] See Nash, R. F., *The Rights of Nature: A History of Environmental Ethics* (Wisconsin University Press 1989); Deveall, B. and Sessions, G., *Deep Ecology: Living as if Nature Mattered* (Gibbs Smith 1985).

[6] Serres, M., *Le contrat naturel* (Flammarion 1987).

[7] Naess, A., 'The Shallow and the Deep, Long-Range Ecology Movement: A Summary' (1976) *Inquiry*, n°16. See also Ost, F., *La nature hors la loi* (La Découverte 1995), 159.

[8] Meyer Abich, K., *Aufstand für die Natur* (Hanser 1990).

by the Declaration, its Principle 4 provides without ambiguity that '[i]n order to achieve sustainable development, environmental protection shall constitute an integral part of the development process and cannot be considered in isolation from it'. There is no better way of saying that Nature and its protection do not exist for themselves. On the contrary, it would not be an overstatement to conclude that, given such a principle, the chance for environmental protection lies for the promoters of the Declaration in its economic dimension, in the sense that damage to the environment creates costs jeopardizing the cost-effectiveness of the activities responsible for the harm. If this is really the case, the limits of the environmentalist perspective of the text are clear. Its relatively traditional concept of progress connects it more to the nineteenth century than to the alarmist concerns of the 'Club of Rome' towards growth, although barely more than a decade old at the time of the meeting of the 'Earth Summit'.[9] At best, it is the idea that progress cannot be achieved 'at all cost' that can be identified in the attempt to reconcile development and the environment. As a result, Principle 8 seeks to eliminate 'unsustainable patterns of production and consumption'.

Such an assertion is probably important enough to justify the authority that we still grant the Declaration twenty years after its adoption—and even more so considering that it advocates a universal duty of solidarity on this basis.

## III) A Duty of Collective Solidarity

The Declaration has remained up to date as none of its key concepts have lost relevance until now: if not, it is the opposite, given that, since its adoption, the state of the terrestrial environment has generally worsened. As a result, the call for a 'global partnership'—based on solidarity between all the elements of the human community in the face of this collective threat—supposedly relies today, as before, on a shared feeling of collective responsibility that focuses more on the future than on the past. It also encourages the development of a normative framework with a universal aim—although, admittedly, the key challenge today lies more in the implementation of existing norms rather than in their formulation.

### 1. A call for collective responsibility

While Nature had originally been the source of so much wealth for man, it gradually became its victim. As a result, the reversal of the relationship between man and Nature and the ever-growing threats of the destruction of Nature encourage humanity to engage in collective action.

The reading of a text elaborated during the penultimate decade of the last century and expressing a new sentiment of responsibility provoked by a certain 'heuristic of fear' might naturally lead us to find its inspiration in one widely read book of the time, '*Das Prinzip Verantwortung*', 'The Imperative of Responsibility'[10] of Hans Jonas, published in German in 1979 and soon after translated into English and other languages. While its influence on the Declaration is highly likely, it also knows some limits, paralleling the criticism levelled against the author regarding his deliberately anti-technical tendencies and critical stance

[9] Meadows, D. H. et al, *The Limits to Growth* (A Report of the Club of Rome 1972).

[10] Jonas, H., *The Imperative of Responsibility: In Search of Ethics for the Technical Age* (University of Chicago Press 1979).

towards the rationalism of the Enlightenment.[11] Here again, even if the philosophy of the Declaration remains implicit, if not unknown by a number of its authors, the 'return to Kant'[12] movement might be more at ease with explaining why the Declaration encourages an increase in global legislation relative to the protection of the environment.

Given that modern technology now allows man to wipe out the planet, Jonas wonders why 'humanity should exist'. He discredits traditional morals, too centred on instantaneousness. We are henceforth responsible for the future. The mission of humanity is thus to safeguard future generations even more than the present ones. Jonas considers that it has become urgent to overcome the abyss originally formulated by David Hume between what is and what ought to be. It is today that we should commit to what is, as it is on this reality that weighs a prophecy of apocalypse. At the opposite of Descartes' project, which considered that man is the 'master and owner of nature', we should now become the 'servants and hostages' of nature; a silent nature but, taken hostage and at the mercy of man, even more so weakened. More than 20 years later, the dramatic warming of the planet, considerably more important than originally predicted by the scientists, and the rapid melting of the Arctic ice cap at the source of new territorial greed, have not at all disqualified the gloomy visions of the heir of Heidegger. In his wake, but in a more positive manner, Paul Ricoeur underlined how these new ethics of the future call for collective responsibility in the form of a 'mission to be fulfilled' rather than as a mistake that requires reparation of its consequences:[13] responsibility, yes, but turned towards the future.

We should therefore note that one of the most fundamental provisions of the Stockholm Declaration, enunciated in Principle 21, appears earlier in the text of the Rio Declaration, at Principle 2:

> States have, in accordance with the Charter of the United Nations and the principles of international law, the sovereign right to exploit their own resources pursuant to their own environmental and development policies and the responsibility to ensure that activities within their jurisdiction or control do not cause damage to the environment of other States or of areas beyond the limits of national jurisdiction.

Nevertheless, this principle, which the International Court of Justice has since reaffirmed several times as part of positive international law, reflects for the most part a classical conception of responsibility. Indeed, it formulates a 'primary obligation' which, if disregarded, would engage responsibility for failure to meet the duty of due diligence. In any case, it is its breadth that opens the principle to a dynamic conception of prevention of harm, widening up to a precautionary approach often inspired by the work of Hans Jonas itself, and found explicitly in the wording of Principle 15 of the Rio Declaration, according to which '[w]here there are threats of serious or irreversible damage, lack of full scientific certainty shall not be used as a reason for postponing cost-effective measures to prevent environmental degradation'.

The criticisms often levelled against the thinking of Jonas by 'egalitarian' authors claiming to concur with the contractualist logic of John Rawls appear here to be only very

[11] See in particular Sève, L., *Pour une critique de la raison bioéthique* (Odile Jacob 1997).

[12] See Renaut, A., *Kant aujourd'hui* (Flammarion 1990).

[13] Ricoeur, P., 'La responsabilité et la fragilité de la vie' (1991) 5 *Le Messager européen* 203, at 203ff, referred to by Ost, *La nature hors la loi*, 285. See also Ricoeur, P., *Soi-même comme un autre* (Seuil 1990), seventh and eighth studies.

partially warranted.[14] In practice, and as the evolution of comparative positive law systems relative to the environment has actually demonstrated, we always legislate for the future and not only for the present, therefore not only for the contemporaries but also for the unborn subjects. There is no conceptual obstacle, unless we limit ourselves with a narrow concept of the law simplified as a contract between equals, to legislating for the protection of future generations. This is even more so if we consider that the revocability of international conventions and their conditions of periodic revision could suffice to ensure their necessary adaptation to the passing of time.[15]

## 2. Return to Kant

On the other hand, the Declaration seems to depart from the possibly too radical ideas of Hans Jonas on responsibility by introducing two determining elements—implying an equitable division of duties and providing for differential treatment according to economic capabilities. Once more, Principle 7 is here enlightening. The provision ends on the statement that: 'the developed countries acknowledge the responsibility that they bear in the international pursuit to sustainable development in view of the pressures their societies place on the global environment', whereas it started by affirming that 'States shall cooperate in a spirit of global partnership to conserve, protect and restore the health and integrity of the Earth's ecosystem'.

This idea of a global partnership remains relatively blurry; however, it clearly establishes the framework of reciprocal solidarity within which cooperation between the 'North' and the 'South' should operate. Notwithstanding their developmental differences, States are all interested in safeguarding their common planetary residence. Therefore, far from breaking away from the ideas of the *Aufklärung*, the Declaration is inscribed in the rationalist tradition that had already inspired the drafting of the Charter of the United Nations, that is, a tradition recognizing the necessity of having a universal constitution to move beyond the state of nature, even though, and contrary to the perspective taken by some contemporary currents, it would be wrong to take the term 'constitution' literally by understanding it as a formal legal instrument. In any case, this idea can easily be transposed from concerns over the establishment of political peace to the fight against pollution; and this in particular given that Principle 25 of the Declaration clearly tells us that 'Peace, development and environmental protection are interdependent and indivisible'.

The reference to humanity, also present in the last paragraph of the Declaration and envisaged by the author of *Perpetual Peace: A Philosophical Sketch*,[16] is what allows man to think of universality imposed by moral law. Humanity, in addition to being trans-temporal by extending to future generations, is also trans-State given its cosmopolitan dimension; it creates a requirement of universality applicable not only to moral law but also to its formalization in the form of law. In the aforementioned *Sketch*, Kant was already blackening the attitude of occidental metropolises for remaining considerably below the

[14] See in particular Barry, B., 'Justice between Generations', in Hacker, P. M. S. and Raz, J. (eds), *Law, Morality and Society, Essays in Honour of H.L.A. Hart* (Clarendon Press 1979), 272. See also Ost, *La nature hors la loi*, at 288ff.

[15] See Brown Weiss, E., *In Fairness to Future Generations: International Law, Common Patrimony and Intergenerational Equity* (Transnational Publishers 1988).

[16] See Kant, I., *Political Writings* (Cambridge University Press 1991), 93–130.

requirements posed by cosmopolitan law and involving 'the right to a common ownership of the surface of the Earth'.

As a result, the Declaration assigns different objectives, more or less general, to the participants in this global partnership: improvement of scientific cooperation relative to the environment (Principle 9); promotion of 'a supportive and open international economic system that would lead to economic growth in all countries' (Principle 12); cooperation to prevent the relocation and transfers towards other States of activities or substances likely to cause 'severe environmental degradation' (Principle 14); international notification in cases of natural catastrophes (Principle 18); or of activities likely to cause transboundary damages (Principle 19). In addition, it is expected that these objectives are carried out in 'a spirit of partnership' (Principle 27).

Contrary to the Stockholm Declaration, the Rio Declaration makes only a shy reference to future generations in Principle 3, devoted to the right to development. We might however consider that the normative programme adopted in 1992, although in principle turned towards the future, is primarily defined by reference to the truly Kantian idea that provides that we need a law common to all the peoples of the Earth to coordinate efforts in order to avoid that the pursuit of economic development transforms into an ecological catastrophe. The adoption, simultaneous to that of the Declaration, of the Framework Convention on Climate Change and of the Convention on Biological Diversity corroborates the existence of a common universal support for this powerful norm to save Nature by leaving the 'state of nature', ie the unorganized coexistence of rival sovereignties. The joint acceptance of Agenda 21, aiming in particular to include regional authorities and all the other stakeholders of economic development in the promotion of sustainable development, also underlines the cosmopolitan dimension of the normative encouragement addressed by the 173 heads of States and governments to the totality of the peoples of the Earth, under the watchful eye of the representatives of international civil society.

## IV) Conclusion

In conclusion, if we accept to step back and consider the temporal dimension of the event that was the Earth Summit, we can observe that, for the first time in the history of humanity, and beyond the movement already initiated in 1972 at Stockholm, all the representatives of those who inhabit the globe gathered together to affirm their common will to save their planet. At the cosmic scale, this planet is only one amongst thousands or billions of others. While it is not possible to confirm our monopoly, this planet is however characterized not only by the existence of life but also by the existence, perhaps progressive, of conscience. To speak like Pierre Teilhard de Chardin, as he was at the beginning of the first quarter of the last century, a 'noosphere' appears as a result, made of the growing interconnection of individual consciences, closely connected to the terrestrial biosphere.[17]

[17] See, among others, his *Hymn for the Universe*, published in 1965; or *The Human Phenomenon*, in a new translation, Appleton-Weber, S. (trans), (Sussex Academic Press 2003). On P. Teilhard de Chardin, see King, U., *Spirit of Fire, The Life and Vision of Teilhard* (Orbis Books 1996).

This leads us to wonder whether, despite its shortcomings and imperfections, the Rio Declaration does not constitute, on the scale of evolution, the most accomplished—up to now—affirmation of the growing awareness that humanity is just a passenger on an Earth in distress.

Any reference to Evolution however designates the implacable arrow of time. Let us nurture the hope that this catalogue of resolutions, while clumsy and perhaps relatively empty promises, will not prove to have been formulated too late.

# 3. Changing Conceptions of Environmental Risk

Jacqueline Peel*



## I) Introduction

Two decades on, the Rio Declaration on Environment and Development still stands as a remarkable milestone in the development of international environmental law.[1] While the Rio Declaration has made many important contributions to international environmental law and the law on sustainable development, perhaps its most transformative contribution lies in its international endorsement of the principle of precaution. As the later chapter in this commentary on Principle 15 discusses, the precautionary principle gives effect to the notion that scientific uncertainty over the nature and extent of environmental harms should not be used as a reason for postponing protective measures.[2] That principle stands in opposition to the idea—well-accepted in international environmental law prior to that point—that measures to address environmental threats ought to be adopted only where there exists firm scientific evidence establishing a likelihood of harm.[3] The Rio Declaration's endorsement of precaution in Principle 15 introduced into international environmental law a new discourse over the proper evidentiary foundations of global environmental regulation. It has thus played an important role in changing conceptions of what amounts to an environmental 'risk' necessitating an international legal response.[4] At the same time the principle continues to generate disagreement over its meaning and effect, including the extent of scientific evidence and (un)certainty that is required to justify environmentally protective measures.

This chapter introduces the competing themes in this discourse as a backdrop to the book's discussion of relevant principles of the Rio Declaration, in particular: Principle 9 (endogenous capacity for sustainable development); Principle 12 (trade and environment);[5]

* Professor of Law at Melbourne Law School.

[1] Rio Declaration on Environment and Development, A/CONF.151/26 (vol I) (1992).

[2] See the chapter by A. A. Cançado Trindade in this commentary.

[3] Sands, Ph. and Peel, J., *Principles of International Environmental Law* (3rd edn, Cambridge University Press 2012), 218–19.

[4] The term 'risk' here is used in the broad sense of a possibility of harm. The term has also acquired a narrower technical meaning as the product of the probability of an adverse event and the magnitude of its harmful consequences: see further Adams, J., *Risk* (UCL Press 1995), 8.

[5] International trade law has been an important forum for testing the permissible extent of precautionary measures to address environmental risks, where such measures also impact international trade. For discussion

and Principle 15 (precaution). It begins with a discussion of the place of science in international environmental law and the central importance of scientific evidence to our understanding of environmental risk. The chapter then considers the challenge that the precautionary principle poses to traditional approaches to international environmental regulation, which limit international action to circumstances where there is strong scientific evidence that significant environmental damage will or is likely to occur. However, in some international treaties dealing with environmental risks, provisions calling for a 'precautionary approach' are juxtaposed with quantitative standard setting measures based on 'present knowledge',[6] or requirements to undertake scientific risk assessment. This raises questions as to the relationship between science-based and precautionary conceptions of environmental risk and associated regulatory approaches. Such tensions are not easily resolved by international law, given underlying differences in environmental values and cultural sensitivities to risk and uncertainty.[7]

## II) Place of Science in International Environmental Law

Since the emergence of the earliest treaty instruments addressing environmental and natural resource management issues, science has played a special role in the development and implementation of international environmental law. State action to address environmental threats has generally been closely tied to scientific discoveries of harm, albeit that the international response may follow some time later and be strongly shaped by other factors, such as economic considerations.[8]

There are at least three reasons that explain the central place that science has occupied, and continues to occupy, in the rules and institutions of international environmental law. First, widespread environmental risks, which require international cooperative action to resolve, are often 'invisible' risks. Their causes are imperceptible to the untrained eye, requiring study and the 'sensory organs' of science for detection.[9] Transboundary pollution problems, such as that in issue in the seminal international environmental case of *Trail Smelter*, are a leading example. In the *Trail Smelter Arbitration*, the Arbitral Tribunal relied on scientific advice and expertise in making its findings about the mechanism of atmospheric distribution of sulphur dioxide gas emitted from the zinc smelter at Trail in British Columbia and the extent of the detrimental effects on property and the environment in neighbouring Washington State.[10] Likewise, contemporary environmental risk problems, such as persistent organic pollutants, ozone depletion, and climate change, depend to an even greater extent upon sophisticated structures of scientific research and modelling to inform policy-makers of the extent of the risks at issue.

see Herwig, A. and Joerges, C., 'The Precautionary Principle in Conflicts Law Perspectives', in Van Calster. G. and Prévost, D. (eds), *Research Handbook on Environment, Health and the WTO* (Edward Elgar 2013) 3; Wagner, M., 'Taking Interdependence Seriously: The Need for a Reassessment of the Precautionary Principle in International Trade Law' (2012) 20(3) *Cardozo Journal of International and Comparative Law* 713.

6 See eg Protocol to the 1979 Convention on Long-Range Transboundary Air Pollution to Abate Acidification, Eutrophication and Ground-Level Ozone (Gothenburg), 30 November 1999, in force 17 May 2005, UN Doc EB.AIR/1999, art 1 ('Gothenburg Protocol').

7 See generally, Peel, J., *Science and Risk Regulation in International Law* (Cambridge University Press 2010), ch 3.

8 Sands and Peel, *Principles of International Environmental Law*, 6–7.

9 Beck, U., *Risk Society: Towards a New Modernity* (SAGE Publications 1992), 27.

10 *Trail Smelter Arbitration (United States v. Canada)*, 16 April 1938, 11 March 1941, 3 RIAA 1907 (1941).

Second, in the 'risk society', as famously postulated by Beck and Giddens, it is these hidden risks of technological or human origin that are of greatest societal concern.[11] The focus on risk in modern society has led to risk management becoming a central feature of government activity at the national and international levels.[12] A focus on risk necessarily requires mechanisms for risk identification, risk assessment, and risk control.[13] These mechanisms are dominated by scientists and other 'risk professionals', who bring a self-consciously 'technical' approach to their work that is seen as being more objective.[14]

Third, as international environmental law has expanded its focus and penetrated more deeply into national regulatory efforts to address risks, its legitimacy has begun to come under challenge.[15] In some cases this has led to attempts to integrate civil society views more effectively in decision-making processes.[16] In other cases, treaty regimes have sought to bolster the scientific foundations of standard-setting and decision-making, using the authority of science and experts to sustain the legitimacy of international environmental risk governance.

The close association between scientific and legal developments in the international environmental field was recognized by States meeting at the United Nations Conference on Environment and Development (UNCED), albeit not explicitly in the Rio Declaration itself. Instead *Agenda 21*, the policy framework for achieving sustainable development formulated at UNCED, states 'the sciences are increasingly being understood as an essential component in the search for feasible pathways toward sustainable development'.[17] A key role for science in this regard was said to be 'to provide information to better enable formulation and selection of environment and development policies in the decision-making process'.[18] This view underpins Principle 9 of the Rio Declaration, which calls, *inter alia*, for States to 'cooperate to strengthen endogenous capacity-building for sustainable development by improving scientific understanding through exchanges of scientific and technological knowledge...'.

Today it is rare to find an international instrument or multilateral treaty dealing with matters of environmental risk that does not make reference to science or technical considerations.[19] At the very least, most international environmental treaties provide for

[11] See generally Beck, *Risk Society*; and Giddens, A., *The Consequences of Modernity* (Stanford University Press 1990).

[12] Jaeger, C. et al, *Risk, Uncertainty, and Rational Action* (London: Earthscan Publications Ltd 2001), 19; Jasanoff, S., *Science and Public Reason* (Routledge 2012), 133.

[13] National Research Council, *Risk Assessment in the Federal Government: Managing the Process* (National Academy Press 1983); Royal Society, *Risk Assessment: Report of a Royal Society Study Group* (Royal Society 1983). See also Jasanoff, S., *Designs on Nature: Science and Democracy in Europe and the United States* (Princeton University Press 2005), 267, noting the wide acceptance of risk assessment as 'a principled approach to ordering knowledge and weighing alternatives'.

[14] Adams, *Risk*, 26.

[15] Bodansky, D., 'The Legitimacy of International Governance: A Coming Challenge for International Environmental Law?' (1999) 93 *AJIL* 596.

[16] A leading example in this regard is the Aarhus Convention on Access to Information, Public Participation and Decision-making and Access to Justice in Environmental Matters, 25 June 1998, in force 30 October 2001, (1998) 38 ILM 517.

[17] UNCED, *Agenda 21: Programme of Action for Sustainable Development* (1993), para 35.2.

[18] UNCED, *Agenda 21*, para 35.1. The relevant paragraph goes on to say that it will therefore be essential to enhance scientific understanding, improve long-term scientific assessments, and strengthen scientific capacities in all countries.

[19] House of Lords Science and Technology Committee, *Science and Treaties* (2004, HL 110-I, London). See also the catalogue of institutions 'for the performance of science policy functions' within multilateral

the transfer of necessary technologies to developing countries, the exchange of scientific information and the allocation of funds for technical assistance and capacity building.[20] A significant number of multilateral environmental treaties also have standing scientific or technical advisory bodies made up of experts from a variety of disciplines who act independently of the governments appointing them.[21] Key functions performed by such bodies include the receipt and audit of national reports, the review of parties' compliance with technical obligations, the issue of guidelines for activities such as environmental monitoring, and performing assessments of environmental health or quality. Treaty-based scientific bodies in turn often have strong linkages with non-governmental or inter-governmental scientific organizations, such as the International Council for Exploration of the Seas, the Group of Experts on the Scientific Aspects of Marine Pollution, the Intergovernmental Platform on Biodiversity and Ecosystem Services and the Intergovernmental Panel on Climate Change. In sum, scientific research in contemporary international environmental regimes is viewed as 'a major supplier of relevant knowledge', which is drawn on by

environmental treaty regimes listed in Haas, P., 'Science Policy for Multilateral Environmental Governance' in Kanie, N. and Haas, P. (eds), *Emerging Forces in Environmental Governance* (United Nations University 2004), 115, appendix.

[20] Examples include the Convention on Wetlands of International Importance especially as Waterfowl Habitat, Ramsar, 2 February 1971, in force 17 December 1975, 996 UNTS 245, art 4(3); Convention for the Protection of the World Cultural and Natural Heritage, Stockholm, 16 November 1972, in force 17 December 1975, 1037 UNTS 151, art 22; Convention on the Prevention of Marine Pollution by Dumping of Wastes and Other Matter, London, 13 November 1972, in force 30 August 1975, 1046 UNTS 120, art IX; Convention on the Conservation of Antarctic Marine Living Resources, Canberra, 5 May 1980, in force 7 April 1982, 1329 UNTS 48 (CCAMLR) art XX; Vienna Convention for the Protection of the Ozone Layer, Vienna, 22 March 1985, in force 22 September 1988, 1513 UNTS 293, arts 3, 4; Montreal Protocol on Substances that Deplete the Ozone Layer, Montreal, 16 September 1987, in force 1 January 1989, 1522 UNTS 3, arts 9, 10, 10A; Basel Convention on the Control of Transboundary Movements of Hazardous Wastes and their Disposal, Basel, 23 March 1989, in force 5 May 1992, 1673 UNTS 57, arts 10(2), 14(1); Protocol on Environmental Protection to the Antarctic Treaty, Madrid, 4 October 1991, in force 14 January 1998, 30 ILM 1455, art 6(1); United Nations Framework Convention on Climate Change, Rio De Janeiro, 9 May 1992, in force 24 March 1994, 1771 UNTS 164 (UNFCCC), arts 4, 11; Convention on Biological Diversity, Rio De Janeiro, 5 June 1992, in force 29 December 1993, 1760 UNTS 79, (CBD) arts 12, 16–18, 21; United Nations Convention to Combat Desertification in those Countries Experiencing Serious Drought and/or Desertification, Particularly in Africa, Paris, 14 October 1994, in force 16 December 1996, 1954 UNTS 3, arts 12, 16–18, 19; Agreement for the Implementation of the Provisions of the United Nations Convention on the Law of the Sea of 10 December 1982 relating to the Conservation and Management of Straddling Stocks and Highly Migratory Fish Stocks (Straddling Stocks Agreement), New York, 4 December 1995, in force 11 December 2001, 2167 UNTS 3, arts 10, 14, 25; Kyoto Protocol to the United Nations Framework Convention on Climate Change, Kyoto, 11 December 1997, in force 16 February 2005, 2303 UNTS 148, art 10(d); Rotterdam Convention on Prior Informed Consent Procedure for Certain Hazardous Chemicals and Pesticides in International Trade, Rotterdam, 11 September 1998, in force 24 February 2004, 2244 UNTS 337, arts 14(1)(a), 16; Cartagena Protocol on Biosafety to the Convention on Biological Diversity (Biosafety Protocol), Cartagena, 29 January 2000, in force 11 September 2003, 2226 UNTS 208, arts 20, 22; Convention on Persistent Organic Pollutants, Stockholm, 23 May 2001, in force 17 May 2004, (2001) 40 ILM 532 (POPs Convention), arts 11(2)(b), 12, 13; International Convention for the Safe and Environmentally Sound Recycling of Ships, Hong Kong, 11 May 2009, not in force, IMO Doc SR/CONF/45, art 13; Protocol on Access to Genetic Resources and the Fair and Equitable Sharing of Benefits Arising from their Utilization to the Convention on Biodiversity Diversity, Nagoya, 29 October 2010, not in force, C.N.782.2010.TREATIES-1, art 23.

[21] Examples include the Convention on the Conservation of Migratory Species of Wild Animals, Bonn, 23 June 1979, in force 1 November 1983, 1651 UNTS 333, art VIII; CCAMLR, arts XIV, XV; Ozone Convention, Decision VCI/6; Antarctic Treaty Protocol, arts 11, 12; UNFCCC, art 9; CBD, art 12; Desertification Convention, art 24; Rotterdam Convention, art 18(6); POPs Convention, arts 8, 19(6); International Convention for the Safe and Environmentally Sound Recycling of Ships (Hong Kong) 11 May 2009, not in force, IMO Doc SR/CONF/45, Annex, Regulation 6.

decision-makers 'for problem identification and diagnosis, and in some cases also for explicit policy advice'.[22]

## III) Precautionary Challenge

In traditional international environmental law-making, the ease with which a cogent case can be made for international regulation generally turns on the ability to show that lack of action by the international community is likely to result in significant adverse effects.[23] Measures to address such 'known' risks can then be instituted in order to prevent or mitigate predicted harms.[24] The precautionary principle represents a fundamental challenge to this process of global environmental regulation. Its basis is not known predictable harms, but rather those risks that are uncertain but yet carry with them the potential for serious or irreversible damage.

The precautionary principle recognizes the inherent limitations of scientific research, which requires a high level of confidence in available data before an adverse effect will be definitively declared.[25] However, uncertainties—whether conceptually or methodologically based[26]—may mask a diagnosis of adverse effect, even where harm is actually occurring. By the time scientific knowledge improves to the point where harm is detected, significant environmental degradation may have already occurred.[27] To avoid this situation, the precautionary principle calls for preventative measures not to be postponed where there are threats of serious or irreversible damage, albeit not demonstrated by conclusive scientific evidence. International regulatory action in such circumstances is based on scientific or other evidence sufficient to demonstrate a potential risk but not meeting the high standards of confidence or 'certainty' required in scientific research.[28]

Since the Rio Declaration, this 'precautionary approach' to regulation has been endorsed in several treaties and by international courts and tribunals.[29] While the

[22] Andresen, S. et al, *Science and Politics in International Environmental Regimes: Between Integrity and Involvement* (Manchester University Press 2000), 182–3.

[23] Sands and Peel, *Principles of International Environmental Law*, 6.

[24] Freestone, D. and Hey, E., 'Origins and Development of the Precautionary Principle', in Freestone, D. and Hey E. (eds), *The Precautionary Principle and International Law: the Challenge of Implementation* (Kluwer Law International 1996), 3, 13.

[25] Kriebal, D. et al, 'The Precautionary Principle in Environmental Science' (2001) 109(9) *Environmental Health Perspectives* 871. Conventionally scientific research guards against Type 1 error—the mistake of concluding that a phenomenon or association exists when in truth it does not—by setting that error rate low, usually 5%.

[26] For a useful discussion of different uncertainties in scientific research that may affect regulatory conclusions see Walker, V., 'The Siren Songs of Science: Toward a Taxonomy of Scientific Uncertainty for Decisionmakers' (1991) 23 *Connecticut Law Review* 567.

[27] The European Environment Agency has issued two reports documenting 'late lessons' from such from 'early warnings'. The reports canvass diverse case studies from fisheries collapse to asbestos and nanotechnology. See European Environment Agency, *Late Lessons from Early Warnings: Science, Precaution, Innovation* (European Union 2013); European Environment Agency, *Late Lessons from Early Warnings: the Precautionary Principle 1896–2000* (European Union 2011).

[28] The phrase 'lack of full scientific certainty' in Principle 15 of the Rio Declaration is problematic in this regard as there is no such thing as absolute certainty in science. A better interpretation would treat the word 'full' in this context as equating to the usual 95% confidence limit applied in scientific research. See further Kriebal et al, 'The Precautionary Principle in Environmental Science'.

[29] See Cançado Trindade, Ch 19. See also Sands and Peel, *Principles of International Environmental Law*, 217–28.

utility of applying 'prudence and caution' when dealing with uncertain environmental risks has been widely recognized,[30] more difficult issues remain as to how this general notion should be operationalized in practice.[31] These include questions over the extent of scientific uncertainty that triggers precautionary action, the degree of 'hard' scientific support required and, in dispute settlement settings, which party bears the onus for demonstrating that precautionary measures are or are not appropriate. Increasingly it is recognized that scientific knowledge about environmental risks represents a spectrum running from well-documented, oft repeated studies to highly uncertain theories, which may or may not be the first signs of a coming paradigm shift in the relevant field of research.[32] Not surprisingly, States and international institutions have differed strongly as to where, along this spectrum, the appropriate domain of precautionary measures lies.

## IV) Competing Conceptions of Environmental Risk

Although a precautionary approach to international environmental regulation has achieved broad support during the past two decades, vigorous debate continues over competing claims of the degree of scientific evidence and certainty required to justify precautionary restrictions. This debate has been facilitated by developments in regulatory science that have focused ever greater attention on complex, 'invisible' risks that afford decision-makers a wider margin of discretion in determining the appropriate regulatory response. In the 1960s *Silent Spring* era,[33] the regulatory focus was on pollutants with direct toxicity to humans or the environment for which an environmental 'assimilative capacity' could be ascertained and employed as a basis for standard-setting.[34] Over time, the focus shifted to issues of carcinogenicity (eg hormone residues in beef) and more recently to indirect, cumulative risks such as endocrine disrupting substances or loss of genetic diversity.[35] For these less direct, less tangible risks scientific uncertainties are often

[30] The 'prudence and caution' formula has been used by courts in several decisions without direct mention of the precautionary principle. See further Cançado Trindade, Ch 19.

[31] For discussion see Peel, J., *The Precautionary Principle in Practice: Environmental Decision-making and Scientific Uncertainty* (Federation Press 2005); Trouwborst, A., *Precautionary Rights and Duties of States* (Brill 2006).

[32] See eg the discussion of the precautionary principle and concepts of sufficiency/insufficiency of scientific knowledge in *Responsibilities and Obligations of States Sponsoring Persons and Entities with Respect to Activities in the Area* (Advisory Opinion) (Seabed Disputes Chamber of the International Tribunal for the Law of the Sea, ITLOS Case No 17, 1 February 2011), para 131; *United States—Continued Suspension of Obligations in the EC-Hormones Dispute*, Report of the WTO Appellate Body, WT/DS320/AB/R, 16 October 2008, para 703.

[33] Rachel Carson's 1962 book *Silent Spring* (Houghton Mifflin 1962) focused global attention on the detrimental effects of pesticides such as DDT on the environment. It is widely credited with having helped to launch the environmental movement in the United States.

[34] The assimilative capacity approach, which bears strong similarities to the notion of critical loads used in treaties such as the Gothenburg Protocol, is based on the assumption that there is a safe level of pollution or emissions that is quantifiable. The precautionary principle implicitly rejects this approach as a basis for environmental policy. See further Barton, C., 'The Status of the Precautionary Principle in Australia: its emergence in legislation and as a common law doctrine' (1998) 22 *HELR* 509.

[35] Joerges, C., 'Law, Science and the Management of Risks to Health the National, European and International Level—Stories on Baby Dummies, Mad Cows and Hormones in Beef' (2001) 7 *Columbia Journal of European Law* 1.

more prevalent, inviting application of the precautionary approach. Conversely, in the face of uncertainty there may be reluctance to put in place regulations to control such risks where the costs will be significant but the health and environmental benefits are difficult to quantify.[36]

Strong differences of perspective on this issue have emerged between the United States—which favours basing regulatory decisions on 'sound' or 'hard' science[37]—and the European Union (EU)—which, in line with the adoption of the precautionary principle in EU law,[38] advocates allowing decision-makers a greater 'margin of appreciation' in the face of scientific uncertainty.[39] These positions in turn reflect strong cultural differences regarding risk, uncertainty, and innovation in the two jurisdictions. The domestic US risk regulatory system has evolved over time to require strong scientific (and economic) support for risk prevention measures.[40] By contrast, the EU, since a series of food safety crises in the 1990s, has taken a progressively more cautious approach to risk management in circumstances of scientific uncertainty.[41]

The transatlantic debate over competing ideas of environmental risk has been particularly intense in the international trade sphere where EU precautionary measures banning or limiting the use of products have been challenged by the United States for breaching rules under agreements of the World Trade Organization (WTO). As discussed in more depth in the chapter on Principle 12 (trade and environment), this conflict has led to a series of cases that has placed the dispute settlement bodies of the WTO in the invidious position of choosing between the merits of different risk conceptions. Prominent disputes have concerned the lawfulness of restrictions on the imports of meat products containing residues of growth hormones (which may be linked to cancer in humans), and the EU's ban on genetically modified crops and foods (which may be linked to a range of health and environmental risks including biodiversity loss and antibiotic resistance of disease-causing organisms).[42] Another dispute looms over recent precautionary measures taken by the EU to ban certain pesticides, which are believed to be contributing to a global die-off in bee populations.[43] Concerns over the rapid decline of bee populations have also been raised in the United States, but the response of government agencies has been to stress the lack of scientific research clearly linking

[36] Sunstein, C., *Laws of Fear: Beyond the Precautionary Principle* (Cambridge University Press 2005).

[37] McGarity, T., 'Our Science is Sound Science and Their Science is Junk Science: Science-Based Strategies for Avoiding Accountability and Responsibility for Risk-Producing Products and Activities' (2004) 52 *University of Kansas Law Review* 897.

[38] Treaty on European Union, Official Journal C 191, 29 July 1992, in force 1 November 1993 required EU action on the environment to 'be based on the precautionary principle', with further amendments under the 1997 Amsterdam Treaty to apply the principle to Community policy on the environment (art 174(2)). For the relevant provisions in the consolidated EU Treaty see Consolidated Version of the Treaty on the Functioning of the European Union, Official Journal C 83/47, 30 March 2010, art 191(2).

[39] Segnana, O., 'Precautionary Principle: New Developments in the Case Law of the Court of First Instance' (2002) 3 *German Law Journal* 68.

[40] For a seminal work on this topic see Jasanoff, S., *The Fifth Branch: Science Advisors as Policymakers* (Harvard University Press 1990). See also Jasanoff, *Designs on Nature*.

[41] Alemanno, A., 'Regulating the European Risk Society', in Alemanno, A. et al (eds), *Better Business Regulation in a Risk Society* (Springer 2013), 37.

[42] See Ch 16 by Margaret Young in this commentary.

[43] European Commission Implementing Regulation No 485/2013 of 24 May 2013, Official Journal L139/12, 25 May 2013, available at <http://ec.europa.eu/food/animal/liveanimals/bees/neonicotinoids_en.htm>.

bee health declines to pesticide use.[44] As one US agency official explained, 'we let the science lead our regulatory decision-making, and we want to make sure that we make accurate and appropriate regulatory decisions as opposed to things that could lead to meaningful societal cost without any benefit whatsoever'.[45]

Conflict between competing 'sound science' and 'precautionary' conceptions of environmental risk is also evident in several treaties concluded since the Rio Declaration.[46] For example, the 2000 Biosafety Protocol to the Convention on Biological Diversity calls for biosafety risk assessments of transboundary movements of 'living modified organisms' (LMOs), which are to be 'carried out in a scientifically sound manner'.[47] At the same time, the Protocol gives a prominent place to the precautionary principle in both its preamble and objective.[48] Parties are also permitted to refuse a proposed import of LMOs on a precautionary basis by way of a provision that states:

> Lack of scientific certainty due to insufficient relevant scientific information and knowledge regarding the extent of the potential adverse effects of a living modified organism on the conservation and sustainable use of biological diversity in the Party of import, taking also into account risks to human health, shall not prevent that Party from taking a decision, as appropriate, with regard to the import of the living modified organism in question... in order to avoid or minimize such potential adverse effects.[49]

In WTO law, similar conflicts arise under the Sanitary and Phytosanitary Measures Agreement (SPS Agreement), which requires SPS measures adopted for the purpose of protecting human, animal or plant life or health to be based on sufficient scientific evidence and a scientific risk assessment.[50] Nonetheless, article 5.7 of the SPS Agreement—characterized by the WTO Appellate Body as 'reflecting' the precautionary principle[51]—permits temporary restrictive measures to be maintained by parties in circumstances where relevant scientific evidence is 'insufficient'.

Resolving the tension between competing conceptions of environmental risk under treaty provisions or in international adjudication creates 'some acute difficulties'.[52] Arguably, where these conflicts arise there is no correct answer and certainly not one that can be diagnosed by reference to the purportedly objective knowledge of science. Rather such conflicts reveal the importance of value considerations to our notions of environmental risk, values that may well diverge across a diverse international community.

[44] United States Department of Agriculture, *Report on the National Stakeholders Conference on Honey Bee Health* (2012, National Honey Bee Health Stakeholder Conference Steering Committee, Alexandria).

[45] Plumer, B., 'Why are the bees dying? The U.S. and Europe have different theories.' *Washington Post* (Washington DC), 3 May 2013, available at <http://www.washingtonpost.com/blogs/wonkblog/wp/2013/05/03/why-are-bees-dying-the-u-s-and-europe-have-different-theories/>.

[46] eg Gothenburg Protocol; POPs Convention, preamble, arts 1 and 8, Annex E. Even a highly precautionary treaty such as the Straddling Stocks Agreement, which requires application of a precautionary approach (art 6), also includes the principle that conservation and management measures should be 'based on the best scientific evidence available and are designed to maintain or restore stocks at levels capable of producing maximum sustainable yield' (art 5).

[47] Biosafety Protocol, art 15.1, Annex III, paras 3 and 9.

[48] Biosafety Protocol, preamble, art 1.

[49] Biosafety Protocol, art 10(6).

[50] Agreement on the Application of Sanitary and Phytosanitary Measures, Marrakesh, 15 April 1994, in force 1 January 1995, 1867 UNTS 493, arts 2.2 and 5.1.

[51] *EC—Measures Concerning Meat and Meat Products* (Hormones), Report of the WTO Appellate Body, WT/DS26/AB/R and WT/DS48/AB/R, 16 January 1998, para 124.

[52] Sands and Peel, *Principles of International Environmental Law*, 7.

## V) Conclusion

With its nod to the importance of science as a component of policy-making for sustainable development while also calling for wide application of a precautionary approach, the Rio Declaration both recognized traditional notions of environmental risk and provided the foundations for a fundamental challenge to them. Our conceptions of environmental risk have been unalterably changed as a result. Acting on the basis of uncertain evidence of threats of environmental harm is now accepted as an important precept—perhaps even a general principle—of international environmental law. Yet debate continues as to how far the international community should go in regulating potential environmental harms in the face of scientific uncertainty. In the decades ahead, these questions are likely to persist as international environmental law moves to tackle a range of pressing environmental problems including climate change and possible technological responses to it such as carbon capture and storage and geo-engineering.

# 4. The Preamble of the Rio Declaration

Francesco Francioni*

The United Nations Conference on Environment and Development, Having met at Rio de Janeiro from 3 to 14 June 1992,

Reaffirming the Declaration of the United Nations Conference on the Human Environment, adopted at Stockholm on 16 June 1972, and seeking to build upon it,

With the goal of establishing a new and equitable global partnership through the creation of new levels of cooperation among States, key sectors of societies and people,

Working towards international agreements which respect the interests of all and protect the integrity of the global environmental and developmental system,

Recognizing the integral and interdependent nature of the Earth, our home, Proclaims that:



## I) Introduction

Departing from an established practice of lengthy and inspirational texts introducing the most important environmental law proclamations, the Rio Declaration presents a very short and subdued Preamble. Of the five incidental clauses of which the Preamble is composed, the first simply recalls the Rio meeting from 3 to 14 June 1992, the second reaffirms the 1972 Stockholm Declaration and the intention to build upon it. The other clauses set forth the basic goals and aspirations of the Declaration. These goals are: the establishment of 'a new and equitable global partnership based' on international cooperation among States, key sectors of society, and people; and the promotion and conclusion of international agreements for the protection of the 'integrity of the global environment and developmental system.' The last sentence underscores the integral and interdependent nature of the Earth, the 'home' of humankind.

This rather plain and unambitious tone of the Preamble is the mirror of the difficulties encountered at the Rio meeting in balancing diverging interests and demands of the developing countries (the 'South'), on the one side, and the industrialized countries (the 'North') on the other side, with regard to the respective competing priorities of economic

* Professor of International Law, Emeritus, European University Institute, Florence, and LUISS University, Rome. Member (associate) of the Institut de Droit International. Previously he held the chair of international law at the Law Faculty of the University of Siena.

development and of reaching a global deal on the protection of the environment. These difficulties, and the attendant necessity of reaching a political compromise between the two camps, underlie all the clauses of the preamble and influence most of the Principles laid down in the Declaration.

The text itself was drafted after the contents of all the Principles had been agreed. At the fourth session of the Preparatory Committee the G77 and China managed to avoid negotiations on the Preamble and focus on the actual Principles. They feared that discussions on the Preamble would consume most of the time and result in a Declaration which would in fact be limited to the Preamble, as some developed countries, including the United States, had suggested.[1] Instead, a focus on the content of Principles would allow for a proper place to be given to developmental (not only environmental) considerations. The language of the Preamble is mostly the contribution of the chairman of the PrepCom, Tommy Koh, who drafted it at the end of the informal consultations within the contact group it had established with representatives of a small group of States (seven developed and seven developing countries). In what follows, the five preambular clauses are placed in their broader policy context, highlighting when relevant their legal implications.

## II) Reaffirming the Stockholm Declaration

In the twenty years since the adoption of the Stockholm Declaration on the Human Environment,[2] several critical developments had taken place, which the Rio Declaration could not ignore. In 1982, under the strong impulse of the International Union on the Conservation of Nature ('IUCN'), the UN General Assembly had adopted the World Charter for Nature,[3] a soft-law document focusing on the conservation and sustainable utilization of living natural resources. In 1987, the World Commission on Environment and Development produced the influential 'Bruntland report', *Our Common Future*,[4] further building upon the Stockholm Declaration and outlining a number of legal principles intended to form the backbone of a new normative order on environmental protection and sustainable development. In 1990, as a follow-up to the 1989 Paris declaration of the G7, Italy organized the Siena Forum on International Law of the Environment, with the participation of governmental experts, scholars, scientists, and representatives of international organizations,[5] with the aim of elaborating a legal framework of environmental principles to be presented at the following G7 meeting in Houston, in the United States, and to the UN. The Final Document of the Forum was presented and circulated as a

[1] See UN Doc A/CONF.151/PC/WG.III/L.21 ('L.21'), proposing that the declaration be incorporated as a 'prologue to Agenda 21'. See also Ling, C.Y., *The Rio Declaration on Environment and Development: An assessment* (Third World Network 2012), 24–8; Kovar, J., 'A Short Guide to the Rio Declaration' (1993) 4 *Colorado Journal of International Environmental Law and Policy* 119, 122–4.

[2] 'Declaration of the United Nations Conference on the Human Environment', Stockholm, 16 June 1972, UN Doc A/CONF 48/14/Rev.1 ('Stockholm Declaration').

[3] 'World Charter for Nature', UNGA Res. 37/7, 28 October 1982.

[4] Report of the World Commission on Environment and Development, *Our Common Future*, 10 March 1987 ('Brundtland Report').

[5] The present writer coordinated the organization of the Forum at the University of Siena and participated in the drafting of the Final Document. The Final Document is published in Presidenza del Consiglio dei Ministri, *Vita Italiana*, n. 1, 1990, 10–72.

document of the UN General Assembly at its 45th session.[6] Through these and other initiatives, the Stockholm Principles were fleshed out and increasingly adapted to changing circumstances.

In this context, one may ask to what extent does the solemn 'reaffirmation' of the Stockholm Principles in the Preamble of the Rio Declaration effectively amount to an incorporation of those Principles in the new document? And to what extent does the Rio Declaration really 'build upon' Stockholm, and take into account the substantive developments produced by the normative instruments adopted in the 20 years that separate Stockholm from Rio?

To answer these questions one has to take into account that both the Stockholm Declaration and the Rio Declaration are soft-law instruments. Therefore, they are not to be treated as binding successive treaties, the relationship between which would have to be assessed under article 30 of the 1969 Vienna Convention on the Law of Treaties.[7] At the same time, the reaffirmation of the Stockholm Declaration by the Preamble does not have the effect of consolidating the two declarations into a single normative text. The two declarations remain separate and the Rio Declaration must be considered in light of a new general perspective on environmental governance and also in light of new principles which were absent from the Stockholm text. These include the principle of sustainable development[8] and the strategically important new Principle 7 on common but differentiated responsibilities,[9] as well as Principle 10 on procedural obligations concerning information and public participation in environmental matters.[10] At the same time, the distinct and separate nature of the two documents becomes evident when we consider the modification brought by the Rio Declaration to some established principles of the Stockholm era. This is the case with Principle 21, widely considered to have attained customary law status, which in the new Rio formulation of Principle 2[11] undergoes a substantive modification by the addition of the words 'and developmental policies' to the original Stockholm text, which speaks only of 'environmental policies' pursuant to which States have a sovereign right to exploit their own natural resources. This addition introduces an entirely new dimension but certainly makes sense in a document intended to address environment and development as inseparable components of the international political agenda.

## III) Environment and Human Rights

In one respect the Preamble of the Rio Declaration marks a regressive step as compared to the Stockholm Declaration. The latter text contained an important acknowledgment of the human rights dimension of environmental law and policy. The first paragraph

6 See UN Doc A/45/666, 24 October 1990.

7 Vienna Convention on the Law of Treaties, 23 May 1969, 1155 UNTS 331.

8 References to sustainable development pervade the text of the Rio Declaration, but its clearest statement is in Principle 4. See the chapter by Pierre-Marie Dupuy and Virginie Barral in this commentary.

9 See Chapter 11 by Philippe Cullet in this commentary. This principle was a key claim of developing countries, perhaps the core demand made by them at Rio in connection with environmental management. See Sand, P. H., 'UNCED and the Development of International Environmental Law' (1992/1993) 8 *Journal of Natural Resources and Environmental Law* 209, at 216.

10 See the chapter by J. Ebbesson in this commentary. This principle was a key demand of developed countries. See Sand, 'UNCED and the Development of International Environmental Law', 216.

11 See the chapter by L.-A. Duvic-Paoli and J. E. Viñuales in this commentary.

of its preamble affirmed that the environment is 'essential to... the enjoyment of basic human rights—even the right to life itself'.[12] This human rights perspective of environmental protection was projected also in Principle 1 of the Stockholm Declaration, which stipulated that '[m]an has the fundamental right of freedom, equality and adequate conditions of life in an environment of a quality that permits a life of dignity and well being'.

It was precisely with a view to giving full legal content to this principle that several initiatives had already taken place in the period immediately preceding the UN Conference on Environment and Development. The World Commission on Environment and Development elaborated, through its expert group on environmental law, a draft provision stipulating that 'all human beings have the fundamental right to an environment adequate for their health and well being'.[13] Similarly, the Final Document of the 1990 Siena Forum on International Law of the Environment dedicated an entire section (section 13)[14] to the practices and techniques to be adopted in order to guarantee respect for individual and collective rights with regard to access to information on environmental issues, public participation at appropriate stages of environmental decision-making processes, access to environmental justice, the right to education, and the legitimate interest of future generations in environmental quality. None of these proposals found their way into the Preamble of the Rio Declaration. A faint echo of them can be found in Principle 10 on citizens' participation and information. But the text of Principle 10 carefully shuns the language of 'rights' in favour of a logic of expediency and efficiency: 'Environmental issues *are best handled*[15] with the participation of all concerned citizens, at the relevant level'. One cannot help noting the striking contrast with the adoption of 'rights' language in Principle 3, which speaks of the 'right to development'.

This is particularly unfortunate because the interconnected nature of human rights and environmental protection has become one of the dominant themes in the post-Rio development of environmental law and in the jurisprudence of the human rights courts.[16] Suffice it to think of the far-reaching impact of the 1998 Aarhus Convention[17] or the robust articulation of an environmental dimension of human rights in the judicial practice implementing the European Convention (especially articles 2, 8, and 6) and the American Convention on human rights (especially article 21), which has gone beyond individual entitlements to construe collective environmental rights.[18] Finally, one must consider the contemporary attempts at adopting a human rights approach to the impending global disaster of climate change.[19]

[12] Stockholm Declaration.

[13] Text reproduced in Munro, R. and Lammers, J., *Environmental Protection and Sustainable Development: Legal Principles and Recommendations* (Graham and Trotman 1987), 38.

[14] See Forum at the University of Siena, Final Document.

[15] Our italics.

[16] See *amplius* on this point in our commentary on Principle 1.

[17] Aarhus Convention on Access to Information, Public Participation in Decision-making and Access to Justice in Environmental Matters, 25 June 1998, 2161 UNTS 447 ('Aarhus Convention').

[18] For a critical analysis of this practice, see Francioni, F., 'International Human Rights in an Environmental Horizon' (2010) 21 *EJIL* 41; Boyle, A., 'Human Rights and the Environment: Where Next?' (2012) 23 *EJIL* 613.

[19] See Office of the High Commissioner for Human Rights ('OHCHR'), *Report of the Office of the United Nations High Commissioner for Human Rights on the relationship between climate change and human rights*, 15 January 2009, UN Doc A/HRC/10/61.

## IV) New Levels of Cooperation

The third paragraph of the Preamble sets the aim of a 'new equitable global partnership' and indicates that the means to achieve this goal is the establishment of 'new levels of cooperation among States, key sectors of society and people'. This commitment has some resonance with the Action Plan for the Human Environment adopted at Stockholm in 1972,[20] which covered the three areas of (1) a global assessment programme, (2) environmental management, and (3) international supporting measures. It contained also provisions on institutional arrangements that formed the basis of the General Assembly's resolution establishing the United Nations Environment Programme (UNEP).

However, the goal of a new equitable global partnership set in the Rio Preamble is more ambitious. It includes the basic framework of Agenda 21[21] with its four sections covering (1) social and economic matters, (2) conservation and management of resources, (3) strengthening the role of major actors, and (4) means of implementation. It is interesting to note that the first section on social and economic matters indirectly reintroduces the human rights dimension of environmental protection, which is missing in the Preamble. It targets poverty as a cause of environmental degradation and links the objective of its eradication to the progressive realization of the right to food, the promotion of the right to health and of the right to adequate lodging, in a world of steady patterns of urbanization that create new challenges and needs for safe shelter.

A strong resonance of the link between human rights and environmental sustainability comes also from the third section of Agenda 21 on the role of major groups. This section recognizes that a fundamental prerequisite of sustainable development is broad public participation in environmental decision-making. The groups whose role is identified as critical in such participation are women, youths, indigenous peoples, NGOs, local authorities, trade unions, business and scientific communities, and farmers. For some of these actors international law has already achieved a codification of basic rights. This is the case for women,[22] and also for indigenous peoples, particularly with the 2007 UN Declaration on the Rights of Indigenous Peoples.[23] For others, such as local authorities, business and scientific communities, farmers, and traditional local communities, their participatory rights have been more recently recognized in special agreements, such as the Nagoya Protocol, additional to the bio-diversity convention, on access and benefit sharing in the commercial exploitation of biological resources.[24] These and other developments can be seen as implied in the programme called for by the third paragraph of the Preamble.

[20] 'Action Plan for the Human Environment', 16 June 1972, UN Doc A/CONF 48/14, 10–62.

[21] Report of the United Nations Conference on Environment and Development, A/CONF.151/26/Rev.l (vol l), Resolution 1, Annex 2: Agenda 21 ('Agenda 21').

[22] Convention on the Elimination of All Forms of Discrimination Against Women, 18 December 1979, 1249 UNTS 455 ('CEDAW').

[23] 'United Nations Declaration on the Rights of Indigenous Peoples', of 2 October 2007, UN Doc A/RES/61/295, Annex. See also Convention (No. 169) concerning Indigenous and Tribal Peoples in Independent Countries, 27 June 1989, (1989) 28 ILM 1382.

[24] The Nagoya Protocol on Access to Genetic Resources and the Fair and Equitable Sharing of Benefits Arising from their Utilization to the Convention on Biological Diversity, 29 October 2010, available at: <http://www.ecolex.org> (TRE-155959) ('Nagoya Protocol'). See Morger, E. E., *Tsiunami and M. Buck, Unraveling the Nagoya Protocol. A Commentary on the Nagoya Protocol on Access and Benefit-sharing to the Convention on Biological Diversity* (Brill 2014).

## V) Working Towards International Agreements

The fourth paragraph of the Preamble expresses the commitment to promoting international agreements 'which respect the interests of all and protect the integrity of the global environment and developmental system'. This formula is innovative with its reference to the global environment but, obviously it remains rather vague and does not offer much guidance as to how such international agreements will be made and how they will be able to satisfy the 'interest of all', assuming that 'all' includes industrial countries and less developed countries, environmentalists and the business community, supporters of new technologies and naturalists, who advocate a conservationist approach.

Be that as it may, the international agreements referred to in this clause comprise the main body of international environmental law. Some important agreements, such as the 1987 Montreal Protocol on Substances that Deplete the Ozone Layer,[25] and the 1989 Basel Convention on the Transboundary Movements of Hazardous Wastes[26] preceded the Rio Declaration. Others followed as part of the package agreed at the Earth Summit. The UN Framework Convention on Climate Change,[27] the Convention of Biological Diversity (CBD),[28] and the Desertification Convention[29] belong to this category, and they all address global environmental problems. At the same time, they all represent a work in progress: the CBD has been complemented by the 2000 Cartagena Protocol on Biosafety[30] and by the two Protocols on access and benefit sharing (Nagoya 2010)[31] and on liability (Nagoya-Kuala Lumpur 2010).[32] The most intractable issue, however, continues to be climate change. The original framework convention adopted in 1992 remains an important source of general principles, but it has proven difficult to translate into operational agreements capable of stemming the increase of greenhouse gases in the atmosphere and reducing the risk of the imminent catastrophe of global warming. The 1997 Kyoto Protocol[33] has proven to be unable to provide a truly universal solution, and the post-Kyoto agenda remains contested.[34]

[25] Montreal Protocol on Substances that Deplete the Ozone Layer, 16 September 1987, 1522 UNTS 29 ('Montreal Protocol').

[26] Basel Convention on the Control of Transboundary Movements of Hazardous Wastes and their Disposal, 22 March 1989, 1673 UNTS 57 ('Basel Convention').

[27] United Nations Framework Convention on Climate Change, 9 May 1992, 31 ILM 849 ('UNFCCC').

[28] Convention on Biological Diversity, 5 June 1992, 1760 UNTS 79 ('CBD').

[29] United Nations Convention to Combat Desertification in those Countries Experiencing Serious Drought and/or Desertification, Particularly in Africa, 17 June 1994, 33 ILM 1328 ('UNCCD').

[30] Cartagena Protocol on Biosafety to the Convention on Biological Diversity, 29 January 2000, (2000) 39 ILM 1027 ('Cartagena Protocol').

[31] The Nagoya Protocol, available at: <http://www.ecolex.org>.

[32] The Nagoya-Kuala Lumpur Supplementary Protocol on Liability and Redress to the Cartagena Protocol on Biosafety, 16 October 2010, available at: <http://www.ecolex.org> [TRE-156245].

[33] Kyoto Protocol to the United Nations Convention on Climate Change, 11 December 1997, 2302 UNTS 148 ('Kyoto Protocol').

[34] See Rajamani, L., 'The Durban Platform for Enhanced Action and the Future of the Climate Regime' (2012) 61 *ICLQ* 501; Francioni, F. and Bakker, C. (eds), *The EU, the US and Global Climate Change* (Aldershot: Ashgate 2014).

## VI) The Integral and Interdependent Nature of the Earth

This is the only clause of the Preamble that appears to depart from the anthropocentric approach of the Declaration. It was introduced on the initiative of the United States representative, which followed the communications presented by civil society groups.[35]

Recognition of the integral and interdependent nature of the Earth would entail, first, the necessity of an ecosystem approach to the protection of nature; that is, an approach that does not isolate single sectors of the natural environment as a distinct object of protection, but proceeds from the knowledge of the complex interaction between the biological and geological components of each ecosystem. Second, it would require recognition that human beings should act not as the conquerors of nature but as custodians that respect the natural heritage and natural processes that permit life on the planet. This second implication becomes problematic when we read it in conjunction with Principle 1 of the Rio Declaration, which abruptly shifts the focus from an ecosystem approach to an anthropocentric approach by placing human beings 'at the centre of concerns for sustainable development' and by making the goal of 'life in harmony with nature' subordinate to the overriding 'entitlement' to a healthy and productive life.

Twenty years on, the incessant aggravation of the effects of climate change, the desertification of vast areas of the planet, loss of biodiversity, and severe pollution of the inhabited areas on the land and of the oceans, bear witness to the failed promise of the Preamble to reconcile developmental goals and respect of the integrity and interdependence of the Earth ecosystem.

[35] Kovar, 'A Short Guide to the Rio Declaration', 124.

# 5. Principle 1

## *Human Beings and the Environment*

Francesco Francioni*

**Principle 1**

Human beings are at the centre of concerns for sustainable development. They are entitled to a healthy and productive life in harmony with nature.



## I) Origins and Rationale of the Principle

The opening statement of Principle 1 leaves no doubt as to which of the two possible approaches—anthropocentric and ecocentric—did prevail in the final document of the UN Conference on Environment and Development (UNCED): 'Human beings are at the centre of concerns for sustainable development.' This sentence does not include the term 'environment' and does not refer to it as a major concern of the international community. The focus is on sustainable development. This idea is reinforced by the second sentence of Principle 1, which reiterates that '[human beings] are entitled to a healthy and productive life in harmony with nature.'[1]

* Professor of International Law, Emeritus, European University Institute, Florence, and LUISS University, Rome. Member (associate) of the Institut de Droit International. Previously he held the chair of international law at the Law Faculty of the University of Siena.

[1] There is wide consensus on the anthropocentric focus on Principle 1. See *Rio Declaration on Environment and Development. Report of the Secretary-General*, 10 February 1997, UN Doc E/CN.17/1997/8 ('UNSG Report'), para 16; UN Department of Social and Economic Affairs, Division for Sustainable Development, *Review of implementation of Agenda 21 and the Rio Principles*, December 2011 ('UNDESA Report'), 5.

This language falls short of recognizing the intrinsic value of the environment as such and independently of its productive capacity. It avoids any reference to the moral and legal responsibility that human beings have toward the natural environment, their 'home', as proclaimed in the Preamble of the Declaration.[2] Principle 1 speaks of an entitlement to a 'healthy and productive life' and this might be taken as human rights language, even though the text shies away from openly recognizing a human right to a safe and healthy environment. Although the human entitlement to 'a healthy and productive life' is qualified by the phrase 'in harmony with nature', this reference is vague and has hardly any normative significance. Besides, surprisingly enough, the word 'nature' does not reappear in any other principle of the Rio Declaration, where, instead, references to development abound.

This utilitarian approach to nature represents a departure from the text and the spirit of the Stockholm Declaration.[3] Principle 1 of the 1972 text opened with the proclamation that '[m]an has the fundamental right to freedom, equality and adequate conditions of life' and at the same time recognized that 'he bears the solemn responsibility to protect and improve the environment for present and future generations'.

The difference in the general approach of Principle 1, and indeed of the whole Declaration—the environment at the service of human beings—as compared to the approach taken at Stockholm[4]—human beings as responsible custodians of the environment—reflects the deep ideological divide that marked the UNCED negotiations and the adoption of the Rio Declaration.[5]

## II) The Principle as Enshrined in the Rio Declaration

### 1. Preparatory work and context

This divide followed the traditional North-South fault line and the relative division of interests. But with respect to Principle 1 and in the broader context of the UNCED negotiations this divide acquired a character of its own thanks to two new factors. On the one hand, the block of the industrialized states of the North had come to the Rio meeting with the expectation that the new spirit of globalization would produce an Earth Charter in which all nations and peoples would recognize their individual and collective responsibility toward the preservation of the planet for present and future generations. This approach entailed the formulation of the concept of 'sustainable development' in terms that, implicitly, would discourage less developed countries of the South from pursuing the same developmental policies of the industrial North, which were at the origin of the major environmental crises of the time. This ideological hubris of the North was fed also by some significant global environmental successes that had preceded the Rio conference: among them, the conclusion of the 1987 Montreal Protocol on Substances that

[2] 'Rio Declaration on Environment and Development', 13 June 1992, UN Doc A/CONF.151/26.Rev.1, ('Rio Declaration'), preamble, sixth recital.

[3] 'Declaration of the United Nations Conference on the Human Environment', Stockholm, 16 June 1972, UN Doc A/CONF 48/14/Rev.1 ('Stockholm Declaration').

[4] On the Stockholm Declaration see Sohn, L. B., 'The Stockholm Declaration on the Human Environment' (1973) 14 *HILJ* 423.

[5] See Khor, M., 'The North-South Battles that dominate Earth Summit' (1992) 1 *Earth Summit Briefings* 7. For a detailed commentary on the preparatory work of the Rio Summit, see Johnson, S., *The Earth Summit. The United Nations Conference on Environment and Development (UNCED)* (Graham & Trotman/Martinus Nijhoff 1993).

Deplete the Ozone Layer,[6] the 1989 Basel Convention on the Control of Transboundary Movements of Hazardous Wastes and their Disposal,[7] and the 1991 Madrid Protocol on the Environmental Protection of Antarctica.[8] The latter instrument, in particular, had seen the ability of a largely spontaneous environmental movement in the developed world to block the opening of Antarctica to oil and gas extraction, as well as the ability of the Antarctic Treaty Parties to curb the appetite for Antarctic minerals by setting aside the 1988 Convention on the Regulation of Antarctic Mineral Activities,[9] and adopting a 50-year ban on such activities together with a comprehensive environmental regime of Antarctica as a global common 'dedicated to peace and science'.[10]

The second factor that contributed to deepening the North-South divide and shifting the focus from nature protection to development was the reinvigorated position of the developing world in rejecting an environmental agenda disconnected from their priority of fighting poverty and promoting economic growth and development. Signs that the developing countries were looking with distrust at the industrial world's motives for a new global environmental compact had already arisen on the eve of the Rio summit. In the notorious 1991 dispute between Mexico and the United States over the latter's restrictions on import of Mexican tuna, the resistance of Mexico to the unilateral, even if well-intentioned, action of the United States came to symbolize the opposition of the developing world to what was perceived as a new form of colonialism under the seductive garb of global ecologism.[11] Of course, the reality of the diplomatic positions within the large group of countries represented at that time by the G77 was much more complex and diversified than the above dichotomy would suggest. But the differences in the level of economic development, political regime, and degree of influence in international affairs were bound to fade when faced with the perceived threat that the environment could be used by the developed world to set limits to the pursuit of their much needed economic and social development.

Given this general background, it is no surprise that the first principle of the Declaration ended up being so brief. Its text is the same as the one that had been approved at the last preparatory negotiation (PrepCom IV) held in New York from 2 March to 3 April 1992.[12]

[6] Montreal Protocol on Substances that Deplete the Ozone Layer, 16 September 1987, 1522 UNTS 3 ('Montreal Protocol').

[7] Basel Convention on the Control of Transboundary Movements of Hazardous Wastes and their Disposal, 22 March 1989, 1673 UNTS 57 ('Basel Convention').

[8] Protocol on Environmental Protection to the Antarctic Treaty, 4 October 1991, 30 ILM 1455 ('Madrid Protocol').

[9] Convention on the Regulation of Antarctic Mineral Resource Activities, 27 ILM 868 (1988) ('CRAMRA'), concluded in Wellington on 2 June 1988 and never entered into force.

[10] Madrid Protocol, art 2. For a commentary, see Francioni, F., 'The Madrid Protocol on the Protection of the Antarctic Environment' (1993) 28 *Texas International Law Journal* 47.

[11] The United States import ban had been prompted by judicial action of environmental NGOs in US courts to enforce US regulations on the conservation of marine-living resources, in that case, the life of dolphins which were caught and killed in the nets of the Mexican fleets fishing for tuna. See Panel Report, *United States—Restrictions on Imports of Tuna*, ('Tuna-Dolphin I') DS21/R-39S/155 (3 September 1991). See Kingsbury, B., 'The Tuna-Dolphin controversy, the World Trade Organization, and the Liberal Project to Reconceptualize International Law' (1994) 5 *YbIEL* 1; Francioni, F., 'Environment, Human Rights and the Limits of Free Trade', in Francioni, F. (ed), *Environment, Human Rights and International Trade* (Hart 2001) 1–26.

[12] 'Principles on general rights and obligations. Draft principles proposed by the Chairman. Rio Declaration on Environment and Development', 2 April 1992, UN Doc A/CONF.151/PC/WG.III/L.33/Rev.1 ('L.33'), Principle 1.

Its brevity appears to be the price that had to be paid for finding an acceptable balance between the conflicting policy concerns of the North and of the South. During PrepCom IV, the discussions in Working Group III, tasked *inter alia* with drafting a set of 'Principles on general rights and obligations', there were heated debates between the G77 and several delegations of developed countries regarding the emphasis and phrasing of this principle. Several draft decisions were submitted in this regard, most notably by the G77,[13] the US,[14] the EC countries,[15] and Nordic States.[16] The phrasing of the principle that was eventually retained for the draft adopted at PrepCom IV largely reflects the G77 draft.[17]

At Rio, even the United States, the only country that proposed, during the UNCED, to reopen negotiations on some substantive parts of the Declaration, did not express any reservation on the text of Principle 1.[18] However, under the mantle of the conference consensus, the brevity and vagueness of Principle 1 speak volumes for what it does not say: that is, the need to avoid a dismal failure of the UNCED Conference as a consequence of the radical divergence of views as to how to conjugate protection of the global environment and economic growth and how to accommodate radical ecocentric views with the alternative idea that 'human beings are at the centre of concerns for sustainable development'. In substance, one may see in this text a victory for the developing countries block and of their uncompromising assertion of the priority of economic development over the global environmental agenda. With the wisdom of hindsight, one wonders whether this was a Pyrrhic victory.

## 2. Scope and dimensions

### *2.1. Human beings and the temporal scope of sustainable development*

Key to the political compromise of Principle 1 is the formulation of the concept of 'sustainable development'. As already indicated, this Principle places human beings 'at the centre of concerns for sustainable development'. However, nowhere in the Declaration can we find a definition of this concept. Five years before the Rio Meeting sustainable development had been defined in the Brundtland Report, *Our Common Future*,[19] as the type of development that takes into account the need of present generations without compromising the needs of future generations. This definition contains the idea of a moral-political platform to identify environmental conditions for a long-term economic development. It is not a legal definition, but evokes Principle 1 of the Stockholm Declaration, which, without mentioning sustainable development, proclaimed man's 'solemn responsibility to protect and improve the environment for present and future generations'.

[13] 'Rio de Janeiro Charter/Declaration on Environment and Development', UN Doc A/CONF.151/PC/WG.III/L.20/Rev.1 ('L.20').

[14] UN Doc A/CONF.151/PC/WG.III/L.21 ('L.21'), proposing that the declaration be incorporated as a 'prologue to Agenda 21'.

[15] 'Elements for the Earth Charter', UN Doc A/CONF.151/PC/WG.III/L.25 ('L.25').

[16] 'Earth Charter. Elements for Consideration', UN Doc A/CONF.151/PC/WG.III/L.27 ('L.27').

[17] Principle 1 of L.20 stated: 'Human beings are at the centre of environmental concerns. They are entitled to a life of well-being and dignity which allows them to live in harmony with the environment'.

[18] The principles on which the United States delegation maintained reservations were: Principle 3, on the right to development; Principle 7, on common but differentiated responsibilities; Principle 12, on trade related environmental measures; and Principle 23, on occupied territories.

[19] Report of the World Commission on Environment and Development, *Our Common Future*, 10 March 1987 ('Brundtland Report').

Principle 1 of the Rio Declaration, on the contrary, does not contain any reference to future generations. Such a reference can be found, instead, in Principle 3. But this Principle deals with the 'right to development', which, as the text goes on to state, 'must be fulfilled so as to equitably meet developmental and environmental needs of present and future generations'. This is the only reference to 'future generations' in the entire text of the Declaration. Its formulation gives the prevailing weight to development rather than to environmental protection. This indicates that the omission of the reference to future generations in Principle 1 was not a mere oversight, but was the result of a deliberate choice to articulate the concept of sustainable development essentially in the horizontal dimension of redistributive justice and not in terms of intergenerational equity.

This interpretation of Principle 1 is confirmed by the language of Principle 5, which places the commitment to sustainable development in the context of the fight against poverty and of the effort at decreasing disparities in standards of living, so as 'to better meet the needs of the majority of the people of the world'. Principle 5 would have been an ideal *locus* for the insertion of a reference to future generations. But such reference is missing again. This omission is regrettable because it is difficult to conceptualize the idea of sustainability divorced from the consideration of the need of future generations, that is, simply as a model of development that helps to eradicate poverty and diminish the disparities of wealth and development among the present generations worldwide. This objective was a priority in the international agenda at the time of the 'new international economic order' (1974),[20] at the time of the Rio Summit, and remains even more so today.[21] But it is part of an agenda of economic policy and social justice, not necessarily of environmental sustainability. Once again, this narrow concept of sustainable development reflects the successful effort of developing countries to shift the focus from global environmental problems to sustainable development as a tool of social justice.

## 2.2. *Sustainable development and human rights*

The second clause of Principle 1 states that human beings 'are entitled to a healthy and productive life in harmony with nature.' This language introduces an important new perspective, which is the link between the preservation of a decent environment and human rights. The text does not explicitly use the expression 'human rights'. However, the words 'entitled', 'human beings', and 'healthy life' conjure up the idea that sustainable development is inseparable from human health, human welfare, and the right to life itself.[22]

This is an important development of the Rio Declaration. It builds upon the groundbreaking Preamble of the Stockholm Declaration, which proclaimed the environment as an essential condition for 'the enjoyment of basic human rights, even the right to life'.[23]

[20] 'Declaration on the Establishment of a New International Economic Order', 1 May 1974, UN Doc A/RES/S-6/3201.

[21] Although 'future generations' are mentioned in the first and last paragraphs (1 and 13) of the 'common vision' expressed in the outcome document of the Rio 2012 Summit (*The future We Want*, 11 September 2012, UN Doc A/Res/66/288), the emphasis on the fight against poverty eradication as the 'greatest global challenge facing the world today' (para 2) focuses on the present. Paragraph 6 reaffirms that 'people are at the centre of sustainable development' and places 'environmental protection' as the third priority of sustainable development. The order in which these objectives are mentioned seem to convey order of priority if one judges by paragraph 4, where 'poverty eradication' is mentioned first. On this trend see Viñuales, J. E., 'The Rise and Fall of Sustainable Development' (2013) 22 *RECIEL* 3.

[22] In this sense see *UNSG Report*, paras 16–20; *UNDESA Report*, 5.

[23] Stockholm Declaration, preamble, recital 1.

It anticipates the subsequent developments of the environmental jurisprudence of human rights courts and human rights treaty bodies.[24] This jurisprudence has developed in the absence of specific environmental provisions in the applicable human rights treaties.[25] At the same time, it has helped achieve a certain 'greening' of human rights by identifying environmental impacts that constitute breaches of established human rights, such as the right to life, health, private and family life, property, and the right to information and participation with regard to environmental decisions.

In this sense, Principle 1 has contributed to the progressive development of customary international law and has opened the way to the contemporary attempts at reforming the system of human rights law to better incorporate concerns for sustainability and environmental protection. So far, such attempts have not resulted in the codification of a new human right to a decent environment. But they have prompted, at the judicial and inter-state level, careful consideration of the implications that the many aspects of environmental degradation have on the enjoyment of human rights.

## 3. Normative impact

### *3.1. Human rights and the environment*

Principle 1 has fostered a number of international initiatives to spell out the link between human rights and the environment. In 2005 the UN Commission on Human Rights referred to the Principles of the Rio Declaration as a starting-point to address the connection between human rights, environmental protection, and sustainable development.[26]

The Human Rights Council, the successor of the Commission, subsequently expanded its investigation to the more general question of the relations between human rights and the environment. In 2011, it requested the OHCHR to prepare an analytical study on this topic.[27] The study, published in late 2011, puts forward the idea that human rights 'have the potential to inform and strengthen the international, regional, and national policy making in the area of environmental protection'.[28]

Pursuing its work on this topic, in 2012 the Council appointed an Independent Expert on human rights obligations relating to the enjoyment of a safe, clean, healthy, and sustainable environment. Professor John Knox, a national of the United States, was entrusted with this mandate. In December 2012, he published his first report on this topic.[29]

[24] See further n 40 in this chapter.

[25] The only exceptions are art 24 ('right to a generally satisfactory environment') of the African Charter on Human and Peoples' Rights, 27 June 1981, 21 ILM 58 (1982), and art 11 ('right to a healthy environment') of the Additional Protocol to the American Convention on Human Rights in the Area of Economic, Social and Cultural Rights, 16 November 1988, OAS Treaty Series No. 69.

[26] UN Human Rights Commission, Resolution 2005/60 (2005). The Resolution 'encourages all efforts toward the implementation of the principles of the Rio Declaration on Environment and Development'. An earlier initiative prompted by a decision of the Sub-Commission on Prevention of Discrimination and Protection of Minorities, adopted in 1989, had already led to elaboration of a report: *Human Rights and the Environment. Final report presented by Mrs Fatma Zohra Ksentini, Special Rapporteur*, 6 July 1994, UN Doc E/CN.4/Sub.2/1994/9 ('Ksentini Report').

[27] UNHRC, Resolution 16/11 (2011), 'Human Rights and the Environment', para 1.

[28] OHCHR, *Analytical study on the relationship between human rights and the environment*, 16 December 2011, UN Doc A//HRC/19/34 ('OHCHR Analytical Study'), para 2.

[29] Report of the Independent Expert on the issue of human rights obligations relating to the enjoyment of a safe, clean, healthy and sustainable environment, John H. Knox, 24 December 2012, UN Doc A/HRC/22/43; Report of the Independent Expert on the issue of human rights obligations relating to the enjoyment of a safe, clean, healthy and sustainable environment, John H. Knox, 30 December 2013, UN Doc A/HRC/25/53.

### *3.2. Human rights and climate change*

In 2009 the Human Rights Council referred explicitly to the Declaration and used the consecrated terminology that 'human beings are at the centre of concerns for sustainable development', albeit in connection with 'right to development'.[30] On this basis, it went on to request the Office of the High Commissioner for Human Rights ('OHCHR') to prepare an analytical study on the relations between climate change and human rights.[31]

This study was presented in 2009[32] and it prompted other action from the Council,[33] particularly Resolution 10/4 (2009), which notes *inter alia* that:

> climate change-related impacts have a range of implications, both direct and indirect, for the effective enjoyment of human rights including, inter alia, the right to life, the right to adequate food, the right to the highest attainable standard of health, the right to adequate housing, the right to self-determination and human rights obligations related to access to safe drinking water and sanitation, and recalling that in no case may a people be deprived of its own means of subsistence...[34]

The Council did not feel the need to appoint an independent expert on the topic, probably because there was no space to add a voice to the highly political climate negotiations. But it convened a seminar to raise awareness on this question,[35] which was held in Geneva in February 2012. The Council has gone a step further for other questions, appointing an independent expert or a special rapporteur.

### *3.3. Business and human rights*

In 2011 the UN Secretary-General's Special Representative on the issue of human rights and business corporations (Professor John Ruggie) issued his report and the annexed 'Guiding Principles' on business and human rights, which were adopted by the Human Rights Council in March 2011.[36] The legal framework developed therein on the responsibility 'to protect, respect and remedy' is relevant to the understanding of the human rights implications of environmental protection and sustainable development.

While the Framework and Guiding Principles maintain the traditional perspective that States have the primary responsibility to protect human rights from environmental harm, they also bring into focus the adverse impacts of corporate behaviour on human rights and the environment, and the duty of these non-State actors to exercise due diligence in preventing such adverse impacts, as well as in avoiding situations of complicity with governmental encroachments on human rights.

[30] UNHRC, Resolution 7/23 (2008), 'Human Rights and Climate Change', preamble, recitals 6–7.

[31] UNHRC, Resolution 7/23 (2008), para 1.

[32] OHCHR, *Report of the Office of the United Nations High Commissioner for Human Rights on the relationship between climate change and human rights*, 15 January 2009, UN Doc A/HRC/10/61.

[33] See World Bank, *Human Rights and Climate Change. A Review of the International Legal Dimensions* (Washington DC: The World Bank 2011).

[34] UNHRC, Resolution 10/4 (2009), 'Human Rights and Climate Change', preamble, recital 7.

[35] UNHRC, Resolution 18/22 (2011), 'Human Rights and Climate Change', para 2.

[36] *Report of the Special Representative of the Secretary-General on the issue of human rights and transnational corporations and other business enterprises—Guiding Principles on Business and Human Rights: Implementing the United Nations 'Protect, Respect and Remedy' Framework*, 21 March 2011, UN Doc A/HRC/17/31. The 'Protect, Respect and Remedy' Framework had been developed in an earlier report to the Human Rights Council: *Protect, Respect and Remedy: a Framework for Business and Human Rights. Report of the Special Representative of the Secretary-General on the issue of human rights and transnational corporations and other business enterprises*, John Ruggie, 7 April 2008, UN Doc A/HRC/8/5.

According to the Guiding Principles it is irrelevant that a government is not itself the operator of a business enterprise that causes an environment-related breach of human rights: its responsibility may arise from its failure to regulate a private business that exposes people to environmentally-induced harm, or from its inability or unwillingness to provide appropriate remedies for the resulting injury.

### *3.4. Other topics: water and toxic waste*

Aside from the abovementioned topics, the Council has also undertaken work on other more specific topics, such as the right to safe drinking water and sanitation[37] or the effects on human rights of dangerous or toxic products and wastes.[38] In both cases, a special rapporteur has been appointed.

Although Principle 1 is not specifically referred to in the relevant resolutions or reports, these initiatives consistently make reference to the Rio Declaration and its principles as part of their foundations.

## 4. Jurisprudential relevance

The work of the Human Rights Council, the independent experts, and special rapporteurs follows in the footsteps of the much more substantial contribution by human rights courts to the analysis and clarification of the link between human rights and the environment.[39] It provides a framework of principles to pursue the policy objective of sustainable development endorsed in Principle 1 of the Rio Declaration. This is important in a world where unbridled trade[40] and unregulated foreign investments[41] have often resulted in harm to the health of the local population and to the local environment.

[37] The UNHCR has adopted many resolutions regarding the human right to safe drinking water and sanitation, including Resolutions 7/22 (2008), 12/8 (2009), 15/9 (2010), 16/2 (2011), 18/1 (2011), 21/2 (2012), 24/3 (2013). A Special Rapporteur, Mrs Catarina de Albuquerque, a national of Portugal, was appointed.

[38] UNHCR, Resolutions 9/1 and 12/18 on the 'Adverse effects of the movement and dumping of toxic and dangerous products and wastes on the enjoyment of human rights', and Resolution 18/11 on the 'Mandate of the Special Rapporteur on the implications for human rights of the environmentally sound management and disposal of hazardous substances and wastes'. The Special Rapporteur is Professor Marc Pallemaerts, a national of Belgium.

[39] There is a substantial body of literature on this link: Boyle, A. and M. Anderson (eds), *Human Rights Approaches to Environmental Protection* (Oxford University Press 1996); Dejeant-Pons, M. and Pallemaerts, M., *Droits de l'homme et environnement* (Council of Europe 2002); Loucaides, L., 'Environmental Protection through the Jurisprudence of the European Convention on Human Rights' (2004) 75 *BYIL* 249; Francioni, F., 'International human rights in the environmental horizon' (2010) 21 *EJIL* 41; Anton, D. K. and Shelton, D., *Environmental Protection and Human Rights* (Cambridge University Press 2011); Inter-American Commission on Human Rights, *Indigenous and Tribal Peoples' Rights over their Ancestral Lands and Natural Resources: Norms and Jurisprudence of the Inter-American Human Rights System*, doc OEA/Ser.L/V/II, doc 56/09, 30 December 2009; Boyle, A., 'Human Rights and the Environment: Where Next?' (2012) 23 *EJIL* 613; Pavoni, R., *Interesse pubblico e diritti individuali nella giurisprudenza ambientale della Corte europea dei diritti umani* (Editoriale scientifica 2013); Chuffart, S. and Viñuales, J. E., 'From the Other Shore: Economic, Social and Cultural Rights from an International Environmental Law Perspective', in Reidel, E., Giacca, G., and Golay, C. (eds), *Economic, Social and Cultural Rights: Current Issues and Challenges* (Oxford University Press 2014) 286–307.

[40] On this link see Francioni, 'Environment, Human Rights and the Limits of Free Trade'; Gehring, M. and Cordonnier-Segger, M.-C. (eds), *Sustainable Development in World Trade Law* (Kluwer 2005).

[41] On this link see Viñuales, J. E., *Foreign Investment and the Environment in International Law* (Cambridge University Press 2012); Cordonnier-Segger, M.-C., Gehring, M., and Newcombe, A. (eds), *Sustainable Development in World Investment Law* (Kluwer 2010).

The current effort to promote mutual supportiveness between human rights and environmental protection may also help overcome the limits of the current environmental jurisprudence of human rights courts, especially the European Court of Human Rights ('ECtHR'), which is still dependent on a narrow 'individualistic' approach to environment-related human rights breaches.[42] This limitation is epitomized by the ECtHR's observation in *Fadeyeva v. Russia* according to which:

Article 8 [right to private and family life] has been relied on in various cases involving environmental concern, yet it is not violated every time that environmental deterioration occurs: no right to nature preservation is as such included among the rights and freedoms guaranteed by the Convention... Thus, in order to raise an issue under Article 8 the interference must directly affect the applicant's home, family or private life.[43]

A similarly limitative approach arises from a decision of the Inter-American Commission on Human Rights in a case concerning the construction of a motorway through a natural preserve:

The Commission... holds the present complaint to be inadmissible since it concerns abstract victims represented in an *actio popularis* rather than specifically identified and defined individuals. The Commission does recognize that given the nature of the complaint, the petition could hardly pinpoint a group of victims with particularity since all the citizens of Panama are described as property owners of the Metropolitan Nature Reserve. The petition is inadmissible, further, because the environmental, civic, and scientific groups considered most harmed by the alleged violations are legal entities and not natural persons, as the Convention stipulates. The Commission therefore rules that it has not the requisite competence *ratione personae* to adjudicate the present matter in accordance with jurisprudence establishing the standard of interpretation for Article 44 of the Convention as applied in the aforementioned cases...[44]

Hopefully, the codification and progressive development work of human rights bodies may be the springboard to begin considering environmental protection as part of the general public interest, as a common good indispensable for the fulfilment of sustainable development, rather than only for the enjoyment of an individual human right.

## III) Relations with Other Principles

The above considerations leave open the question of the definition of what sustainable development means in the context of a human rights and environmental protection agenda. Principle 1 does not provide any legal definition. However, other international law sources may assist understanding of its meaning and function.

The International Court of Justice has characterized sustainable development as a 'concept' in the *Gabčíkovo-Nagymaros* case.[45] Later, the same Court has spoken of sustainable

[42] See Francioni, 'International human rights in the environmental horizon'.

[43] *Fadeyeva v. Russia*, ECtHR Application no 55723/00, Judgment (30 November 2005), para 68. See also *Kyrtatos v. Greece*, ECtHR Application no. 41666/98, Judgment (22 May 2003), para 52 (relating to art 8); *Athanassoglou and others v. Switzerland*, ECtHR Application no 27644/95, Judgment (6 April 2000), para 52 (relating to art 6); *Oneryildiz v. Turkey*, ECtHR Application no 48939/99, Judgment (30 November 2004), para 91–6 (relating to art 2). For an overview of the case law see *Ivan Atanasov v. Bulgaria*, ECtHR Application no 12853/03, Judgment (11 April 2011), paras 66–75.

[44] *Metropolitan Nature Reserve v. Panama*, Case 11.533, Report No 88/03, ICommHR, OEA/Ser.L/V/II.118 Doc 70 rev 2 at 524 (2003), para 34.

[45] *Case Concerning The Gabčíkovo-Nagymaros Project* (Hungary/Slovakia), Judgment, ICJ Reports 1997, 7 ('*Gabčíkovo-Nagymaros*'), para 140.

development as an 'objective' in the *Pulp Mills* case between Argentina and Uruguay.[46] Both of these definitions capture elements of sustainable development but they are not very helpful in understanding what kind of obligations the 'concept' or 'objective' of sustainable development entails for the State. In addition, terms such as 'concepts' and 'objectives' evoke the idea of something static and permanent. But in the context of environmental law sustainable development should be understood as a method of dynamic adaptation of decision-making processes to the variable exigencies of environmental governance and economic policy in a world of limited resources. In this perspective the important question raised by the reference to sustainable development in Principle 1 is 'who will decide' whether a given development project is 'sustainable', and whether, if its sustainability is in question, the project should nevertheless proceed or not. Principle 1 does not provide any concrete indication on how this question should be answered. But an answer can be found, albeit indirectly, in Principles 10, 2, and 3 of the Declaration.

A first aspect of this answer concerns the 'internal' exercise of sovereignty by requiring that environmental issues be handled with the participation and information of all concerned citizens. The 1998 Aarhus Convention is the most advanced normative instrument for the implementation of this principle.[47] The second aspect of the answer concerns sovereignty in its 'international' dimension. Principle 2 reaffirms in this respect that 'States have the sovereign right to exploit their own resources pursuant to their own environmental and developmental policies'. This reassertion of State sovereignty over natural resources in the face of global environmental challenges certainly tells us that States remain the arbiters of first instance in the decisions concerning the use of their natural resources and in the final assessment of the sustainability of relative projects. This conclusion is further confirmed by the language used in Principle 3, which speaks of a 'right to development'. Of course, depending on whether this is understood as a right of States or as a human right the answer may be to some extent different. But contrasting the formulation of Principle 3 with that of Principle 10, which clearly identifies individuals as the right-holders, suggests that it is for the sovereign State to decide on the sustainability of the use of its resources.

Should this reliance on sovereignty lead us to conclude that nothing has changed in international law in the more than fifty years that have passed since the proclamation in the 1960s of the post-colonial principle of 'permanent sovereignty over natural resources'[48] and its reaffirmation in 1992?

## IV) Assessment: Sovereignty, Then and Now

We believe that much has changed in international law in this period. Environmental law has become a major branch of international law and has gradually imposed restrictions

[46] *Pulp Mills on the River Uruguay (Argentina v. Uruguay)*, Judgment, ICJ Reports 2010, 14, paras 75–7 and 177.

[47] Aarhus Convention on Access to Information, Public Participation in Decision-making and Access to Justice in Environmental Matters, 25 June 1998, 2161 UNTS 447 ('Aarhus Convention'). See *The Aarhus Convention: An Implementation Guide*, available at: <http://www.unece.org/env/pp/implementation%20guide/english/part2.pdf> (visited 10 April 2014) ('Implementation Guide').

[48] See 'Permanent Sovereignty over Natural Resources', 14 December 1962, UN Doc A/RES/1803/XVII, ('*resolution 1803*'); 'Permanent Sovereignty over Natural Resources', 17 December 1973, UN Doc A/RES/3171/XXVIII.

on the freedom of States to use natural resources,[49] not only in a transboundary context but also with regard to many aspects of their economic activities within the national territory (hazardous waste, banned chemicals, conservation of endangered species, etc). Globalization has increased the opportunities for efficient use of natural resources at the service of economic and social development. At the same time, degradation of the natural environment has continued unabated and new global problems have emerged: in particular, climate change. In view of this, a concept such as 'sovereignty over natural resources' must be understood in light of present realities and in accordance with the evolving interpretation required by article 31(3) of the Vienna Convention on the Law of Treaties.[50]

The concept of 'permanent sovereignty', as proclaimed in the post-colonial period of the 1960s and in the context of the 'new international economic order' of the 1970s, had the pre-eminent legal and political function of enabling newly independent countries to be free from obligations owed to the former colonial power. It had also the function of enabling them to recover full control over their natural resources, which in many cases had been lost to foreign investors in a context of colonial domination.

Principle 1 belongs to a different era. Even with its 'development' focus it must be interpreted in the context of the worldwide movement toward more effective governance of global environmental problems that the Rio Summit epitomized. This movement did not stop with the 1992 Declaration. It has continued with both success and failure until today, hand in hand with the increasing severity of environmental degradation. At Rio, the main block of the industrial countries of the North did not succeed in the project of 'globalizing' the environment: hence, the persistence in the Declaration of the reference to the 'sovereign right' to exploit their natural resources; hence, the failure to establish a global institution capable of overseeing States' compliance with international environmental obligations.[51] If this is understandable in light of the negotiating history of the Rio Declaration, it should nevertheless not obliterate the need to interpret the Rio Declaration in light of the present realities and of the contemporary evolution of international law.

One of the important implications of Principle 1, and indeed of the whole Declaration and of contemporary international law, is the need to look at sovereignty in a different normative perspective: that is, a perspective in which sovereignty and sovereign rights no longer imply an unlimited power of a State over the physical space that the vicissitudes of history have apportioned to it. A modern conception of sovereignty implies instead the idea of a governmental 'function' to be exercised within the limits of international law and under the conditions set by the general interest of the international community. It is in the context of this 'functionalization' of sovereignty and sovereign rights that one can understand the impact of the novel concept of 'common concern of humankind', which also emerged from the work leading to

[49] For an early study of how the exercise of permanent sovereignty over natural resources has been brought within increasingly demanding legal bounds see Schrijver, N., *Sovereignty Over Natural Resources. Balancing Rights and Duties* (Cambridge University Press 1997).

[50] Vienna Convention on the Law of Treaties, 23 May 1969, 1155 UNTS 331.

[51] The absence of global institutions for environmental governance and for the compulsory settlement of environmental disputes still characterizes international environmental law and is also a reason for the weakness of this branch of the law as compared to other branches such as trade, foreign investment, and even human rights. On this see further Francioni, F., 'The Private Sector and the Challenge of Implementation', in Dupuy, P.-M. and Viñuales, J. E. (eds), *Harnessing Foreign Investment to Promote Environmental Protection: Incentives and Safeguard* (Cambridge University Press 2013), 24–49.

the Rio Summit and has been codified in the treaties on the protection of biodiversity[52] and the global climate.[53] It is also in this context that one can understand the meaning and impact of Principe 7 of the Rio Declaration on 'common but differentiated responsibilities', which entails that developing countries can only be asked to place their environmental resources (eg forests and biodiversity) at the service of global goals (eg combating climate change) if corresponding 'differentiated' limitations on their sovereignty, especially in the form of obligations to cooperate, are accepted by the industrial countries that advocate global ecologism.

If the restatement of developmental priorities and of sovereign rights in the Rio Declaration confirms that States remain in control of the use of their natural resources, the imperative of sustainability in Principle 1 should ensure that the exercise of sovereignty over such resources remains responsible and functional to the achievement, not only of 'a productive life' for all human beings, but, more importantly, of the goal of preserving the global environment in such a way as to permit the very continuing existence of human beings on Earth, if not the unrealistic goal of a 'life in harmony with nature'.

## V) Select Bibliography


Anton, D. K. and Shelton, D., *Environmental Protection and Human Rights* (Cambridge University Press 2011).

Boyle, A. and Anderson, M., (eds), *Human rights approaches to environmental protection* (Oxford University Press 1996).

Boyle, A., 'Human Rights and the Environment: Where Next?' (2012) 23 *EJIL* 613.

Chuffart, S. and Viñuales, J. E., 'From the Other Shore: Economic, Social and Cultural Rights from an International Environmental Law Perspective', in Reidel, E., Giacca, G., and Golay, C. (eds), *Economic, Social and Cultural Rights: Current Issues and Challenges* (Oxford University Press 2014), 286–307.

Dejeant-Pons, M. and Pallemaerts, M., *Droits de l'homme et environnement* (Strasbourg: Council of Europe 2002).

Francioni, F. (ed), *Environment, Human Rights and International Trade* (Oxford: Hart 2001).

Francioni, F., 'International human rights in the environmental horizon' (2010) 21 *EJIL* 41.

Francioni, F., 'The Private Sector and the Challenge of Implementation', in Dupuy, P.-M. and Viñuales, J. E. (eds), *Harnessing Foreign Investment to Promote Environmental Protection: Incentives and Safeguard* (Cambridge University Press 2013), 24–49.

Inter-American Commission on Human Rights, *Indigenous and Tribal Peoples' Rights over their Ancestral Lands and Natural Resources: Norms and Jurisprudence of the Inter-American Human Rights System*, doc OEA/Ser.L/V/II, doc 56/09, 30 December 2009.

Ksentini, F. Z., *Human Rights and the Environment. Final report presented by Mrs Fatma Zohra Ksentini, Special Rapporteur*, 6 July 1994, UN Doc E/CN.4/Sub.2/1994/9.

Loucaides, L., 'Environmental Protection through the Jurisprudence of the European Convention on Human Rights' (2004) 75 *BYIL* 249.

Office of the High Commissioner for Human Rights, *Analytical study on the relationship between human rights and the environment*, 16 December 2011, UN Doc A//HRC/19/34.


[52] Convention on Biological Diversity, 5 June 1992, 1760 UNTS 79, preamble, para 3.

[53] United Nations Framework Convention on Climate Change, 9 May 1992, 31 ILM 849, preamble, para 1.

Office of the High Commissioner for Human Rights, *Report of the Office of the United Nations High Commissioner for Human Rights on the relationship between climate change and human rights*, 15 January 2009, UN Doc A/HRC/10/61.

Pavoni, R., *Interesse pubblico e diritti individuali nella giurisprudenza ambientale della Corte europea dei diritti umani* (Naples: Editoriale scientifica 2013).

Ruggie, J., *Protect, Respect and Remedy: a Framework for Business and Human Rights. Report of the Special Representative of the Secretary-General on the issue of human rights and transnational corporations and other business enterprises*, 7 April 2008, UN Doc A/HRC/8/5.

Ruggie, J., *Report of the Special Representative of the Secretary-General on the issue of human rights and transnational corporations and other business enterprises—Guiding Principles on Business and Human Rights: Implementing the United Nations 'Protect, Respect and Remedy' Framework*, 21 March 2011, UN Doc A/HRC/17/31.

United Nations Secretary-General, *Rio Declaration on Environment and Development. Report of the Secretary-General*, 10 February 1997, UN Doc E/CN.17/1997/8 ('UNSG Report').

United Nations Department of Social and Economic Affairs, Division for Sustainable Development, *Review of implementation of Agenda 21 and the Rio Principles*, December 2011.

Viñuales, J. E., 'The Rise and Fall of Sustainable Development' (2013) 22 *Review of European, Comparative and International Environmental Law* 3.

World Bank, *Human Rights and Climate Change. A Review of the International Legal Dimensions* (Washington DC: The World Bank 2011).

# 6. Principle 2

## *Prevention*

Leslie-Anne Duvic-Paoli* and Jorge E. Viñuales**

**Principle 2**

States have, in accordance with the Charter of the United Nations and the principles of international law, the sovereign right to exploit their own resources pursuant to their own environmental and developmental policies, and the responsibility to ensure that activities within their jurisdiction or control do not cause damage to the environment of other States or of areas beyond the limits of national jurisdiction.

---




* PhD candidate and teaching assistant, Graduate Institute of International and Development Studies, Geneva.

** Harold Samuel Professor of Law and Environmental Policy, University of Cambridge.

## I) Origins and Rationale of the Principle

Principle 2 of the Rio Declaration on Environment and Development[1] provides that States shall exercise their sovereignty over natural resources within environmental bounds. As such, it embodies the *raison d'être* of international environmental law. Indeed, based on the idea that the protection of the environment is best ensured by preventing harm from occurring rather than by attempting to repair the damages afterwards, international environmental law aims to organize environmental protection through a diverse body of preventive duties. The rationale underpinning international environmental law differs from the perspective of general international law, with its emphasis on State responsibility and reparation.

However, the prevention principle, as formulated in Principle 21 of the Stockholm Declaration[2] and, later, in Principle 2 of the Rio Declaration, does not stem from a direct concern over the protection of the environment, but rather from a desire to respect the territorial sovereignty of neighbouring States when exploiting natural resources.[3] Before the emergence of an environmental consciousness in the 1960s, the 'environment' was perceived through the lenses of 'natural resources' and, to a far lesser extent, of 'conservation'.[4] Environmental harm was only a concern inasmuch as the exploitation of natural resources would have damaging consequences on a neighbouring State and would therefore encroach on the territorial sovereignty of another State. The international legal response to such damage rested on the rules of State responsibility for internationally wrongful act. The focus on reparation and compensation in the case of environmental harm was an application of the traditional legal concepts protecting State sovereignty—these included in particular the principle *sic utere tuo ut alienum non laedas* rule ('use your own property so

[1] Rio Declaration on Environment and Development, 13 June 1992, (1992) 31 ILM 874 ('Rio Declaration').

[2] Declaration of the United Nations Conference on the Human Environment, Stockholm, 16 June 1972, UN Doc A/CONF 48/14/Rev.1 ('Stockholm Declaration').

[3] See generally Xue, H., *Transboundary Damage in International Law* (Cambridge University Press 2003); Bratspies, R. M. and Miller, R. A. (eds), *Transboundary Harm in International Law. Lessons from the Trail Smelter Arbitration* (Cambridge University Press 2006).

[4] On the evolution of international efforts to protect the environment and their different approaches see Viñuales, J. E., 'The Rise and Fall of Sustainable Development' (2013) 22 *RECIEL* 3.

as not to harm that of another'), the prohibition of *abus de droit* and the rules on good neighbourliness.[5] These concepts translated the idea that, in an interdependent world, sovereignty can only be relative and is limited by the obligation to respect the sovereignty of other States. Such recognition crystallized in the 'no-harm rule', the obligation of States not to cause transboundary environmental harm.

Yet, as environmental problems with their local, transboundary, and global dimensions became better understood, the transboundary perspective of the no-harm rule appeared insufficient. The 1960s witnessed a fundamental change in human perceptions of life on Earth and the ensuing necessity to protect nature, which, in turn, provided the socio-political foundations for a shift in the legal paradigm. Reparation of environmental damage appeared as an ancillary approach whilst prevention became the *raison d'être* of international environmental law. As a result, the understanding of the no-harm rule evolved towards the more comprehensive principle of prevention.

The prevention principle in its contemporary form was formulated at the Stockholm Conference on the Human Environment, in Principle 21 of the Stockholm Declaration:

> States have, in accordance with the Charter of the United Nations and the principles of international law, the sovereign right to exploit their own resources pursuant to their own environmental policies, and the responsibility to ensure that activities within their jurisdiction or control do not cause damage to the environment of other States or of areas beyond the limits of national jurisdiction.

The Stockholm Conference placed environmental problems within the remit of the United Nations Organization and, importantly, it framed cooperation in this area through the lenses of prevention and not of reparation. In the aftermath of Stockholm, several treaties and soft-law documents were adopted concerning different areas of international environmental law, all reaffirming explicitly[6] or implicitly[7] Principle 21.

Principle 21 embodies a compromise between seemingly contradictory aspects: (i) the principle of sovereignty over natural resources; (ii) the prohibition against causing

[5] See Andrassy, J., 'Les relations internationales de voisinage', in *Collected Courses of the Hague Academy of International Law* (vol 79, Martinus Nijhoff 1951); Kiss, A., *L'abus de droit en droit international* (Librairie générale de droit et de jurisprudence 1952); Pop, I., *Voisinage et bon voisinage en droit international* (Pedone 1980).

[6] See, *inter alia*, texts reaffirming almost *verbatim* principle 21: Convention on the Prevention of Marine Pollution by Dumping of Wastes and Other Matter, London, 29 December 1972, in force 30 August 1975, (1972) 11 ILM 1294, Preamble; Charter of Economic Rights and Duties of States, UNGA Res. 3281 (XXVII) (1974), art 30; Final Act of the Helsinki Conference on Security and Co-operation in Europe, Helsinki, 1 August 1975, (1975) 14 ILM 1292, section 5; Convention on Long-Range Transboundary Air Pollution, Geneva, 13 November 1979, in force 16 March 1983, (1979) 18 ILM 1442, Preamble; Principles on Conservation and Harmonious Utilisation of Natural Resources Shared by Two or More States, UNEP Governing Council Decision, UNEP/IG12/2 (1978), principle 3, para 1; World Charter for Nature, UNGA Res. 37/7 (XXXVII) (30 October 1980), para 21(d); United Nations Convention on the Law of the Sea, Montego Bay, 10 December 1982, in force 16 November 1994, 1833 UNTS 3 ('UNCLOS'), arts 192–4.

[7] The rationale of prevention underpins the following instruments: Convention on International Trade in Endangered Species of Wild Fauna and Flora, Washington, 3 March 1973, in force 1 July 1975, 993 UNTS 243; UNESCO Convention for the Protection of the World Cultural and Natural Heritage, Paris, 16 November 1972, in force 17 December 1975, (1972) 11 ILM 1358; Convention for the Conservation of Antarctic Seals, London, 1 June 1972, in force 11 March 1978, (1972) 11 ILM 251; Convention on the Conservation of European Wildlife and Natural Habitats, Berne, 19 September 1979, in force 1 June 1982, (1982) UKTS 56 Cmnd 8738; Convention on the Conservation of Migratory Species of Wild Animals, Bonn, 23 June 1979, in force 1 November 1983, (1980) 19 ILM 15; Convention on the Conservation of Antarctic Marine Living Resources, Canberra, 20 May 1980, in force 7 April 1982, (1980) 19 ILM 841.

transboundary damage; and (iii) the obligation to protect the environment beyond national jurisdiction. The loose combination of these three components allows for a flexible principle and gives States enough freedom to interpret the norm in different ways—explaining in part the widespread acceptance of the principle. Since its inclusion in the Stockholm Declaration, the prevention principle has been considered as the 'golden rule' of international environmental law.[8]

## II) The Principle as Enshrined in the Rio Declaration

### 1. Preparatory work and context

#### *1.1. Overview*

In the twenty years following the Stockholm Conference, the prevention principle became clearly established as a cornerstone of international environmental law. As a result, there was little controversy on the need to include the 'Stockholm principle' in the Rio Declaration. The negotiations on this principle focused instead on the specific wording of Principle 21 and, particularly, on whether to reaffirm or, on the contrary, delete certain components of the principle.

#### *1.2. Proposals included in 'L.8'*

At the third meeting of the Preparatory Committee ('PrepCom III'), different formulations of the prevention principle were proposed by delegations and consolidated by the Chairman of Working Group III, Dr Bedrich Moldan, into a draft referred to as 'L.8'.[9] Despite Dr Moldan's efforts to this effect, L.8 was not the basis of the negotiations during PrepCom IV that led to the formulation of Principle 2,[10] subsequently adopted without changes at the Rio Summit. However, a survey of the proposals included in L.8 provides a useful overview of the range of views expressed by States.

At PrepCom III, the G77 proposed a text emphasizing the sovereignty component of Principle 21 but not mentioning a corresponding duty.[11] On the other hand, Burkina Faso and the G22 wanted to delete the first part of Principle 21 on permanent sovereignty over natural resources and to concentrate on the two environmental components.[12] Interestingly, Nigeria and the G22 also 'recognized, reaffirmed and defended' the right to sovereignty over natural resources while promoting an obligation of prevention of environmental harm over the domestic territory of States—thereby going further in the protection of the environment and moving away from the transboundary perspective of prevention.[13]

[8] de Sadeleer, N., *Environmental Principles: From Political Slogans to Legal Rules* (Oxford University Press 2002), 89; Kiss, A. and Beurier, J.-P., *Droit international de l'environnement* (4e édn, Pedone 2010); Sands, P. and Peel, J., *Principles of International Environmental Law* (3rd edn, Cambridge University Press 2012), 191; Kiss, A. and Shelton, D., *International Environmental Law* (3rd edn, Transnational Publishers 2004), 113.

[9] Chairman's consolidated draft entitled 'Earth Charter. The Rio de Janeiro Declaration on Environment and Development', UN Doc A/CONF.151/PC/WG.III/L.8/Rev.1 and Add. 1 and 2 ('L.8').

[10] 'Principles on general rights and obligations. Draft principles proposed by the Chairman. Rio Declaration on Environment and Development', 2 April 1992, UN Doc A/CONF.151/PC/WG.III/L.33/Rev.1 ('L.33'), Principle 2.

[11] 'Principles on general rights and obligations', para 43.

[12] 'Principles on general rights and obligations', para 37.

[13] 'Principles on general rights and obligations', para 45.

A number of States sought to broaden the obligation of prevention by confirming its applicability beyond the transboundary perspective. For instance, Canada and Austria adopted a very broad perspective to prevention by creating an obligation for States but also individuals and organizations to protect the planet:

> All individuals, organizations and States shall respect the environment of other individuals, organizations and States, and the Earth's ecosystem; and treat the global commons of the Earth in a manner at least as favourable as their own environment, keeping in mind the interests of human kind as a whole.[14]

The proposal differed from Principle 21 by its departure from the sovereignty referential and the use of non-traditional concepts such as 'ecosystems', 'global commons', and 'human kind'. By providing that States should treat the global environment no worse than their own environment, the proposal also attempted to renew the relationship between sovereignty and environmental protection. Chile's proposal regarding the prevention principle was also broader in that it introduced an obligation of prevention for non-State actors such as international organizations, transnational enterprises, or individuals:

> National sovereignty of States shall not be an obstacle to the interdependent resolution of the global problems of development and environment by the international community.
>
> This will require action in solidarity, inter alia, to avoid the degradation of natural resources, infringement of global international security, and to contribute to the eradication of extreme poverty. States, international organizations and transnational corporations shall prevent transfrontier damage and shall protect the global commons.[15]

The European approach was more concerned with the procedural aspect of prevention rather than with its application to non-State actors. The European Economic Community focused on the obligation of information and consultation in order to prevent environmental harm.[16] Such an approach hints at the fact that the implementation, rather than the acceptance, of the prevention principle was the key challenge. In addition, it was a reminder of the Chernobyl disaster, still fresh in delegates' minds, and the subsequent emergence of an obligation of information sharing in order to avoid or mitigate environmental harm.

In sum, industrialized States focused on proposals that would contribute to the progressive development of Principle 21, whereas developing countries were eager to highlight the sovereignty component of Principle 21.

### 1.3. *The 'Stockholm principle' in PrepCom IV*

As noted earlier, the negotiations of WG III at PrepCom IV were not based on the chairman's consolidated draft or his own 'compromise draft', but took a different course with several new drafts being submitted by major groups, particularly after the G77+China decided to submit their new text ('L.20').[17] The atmosphere of the negotiations on the

[14] L.8, para 38. [15] L.8, paras 39–40.

[16] L.8, para 44: 'States shall provide prior and timely notification and relevant information to other concerned States on activities which may have a significant international or transboundary effect and shall consult with those States at an early state and in good faith' (Netherlands/EEC).

[17] 'Rio de Janeiro Charter/Declaration on Environment and Development', UN Doc A/CONF.151/PC/WG.III/L.20/Rev.1 ('L.20'). See also the draft presented by: the United States, UN Doc A/CONF.151/PC/WG.III/L.21 ('L.21'); Japan, 'Rights and Obligations', UN Doc A/CONF.151/PC/WG.III/L.22 ('L.22'); Canada, UN Doc A/CONF.151/PC/WG.III/L.23 ('L.23'); Australia, UN Doc A/CONF.151/PC/WG.III/L.24 ('L.24'); EC countries, 'Elements for the Earth Charter', UN Doc A/CONF.151/PC/WG.III/L.25 ('L.25'); Nordic countries, 'Earth Charter. Elements for Consideration', UN Doc A/CONF.151/PC/WG.III/L.27 ('L.27').

prevention principle in the first days is well captured by the Earth Summit Bulletin, which reported that:

Many governments were of the view that [Principle 21 of the Stockholm Declaration] would be best suited for inclusion in the preamble. Some thought it should be restated verbatim, while others argued for greater elaboration which would take into account the important fact that UNCED, unlike Stockholm, is charged with the mandate to consider development as well as environmental problems.[18]

The prevention principle featured prominently in the different drafts.[19] Whereas some formulations introduced significant variations with respect to the language of the 'Stockholm principle', others—including the one that eventually prevailed—followed such language closely with only minor variations.

Examples of the first category include the proposals by Japan and Canada. Principle 5 of Japan's draft stated:

Each State has the sovereign right to exploit its own resources in accordance with its own environmental policies. *However, this right should not be exercised in a manner inconsistent with the goal of integrating development and environmental protection.* States have the responsibility to ensure that activities within their jurisdiction or control do not cause damage to the environments of other States. *They should therefore conduct environmental impact assessments on any projects whose effects may be felt beyond their own national boundaries, the results to be provided promptly to the States concerned* (italics added).

Japan's proposal thus blends the prevention principle with the so-called principle of integration, appearing in Principle 4 of the Rio Declaration, as well as with the requirement to conduct an environmental impact assessment, later formulated in Principle 17 of the Rio Declaration. As for Canada's proposal, Principle 4 of its draft took a different perspective using a 'national treatment' approach:

All States and people shall treat the environment of other States and people, the global commons, as well as the Earth's ecosystem, in a manner at least as favourable as their own environment and consistent with international law and this Charter.

Other formulations were much closer to the Stockholm principle, including those proposed by the G77+China, the United States, Australia, and the Nordic countries. The main bone of contention between the formulations of this second category was the qualification of the exercise of sovereignty over natural resources. Whereas Principle 2 of the draft tabled by the G77+China referred to the sovereign right to exploit natural resources pursuant to their own environmental 'and developmental policies', the US and Nordic drafts omitted any such qualification, including the one appearing in Principle 21 of the Stockholm Declaration ('pursuant to their own environmental policies'). The Australian draft referred, in its Principle 5, to the right to exploit natural resources 'in a sustainable manner'.

Eventually, a compromise was found between the two perspectives. Suggestions to substantially reword Principle 21 were rejected and the Stockholm formulation was only modified to add that States have 'the sovereign right to exploit their own resources pursuant

[18] 'Earth Summit Bulletin', vol 1–6, from UNCED-Prep Com IV, 8 March 1992.

[19] See L.20, principle 2; L.21, principle 5; L.22, principle 5; L.23, principle 4; L.24, principle 5; L.27, principle 7.

to their own environmental *and developmental policies*'. This minor change, introduced by the draft of the G77+China, was deemed necessary to integrate the development perspective advocated by developing countries.

The difference between Principle 21 of the Stockholm Declaration and Principle 2 of the Rio Declaration is subtle but nevertheless revealing. On the one hand, Principle 21 was reaffirmed as the cornerstone of international environmental law and was not replaced by another concept. As expressed in the Preamble of the Declaration, the Rio Declaration is to be seen as a continuation of the Stockholm Declaration, and the reaffirmation of Principle 21 stresses such continuity. Yet, its inclusion in the Declaration and the focus on developmental policies strengthens the position of the first component of the principle (sovereignty over natural resources) as compared to the environmental protection components.

## 2. Scope and dimensions

### *2.1. The normative components of the prevention principle*

#### 2.1.1. From no-harm to prevention

Some early codification works have tended to assimilate the no-harm rule and the prevention principle. As will be discussed in section II) 3.2.1 of this chapter, the work of the ILC on prevention adopted an exclusively transboundary perspective. In an earlier attempt, the legal principles appended as an annex to the 1987 report of the World Commission on Environment and Development had also focused on the transboundary dimension of prevention.[20] Similarly, the expert group convened by the Commission of Sustainable Development in 1995 to report on the legal principles of sustainable development, identified three different principles conveying prevention without clarifying the differences between no-harm and prevention.[21]

There are, however, noticeable differences between the no-harm rule, as it still operates in an area such as shared watercourses,[22] and the prevention principle. The first and perhaps most obvious is the focus of the latter on preventing harm rather than on imposing a horizontal tort-like duty on States.

The second is the emphasis of the prevention principle on preventing harm to the environment as such, rather than to other States. This apparently innocuous difference in formulation may become relevant when it comes to determining who may bring a claim for environmental harm. In a pure no-harm context, it is the sovereignty of the affected State, which is at stake and, logically, the entitlement to bring a claim belongs to the State itself. In the context of prevention, other voices (eg individuals, collective subjects such as an indigenous or tribal people, communities, civil society groups or, perhaps, international organizations) may speak for the protection of the environment. The distinction may have significant consequences. By way of illustration, in *Chevron v. Ecuador*, a significant part of the case turned on whether Ecuador was the only entity capable of exercising diffuse

[20] Commission on Sustainable Development, Report of the Expert Group Meeting on Identification of Principles of International Law for Sustainable Development, Geneva, Switzerland, 26–28 September 1995 ('Report-principles'), principle 14.

[21] See Section II) 3.2.2 of this chapter.

[22] Convention on the Law of the Non-Navigational Uses of International Watercourses, New York, 21 May 1997, in force 17 August 2014, (1997) 36 ILM 700, art 7. See also, McCaffrey, S.C., *The Law of International Watercourses* (2nd edn, Oxford University Press 2007), chs 10–12.

rights to environmental protection and, as a result, was entitled to release Texaco and Chevron from any liability in this connection.[23] Conversely, in the context of the World Heritage Convention, the World Heritage Committee is entitled to speak for the environment in that it can propose that a listed site be moved to the list of World Heritage in danger, which has sometimes led to significant tensions with the States where the site is located.[24] The distinction is also relevant for the potential invocation of the prevention principle to support human rights applications (brought by individual or collective subjects) for extraterritorial environmental harm.[25]

The third difference between the no-harm and the prevention principles concerns their respective spatial scope. Whereas the no-harm principle only concerns transboundary damage, the prevention principle also applies to harm to areas beyond national jurisdiction and potentially also to environmental harm within a State's territory.

### 2.1.2. The three components of the prevention principle

#### *2.1.2.1. Overview*

The prevention principle as formulated in Principle 2 of the Rio Declaration has three main components: (i) permanent sovereignty over natural resources; (ii) prohibition against causing harm to the environment of other States; and (iii) prohibition against causing harm to the environment beyond national jurisdiction. The following sections examine each component in turn.

#### *2.1.2.2. Sovereignty over natural resources*

The concept of permanent sovereignty over natural resources is not an environmental concept at its core but it provides the backdrop of prevention because it assigns legal powers over natural resources. Its subsequent adaptation to the environmental sphere has shaped the prevention principle in such a way as to create a dynamic balance between sovereignty and environmental protection.

The concept itself emerged from the affirmation of the rights to self-determination of colonial peoples and to economic development of newly independent States. For peoples under colonial rule, the main objective was to protect and preserve their natural resources from the colonial power. Once their right to self-determination was exercised, newly independent States further sought to ensure their economic emancipation against encroachments by foreign companies exploiting their resources. The concept of permanent sovereignty over natural resources emerged to secure both claims. Resolution 523 (VI) was the first resolution mentioning the States' 'right to determine freely the use of their natural resources'. It did not refer to permanent sovereignty over natural resources, nor did it characterize the principle as permanent and inalienable.[26] Resolution 626 (VII) confirmed that 'the right of peoples freely to use and exploit their natural wealth and resources is inherent in their sovereignty'.[27] Resolution 1314 (XIII) recognized that the

[23] See *Chevron Corporation and Texaco Petroleum Corporation v. The Republic of Ecuador*, UNCITRAL, PCA Case No. 2009-23, First Partial Award on Track 1 (17 September 2013), para 106.

[24] See Affolder, N., 'Mining and the World Heritage Convention: Democratic Legitimacy and Treaty Compliance' (2007) 24 *Pace Environmental Law Review* 35.

[25] On extra-territorial environmental harm, see, Boyle, A., 'Human Rights and the Environment: Where Next?' (2012) 23 *EJIL* 613; Viñuales, J. E., 'A Human Rights Approach to Environmental Protection? An Assessment', in Bhuta, N. (ed), *The Frontiers of Human Rights: Extraterritoriality and its Challenges* (Oxford University Press, forthcoming 2015).

[26] UNGA Res. 523 (VI) (12 January 1952).

[27] UNGA Res. 626 (VII) (21 December 1952).

concept was a 'basic constituent of the right to self-determination'.[28] Finally, the work culminated in the adoption of Resolution 1803 (XVII) on 'Permanent Sovereignty over Natural Resources'.[29]

Although the emphasis of this resolution is on the use of 'natural resources' (not on the protection of the 'environment'), the exercise of sovereignty is not unbridled, because it 'must be exercised in the interest of their national development and of the well-being of the people of the state concerned'. Such limitations were further specified by the reference to sovereignty over natural resources in Principle 21 of the Stockholm Declaration with the explicit qualification that it must not be exercised to the detriment of the environment. At the same moment, however, the UN General Assembly further strengthened the first component of the principle by emphasizing, in Resolution 3281 (XXVII), the right of States to use their natural resources as they see fit.[30]

The concept of sovereignty over natural resources is at the centre of Principle 2, perhaps to a greater extent than it was for Principle 21, since it is the developmental dimension of the principle that received further support at the Rio Summit. Developing countries, fearing that environmental protection would be used as an argument to curtail their development efforts, sought to ensure that environmental and development policies remain in the hands of States.[31] They felt that if the classical concept of sovereignty was 'no longer beneficial to developed countries it must now be beneficial to [developing countries]'[32] and that they were entitled to pollute if necessary for their economic development.

Today, the concept of sovereignty over natural resources remains at the heart of the prevention principle. Most often, it is invoked to limit the demands of environmental protection 'when states wish to resist international pressure to protect their natural resources from overuse and depletion'.[33] Yet, sovereignty and environmental protection may not necessarily be seen as competing considerations. In recent years, there have been some attempts at reconceptualizing sovereignty in 'functional' terms or as powers held in trust to the benefit of present and future generations.[34]

### *2.1.2.3. Preventing harm to the environment of other States*

The prohibition against causing harm to the environment of other States is widely recognized in international law. It predates the Stockholm Conference and is based on the

[28] UNGA Res. 1314 (XIII) (12 December 1958).

[29] UNGA Res. 1803 (XVII) (14 December 1962).

[30] Charter of Economic Rights and Duties of States, UNGA Res. 3281 (XXVII) (1974), art 2(1).

[31] In this respect, Bekhechi notes: 'L'un des résultats les plus significatifs du sommet de Rio est constitué par la réaffirmation du principe de souveraineté que d'aucuns avaient cru battu en brèche au nom d'un nouveau globalisme qui implique l'engagement sans réserve de tous les Etats à lutter contre les atteintes à l'environnement'. Bekhechi, M.A., 'Le droit international à l'épreuve du développement durable. Quelques réflexions à propos de la Déclaration de Rio sur l'environnement et le développement' (1993) *Hague Yearbook of International Law* 59, 68.

[32] Porras, I., 'The Rio Declaration: A New Basis for International Co-operation' (1992) 1 *RECIEL* 245–53, 251.

[33] Perrez, F. X., *Cooperative Sovereignty: From Independence to Interdependence in the Structure of International Environmental Law* (Kluwer 2000), 95.

[34] See in particular Perrez, *Cooperative Sovereignty*, 28 (on 'positive sovereignty'); Francioni, F., 'The Private Sector and the Challenge of Implementation', in Dupuy, P.-M. and Viñuales, J. E. (eds), *Harnessing Foreign Investment to Promote Environmental Protection: Incentives and Safeguards* (Cambridge University Press 2013), 30 (on 'functional sovereignty'). See also the chapters by Francioni (Principle 1), Molinari (Principle 3) and Sand (Principle 27) in this commentary.

understanding that territorial sovereignty has its limitations: a State can enjoy sovereignty over natural resources as long as it does not cause transboundary harm.

Particularly well developed in early watercourse treaties,[35] the no-harm rule was recognized in 1941 in the *Trail Smelter* arbitration. The case concerned the harm caused in the United States by the emissions from a lead smelter based in Canada. The tribunal famously noted that:

> under the principles of international law, as well as of the law of the United States, no State has the right to use or permit the use of its territory in such a manner as to cause injury by fumes in or to the territory or the properties therein, when the case is of serious consequences and the injury is established by clear and convincing evidence.[36]

This approach was later confirmed by the International Court of Justice in the *Corfu Channel* case, where the Court noted that States have the 'obligation not to allow knowingly its territory to be used for acts contrary to the rights of other states'.[37] Such an approach, focusing on an obligation of good neighbourliness, was confirmed in the *Lac Lanoux* arbitration in which the arbitral tribunal affirmed that a State is entitled to exercise its rights so long as it does not 'ignore' the interests of the neighbouring State.[38]

Although the existence of an obligation not to cause harm to the territory of another State is not a matter of controversy, the definition of 'transboundary damage' and the 'threshold' that triggers the violation of the obligation of prevention is disputed. It is generally recognized that not 'any' environmental damage is prohibited, but only 'significant' environmental harm, a threshold recognized in treaty-law,[39] case law[40] and in the ILC Prevention articles.[41] The ILC Prevention articles define the 'risk of causing significant transboundary harm' as including 'risks taking the form of a high probability of causing

[35] See in particular the resolution of the Institut de droit international, 'International Regulation regarding the Use of International Watercourses for Purposes other than Navigation', Session of Madrid, 1911.

[36] *Trail Smelter Arbitration* decision (*United States v. Canada*) (16 April 1939 and 11 March 1941), (1941) 3 RIAA 1905 *('Trail Smelter')*, 1965.

[37] *Corfu Channel* (United Kingdom/Albania) ICJ Reports 1949, 4, 22.

[38] *Lac Lanoux Arbitration* (*France v. Spain*) (1957) 24 ILR 101, 40.

[39] See, *inter alia*, Convention for the Protection of the Ozone Layer, Vienna, 22 March 1985, in force 22 September 1988, (1985) 26 ILM 1529, art 1(2); Convention on the Regulation of Antarctic Mineral Resource Activities, Wellington, 2 June 1988, not in force, (1988) 27 ILM 868, art 4(2); Convention on Environmental Impact Assessment in a Transboundary Context, Espoo, 25 February 1991, in force 10 September 1997, (1991) 30 ILM 802, art 2(1)–(2); Convention on the Protection and Use of Transboundary Watercourses and International Lakes, Helsinki, 17 March 1992, in force 6 October 1996, (1992) 31 ILM 1312, art 1(2); United Nations Framework Convention on Climate Change, New York, 9 May 1992, in force 24 March 1994, 1771 UNTS 107 ('UNFCCC'), art 1(1); Convention on Biological Diversity, Nairobi, 22 May 1992, in force 29 December 1993, (1992) 31 ILM 822, art 14(1)(a); and Convention on the Law of the Non-navigational Uses of International Watercourses, art 7.

[40] See in particular, *Iron Rhine Railway* (*Belgium v. Netherlands*), Permanent Court of Arbitration, (2005) 27 RIAA 35, para 222 ('*Iron Rhine*'); *Pulp Mills on the River Uruguay* (*Argentina v. Uruguay*) (Judgment) (2010) ICJ Rep 14 ('*Pulp Mills*'), para 101; *Indus Waters Kishenganga Arbitration* (*Pakistan v. India*), ('*Kishenganga Arbitration*') Permanent Court of Arbitration, Partial Award, 18 February 2013, para 451, and Final Award, 20 December 2013, para 112. Although there is a currently a consensus on the 'significant' threshold, the earlier jurisprudence had dealt with other thresholds: see the *Trail Smelter* award, which used the words 'serious consequence[s]' (at 716); and the *Lac Lanoux* arbitration award, in which the tribunal highlighted the prohibition to 'seriously' prejudice a neighbouring State (at 129).

[41] International Law Commission, 'Draft Articles on Prevention of Transboundary Harm from Hazardous Activities (with Commentaries)' (2001) *Yearbook of the International Law Commission* (vol II, part 2) 148 ('ILC Prevention articles' and 'ILC Prevention Commentaries'), art 1.

significant transboundary harm and a low probability of causing disastrous transboundary harm'.[42] The commentaries to the ILC Articles additionally note that:

> [t]he term 'significant' is not without ambiguity and a determination has to be made in each specific case. It involves more factual considerations than legal determination. It is to be understood that 'significant' is something more than 'detectable' but need not be at the level of 'serious' or 'substantial'.[43]

It remains that the determination of whether the prohibition applies is very much dependent on the circumstances. In addition, the significant harm threshold fails to address the issue of cumulative harm, that is, low impact damage that accumulates over time and creates significant harm, which seems particularly relevant for contexts such as climate change.

Aside from the 'significance' of the harm, another important point concerns its 'nature'. Article 2(b) of the ILC Prevention articles defines 'harm' as 'harm caused to persons, property or the environment'. This definition must be read in the light of article 1, which limits the scope of the prevention duty in the ILC Prevention articles to 'physical consequences'. It therefore does not cover 'transboundary harm which may be caused by State policies in monetary, socioeconomic or similar fields'.[44] This limitation of the nature of harm is explained in the commentary as an attempt to keep the codification work within manageable bounds.[45] As a result, this limitation does not entail that the customary prevention principle is equally limited. The distinction is not a purely academic point, as it is relevant to assess whether policies that restrict access to low-carbon technology in other countries or sanctions that force affected communities to behave in an environmentally adverse manner may come under the remit of the prevention principle.

#### 2.1.2.4. *Preventing harm to the environment beyond national jurisdiction*

The third component of Principle 2 is the prohibition against causing damage to the environment beyond national jurisdiction. By moving beyond the transboundary approach, Principle 2 calls for a redefinition of traditional international law as it was originally conceived, ie with a focus on the 'State' and its territorial sovereignty. Indeed, the obligation not to cause harm to the environment beyond national jurisdiction changes the perspective of the obligation: the State is not only required to prevent transboundary harm in order to respect the sovereignty of other States but is also obliged to protect the environment as such, including those areas such as the global commons which have no connection to State sovereignty. As such, the last component clarifies the specificity to the prevention principle. The evolution from no-harm to prevention is particularly important as it favours a non-spatial approach to environmental protection.

The third component of prevention finds expression in provisions creating an obligation of environmental protection applicable to areas beyond the national jurisdiction of States, such as the high seas,[46] international air space[47] or the Antarctic.[48] It remains nevertheless

[42] ILC Prevention articles, art 2(a).

[43] ILC Prevention Commentaries, Commentary to Article 2, para 4.

[44] ILC Prevention Commentaries, Commentary to Article 1, para 16.

[45] ILC Prevention Commentaries, Commentary to Article 1, para 16.

[46] UNCLOS, arts 116–18 (on conservation and management of the living resources of the high seas) and art 192 (on a general obligation to protect and preserve the marine environment).

[47] The right to take environmental measures to protect the international air space was recognized in *Air Transport Association of America and others v. Secretary of State for Energy and Climate Change, Judgment of the Court*, C-366/10, Court of Justice of the European Union, Grand Chamber (21 December 2011).

[48] Protocol on Environmental Protection to the Antarctic Treaty, Madrid, 4 October 1991, in force 14 January 1998, (1991) 30 ILM 1461, art 2.

that the spatial referential is still present in many of these provisions: the global commons are envisaged by contrast to areas under State jurisdiction. However, certain references to prevention have been formulated from an a-territorial perspective. For instance, article 192 of the 1982 United Nations Convention on the Law of the Sea (UNCLOS) creates a general obligation to protect and preserve the marine environment by providing that 'States have the obligation to protect and preserve the marine environment'. A similar obligation is stated in article 20 of the 1997 United Nations Convention on the Law of the Non-Navigational Uses of International Watercourses, which not only refers to an obligation not to cause harm[49] but also to a broader obligation to protect the ecosystems of international watercourses: '[w]atercourse States shall, individually and, where appropriate, jointly, protect and preserve the ecosystems of international watercourses'.

Such provisions, and others referring to the protection of ecosystems or nature in general,[50] can be seen as an extension of the third component of Principle 2. They move beyond the anchor of Principle 2 on sovereignty and highlight the duty to prevent damage to the environment *tout court*.

### 2.1.3. Prevention and due diligence

The prevention principle imposes a duty of due diligence on States with respect to the environment. The concept of due diligence is important in this context for two main reasons. First, by referring to 'due diligence', the nature of the duty is further clarified as one of means or conduct and not one of result. Second, the content of the 'diligence' required from States is further clarified and therefore made more concrete and capable of application.

In the *Pulp Mills on the River Uruguay* case ('*Pulp Mills*'), the ICJ elaborated on this concept. Although the Court's analysis relates to the provisions of the Statute of the River Uruguay, its reasoning suggests that the prevention principle requires: (i) an obligation of conduct and, more particularly, of cooperation for the implementation and application of appropriate measures for the preservation of the environment;[51] as well as (ii) the obligation to conduct an environmental impact assessment where the proposed activity is likely to have a significant adverse impact in a transboundary context, especially with respect to a shared resource.[52]

This understanding has been confirmed by the advisory opinion of the Seabed Chamber of the International Tribunal for the Law of the Sea ('ITLOS') on the *Responsibilities and Obligations of States sponsoring Persons and Entities with respect to Activities in the Area* ('Advisory Opinion on the Area').[53] According to the Seabed Chamber, the 'due diligence' obligation encompasses: (i) the obligation of States to adopt appropriate measures and ensure that they are reasonably enforced;[54] (ii) the obligation (based both on

49 Convention on the Law of the Non-Navigational Uses of International Watercourses, art 7.

50 See for instance Principle 1 of the World Charter for Nature, UNGA Res. 37/7 (XXXVII), which reads as follows: 'Nature shall be respected and its essential processes shall not be impaired'.

51 *Pulp Mills*, paras 101–2 and 181–9. The obligation of conduct is also recognized in the ILC Prevention Commentaries, Commentary to art 3, para 7.

52 *Pulp Mills*, para 204.

53 *Responsibilities and Obligations of States sponsoring Persons and Entities with respect to Activities in the Area*, Case No. 17, ITLOS (Seabed Dispute Chamber), Advisory Opinion of 1 February 2011 ('Advisory Opinion on the Area').

54 Advisory Opinion on the Area, para 115 (referring to the interpretation of the obligation of 'due diligence' provided by the ICJ in the *Pulp Mills* case), 116 (referring to the ILC Project on Prevention) and 117–20 (referring, in para 120, to the more detailed answer given by the Chamber in response to the third question put to it).

the UNCLOS and in customary international law) to conduct an environmental impact assessment;[55] and (iii) the obligation to apply the precautionary approach not only as a requirement of the applicable regulations of the Seabed Authority but also as a component of the 'due diligence' obligation and, possibly, of customary international law.[56]

### 2.1.4. Prevention in a domestic context

One important question is whether customary international law requires States to prevent harm to the environment within their territory or jurisdiction even when no external impact can be reasonably foreseen. Aside from the obligations that may arise from treaty law, there are four main considerations suggesting that such obligation exists.

The first has been already discussed in connection with the distinction between no-harm and prevention. The focus of the prevention principle on environmental protection per se irrespective of spatial considerations provides a strong indication that States must protect their own environment.

The second and related consideration concerns the existence of a sophisticated framework for environmental protection in many States and the emphasis placed, during the negotiation of the Rio Declaration, on the need to adopt domestic environmental policies.[57] Canada's proposal during PrepCom IV illustrates this point to the extent it framed 'external' prevention as a reflection of 'internal' prevention, through a sort of national treatment rule requiring States to protect the environment abroad to the same degree as their own environment.[58]

The third consideration is specifically legal. The principle of sovereignty over natural resources is qualified by the requirement that sovereignty 'must be exercised in the interest of their national development and of the well-being of the people of the state concerned'.[59] Although this requirement is difficult to implement in practice, it clearly imposes on States a duty to use resources in a way that is not harmful to its population.

Fourth, the vagueness of the foregoing requirement is offset by the existence of specific human rights obligations with environmental components. Irrespective of whether provisions such as article 24 (peoples' right to a generally satisfactory environment) of the African Charter on Human and Peoples' Rights[60] have customary grounding or not, even basic human rights, the customary grounding of which is less controversial,[61] such as the human rights to life, health, private and family life, or individual and collective cultural rights entail a proactive duty of the State to protect individuals from deprivation by activities conducted by third parties or even natural disasters.[62] The relevant case law on this point is discussed in section II) 4.4. of this chapter.

[55] Advisory Opinion on the Area, para 145.

[56] Advisory Opinion on the Area, paras 125–35, particularly at 131 and 135.

[57] See the chapter by Kunz in this commentary. [58] See L.23. [59] See L.23, principle 4.

[60] African Charter on Human and Peoples' Rights, Banjul, 27 June 1981, in force 21 October 1986, (1982) 21 ILM 58.

[61] On human rights threatened by environmental harm, see the 'Report of the Independent Expert on the issue of human rights obligations relating to the enjoyment of a safe, clean, healthy and sustainable environment, John H. Knox: Preliminary report', A/HRC/22/43, 24 December 2012, paras 18–24.

[62] The obligations to be respected in order to fulfil this proactive duty are detailed in the 'Report of the Independent Expert on the issue of human rights obligations relating to the enjoyment of a safe, clean, healthy and sustainable environment, John H. Knox: Mapping Report', A/HRC/25/53, 30 December 2013, paras 26–68.

## 2.2. Legal nature

### 2.2.1. Nature and functions

There is much discussion as to whether different concepts regularly used in international environmental law operate as 'concepts', 'principles', 'rules', or 'decision-making processes'. As noted by the arbitral tribunal in the *Iron Rhine Railway* case '[t]here is considerable debate as to what, within the field of environmental law, constitutes "rules" or "principles"'.[63] Leaving aside the important theoretical dimension of this debate, for the purpose of this commentary the main question relates to the functions that the 'statement' appearing in Principles 21 of the Stockholm Declaration and 2 of the Rio Declaration may perform. The word 'statement' is used as a neutral term.

The different statements appearing in the Rio Declaration may perform a variety of functions. First, they may drive the contents of a treaty or a section of a treaty (eg Part XII of the UNCLOS[64]) in what can be called an architectural function. Second, statements may also perform an interpretive function: to clarify or develop the meaning of a provision, or to conciliate the requirements of two conflicting norms. Third, statements can also perform a decision-making function determining the conformity of a given act with what is legally required, prohibited, or authorized. Such requirement, prohibition or authorization can be more or less clear according to the formulation of the statement. A statement is considered to be a principle if it can perform these three functions.

Under this definition, the statement included in Principle 2 of the Rio Declaration is indeed a 'principle'. Its architectural function can be illustrated by reference to numerous environmental treaties covering matters such as transboundary air pollution or the protection of the marine environment.[65] Prevention performs also an important interpretive function of treaty provisions relating to other matters: to clarify[66] or update their content,[67] or to conciliate different considerations.[68] Finally, despite its broad formulation, the prevention principle is precise enough to perform a decision-making function as illustrated by the classic *Trail Smelter* case.[69]

### 2.2.2. Legal grounding

The prevention principle is well-established as a customary norm of international law. In addition to the Stockholm and the Rio Declarations, the relevant practice embodying this norm encompasses not only many environmental treaties[70] but also major codification initiatives under the aegis of the UN International Law Commission ('ILC'),[71] the Commission on Sustainable Development ('CSD'),[72] the Institut de Droit International ('IDI')[73] or the

[63] *Iron Rhine*, para 58. [64] See Section II) 3.1 of this chapter.

[65] See Section II) 3.1 of this chapter. [66] See eg Advisory Opinion on the Area, paras 110–16.

[67] See eg *Iron Rhine*, para 58; Report of the Appellate Body, *United States—Import Prohibition of Certain Shrimp and Shrimp Products*, 12 October 1998, WT/DS58/AB/R ('*Shrimp-Turtle* case'), paras 129–31, 152–3; *Kishenganga Arbitration*, Partial award, para 452.

[68] See eg *S.D. Myers Inc. v. Canada, NAFTA Arbitration* (UNCITRAL Rules), Partial Award (13 November 2000), para 247.

[69] *Trail Smelter*, 1965. See also *Corfu Channel*, 22 (although this case does not concern environmental matters, the ICJ has equated the prevention principle applied in it with the modern prevention principle, see *Pulp Mills*, para 101).

[70] See Section II) 3.1 of this chapter. [71] See Section II) 3.2.1 of this chapter.

[72] See Section II) 3.2.2 of this chapter. [73] See Section II) 3.2.3 of this chapter.

International Law Association ('ILA').[74] There is also wide agreement among commentators on the customary nature of the prevention principle.[75]

With respect to jurisprudential decisions, the International Court of Justice ('ICJ') has recognized the customary grounding of the prevention principle on several occasions, explicitly referring to Principles 21 of the Stockholm Declaration and 2 of the Rio Declaration as a codification of general international law. In its *Advisory Opinion on the Legality of the Threat or Use of Nuclear Weapons* the ICJ noted, by reference to Principles 21 and 2, that:

> The existence of the general obligation of States to ensure that activities within their jurisdiction and control respect the environment of other States or of areas beyond national control is now part of the corpus of international law relating to the environment.[76]

The following year, in its judgment on the *Gabčíkovo-Nagymaros* case, the ICJ further stated that:

> in the field of environmental protection, vigilance and prevention are required on account of the often irreversible character of damage to the environment and of the limitations inherent in the very mechanism of reparation of this type of damage.[77]

In another judgment rendered in 2010 on the *Pulp Mills* case, the ICJ further confirmed this principle and linked it to its origins in the no-harm principle.[78]

Taken together, the foregoing authorities clearly establish the customary nature of the prevention principle with its different components.

## 3. Normative impact

### *3.1. Treaty law*

The prevention principle pervades international environmental law, and it has been stated in terms that are very similar to Principle 2 of the Rio Declaration or, its predecessor, Principle 21 of the Stockholm Declaration, in many instruments predating but also following the 1992 Earth Summit. For present purposes, it will suffice to refer to some of the most important environmental treaties that are expressly based on the prevention principle.

One major feature of UNCLOS, adopted in 1982,[79] is the inclusion of an entire part (Part XII) specifically devoted to the protection and preservation of the marine environment. Part XII is anchored in the prevention principle, the components of which are stated

[74] See Section II) 3.2.4 of this chapter.

[75] Birnie, P., Boyle, A., and Redgwell, C., *International Law and the Environment* (3rd edn, Oxford University Press 2009), 109; Boisson de Chazournes, L. and Maljean-Dubois, S., 'Les principes du droit international de l'environnement', *fascicule du Jurisclasseur Environnement et développement durable*, 146–15, September 2010, 11–12; Dupuy, P.-M., 'Où en est le droit international de l'environnement à la fin du siècle?' (1997) 28 *RGDIP* 886, 879–81; Kiss, A. and Beurier, J.-P., *Droit international de l'environnement* (3rd edn, Pedone 2004), 124; Kiss, A. and Shelton, D., *International Environmental Law* (Graham and Trotman 1991), 106–7; Sand, P. H., 'UNCED and the Development of International Environmental Law' (1992/1993) 8 *Journal of Natural Resources and Environmental Law* 209, 216; Sands and Peel, *Principles of International Environmental Law* 200; Viñuales, J. E., 'The Contribution of the International Court of Justice to the Development of International Environmental Law' (2008) 32 *Fordham International Law Journal* 232, 246–9.

[76] *Legality of the Threat or Use of Nuclear Weapons* (Advisory Opinion) (1996) ICJ Rep 226 ('Nuclear Weapons Advisory Opinion'), para 29.

[77] *Gabčíkovo-Nagymaros Project* (Hungary/Slovakia) (1997) ICJ Rep 7, para 140.

[78] *Pulp Mills*, paras 101 and 185. [79] UNCLOS.

in articles 193 (sovereignty over natural resources) and 194 (limitation of such sovereignty in order to protect the environment). According to article 194(2):

States shall take all measures necessary to ensure that activities under their jurisdiction or control are so conducted as not to cause damage by pollution to other States and their environment, and that pollution arising from incidents or activities under their jurisdiction or control does not spread beyond the areas where they exercise sovereign rights in accordance with this Convention.

References to prevention also appear in other major treaties, including the three conventions that arose from the Rio 1992 process, namely, the United Nations Framework Convention on Climate Change,[80] the Convention on Biological Diversity[81] and the Convention to Combat Desertification.[82] Later treaties also make reference to the principle. One major example is the Stockholm Convention on Persistent Organic Pollutants, adopted in 2001.[83]

At the regional level, the prevention principle is referred to *inter alia* in the 1993 North American Agreement on Environmental Cooperation,[84] the 2003 African Convention on the Conservation of Nature[85] as well as in some of the Protocols to the 1979 UNECE Convention on Long-Range Transboundary Air Pollution, including the 1998 Aarhus Protocol on Persistent Organic Pollutants,[86] the 1998 Heavy Metals Protocol,[87] and the 1999 Gothenburg Protocol.[88]

## 3.2. *Codification work*

### 3.2.1. Prevention in the International Law Commission (1978–2001)

Prevention has also been at the centre of the work of the International Law Commission ('ILC') on international liability for injurious consequences arising out of acts not prohibited by international law. After years of hesitation as to the proper angle for the topic, the ILC set two separate tracks, one focusing on the definition of prevention of environmental harm as a duty of States ('ILC Prevention articles' adopted in 2001[89]) and another setting parameters for the allocation of loss in the event harm occurs ('ILC Principles on the allocation of loss' adopted in 2006[90]). The first reads as an elaboration of the primary norm

[80] UNFCCC, Preamble, para 8. [81] Convention on Biological Diversity, art 3.

[82] Convention to Combat Desertification in Those Countries Experiencing Serious Drought and/or Desertification, Particularly in Africa, Paris, 17 June 1994, in force 26 December 1996, (1994) 33 ILM 1328, preamble, para 15.

[83] Convention on Persistent Organic Pollutants, Stockholm, 22 May 2001, in force 17 May 2004, (2001) 40 ILM 532, preamble, para 10.

[84] North American Agreement on Environmental Cooperation, Ort der Annahme, 13 September 1993, in force 1 January 1994, available <http://www.cec.org/Page.asp?PageID=1226&SiteNodeID=567>, Preamble.

[85] African Convention on the Conservation of Nature and Natural Resources (Revised Version), Maputo, 11 July 2003, not in force, available on the AU website <http://www.au.int/en/content/african-convention-conservation-nature-and-natural-resources-revised-version>, Preamble.

[86] Protocol to the 1979 Convention on Long Range Transboundary Air Pollution on Persistent Organic Pollutants, Aarhus, 24 June 1998, in force 23 December 2003, (1998) 37 ILM 505, Preamble.

[87] Protocol to the 1979 Convention on Long Range Transboundary Air Pollution on Heavy Metals, Aarhus, 24 June 1998, in force 29 December 2003, available on the UNECE website <http://www.unece.org/env/lrtap/hm_h1.html>, Preamble.

[88] Protocol to the 1979 Convention on Long Range Transboundary Air Pollution to Abate Acidification, Eutrophication and Ground-Level Ozone, Gothenburg, 30 November 1999, in force 17 May 2005, UN Doc EB/AIR/1999, Preamble.

[89] ILC Prevention articles.

[90] ILC, 'Draft Principles on the Allocation of Loss in the Case of Transboundary Harm Arising out of Hazardous Activities (with Commentaries)' (2006) (UN Doc A/63/10).

or duty of prevention, as stated in Principle 21 of the Stockholm Declaration and Principle 2 of the Rio Declaration, although with a narrower focus. The second provides guidance on how to organize the consequences of damage to the environment at the national and international level, much as a civil liability treaty would.

Importantly, the preamble of the ILC Prevention articles makes it clear that they are intended as an elaboration of the Rio Principles, particularly of the balance between sovereignty over natural resources and its limits.[91] To assess the scope of this normative development, two main questions must be addressed, namely the content of the obligation of prevention as defined in the ILC Prevention articles and the relationship between this instrument and the customary rules of prevention embodied *inter alia* in Principle 2 of the Rio Declaration. The two are of course intertwined.

Regarding the contents of the ILC Prevention articles, the focus is narrower than Principle 2 of the Rio Declaration, as the ILC carefully circumscribed the scope of its work according to several parameters.[92] Compared to Principle 2, the main differences are the strictly transboundary scope of the ILC Prevention articles (thus excluding areas beyond national jurisdiction and its application to purely domestic environmental harm) and the pragmatic recognition that in some cases harm may be admissible if it is minimized.[93] The risk of significant transboundary harm is defined in a non-limitative manner, as 'includ[ing] risks taking the form of a high probability of causing significant transboundary harm and a low probability of causing disastrous transboundary harm'.[94] Within these bounds, the duty of prevention is characterized by reference to several interrelated obligations, much in the same way as (and by reference to) the Rio Declaration. Inter-State or 'horizontal' obligations include prevention (art 3), cooperation in prevention and response (arts 4, 8, 9, 11, 12, 16, and 17), and information and protection to the public concerned (arts 13 and 15). Intra-State or 'vertical' obligations include adopting domestic legislation (art 5) and, more specifically, a system of authorization of potentially harmful activities (art 6) involving an environmental impact assessment (art 7). This array of obligations amounts to different expressions of the prevention principle but they also have a more specific grounding in other well-established principles, such as cooperation (Principles 18 and 19 of the Rio Declaration), the conduct of an environmental impact assessment (Principle 17 of the Rio Declaration), or public participation requirements (Principle 10). The articles also include a provision on the settlement of disputes (art 19) and another on the relations with other rules of international law (art 18).

The latter provision raises the question of the relationship between the ILC Prevention articles and the customary duty of prevention. The question has sometimes been asked from a different perspective, namely what is the customary status of the ILC Prevention articles. Clearly, the core system (prevention, cooperation, and environmental impact assessment) of this instrument rests on customary law, as it overlaps with the second pillar of the prevention principle (the transboundary duty of prevention). It is also clear that some provisions of the ILC Prevention articles, particularly the detail of the procedures set out in articles 11 and 19, do not rest on a customary basis. As for the requirements of

[91] The ILC Prevention Commentaries refer explicitly to Principle 2 of the Rio Declaration (general commentary, paras 3 and 4).

[92] See ILC Prevention Commentaries, Commentary to arts 1 and 2.

[93] See ILC Prevention Commentaries, Commentary to art 3, para 7, and to art 10(b), para 4.

[94] ILC Prevention articles, art 2(a).

public participation, there is increasing support for the proposition that some measure of non-discriminatory participation is required by customary international law, as a result of State environmental and human rights practice.[95] Beyond the specific status of different provisions of the ILC Prevention articles, which in many ways convey the 'transboundary' no-harm rule, it is important to note that the customary prevention principle operates in parallel (as regards transboundary matters) and may have a broader scope, not only spatial but also substantive. Specifically, the customary prevention principle applies to environmental harm beyond national jurisdiction and, perhaps also within the territory of the State conducting the activity. Moreover, its focus is not specifically on 'activities' with 'physical consequences' and may potentially encompass 'policies' with other types of consequences (eg socio-economic). The difference in scope and content is clearly preserved by article 18 of the ILC Prevention articles.

### 3.2.2. Prevention in the Commission on Sustainable Development (1995)

In 1995, the Commission on Sustainable Development ('CSD') (which ceased its activities in 2012 and has since then been replaced with a High Level Political Forum) convened a meeting of experts to examine the legal principles on sustainable development. The expert group issued a Report, which was understood as a study intervening:

> within the framework established by the Rio Declaration on Environment and Development and Agenda 21. It was agreed that these instruments provided the essential basis for identifying and assessing principles and concepts of international law for sustainable development, and that the delicately crafted packages they represent should not be unravelled...[96]

The Report devotes several paragraphs to what it calls the 'Sovereignty over natural resources and responsibility not to cause damage to the environment of other States or to areas beyond', 'the principle of sustainable use of natural resources', and 'prevention of environmental harm'. These are presented as three distinct principles, although the Report does not provide a clear conceptual or legal distinction. In the three cases, the legal foundations referred to are Principles 21 of the Stockholm Declaration and 2 of the Rio Declaration and the need to limit the exercise of sovereignty over natural resources arising from a variety of sources.

It is true that the formulation of the prevention principle leaves the question of prevention within the territory of a State unaddressed. But this is not to say that three different principles exist and place distinct requirements on States. With the benefit of almost twenty years of hindsight, the better view is that there is a single customary obligation of prevention of environmental harm, with a spatial scope that is well established in the transboundary context and beyond national jurisdiction and which is becoming increasingly clear in a purely domestic context, not only as a result of treaty obligations but also as a matter of human rights obligations.

### 3.2.3. Prevention in the Institut de Droit International (1997)

The Institut de Droit International ('IDI') examined the question of prevention of environmental harm both in specific areas[97] and, later, more generally. In three resolutions adopted in 1997 at the session of Strasbourg, the IDI characterized the duty of

[95] See the chapter by Ebbesson in this commentary.

[96] Commission on Sustainable Development, Report-principles.

[97] Institut de Droit International ('IDI'), 'The Pollution of Rivers and Lakes and International Law', Session of Athens, 1979; 'Transboundary Air Pollution', Session of Cairo, 1987.

prevention[98] and the relevant secondary rules (responsibility and liability),[99] and provided guidance on the process of implementation.[100] Although the first resolution does not refer to the Rio Declaration explicitly, the second does so and, more specifically, it is premised on Principle 21 of the Stockholm Declaration and Principle 2 of the Rio Declaration.[101]

The contents of the IDI Resolution on prevention are broadly similar to those subsequently adopted, in 2001, by the ILC. Article 6 defines the duty of prevention as follows:

> Every State, when intervening on the basis of decisions taken in the exercise of its sovereignty in fields of activity where the effects of such decisions on the environment are clear, has the responsibility to ensure that activities within its jurisdiction or under its control do not cause damage which may affect the lives of the present and future generations.

The scope of the duty is closer to Principle 2 of the Rio Declaration than to the formulation retained in the ILC Prevention articles, which only concern transboundary harm. Indeed, the reference to 'present and future generations' may encompass harm to areas beyond national jurisdiction, particularly if read in the light of the ICJ's *Advisory Opinion on Nuclear Weapons*[102] rendered the year before the IDI Resolution was adopted.

The IDI Resolution further refers to duties of cooperation[103] and to the conduct of environmental impact assessments of activities which may have consequences on the environment.[104] The language used in the Resolution is broader than in the ILC Prevention articles or Principle 2 of the Rio Declaration as it applies to 'any project, whether international, national or local, which may have consequences for the environment'. The second IDI Resolution (on Responsibility and Liability) adds, in connection with the level of diligence required from States in discharging their duties, that:

> When due diligence is utilized as a test for engaging responsibility it is appropriate that it be measured in accordance with objective standards relating to the conduct to be expected from a good government and detached from subjectivity. Generally accepted international rules and standards further provide an objective measurement for the due diligence test.[105]

This specification clarifies the primary norm defined in the first IDI Resolution, thus completing the definition of the conduct required.

### 3.2.4. Prevention in the work of the International Law Association (1992–2012)

Between 1992 and 2002, the International Law Association ('ILA') undertook a codification effort on the 'Legal Aspects of Sustainable Development'. This work has been subsequently developed through two other Committees ('International Law on Sustainable Development', 2003–2012, and 'Role of International Law in Sustainable Natural Resource Management for Development', 2012–current). The main outcome of these initiatives so far is the adoption, in April 2002, of the New Delhi Declaration of Principles relating to Sustainable Development.[106]

[98] IDI, 'Environment', Session of Strasbourg, 1997.

[99] IDI, 'Responsibility and Liability under International Law for Environmental Damage', Session of Strasbourg, 1997.

[100] IDI, 'Procedures for the Adoption and Implementation of Rules in the Field of Environment', Session of Strasbourg, 1997.

[101] IDI, 'Responsibility and Liability', Preamble.

[102] *Nuclear Weapons Advisory Opinion*, para 36.

[103] IDI, 'Environment', arts 6(3) and 7.

[104] IDI, 'Environment', art 5.

[105] IDI, 'Responsibility and Liability', art 3(2).

[106] International Law Association, Committee on the Legal Aspects of Sustainable Development, 'New Delhi Declaration of Principles of International Law Relating to Sustainable Development' (New Delhi, 70th session, 2002) ('ILA New Delhi Declaration').

As acknowledged in the preamble, the New Delhi Declaration takes specifically into account the Rio Declaration.[107] Article 1(1) of the New Delhi Declaration states:

> It is a well-established principle that, in accordance with international law, all States have the sovereign right to manage their own natural resources pursuant to their own environmental and developmental policies, and the responsibility to ensure that activities within their jurisdiction or control do not cause significant damage to the environment of other States or of areas beyond the limits of national jurisdiction.[108]

The wording used is, with only slight variations, that of the Principle 2 of the Rio Declaration, including the reference to 'and developmental policies', which does not appear in Principle 21 of the Stockholm Declaration. Unlike Principle 2, however, article 1(1) qualifies the term damage with the adjective 'significant' and speaks of 'natural' resources. The centre of gravity of article 1(1) is therefore closer to development than that of Principle 2, itself a departure of Principle 21. This variation in tone is recalled by the title of article 1 ('The duty of States to ensure sustainable use of natural resources'), which takes as a basis the first pillar of the prevention principle, namely the use of resources.

In 2012, the ILA adopted the Sofia Guiding Statements, which attempt to clarify the content of the New Delhi Declaration to foster their use in judicial practice. The statement on article 1 notes that:

> As a matter of common concern, the sustainable use of all natural resources represents an emerging rule of general customary international law, with particular normative precision identifiable with respect to shared and common natural resources.[109]

The formulation is ambiguous. As a statement addressed to adjudicators, it cannot be understood as detracting from the well-established principle of prevention of environmental harm whether in a transboundary context or in the global commons. This is what the last sentence seeks to convey. Yet, the attempt to derive a rule on the use of 'all' natural resources (including, presumably, the resources located in the territory or under the jurisdiction of a State) as a matter of 'common concern' is misguided, as the application of the latter concept has been confined so far to 'resources' such as the climatic system or biological diversity. The ambiguity is perhaps due to the ILA's attempt at finding a legal basis to support article 1(2)–(3) of the New Delhi Declaration, which calls for the rational use of natural resources, including those located within the territory or jurisdiction of a State and the 'natural environment' as a common concern. Yet, a more solid legal basis, implicitly referred to in article 1(2), would be reference to human rights duties,[110] which amounts in fact to the exercise of due diligence within their territory (see above section II) 2.1.4).

## 4. Jurisprudential relevance

### *4.1. The International Court of Justice*

Whereas in the period between Stockholm 1972 and Rio 1992 the prevention principle provided the foundations of most environmental treaties, the post-Rio period saw the

[107] ILA New Delhi Declaration, eleventh preambular clause.

[108] ILA New Delhi Declaration, art 1(1).

[109] International Law Association, Committee on International Law on Sustainable Development, 'Sofia Guiding Statements on the Judicial Elaboration of the 2002 New Delhi Declaration of Principles of International Law Relating to Sustainable Development' (Sofia, 75th session, 2012) ('ILA Sofia resolution'), para 3.

[110] See eg Commission on Sustainable Development, Report-principles, para 51.

beginning of an era of inter-State environmental disputes. Before 1992, environmental issues had only given rise to a handful of environmental cases but as environmental concerns grew, States became more inclined to resort to adjudication to solve environmental disputes.

The *Phosphate Lands in Nauru* case is illustrative of this trend. Although the case was settled at an early stage, it nevertheless provides an illustration of a reference to the first component of prevention—right to sovereignty over natural resources—which according to Nauru had been breached by Australia as a result of massive resource depletion.[111] Since then, the ICJ has recognized in several occasions the prevention principle, as discussed in section II) 2.2.2. of this chapter. In this section, in addition to a brief reference to such cases, we also refer to cases where the prevention principle was mobilized in a litigation context.

The issue of prevention came again before the ICJ in 1995, in the context of the *Request for a Reexamination of the Nuclear Tests* case. Although the Court rejected the request, it left the door open for the subsequent recognition of the prevention principle when it noted that its decision was 'without prejudice to the obligations of States to respect and protect the natural environment'.[112] The following year, in the *Advisory Opinion on Nuclear Weapons*, the Court recognized the customary nature of the prevention principle codified in Principles 21 of the Stockholm Declaration and 2 of the Rio Declaration.[113]

As already noted, this position was subsequently confirmed in two other cases. In the 1997 *Gabčíkovo-Nagymaros* case, the Court recognized the specificity of environmental law by highlighting the importance of prevention over reparation.[114] In the 2010 *Pulp Mills* case, the Court went further and developed the content of the prevention principle. It recognized that the principle of prevention has its 'origins in the due diligence that is required of a state in its territory'[115] and observed that the obligations to carry out an environmental impact assessment ('EIA')[116] and to cooperate[117] are central components of the duty to avoid or minimize the occurrence of transboundary environmental harm.

### *4.2. Inter-State arbitration*

One early application of the prevention principle or, more accurately, of the no-harm principle in an environmental context appears in the *Trail Smelter* case. The United States complained of emissions of sulphur dioxide released by a smelter based in Canadian territory, which caused damage to the neighbouring state of Washington. By a treaty of 15 April 1935, the question was submitted to arbitration. In its decision of 11 March 1941, the arbitral tribunal concluded that according to the principles of international law:

> no State has the right to use or permit the use of its territory in such a manner as to cause injury by fumes in or to the territory of another or the properties or persons therein, when the case is of serious consequence and the injury is established by clear and convincing evidence.[118]

The prevention principle has also played an important role in two more recent inter-State arbitrations conducted under the aegis of the Permanent Court of Arbitration ('PCA'). In

111 *Certain Phosphate Lands in Nauru (Nauru v. Australia)* (1992) (Preliminary Objections) ICJ Rep 240, para 5.

112 *Request for an Examination of the Situation in Accordance with the Court's Judgment of December 1974 in the Nuclear Tests (New Zealand v. France)* (1995) ICJ Rep 288, para 64.

113 *Nuclear Weapons Advisory Opinion*, para 29.

114 *Gabčíkovo-Nagymaros Project*, para 140.

115 *Pulp Mills*, para 101.

116 *Pulp Mills*, para 204.

117 *Pulp Mills*, para 102.

118 *Trail Smelter*, 1965.

the 2005 *Iron Rhine Railway* Arbitration, the tribunal considered that economic activities (*in casu* the reactivation of a railway passing through Dutch territory) had to be planned so as to prevent environmental damage. It noted, in this context, that the 'duty of prevention' is now 'a principle of general international law' that 'applies not only in autonomous activities but also in activities undertaken in implementation of specific treaties between the Parties'.[119] Relying on the ICJ's *Advisory Opinion on Nuclear Weapons*, it recognized that:

> [t]oday, in international environmental law, a growing emphasis is being put on the duty of prevention. Much of international environmental law has been formulated by reference to the impact that activities in one territory may have on the territory of another.[120]

It must be noted that, in referring to prevention, the tribunal did not make a clear distinction between the related concepts of sustainable development and the principle of integration (formulated in Principle 4 of the Rio Declaration) and seemed to apply them together.

In another PCA arbitration, decided in 2013 in the *Indus Waters Kishenganga* case, the tribunal also referred in its Partial Award to the prevention of environmental harm and sustainable development as formulated in Principle 21[121] and earlier jurisprudence—the *Trail Smelter* case[122] and the *Pulp Mills* case.[123] The case concerned the interpretation of the 1960 Indus Waters Treaty and, specifically, the effects of a hydroelectric project pursued by India on the water flowing to Pakistan. The prevention principle was referred to in this context as 'a foundational principle of customary international environmental law' to buttress the Tribunal's conclusion that 'hydro-electric projects... must be planned, built and operated with environmental sustainability in mind'.[124] In the Final Award, the tribunal reaffirmed the customary nature of the 'duty to prevent, or at least mitigate significant harm to the environment when pursuing large-scale construction activities.'[125]

### 4.3. *The International Tribunal for the Law of the Sea*

In addition to ruling on cases of transboundary harm, the jurisprudence has also contributed to the application of the prevention principle to the global commons.

An important jurisprudential contribution in this regard is provided by the 2011 ITLOS Advisory Opinion on the Area. In this case, the Seabed Chamber referred to the case law of the ICJ and, more specifically, to paragraph 187 of the ICJ's judgment in the *Pulp Mills* case in order to characterize the obligation 'to ensure' arising from article 139(1) of the UNCLOS as an obligation 'of conduct' or 'due diligence'.[126] The obligation was subsequently assimilated to the prevention duty stated in article 194(2) of the UNCLOS.[127] Importantly, the Chamber construed States' 'due diligence' obligations as encompassing: (i) the obligation to adopt appropriate measures and ensure that they are reasonably enforced;[128] (ii) the obligation (arising from the UNCLOS and customary international

[119] *Iron Rhine*, para 59. [120] *Iron Rhine*, para 222.

[121] *Kishenganga Arbitration*, Partial Award, para 448.

[122] *Kishenganga Arbitration*, paras 448–9. [123] *Kishenganga Arbitration*, para 450.

[124] *Kishenganga Arbitration*, para 454. [125] *Kishenganga Arbitration*, Final Award, para 112.

[126] *Advisory Opinion on the Area*, paras 110–11. [127] *Advisory Opinion on the Area*, para 113.

[128] *Advisory Opinion on the Area*, para 115 (referring to the interpretation of the obligation of 'due diligence' provided by the ICJ in the *Pulp Mills* case), para 116 (referring to the ILC Project on Prevention) and

law) to conduct an environmental impact assessment;[129] and (iii) the obligation to apply the precautionary approach not only as required by the applicable regulations of the Seabed Authority but also as part of the 'due diligence' obligation and, possibly, of customary international law.[130]

Another potentially important case currently pending before the ITLOS is the request for an advisory opinion filed by the Sub-Regional Fisheries Commission ('SRFC'), an international organization based in Senegal. The advisory opinion could potentially shed light on the responsibility of flag and coastal States (as well as international agencies) in preventing harm to the fish stocks in the exclusive economic zone of other States as well as to 'shared stocks and stocks of common interests'.[131] Several States and international organizations (including the UN and the FAO) have submitted their views on the questions formulated by the SRFC. Irrespective of the results of this request, it provides a useful occasion to clarify the contours of the prevention principle as applied to the issue of illegal, unreported, or unregulated ('IUU') fishing.[132]

### *4.4. Human rights fora*

Human rights fora have made a significant contribution to an often neglected aspect of the duty of prevention, namely the State's obligations to prevent domestic environmental harm when such harm amounts to an impairment of a human right. The relevant case law in this regard is discussed in the chapters of this commentary devoted to Principles 1, 10, and 22. The focus here is therefore on reconceptualizing the obligations arising from human rights, particularly the obligation of States to protect individuals from deprivation of their human rights by third parties causing environmental harm or, more rarely, against natural disasters. In addition, the prevention principle has been referred to in order to buttress the argument that States have extraterritorial human rights obligations not to cause harm to the environment of other States resulting in human rights violations in the territory of such other States.

The first hypothesis is the traditional province of human rights approaches to environmental protection. In their contemporary understanding, human rights entail three correlative obligations for States, namely to respect (not to interfere directly with human rights), to protect (against interference by third parties) and to fulfil (to progressively realize the conditions for the enjoyment of human rights).[133] The second obligation has been viewed by the European Court of Human Rights ('ECtHR') as a proactive duty to

paras 117–20 (referring, in paragraph 120, to the more detailed answer given by the Chamber in response to the third question put to it).

[129] *Advisory Opinion on the Area*, para 145.

[130] *Advisory Opinion on the Area*, paras 125–35, particularly at 131 and 135.

[131] *Request for an advisory opinion submitted by the Sub-Regional Fisheries Commission (SRFC)*, ITLOS Case No 21, Institution of Proceedings 27 March 2013.

[132] The written and oral proceedings are available online: <http://www.itlos.org/index.php?id=252&L=0> (last accessed October 2014).

[133] See *Report on the right to adequate food as a human right. Final report presented by the Special Rapporteur Asbjørn Eide*, 7 July 1987, UN Doc E/CN.4/Sub.2/1987/23 (1987), paras 66–9; Committee on economic, social and cultural rights, *General comment no. 12: The right to adequate food (art 11)*, 12 May 1999, UN Doc E/C.12/1999/5 (1999), para 15; Human Rights Committee, *General comment no. 6: art 6 (Right to life)*, 30 April 1982, UN Doc HRI/GEN/1/Rev.9 (vol I), paras 3–5; *Social and Economic Rights Action Center (SERAC) and others v. Nigeria*, African Commission Application no. 155/96 (2001–2002) ('*Ogoni* case'), paras 44–7 (structuring this set of obligations as four duties).

regulate the activities of third parties,[134] similar to the 'vertical' obligations identified in the ILC Prevention articles.[135] The difference between the two lies in the spatial scope. Whereas the ILC Prevention articles and the customary prevention principle require due diligence to prevent environmental harm abroad, the positive duty of due diligence arising from human rights requires the regulation of activities within the State's territory. Although environmental degradation only amounts to a violation of a human right if there is a direct and serious link between the two,[136] the proactive duty remains relevant because it requires regulation (ie a regulatory framework and its implementation) of activities that may potentially lead to environmental degradation with ensuing consequences on human rights.

The second hypothesis also concerns the obligation to protect from deprivation but differs in that the impairment of human rights stems from natural disaster or, more specifically, from the State's failure to provide adequate protection against it. The ECtHR examined this situation in *Budayeva v. Russia* in connection with a claim brought by several Russian citizens alleging a failure by Russian authorities to mitigate the consequences of a mudslide and provide effective domestic remedies.[137] The Court recognized the existence of a positive obligation entailing 'above all a primary duty on the State to put in place a legislative and administrative framework designed to provide effective deterrence against threats to the right to life.'[138] Importantly, the Court considered that, under the circumstances, the duties arising from article 8 in connection with dangerous activities were also applicable in the context of article 2, although a significant degree of deference had to be granted to domestic authorities due to the nature of the threat *in casu*.[139] The Court defined the content of the duty of prevention as follows:

> [I]n the particular context of dangerous activities the Court has found that special emphasis must be placed on regulations geared to the special features of the activity in question, particularly with regard to the level of the potential risk to human lives. They must govern the licensing, setting up, operation, security and supervision of the activity and must make it compulsory for all those concerned to take practical measures to ensure the effective protection of citizens whose lives might be endangered by the inherent risks. Among these preventive measures, particular emphasis should be placed on the public's right to information, as established in the case-law of the Convention institutions. The relevant regulations must also provide for appropriate procedures, taking into account the technical aspects of the activity in question, for identifying shortcomings in the processes concerned and any errors committed by those responsible at different levels.[140]

Applying this standard, the Court concluded that Russia had breached its obligations under article 2 as a result of its failure to protect the applicants from the disaster in question.

The third hypothesis concerns the combination of the prevention principle with the rights of individuals beyond the territory of the State of origin of transboundary or global environmental harm. The question that arises is the extent to which such State may breach

[134] See *Tatar v. Romania*, ECtHR Application no. 67021/01, Judgment (6 July 2009), paras 85–8 (and the overview of authorities cited therein). See also for the African and Inter-American contexts the following cases (and the overview of authorities cited therein): *Ogoni* case, paras 52–3; *Indigenous People Kichwa of Sarayaku v. Ecuador*, ICtHR Series C No 245, Judgment (merits and compensation) (27 June 2012), paras 145–7 (right to property) and 159–68 (participatory rights).

[135] See Section II) 3.2.1 of this chapter.

[136] *Fadeyeva v. Russia*, ECtHR Application no. 55723/00, Judgment (30 November 2005), paras 68–70.

[137] *Budayeva and others v. Russia*, ECtHR Applications no. 15339/02, 21166/02, 20058/02, 11673/02 and 15343/02, Judgment (29 September 2008) ('*Budayeva*').

[138] *Budayeva*, para 129. [139] *Budayeva*, paras 128–37. [140] *Budayeva*, para 132.

their human rights obligations for environmental harm occurring abroad. This argument was made in the now settled case between Ecuador and Colombia before the ICJ relating to the aerial spraying of herbicides.[141] So far, none of the cases before human rights fora dealing with the extraterritorial application of human rights obligations have addressed environmental threats.[142] The Inter-American Commission on Human Rights held, however, two hearings in connection with petitions for climate change-related extraterritorial violations of human rights, one brought by the Inuit people[143] and the other by Bolivian farmers.[144] Both claims were dismissed as inadmissible. The main hurdles that such claims would have to overcome are (i) the proof of a direct link between an environmental threat and an impairment of a human right abroad (causality) and (ii) the establishment of responsibility of the source State despite the effective control exercised by the affected State over the victim of the breach (responsibility).[145]

## *4.5. The WTO Dispute Settlement Body*

The prevention principle has not, as such, been raised or discussed by WTO panels or by the Appellate Body ('AB').

However, in the *Shrimp-Turtle* case, the AB made reference to the preamble of the WTO Agreement, which links international trade with 'sustainable development' and the protection and preservation of the environment, in order to interpret article XX(g), and specifically the term 'natural resources', as encompassing biological resources[146] and the policies adopted by the United States as 'relating to' a prevention objective.[147]

WTO panels and the AB have also discussed the exceptions provided for in article XX(a),[148] (b),[149] and (g)[150] from an environmental perspective in other cases. This body of decisions will be analysed in the chapter of this commentary devoted to Principle 12. Of particular note is the reference by the panel in *China—Raw materials* to

[141] *Aerial Herbicide Spraying (Ecuador v. Colombia)*, ICJ, removed from the docket list on 13 September 2013. See Boyle, 'Human Rights and the Environment: Where Next?', 635.

[142] For an analysis of the case law see Milanovic, M., *Extraterritorial Application of Human Rights Treaties. Law, Principles and Policy* (Oxford University Press 2011).

[143] See Inuit Circumpolar Conference, *Petition to the Inter-American Commission on Human Rights Seeking Relief from Violations Resulting from Global Warming Caused by Acts and Omissions of the United States* (2005), available at: <http://www.inuitcircumpolar.com/inuit-petition-inter-american-commission-on-human-rights-to-oppose-climate-change-caused-by-the-united-states-of-america.html> (accessed in January 2014). On this case see Shelton, D., 'Human Rights Violations and Climate Change: The Last Days of the Inuit People' (2010) 37 *Rutgers Law Record* 182.

[144] See 'Inter-American Commission on Human Rights hears testimony on freshwater loss due to climate change', 28 March 2011, available at: <http://www.earthjustice.org>.

[145] See Viñuales, 'A Human Rights Approach to Extraterritorial Environmental Protection? An Assessment'.

[146] *Shrimp-Turtle* case, para 129.

[147] *Shrimp-Turtle* case, para 135: 'It is well to bear in mind that the policy of protecting and conserving the endangered sea turtles here involved is shared by all participants and third participants in this appeal, indeed, by the vast majority of the nations of the world. None of the parties to this dispute question the genuineness of the commitment of the others to that policy'.

[148] See eg *European Communities—Measures Prohibiting the Importation and Marketing of Seal Products*, Panel report, 25 November 2013, WT/DS400 and WT/DS401, para 7.625–7.639.

[149] See eg *United States—Restrictions on Imports of Tuna*, ('Tuna-Dolphin I') DS21/R-39S/155 (3 September 1991), para 5.24–5.29; *United States—Measures Concerning the Importation, Marketing and Sale of Tuna and Tuna Products* ('Tuna-Dolphin II'), DS29/R (16 June 1994), para 5.28–5.39.

[150] See eg *United States—Standards for Reformulated and Conventional Gasoline*, Report of the Panel, 29 January 1996, WT/DS2/R, 43–6; *United States—Standards for Reformulated and Conventional Gasoline*, Report of the Appellate Body, 29 April 1996, WT/DS2/AB/R (appeal limited to the application of art XX(g)).

the customary principle of sovereignty over natural resources as a norm to be taken into account in interpreting article XX(g).[151]

## *4.6. Investment arbitration tribunals*

There is a significant and growing body of investment awards involving environmental components.[152] In this jurisprudential body, the protection of the environment is analysed from different perspectives, including as a legitimate goal for the exercise of a State's police powers,[153] as a factor capable of justifying different treatment of two projects,[154] as an essential interest capable of being protected by the necessity defence,[155] as a concern that must be taken into account by investors in forming their legitimate expectations[156] or by tribunals in determining compensation.[157] Reference to the prevention principle is therefore not explicit.

There is however a case, *S.D. Myers v. Canada*,[158] where the tribunal explicitly referred to the principles of the Rio Declaration (and to instruments referring to the Stockholm and Rio Declarations) as part of the context that had to be taken into account to interpret the provisions of chapter 11 of the North American Free Trade Agreement ('NAFTA').[159] The case concerned a trade ban imposed by Canada, which harmed the operations of a foreign investor active in the waste treatment sector. As part of the relevant context for the interpretation of article 1102 of the NAFTA, the tribunal referred to:

> [T]he various provisions of the NAFTA, its companion agreement the NAAEC and principles that are affirmed by the NAAEC (including those of the Rio declaration). The principles that emerge from that context, to repeat, are as follows... states have the right to establish high levels of environmental protection. They are not obliged to compromise their standards merely to satisfy the political or economic interests of other States... states should avoid creating distortions to trade... environmental protection and economic development can and should be mutually supportive.[160]

The tribunal concluded eventually that Canada had indeed breached the NAFTA, but its reference to certain applications of the prevention principle (eg establishing high levels

[151] *China—Measures Related to the Exportation of Various Raw Materials—Reports of the Panel*, WT/DS394/R; WT/DS395/R; WT/DS398/R (5 July 2011), para 7.381 stating that '[t]he principle of sovereignty over natural resources affords Members the opportunity to use their natural resources to promote their own development while regulating the use of these resources to ensure sustainable development.'

[152] See Viñuales, J. E., *Foreign Investment and the Environment in International Law* (Cambridge University Press 2012), ch 1.

[153] *Methanex Corporation v. United States of America*, NAFTA (UNCITRAL), Award (3 August 2005), Part IV, ch D, para 7; *Chemtura Corporation (formerly Crompton Corporation) v. Government of Canada*, UNCITRAL, Award (2 August 2010), para 266.

[154] *Parkerings-Compagniet AS v. Republic of Lithuania*, ICSID Case No ARB/05/8, Award (11 September 2007), para 392.

[155] *Suez, Sociedad General de Aguas de Barcelona S.A. and InterAguas Servicios Integrales del Agua S.A. v. The Argentine Republic*, ICSID Case No. ARB/03/17, para 238; *Suez, Sociedad General de Aguas de Barcelona, S.A. and Vivendi Universal, S.A. v. The Argentine Republic*, ICSID Case No. ARB/03/19, para 260.

[156] *Plama Consortium Ltd v. Republic of Bulgaria*, ICSID Case No. ARB/03/24, Award (27 August 2008), paras 219–21; *Chemtura Corporation v. Government of Canada*, para 149.

[157] *Southern Pacific Properties (Middle East) Limited (SPP) v. Arab Republic of Egypt*, ICSID Case No. ARB/84/3, Award (20 May 1992), paras 191, 250.

[158] *SD Myers Inc. v. Canada, NAFTA Arbitration* (UNCITRAL Rules), Partial Award (13 November 2000) ('*SD Myers v. Canada*').

[159] North American Free Trade Agreement, 17 December 1992, 32 ILM 296 ('NAFTA').

[160] *SD Myers Inc. v. Canada*, para 247.

of environmental protection) illustrates how the latter can be relevant for the settlement of investment disputes.

## *4.7. Court of Justice of the European Union*

The prevention principle has also featured in the jurisprudence of the Court of Justice of the European Union ('CJEU'). In a decision prompted by a referral by a British court, *Air Transport Association America v. Secretary of State for Energy and Climate Change*,[161] the Court examined the legality of preventive measures applicable to areas beyond national jurisdiction.

The case concerned the extension of the Emissions Trading Directive[162] to aviation and, more specifically, to flights departing or landing in EU territory. The companies operating such flights were required to present carbon allowances for emissions produced beyond EU territory, in international air space. The Court upheld the legality of the measure. Although it did not discuss the prevention principle explicitly, for present purposes, the extension of the EU Emissions Trading System ('EU ETS') could be construed as a measure to prevent environmental harm beyond national jurisdiction. Of course, such interpretation would not be entirely accurate as emissions of carbon dioxide have a global impact, irrespective of where they were produced. Therefore, the harm is occurring not just beyond national jurisdiction but everywhere, by reason of the contribution of such emissions to climate change.

## *4.8. Domestic courts*

The customary prevention principle has been discussed in some domestic cases concerning environmental harm. In the *Reinwater* case, before Dutch courts, the principle *sic utere tuo* (no-harm) was recognized by a Rotterdam court of first instance as a sufficient basis to hold the defendant, the mining company Mines de Potasse d'Alsace, liable for having discharged saline waste into the Rhine.[163] Although the finding was reversed by the Appeals Court of The Hague, on the grounds that the principle cannot be applied in the relations between private parties,[164] the case provides an early illustration of the jurisprudential relevance of the customary prevention principle.

The principle has also been invoked before the federal courts of the United States. In *Amlon Metals v. FMC*,[165] the plaintiffs alleged that the shipping of copper waste residues containing dangerous chemicals from the US to the UK amounted to a violation of the customary prevention principle reflected in Principle 21 of the Rio Declaration. This claim was rejected on the grounds that the Stockholm principles:

> do not set forth any specific proscriptions, but rather refer only in a general sense to the responsibility of nations to ensure that activities within their jurisdiction do not cause damage to the environment beyond their borders.[166]

[161] *Air Transport Association of America and others v. Secretary of State for Energy and Climate Change.*

[162] Directive 2003/87/EC, 'EU Emissions Trading Directive' (Consolidated version of July 2013).

[163] *Reinwater v. Mines de Potasse d'Alsace*, District Court of Rotterdam (8 January 1979), NJ 1979, no 113, cited in Nollkaemper, A., 'International Environmental Law in the Courts of The Netherlands', in Anderson, M. and Galizzi, P. (eds), *International Environmental Courts in National Courts* (British Institute of International and Comparative Law 2002), 183, 187.

[164] Appeals Court of The Hague (10 September 1986), the Hoge Raad (23 September 1989), NJ 1989, no 743, cited in Nollkaemper, 'International Environmental Law in the Courts of The Netherlands'.

[165] *Amlon Metals v. FMC*, 775 F Supp 668 (SDNY 1991).

[166] *Amlon Metals v. FMC*, 671, cited in Bodansky, D. and Manous, M., 'International Environmental Law in US Courts', in Anderson and Galizzi, *International Environmental Courts in National Courts*, 233, 243–4.

Another case where the prevention principle, in the formulation of Principle 2 of the Rio Declaration, was invoked is *Aguinda v. Texaco*.[167] The case concerned a claim brought by Ecuadorian plaintiffs for environmental harm caused by Texaco. The District Court seemed initially sympathetic to the claim, denying Texaco's motion to dismiss and considering that further discovery had to be ordered to assess whether Texaco had breached customary international law. However, the case was subsequently dismissed on the grounds that Ecuadorian courts were the proper forum.

## III) Relations with Other Principles

### 1. Overview

As a foundational principle of international environmental law, prevention acts as the bedrock on which other principles and rules are based. The location of Principle 2 at the beginning of the Rio Declaration highlights the fact that several other principles are extensions or more specific implementations of Principle 2.

### 2. Prevention and cooperation

Some commentators have expressed the view that '[i]f due diligence is the first rule of transboundary environmental risk management, cooperation is the second'.[168] Prevention and cooperation are indeed closely linked given their common origin in good neighbourliness considerations. Their connection predates the recognition of prevention as a principle of international environmental law. Much as the no-harm rule emerged to preserve the territorial integrity of a neighbouring State, a duty of cooperation also emerged to facilitate the management of shared natural resources.

The idea of cooperation largely developed in the law of international watercourses. As early as 1929, the Permanent Court of International Justice reasoned in the *River Oder* case that a 'community of interest' in navigation among all riparian States was required, based on equality of rights over the whole navigable course of the river without accepting 'any preferential privilege of any one ... State in relation to the others'.[169] The concept of 'community of interest' entails that cooperation is required in order to take into account the interest of all the States concerned. An obligation to consult riparian States when exploiting the shared resources is one expression of such understanding. In the *Lac Lanoux* case, for instance, the tribunal recognized that while France could carry out diversion works entirely within its own territory, it had an obligation to consult Spain and to safeguard its rights in the watercourse.[170]

The expressions of cooperation have evolved significantly since then. The close link between prevention and cooperation is made clear in the ILC Prevention articles. The prevention obligation stated in article 3 is subsequently implemented by article 4, which requires States to 'cooperate in good faith ... in preventing significant transboundary harm or at any event in minimizing the risk thereof'. This close relationship was highlighted in

[167] *Aguinda v. Texaco*, 945 F Supp 625 (SDNY 11 Apr 1994).

[168] Birnie, Boyle, and Redgwell, *International Law and the Environment*, 175.

[169] *Territorial Jurisdiction of the International Commission of the River Oder* (Czechoslovakia, Denmark, France, Germany, Great Britain, Sweden/Poland) (1929) PCIJ Series A No. 23, 27.

[170] *Lac Lanoux* arbitration, 140.

the ITLOS *MOX Plant* case in which the Tribunal held that 'the duty to co-operate is a fundamental principle in the prevention of pollution of the marine environment under Part XII of the Convention and general international'[171] as well as in the *Pulp Mills* case where the Court held that the parties had an obligation to inform[172] and notify[173] in order to cooperate in a successful manner to 'jointly manage the risks of damage to the environment'.[174]

## 3. Prevention and the requirement to conduct an environmental impact assessment

Principle 17 of the Rio Declaration concerning the requirement to conduct an EIA makes a direct reference to the obligation to prevent significant damage to the environment. Despite some scepticism in legal commentary as to the specificity of the obligations arising from the prevention principle,[175] it is now well-established that, at the very least, prevention requires the conduct of a prior EIA. The connection between prevention and its expression through the EIA requirement is further acknowledged in the codification work conducted by the ILC[176] and the ILA.[177]

Moreover, in the *Pulp Mills* case, after noting that the requirement to carry out an EIA in a transboundary context had become part of customary law, the ICJ noted that:

> due diligence, and the duty of vigilance and prevention which it implies, would not be considered to have been exercised, if a party planning works liable to affect the régime of the river or the quality of its waters did not undertake an environmental impact assessment on the potential effects of such works.[178]

Subsequently, the ITLOS Seabed Chamber broadened the application of the EIA requirement to the global commons on the basis of the ICJ's comment on the relationship between prevention and EIA.[179]

## 4. Prevention and precaution

After its recognition in the Rio Declaration, the precautionary approach has received much attention.[180] The relationship between prevention and precaution can be interpreted in different ways.

Precaution can be understood as an extension of the obligation of prevention. In this sense, both concepts follow the same logic of harm avoidance and precaution is considered to be a more advanced form of the idea of prevention, advocating prudence even in cases of scientific uncertainty.[181] The ITLOS Seabed Chamber has followed this line of reasoning

[171] *MOX Plant* case (*Ireland v. United Kingdom*) (provisional measures) ITLOS No. 10 (3 December 2001), para 84.

[172] *Pulp Mills*, para 102. [173] *Pulp Mills*, para 113. [174] *Pulp Mills*, para 77.

[175] For instance, Vessey notes that 'The abstract principle of prevention is seemingly well-settled but the issue of translating that principle into specific obligations is not' (Vessey J., 'The Principle of Prevention in International Law' (1998) 3 *Austrian Review of International and European Law* 181, at 183).

[176] ILC Prevention articles, art 7. [177] ILA Sofia resolution, guiding statement 10.

[178] *Pulp Mills*, para 204. [179] Advisory Opinion on the Area, para 148.

[180] See the chapter by Cançado Trindade in this commentary.

[181] The precautionary approach was presented as a continuum to prevention during the oral proceedings of the *Gabčíkovo-Nagymaros Project* case, as Hungary argued that 'le principe de précaution a émergé comme la forme la plus développée de la règle générale qui impose la prévention' (Oral Proceedings, CR/1997/2, para 23).

when noting that both prevention and precaution are expressions of the States' due diligence duty. According to the Chamber, like prevention, precaution:

> is also an integral part of the general obligation of due diligence of sponsoring States, which is applicable even outside the scope of the [Nodules] Regulations. The due diligence obligation of the sponsoring States requires them to take all appropriate measures to prevent damage that might result from the activities of contractors that they sponsor. This obligation applies in situations where scientific evidence concerning the scope and potential negative impact of the activity in question is insufficient but where there are plausible indications of potential risks.[182]

Given the close proximity between the two principles, some commentators have argued precaution is the cornerstone of international environmental law because an obligation of precaution would inevitably imply an obligation of prevention.[183] However, despite their similarities, the two norms operate in distinct spheres.[184] On the one hand, prevention is a legal principle that aims to better respond to the notion of 'risk' (a negative outcome the probability of which can be assessed). On the other hand, precaution emerged out of the realization that it is not always possible to assess the consequences of some activities in advance (particularly whether an activity entails even a small probability of serious or irreversible damage) and that such uncertainties cannot be an excuse for inaction.

The relationship between the two principles is well captured in the 2012 report of the ILA on Legal Principles relating to Climate Change:

> In EU environmental law, the prevention principle and the precautionary principle are widely understood as elements of one principle, in that they form part of a continuum. Locating a dispute on the precaution-prevention continuum depends on the extent of scientific uncertainty; only when there is very strong scientific evidence will the prevention principle be engaged... In international law, it appears that the prevention principle and the precautionary principle are regarded as two different principles, having a different legal background, although in some cases working along a continuum.[185]

It must be added that what the Report characterizes as a 'different legal background' introduces a very important distinction between the two principles. Simply stated, while the customary grounding of prevention is well-established, that of precaution remains controversial.

## IV) Assessment

The prevention principle is in many ways the cornerstone of modern international environmental law. Its grounding in both customary and treaty law is uncontroverted and its operation as an architectural, interpretive and decision-making norm is well-established. The three main challenges it faces help to understand both its foundational role and its limitations.

[182] Advisory Opinion on the Area, para 131.

[183] See, eg Troubworst, A., *Precautionary Rights and Duties of States* (Martinus Nijhoff 2006).

[184] See Viñuales, J.E., 'Legal Techniques for Dealing with Scientific Uncertainty in Environmental Law' (2010) 43 *Vanderbilt Journal of Transnational Law* 437; *Pulp Mills*, Separate Opinion of Judge Cançado Trindade.

[185] International Law Association, Committee on Legal Principles relating to Climate Change, 'Second Report' (Sofia, 75th session, 2012), 28.

The first challenge is one of specificity. The broad formulation of the prevention principle in customary international law allows for significant controversy in its actual implementation. In customary law, its main expressions are the duty of cooperation and the requirement to conduct an environmental impact assessment, which are analysed in detail in other chapters of this volume.[186] There are, in addition, numerous treaties and codification initiatives spelling out the contents of the prevention principle both in a transboundary and a global context. In addition, there is some authority for the proposition that the prevention obligation also applies in a purely domestic context.

The second challenge comes from the nature of environmental problems, which normally entail a significant measure of scientific uncertainty. Whereas the sphere of operation of the prevention principle is risk, its impact on questions subject (at a given point in time) to scientific uncertainty remains limited. In this regard, the precautionary approach/principle adds a useful contribution to preventive efforts, requiring or authorizing States to take action despite the lack of sufficient information. Precaution performs, in many ways, a scouting function, mapping future threats that, once known, enter the realm of prevention. By way of illustration, the international legal regime on climate change, which was initially premised on the precautionary principle, is nowadays an example of preventive action.

The third challenge concerns differentiation. Principle 2 of the Rio Declaration sought to capture this fundamental consideration by adding a reference to the 'developmental policies' of States. Yet, such a reference is insufficient to capture the extent to which differentiation weighs on domestic, regional, and global efforts to protect the environment. Principle 2 must therefore be read as the driver of international environmental law within a Declaration that also addresses distributional questions, among different stakeholders (primarily developing and developed States) but also among different considerations (social, economic, and environmental). Whereas Principle 2 guides the development of international environmental law as a branch of international law, the Rio Declaration in its entirety recalls that environmental protection is not merely a branch but a perspective to be integrated in all human activities, according to appropriate distributional criteria.

## V) Select Bibliography

Abi-Saab, G., 'La souveraineté permanente sur les ressources naturelles', in Bedjaoui, M. (ed), *Droit international: Bilan et perspectives* (Paris: Pedone 1991), 639.

Anderson, M. and Galizzi, P. (eds), *International Environmental Law in National Courts* (London: British Institute of International and Comparative Law 2002).

Bowman, M. and Boyle, A., *Environmental Damage in International and Comparative Law: Problems of Definition and Valuation* (Oxford University Press 2002).

Boyle, A., 'Human Rights and the Environment: Where Next?' (2012) 23 *EJIL* 613.

Bratspies, R. and Miller, R. (eds), *Transboundary Harm in International Law: Lessons from the 'Trail Smelter' Arbitration* (Cambridge University Press 2006).

Francioni, F. and Scovazzi, T. (eds), International Responsibility for Environmental Harm (London: Graham & Trotman 1991).

[186] See the chapters by Craik (Principle 17), Okowa (Principle 18), and Boisson de Chazournes/Sangbana (Principle 19) in this commentary.

Koivurova, T., 'Due diligence', *Max Planck Encyclopedia of Public International Law* (Oxford University Press 2008).

Lefeber, R., *Transboundary Environmental Interference and the Origin of State Liability* (Leiden: Martinus Nijhoff 1996).

Okowa, P., *State Responsibility for Transboundary Air Pollution in International Law* (Oxford University Press 2000).

Perrez, F. X., 'The Relationship between "Permanent Sovereignty" and the Obligation not to Cause Transboundary Environmental Damage' (1996) 26 *Environmental Law* 1190.

Perrez, F. X., *Cooperative Sovereignty: From Independence to Interdependence in the Structure of International Environmental Law* (The Hague: Kluwer 2000).

Plakokelafos, I., 'Prevention Obligations in International Environmental Law' (2012) 23 *YbIEL* 3.

Pop, I., *Voisinage et bon voisinage* (Paris: Pedone 1980).

Sadeleer, N. de, *Environmental Principles: From Political Slogans to Legal Rules* (Oxford University Press 2002).

Schrijver, N., *Sovereignty over Natural Resources: Balancing Rights and Duties* (Cambridge University Press 1997).

Soljan, L., 'The General Obligation to Prevent Transboundary Harm and its Relation to Four Key Environmental Principles' (1998) 3 *Austrian Review of International and European Law* 209.

Vessey, J., 'The Principle of Prevention in International Law' (1998) 3 *Austrian Review of International and European Law* 181.

Viñuales, J. E., 'The Contribution of the International Court of Justice to the Development of International Environmental Law' (2008) 32 *Fordham International Law Journal* 232.

Viñuales, J. E., 'Legal Techniques for Dealing with Scientific Uncertainty in Environmental Law' (2010) 43 *Vanderbilt Journal of Transnational Law* 437.

Viñuales, J. E., 'The Rise and Fall of Sustainable Development' (2013) 22 *Review of European, Comparative and International Environmental Law* 3.

Viñuales, J. E., 'A Human Rights Approach to Extraterritorial Environmental Protection? An Assessment', in Bhuta, N. (ed), *The Frontiers of Human Rights: Extraterritoriality and its Challenges* (Oxford University Press, forthcoming 2015).

Xue, H., *Transboundary Damage in International Law* (Cambridge University Press 2009).

# 7. Principle 3

## *From a Right to Development to Intergenerational Equity*

Claire Molinari*

**Principle 3**

The right to development must be fulfilled so as to equitably meet developmental and environmental needs of present and future generations.



## I) Origins and Rationale of the Principle

It is clear that environmental harm done now can have an impact on future generations. Environmental damage can be long lasting or irreversible. For example, nuclear testing in the Bikini Atoll during the middle of the twentieth century has had a severe impact on several generations. Environmental damage can result long after the practices that cause

* Analyst at investment manager Sarasin & Partners, specializing in evaluating environmental, social, and governance issues in investment decision-making.

it have ceased: damage resulting from climate change in the future will be caused in part by greenhouse gas emissions dating from the beginning of the Industrial Revolution.[1] Although the notion of intergenerational equity is not related exclusively to environmental issues, the promotion of intergenerational equity does require, at a fundamental level, the appropriate management of natural resources and concern more broadly for the environment. Whereas many principles of international environmental law address the geographic implications of environmental problems (eg polluter-pays, transboundary pollution), the concept of intergenerational equity focuses on the temporal dimension: balancing the needs of the present generation with those of future generations.

The notion of preserving natural resources for the benefit of future generations was first expressed in an international legal context in the *Pacific Fur Seals Arbitration*,[2] when the United States called for a limit to seal hunting. In the latter half of the twentieth century, the interests of future generations were mentioned explicitly in a number of international instruments. The 1972 Stockholm Declaration[3] refers twice to 'future generations' (in Principles 1 and 2), each time together with the 'present generation'. Stockholm's Principle 1 describes man's 'solemn responsibility to protect and improve the environment for present and future generations', while Principle 2 states that the 'natural resources of the earth...must be safeguarded for the benefit of present and future generations'. During the Preparatory Committee for Stockholm, the Intergovernmental Working Group was given a suggestion by the Secretary-General of the United Nations that the Declaration should refer to the 'duty of all nations to carefully husband their natural resources and to hold in trust for present and future generations the air, water, lands and communities of plants and animals on which all life depends.'[4] However, this stronger language did not survive beyond the first draft of the Working Group.[5] In the Preparatory Committee for Stockholm, there was a tension between economic development and environmental protection,[6] a theme that would reappear in Rio twenty years later.

The idea that the interests of present and future generations might conflict is not made explicit in the Stockholm Declaration, where there is no mention of 'equitably' meeting the needs of both present and future generations. In this sense, the Rio Declaration has more in common with the definition of sustainable development put forward in the 1987 Report of the World Commission on Environment and Development Report: 'development that meets the needs of the present generation without compromising the ability of future generations to meet their own needs.'[7] Arguably, in recognizing that the interests of present and future generations may diverge, the language of Principle 3 of the

[1] The greenhouse effect is caused by the build-up of greenhouse gases over many years. Prior to the Industrial Revolution, CO2 concentrations in the atmosphere had been constant at 280ppm (parts per million) for the past 500,000 years. CO2 concentrations rose steeply since the middle of the nineteenth century to approximately 380ppm in 2005: IPCC, *Climate Change 2007: Working Group I: The Physical Science Basis* (2007), 511.

[2] Sands, P. and Peel, J., *Principles of International Environmental Law* (3rd edn, Cambridge University Press 2012), 206.

[3] 'Declaration of the United Nations Conference on the Human Environment', Stockholm, 16 June 1972, UN Doc A/CONF 48/14/Rev.1 ('Stockholm Declaration').

[4] UN Doc A/CONF.48/PC/SG.1/CRP.4, 13 (1971), cited by Redgwell, C., *Intergenerational Trusts and Environmental Protection* (Manchester University Press 1999), 119.

[5] Redgwell, *Intergenerational Trusts*, 119.

[6] Sohn, L.B., 'The Stockholm Declaration on the Human Environment' (1973) 14 *HILJ* 423, 456–7.

[7] Report of the World Commission on Environment and Development, *Our Common Future*, 10 March 1987 ('Brundtland Report').

Rio Declaration highlights the need to address this tension. As will be discussed next, although the preparatory work shows that the formulation of Principle 3, read in its historical context, was intended to stress the importance of present generations (with their 'right to development') rather than future ones, over time, the emphasis has progressively moved away from development as a merely present concern and towards a conception more sensitive to the temporal dimension.

## II) The Principle as Enshrined in the Rio Declaration

### 1. Preparatory work and context

#### *1.1. Overview*

The temporal focus of Principle 3, now central to the concept of intergenerational equity, was overshadowed by its development focus in the early stages of the Rio drafting process. The final formulation of Principle 3 of the Rio Declaration is a compromise between the right to development advocated by the G77 countries and the preservation of the environment for the future generations, advocated by the North. In the lead-up to the Rio Conference, the G77 and China argued strongly for the inclusion of a principle of the 'inalienable right to development' in the Declaration, which they felt must not be subordinated to the environmental interests of the North.[8] The North staunchly opposed the inclusion of a right to development until the final days of the final Preparatory Committee. Eventually the Nordic countries proposed a compromise: the reference to the needs of future generations would limit the right to development.[9] In the final week of Preparatory Committee IV, the North agreed that it could accept each State's right to development, provided that it accounted for the needs of present and future generations.[10]

A wide range of statements relating to development and/or future generations were proposed at Preparatory Committee IV.[11]

#### *1.2. The G77+China's proposals*

The early G77+China proposal (5 March) included a principle stating that 'the right to development is an inalienable right and therefore the development needs of all developing countries shall be treated as a matter of priority.'[12] Separately, the proposal included a principle on 'Equity', which stated that 'to meet the needs of present and future generations, considerations of equity must include damage caused to the environment in the past, the growth and development needs of the present generation and the apportionment of equal shares of global environmental space.'[13] The proposal's temporal focus was on the past: addressing historical responsibility for environmental damage, which would lie mainly with the industrialized North. It also suggested redistribution of natural capital.

8 *Earth Negotiations Bulletin*, vol 1(13), 24 March 1992.

9 Ling, C.Y., *The Rio Declaration on Environment and Development: An assessment* (Third World Network 2012), 30.

10 Halpern, S., *United Nations Conference on Environment and Development: Process and documentation* (Academic Council for the United Nations System 1993).

11 See UN Doc A/CONF.151/PC/128.

12 UN Doc A/CONF.151/PC/WG.III/L.20 ('L.20'), principle 3.

13 L.20, principle 6.

The revised G77+China Principle 3 stated:

The inalienable right of States and people to development must be fulfilled in order to meet the environmental needs of present and future generations. Equity within the present generation shall take into account environmental damage caused in the past, as well as the developmental and environmental needs of present and future generations.[14]

At this point the notion of equity had been subsumed into the right to development rather than forming a separate principle. The notion of historical responsibility for past environmental damage remained, but the redistributive component had been removed.

### *1.3. Northern proposals*

By contrast, the Northern countries stressed the need to protect the environment for future generations in their proposals. The United States' proposal stated that 'all people should share in the benefits of a clean environment' and recognized 'the need to preserve those benefits for future generations.'[15] Canada's proposal stated that '[a]ll States and people shall, for the benefit of future as well as present generations, have the opportunity to achieve full development and equity, while living within the capacities of the Earth's ecosystem.'[16] Japan's proposal stated that:

[t]oday and in the future, the individual has both a fundamental right to benefit from the common resources of humankind, which constitute the global environment, and at the same time a responsibility to protect, restore and improve them for present and future generations.[17]

No Northern country supported a right to development. Some Northern countries made reference to 'the benefits of development'[18] (United States), 'a common goal'[19] of sustainable development (Norway), or 'a right to benefit from the common resources of humankind'[20] (Japan). Australia's proposal completely omitted referring to development.[21] Norway separated ideas relating to development and future generations into two separate principles.[22]

### *1.4. The compromise*

In the final stages of the fourth Preparatory Committee, all of the Northern countries opposed the G77's revised proposal in its entirety.[23] The Netherlands, speaking on behalf of the EU, argued that development could not be unlimited, so a right to development was not acceptable.[24] The G77 argued that millions of people in the South lived in absolute poverty, and that development was necessary to meet basic needs. In the end, the Nordic countries agreed to accept a right to development, as long as it was tempered by reference to the needs of future generations.[25] The final wording of the principle reflects this compromise.

At the time, Principle 3 was seen as something of a *coup* for the G77, as it represented the first time that the 'right to development' had been 'affirmed in an international instrument of consensus.'[26] Interestingly, although the Declaration was not intended to

[14] UN Doc A/CONF.151/PC/WG.III/L.20/Rev.1, Principle 3.
[15] UN Doc A/CONF.151/PC/WG.III/L.21 ('L.21'), Principle 4.
[16] UN Doc A/CONF.151/PC/WG.III/L.23 ('L.23'), Principle 2.
[17] UN Doc A/CONF.151/PC/WG.III/L.22 ('L.22'), Principle 4.
[18] L.21, Principle 4.
[19] UN Doc A/CONF.151/PC/WG.III/L.27 ('L.27'), Principle 2.
[20] L.22, Principle 4.
[21] See for example Australia: UN Doc A/CONF.151/PC/WG.III/L.24, in particular Principle 4.
[22] L.27, Principles 2 and 8.
[23] Ling, *The Rio Declaration*, 30.
[24] Ling, 30.
[25] Ling, 31.
[26] Sands, P., *Principles of International Environmental Law* (2nd edn, Cambridge University Press 2003), 55.

be a binding instrument, the United States made a reservation with respect to Principle 3 expressing its:

> long-standing opposition to the so-called 'right to development'. Development is not a right... The United States understands and accepts the thrust of principle 3 to be that economic development goals and objectives must be pursued in such a way that the development and environmental needs of present and future generations are taken into account. The United States cannot agree to, and would disassociate itself from, any interpretation of principle 3 that accepts a 'right to development', or otherwise goes beyond that understanding.[27]

Contemporaneous commentators noted the emphasis placed on development in the wording of Principle 3. David Wirth, writing in 1995, noted that the principle required the 'fulfilment' of the right to development, but made no express requirement that protection of the environment be fulfilled. If a conflict arose between environmental and development requirements, he conjectured, the language of Principle 3 suggested that development needs would be prioritized.[28]

## 2. Scope and dimensions

### 2.1. *From a right to development to intergenerational equity*

The G77's position during the lead-up to the Rio Conference reflected a continuing hope in developing nations at the time for a New International Economic Order ('NIEO'). During the 1970s and 1980s, developing nations put forward a series of proposals to the United Nations attempting to restructure the international economic system in a way that would empower developing countries vis-à-vis the industrialized countries. The elements of the NIEO were set out in the UN General Assembly's Declaration on the Establishment of a New International Economic Order in 1974,[29] according to which:

> the developing countries, which constitute 70 per cent of the world's population, account for only 30 per cent of the world's income. It has proved impossible to achieve an even and balanced development of the international community under the existing international economic order...[30]

The General Assembly went on to set out founding principles for a NIEO. These included a demand for 'sustained improvement' of the terms of trade for the producers of raw materials and primary commodities;[31] 'preferential and non-reciprocal treatment for developing countries, wherever feasible, in all fields of international economic co-operation whenever possible';[32] and 'securing favourable conditions for the transfer of financial resources to developing countries.'[33] There were clear financial demands associated with the NIEO development aims. Very little practical progress was made on them, however, and in the twenty years since the Rio Declaration, the pursuit of an international law right to development (and its financial implications) has lost impetus.[34]

[27] UN Doc A/CONF.151/12/Rev.l (vol II), Ch. III (B), para 16.

[28] Wirth, D.A., 'The Rio Declaration on Environment and Development: Two Steps Forward and One Back, or Vice Versa?' (1995) 29 *Georgia Law Review* 599, 627.

[29] 'Declaration on the Establishment of a New International Economic Order', 1 May 1974, UN Doc A/RES/S-6/3201 ('NIEO Declaration').

[30] NIEO Declaration, para 1.

[31] NIEO Declaration, para 4, Principle j.

[32] NIEO Declaration, para 4, Principle n.

[33] NIEO Declaration, para 4, Principle o.

[34] See eg Saloman, M. E., 'From NIEO to Now and the Unfinishable Story of Economic Justice' (2013) 62 *ICLQ* 31, 31.

It is perhaps not surprising, then, that in recent years commentators have focused on the interests of future generations expressed in Principle 3. Despite the sense at the time that Principle 3 was a 'victory' for the G77,[35] Principle 3 has become increasingly perceived as a statement of intergenerational equity rather than of the right to development. For example, the relevant section of a major textbook states that 'inter-generational equity is explicitly referred to in Principle 3 of the 1992 Rio Declaration.'[36] Another commentator makes the same observation.[37] While many commentators acknowledge the tension between development and the environment present in Principle 3,[38] this tension is rarely the focus of modern commentary. Instead, the temporal element of Principle 3 (the interests of future generations) has come to overshadow the G77's original intent that it express a pure right to development.

While international environmental law commentators today pay little attention to the financial implications that were associated with a pure right to development in the early 1990s, they do see Principle 3 as underpinning the concept of 'sustainable development'. For example, the last edition of another major textbook describes intergenerational equity as one of the 'legal elements of the concept of "sustainable development", as reflected in international legal agreements.'[39] The relationship between intergenerational equity and sustainable development is discussed later in section II) 4.1 of this chapter.

### *2.2. Legal nature*

There is still limited support for the proposition that intergenerational equity is a 'hard law' principle of international law. Reference to the needs of future generations can be found in a number of international declarations aside from the Rio Declaration, including the Stockholm Declaration[40] and the UNESCO Declaration on the Responsibilities of the Present Generations towards Future Generations.[41] However, while these international declarations 'indicate the importance now attached in international policy to the protection of the environment for future generations',[42] they are not enforceable. Nor can intergenerational equity be described categorically as a legal 'principle' in the narrow, strong sense described by Ronald Dworkin, where a principle is 'one which officials must take into account, if it is relevant, as a consideration inclining in one direction or another.'[43]

Instead, it is more likely to be construed as a concept or principle in a broader sense: one that guides interpretation and provides context for decisions in international environmental law, and informs the development of new law. Along these lines, Alan Boyle argues that intergenerational equity may be seen as a principle but not a rule:

> [s]ustainable development, intergenerational equity, or the precautionary principle are all more convincingly seen in this sense: not as binding obligations which must be complied with, but as

[35] Sands, *Principles of International Environmental Law* (2nd edn), 55.
[36] Birnie, P., Boyle, A., and Redgwell, C., *International Law and the Environment* (3rd edn, Oxford University Press 2009), 120.
[37] Fitzmaurice, M., *Contemporary Issues in International Environmental Law* (Edward Elgar 2009), 72.
[38] See Fitzmaurice, *Contemporary Issues*, 68.
[39] Sands and Peel, *Principles of International Environmental Law* (3rd edn), 207.
[40] Stockholm Declaration, Principles 1 and 2.
[41] UNESCO Declaration on the Responsibilities of the Present Generations towards Future Generations, adopted on 12 November 1997 by the General Conference of UNESCO at its 29th session.
[42] Birnie et al, *International Law and the Environment*, 120.
[43] Dworkin, R., *Taking Rights Seriously* (Harvard University Press 1977), 26.

principles, considerations or objectives to be taken account of—they may be soft, but they are still law.[44]

Catherine Redgwell has pointed to the generality of this principle: 'intergenerational equity may be said to constitute a "guiding principle" in the application of substantive norms, including existing treaty obligations, under international law.'[45]

However, there is some authority in the jurisprudence of the International Court of Justice ('ICJ') for the proposition that intergenerational equity may be becoming more than mere guidance. In his dissenting opinion in the *Nuclear Tests* case, Judge Weeramantry described intergenerational equity as 'an important and rapidly developing principle of contemporary international law'.[46] A year later, in his dissent to the ICJ's *Advisory Opinion on the Legality of the Threat or the Use of Nuclear Weapons*, Weeramantry went further:

[t]he rights of future generations have passed the stage when they were merely an embryonic right struggling for recognition. They have woven themselves into international law through major treaties, through juristic opinion and through general principles of law recognized by civilized nations.[47]

More recently, in two cases before the ICJ, Judge Cançado Trindade has expressed similar views. In his separate opinion in the *Pulp Mills* case, Judge Cançado Trindade noted that '[n]owadays, in 2010, it can hardly be doubted that the acknowledgement of inter-generational equity forms part of conventional wisdom in International Environmental Law'.[48] In another opinion appended to the ICJ's decision on *Whaling in the Antarctic*, Judge Cançado Trindade reaffirmed his prior opinion and added, further, that 'intergenerational equity marks presence nowadays in a wide range of instruments of international environmental law, and indeed of contemporary public international law'.[49] The language is certainly cautious, but it moves a step further than international environmental law to public international law at large, which suggests that the principle may have some grounding in general international law.

Some domestic decisions also lend support to the proposition that intergenerational equity is a justiciable principle. In *Intellectuals Forum, Tirupathi v. State of A.P. & Ors*,[50] an Indian appeals court held that:

The principles mentioned above [intergenerational equity] wholly apply for adjudicating matters concerning environment and ecology. These principles must, therefore, be applied in full force for protecting the natural resources of this country… It is now an accepted social principle that all human beings have a fundamental right to a healthy environment, commensurate with their well

[44] Boyle, A. E., 'Some Reflections on Relationship of Treaties and Soft Law' (1999) 48 *ICLQ* 901, 908–9.

[45] Redgwell, *Intergenerational Trusts*, 123.

[46] *Request for an Examination of the Situation in Accordance with Paragraph 63 of the Court's Judgment of 20 December 1974 in the Nuclear Tests (New Zealand v. France) Case*, ICJ Reports 1995, 288, dissenting opinion of Judge Weeramantry, 341.

[47] *Legality of the Threat or Use of Nuclear Weapons* (Advisory Opinion) (1996) ICJ Rep 226, para 29 ('Legality of Nuclear Weapons'), dissenting opinion of Judge Weeramantry, 455.

[48] *Pulp Mills on the River Uruguay (Argentina v. Uruguay)*, Judgment, ICJ Reports 2010, 14, Separate Opinion of Judge Cançado Trindade, para 122.

[49] *Whaling in the Antarctic (Australia v. Japan; New Zealand intervening)*, Judgment (31 March 2014) (unreported), Separate Opinion of Judge Cançado Trindade, para 47.

[50] *Intellectuals Forum, Tirupathi v. State of A.P. & Ors* [2006] 3 SCC 549, cited in Ramlogan, R., *Sustainable Development: Towards a Judicial Interpretation* (Martinus Nijhoff 2011), 225.

being, coupled with a corresponding duty of ensuring that resources are conserved and preserved in such a way that present as well as the future generations are aware of them equally...[51]

In another case, *State of Himachal Pradesh and others v. Ganesh Wood Products and others*,[52] intergenerational equity was referred to as a ground to refuse a permit to the extent the operations contemplated by the company could have depleted the relevant natural resources because '[a]fter all, the present generation has no right to deplete all the existing forests and leave nothing for the next and future generations'.[53] Another case before Indian courts, *S. Jagannath v. Union of India & Ors*,[54] suggested that intergenerational equity may be grounded in customary international law because of its ties with sustainable development:

> We have no hesitation in holding that 'Sustainable Development' as a balancing concept between ecology and development has been accepted as a part of the Customary International Law though its salient features have yet to be finalised by the International Law Jurists. Some of the salient principles of 'Sustainable Development', as culled out from Brundtland Report and other international documents, are Inter-Generational Equity...[55]

As will be discussed later in section II) 4 of this chapter, intergenerational equity has also played a role in the jurisprudence of other States.

## 3. Normative impact

### *3.1. International instruments*

In addition to the Stockholm and Rio Declarations, a number of other international instruments refer to the interests of future generations. Examples include[56] the 1946 Whaling Convention,[57] the 1972 World Heritage Convention,[58] the 1993 Vienna Declaration of the World Conference on Human Rights,[59] and the 1992 UN Framework Convention on Climate Change.[60] These instruments 'indicate the importance now attached in international policy to the protection of the environment for future generations',[61] but so far they have not been construed as creating enforceable rights relating to future generations.[62]

Along these lines, Catherine Redgwell argues that 'while intergenerational equity has not yet achieved the status of a binding rule (or perhaps more accurately, set of rules)

[51] Cited in Ramlogan, *Sustainable Development*, 225–6.

[52] *State of Himachal Pradesh and others v. Ganesh Wood Products and others*, 1995 (6) SCC 363, cited in Ramlogan, *Sustainable Development*, 226.

[53] Ramlogan, *Sustainable Development*, 226.

[54] *S. Jagannath v. Union of India & Ors* 1997 (2) SCC 87, cited in Ramlogan, *Sustainable Development*, 226.

[55] Cited in Ramlogan, *Sustainable Development*, 227.

[56] For a preliminary list see: Commission on Sustainable Development, *Report of the Expert Group Meeting on Identification of Principles of International Law for Sustainable Development*, Geneva, Switzerland, 26–28 September 1995 ('Report-principles'), para 46. An updated list appears in UN Secretary-General, *Intergenerational Solidarity and the Needs of Future Generations. Report of the Secretary-General*, 15 August 2013, UN Doc A/68/322 ('UNSG Report'), paras 33–5.

[57] International Convention for the Regulation of Whaling, 2 December 1946, 161 UNTS 361, Preamble, first recital.

[58] Convention Concerning the Protection of the World Cultural and Natural Heritage, 16 November 1972, 1037 UNTS 151, art 4.

[59] 'Vienna Declaration and Program of Action', 12 July 1993, UN Doc A/CONF.157/23, para 11.

[60] United Nations Framework Convention on Climate Change, 9 May 1992, 31 ILM 849 ('UNFCCC'), art 3(1).

[61] Birnie et al, *International Law and the Environment*, 120.

[62] Birnie et al, *International Law and the Environment*, 120.

under international law, a process of "creeping intergenerationalisation" may be observed within international law'.[63] According to Redgwell, an increasing focus on intergenerational issues is entering international law in two ways. First, many preambles to international treaties make reference to future generations.[64] While such references are not in themselves legally binding, judges are able to use them in the interpretation and application of substantive treaty provisions. Second, elsewhere in international environmental law there are substantive principles that contain an intertemporal dimension. In addition to sustainable development, Redgwell argues[65] that intergeneralization may be seen within the common heritage of humankind principle,[66] the principle of custodianship or stewardship,[67] the precautionary principle[68] and the principle of common but differentiated responsibilities.[69]

It is worth noting that not all of these references to the concept of intergenerational equity are completely consistent.[70] These inconsistencies could affect the way in which intergenerational equity comes to be applied. It may be that intergenerational equity as a legal entity is still too immature to be confined to a particular term, and that any reference in an international law instrument to future generations may be taken as evidence of an emerging principle of intergenerational equity. If this is the case, though, it does not do much to clarify the term's meaning, or intensify its impact.

### *3.2. Ombudsman for future generations*

During the third meeting of the Preparatory Committee, Malta proposed the following with respect to Principle 4 of the *Chairman's Consolidated Draft* of *Principles on General Rights and Obligations*:

> Each generation has, in particular, the responsibility to ensure that in any national or international forum where it is likely that a decision be taken affecting the interest of future generations, access be given to an authorized person appointed as 'guardian' of future generations to appear and make submissions on their behalf.[71]

While the Maltese proposal does not appear in the final text of the Rio Declaration, a number of countries took action at the domestic level to give a voice to future generations.[72] Israel and Hungary implemented an ombudsman for future generations, though neither office remained in place as initially planned. Hungary appointed a parliamentary commissioner for future generations, for a six-year term commencing in 2008.[73] The Hungarian ombudsman for future generations largely functioned as an environmental ombudsman. However, the office of the commissioner for future generations was abolished by a parliamentary act in 2011, and the interests of future generations have been subsumed under the Office of the Commissioner for Fundamental Rights.[74] In that office, there is a Deputy

[63] Redgwell, *Intergenerational Trusts*, 126.
[64] Redgwell, *Intergenerational Trusts*, 126.
[65] Redgwell, *Intergenerational Trusts*, 127.
[66] Redgwell, *Intergenerational Trusts*, 129–32.
[67] Redgwell, *Intergenerational Trusts*, 132–8.
[68] Redgwell, *Intergenerational Trusts*, 138–40.
[69] Redgwell, *Intergenerational Trusts*, 140–2.
[70] See Wirth, 'The Rio Declaration', 627–9.
[71] UN Doc A/CONF.151/PC/WG.III/L.8/Rev.1, para 33.
[72] See UNSG Report, paras 39–48, discussing the mechanisms established in Canada, Finland, Germany, Hungary, Israel, New Zealand, Norway, and Wales (UK).
[73] House of Commons Environmental Audit Committee, *Embedding Sustainable Development across Government, after the Secretary of State's Announcement on the Future of the Sustainable Development Commission* (first report of session 2010–11), Ev. 47.
[74] See <http://jno.hu/en/> (accessed on 8 February 2014).

Commissioner for Fundamental Rights responsible for the protection of the interests of future generations. In Israel, the first Commissioner for Future Generations, Judge Schlomo Shaham, served from 2001 to 2006. At the end of the Commissioner's first term, the Knesset declined to appoint a new commissioner for four years. Legal proceedings ensued, and the High Court eventually found that the Knesset was not bound to make a new appointment. The Knesset then abolished the office, citing budget constraints and duplication of roles.

More recently, as part of the discussions leading to the Rio 2012 Summit, the idea of a UN High Commissioner for Future Generations has been put forward by civil society.[75] The outcome document of the Summit, *The Future We Want*, requested the UN Secretary-General to prepare a report on how to promote intergenerational solidarity.[76] The Secretary-General submitted his Report in August 2013.[77] Interestingly, the Report discusses a number of conceptual issues such as the identification of future generations and the possibility of obligations without specific right-holders. More practically, it puts forward four basic options to give future generations a more institutionalized backing, namely a 'High Commissioner' for future generations, a 'Special Envoy' of the Secretary-General, a regular 'agenda item' to be discussed by the High political forum called for by the same paragraph of the Outcome document, or a system of inter-agency coordination with regard to the rights of future generations.[78]

## 3.3. *Intergenerational trust*

Some commentators have suggested that intergenerational equity can be achieved through the use of an intergenerational trust. According to Edith Brown Weiss, the primary exponent of this approach, there is an implied 'planetary trust' established by 'an implied declaration by each generation that it holds the resources of the planet in trust for future generations.'[79] In order for the planetary trust to be enforceable, each generation would have to enact and enforce 'positive laws affirming their obligation to future generations.'[80] Brown Weiss states that intergenerational equity requires the conservation of options, quality, and access for future generations with respect to the world's resources.[81]

Malgosia Fitzmaurice has expressed the view that the Marshall Islands' agreement with the US regarding nuclear testing has an intergenerational element akin to the intergenerational trust described by Weiss: trust funds were set up to compensate the people of the Marshall Islands for past, present, and future losses caused by nuclear testing.[82] She argues that while the concept of intergenerational equity faces significant obstacles in its practical implementation, it nonetheless 'is alive':

[75] Ward, H., *Committing to the future we want: a High Commissioner for Future Generations at Rio+20*, Discussion paper, March 2012.

[76] Para 86, second sentence, of the Outcome document states: 'We will also consider the need for promoting intergenerational solidarity for the achievement of sustainable development, taking into account the needs of future generations, including by inviting the Secretary-General to present a report on this issue', *The Future We Want*, 11 September 2012, UN Doc A/Res/66/288.

[77] UNSG Report, UN Doc A/68/322.

[78] UNSG Report, paras 63–7.

[79] Brown Weiss, E., 'The Planetary Trust: Conservation and Intergenerational Equity', (1984) 11 *Ecology Law Quarterly* 495, 504.

[80] Brown Weiss, 'The Planetary Trust', 504.

[81] Brown Weiss, E., *In Fairness to Future Generations: International Law, Common Patrimony and Intergenerational Equity* (United Nations University 1989), 198–9.

[82] Fitzmaurice, *Contemporary Issues in International Environmental Law*, 156–7.

The legal processes taking place in the Republic of the Marshall Islands are of paramount importance, most notably the legal proceedings before the Nuclear Claims Tribunal, which in its legal settlements accounts for generations unborn and their well-being.[83]

As discussed next, intergenerational equity may find expression in less legal manners, some of which are very important in practice.

### *3.4. Sustainable investing*

In the twenty years since the Rio Declaration, there has been an increase in sustainable or socially responsible investing. As of April 2013, more than 1200 institutional investors (banks, pension funds, investment managers, and charities)—representing more than $34 trillion—had committed to the United Nations-sponsored Principles of Responsible Investment, a set of six voluntary[84] principles intended to help institutional investors to invest their considerable funds in a way that encourages investee companies to manage environmental, social, and corporate governance issues in a responsible and long-term way.[85]

Underlying many of the forms of sustainable investing[86] is the idea that investors should contribute to maintaining a viable economic system over the long-term: sustainable investing implies 'ensuring that the *conditions* for [corporate and investor] responsibility remain intact.'[87] Sustainable investing encompasses both the manner of investment (longer-term and considered), and stock selection (investing in appropriate companies). Thus sustainable investing is likely to involve investing in socially useful companies over a long time frame, rather than making short-term bets on share price fluctuation. From an environmental and social perspective, large institutional investors decide how to allocate funds to companies that will have a significant impact (positive or otherwise) on the lives of current and future generations. Some industry pension funds, for example, are particularly concerned about the labour conditions for workers within the companies in which they invest. Charity endowments may wish to avoid investing in companies that produce products or behave in ways that offend their charitable aims. Other investors may wish to avoid taking a moral stance on any particular issue, but see responsible business practice as increasing the likelihood that the economy will remain workable for future investment. Infusing these divergent investment approaches are social preferences that reflect the sort of world these investors wish to create for future generations.

Intergenerational equity is also relevant within institutional investment funds themselves. As the burden for planning for retirement falls increasingly on individuals within our ageing populations, the equitable distribution of funds becomes a tangible concern for many people. Long-term investors, such as pension funds, have investment time horizons of thirty years or longer: in human terms, a generation. On a purely financial level, institutional investors must tailor their investment strategy to meet the needs of their beneficiaries. Old and young beneficiaries within the same pension fund have very different needs. An older beneficiary on the cusp of retirement will benefit most from a lower

[83] Fitzmaurice, *Contemporary Issues*, 169.

[84] Signatories must report annually their progress in implementing the six principles: <http://www.unpri.org/areas-of-work/reporting-and-assessment/reporting-framework/> (accessed on 8 February 2014).

[85] See <http://www.unpri.org/introducing-responsible-investment/> (accessed on 8 February 2014).

[86] See generally Woods, C. and Urwin, R., 'Putting Sustainable Investing into Practice: A Governance Framework for Pension Funds' (2010) 92 *Journal of Business Ethics* 1.

[87] Woods and Urwin, 'Putting Sustainable Investing into Practice', 5.

risk approach, whereas a younger beneficiary stands to gain more from higher return (and higher risk) strategy. Failing to negotiate the competing requirements of different generations of beneficiaries could have serious implications.[88] For pension funds and long-term focused investment managers practicing sustainable investing, the concept of intergenerational equity becomes very real.

### 3.5. *Economics and generational accounting*

The development of the concept of intergenerational equity at international environmental law has occurred alongside the development of greater interest in the question of justice between generations in philosophy and economics. As Janna Thompson notes:

> theories of justice... centre on the interests and relationships of co-temporal adult individuals. They concentrate on determining the bargains or agreements that would be endorsed by these individuals, the rights that they can claim or on the responsibilities that arise from their collective political actions. Such accounts cannot easily encompass intergenerational relationships.[89]

Only relatively recently have Western philosophers attempted to answer questions such as: how do we decide what is just for people who do not yet exist?[90] Or, when and how do we prioritize justice for future generations when there is so much injustice between members of the current generation?[91]

What constitutes an 'equitable relationship' in an intergenerational context is a matter for debate. For example, should future generations' interests be discounted? If so, to what extent? What distributive principles should apply between generations? Economists have addressed the question by focusing on how discount rates should be set in order to compare policies whose effects will be felt over long time frames, by many generations.[92] This is problematic, though, as using even a reasonably low discount rate, a future life is worth very little compared to a present life. Not surprisingly, as Paul Portney and John Weyant note, 'even the best minds in the [economic] profession' feel a sense of 'unease' about discounting.[93] The difficulty that economists face in selecting an appropriate discount rate is a testament to the complex ethical and practical issues surrounding the concept of intergenerational equity.

While discounting the value of the future has deep ethical implications,[94] discount rates can provide a tool for policy evaluation. Norway and the Netherlands, for example, use 'generational accounts' to help determine the fiscal sustainability of current government

[88] Though it occurred in a family trust rather than an institutional investment setting, *Nestle v. National Westminster Bank plc* [1993] 1 WLR 1260 is instructive: in that case, the young beneficiary of a family trust sued the trustees, who had made investments that benefited her father (also a beneficiary), to his daughter's detriment.

[89] Thompson, J., *Intergenerational Justice: Rights and Responsibilities in an Intergenerational Polity* (Taylor & Francis 2009), 3.

[90] See eg Parfit, D., *Reasons and Persons* (Oxford University Press 1984), 377 and 451.

[91] Gaspart, F. and Gosseries, A., 'Are Generational Savings Unjust?' (2007) 6 *Politics, Philosophy and Economics* 193, 204.

[92] Solow, R. M., 'Foreword', in Portney, P. R. and Weyant, J. P. (eds), *Discounting and Intergenerational Equity* (Resources for the Future 1999), vii, vii–ix.

[93] Portney, P. R. and Weyant, J. P., 'Introduction', in Portney and Weyant (eds), *Discounting and Intergenerational Equity*, 1–12, 5.

[94] Parfit, D. and Cowen, T., 'Against the Social Discount Rate', in Laslett, P. and Fishkin, J. S. (eds), *Justice between Age Groups and Generations* (Yale University Press 1992) 144, T 144.

projects.[95] In generational accounting, the ethical implications of discount rates become practical.

## 4. Jurisprudential relevance

### 4.1. *A component of sustainable development?*

Intergenerational equity is sometimes viewed as forming a part of sustainable development. Sands and Peel describe intergenerational equity as 'an important aspect of the concept of sustainable development'.[96] Similarly, Bell and McGillivray argue that the concept of intergenerational equity forms part of the principle of sustainable development.[97] The Expert Group convened in 1995 by the Commission of Sustainable Development locates intergenerational equity within a broader notion of equity, but it recognizes its conceptual links with sustainable development.[98]

The ICJ views sustainable development as a 'concept'[99] or an 'objective'.[100] However, this conception was criticized by Judge Weeramantry in his separate opinion in the *Gabčíkovo-Nagymaros* case.[101] Weeramantry considered that sustainable development is 'more than a mere concept, but... a principle with normative value',[102] and an 'integral part of modern international law.'[103] In his opinion, Weeramantry viewed intergenerational equity as a component of sustainable development not only as a principle but as 'one of the most ancient ideas in the human heritage'.[104] In a similar vein, in his separate opinion to the *Pulp Mills* case, Judge Cançado Trindade considered intergenerational equity as the temporal dimension of sustainable development.[105]

Without further application to practical situations, however, it is difficult to predict what intergenerational equity as part of sustainable development will require in the context of future adjudication.

### 4.2. *Future generations' rights*

The concept of intergenerational equity has been invoked explicitly only a handful of times before the ICJ. The most significant international legal treatment of the concept thus far has been in the *Nuclear Weapons Advisory Opinion*.[106] In that case, the ICJ found that:

> in order correctly to apply to the present case the Charter law on the use of force and the law applicable in armed conflict, in particular humanitarian law, it is imperative for the Court to take account of the unique characteristics of nuclear weapons, and in particular their destructive capacity, their

[95] Anderson, B. and Sheppard, J., 'Fiscal Futures, Institutional Budget Reforms, and Their Effects: What can be learned?' (2009) 9 *OECD Journal on Budgeting* 1, 28.

[96] Sands and Peel, *Principles of International Environmental Law*, 210.

[97] Bell, S. and McGillivray, D., *Environmental Law* (7th edn, Oxford University Press 2008), 58. See also Birnie et al, *International Law and the Environment*, 121; Sands and Peel, *Principles of Environmental Law*, 210.

[98] Report-principles, para 46.

[99] *Case Concerning The Gabčíkovo-Nagymaros Project* (Hungary/Slovakia), Judgment, ICJ Reports 1997, 7 ('*Gabčíkovo-Nagymaros*'), para 140.

[100] *Pulp Mills on the River Uruguay*, paras 75–7 and 177.

[101] *Gabčíkovo-Nagymaros*, Separate Opinion of Vice-President Weeramantry.

[102] *Gabčíkovo-Nagymaros*, (V-P Weeramantry), 85.

[103] *Gabčíkovo-Nagymaros*, (V-P Weeramantry), 86.

[104] *Gabčíkovo-Nagymaros*, (V-P Weeramantry), 107.

[105] *Pulp Mills on the River Uruguay*, (Judge Cançado Trindade), paras 123–4.

[106] *Legality of Nuclear Weapons*.

capacity to cause untold human suffering, and their ability to cause damage to generations to come.[107]

While the Court stressed the importance of considering the interests of future generations, its decision 'falls far short' of explicitly recognizing a principle of intergenerational equity or rights of future generations.[108]

Judge Weeramantry's dissenting opinion referred directly to intergenerational equity and strongly advocated for the recognition of the rights of future generations. He noted that, given the particularly long-lasting health and environmental effects of nuclear warfare, the ICJ was under an obligation to 'pay due recognition to the rights of future generations.'[109] He went on to stress that:

> the rights of future generations have passed the stage when they were merely an embryonic right struggling for recognition. They have woven themselves into international law through major treaties, through juristic opinion and through general principles of law recognized by civilized nations. Among treaties may be mentioned, the 1979 London Ocean Dumping Convention, the 1973 Convention on International Trade in Endangered Species, and the 1972 Convention Concerning the Protection of the World Cultural and Natural Heritage. All of these expressly incorporate the principle of protecting the natural environment for future generations, and elevate the concept to the level of binding State obligation.[110]

His argument was focused on the rights of future generations, rather than on the concept of intergenerational equity per se. However, he did state explicitly that the concept of intergenerational equity was 'academically well established'[111] and presented it as a concept that supported the rights of future generations.

One important question in this regard is: who may exercise the rights of future generations? As discussed next, in the absence of an ombudsman for future generations, the main avenue is to allow for the representation of future generations by present ones.

### *4.3. Jus standi*

At a national level, the most prominent case involving intergenerational equity is the Philippines Supreme Court case, *Minors Oposa v. Secretary of the Department of Environment and Natural Resources* (*DENR*).[112] In that case, a group of petitioners sued the DENR to prevent the granting of timber licences. The petitioners claimed to represent unborn generations as well as themselves. The Supreme Court found in favour of the petitioners that (amongst other things) the DENR had failed in its duty to preserve the environment for future generations, and referred the case to the court of first instance to review the grant of the timber licences in question.

[107] *Legality of Nuclear Weapons*, para 36.

[108] Brown Weiss, E. 'Opening Doors to the Environment and to Future Generations', in Boisson de Chazournes, L. and Sands, Ph. (eds), *International Law, the International Court of Justice and Nuclear Weapons* (Cambridge University Press 1999) 338, 349–50.

[109] *Legality of Nuclear Weapons*, Dissenting Opinion of Judge Weeramantry, 455.

[110] *Legality of Nuclear Weapons*, (Weeramantry J), 455.

[111] *Legality of Nuclear Weapons*, (Weeramantry J), 455. Weeramantry J referred to Brown Weiss, E., *In Fairness to Future Generations: International Law, Common Patrimony and Intergenerational Equity* (United Nations University 1989).

[112] *Minors Oposa v. Secretary of the Department of Environment and Natural Resources* (DENR) 33 ILM (1994) 173 (30 July 1993) (Phil.) ('*Minors Oposa*').

The *Minors Oposa* case is often cited as an example of the implementation of a principle of intergenerational equity at a national level.[113] The Supreme Court found that the petitioners could file a class suit 'for themselves, for others of their generation and for the succeeding generations',[114] stressing that '[t]heir personality to sue on behalf of the succeeding generations can only be based on the concept of intergenerational responsibility insofar as the right to a balanced and healthful ecology is concerned.'[115] However, critics argue that the decision provides little more than coincidental support for the concept.[116] The rights of future generations were already recognized in the law of the Philippines prior to the case, so the decision did not create a new precedent in that regard.[117] In a separate opinion, Judge Feliciano found that the class of potential petitioners was too wide to be practicable: it encompassed 'everyone living in the country, whether now or in the future.'[118]

## 4.4. *Environmental impact assessment*

In Australia, two decisions from the New South Wales Land and Environment Court provide a more detailed view of how the concept of intergenerational equity might be applied in practice. *Gray v. Minister for Planning*[119] and *Taralga Landscape Guardians Inc v. Minister for Planning*[120] relate to administrative decisions affecting the environment.

In *Gray*, a case involving an environmental impact assessment for a new coalmine, Justice Pain found that the principle of intergenerational equity required, in the context of environmental impact statements, 'the assessment of cumulative impacts of proposed activities on the environment.'[121] Here, the environmental impact assessment for the coal mine should include estimations of greenhouse gas emissions from not only the construction of the coal mine but also from the end-uses of the coal to be mined there.[122]

*Taralga* involved a dispute between a group of rural residents and a wind energy company over the company's development proposal for a wind farm that would be visible from the residents' properties. In that case, Chief Justice Preston reasoned that in the context of energy production, intergenerational equity requires two things: first, sustainable extraction and use, with respect to both the resource and the environment surrounding the

[113] See eg Popovic, N.A.F., 'In Pursuit of Environmental Human Rights' (1996) 27 *Columbia Human Rights Law Review* 487, 513.

[114] *Minors Oposa*, 185. [115] *Minors Oposa*, 185.

[116] See eg Gatmayan, D. B., 'The Illusion of Intergenerational Equity: Oposa v Factoran as Pyrrhic Victory' (2003) 15 *GIELR* 457, 458–60, arguing that the decision to grant standing to unborn generations in this case was *obiter dictum*.

[117] Gatmayan, 'The Illusion of Intergenerational Equity', 458–60. This point seems to be confirmed by the position of a Bangladesh court in *Farooque v. Government of Bangladesh* (WP 998 of 1994, CA of 1995 (1996.07.25) (*Flood Action Plan* case)): '[w]e have given reasons of our own why the appellant is a person aggrieved, but we have to say specifically that we do not accept Dr. Farooque's submission that the association represents not only the present generation but also the generation yet unborn. This claim is based on a case of Philippines Supreme Court… The minors' locus standi was allowed because "the right to a balanced and healthful ecology" was fundamental right and several laws declaring the policy of the State to conservation of the country's forest "not only for the present generation but for the future generation as well" were guaranteed… Our Constitution does not contain an analogous provision', cited in Ramlogan, *Sustainable Development*.

[118] *Minors Oposa*, Concurring Opinion of Judge Feliciano, 200–1.

[119] *Gray v. Minister for Planning* [2006] NSWLEC 720 ('*Gray*').

[120] *Taralga Landscape Guardians Inc v. Minister for Planning* [2007] NSWLEC 59 ('*Taralga*').

[121] *Gray*, para 122. [122] *Gray*, para 100.

resource; and second, the increasing substitution of cleaner energy sources for existing, dirtier ones.[123]

Both of these cases were decided under the New South Wales Land and Environment Court's special merits review jurisdiction, and it is unclear to what extent decisions made under this special jurisdiction can be deemed to contribute to the development of jurisprudence.[124] Nonetheless, the cases paint a clearer picture of the potential for intergenerational equity to have a substantial practical legal effect.

The courts of other States have also referred to intergenerational equity in the context of environmental impact assessment. In *Tikiri Band Bulankulama and others v. The Secretary, Ministry of Industrial Development and others*,[125] a Sri-Lankan court considered that:

> The right to development must be fulfilled so as to equitably meet developmental and environmental needs of present and future generations. (Principle 3, Rio de Janeiro Declaration). The inter-generational principle, in my view, should be regarded as axiomatic in the decision making process in relation to matters concerning the natural resources and the environment of Sri Lanka in general, and particularly in the case before us...[126]

Similar positions have been taken by the courts of India, in cases such as *A. P. Pollution Control Board v. Nayudu*,[127] *State of Himachal Pradesh v. Ganesh Wood Products* or *Jagannath v. Union of India*.[128]

## III) Relations with Other Principles

As noted at the outset of this chapter, Principle 3 of the Rio Declaration bears a strong resemblance with the definition of sustainable development provided by the World Commission on Environment and Development. It comes therefore as no surprise that Principle 3 is closely related to Principle 4, which bears directly upon sustainable development. According to Sands (2003):

> The heart of the Rio Declaration is found in Principles 3 and 4, which should be read together to understand the political context in which they were negotiated and the trade-off they represent. Both Principles were initially controversial... In return for Principle 3, the developed countries extracted Principle 4, which provides that '[i]n order to achieve sustainable development, environmental protection shall constitute an integral part of the development process and cannot be considered in isolation from it.' This reflects a commitment to moving environmental considerations and objectives from the periphery of international relations to its economic core.[129]

[123] *Taralga*, para 74.

[124] See Justice Jagot in *Drake-Brockman v. Minister for Planning* [2007] NSWLEC 490, para 124: 'care must be taken in applying observations about the level or extent of issues found to be appropriate in merits appeals to other contexts.' Contrast Elizabeth Fisher who argues (in the context, particularly, of Australian specialist environmental tribunals) that merits review has more precedential value than is commonly recognized: Fisher, E., 'Administrative Law, Pluralism and the Legal Construction of Merits Review in Australian Environmental Courts and Tribunals', in Pearson, L., Harlow, C., and Taggart, M. (eds), *Administrative Law in a Changing State: Essays in Honour of Mark Aronson* (Hart 2008) 325, 332–48.

[125] *Tikiri Band Bulankulama and others v. The Secretary, Ministry of Industrial Development and others*, SC Application No. 884/99 (F.R.), cited in Ramlogan, *Sustainable Development*, 227.

[126] Cited in Ramlogan, *Sustainable Development*, 228.

[127] *A. P. Pollution Control Board v. Nayudu*, CA 368–71 of 1999 (1999.01.27), cited in Ramlogan, *Sustainable Development*, 224–5.

[128] Cited in Ramlogan, *Sustainable Development*, 226.

[129] Sands, *Principles of International Environmental Law*, 55.

For other commentators, the relationship between intergenerational equity and sustainable development goes further than mere resemblance. In these accounts, intergenerational equity would be best viewed as a component of sustainable development.[130]

The main practical implications of siding with one view or the other may lie in either the legal materials to which one could refer to assess the legal character of intergenerational equity or the institutions that could potentially claim a voice in connection with the respect of the rights of future generations. Sustainable development may offer a wider and more solid basis of legal instruments and institutions, but specific reference to and action on intergenerational equity may not be easily grounded on unspecific texts and mandates.

## IV) Assessment

For a principle that was at its inception seen primarily as a 'right to development', the focus of Principle 3 of the Rio Declaration has changed significantly. It is now regarded as the principal statement of the concept of intergenerational equity at international law. Far from conferring a right to economic development and any financial benefits such a right might infer, Principle 3 has come to be seen by judges and commentators alike as providing protection to the environment in the interests of future generations.

In practical terms, the decisions involving intergenerational equity are too few for a detailed and definitive picture of its influence to emerge. One might say that the concept of intergenerational equity has been referred to, rather than applied, in international law. Nonetheless, the few exemplars that do exist indicate that the concept might be used to defend the interests of future generations, or as a temporally-focused component of the international environmental law principle of sustainable development. In the *Nuclear Weapons Advisory Opinion*, Judge Weeramantry's dissenting opinion drew on the concept to bolster his complete opposition to any form of nuclear warfare, stressing that future generations, and not just contemporary people, would suffer the consequences of the bomb. In the Philippines Supreme Court case, *Minors Oposa*, the court allowed a lawsuit on behalf of future generations in the context of contested timber permits and deforestation, but only in a limited setting. In Australia, the New South Wales Land and Environment Court has used the concept to extend the time horizon over which administrative decision-makers must consider environmental impacts, requiring them to look at cumulative environmental impacts in one case, and at the longer-term sustainability of energy sources in another. As merits review cases, the precedential value of these Australian cases is controversial, but they nonetheless give a glimpse of the substantive and even radical way that intergenerational equity might be applied in the future.

## V) Select Bibliography

Agius, E. and Busuttil, S. (eds), *Future Generations and International Law* (London: Earthscan 1998).

Bell, S. and McGillivray, D., *Environmental Law* (7th edn, Oxford: Oxford University Press 2008).

Birnbacher, D., *La responsabilité envers les générations futures* (Paris: Presses universitaires de France 1994).

[130] Sands and Peel, *Principles of International Environmental Law*, 210; Birnie et al, *International Law and the Environment*, 121; Bell and McGillivray, *Environmental Law*, 58; Report-principles, para 46.

Birnie, P., Boyle, A., and Redgwell, C., *International Law and the Environment* (3rd edn, Oxford: Oxford University Press 2009).

Brown Weiss, E., 'The Planetary Trust: Conservation and Intergenerational Equity' (1984) 11 *Ecology Law Quarterly* 495.

Brown Weiss, E., *In Fairness to Future Generations: International Law, Common Patrimony and Intergenerational Equity* (Tokyo: United Nations University 1989).

Brown Weiss, E., 'Our Rights and Obligations to Future Generations for the Environment' (1990) 94 *AJIL* 198.

Commission on Sustainable Development, *Report of the Expert Group Meeting on Identification of Principles of International Law for Sustainable Development*, Geneva, Switzerland, 26–28 September 1995.

Fitzmaurice, M., *Contemporary Issues in International Environmental Law* (Cheltenham: Edward Elgar 2009).

Gatmayan, D.B., 'The Illusion of Intergenerational Equity: Oposa v Factoran as Pyrrhic Victory' (2003) 15 *GIELR* 457.

Laslett, P. and Fishkin, J. S. (eds), *Justice between Age Groups and Generations* (New Haven CT: Yale University Press 1992).

Ling, C.Y., *The Rio Declaration on Environment and Development: An assessment* (Penang: Third World Network 2012).

Parfit, D., *Reasons and Persons* (Oxford: Oxford University Press 1984).

Portney, P.R. and Weyant, J.P. (eds) *Discounting and Intergenerational Equity* (Washington DC: Resources for the Future 1999).

Ramlogan, R., *Sustainable Development: Towards a Judicial Interpretation* (Leiden: Martinus Nijhoff 2011).

Redgwell, C., *Intergenerational Trusts and Environmental Protection* (Manchester: Manchester University Press 1999).

Sands, P., *Principles of International Environmental Law* (2nd edn, Cambridge: Cambridge University Press 2003).

Sands, P. and Peel, J., *Principles of International Environmental Law* (3rd edn, Cambridge: Cambridge University Press 2012).

Supanich, G., 'The Legal Basis of Intergenerational Responsibility: An Alternative View—The Sense of Intergenerational Identity' (1992) 3 *YbIEL* 94.

Thompson, J., *Intergenerational Justice: Rights and Responsibilities in an Intergenerational Polity* (London: Taylor & Francis 2009).

UN Secretary-General, *Intergenerational Solidarity and the Needs of Future Generations. Report of the Secretary-General*, 15 August 2013, UN Doc A/68/322.

Ward, H., *Committing to the future we want: a High Commissioner for Future Generations at Rio+20*, Discussion paper, March 2012.

Wirth, D.A., 'The Rio Declaration on Environment and Development: Two Steps Forward and One Back, or Vice Versa?' (1995) 29 *Georgia Law Review* 599.

Woods, C. and Urwin, R., 'Putting Sustainable Investing into Practice: A Governance Framework for Pension Funds' (2010) 92 *Journal of Business Ethics* 1.

Woods, C., *The Environment, Intergenerational Equity and Long-term Investments* (doctoral dissertation, University of Oxford 2011).

# 8. Principle 4

## *Sustainable Development through Integration*

Virginie Barral* and Pierre-Marie Dupuy**

**Principle 4**

In order to achieve sustainable development, environmental protection shall constitute an integral part of the development process and cannot be considered in isolation from it.




* Senior lecturer at the School of Law of the University of Hertfordshire.

** Emeritus professor of international law at the University Panthéon-Assas (Paris 2) and at the Graduate Institute of International and Development Studies, Geneva.

## I) Origins and Rationale of the Principle

Principle 4 of the Rio Declaration is a key principle in the operation of sustainable development. The idea it enshrines, that of integration of economic and environmental concerns, predates Rio however and can be traced back to the early 1970s.

The importance of integrating environmental concerns into the development process was first underlined in the 1971 Founex Report.[1] This report was the result of a meeting of experts arranged by Maurice Strong, the Secretary-General to the Stockholm Conference, and it contributed to persuading many Southern nations to attend the Conference. The document, which was primarily aimed at helping developing countries design and plan development programmes, highlighted that environmental deterioration arose both out of the process of development and out of the lack of development itself. It insisted in particular that in order to avoid repeating the past mistakes of the industrialized nations in their development patterns, a broader, more integrated approach to development should be adopted;[2] an approach where 'environmental policies are integrated with development planning and regarded as part of the overall framework of economic and social planning'.[3]

For the Founex experts, the objective for developing countries should be to 'regard environmental improvement as one of the multiple goals in a development plan'.[4] It is thus little surprise that this use of the language of integration can also be found in the text of the Stockholm Declaration on the Human Environment.[5] In particular, Principle 13 states that:

> In order to achieve a more rational management of resources and thus to improve the environment, States should adopt an integrated and coordinated approach to their development planning so as to ensure that development is compatible with the need to protect and improve the environment for the benefit of their population.

Principle 14 states for its part that: 'Rational planning constitutes an essential tool for reconciling any conflict between the needs of development and the need to protect and improve the environment.'

At both Founex and Stockholm, however, the idea of 'integration' was closely associated to that of 'planning', which partly due to its socialist overtones and the realities of the world economy has then disappeared from the Rio documents. Furthermore, if by 1972 the link between environmental deterioration and economic development was fully acknowledged, these concerns were still viewed, to some extent, as opposites that needed to be reconciled. The close and intimate interdependence between the environment and economic and social development put to the fore by global environmental threats such as climate change and the loss of biological diversity had not yet, at Stockholm, sunk into the conscience of humanity, and State representatives. This element, which is missing from Stockholm but which is a central feature of the Rio process, is essential in understanding the meaning of Principle 4.

1 *The Founex Report on Development and Environment*, Founex, Switzerland, 4–12 June 1971.

2 *The Founex Report*, 3–5. 3 *The Founex Report*, 19. 4 *The Founex Report*, 19.

5 'Declaration of the United Nations Conference on the Human Environment', Stockholm, 16 June 1972, UN Doc A/CONF 48/14/Rev.1 ('Stockholm Declaration').

In the twenty years separating Stockholm from Rio, the increased recognition of the close interconnectedness between environmental and economic concerns, together with the need to adopt an integral approach to these issues, has grown apace. The Helsinki Final Act in 1975 viewed protection of the environment as a task of major importance for the economic development of all countries.[6] In 1982 the United Nations Environment Programme in its Nairobi Declaration advocated an integrated approach to environment, development, population, and resources emphasizing their interrelationship in order to lead to sustainable development.[7] Nature conservation and/or environmental protection was also viewed as an integral part of economic development activities in many high level international documents such as the 1982 World Charter for Nature,[8] the UN General Assembly's 1987 Environmental Perspective to the Year 2000 and Beyond,[9] the 1987 WCED proposed Legal Principles,[10] the 1989 Commonwealth Langkawi Declaration,[11] or the 1991 World Conservation Strategy.[12]

The idea that environmental protection needed to form an integral part of economic development and economic decision-making also started making its way into formally binding international law even before Rio and it is primarily in the area of marine protection that some articulation of the concept of integration can first be found. Several regional conventions dedicated a paragraph in their preamble recognizing either the need to adopt an integrated approach to the use of the marine environment in order to achieve both environmental and developmental goals,[13] or the threat posed to the marine environment by the very absence of such integration of environment and development.[14] The 1974 OSPAR Convention even referred to the idea of integration within its substantive provisions as article 6(2)(d) requests the parties to take into account the 'need for an integrated planning policy consistent with the requirement of environmental protection'.[15] Though it never came into force, article 2 of the ASEAN Agreement on the Conservation of Nature and Natural Resources[16] also placed, as early as 1985, an obligation of means on its Parties to 'ensure that conservation and management of natural resources are treated as an integral part of development planning at all stages and at all levels'. When States came to the negotiating table at Rio they were thus not faced with an entirely new idea, but one which had emerged and developed over the preceding twenty years.

[6] Conference on Security and Cooperation in Europe, Final Act, Helsinki, 1 August 1975, Section 5 Environment, preamble.

[7] Nairobi Declaration, adopted at the 13th meeting of the session on 18 May 1982, para 3.

[8] 'World Charter for Nature', UN Doc A/RES 37/7, 1982.

[9] 'Environmental Perspective to the Year 2000 and Beyond', UN Doc A/RES 42/186, 1987.

[10] Report of the World Commission on Environment and Development, *Our Common Future*, 10 March 1987 ('Brundtland Report'), Annex 1: Summary of Proposed Legal Principles for Environmental Protection and Sustainable Development Adopted by the WCED Experts Group on Environmental Law, Sustainable Development and Assistance, para 7.

[11] Langkawi Declaration on Environment, Heads of Government of the Commonwealth, Langkawi (Malaysia), 21 October 1989, para 8.

[12] World Conservation Strategy, 1980, joint IUCN/WWF/UNEP document.

[13] Kuwait Regional Convention for Co-operation on the Protection of the Marine Environment from Pollution 24 April 1978, 1140 UNTS 133; Jeddah Regional Convention for the Conservation of the Red Sea and the Gulf of Aden Environment, 14 February 1982, (1982) 9 EPL 56.

[14] Abidjan Convention for Co-operation in the Protection and Development of the Marine and Coastal environment of the West and Central African Region and Protocol, 23 March 1984, (1981) 20 ILM 746; Nouméa Convention for the Protection of the Natural Resources and Environment of the South Pacific Region, 24 November 1986, (1986) 26 ILM 38.

[15] Convention for the Protection of the Marine Environment of the North East Atlantic, 22 September 1992, 2354 UNTS 67.

[16] 9 July 1985, (1985) 15 EPL 64.

## II) The Principle as Enshrined in the Rio Declaration

### 1. Preparatory work and context

In view of the intensely polarized negotiations of the Rio Declaration, it is no surprise that the text of Principle 4, as it stands today, has been the subject of wide variations in terms of content, location, or even inclusion in the Declaration proper in the weeks running up to the Conference at PrepCom IV. At PrepCom III, the chairman of Working Group 3 proposed a consolidated draft based on States delegations' proposals.[17] Within this document, the first principle to appear is that of 'integration of environment and development'. It is a rather long principle with an unsurprisingly—as it consolidates various delegations' proposals—wordy content. It essentially provides that States 'shall address environmental issues in the process of development by integrating environmental concerns with the imperatives of economic growth and development'.[18] Mention is also made of the establishment of a global partnership for environmental protection and sustainable development through the implementation of the principles. Recognition of the right to development is then proposed within the same principle but in a subsequent paragraph, whereas another option stresses the need to integrate environmental considerations within planning and policy making as well as the need to stabilize the world's population.

This very dense consolidated draft however did not serve as a basis for negotiation for Working Group 3's work on agenda item 3 during PrepCom IV, where most of the drafting of the Declaration took place. Instead, in the G77 and China's 'Rio de Janeiro Charter/Declaration on Environment and Development' proposal, the principle of integration was relegated from the first to the fourth position and became the following:

> States and international organizations shall address environmental issues in the process of development by integrating environmental concerns with the imperatives of economic growth and development.[19]

While the environment is seen as an issue or a concern, economic growth and development are viewed as imperatives. Such phrasing emphasizes the primacy given to economic development over environmental protection, which also, it seems, needs to be dealt with within the overarching aim of development.

Following criticism and in an effort by the developing countries to found their proposal as the basis for negotiation, the G77 soon proposed a revised version of its Principle 4 which lost its title in the process and now read: 'Environmental protection shall be viewed as an integral part of the development process and cannot be considered in isolation from it'.[20] Although very close to the final text's wording, it was still met with a number of counterproposals.

At the same meeting, on 5 March 1992, the United States proposed that the reference to integration be stated in the first principle which should read:

[17] Principles on General Rights and Obligations, Chairman's Consolidated Draft, A/CONF.151/PC/WG.III/L.8/Rev.1.

[18] Principles on General Rights and Obligations, Chairman's Consolidated Draft, 3.

[19] See Report of the Preparatory Committee for the United Nations Conference on Environment and Development on the Work of its Fourth session, A/CONF.151/PC/128, 83.

[20] Report of the Preparatory Committee for the United Nations Conference on Environment and Development on the Work of its Fourth session, 88.

Environmental protection and economic and social development ultimately cannot be achieved at the expense of each other. Environment and development goals should be pursued simultaneously, in an integrated fashion.[21]

As opposed to the G77's proposal, such phrasing clearly places environment and development on an equal footing. Japan also introduced a proposal devoting its first principle to the issue of integration but added a reference to sustainable development and to the need to adopt a long-term perspective.[22] To the contrary, in Canada's tabled proposal for an 'Earth Charter' the reference to integration disappears altogether.[23] Australia for its part preferred to view integration as a goal rather than a principle and accordingly located its reference to integration in the preamble to the document.[24] Lastly, in the EU's proposal, the reference to integration would be located in a second principle entitled 'sustainable development'. This read:

In order to ensure sustainable development in all countries, environmental considerations shall be integrated into the formulation of policies and into decision-making processes at local, national and international levels.

This variety of phrasing reflects the disagreements pervading the negotiations of the Rio Declaration altogether, although disagreements on the issue of integration were less intense than as regards other principles such as, for example, the right to development. In fact, because of the industrialized world's reluctance towards that principle, attempts were made to combine it with the principle of integration, but such attempts were firmly rejected by the G77 and China.[25] Eventually, an informal contact group had been formed to try and overcome the opposition between developed and developing countries and this group agreed to work on the basis of the G77 and China's proposal.[26] Although a reference to sustainable development was later added, it is this phrasing that the formal contact group later established to solve the remaining divergences finally adopted. This contact group managed to put together a final text including the current version of Principle 4 adopted without change at the Conference itself.

## 2. Scope and dimensions

### *2.1. Conceptual nature*

Beyond any question relating to their formally binding character,[27] it is not enough to conclude that because the Rio Declaration is made up of 27 'principles', these 27 enactments do actually reflect legal 'principles' rather than goals, rules, or procedures.

A generally accepted distinction between principles and rules revolves around the degree of precision of the provision in question. If the wording of the provision is sufficiently specific to allow for immediate application with well-defined consequences, then

[21] Report of the Preparatory Committee, 92. Such phrasing and location was also adopted in the proposal of 11 March 1992 of Denmark, Iceland, Norway, and Sweden.

[22] See Report of the Preparatory Committee, 96.

[23] Report of the Preparatory Committee, 97–9.

[24] Report of the Preparatory Committee, 99.

[25] Del Lujan Flores, M., 'Algunas Reflexiones en torno a la Declaración de Rio sobre el Medio Ambiente y el Desarrollo', in *Le droit international dans un monde en mutation.* Liber Amicorum *en hommage au professeur Jiménez de Aréchaga* (Montevideo: Fundación de cultura universitaria 1994, vols I and II), 815, 828.

[26] While at the same time keeping other proposals on an equal footing. See Del Lujan Flores, 'Algunas Reflexiones en torno a la Declaración de Rio', 826.

[27] See section II) 2.4 of this chapter. (Legal nature).

it may be characterized as a rule. Often such rule may be a 'practical formulation'[28] of a more abstract and general 'principle'. Indeed, principles are characterized by their high level of abstraction and the generality of their formulation.[29] Legal principles may even be so abstractly formulated that they can be expressed as a concept, with no practical reference whatsoever to the circumstances in which they may be applied.[30]

As far as 'Principle' 4 is concerned, its wording might not be sufficiently specific to fall in the category of 'rules'. In fact, whereas the Tribunal in the *Iron Rhine Railway* arbitration accepted that there was a distinction in international law between rules and principles,[31] it then referred to Principle 4 as a 'principle'.[32] Principle 4 does reflect a relatively high degree of generality and abstraction which indeed suits the category of principles. It is however more than a goal or concept with no legal grounding. Australia's failure to have it included as a goal in the preamble rather than the text of the Declaration itself is testimony to the international community's consensus as to its 'principled' nature.

Another distinction that can be subject to debate with respect to the nature of Principle 4 is whether it reflects a process or an outcome. In other words, by integrating environmental considerations into the development process does the principle require States to achieve a specific environment-related result or outcome? That is, does the principle have an autonomous and substantive content? Or does it simply require States to take environmental considerations into account in the process of development decision-making (or vice versa), irrespective of the outcome achieved?

There is ample recognition of the procedural nature of Principle 4 in that the very action of integration of environmental and socio-economic considerations is primarily located within the process of decision-making.[33] It is also on the decision-making process that Chapter 8 of Agenda 21, the 'how to'[34] guide for the integration of environment and development, focuses. Agenda 21 thus indicates that States should:

> improve the processes of decision-making so as to achieve the progressive integration of economic, social and environmental issues in the pursuit of development that is economically efficient, socially equitable and responsible and environmentally sound.[35]

And according to Agenda 21 the principle of integration may well be limited to its procedural dimension, requiring a process to be put in place rather than an outcome to be achieved. This is so because in suggesting activities that States may pursue to achieve

[28] See Cheng, B., *General Principles of Law as Applied by International Courts and Tribunals* (Cambridge University Press 1953), 376, referring to the opinion of the umpire in the *Gentini* case (*Italy v. Venezuela*) 10 RIAA 551.

[29] See Dupuy, P.-M. and Kerbrat, Y., *Droit international public* (10th edn, Dalloz 2010), 376.

[30] Virally, M., 'Le rôle des "principes" dans le développement du droit international', in *Recueil d'études de droit international en hommage à Paul Guggenheim* (Institut universitaire des hautes études internationales/Faculté de Droit de l'Université de Genève 1968), 531, 534.

[31] *Award in the Arbitration regarding the Iron Rhine ('Ijzeren Rijn') Railway between the Kingdom of Belgium and the Kingdom of the Netherlands*, 27 RIAA (2005) 35, para 58.

[32] *Award in the Arbitration regarding the Iron Rhine ('Ijzeren Rijn') Railway*, para 59.

[33] See eg Boyle, A. and Freestone, D., 'Introduction', in Boyle, A. and Freestone, D. (eds), *International Law and Sustainable Development. Past Achievements and Future challenges* (Oxford University Press 1999), 1–18, 10–11, 17; Jodoin, S. 'The Principle of Integration and Interrelationship in Relation to Human Rights and Social, Economic and Environmental Objectives', Draft working paper, CISDL, *Recent Developments in International Law Related to Sustainable Development* Series, 9 and 20.

[34] Jodoin, 'The Principle of Integration and Interrelationship', 19.

[35] Report of the United Nations Conference on Environment and Development, A/CONF.151/26/Rev.1 (vol I), Agenda 21, 9–480 ('Agenda 21'), 96, para 8.4.

an integrated decision-making process it specifies that: 'Countries will develop their own priorities in accordance with their national plans, policies and programmes'.[36] In other words, States need to integrate environmental considerations in the development decision-making process but the outcome of this integration falls within the realm of State sovereignty.

There is an argument however that the principle of integration may require more than a process to be followed and actually impinge on the outcome to be achieved, thus vesting it with substantive content. This is apparent in both the meaning and the mode of application of the principle.[37]

## *2.2. Meaning*

A simple textual interpretation of Principle 4 generates a number of remarks as to its meaning. Principle 4, like most principles of the Rio Declaration, is laid out in mandatory language as it stipulates that 'environmental protection *shall* constitute an integral part of the development process.' It thus intends to lay down an obligation on its recipients, an obligation to integrate the environmental component within the development process. There is no priority granted to environmental protection over the development process or vice versa. Although, via their integration, environmental considerations may limit or impinge on the development process, it is also added that environmental protection cannot be considered in isolation from it. Environmental policies may thus not be developed at the expense of development needs. A fine balance is struck between environmental and developmental considerations. As Sands puts it:

> The principle might mean that development decisions which failed to take any, or adequate account of the environmental consequences could not contribute to sustainable development. Or it might mean that environmental decisions should not be used to limit developmental decisions which aim to address fundamental human needs, such as the provision of clean water or adequate housing.[38]

It is also clear that the concept of development referred to is a wide one embodying both the economic and social pillars, as confirmed by chapter 8 of Agenda 21.[39] Chapter 8 also confirms that it is primarily, though not only, at the decision-making level that integration should happen.[40]

One crucial question that remains however is that of the kind of actions that will be sufficient to qualify as adequate integration of environmental and development considerations for the purpose of Principle 4. Does Principle 4 merely require environmental protection to be 'taken into account' in the development decision-making process (or vice versa), or does it require more and imply a modification of the contents of the decisions made? As underlined earlier, if such considerations only need to be taken into account, without necessarily having an impact on the outcome, then Principle 4 would essentially lay down a procedural rather than a substantive obligation. And that could be so if the

[36] Agenda 21, para 8.4.

[37] See also Nollkaemper, A., 'Three Conceptions of the Integration Principle in International Environmental Law', in Lenschow, A. (ed) *Environmental Policy Integration: Greening Sectoral Policies in Europe* (Earthscan Publications 2002), 22, 29–31.

[38] Sands, P., 'International Law in the Field of Sustainable Development' (1994) 64 *BYIL* 303, 338.

[39] Agenda 21.

[40] On the various manners in which integration may happen, see section II) 2.3 in this chapter (Modus operandi).

principle simply read: 'Environmental protection shall constitute an integral part of the development process and cannot be considered in isolation from it'.

However the drafters have decided not to lay down this principle in the abstract without reference to the context in which it is to take place. If integration must happen, it is 'in order to achieve sustainable development' as specified by the first part of Principle 4. It is thus integration for a purpose, integration as an effort, a contribution, in the achievement of an objective, the objective of sustainable development. In that sense, rather than being sustainable development itself,[41] the principle of integration is an essential tool for its realization.[42] And this anchoring of integration within the broader matrix of sustainable development in Principle 4 can actually confer a substantive content to the obligation to integrate.

A purely formal process of integration whereby environmental considerations are simply 'taken into account' within the development decision-making process with no actual impact on the decision outcome may well fall short of being considered a sufficient effort in striving to achieve sustainable development.[43] Surely, if the principle of integration were to have solely a procedural content, the *status quo* may be forever perpetuated and progress towards sustainable development never be achieved. In fact, the principle could altogether be meaningless as States could formally 'take into account', say, environmental considerations, but then discard them as irrelevant or not sufficiently relevant to modify the development decision. States could thus continue with their business as usual, continue ignoring the intimate interdependence between socio-economic development and environmental protection, and frustrate the attainment of the objective of sustainable development.[44] By positing sustainable development as an objective to be achieved via the medium of integration, the drafters of the Rio Declaration have thus opted to confer a substantive content to the principle of integration and the process of integration may, as a result, require more than considerations being 'taken into account'; it may indeed require a modification of the outcome of decisions.

Beyond any reference to sustainable development, an interpretation of the principle of integration in the light of current environmental standards would lead to the same conclusion.[45] It is indeed unlikely that an 'integrative' decision-making process that allows for development decisions to remain unchallenged by environmental considerations would not conflict with accepted international standards regarding say acceptable noise levels or the protection of endangered species. Certainly the alternative may not be between the decision to build a new railway line or not (though in certain circumstances it could), but it may be between deciding to build a new railway line with no mitigating environmental measures and the decision to build a new railway line provided certain mitigating environmental measures are adopted. Yet, the integrative decision-making

[41] See Fitzmaurice, M., 'International Protection of the Environment' (2001) 293 *RCADI* 9, 52.

[42] See Barral, V., 'Sustainable Development in International Law: Nature and Operation of an Evolutive Legal Norm' (2012) 23 *EJIL* 377, 381. For Dupuy it is 'à la base du développement durable', see Dupuy, P.-M., 'Où en est le droit international de l'environnement à la fin du siècle?' (1997) 101 *RGDIP* 873, 891.

[43] Although the level of balancing required can still depend on the specific circumstances of each State.

[44] In the context of discarding the relevance of environmental considerations though formally they have been taken into account, environmental deterioration could go unabated. The reverse may also apply by rejecting the relevance of basic human needs in the making of environmental policies and thus hampering economic and social development.

[45] As permitted by art 31(3)(c) of the Vienna Convention on the Law of Treaties, 23 May 1969, 1155 UNTS 331 ('VCLT').

process would still have modified the decision outcome. Such conclusion is confirmed by the Arbitral Tribunal's interpretation of the meaning of the principle of integration in the *Iron Rhine Railway* case as it indicated, after citing Principle 4, that:

> Importantly, th[ese] emerging principle[s] now integrate environmental protection into the development process. Environmental law and the law on development stand not as alternatives but as mutually reinforcing, integral concepts, which require that where development may cause significant harm to the environment there is a duty to prevent, or at least mitigate, such harm.[46]

In other words, through the process of integration of environmental and development considerations, States are required at a minimum to mitigate environmental harm. This reading of integration by the Arbitral Tribunal does not seem to be in tension with Principle 4 of the Rio Declaration. After all, if its drafters had intended that environmental or development considerations be only 'taken into account' in the decision-making process, that is what they would have provided for rather than insisting on the need that they be 'integrated'.[47]

## 2.3. *Modus operandi*

### 2.3.1. Overview

There are different dimensions to the realization of the principle of integration. One such dimension is organizational in nature. To achieve better-integrated outcomes, adequately organized institutions are paramount, be it at the local, domestic, or international level. This means that specific institutions may need to be created, or existing institutions reorganized and restructured, for example via the 'appointment of personnel skilled in environmental and/or social policy in traditionally economic-growth focused organizations.'[48] It also means that institutions at different levels (vertical integration) or across sectors (horizontal integration) will need to cooperate to achieve the integration of the economic, social and environmental dimensions of development.

Reorganization and cooperation however is only a small aspect of what the principle of integration involves. Another key dimension of the principle is substantive integration as opposed to institutional (ie organizational) integration, substantive integration at the decision-making level, at the norm-creation level, and at the norm application/interpretation level. These will be the focus of this section.

### 2.3.2. Integrative decision-making

One essential way in which integration of economic, environmental, and social factors can happen is through the decision-making process. As pointed out by the ILA and evidenced by the focus of Agenda 21, chapter 8,[49] it is probably 'what Principle 4 of the Rio Declaration had principally in mind'.[50]

Concretely this means for example that before the decision to build a dam is made, or before approving the operation of pulp mills on the banks of a river, the institutions involved in that decision will have to carefully balance all relevant, economic, social, and

[46] *Iron Rhine ('Ijzeren Rijn') Railway*, para 59.

[47] Note that according to the *Concise Oxford English Dictionary* (11th edn, Oxford University Press 2006), the verb to integrate is defined as: 'combine or be combined to form a whole', which suggests a merging of elements to create a unique result, hence a specific outcome.

[48] ILA, Toronto Conference (2006), International Law on Sustainable Development ('ILA 2006'), 12.

[49] Entitled 'integrating environment and development in decision-making'.

[50] ILA 2006, 8.

environmental factors at stake. Environmental and social impact assessments will need to be carried out. Additionally, the decision-making institution(s) will need to cooperate with other institutions with specific competences or attributions relating to such factors; adequate information should be disseminated to the public; and those potentially affected by the decision should be given an opportunity to participate in the decision-making process.[51] This is because not only must all relevant factors be considered but also because all relevant actors must be involved.[52]

Integrative decision-making ensuring a balancing of environmental, economic, and social factors and adequate involvement of concerned actors may take place at the project-specific level, as well as at the level of policy-making or even broader levels such as the setting-up of long term national or international programmes.[53] Irrespective of the level at which it happens however, the actual weighing of the different factors will depend upon the circumstances of each case and the socio-economic and cultural specificities of each State.

Undoubtedly in this respect States retain a significant level of sovereignty in determining their development priorities.[54] Sustainable development, which, as emphasized by Principle 4, integration aims to achieve, is also evolutive in nature and what it requires may vary in time, space and content. These considerations necessarily add some uncertainty as to what the outcome of an integrated decision-making process will be. This level of uncertainty is slowly narrowing though as States are increasingly constrained by internationally accepted environmental and social standards and as the requirements of sustainable development become more specific.

### 2.3.3. Normative integration 1: norm-creation

The principle of integration implies that in areas that impinge on the achievement of sustainable development, when new norms are created, they should reflect an adequate weighing of economic, social, and environmental factors, whether at the national or international level.

At the international level this may take place when new treaties are negotiated (or potentially when new customary rules are developed). Integration can also take place through the renegotiation of pre-existing regimes whether via amendment or other means of renegotiation.[55] The scope of existing treaty systems can thus be broadened to incorporate previously neglected dimensions such as environmental or social factors.

Trade-related treaties incorporating an environmental chapter within their provisions are examples of integration at work.[56] So is the inclusion of environmental considerations within energy law, investment law, or the law of commodities. Conversely, primarily environmental regimes may widen their scope by incorporating economic concerns, such as for example the efforts made by the COP within the Ramsar Convention on wetlands' regime.[57]

[51] In line with the principle of public participation in the decision-making process.

[52] See ILA 2006, 9.

[53] Such as the Millennium Development Goals or Agenda 21. For an account of the specific tools available to achieve integration at each level see ILA 2006, 10–12.

[54] As confirmed by Principle 2 of the Rio Declaration.

[55] Such as decisions of the Conference of the Parties ('COP').

[56] See eg U.S.-Morocco Free Trade Agreement 15 June 2004, (2005) 44 ILM 544.

[57] On the incorporation of sustainable development concerns within the Montreal Protocol, Basel Convention and Ramsar Convention, see Barral, V., *Le développement durable en droit international: Essai sur les incidences juridiques d'une norme évolutive* (Bruylant: Bruxelles, forthcoming).

According to the ILA however, progress in environmental regimes with integration of economic and social factors remains rather slow.[58] Nonetheless, the increasing inclusion of extraneous considerations (ie environmental and social) within traditionally closed regimes such as the WTO system or other free trade agreements are testament to the substantive effect of the principle of integration.

### 2.3.4. Normative integration 2: norm-application and interpretation

Because of its transversal nature, the principle of integration may also be used as an instrument to facilitate inter-normative relations across legal regimes.[59] Integration of environmental and social considerations into a rule with a strong economic focus for example can thus happen through the application and interpretation of that norm (rather than via the creation of a wholly new norm). As far as interpretation is concerned, such integration could be the result of an authentic interpretation of the parties.[60] It could also be the result of a judicial pronouncement.

The principle of integration, as a means to achieve sustainable development, can indeed be a useful tool in the hands of judges to resolve a conflict of norms or to found a balancing exercise between considerations that are in tension. This is in fact how the principle was used by the arbitral Tribunal in the *Iron Rhine Railway* case. Whereas Belgium was relying mainly on a Treaty-based right to reactivate an old railway line passing through the Netherlands, the Netherlands argued that such reactivation was to be subject to a range of environmental protection measures to be borne financially by Belgium. By relying on the principle of integration, the Tribunal argued that Belgium's economic interests and the Netherlands' environmental concerns had to be reconciled.[61] It also concluded that each parties' interests were legitimate, and that meant that Belgium had a right to reactivate the railway line, but that appropriate mitigating environmental measures also had to be adopted. This led it to conclude that in view of the legitimacy of each party's interests and the need to reconcile them, the associated financial costs of the environmental measures had to be carefully balanced between the parties.[62]

On other occasions, judges have invoked the objective of sustainable development rather than the principle of integration to justify a balancing exercise or the need to reconcile economic and environmental considerations.[63] In these circumstances, even if no reference is made to the principle as such, it is via their integration that economic and environmental considerations are to be reconciled or balanced, (whether the judges engage with the balancing themselves[64] or enjoin the parties to do so[65]) as integration is the mechanism 'par excellence' to achieve sustainable development.[66]

[58] It notes that 'whilst non-environmental treaties have begun to be modified to take greater account of conservation and environmental protection concerns, the same has not necessarily been true of nature conservation treaties', ILA 2006, 18.

[59] See Rodrigo Hernández, A., 'El Principio de Integración de los Aspectos Económicos, Sociales y Medioambientales del Desarrollo Sostenible' (2012) 64 *REDI* 133, 138.

[60] Under art 31(3)(a) or 31(3)(b) of the VCLT. Arguably, decisions, recommendations, and resolutions of COPs or MOPs widening the scope of the treaty basis could fall under that banner, see Barral, *Le développement durable en droit international.*

[61] *Iron-Rhine*, para 221. [62] *Iron-Rhine*, para 220.

[63] See *Gabčíkovo-Nagymaros Project (Hungary/Slovakia)*, Judgment, ICJ Reports 1997, 7, paras 140–1; *Pulp Mills on the River Uruguay (Argentina v. Uruguay)*, Judgment, ICJ Reports 2010, 14, para 177.

[64] As they did in *Iron Rhine.* [65] As they did in *Gabčíkovo-Nagymaros Project.*

[66] See section III) of this chapter.

## *2.4. Legal nature*

Beyond the existence of treaty-based obligations of integration, there is some authority for the proposition that the principle of integration also reflects customary or general international law.

It is well accepted that the fact that Principle 4 is inserted in a formally non-binding legal instrument is not an obstacle to the recognition of the customary nature of the principle it embodies. So long as 'evidence of a general practice accepted as law'[67] relating to the principle is ascertained, that is, that both *opinio juris* and consistent practice can be proven, then it will meet the criteria of customary norms.

As far as the subjective element is concerned, the Rio Declaration itself can be viewed as evidence of an emerging *opinio juris* of the international community in respect of Principle 4. This is because it has been adopted by consensus, without any State objection; because it is laid down in mandatory language, thus confirming its norm-creating capacity; and because mechanisms have been put in place to monitor the implementation of its provisions.[68] Aside from the Rio Declaration, the principle of integration has also been repeated many times in a vast number of international legal instruments whether treaties or soft-law instruments,[69] all reflecting the consolidation of the required *opinio juris*.

Regarding the objective or material element, the existence of a consistent practice of States relating to the principle of integration is somewhat more difficult to ascertain. Proving the existence of a practice as such is unproblematic. At the domestic level many States have adopted national sustainable development strategies or other tools endeavouring to integrate economic, social, and environmental considerations. Some have created specific institutions to this effect. The generalization of the use of environmental impact assessments and public participation in the decision-making process are also concrete examples of an integrative decision-making process. Instances of integration at work are also notable at the international level, for example at the World Bank where environmental considerations have been widely incorporated in the Bank's lending practices. The negotiation or renegotiation of international instruments including previously-ignored considerations, be they environmental, social, or economic, are also evidence of practice relating to the principle of integration. However, the wide divergence in the situations in which such action takes place means that it is more difficult to prove that they reflect an effective practice, that is, a practice that is uniform and coherent.

Because of the difficulties that come with proving the existence of a custom, the international community relies heavily on judicial pronouncements in this regard. In fact, a judicial affirmation of the existence of a customary rule will often be considered as the most authoritative evidence of the existence of norms of general international law.[70]

With respect to the principle of integration, the findings in the *Iron Rhine Railway* case are particularly noteworthy. According to the Tribunal, 'both international and EC law require the integration of appropriate environmental measures in the design and implementation of economic development activities'.[71] This statement stands for the proposition

[67] Article 38(1)(b) of the Statute of the ICJ, 24 October 1945, 33 UNTS 993.

[68] Such as Agenda 21 and the Commission on Sustainable Development.

[69] See section II) 3 (Normative impact) of this chapter.

[70] See Jennings, R., 'What is international law and how do we tell when we see it?' (1981) 37 *Annuaire suisse de droit international* 59, 74.

[71] *Iron-Rhine*, para 59.

that the principle of integration is vested with binding nature in international law. The Tribunal further specified that:

> Environmental law and the law on development stand not as alternatives but as mutually reinforcing, integral concepts, which require that where development may cause significant harm to the environment there is a duty to prevent, or at least mitigate, such harm [and that] [t]his duty, in the opinion of the Tribunal, has now become a principle of general international law.[72]

Although it may seem that the Tribunal is here referring to the duty of prevention, a closer look would suggest a different interpretation. At the time of the Award the customary nature of the duty of prevention had indeed already been ascertained by the ICJ in the *Legality of the Threat or Use of Nuclear Weapons* advisory opinion of 1996,[73] as acknowledged by the Tribunal itself.[74] It thus appears unlikely that the Tribunal would choose to use language indicating judicial innovation[75] to refer to the customary status of an already well-established principle of general international law. Rather, the language used suggests that it is in fact to the principle of integration that the Tribunal is referring. Thus, it is the principle of integration that has now, in the eyes of the Tribunal, become a principle of general international law.

## 3. Normative impact

### 3.1. Overview

The principle of integration has deeply influenced the content of treaties, as demonstrated by the substantial number of international conventions that have either incorporated environmental considerations or expressly adopted an integrated approach to govern the areas/resources they aim to regulate. Beyond this impact on international instruments, the principle of integration has also started to exert its influence on international jurisprudence, as will be discussed in section II) 4 in this chapter.

### 3.2. Environmental clauses in non-environmental treaty contexts

Certain instruments have given effect to the principle of integration by incorporating traditionally extraneous considerations within their text or treaty system.

This is the case where, for example, classic economic-growth oriented treaties, such as free trade agreements, have been negotiated or renegotiated to include an environmental chapter. Similarly, bilateral investment treaties and investment chapters in free trade agreements increasingly refer to environmental considerations in their text.[76] Another example concerns international humanitarian law instruments, which, in some cases, expressly refer to the protection of the natural environment.[77] Still another illustration is, arguably, the reference to environmental protection in some human rights treaties, particularly those concluded after the Stockholm Conference.[78] Although in the two latter

[72] *Iron-Rhine*, para 59.

[73] *Legality of the Threat or Use of Nuclear Weapons, Advisory Opinion*, ICJ Reports 1996, 226, para 29.

[74] *Iron-Rhine*, para 222.

[75] As suggested by the use of the expression 'in the opinion of the Tribunal'.

[76] See Viñuales, J. E., *Foreign Investment and the Environment in International Law* (Cambridge University Press 2012), ch 1.

[77] Protocol Additional to the Geneva Conventions of 12 August 1949, and Relating to the Protection of Victims of International Armed Conflicts, 6 August 1977, 1125 UNTS 3, art 35(1).

[78] African Charter on Human and Peoples' Rights, 27 June 1981, 21 ILM 58 (1982), art 24; Additional Protocol to the American Convention on Human Rights in the Area of Economic, Social and Cultural

examples the principle of integration was implemented *avant la lettre*, they are nevertheless noteworthy because they show the wide span of integration as a concept.

Even in those cases where the treaty body does not explicitly refer to environmental protection, some treaty regimes have expanded to include such previously extraneous considerations through 'secondary' decision-making or legislation.[79]

In all of these examples, the principle of integration is not referred to as such, but it is, in fact, directly implemented by the very fact that environmental considerations are specifically taken into account. Exceptionally, the principle of integration may be expressly stated in this type of treaty. An example is the preamble of the Convention on the Rights of Persons with Disabilities.[80]

### 3.3. *Integration in multilateral environmental agreements*

The principle of integration has been expressly incorporated into the body of numerous multilateral environmental agreements.

Not surprisingly it is included in the 'Rio treaties'. The United Nations Framework Convention on Climate Change[81] thus states in its article 3(4) that:

> Policies and measures to protect the climate system against human-induced change should be...integrated with national development programmes, taking into account that economic development is essential for adopting measures to address climate change.

Similarly, under the Convention on Biological Diversity, parties are required, according to their capacities, to: '[i]ntegrate, as far as possible and as appropriate, the conservation and sustainable use of biological diversity into relevant sectoral or cross-sectoral plans, programmes and policies'[82] and '[i]ntegrate consideration of the conservation and sustainable use of biological resources into national decision-making'.[83] Integration is also a central feature of the Convention to Combat Desertification. It is through an integrated approach 'addressing the physical, biological and socio-economic aspects of the processes of desertification and drought' that the objective to combat desertification is to be achieved.[84]

As 'sustainable development' treaties negotiated over the same period as the Rio Declaration, the inclusion of integration in the text of these conventions will not come as a surprise.

### 3.4. *Integration in mixed regimes*

The principle of integration also finds its way into a number of treaties aimed at governing areas where both socio-economic as well as environmental considerations naturally arise, such as the management of international watercourses, lakes, regional seas, or mountain areas. Because they will necessarily involve a balancing between the economic uses of

Rights, 16 November 1988, OAS Treaty Series No. 69, art 11(1); ASEAN Human Rights Declaration, 19 November 2012, available at: <http://www.asean.org> (accessed on 3 February 2014), art 28(f).

[79] See eg the legislative activity of the EU that has over the years expanded its legal regime to social and environmental considerations. On these points, see section II) 2 of this chapter (Scope and dimensions).

[80] Convention on the Rights of Persons with Disabilities, 13 December 2006, 2515 UNTS 3, Preamble, recital (g).

[81] United Nations Framework Convention on Climate Change, 9 May 1992, 1771 UNTS 107.

[82] Convention on Biological Diversity, 5 June 1992, 1760 UNTS 79, art 6(b).

[83] Convention on Biological Diversity, art 10(a).

[84] United Nations Convention to Combat Desertification in those Countries Experiencing Serious Drought and/or Desertification, Particularly in Africa, 17 June 1994, 33 ILM 1328, art 4 (2)(a) (general obligations). See also art 2(1) and 2(2).

these areas and the preservation of their often fragile ecosystem, they are typical examples of why an integrated approach to the management of these resources and ecosystems needs to be adopted in order to achieve sustainable development.

Integration is thus key to the Protocol on the Integrated Coastal Zone Management in the Mediterranean,[85] which is no less than the principle of integration made operational at the ecosystem management level. Not only does the Protocol dwell upon the necessary elements to an integrated management approach (Part II), but it also defines the necessary instruments for its achievement (Part III), which include environmental assessments and economic and financial instruments.[86] An integrated approach is also prominent in the Escaut and Meuse Protection Agreements,[87] the Southern African Development Community ('SADC') Protocol on Shared Watercourses,[88] the Convention on the Sustainable Management of Lake Tanganyika,[89] the Framework Agreement on the Sava River Basin,[90] the Carpathian Convention,[91] the Mountain Farming Protocol to the Alpine Convention,[92] and the Spatial Planning and Sustainable Development Protocol to the Alpine Convention.[93]

### 3.5. *Integration in natural resource treaties*

Beyond sustainable development treaties or treaties that specifically call for an integrated approach, the principle of integration also appears in treaties regulating the use of natural resources.

Examples include the International Tropical Timber Agreement,[94] and the International Treaty on Plant Genetic Resources;[95] in nature protection conventions such as the SADC Protocol on Wildlife or the European Landscape Convention;[96] pollution prevention treaties such as the Stockholm Convention on Persistent Organic Pollutants and the Aruba Protocol Concerning Pollution from Land-Based Sources and Activities;[97]or procedural treaties such as the Kiev Protocol on Strategic Impact Assessment to the Espoo Convention.[98] Instruments at the junction between environmental and Human Rights protection have also made reference to the principle of integration. This is for example the case of the Aarhus Convention and its Kiev Protocol

[85] 21 January 2008, (2009) OJ 434/19.

[86] Protocol on the Integrated Coastal Zone Management in the Mediterranean, arts 19 and 21.

[87] 3 December 2002, (2005) 116 JORF 8731, art 2; and 3 December 2002, (2005) 116 JORF 8731, art 2 respectively.

[88] 7 August 2000, 40 ILM 321, art 2(c).

[89] 12 June 2003, FAOLEX (FAO legal database online), arts 2(1) and 13.

[90] 3 December 2002, FAOLEX (FAO legal database online), arts 11 and 12.

[91] Framework Convention on the Protection and the Sustainable Development of the Carpathians, 22 May 2003, available at: <http://www.carpathianconvention.org/tl_files/carpathiancon/Downloads/01%20The%20Convention/1.1.1.1_CarpathianConvention.pdf> (accessed on 12 May 2014), arts 2(e), 3, and 4(4).

[92] 20 December 1994, (2006) OJEU L271/63, art 13.

[93] 20 December 1994, (2006) 32 JORF 1960, art 10. The principle also appears in the preamble of the Protocol for the Sustainable Development of the Lake Victoria Basin.

[94] 27 January 2006, 2801 UNTS Doc TD/TIMBER.3/12, art 24(1).

[95] 3 November 2001, 2400 UNTS 303, art 5.

[96] 14 August 1999 available at: <http://www.sadc.int/documents-publications/show/Protocol%20on%20Wildlife%20Conservation%20and%20Law%20Enforcement%20%281999%29> (accessed on 12 May 2014), arts 7(1) and 20 October 2000, CETS 176, art 5(d) respectively.

[97] 22 May 2001, 2256 UNTS 119, art 7(3) and 6 October 1999, available at: <http://www.cep.unep.org/cartagena-convention/lbs-protocol/lbs-protocol-english> (accessed on 12 May 2014) III(2) respectively.

[98] 21 May 2003, Doc ECE/MP.EIA/2003/2, Preamble.

on Pollutant Release and Transfer Registers;[99] as well as of the Protocol on Water and Health to the Helsinki Convention.[100]

### 3.6. *Integration in European law*

Another noteworthy treaty system to have widely incorporated the principle of integration is the EU legal order.

Beyond its trickle down effect in secondary legislation, the principle appears at article 11 of the TFEU which states that:

> Environmental protection requirements must be integrated into the definition and implementation of the Union policies and activities, in particular with a view to promoting sustainable development.[101]

It is also stated in article 37 of the Charter of Fundamental Rights, according to which:

> A high level of environmental protection and the improvement of the quality of the environment must be integrated into the policies of the Union and ensured in accordance with the principle of sustainable development.[102]

Integration also features throughout the EU-ACP Cotonou Partnership Agreement, which equally incorporates economic, social, and environmental considerations.[103]

## 4. Jurisprudential relevance

### 4.1. *Overview*

As for Treaties, international courts and tribunals have on occasions, though still rather rarely, expressly referred to the principle of integration and used it in their reasoning process to come to a specific conclusion. However, even where judicial bodies do not use the language of integration in their findings, such findings may still, in practice, be an application of integration.

### 4.2. *The jurisprudence of the ICJ*

The ICJ itself has given effect to some extent to the principle of integration on two occasions.

In the *Gabčíkovo-Nagymaros Project* case, the Court recognized the need to reconcile economic development with the protection of the environment. Specifically, it considered that new environmental norms and standards have to be given proper weight when States: 'contemplate new activities [and] [...] when continuing with activities begun in the past'; and concludes that this means that 'the Parties should look afresh at the effects on the environment of the operation of the Gabcikovo power plant...'[104] Thus, the Court did nothing less than enjoin the parties to give effect to the principle of integration by negotiating an agreed solution incorporating such considerations into the

[99] Convention on Access to Information, Public Participation in Decision-Making and Access to Justice in Environmental Matters, 25 June 1998, 2161 UNTS 447 and 21 May 2003, Doc MP.PP/2003/1, Preamble in both cases.

[100] 17 June 1999, 2331 UNTS 202, arts 4(1), 5(j) and 6(2).

[101] 1 December 2009, (2012) OJEU C 326/47, art 11.

[102] 7 December 2000, (2000) OJEC C 364/1, art 37.

[103] 4 November 2010, OJEU L 287.

[104] *Gabčíkovo-Nagymaros Project*, para 140.

original treaty. In fact the Court does actually go so far as using the language of integration and adds that:

> It is for the Parties themselves to find an agreed solution that takes account of the objectives of the Treaty, which must be pursued in a joint and *integrated* way, as well as [of] the norms of international environmental law…[105]

In the *Pulp Mills* case[106] again, by recalling its findings on the need to reconcile economic development and environmental protection in the *Gabčíkovo-Nagymaros Project* case[107] and requesting the Parties to cooperate in order to 'jointly manage the risks of damage to the environment',[108] it in effect asks the parties to apply the principle of integration.

Although the recent *Whaling in the Antarctic* decision[109] does not mention either the principle of integration or sustainable development, it confirms that the conservation of whales, together with their sustainable exploitation, forms part and parcel of the object and purpose of the International Convention for the Regulation of Whaling ('ICRW').[110] This reading of the object and purpose thus endorses the evolution of the ICRW from a treaty regime originally intended for the development of the whaling industry to one that now integrates nature protection and conservation considerations.

### *4.3. The Iron-Rhine Arbitration*

The clearest and boldest application of the principle of integration however is attributable to the Permanent Court of Arbitration in the *Iron Rhine Railway* case. The Tribunal indeed not only affirms that 'international and EC law require the integration of appropriate environmental measures in the design and implementation of economic development activities'[111] but it then immediately adds that Principle 4 of the Rio Declaration reflects this trend. It then goes on to clarify the specific implications of the principle by adding that:

> these emerging principles now integrate environmental protection into the development process. Environmental law and the law on development stand not as alternatives but as mutually reinforcing, integral concepts, which require that where development may cause significant harm to the environment there is a duty to prevent, or at least mitigate, such harm.[112]

Importantly, it is later on the basis of this requirement that the solution to the dispute is founded. In a pure application of the principle of integration and of the requirement of sustainable development, the Tribunal finds both Belgium's economic interests and the Netherlands' environmental preoccupations to be legitimate and in need of reconciliation, thus necessitating a careful balancing.[113] However this time, the balancing is carried out by the Tribunal itself, rather than by the parties as was the case in the *Gabčíkovo-Nagymaros Project* decision. And in fact the Tribunal concludes that even though Belgium has the right to reactivate the Iron Rhine, such reactivation may well necessitate environmental protection measures since:

[105] *Gabčíkovo-Nagymaros Project*, para 141 (emphasis added).
[106] *Pulp Mills on the River Uruguay.*
[107] *Gabčíkovo-Nagymaros Project*, para 76.
[108] *Pulp Mills*, para 77.
[109] *Whaling in the Antarctic (Australia v. Japan: New Zealand intervening)*, Judgment, ICJ, 31 March 2014, not yet reported, available at <http://www.icj-cij.org/docket/files/148/18136.pdf> (accessed on 12 May 2014).
[110] International Convention on the Regulation of Whaling, 2 December 1946, 161 UNTS 72. See in particular *Whaling in the Antarctic* case, para 56.
[111] *Iron-Rhine*, para 59. [112] *Iron-Rhine*, para 59. [113] *Iron-Rhine*, para 220–1.

The reactivation of the Iron Rhine railway cannot be viewed in isolation from the environmental protection measures necessitated by the intended use of the railway line. These measures are to be fully integrated into the project and its costs.[114]

Not only does the tribunal, on this basis, integrate the required Dutch environmental measures into the project, but it also further allocates the financial burdens of such measures by balancing out each Party's legitimate interests and benefits from the railway, thus reintegrating economic interests in the apportionment of costs.[115]

### *4.4. The jurisprudence of the WTO Dispute Settlement Body*

Express references to the principle of integration can also be found in the WTO's Appellate Body ruling on the *Shrimp-Turtle* case when the Appellate Body refers to the concept of sustainable development and the Ministerial Decision on Trade and Environment.[116]

More significantly, by incorporating a definition of natural resources based on modern environmental instruments into the WTO Agreement text, it does in practice integrate environmental considerations into a primarily economic treaty. This is all the more so as this evolutive interpretation is grounded in the acknowledgement of the objective of sustainable development in the Preamble to the WTO Agreement, which the Appellate Body defines as the integration of economic and social development and environmental protection.[117]

The objective of sustainable development, and the integration of the various considerations that it requires, also informed the interpretation of the notion of conservation in article XX(g) of the GATT in the *Raw Materials* case.[118] The acknowledgment of this objective in the Preamble to the WTO Agreement meant for the Panel that:

a proper reading of Article XX(g) in the context of the GATT 1994 should take into account the challenge of using and managing resources in a sustainable manner that ensures the protection and conservation of the environment while promoting economic development.[119]

This, in turn, required the making of policy choices and prioritization among different objectives (economic, social, environmental) which could not be viewed in isolation as they were 'related facets of an integrated whole'.[120] In the same dispute, the Appellate Body also noted that in view of the various objectives listed in the Preamble to the WTO Agreement (including the preservation of the environment and the objective of sustainable development), the WTO Agreement as a whole should be understood to reflect the balance struck between trade and non-trade related concerns.[121]

[114] *Iron-Rhine*, para 223. [115] *Iron-Rhine*, paras 224–34.

[116] See *United States—Import Prohibition of certain Shrimp and Shrimp Products*, WT/DS58/AB/R, 1998, at footnotes 107 and 147.

[117] *United States—Import Prohibition of certain Shrimp and Shrimp Products*, para 129.

[118] *China—Measures Related to the Exportation of Various Raw Materials*, Panel Report, WT/DS 394/12, 2011.

[119] *China—Measures Related to the Exportation of Various Raw Materials, Panel Report*, para 7.375.

[120] *China—Measures Related to the Exportation of Various Raw Materials, Panel Report*, para 7.376. The Panel also concluded that article 31(3)(c) of the Vienna Convention on the Law of Treaties meant that in interpreting article XX(g) of the GATT it had to take into account the principle of sovereignty over natural resources which 'affords Members the opportunity to use resources to promote their own development while regulating the use of these resources to ensure sustainable development' at para 7.381.

[121] *See China—Measures Related to the Exportation of Various Raw Materials*, Appellate Body Report, WT/DS 394/AB/R, 2012, at para 306.

The definition of the notion of conservation in the light of these considerations was then further elaborated in the *Rare Earth* case.[122] In this dispute, the Panel confirmed that the principles of sovereignty over natural resources and sustainable development embodied in Principles 2 and 4 of the Rio Declaration needed to be taken into account when interpreting article XX(g) and the notion of conservation.[123] According to the Panel, a definition of conservation in the light of these principles meant that conservation could not be read as being limited to the mere preservation of natural resources but also included the need to use them in a sustainable manner.[124] Interestingly, the Panel carefully added that the definition of conservation thus adopted:

> strikes an appropriate balance between trade liberalization, sovereignty over natural resources, and the right to sustainable development.[125]

It is, in other words, the product of an integrative judicial decision-making process.

## 4.5. *The jurisprudence of Investment Tribunals*

In contrast to trade-related disputes the principle of integration is at pains to find its way into the jurisprudence of arbitral tribunals adjudicating on investment related disputes. In fact, these are mostly silent about either integration or sustainable development. A notable exception is that of the *SD Myers v. Canada* case[126] where the Tribunal considered that the legal context of article 1102 (on national treatment) included the various provisions of the NAFTA, the NAAEC, and principles that are affirmed by the NAAEC, including those of the Rio Declaration, and notably the principle that 'environmental protection and economic development can and should be mutually supportive'.[127]

## 4.6. *The jurisprudence of the European Court of Justice*

The principle of integration also finds expression in European jurisprudence. As one of the treaty-based principles of EU law[128] it is not surprising that it has been applied and made operational by the European Court of Justice.

In its *Greece v. Council* case the Court first made clear that what is now article 11[129] meant that 'all Community measures must satisfy the requirements of environmental protection'[130] and that this obligation implied more than merely taking such requirements into consideration, since it added that this: 'implies that a Community measure cannot be part of Community action on environmental matters merely because it takes account of those requirements.'[131]

[122] *China—Measures Related to the Exportation of Rare Earths, Tungsten, and Molybdenum*, Panel Report, WT/DS 431/R, 2014.

[123] See *China—Measures Related to the Exportation of Rare Earths, Tungsten, and Molybdenum*, Panel Report, para 7.262.

[124] See *China—Measures Related to the Exportation of Rare Earths, Tungsten, and Molybdenum*, Panel Report, para 7.267.

[125] *China—Measures Related to the Exportation of Rare Earths, Tungsten, and Molybdenum*, Panel Report, para 7.277.

[126] *SD Myers, Inc. v. Canada*, UNCITRAL case, Partial Award, 13 November 2000, 121 ILR 173.

[127] See *SD Myers, Inc. v. Canada*, para 247.

[128] See TFEU, art 11.

[129] The Court was then referring to article 130 (r)(2), which read 'Environmental protection requirements shall be a component of the Community's other policies.'

[130] *Hellenic Republic v. Council of the European Communities*, Case C-62/88, 29 March 90, para 20.

[131] *Hellenic Republic v. Council of the European Communities*, para 20.

This reading of the principle of integration was soon confirmed in the *Titanium dioxide* case where the Court clarified that: 'That principle implies that a Community measure cannot be covered by Article 130s merely because it also pursues objectives of environmental protection.'[132] According to EU case law, the principle of integration thus seems to require more than environmental protection to be taken into account but that it be satisfied. In the words of one Advocate General, it may even be vested with direct effect.[133]

As far as its application is concerned, an example can be found in the *Concordia* case where it was used to allow the integration of environmental considerations in a public procurement directive that was silent on the matter.[134]

## *4.7. The jurisprudence of the European Court of Human Rights*

The idea of integration, if not the word as such, can also be found in European human rights case law. The requirement by the ECtHR that a fair balance be struck between individual rights and the State's general interest, could indeed, in cases involving individuals' environmental concerns,[135] reflect a variant of the principle of integration. In the *Hatton* case, the Court noted that:

> a governmental decision-making process concerning complex issues of environmental and economic policy... must necessarily involve appropriate investigations and studies in order to allow them to strike a fair balance between the various conflicting interests at stake.[136]

In such situations however the Court does not carry out the balancing itself, rather, as confirmed in *Fadeyeva*, it controls whether such balancing has taken place at the State level and whether in doing so the State has not exceeded its margin of appreciation.[137] Although there are clear practical connections between the fair balance requirement and the principle of integration, viewing this case law as an example of integration per se may be an overstretch. At the time of the recognition of the principle of integration in the Rio Declaration, the balancing of competing rights and interests had already long been an element of the ECtHR's jurisprudence.

[132] *Commission of the European Communities v. Council of the European Communities*, Case C-300/89, 11 June 91, para 22.

[133] Advocate General Cosmas, Opinion in Case C-321/95P *Greenpeace v. Council*, delivered on 23 September 97, para 62.

[134] See *Concordia Bus Finland Oy Ab v. Helsingin Kaupunki and HKL-Bussiliikenne*, Case C-513/99, 17 September 2002, para 57.

[135] Under art 8 generally.

[136] *Hatton v. UK*, Grand Chamber, ECtHR Application no. 36022/97, Judgment (8 July 2003), para 128.

[137] See *Fadeyeva v. Russia*, ECtHR Application no. 55723/00, Judgment (9 June 2005), para 128: 'it is not the Court's task to determine what exactly should have been done in the present situation to reduce pollution in a more efficient way. However, it is certainly within the Court's jurisdiction to assess whether the Government approached the problem with due diligence and gave consideration to all the competing interests', and at para 134: 'The Court concludes that, despite the wide margin of appreciation left to the respondent State, it has failed to strike a fair balance between the interests of the community and the applicant's effective enjoyment of her right to respect for her home and her private life'. See also *Hatton v. UK*, para 129: 'In these circumstances the Court does not find that, in substance, the authorities overstepped their margin of appreciation by failing to strike a fair balance between the right of the individuals affected by those regulations to respect for their private life and home and the conflicting interests of others and of the community as a whole'.

In practice however, the principle of integration and the fair balance requirement may well pursue the same objectives, that is, a reconciliation of economic and environmental considerations.[138]

## III) Relations with Other Principles

Certain key principles of the Rio Declaration are intimately connected to the integration principle in that they serve as integrative tools and their application thus forms part and parcel of any duty to integrate environmental protection and socio-economic development.

This is most notably the case for Principle 17 on environmental impact assessments. The conduct of an EIA of an economic development project is indeed central to an integrative decision-making process and has even been referred to as 'one of the most powerful integrative tools currently available to decision-makers'.[139]

Probably on an equal footing with Principle 17 is Principle 10 on participative decision-making. An integrative decision-making process clearly involves the adequate participation of all concerned actors and the collection and dissemination of all necessary information. Compliance with Principle 10 is thus also necessary to comply with Principle 4.

Beyond EIAs and participative decision-making, an integrative decision-making process may also involve compliance with Principle 16 establishing the polluter-pay principle; Principle 15 on the precautionary approach; or Principle 19 on notification and consultation with other States on activities that may have a significant adverse transboundary environmental effect.

The principle of integration finally entertains a special relationship with the objective of sustainable development. Although not technically one of the principles of the Rio Declaration, the Declaration can still overall be understood as being about sustainable development, and in particular Principle 4 is commonly seen as the core philosophy underlying the concept.[140] For some commentators:

> Principle 4 is the closest the Rio Declaration comes to a definition of 'sustainable development', generally succeeding at finding the balance between development and environment considerations. At its best, the principle reflects a more action-oriented approach toward defining sustainable development than many of the Declaration's other principles.[141]

Although it would be unduly restrictive to conclude that integration is neither more nor less than sustainable development, as it would make most of the other principles of the Declaration redundant, it is still the essential means by which sustainable development may be achieved. A useful way to describe the relationship between sustainable

[138] The fair balance requirement remains nevertheless much wider in scope than the principle of integration as its application is not limited to environmental cases but is meant to apply to all the qualified rights of the ECHR, beyond their potential environmental implications.

[139] See ILA (2006), 8 and ILA, Sofia Conference (2012) International Law on Sustainable Development, 34.

[140] See Maljean-Dubois, S. and Mehdi, R., 'Environnement et développement, Les Nations Unies à la recherche d'un nouveau paradigme', in Maljean-Dubois, S. and Mehdi, R. (eds), *Les Nations Unies et la protection de l'environnement: La promotion d'un développement durable* (Pedone 2000), 9, 24; Boyle and Freestone, *International Law and Sustainable Development*, 10–12; Fitzmaurice, 'International Protection of the Environment', 52; French, D., *International Law and Policy of Sustainable Development* (Manchester University Press 2005), 54; ILA 2006, 2.

[141] Kovar, J. D., 'United Nations Conference on Environment and Development (UNCED). A Short Guide to the Rio Declaration' (1993) 4 *Colorado Journal of International Environmental Law and Policy* 119, 127.

development and integration is to see sustainable development as the substantive objective to be achieved and integration as the technique for the realization of this objective. As such the assessment of whether adequate integration of socio-economic and environmental considerations took place provides a useful standard of measure of the efforts States make towards achieving sustainable development.

## IV) Assessment

Whether integration as embodied in Principle 4 of the Rio Declaration proves to be an effective technique in achieving sustainable development will ultimately depend on whether States, and relevant institutions at the domestic level, apply the principle properly. In most circumstances, integration should require a modification of the outcomes of decisions reflected by an inclusive decision-making process, rather than by merely taking all considerations into account.

The principle of integration also reflects a potentially powerful tool in the hands of judges, both at the domestic and international level, to review the outcome of decisions impinging on sustainable development. The effectiveness of the principle of integration as a standard of review however will depend on the extent to which judges are willing or able to make use of it. Despite a few applications of the principle of integration, it has yet to take off in international jurisprudence. Will courts and tribunals be willing to control the application of the principle of integration in terms of outcome rather than merely in terms of process? Should judges only review whether a balancing of different considerations took place or should they go further and review the adequacy of such balancing? In other words are judges to review whether all considerations have been given proper weight? Or should they go even further and carry out the balancing themselves, as they seem to have done in the *Iron Rhine Railway* arbitration?

There is little indication of any consistent approach in international case law so far. Inspiration could however be drawn from the standards followed by the ECtHR when reviewing the legitimacy of a State interference with a qualified right.[142] The crux of this standard of review is that of the proportionality of the interference in the light of the objective pursued. In such matters, although the Court does not purport to carry out the balancing itself, it does review and scrutinize closely the weight attributed to each relevant consideration by the State and not only whether they have been taken into account. It is also for the Court to determine whether, in each particular case, a fair balance has been struck or not.[143]

As far as the principle of integration is concerned, the greater the intensity of the review, the more effective the principle will be in achieving sustainable development. And arguably, the flexibility of the objective of sustainable development correlatively grants judges a wide margin of discretion in determining whether adequate efforts have been demonstrated or not. In that sense the principle of integration could indeed be a powerful tool in the hands of judges in reviewing whether a fair balance has been struck between competing interests, that is obviously, should judges be willing to make use of it.

[142] A human right that States may interfere with provided that this interference is in accordance with law, for a legitimate aim and necessary in a democratic society.

[143] See *Fadeyeva v. Russia* and *Hatton v. UK*, cited above in nn 136 and 137.

## V) Select Bibliography

Barral, V., *Le développement durable en droit international: Essai sur les incidences juridiques d'une norme évolutive* (Bruylant: Bruxelles, forthcoming).

Barral, V., 'Sustainable Development in International Law: Nature and Operation of an Evolutive Legal Norm' (2012) 23 *EJIL* 377.

Boyle, A. and Freestone, D., 'Introduction', in Boyle, A. and Freestone D. (eds.), *International Law and Sustainable Development. Past Achievements and Future challenges* (Oxford: Oxford University Press 1999).

Del Lujan Flores, M., 'Algunas Reflexiones en torno a la Declaración de Rio sobre el Medio Ambiente y el Desarrollo', in *Le droit international dans un monde en mutation.* Liber Amicorum *en hommage au professeur Jiménez de Aréchaga* (vols I–II, Montevideo: Fundación de cultura universitaria 1994), 815.

Dupuy, P.M., 'Où en est le droit international de l'environnement à la fin du siècle?' (1997) 101 *Revue générale de droit international public* 873.

Dupuy, P.M. and Kerbrat, Y., *Droit international public* (10th edn, Paris: Dalloz 2010).

Fitzmaurice, M., 'International Protection of the Environment' (2001) 293 *RCADI* 9.

French, D., *International Law and Policy of Sustainable Development* (Manchester: Manchester University Press 2005).

International Law Association, International Law on Sustainable Development, Toronto Conference (2006).

International Law Association, International Law on Sustainable Development, Sofia Conference (2012).

Jennings, R., 'What is international law and how do we tell when we see it?' (1981) 37 *Annuaire suisse de droit international* 59.

Jodoin, S., 'The Principle of Integration and Interrelationship in Relation to Human Rights and Social, Economic and Environmental Objectives', Draft working paper, CISDL, *Recent Developments in International Law Related to Sustainable Development* Series.

Kovar, J. D., 'United Nations Conference on Environment and Development (UNCED). A Short Guide to the Rio Declaration' (1993) 4 *Colorado Journal of International Environmental Law and Policy* 119.

Maljean-Dubois, S. and Mehdi, R., 'Environnement et développement, Les Nations Unies à la recherche d'un nouveau paradigme', in Maljean-Dubois, S. and Mehdi, R. (eds), *Les Nations Unies et la protection de l'environnement: La promotion d'un développement durable* (Paris: Pedone 2000), 9.

Nollkaemper, A., 'Three Conceptions of the Integration Principle in International Environmental Law', in Lenschow, A. (ed), *Environmental Policy Integration: Greening Sectoral Policies in Europe* (London: Earthscan Publications 2002), 22.

Rodrigo Hernández, A., 'El Principio de Integración de los Aspectos Económicos, Sociales y Medioambientales del Desarrollo Sostenible' (2012) 64 *Revista española de derecho internacional* 133.

Sands, P., 'International Law in the Field of Sustainable Development' (1994) 64 *BYIL* 303.

Viñuales, J. E., *Foreign Investment and the Environment in International Law* (Cambridge University Press 2012).

Virally, M., 'Le rôle des "principes" dans le développement du droit international', in *Recueil d'études de droit international en hommage à Paul Guggenheim* (Geneva: Institut universitaire des hautes études internationales/Faculté de Droit de l'Université de Genève 1968), 531.

# 9. Principle 5

## *Poverty Eradication*

Takhmina Karimova* and Christophe Golay**

**Principle 5**

All States and all people shall cooperate in the essential task of eradicating poverty as an indispensable requirement for sustainable development, in order to decrease the disparities in standards of living and better meet the needs of the majority of the people of the world.




* Human Rights Officer at the Office of the High Commissioner for Human Rights.

** Research Fellow and Coordinator of the Project on Economic, Social and Cultural Rights at the Geneva Academy of International Humanitarian Law and Human Rights, and Lecturer at the Geneva Centre for Education and Research in Humanitarian Action.

# I) Origins and Rationale of the Principle

## 1. Introduction

Principle 5 reflects, in essence, an intragenerational equity value of the Rio Declaration. It is one of the three cardinal points (together with Principles 3 and 7) around which the concern of the developing states revolved at United Nations Conference on Environment and Development (UNCED). This principle, albeit indirectly, is also expressed in other development-oriented elements of the Rio Declaration, for poverty eradication has always been approached as the prime purpose of development since internationalization of 'social' domain as the major international problem.[1]

Within the United Nations framework, the concept, formulated broadly as *improvement of standards of living*, constitutes one of the main constructs of the UN Charter. In the 1970s, the poverty agenda of development institutions was assumed under the basic needs approach, followed later by structural adjustment policies. However, the 1990s witnessed a renewed focus on poverty. The international declarations and texts invited the international community to assign a high priority to this goal. Since its rediscovery, the fight against poverty has become an established objective of the international community and a working principle of all development interventions.

## 2. Precedents of the Principle in the Stockholm Declaration

Poverty eradication figures in all the texts leading to the Rio Declaration. Formulations very similar to Principle 5 as it appears in the Rio Declaration are found in previous *environmental* instruments. Principles 1 and 8 of the Stockholm Declaration on the Human Environment, among others, are direct predecessors of Principle 5. The text of these principles reads:

Principle 1

Man has the fundamental right to freedom, equality and adequate conditions of life, in an environment of a quality that permits a life of dignity and well-being, and he bears a solemn responsibility to protect and improve the environment for present and future generations. In this respect, policies promoting or perpetuating apartheid, racial segregation, discrimination, colonial and other forms of oppression and foreign domination stand condemned and must be eliminated.

and

Principle 8

Economic and social development is essential for ensuring a favorable living and working environment for man and for creating conditions on earth that are necessary for the improvement of the quality of life.

[1] See in particular President Truman's Point Four in Rist, G., *The History of the Development: from Western Origins to Global Faith*, (Zedbooks 2002), 69. An official publication of the WB recounts: 'In the 1960s, the Bank focused on economic growth as the key to poverty reduction. During the 1970's attention shifted first to redistribution with growth and later to satisfaction of basic human needs. In the early 1980s policy-based adjustment lending overshadowed the Bank's poverty reduction objectives... In 1987 and 1988, the primacy of the Bank's poverty reduction objective was reemphasized in task force reports...' in *The World Bank, 1992*, 51–2.

The first sentence of Principle 1 Stockholm Declaration may be interpreted in several ways. Read restrictively, it restates 'pre-existing international human rights guarantees of liberty, equality and an adequate standard of living, but innovates in adding that the exercise of these rights depends upon environmental conditions, reflecting the perception that environmental degradation can impair the full enjoyment of human rights'.[2] These references to the human rights treaty text would be further omitted in formulation of the Rio Declaration. In effect, the Rio Declaration states simply 'Human beings are at the centre of concerns for sustainable development. They are entitled to a healthy and productive life in harmony with nature'.[3]

The relationship of poverty (as well as its tensions) with environment has been most prominently phrased in the Brundtland report in the following terms: '[s]ustainable development requires meeting the basic needs of all and extending to all the opportunity to fulfill their aspirations for a better life . . . a world in which poverty is endemic will always be prone to ecological and other catastrophes'.[4] Thus, defining poverty as environmentally unsustainable has led the objective of its eradication to become one of the pillars of the sustainable development agenda.

## II) The Principle as Enshrined in the Rio Declaration

### 1. Travaux préparatoires

#### *1.1. Poverty eradication as a condition for sustainable development*

The question of poverty eradication was a very important issue during the preparations for the United Nations Conference on Environment and Development ('UNCED') and at the conference itself. In deciding to convene the UNCED, the General Assembly specified that the Conference should address the issue of 'improvement of the living and working environment of the poor in urban slums and rural areas, through the eradication of poverty by inter alia, implementing integrated rural and urban development programmes, as well as taking other appropriate measures at all levels necessary to stem the degradation of the environment'.[5] In addition, General Assembly Resolution 44/228 also identified '. . . protection of human health conditions and improvement of quality of life' as an important environment-related problem. At its first session, the Preparatory Committee for the United Nations Conference on Environment and Development decided that these questions would be dealt with as cross-cutting issues.

The extensive documentation presented within UNCED reiterated the basic ideas on the relationship between environment and poverty as reflected in the Brundtland report. The preamble of Agenda 21 stated 'integration of environment and development concerns and greater attention to them will lead to the fulfilment of basic needs, improved living standards for all, better protected and managed ecosystems and a safer, more prosperous future. No nation can achieve this on its own; but together we can—in a global partnership for sustainable development'.[6]

2 Shelton, D., *Stockholm Declaration*, MPEPIL, available at <http://www.mpepil.com>.

3 Principle 1 of Rio Declaration on Environment and Development.

4 UN, 'Our Common Future: Report of the World Commission on Environment and Development', 1987, United Nations publication A/42/427.

5 UNGA Resolution 44/228.

6 Agenda 21, Preamble 1.1.

In effect, the poverty reduction focus and the principle of cooperation as a vehicle to realize this task is woven into the very fabric of the Rio Declaration and Agenda 21. Combating poverty is an issue closely interlinked to many areas of environmental concerns, such as food, water, quality of environment, and so on. Agenda 21 included social and economic dimension as a major area of action dealing explicitly with combating poverty in chapter 3, and further specifying poverty reduction-related operational guidance in many programme areas including changing of consumption patterns, demographic dynamics and sustainability, protecting and promoting human health conditions, and promoting sustainable human settlement development—all of which relate directly to economic and social rights.

Furthermore, as far as cooperation for poverty reduction was concerned it was stated that '[t]he linkage between environment and development will often reduce or remove the distinction between environment and development costs as environmental needs are seen as important in development terms. These needs must include the alleviation of poverty which is as important in environmental terms as it is in development and humanitarian terms'.[7]

### *1.2. Preparatory committees*

The theme of poverty reduction featured in all four sessions in Nairobi in August 1991 (PrepCom I), in Geneva in March 1991 (PrepCom II), in August (PrepCom III), and finally in March 1992, at the United Nations Headquarters in New York (PrepCom IV) [in cross sectoral issues, general rights and obligations, and Agenda 21]. The UNCED Secretariat drew upon several elements of relevance to Principle 5 in its proposal on elements for the General Rights and Obligations. In particular, in the context of basic duties it considered under element 5 (protection of individual rights to environment and development), article 12 of ICESCR on right to health and Principle 1 of the Stockholm Declaration,[8] and article 1 of the Declaration of the Right to Development, both of which were of much broader remit, including the right of individuals to 'adequate conditions of life'. Although these areas have a direct bearing upon the problem of poverty, the priority of poverty alleviation appeared separately under principles related to decision making.[9]

Within the PrepCom, various proposals were put before Working Group III on legal and institutional issues and more substantive elaboration of the various rationales and parameters of Principle 5 appear for the first time in the Chairman's Consolidated Draft.[10] The seeds of the ideas on poverty reduction-related proposals were made in the context of the preamble, but proposals were also made under Principle 3 [the right to development] which interestingly integrated several individual rights such as right to life, food, shelter,

[7] Cross-Sectoral Issues, Progress Report on Financial Resources Report of the Secretary-General of the Conference, A/CONF.151/PC/18, 31 January 1991, 5.

[8] eg 'Man has the fundamental right to freedom, equality and adequate conditions of life, in an environment of a quality that permits a life of dignity and well-being, and he bears a solemn responsibility to protect and improve the environment for present and future generations'.

[9] Note by the Secretariat on Annotated Check-List of Principles on General Rights and Obligations, UN Doc A/CONF.151/PC/78, 26 July 1991.

[10] Chairman's Consolidated Draft, Principles on General Rights and Obligations, A/CONF.151/PC/WG.III/L.8, 24 August 1991.

healthy environment,[11] the right to development,[12] and the rights of women and indigenous peoples.[13] Similarly, the need for States to cooperate and the legal obligation for that are enunciated in the preamble,[14] but more strongly, and in relation to the preservation of the environment under Principle 7,[15] and cooperation for creation of the necessary economic environment under Principle 9, which all have direct and indirect relation to poverty reduction.[16] However, more concrete proposals such as 'a united struggle against poverty' and cooperation 'in good faith and in a spirit of partnership in the effort to eradicate poverty' appeared under Principle 16.[17] These elements remained unaltered in the second Consolidated Draft.[18]

As Kovar notes, Principle 5 was 'another touchstone for the G77 and China during negotiations' after negotiations over Principle 3 on the right to development.[19] The concerns of the developing States gravitated mainly around their priority of fighting poverty and promoting economic development. Indeed, the G77 proposal for the draft Rio Declaration on Environment and Development expresses the overriding priority needs of developing countries by integrating the poverty focus in several principles, including the human-centred sustainable development that depended 'on the satisfaction of basic human needs' and that human beings should be guaranteed 'a healthy life, free from hunger, disease and poverty' as well as emphasizing the right to development.[20]

Substantive work on the Principle was carried out in the framework of PrepCom IV, where the WG III had many proposals before it,[21] including the proposal of China and Pakistan on behalf of G77[22] and the proposal by the US.[23] Both proposals included

[11] Chairman's Consolidated Draft, Principles on General Rights and Obligations, Australia, para 23; Burkina Faso/22, para 24 on right to health and food; and Peru, para 35. G77's proposal read as follows: 'The human person should be protected through guaranteeing him the right to development and freedom from hunger, disease and poverty, underlining that no environment can be safe if the human state is in misery'.

[12] Chairman's Consolidated Draft, Principles on General Rights and Obligations, G77, para 31; also New Zealand, para 22.

[13] Australia, para 23; Norway, para 34.

[14] Chairman's Consolidated Draft, Principles on General Rights and Obligations, Chile, preamble; and India, para 5.

[15] Chairman's Consolidated Draft, Principles on General Rights and Obligations, paras 66–76.

[16] Chairman's Consolidated Draft, paras 83–9.

[17] Chairman's Consolidated Draft, paras 142–3 [Principle 16] Tanzania and Colombia. In the second Chairman's Consolidated Draft [Suggested headings of draft principles] of PrepCom III, 'poverty' appears under Principle 16, while individual and group rights appear under Principle 3. See Chairman's Consolidated Draft on Suggested headings of draft principles, UN Doc A/CONF.151/PC/WG.III/L.8/Add.1, 26 August 1991.

[18] Chairman's Consolidated Draft, UN Doc A/CONF.151/PC/WG.III/L.8/Rev.1, 30 August 1991.

[19] Kovar, J. D., 'A Short Guide to the Rio Declaration' (1993) 4 *Colorado Journal of International Environmental Law and Policy* 119, 127.

[20] Principle 2, Proposal submitted by China and by Pakistan on behalf of the States Members of the United Nations that are members of the Group of 77, UN Doc A/CONF.151/PC/WG.III/L.20, 4 March 1992.

[21] See Earth Charter Proposal submitted by Canada, UN Doc A/CONF.151/PC/WG.III/L.23, 4 March 1992; Proposal submitted by Portugal on behalf of the States members of the European Community, UN Doc A/CONF.151/PC/WG.III/L.25, 6 March 1992; Proposal submitted by Australia, Structure and Outline of the Rio de Janeiro Declaration/Earth Charter and Comments on A/CONF.151/PC/WG.III/L.8/Rev.1, UN Doc A/CONF.151/PC/WG.III/L.24, 5 March 1992; and Proposal submitted by Denmark, Iceland, Norway and Sweden: Earth Charter. Elements for Consideration, UN Doc A/CONF.151/PC/WG.III/L.27, 9 March 1992.

[22] Proposal submitted by China and by Pakistan on behalf of the States Members of the United Nations that are members of the Group of 77, UN Doc A/CONF.151/PC/WG.III/L.20, 4 March 1992.

[23] Principles on General Rights and Obligations, Proposal submitted by the United States of America, UN Doc A/CONF.151/PC/WG.III/L.21, 4 March 1992. Other proposals included by Japan, contained

poverty eradiation as a principle, with a difference of emphasis by G77 on a formula with a distinctly legal flavour compared to the US wording that seemed to exclude any connotation of binding force.[24] The subsequent Chairman's draft proposed the formula that served as a basis of the Principle 5, which was a compromise between different proposals combining the mandatory form of cooperation expressed in 'shall' but retaining the eradication of poverty as an 'essential task'.[25] The draft Rio Declaration on Environment and Development proposed by the Chairman included Principle 5 in its current wording:

> All States and all people shall cooperate in the essential task of eradicating poverty as an indispensable requirement for sustainable development, in order to decrease the disparities in standards of living and better meet the needs of the majority of the people of the world.[26]

The text was soon passed without much discussion at the UNCED. In the final text of the Declaration, as adopted, references to poverty were omitted from the preamble: Principle 1 and Principle 6. And perhaps more significant still is the fact that all the important acknowledgements of the human rights perspective of poverty expressed by references to human well-being and the right of individuals to adequate conditions of life, including the rights to food, to shelter, and to health figuring in many of the proposals and earlier drafts of the Declaration withered away in the final text.

Notwithstanding, the focus on poverty reintroduces indirectly the human rights dimension of the Rio Declaration. This is particularly evident in the social and economic dimension of Agenda 21's programme areas, which tie the objective of poverty eradication to realization of certain components of the right to food, to health and healthy environment, to housing, to education, and to a livelihood. Thus, the *task* of poverty eradication, albeit lacking human rights perspective, remains the most explicit and structuring principle in the Declaration and cooperative framework for action by States to strive for a minimum essential for a dignified existence.

## 2. Scope and dimensions

### *2.1. Nature*

Although Principle 5 appears as a separate principle, the objective of eradication of poverty is already included in the very notion of sustainable development.[27] It is fair to say that poverty eradication is formulated more as a political postulate, a policy guideline (hence defined as 'a *task*') than as a principle of law linked with the development of environmental

in Rights and obligations: Proposal submitted by Japan, UN Doc A/CONF.151/PC/WG.III/L.22, 4 March 1992.

[24] G77 proposal of Principle 6 read as 'States, organizations and individuals shall cooperate in good faith and in a spirit of partnership in the effort to eradicate poverty' and the US proposed under Principle 16 the wording such as 'In addition to its corrosive effects on social and economic well-being and development, poverty is a major contributor to environmental degradation. All States and all people should make the elimination of poverty an essential task of their efforts to achieve sustainable development'.

[25] Principle 6, Draft principles proposed by the Chairman, A/CONF.151/PC/WG.III/L.33, 31 March 1992 which read as 'All States and all people [shall] [should] cooperate in the essential task of eradicating poverty as an indispensable requirement for sustainable development. [Any international regime cannot be considered equitable and just if it ignores the disparities in standards of living between nations and is insensitive to the development needs of the majority of the people of the world.]'

[26] Draft principles proposed by the Chairman Rio Declaration on Environment and Development, UN Doc A/CONF.151/PC/WG.III/L.33/Rev.1, 2 April 1992.

[27] See Francioni, chapter on Principle 1, in this commentary.

law. Added to this, the very formulation of the principle confirms that the Rio Declaration is more preoccupied with economic concerns, therefore reduction of poverty is only identified as *'an indispensable requirement for sustainable development'* rather than an objective *eo ipso.*

Legal rules in the area of curbing poverty and socio-economic inequalities did not develop in the same way as in the area of environment.[28] Although such a goal is proclaimed through engaging statements, poverty reduction is depicted mostly as a common political responsibility and imposes a moral responsibility to combat it. The origin of such an outcome goes partly back to the relationship between development and law, which has always been uncertain. More particularly, attempts to canvass the legal landscape of development failed by definition, because there is no consensus as to whether this law should capture the reality of development as it *is* or should be instead oriented towards what it *should be.*[29]

Within this framework, the alleviation of poverty discourse provided the leitmotif for development praxis since the discovery of the problem of 'underdevelopment'. Alleviation of poverty formed a backbone for decades of development within the United Nations, in the formulation of the New International Economic Order and still remains a blueprint for international development cooperation, as expressed by the Millennium Development Goals.

As a result, the ensemble of legal principles and practices that formed the basis of the law of development, as aptly described, were 'insufficiently legalized', 'never fully accepted' and have been described in terms of ethical obligations rather than legal.[30] Notwithstanding their legal quality, major international development policies, at the heart of which is poverty reduction, are major instruments for achieving some essential components of economic, social, and cultural human rights. Importantly, as far as cooperation between States for combating poverty is concerned, there is a positive attitude towards provision of assistance to developing countries to achieve this task.

The principle of poverty eradication changes its legal nature if it is phrased as a human rights *problematique*. It is important to note that the problem of poverty as such has never been articulated in human rights-standards terms. Nonetheless, the policy objective of poverty reduction and the attendant activities overlap with material provisions of the treaties protecting economic, social, and cultural rights. Normatively, therefore, the basis of poverty can be sought within a composite legal framework.

## 2.2. *Elements of Principle 5*

### 2.2.1. The task of 'poverty eradication'

Neither the wording of Principle 5 nor that of any other principle of the Rio Declaration gives any indication as to the concrete meaning of the term 'poverty eradication'. During the preparatory work preference was given to alternative technical conceptions such as poverty, which was predominantly used in the development institutions' practice instead

28 The legal rules and principles that have been developed, such as the precautionary principle, the principle of common but differentiated responsibilities, and polluter-pays principle—almost exclusively deal with the environmental issues and do not apply to the 'human' dimension of development activities.

29 Tomasevski, K., 'Monitoring Human Rights Aspects of Sustainable Development' (1992) 8 *American University Journal of Law and Policy* 89.

30 Jouannet, E., 'How to Depart from the Existing Dire Condition of Development', in Cassese, A. (ed), *Realizing Utopia: The Future of International Law* (Oxford University Press 2012), 392, 404.

of the traditional terminology used in the legal texts such as better conditions of life or standards of living. Some available definitions of what constitutes poverty have been defined in absolute terms. For example, The World Bank has defined a new international poverty line as 1.25 USD a day for 2005 (equivalent to 1.00 USD a day in 1996 US prices).[31]

The Copenhagen Declaration on Social Development and Programme of Action of the World Summit for Social Development of 1995 defined absolute poverty as 'a condition characterized by severe deprivation of basic human needs, including food, safe drinking water, sanitation facilities, health, shelter, education and information'.[32] It further specified that poverty depends not only on income but also on access to social services. The report on human rights and extreme poverty, submitted by the Special Rapporteur, Mr Leandro Despouy, defined poverty in terms of rights and responsibilities, more specifically as:

> The lack of basic security connotes the absence of one or more factors enabling individuals and families to assume basic responsibilities and to enjoy fundamental rights. The situation may become widespread and result in more serious and permanent consequences. The lack of basic security leads to chronic poverty when it simultaneously affects several aspects of people's lives, when it is prolonged and when it severely compromises people's chances of regaining their rights and of reassuming their responsibilities in the foreseeable future.[33]

At the regional level, the European Committee of Social Rights ('ECSR') has established a definition of poverty which it initially defined as meaning 'deprivation due to the lack of resources'.[34] This rather short definition has been further developed by the Committee and phrased in human rights terms. Thus, the ECSR stated that '[t]he fact of living in a situation of poverty and social exclusion violates the dignity of human beings'.[35]

The current focus of poverty reduction as the prime objective of development began in the early 1990s.[36] Since then, policy frameworks such as the Millennium Development Goals aim to halve poverty. The operational tools of the IFIs aim to reduce poverty (Poverty Reduction Strategies) and deal with the debt problems of the highly indebted poor countries (HIPC initiative). At the international level, days and decades are dedicated to the issue of poverty.[37] Development aid *no longer serves* the 'modernization'

[31] See Ravallion, M., Chen, S., and Sangraula, P., *Dollar a Day Revisited*, WB, (2008) Policy Research Working Paper 4620.

[32] Copenhagen Declaration on Social Development and Programme of Action of the World Summit for Social Development, Copenhagen, 6–12 March 1995, para 19.

[33] Final report on human rights and extreme poverty, submitted by the Special Rapporteur, Mr Leandro Despouy, UN Doc E/CN.4/Sub.2/1996/13, 28 June 1996, Annex III.

[34] ESCR Conclusions 2003, Statement of Interpretation on Article 30.

[35] ESCR, *International Movement ATD Fourth World v. France*, Complaint no 33/2006, Decision on the merits, 5 December 2007, para 163.

[36] Focus on human well-being was situated already in 1960s in the framework of the UN Development Decades launched for the first time in 1961. Similarly, when underlying assumptions of the modernization approach to development were widely criticized, particularly by dependency theorists in the late 1960s and 1970s, the idea of 'basic needs' started to gain support among development institutions. See Jacoby, E. H., 'Dilemma of the World Bank: Comment to the Annual Report 1972', 4(3) *Development and Change* 95.

[37] The UN launched the First United Nations Decade for Eradication of Poverty in 1995, UNGA, UN Doc A/RES/50/107, 20 December 1995; but the commitment to eradicate poverty was already highlighted in the Copenhagen Summit on Social Development, Report of the World Summit for Social Development, UN Doc A/CONF.166/9, 19 April 1995, para 13; the Copenhagen commitments were reviewed by UNGA, UN Doc A/RES/S-24/2, 15 December 2000, para 25. The year 2010 was proclaimed as the European Year for Combatting Poverty. A second UN Decade for the Eradication of Poverty 2007–2017 was proclaimed by GA in 2007, UN Doc A/RES/62/205, 10 March 2008.

purpose but instead aims at fighting poverty.[38] Foreign policies goals are defined in terms of overcoming poverty. The fact that poverty was problematized and became an organizing principle of development was not new; what is thought to be new is its rediscovery as a goal for development, its ascension to a top priority for development aid.

When compared to the formative stages of the international development 'law' principles and practices, it becomes clear that the current project of fighting against poverty is consensus-based, and, as many scholars point out, is 'much less' revolutionary. The focus is on precisely formulated targets disguising the underlying and systemic factors that contributed to the current persisting inequalities.[39] Initially, many of the claims of developing States have been de-radicalized subsequent to the NIEO movement, and the current focus on poverty eradication is far more consensual and does not generally question the underlying logic of the established international economic order.[40]

Seen in these terms, the return to the 'poverty' agenda is considered as a failure of previous development paradigms: a departure from the structural and systemic transformation to a narrow set of rules which equates to 'endorsing the idea that it is impossible to find political and legal solutions for the all-round development of developing countries.'[41] It has been suggested in particular that poverty reduction (as an obstacle to 'survival') is about 'lowering of ambitions' as opposed to accepting a broader concept of development.[42] The turn to poverty in a way embodies 'a sense of helplessness and of the inefficiency of certain legal and economic principles and rules that also led to this focus on poverty alone, and on humanitarian action alone.'[43]

38 Jouannet, E., 'How to Depart from Dire Conditions of Development', in Cassese, A. (ed), *Realizing Utopia: The Future of International Law* (Oxford University Press 2012), 402.

39 Saith holds that MDGs are 'a clear shift in the perspective in favour of a narrower frame focusing essentially on absolute aspects of some key measurable facets of poverty and deprivation, and away from a broader, more essentialist rights-based approach' in Saith, A., 'From Universal Values to Millennium Development Goals: Lost in Translation' (2006) 37(6) *Development and Change* 1170.

40 In terms of policy measures required to attain the objective of poverty reduction, the consensus reached is reflected in the Monterrey Consensus on Financing for Development. The outcome produced six areas of financing for development, whereby the development cooperation is only one of the components: 1) mobilizing domestic financial resources; 2) mobilizing international resources: foreign direct investment and private financial flows; 3) international trade as an engine of development; 4) increasing international financial and technical cooperation for development (ODA); 5) sustainable debt financing and external debt relief, and 6) addressing the structural issues, namely enhancing the coherence and consistency of the international monetary, financial and trading systems.

41 Jouannet, E., 'How to Depart from Dire Conditions of Development', in Cassese, A. (ed), *Realizing Utopia: The Future of International Law* (Oxford University Press 2012), 402. Criticism also comes from governments. See, eg the Advisory Council on Governmental Policy of the Netherlands stating: '[h]owever, the MDGs are largely static goals which are strongly oriented around alleviating emergencies. They say nothing of the resources, the strategy and underlying mechanisms required to achieve the goals, nor about the capacities of societies to develop, and from a macroeconomic perspective they are rather vacuous. In that sense they are not very development related. Economic growth is not included as a final or intermediary goal in the MDGs, and important issues like transformation of the productive sectors are not even referred to. Although MDG 8 does refer to the need for a fair trade system, this can only make a very limited contribution to the creation of productive national economic sectors. The MDGs are inspiring but also problematic in that they detract attention away from structural changes and the strengthening and transformation of agriculture and other productive sectors...' in Advisory Council on Government Policy (WRR), *Less Pretension, More Ambition; Development Policy in Times of Globalization* (Amsterdam University Press 2010), 110, available at <http://dare.uva.nl/cgi/arno/show.cgi?fid=210419>.

42 Minority Rights Group, Minority Rights in Development Aid Policies, November 2000, 15.

43 Jouannet, 'How to Depart from Dire Conditions of Development', 403.

Added to scholarly critique, the UN Conference on Trade and Development (UNCTAD) examined the efficiency of the current development structure under a big question mark. It contends that the existing international economic architecture is not conducive to the development of States, including the goal of poverty reduction. Even if the current—weak in design and implementation—special support measures (aid, debt relief, etc) are strengthened considerably, they would still be insufficient to promote more sustained development.[44]

### 2.2.2. Poverty in light of international human rights law

There is a consensus that poverty is a human rights problem.[45] The preamble to the Universal Declaration of Human Rights and the preamble common to both the International Covenant on Civil and Political Rights and the International Covenant on Economic, Social and Cultural Rights designated 'freedom from...want' as a human rights issue. The goal of poverty eradication is also reflected in the concept of the right to development. The Vienna Declaration and Programme of Action of the World proclaimed that the existence of widespread extreme poverty constituted a violation of human dignity.[46] Similarly, the Committee on Economic, Social and Cultural Rights, acknowledged that the rights to work, an adequate standard of living, housing, food, health, and education are areas 'which lie at the heart of the Covenant' and although, traditionally, dealt with as a poverty issue, constitute 'a denial of human rights'.[47] Poverty is both a cause and consequence of human rights violations and the condition creating the environment for other violations.[48]

There is as yet no conceptual framework to define precisely the poverty and ESC rights interface. The 1993 Vienna Declaration on Human Rights has only underlined that the existence of extreme poverty inhibits the full and effective enjoyment of human rights and that its immediate alleviation and eventual elimination must remain *a high priority*. In effect, there are obvious cognate links between poverty and ESC rights. A great degree of overlap exists between the two on substantive level: both deal with education, living standards, health, social protection, and so on. However, at the practical level, it is not clear how the basic needs approach underlying the fight against poverty logically corresponds to core economic, social, and cultural rights. More specifically, the predominant 'trade-off' approach of the development praxis to give priority to certain issues only, does not offer, from a legal point of view, sound legal or policy guidelines for selecting which human right may qualify as a basic need.[49]

[44] UNCTAD, *The Least Developed Countries Report 2010: Towards a New International Development Architecture for LDCs* (2010), 84 et seq.

[45] Statement on Poverty and the International Covenant on Economic, Social and Cultural Rights, UN Doc E/2002/22 -E/C.12/2001/17, 10 May 2001; See also eg UNGA Resolution 55/106 of 4 December 2000 on Human Rights and Extreme Poverty, and Commission on Human Rights Resolution 2001/31 of 23 April 2001 on the same subject matter.

[46] Vienna Declaration and Programme of Action, as adopted by the World Conference on Human Rights, UN Doc A/CONF.157/23, 12 July 1993, paras 14, 25.

[47] Statement on Poverty and the International Covenant on Economic, Social and Cultural Rights, para 1.

[48] Report of the SG, In Larger Freedom: towards Development, Security and Human Rights for All, UN Doc A/59/2005/Add.3, 26 May 2005, para 10.

[49] See Rajagopal, B., *International Law from Below: Development, Social Movements and Third World Resistance* (Cambridge University Press 2003).

Furthermore, poverty defines a relative state or condition, whereas economic and social rights embody a set of claims and obligations that are assigned to specific actors. An essential factor in understanding commonalities and divergences between poverty and ESC rights is the non-material dimension of poverty which is better captured by human rights. For this reason, poverty is considered not only as an economic issue but 'a multidimensional phenomenon that encompasses a lack of both income and the basic capabilities to live in dignity'.[50] The Committee on Economic, Social and Cultural Rights stated that poverty was 'a human condition characterized by the sustained or chronic deprivation of the resources, capabilities, choices, security and power necessary for the enjoyment of an adequate standard of living and other civil, cultural, economic, political and social rights'.[51] The *Guiding Principles on Extreme Poverty and Human Rights* further developed this idea by identifying a number of civil and political rights to be relevant to the questions of poverty such as right to life and physical integrity, rights to liberty and security of the person, right to equal protection before the law, access to justice and effective remedies, right to recognition as a person before the law, the right to privacy, and to protection for home and family.[52]

The non-economic dimension of poverty phenomenon has equally been recognized by the major development actors. In *Voices of the Poor*, the World Bank series, empowerment of the poor is one of the persistent themes.[53] Subsequently, this concept has been integrated under the umbrella concept of 'rights-based approach' to development at the operational level.[54]

### 2.2.3. 'states shall cooperate' for the task of poverty eradication

Although as stated before, Principle 5 is a policy goal, it nevertheless contains elements pertaining to the general obligation of cooperation under the UN Charter. There is a considerable uncertainty as to whether, outside express obligations under the UN Charter, there is a legally binding obligation on States to cooperate for development, and by extension for poverty reduction. Normatively, attempts to answer this question have been addressed in the realm of the 1970 Declaration on Principles of International Law Concerning Friendly Relations and Cooperation among States, the 1974 Declaration on the Establishment of a New International Economic Order, the 1974 Charter of

[50] 'Final draft of the guiding principles on extreme poverty and human rights, submitted by the Special Rapporteur on extreme poverty and human rights', Magdalena Sepúlveda Carmona, UN Doc A/HRC/21/39, 18 July 2012, para 2.

[51] 'Statement on Poverty and the International Covenant on Economic, Social and Cultural Rights', para 8.

[52] The Human Rights Council adopted the Guiding Principles at its 21st session in September 2012 contained in 'Final draft of the guiding principles on extreme poverty and human rights', submitted by the Special Rapporteur on extreme poverty and human rights, Magdalena Sepúlveda Carmona, UN Doc A/HRC/21/39, 18 July 2012.

[53] Narayan, D., Chambers, R., Shah, M. K., and Petesch, P., *Voices of the Poor: Crying Out for Change*, World Bank (Oxford University Press 2000).

[54] The OECD policy paper notes that '[t]here is growing consensus on the value of human rights principles—such as participation, non-discrimination and accountability—for good and sustainable development practice' as their application builds on and strengthens good and sustainable development practice. See OECD, *DAC Action-Oriented Policy Paper on Human Rights and Development*, OECD: 2007, 3. See also United Nations, *The Human Rights Based Approach to Development Cooperation: Towards a Common Understanding Among UN Agencies (Stanford Statement)*, 2003.

Economic Rights and Duties of States,[55] and the 1990 Declaration on International Economic Cooperation, in particular the Revitalization of Economic Growth and Development of the Developing Countries.[56]

While the text of the Declaration on Principles of International Law Concerning Friendly Relations and Cooperation among States endorses the obligation to cooperate for 'universal respect for, and observance of, human rights' as a statement of a binding rule, it falls short of according the same quality a 'general legal obligation to cooperate' for development.[57] Nonetheless, a theoretically conceivable argument for the existence of an obligation to cooperate for development and for poverty reduction can be developed on the basis of the UN Charter and interpretations given to the provisions of the Covenant on Economic, Social and Cultural Rights and the Convention on the Rights of the Child.[58] This is because human rights treaties dealing with economic, social, and cultural rights have incorporated cooperation for development as a means for States to fulfil their obligations on those rights.

## 3. Legal basis

The basic coordinates of Principle 5 draw from a broad normative framework, viz the UN Charter, Declaration on Principles of International Law Concerning Friendly Relations and Co-operation among States, 1966 International Covenants on human rights, the right to development discourse.

### *3.1. UN Charter, UN Declarations on Socio-Economic Development*

The preamble to the UN Charter, *inter alia*, determined that in order:

> to reaffirm faith in fundamental human rights, in the dignity and worth of the human person, in the equal rights of men and women and of nations large and small, and...
> to promote social progress and better standards of life *in larger freedom*,
> [member states shall]
> employ international machinery for the promotion of the economic and social advancement of all peoples....[59]

Furthermore, article 55 states that with a view to the creation of conditions of stability and well-being which are necessary for peaceful and friendly relations among nations based

[55] Art 17 of the Charter provides that international cooperation for development is the shared goal and common duty of all States, UNGA Res. 3281 (XXIX), Charter of Economic Rights and Duties of States, 12 December 1974.

[56] While the legally binding nature of these instruments has been contested, Wolfrum has opined that such an outcome does not 'preclude the use of individual provisions of these instruments as evidence of the existence of corresponding rules of international law' in Commentary by Wolfrum, R., 'Article 55', in Simma et al (eds), *The Charter of the United Nations. A Commentary* (2nd edn, Oxford University Press 2002), 897, 907.

[57] Delbruck, J. (ed), *International Law of Cooperation and State Sovereignty: Proceedings of an International Symposium of the Kiel Walther-Shucking-Institute of International Law, May 23–26, 2001* (Dunker and Humbold 2001), 96; See also Arangio-Ruiz, G., *The UN Declaration on Friendly Relations and the System of the Sources of International Law* (Sijthoff & Noordhoff 1979), 144; and Wolfrum, R., 'International Law of Cooperation', *Max Planck Encyclopedia of International Law*, <http://www.mpepil.com>, para 17.

[58] Louis Henkin suggests that 'The Covenant serves as justification for demands for international economic change...and for assistance from international institutions and from other States.' Henkin, L., 'International Law: Politics, Values and Functions' (1989) 216 *Recueil des Cours* 270.

[59] Preambular paras 2, 4 and 8, UN Charter, [emphasis added]. See also arts 55 (a)(b) and 56 of the UN Charter.

on respect for the principle of equal rights and self-determination of peoples, the United Nations shall promote:

a) higher standards of living, full employment, and conditions of economic and social progress and development;
b) solutions of international economic, social, health, and related problems; and international cultural and educational cooperation; and
c) universal respect for, and observance of, human rights and fundamental freedoms for all without distinction as to race, sex, language, or religion.

The interpretation of article 55 in conjunction with article 56 is maintained as creating basic obligations that all members must fulfil in good faith. Article 56 reads:

All members pledge themselves to take joint and separate action in co-operation with the Organization for the achievement of the purposes set forth in Article 55.

This interpretation has been advanced however only in relation to human rights and not socio-economic issues, which includes, among others, eradication of poverty. As the UN Charter commentaries make clear, articles 55 and 56 are 'rarely mentioned in regard to the issues addressed in Art. 55(a) and (b)', that is, in the economic and social fields.[60] In effect, the majority of references to article 56 and debates surrounding the import of the provision relate to the question of human rights. This dividing line between human rights and development at the level of obligations becomes blurred, when socio-economic human rights treaties require States, to use the wording of the UN Charter, 'to employ international machinery for the promotion of the economic and social advancement' for the fulfilment of their obligations.

## 3.2. *International treaties in the area of economic, social and cultural rights*

### 3.2.1. Relevant ESCR

The most important international treaties recognizing economic, social, and cultural rights ('ESCR') are the International Covenant on Economic, Social and Cultural Rights ('ICESCR'),[61] the Convention on the Elimination of All Forms of Discrimination against Women,[62] and the Convention on the Rights of the Child.[63] They all enshrine ESCR and recognize correlative States' obligations that have been further defined through the practice of treaty monitoring bodies. The adoption of Optional Protocols to the three instruments in the last decade gives victims of violations of ESCR—under certain conditions—the possibility to send communications to these treaty-monitoring bodies and seek redress at the international level.

Article 11 of the ICESCR is particularly important in recognizing the right to an adequate standard of living and the fundamental right to be free from hunger:

[60] Stoll, T., 'Article 55 (a) and (b)', in Simma, B., Khan, D.-E., Nolte, G., and Paulus, A. (eds), *The Charter of the United Nations A Commentary* (3rd edn, Oxford University Press 2013), para 29. Stoll at the same time states that since art 55 (a) and (b) 'is very broad and abstract, however, such use of the terms of the provision is not very significant in legal terms.'

[61] The International Covenant on Economic, Social and Cultural Rights ('ICESCR') was adopted by the UN General Assembly, Resolution 2200 A (XXI), 16 December 1966. It entered into force 3 January 1976.

[62] Adopted by the General Assembly 18 December 1979, Resolution 34/180; entered into force 3 September 1981.

[63] Adopted by the General Assembly 20 November 1989, Resolution 44/25; entered into force 2 September 1990.

1. The States Parties to the present Covenant recognize the right of everyone to an adequate standard of living for himself and his family, including adequate food, clothing and housing, and to the continuous improvement of living conditions. The States Parties will take appropriate steps to ensure the realization of this right, recognizing to this effect the essential importance of international co-operation based on free consent.
2. The States Parties to the present Covenant, recognizing the fundamental right of everyone to be free from hunger, shall take, individually and through international co-operation, the measures, including specific programmes, which are needed: (a) To improve methods of production, conservation and distribution of food by making full use of technical and scientific knowledge, by disseminating knowledge of the principles of nutrition and by developing or reforming agrarian systems in such a way as to achieve the most efficient development and utilization of natural resources; (b) Taking into account the problems of both food-importing and food-exporting countries, to ensure an equitable distribution of world food supplies in relation to need.

It is worth noting that the language used in article 11 of the ICESCR reflects several elements of Principle 5, including the essential importance of international cooperation, the need to improve living conditions, and the necessity to ensure an equitable distribution of goods to meet people's needs. If the ICESCR enshrines the ESCR of everyone, it also implies that States must take targeted measures to protect the rights of the most vulnerable members of society, among whom are infants, young children, the aged, persons with disabilities, the terminally ill, the chronically ill, the mentally ill, small peasants without land, indigenous populations, and victims of natural disasters.[64]

While article 11 protects the right to food,[65] the right to housing,[66] and the right to water and sanitation,[67] other articles of the ICESCR are also relevant to Principle 5, including article 9 on the right to social security,[68] article 12 enshrining the right to health,[69] and article 13 recognizing the right to education.[70] More than 160 countries have ratified the ICESCR,[71] which makes it a major source of protection of ESCR at the international level.

The Convention on the Elimination of All Forms of Discrimination against Women recognizes many ESCR of women, including their rights to education, health, employment, and economic and social benefits in its articles 9 to 13. It also puts emphasis on the need to combat discrimination against women living in rural areas, who are among

[64] See for example Committee on Economic, Social and Cultural Rights ('CESCR'), *General Comment 12: The right to adequate food (art 11)*, UN Doc E/C.12/1999/5, 12 May 1999, para 13; CESCR, *General Comment 6: The economic, social and cultural rights of older persons*, UN Doc E/1996/22, 8 December 1995; CESCR, *General Comment N° 5: Persons with Disabilities*, UN Doc E/1995/22, 9 December 2004.

[65] CESCR, *General Comment 12: The right to adequate food (art 11)*, UN Doc E/C.12/1999/5, 12 May 1999.

[66] CESCR, *General Comment 4: The right to adequate housing (art 11 (1) of the Covenant), (Sixth session, 1991)*, UN Doc E/1992/23, 13 December 1991.

[67] CESCR, *General Comment N° 15 (2002): The right to water (arts 11 and 12 of the International Covenant on Economic, Social and Cultural Rights)*, UN Doc E/C.12/2002/11, 20 January 2003. CESCR, *Statement on the right to sanitation*, UN Doc E/C.12/2010/1 18 March 2011.

[68] CESCR, *General Comment N° 19: The right to social security (art 9)*, UN Doc E/C.12/GC/19, 4 February 2008.

[69] CESCR, *General Comment N° 14 (2002): The right to the highest attainable standard of health (Article 12 of the International Covenant on Economic, Social and Cultural Rights)*, UN Doc E/C.12/2000/4, 11 August 2000.

[70] CESCR, *General Comment N° 13 (2002): The right to education (Article 13 of the Covenant)*, UN Doc E/C.12/1999/10, 8 December 1999.

[71] 162 States were parties to the ICESCR when this contribution was finalized (31 October 2014). The lists of States parties to the various international human rights instruments are available online at: <http://treaties.un.org/Pages/Treaties.aspx?id=4&subid=A&lang=en&clang=_en> (last accessed 31 October 2014).

the poorest in the world and the first victims of ESCR violations.[72] To this aim, its article 14 protects the rights of rural women against discrimination, including in access to productive resources and social security programmes.[73] Other rights recognized in the Convention complete the protection of women's ESCR, such as the right to equality in marriage and family relations, enshrined in article 16.[74] All of these articles offer a complete protection of women's ESCR, within the framework of an instrument ratified by almost 190 states.[75]

In a similar vein, the Convention on the Rights of the Child accords an important place to the protection of children's ESCR and is based on the principle that States are not the sole guarantors of the fulfilment of the protected rights.[76] Children's ESCR are explicitly protected in article 24 of the Convention, which enshrines the right to health, article 26 recognizing the right of the child to the benefit of social security, article 27 enshrining the right to an adequate standard of living, and articles 28–9 on the right to education.

### 3.2.2. Obligations of States and the practice of treaty monitoring bodies

An 'umbrella' provision of the Covenant on Economic, Social and Cultural Rights in article 2(1) on States Parties' obligations reads as follows:

> Each State Party to the present Covenant undertakes to take steps, *individually and through international assistance and co-operation*, especially economic and technical, to the maximum of its available resources with a view to achieving progressively the full realisation of the rights recognized in the presented Covenant.[77]

The obligation stipulated in ICESCR article 2(1) can be divided into three subsidiary obligations: the obligation to take steps through all appropriate means, including and especially legislative measures; the obligation to take steps with a view to progressively achieving the full realization of ESCR; and the obligation to take steps, to the maximum of all available resources, both those within a country and those available from the international community through international cooperation and assistance.

[72] Frostell, K. and Scheinin, M., 'Women', in Eide, A., Krause, C., and Rosas, A. (eds) *Economic, Social and Cultural Rights: A Textbook* (2nd revised edn, Kluwer Law International 2001) 331, at 338–49.

[73] The second paragraph of this article states: 'States Parties shall take all appropriate measures to eliminate discrimination against women in rural areas in order to ensure, on a basis of equality of men and women, that they participate in and benefit from rural development and, in particular, shall ensure to such women the right:... c. to benefit directly from social security programmes;... g. to have access to agricultural credit and loans, marketing facilities, appropriate technology and equal treatment in land and agrarian reform as well as in land resettlement schemes.'

[74] In its General Recommendation 21, the Committee on the Elimination of All Forms of Discrimination against Women clarified that the convention's art 16 was essential for women's ESCR, stating: 'The right to own, manage, enjoy and dispose of property is central to a woman's right to enjoy financial independence, and in many countries will be critical to her ability to earn a livelihood and to provide adequate housing and nutrition for herself and for her family.' para 26.

[75] One hundred and eighty-eight States were parties to the Convention on the Elimination of All Forms of Discrimination against Women when this book was finalized (31 October 2014).

[76] Children being the most vulnerable members of society, it is essential that responsibility for their rights not be incumbent only on the State. The persons who have custody of the child thus have very clear obligations under the Convention. As stipulated in the Convention on the Rights of the Child, art 3, para 2: 'States Parties undertake to ensure the child such protection and care as is necessary for his or her well-being, taking into account the rights and duties of his or her parents, legal guardians, or other individuals legally responsible for him or her, and, to this end, shall take all appropriate legislative and administrative measures.'

[77] Emphasis added.

For the Committee on ESCR ('CESCR'), article 2 (1) of ICESCR imposes a first obligation for the States parties, which is to take steps, an obligation 'which in itself, is not qualified or limited by other considerations'.[78] The measures that the States must take to achieve the fulfilment of ESCR are varied; they include, notably, legislative, administrative, judicial, economic, social and educational measures.[79] The obligation to take steps 'must be read in the light of the overall objective, indeed the *raison d'être*, of the *Covenant* which is to establish clear obligations for States parties in respect of the full realization of the rights in question in the *Covenant*'.[80] States thus have the obligation to act in a deliberate way, concretely, working as fast as possible to assure the full enjoyment of ESCR.[81] ESCR have seen momentous developments in terms of interpretation of their normative content,[82] which evolved in the general comments of the treaty bodies, dialogue with States, and concluding observations, and in the work of Special Rapporteurs.

By becoming parties to the ICESCR, States commit themselves to taking steps using the maximum of their available resources to realize the ESCR of their populations, giving priority to the most vulnerable groups in the allocation of these resources. According to the ICESCR, a state's available resources include both its own resources and those of the international community.[83] A State must thus also demonstrate that it has attempted to obtain international support to assure the full realization of ESCR.[84] The corollary of this obligation is the obligation of international assistance and cooperation incumbent on States parties to the ICESCR. The CESCR has provided useful guidance but has not yet clarified these aspects comprehensively or systematically so that they can be applied in a uniform manner in any given situation. It had, however, clarified that:

> [I]n accordance with Articles 55 and 56 of the Charter of the United Nations, with well-established principles of international law, and with the provisions of the Covenant itself, international cooperation for development and thus for the realization of economic, social and cultural rights is an obligation of all States. It is particularly incumbent upon those States which are in a position to assist others in this regard. The Committee notes in particular the importance of the Declaration on the Right to Development adopted by the General Assembly in its resolution 41/128 of 4 December 1986 and the need for States parties to take full account of all of the principles recognized therein. It emphasizes that, in the absence of an active programme of international assistance and cooperation on the part of all those States that are in a position to undertake one, the full realization of economic, social and cultural rights will remain an unfulfilled aspiration in many countries.[85]

One understanding of the international assistance and cooperation provision by the treaty monitoring bodies of both the ICESCR and Convention on the Rights of the Child comes

[78] CESCR, *General Comment 3: The nature of States parties obligations (Art 2, para 1 of the Covenant)*, UN Doc E/1991/23, 14 December 1990, para 2.

[79] CESCR, *General Comment 3*, para 7.

[80] CESCR, *General Comment 3*, para 9.

[81] CESCR, *General Comment 3*, paras 2, 9.

[82] The CESCR's efforts equilibrated to a certain extent the imbalance between civil and political and socio-economic rights in terms of their normative substance. The CESCR posited that 'there is no Covenant right which could not, in the great majority of systems, be considered to possess at least some significant justiciable dimensions.' CESCR, General Comment No 9: 'The domestic application of the Covenant', E/C.12/1998/243 December 1998, at para 10. For a nuanced analysis of the question of justiciability particularly in light of the 'progressive realization' of ESC rights, see Pisillo Mazzeschi, R., 'Responsabilité de l'état pour violation des obligations positives relatives aux droits de l'homme' (2008) 333 *Recueil des Cours* 455.

[83] CESCR, *General Comment No 9: The domestic application of the Covenant*, para 13.

[84] CESCR, *General Comment No 9: The domestic application of the Covenant*, para 13.

[85] CESCR, *General Comment No 3, The Nature of States Parties' Obligations*, UN Doc E/1991/23, 14 December 1990, para 14.

very close to the meaning of the right to development, that is, when it links the provision with cooperation for development. The CESCR's view in this regard is that 'international cooperation *for development and thus for* the realization of economic, social and cultural rights is an obligation for all States.'[86] Perhaps a somewhat far-fetched, but nonetheless theoretically conceivable, argument for the existence of an obligation to cooperate for development *via* human rights can be developed on the basis of the UN Charter and interpretations given by the treaty monitoring bodies. To put it in the context of Principle 5, and read through the provisions of the ICESCR, cooperation of States to eradicate poverty stipulates legally binding consequences.

The Covenant has defined only the objective of obligation to cooperate and assist, in general, for the full realization of human rights. It would seem logical to suggest that the first responsibility of States Parties to ICESCR is *to define* the obligations incumbent upon them in accordance with article 2(1) on international assistance and cooperation.[87] In the absence of this definition agreed by States Parties, the Committees on Economic Social and Cultural Rights, and on the Rights of the Child, have (rightly or wrongly) on occasion, where appropriate, referred to State pledges for development cooperation in outcome documents of UN summits.[88] The CESCR has consistently requested States to report on their efforts on the ODA target of 0.7%, the volume of aid defined as a standard of achievement (as opposed to a legal obligation) in the area of development. In any event, the primary obligation rests with the domestic State.[89] States have an obligation to seek assistance and cooperation.[90] Hence, international assistance, depending on the circumstances, may either be subsidiary (the most common case), or concurrent.[91] On one occasion, the CESCR clarified that when a State is *clearly lacking* in financial or technical resources, 'the international community has a clear obligation to assist.'[92] Over the past

[86] Emphasis added. The Committee repeated its position regarding an obligation to cooperate for development in General Comment No 17, 'The right of everyone to benefit from the protection of the moral and material interests resulting from any scientific, literary or artistic production of which he or she is the author' (art 15), UN Doc E/C.12/GC/17, 12 January 2006, para 37.

[87] Similarly, the Report on the Secretary General on *Progressive Development of the Principles and Norms of International Law Relating to the New International Economic Order* suggested that the normative prescription of the duty to cooperate 'can at most, in addition to defining the objective in general, create a duty or an obligation to negotiate with a view to defining more precisely the targets to be reached and the ways and means of reaching them.' However, as the Report admits, 'such a normative prescription is not sufficient by itself to constitute a normative proposition. In other words, the purely normative approach reaches its limits in the context of the international law of cooperation, which, by modulating the legal regulation closely to its subject-matter, is rich in specific applications that do not, or not yet, lend themselves to normative generalizations' in UN Doc A/39/504/Add.1, 23 October 1984, paras 134–5.

[88] The CESCR has made references to the agreements reached at Rome Declaration of the World Food Summit, the Alma-Ata Declaration on Primary Health Care, and the Committee on the Rights of the Child has made references to the Millennium Development Goals.

[89] See CESCR, General Comment No. 3, para 11. Similarly '[w]hile development facilitates the enjoyment of all human rights, the lack of development may not be invoked to justify the abridgement of internationally recognized human rights' in UNGA, *Vienna Declaration and Programme of Action*, UN Doc A/CONF.157/23, 12 July 1993, para 10.

[90] See eg CESCR, Statement: An evaluation of the obligation to take steps to the 'Maximum of available resources' under an optional protocol to the Covenant, UN Doc E/C.12/2007/1, 10 May 2007, para 10.

[91] For instance, in the context of the right to food, the CESCR clarified that States 'have a joint and individual responsibility, in accordance with the Charter of the United Nations, to cooperate in providing disaster relief and humanitarian assistance in times of emergency, including assistance to refugees and internally displaced persons.' CESCR, General Comment No. 12, The Right to Adequate Food, UN Doc E/CN.12/1999/5, 12 May 1999, para 38.

[92] CESCR, General Comment No. 11, Plans of action for primary education, UN Doc E/C.12/1999/4, 10 May 1999, para 9.

few years there has been considerable development in the understanding of the core issues concerning the obligation of international cooperation and assistance,[93] not least on the extent to which we can stretch the notion.[94]

In addition to general obligations reflected in article 2(1), States bear specific obligations to respect, protect, and fulfil economic, social and cultural rights.[95] In the context of poverty reduction, the Committee on ESCR has stated that, any activities of States and international actors undertaken for the task of poverty reduction must respect human rights. The Committee on Social, Economic and Cultural Rights has stressed that:

> the core obligations of economic, social and cultural rights have a crucial role to play in national and international developmental policies, including anti-poverty strategies. When grouped together, the core obligations establish an international minimum threshold that all developmental policies should be designed to respect... [i]f a national or international anti-poverty strategy does not reflect this minimum threshold, it is inconsistent with the legally binding obligations of the State party.[96]

Consequently, the issue of poverty frequently arises in the course of the CESCR's constructive dialogue with State parties, and the Committee has effectively integrated the State pledges for poverty eradication in the review of State parties commitments arising from the Covenant.[97] The issue is also systematically taken up in relation to compliance with article 2(1) of the ICESCR which requires States to cooperate for the achievement of the full realization of economic, social, and cultural rights. State parties are frequently requested to report on provision of development assistance, on the way the development policies of a State concerned contributed to realization of ESC rights in developing countries, and measures States take as members of international financial institutions to ensure their policies are in compliance with the Covenant. Apart from very rare exceptions, generally the response of State parties to the Committee's requests are positive and absence of refutation in the context of monitoring compliance with international obligations may amount to endorsement of the existence of an obligation to cooperate in the task of poverty eradication particularly through provision of development assistance and ensuring compliance of the policies and programmes with economic, social, and cultural rights.[98]

[93] There are signs that some States are beginning to recognize their international obligations under the IESCR. For the Czech Republic, for example: 'If core obligations under ICESCR are not met due to resource constraints, then international assistance and cooperation should be provided, in keeping with the Charter of the United Nations and Article 2, Para 1, of ICESCR'. (Open-ended working group on an optional protocol to the ICESCR, *Report of the Secretary-General in response to Commission resolution 2003/18*, UN Doc E/CN.4/2004/WG.23/2, 17 November 2003, para 8.)

[94] Pisillo Mazzeschi has given a critical analysis of the extent to which international assistance and cooperation can be identified as an autonomous obligation. See Pisillo Mazzeschi, R., 'Responsabilité de l'état pour violation des obligations positives relatives aux droits de l'homme' (2008) 333 *Recueil des Cours*. See also a complex approach adopted by the Maastricht Principles on Extraterritorial Obligations of States in the area of Economic, Social and Cultural Rights, Maastricht University, September 2011.

[95] See for example, Committee, *General Comment 15: The Right to Water (Arts 11 et 12)*, UN Doc E/C.12/2002/11, 20 January 2003, paras 17–29; Committee, *General Comment 18: The Right to Work (art 6)*, UN Doc E/C.12/GC/18, 6 February 2006, paras 19–28; Committee, *General Comment 19: The Right to Social Security (art 9)*, UN Doc E/C.12/GC/19, 4 February 2008, paras 40–51.

[96] CESCR, Statement on Poverty and the International Covenant on Economic, Social and Cultural Rights, UN Doc E/2002/22-E/C.12/2001/17, annex VII, para 17.

[97] See note 88.

[98] Response of States to the CESCR: Italy (UN Doc HR/CESCR/NONE/2004/3), Finland (UN Doc E/C.12/FIN/Q/5/Add.1), Netherlands (UN Doc E/C.12/NLD/Q/3/Add.1), Belgium (UN Doc E/C.12/BEL/Q/3/Add.1), Sweden (UN Doc E/C.12/SWE/Q/5/Add.1), UK (UN Doc E/C.12/GBR/Q/5/

### 3.2.3. ESCR Enforcement Mechanisms

Compliance with the international human rights treaties in relation to ESCR is monitored by treaty bodies composed of independent experts.[99] All these bodies receive periodic reports from State parties on the measures taken to implement their obligations.[100] Further, several treaty bodies have the authority to receive communications alleging violations of the rights enshrined in the treaty, thus benefiting from a quasi-judicial status.

Among the treaties recognizing ESCR, two benefit from a quasi-judicial procedure: the Convention on the Elimination of All Forms of Discrimination against Women, under its optional protocol,[101] and the ICESCR, under its optional protocol which entered into force on 5 May 2013.[102] This means that it is possible for victims of ESCR violations to invoke violations of the provisions of these two treaties.[103] The Optional Protocol to the ICESCR also provides for interstate communication procedures through which a State may accuse another State of the violation of one of the enshrined rights.[104] No such communications, however, have ever been sent to any of the treaty bodies.[105]

The Committee on the Elimination of Discrimination against Women can carry out investigations if it is informed through credible information that a State party is seriously or systematically violating rights set forth in the Convention.[106] It can also at any time request that a State party take precautionary measures when such measures are necessary to avoid irreparable harm to the victims of the presumed violation.[107] These two powers have also been attributed to the Committee on ESCR through the Optional Protocol to the ICESCR, the first being subject to a declaration accepting jurisdiction by the State party concerned.[108]

Add.1), Australia (UN Doc E/C.12/AUS/Q/4/Add.1), Switzerland (UN Doc E/C.12/CHE/Q/2-3/Add.1), New Zealand (UN Doc E/C.12/NZL/Q/3/Add.1), Spain (UN Doc E/C.12/ESP/Q/5/Add.1).

[99] Regarding the composition and workings of these treaty bodies, see Vandenhole, W., *The Procedures Before the UN Human Rights Bodies: Divergence or Convergence?* (Intersentia 2004), 7–73. See also Alston, P., 'The Committee on Economic, Social and Cultural Rights', in Alston, P. (ed), *The United Nations and Human Rights. A Critical Appraisal* (Clarendon Press 1995), 473–508; Craven, M. C. R., *The International Covenant on Economic, Social and Cultural Rights. A Perspective on its Development* (Clarendon Press 1995), 30–105.

[100] Rosas, A. and Scheinin, M., 'Implementation Mechanisms and Remedies', in Eide, A., Krause, C., and Rosas, A. (eds), *Economic, Social and Cultural Rights: A Textbook* (2nd edn, Kluwer Law International 2001), 426–34.

[101] Adopted as General Assembly Resolution 54/4, 6 October 1999; entered into force 22 December 2000.

[102] Adopted as General Assembly Resolution A/RES/63/117, 10 December 2008, entered into force 5 May 2013. On the Optional Protocol to the ICESCR, see Golay, C. and Biglino, I., *The Optional Protocol to the International Covenant on Economic, Social and Cultural Rights* (Geneva Academy of International Humanitarian Law and Human Rights 2013).

[103] The optional protocol creating a communication mechanism for the Convention on the Rights of the Child was adopted on 19 December 2011 but is not yet in force. It is thus not yet possible to seek redress before the Committee on the Rights of the Child in the event of a violation of ESCR.

[104] Optional Protocol to the ICESCR, art 10.

[105] Golay and Biglino, *The Optional Protocol to the International Covenant on Economic, Social and Cultural Rights*, 42. In one instance, an inter-State complaint was brought before the International Court of Justice based on a complaint of a violation of the Convention on the Elimination of All Forms of Racial Discrimination. ICJ, *Application of the International Convention on the Elimination of All Forms of Racial Discrimination (Georgia v. Russian Federation),* Judgment of 1 April 2011.

[106] Optional Protocol to the Convention for the Elimination of All Forms of Discrimination against Women, art 8.

[107] Optional Protocol to the Convention on the Elimination of All Forms of Discrimination against Women, art 5.

[108] Optional Protocol to the ICESCR, arts 5, 11.

The Optional Protocol to the ICESCR has two main particularities.[109] The first is that it provides that the CESCR, when reviewing a communication, should consider the reasonableness of the measures taken by the State party under article 2, § 1 of the ICESCR, while keeping in mind that the State party may adopt a variety of measures to implement the rights set forth in the ICESCR.[110] The second particularity of this protocol is that its article 14 provides for the possibility of the CESCR to make recommendations to United Nations agencies and programmes, with the consent of the State party concerned, so that these international institutions may support the State in the implementation of the Committee's recommendations.[111] The same article also provides for the creation of a fund to aid the State parties in fulfilling the rights enshrined in the ICESCR.[112]

## *3.3. Global policies on poverty reduction*

### 3.3.1. MDGs

The Millennium Development Goals (MDGs) have dominated the last decade as the most prominent initiative on the international development agenda. The United Nations Millennium Summit, from which the MDGs emerged, was an unparalleled event in which 198 world leaders signed the Millennium Declaration, committing their nations to combating 'abject and dehumanizing conditions of extreme poverty' and 'making the right to development a reality for everyone'.[113]

The MDGs call for achievement of concrete results: eight quantifiable goals to reduce poverty by 2015. The eight MDGs are designed to: halve extreme poverty and hunger (MDG 1); achieve universal primary education (MDG 2); promote gender equality and empower women (MDG 3); reduce child mortality (MDG 4); improve maternal health (MDG 5); combat HIV/AIDS, malaria, and other diseases (MDG 6); ensure environmental sustainability (MDG 7); develop a global partnership for development (MDG 8). The global partnership for development as stipulated in MDG 8 requests States in a position to provide assistance to conclude a global development compact with developing countries in order to facilitate the implementation of the MDGs 1 to 7. In order to define the goals with greater precision and make their attainment quantifiable, a set of corresponding targets and indicators have been inserted in each goal.

With less than a year to go to the MDGs' target date of 2015, the picture to be sketched from the extant analysis can be considered to be all but homogeneous. While progress has been achieved on a number of goals, including the fight against poverty and several health-related goals, setbacks have been identified on a number of others, including the fight against hunger, gender equality, and access to improved sanitation facilities.[114] In addition, gains from some progress in areas of access to markets and efforts on debt relief were compromised by the financial crises. According to the latest reviews, conflict-affected countries are likely not to achieve any of the MDG goals.[115] Experts argue that the results at any rate need to be put in

[109] Golay and Biglino, *The Optional Protocol to the International Covenant on Economic, Social and Cultural Rights*, 22–38.

[110] Optional Protocol to the ICESCR, art 8, para 4.

[111] Optional Protocol to the ICESCR, art 14, paras 1, 2.

[112] Optional Protocol to the ICESCR, art 14, para 3.

[113] General Assembly, *UN Millennium Declaration*, UN Doc A/RES/55/2, 18 September 2000, para 25.

[114] United Nations, *The Millennium Development Goals Report 2013* (United Nations 2013), 4–5, available at <http://www.un.org/millenniumgoals/pdf/report-2013/mdg-report-2013-english.pdf>.

[115] WB, *World Development Report 2011: Conflict, Security and Development*, in particular 61–3, available at <http://web.worldbank.org/WBSITE/EXTERNAL/EXTDEC/EXTRESEARCH/EXTWDRS/0,,contentMDK:23256432~pagePK:478093~piPK:477627~theSitePK:477624,00.html>.

perspective.[116] Despite the fact that all MDGs will not be met by 2015, the United Nations Secretary-General has described the MDGs as 'the most successful global anti-poverty push in history'.[117]

### 3.3.2. Johannesburg Declaration on Sustainable Development

To mark the 10th anniversary of the Rio Declaration, the UN convened the World Summit on Sustainable Development ('WSSD') in 2002 to 'reaffirm commitment of the Rio Principles, the full implementation of Agenda 21 and the Programme for the Further Implementation of Agenda 21'. The outcome document, Declaration on Sustainable Development, affirmed the will of the States to 'assume a collective responsibility to advance and strengthen the interdependent and mutually reinforcing pillars of sustainable development—economic development, social development and environmental protection—at local, national, regional and global levels'.[118] In the WSSD, the emphasis of efforts in the field of sustainable development shifted from environmental concerns to poverty eradication, albeit the Declaration recognized the problems of global environment.

### 3.3.3. Rio+20

The outcome document of Rio+20, *The Future We Want*, while reaffirming the commitment of States to sustainable development in its various dimensions, states in the first place that

> Poverty eradication is the greatest global challenge facing the world today and an indispensable requirement for sustainable development. In this regard, we are committed to freeing humanity from poverty and hunger as a matter of urgency.[119]

The outcome document further links poverty eradication with the commitment 'to make every effort to accelerate the achievement of the internationally agreed development goals, including the Millennium Development Goals by 2015'.[120] The Rio+20 outcome document also specifies that the process of elaboration of the Sustainable Development Goals 'be coordinated and coherent with the processes to consider the post-2015 development agenda'.[121]

As the process from Stockholm evolved through Rio, Johannesburg, and Rio+20, and the international community is heading towards formulating a new post-2015 framework, distributional, social justice, and equity concerns are becoming more pronounced. The tension between growth and the need to preserve the environment is more acute than ever.

116 Pogge, T., 'The First United Nations Development Goal: A Cause for Celebration', 5(3) *Journal of Human Development and Capabilities* (2004), 337–97.

117 United Nations, *The Millennium Development Goals Report 2013*, New York, United Nations, 2013, 3.

118 Johannesburg Declaration on Sustainable Development, para 5.

119 GA Resolution 66/288, *The Future We Want*, UN Doc A/RES/66/288, 11 September 2012, para 2.

120 GA Resolution 66/288, *The Future We Want*, para 5.

121 To this end, a 30 member intergovernmental Open Working Group ('OWG') was established in January 2013 with a task to submit a report by September 2014 with their proposal on the Post-2015 Agenda and SDGs (see A /67/L.48/Rev.1). In the outcome document, the OWG defined the goal of 'Ending poverty in all its forms everywhere' as a SDG 1 accompanied with seven targets that will be further elaborated through indicators. See *Outcome Document—Open Working Group on Sustainable Development Goals*, available at <http://sustainabledevelopment.un.org/focussdgs.html>.

## 4. Normative impact

The general view, widely shared among scholars, is that international law concerned with combating poverty and the development as it emerged in the immediate post-war period, particularly within the framework of the United Nations, has 'virtually come to a halt if it has not in fact already withered away'.[122]

The reasons behind this outcome are very complex, but they broadly can be reduced to three sets of factors. First, the core of the poverty reduction logic was based on the ensemble of principles and practices of earlier development paradigm. Second, reliance has been exclusively on general mechanisms like market mechanisms or improved terms of trade, which is particularly problematic within the time horizon set for achieving the MDGs. Third, the composite nature of sustainable development carries the risk of inevitable tension and contradiction between different objectives. Instead eradication of poverty has engendered a wealth of soft-law instruments and practices. Principle 5 can be said to have a major impact on the international and national policy frameworks all of which without exception aim to halve poverty. Added to this, development aid and foreign policy goals are defined in terms of overcoming poverty. The main problem is that those principles and practices developed on 'poverty' have had a very limited effectiveness so far.

The situation seems to be nuanced at the regional level. In recognition of the problem of poverty the Revised European Social Charter adopted in 1996 extended the protection of individuals in the socio-economic terms by providing a specific right to protection from poverty and social exclusion. Article 30 of the Charter stipulates that 'with a view to ensuring the effective exercise of the right to protection against poverty and social exclusion' State Parties undertake 'to take measures within the framework of an overall and co-ordinated approach to promote the effective access of persons who live or risk living in a situation of social exclusion or poverty, as well as their families, to, in particular, employment, housing, training, education, culture and social and medical assistance'.[123] Protection against poverty, thus, requires measures to be taken to provide access to employment, housing, training, education, culture, and social and medical assistance.

## 5. Jurisprudential relevance

As noted before, the content of poverty eradication as envisaged in Principle 5 materially overlaps with the economic, social, and cultural rights guaranteed by international human rights treaties. In this sense, protection of the economic, social, and cultural rights, per se, serves the purpose of poverty eradication. Today, a number of ESC rights cases have been adjudicated and the trend is indicating growth in this area. These cases emerge from various jurisdictions representing different legal systems developing both positive and negative dimensions of States' obligations vis-à-vis ESC rights. Similarly, the European, African, and Inter-American human rights systems have contributed to a growing body of jurisprudence in this area.

In addition, socio-economic components of civil and political rights have been adjudicated through human rights mechanisms. The practice of the Inter-American Court of Human Rights ('IACtHR') is particularly interesting as it has adopted a broad approach

[122] Schrijver, N., *The Evolution of Sustainable Development in International Law: Inception, Meaning and Status* (Martinus Nijhoff 2008), 30.

[123] Art 30, Revised European Social Charter, 3 May 1996.

in defining the content of the right to life to encompass creation of decent conditions of life in the case of *Street Children*.[124] In this case, with reference to article 4 of the American Convention, the IACtHR held that:

In essence, the fundamental right to life includes not only the right of every human being not to be deprived of his life arbitrarily, but also the right that he will not be prevented from having *access to the conditions that guarantee a dignified existence.* States have the obligation to guarantee the creation of the conditions required in order that violations of this basic right do not occur and, in particular, the duty to prevent its agents from violating it.

In this case, the Court, with reference to article 19 on the rights of the child, found a violation in particular when States 'do not prevent them [eg children] from living in misery, thus depriving them of the minimum conditions for a dignified life and preventing them from the 'full and harmonious development of their personality', even though every child has the right to harbour a project of life that should be tended and encouraged by the public authorities so that it may develop this project for its personal benefit and that of the society to which it belongs.'[125] Similarly, in the case of the *Yakye Axa Indigenous Community*, the Court confirmed that the right to life comprises 'not only the right of every human being not to be arbitrarily deprived of his life, but also the right that conditions that impede or obstruct access to a decent existence',[126] and that the State has an obligation of 'generating minimum living conditions that are compatible with the dignity of the human person and of not creating conditions that hinder or impede it.'[127] The Court went to conclude that the right to life has been abridged 'for not taking measures regarding the conditions that affected their possibility of having a decent life.'[128]

The jurisprudence of the European Committee of Social Rights ('ECSR') has applied Principle 5 of the Rio Declaration in a much more integrated fashion. As already noted, the Revised European Social Charter provides for a right to protection from poverty that integrated several socio-economic rights. In the case *International Fourth World Movement v. France*, the Committee has developed in a fairly comprehensive manner the scope of States' obligations under the right to protection from poverty and social exclusion. The relevant passages merit being reproduced here in full:

With a view to ensuring the effective exercise of the right to protection against poverty and social exclusion, Article 30 requires States Parties to adopt an overall and coordinated approach, which should consist of an analytical framework, a set of priorities and measures to prevent and remove obstacles to access fundamental social rights. There should also exist monitoring mechanisms involving all relevant actors, including civil society and persons affected by poverty and exclusion. This approach must link and integrate policies in a consistent way, moving beyond a purely sectoral or target group approach.

[124] ICtHR, *Case of the 'Street Children' (Villagrán-Morales* et al*) v. Guatemala*, Judgment of 19 November 1999, Series C. No. 63, para 144.

[125] ICtHR, *Case of the 'Street Children'*, para 191.

[126] ICtHR, *The Yakye Axa Indigenous Community v. Paraguay*, Judgment of 17 June 2005, Series C. No. 125, para 161.

[127] ICtHR, *The Yakye Axa Indigenous Community v. Paraguay*, para 162.

[128] ICtHR, *The Yakye Axa Indigenous Community*, para 176. In the practice of the European Court of Human Rights, certain cases can be identified where the protection of the right to life implied prevention of dangers to health of a person. These include *L.C.B. v. UK*, Judgment of 9 June 1998, Reports 1998-III, para 36; *Velikova v. Bulgaria*, Judgment of 18 May 2000, Reports 2000-VI; *Anguelova v. Bulgaria*, Judgment of 13 June 2002, Reports 2002-IV.

> The measures taken for such a purpose must promote and remove obstacles to access to fundamental social rights, in particular employment, housing, training, education, culture and social and medical assistance. It should be noted that this is not an exhaustive list of the areas in which it is necessary to take initiatives in order to address the multidimensional phenomena of poverty and exclusion.
>
> The measures should strengthen access to social rights, their monitoring and enforcement, improve the procedures and management of benefits and services, improve information about social rights and related benefits and services, combat psychological and socio-cultural obstacles to accessing rights and where necessary specifically target the most vulnerable groups and regions. Access to fundamental social rights is assessed by taking into consideration the effectiveness of policies, measures and actions undertaken.
>
> Adequate resources are one of the main elements of the overall strategy to fight social exclusion and poverty, and should consequently be allocated to attain the objectives of the strategy.[129]

In addition to concluding that provision of access to employment, housing, training, education, culture, social and medical assistance constituted fundamental social rights, the ECSR set forth a set of essential elements for poverty eradication measures. States are under an obligation to adopt coordinated and coherent policies and programmes supported by adequate resources and envisage monitoring and enforcement for such policies to be effective. Importantly, the ECSR elaborated the procedural aspects of the right to protection from poverty by requiring that monitoring mechanisms should involve all relevant actors and persons affected by poverty and exclusion.

This principle of participation has been given prominence in the cases decided by the African Commission of Human and Peoples' Rights ('ACmHPR') particularly in the context of balancing of States' development objectives and plans with the protection of the rights of individuals. In the case of *SERAC and CESR v. Nigeria*, the African Commission found that the failure to involve the Orgoni people in the decisions that affected their development as well as lack of access to information on health and environmental risks of major industrial activities constituted violation of the right of peoples to the right to a general satisfactory environment favourable to their development.[130] In another case concerning the Endorois indigenous community, the Commission concluded that the failure of the State to adequately involve the Endorois in the development process that affected them constituted a violation of the right to development provided for in article 22 of the African Charter of Human and Peoples' Rights.[131]

## III) Relations with Other Principles

The objective of poverty eradication suggests a close relationship with Principle 1, that puts human beings at the centre of concerns for sustainable development. In addition Principle 5 stands in the context of Principle 3 on the right to development. This is particularly so, since the Vienna Declaration and Programme of Action links the right to development

[129] ECSR, *International Movement ATD Fourth World v. France*, Complaint no. 33/2006, Decision on the merits, 5 December 2007, paras 164–8.

[130] African Commission, *The Social and Economic Rights Action Center and the Center for Economic and Social Rights v. Nigeria*, Communication No. 155/96 (2001), paras 53–5.

[131] African Commission, *Centre for Minority Rights Development (Kenya) and Minority Rights Group International on behalf of Endorois Welfare Council v. Kenya*, 276/2003, 4 February 2010.

with the sustainable development.[132] Such a merger signifies that the right to development should be oriented first and foremost towards the eradication of poverty. Together these three principles bear witness to a legal order designed to define 'a level of indigence and of lack of ability to fulfil basic needs which is unacceptable for the world order'.[133]

## IV) Assessment

While the concept of sustainable development itself is based on a delicate balance between various, sometimes conflicting, interests, in practice socio-economic inequality *between* and *within* States has received limited attention in terms of legal articulation of principles. The unanimous support among States and the focus of major development agencies on poverty eradication, have so far failed to ensure a firm basis for international action in this field.

The challenge ahead for international lawyers is to analyse which parts of the traditional law of international development can and should be reinforced, where and how it is to take new directions through normative developments and practice, and to what extent international law can contribute to social justice. The further challenge lying ahead for the international community is how to articulate a genuinely universal global post-2015 framework applicable to all people everywhere, from the US and Europe through to Small Island States and Least Developed Countries ('LDCs'), with due regard to the principles of Rio Declaration.

Notwithstanding, the broad support for the declarations, the detailed programmes of actions, the frequent incantation of the goals of the poverty reduction at the highest levels, and a concrete follow-up at the operational level have created a political and moral commitment from States and engendered the development agenda as an ambitious but generally accepted and achievable reform agenda. This wide spectrum of commitments provide a framework for the UN system and the international community to work together towards promoting social progress and better standards of life in larger freedom.

It is suggested that international human rights law is a key ingredient in the reconstruction of the body of principles concerned with the problems of poverty eradication, not least because human rights are one of the many definitions of sustainable development, but also because there is at least a minimal consensus across all disciplines that the ultimate objective of poverty eradication is to improve the human condition. The potential of this corpus of legal norms may lie in introducing legal rules and principles into poverty eradication policies and practices, but ultimately to ensure that these frameworks are respectful of the rights of individuals.

[132] Paragraph 11 of Vienna Declaration and Programme of Action, as adopted by the World Conference on Human Rights on 25 June 1993 states: 'The right to development should be fulfilled so as to meet equitably the developmental and environmental needs of present and future generations'.

[133] Bothe, M., 'Environment, Development, Resources' (2005) 318 *Recueil des Cours* 380.

## V) Select Bibliography

*UN documents*

CESCR, Statement on Poverty and the International Covenant on Economic, Social and Cultural Rights, UN Doc E/2002/22-E/C.12/2001/17, 10 May 2001.

CESCR, Globalization and Its Impact on the Enjoyment of Economic, Social and Cultural Rights, 18th Session, UN Doc E/1999/22-E/C.12/1998/26, 27 April–15 May 1998.

CESCR, Statement on the importance and relevance of the right to development, adopted on the occasion of the twenty-fifth anniversary of the Declaration on the Right to Development, UN Doc E/C.12/2011/2, 13 July 2011.

*Selected literature*

Abi-Saab, G., 'The Legal Formulation of the Right to Development', in Dupuy, R-J. (ed), *The Right to Development at the International Level* (The Hague Academy of International Law 1980), 159.

de Feyter, K., *World Development Law: Sharing Responsibility for Development* (Intersentia 2001).

Eide, A., Krause, C., and Rosas, A. (eds), *Economic, Social and Cultural Rights. A Textbook* (Dordrecht 1995).

Jouannet, E., 'How to Depart from the Existing Dire Condition of Development', in Cassese, A. (ed), *Realizing Utopia: The Future of International Law* (Oxford University Press 2012), 392.

Jouannet, E., *The Liberal-Welfarist Law of Nations: A History of International Law* (Cambridge University Press 2012).

Pisillo Mazzeschi, R., 'Responsabilité de l'état pour violation des obligations positives relatives aux droits de l'homme' (2008) 333 *Recueil des Cours* 175.

Schrijver, N., 'The Evolution of Sustainable Development in International Law: Inception, Meaning and Status' (2007) 329 *Recueil de Cours* 217.

# 10. Principle 6

## *Special Situation of Developing Countries*

Mamadou Hébié*

**Principle 6**

The special situation and needs of developing countries, particularly the least developed and those most environmentally vulnerable, shall be given special priority. International actions in the field of environment and development should also address the interests and needs of all countries.



* Lecturer in International Law at The Graduate Institute, Geneva.

## I) Origins and Rationale of the Principle

Article 2, paragraph 1 of the United Nations Charter states the principle of the sovereign equality of States before international law. As a foundational principle of the contemporary international legal order, the principle of sovereign equality of States calls for the equal treatment of all States in general international law. However, this equality before international law does not entail equality in other respects, including States' socio-economic conditions. Irrespective of their formal equality before international law, States with uneven capabilities face environmental, economic, and social challenges that are often different both in nature and in scope. This structural inequality among States places certain constraints on international cooperation, including setting the agenda, assigning an order of priority to its different items, as well as paying sufficient regard to parties' capacities to implement their obligations. International actions being based on consent, accounting insufficiently for the heteroclite composition of the international community is likely to make States reluctant to adopt international commitments or incapable of implementing them. Multilateral participation in international regimes, as well as their effectiveness and equity, requires addressing the socio-economic differences among States and modulating the provisions of treaties according to their different capacities, needs, and interests.

In international negotiations, States use differentiation, either through contextualization or differential treatment, to tackle the challenges arising from the heterogeneity of needs and interests. Under provisions stipulating differential treatment, 'formal legal equality and reciprocity are sidelined to accommodate extraneous factors',[1] in order to grant a presumably more favourable treatment to certain categories of States while excluding others.[2] In this respect, differential treatment norms are different from 'contextual norms'. A contextual norm is 'a norm that on its face stipulates an identical treatment to all States falling within its scope of application. However, its implementation requires (or at least permits) consideration of characteristics that might vary from country to country.'[3] Contextual and differential treatment norms are both distinct from absolute norms, which provide identical treatment to all countries and neither require nor permit consideration of factors that vary among them.[4]

Principle 6 of the Rio Declaration embodies the consensus of the international community to consider the diversity of States' situations and needs when undertaking actions in the field of the environment and development. On the one hand, it specifies that the special needs of environmentally vulnerable States and developing States, especially least developed countries, shall be addressed as a matter of priority. On the other hand, it requires addressing the interests and needs of other States.

[1] Cullet, Ph., 'Common but Differentiated Responsibilities', in Fitzmaurice, M., Ong, D. M., and Merkouris, P. (eds), *Research Handbook on International Environmental Law* (Edward Elgar 2010), 165.

[2] Magraw, D. B., 'Legal Treatment of Developing Countries: Differential, Contextual, and Absolute Norms' (1990), 1 *Colorado Journal of International Environmental Law and Policy* 69, 73.

[3] Magraw, 'Legal Treatment of Developing Countries', 74.

[4] Magraw, 'Legal Treatment of Developing Countries', 76.

## II) The Principle as Enshrined in the Rio Declaration

### 1. Preparatory work and context

#### *1.1. Precedents*

So long as environmental instruments were bilateral or regional in scope and involved only States having approximately the same level of development, differentiation was mainly operated through contextualization to account for the capacity of the parties to implement their obligations. However, the need for cooperation brought together developed and developing countries around global environmental issues.

The Stockholm Declaration constitutes a starting point of the use of differential treatment as a technique to tackle the differences among participants in international environmental actions. Principle 12 of the Stockholm Declaration acknowledged developing countries' needs for 'additional financial aids and transfer of technology.' Principle 23 stressed that it is essential in adopting environmental standards, both international and domestic:

> to consider the systems of values prevailing in each country, and the extent of the applicability of standards which are valid for the most advanced countries but which may be inappropriate and of unwarranted social cost for the developing countries.[5]

Under article 30 of the Charter on the Economic Rights and Duties of States of 1974, '[t]he environmental policies of all states should enhance and not adversely affect the present and future development potential of developing countries.'[6]

Differentiation clauses were also included in environmental treaties, and appeared either in their preamble—as an element of interpretation of their provisions—or in substantive provisions to qualify their implementation by developing countries. The preamble of the 1985 Vienna Convention on the Protection of the Ozone Layer refers to 'the circumstances and particular requirements of developing countries'.[7] Dealing with implementation, article 207 paragraph 4 of the United Nations Convention on the Law of the Sea provides that States must collectively and individually adopt binding and non-binding norms to combat pollution of the marine environment from land-based sources, 'taking into account characteristic regional features, the economic capacity of developing states and their need for economic development.'[8]

Other treaties called for cooperation in order to provide financial and technical assistance to developing countries.[9] The 1987 Montreal Protocol went a step further by granting extended deadlines to developing countries—10 years—to comply with control measures,[10] and authorizing them to use a subsequent base year.[11] Under article 10 paragraph 3 of the Basel Convention, the parties were called to cooperate 'in order

[5] Declaration of the United Nations Conference on the Human Environment, Stockholm, 5–16 June 1972, A/CONF.48/14/Rev.1.

[6] UNGA Doc A/RES/29/3281(XXIX), *Charter of Economic Rights and Duties of States*, art 30.

[7] See also the preamble of the Basel Convention and para 5 of the preamble of UNCLOS.

[8] United Nations Convention on the Law of the Sea, 10 December 1982, 1833 UNTS 397.

[9] Convention for the protection of the Mediterranean Sea against pollution, 16 February 1976, 1102 UNTS 45, art 11 para 3; Montreal Protocol on Substances that Deplete the Ozone Layer, 16 September 1987, 1522 UNTS 29, art 10 A.

[10] Montreal Protocol, arts 2A–2I.

[11] Montreal Protocol, art 5(3)(a).

to assist developing countries in the implementation of subparagraphs a, b, c, and d of paragraph 2 of Article 4'.[12] Article 11 of the Convention foreshadows the mechanism of Principle 6 by imposing on future bilateral or multilateral conventions concluded by the parties regarding transboundary movement of hazardous wastes or other wastes not to derogate to the provisions of the Basel Convention and to take into account the interests of developing countries.

Special treatment on the basis of States' level of development and capacities also figured in non-governmental initiatives, such as the work of the Institut de Droit International.[13] Unsurprisingly, one early attempt to codify the principles of international environmental protection beyond sectoral lines emphasized the importance of differentiation. According to paragraph 2, first line of article 7 of the codification project conducted by the legal expert panel of the Brundtland Commission, '[p]articular attention shall be paid to environmental problems arising in developing countries and to the need to incorporate environmental considerations in all development assistance programmes.' The commentary to this provision stresses that:

> the very condition of underdevelopment is likely to involve, in its own way, a great danger to the proper conservation of natural resources and the environment. In their efforts to close or at least narrow the development gap between the rich and the poor countries the developing countries may well be inclined to give secondary consideration to environmental concerns.[14]

Accordingly:

> States shall make available to other states and especially to developing countries upon their request and under agreed terms scientific and technical information and expertise, results of research programmes, training opportunities and specialized equipment and facilities which are needed by such other states to promote rational use of natural resources and the environment or to prevent or abate interference with natural resources or the environment, in particular in cases of environmental emergencies.[15]

Principle 6 of the Rio Declaration stands out from pre-Rio approaches by its generality and its scope. Like the Brundtland principles, Principle 6 sought to operate by way of generalization as an autonomous provision different and—at the same time—complementary of specific actions adopted in favour of developing countries, such as the transfer of technologies and the provision of development assistance. Neither the Abidjan Declaration on Environment and Development, nor developing countries' first proposal at New York PrepCom IV, had conceptualized it as a general principle distinguishable from these concrete actions. In addition, Principle 6 is not limited to any treaty subject matter. Instead, it applies to any international action undertaken not only in the field of environment, but also in that of development, and possibly also beyond. Furthermore, Principle 6 broadens and specifies the beneficiaries of special attention by including

[12] Basel Convention on the Control of Transboundary Movements of Hazardous Wastes and their Disposal, 22 March 1989, 1673 UNTS 57, art 10(3).

[13] Institute of International Law, Resolution on the Pollution of Rivers and Lakes and International Law, Session of Athens 1979 (art VIII).

[14] *Elements for a Draft Convention on Environmental Protection and Sustainable Development*, adopted by the Expert Group on Environmental Law, June 1986, in *Environmental Protection and Sustainable Development. Experts Group on Environmental Law of the World Commission on Environment and Development*, (Nijhoff 1987), 66.

[15] *Elements for a Draft Convention on Environmental Protection and Sustainable Development*, 68.

environmentally vulnerable countries and by singling out least developing countries. A reference to 'other States' was also inserted in allusion to the needs and interests of States transitioning towards a free-market economy.

## *1.2. Travaux préparatoires*

### 1.2.1. Overview

Unlike Principle 7, its sister provision, negotiations on the need to recognize the special needs of developing countries raised limited controversy. Principle 6 benefited from the decision to adopt G77+China's proposal, which emphasized greatly the special situations, needs, and interests of developing countries, as a basis for the negotiations.[16] When the different proposals were summarized according to their essence,[17] the principle on the special needs of developing countries was characterized as one of the 'easy principles' and benefitted from the early adoption process.[18] What became more controversial was the determination of the categories of States entitled to special treatment.

### 1.2.2. A consensus on the need for differentiation

Both developed and developing countries' proposals at PrepCom IV contain elements which indicated their awareness of the variety of needs and situations in the international community. Accordingly, they proposed differential treatment or contextualization. Not surprisingly, G77+China's proposals at the Conference emphasized the importance of recognizing the special situation and needs of developing countries. Principle 3 of their first proposal considered that their inalienable right to development shall be treated as a matter of priority.[19] Principle 7 called for the provision of technological and new and additional financial resources to developing countries to help them attain sustainable development.[20] Principle 9 noted that:

> [e]nvironmental standards that are valid for the most advanced countries may be inappropriate and of unwarranted economic and social cost for the developing countries. Therefore, environmental management objectives and priorities for the developed and developing countries, based on living standards, social and economic conditions as well as natural resources endowments, will be different.[21]

In Principle 16 of their proposal, developing countries also stressed that full consideration should be given to their special situation regarding the implementation of the future Rio declaration.[22]

This first proposal of G77+China submitted at PrepCom IV received mixed reactions. Whereas certain delegations stressed 'the importance of ensuring that the special needs of developing countries are sufficiently reflected' in the project,[23] others found it

16 *Earth Summit Bulletin*, vol 1, n° 6 UNCED-PC IV, 8 March 1992, at 1.

17 *Earth Summit Bulletin*, vol 1, n° 20 UNCED-PC IV, 27 March 1992, at 1.

18 *Earth Summit Bulletin*, vol 1, n° 19 UNCED-PC IV, 26 March 1992, at 2.

19 Principle 3, 'Right to Development', of the *Proposal submitted by China and by Pakistan on behalf of the States Members of the United Nations that are members of the Group of 77*, A/CONF.151/PC/WG.III/L.20, 4 March 1992.

20 Principle 7, 'Special needs of developing states', *Proposal submitted by China and by Pakistan on behalf of the Group of 77*, 4 March 1992.

21 Principle 9, 'Environmental, economic, social and cultural diversity', *Proposal submitted by China and by Pakistan on behalf of the Group of 77*, 4 March 1992.

22 During the discussions, Principle 16 was perceived as redundant; the other principles having sufficiently covered the position of the South. (*Earth Summit Bulletin*, vol 1, n° 11 UNCED-PC IV, 15 March 1992).

23 *Earth Summit Bulletin*, vol 1, n° 6 UNCED-PC IV, 8 March 1992.

imbalanced.[24] Developing countries tabled a second more concise proposal. It addressed the specific situation of developing States in four manners. First, it placed special emphasis on developing countries' situation in order to contextualize norms of general applicability.[25] Second, it took into account developing countries' capabilities and responsibilities when determining their duty to provide technological and financial assistance.[26] A third method consisted in highlighting the unfairness and unsustainability of any international action that would ignore the differences among developed and developing States.[27] A last technique proposed by the G77+China called for considering the special situations of certain groups of States, such as those affected by desertification, and 'small island states and of low-lying coastal, arid and semi-arid areas.'[28]

Foreshadowing the actual Principle 6 of the Rio declaration, Principle 6 of G77+China's second proposal stipulated that:

> The special situation and needs of developing countries, particularly the least developed countries, their right to achieve their full economic potential, and the eradication of poverty shall be fully taken into account in any international action taken with respect to the environment and development.

Developed countries rejected again this second proposal. They characterized it as 'too detailed, too accusatory and far too politicized'.[29] Nonetheless, these countries also shared the view that pervasive differences among countries required differentiation in the elaboration of environmental regimes. However, unlike the proposals submitted by G77+China, developed countries' draft articles did not consecrate differentiation as a binding principle to guide the elaboration of future international environmental actions. Proposals suggested mentioning the needs or special situations of developing countries in the preamble of the Declaration.[30] Provisions aiming to address developing countries' needs of technical and financial assistance were often merely hortatory.[31] The EC countries took the special status of developing countries into consideration by requiring cooperation 'on the basis of a global partnership reflecting equitable burden sharing between developed and developing countries'.[32] Their proposal also suggested a specific obligation

[24] *Earth Summit Bulletin,* vol 1, n° 13, UNCED-PC IV.

[25] See for instance, Principle 8, 'Rio de Janeiro Charter/Declaration on Environment and Development', *Proposal submitted by China and by Pakistan on behalf of the States Members of the United Nations that are members of the Group of 77,* A/CONF.151/PC/WG.III/L.20.Rev.1., 19 March 1992.

[26] This was criticized by certain States that emphasized that it was inappropriate to refer to these elements, as they were being dealt with under separate Agenda 21 chapters. For developing countries however, transfer of technology on concessional terms and new and additional financial resources were 'the two fundamental components of the new form of international cooperation called for in this Principle.' *Earth Summit Bulletin,* vol 1, n° 9, UNCED-PC IV, March 12 1992.

[27] Principle 24, *Earth Summit Bulletin,* vol 1, n° 9, UNCED-PC IV, 12 March 1992; See also Principle 13.

[28] Principle 18, *Earth Summit Bulletin,* vol 1, n° 9, UNCED-PC IV, 12 March 1992.

[29] *Earth Summit Bulletin,* vol 1, n°. 15, UNCED-PC IV.

[30] Principle 6 of the 'Earth Charter. Elements for Consideration', *Proposal submitted by Denmark, Iceland, Norway and Sweden,* A/CONF.151/PC/WG.III/L.27, 9 March 1992; 'Principles on General Rights and Obligations', *Proposal submitted by Denmark and the United Kingdom of Great Britain and Northern Ireland on the basis of the work of several non-governmental organizations from around the world,* A/CONF.151/PC/WG.III/L.28, 9 March 1992.

[31] Principles 8 and 17 of the 'Principles on General Rights and Obligations', *Proposal submitted by the United States of America,* A/CONF.151/PC/WG.III/L.21, 4 March 1992. See also, Point 8 [Special needs of developing countries], 'Principles on General Rights and Obligations', *Proposal submitted by Japan,* A/CONF.151/PC/WG.III/L.22, 4 March 1992.

[32] Point 3, 'Elements for the Earth Charter', *Proposal submitted by Portugal on behalf of the States members of the European Community Elements for the Earth Charter,* A/CONF.151/PC/WG.III/L.25, 6 March 1992.

imposing to all States to combat poverty.[33] Other States preferred using contextualization to address differences among States. Canada proposed that the implementation of its draft principles, which were binding on all States, be done through cooperation and 'in accordance with their respective responsibilities and capabilities.'[34]

In sum, whereas developed countries acknowledged that the situation and needs of developing countries deserved special consideration, they limited their impact to non-binding stipulations regarding compliance assistance.

### 1.2.3. A consensus on developing and environmentally vulnerable States

Our survey of the proposals submitted at PrepCom IV revealed that all of them in some manner addressed the special situation and needs of developing States. However, least developed countries were rarely singled out as a separate category. Level of development and capabilities were the main criterion for identifying States whose needs and interests deserved special attention.[35]

Environmentally vulnerable States were mentioned in few proposals submitted at PrepCom IV. Before the Conference, Amazonian countries had drawn attention to their special situation through the Manaus declaration on the relation between the environment and development.[36] Pacific Island Developing Countries also addressed a letter to the Chairman identifying climate change and associated sea level rise as the heart of the obstacles they faced in their journey towards sustainable development.[37] On this basis, they emphasized that '[i]ndividual island countries, and the South Pacific region as a whole, have a uniqueness and a significance that must be reflected in the preparation and outcomes of UNCED.'[38] Principle 18 of G77+China's second proposal lent support to environmentally vulnerable States:

> States shall give urgent attention to and shall embark promptly on innovative measures, including legal instruments, to halt and reverse the process of desertification, as well as to alleviate the threat to the survival of some small island states and of low-lying coastal, arid and semi-arid areas.[39]

Among developed countries, Australia highlighted the 'particular vulnerability of some states to environmental change'.[40] Accordingly, a special mention of these countries was not very controversial.

### 1.2.4. The reference to 'other states'

PrepCom IV took place two years after the fall of the Berlin Wall and the breakdown of the USSR. New States created in this process were transitioning towards a market

[33] Point 3, 'Elements for the Earth Charter', *Proposal submitted by Portugal*, 6 March 1992.

[34] Point 12, 'Earth Charter', *Proposal submitted by Canada*, A/CONF.151/PC/WG.III/L.23, 4 March 1992; See also, Principle 2, 'Principles on General Rights and Obligations', *Proposal submitted by Australia*, A/CONF.151/PC/WG.III/L.24, 5 March 1992.

[35] This could already be inferred from the UN General Assembly Resolution 44/228 which refers in several respects to the situations, needs and interests of developing countries. UN Doc GA RES/44/228.

[36] *Manaus Declaration on the United Nations Conference on Environment and Development*, A/CONF.151/PC/123, 24 February 1992, at 5.

[37] *Manaus Declaration*, 5.

[38] Letter from the Chairman of the Fourth SPREP International Governmental Meeting, A/CONF.151/PC/126, 4 March 1992.

[39] Principle 8 of the 'Rio de Janeiro Charter/Declaration on Environment and Development', *Proposal submitted by China and by Pakistan on behalf of the States Members of the United Nations that are members of the Group of 77*, A/CONF.151/PC/WG.III/L.20.Rev.1, 19 March 1992.

[40] Point 8 of the 'Principles on General Rights and Obligations', *Proposal submitted by Australia*, A/CONF.151/PC/WG.III/L.24, 5 March 1992.

economy and refused to be characterized as 'developing states' during the negotiations on 'financial resources'. They preferred the more descriptive and neutral term of 'transitional countries'.[41] According to Jeffrey Kovar, who was part of the US delegation, the reference to the 'interests and needs of all countries' in Principle 6 arose from G77+China's opposition to any express mention of the special needs of 'states with economies of transition'. Developing countries feared that 'recognition of priority of these states would detract from the special efforts due the G77+China and could lead to reduced assistance levels.'[42] However, former Soviet bloc countries were adamant that 'they would not support the Declaration without the recognition of their need for international assistance'.[43] Eventually, the Chairman of the PrepCom, Tommy Koh, stepped in and brokered the following compromise: no specific mention of 'transitional economies' would be made, but a general reference in Principle 6 would ensure that the special needs and situations of all States, including those transitioning towards a market economy, would be addressed.[44]

Although Russia's draft did not address the special treatment for States transitioning towards a market economy,[45] the *Earth Summit Bulletin*'s account of the negotiations reveals that the Russian Federation called for a complete revision of G77+China's first proposal in order to take into account the special needs of countries transitioning towards a market economy.[46] Russia's presence in the restricted contact group that negotiated the final text of the Declaration may have therefore played a role in the inclusion of this reference to 'other states'.[47]

Kovar's account of the discussions surrounding the inclusion of the second sentence of Principle 6 is confirmed by the positions taken by developing and transitional States during the negotiations of Agenda 21.[48] Some provisions of draft Agenda 21, such as its chapter 20, had listed developing and transitional States as equal recipients of technical and financial assistance. G77+China challenged this extension of the beneficiaries of this special treatment. After consultations under the direction of Algeria, reference to transitional countries was removed from the text of Agenda 21. Only a general mention of their special needs was kept in Point 1.5 of the preamble of Agenda 21.[49]

## 2. Scope and dimensions

### 2.1. Overview

The normative content of Principle 6 can be established by contrasting its actual formulation with other proposals available during New York PrepCom IV. In addition, other instruments adopted or opened for signature at Rio, such as Agenda 21, the UN Framework Convention on Climate Change, the Convention on Biological diversity, and

[41] *Earth Summit Bulletin*, vol 1, n° 19, UNCED-PC IV, 26 March 1992.

[42] Kovar, J. D., 'A Short Guide to the Rio Declaration' (1993) 4 *Colo J Int'l E L & Pol'y* 119, 127–8.

[43] Kovar, 'A Short Guide to the Rio Declaration', 128.

[44] Kovar, 'A Short Guide to the Rio Declaration', 128.

[45] See 'Principles on General Rights and Obligations'. *Proposal Submitted by the Union of Soviet Socialist Republics*, UNGAOR 1st Sess, Agenda Item 2, UN DOC A/CONF.151/PC/CRP.8 (1992).

[46] *Earth Summit Bulletin*, vol 1, n° 6, UNCED-PC IV, 8 March 1992; See also *Earth Summit Bulletin*, vol 1, n° 13, UNCED-PC IV 17 March 1992.

[47] *Earth Summit Bulletin*, vol 1, n° 26, UNCED-PC IV, 5 Apr 1992. (This group was composed of seven developed countries, seven developing countries, plus Russia.)

[48] *Earth Summit Bulletin*, vol 2, n°6, 6 June 1992.

[49] *Earth Summit Bulletin*, vol 2, n°6, 6 June 1992.

the 'Non Legally Binding Authoritative Statement of Principles for a Global Consensus on the Management, Conservation and Sustainable Development of All Types of Forests' can also help to unveil the shared views of the parties on its scope.

## *2.2. The subject-matter of Principle 6: 'any international action in the field of environment and development'*

The scope of application of Principle 6 is broad. Covering 'any international action in the field of environment and development', its wording leaves out only domestic measures.

Principle 6 is applicable at the moment of allocation of the rights and obligations of the parties, as well as that of determining the modalities of their implementation. During negotiations regarding the allocation of rights and obligations of the parties, material inequality among States can be adjusted through differentiation to take into account their level of development or the economic or social costs that may be imposed by uniform international standards upon them. As a consequence, differentiation is not limited merely to economic and technical assistance.

However, financial and technical assistance enhances the capacity of developing countries to respect their obligations. In this specific context, Principle 6 refers equally to cases where technical and financial assistance is provided as part of compliance assistance—limited to ensure compliance with certain environmental treaty obligations—or those where such assistance is channelled through 'development programmes'. Embracing both fields of 'development and environment', Principle 6 blurs these boundaries. In addition, Principle 6 requires that both environmental and development initiatives address developing countries' development needs. Although it may seem tautological to require development actions to address development needs, expecting environmental actions also to address them was a significant dimension of the Rio process.[50] The clean development mechanism instituted under article 12 the Kyoto Protocol is the most remarkable expression of this form of linkage between environment and development. Through this mechanism, developed countries investing in projects resulting in certified emission reduction in developing countries obtain credits that can be used to achieve compliance with their quantified emission limitation and reduction commitments under article 3 of the Protocol.[51]

## *2.3. Distinguishing obligations according to groups of States*

### 2.3.1. Developing States and those environmentally vulnerable

#### *2.3.1.1. Identifying environmentally vulnerable and developing countries' situation and needs*

Development and fighting against poverty are the main priorities of developing countries. This appears both from the Common African Position on Environment and

[50] Galizzi, P. and Herklotz, A., 'Environment and Development: Friends or Foes in the 21st Century', in Fitzmaurice, M., Ong, D. M., Merkouris, P. (eds), *Research Handbook on International Environmental Law* (Edward Elgar 2010), 69, 81.

[51] See art 12 of the Kyoto Protocol.

Development,[52] and from G77+China's proposals in New York.[53] In this respect, technological, as well as new and additional financial assistance, was considered of paramount importance.[54] Developed countries mentioned more generally 'the special situation and needs of developing countries in achieving sustainable development',[55] 'to combat poverty',[56] their 'special economic and other circumstances of developing countries and their need for capacity-building'.[57] Any doubt on the nature of developing countries' priorities is clarified by the preamble and article 20 of the Convention on Biological Diversity which restate that 'economic and social development and eradication of poverty are the first and overriding priorities of the developing country Parties.'[58]

Regarding the special situation of 'environmentally vulnerable states', it covered a variety of hypotheses. The majority of proposals submitted in this respect at PrepCom IV focused on vulnerability to climate change, desertification, and drought.[59] The negotiation of the UNFCCC suggested that participants had a broader notion of environmentally vulnerable States in mind. Vulnerability is no longer defined by reference to the adverse effects of climate change. It encompasses also vulnerability to response measures adopted to combat them.[60] In implementing this broad definition of environmental vulnerability, the parties identified certain groups of States perceived as deserving special attention. The list includes:

> (a) Small island countries; (b) Countries with low-lying coastal areas; (c) Countries with arid and semi-arid areas, forested areas and areas liable to forest decay; (d) Countries with areas prone to natural disasters; (e) Countries with areas liable to drought and desertification; (f) Countries with areas of high urban atmospheric pollution; (g) Countries with areas with fragile ecosystems, including mountainous ecosystems; (h) Countries whose economies are highly dependent on

[52] *African Common Position on Environment and Development*, A/CONF.151/PC/120, 26 March 1992, 13, para 27. See also 17, para 34.

[53] Principle 3, 'Right to Development', and Principle 16, 'Special situation of the developing countries', of the *Proposal submitted by China and by Pakistan on behalf of the States Members of the United Nations that are members of the Group of 77*, A/CONF.151/PC/WG.III/L.20, 4 March 1992; See also Principle 5 of the 'Rio de Janeiro Charter/Declaration on Environment and Development', *Proposal submitted by China and by Pakistan on behalf of the States Members of the United Nations that are members of the Group of 77*, A/CONF.151/PC/WG.III/L.20.Rev.1., 19 March 1992.

[54] Principle 6, 'Special needs of the developing countries', of the *Proposal submitted by China and by Pakistan on behalf of the States Members of the United Nations that are members of the Group of 77*, A/CONF.151/PC/WG.III/L.20, 4 March 1992.

[55] Principle 8, 'Principles on General Rights and Obligations', *Proposal submitted by the United States of America*, A/CONF.151/PC/WG.III/L.21, 4 March 1992.

[56] Point 8 of the 'Principles on General Rights and Obligations', *Proposal submitted by Japan*, A/CONF.151/PC/WG.III/L.22, 4 March 1992.

[57] Point 8 of the 'Principles on General Rights and Obligations', *Proposal submitted by Australia*, A/CONF.151/PC/WG.III/L.24, 5 March 1992.

[58] See in this regard, the Convention on Biological Diversity, 5 June 1992, 1760 UNTS 79; See also art 4 para 7 United Nations Framework Convention on Climate Change, 9 May 1992, 31 ILM 849. See also art 20 para 4 of the United Nations Convention to Combat Desertification in those Countries Experiencing Serious Drought and/or Desertification, Particularly in Africa, UN Doc A/AC.241/15/Rev. 7 (1994), 17 June 1994, 33 ILM 1328.

[59] See for instance, Letter from the Chairman of the Fourth SPREP International Governmental Meeting, A/CONF.151/PC/126, 4 March 1992, 5; Principle 18 of the of the 'Rio de Janeiro Charter/Declaration on Environment and Development', *Proposal submitted by China and by Pakistan on behalf of the States Members of the United Nations that are members of the Group of 77*, A/CONF.151/PC/WG.III/L.20.Rev.1, 19 March 1992. 'Principles on General Rights and Obligations', *Proposal submitted by Australia*, A/CONF.151/PC/WG.III/L.24, 5 March 1992.

[60] See art 4 of the Convention on Climate Change.

income generated from the production, processing and export, and/or on consumption of fossil fuels and associated energy-intensive products; and (i) Land-locked and transit countries.

A sub-category of environmentally vulnerable States, that is to say small islands, was identified in chapter 17 of Agenda 21 devoted to the 'Sustainable development of small islands'. In addition to their vulnerability to global warming and seal level rise, their vulnerability to frequent cyclones, storms, and hurricanes was also emphasized.[61]

In sum, the concept of environmental vulnerability under Principle 6 was interpreted in reference both to vulnerability to the effects of climate change and to the corrective measures adopted to fight them. It also includes vulnerability to natural disasters. The groups of States listed under the UNFCCC are merely illustrative and serve as auxiliary means to interpret the notion of 'state environmentally vulnerable' under Principle 6. Principle 6 is applicable to any State demonstrating a particular vulnerability to certain environmental problems or to their response measures, irrespective of whether the latter is related or not to climate change. In addition, level of development is not decisive for determining environmental vulnerability. Principle 6 of the Rio Declaration, and article 4 of the UNFCCC single out least developed countries and those environmentally vulnerable within the broader category of developing countries. It is however doubtful that all environmentally vulnerable States are necessarily developing countries. Oil-rich countries, such as Saudi Arabia, are environmentally vulnerable, without being necessarily developing countries. Admittedly, their environmental problems may not enjoy a special consideration only because of the fact that they possess sufficient means to address them. However, reference to capabilities is just one level where differentiation can be applied. Differentiation could imply different substantive legal obligations.

#### *2.3.1.2. The content of the obligation to give 'special priority' to the situation and the needs of developing countries*

Giving special priority to the situation and needs of environmentally vulnerable and developing countries imposes certain behaviour when devising 'international actions in the field of environment and development'. First of all, it requires addressing these countries' needs and interests *as a matter of priority*. The UNFCCC referred to small islands' concerns that were specifically affected by consequences of climate change, such as sea-level rise.[62] Later, in 1994, the UN Convention on Desertification was adopted to address an issue affecting particularly developing countries, and respond to the obligation to address their issues as a matter of priority.[63]

Second, Principle 6 highlights that developing countries possess limited resources and calls for the understanding of their priorities when allocating such resources. At the same time, it justifies international solidarity irrespective of the limited resources that developing countries may invest in the protection of the environment.[64] Accordingly, differential

[61] Agenda 21, ch 17, point 17.126. See also 17.132.

[62] See the preamble of the United Nations Framework Convention on Climate Change, 9 May 1992, 31 ILM 849.

[63] See the preamble of the United Nations Convention to Combat Desertification in those Countries Experiencing Serious Drought and/or Desertification, Particularly in Africa, UN Doc A/AC.241/15/Rev. 7 (1994), 17 June 1994, 33 ILM 1328.

[64] See for a clear statement of this idea, Principle 9 a) of the Non Legally Binding Authoritative Statement of Principles for a Global Consensus on the Management, Conservation and Sustainable Development of All Types of Forests, A/CONF.151/26 (vol III), 14 August 1992.

treatment or contextualization should be applied to assist them to meet their obligations under the conventions.[65] This includes tailoring their obligations accordingly, either by exempting them completely of certain obligations or imposing on them obligations that are partially or totally different from those of developed countries. Other possibilities include granting developing countries transitioning periods or extended deadlines to comply with their international environmental obligations. Among treaties opened for signature at Rio, article 12(5) UNFCCC delayed developing countries' reporting obligations.[66] Core obligations of the Kyoto Protocol to the UNFCCC are exclusively applicable to developed countries, whereas developing countries were subjected only to reporting obligations.[67] In addition, developing countries enjoyed delayed compliance schedules,[68] and benefited from a softer approach to compliance.[69]

Treaties concluded under the aegis of the Rio Conference readily acknowledged that socio-economic development and the fight against poverty are the first priorities of developing countries.[70] In addition, developing countries' needs for financial and technological assistance were acknowledged in the preambles of all three 'Rio treaties'.[71] Parties were often reminded that developing countries' compliance with their treaty obligations was conditional upon the provision of financial and technical assistance by developed countries.[72] Compliance assistance through financial and technical assistance helps developing and environmentally vulnerable States to face adaptation and incremental costs required by the implementation of their international environmental obligations. Under compliance assistance provisions, developing countries' 'specific interests were not only considered as contextual background, as a reason for the different interpretation of the same provision, or as the basis for differing obligations, but gave rise to specific obligations for compliance assistance to developing countries.'[73] Special provisions of the Rio treaties were devoted to compliance assistance, even though they rarely established firm commitments to provide technical and financial assistance.[74]

[65] Agenda 21, para 39.3. d).

[66] United Nations Framework Convention on Climate Change, 9 May 1992, 31 ILM 849.

[67] See the division of obligations between Annex I and Annex II countries. Art III of the Kyoto Protocol.

[68] Revision of the UNFCCC reporting guidelines on annual inventories for Parties included in Annex I to the Convention, in Report of the Conference of the Parties on its seventeenth session, held in Durban from 28 November to 11 December 2011, Addendum Part Two: Action taken by the Conference of the Parties at its seventeenth session, FCCC/CP/2011/9/Add.2 (2014).

[69] Procedures and mechanisms relating to Compliance under the Kyoto Protocol, in report of the Conference of the Parties on its Seventh Session, Addendum, Part Two: Action taken by the Conference of the Parties at its Seventh Session, vol III, FCCC/CP/2001/13/Add.3 (2002).

[70] See the preamble and art 20 § 4 of the Convention on Biological Diversity; art 4 para 7 of the UN Framework Convention on Climate Convention; art 20 para 7 of the 1994 Convention on Desertification.

[71] Art 20 para 2 of the Convention on Biological Diversity; United Nations Convention to Combat Desertification in those Countries Experiencing Serious Drought and/or Desertification, Particularly in Africa, 33 ILM 1328.

[72] Art 20 para 4 of the Convention on Biological Diversity; art 4 para 7 of the UNFCCC; art 3 (5), Kyoto Protocol 1997.

[73] Beyerlin, U. and Marauhn, T., *International Environmental Law* (Hart 2011), 344.

[74] See Art 27 para 7 of the United Nations Convention to Combat Desertification in those Countries Experiencing Serious Drought and/or Desertification, Particularly in Africa, 17 June 1994, 33 ILM 1328; art 4 paras 3–4 UNFCCC; art 26 para 7 Convention on Desertification: Principles 7 b) and 10 of the Non Legally Binding Authoritative Statement of Principles for a Global Consensus on the Management, Conservation and Sustainable Development of All Types of Forests, A/CONF.151/26 (vol III), 14 August 1992.

Finally, addressing developing countries' special needs and interests as a matter of priority was interpreted as requiring an increase of official development assistance ('ODA'). But no firm commitment was made in Rio. Acknowledging that development and eradication of poverty are the overriding priorities of developing countries,[75] Agenda 21 stressed the need of 'substantial new and additional financial resources'[76] and the difficulties that developing countries would face to implement Agenda 21 by their own means.[77] Agenda 21 assessed the financial needs of developing countries for implementing Agenda 21 at approximately 125 million dollars.[78]

Agenda 21 reaffirmed the UN target of 0.7% GNP for official development assistance for those States having already committed to reach it. The United States and Switzerland, which had never made this commitment, were therefore excluded.[79] No firm deadline was established for reaching the 0.7% target, although some States committed to reach it by the year 2000. However, nothing concrete was adopted in Rio. Agenda 21 merely suggested that '[d]eveloped countries and others in a position to do so should make initial financial commitments to give effect to the decisions of the Conference. They should report on such plans and commitment to the United Nations General Assembly in the Fall of 1992 at its forty-seventh session.'[80] Other States, 'in line with their support for reform effort in developing countries, agree to make their best efforts to increase their level of ODA'.[81] Eventually, 'other countries, including those undergoing the process of transition to a market economy, may voluntarily augment the contributions of the developed countries'.[82]

### 2.3.2. Other States

#### *2.3.2.1. States transitioning towards market economy*

The reference to 'other states' in Principle 6 of the Rio declaration was essentially directed to States transitioning towards a market economy. As mentioned above, developing countries opposed the inclusion of transitional States to avoid spreading the financial aid and technical assistance to many beneficiaries. However, transitional countries appear in the Rio treaties. Under article 21 of the Convention on Biological Diversity, they could freely choose to be subjected to the same obligations as developed countries. Under article 4 paragraph 2 of the UNFCCC, they were listed under annex I, and therefore subjected to the more onerous obligations of the Convention. However, article 4 paragraph 6 of the Convention made a caveat affording them flexibility 'in order to enhance the ability of these Parties to address climate change, including with regard to the historical level of anthropogenic emissions of greenhouse gases not controlled by the Montreal Protocol chosen as a reference.' Unlike developed States under UNFCCC and the Convention on Biological Diversity, transitioning States were not obliged to provide financial assistance to developing countries.[83]

The reference to 'other states' in Principle 6 was designed to cover the special status of transitional countries. However, its inclusive formulation suggests that other categories

[75] Agenda 21, point 33.3. [76] Agenda 21, point 33.10; Agenda 21, point 33.13.
[77] Agenda 21, point 33.3. [78] Agenda 21, point 33.18.
[79] See on this issue Johnson, S. P., *The Earth Summit: The United Nations Conference on Environment and Development (UNCED)* (Graham & Trotman 1993), 375, 448.
[80] Agenda 21, point 33.21. [81] Agenda 21, point 33.15. [82] Agenda 21, point 33.15.
[83] See arts 4 (3) and 4 (5) of UNFCCC; see also art 20 para 2 of the Convention on Biological Diversity.

of States can fall within its scope of application. At minimum, nothing in the context or in the different proposals submitted during PrepCom IV suggests a restrictive interpretation. It is noteworthy that in *The Future We Want*, the outcome document of Rio 2012 Summit, new categories of States deserving special attention were included. Participants called for special attention to be paid to 'the special challenges facing the most vulnerable countries and in particular African countries, least developed countries, landlocked developing countries, and small island developing States, as well as the specific challenges facing the middle-income countries', and also '[c]ountries in situations of conflict.'[84] Accordingly, the needs and interests of any State which can justly claim to be in a special situation in the field of environment and development should also be addressed.

#### *2.3.2.2. Content of the second sentence of Principle 6: 'all countries'*

The broad scope of the second sentence of Principle 6 seems counterbalanced by the vagueness of its content: '[i]nternational actions in the field of environment and development should also address the interests and needs of all countries'.

The second sentence of Principle 6 differs in many respects from the first sentence, consecrating the obligation to grant special priority to the situation and needs of developing and environmentally vulnerable States. The conditional tense evidenced by the term 'should' signals that the required conduct is not as such binding. In addition, its substance is not precisely defined. States are merely required not to ignore, but to 'address the interests and needs of all countries'. In this regard, the normative added value of Principle 6, besides negotiations in good faith, remains somewhat mysterious. Arguably, irrespective of the field, States always aim at addressing their respective needs and interests when participating in international actions. At best, the second sentence of Principle 6 makes it praiseworthy to address the needs and interests of all States when devising international actions in the field of environment and development.

### *2.4. Nature of the principle*

Each of the two sentences constituting Principle 6 of the Rio Declaration embodies a different norm. As mentioned above, the second sentence of Principle 2 is hortatory. It merely encourages addressing needs and interests of States, other than developing and environmentally vulnerable ones. Conversely, under the first sentence of Principle 6, it is mandatory to take into account the situation, needs, and interests of these two categories of States as a matter of priority.[85] One indication is the fact that proposals tabled by the UK and the Nordic countries, suggesting a reference to the special needs and interests of developing countries in the preamble (which would have relegated them to an element of interpretation of the Declaration), were not followed. In addition, the first sentence of Principle 6 is not merely hortatory. The use of the future tense 'shall' goes against any such interpretation. Again, formulas proposed by developed countries' proposals, which were phrased in the conditional tense and would have had this effect, were rejected in favour for the binding formula of G77+China's proposal.

[84] UNGA A/RES/66/288, Annex, *The Future We Want*, para 32.

[85] See on the distinction between hortatory and binding provisions, *Application of the Convention on the Prevention and Punishment of the Crime of Genocide (Bosnia and Herzegovina v. Serbia and Montenegro)*, Judgment, ICJ Reports 2007, para 162.

The substance of the first sentence of Principle 6 is rather weak. It imposes a binding obligation of conduct—*obligation de comportement*—stipulating that special priority shall be given to developing and environmentally vulnerable States' needs and interests.[86] Somewhat abstract and general, the first sentence of Principle 6 operates therefore as a 'framework principle'. It imposes a standard of behaviour to guide future international negotiations regarding the environment and development. It also provides the rationale running through more specific provisions of the Rio Declaration, such as those stipulating granting technological and financial assistance to developing countries.

## 3. Normative impact

The impact of Principle 6 after Rio can be assessed in accordance with the different stages at which the principle intervenes.

### 3.1. *Prioritizing the interests of developing and environmentally vulnerable countries when setting up the international agenda for cooperation*

Many conventions and other international instruments, falling under the rubric of 'international actions in the field of the environment and development', have been adopted to deal with issues specific to these countries. Regarding the field of the environment, several conventions dealing with environmental issues of particular relevance for developing countries were adopted, starting with the Convention on Desertification. Concerns specific to environmentally vulnerable countries were also dealt with through treaties, including the UNFCCC and the Kyoto Protocol, and other instruments such as the Programme of Action for the Sustainable Development of Small Island Developing States (Barbados Programme of Action),[87] and the Mauritius Strategy for the Further Implementation of the Programme of Action for the Sustainable Development of Small Island Developing States.[88]

In the field of development, several initiatives have been adopted to tackle the needs of developing countries, especially least developing ones, including the Programme of Action for the Least Developed Countries 2011–2020 (Istanbul Programme of Action), the Heavily Indebted Poor Countries Initiative, the Political Declaration on Africa's Development Needs, the New Partnership for Africa's Development, and the Almaty Programme of Actions addressing the Special Needs of Landlocked Developing Countries within a New Global Framework for Transit Transport Cooperation for Landlocked and Transit Developing Countries.

### 3.2. *Granting special treatment to developing countries according to their needs*

Preambles of treaties concluded after the 1992 Rio Conference invariably acknowledged the special needs and interests of developing countries, elevating these elements to the status of means of interpretation of their provisions. For instance, the Cartagena Protocol acknowledged 'the limited capabilities of many countries, particularly developing

[86] For a similar obligation of conduct, which the Court found breached, see *Application of the Interim Accord of 13 September 1995 (the former Yugoslav Republic of Macedonia v. Greece)*, ICJ Reports 2011, paras 70, 81–2.

[87] United Nations General Assembly A/CONF.167/9, October 1994.

[88] Mauritius Strategy for the Further Implementation of the Programme of Action for the Sustainable Development of Small Island Developing States, A/60/401, 3 October 2005.

countries, to cope with the nature and scale of known and potential risks associated with living modified organisms'.[89] Other treaties stressed that 'the capacity of developing countries and countries with economies in transition to undertake such tasks needs urgently to be reinforced'.[90]

Some provisions of treaties imposed to interpret and apply their provisions in light of the status of developing countries. For instance, article 4.7 of the Stockholm Convention on Persistent Organic Pollutants stipulates that the Conference of the Parties should consider a State's status as a developing country when deciding to extend or not its exemption periods.[91] Other conventions posterior to Rio imposed differential obligations to developing countries, including by granting them delayed compliance or reporting schedules,[92] adopting softer approaches to non-compliance with respect to them,[93] or making allowance for the absence of domestic legislation on new technological issues.[94] Another type of provisions granted compliance assistance, either financial or technological, to developing countries. [95] However, compliance assistance provisions either merely requested cooperation for financial assistance or were made dependent on developed countries' capabilities. Despite their imprecision and indeterminacy, which make their implementation and its monitoring difficult, these provisions nonetheless constitute binding obligations requiring cooperation to provide financial and technological assistance to developing countries.

Adopted in 1997, the provisions of the Kyoto protocol remain a special case of differential treatment for two reasons. First, the Protocol implemented, through the clean development mechanism, the aspect of Principle 6 requiring international actions in the field of the environment to also address the needs of developing countries.[96] In practice, however, only a few developing countries, especially Latin-American countries and India, took advantage of this mechanism. The clean development mechanism impact on least

[89] See Cartagena Protocol on Biosafety to the Convention on Biological Diversity, 29 January 2000, 39 ILM 1027 (2000), preamble; See also Agreement for the Implementation of the Provisions of the United Nations Conventions on the Law of the Sea of 10 December 1982 Relating to the Conservation and Management of Straddling Fish Stocks and Highly Migratory Fish Stocks, 4 August 1995, 2167 UNTS 88, preamble.

[90] International Treaty on Plant Genetic Resources for Food and Agriculture, 3 November 2001, 2400 UNTS 379, preamble. See also Stockholm Convention on Persistent Organic Pollutants, 22 May 2001, 40 ILM 532 (2001) (as amended in 2009), preamble.

[91] Art 4.7 of the Stockholm Convention on Persistent Organic Pollutants, 22 May 2001, 40 ILM 532 (2001) (as amended in 2009); See also arts 3 and 5 of the Agreement for the Implementation of the Provisions of the United Nations Conventions on the Law of the Sea of 10 December 1982 Relating to the Conservation and Management of Straddling Fish Stocks and Highly Migratory Fish Stocks, 4 August 1995, 2167 UNTS 88.

[92] United Nations Framework Convention on Climate Change, 9 May 1992, 31 ILM 849.

[93] Procedures and mechanisms relating to Compliance under the Kyoto Protocol, in report of the Conference of the Parties on its Seventh Session, Addendum, Part Two: Action taken by the Conference of the Parties at its Seventh Session, vol III, FCCC/CP/2001/13/Add.3 (2002).

[94] Art 11 para 6 Cartagena Protocol.

[95] Art 16 of the Rotterdam Convention on the Prior Informed Consent Procedure for Certain Hazardous Chemicals and Pesticides in International Trade; arts 22 and 28 of the Cartagena Protocol on Biosafety; art 28 on Financial Assistance; arts 12–13 of the Stockholm Convention on Persistent Organic Pollutants; arts 8 and 18.5 of the International Treaty on Plant Genetic Resources for Food and Agriculture. arts 24–6 of the Agreement for the Implementation of the Provisions of the United Nations Conventions on the Law of the Sea of 10 December 1982 Relating to the Conservation and Management of Straddling Fish Stocks and Highly Migratory Fish Stocks, 4 August 1995, 2167 UNTS 88.

[96] See also art 1 g) of the International Tropical Timber Agreement, considering, as part of the objectives of the agreement to contribute to sustainable development and to poverty alleviation.

developed countries was rather limited because of the types of activities for which emission reduction certificates are granted.[97]

The Kyoto protocol is also different from other instruments by the type of differential treatment it institutes in favour of developing countries.[98] Instead of traditionally differentiating with respect to the implementation, it exempted developing countries from some of its core, and arguably, more burdensome provisions. As a concrete consequence, the Protocol remained unpopular with developed countries, and the United States refused to ratify it. More recently, the United States and other developed countries have advocated for more equality in the climate change regime established by the Protocol. This emerging trend towards equality in the climate change regime was interpreted as signalling the swan song of differential treatment in international environmental law.[99] From a different perspective, Pauwelyn maintains that only differential norms are disappearing from practice, in favour of contextual norms.[100] According to this author, more differentiation on the basis of objective criteria—and not only on the status of 'developing country'—is to be expected in the future.[101]

Being the most recently signed multilateral environmental treaty, the 2013 Minamata Convention on Mercury provides insights into the current status of differentiation in contemporary international environmental law. This is particularly the case because as of 11 February 2014, the United States is the first and only State to have ratified the Convention. Its preamble reaffirms differentiation in favour of developing countries, while emphasizing at the same time the needs of least developed countries and countries with economy in transition of 'financial, technological, technical and capacity building support'.[102] More generally, it acknowledged 'states' respective circumstances and capabilities and the need for global action'.[103] Furthermore, the convention makes it conditional upon the provision of compliance assistance by developed countries the implementation by 'developing country Parties, in particular the least developed countries and small island developing states, and Parties with economies in transition' of their obligations under the Convention.[104]

The provisions of the Minamata Convention suggest a continuing relevance of differential treatment based on needs and circumstances as an important principle of contemporary international environmental law. In this regard, a distinction should be made between the climate change regime and its special form of differential treatment and other international environmental regimes. The backlash against the UNFCCC and the Kyoto protocol is attributable to several causes, completely unrelated to a wholesale rejection of the use of differentiation in international environmental law. Perhaps, the most obvious of these reasons is the perceived inequity of allocating responsibilities regarding the core obligations of the Protocol, exclusively on the basis of countries' historical contribution

[97] Behn, D., 'Linking Climate Change Mitigation and Poverty Reduction. Continued Reformed of the Clean Development Mechanism in the Post-Kyoto Era to Promote Sustainable Energy Development on the African Continent', in Bouthillier, Y. Le et al (eds), *Poverty Alleviation and Environmental Law* (Edward Elgar 2012), 273.

[98] Rajamani, L., 'The Changing Fortunes of Differential Treatment in the Evolution of International Environmental Law' (2012) 88 *International Affairs* 605, 611.

[99] Rajamani, 'The Changing Fortunes of Differential Treatment', 622.

[100] Pauwelyn, J., 'The End of Differential Treatment for Developing Countries? Lessons from the Trade and Climate Change Regimes' (2013) 22 (1) *RECIEL* 29, 41.

[101] Pauwelyn, 'The End of Differential Treatment for Developing Countries?' 41.

[102] Preamble of the Minamata Convention.

[103] Art 14 para 2 of the Minamata Convention.

[104] Art 14 of the Minamata Convention.

to the degradation of the planet, and not on the basis of their current contribution. This allows several countries with high environmental footprints, such as Brazil, South Africa, India, and China, to get off the hook.[105] Caution should therefore guide any extrapolation on the status of differentiation in environmental law exclusively in light of the Kyoto protocol regime. Admittedly, provisions granting effect to the principle can be contested, as inappropriate or excessive, while no challenge is addressed to the principle itself. In addition, as differentiation can rest on several rationales, some of its rationales embodied in certain treaties can be contested, while others remain unaffected.

From this perspective, as long as pervasive differences relevant for the adoption or the implementation of international environmental obligations will persist, a certain form of differentiation, either through differential treatment or contextualization, is required. Actually, differentiation has been upgraded to the status of a binding principle of environmental law, even for States transitioning towards a market economy. After Rio, these States achieved parity with developing countries regarding special treatment, as evidenced by documents and plans of actions adopted in Rio+5 and Rio+10, as well as in the 2005 World Summit. The two categories appear systematically one after the other in provisions stipulating special attention to the needs and interests of certain States. However, it is noteworthy that transitioning countries have completely disappeared as a special category in the 2012 Rio Declaration. Middle-income countries were mentioned at their expense, if not to encompass them.[106]

In the majority of treaties concluded after Rio, transitional countries are treated on equal footing with developing countries, as deserving equal consideration. In fact, recent environmental treaties elevate the needs and circumstances of both developing and States transitioning towards a market economy to the status of elements of interpretation of their provisions. Substantive provisions of these conventions call for cooperation in order to grant financial and technical provisions to these countries.[107] This is a significant departure from the text of Principle 6, which formulation aimed at excluding transitional States from entitlement to financial and technical assistance, to avoid excessively wide dispersion.

### 3.3. *Taking into account the special situation of developing countries through development assistance*

Through Agenda 21 adopted in Rio, developed countries reaffirmed their commitment—for those of them having already done so—to grant 0.7% of their GDP to developing countries as development assistance. At the 2001 Third UN Conference on Least Developed Countries, developed countries agreed to increase their official development assistance from 0.15 to 0.20% for Least Developed Countries.[108] None of these two commitments has been satisfactorily implemented, as noticed by a UN 2012 assessment of the implementation of Agenda 21.[109] Just five years after Rio, developing countries pointed out

[105] The Bali Plan of Action seems designed to redress this situation.

[106] See for instance, *The Future We Want*, UNGA RES/66/288, 11 September 2001, para 32.

[107] Art 16 of the Rotterdam Convention; art 11 para 6, and 22.2 and 28.4 of the Cartagena Protocol; arts 12–13 of the Stockholm Treaty.

[108] Brussels Declaration, A/CONF./192/12, 2 July 2001, point 8.

[109] See the *Review of Implementation of Agenda 21 and the Rio Principles*, January 2012, UN Department of Economic and Social Affairs, Division for Sustainable Development, 13.

developed countries' failures to deliver on their promises on development assistance.[110] In 1997, resolution A/RES/S-19/2 of the General Assembly on the further implementation of Agenda 21 stressed that 'while some progress has been made, much remains to be done to activate the means of implementation set out in Agenda 21, in particular in the areas of finance and technology transfer, technical assistance and capacity-building.'[111] More specifically, it stressed the failure of most developed countries to reach the target of committing 0.7% of their GDP to official development assistance.[112] Similar criticisms were reiterated at Rio+10.[113]

At Rio+20, the 0.7% of GNP for ODA target was still not met, prompting the participants to 'reaffirm that developing countries need additional resources for sustainable development'.[114] They also reiterated that the 'fulfilment of all commitments related to ODA is crucial, including the commitments by many developed countries to achieve the target of 0.7 per cent of gross national product (GNP) for ODA to developing countries by 2015, as well as a target of 0.15 to 0.20 per cent of GNP for ODA to the least developed countries'.[115] Concerning Africa specifically, participants noted that aid to Africa 'still lags behind commitments that were previously made' despite recent increase.[116]

## III) Relations with Other Principles

Unlike the second sentence of Principle 6 which seems not to bear any particular relation to other provisions of the Declaration, the first sentence of Principle 6 on the needs and interests of environmentally vulnerable and developing countries should not be read in isolation from other provisions of this instrument. The relationship between the first sentence of Principle 6 and some principles of the Rio Declaration are quite straightforward. Principle 9 dealing with endogenous capacity building and transfer of technology is merely a means to implement the first sentence of Principle 6.[117] Principles 11 and 6 share the same rationale. Both principles emphasize the non-existence of universal environmental standards to be applied equally in all countries. However, the focus of Principle 11 is on environmental standards adopted domestically. It does not deal with international standards that could be adopted within the framework of 'international actions in the field of environment and development'.[118] The relation with Principle 12 is also evident. Measures decided on the basis of an international consensus to deal with transboundary

[110] Sustainable Development Commission—4—Press Release ENV/DEV/409 2nd Meeting (PM) 8 April 1997: *Lack of Financial Aid will kill Dream of Sustainable Development in Developing Countries, Group of 77 tells Sustainable Development Commission*; See also General Assembly Plenary—8—Press Release GA/9266 Nineteenth Special Session ENV/DEV/432 4th Meeting (PM) 24 June 1997, *General Assembly is told Alleviation of Global Poverty Essential of Sustainable Development Goals are to be Reached.*

[111] *Programme for the Further Implementation of Agenda 21*, Resolution A/RES/S-19/2, 19 September 1997, para 17.

[112] *Programme for the Further Implementation of Agenda 21*, para 18.

[113] *Plan of Implementation of the World Summit on Sustainable Development*, Annexed to Resolution 2 on Plan of Implementation of the World Summit on Sustainable Development of Report of the World Summit on Sustainable Development Johannesburg, South Africa, 26 August–4 September 2002, para 85.

[114] UNGA A/RES/66/288, Annex, *The Future We Want*, para 252.

[115] UNGA A/RES/66/288, Annex, *The Future We Want*, para 258.

[116] UNGA A/RES/66/288, Annex, *The Future We Want*, para 35.

[117] See commentary to Principle 9 in this volume.

[118] See commentary to Principle 11 in this volume.

or global environmental problems, shall give special priority to the needs and interests of developing and environmentally vulnerable States.[119]

The relation between Principle 6 and other principles of the Rio Declaration deserves more comment. First in line is the relation with Principle 4, which states the principle of integration.[120] The possibility of a conflict between the two provisions arises from the underlying consensus, under Principle 6, that poverty and social and economic development are the most pressing priorities of developing countries. A captious extrapolation of this acknowledgment would consider environmental protection as a secondary priority of developing countries and assign to it a subordinate role. Such an interpretation could defeat, in some respects, the integration approach under Principle 4. However, Principle 6 does not subordinate environmental protection to development or to the fight against poverty. It simply qualifies developing countries' use of their personal resources. In this way, provisions imposing new and additional financial assistance make completely sense. They implement the principle of solidarity by providing for compliance assistance.

The relation between Principles 6 and 7 of the Rio declaration also calls for clarification. Manuals and monographs on international environmental law often address these two principles simultaneously under the heading 'Common But Differentiated Responsibility' (hereafter CBDR).[121] Both principles are perceived as embodying CBDR, although they do not have the same content. However, this interpretation of Principle 6 runs the risk of turning it into a redundant provision, in contradiction with the principle *ut res magit pereat*. This should not be lightly presumed. Principle 7 allocates States' environmental responsibilities according to their respective contribution to the degradation of the global environment and their capacities.[122] To the contrary, differentiation under Principle 6 finds its rationale in the special needs and interests of environmentally vulnerable and developing countries.[123] Very interestingly, the United States of America attached an 'interpretative statement' to Principle 7, leaving untouched Principle 6. This speaks volumes regarding the difference of rationale between the two provisions. Whereas the United States accepted differential treatment and contextualization on the basis of the special needs and interests of developing countries and those environmentally vulnerable, it was reluctant to acknowledge any enhanced responsibility arising from its contribution to environment damage or from its greater financial and technological resources.[124] The adoption process of the two principles also reflects the perception of the drafters of the Rio declaration that their legal effects were different. While Principle 6 was adopted in New York as part of the 'easy principles', Principle 7 remained contentious, prompting the US last minute 'interpretative statement'. Principle 7 can therefore hardly be described as a 'practical consequence of Principle 6'[125] or merely as an elaboration of this provision.[126] It provides a different and separate rationale for differentiation.

[119] See commentary to Principle 12 in this volume.

[120] See commentary to Principle 4 in this volume.

[121] See among others, Hunter, D., Salzman, J., and Zaelke, D., *International Environmental Law and Policy* (4th edn, Foundation Press 2011), 464–5; Birnie, P. and Boyle, A., *International Law & the Environment* (2nd edn, Oxford University Press 2002), 101–4; Beyerlin, U. and Marauhn, T., *International Environmental Law*, 344.

[122] See the commentary to Principle 7 in this volume.

[123] French, D., 'Developing States and International Environmental Law: The Importance of Differentiated Responsibilities' (2000) 49 (1) *ICLQ* 35, at 46, 52.

[124] A/CONF.151/26/Rev.1 (vol II) 18 (1993).

[125] Kiss, A. and Beurier, J.-P., *Droit international de l'environnement* (2nd edn, Pedone 2000), 40.

[126] Nanda, P. and Pring, G., *International Environmental Law & Policy for the 21st Century* (Transnational Publishers 2003), 39.

## IV) Assessment

Principle 6 is based on a classification of States' needs according to their level of development and their vulnerability to environmental challenges. This classification triggers a special treatment in favour of these States in international negotiations in the field of the environment and development. A link exists therefore between the special treatment granted to developing countries and the circumstances and needs that are to be addressed through international action. However, this link can be easily severed when the situation of a country does not call for special treatment on the issue at stake. Indeed, equity no longer compels granting special treatment when there is no difference between parties or when an existing difference is irrelevant in light of the particular circumstances. Scholars have criticized the continuing relevance of systematically distinguishing between developing and developed countries.[127] More generally, defining developing countries through participation in the G77 group and developed countries by membership in OECD is neither reflective of the real needs of these countries nor of their capacities to assume more or less burdensome obligations.[128]

The criticisms directed to certain forms of implementation of Principle 6 should not however distract from the soundness of its rationale. Principle 6 does not as such make differential treatment dependent upon the status of a State as developing, environmentally vulnerable, or transitioning towards a market economy. To the contrary, the rationale of Principle 6 lies in the specific needs and circumstances that are entailed by this status with regard to the specific question under examination. Although the qualification as a developing country or an environmentally vulnerable State can justify certain presumptions in this regard, it does not establish in a definitive manner the existence of the special needs and circumstances that call for special treatment. In this respect, legitimate differentiation is not necessarily limited to contextualization but can require imposing a completely different set of obligations upon the parties. Conversely, it can call for distinguishing between developing countries when this is relevant, as already exemplified by certain treaties.[129] In fact, Principle 6 points both to the relevance of the subject matter at stake—when it referred to the special needs of environmentally vulnerable countries—and to the possibility to distinguish even between developing countries according to their special circumstances—when it laid emphasis on least developed countries. In this regard, divergences on classifying certain States as developing countries should not delay addressing, as a matter of priority, the needs of States which are clearly identified and not contentious, such as least developing countries.

## V) Select Bibliography

Cullet, Ph., 'Common but Differentiated Responsibilities', in Fitzmaurice, M., Ong, D.M., and Merkouris, P. (eds), *Research Handbook on International Environmental Law* (Cheltenham/ Northampton: Edward Elgar 2010), 161.

Cullet, Ph., *Differential Treatment in International Environmental Law* (Ashgate 2003).

[127] See eg Maljean-Dubois, S. and Rajamani, L., 'The Current State of Research Carried Out by the English-speaking and the French-speaking Sections—Report of the Directors of Studies', in Maljean-Dubois, S. and Rajamani, L. (eds), *Implementation of International Environmental Law* (Nijhoff 2011), 153–4; Cullet, 'Common but Differentiated Responsibilities', 175–6.

[128] Maljean-Dubois and Rajamani, 'The Current State of Research', 154.

[129] See for instance art 32 of the International Timber Treaty (granting special treatment to 'developing members which are timber consumer countries').

Cullet, Ph., 'Differential Treatment in International Law. Towards a New Paradigm of Inter-State Relations', in Qureshi, A.H. and Gao, X. (eds), *International Economic Law. Critical Concepts in Law*, vol 1, (Routledge 2011), 304.

French, D., 'Developing States and International Environmental Law: The Importance of Differentiated Responsibilities' (2000) 49 (1) *ICLQ* 35.

Galizzi, P. and Herklotz, A., 'Environment and Development: Friends or Foes in the 21st Century', in Fitzmaurice, M., Ong, D. M., and Merkouris, P. (eds), *Research Handbook on International Environmental Law* (Cheltenham/Northampton: Edward Elgar 2010), 69.

Halvorssen, A. M., *Equality among Unequals in International Environmental Law: Differential Treatment for Developing Countries* (Westview Press 1999).

Kovar, J. D., 'A Short Guide to the Rio Declaration' (1993) 4 *Colo J Int'l E L & Pol'y* 119.

Magraw, D. B., 'Legal Treatment of Developing Countries: Differential, Contextual, and Absolute Norms' (1990) 1 *Colo J Int'l Envtl L & Pol'y* 69.

Pauwelyn, J., 'The End of Differential Treatment for Developing Countries? Lessons from the Trade and Climate Change Regimes' (2013) 22 (1) *RECIEL* 29.

Rajamani, L., *Differential Treatment in International Environmental Law* (Oxford: Oxford University Press 2006).

Rajamani, L., 'The Changing Fortunes of Differential Treatment in the Evolution of International Environmental Law' (2012) 88 *International Affairs* 605.

# 11. Principle 7

## *Common but Differentiated Responsibilities*

Philippe Cullet*

**Principle 7**

States shall cooperate in a spirit of global partnership to conserve, protect and restore the health and integrity of the Earth's ecosystem. In view of the different contributions to global environmental degradation, States have common but differentiated responsibilities. The developed countries acknowledge the responsibility that they bear in the international pursuit of sustainable development in view of the pressures their societies place on the global environment and of the technologies and financial resources they command.



## I) Origins and Rationale of the Principle

The principle of common but differentiated responsibilities ('CBDR') has been since the late 1980s one of the key principles of international environmental law. Its central role is linked to the fact that the adoption of international environmental legal instruments has been largely conditional on the inclusion of some form of differentiation. This is confirmed

* Professor of International and Environmental Law at SOAS, University of London, the Convenor of the International Environmental Law Research Centre (IELRC) and a Senior Visiting Fellow at the Centre for Policy Research (CPR), New Delhi.

by the fact that today one of the biggest stumbling blocks in the context of the revision of the climate change treaties is the place and understanding of CBDR.[1]

CBDR in its presently accepted form is found at Principle 7 of the Rio Declaration.[2] Yet, its origins can be traced back to the very beginnings of international environmental law. Indeed, Principle 12 of the Stockholm Declaration already recognized the need for taking into account the 'circumstances and particular requirements of developing countries' and provided for 'additional international technical and financial assistance' to ensure that sufficient resources would be available to preserve and improve the environment.[3] In effect, the Stockholm Declaration recognized the need to consider the different situation in which developing countries find themselves but it did not go as far as calling for the traditional reciprocity of obligations to be curtailed or cast aside.

The Stockholm Declaration also recognized that there should be a balance between development and environmental protection. Principle 11 thus stated that the present or future development potential of developing countries should not be hampered by environmental policies.[4] This constituted in a sense the starting point of the evolution that led to the development of the notion of sustainable development in the 1980s. It is sustainable development as defined in the Brundtland report that then opened the way for the development of the principle of CBDR.

The Brundtland report was instrumental in bringing to the attention of the world the need to conceive environmental policy within the context of a development path that gives 'overriding priority' to the needs of the world's poor and is conceived in what we today understand as intra- and intergenerational equity.[5] Sustainable development may never have been given a generally accepted legal definition but its central position in international environmental policy has never been questioned since 1987. Its central premise was and remains the need to consider environmental policy in the context of poverty eradication. This calls, at the very least, for considering the situation of diverse countries differently.

The preparation of the Brundtland report took place alongside the negotiations concerning what was in effect the first global environmental regime, that of the depletion of the ozone layer. While neither the Vienna Convention[6] nor the Montreal Protocol[7] refer specifically to common but differentiated responsibilities, the evolution of the regime parallels developments that lead to the adoption of Principle 7 of the Rio Declaration. Firstly, article 5 of the Montreal Protocol provides that developing countries with a low per capita consumption of controlled substances are given a decade to implement commitments taken under the Protocol. This is a direct manifestation of common but differentiated responsibilities although the wording is not used yet. Further developments in the ozone regime confirm the differentiated rationale of the Montreal Protocol. Indeed, it became the first major global environmental regime to establish a financial mechanism specifically

[1] See eg Deleuil, T., 'The Common but Differentiated Responsibilities Principle: Changes in Continuity after the Durban Conference of the Parties' (2012) 21(3) *RECIEL* 271.

[2] 'Rio Declaration on Environment and Development', 14 June 1992, Doc A/CONF.151/26/Rev.1 (Vol I), Annex II (1992).

[3] Declaration of the United Nations Conference on the Human Environment, Stockholm, 16 June 1972, ('the Stockholm Declaration') Principle 12.

[4] The Stockholm Declaration, Principle 11.

[5] Report of the World Commission on Environment and Development, Our Common Future, UN Doc A/42/427 (1987), 54.

[6] Vienna Convention on the Protection of the Ozone Layer, 22 March 1985, 1513 UNTS 293.

[7] Montreal Protocol on Substances that Deplete the Ozone Layer, 16 September 1987, 1522 UNTS 29, art 5.

tasked with providing financial and technical cooperation, including technology transfer to countries operating under article 5 of the Protocol.[8]

The ozone regime thus established a framework based on common but differentiated responsibilities before the principle of CBDR was coined in the Rio Declaration. The shared nature of the measures taken under the Montreal Protocol and CBDR become more evident when comparing later actions of the Parties to the Protocol that have repeatedly mentioned the principle and, for instance, confirmed in 2007 that the Montreal Protocol 'operates on the concept of shared but differentiated responsibilities of the Parties'.[9]

Developments in the Montreal Protocol are symptomatic of the twin bases for CBDR in international environmental law. On the one hand, CBDR is a manifestation of equity.[10] It reflects the broad division of the world into richer and poorer countries, countries with higher and lower levels of human development, as well as technological and economic endowments. The acknowledgement of deep inequalities among countries provides the basis for the call for redistributive measures.[11] Distributive justice is thus at the centre of CBDR. It constitutes a compelling political and moral call on States to ensure that the legal framework takes into account the situation of developing countries. On the other hand, CBDR is a reflection of the special nature of certain global environmental issues in policy terms that provides a new basis for compromises between developed and developing countries. This was the case with the depletion of the ozone layer. While the global nature of the problem was easily established since ozone depleting substances emitted from any part of the world had the same capacity to harm the ozone layer, the location of the holes around polar areas happened to make developed countries the first targets. As a result, developing countries were able to extract a number of non-reciprocal concessions in the negotiations of the agreement that may not have been possible otherwise.

The principle of CBDR is thus based on two pillars that are largely distinct, if not opposed. From an analytical point of view, the distributive justice basis is what makes CBDR such a potent source of change in international law. The very idea of non-reciprocity in a legal framework that had been based nearly exclusively on reciprocal obligations between theoretically equal States has the potential to bring significant structural changes to international law. From a pragmatic point of view, what has made CBDR an inescapable part of present international environmental law is the meeting of different interests that coalesce around what is in essence the concept of sustainability. The challenge that international environmental law faces today is that the distinct but complementary interests that provided the basis for the successful conclusion of various negotiations in the 1980s and 1990s are changing. This is particularly visible in the climate change context where there have been increasing calls for putting an end to differentiation as conceived under the Kyoto Protocol.[12] This does not signal that the rationale

[8] Decision II/8: Financial Mechanism, Second Meeting of the Parties to the Montreal Protocol on Substances that Deplete the Ozone Layer, London, 27–9 June 1990.

[9] Montreal Declaration, Annex IV of the report of the Nineteenth Meeting of the Parties to the Montreal Protocol on Substances that Deplete the Ozone Layer, Montreal, 17–21 September 2007.

[10] See Commission on Sustainable Development, *Report of the Expert Group Meeting on Identification of Principles of International Law for Sustainable Development*, Geneva, Switzerland, 26–8 September 1995 ('Report-principles'), para 38.

[11] eg Cullet, Ph., *Differential Treatment in International Environmental Law* (Ashgate 2003).

[12] eg Submission of the United States, ADP Workstream 1: 2015 Agreement, 11 March 2013, 2, available at <http://unfccc.int/files/documentation/submissions_from_parties/adp/application/pdf/adp_usa_workstream_1_20130312.pdf>, acknowledging differentiation but suggesting that 'contributions identified by Parties would naturally fall along a spectrum or continuum'.

for differentiation has disappeared. It rather signifies that certain realignments are necessary in view of the evolving situation of some big countries. At the same time, if the aggregate contribution of some countries to environmental degradation like China and India has increased substantially over the past two decades, the basic underlying situation that made CBDR relevant in the first place has not changed and the overwhelming majority of developing countries are comparatively in no better shape than they were in 1992.

## II) The Principle as Enshrined in the Rio Declaration

### 1. Preparatory work and context

The genesis of Principle 7 can be identified in the General Assembly resolution that called for the Rio Conference.[13] Indeed, the preamble specifically affirmed that:

> the responsibility for containing, reducing and eliminating global environmental damage must be borne by the countries causing such damage, must be in relation to the damage caused and must be in accordance with their respective capabilities and responsibilities.[14]

Further, the resolution recognized that all States have a role to play in protecting the environment, 'in accordance with their capacities and specific responsibilities', that developed countries 'have the main responsibility' for combating pollution, and linked developing countries' debt and their capacity to contribute to global efforts to protect and enhance the environment.[15]

Despite these clear statements in Resolution 44/228, the actual drafting of Principle 7 followed a convoluted process. The first compilation of elements to be considered in elaborating a declaration did include a section on common responsibility for the preservation of the Earth.[16] It also included a section on '[e]quitable sharing of responsibilities and benefits'. However, in this section, of the three statements cited as relevant, two of them—the Stockholm Declaration and the Brundtland Report—focused on overall sustainable use of resources and only the last instrument cited, the Langkawi Declaration emphasized the need to take into account the ability of developing countries to take measures to protect the environment.[17]

Even an early draft of the Principles on General Rights and Obligations included proposals for a Principle 7 that focused mostly on cooperation and partnership and proposals for a Principle 8 that included a proposal by China for the recognition of the 'special situation and needs of the developing countries', a proposal by Chile for increased technical and financial assistance to foster developing country participation in international environmental law and a proposal by the G77 to stress responsibility of developed countries in the improvement of the international economic environment.[18]

[13] UN General Assembly Resolution 44/228, United Nations Conference on Environment and Development, 22 December 1989, UN Doc A/RES/44/228.

[14] UN General Assembly Resolution 44/228, preamble.

[15] UN General Assembly Resolution 44/228, paras 7, 9, 11.

[16] Preparatory Committee for the UN Conference on Environment and Development, Third Session, Annotated Check-List of Principles on General Rights and Obligations, UN Doc A/CONF.151/PC/78 (1991).

[17] Langkawi Declaration on Environment, Heads of Government of the Commonwealth, Langkawi (Malaysia), 21 October 1989, para 5.

[18] Principles on General Rights and Obligations—Chairman's Consolidated Draft, Preparatory Committee for the UN Conference on Environment and Development, Third Session, Working Group III, UN Doc A/CONF.151/PC/WG.III/L.8 (1991).

By the time of the last session of Working Group III in March 1992, positions had become more entrenched and sharp differences between developed and developing countries were visible. On the one hand, a proposal from China and Pakistan would have given Principle 7 a strong focus on the responsibility of developed countries and singled out their duties to provide the resources and technologies that would allow developing countries to achieve sustainable development. This draft included three paragraphs, two of which specifically calling on developed countries to take action. It read:

> All States share a common but differentiated responsibility for containing, reducing and eliminating global environmental damage and for restoring the ecological balance of the Earth, in accordance with their respective responsibilities and capabilities.
>
> The major cause of the continuing deterioration of the global environment is the unsustainable patterns of production and consumption, particularly in developed countries. All countries, particularly developed ones, shall make commitments to address their unsustainable patterns of production and consumption.
>
> In view of their main historical and current responsibility for global environmental degradation and their capability to address this common concern, developed countries shall provide adequate, new and additional financial resources and environmentally sound technologies on preferential and concessional terms to developing countries to enable them to achieve sustainable development.[19]

This relatively extensive proposal was countered, for instance, by a proposal from the United States that included a Principle 7 emphasizing only the partnership dimension of what we know as CBDR. It proposed that '[a]ll people should cooperate in good faith and in a spirit of global partnership at the local, national, regional and international levels to achieve sustainable development'.[20] It then included a Principle 8, which was the equivalent of a much weaker Principle 6 of the Rio Declaration that simply stated that States 'should consider the special situation and needs of developing countries in achieving sustainable development and provide appropriate assistance'.[21] A proposal by Japan included a provision on aid to developing countries but no reference to partnership or responsibility.[22]

The European Economic Community introduced a proposal, which put the principle of CBDR at the very beginning of the proposed Earth Charter. This document proposed a framework that started from the recognition of the commonality of responsibilities translating into a global partnership to address the global environment 'reflecting equitable burden sharing between developed and developing countries'.[23] This proposal thus provided

[19] Principles on General Rights and Obligations—China and Pakistan—Draft Decision, Preparatory Committee for the UN Conference on Environment and Development, 4th session, UN Doc A/CONF.151/PC/WG.III/L.20/Rev.l (1992).

[20] United States proposal on principles on general rights and obligations, *in* Report of the Preparatory Committee for the UN Conference on Environment and Development, 4th session, UN Doc A/CONF.151/PC/128 (1992), 94.

[21] United States proposal on principles on general rights and obligations, 94.

[22] Japan proposal on rights and obligations, *in* Report of the Preparatory Committee for the UN Conference on Environment and Development, 4th session, UN Doc A/CONF.151/PC/128 (1992), 95.

[23] European Economic Community, Elements for the Earth Charter, *in* Draft Report, Preparatory Committee for the UN Conference on Environment and Development, 4th session, Working Group III, UN Doc A/CONF.151/PC/WG.III/L.34 (1992), 30.

recognition of historical responsibilities that did not translate into legal obligations for developed countries towards developing countries.

By the end of the session, the draft principles proposed by the chairperson included a heavily bracketed Principle 7 that still included six different paragraphs. The first one focused on the recognition of common but differentiated responsibilities for global environmental damage to be addressed through a global partnership. The second and third paragraphs focused on the causes of global environmental damage, emphasizing the fact that all countries share a responsibility for this and must make commitment to address it. The second paragraph focused on the particular commitments that developed countries should make while the third one specified that all countries should address the problem in accordance with their responsibilities and capabilities. The fourth and the fifth paragraphs were admonitions to all countries to eliminate, reduce, or avoid unsustainable patterns of production and consumption and in the stronger of the two versions to 'slow rapid population growth'. The last paragraph called on developed countries to provide additional financial resources and environmentally sound technologies on the basis of their historical and current responsibility for global environmental degradation.[24]

## 2. Scope and Dimensions

### 2.1. *Partnership and equity*

Principle 7 as adopted in the Rio Declaration is built on a twin foundation of partnership and equity. Its three sentences reflect these different dimensions. The first sentence emphasizes the duty of all States to cooperate to ensure the conservation, protection, and restoration of the global ecosystem. In subsequent reports, this sentence has been approached from the perspective of chapter IX of the United Nations Charter ('International Economic and Social Cooperation') as well as on the broader duty of cooperation well established in general international law.[25] States are thus called upon to participate in regimes that seek to address the health and integrity of the Earth's ecosystem, or in other words, global environmental issues.

The second sentence acknowledges that States have historically made and still make different contributions to global environmental degradation. This highlights the twin intergenerational and intragenerational equity dimension of Principle 7, which provides the foundation for the reiteration that States have common responsibilities and the recognition that there are also differentiated responsibilities. Principle 7 thus rests on this dichotomy between the recognition of commonality and differentiation but fails to indicate whether one prevails over the other.

The third sentence elucidates the extent of differentiation by focusing on the responsibilities of developed countries. It shifts the focus from environmental integrity to sustainable development and provides an acknowledgment by developed countries that they bear a

[24] Draft Principles Proposed by the Chairman, Preparatory Committee for the UN Conference on Environment and Development, 4th session, Working Group III, A/CONF.151/PC/WG.III/L.33 (1992), 2.

[25] United Nations Commission on Sustainable Development, Report of the Secretary-General, Rio Declaration on Environment and Development—Application and Implementation, UN Doc E/CN.17/1997/8 (1997), para 44. See also the chapters on Principles 19 and 27 in this commentary; UN Department of Social and Economic Affairs, Division for Sustainable Development, Review of Implementation of the Rio Principles (2011), 53.

special responsibility because they cause more damage to the global environment and have more technological and financial resources at their disposal to address the problems caused.

Principle 7 thus acknowledges a 'responsibility' of developed countries linked to their contribution to global environmental harm, mostly turned towards the future.[26] It also provides a basis for considering the situation of different countries based on capabilities. Principle 7 does not, however, provide a direct basis for holding developed countries legally responsible for global environmental damage or an obligation of compensation for damage to the environment, as proposed in the Pakistan/China proposal. At the same time, Principle 7 provides a framework for the adoption of differential norms that may include specific obligations laid at the door of developed countries, as has in fact happened in the context of some treaties.

The scope of Principle 7 is in principle relatively broad since it does not mention specific environmental problems that fall within its scope. At the same time, it is specifically geared towards problems that are defined as global. It thus lends itself particularly well to application in the case of climate change. Here, the 'differentiated' responsibility dimension is particularly easy to identify since developed countries had contributed by 1992 the biggest share to the problem in historical and present terms.[27] This overlapping dimension between developed countries and responsibility for climate change has led to the debate around CBDR being largely reduced to an opposition between developed and developing countries. This was probably never appropriate but with divergent development trajectories within the group of 'developing countries', this has become largely untenable from an environmental perspective. The positive element is that the vagueness of Principle 7 on this count ensures that it does not impose on international law makers to look at the world only in terms of an opposition between two groups of countries.[28]

Another interesting dimension of Principle 7 is that its third sentence moves away from an environmental focus to a mention of sustainable development. While this is not particularly surprising in the context of a declaration on 'environment and development', such reference constitutes an important acknowledgment that the context within which CBDR is to be understood is one that includes development concerns. This happens to be crucial when Principle 7 is seen in a longer-term perspective. From the Stockholm Conference to the Johannesburg Summit, a progressive strengthening of the development dimension can be identified.[29] This confirms that CBDR participates in a trend that understands the environment in a broader context. This historical perspective also confirms the challenges that CBDR faces today in a context where the Rio+20 Conference went back to generally equating economic development with economic growth,[30] a throwback to an earlier era where growth was seen as the primary determinant of development.

26 Bartenstein, K., 'De Stockholm à Copenhague—Genèse et évolution des responsabilités communes mais différenciées dans le droit international de l'environnement' (2010) 56(1) *McGill Law Journal—Revue de droit de McGill* 177, 187.

27 For an analysis of differential treatment focused on climate change, eg Prost, M. and Torres Camprubi, A., 'Against Fairness? International Environmental Law, Disciplinary Bias, and Pareto Justice' (2012) 25 *Leiden Journal of International Law* 379, 392.

28 cf Pauwelyn, J., 'The End of Differential Treatment for Developing Countries? Lessons from the Trade and Climate Change Regimes' (2013) 22/1 *RECIEL* 29, 41.

29 eg Rajamani, L., 'The Changing Fortunes of Differential Treatment in the Evolution of International Environmental Law' (2012) 88(3) *International Affairs* 605, 614.

30 eg UN General Assembly Resolution 66/288, *The Future We Want*, UN Doc A/RES/66/288 (2012), para 6. On this trend see Viñuales, J. E., 'The Rise and Fall of Sustainable Development' (2013) 22 *RECIEL* 3.

## 2.2. Nature of the principle

While CBDR has been repeatedly included in international environmental instruments over the past two decades and has become an integral part of international environmental law, there remains significant debate concerning its legal status as an independent principle. The controversial nature of the principle can be traced back to the Rio Declaration itself. Indeed, the United States was sufficiently concerned by the adoption of Principle 7 to attach a specific interpretative statement to highlight that it did not:

> accept any interpretation of Principle 7 that would imply a recognition or acceptance by the United States of any international obligations or liabilities, or any diminution in the responsibilities of developing countries.[31]

On the whole, secondary literature adopts the view that CBDR is not a customary principle. Yet, this broad conclusion must not hide the diverse positions that have been expressed on this point. An early commentator like Pallemaerts found that differentiation seemed to emerge as a new general principle of international environmental law.[32] More recent analyses have ranged from denying it customary status to cautious endorsement of its legal impacts. Stone finds that CBDR has not 'been elevated to the status of a customary principle of international law'.[33] Rajamani, reviewing doctrinal positions asserts that '[t]he reluctance to stop short of characterizing this principle as one of customary international law is perhaps justified'.[34] Elsewhere, Hey finds that while CBDR is 'unlikely to qualify as a rule, given that it cannot apply in an all or nothing fashion', it is 'most likely to qualify as a principle of international environmental policy'.[35] At the same time, she finds that it has affected international environmental law in a 'fundamental manner'.[36] Bartenstein on her part finds that CBDR has a certain normative value and labels it a structuring principle that plays a central role in the systematization of legal rules.[37]

On the whole, the weight of the doctrine is to deny customary status to the principle. However, the main significance of CBDR lies in the extent to which it can be linked to a reform of the structure of international obligations in the context of international environmental law. In a context where most of the differentiation that exists in international environmental law can be linked to the principle of CBDR, the key issue is not its status as a separate customary principle but the extent to which it has provided the basis for the development of a fresh approach to international legal obligations that need not be based strictly and exclusively on reciprocity. In a context where the whole of international environmental law has been infused by differentiation over the past two decades, it is difficult to find an exact marker of the legal significance of CBDR. At the same time, there is no denying the transformative potential it unleashed.

[31] Report of the United Nations Conference on Environment and Development, Doc A/CONF.151/26 (vol IV) (1992), para 16.

[32] Pallemaerts, M., 'La Conference de Rio: Grandeur ou décadence du droit international de l'environnement?' (1995) 28(1) *Revue belge de droit international* 175, 201.

[33] Stone, C. D., 'Common but Differentiated Responsibilities in International Law' (2004) 98 *AJIL* 276, 299.

[34] Rajamani, L., *Differential Treatment in International Environmental Law* (Oxford University Press 2006), 159.

[35] Hey, E., 'Common but Differentiated Responsibilities', in Wolfrum. R. (ed), *Max Planck Encyclopedia of Public International Law—Volume II* (Oxford University Press 2012), at 444, 447.

[36] Hey, 'Common but Differentiated Responsibilities', 444, 447.

[37] Bartenstein, 'De Stockholm à Copenhague—Genèse et évolution des responsabilités communes', 199.

## 3. Normative impact

### *3.1. Overview*

Since the adoption of the Rio Declaration, Principle 7 has been directly integrated into a variety of legal instruments. In addition, its realization through a variety of legal techniques has become so pervasive that current international environmental law cannot be explained without reference to differentiation. As noted by a report prepared in 1997 by the UN Secretary-General:

> In practical terms, the principle of common but differentiated responsibilities is translated into the explicit recognition that different standards, delayed compliance timetables or less stringent commitments may be appropriate for different groups of countries, to encourage universal participation. The developed countries acknowledge their responsibility because of the pressure on the global environment, and because of the technologies and financial resources they command. A number of international agreements recognize a duty on the part of industrialized countries to contribute to the efforts of developing countries to pursue sustainable development and to assist developing countries in protecting the global environment. Such assistance may entail, apart from consultation and negotiation, financial aid, transfer of environmentally sound technology and cooperation through international organizations.[38]

At the same time, it was never well accepted by some developed countries and, as noted in the previous section, its customary status consequently remains doubtful to date. Further, since it is one of the principles of international environmental law that has the biggest potential to bring change to the way international law is structured, it has also been at the centre of increasing attacks in the context of the climate change regime, which has been the most visible and politically sensitive environmental regime over the past decade.

### *3.2. Non-reciprocity*

The principle of CBDR has had significant influence on the development of international environmental law over the past two decades. At the most general level, it has become nearly inconceivable to adopt environmental legal instruments that do not recognize the dichotomy between developed and developing countries. This translates into a variety of mechanisms that differentiate between different groups of countries, most often developed and developing countries. The most differential instrument is where the principle of reciprocity of obligations is abandoned in favour of different obligations for different groups of countries. This has been applied in a limited number of treaties, such as the Kyoto Protocol and Desertification Convention where developed and developing countries take on different commitments.[39]

Beyond this, a number of differential instruments have been used in recognition of the different responsibilities and capabilities of developing countries, such as delayed compliance timetables.[40] A number of treaties include provision for facilitated access to environmentally sound technologies and financial resources.[41] Such provisions, which reflect

[38] Commission on Sustainable Development UN Doc E/CN.17/1997/8 (1997), para 46.

[39] See respectively Kyoto Protocol to the United Nations Framework Convention on Climate Change, Kyoto, 11 December 1997, art 3 and Convention to Combat Desertification in Those Countries Experiencing Serious Drought and/or Desertification, Particularly in Africa, Paris, 17 June 1994, UN Doc A/AC.241/15/ Rev. 7, art 6.

[40] eg Montreal Protocol on Substances that Deplete the Ozone Layer, 16 September 1987, 1522 UNTS 29, art 5.

[41] eg Convention on Biological Diversity, Rio de Janeiro, 5 June 1992, 1760 UNTS 79.

Principle 9 of the Rio Declaration promoting the diffusion and transfer of technology, are in fact by now among the standard clauses that are a necessary part of the negotiation of an international environmental regime. At the same time, with certain exceptions like in the case of the Montreal Protocol,[42] the implementation of technology transfer clauses remain often behind expectations, in particular where technology is protected by intellectual property rights. It is, in fact, in response to concerns about technology transfer that certain treaties go further and make developing country compliance dependent on developed countries' implementation of their financial and technology transfer commitments.[43]

### 3.3. *Contextualized reciprocity*

Beyond the above techniques that specifically provide developing countries with certain forms of non-reciprocity, international environmental law is now replete with clauses that contextualize reciprocal commitments. This provides a context for countries taking on formally reciprocal obligations to take into account respective capabilities in the implementation of these commitments. This is, for instance, what article 6 of the Biodiversity Convention does when the binding commitments taken by a member State are 'in accordance with its particular conditions and capabilities'.[44]

This contextualization has often been criticized as weakening the law because of a loss of certainty in the obligations contained in the treaty.[45] This is not the real issue since, in international environmental law, States have generally shown willingness to implement their commitments but have not always had the capacity to do so. This is not a problem that can be solved by threatening States with the consequences of State responsibility for failing to comply.[46] This is confirmed by the development of non-compliance procedures that reflect an understanding that States who fail to comply most often do so because they have not been able to do so rather than because they are unwilling.[47]

### 3.4. *Restatement of CBDR*

Beyond provisions that implement the principle of CBDR, international environmental law also includes a number of binding and non-binding instruments that restate the principle itself. The best known is the Climate Change Convention in whose context CBDR is one of the basic principles on which the whole regime is based.[48] The Convention adds the additional concept of 'respective capabilities', which comes to complement 'differentiated responsibilities'.[49] In addition to being a basic principle of the framework convention, CBDR also underlies the main commitments that member States take since it provides the contextualization for all commitments taken.[50] As noted above, the general context

[42] eg Fahey, D. W., 'The Montreal Protocol Protection of Ozone and Climate' (2013) 14 *Theoretical Inquiries in Law* 21.

[43] eg Report of the Expert Group Meeting on Identification of Principles of International Law for Sustainable Development, Geneva, Switzerland, 26–8 September 1995, para 92, *in* United Nations Commission on Sustainable Development, Background paper for the Fourth Session, 1996.

[44] Convention on Biological Diversity, Rio de Janeiro, 5 June 1992, 1760 UNTS 79.

[45] eg Akehurst, M., 'Equity and General Principles of Law' (1976) 25(4) *ICLQ* 801, 809.

[46] eg Victor, D. G., 'Enforcing International Law: Implications for an Effective Global Warming Regime' (1999) 10 *Duke Environmental Law & Policy Forum* 147.

[47] For a list of obstacles to compliance, para 5, Guidelines for Strengthening Compliance with and Implementation of Multilateral Environmental Agreements (MEAs) in the ECE Region, Fifth Ministerial Conference Environment for Europe, Kiev, Ukraine 21–3 May 2003, UN Doc ECE/CEP/107.

[48] United Nations Framework Convention on Climate Change, 9 May 1992, art 3(1).

[49] Rajamani, 'The Changing Fortunes of Differential Treatment', 137.

[50] United Nations Framework Convention on Climate Change, 9 May 1992, art 4(1).

provided by CBDR translated in the context of the Kyoto Protocol into one of the few treaty provisions whereby developed and developing countries take on separate commitments.[51] In addition, CBDR is also specifically restated in the context of the compliance regime instituted under the Kyoto Protocol. Indeed, with regard to the Facilitative Branch, CBDR is the principle that guides it in its general 'advice and facilitation' function and in the 'consequences' it applies.[52] The latter is not surprising since one of the consequences applied is the facilitation of financial and technical assistance, including technology transfer, that happen to be two of the techniques highlighted above as being some of the most frequent differential provisions in environmental treaties.

The extensive reference to CBDR in the climate change regime has made it a hallmark of the existing regime and given Principle 7 visibility much beyond the circles of environmental law and policy-makers. This is also what has put it at the centre of controversy in the context of negotiations for the future of the climate change regime after the end of the first or the second commitment periods under the Kyoto Protocol. In a context where the exemption that large fast-growing economies in the South can claim as 'developing countries' has become a bone of contention, it is in effect the principle of CBDR that has been under attack,[53] particularly in the context of the negotiations under the Durban Platform on Enhanced Action.[54] As a result, there has been in recent years a visible erosion of the support for the kind of measures adopted under the Kyoto Protocol for the benefit of developing countries.[55] While this is a significant development in a context where the climate change regime has been the most visible environmental regime in recent years, this does not per se indicate that CBDR is on the wane in international environmental law.[56]

Besides the climate change regime, CBDR has been restated in other treaties. The 2001 Stockholm Convention includes, for instance, in its preamble a specific restatement of CBDR and of the Rio Declaration.[57] Similarly the 2013 Minamata Convention's preamble recalls the reaffirmation of the Rio Declaration at the Rio+20 Conference and the only principle singled out in this provision is CBDR.[58] CBDR has also been explicitly restated in the context of the development of other environmental regimes. This is, for instance, the case of the 1987 Montreal Protocol that does not mention CBDR since it predated the Rio Declaration. In this case, mention of CBDR is found, for instance, in

51 Kyoto Protocol to the United Nations Framework Convention on Climate Change, Kyoto, 11 December 1997, 2303 UNTS 148, art 3.

52 Decision 27/CMP.1, 'Procedures and mechanisms relating to compliance under the Kyoto Protocol', Report of the Conference of the Parties serving as the meeting of the Parties to the Kyoto Protocol on its first session, held at Montreal from 28 November to 10 December 2005, UN Doc FCCC/KP/CMP/2005/8/Add.3, paras IV and XIV.

53 eg Prost, M. and Torres Camprubi, A., 'Against Fairness? International Environmental Law, Disciplinary Bias, and Pareto Justice' (2012) 25 *Leiden Journal of International Law* 379.

54 Establishment of an Ad Hoc Working Group on the Durban Platform for Enhanced Action, Decision 1/CP.17, 15 March 2012, Doc FCCC/CP/2011/9/Add.1, 2.

55 Rajamani, L., 'Differentiation in the Emerging Climate Regime' (2013) 14 *Theoretical Inquiries in Law* 151.

56 eg Cullet, Ph., 'Le principe des responsabilités communes mais différenciées en droit international de l'environnement: enjeux et perspectives' (2014) 55 *Cahiers de droit* 9.

57 Stockholm Convention on Persistent Organic Pollutants, 22 May 2001, available at <http://www.pops.int/documents/convtext/convtext_en.pdf>, preamble.

58 Minamata Convention on Mercury, Kumamoto, 10 October 2013, available at <http://www.mercuryconvention.org/Portals/11/documents/conventionText/Minamata%20Convention%20on%20Mercury_e.pdf>, preamble.

a decision of 2004 concerning trade in products and commodities treated with methyl bromide.[59]

In addition, CBDR has been restated on various occasions in non-binding instruments. Thus, the plan of action of the 2002 World Summit on Sustainable Development includes various references to CBDR and a specific reproduction of Principle 7, which was the only principle of the Rio Declaration singled out in the context of the search for new ways to better implement Agenda 21.[60] A decade later, the section on renewing political commitments of the outcome document of the Rio+20 Conference similarly reaffirms the Rio Principles, in whose context the only principle singled out is CBDR.[61] The principle of CBDR has also been included, for instance, as a separate principle by the International Law Association (ILA) in its Declaration of Principles of Sustainable Development.[62]

## 4. Jurisprudential relevance

CBDR constitutes an extension of judicial equity that has been widely applied at the international level for a long time.[63] At the same time, it goes further than traditional judicial equity that focuses on ensuring that the application of a reciprocal rule in a specific case yields results that are just.[64] This has two consequences. On the one hand, judicial equity can be seen as directly related to CBDR. On the other hand, since court decisions are usually concerned with individual States, CBDR is not often directly brought into judicial proceedings.

A few instances of references to CBDR can nevertheless be identified. There is, for instance, the case of the Advisory Opinion ITLOS Seabed Chamber on *Activities in the Area*.[65] In this case, when addressing the question of the legal responsibilities of States with respect to the sponsorship of activities in the Area, the Chamber specifically considered the situation of developing countries and examined the extent to which developing sponsoring States enjoy preferential treatment compared to developed sponsoring countries.[66]

In the context of the WTO dispute settlement body, CBDR has been referred to in several cases.[67] In a relatively early case, *India—Quantitative Restrictions*, the Panel indicated that article XVIII:B of GATT 1994, which allows developing countries to maintain, under certain conditions, temporary import restrictions for balance of payments purposes,

[59] Decision XVI/7, 'Trade in Products and Commodities Treated with Methyl Bromide', Sixteenth Meeting of the Parties to the Montreal Protocol on Substances that Deplete the Ozone Layer, Prague, 22–6 November 2004.

[60] World Summit on Sustainable Development—Plan of Implementation, UN Doc A/CONF.199/20 (2002), para 75.

[61] UN General Assembly Resolution 66/288, *The Future We Want*, UN Doc A/RES/66/288 (2012), para 15.

[62] International Law Association, New Delhi Declaration of Principles of International Law Relating to Sustainable Development, Resolution 3/2002, Principle 3.

[63] eg Chemillier-Gendreau, M., 'La signification des principes équitables dans le droit international contemporain' (1981) 16 *Revue belge de droit international* 509.

[64] eg Janis, M. W., 'The Ambiguity of Equity in International Law' (1983) 9 *Brooklyn J Int'l L* 7.

[65] Responsibilities and Obligations of States Sponsoring Persons and Entities with Respect to Activities in the Area, Advisory Opinion, Seabed Disputes Chamber of the International Tribunal for the Law of the Sea, 1 February 2011.

[66] Advisory Opinion ITLOS Seabed Chamber on *Activities in the Area*, para 152.

[67] Mitchell, A. D., 'A Legal Principle of Special and Differential Treatment for WTO Disputes' (2006) 5(3) *World Trade Review* 445.

reflects an acknowledgment of the specific needs of developing countries and thus embodies special and differential treatment.[68] Another example concerns the Enabling Clause case wherein India complained against the European Communities (EC) regarding the conditions under which the EC accorded tariff preferences to developing countries.[69] While the Enabling Clause constitutes a weak form of differentiation since it is a unilateral measure of developed countries, the case raised interesting issues concerning the way in which this differentiation must be implemented. The Appellate Body found, for instance, that the Enabling Clause does not prohibit granting differential tariffs to different sub-categories of beneficiaries.[70]

On the whole, CBDR has relevance in many judicial proceedings. However, the largely bilateral nature of most proceedings limits the frequency of its use.

## III) Relations with Other Principles

The Rio Declaration includes two main principles concerned with differentiation. Principle 6, analysed in the previous chapter, provides the general recognition of categories of States (developing countries, environmentally vulnerable countries, States in transition to a market economy) and the need to consider their special situation and needs.

Principle 7 then provides the policy context for taking measures on global environmental problems based on the division of the world into developing and developed countries, taking as its starting point that the latter have contributed more to environmental degradation and can mobilize more financial and technological resources. As with Principle 6, the means to implement differentiation under Principle 7 are further spelt out in other principles, most notably in Principle 9 (transfer of technology), Principle 11 (variations in the applicable standards) and Principle 12 linking trade and environmental policy, even though the latter does not even specifically refer to special and differential measures existing under GATT.

Although Principles 6 and 7 are often equated, their differing rationales must not be overlooked. Both aim at introducing differentiation but not on the same basis and with the same objectives. Specifically, unlike Principle 6, Principle 7 targets different contributions to environmental degradation and different capabilities, and it suggests that developed countries must carry a heavier burden as a result. This difference explains why, unlike Principle 6, Principle 7 could not be placed within the set of 'easy' principles requiring less discussion during the preparatory works, as well as why the United States decided to add an interpretive statement to it and not to Principle 6.

Thus, the better view is that Principles 6 and 7 together, as further spelled out in other principles, provide the framework within which differentiation is taken up in the Rio Declaration. While Principle 6 is the broader principle that sets out the generic parameters for differentiation, it is Principle 7 that has attracted most of the scholarly and policy-making attention. It is also Principle 7 that has been extensively used and repeated in various subsequent legal instruments.

[68] *India—Quantitative Restrictions on Imports of Agricultural, Textile and Industrial Products*, Report of the Panel, WTO Doc WT/DS90/R, para 5.155.

[69] *European Communities—Conditions for the Granting of Tariff Preferences to Developing Countries*, Report of the Appellate Body, WTO Doc WT/DS246/AB/R (2004).

[70] *European Communities—Conditions for the Granting of Tariff Preferences to Developing Countries*, para 175.

## IV) Assessment: Principle 7 as a Linchpin of International Environmental Law

The principle of CBDR has been and remains at the centre of significant attention. This is due to the fact that it encapsulates some of the transformative energy of international environmental law that makes it a beacon for other, more settled, areas of law. Other principles of the Rio Declaration, such as Principle 15 recognizing the precautionary principle, are more important from the point of view of advancing environmental protection per se. The novel dimension of Principle 7 lies in its underlying acknowledgment that the traditional structure of international legal obligations is not suited for some of the most pressing environmental challenges that the world faces.

The significance of CBDR does not lie in the development of non-reciprocal commitments, something that had already been developed a couple of decades earlier in international economic law.[71] Rather, it lies in providing a framework generally acceptable to all States within which distortions to reciprocity have been accepted not just in a limited number of cases but also in a manner that pervades most of international environmental law. Indeed, as noted above, CBDR has been directly used or reflected in the majority of environmental instruments adopted over the past two decades.

This is not to say that CBDR constitutes the magic wand to address all equity issues in international environmental law. Its relatively narrow scope is what made it politically acceptable in the first place and what limits its transformative potential. One of the limits of CBDR is the type of environmental issues to which it applies easily. Whereas climate change fits perfectly the wording of Principle 7, this is, for instance, not the case with forests. In this case, a narrow reading of deforestation that does not take into account the export market dimension may end up ascribing most of the blame to developing countries. Similarly in the case of water, as long as increasing water scarcity is not linked to the global water cycle, developing countries may be blamed for their water woes as being caused by population growth.[72] The broader point is that most environmental issues today have a transboundary dimension and thus deserve international attention. All such issues have a differential component but CBDR is not always an appropriate starting point for addressing it.

Another difficulty with CBDR is the way in which the environment and development dimensions are conjoined. In the version of CBDR adopted in Principle 7, the emphasis in terms of responsibility is on contributions to global environmental degradation. While this seems straightforward, it hides the fact that the 'different' contributions are allocated in terms of groups of countries defined in terms of economic development status. This partly hidden dimension is indirectly acknowledged in the version of CBDR found in the ILA Declaration of Principles stating that differentiation is principally based on contributions to environmental degradation but 'must also take into account the economic and developmental situation of the State'.[73] This indicates an underlying tension between the

[71] eg Kofele-Kale, N., 'The Principle of Preferential Treatment in the Law of GATT: Toward Achieving the Objective of an Equitable World Trading System' (1987/88) 18 *California Western International Law Journal* 291.

[72] cf Chartres, C. J., 'Water and Food Security', in Rayfuse, R. and Weisfelt, N. (eds), *The Challenge of Food Security—International Policy and Regulatory Frameworks* (Edward Elgar 2012), 128, stating at 130 that '[t]he first and most critical driver of water scarcity is population growth'.

[73] International Law Association, New Delhi Declaration of Principles, Resolution 3/2002, Principle 3(2).

environmental and developmental objectives, which is not specific to CBDR but pervades the law of sustainable development. It is, however, particularly prominent in the context of CBDR because contribution to environmental damage is often proportional to the speed or kind of economic growth experienced in a given country. While this may be seen as potentially threatening the environmental objectives of a particular treaty regime, CBDR needs to be seen in a different manner. Indeed, the central benefit of CBDR is to ensure the possibility of an agreement in the first place. The baseline against which CBDR needs to be measured is thus the no-agreement option. In the first few years before differentiation became an integral part of international environmental negotiations, the no-agreement option was indeed a weapon that was wielded in the case of the Montreal Protocol by India and China, which demanded a specific increase in the funds available as a condition of their ratification.[74]

The central role of CBDR in international environmental law has not abated. At the same time, as noted above, it has come under increasing attack in the context of the negotiations for a successor agreement to the Kyoto Protocol. This should not be dismissed as irrelevant given the central place of the climate change regime in international environmental law. Yet, this needs to be put in perspective. Firstly, as noted above, the Rio+20 Conference clearly reaffirmed the central role of CBDR. Secondly, the attacks against CBDR need to be put in a context that has seen stagnation and some regression in environmental law generally since the beginning of the century. Finally, in the current socio-economic context that characterizes the world, the crucial nature of CBDR is illustrated by the fact that in terms of human development, the structural gaps that were the bedrock of the distinction between developed and developing countries in the early 1990s has remained essentially unchanged. Indeed, while the Human Development Index progressed from 0.315 in 1980 to 0.466 in 2012 for countries with low human development, it progressed from 0.773 to 0.905 for countries with high human development during the same period.[75] There has thus been no significant relative improvement in the situation of countries with low human development that would warrant any change in the principle of CBDR. Current debates around large countries that identify as developing countries such as Brazil, China, and India simply indicate that the division of the world into two amorphous categories is likely inappropriate and needs to be further refined. This is not particularly new or surprising since there have been various attempts to take into account other factors, such as vulnerability, and there are situations where countries are individually assessed, such as in the context of their contribution to the budget of the UN.[76]

CBDR may be in the eye of the storm in the climate change regime but it has lost none of its relevance. The challenge is thus to make sure that it can be further refined to ensure that it maintains its transformative potential without leading to a fragmentation of the G77 that would then affect the poorest countries' ability to negotiate regimes that take into account at least some of their environmental and development concerns.

[74] eg Hurlbut, D., 'Beyond the Montreal Protocol: Impact on Nonparty States and Lessons for Future Environmental Protection Regimes' (1993) 4 *Colorado Journal of International Environmental Law and Policy* 344, 352.

[75] UNDP, Human Development Report 2013 (UNDP 2013).

[76] UN General Assembly Resolution 67/238, Scale of Assessments for the Apportionment of the Expenses of the United Nations, 24 December 2012, UN Doc A/RES/67/238.

## V) Select Bibliography


Akehurst, M., 'Equity and General Principles of Law' (1976) 25 *ICLQ* 801.

Bartenstein, K., 'De Stockholm à Copenhague—Genèse et évolution des responsabilités communes mais différenciées dans le droit international de l'environnement' (2010) 56 *McGill Law Journal—Revue de droit de McGill* 177.

Chemillier-Gendreau, M., 'La signification des principes équitables dans le droit international contemporain' (1981) 16 *Revue belge de droit international* 509.

Cullet, Ph., *Differential Treatment in International Environmental Law* (Aldershot: Ashgate 2003).

Cullet, Ph., 'Le principe des responsabilités communes mais différenciées en droit international de l'environnement: enjeux et perspectives' (2014) 55 *Cahiers de droit* 9.

Deleuil, T., 'The Common but Differentiated Responsibilities Principle: Changes in Continuity after the Durban Conference of the Parties' (2012) 21 *Review of European, Comparative and International Environmental Law* 271.

Hey, E., 'Common but Differentiated Responsibilities', in Wolfrum, R. (ed), *Max Planck Encyclopedia of Public International Law—Volume II* (Oxford: Oxford University Press 2012), 444.

Janis, M. W., 'The Ambiguity of Equity in International Law' (1983) 9 *Brooklyn J Int'l L* 7.

Kofele-Kale, N., 'The Principle of Preferential Treatment in the Law of GATT: Toward Achieving the Objective of an Equitable World Trading System' (1987/88) 18 *California Western International Law Journal* 291.

Mitchell, A.D., 'A Legal Principle of Special and Differential Treatment for WTO Disputes' (2006) 5(3) *World Trade Review* 445.

Pallemaerts, M., 'La Conférence de Rio: Grandeur ou décadence du droit international de l'environnement?' (1995) 28 *Revue belge de droit international* 175.

Pauwelyn, J., 'The End of Differential Treatment for Developing Countries? Lessons from the Trade and Climate Change Regimes' (2013) 22 *Review of European, Comparative and International Environmental Law* 29.

Prost, M. and Torres Camprubi, A., 'Against Fairness? International Environmental Law, Disciplinary Bias, and Pareto Justice' (2012) 25 *Leiden Journal of International Law* 379.

Rajamani, L., *Differential Treatment in International Environmental Law* (Oxford: Oxford University Press 2006).

Rajamani, L., 'The Changing Fortunes of Differential Treatment in the Evolution of International Environmental Law' (2012) 88 *International Affairs* 605.

Rajamani, L., 'Differentiation in the Emerging Climate Regime' (2013) 14 *Theoretical Inquiries in Law* 151.

Stone, C.D., 'Common but Differentiated Responsibilities in International Law' (2004) 98 *AJIL* 276.

United Nations Commission on Sustainable Development, Report of the Secretary-General, Rio Declaration on Environment and Development—Application and Implementation, UN Doc E/CN.17/1997/8 (1997).

United Nations Department of Social and Economic Affairs, Division for Sustainable Development, Review of Implementation of the Rio Principles (2011).

Viñuales, J.E., 'The Rise and Fall of Sustainable Development' (2013) 22 *Review of European, Comparative and International Environmental Law* 3.

# 12. Principle 8

## *Sustainable Patterns of Production and Consumption and Demographic Policies*

Christina Voigt*

**Principle 8**

To achieve sustainable development and a higher quality of life for all people, States should reduce and eliminate unsustainable patterns of production and consumption and promote appropriate demographic policies.



* Professor at the Department of Public and International Law, University of Oslo, Norway.

## I) Origins and Rationale of the Principle

Principle 8 of the Rio Declaration recognizes the direct link between sustainable development and a higher quality of life on the one hand and the underlying patterns of which societies produce and consume on the other. The deeply interlinked economic, social, and environmental crises that societies are facing stem, in large part, from current unsustainable patterns of consumption and production, and pose serious threats to human development. The environment, human health, education, equity, and empowerment are all adversely affected. Consumption of resources is higher than ever, both per person and in absolute terms, exceeding by far the planet's regenerative capacity. Former UN Secretary-General, Kofi Annan, aptly summarized this situation: 'Unsustainable practices are woven deeply into the fabric of modern life.'[1] In fact, it can be said that unsustainable patterns of production and consumption are *the* major impediment to sustainable development.

At UNCED in 1992, the reduction and elimination of sustainable consumption and production ('SCP') was recognized as an overarching theme to link environmental and development challenges. Agenda 21 states that the major cause of the continued deterioration of the global environment is the unsustainable patterns of consumption and production.

The main goal of Principle 8 is thus to 'decouple' economic growth and environmental degradation by increasing the efficiency of resource use in the production, distribution and use of products, aiming to keep the energy, material and pollution intensity of all production and consumption within the carrying capacities of natural ecosystems.[2]

Ten years after the Rio Conference, world leaders signed the Johannesburg Plan of Implementation ('JPOI') at the World Summit on Sustainable Development (WSSD) in 2002, declaring that 'fundamental changes in the way societies produce and consume are indispensable for achieving global sustainable development. All countries should promote sustainable consumption and production patterns',[3] recognizing that 'poverty eradication, changing unsustainable patterns of production and consumption and protecting and managing the natural resource base of economic and social development are overarching objectives of, and essential requirements for, sustainable development.'[4]

The JPOI also called for the development of a 10-Year Framework of Programmes ('10 YFP') to accelerate the shift towards sustainable consumption and production, and to promote social and economic development within the carrying capacity of ecosystems by delinking economic growth from environmental degradation. The Marrakech Process which was initiated in 2003 responded to this call of the JPOI by supporting the implementation of SCP programmes, projects and policies, and helping to construct the 10YFP. At the Rio+20 Summit in 2012, the 10YFP was finally adopted.

[1] Address by Secretary-General Kofi Annan to the World Summit on Sustainable Development in Johannesburg, 2 September 2002, UN Press Release SG/SM/8358, AFR/468, ENV/DEV/693, 03.09.2002.

[2] UNEP, *ABC of SCP—Clarifying Concepts on Sustainable Consumption and Production*, 2010. Available at: <http://www.uneptie.org/scp/marrakech/pdf/ABC%20of%20SCP%20%20Clarifying%20Concepts%20on%20SCP.pdf>.

[3] Plan of Implementation of the World Summit on Sustainable Development, Johannesburg, 2002, ('JPOI') para 14. Available at: <http://www.un.org/esa/sustdev/documents/WSSD_POI_PD/English/WSSD_PlanImpl.pdf>.

[4] JPOI, para 2.

Sustainable consumption and production is about providing goods and services to meet basic needs of the world population without further burdening the already burdened environment and thereby compromising future generations to meet their own needs. The principle expresses the necessity of a shift in the way goods and services are produced and consumed in order to avoid worsening development and environmental degradation. To meet the Millennium Development Goals ('MDG'), the world needs to produce goods and services more efficiently, using fewer resources and generating less waste and pollution. Achieving SCP patterns will sustain improvements in economic development and human welfare that humans depend on, including improvements in health and education. In other words, SCP aims at doing more and better with less—across the entire life cycle of products, while increasing quality of life for all. 'More' delivered in terms of goods and services, with 'less' impact in terms of resource use, environmental degradation, waste, and pollution.[5] In this respect, SCP provides policies, tools, measures, infrastructure, and behaviour change support leading to green, resource efficient economies that ensure well-being, quality of life, and social development for all, while minimizing environmental degradation along the whole life cycle.

However, while attention to sustainable consumption and production patterns has increased in the two decades since the Rio Declaration, resource-intensive consumption and production of goods and services has continued to rise. This growth has occurred at a steady rate in developed and industrialized countries and has accelerated significantly in developing nations, particularly emerging economies.[6] Whilst part of this increase can be attributed to an increasing global human population, much of the rise is a result of advancing levels of prosperity across a number of nations. Rapid levels of economic growth have further stimulated the demand for resources, such as food, fuel, electronic goods, land, and increasing areas of space for the disposal of waste. Such demand now requires resources to be sourced from outside national borders and has led to increasing levels of environmental degradation.[7]

## II) The Principle as Enshrined in the Rio Declaration

### 1. Preparatory work and context

#### *1.1. Conceptual evolution*

The concept of sustainable consumption and production evolved over a long time. During the rise of environmentally-focused legislation in the late 1960s and early 1970s, policy solutions were generally characterized by being single-issue, reactive, site-specific, and end-of-pipe. For this reason, the concept as such is not mentioned in the Stockholm Declaration of 1972.

[5] UNEP (2012), *Global Outlook on SCP Policies: taking action together*, 12.

[6] United Nations Department of Economic and Social Affairs, Division for Sustainable Development, Sustainable Development in the 21st century (SD21), *Review of implementation of Agenda 21 and the Rio Principles*, Synthesis, January 2012. Available at: <http://www.uncsd2012.org/content/documents/194Synthesis%20Agenda%2021%20and%20Rio%20principles.pdf>. See also Stakeholder Forum for a Sustainable Future, December 2011, *Review of Implementation of the Rio Principles*, 57. Available at: <http://www.stakeholderforum.org/fileadmin/files/SD21%20Rio%20principles.pdf>.

[7] Stakeholder Forum for a Sustainable Future, December 2011, *Review of Implementation of the Rio Principles*, 58.

In the 1980s, 'cleaner production' ('CP') was a policy-making approach with growing importance in environmental policy. This was the result of several parallel trends, including the application of a systems perspective to environmental policy.[8] CP has seen a number of shifts in approach, including from reactive to preventative measures, from ad hoc and acute to chronic problems and sources of impacts, from single-pollutant or single-media to multimedia and multi-impact pollutants, from site-specific to supply chains, and from throughput to material cycles.[9]

CP was promoted as a strategy for increasing the efficiency of natural resource use (eco-efficiency) and minimizing waste. Importantly, it implied the preventative and precautionary approach that was eventually endorsed by the Rio Declaration on Environment and Development. This meant reducing pollution and health risks at their point of generation, rather than the end of the production process—the 'end-of-pipe' stage.

The SCP concept as endorsed in Principle 8 of the Rio Declaration is recognizant of the fact that moving towards sustainable consumption and production is a systemic and long-term challenge—but at the same time a fundamental prerequisite for sustainable development. The approach to sustainable consumption and production has therefore evolved to require an integrated, holistic lifecycle approach, cooperation across all actors of society, and a mix of policies and tools that will be adapted to each country based on their levels of development.

SCP is now understood to require a product and service 'lifecycle perspective' to ensure sustainable management of natural resources from the extraction, to the production, distribution, consumption, and disposal/reuse phases.[10] With this life cycle perspective, SCP goals and actions could become powerful levers to accelerate the transition to eco-efficient economies and turn global, regional, and national environmental and social challenges into business and employment opportunities, while decoupling economic growth from environmental degradation—political will provided.

Decoupling can generally be understood as having rates of increasing wealth greater than the rates of increasing impacts. When used in this way, it refers to the ability of an economy to grow without corresponding increases in environmental pressure. An economy that is able to sustain GDP growth without having a negative impact on environmental conditions is said to be decoupled. The OECD has made decoupling a major focus of the work of its Environment Directorate. The OECD defines the term as breaking the link between 'environmental bads' and 'economic goods'.[11]

The antecedents of decoupling were represented in 'Limits to Growth' which outlined a series of scenarios within which the planet's stock of natural capital, being finite, would, if degraded and depleted, eventually have an impact on economic growth and economic well-being.[12] Decoupling refers typically to the ability of breaking the long-held causal relationship between economic growth and the growth in the consumption of natural resources. It goes beyond simple price adjustments or marginal policy shifts but strikes a blow at the

[8] UNEP (2012a), *Global Outlook on SCP Policies: taking action together*, 20.

[9] UNEP (2012a), *Global Outlook on SCP Policies: taking action together*, 18.

[10] *Proposed input to CSD 18 and 19 on a 10 Year Framework of Programmes on Sustainable Consumption and Production (10YFP on SCP)*, Revised Draft (7 April 2010) Document prepared by the Marrakech Process Secretariat: UNDESA and UNEP.

[11] OECD 2002, *Indicators to Measure Decoupling of Environmental Pressure from Economic Growth*, <http://www.oecd.org/dataoecd/0/52/1933638.pdf>.

[12] Meadows, D. H., Meadows, D. L., Randers, J. and Behrens, W. III, *The Limits to Growth: A report of the Club of Rome's Project on the Predicament of Mankind* (Potomac Associated Press 1972).

heart of the fundamental yet mistaken belief that economic growth and natural resource use are the two sides of the same coin, joined forever in a mutually reinforcing manner.

One of the earliest proponents of decoupling was the ecological economist Herman Daly, who suggested the economic approach of a steady state: a system that permits qualitative development but not aggregate quantitative growth.[13] Tim Jackson, another important proponent of decoupling, stresses the importance of differentiating between relative and absolute decoupling when using the term.[14] Relative decoupling refers to a decline in the ecological intensity per unit of economic output. In this situation, resource impacts decline relative to the GDP, which could itself still be rising. Absolute decoupling refers to a situation in which resource impacts decline in absolute terms. Resource efficiencies must increase at least as fast as economic output does and must continue to improve as the economy grows, if absolute decoupling is to occur. Jackson points out that an economy can correctly claim that it has relatively decoupled its economy in terms of energy inputs per unit of GDP. However, in this situation, total environmental impacts would still be increasing, albeit at a slower pace of growth than in GDP.

In 2011, the International Resource Panel, hosted by the United Nations Environment Programme ('UNEP') warned that by 2050, the human race could devour 140 billion tons of minerals, ores, fossil fuels, and biomass per year—three times its current appetite—unless nations can start decoupling economic growth rates from the rate of natural resource consumption.[15]

Recently, the Club of Rome announced its plan to develop the idea of decoupling into a major work programme by explaining: 'The essential rationale is that, under any plausible assumptions about the limits we face, decoupling is required to move us towards a safer and sustainable world. There are cases where absolute decoupling will be required at a point in time: our move towards a no-carbon society at some point in the future is almost certain.'[16]

## *1.2. From Rio 1992 to Rio 2012*

### 1.2.1. The 1992 Earth Summit

The key debate underlying Principle 8 during the last week of PrepCom IV concerned developing countries' emphasis on the unsustainable character of the consumption and production patterns of developed countries and the latter's view that the demographic policies of developing countries were themselves unsustainable. The convoluted negotiation process during PrepCom IV kept this question open until the informal contact group chaired by Tommy Koh (the chairman of the PrepCom) managed to combine these two propositions within one single principle.[17] The connection between them is easily grasped: if population drives consumption, and consumption drives production, then sustainability policies must address unsustainable patterns of consumption and production but also demographic growth. With this context in mind, it is unsurprising that Agenda 21 devoted its chapter 4 to 'Changing consumption patterns' and, immediately after,

[13] Daly, H. E., *Steady State economics* (Island Press 1977).

[14] Tim, J., *Prosperity without Growth: Economics for a Finite Planet* (Earthscan 2009).

[15] *Decoupling: natural resource use and environmental impacts of economic growth* (International Resource Panel report 2011).

[16] 'Decoupling—A Response to Limits to Growth': A Project Proposed by the Club of Rome, September 2013. Available at: <http://clubofromeagm2013.files.wordpress.com/2013/09/background_note_for_the_decoupling_session-2.pdf>.

[17] See Kovar, J., 'A Short Guide to the Rio Declaration' (1993) 4 *Colorado Journal of International Environmental Law and Policy* 119, 130.

chapter 5 to 'Demographic dynamics and sustainability'. This is, at the same time, a useful indication of where to look for the implications of the laconic language used in Principle 8.

Regarding chapter 4, it places consumption and production as one of the major conditions for the mitigation of global environmental deterioration and the sustainable improvement of human welfare. According to paragraph 4.3:

> The major cause of the continued deterioration of the global environment is the unsustainable pattern of consumption and production, particularly in industrialized countries, which is a matter of grave concern, aggravating poverty and imbalances...[18]

Reference was also made to the importance of consumption and production in particular issue areas—such as energy, transportation, waste—and implementation tools—such as economic instruments and the transfer of technology. This created the basis for SCP to be reflected in the national strategies for sustainable development and local Agenda 21 strategies that parties had agreed to establish. Importantly, Agenda 21's emphasis on *consumption* patterns marked a significant change in environmental policymaking, which had previously focused more on production. This stimulated a number of countries in the 1990s to convene symposia on the environmental implications of consumption. The Organisation for Economic Co-operation and Development (OECD), the United Nations Commission on Sustainable Development, and the United Nations Environment Programme (UNEP) launched work programmes around this theme.[19]

As for chapter 5, it has three objectives, namely: to develop knowledge regarding the connection between population and environmental degradation; to formulate policies to address this link: and to implement them. In line with the position taken by developing countries during the negotiations, paragraph 5.3 nuances the causal effect of the unsustainable patterns of consumption and production decried by developing countries:

> The growth of world population and production combined with unsustainable consumption patterns places increasingly severe stress on the life-supporting capacities of our planet. These interactive processes affect the use of land, water, air, energy and other resources.

However, population policy is a particularly sensitive area of governmental intervention because of its 'Malthusian' tones and the potential tensions with human rights, particularly the right to private and family life. Thus, while the objective of increasing knowledge and awareness set out in programme area A of chapter 5 may provide a useful starting point for policy formulation and implementation, in practice, such policies are as necessary as they are difficult—politically—to materialize.

### 1.2.2. WSSD (2002) and the Marrakesh Process

The WSSD, held in Johannesburg, South Africa, in 2002 was crucial in establishing the vital importance of establishing SCP patterns at a global level to achieve sustainable development. The Johannesburg Declaration on Sustainable Development recognized that:

> poverty eradication, changing consumption and production patterns and protecting and managing the natural resource base for economic and social development are overarching objectives of and essential requirements for sustainable development.[20]

[18] Agenda 21, ch 4.3. [19] UNEP (2012a), *Global Outlook on SCP Policies: taking action together*, 18.

[20] United Nations Department of Economic and Social Affairs (2004, December 15), Johannesburg Declaration on Sustainable Development, para 11. Available at: <http://www.un.org/esa/sustdev/documents/WSSD_POI_PD/English/POI_PD.htm>.

The same text is included in the more detailed JPOI, also adopted by governments at the summit, along with an entire chapter devoted to unsustainable patterns of consumption and production. This chapter opens by declaring that '[f]undamental changes in the way societies produce and consume are indispensable for achieving global sustainable development'.[21]

Recognizing that consumption patterns often undermine progress made in improving resource efficiency in production, the text placed the term 'consumption' ahead of the term 'production' resulting in the consistent reference to 'sustainable consumption and production' from then on.[22] This term also sought to recognize the interrelation between consumption and production, between supply and demand, and the need to move beyond the tendency at the time to treat these aspects in isolation from each other.[23]

The JPOI also laid the groundwork for follow-up in the longer term, with States agreeing to:

> Encourage and promote the development of a 10-Year Framework of Programmes in support of regional and national initiatives to accelerate the shift towards sustainable consumption and production to promote social and economic development within the carrying capacity of ecosystems by addressing and, where appropriate, delinking economic growth and environmental degradation through improving efficiency and sustainability in the use of resources and production processes and reducing resource degradation, pollution and waste. All countries should take action, with developed countries taking the lead, taking into account the development needs and capabilities of developing countries, through mobilization, from all sources, of financial and technical assistance and capacity-building for developing countries.[24]

Launched in 2003, the global, multi-stakeholder Marrakech Process was the response to this call. Its main objectives were to support the implementation of SCP in all regions of the world and to develop inputs for the elaboration of a 10-Year Framework of Programmes ('10YFP') on sustainable consumption and production, as called for by the WSSD Johannesburg Plan of Action.[25]

The goals of the Marrakech Process were to assist countries in their efforts to green their economies, to help corporations develop greener business models, and to encourage consumers to adopt more sustainable lifestyles.[26] UNEP and United Nations Department of Economic Affairs ('UNDESA') were the lead agencies of this global process, with an active participation of national governments, development agencies, and civil society.

The Marrakech Process produced a number of outputs. The results include the establishment of seven Marrakech Task Forces as key implementation mechanisms that are developing policy toolkits and building North-South cooperation in all the regions. Importantly, an outline of the 10YFP was developed.[27]

[21] United Nations Department of Economic and Social Affairs (15 December 2004), Johannesburg Plan of Implementation. ch 3. Changing unsustainable patterns of consumption and production. Available at: <http://www.un.org/esa/sustdev/documents/WSSD_POI_PD/English/POIChapter3.htm> (further JPOI).

[22] UNEP (2012), *Global Outlook on SCP Policies: taking action together*, 25.

[23] UNEP (2012), *Global Outlook on SCP Policies: taking action together*, 25.

[24] JPOI, para 14.

[25] For more information on the Marrakesh Process, see: <http://esa.un.org/marrakechprocess/index.shtml>.

[26] United Nations Sustainable Development Platform: <http://sustainabledevelopment.un.org/index.php?menu=1546>.

[27] See the development of the various drafts here: <http://esa.un.org/marrakechprocess/draft10YFPInput.shtml>.

The outline reflects the need for a common global framework and international cooperation to support regional and national shifts in the medium and long term towards SCP, and to bridge the gaps between developed and developing countries. It recognizes that only joint efforts can reverse the worsening social and ecological trends and promote a rapid transition towards resource efficient, equitable, low-carbon economies and societies that operate within the carrying capacity of ecosystems, while enhancing our cultural and natural heritage, and decreasing the disparities in standards of living.[28]

The 10YFP was considered by the Commission on Sustainable Development ('CSD') during its 2010–11 implementation cycle.[29] The negotiations in the course of the nineteenth session of CSD ('CSD19') in May 2011 resulted in an agreed-upon text establishing the 10YFP, comprising a vision, goals, objectives, functions, an institutional structure, and an initial, open list of programmes for inclusion in the framework. The work of the Marrakech Process was duly acknowledged by the eighteenth and nineteenth sessions of CSD, where it was recognized as a sound basis to develop a 10YFP. At CSD19, 'Delegations reached full agreement on elements of a decision on a 10-year framework of programmes on sustainable consumption and production . . .'.[30] However, disagreements over other issues, such as the preamble regarding the thematic cluster of transport, chemicals, and mining, and the means of implementation in chemicals and waste management, prevented CSD19 from adopting an official decision.[31]

As an outcome of CSD19, SCP and the 10YFP have gained more visibility and were reiterated in various regional meetings and the national submissions for the 2012 United Nations Conference on Sustainable Development (Rio+20). In the meantime, several countries were requesting the adoption of a 10YFP including: Australia, Croatia, the Dominican Republic, Indonesia, Japan, Mexico, Singapore, the European Union, CARICOM, the G77, and the entire African region.

### 1.2.3. Rio 2012 and the 10YFP

At the United Nations Conference on Sustainable Development (Rio+20), the Heads of State reaffirmed that promoting sustainable patterns of consumption and production is one of the three overarching objectives of, and essential requirements for sustainable development. They also reiterated that fundamental changes in the way societies consume and produce are indispensable for achieving global sustainable development. They recognized that:

> poverty eradication, changing unsustainable and promoting sustainable patterns of consumption and production and protecting and managing the natural resource base of economic and social development are the overarching objectives of and essential requirements for sustainable development.[32]

[28] Proposed input to CSD 18 and 19 on a 10 year Framework of Programmes on Sustainable Consumption and Production (10YFP on SCP), revised draft (7 April 2010), document prepared by the Marrakech Process secretariat: UNDESA and UNEP.

[29] Available at: <http://sustainabledevelopment.un.org/csd.html>.

[30] Commission on Sustainable Development, Report of the 19th session (14 May 2010 and 2–13 May 2011), paras 65–7.

[31] International Institute for Sustainable Development (2011, 7 March). *Summary of the Intergovernmental Preparatory Meeting for the Nineteenth Session of the Commission for Sustainable Development: 28 February–4 March 2011*. Available at: <http://www.iisd.ca/download/pdf/enb05293e.pdf>.

[32] General Assembly, *The Future We Want*, A/RES/66/288,11. September 2012, para 4.

Further, they recognized that:

> urgent action on unsustainable patterns of production and consumption where they occur remains fundamental in addressing environmental sustainability and promoting conservation and sustainable use of biodiversity and ecosystems, regeneration of natural resources and the promotion of sustained, inclusive and equitable global growth.[33]

Importantly, at Rio 2012, Heads of State strengthened their commitment to accelerate the shift towards SCP patterns with the adoption of the 10-Year Framework of Programmes on Sustainable Consumption and Production Patterns—as stated in paragraph 226 of the Rio+20 Outcome Document *The Future We Want* which references to document A/CONF.216/5.[34] The adoption was based on the recognition 'that fundamental changes in the way societies consume and produce are indispensable for achieving global sustainable development.'[35]

The 10YFP is a very concrete and operational outcome of Rio+20. It responds to the 2002 Johannesburg Plan of Implementation. It recalls the commitments made in the Rio Declaration, Agenda 21 and the Johannesburg Plan of Implementation on sustainable consumption and production and, in particular, the request in chapter III of the Johannesburg Plan of Implementation to encourage and promote the development of a ten-year framework of programmes. It builds on the 8 years work of the Marrakech Process, on regional SCP strategies and initiatives, as well as on the national cleaner production centres and other SCP best practices engaging a wide range of SCP stakeholders.

The 10YFP is now a global framework of action to enhance international cooperation to accelerate the shift towards SCP in both developed and developing countries. The framework aims at supporting capacity building, and providing technical and financial assistance to developing countries for this shift. The 10YFP will develop, replicate, and scale up SCP and resource efficiency initiatives, at national and regional levels, decoupling environmental degradation and resource use from economic growth, and thus enhance the net contribution of economic activities to poverty eradication and social development. The framework encourages innovation and cooperation among all stakeholders.

The A/CONF.216/5 adopted document provides the vision, goals, and values of the 10YFP as well as its functions, organizational structure, means of implementation, criteria for programmes design and an initial, non-exhaustive list of five programmes. The 10YFP includes: a Secretariat, a UN Interagency Coordination Group, a 'small' Board, National Focal Points, and a review/reporting body.[36] UNEP has been requested to act as the 10YFP Secretariat and to establish and administer a Trust Fund to support SCP implementation in developing countries. The 10YFP-adopted text includes an indicative and open list of programmes, which build primarily on the experience gained through the Marrakech Process, including its Task Forces and regional SCP roundtables and strategies. The five initial programmes are: i) consumer information; ii) sustainable lifestyles and education; iii) sustainable public procurement (SPP); iv) sustainable buildings and construction; and v) sustainable tourism, including ecotourism.

The ambition is that the 10YFP will bring together existing initiatives and partnerships working in similar areas, building synergies and cooperation between stakeholders to

[33] General Assembly, *The Future We Want*, 61.
[34] General Assembly, *The Future We Want*.
[35] General Assembly, *The Future We Want*, 224.
[36] For more information, see UNEP website: <http://www.unep.fr/scp/marrakech/10yfp.htm>.

leverage resources towards mutual objectives and minimize duplication of ongoing efforts. The programmes aim at contributing to meeting the goals and principles of the 10YFP responding to national and regional needs, priorities, and circumstances. Through providing a mix of policy instruments and setting clear objectives, activities, and indicators of success. it is hoped that they will encourage the involvement of governments, business, civil society, and all relevant stakeholders.

Means of implementation are through voluntary contributions from all sources, and a Trust Fund to be administered by UNEP. The voluntary nature of contributions and the soft-policy oriented focus (ie information, education) of the YFP, however, raise questions as to its effectiveness and political relevance.

## 2. Barriers

Despite its long history, the movement towards sustainable production and consumption is still in its infancy. Initiatives such as sustainable procurement, ecological tax reforms, and regulation to improve energy conservation and energy and resource efficiency, whilst crucial to enabling and achieving sustainable production and consumption, still remain ad hoc, fragmented, and limited to national and regional levels.[37]

At the international level, the discussion on SCP has been occupied mostly by academics and think tanks, with no real traction on policy-making. Alongside a dearth of comprehensive, joined-up national strategies for sustainable consumption and production, a range of other drivers further complicate the implementation of Principle 8.

The Stakeholder Forum on Sustainable Development identified a number of barriers to moving towards sustainable consumption and production patterns. One such barrier is the increasing globalization of markets. 'Globalisation has facilitated the relative decoupling of economic activities from resource impacts and waste generation in developed countries, as increasingly, the majority of energy- and resource-intensive activities take place in developing nations, with cheap production and labour costs. However, when taking into account the lifecycle of products, the intensity of resource use and waste generation remain unchanged. Globalisation has thus promoted the outsourcing of unsustainable production systems to developing countries, transferring production emissions to outsourced nations' production activities whilst exporting products to developed countries.'[38]

Another barrier is the so-called 're-bound principle', whereby increased efficiency is used to produce and consume even more products, thus leading to increased production and consumption and nullifying the effect of more efficient production patterns. The Forum noted that 'Improvements such as better national and international transportation links and other technological advancements have increased the capacity to exploit an enormous concentration of natural resources with reduced expense. In turn low cost products become available to the market. Consequently production efficiencies can actually uphold the vast levels of consumption that have become commonplace.'[39] Such development is particularly worrisome in the context of a new generation of affluent consumers in emerging economies. Such production efficiencies remain ineffective or even actively compromise sustainability without a step-change in consumer attitudes to the products, and the quantities of those products, that are being consumed.

[37] Stakeholder Forum (2011), 60.
[38] Stakeholder Forum (2011), 60.
[39] Stakeholder Forum (2011), 60.

Another barrier, and perhaps the most significant one, is lack of political will and action. Commentators have noted a lack of responsibility in taking action, from both public and private sides. There is a tendency from those outside government to downplay the importance of States' roles, and a tendency from governments to push much of the responsibility for action and change on to non-State institutions. Both tendencies are symptomatic of slow progress on these issues.[40]

## 3. Scope and dimensions

### 3.1. *Legal nature*

The Rio Declaration is a non-binding, soft law document. While some of its principles are binding as customary or general principles of law, Principle 8 in the Rio Declaration does not hold such legally binding character. Despite the longstanding and ongoing activities at the international level to set up a framework for SCP, the barriers mentioned above make it difficult to argue for a legal conscience or an *opinio juris*.

Already *Grotius* suggested a *tacitus consensus populorum* as necessary for any norm based on custom.[41] The classical judicial *locus classicus* on this point is the *North Sea Continental Shelf* Judgment by the ICJ:

> Not only must the acts concerned amount to a settled practice, but they must also be such, or to be carried out in such a way, as to be evidence of a belief that this practice is rendered obligatory by the existence of a rule of law requiring it. The need for such a belief, i.e., the existence of a subjective element, is implicit in the very notion of the *opinio jure sive necessitatis*.[42]

It is thus the *belief* of the existence of the normative statement coupled with the *will* to comply with it, which transposes a concept into a customary norm (state practice provided). What is required therefore is a psychological element: the consciousness of conforming to a norm.

The barriers mentioned above give little proof of an emerging *opinio juris* as to the obligation to implement sustainable consumption and production patterns. More importantly and sadly, global trends show little alignment with SCP and state practice is thus rather rare. However, Principle 8 laid the foundation for many subsequent international and regional agreements, as well as domestic policies that have bound parties to specific actions contributing to the shift to SCP patterns.

### 3.2. *SCP and the three pillars of sustainable development*

Sustainable consumption and production is inseparably intertwined with sustainable development. SCP depends on a clear conceptual understanding of sustainable development in order to work, and, if so, may be its best example. Importantly, SCP is also a vital prerequisite for sustainable development and the quality of life for all people. In other words SCP's *purpose* is that of sustainable development. It is the fundament on which sustainable societies can be built.

Moreover, underlying the holistic, life-cycle SCP-approach—from conception through consumption and to the end of its life—is the call for better *integration* across all three

[40] Stakeholder Forum (2011), 61.

[41] On the development of customary law see: Guggenheim, P. and Kappeler, D., *Traité de Droit International Public; Avec mention de la practique internationale et suisse*, vol I (2nd edn, Librairie de l'Université 1967), 94.

[42] ICJ Reports 1969, 3, para 177.

pillars of sustainable development: economic development, social development, and environmental protection. Only when all aspects of a product's life can be taken into account, might a shift to more sustainable patterns be possible. This approach, however, requires that social, environmental, and economic dimensions are considered and applied simultaneously, holistically and in an integrated manner.

The challenge for sustainable development is to delimit the frame for integration. Integration in the context of sustainable development raises the fundamental question of whether the economy, social interests, and the environment are of equal importance or whether their obvious connectedness needs to be brought into some sort of *systematic relationship*—a priority order—in order to give the concept meaning.

The standard view is to accord the divergent elements equal importance ('pillars'). As a result, integration is perceived as a balancing act with supposedly unavoidable trade-offs—often on the environmental side. While there is no doubt that integrating environmental, economic, and social factors is pivotal for sustainable development, it does not necessarily mean treating all three in the same manner or giving them the same weight. Equal treatment can be no more than an illusory or idealized goal in the absence of conceptual clarity. Integration can be defined as 'mak[ing] whole or becoming complete; bring[ing] (parts) together into a whole.'[43] The desired outcome of this process is integrity—generally defined as completeness, wholeness, or unimpaired condition.

In the context of sustainable development it is and must be: *environmental integrity* which can be defined as: Human activities that (at a minimum) sustain important biophysical processes which support plant, animal, and human life and which must be allowed to continue without significant change. The objective is to assure the continued health of essential life support ecological systems, including air, water, and soil, by protecting their resilience, diversity, and purity.

Here, the importance of SCP in the understanding of sustainable development plays a significant role. As said above, the main goal of Principle 8 of the Rio Declaration is to 'decouple' economic growth and environmental degradation in order to keep the energy, material, and pollution intensity of all production and consumption *within the carrying capacities of natural ecosystems*.[44] These ecological limits—or planetary boundaries—are not unknown. There is a wealth of scientific data and knowledge.[45]

This goal of SCP makes clear the priority of not endangering the capacities of natural ecosystems. This was something the World Commission on Environment and Development ('WCED') called for and it is essential still. 'At *a minimum*' the Commission stated, 'sustainable development must not endanger the natural systems that support life on Earth'.[46] Integration in the context of SCP and sustainable development thus means to respect these functions as an absolute priority. They are irreplaceable on a local, regional, and global, as well as temporal, scale: neither knowledge, technology, nor economic wealth could provide

[43] *Webster's New Dictionary and Thesaurus*, 2004, 354.

[44] UNEP, *ABC of SCP—Clarifying Concepts on Sustainable Consumption and Production*, 2010. Available at: <http://www.uneptie.org/scp/marrakech/pdf/ABC%20of%20SCP%20-%20Clarifying%20Concepts%20on%20SCP.pdf>.

[45] See, eg Millennium Ecosystem Assessment; Rockström, J. et al, 'Planetary Boundaries: Exploring the Safe Operating Space for Humanity' (2009)14:2 *Ecology and Society* 32.

[46] WCED, *Report of the World Commission on Environment and Development: Our Common Future*,1987, 44–5. Available at <http://www.un-documents.net/wced-ocf.htm>.

any substitute.[47] Integration in the context of SCP and sustainable development therefore demands that ecological thresholds are respected.

## *3.3. Sustainable production and consumption patterns*

### 3.3.1. Definition

The most widely accepted definition of SCP, as developed at the multi-stakeholder workshop hosted by the Norwegian Ministry of Environment at the Oslo Symposium on Sustainable Consumption in 1994, is:

> the use of services and related products, which respond to basic needs and bring a better quality of life while minimizing the use of natural resources and toxic materials as well as the emissions of waste and pollutants over the life cycle of the service or product so as not to jeopardize the needs of future generations.[48]

### 3.3.2. Scope

The fundamental objective of SCP is to decouple economic growth from environmental degradation.

Achieving SCP requires a holistic approach. At its core is the life-cycle perspective. Accordingly, it considers the total use of resources as well as the resulting emissions, effluents, and waste; aiming to minimize negative environmental impacts; and promoting inclusive well-being. Its focus on the sustainable and efficient management of resources at all stages of value chains of goods and services encourages the development of processes that use fewer resources and generate less waste, including hazardous substances, while yielding environmental benefits and frequently productivity and economic gains.[49] Such improvements can also increase the competitiveness of enterprises, turning solutions for sustainability challenge into business, employment, and export opportunities. SCP also encourages capturing and reusing or recycling valuable resources, thereby turning waste streams into value streams ('cradle-to-cradle'). Central to life-cycle management are precautionary and preventive approaches.

Finally, it analyses the impacts of products when recycled, reused, or disposed of. A life-cycle approach also assesses the value chain from an environmental and social perspective, identifying impacts on local communities; access to material and non-material resources; cultural heritage; safety and living conditions; as well as considering the rights of indigenous people, community engagement, and local employment. Hence it evaluates the true cost of a product over its full life cycle and points to benefits distributed along the whole value chain.

SCP's main goal to 'decouple' economic growth and environmental degradation is a 'journey' to increasing the efficiency of resource use, supporting sustainable lifestyles and

[47] See Daily, G. D., *Nature's Services: Societal Dependence on Natural Ecosystems* (Island Press 1997). A preliminary estimation of the economic value of the services provided to humans by ecological systems and the global natural capital stock which produces them ranges them at a price level of US$54 trillion annually, compared to a gross global product of US$18 trillion p.a. See Constanza. R. et al, *The Value of the World's Ecosystem Services and Natural Capital* (1997) 387 *Nature* 253–60.

[48] Norwegian Ministry of Environment, 1994.

[49] For more detailed information on the life-cycle approach, see Annex IV to the 'Proposed input to CSD 18 and 19 on a 10 year framework of programmes on sustainable consumption and production (10YFP on SCP), Revised draft' (7 April 2010), Document prepared by the Marrakech Process Secretariat: UNDESA and UNEP.

livelihoods for all, sustainable infrastructure, green jobs, and better quality of life and equity.

### *3.4. Appropriate demographic policies*

The growth of world population and production combined with unsustainable consumption patterns places increasingly severe stress on the life-supporting capacities of the planet. These interactive processes affect the use of land, water, air, energy, and other resources. Rapidly growing cities, unless well-managed, face major environmental problems. This issue alone is deserving of an entire chapter in this book. Due to spatial constraints, a few comments will have to suffice, though the author is well aware of the fact that these do not appropriately address this issue.

Access to contraception, women's rights, and maternal and child health are the more accepted and recognizably important determinants of demographic change and reproductive behaviour, and to date have been the key means offered for tackling population growth in international fora and national government policy.

At an international level, the 1994 International Conference on Population and Development ('ICPD') held in Cairo was devoted to female health. Integrating family planning and women's health services and promoting the rights of women were key issues on the agenda discussed at the conference. The Programme of Action strongly urged Governments to make reproductive health services available to 'all individuals of appropriate ages'.

All Governments were encouraged to assess the unmet need for good-quality family-planning services and to take steps to meet this need. They were also encouraged to expand the provision of maternal and child health services in the context of primary health care. Some of the points from the Cairo Conference were incorporated into the MDG targets.

## 4. Normative impact

### *4.1. Overview*

One way in which governments have promoted SCP has been through the negotiation, adoption and implementation of multilateral environmental agreements ('MEAs'), which in some cases involve efforts to change production and consumption patterns.

The term 'sustainable consumption and production' as such does not occur in convention texts. Nevertheless, some SCP aspects and policies to altering consumption and production patterns have been addressed by a number of treaties, such as the waste-related Basel, Stockholm, and Rotterdam Conventions.

### *4.2. Vienna Convention for the Protection of the Ozone Layer*

The Vienna Convention for the Protection of the Ozone Layer, negotiated in 1985 and in force since 1988 is a prominent example of how SCP has been addressed and promoted directly or indirectly in a holistic manner or in some stages of the life cycle. The Convention as a framework agreement for global efforts to protect the ozone layer does not make an explicit reference to SCP or an SCP approach. However, its Montreal Protocol, which sets out legally binding reduction targets for ozone-depleting substances ('ODS'), has in practice required interventions across the consumption and production chains for a number of goods.

The Montreal Protocol's Multilateral Fund, which promotes cleaner and more sustainable products, as well as providing information to consumers and households, has successfully disbursed billions of U.S. dollars for industrial conversion to switch to sustainable production technologies and practices and other activities to protect the ozone layer.

### *4.3. MEAs on waste: Basel, Rotterdam, and Stockholm*

Adopted in 1989, the Basel Convention on the Control of Transboundary Movements of Hazardous Wastes and their Disposal, was originally focused principally on the transboundary movement of hazardous waste. Since 2000, however, it has also emphasized the minimization of waste through environmentally sound management that addresses virtually all stages in its production and consumption, including generation, storage, transport, treatment, reuse, recycling, recovery, and final disposal, thereby adopting an integrated life-cycle approach. The Basel Convention obliges parties to implement and enforce its provisions, has requirements for monitoring and compliance and measures for encouraging compliance.

Its partnership programme has also encouraged the promotion of SCP in a number of sectors, for example, establishing guidelines on the sound management of end-of-life mobile phones and computing equipment. In particular the environmentally sound management of electrical and electronic waste (e-waste) and the recovery of shipwrecks can be identified as two examples of policy areas where the Basel Convention attempts to adopt a life-cycle approach. The current discussions about extended producer responsibility ('EPR') for e-waste highlights the SCP importance of the Convention.

EPR is an environmental policy approach in which a producer's responsibility for a product is extended to the post-consumer stage of a product's life cycle. An EPR policy is characterized by: (1) the shifting of responsibility (physically and/or economically; fully or partially) upstream toward the producer and away from municipalities; and (2) the provision of incentives to producers to take into account environmental considerations when designing their products. While other policy instruments tend to target a single point in the production chain, EPR seeks to integrate signals related to the environmental characteristics of products and production processes throughout the product chain.[50]

The Rotterdam Convention, adopted in 1998, complements the Basel Convention by establishing mandatory rules regarding the import and export of hazardous chemicals and pesticides, creating mechanisms for information sharing and encouraging the environmentally sound management of permitted chemicals.

The Stockholm Convention on Persistent Organic Pollutants ('POPs'), adopted in 2001, addresses both production and waste treatment processes in order to minimize, and in some cases eliminate, the release of long-lasting chemical pollutants, as well as promoting the development of substitute materials, products, and processes. Although it does not refer to SCP explicitly, by recognizing the need to address the creation of POPs throughout different stages in the life cycle of goods, it implicitly recognizes the need for a holistic analysis of product life cycles.

Together, the three treaties represent a framework for the life-cycle management of hazardous chemicals.[51]

[50] For example in the EU, Extended Producer Responsibility for e-waste is implemented through Directive 2012/19/EU on Waste Electrical and Electronic Equipment ('new WEEE Directive').

[51] UNEP (2012), in particular the overview over MEAs with SCP relevance, 31–3.

### *4.4. Convention on Biological Diversity*

The Convention on Biological Diversity ('CBD')'s triple objective is the conservation of biological diversity, the sustainable use of its components and the fair and equitable sharing of the benefits arising out of the utilization of genetic resources, including by appropriate access to genetic resources and appropriate transfer of relevant technologies, taking into account all rights over those resources and to technologies, and by appropriate funding (article 1).

Further, the CBD sets out the principle that, although States have the right to exploit natural resources for the benefit of their people, the conservation of biodiversity is a common concern of humankind and that member States are responsible for the biological resources in their jurisdiction. It made new and additional funding available to developing countries for this purpose, to be managed by the Global Environment Facility ('GEF'). It has significant implications for SCP given the direct and indirect impacts on ecosystems that are caused by resource extraction, production processes, consumption, and waste.

In 2010, Parties to the Convention agreed on the Nagoya Protocol on Access to Genetic Resources and the Fair and Equitable Sharing of Benefits Arising from their Utilization to the Convention on Biological Diversity ('ABS'). The protocol establishes that access to genetic resources should be based on a country's prior informed consent and the equitable sharing of benefits. The adoption of the protocol on ABS in 2010 is widely regarded as a critical step in promoting SCP, as its requirement for countries to equitably share the benefits of economic resources will enable countries to capture some of the economic value of biodiversity, thus incentivizing conservation. Decision X/44 on incentive measures, also taken at the Nagoya COP, explicitly invited countries to foster 'sustainable consumption and production patterns for the conservation and sustainable use of biodiversity'.

### *4.5. United Nations Framework Convention on Climate Change*

The United Nations Framework Convention on Climate Change ('UNFCCC') has perhaps the greatest potential to stimulate a revolution in consumption and production. In fact, SCP is a prerequisite for meeting the ultimate objective of the Convention: to avoid dangerous interference with the climate system (article 2).

Nothing short of effective SCP can achieve the reduction in atmospheric levels of greenhouse gas ('GHG') concentrations recommended by scientific assessments. An SCP approach is fundamental to this goal throughout the different stages of the life cycles of many goods and services.

As part of the UNFCCC process, recent decisions by the COP show that climate change mitigation is an issue deeply intertwined with consumption and production patterns. These decisions cover a multitude of issues, such as quantified emission reduction targets, Nationally Appropriate Mitigation Actions on GHG emissions; Reducing Emissions from Deforestation and Forest Degradation ('REDD+'); financing; technology transfer and capacity-building and the monitoring, reporting. and verification ('MRV') of emissions. The evolution of the climate regime can be seen as a step toward facilitating the implementation of SCP, particularly by addressing economy-wide emissions from all major emitters, committing additional finance and representing progress towards a new agreement to be adopted in 2015.

### *4.6. The nature of MEAs and SCP*

MEAs have been implemented most effectively when they include flexible mechanisms for implementation at a national level, and mechanisms for financial support. This is particularly important in developing countries, which often face financial and institutional barriers to compliance. Where financial mechanisms exist as a part of other MEAs, they have also proven to be significant in enabling countries to take action.

In general, flexibility mechanisms have also been key in allowing States to achieve progress within the bounds of their national constraints while still complying with international targets. With many global policy agreements, mechanisms are needed to promote national implementation, taking into account differing national capacities.

Despite the significant progress represented by the number of MEAs that have been agreed since the Stockholm Conference on the Human Environment in 1972, today the large number of agreements (over 500) and their relative fragmentation is increasingly being recognized as an operational problem.[52] This is further complicated by the fact that agreements are forged during long and difficult negotiations, under the different organizations, frequently of diverse institutional natures, memberships, and regional coverage.[53]

There is the fear that this complexity leads to normative conflicts and overlapping competencies between agreements, a neglect of the linkages between the ecological problems being addressed by different MEAs and inefficient deployment of financial resources, as well as placing significant administrative and financial burdens on national governments.[54]

In recognition of this, the three major treaties on waste—the Basel, Rotterdam, and Stockholm Conventions—have recently experimented with coordinating their Conferences of Parties ('COPs'), and, judging it a success, initiated processes to further coordinate a number of operational functions. It should also be noted that MEAs are only one part of a web of international agreements.

As a significant area of global policymaking, international trade agreements have very important implications for SCP, as life cycles in a globalized economy often span a number of nations. Materials extraction, processing, manufacturing, packing, and transportation of a product, a product's useful life and its end-of-life stage may all take place in different countries. Interventions that lead to cost increases in one country may simply lead companies to shift the location of unsustainable life-cycle stages to other countries.[55]

This implies the need for coordination, cooperation, and agreements among States and between stakeholders across all areas of policymaking. It also implies ensuring that policies in *non-environmental* areas are nonetheless aligned with countries' environmental priorities.

Alternatively, it might take the form of agreements allowing States to impose environmentally related taxes on imported products, or the provision of technical assistance and capacity-building to developing countries and small and medium-size enterprises ('SMEs')

[52] See, for example, Stephens, T., 'Multiple International Courts and the "Fragmentation" of International Environmental Law' (2007) 25 *Australian Yearbook of International Law* 227; Carlarne, C., 'Good Climate Governance: Only a Fragmented System of International Law Anyway?' (2008) 30 *Law and Policy* 450; Biermann, F., Pattberg, P., van Asselt, H., and Zelli, F., 'The Fragmentation of Global Governance Architectures: A Framework for Analysis' (2009) 9 *Global Environmental Politics* 14; Van Asselt, H., Sindico, F., and Mehling, M., 'Global Climate Change and the Fragmentation of International Law' (2008) 30 *Law and Policy* 423.

[53] Najam, A., Papa, M., and Taiyab, N., *Global Environmental Governance: A Reform Agenda.* Available at: <http://www.iisd.org/pdf/2006/geg.pdf>.

[54] Wolfrum, R. and Matz, N., *Conflicts in International Environmental Law* (Springer 2003).

[55] UNEP, 2012, 25.

to enable them to secure certification to environmental standards so as to secure access to international markets. For the successful promotion of SCP patterns, therefore, it is vital that both trade and environmental policies facilitate a rational, equitable and integrated approach to addressing life-cycle impacts of products, which must be reflected in the relevant international agreements.[56]

A full life-cycle analysis is now accepted as good practice in assessing the potential of policy interventions, from investments in renewable energy technologies to increased sustainable public procurement—as reflected in many MEAs. Despite the lack of a holistic international framework on sustainable consumption and production, MEAs remain important for their future potential to promote SCP. For example, the emerging climate governance framework for reducing GHG emissions in line with scientific recommendations would require a fundamental change to production and consumption patterns worldwide. However, if intergovernmental agreements are to contribute to resource efficiency and promote SCP effectively, the focus of intergovernmental activity must shift away from the negotiation of goals—the 'what'—to mechanisms for inducing effective implementation—the 'how'.

## III) Relations with Other Principles

### 1. SCPs many inter-linkages with other Rio Principles

Principle 8 of the Rio Declaration is closely linked to other principles, such as sustainable development (see section II) 3.2 of this chapter), common but differentiated responsibilities (Principle 7), and free trade and economic growth (Principle 12), which will be discussed in more detail below. However, Principle 8 can be said to be a major component of or even prerequisite for the implementation of *all* other principles. Given the globalization of production processes, the global sourcing of resources and the international trade in goods for consumption and given the interlinked nature of the global environment, SCP processes cannot be ensured by any single State, neither by fragmented, sectoral action. What is needed is coordinated, global action in all sectors and on all levels, both by State and non-State actors, businesses, and individuals to keep consumption and production patterns within the carrying capacity of ecological systems. A healthy and productive life in harmony with nature (Principle 1), the right to development that equitably meets developmental and environmental needs of present and future generations (Principle 3) the eradication of poverty (Principle 5), avoiding damages to other States and to areas beyond national jurisdiction (Principle 2), all remain illusory goals without the transition to sustainable consumption and production patterns.

At the same time, in order to be effective, SCP policies require preventive and precautionary approaches (Principle 15), they need the integration of environmental protection as an integral part of the development process (Principle 4), capacity-building, knowledge, and science transfer (Principle 9), information flows (Principles 10 and 19), effective environmental legislation (Principle 11), internalization of environmental costs (Principle 16), environmental impact assessments (Principle 17), and the participation of all parts of society, including women, youth, indigenous peoples and local communities (Principles 19–22).

[56] UNEP, 2012, 25.

## 2. Common but differentiated responsibilities (Principle 7)

Principle 8 is based on the understanding that all countries should promote sustainable consumption and production patterns, with the developed countries expected to take the lead and with all countries benefiting from the process ('quality of life for all human beings'). The responsibility of developed countries is derived from the principle of common but differentiated responsibilities as set out in Principle 7 of the Rio Declaration, where it is noted that 'developed countries acknowledge the responsibility that they bear in the international pursuit to sustainable development in view of the pressures their societies place on the global environment and of the technologies and financial resources they command.' The common understanding of Principle 7 is that it puts developed countries in the lead due to their historic contribution to environmental degradation and unsustainable resource use and the means they command to address these. Since the Rio Declaration, differentiation has therefore been along the dividing line of 'developed' and 'developing' States and according to historical contributions of developed countries to environmental degradation, as well as developed countries capability to engage in cost-intensive environmental mitigation action. These factors (criteria) have led to substantively stronger obligations of developed countries, with developing countries having no or milder obligations as well as rights to financial transfers as well as transfer of technology and know-how from developed countries.

Based on these criteria, 'positive discrimination' in favour of developing countries has led to highly asymmetric environmental obligations coupled with mechanisms for capacity building, transfer of financial resources and technology as well as compliance assistance.

While such a 'binary view' holds true historically, the current state of affairs is more complex. Unsustainable consumption patterns have continued to rise, at a steady pace both in industrialized and developing countries. The BRIC countries (Brazil, Russia, India, and China) are seeing blooming consumer classes that aspire to high per capita consumption levels and other developing countries will follow suit in time. Population projections for developing countries are estimating a 30% rise in population by 2050. These trends are compounding each other and increasing the unsustainable impacts of human activities beyond the ability of ecosystems to recover.

The immense current global challenges all States commonly face can only be tackled by taking cooperative large-scale remedial action. However, the factual preconditions under which States are acting still differ considerably. Yet, the 'landscape of similarities and differences' has changed since its perception more than 40 years ago. The world is characterized by disparities in resources and capabilities in different ways now. The antagonistic dividing line between developed and developing countries is becoming increasingly blurred. Any of the two groups, if they can be identified at all,[57] is no longer homogenous but marked by stark internal differences. In addition, the international landscape undergoes changes and fluctuations. Any attempt of categorization might be insufficient to capture

[57] See, for example, the classification by the International Monetary Fund ('IMF') in 'advanced economies' and 'emerging market and developing economies'. (IMF, *World Economic Outlook*, October 2012, 179). The IMF notes: 'This classification is not based on strict criteria, economic or otherwise, and it has evolved over time.' (*World Economic Outlook*, 177). According to the United Nations Statistics Division, 'There is no established convention for the designation of 'developed' and 'developing' countries or areas in the United Nations system.' See: UNSD, *Composition of macro geographical (continental) regions, geographical sub-regions, and selected economic and other groupings (fn C)*, revised 11 October 2012, available at: <http://unstats.un.org/unsd/methods/m49/m49regin.htm#ftnc>.

such dynamism. For that reason, differentiation should be flexible and dynamic and only be granted on a temporary basis.

In order to approach SCP from the principle of common but differentiated responsibilities, new and more flexible and dynamic ways of differentiation between States need to be developed. Having said that, finding reliable, but flexible and dynamic, criteria or means to defining various (groups of) 'equals' and allocating rights and responsibilities accordingly, may thus be the main and toughest task in multilateral environmental treaty making.

## 3. Growth and free trade (Principle 12)

A potential contradiction has been identified between Principle 12 (growth and free trade as the model) and Principle 8 (addressing unsustainable consumption patterns). The United Nations Department of Economic and Social Affairs Division for Sustainable Development noted recently, that 'Over the last two decades it has become increasingly apparent that where and when trade and a need for rethinking of consumption patterns come up against one another, trade wins. This results in an undermining of the practice of sustainable development. Overall, Principle 8 remains largely unaddressed. Instead a "business-as-usual, growth at all costs" paradigm has continued to dominate.'[58]

In other words, the international developments on sustainable development have given rise to a contradiction. On the one hand, the Brundtland Commission put on the fore two critical dimensions in its report and definition on sustainable development: 1) caring about future generations (translated in Rio Principle 3); and 2) addressing unsustainable consumption patterns of the rich (translated in Rio Principle 8). Principles 15 and 16 of the Rio Declaration (the so-called 'polluter pays' and precautionary principles) provided general guidance for a prudent management of resources and sinks.

On the other hand, some of the Rio Principles put forward a 'business as usual plus (BAU+)' argument, which contradicts the above-mentioned principles. In the Rio declaration, the fundamental assumptions of post-war neo-liberal economics (ie economic growth coupled with free trade) were left unchallenged. Commentators have noted that the principles were both 'adorned' by 'safeguards' that satisfied both North and South.[59] The result of this were 'environmental safeguards' which ensured that discreet environmental issues of concern for the North were managed, and 'development safeguards' which ensured economic development of the South could continue unimpeded.[60] However, without any conceptual link and a holistic framework to integrate these perspectives, they remained, at best, conflict-prone cohabitants.

It was hoped that a BAU+ model was able to deliver sustainable consumption and production patterns and longer-term decision-making, and that these were compatible in practice through decoupling of resource use from consumption. Commentators noted that there was quickly no doubt left about which of the two would prevail when conflict arose or absolute decoupling proved to be difficult to achieve. Business as usual has prevailed and unsustainable

[58] United Nations Department of Economic and Social Affairs, Division for Sustainable Development, Sustainable Development in the 21st century ('SD21'), Review of implementation of Agenda 21 and the Rio Principles, Synthesis, January 2012. Available at: <http://www.uncsd2012.org/content/documents/194Synthesis%20Agenda%2021%20and%20Rio%20principles.pdf>.

[59] Dodds, F., Strauss, M., and Strong, M., *Only One Earth: The Long Road via Rio to Sustainable Development* (Routledge 2012), 229.

[60] Dodds, Strauss, and Strong, *Only One Earth: The Long Road via Rio to Sustainable Development*, 229.

patterns of consumption and production persist. This in turn means that global commons (eg forests, atmosphere, biodiversity, oceans) are still managed unsustainably, and worse, are being degraded beyond their ability to recover unless pressure is lessened. As noted by some commentators:

> It has now become clear that humanity's environmental impact is increasing, and in the future, rising population and increased affluence will compound this impact. Historically, reductions of impacts (eg CO2 emissions) through improved technology have been insufficient to counterbalance increases linked with those factors, as per the IPAT equation whereas human impact (I) on the environment equals the product of P = population, A = affluence, T = technology (I = P + A + T). Thus, based on historical evidence, it is unlikely that action on technology alone can keep environmental damage in check in the future.[61]

### 4. Tensions

In addition, there are a number of tensions between different principles included in the Rio declaration that will need to be addressed. According to the Stakeholder Forum on Sustainable Development, these include:

- Sovereignty versus global goods—ensuring that the sovereign right to exploit resources (Rio Principle 2) is balanced against the global partnership to conserve, protect, and restore the health and integrity of the Earth's ecosystem (Rio Principle 7);
- Precaution versus free trade markets—resolving the tensions between the precautionary approach (Rio Principle 15) and unfettered use and diffusion of new technologies with unknown potential impacts, and better incorporating risk in decision-making procedures. This spans a number of areas, including chemicals, agriculture, nano-technologies, to investment decision tools and climate change;
- Polluter pays versus global markets– ensuring that the polluter should bear the cost of pollution, with due regard to the public interest and without distorting international trade and investment (Rio Principle 16).[62]

Based on the detailed assessment of Rio Principles and Agenda 21 chapters, it seems clear that the 'market' outcomes have to be more regulated based on value-oriented principles (eg the fundamental principles enunciated in the Millennium Declaration: freedom, equality, solidarity, tolerance, respect of nature, and shared responsibility). Dobbs, Strauss, and Strong aptly summarized the position:

> Currently there is a lack of linkage between commonly agreed values and principle and market practices. This has clear links to the underdeveloped social dimension within the Rio Principles. Further development of such values could help shift behaviours, drive practices and ultimately achieve sustainable outcomes.[63]

## IV) Assessment

Principle 8—sustainable production and consumption, and the promotion of appropriate demographic policies—is deemed to have been unsuccessful in achieving its intended goal.

[61] Dodds, Strauss, and Strong, 229.
[62] Stakeholder Forum, 2012, 16.
[63] Dodds, Strauss, and Strong, 230.

Unsustainable consumption patterns have continued to rise at a steady pace in industrialized and developing countries, particularly in emerging economies. Population projections are estimating a 30% rise in population by 2050. These trends are compounding each other and increasing the unsustainable impacts of human activities beyond the ability of ecosystems to recover. The pressures that nations collectively put on the Earth's resources and sinks are growing and may soon overwhelm the capacity of natural ecosystems.[64]

SCP is recognized by many commentators and actors as a cornerstone of sustainable development. As such, it should not be treated in isolation but incorporated within current concepts of a 'green economy'. Discussions on the way forward for sustainable production and consumption should acknowledge the barrier that current consumption patterns and behaviours in developed countries present to sustainability, and include facilitation for developing economies for implementing SCP activities. Furthermore, there must be greater partnership between national governments and other actors including civil society organizations and NGOs on promoting sustainable production and consumption at a local level.

Prospects for action on the SCP front seem linked to a shift in political will, yet the current political environment does not seem ripe for such a shift.

## V) Select Bibliography

Club of Rome, *'Decoupling—A Response to Limits to Growth': A Project Proposed by the Club of Rome*, (September 2013).

Constanza, R. et al, 'The Value of the World's Ecosystem Services and Natural Capital' (1997) 387 *Nature* 253.

Daily, Gretchen C. (ed), *Nature's Services: Societal Dependence on Natural Ecosystems* (Island Press 1997).

Daly, Herman E., *Steady State Economics* (Island Press 1977).

Dodds, F., Strauss, M., and Strong, M., *Only One Earth: The Long Road via Rio to Sustainable Development* (Routledge 2012).

General Assembly, *The Future We Want*, A/RES/66/288, 11 September 2012.

International Institute for Sustainable Development (7 March 2011). *Summary of the Intergovernmental Preparatory Meeting for the Nineteenth Session of the Commission for Sustainable Development*, 28 February–4 March 2011.

International Resource Panel, (2011), *Decoupling: natural resource use and environmental impacts of economic growth.*

Jackson, T., *Prosperity without Growth: Economics for a Finite Planet* (London: Earthscan 2009).

Kovar, J., 'A Short Guide to the Rio Declaration' (1993) 4 *Colorado JIELP* 119.

Meadows, D. H., Meadows, D. L., Randers, J., and Behrens, W. III, *The Limits to Growth: A report of the Club of Rome's Project on the Predicament of Mankind* (Potomac Associated Press 1972).

OECD (2002), *Indicators to Measure Decoupling of Environmental Pressure from Economic Growth.*

Stakeholder Forum for a Sustainable Future (December 2011), Review of Implementation of the Rio Principles.

United Nations Department of Economic and Social Affairs, Division for Sustainable Development (January 2012), *Sustainable Development in the 21st century (SD21), Review of implementation of Agenda 21 and the Rio Principles*, Synthesis Report.

[64] Stakeholder Forum, 2012, 11.

United Nations Department of Economic and Social Affairs (15 December 2004), *Johannesburg Plan of Implementation. Chapter 3. Changing unsustainable patterns of consumption and production.*

United Nations Department of Economic and Social Affairs (15 December 2004), *Johannesburg Declaration on Sustainable Development.*

UNEP (2012), *Global Outlook on SCP Policies: taking action together.*

UNEP (2011), *Life Cycle Initiative.*

UNEP (2010), *ABC of SCP—Clarifying Concepts on Sustainable Consumption and Production.*

United Nations Sustainable Development Platform: <http://sustainabledevelopment.un.org/index.php?menu=1546>.

# 13. Principle 9

## *Science and Technology*

Sandrine Maljean-Dubois*

**Principle 9**

States should cooperate to strengthen endogenous capacity-building for sustainable development by improving scientific understanding through exchanges of scientific and technological knowledge, and by enhancing the development, adaptation, diffusion and transfer of technologies, including new and innovative technologies.



## I) Origins and Rationale of the Principle

The term 'capacity-building' emerged in the lexicon of international organizations during the 1990s. Today, it is commonly used in the United Nations language and mentioned in the programmes of most international organizations working on development, such as

* Director of research at the Centre National pour la Recherche Scientifique, Director of CERIC (CNRS & University of Aix-Marseille, UMR7318).

the World Bank. It stands for the strengthening of skills, competencies and capabilities of States—or, at another level, of people, communities, and individuals—in their self-development. The United Nations Development Programme ('UNDP') explains, for instance, that it aims at helping developing countries to strengthen:

> their own capacities to design and implement development strategies that reflect specific national circumstances and national objectives, within the overall framework of the internationally agreed development goals. This work is . . . always aimed at strengthening national institutions, governance capabilities and citizen participation.[1]

Moreover, the United Nations Environment Programme ('UNEP') has stressed that:

> Instead of being regarded as merely a component or by-product of development programmes and products, capacity building has become a principal and explicit priority of all United Nations activities.[2]

Under these circumstances, it is not surprising that the Rio Declaration devotes one of its 27 principles to capacity-building for *sustainable development.* Capacity-building also helps reinterpret major international concepts and principles in the light of sustainable development. From this point of view, Principle 9 underscores the need to develop international cooperation to that end. More precisely, it aims at encouraging scientific and technical cooperation between States in order to 'strengthen endogenous capacity-building for sustainable development'. Thus the main goal of this provision is to enhance States' capacities. Scientific and technical cooperation are identified as two means serving this same end. One must note the fact that the text refers to cooperation and not to assistance, which is broader.

Rio Principle 9 builds upon Stockholm Declaration Principle 20[3] to cover the same subject matter. The 1992 wording is, however, softer. In 1972, Principle 20 of the Stockholm Declaration had been strongly influenced by calls for a new international economic order. Indeed, the Stockholm Declaration used the word 'must' where the Rio Declaration uses 'should'. Moreover, it referred to a 'free flow' of scientific information and transfer of experience, a 'wide dissemination' or even to the need not to cause 'an economic burden on the developing countries'. Principle 9 of the Rio Declaration reflects a more balanced vision between expectations and claims of the North and the South.

## II) The Principle as Enshrined in the Rio Declaration

### 1. Preparatory work and context

When convening the United Nations Conference on Environment and Development, in its Resolution 44/228 of 1989, the UN General Assembly emphasized:

> the crucial role of science and technology in the field of environmental protection and . . . the need of developing countries, in particular, for favourable access to environmentally sound technologies,

[1] UNDP, *UNDP strategic plan, 2008–2011 Accelerating global progress on human development*, DP/2007/43, 18 July 2007.

[2] UNEP, *Capacity building for sustainable development: An Overview of UNEP environmental capacity development initiatives* (UNEP 2002) at 15.

[3] 'Declaration of the United Nations Conference on the Human Environment', Stockholm, 16 June 1972, UN Doc A/CONF 48/14/Rev.1 ('Stockholm Declaration'), Principle 20: 'Scientific research and development in the context of environmental problems, both national and multinational, must be promoted in all countries, especially the developing countries. In this connection, the free flow of up-to-date scientific information and

processes, equipment and related research and expertise through international co-operation designed to further global efforts for environmental protection, including the use of innovative and effective means...[4]

It also 'reaffirm[ed] the need to strengthen international cooperation' to this end.[5]

The *travaux préparatoires* show the difficult negotiations between, broadly speaking, the North and the South about the content of this provision in the future Declaration. For instance, during PrepCom II, with regard to transfers of technology, the G77 supported concessional and preferential terms, but the US argued that intellectual property rights, owned by private companies, would limit such transfers. Furthermore, the US stressed that the same topic was being discussed at the Uruguay Round of the GATT.[6] During PrepCom III, Chile emphasized the need for States capable of doing so, as well as for international organizations, to provide the necessary technical assistance. More generally, the G77 reaffirmed that the Declaration should promote access to, and transfer of environmentally sound technology, at preferential concessional terms, thus striving for endogenous capacity building.

In the section entitled 'Principles on general rights and obligations' of the Chairman's consolidated draft of 30 August 1991, the wording was clearly much more supportive of the position of Southern countries. It provided that:

States shall strengthen endogenous capacity-building in order to promote sustainable development, particularly in developing countries. Effective international cooperation in research, development and application of environmentally sound technologies is crucial for environmental protection. The free access to, and transfer of, state-of-the-art scientific and technical knowledge, experience and information shall therefore be supported and ensured to strengthen national scientific, technical and technological capabilities in the field of environment and development.[7]

One year later, the—much shorter—text eventually adopted used the wording 'should' instead of the stronger 'shall'. It no longer referred to the specific mention 'particularly in developing countries' or to the necessary effectiveness of the cooperation or the 'free access to, and transfer of, state-of-the-art' information. Indeed, the final version is far less precise and places far looser demands on developed countries. In fact, during the last year of the negotiations, the project underwent major changes. The principle was split into two separate provisions, one devoted to scientific cooperation (Principle 10), and the other to capacity-building (Principle 11). The wording is quite close to the final Principle 9 of the Rio Declaration.[8] This progressive shift must be seen as the result of the continued pressure exercised by industrialized countries, in particular the US. The US strongly advocated

transfer of experience must be supported and assisted, to facilitate the solution of environmental problems; environmental technologies should be made available to developing countries on terms which would encourage their wide dissemination without constituting an economic burden on the developing countries.'

[4] UNGA Resolution 44/228, 'United Nations Conference on Environment and Development', 22 December 1989, Preamble, recital 19.

[5] UNGA Resolution 44/228, 'United Nations Conference on Environment and Development', para 14.

[6] Halpern, S., 'United Nations Conference on Environment and Development: Process and documentation' (Academic Council for the United Nations System 1992).

[7] Working Group III, Chair's consolidated draft of August 30, A/CONF.151/PC/WG.III/L.8/Rev.1, 30 August 1991.

[8] Preparatory Committee for the United Nations Conference on Environment and Development, Fourth session, New York, 2 March–3 April 1992, *Report of the Preparatory Committee for the United Nations Conference on Environment and Development on the work of its fourth session*, A/CONF.151/PC/128, 12 May 1992, 84.

until the very end of the Rio Conference in favour of the protection of intellectual property rights as an 'essential component of any international technology cooperation... essential to provide incentives for innovation in the development of environmentally sound and appropriate technologies.'[9]

## 2. Scope and dimensions

### 2.1. *The two dimensions of the principle*

#### 2.1.1. Overview

Progressively stripped of its content during the *travaux préparatoires* for the Conference, Principle 9 sets out in its final wording nothing more than a very general principle. Although it is built on an even more general principle—the principle of cooperation[10]—it does little to further specify it. It is formulated in a hortatory language ('should') and it therefore operates 'on the basis of persuasion rather than on legal obligation'.[11]

States are encouraged to cooperate in two manners: through 'exchanges of scientific and technological knowledge' and 'by enhancing the development, adaptation, diffusion and transfer of technologies, including new and innovative technologies'. Even if both areas of cooperation are quite close, scientific and technical cooperation differ in practice. Nevertheless, they are referred to in the same provision, perhaps for the sake of brevity or, more likely, as the result of the willingness to water down developed States' commitments in matters of technological cooperation, which thus remain at the same very broad level as scientific cooperation.

#### 2.1.2. Scientific cooperation

Principle 9 encourages States to cooperate 'to strengthen endogenous capacity-building for sustainable development by improving scientific understanding through exchanges of scientific and technological knowledge'. Such cooperation is very important for enhancing capacity-building and decision-making processes. Improving the availability of information on the state of the environment, on activities that have adverse effects on it or on technical means to deal with them is a well-established objective of international environmental law since its inception. Information is widely recognized as a prerequisite for effective national and international environmental management, protection, and cooperation.[12] And, as far as scientific activities are concerned, economies of scale and other efficiency gains can be achieved through increased cooperation.

The call made in Principle 9 is not new. In 1972, the principle was sharply worded in the Stockholm Declaration, incorporating the demands of Southern countries. In 1982, the World Charter for Nature broadened the scope and extent of obligations relating to scientific cooperation, stating that '[c]onstant efforts shall be made to increase knowledge of

[9] See *Report of the United Nations Conference on Environment and Development*, A/CONF.151/26/Rev.1, Vol II, *Proceedings of the Conference*, ONU, New York, 1993, 18.

[10] See eg Principle 24 of the Stockholm Declaration which reflects a general political commitment to international cooperation in matters concerning the protection of the environment. See also the 'Declaration on Principles of International Law concerning friendly relations and cooperation among States in accordance with the Charter of the United Nations', UN General Assembly, Resolution 2625 (XXV), 24 October 1970.

[11] Boon, K., 'The Rio Declaration and its influence on international environmental law' (1992) *Singapore Journal of Legal Studies* 351.

[12] Sands, Ph., Peel, J., Fabra, A., and MacKenzie, R., *Principles of International Environmental Law* (Cambridge University Press 2012), 204.

nature by scientific research and to disseminate such knowledge unimpeded by restrictions of any kind'.[13] Ten years later, an entire chapter of Agenda 21 (chapter 35) was devoted to 'Science for Sustainable Development' and divided in four sections: 'Strengthening the scientific basis for sustainable management'; 'Enhancing scientific understanding'; 'Improving long-term scientific assessment'; 'Building up scientific capacity and capability'. Agenda 21 is comprehensive and ambitious, but again, very general and soft in its wording, going probably in too many directions to be genuinely effective.

In practice, States and international organizations have played a leading role in encouraging international scientific cooperation among scientists, even at a non-governmental level. The Stockholm Conference called for the establishment of the Earthwatch system to keep the global environment under review. At that time, comprehensive and relevant data on the global environment were scarce. Shortly after its establishment, UNEP created the Global Environment Monitoring System ('GEMS') programme and tried to harmonize existing efforts for global overviews. UNEP also created INFOTERRA, an environmental information reference service, connecting different national focal points into a network. In early 1992, in the run-up to UNCED, UNEP instituted a UN system-wide Earthwatch Coordination function to coordinate, harmonize, and integrate monitoring, assessment, and reporting activities across the UN system.[14] This function provides the basis for the drafting of its Global Environmental Outlook (GEO) Reports. But after UNCED, UNEP was also faced with a major decline in funds, which adversely affected the performance of its work programme, including its monitoring and assessment activities. At the same time, many intergovernmental organizations—World Bank, UNDP, regional organizations, development banks, etc—and non-governmental organizations have engaged in global and regional environmental data collection and evaluation activities.[15] Such efforts lack coordination, which has taken a toll in terms of efficiency; and all the more so due to the fact that inter-State scientific cooperation is developing also in a wide range of specific areas, most often under international environmental regimes. In a complex and uncertain field, States and international organizations feel the need to 'develop . . . a stronger scientific basis for the improvement of environmental and developmental policy formulation consistent with long-term goals of sustainable development'.[16]

In most cases, international environmental agreements have their own arrangements.[17] In other cases, this problem has been addressed through the design of over-arching institutional mechanisms, such as the Intergovernmental Panel on Climate Change ('IPCC', 1988) or the Intergovernmental Platform on Biodiversity and Ecosystem Services ('IPBES', 2012), with a mandate to provide policy-relevant analysis and thereby improve the science-policy interface. Throughout its five assessment reports published to date, the IPCC has made a major contribution to the building of an international consensus on climate science. As to the IPBES, it seeks to shed some light in the cacophony of biodiversity-related scientific information. Preliminary studies had highlighted such cacophony and shown a gap with respect to policy impact:

> Various mechanisms synthesize, present and communicate knowledge to inform policy. There is, however, a lack of regular processes providing periodic, timely and policy-relevant information

[13] AG UN, A/RES/37/7, 28 October 1982, 'World Charter for Nature', para 18.
[14] UN, *Earthwatch homepage, Review of Past Activities, Present Gaps and Lessons Learned* (UN 2013).
[15] UN, *Earthwatch homepage, Review of Past Activities, Present Gaps and Lessons Learned* (UN 2013).
[16] *Agenda 21*, Chapter 35. [17] See *infra* section 3.1 of this chapter.

covering the full range of biodiversity and ecosystem service issues to the broader development community. This information and knowledge is not always translated and communicated in the most efficient way or the most useful format [to decision-makers]...[18]

However it is still too early to assess the contribution of the IPBES. This body has been established in April 2012 as an independent intergovernmental body open to all member countries of the United Nations and its institutional development is still ongoing.

Beyond these two examples, the science-policy interface remains a major concern in international policy making. Such concern was reaffirmed in the Outcome document of the 2012 Rio Summit, which asks UNEP to:

Promote a strong science-policy interface, building on existing international instruments, assessments, panels and information networks, including the Global Environment Outlook, as one of the processes aimed at bringing together information and assessment to support informed decision-making.[19]

### 2.1.3. Transfer of technologies

Principle 9 refers to 'development, adaptation, diffusion and transfer of technologies', that is to say to technology transfer in the broad sense. The IPCC has characterized this term as follows:

the broad and inclusive term 'transfer' encompasses diffusion of technologies and technology cooperation across and within countries. It covers technology transfer processes between developed countries, developing countries, and countries with economies in transition. It comprises the process of learning to understand, utilize and replicate the technology, including the capacity to choose and adapt to local conditions and integrate it with indigenous technologies.[20]

Several methods act as pathways for technology transfer: foreign direct investment, public knowledge, licensing, and international trade. Companies are the main suppliers and recipients of technology. In this context, governments are expected to adopt:

supportive measures that promote technology cooperation and that should enable transfer of necessary technological know-how as well as building up of economic, technical, and managerial capabilities for the efficient use and further development of transferred technology.'[21]

The main goal of Rio Declaration Principle 9 is to encourage the transfer of technologies including 'new and innovative' ones. To be encouraged is, of course, not the same as to be required. This nuance is conveyed by the use of the modal verb 'should' (instead of 'shall'), despite the high expectations of developing countries. But, as noted by one commentator:

given the political climate resulting from the North-South divide at Rio and the somewhat controversial stance adopted by the American government of President George Bush, this provision for technological transfer was probably the best that could be achieved.[22]

[18] UNEP, *Gap analysis for the purpose of facilitating the discussions on how to improve and strengthen the science-policy interface on biodiversity and ecosystem services*, UNEP/IPBES/2/INF/1, 19 August 2009, 6.

[19] AG UN, A/RES/66/288, *The Future We Want*, 27 July 2012, para 89.

[20] IPCC, *Methodological and Technological Issues in Technology Transfer* (IPCC 2000).

[21] *Agenda 21*, Chapter 34, paras 2–3.

[22] Panjabi, R. K. L., 'From Stockholm to Rio: A Comparison of the Declaratory Principles of International Environmental Law' (1992–1993) 21 *Denver Journal of International Law & Policy* 245.

Complementing Principle 9, Agenda 21 devotes its chapter 34 to 'Transfer of Environmentally Sound Technology Discussion' and chapter 37 to 'Cooperation for Capacity Building in Developing Countries'. It defines environmentally sound technologies as 'process and product technologies that generate low or no waste, for the prevention of pollution', including 'end of the pipe technologies for treatment of pollution after it has been generated'.[23] Agenda 21 further states that these 'are not just individual technologies, but total systems which include know-how, procedures, goods and services, and equipment as well as organizational and managerial procedures'. It highlights the importance of technology in achieving environmental goals and the need to make this technology accessible by calling for favourable access to and transfer of such technologies to developing countries.[24] The promotion and use of environmentally sound technologies was expected to become a key objective of the international community. As noted in a report prepared by the IPCC:

> to a large extent, the state of the environment today is the result of technological choices of yesterday. The state of the environment in the 21st century will be determined largely by the technologies we choose today.[25]

Of course, transfer of technologies is not an invention of the Rio Declaration. In the 1970s, it was a core claim of developing countries in their efforts to establish a new international economic order ('NIEO').

### *2.2. Legal nature*

The Rio Declaration contains several principles touching upon different aspects of cooperation, whether relating to the protection of the environment or, more broadly, to sustainable development. But the legal scope of these obligations has to be considered on a case-by-case basis.

Regarding scientific and technical cooperation, there is no clear support for the proposition that it is a customary obligation. Developed countries have always resisted such demands from developing countries as illustrated by the soft wording of Principle 9. Beyond treaty-based obligations, international law thus only encourages cooperation in this field. As the law stands today, no State can be considered as being responsible or sanctioned for a failure to respect Principle 9 as an expression of an international customary rule.

The legal basis for such cooperation is rather to be found in international treaties, complemented with programme agreements negotiated and adopted at different levels, depending on the extent of the concerns.[26]

## 3. Normative impact

### *3.1. Scientific cooperation*

#### 3.1.1. Overview

Aside from provisions focusing specifically on cooperation to prevent or manage transboundary harm,[27] virtually every MEA provides for more general scientific and technical cooperation.

[23] *Agenda 21*, Chapter 34, paras 2–3. [24] *Agenda 21*, Chapter 34, para 4.

[25] IPCC, *Methodological and Technological Issues in Technology Transfer* (IPCC 2000).

[26] Salmon, J. (ed), *Dictionnaire de droit international* (Bruylant 2001), 271.

[27] See the commentary to Principles 18 and 19 in this volume.

In order to enhance information exchange and scientific cooperation, the institutionalization of cooperation, and particularly the design of scientific and/or technical bodies within treaty-regimes, is very useful. It helps to overcome the stage of a basic bilateral exchange of information and to further develop the system under conditions of evolving scientific and technical knowledge.[28]

### 3.1.2. The Convention on Migratory Species

The Convention on the Conservation of Migratory Species ('CMS')[29] provides a good example. The Convention states that Parties 'should promote, co-operate in and support research relating to migratory species' (Fundamental Principles, article II). It establishes a Scientific Council composed of 'qualified expert[s]' 'to provide advice on scientific matters' (article VIII), with a broad range of tasks.

In practice it is a very active body, which has contributed to improve scientific understanding of migratory species and operated as a useful science-policy interface with Parties. Moreover, the CMS acts as a framework Convention, to be completed by other instruments ranging from legally binding treaties ('agreements') to less formal instruments (as memoranda of understanding). Each of them devotes more precise and detailed provisions to scientific cooperation regarding its specific topic (African-Eurasian Waterbirds, European Bats, Siberian Crane, etc).

### 3.1.3. The Convention on Biological Diversity

Another example is given by article 18 of the Convention on Biological Diversity,[30] first subparagraph:

> The Contracting Parties shall promote international technical and scientific cooperation in the field of conservation and sustainable use of biological diversity, where necessary, through the appropriate international and national institutions.

This provision is closely linked to Principle 9 of the Rio Declaration, sharing with it the same inspiration and even some of its wording. It can be seen as an implementation of Principle 9 in the area of biodiversity.

Such mandate has been actively pursued in this field, mainly through its Subsidiary Body on Scientific, Technical and Technological Advice (article 25) and its clearing-house mechanism, established by the Conference of the Parties' decision I/3 in 1994.[31] It is now complemented by the aforementioned IPBES.

## *3.2. Transfer of technologies*

### 3.2.1. Policy documents

Promoting environmentally sound technologies has been at the top of the agenda of all major United Nations conferences since the 1992 Rio Summit. At the World Summit on Sustainable Development in Johannesburg, South Africa (2002), governments adopted

[28] See Viñuales, J. E., 'Legal Techniques for Dealing with Scientific Uncertainty in Environmental Law' (2010) 43 *Vanderbilt Journal of Transnational Law* 437.

[29] Convention on the Conservation of Migratory Species of Wild Animals, Bonn, 23 June 1979, United Nations—Treaties Series, vol 1651, 356.

[30] Convention on Biological Diversity, Rio, 5 June 1992, United Nations—Treaties Series, vol 1760, 79.

[31] On the functioning of this mechanism, see UNEP, Information Services of the Central Clearing-House Mechanism, UNEP/CBD/CHM/IAC/2010/1/3, 27 September 2010, Nagoya, Japan, 17 October 2010.

a Plan of Implementation, which recognized that one of the means of maintaining and increasing global progress towards sustainable development is:

> access to and the development, transfer and diffusion of environmentally sound technologies and corresponding know-how, in particular to developing countries and countries with economies in transition on favourable terms, including on concessional and preferential terms, as mutually agreed.[32]

Moreover, the Plan of Implementation highlighted the link between liberalizing trade in environmental goods and services and promoting access to and transfer of environmentally sound technology.[33]

### 3.2.2. Multilateral environmental agreements

Many clear commitments and arrangements on technology transfer are laid out in specific international instruments. In fact most multilateral environmental agreements contain provisions on technology transfer as part of the incentive packages for developing countries to meet their obligations under the treaty. The Basel Convention on the Control of Transboundary Movements of Hazardous Wastes and their Disposal,[34] the Montreal Protocol on the Ozone Layer,[35] the Convention on Biological Diversity,[36] and the United Nations Framework Convention on Climate Change[37] and its related Kyoto Protocol[38] all refer to technology transfer as a critical method for achieving concrete environmental improvements and devote provisions to identifying appropriate technology as well as facilitating access to and encouraging the transfer of technology.[39] Moreover, many MEAs include explicit provisions for making these technologies accessible to developing countries and countries with economies in transition. But even technology transfer provisions that contain binding language generally do not require the direct transfer of technology, which may be proprietary in nature. Instead, such provisions envisage the use of government incentive measures aimed at facilitating technical cooperation.[40] Here again, a clearing-house mechanism could play a central role, helping to document and share expertise, experience, and best practices and to facilitate information exchange between Parties on needs and sources of financial and technical assistance. Many international environmental agreements have established such mechanisms, with varying degrees of success.

[32] WSSD, *Plan of Implementation*, para 105.

[33] WSSD, *Plan of Implementation*, paras 47(e), 48, or 90(c).

[34] Basel Convention on the Control of Transboundary Movements of Hazardous Wastes and their Disposal, Basel, 22 March 1989, United Nations—Treaties Series, vol 1673, 57, art 10.

[35] Montreal Protocol on Substances that Deplete the Ozone Layer, United Nations—Treaties Series, vol 1522, 3, art 10A.

[36] Convention on Biological Diversity (CBD), Rio, 5 June 1992, United Nations—Treaties Series, vol 1760, 79, art 16.

[37] United Nations Framework Convention on Climate Change, United Nations—Treaties Series, vol 1771, 107, art 4.

[38] Kyoto Protocol to the United Nations Framework Convention on Climate Change, United Nations—Treaties Series, vol 2303, 148, art 10.

[39] Esty, D. C., Ivanova, M. H., 'Revitalizing Global Environmental Governance: A Function-Driven Approach', in Esty, D. C. and Ivanova, M. H. (eds), *Global Environmental Governance: Options & Opportunities* (Yale School of Forestry & Environmental Studies 2002), 16.

[40] UNEP-UNCTAD, 'A Preliminary Analysis of MEA Experiences in Identifying and Facilitating the Transfer of Technology What Insights Can Be Drawn for the WTO EGS Negotiations?' (UNEP-UNCTAD 2007), 1.

In practice, depending on their history, subject matter, and objectives, different MEAs approach technology transfer in different ways. While some MEAs include specific procedures to identify, adopt, and disseminate technologies, others contain provisions setting out more general practices for exchanging information on technologies. A number of MEAs also include provisions aimed to ensure that technology is accessible to all Parties, in particular developing and transition countries. Consequently, projects and initiatives carried out under MEAs often include a technology component.[41] In some cases, environmental regimes even led to the development of very comprehensive and sophisticated mechanisms. MEA Secretariats and Parties:

> often adopt a 'package' approach to technology and technology transfer, where the transfer of the technology is complemented by capacity building, technical assistance, training of personnel, sharing of know-how, and exchange of information.[42]

Conventional provisions are often built on the Rio Declaration Principle 9, but their wording is more detailed and encompassing, as illustrated by article 16 of the CBD. This provision recognizes that both—access to technology and technology transfer among Parties—are 'essential elements for the attainment of the objectives of this Convention'. On this basis, it requires Parties to:

> provide and/or facilitate access for and transfer to other Contracting Parties of technologies that are relevant to the conservation and sustainable use of biological diversity or make use of genetic resources and do not cause significant damage to the environment.

The Convention also provides that access to, and transfer of, technology:

> 'shall be provided and/or facilitated under fair and most favourable terms, including on concessional and preferential terms where mutually agreed', and in a way 'consistent with the adequate and effective protection of intellectual property rights'.[43]

In practice, numerous measures and activities have been introduced to that end within the CBD. The Subsidiary Body on Scientific, Technical and Technological Advice was established by the Parties in order, *inter alia*, to:

> identify innovative, efficient and state-of-the-art technologies and know-how relating to the conservation and sustainable use of biological diversity and advise on the ways and means of promoting development and/or transferring such technologies.[44]

The CBD Secretariat also established an Expert Group on Technology Transfer and Scientific and Technical Cooperation, it developed options for applying measures and mechanisms to facilitate access to and adaptation of technologies, included the aforementioned clearing-house mechanism, and it established mechanisms for cooperation with other Conventions and international organizations. The Secretariat compiled information on technology needs assessment methodologies and case studies on institutional, administrative, legislative, and policy frameworks to facilitate access to and adaptation of technologies within the public domain. But, according to a study from the Secretariat (2007), based on 22 national reports submitted by Parties, nearly half of the reporting countries

[41] UNEP-UNCTAD, 'A Preliminary Analysis of MEA Experiences', 7.
[42] UNEP-UNCTAD, 'A Preliminary Analysis of MEA Experiences', xi.
[43] CBD, art 16 (2). [44] CBD, art 25.

indicated that they had not achieved the outcomes identified in the work programme through transfer of technology or technology cooperation.[45] Another significant element is the link between such transfers and the extent of the obligations of developing countries. The Convention states in this regard that:

> [t]he extent to which developing country Parties will effectively implement their commitments under this Convention will depend on the effective implementation by developed country Parties of their commitments under this Convention related to financial resources and transfer of technology.[46]

### 3.2.3. The link between finance and technology

Bilateral and multilateral financial assistance programmes also play a key role in the diffusion of technology which can be financed through several channels like national development and investment initiatives, foreign direct investment, official development assistance (multilateral or bilateral) or commercial lending.

The Global Environmental Facility ('GEF') plays here an important role in facilitating technology transfer to help developing countries,[47] but some multilateral agreements set up also their own institutional arrangements. From this perspective, the protection of the ozone layer serves as a perfect example of a comprehensive and effective approach. Indeed, substitutes for ozone-depleting substances ('ODS') and the products that incorporate them are predominantly made out of privately-owned technologies. Widespread adoption of substitute technologies entails significant costs, including the purchase of access and the rights to use technology.

Under the Montreal Protocol,[48] a Fund has been established through which financial and technical assistance is provided in the form of grants or concessional loans. Funds are used, for instance, to finance the conversion of existing manufacturing processes, train personnel, pay royalties and patent rights on new technologies, and establish national Ozone Units.[49] Thus, the availability of dedicated funds to pay the incremental costs of transition, a mechanism unique to the Montreal Protocol, has been a significant driver for transfer of technological know-how and investments related to ODS substitutes.[50]

### 3.2.4. Market mechanisms

Another original tool to be mentioned is the Clean Development Mechanism (CDM) of the Kyoto Protocol (1997), in the field of climate change.

Although the CDM does not have an explicit technology transfer mandate, it may contribute to technology transfer by financing emission reduction projects using technologies currently not available in the host countries. A study prepared for the secretariat of the UNFCCC concluded that roughly 36% of the projects accounting for 59% of the annual emission reductions claim to involve technology transfer.[51]

45 UNEP-UNCTAD, 'A Preliminary Analysis of MEA Experiences', 13.
46 CBD, art 20(4).
47 GEF, *Transfer of Environmentally Sound Technologies, Case Studies from the GEF Climate Change Portfolio*, 2010, 48.
48 Montreal Protocol on Substances that Deplete the Ozone Layer, United Nations—Treaties Series, vol 1522, p. 3, art 10.
49 UNEP-UNCTAD, 'A Preliminary Analysis of MEA Experiences', 17.
50 UNEP-UNCTAD, 'A Preliminary Analysis of MEA Experiences', 17.
51 Haites, E., Duan, M., and Seres, S., 'Technology transfer by CDM projects' (2006) 6 *Climate Policy* 327.

### 3.2.5. Technology, intellectual property rights, and trade

Lastly, as international trade provides a means for creating incentives to transfer environmentally sound technology, one important issue is the link between trade law and the promotion of these technologies.

The Johannesburg Plan of Implementation adopted at WSSD called on countries to 'promote mutual supportiveness between the multilateral trading system and the multilateral environmental agreements', and more specifically, to 'complement and support the Doha Ministerial Declaration' by encouraging 'market based initiatives for the creation and expansion of domestic and international markets for environmentally friendly goods and services'.[52] As stated previously, Agenda 21 recognized that '[p]roprietary technology is available through commercial channels, and international business is an important vehicle for technology transfer'.[53] The successful completion of the WTO negotiations on environmental goods and services could have contributed to current efforts to make environmentally sound technologies accessible to all countries. But negotiations are at a deadlock, and many problems are still unresolved.

For instance, it is widely acknowledged that technology and technology transfer in the context of climate-change mitigation and adaptation are key. Technological innovation, together with the transfer and widespread implementation of climate-friendly technologies, will be central to global efforts for handling the many challenges associated with climate change. A broad spectrum of technological measures will be required, covering both greenhouse gas emission mitigation technologies and climate change adaptation technologies, and will include 'soft' as well as 'hard' technologies.[54] There is an ongoing debate—academic as well as diplomatic—on whether the protection of intellectual property rights, in particular patents, impedes or facilitates the transfer of technologies to developing countries.[55] On the one hand, enforceable intellectual property rights are an essential catalyst for the development of climate-friendly goods and technologies. They play an important role in ensuring economic returns for investors, including resources for research and development that have been devoted to developing and improving a technology, and enabling its transfer and diffusion. But, on the other hand, stronger protection of intellectual property rights—as called by the WTO Agreement on Trade Related Aspects of Intellectual Property Rights ('TRIPS')[56]—might act as an impediment to the acquisition of new technologies and innovations in developing countries.[57] Intellectual property protection should certainly:

> contribute to the promotion of technological innovation and to the transfer and dissemination of technology, to the mutual advantage of producers and users of technological knowledge and in a manner conducive to social and economic welfare, and to a balance of rights and obligations.[58]

But it must be clarified how to implement this provision, and from this point of view multilateral trade negotiations remain at an impasse.

[52] WSSD Plan of Implementation, para 99(b).
[53] *Agenda 21*, ch 34, para 11.
[54] WTO-UNEP, Trade and Climate Change (WTO 2009), 42; Philibert, C., *Technology, Innovation, Development and Diffusion*, OECD and IEA Information Paper, COM/ENV/EPOC/IEA/SLT (OECD&IEA 2003).
[55] WTO-UNEP, Trade and Climate Change (WTO 2009), 43.
[56] WTO Agreement on Trade Related Aspects of Intellectual Property Rights, *The Results of the Uruguay Round of Multilateral Trade Negotiations. The legal texts* (Cambridge University Press 2007), 321.
[57] WTO-UNEP, Trade and Climate Change (WTO 2009), 43.
[58] TRIPS, art 7.

Biotechnology demonstrates also how in practice the soft wording of Rio Declaration Principle 9 itself is powerless in the face of the gradual development of intellectual property rights, such as encouraged by WTO law. Potential problems indeed arise from intellectual property rights, in particular, with technological developments in biotechnology engineering, regarding the protection of indigenous peoples' right to their genetic resources. International law appears somewhat fragmented in its treatment of genetic resources and biotechnology.

The CBD includes technology transfer provisions related to the fair and equitable sharing of benefits arising out of the utilization of genetic resources. The access and benefit sharing aspects of technology transfer are quite unique to the context of the CBD, where the Parties:

> recognizing that patents and other intellectual property rights may have an influence on the implementation of this Convention, shall cooperate in this regard subject to national legislation and international law in order to ensure that such rights are supportive of and do not run counter to its objectives.[59]

A specific instrument has been adopted on this question, namely the Nagoya Protocol on Access to Genetic Resources and the Fair and Equitable Sharing of Benefits Arising from their Utilization (2010). But it is not, as such, sufficient to effectively address this controversial issue. The interests channelled through a number of other regimes, such as the CBD, TRIPS, the International Treaty on Plant Genetic Resources (Rome, 2001),[60] the International Union for the Protection of New Varieties of Plants ('UPOV')[61] or the World Intellectual Property Organization (WIPO) are potentially in conflict, with vast implications for the environment, but also for the biotechnology, pharmaceutical, and agricultural industries.

The CBD could have been seen as a threat to the biotechnology industry.[62] But in fact, torn between conflicting tendencies, it does not succeed in providing a framework which is coherent and strong enough to face current issues. Weak and ambiguous, the CBD endeavours to resist the WTO's force of attraction. The Nagoya Protocol does not address the issue of the linkages between the Convention, the WIPO and the WTO. In itself, it constitutes the main barrier. Indeed, most of the Nagoya Protocol provisions refer to simple 'agreements' to be negotiated from case to case, and it leaves to the good will of States the design of domestic legislations to regulate these agreements, as well as the monitoring of resource collection and allocation. Intellectual rights of the ones and the others should be balanced; the cultural and thus economic value of innovation has to be balanced by the cultural and thus economic value of its transmission.[63] The WIPO is currently working on draft articles on the protection of traditional cultural expressions, but it is still very controversial, as evidenced by the number of brackets remaining in the working draft.[64]

[59] CBD, art 16 (5).

[60] International Treaty on Plant Genetic Resources, <http://www.planttreaty.org/content/texts-treaty-official-versions> [17 April 2014].

[61] International Union for the Protection of New Varieties of Plants, UNTS vol 815, 109.

[62] Panjabi, 'From Stockholm to Rio: A Comparison of the Declaratory Principles of International Environmental Law' 245.

[63] Hermitte, M. H., Maljean-Dubois, S., and Truilhé-Marengo, E., 'Actualités de la Convention sur la diversité biologique: Science et politique, Équité, Biosécurité' (2011) *Annuaire français de droit international* 425.

[64] WIPO, *The Protection of Traditional Cultural Expressions: Draft Articles* (Rev.2), WIPO/GRTKF/IC/25/WWW/FACILITATORS DOCUMENT REV. 2, 19 July 2013.

### 4. Jurisprudential relevance

Although, to our knowledge, there are no decisions specifically relating to Principle 9 of the Rio Declaration, the recognition of the need to transfer technology remains relevant from a jurisprudential perspective in at least in two respects.

First, it should be mentioned that non-compliance procedures established under multilateral environmental agreements are sometimes called upon to deal with the assessment of the causes of non-compliance and offer financial and technical assistance to tackle them.[65] The extent of actual 'technology transfer' remains limited as technologies are usually in the hands of private entities and protected by proprietary rights. It is perhaps more accurate to speak of 'technical' assistance or capacity-building, which can indeed be mobilized or facilitated by compliance bodies.[66]

A second area of potential jurisprudential relevance is the tension between the application of non-differential standards of intellectual property protection (most notably through the TRIPs agreement) and the principle of common but differentiated responsibilities (Principle 7 of the Rio Declaration), which Principle 9 seeks to implement. Although there are no specific cases raising this tension, there have been two instances in which India and Brazil started consultations under the WTO dispute settlement mechanisms as a result of the seizure in The Netherlands of generic drugs in transit.[67] Irrespective of the specific products at stake, developing countries have insisted over the past years that a system for clean technology diffusion should be established on a basis similar to the one applied under a 2001 agreement to drugs against AIDS and malaria.

Aside from the foregoing areas, the fact that most technology is in the hands of private operators has the consequence that disputes over technology transfer (aside from its trade dimension), specifically in connection with licensing or foreign direct investment, will follow either company/company arbitration (either normal commercial arbitration or WIPO arbitration[68]) or company/State arbitration (investment disputes).

## III) Relations with Other Principles

Principle 9 is closely linked to Principle 7. The latter provides that:

> States shall cooperate in a spirit of global partnership to conserve, protect and restore the health and integrity of the Earth's ecosystem. In view of the different contributions to global environmental degradation, States have common but differentiated responsibilities. The developed countries acknowledge the responsibility that they bear in the international pursuit to sustainable development

[65] See eg Decision 27/CMP.1 Procedures and mechanisms relating to compliance under the Kyoto Protocol, FCCC/KP/CMP/2005/8/Add.3, 92 (para XIV, *Consequences applied by the Facilitative Branch*). For a comprehensive analysis of non-compliance procedures see Treves, T. et al, *Non-Compliance Procedures and Mechanisms and the Effectiveness of International Environmental Agreements* (TMC Asser Press 2009).

[66] See Urbinati, S., *Les mécanismes de contrôle et de suivi des conventions internationales de protection de l'environnement* (Milano: Giuffré 2009), 255–60, referring to the decision of the Compliance Committee established under the Aarhus Convention: Findings and recommendations with regard to compliance by Albania, 31 July 2007, Doc ECE/MP.PP/C.1/2007/4/Add.1. (indicating specific measures as guidance and facilitating assistance by NGOs).

[67] *European Union and a Member State—Seizure of Generic Drugs in Transit*, DS/408 (Complainant: India), DS/409 (Complainant: Brazil).

[68] See the website of WIPO's Alternative Dispute Resolution (ADR) on Research Development/Technology Transfer: <http://www.wipo.int/amc/en/center/specific-sectors/rd/> (accessed on 15 April 2014).

in view of the pressures their societies place on the global environment and of the technologies and financial resources they command.

Principle 9 could be viewed as implementing Principle 7, first sentence, in the specific field of technical and scientific cooperation. Broader in scope, Principle 7 is inevitably also more general in its wording. The use of the term 'shall' in this context (by contrast with 'should' in Principle 9) makes no significant difference. A similar relationship can be established between the second and third sentences of Principle 7, which refer to the common but differentiated responsibilities principle, and Principle 9. The latter is, again, intended to implement the former in connection with scientific and—even more—technical cooperation.

Principle 9 should be read also in conjunction with Principle 12, which provides that:

> States should cooperate to promote a supportive and open international economic system that would lead to economic growth and sustainable development in all countries, to better address the problems of environmental degradation.

Promoting technology transfer is a way of implementing the first sentence of Principle 12. Such a balanced international economic system is in turn necessary for a broad diffusion of environmentally sound technologies.

Lastly, Principle 22 of the Rio Declaration, devoted to indigenous peoples and their communities, is also relevant in this context as it highlights their 'vital role' in sustainable development 'because of their knowledge and traditional practices'. Indeed the protecting of the knowledge and the practices of indigenous peoples should not be sacrificed in the name of efforts to promote the diffusion and transfer of technology.

## IV) Assessment

The Rio Conference strongly encouraged through Agenda 21 and Principle 9 of the Rio Declaration the development of technical and scientific cooperation to build endogenous capacities. This need has been reaffirmed several times, for instance by the Plan of Implementation of the World Summit on Sustainable Development (Johannesburg, 2002)[69] or more recently by the Rio+20 Declaration *The Future We Want*.

Although the impact of such general principles is difficult to assess, the 'scientific understanding through exchanges of scientific and technological knowledge' and the science-policy interface have been significantly expanded in the last twenty years. Several mechanisms have been established, within the main international environmental agreements or beyond, like the IPBES. However, 'enhancing the development, adaptation, diffusion and transfer of technologies, including new and innovative technologies' has proved to be more difficult. The process of selecting and operating environmentally sound technologies is not a simple one. Indeed, as noted by two commentators:

> Selecting a technology that is suitable for local needs, adapting it to local conditions, and maintaining it require substantial skills and information. Yet, the recipients of technology transfers have limited access to information and limited technical capacity, underscoring the need for an information clearinghouse on various abatement technologies.[70]

69 WSSD Plan of Implementation, in particular paras 15(c), 18 and 137.

70 Esty and Ivanova, 'Revitalizing Global Environmental Governance: A Function-Driven Approach', 29.

The diffusion of such technologies represents still another stage. Economic actors seek, quite naturally, to protect their own interests. And international institutions suffer from weak and overlapping mandates. Interactions between the scientific bodies of the various MEAs are still insufficiently streamlined, with some duplication in the reporting, monitoring and assessment efforts.

Yet, capacity-building and technology transfer to developing countries are key for the green economy policies promoted by the Rio+20 Outcome *The Future We Want*.[71] From Rio 1992 to Johannesburg, and from Johannesburg to Rio 2012, the call to effectively transfer environmentally sound technologies[72] has been reiterated once and again with little success.

## V) Select Bibliography


Aslam, M. A., 'Technology Transfer under the CDM: Materializing the Myth in the Japanese Context?' (2001) 1 *Climate Policy* 451.

Barton, J. H., *Intellectual Property and Access to Clean Energy Technologies in Developing Countries. An Analysis of Solar Photovoltaic, Biofuel and Wind Technologies* (Geneva: ICTSD Programme on Trade and Environment 2007).

Batt, J. and Short, D. C., 'The Jurisprudence of the 1992 Rio Declaration on Environment and Development: A Law, Science, and Policy Explication of Certain Aspects of the United Nations Conference on Environment and Development' (1992–1993) 8 *Journal of Natural Resources & Environmental Law* 270.

Boisson de Chazournes, L., 'Technical and Financial Assistance', in Bodansky, D., Brunnee, J., Hey, H., *The Oxford Handbook of International Environmental Law* (Oxford University Press 2007), 947.

Boon, K., 'The Rio Declaration and its Influence on International Environmental Law' (1992) *Singapore Journal of Legal Studies* 347.

Coninck, H., de Haake, F., van der Linden N. H., 'Technology Transfer in the Clean Development Mechanism' (2008) 7 *Climate Policy* 443.

Dechezleprêtre, A., Glachant, M., Ménière, Y., 'Technology Transfer by CDM projects: a Comparison of Brazil, China, India and Mexico' (2009) 37 *Energy Policy* 703.

Dupuy, P.-M., Vinuales, J. E., *Harnessing Foreign Investment to Promote Environmental Protection: Incentives and Safeguards* (Cambridge University Press 2013).

Eiadat, Y., Kelly A., Roche, F., Eyadat, H., 'Green and Competitive? An Empirical Test of the Mediating Role of Environmental Innovation Strategy' (2008) 43 *Journal of World Business* 131.

Esty, D. C. and Ivanova, M. H., 'Revitalizing Global Environmental Governance: A Function-Driven Approach', in Esty, D. C. and Ivanova M. H. (eds), *Global Environmental Governance: Options & Opportunities* (Yale School of Forestry & Environmental Studies 2002).

Foxon, T. and Pearson, P. 'Overcoming Barriers to Innovation and Diffusion of Cleaner Technologies: some Features of a Sustainable Innovation Policy Regime' (2008) 16 *Journal of Cleaner Production* 148.

Global Environmental Facility, *Transfer of Environmentally Sound Technologies, Case Studies from the GEF Climate Change Portfolio* (GEF 2010).

Greiner, M. A. and Franza, R.M., 'Barriers and Bridges for Successful Environmental Technology Transfer' (2003) 28 *Journal of Technology Transfer* 167.

Haites, E., Duan, M., and Seres, S., 'Technology Transfer by CDM projects' (2006) 6 *Climate Policy* 327.


[71] *The Future We Want*, AG UN, A/RES/66/288, 27 July 2012, paras 58, 65–6, 73–4, 277.

[72] *The Future We Want*, para 73.

Halpern, S., 'United Nations Conference on Environment and Development: Process and Documentation' (New York: Academic Council for the United Nations System 1992).

Hassan, H. M. and Hutchinson, C., *Natural Resource and Environmental Information for Decision Making* (Washington DC: World Bank 1992).

Hermitte, M. H., Maljean-Dubois, S. and Truilhé-Marengo, E., 'Actualités de la Convention sur la diversité biologique: Science et politique, Équité, Biosécurité' (2011) [57] *Annuaire français de droit international* 399.

Hutchison, C., 'Does TRIPS Facilitate or Impede Climate Change Technology Transfer into Developing Countries?' (2006) 3 *Law & Technology Journal* 537.

IPCC, *Managing Technological Change in Support of the Climate Change Convention: Framework for Decision-Making, Methodological and Technological Issues In Technology Transfer*, IPCC Special Report on Climate Change (IPCC 1991).

IPCC, *Methodological and Technological Issues in Technology Transfer* (IPCC 2000).

Kiss, A., 'The Rio Declaration on Environment and Development', in Campiglio, L., Pineschi, L., Siniscalco, D., and Treves, T. (eds), *The Environment after Rio: International Law and Economics* (The Hague: Kluwer Law International 1994).

Martyniuk, A. O, Jain, R. K., and Stone, H. J., 'Critical Success Factors and Barriers to Technology Transfer: Case Studies and Implications' (2003) 2 *International Journal of Technology Transfer and Commercialisation* 306.

Panjabi, R. K. L., 'From Stockholm to Rio: A Comparison of the Declaratory Principles of International Environmental Law' (1993) 21 *Denver Journal of International Law & Policy* 215.

Philibert, C., *Technology, Innovation, Development and Diffusion*, OECD and IEA Information Paper, COM/ENV/EPOC/IEA/SLT (OECD&IEA 2003).

Preparatory Committee for the United Nations Conference on Environment and Development, *Report of the Preparatory Committee for the United Nations Conference on Environment and Development on the work of its fourth session*, Fourth session, New York, 2 March–3 April 1992, A/CONF.151/PC/128, 12 May 1992.

Salmon, J. (ed), Dictionnaire de droit international public (Bruxelles: Bruylant 2001).

Sand, P., 'UNCED and the Development of International Environmental Law' (1992–1993) 8 *Journal of Natural Resources & Environmental Law* 209.

Sands Ph., *Principles of International Environmental Law* (2nd edn, Cambridge University Press 2003).

Sands, Ph., Peel, J., Fabra, A., and MacKenzie, R., *Principles of International Environmental Law* (3rd edn, Cambridge University Press 2012).

Shelton, D., 'Stockholm Declaration (1972) and Rio Declaration (1992)', in *Max Planck Encyclopedia of Public International Law* (Oxford University Press 2012).

Tébar Less, C. and McMillan, S., *Achieving the Successful Transfer of Environmentally Sound Technologies: Trade Related Aspects* (Paris: OECD 2005).

United Nations Conference on Environment and Development, *Report of the United Nations Conference on Environment and Development*, A/CONF.151/26/Rev.1, vol II, *Proceedings of the Conference* (New York: ONU 1993).

United Nations Development Programme, 'UNDP Strategic Plan, 2008–2011 Accelerating Global Progress on Human Development', DP/2007/43, 18 July 2007.

United Nations Environment Programme-United Nations Commission on Trade and Development, 'A Preliminary Analysis of MEA Experiences in Identifying and Facilitating the Transfer of Technology What Insights Can Be Drawn for the WTO EGS Negotiations?' (United Nations Environment Programme and United Nations Conference on Trade and Development 2007).

United Nations Environment Programme, *Capacity Building for Sustainable Development: An Overview of UNEP Environmental Capacity Development Initiatives* (UNEP 2002).

United Nations Environment Programme, *Information Services of the Central Clearing-House Mechanism*, UNEP/CBD/CHM/IAC/2010/1/3, 27 September 2010, Nagoya, Japan, 17 October 2010.

United Nations, *Earthwatch homepage, Review of Past Activities, Present Gaps and Lessons Learned* (UNO 2013).

World Intellectual Property Organization, *Climate Change and the Intellectual Property System: What Challenges, What Options, What Solutions?*, Draft 5.0 (WIPO 2008).

Worrell, E., van Berkel, R., Fengqi, Z., Menke, C., Schaeffer, R., and Williams, R.O., 'Technology Transfer of Energy Efficient Technologies in Industry: A Review of Trends and Policy Issues' (2001) 1 *Energy Policy* 29.

# 14. Principle 10

## *Public Participation*

Jonas Ebbesson*

**Principle 10**

Environmental issues are best handled with the participation of all concerned citizens, at the relevant level. At the national level, each individual shall have appropriate access to information concerning the environment that is held by public authorities, including information on hazardous materials and activities in their communities, and the opportunity to participate in decision-making processes. States shall facilitate and encourage public awareness and participation by making information widely available. Effective access to judicial and administrative proceedings, including redress and remedy, shall be provided.



* Dean, Professor of Environmental Law, and Director of Stockholm Environmental Law and Policy Centre, at the Faculty of Law, Stockholm University; and Chairperson of the Aarhus Convention Compliance Committee. Useful for the writing of this article was my paper 'Participatory and Procedural Rights in Environmental Matters: State of Play' commissioned by UNEP for the High Level Meeting of the New Future of Human Rights and Environment: Moving the Global Agenda Forward, co-organized by UNEP and OHCHR in Nairobi, 30 November–1 December 2009.

# I) Origins and Rationale of the Principle

## 1. Origins

Despite the influence of Principle 10 of the Rio Declaration on the development of international and national laws on public participation, this development did not originate in one event or document. Public participation in environmental matters—usually understood as including access to information, participation in decision-making and access to justice—has been debated and legislated in various domestic contexts, in some parts of the world, at least since the early 1970s.[1] To some extent, the international debate on participatory rights in environmental matters also stems from international human rights law, predating UNCED, in particular with respect to access to justice.

Public participation was not highlighted in the *1972 Stockholm Declaration on the Human Environment*, but it was addressed by the *Stockholm Action Plan for the Human Environment*:

> It is recommended that Governments and the Secretary-General provide equal opportunities for everybody, both by training and by ensuring access to relevant means of information, to influence their own environment by themselves. (Recommendation 39(a))[2]

The 1972 recommendation pertains to access to information and opportunities for everybody to influence their own environment; two of the elements in the international debate and legal development on public participation. Ten years later, through the *1982 World Charter for Nature*, the UN General Assembly was more straightforward in prescribing opportunities for participation. It also highlighted the third element in the international debate and legal development on public participation in environmental matters, access to justice:

> All persons, in accordance with their national legislation, shall have the opportunity to participate, individually or with others, in the formulation of decisions of direct concern to their environment, and shall have access to means of redress when their environment has suffered damage or degradation. (Principle 23)[3]

The 1972 and 1982 UN documents had limited, if any, immediate impact on international law and policy on public policy. Still, in parallel to developments in national laws and EU law, they were supportive to the increasing international debate on environmental

[1] See Ebbesson, J., 'The Notion of Public Participation in International Environmental Law' (1997) 8 *YbIEL* 51.

[2] 'Declaration of the United Nations Conference on the Human Environment', Stockholm, 16 June 1972, UN Doc A/CONF 48/14/Rev.1 ('Stockholm Declaration').

[3] 'World Charter for Nature', GA Res. 37/7, UN Doc A/37/51 (1982).

and participatory rights, and thus helped paving the way for Principle 10 of the Rio Declaration. So did some regional conventions and OECD decisions on equal access and non-discrimination in transboundary environmental contexts, adopted in the 1970s and 1980s.[4]

So, the issues covered by Principle 10 were not entirely novel. Yet, it had a huge impact on international law and policy. A likely reason is the timing—this was 1992—combined with the major attention given to UNCED in general. UNCED took place and the Rio Declaration was adopted at a time of huge political changes in Europe and elsewhere, only shortly after the fall of the Berlin Wall and the Cold War. These changes influenced, if not transformed, the perception of what are international and national legal issues. Thus, a window was opened for new issues of civic society, such as democratization, environmental human rights and globalization, to transcend state borders and expand into international discourse, law, and policy-making in a way that had previously not been possible.

Even though most environmental treaties adopted prior to UNCED contain provisions on information exchange, they essentially focus on inter-state communications. The lack of provisions on participation in decision-making, access to information held by public authorities, and access to review procedures reflects the then dominant perception that these issues were part of domestic law only.

## 2. Rationale

In most countries, laws and policies for ensuring the protection of human health and the environment rely heavily on governments and public administrations. Despite this expectation—indeed duty—for the state and public administration to ensure the protection of human health and the environment, such protection not only depends on the public administration; it is also shaped by the rights, responsibilities and powers of members of the public, as well as the corporate sector, in the performance, control and decision-making related to environmental activities.

The statement in *Agenda 21*, also adopted at UNCED, that '[o]ne of the fundamental prerequisites for the achievement of sustainable development is broad public participation in decision-making', is too abstract to explain why public participation in environmental matters was—and should be—supported in international law and policy. In other writings,[5] I have argued that the main rationales and justifications of law for public participation are found in 'straightforward environmental arguments', the adaptation and furtherance of human rights law, and the enhancement of the legitimacy of decision-making.

The protection of health and the environment may benefit from public participation through more effective enforcement and application of existing environmental laws. Thus, members of the public can challenge decision-making and also bring up environmental

[4] 1974 Nordic Environment Protection Convention, 13 ILM (1974) 591; 1977 OECD Recommendation on the Implementation of a Regime of Equal Right to Access and Non-discrimination in Relation to Transfrontier Pollution, C(77)28 Final, (1977), 16 ILM (1977) 977; 1988 OECD Decision-Recommendation of the Council concerning Provisions of Information to the Public and Public Participation in Decision-making Processes related to the Prevention of, and Response to, Accidents Involving Hazardous Substances, C(88)85/Final, 8 July 1988. Available at <http://www.oecd.org>. (accessed 1 February 2014).

[5] See Ebbesson, 'The Notion of Public Participation in International Environmental Law'; Ebbesson, J., 'Public Participation', in Bodansky, D., Brunnée, J., and Hey, E. (eds), *The Oxford Handbook of International Law* (Oxford University Press 2007), 681–703; Ebbesson, J., 'Public Participation and Privatisation: An Assessment of the Aarhus Convention' (2011) 4 *Erasmus Law Review* 71.

issues, interests or aspects that would otherwise risk being ignored. Moreover, public participation helps in shaping which issues are seen or identified as environmental or health issues in the first place, and it affects the perception of what is a problem.

As to human rights arguments, participatory rights in environmental matters adapt existing notions and norms to new circumstances and contexts. The right to participate in environmental decision-making furthers and specifies the already established human right to political participation. The right to judicial and administrative proceeding, including redress and remedy, in environmental matters draws on the right to a fair trial, and expands it, for example, by pertaining to non-governmental organizations.

Finally, public participation in decision-making serves to legitimize environmental decisions, which engage a mix of private and public interests. While the notion of public participation in environmental decision-making presupposes a responsibility on the government and the public administration to take an active role in protecting human health and the environment, it also reveals, if not an actual distrust in government, cognizance that the public administration cannot effectively or legitimately carry out these functions without due transparency and control, and the participation of members of the public in decision-making procedures.

Different reasons of trust in public authorities, legitimacy, justice, and effectiveness in environmental decision-making have motivated the promotion of public participation in environmental matters. The three main elements reflected in Principle 10 are also supportive for environmental democracy in general.[6] Although public participation remains particularly relevant in domestic contexts, given the increased transboundary and international dimensions of environmental effects as well as of environmental discourse and decision-making, the same rationales and justifications explain the development of international law on access to information, public participation, and access to justice in environmental matters.

## II) The Principle as Enshrined in the Rio Declaration

### 1. Preparatory work and context

Public participation was frequently addressed in the preparation of UNCED and the adoption of the Rio Declaration. According to the World Commission on Environment and Development ('WCED'), which was influential for the conference, sustainable development requires 'a political system that secures effective citizen participation in decision making'.[7] Despite its emphasis on effective participation in relation to equity and common interests,[8] public participation was still not a major theme in the WCED report. Nor was it much addressed by the international legal experts group of the WCED ('WCED Legal Experts'), mandated to reinforce existing principles and to formulate new principles and rules of law 'which reflect and support the mainly anticipatory and preventive strategies which the Commission is committed to developing'.[9] The WCED Legal Experts

[6] See eg Aarhus Convention on Access to Information, Public Participation in Decision-making and Access to Justice in Environmental Matters, 25 June 1998, 2161 UNTS 447 ('Aarhus Convention'), Preamble, para 21.

[7] WCED, *Our Common Future* (Oxford University Press 1987), 65.

[8] WCED, *Our Common Future*, 47.

[9] Expert Group on Environmental law of the WCED, *Environmental Protection and Sustainable Development: Legal Principles and Recommendations* (Graham & Trotman 1987), 1.

emphasized equal access, equal treatment, and non-discrimination,[10] but they were surprisingly modest in proposing anything close to international minimum standard for public participation, including access to information and access to justice.[11]

More ambitious on public participation than the WCED and its Legal Experts were the regional ministerial declarations for, respectively, the UNECE region (including at the time Europe, with Soviet Union, USA, and Canada)[12] and Asia and the Pacific,[13] adopted in the run-up to the Rio Conference. While significantly different from each other, both declarations thus affirmed access to information and public participation as a right of individuals and NGOs.

In the run-up for UNCED, several proposals for a text on public participation, with different ambitions, were also put forth in Working Group III of the UNCED Preparatory Committee (eg by the G77 and China, USA, Japan, Australia, the EU, and the Nordic countries), not least during its fourth and final meeting in spring 1992.[14] The final version was presented as part of the 'Draft Proposal by the Chairman on Principles on General Rights and Obligations', forwarded to the Rio Conference, and finally adopted as the Rio Declaration on Environment and Development.[15]

## 2. Scope and dimensions

### *2.1. Legal issues*

Principle 10 neatly comprises the three closely-related issues of access to information, public participation in decision-making processes, and access to justice, which are all crucial components for effective public participation in environmental contexts. While access to information is a prerequisite for meaningful participation, access to justice is a means to having decisions and decision-making processes reviewed. Although Principle 10 is carefully drafted so as not to include the term 'right', it is reasonably impossible for a state to properly comply with Principle 10 without granting, in some sense, rights to access to information, rights for citizens to participate in decision-making, and rights to access administrative and judicial proceedings, including redress and remedy. In leaving out any reference to civil society organizations, of course Principle 10 does not preclude states from

[10] Expert Group on Environmental law of the WCED, *Environmental Protection and Sustainable Development*, 119–26 (art 20).

[11] Expert Group on Environmental law of the WCED, *Environmental Protection and Sustainable Development*, 63–5 (art 6).

[12] Bergen Ministerial Declaration on Sustainable Development in the ECE Region. Adopted in Bergen, Norway, 16 May 1990. UN Doc A/CONF.151/PC/10, Annex I, para 16.

[13] Bangkok Ministerial Declaration on Environmentally Sound and Sustainable Development in Asia and the Pacific. Adopted in Bangkok, Thailand, 16 October 1990. UN Doc A/CONF.151/PC38, Annex 2, para 27.

[14] Report of the Preparatory Committee for the United Nations Conference on Environment and Development on the Work of its Fourth Session. UN Doc A/CONF.151/PC/128, Annex IV, 12 May 1992; Preparatory Committee for the United Nations Conference on Environment and Development, Principles on General Rights and Obligations: Chairman's Consolidated Draft, Earth Charter/The Rio Declaration on Environment and Development. UN Doc A/CONF.151/PC/WG.III/L.8/Rev.1, 30 August 1991.

[15] *Principles on General Rights and Obligations, Draft principles Proposed by the Chairman, Rio Declaration on Environment and Development.* Preparatory Committee for the United Nation Conference on Environment and development, Fourth Session, New York, 2 March-3 April 1992. UN Doc A/CONF.151/PC/WG.III/L.33/Rev.1. 2 April 1992. For general analyses and comments on the Rio Declaration, see eg Porras, I. M., 'The Rio Declaration: A New Basis for International Co-operation', 1 *Review of European Community and International Environmental Law* 245; and Sand, P.H., 'International Law after Rio' (1993) 4 *EJIL* 377.

also granting informational, participatory, and judicial rights and opportunities to such organizations or to other groups of people (cf Principle 22).

Being addressed to states, Principle 10 limits the duty of providing information to public authorities, without granting opportunities for individuals to make direct requests for information to the enterprises engaged in activities with an environmental impact. A crucial issue therefore is whether 'public authorities' include also private actors when performing public functions or operating under a public responsibility. If not, outsourcing of various services and functions may severely limit the scope and usage of access to environmental information and participation in decision-making.[16] Moreover, in fulfilling the obligation of actively facilitating and encouraging public awareness, states will have to continuously request and gather relevant information, through their public authorities, for example from enterprises engaged with hazardous chemicals and other activities with an impact on human health or the environment. This information should then be made available for appropriate access.

Principle 10 is not limited to certain decision-making relating to the environment. Rather, it pertains to all forms of decision-making with a bearing on the environment, for instance decisions on specific activities, projects, spatial planning, nature conservation and biodiversity, marketing of chemicals and genetically modified products, waste treatment, fishery, emissions trading and infrastructure.

Despite the new thinking in Principle 10, the reference to 'all concerned citizens' instead of all concerned persons appears as narrow and outdated by suggesting that environmental contexts remain domestic and only citizens within a given country may be considered concerned. Given the attention to non-discrimination in various legal documents as well as the increasing awareness of the transboundary dimension of environmental contexts prior to UNCED,[17] it is surprising that neither Principle 10 nor Principle 17 (on Environmental Impact Assessment) or any other principle of the Rio Declaration include any express reference to non-discrimination or transboundary public participation. Indeed, for some environmental issues 'appropriate' public participation would require international, supranational, or transnational procedures for multilevel governance rather than or in addition to national procedures. Despite this shortcoming, Principle 10 does not preclude the promotion of Principle 10 in international fora or a more expansive, transboundary and adequate approach to defining the scope of persons with opportunities to participate in decision-making.[18]

## *2.2. Legal nature*

The impact of Principle 10 on international environmental treaties and the increasing attention given to public participation at the time of UNCED is apparent when comparing treaties adopted prior to and after UNCED. On the one hand, essentially none of the environmental treaties of global reach adopted in the 1970s and 1980s, on matters such

[16] Ebbesson, 'Public Participation and Privatisation: An Assessment of the Aarhus Convention' 74–8; Mason, M., 'Information Disclosure and Environmental Rights: The Aarhus Convention' (2010) 10 *Global Environmental Politics* 3.

[17] See eg OECD Recommendation on the Implementation of a Regime of Equal Right of Access and Non-discrimination in Relation to Transfrontier Pollution, C(77) 28(Final), 16 ILM (1977) 977. On non-discrimination in international environmental law, see Ebbesson, 'The Notion of Public Participation in International Environmental Law'.

[18] See Almaty Guidelines in Promoting the Application of the Principles in the Aarhus Convention in International Forums, Annex to Decision II/4, *Report of the Second Meeting of the Parties*, UN Doc ECE/MO.PP/2005/2/Add.5 (2005), at <http//www.unece.org> (accessed 1 February 2014).

as marine pollution, trade in endangered species, trade in wastes, and ozone layer depletion, obliged the parties to promote, let alone ensure, public access to information or participation in decision-making. On the other hand, most global environmental agreements adopted since UNCED endorse public access to information and public participation by some means.

While there is thus significant support for the Principle 10 issues in international law today, to a considerable degree the legal developments have taken place regionally, and these developments are geographically remarkably asymmetric. Strongest support for Principle 10 in international law is found in Europe and in the Caucasus and Central Asian regions (which were previously parts of the Soviet Union). There is also support for Principle 10 in regional international law of the Americas and Africa. In these regions, provisions on access to information, public participation and access to justice are set out in environmental agreements, and, more importantly, the regional human rights regimes have given significant inputs for the development of participatory and procedural rights in environmental matters. International law on Principle 10 issues is weakest in Asia and the Pacific, where there has hardly been any development in international law at all beyond the global regimes.

The support for Principle 10 in environmental treaties differs also in the degree of details and ambitions, and in the scope of procedural issues. Some agreements essentially aim at improving public awareness about environmental problems and public engagement and participation in these fields, whereas others go further and actually oblige the parties to ensure public access to information and public participation in matters covered by the agreements. Several agreements refer both to access to information and public participation, thus confirming the close link between these aspects. Other agreements refer only to public access to information, and yet others to all three elements, thus including access to justice.

As explained below, some environmental and human rights regimes provide *rights* for members of the public to access to information, participation in decision-making and access to review procedures. Other international regimes, while referring to access to information and public participation, give a greater leeway for the parties in deciding not only how, but also when or even *if* public access to information or public participation should actually be granted to members of the public. Yet other treaties merely require the promotion or facilitation of public awareness and participation in general terms. However, even treaties which do not provide for a right to access or participation are nevertheless supportive rather than neutral to the notions of Principle 10.

Among the elements of Principle 10, public access to information is most widely provided for in environmental agreements. The information to be made publicly available and the opportunities for public participation to be provided depend on the scope and purpose of the agreement itself. In some contexts, the information and scope for participation concern a particular procedure or installation, as in the case of environmental impact assessment procedures, and prevention and emergency planning for hazardous activities, including nuclear activities. In other cases, the information and participatory opportunities refer to particular substances, for instance hazardous chemicals, radioactive wastes, or genetically modified organisms. In some treaty regimes, finally, information on environmental matters to be publically available concern legislation, decisions by administrative authorities, or judgments by courts.

The parallel enhancement of Principle 10 in international human rights law after UNCED does not arise from new treaties. Indeed, few, if any, human rights treaties have been adopted or changed as a result of Principle 10 or the increasing recognition of participatory rights in environmental matters. Instead, Principle 10 issues have been significantly promoted by some international courts and committees in the field of human rights when construing—'greening'—the applicable treaties in light of the new notions of access to information, public participation, and access to justice in environmental contexts. In addition, some treaty bodies mandated to examine compliance and implementation by treaty parties on Principle 10 issues have developed useful jurisprudence in this area.

While this chapter focuses on international law and policy, Principle 10 and the related debate have also influenced national laws and debates, and not only in countries and regions where international law so requires.

## 3. Normative impact

### *3.1. Instruments and regimes of global scope*

#### 3.1.1. Sustainable development policy instruments

The message of Principle 10 was confirmed by the First Global Ministerial Environment Forum, in Malmö 2000,[19] and by the *2002 Johannesburg Plan of Implementation*, adopted at the 2002 Johannesburg World Summit on Sustainable Development.[20] The latter is peppered with references to participation, such as the participation of women, youth, different communities, local enterprises, all stakeholders, and civil society in general, but instead of developing Principle 10 further, it was merely agreed to:

> ensure access, at the national level, to environmental information and judicial and administrative proceedings in environmental matters, as well as public participation in decision-making, so as to further principle 10 of the Rio Declaration on Environment and Development, taking into full account principles 5, 7 and 11 of the Declaration.[21]

Contrary to the 2002 World Summit, which did not really further Principle 10, the outcome of the 2012 Rio Conference on Sustainable Development ('Rio+20'), *The Future We Want*, expanded the application of Principle 10 beyond national contexts. The plan does not call for global action on Principle 10,[22] but it encourages 'action at the regional, national, subnational and local levels to promote access to information, public participation and access to justice in environmental matters, as appropriate'.[23] This stretch of the scope for action beyond state borders and national contexts reflects the increasing focus on multilevel governance and the need for actions and norms for public participation of different scales, scope and levels.

#### 3.1.2. Treaties adopted at UNCED and its aftermath

Some influence of Principle 10 is discerned in the two conventions adopted next to the Rio Declaration at UNCED.

[19] Malmö Ministerial Declaration, Malmö, 31 May 2000, para 16, <http//www.unep.org> (accessed 1 February 2014).

[20] *United Nations Report of the World Summit on Sustainable Development*, Johannesburg, South Africa, 26 August–4 September 2002, UN Doc A/CONF. 199/20.

[21] *United Nations Report of the World Summit on Sustainable Development*, para 128.

[22] See however the submission by Brazil to the Preparatory Process Rio+20 Conference, 1 November 2011, chapter 4, para P8D, <http://www.uncsd2012.org/> (accessed 1 February 2014).

[23] Report of the United Nations Conference on Sustainable Development, Rio de Janeiro, Brazil, 20–2 June 2012, UN Doc A/CONF.216/16, para 99.

The *1992 UN Framework Convention on Climate Change* ('UNFCCC') promotes access to information and public participation, although only in a general manner.[24] The convention parties are essentially obliged to 'promote and facilitate' public access to information on climate change and its effects, and public participation in addressing climate change and its effects, but without further specification or qualification.[25] The 1997 *Kyoto Protocol to the UNFCCC* effectively only repeats what is already required by the UNFCCC.[26] These provisions could be used as a platform for further development of criteria for access to information and public participation, but little has been done so far to that effect.[27]

The *1992 Convention on Biological Diversity* ('CBD') is also rather modest in pushing for Principle 10. Whereas the obligations concerning information are essentially limited to inter-state exchanges,[28] in introducing environmental impact assessment ('EIA') procedures for projects likely to have significant adverse effects on biodiversity, the convention parties shall allow for public participation in such procedures 'where appropriate'.[29] The weak provisions of the CBD are supplemented by several decisions by the CBD conference of the parties, which promote public participation.[30] Moreover, contrary to the UNFCCC, access to information and public participation have been more adequately addressed in the context of the CBD through subsequent protocols (see later in this chapter).

Also established in connection to (although not at) UNCED, the *1994 Convention to Combat Desertification* (UNCCD) is more supportive to Principle 10 than the UNFCCC and CBD. Drawing on several principles of the Rio Declaration, public participation and access to information are important element in the UNCCD. Accordingly, the parties shall promote and facilitate 'the participation of local populations, particularly women and youth, with the support of non-governmental organizations, in efforts to combat desertification and mitigate the effects of drought'[31] and make information on desertification 'fully, openly and promptly available'.[32] Moreover, the UNCCD is more specific than the UNFCCC and CBD by requiring the parties to provide for effective participation at the local, national, and regional levels of non-governmental organizations and local populations in policy planning, decision-making, and implementation and review of national action programmes.[33]

### 3.1.3. Treaties on trade and use of harmful matters

The difference between treaties adopted prior to and after UNCED in addressing Principle 10 issues is most apparent when comparing five treaties of global scope on trade in and the use of different harmful matters. Whereas the *1989 Basel Convention on the Control of Transboundary Movements of Hazardous Wastes and their Disposal* makes no reference at all to public access to information or public participation in decision-making, the

[24] United Nations Framework Convention on Climate Change, 9 May 1992, 1771 United Nations Treaty Series 107.

[25] UNFCCC, art 6. [26] 1997 Kyoto Protocol, art 10(e).

[27] See, however, the Doha work programme on art 6 of the Convention, Decision 15/CP.18, *Report of the Conference of the Parties on its Eighteenth Session, held in Doha from 26 November to 8 December 2012*, UN Doc FCCC/CP/2012/8/Add.2 (2013).

[28] CBD, arts 14(c) and 17. [29] CBD, art 14(a).

[30] See Koester, V., 'The Nature of the Convention on Biological Diversity and its Application of Components of the Concept of Sustainable Development' (2006) 16 *Italian Yearbook of International Law* 57.

[31] UNCCD, art 5(d). [32] UNCCD, arts 16 and 19. [33] UNCCD, art 10.

1998 *Rotterdam Convention on the Prior Informed Consent Procedure for Certain Hazardous Chemicals and Pesticides in International Trade*, 2000 *Cartagena Protocol on Biosafety to the Convention on Biological Diversity*, 2002 *Stockholm Convention on Persistent Organic Pollutants*, and the 2013 *Minamata Convention on Mercury* all contain such provisions.

Concerned with international trade in chemicals, the Rotterdam Convention parties must ensure that the public has appropriate access to information on chemical handling and accident management, and also to information on safer alternatives than the chemicals subject to prescribed prior informed consent procedures.[34] While setting minimum standards for such access to information, however, the Rotterdam Convention does not provide for public participation in any decision-making procedure.

The Stockholm Convention takes Principle 10 further by specifying the requirements on access to information and public participation. Applicable to the control of persistent organic pollutants, the parties shall ensure that the public has access to up-to-date information concerning such pollutants and their effects, and consider the establishment of mechanisms, such as pollutants release and transfer register.[35] In ensuring public participation, opportunities must be given to address responses concerning persistent organic compounds as well as the implementation of the Convention as such.

The Cartagena Protocol to the CBD obliges the parties to promote and facilitate public participation and access to information concerning living modified organisms in general. The parties must indeed grant opportunities for public participation and consultation,[36] and provide information when consulting with the public in decision-making. The result of such decisions shall be made available to the public, while respecting confidential information in accordance with the Protocol.

The Minamata Convention (not yet in force), intended to 'protect human health and the environment from anthropogenic emissions and releases of mercury and mercury compounds', is significantly weaker than the previous three treaties in advancing Principle 10. Rather than setting out clear-cut obligations for public participation or public access to information, it merely obliges the parties to promote and facilitate within their capabilities 'provision to the public of available information' relating to, for example, effects, uses, and emissions of mercury as well as on measures to fulfil the convention requirements. The parties shall also promote and facilitate education, training and public awareness with respect to mercury.[37]

### 3.1.4. Treaties on benefit-sharing and resources

While focusing on indigenous and local communities rather than individuals or members of the public in general, the *2010 Nagoya Protocol on Access to Genetic Resources and the Fair and Equitable Sharing of Benefits Arising from their Utilization to the Convention on Biological Diversity* ('Nagoya Protocol') still promotes the notion of Principle 10 by providing for participation and involvement of indigenous and local communities in procedures of prior informed consent or approval concerning access to genetic resources.[38]

The measures taken in order to raise awareness of the importance of genetic resources and traditional knowledge associated with genetic resources may include the organization of meetings of indigenous and local communities and relevant stakeholders, and information

[34] Rotterdam Convention, art 15.
[35] Stockholm Convention, art 10.
[36] Cartagena Protocol, art 23.
[37] Minamata Convention, art 18.
[38] Nagoya Protocol, art 6.

dissemination.[39] Contrary to the previous treaties, the Nagoya Protocol also addresses participatory processes across state borders: the parties must cooperate in transboundary contexts with the involvement of indigenous and local communities concerned.[40]

### 3.1.5. Treaties on nuclear energy

International law on nuclear activities has never been at the forefront in promoting Principle 10 issues. Yet, it also provides some such support, in particular for public access to information.

The *1994 Nuclear Safety Convention* requires access to appropriate information for emergency planning and response in case of radiological emergency for the affected population,[41] and the *1997 Convention on the Safety of Spent Fuel Management and on the Safety of Radioactive Waste Management* requires procedures to make information on facilities intended for spent fuel or radioactive waste management available to members of the public, for example, through environmental impact assessment procedures.[42] While the push for public access to information and public participation in these conventions is rather modest, they still reflect a move in accordance with Principle 10 compared to conventions and international policies on nuclear policies predating UNCED.

### 3.1.6. The UNEP Bali Guidelines

Although (or because) they are not legally binding, the *2010 UNEP Guidelines for the Development of National Legislation on Access to Information, Public Participation and Access to Justice in Environmental Matters* ('Bali Guidelines')[43] are far more elaborate than any of the mentioned global environmental treaties.

Intended to provide guidance for states on how to promote effective implementation of Principle 10 in their national laws, the Bali Guidelines are also relevant for any new treaty negotiation on Principe 10 issues and, possibly, when construing the provisions for access to information, public participation, or access to justice in existing environmental treaties.

### 3.1.7. Human rights instruments

In addition to the mentioned environmental treaties and policy documents, support for Principle 10 is found in international human rights instruments of global reach, even though they all predate UNCED.

Thus, the *1948 UN Declaration of Human Rights* ('UDHR') as well as the *1966 International Covenant on Civil and Political Rights* ('ICCPR') provide for a right to freedom of opinion and the right to seek, receive, and impart information.[44] As to public participation in decision-making, the UDHR stipulates the right to be part of government, directly or through voting,[45] and the ICCPR a right to take part in the conduct of public affairs.[46] In principle, both versions of the right to political participation can be said to pertain to environmental matters.

[39] Nagoya Protocol, art 21. [40] Nagoya Protocol, art 11.

[41] Nuclear Safety Convention, art 16.

[42] Convention on the Safety of Spent Fuel Management and on the Safety of Radioactive Waste Management, arts 6, 8, 13, and 15.

[43] UNEP, UNEP Guidelines for the Development of National Legislation on Access to Information, Public Participation and Access to Justice in Environmental Matters, adopted by the UNEP Governing Council in decision SS.XI/5, 26 February 2010.

[44] UDHR, art 19; ICCPR, art 19. [45] UDHR, art 21. [46] ICCPR, art 25.

Participatory rights have also been acknowledged as part of the right to health[47] and the right to water (with explicit reference to Principle 10)[48] under the 1966 *International Covenant on Economic, Social and Cultural Rights*. Focusing on tribal and indigenous peoples, the 1989 *ILO Convention Concerning Indigenous and Tribal Peoples in Independent Countries* slightly resembles the Nagoya Protocol to the CBD by providing for public participation through consultations and other means by which these peoples may freely participate at all levels of decision-making as well as in the use, management, and conservation of natural resources.[49]

Access to justice, finally, is supported by the recognized human right to a fair trial, set out, for example, in the UDHR and the ICCPR.[50] Although international human rights jurisprudence has mainly developed through regional human rights bodies (see later in this chapter), Principle 10 has also been promoted and confirmed through resolutions of the UN Commission on Human Rights[51] and the work of the UN Human Rights Council.[52]

#### 3.1.8. The ILC Prevention Articles

In addition to the foregoing survey of global environmental and human rights treaties and instruments, some indication that public participation may become part of general international law is given by the UN International Law Commission's *2001 Articles on Prevention of Transboundary Harm from Hazardous Activities* (ILC Articles).[53]

Partly inspired by the Rio Declaration, the ILC sets out in these Articles that states shall provide the public likely to be affected by a hazardous activity with relevant information relating to the activity, the risks involved, and the harm which might result, and also 'ascertain their views'. While ambiguous and limited to certain categories of activities, this would imply some form of public participation in support of Principle 10.[54]

### *3.2. Instruments and regimes of regional scope*

#### 3.2.1. Europe and Central Asia

No other international treaty—global or regional—furthers Principle 10 as comprehensively as the *1998 Convention on Access to Information, Public Participation in Decision-making and Access to Justice in Environmental Matters* (Aarhus Convention), by transforming and developing it into international law. The Aarhus Convention developed within the

[47] See Committee on Economic, Social and Cultural Rights, *Substantive Issues Arising in the Implementation of the International Covenant on Economic, Social and Cultural Rights, General Comment No. 14 (2000), The Right to the Highest Attainable Standard of Health (Article 12 of the International Covenant on Economic, Social and Cultural Rights)*, UN Doc E/C.12/2000/4 (11 August 2000).

[48] See Committee on Economic, Social and Cultural Rights, *Substantive Issues Arising in the Implementation of the International Covenant on Economic, Social and Cultural Rights, General Comment No. 15 (2002), The Right to Water (Arts. 11 and 12 of the International Covenant on Economic, Social and Cultural Rights)*, UN Doc E/C.12/2002/11 (20 January 2003).

[49] ILO Convention, arts 6 and 15.

[50] UDHR, art 10; ICCPR, art 14.

[51] See UN Commission on Human Rights, *Human Rights Resolution 2005/60: Human Rights and the Environment as Part of Sustainable Development*, 20 April 2005, E/CN.4/RES/2005/60, <http://www.ohchr.org/> (accessed 1 February 2014).

[52] See *Human Rights Council, Report of the Independent Expert on the issue of human rights obligations relating to the enjoyment of a safe, clean, healthy and sustainable environment, John H. Knox*, 24 December 2014, UN Doc A/HRC/22/43, <http://www.ohchr.org/> (accessed 1 February 2014).

[53] UN International Law Commission 'Draft Articles on Prevention of Transboundary Harm from Hazardous Activities', (2001) GAOR 56th Session Supp 10, 370.

[54] ILC Articles, art 13.

United Nations Economic Commission for Europe ('UNECE'), which actively pushed for Principle 10 soon after UNCED. In explicitly referring to Principle 10, the Aarhus Convention stipulates minimum standards on access to information, public participation, and access to justice, to be complied with and implemented by the parties. It also sets general principles with respect to participatory rights for non-governmental organizations,[55] non-discrimination (eg in transboundary contexts),[56] and non-harassment,[57] and it obliges the parties to promote the application of the convention principles in international fora.[58,59]

The convention parties must ensure that public authorities make information available upon request within a given time frame. While access may be refused upon certain listed grounds, these grounds shall be interpreted in a restrictive way, taking into account the public interest served by the disclosure.[60] The convention parties are also requested to gather, update, and disseminate certain environmental information.[61]

In setting minimum standards for public participation, the Aarhus Convention distinguishes between three different categories of decisions and procedures: decisions concerning permits for specific activities; decisions on plans, programmes, and policies relating to the environment; and the preparation of regulations and other normative instruments. The most detailed provisions on public participation apply to permit procedures.[62] The parties have to ensure that the public concerned is adequately, timely, and effectively informed at an early stage, and allowed to participate 'when all options are open and effective participation can take place.' The procedures for public participation must allow the public to submit comments and views that it considers relevant, and in the decision, due account must be taken to the outcome of the participation. Rather similar standards apply to decision-making concerning plans, programmes, and policies,[63] while the requirements for public participation are less strict for the preparation of regulations and generally applicable normative instruments.[64]

In effect, the access to justice requirements pertain to all kinds of decisions, acts, and omissions relating to environmental laws. Specific standards apply for access to judicial procedures concerning requests for environmental information, and decisions, acts, and omissions relating to permits and permit procedures for specific activities. In addition, members of the public shall have access to administrative or judicial procedures to challenge any other act or omission, by private persons and public authorities, which contravene provisions of national law relating to the environment (eg acts and omissions related to, say, city planning, nature conservation, fishing quotas, and the control of chemicals and wastes). In different ways, the convention limits the discretion for the parties in defining the scope of persons with access to review procedures. Moreover, for all these situations, the parties shall ensure that the procedures provide 'adequate and effective remedies, including injunctive relief as appropriate, and be fair, equitable, timely and not prohibitively expensive.'[65]

In addition to setting minimum standards on Principle 10 issues, the Aarhus Convention provides a unique compliance mechanism, through which members of

[55] eg arts 2(5) and 3(4). [56] Art 3(9). [57] Art 3(8) [58] Art 3(7).

[59] For comprehensive information about the Aarhus Convention, see UNECE, *The Aarhus Convention: An Implementation Guide* (2nd edn, United Nations 2014).

[60] Art 4.

[61] Art 5. Within the framework of the Aarhus Convention, the right to access to information is even further developed by the adoption of the *2003 Protocol on Pollutant Release and Transfer Registers* ('PRTR Protocol').

[62] Art 6. [63] Art 7. [64] Art 8. [65] Art 9.

the public may trigger compliance reviews by the independent Aarhus Convention Compliance Committee ('ACCC').[66] In examining compliance by the parties, the ACCC jurisprudence is instrumental also for the implementation of Principle 10 (see later in this chapter).

Principle 10 is confirmed and promoted by some other UNECE environmental treaties as well, adopted during the run up for or after UNCED. While less detailed on public participation than the Aarhus Convention, the *1991 Convention on Environmental Impact Assessment in a Transboundary Context* ('Espoo Convention') obliges the parties to provide access to certain information and to ensure that the public likely to be affected be informed and provided with a possibility to make comments and objections concerning the proposed activity. The EIA documentation must be distributed to the public for comments, and the comments shall be taken into account in the final decision for the proposed activity. Similar provisions in support of Principle 10 are found in the *2003 Protocol on Strategic Impact Assessment* to the Espoo Convention. The *1991 Convention on Transboundary Effects of Industrial Activities* ('Industrial Accident Convention') obliges the parties not only to provide and disseminate adequate information on prevention and emergency preparedness with respect to industrial accidents arising out of hazardous activities. The public capable of being affected by such accidents shall also be given an opportunity to participate in relevant procedures concerning prevention and preparedness measures. Both these conventions also provide for access to information and public participation in transboundary contexts through non-discrimination. Finally, as far as the UNECE is concerned, general support for access to information is found in the *1992 Convention on the Protection and Use of Transboundary Watercourses and International Lakes* ('Helsinki Convention'),[67] and even more advanced and precise provisions on access to information and public participation are set out in the *1999 Protocol on Water and Health* related to the Helsinki Convention.[68] As this survey of treaties reveals, the UNECE maintains an outstanding position in the UN organization in promoting Principle 10.

Besides these UNECE treaties, the most robust support for Principle 10 in international law in the region is provided by the *European Convention on Human Rights* ('ECHR'), which predates UNCED. Although the ECHR does not explicitly address environmental matters, the European Court of Human Rights has construed the provisions of the ECHR, in particular the right to private and family life,[69] and the right to a fair trial,[70] in light of new notions, including Principle 10. Indeed, the European Court of Human Rights has developed the ECHR into an important driver for participatory rights in environmental contexts (see later in this chapter).

The European Union, finally, in adopting legislation and developing jurisprudence intended to meet the Aarhus Convention requirements,[71] also significantly promotes the implementation of Principle 10 in EU member States.

[66] Koester, V., 'Review of Compliance under the Aarhus Convention: A Rather Unique Compliance Mechanism' (2005) 2 *Journal of European Environmental and Planning Law* 31; Koester, V., 'Public Participation and Privatisation: An Assessment of the Aarhus Convention' (2011) 4 *Erasmus Law Review* 71.

[67] Helsinki Convention, art 16. [68] Water and Health Protocol, art 5.

[69] ECHR, art 8. [70] ECHR, art 6.

[71] Pallemaerts, M. (ed), *The Aarhus Convention at Ten: Interactions and Tensions Between Conventional International Law and EU Environmental Law* (Europa Law Publishing 2011).

### 3.2.2. Americas

The *1993 North American Agreement on Environmental Cooperation* ('NAAEC'), the side agreement to the North American Free Trade Agreement between Canada, USA and Mexico, reaffirms the Rio Declaration and addresses all three aspects of Principle 10. Without going as far as the Aarhus Convention, the NAAEC obliges the parties to ensure public access to certain information relating to environmental matters, held by public authorities.[72] The parties must also ensure procedural rights and procedural guarantees that are open to the public,[73] but the agreement does not formulate minimum requirements for public participation in environmental decision-making.[74]

The NAAEC is particularly supportive of access to justice. The NAAEC parties shall not only ensure access to remedies and certain procedural guarantees for private actors.[75] Persons with a legally recognized interest shall have access to judicial and quasi-judicial or administrative procedures for the enforcement of environmental laws. This includes access to remedies, including the right to sue for damages, and seek sanctions and injunctions.[76] The parties shall also ensure fair open and equitable administrative, quasi-judicial or judicial proceedings, and 'comply with due process of law'. These proceedings must not be 'unnecessarily complicated' or 'entail unreasonable charges or time limits or unwarranted delays'.[77] Whereas the parts on access to information and public participation do not meet the Aarhus Convention standards, the NAAEC requirements for domestic remedies are no less advanced than those of the Aarhus Convention.

Apart from the NAAEC and some bilateral agreements,[78] Principle 10 has not yielded much effect in environmental treaties of the Americas. However, at the time of Rio+20 initiatives were taken for some form of regional instruments on Principle 10 issues for Latin America and the Caribbean.[79]

Despite these efforts, thus far the most profound support for Principle 10 in international law of the Americas is found in human rights instruments. Neither the *1948 American Declaration of the Rights and Duties of Man* ('AmDRDM') nor the *1969 American Convention on Human Rights* ('AmCHR') contains any explicit reference to environmental matters. Still, they have become important drivers for Principle 10 through the jurisprudence of the Inter-American Commission on Human Rights and the Inter-American Court of Human Rights when applying established human rights concepts, such as the right to freedom of thought and expression,[80] the right to take part in the conduct of public affairs,[81] the right to property,[82] and right to judicial protection[83] to environmental matters (see later in this chapter). Moreover, the *1988 Additional Protocol to the American Convention on Human Rights in the Area of Economic, Social and Cultural Rights*,

[72] NAAEC, art 4. [73] NAAEC, arts 6 and 7. [74] NAAEC, arts 4 and 7.
[75] NAAEC, arts 6 and 7. [76] NAAEC, art 6. [77] NAAEC, art 7.
[78] See eg the *1993 USA-Mexico Agreement Concerning the Establishment of a Border Environment Cooperation Commission and a North American Development Bank*, available at <http://www.nadbank.org>.
[79] See *Declaration on the application of Principle 10 of the Rio Declaration on Environment and Development*, Annex to the note verbale dated 27 June 2012 from the Permanent Mission of Chile to the United Nations addressed to the Secretary-General of the United Nations Conference on Sustainable Development, Item 10, UN Doc A/CONF.216/13 (25 July 2012); and *Plan of Action to 2014 for the Implementation of the Declaration on the Application of Principle 10 of the Rio Declaration on Environment and Development in Latin America and the Caribbean and its Road Map*, Guadalajara, Mexico, 17 April 2013.
[80] AmCHR, art 13. [81] AmCHR, art 23. [82] AmCHR, art 21. [83] AmCHR, art 25.

which predates UNCED, is exceptional in addressing environmental matters explicitly: 'Everyone shall have the right to live in a healthy environment and to have access to basic public services.'[84] In light of the interpretation of other human rights treaties, this would also appear to promote participatory rights in environmental matters.

### 3.2.3. Africa

Influenced by Principle 10, and possibly by the Aarhus Convention, the *2003 African Convention on the Conservation of Nature and Natural Resources* (2003 African Nature Conservation Convention) contains a provision on participatory and procedural elements in environmental matters, but it is not yet in force.[85] Once (if) in force, the parties will have to ensure 'timely and appropriate' dissemination of and access to environmental information,[86] 'timely and appropriate' participation of the public in decision-making with a potentially significant impact, and 'access to justice in matters related to the protection of environment and natural resources.'[87] Yet, in addition to the slow process of ratification, the convention does not give any detail on how it is to be made available or on how the other procedural arrangements should be established.

So far, the *1981 African Charter on Human and Peoples' Rights* (African Charter) has been far more important for the promotion of Principle 10 in international law in Africa. While the prescribed right of all peoples to a 'general satisfactory environment favourable to their development'[88] is relevant for access to information and public participation in decision-making, also other provisions of the Charter have been interpreted as supporting Principle 10 elements (see later in this chapter). Instead of requiring access to a court, or court-like, independent, and impartial body of law, the African Charter provides for a person's right to be heard and to 'appeal to competent national organs against acts violating his fundamental rights'.[89] The limited case law of the African Commission on Human and Peoples' Rights has been shown to be highly important in promoting Principle 10 for Africa (see later in this chapter).

### 3.2.4. Asia and the Pacific

Despite the affirmation in the 1990 Bangkok Declaration for Asia and the Pacific of the right of individuals and non-governmental organizations to be informed, have access to information, and to participate in environmental decision-making,[90] there has been little development of international law and policy on Principle 10 in the Asian and Pacific region (except for Central Asia through the Aarhus Convention).[91]

Interestingly, the *1985 ASEAN Agreement on the Conservation of Nature and Natural Resources* (ASEAN Agreement), adopted before UNCED, contains provisions for public participation and access to information, but not access to justice, concerning the

[84] Art 11(1).

[85] The 1968 version of the African Convention on the Conservation of Nature and Natural Resources, which is in force, does not contain any provision of this sort.

[86] Art 16. [87] Art 16. [88] African Charter, art 24. [89] African Charter, art 7.

[90] Bangkok Ministerial Declaration on Environmentally Sound and Sustainable Development in Asia and the Pacific. Adopted in Bangkok, Thailand, 16 October 1990. UN Doc A/CONF.151/PC38, Annex 2, para 27.

[91] The 2004 Arab Charter on Human Rights (art 38) as well as the 2012 Human Rights Declaration of the Association of Southeast Asian Nations (art 28(f)) contain provisions on the right to a safe environment as an element of the right to an adequate standard of living. While neither document explicitly links this right to Principle 10 issues, they could be construed similarly to the 1981 African Charter, art 24, as including some form of participatory right.

environment.[92] The parties are requested to circulate information on conservation measures and 'as far as possible' to organize participation of the public in the planning and implementation of such measures. As with the African Nature Conservation Convention, the ASEAN Agreement provides no details on how information is to be circulated to the public. Even more problematic, still after about 30 years, the ASEAN Agreement has not entered into force.

Lacking any regional human rights treaty and any effective regional environmental treaty promoting participatory rights in environmental matters, the support in international law for Principle 10 in Asia and the Pacific derives from the mentioned environmental and human rights treaties of global scope and, possibly, from general international law.

## 4. Jurisprudential relevance

### *4.1. Jurisprudence of global scope*

Despite some support for Principle 10 in environmental treaties of global scope, the jurisprudence in support of public participation has developed regionally and, except for the Aarhus Convention, through human rights regimes. The *International Court of Justice* has not yet addressed public participation in environmental matters in its jurisprudence. While concluding in the *Pulp Mills* case that the obligation to carry out environmental impact assessments in transboundary contexts is today part of general international law, the court did not assert that under general international law public participation should be a necessary element in the EIA process.[93] Nor has any jurisprudence on participatory rights in environmental matters, comparable to that of the regional human right bodies, developed through the *UN Human Rights Committee*, when acting under the Optional Protocol to the ICCPR.[94]

### *4.2. Europe and Central Asia*

The *European Court of Human Rights* has developed important jurisprudence on all aspects of Principle 10, in particular by construing the right to respect for private and family life[95] as creating a right to access to information and to participate in decision-making. In several cases, the court has referred to Principle 10 of the Rio Declaration.[96]

In a landmark case on access to information decided in 1998, the Court concluded that a state violates the right to respect for private and family life if it fails to provide essential information about hazardous activities that enables members of the public to assess the risks they and their families might run.[97] This implies a positive duty of the state to ensure that relevant information is made available, and a corresponding right of members of the

[92] ASEAN Agreement, art 16.

[93] As suggested by Boyle, A., 'Developments in International Law of Environmental Impact Assessments and their Relation to the Espoo Convention' (2011) 20 *RECIEL* 225, 231, this was possibly due to the way in which the parties argued the case.

[94] See, however, *Mikmaq tribal Society v. Canada*, Communication 205/1986, on the modalities of participation in the conduct of public affairs; and *Jouni E. Länsman et al v. Finland*, Communication No. 671/1995, where the Committee examined whether the Sami Community had opportunities for effective participation in decision-making.

[95] ECHR, art 8.

[96] See eg ECtHR, *Okyay et al v. Turkey*, 36220/97 of 12 July 2005; ECtHR, *Taskin et al v. Turkey*, 46117/99 of 10 November 2004; and ECtHR, *Tătar v. Romania*, 67021/01 of 27 January 2009.

[97] ECtHR, *Guerra et al v. Italy*, 14967/89 of 19 February 1998.

public concerned to access such information. The Court has also held that the right to respect for private and family life requires that, where a state determines complex issues of environmental and economic policy, the decision-making process must involve appropriate investigations and studies in order to be able to predict and evaluate the effects. The Court stressed, the '[t]he importance of public access to the conclusions of such studies and to information, which would enable members of the public to assess the danger to which they are exposed is beyond question'. In such contexts, the decision-making processes leading to measures of interference must be fair and such as to afford due respect to the interests of the individual safeguarded by the right to respect for private and family life.[98] In addition, in cases of dangerous activities, the public's right to information may be based on the protection of the right to life.[99] Although access to justice in environmental matters has mainly been considered in relation to the right to a fair trial,[100] the right to respect for private and family life has also been interpreted as including a right for the individuals concerned to appeal to the courts environmental decisions, act or omission where they consider that their interests or comments have not been given sufficient weight in the decision-making process.[101] The parallels to the Aarhus Convention are obvious.

While not a judicial body, but an independent compliance review body, the *Aarhus Convention Compliance Committee* ('ACCC') has received more than 100 communications from members of the public alleging non-compliance by the parties.[102] The ACCC jurisprudence concerning the interpretation of the Aarhus Convention also pertains to all aspects of Principle 10. The endorsement of the ACCC findings of non-compliance by the Meeting of the Parties increases the normative status and impact of its jurisprudence.[103]

Among the issues considered, the ACCC has examined whether parties meet the rather detailed requirements on providing environmental information upon request and making information adequately available.[104] Thus the ACCC has concluded that ignoring requests for environmental information for three months, failing to give reasons for the denial of access to information, and imposing unreasonable fees for copying documents amount to non-compliance with the Convention.[105] The ACCC has also examined whether members of the public, including national and foreign NGOs,[106] have effective opportunities for participation in different forms of decision-making.[107] For example,

[98] ECtHR, *Taskin et al v. Turkey*, 46117/99 of 10 November 2004.

[99] ECtHR, art 2, *Öneryildiz v. Turkey*, 48939/99, of 30 November 2004.

[100] ECHR, art 6. See eg ECtHR, *Zander v. Sweden*, 45/1992/390/468 of 25 October 1993; and *Karin Andersson et al v. Sweden*, 29878/09 of 25 September 2014.

[101] ECtHR, *Taskin et al v. Turkey*, 46117/99 of 10 November 2004; and ECtHR, *Giacomelli v. Italy*, 59909/00, of 2 November 2006.

[102] Information on all communications, with full documentation, and ACCC findings with recommendations in admissible cases are found at the Aarhus Convention website, at <http://www.unece.org> (accessed 1 February 2014).

[103] As argued by Tanzi, A. and Pitea, C., 'The Interplay between EU Law and International Law Procedures in Controlling Compliance with the Aarhus Convention by the EU Member States', in Pallemaerts, M. (ed), *The Aarhus Convention at Ten*, 367, 380, when interpreting the Aarhus Convention 'any decision by the [ACCC], when it is backed by the MOP through adoption by consensus, may be considered as falling within the concept of "subsequent practice" ' under art 31 of the 1969 Vienna Convention on the Law of Treaties.

[104] See eg *ACCC/C/2008/30 (Moldova)*, 8 February 2011.

[105] See eg *ACCC/C/2008/24 (Spain)*, 15–18 December 2009; and *ACCC/C/2009/36 (Spain)*, 18 June 2010. In *ACCC/C/2009/37 (Belarus)*, 24 September 2010, Belarus was held in non-compliance with the Aarhus Convention for having failed to provide requested information.

[106] See *ACCC/C/2004/5 (Turkmenistan)*, 14 March 2005.

[107] See eg ACCC/C/2004/3 *(Ukraine)*, 14 March 2005; *ACCC/C/2004/8 (Armenia)*, 31 March 2006.

it held that a party failed to comply with the convention because it did not inform the public in an adequate, timely, and effective manner about the possibility to participate in the decision-making, because it provided too little time for participation, and because it made the developer rather than public authorities responsible for organizing public participation.[108]

As for access to justice, convention parties have been found non-compliant, for instance, because the costs for judicial appeals were 'prohibitively expensive'[109] and because the national criteria for standing were too strict with respect to individuals and/or non-governmental environmental organizations.[110]

The ACCC also examines the performance of the EU, including whether it provides for access to information, public participation, and access to justice in its legislation addressed to the EU member States. The ACCC thus concluded that the EU had failed to comply with the Convention because it did not have in place a proper regulatory framework and/ or other instructions to ensure implementation of the convention requirements on public participation by its member States with respect to the adoption of so called National Renewable Energy Action Plans. The Committee also found that the EU, in practice, by way of its monitoring responsibility, failed to ensure proper implementation of the relevant provision of the Convention.[111]

Being a party to the Aarhus Convention, the European Union ('EU') has adopted a large set of legislation intended to meet the convention requirements. Based on this legislation and the Aarhus Convention itself the Court of Justice of the European Union ('CJEU') has for instance ruled out, as far too strict, certain national minimum requirements for allowing environmental associations to appeal permit decisions,[112] and on acceptable criteria so as not to make judicial proceedings in environmental matters prohibitively expensive.[113] In addition, the CJEU has considered to what extent the Aarhus Convention shall be directly considered by the national courts of the EU member States.[114] In general, by enforcing the Aarhus Convention, the CJEU has also helped implementing Principle 10 among the EU member States.[115]

In Europe the dynamic interplay and between these three legal regimes (Aarhus Convention, ECHR, and EU) and the respective body mandated to examine compliance (ACCC, ECtHR and CJEU) has had a positive effect not only for implementing Principle 10 elements, but also for keeping the Principle 10 discourse alive.

[108] *ACCC/C/2006/16 (Lithuania)*, 7 March 2008. Public participation issues have also been raised in the mentioned cases *ACCC/C/2008/24 (Spain)*, 15–18 December 2009; and *ACCC/C/2009/37 (Belarus)*, 24 September 2010.

[109] See *ACCC/C/2008/23 (UK)*, 24 September 2010; *ACCC/C/2008/27 (UK)*, 24 September 2010; *ACCC/C/2008/33 (UK)*, 3 December 2010; and *ACCC/C/2011/57 (Denmark)*, 30 March 2012.

[110] See, *ACCC/C/2010/48 (Austria)*, 16 December 2011; and *ACCC/C/2011/63 (Austria)*, 27 September 2013; *ACCC/C/2008/31 (Germany)*, 17-20 December 2013; *ACCC/C/2010/50 (Czech Republic)*, 29 June 2012; and *ACCC/C/2011/58 (Bulgaria)*, 28 September 2012.

[111] *ACCC/C/2010/54 (European Union)*, 29 June 2012.

[112] C-263/08, *Djurgården Lilla Värtan Miljöskyddsförening v. Stockholms kommun* [2009] European Court Reports, 15 October 2009. The judgment resulted in a swift change in the national laws in question (in Sweden), much more in line with the Aarhus Convention.

[113] C-260/11, *David Edwards and Lilian Pallikaropoulos v. Environment Agency et al (UK)*, 11 April 2013.

[114] C-240/09, *Lesoochranárske zoskupenie VLK v. Ministerstvo životného prostredia Slovenskej republiky*, 8 March 2011.

[115] On the relation between the Aarhus Convention, ACCC and jurisprudence of the CJEU, see generally, Pallemaerts (ed), *The Aarhus Convention at Ten*.

### 4.3. Americas

Although the NAAEC provides a review mechanism that is also available for the public, it is primarily intended to ensure enforcement of national environmental protection standards rather than examining compliance with the NAAEC provisions on Principle 10 issues.[116] Instead, robust international jurisprudence in support of Principle 10 is provided by the Inter-American human rights regime, despite the lack of provisions addressing environmental matters in the AmDHR and the AmCHR. Thus, like in the European human rights system, the relevant case law builds on the interpretation of established human rights. Whereas in the European human rights system this largely builds on the right to respect for private and family life, the key for Principle 10 jurisprudence for the Americas is the right to property,[117] in connection to, for instance, the right to judicial protection.[118]

According to the *Inter-American Court of Human Rights* ('IACtHR') the right to property requires, that in cases when concessions are granted for the exploitation and extraction of natural resources within territories of tribal communities, the state ensures effective participation of the members of the community concerned; that is, the state has to actively consult with the community, including by accepting and disseminating information.[119] The *Inter-American Commission on Human Rights* makes a similar interpretation: that failing to provide for effective consultation with indigenous communities, including 'information that must be shared with the communities concerned', amounts to a violation of the right to property.[120] As for access to justice in environmental matters, the Commission's conclusion, that states are not only obliged to provide courts or formal procedures, but also to take affirmative steps to ensure that the remedies are 'truly effective' in establishing possible violations and in providing redress,[121] resembles the notion of access to justice under the Aarhus Convention.

Lacking more precise international standards for transparency in environmental matters, these findings by the Inter-American Court and Commission on Human Rights give profound support for the development of international law in support of Principle 10 in the region.[122]

### 4.4. Africa

In Africa too, international jurisprudence for the implementation of Principle 10 has developed in the context of human rights rather than in relation to any environmental treaty. In particular, the African Commission on Human & Peoples' Rights, operating

[116] See Fitzmaurice, M., 'Public Participation in the North American Agreement on Environmental Cooperation' (2003) 52 *International and Comparative Law Quarterly* 333; and Fitzmaurice, M., 'Environmental Justice through International Complaint procedures? Comparing the Aarhus Convention and the North American Agreement on Environmental Cooperation', in Ebbesson, J. and Okowa, P. (eds), *Environmental Law and Justice in Context* (Cambridge University Press 2009), 211.

[117] AmDRDM, art 23; AmCHR, art 21. [118] AmCHR, art 25.

[119] IACtHR, *Case of the Saramaka People v. Suriname*, Judgment of 28 November 2007 (Merits, Reparations and Costs), Series C No 172, para 133.

[120] Inter-American Commission on Human Rights, *Maya Indigenous Communities of the Toledo District, Belize*, Report No 40/04, Case 12.053, 12 October 2004.

[121] Inter-American Commission on Human Rights, *Maya Indigenous Communities of the Toledo District, Belize*, Case 12.053, Report No 40/04 of 12 October 2004.

[122] See also IACtHR, *Claude-Reyes and Others v. Chile*, Judgment of 19 September 2006 (Merits, Reparations and Costs), Series C No 151, where the Court, in para 81, refers to Principle 10 as well as to the Aarhus Convention.

under the African Charter on Human and Peoples' Rights, has construed the provisions on the right to best attainable state of health and on the right to a satisfactory environment to this end.[123]

According to the Commission, these rights imply a duty on the state to monitor threatened environments, undertake environmental and social impact studies, and provide information to the communities exposed to hazardous materials and activities.[124] This includes a duty on the state to provide relevant information as well as meaningful opportunities for individuals to be heard and to participate in the development decisions that affect their communities.[125] Lacking any specific international regime on Principle 10 issues, this jurisprudence provides important support for the development of regional international law on participatory rights in environmental matters.

### *4.5. Asia and the Pacific*

Lacking any international environmental treaty on participatory rights as well as any international human rights regime for Asia and the Pacific, there is also no regional international jurisprudence relating to Principle 10 for this region. Therefore, in addition to the global environmental treaties, the main support for Principle 10 in Asia and the Pacific has developed in some national laws, not further analysed here.[126]

## III) Connections with Other Principles

Principle 10 connects with several other Principles of the Rio Declaration. The entitlement of a healthy and productive life in harmony with nature, set out in Principle 1, depends on the opportunities and rights for members of the public to access information, participate in decision-making, and to access judicial and administrative procedures with effective redress and remedy.[127]

As mentioned, members of the public may enhance the control of the public administration through access to information, participation in decision-making and access to justice. Such activities are also instrumental for effective environmental legislation, as required by Principle 11, and for effective application of the precautionary approach of Principle 15 in various decision-making procedures.

[123] Art 16 on best attainable status of health, and art 24 on satisfactory environment. In addition, both the right to property, in art 14, and the right to freely dispose of wealth and natural resources, in art 21, include elements of a duty for governments to consult with affected groups; see African Commission on Human & Peoples' Rights, *Centre for Minority Rights Development (Kenya) and Minority Rights Group (on behalf of Endorois Welfare Council) v. Kenya*, Communication 276/03, 25 November 2009.

[124] African Commission on Human & Peoples' Rights, *The Social and Economic Rights Action Center and the Center for Economic and Social Rights v. Nigeria*, Communication 155/96, 13–27 October 2001.

[125] African Commission on Human & Peoples' Rights, *The Social and Economic Rights Action Center and the Center for Economic and Social Rights v. Nigeria*, Communication 155/96, 13–27 October 2001.

[126] See eg Mushkat, R., 'Public Participation in Environmental Law making: A Comment on the International Framework and the Asia-Pacific Perspective' (2002) 1 *Chinese Journal of International Law* 185; Razzaque, J., 'Information, public participation and access to justice in environmental matters', in Alam, S. et al (eds), *Routledge Handbook of International Environmental Law* (Routledge 2012), 137, 144–5; Razzaque, J., 'Participatory Rights in Natural Resources Management: Role of Communities in South Asia', in Ebbesson, J. and Okowa, P. (eds), *Environmental Law and Justice in Context* (Cambridge University Press 2009), 117; and Du, Q., 'Public Participation and Challenges of Environmental Justice in China, in *ibid*, 139.

[127] See Aarhus Convention, art 1.

The development of national and international laws on liability and compensation, as set out in Principle 13, is an important element of the implementation of Principle 10, since laws on liability and compensation may ensure effective redress and remedy.

Conceptually, environmental impact assessments, in Principle 17, should include adequate procedures for public participation; indeed, in many countries the opportunities for public participation are provided as part of the environmental impact assessments. Thus, such assessments are crucial means for effective implementation of Principle 10.

Finally, Principle 10 links with Principles 20, 21, and 22, which all emphasize the participation of different segments of the public, that is, women, youth, and indigenous people and their communities.[128]

## IV) Assessment

Principle 10 has influenced international law in two distinct and remarkable ways.

First, Principle 10 was instrumental for changing the substance of global environmental treaties in support of participatory opportunities for members of the public. Whereas essentially *no* global environmental agreement predating UNCED included any provision on Principle 10 issues, just about *all* such treaties adopted at or after UNCED provide for public access to information and/or public participation, albeit with different degrees of ambition. Many of these treaties have more than 150 parties, thus revealing broad global support to the notions of public awareness, public access to documents, and public participation in environmental matters at a rather abstract level. Lacking effective mechanisms for compliance control, further developments of participatory rights within these global regimes will depend on actions and decisions, for example, action programmes, resolutions and guidelines, by the respective conference of the parties. While not (yet) confirmed by the International Court of Justice, these global treaties and some other indications (eg the ILC Articles) are supportive of the development of a duty under general international law to provide for some form of public consultation, at least in cases where harmful activities entail risks of significant transboundary harm.

Second, Principle 10 has inspired international human rights tribunals to construe existing human rights (eg right to respect for private and family life, right to property, and right to a fair trial) in a new light, thus acknowledging that established human rights provide for access to information, public participation, and access to justice in environmental matters. This development not only confirms these rights as part of international law, but also reveals the fundamental status of participatory rights as part of the human rights legal framework. Yet, this second development is geographically asymmetric. While Principle 10 issues have been embodied in human rights jurisprudence in Europe, the Americas, and Africa, there is not yet any corresponding development in international law for Asia and the Pacific.

No other treaty implements Principle 10 to the same extent as the Aarhus Convention, which merges environmental law and human rights law, and thus reflects the integration of these two dimensions. Possibly, the call at Rio+20 (2012) for action beyond state borders to promote access to information, public participation, and access to justice in environmental

128 See eg the CBD and the Nagoya Protocol as well as the human rights jurisprudence described in this chapter.

matters will stimulate similar legal developments for other parts of the world, and thus help correcting the described geographic asymmetry in support of Principle 10.

## V) Select Bibliography

Du, Q., 'Public Participation and Challenges of Environmental Justice in China', in Ebbesson, J. and Okowa, P. (eds), *Environmental Law and Justice in Context* (Cambridge University Press 2009), 139.

Ebbesson, J., 'The Notion of Public Participation in International Environmental Law' (1997) 8 *YbIEL* 51.

Ebbesson, J., 'Public Participation', in Bodansky, D., Brunnée, J., and Hey, E. (eds), *The Oxford Handbook of International Law* (Oxford University Press 2007), 681.

Ebbesson, J., 'Public Participation and Privatisation: An Assessment of the Aarhus Convention' (2011) 4 *Erasmus Law Review* 71.

Koester, V., 'Review of Compliance under the Aarhus Convention: A Rather Unique Compliance Mechanism' (2005) 2 *Journal of European Environmental and Planning Law* 31.

Koester, V., 'The Convention on Access to Information, Public Participation in Decision-making and Access to Justice in Environmental Matters (Aarhus Convention)', in Ulfstein, G. et al (eds), *Making Treaties Work: Human Rights, Environment and Arms Control* (Cambridge University Press 2007), 179.

Krämer, L., 'Transnational Access to Environmental Information' (2012) 1 *Transnational Environmental Law* 95.

Lee, M. and Abbot, C., 'The Usual Suspect? Public Participation under the Aarhus Convention' (2003) 66 (1) *Modern Law Review* 80.

Malone, L. A. and Pasternack, S., *Defending the Environment: Civil Society Strategies to Enforce International Environmental Law* (Transnational Publishers 2004).

Mushkat, R., 'Public Participation in Environmental Law Making: A Comment on the International Framework and the Asia-Pacific Perspective' (2002) 1 *Chinese Journal of International Law* 185.

Pallemaerts, M. (ed), *The Aarhus Convention at Ten: Interactions and Tensions Between Conventional International Law and EU Environmental Law* (Europa Law Publishing 2011).

Raustiala, K., 'The "Participatory Revolution" in International Environmental Law' (1997) 21 *HELR* 537.

Razzaque, J., 'Participatory Rights in Natural Resources Management: Role of Communities in South Asia', in Ebbesson, J. and Okowa, P. (eds), *Environmental Law and Justice in Context* (Cambridge University Press 2009), 117.

Redgwell, C., 'Access to Environmental Justice', in Francioni, F. (ed), *Access to Justice as a Human Right* (Oxford University Press 2007), 153.

Richardson, B. J. and Razzaque, J., 'Public Participation in Environmental Decision-making', in Richardson, B. J. and Wood, S. (eds), *Environmental Law for Sustainability: A Reader* (Hart 2006), 165.

de Sadeleer, N. et al, *Access to Justice in Environmental Matters and the Role of NGOs: Empirical Findings and Legal Appraisal* (Europa Law Publishing 2005).

Sand, P. H., 'The Right to Know: Freedom of Environmental Information in Comparative and International Law' (2011) 20 *Tulane Journal of International and Comparative Law* 203.

United Nations Economic Commission for Europe, *The Aarhus Convention: An Implementation Guide* (2nd edn, United Nations 2014).

Zillman, D. N., Lucas, A. R., and Pring, G. (eds), *Human Rights in Natural Resource Development: Public Participation in the Sustainable Development of Mining and Energy Resources* (Oxford University Press 2002).

# 15. Principle 11

## *Environmental Legislation*

Martina Kunz*

**Principle 11**

States shall enact effective environmental legislation. Environmental standards, management objectives and priorities should reflect the environmental and development context to which they apply. Standards applied by some countries may be inappropriate and of unwarranted economic and social cost to other countries, in particular developing countries.



## I) Origins and Rationale of the Principle

Principle 11 represents a subtle combination of two main components, each with its own origins and rationale, (i) effective legislation, and (ii) differentiated harmonization.

The first is formulated in the opening statement of Principle 11 and reflects a clause often found in environmental treaties, since as early as 1897,[1] to adopt all necessary national legislative measures in implementation of the treaty and ensure their effectiveness. This is usually linked to an obligation to report on any such measures to the other parties or a

* PhD Candidate, University of Cambridge.

[1] Convention for the preservation of fur seal and sea otter in the North Pacific Ocean and Bering Sea, Washington, 6 November 1897, Unperfected Treaty Series X-4, art I ('The High Contracting Parties agree to prohibit their respective subjects and citizens from killing the fur seal and sea otter in all the waters of the North Pacific Ocean . . . for the period of one year from the date of this Convention; *and they will use their best efforts to make this prohibition effective against their respective subjects and citizens.*' Emphasis added).

treaty organ. However, as there is not yet a treaty encompassing the entire range of 'environmental' questions, such a broad obligation can only be found in non-binding instruments. Neither the 1972 Stockholm Declaration[2] nor the 1982 World Charter for Nature[3] contain a statement equivalent to this first component of Principle 11. A statement with a rather close content can be found in Principle 4 of the set of legal principles drafted by the World Commission on Environment and Development, which stated: 'States shall establish adequate environmental protection standards and monitor changes in and publish relevant data on environmental quality and resource use.'[4] However, the true origin of the first component of Principle 11 is to be found not at a global, but at a regional level, in the extended European context[5] where the 1975 Helsinki Final Act was adopted. The Final Act aimed *inter alia* 'to increase the effectiveness of national and international measures for the protection of the environment',[6] and it specified '[l]egal and administrative measures for the protection of the environment' as one of the areas of cooperation.[7]

The second component, differentiated harmonization, was already present in the Stockholm Declaration, Principle 23 of which stated that:

> Without prejudice to such criteria as may be agreed upon by the international community, or to standards which will have to be determined nationally, it will be essential in all cases to consider the systems of values prevailing in each country, and the extent of the applicability of standards which are valid for the most advanced countries but which may be inappropriate and of unwarranted social cost for the developing countries.[8]

While the language is somewhat similar, Principle 11 strikes a different balance than the Stockholm Declaration, leaning more towards harmonization of environmental regulation.

## II) The Principle as Enshrined in the Rio Declaration

### 1. Preparatory work and context

Contrary to what one might think, Principle 11 gave rise to heated debates during the negotiation process and was among the last to be finalized.[9] As is the case with many principles of the Rio Declaration, it is a juxtaposition of two, very different, proposals, one from the North and one from the South.

[2] Declaration of the United Nations Conference on the Human Environment, Stockholm, 16 June 1972, UN Doc A/CONF 48/14/Rev.1 ('Stockholm Declaration').

[3] World Charter for Nature, 28 October 1982, UN Doc A/RES/37/7 ('World Charter for Nature').

[4] Report of the World Commission on Environment and Development, *Our Common Future*, 10 March 1987 ('Brundtland Legal Principles').

[5] This is a reasonable assumption because the EEC proposed this very sentence of Principle 11. See section II) 1 later in this chapter.

[6] Conference on Security and Cooperation in Europe, Final Act, Helsinki, 1 August 1975, 27.

[7] Conference on Security and Cooperation in Europe, 29.

[8] Stockholm Declaration, Principle 23. The enabling resolution of the Stockholm Conference, Resolution 2849(XXVI) on Development and environment, contained even stronger language, emphasizing that 'notwithstanding the general principles that might be agreed upon by the international community, criteria and minimal standards of preservation of the environment as a general rule will have to be defined at the national level and, in all cases, will have to reflect conditions and systems of values prevailing in each country, avoiding where necessary the use of norms valid in advanced countries, which may prove inadequate and of unwarranted social cost for the developing countries', thus overtly opposing harmonization.

[9] *Earth Negotiations Bulletin*, Vol 1(24), UNCED-PC IV, 2 April 1992.

From the very beginning of discussions on the content of the Rio Declaration at the third Preparatory Committee ('PrepCom') meeting in August/September 1991, India proposed a statement which proved to be largely successful, namely that '[e]nvironmental standards which are valid for the most advanced countries may be inappropriate and of unwarranted economic and social cost for the developing countries', similar to Principle 23 of the Stockholm Declaration discussed above, but instead of reserving international law, it added that 'common international standards can be developed and applied on the basis of provision of full incremental costs to the developing countries concerned'.[10] The latter echoes the London Amendment to the Montreal Protocol the year before, which required the payment of 'agreed incremental costs' to developing countries for their foregone short-term economic advantage of using cheap ozone-depleting substances.[11] However, the issue of finance was met with too much resistance from the developed states[12] and was ultimately abandoned, leaving Principle 11 without any reference to international standards as such. The uncontroversial part of India's proposal appeared again in the draft declaration of G77 and China at the fourth and final PrepCom, in March/April 1992, under the heading of 'Environmental, economic, social and cultural diversity'.[13] The provision first calls on states to respect and conserve this four-fold diversity, followed by a verbatim reproduction of India's Stockholm-inspired statement, and concludes by making explicit that 'environmental management objectives and priorities for the developed and developing countries, based on living standards, social and economic conditions as well as natural resource endowments, will be different.'[14] This last sentence was withdrawn in a revised version of the developing countries' draft declaration,[15] but an injunction for states to duly 'take into account different socio-economic contexts' in the adoption of their environmental measures appeared in the principle on the precautionary approach immediately preceding the principle under consideration,[16] and the core content reappeared in a different shape again in the final version of Principle 11.[17]

[10] Principles on General Rights and Obligations, Chairman's Consolidated Draft, A/CONF.151/PC/WG.III/L.8/Rev.1 ('Chairman's Consolidated Draft'), Principle 2.

[11] Montreal Protocol on Substances that Deplete the Ozone Layer, 16 September 1987, 1522 UNTS 3 ('Montreal Protocol'), Amendment to the Montreal Protocol agreed by the Second Meeting of the Parties (London, 27–29 June 1990), art 10.

[12] Though eg Australia included it in its own proposal at the fourth PrepCom, not as their 'preferred text' but at least as a 'possible element', stating that '[c]ommon international standards can be developed on the basis of assistance to address differences in capacity'. Note that the rationale for assistance is lack of capacity, not historic responsibilities or foregone profit, but equity considerations were addressed in its preferred text ('Responsibilities for combating environmental degradation and pollution should be according to contribution to that damage'). See A/CONF.151/PC/WG.III/L.24, Principle 2 on common but differentiated responsibility ('CBDR').

[13] G77 and China's Proposal, 5 March, A/CONF.151/PC/WG.III/L.20, Principle 9.

[14] G77 and China's Proposal, 5 March, Principle 9.

[15] Thus, Principle 13 of the revised G77 and China draft read: 'States shall respect and conserve ecological, social and cultural diversity. Environmental standards, management objectives and priorities valid for developed countries may be inappropriate and of unwarranted economic and social cost for developing countries.' (A/CONF.151/PC/WG.III/L.20/Rev.1). This text served as negotiating text, on equal footing with other proposals due to lengthy debates on which draft the negotiations should be based. See *Earth Negotiations Bulletin*, Vols 1(5)–(6), UNCED-PC IV, 6–8 March 1992.

[16] G77 and China's Proposal, 5 March, Principle 12.

[17] The second sentence of Principle 11 is similar to the third sentence of this G77 draft, as it emphasizes the need for consideration of both socio-economic and environmental context in the making of law and policy.

As for the global North's contribution to Principle 11, the obligation to enact effective environmental legislation, its current formulation can be traced back to a proposal of the European Economic Community at the fourth PrepCom, which contained a principle entitled 'Environmental legislation and economic instruments':

> States shall enact and implement effective environmental legislation and make full use of economic instruments. Measures of environmental protection shall be coordinated internationally, where possible.[18]

Note that reference to the use of economic instruments later came to be incorporated in what is now Principle 16 on cost internalization and polluter-pays. None of the other draft declarations tabled at PrepCom IV by developed states as competitors to the negotiating text proposed by G77 and China included anything directly relevant to Principle 11.[19]

An apt juxtaposition of a strong obligation to enact effective environmental law with a reminder of the need for differentiation proved to be a successful package in the end.

## 2. Scope and dimensions

### 2.1. *Nature*

While Principle 11 does neither enshrine a legal principle nor an important concept like other principles of the Rio Declaration, it nevertheless contains three normative statements of the kind that could be found in treaties. It is worth starting the analysis with an examination of the type of obligation expressed in the different components of Principle 11, without prejudice to the issue of its *legal* nature under formal sources of international law.[20]

With regard to the normative operator of the three sentences, it is immediately apparent that the first sentence contains an actual obligation ('shall'), whereas the normative content of the second and third statements is less clear when only textual interpretation is used. However, contextual interpretation in light of other principles of the Rio Declaration arguably resolves the ambiguity, leaving trade impacts of environmental legislation to Principle 12, and showing the proper scope of Principle 11 to be the duty of states to adopt effective environmental legislation, which is a common but differentiated responsibility ('CBDR')[21] due to the need for adaptation to the local environmental and developmental context. These two complementary CBDR-like dimensions of Principle 11 will be further specified in the following sections.

### 2.2. *Enactment of effective environmental legislation*

There are three cumulative conditions in this concise but dense first clause of Principle 11, which asserts that 'States shall enact effective environmental legislation'.

First, the requirement to enact legislation is a procedural obligation of result which can be seen as containing two components itself, requiring the measures adopted to take some

[18] EEC Proposal, submitted by Portugal, 11 March 1992, A/CONF.151/PC/WG.III/L.25, Principle 4.

[19] Not even the US proposal, even though the proposal it put forward at the previous PrepCom session and reported in the Chairman's Consolidated Draft featured a principle which held that '[e]nvironmental standards should be developed by each State in a pragmatic and effective fashion to address the particular concerns of its development needs and activities', faintly reminiscent of Principle 4 of the Brundtland Legal Principles discussed above. But this earlier US proposal is weaker than the EEC draft in normative terms.

[20] See section II) 3 later in this chapter.

[21] See Principle 7.

form of law instead of mere policies, action plans, strategies etc, and this legislation must actually be enacted, and not simply contemplated, debated or planned.

Second, the attribute 'environmental' adds an important substantive requirement. However, whether this means that the law should aim at the protection of the environment at all is unclear in light of the six authoritative language versions. While the English and Chinese versions require the law to be 'environmental',[22] the other versions of Principle 11 merely demand it be 'on the environment',[23] for instance solely targeting a social objective such as fair benefit-sharing of natural resources. Nonetheless, what is implied in all language versions is the comprehensive nature of such legislation, compared to a sectoral mandate such as the duty to develop national law regarding liability and compensation for the victims of pollution and other environmental damage, expressed by Principle 13. The need for a comprehensive approach is also emphasized by Agenda 21, which points out that 'although the volume of legal texts in this field is steadily increasing, much of the law-making in many countries seems to be ad hoc and piecemeal'.[24]

Third, the enacted environmental legislation is to be 'effective', in other terms, designed such that it will achieve its objectives. Of course at the moment of enactment it cannot yet be effective, only time may tell whether it will be effective. Environmental law usually requires a number of administrative measures at various levels, for instance withdrawing licenses or imposing new conditions, before it can induce the behavioural change required, such as adopting cleaner production systems or reducing overexploitation of natural resources, which will ultimately bring about the desired environmental outcome, for example, better air quality or populations of endangered species growing again. If the expected result is not forthcoming, the law will have to be readjusted so as to take into account relevant socio-economic and environmental factors which were previously neglected, or simply such that it can be more easily implemented and monitored. Chapter 8 of Agenda 21 contains a whole section entitled 'Providing an effective legal and regulatory framework' with specific guidance as to how laws and regulations can be made more effective and the potential role of international assistance therein.[25]

The fact that express reference to implementation of environmental legislation has been deleted in the course of the drafting process of Principle 11[26] does thus not mean that mere enactment is sufficient, but rather that the attribute 'effective' already provides a focus on the real-world impact of the law. Any law, and especially environmental law, needs to be continuously adapted in line with socio-economic and environmental developments. This emphasis on effectiveness is particularly important given that in the early 1990s many states already had some sort of environmental legislation, but often not effective enough due to design flaws or lack of enforcement.[27] Hence Principle 11 is by no means only targeted at states which did not have any extant environmental law asking them to develop

[22] Chinese: '环境立法'.

[23] Arabic: 'بشأن البيئة', French: 'en matière d'environnement', Russian: 'в области окружающей среды', Spanish: 'sobre el medio ambiente'. Rio Declaration, Report of the United Nations Conference on Environment and Development, A/CONF.151/26/Rev.1 (Vol 1), Annex I.

[24] Agenda 21, Report of the United Nations Conference on Environment and Development, A/CONF.151/26/Rev.1 (Vol 1), Annex II, 9–480 ('Agenda 21'), ch 8, section B, para 13.

[25] Agenda 21, ch 8, section B.

[26] Recall that the EEC proposal originally required states to 'enact *and implement* effective environmental legislation' (emphasis added), see section II.1, earlier in this chapter.

[27] Agenda 21, ch 8, section B, para 13.

such laws, but calls on all states to enact *effective* environmental legislation, including by adopting the necessary amendments in order to make existing law more effective.

Whether or not this (new or amended) environmental legislation is enacted in order to comply with international treaty obligations is not as such addressed by Principle 11, but Agenda 21 points out that the adoption and enforcement of national and sub-national laws and regulations are 'essential for the implementation of most international agreements in the field of environment and development' and that there is space for improvement in this regard.[28]

### 2.3. *Differentiated harmonization of national laws*

Contrary to the first sentence, the second and third sentences provide some guidance with regard to international aspects of environmental law- and policy-making, even though no explicit reference to common international standards is made.

The second statement of Principle 11 seems to contain a duty ('should') to make environmental standards, objectives and priorities reflect the local context, but the duty-bearer can hardly be the concerned (developing) state because its own endogenous standards, objectives, and priorities are naturally shaped by the local context. Moreover, in view of the preamble and the other principles, the Rio Declaration could not be interpreted as precluding a state from setting ambitious environmental targets, at least if these do not lead to a distortion of international trade and investment.[29] Thus, read in conjunction with the third sentence and taking into account the *travaux préparatoires*, this statement simply expresses the need to adapt any exogenous standards and objectives to local conditions and priorities. The external source for such environmental norms and targets could be governmental or non-governmental organizations, think tanks, consultancies, and so forth, and both these actors and the concerned state itself are the addressees of this normative statement. In this sense it is slightly broader than the third sentence which only contemplates uniformization of national laws at the exclusion of, for instance, international 'soft' law standards, such as the non-binding recommendations of the World Health Organization. The third statement is also weaker in its normative content because it merely asserts that wholesale importation of other states' environmental laws *may* be inappropriate. In essence, it provides a ground for refusal of non-differentiated harmonization.

Reading these three statements in the given sequence, Principle 11 articulates an obligation for states to adopt effective environmental law, while conveying at the same time that states are not obliged to harmonize their laws with others' at all costs, and anyone engaged in streamlining environmental standards, management objectives, and priorities in law and policy should pay attention to the need for adaptation to the local environmental and developmental context.

## 3. Legal basis

Principle 11 as a whole is reproduced almost verbatim in the preamble of the United Nations Framework Convention on Climate Change ('UNFCCC') which was drafted

[28] Agenda 21, ch 8, section B, para 15.

[29] See Principle 12 on trade and the environment and Principle 15 on cost internalization, economic instruments and polluter-pays. The relations with other principles will be discussed in section III of this chapter.

shortly after the adoption of the Rio Declaration in April 1992. Besides that, both components of Principle 11 are independently reflected in treaty law.

The obligation to enact environmental legislation in order to implement a treaty is a common feature of international environmental agreements, and the duty to ensure their effectiveness is increasingly emphasized. While at first sight the articulation in treaties of this obligation of implementation through the adoption of national legislative measures may seem superfluous given the fundamental principle of *pacta sunt servanda*,[30] its value lies in the specification of a means of implementation which is easily monitored given the publicity of laws, and which is often thought to be an indispensable part of the treaty implementation process at the national level.[31]

As for the second component of Principle 11, refusal of undifferentiated harmonization is reflected in a few major multilateral environmental treaties. Two types of legal techniques have been used to express the need for differentiation,[32] (i) adjustments of core treaty obligations, and (ii) implementation assistance. As for the former, two kinds of adjustments have been experimented with at the international level, (a) *ratione temporis* (such as a grace period, a different base year, and a slower phase-out of ozone-depleting substances for developing countries under the Montreal Protocol),[33] and (b) *ratione materiae* (exemptions or derogations for certain uses of regulated pollutants under the Stockholm Convention on Persistent Organic Pollutants[34] or of protected species under the Convention on International Trade in Endangered Species[35]). As for the latter, three kinds of assistance are often required: (a) financial assistance (through multilateral funds such as the one established by the Montreal Protocol);[36] (b) technology transfer (specified for instance in the ozone regime and the climate regime);[37] and (c) capacity-building (similarly in a number of regimes).[38] The crux of the matter lies in the link between such assistance and substantive obligations of developing countries, that is, whether lack of assistance may justify non-compliance with environmental protection obligations, and this depends on the specific treaty provisions.[39] Temporal and substantive adjustments of treaty obligations

[30] Vienna Convention on the Law of Treaties, 23 May 1969, in force 27 January 1980, 1155 UNTS 331, 8 ILM 679 ('VCLT'), art 26.

[31] Depending on the substantive obligations in the treaty, see Redgwell, C., 'National Implementation', in Bodansky, D., Brunnée, J., and Hey, E. (eds), *The Oxford Handbook of International Environmental Law* (Oxford University Press 2007), 922, at 929.

[32] For monographs on this issue, see eg Cullet, Ph., *Differential Treatment in International Environmental Law* (Ashgate 2003); Rajamani, L., *Differential Treatment in International Environmental Law* (Oxford University Press 2006). See also the chapter on Principle 6 in this volume.

[33] Montreal Protocol, art 5(1).

[34] Stockholm Convention on Persistent Organic Pollutants, 22 May 2001, in force 17 May 2004, 2256 UNTS 119 ('POP Convention'), art 4.

[35] Convention on International Trade in Endangered Species of Wild Fauna and Flora, 3 March 1973, in force 1 July 1975, 993 UNTS 243 ('CITES'), arts 7 and 23, as well as a number of CoP decisions, eg Dec. 16.17–16.25 'CITES and livelihoods', available on <http://www.cites.org/eng/dec/valid16/185> (last accessed 10 May 2013).

[36] Montreal Protocol, art 10.

[37] Montreal Protocol, art 19A, Kyoto Protocol to the UN Convention on Climate Change, 11 December 1997, 2302 UNTS 148, arts 10(c), 11(2)(b), etc.

[38] Montreal Protocol, arts 2(5) and 2(5)bis, among others. See also the chapter on Principle 9 in this volume.

[39] See eg Montreal Protocol, art 5(5); Convention on Biological Diversity, 5 June 1992, in force 29 December 1993, 1760 UNTS 79 ('CBD'), art 20(4); POP Convention, art 13(4); United Nations Framework Convention on Climate Change, 9 May 1992, in force 21 March 1994, 1771 UNTS 107 ('UNFCCC'), art 4(7).

reflect the need for adaptation to the local environmental and developmental context, while implementation assistance is a response to unwarranted socio-economic costs that may arise from environmental protection measures.

## 4. Normative impact

### *4.1. Effective environmental legislation*

The UN Secretary-General's Report on the implementation of the Rio Declaration presented at the occasion of Rio+5 in 1997 noted that most states adopted new environmental laws or amended existing legislation in the years following the Rio Conference.[40] While many states had already enacted environmental legislation in the two decades after the Stockholm Conference, the UNCED provided new impetus to ensure coherence among different pieces of legislation, filling the gaps and thus establishing a comprehensive legislative framework for environmental protection and sustainable resource management. States enhanced their institutional machinery for environmental law-making by setting up parliamentary bodies dealing with environmental questions and environmental ministries.[41]

Still, the main contribution of Principle 11, together with relevant sections of Agenda 21, was probably the emphasis on the effectiveness of any such legislation, in line with the turn to implementation in environmental law, both at the international and at the national level. One sign of this trend is the increasing reference to effectiveness, compliance, and implementation in treaties concluded in the 1990s as compared to agreements concluded earlier.[42] New reporting and monitoring mechanisms were established within environmental treaty systems, as well as non-compliance procedures to address insufficient implementation. Yet, by definition, such mechanisms are only concerned with the implementation of the treaty at hand, not states' environmental law in general. There is so far no comprehensive global environmental framework convention which would set out general rights and obligations and establish oversight mechanisms, although the drafting of such an instrument was attempted by the International Union for the Conservation of Nature ('IUCN') in the period between the outcome of the WCED and the preparatory work of

[40] Commission on Sustainable Development, 'Rio Declaration on Environment and Development: application and implementation', Report of the Secretary-General, E/CN.17/1997/8, 10 February 1997, 18, para 68.

[41] Inter-Parliamentary Union, World Directory of Parliamentary Bodies for Environment, 1997; and Ecolex contains data on environmental ministries created by national legislation (<http://www.ecolex.org>).

[42] See R. Mitchell's IEA Database Project (<http://iea.uoregon.edu>). Another sign are the publications concerned with implementation and effectiveness that began mushrooming in the 1990s, by academics, IOs and NGOs, eg Sand, P. H., and United Nations Conference on Environment and Development, *The Effectiveness of International Environmental Agreements: A Survey of Existing Legal Instruments* (Grotius Publications 1992); Haas, P. M., Keohane, R. O., and Levy, M. A., *Institutions for the Earth: Sources of Effective International Environmental Protection* (MIT Press 1993); Impériali, C. and Kiss, A. C., *L'effectivité du droit international de l'environnement: contrôle de la mise en oeuvre des conventions internationales* (Economica 1998); Victor, D. G., Raustiala, K., and Skolnikoff, E. B., *The Implementation and Effectiveness of International Environmental Commitments: Theory and Practice* (International Institute for Applied Systems Analysis; MIT Press 1998); Weiss, E. B. and Jacobson, H. K., *Engaging Countries: Strengthening Compliance with International Environmental Accords* (MIT Press 1998); Wolfrum, R., 'Means of Ensuring Compliance with and Enforcement of International Environmental Law' [1998] Recueil des cours de l'Académie de droit international de La Haye—Collected courses of the Hague Academy of International Law 9; Young, O. R., *The Effectiveness of International Environmental Regimes: Causal Connections and Behavioral Mechanisms* (MIT Press 1999).

the UNCED.[43] More recently, the Rio 2012 Summit[44] has launched a process towards the definition of sustainable development goals, the implementation of which will be reviewed by the newly established High-Level Political Forum on Sustainable Development. The specific content of such goals is expected to be known in July 2014, but it is likely that they will capture among other variables the adoption of domestic environmental law.

All kinds of actors, private and public, national and international, have tackled the difficult challenge raised by Principle 11 of assessing to what extent states' environmental legislation is effective and how it could be improved, such as the United Nations Commission on Sustainable Development, UNEP, UNDP, UNDESA, UNITAR, Global Environment Facility, Inter-Parliamentary Union, INTOSAI, IUCN, and many others.[45]

The first component of Principle 11 did have some normative impact, although such impact may not be properly understood as causality between the statement included in the Rio Declaration and subsequent developments. Rather, it is the Rio process and the call for the adoption of appropriate and effective environmental legislation that lies at the roots of such legislative progress.

### *4.2. Differentiated harmonization*

The tension between a drive for uniformization of environmental regulations, not least due to international economic law and the Bretton Woods institutions, and a counter-hegemonic move to more context-specific, 'bottom-up', participatory environmental law-making continued to manifest itself in various ways after UNCED, and Principle 11 is often invoked in this context because it aptly strikes a delicate balance that the Stockholm Declaration and other preceding texts did not achieve. There are two ways in which the international community operationalized this balance, namely regionalization and increasing participation.[46]

The United Nations Convention to Combat Desertification, concluded two years after the Rio Conference, provides perhaps the clearest example of this bottom-up approach in an environmental agreement.[47] The UNCCD has several annexes by region (the most detailed of which concerns Africa), which contextualize the treaty regime to the specific geographical and social situation of each region covered.

[43] See Munro, R. D. (Chairman) and Lammers, J. G. (Rapporteur), *Environmental Protection and Sustainable Development. Legal Principles and Recommendations Adopted by the Experts Group on Environmental Law of the World Commission on Environment and Development* (Graham & Trotman/Martinus Nijhoff 1987). This work was subsequently taken up by the IUCN and introduced into the preparatory work of the UNCED through the delegation of Iceland: UN Doc A/CONF.151/PC/WG.III/4. On the state of this project see IUCN, *Draft International Covenant on Environment and Development* (4th edn, IUCN 2010).

[44] *The Future We Want*, 11 September 2012, UN Doc A/RES/66/288, paras 245–51.

[45] See eg Kaniaru, D. et al, 'UNEP's Programme of Assistance on National Legislation and Institutions', as well as Wilson, P. et al, 'Emerging Trends in National Environmental Legislation in Developing Countries', in *UNEP's New Way Forward: Environmental Law and Sustainable Development* (UNEP 1995); IPU-UNITAR, *Global capacity-building initiative for parliaments on sustainable development* (Inter-Parliamentary Union 2005); UNCSD, *Regional, national and local level governance for sustainable development*, Rio 2012 Issue Briefs, December 2011; *Auditing the Implementation of Multilateral Environmental Agreements (MEAs): A Primer for Auditors*, prepared by UNEP in cooperation with INTOSAI-WGEA (Working Group on Environmental Auditing of the International Organisation of Supreme Audit Institutions), (UNEP 2010); Global Environment Facility, *Capacity Development Study—CB2*, Final report, December 2013.

[46] See the chapter on Principle 9 in this volume.

[47] United Nations Convention to Combat Desertification, 17 June 1994, 1954 UNTS 3 ('UNCCD').

## 5. Jurisprudential relevance

Although Principle 11 as such does not appear to have been expressly referred to in international jurisprudence, its two components have featured in a number of cases.

The duty to enact effective environmental legislation has been identified as part of the obligations arising for States from human rights provisions with environmental content. Indeed, the positive obligation to protect from deprivation of human rights as a result of activities conducted by third parties requires States to regulate certain activities and to do so effectively.[48] However, unlike the formulation of Principle 11, such a duty is not an obligation of result but only one of conduct or, in other terms, of due diligence.

Another illustration of how the call for 'effective' environmental legislation may be relevant from a jurisprudential perspective is provided by the system of citizen submissions on enforcement matters ('SEMs') established under the 1992 North American Agreement on Environmental Cooperation ('NAAEC').[49] The NAAEC is intended to enhance compliance with domestic environmental law as well as transparency and public participation.[50] In its broader context, as a side agreement to the well-known North American Free Trade Agreement ('NAFTA'), the NAAEC is also intended as a check against regulatory competition or, more specifically, against the lowering of environmental standards either *de jure* or *de facto* as a way of attracting investment. Since the beginning of its operations, several dozens of communications have been brought by civil society.[51] In some cases, it is the effective enforcement of existing environmental legislation that is at stake. One illustration is provided by the 2005 *Tarahumara* case,[52] concerning the denial of access to justice to an indigenous community in Mexico, which, as a result, runs against the effective implementation of environmental laws.

Regarding the second component of Principle 11, a significant degree of deference has been granted to States to adopt the environmental measures that they see as the most appropriate to their own realities. Again, Principle 11 has seemingly not been referred to as such, but deference has been ensured through references to concepts such as the margin of appreciation doctrine[53] or the police powers doctrine.[54] Of course, the deference given to the State is not without limits and, in some cases, the measures adopted

[48] See eg *Tatar v. Romania*, ECtHR Application no. 67021/01, Judgment (6 July 2009), paras 85–8 (and the overview of authorities cited therein); *Social and Economic Rights Action Center (SERAC) and others v. Nigeria*, African Commission Application no. 155/96 (2001–2002), paras 52–3; *Indigenous People Kichwa of Sarayaku v. Ecuador*, ICtHR Series C No 245, Judgment (merits and compensation) (27 June 2012), paras 145–7 (right to property) and 159–68 (participatory rights).

[49] North American Agreement on Environmental Cooperation, 17 December 1992, 32 ILM 1480 (1993) ('NAAEC'), arts 14 and 15.

[50] NAAEC, art 1(g)–(h).

[51] The registry is available at: <http://www.cec.org/Page.asp?PageID=751&SiteNodeID=250> (accessed on 1 May 2014).

[52] Final Factual Record regarding the *Tarahumara* Submission (SEM-00-006), Commission for Environmental Cooperation, July 2005, Record released 9 January 2006.

[53] The doctrine has been spelled out in *Handyside v. United Kingdom*, ECtHR Application No. 5493/72, Judgment (7 December 1976), A 24, para 48. In the environmental context *see Turgut v. Turkey*, ECtHR Application No. 1411/03, Judgment—Merits (8 July 2008), para 90.

[54] See eg *Methanex Corporation v. United States of America*, NAFTA (UNCITRAL), Award (3 August 2005), part IV, ch D, para 7; *Chemtura Corporation (formerly Crompton Corporation) v. Government of Canada*, UNCITRAL, Award (2 August 2010) ('*Chemtura v. Canada*'), para 266.

have been found in breach of a treaty despite their environmental purpose. An apposite illustration is provided by the *Shrimp-Turtle* case. Interestingly, in this case, the US measure challenged was found to be in breach of the chapeau of article XX of the GATT precisely because it sought to impose extraterritorially a domestic environmental policy upon third countries.[55]

## III) Relations with Other Principles

Principle 11 is best conceptualized as a connecting node in a web of principles, or as a bridge between the environmental, social, and economic pillars of sustainable development. In a way, it is a concretization of the principle of common but differentiated responsibilities (CBDR), but differentiating on the side of the global South, on the basis of the right to development (Principle 3) and poverty eradication (Principle 5). The recognition and justification of different priorities in Principle 11 is in turn reflected in Principle 15 on the precautionary approach ('according to their capabilities'), Principle 16 on cost-internalization ('with due regard to the public interest and without distorting international trade and investment'), and Principle 17 on environmental impact assessments ('subject to a decision of a competent national authority'). This kind of qualifying language is absent in other national-level legislative requirements, including liability and compensation for the victims of environmental damage (Principle 13), public participation (Principle 10), and major stakeholders (Principles 20–2 on women, youth, and indigenous people), perhaps because these principles are human-centred whereas the former three focus on environmental protection.

## IV) Assessment

Aside from any explicit references to Principle 11 in international instruments and processes, it is above all the influence of the two components of this principle in both international environmental law and in other areas of international law (eg human rights, trade, investment) that must be highlighted. In this regard, the operation of Principle 11 as a 'connecting node' extends also to the variety of instruments that call for the adoption of domestic environmental legislation duly adjusted to take into account domestic circumstances.

This call is likely to be strengthened by the development of 'Sustainable Development Goals' ('SDGs') currently in the process of being elaborated. The adoption of duly adjusted environmental legislation is an indispensable step in realizing the programme conveyed by the Rio Declaration and spelled out in Agenda 21. The possibility of review by a High-Level Political Forum on Sustainable Development adds a very useful complement, which brings the adoption of environmental protection legislation a step closer to efforts to protect human rights, which are themselves subject to a 'Universal Periodic Review' by the Human Rights Council.[56]

[55] See eg *United States—Import Prohibition of Certain Shrimp and Shrimp Products*, Report of the Appellate Body, 12 October 1998, WT/DS58/AB/R, paras 167–9 (concluding that a measure genuinely adopted for environmental purposes was nevertheless in breach of the chapeau of art XX of the GATT *inter alia* because of the insufficient attempts at finding a multilateral solution).

[56] See 'Human Rights Council', 3 April 2006, UN Doc A/60/251, para 5(e).

## V) Select Bibliography


Andreen, W.L., 'Environmental Law and International Assistance: The Challenge of Strengthening Environmental Law in the Developing World' (2000) 25 *Colum J Envtl L* 17.

Beyerlin, U. (ed), *Ensuring Compliance with Multilateral Environmental Agreements: A Dialogue between Practitioners and Academia* (Martinus Nijhoff Publishers 2006).

Blomberg, A. B., 'European Influence on National Environmental Law Enforcement: Towards an Integrated Approach' (2008) 1 *Review of European Administrative Law* 39.

Cullet, P., *Differential Treatment in International Environmental Law* (Ashgate 2003).

Dernbach, J. C., 'Reflections on Comparative Law, Environmental Law, and Sustainability' (1998) 3 *Widener Law Symposium Journal* 279.

Goeteyn, N. and Maes, F., 'Compliance Mechanisms in Multilateral Environmental Agreements: An Effective Way to Improve Compliance?' (2011) 10 *Chinese Journal of International Law* 791.

Haas, P. M., Keohane, R. O., and Levy, M. A., *Institutions for the Earth: Sources of Effective International Environmental Protection* (MIT Press 1993).

Helm, C. and Sprinz, D., Measuring the Effectiveness of International Environmental Regimes (PIK 1999).

Impériali, C. and Kiss, A. C., *L'effectivité du droit international de l'environnement: contrôle de la mise en oeuvre des conventions internationales* (Economica 1998).

International Court of Environmental Arbitration and Conciliation, Ojeda Mestre, R. A., and Loperena, D., *Cases and Materials on International and Comparative Environmental Law* (Editora Laguna, SA de CV 2001).

Kelly, M. J., 'Overcoming Obstacles to the Effective Implementation of International Environmental Agreements' [1997] *The GIELR* 447.

Kiss, A., 'Reporting Obligations and Assessment of Reports', in Beyerlin, U., Stoll, P. T., and Wolfrum, R. (eds), *Ensuring Compliance with Multilateral Environmental Agreements* (Martinus Nijhoff Publishers 2006).

Lutz, R. E., 'The Laws of Environmental Management: A Comparative Study' (1976) 24 *The American Journal of Comparative Law* 447.

Magraw, D. B., 'Legal Treatment of Developing Countries: Differential, Contextual, and Absolute Norms' (1990) 1 *Colorado Journal of International Environmental Law and Policy* 69.

Maljean-Dubois, S. and Rajamani, L., *La mise en oeuvre du droit international de l'environnement* (Martinus Nijhoff Publishers 2011).

McCutcheon, E. D., 'Think Globally, (en)act Locally: Promoting Effective National Environmental Regulatory Infrastructures in Developing Nations' [1998] *Cornell International Law Journal* 395.

Morrison, F. L., 'The Relationship of International, Regional, and National Environmental Law', in Morrison, F.L. and Wolfrum, R. (eds), *International, Regional and National Environmental Law* (Kluwer Law International 2000).

Paddock, L. C. (ed), *Compliance and Enforcement in Environmental Law: Toward More Effective Implementation* (Elgar 2011).

Rajamani, L., *Differential Treatment in International Environmental Law* (Oxford University Press 2006).

Redgwell, C., 'National Implementation', in Bodansky, D., Brunnée, J., and Hey, E. (eds), *The Oxford Handbook of International Environmental Law* (Oxford University Press 2007).

Robinson, N. A., 'Comparative Environmental Law Perspectives on Legal Regimes for Sustainable Development' (1998) 3 *Widener Law Symposium Journal* 247.

Robinson, N.A., Lin Heng, L., and Burleson, E., *Comparative Environmental Law and Regulation* (West 2011).

Sand, P. H. and United Nations Conference on Environment and Development, The Effectiveness of International Environmental Agreements: A Survey of Existing Legal Instruments (Grotius Publications 1992).

Schachter, O. and Baldwin, M., 'Post-Stockholm: Influencing National Environmental Law and Practice Through International Law and Policy' (1972) 66 *AJIL* 1.

Schroth, P. W., 'Comparative Environmental Law: A Progress Report' (1976) 1 *HELR* 603.

Seerden, R. and Heldeweg, M., *Comparative Environmental Law in Europe: An Introduction to Public Environmental Law in the EU Member States* (Maklu Uitgevers; METRO 1996).

Tarlock, A. D. and Tarak, P., 'An Overview of Comparative Environmental Law' (1983) 13 *Denver Journal of International Law and Policy* 85.

Victor, D. G., Raustiala, K., and Skolnikoff, E. B., *The Implementation and Effectiveness of International Environmental Commitments: Theory and Practice* (International Institute for Applied Systems Analysis; MIT Press 1998).

Viñuales, J. E., 'Managing Abidance by Standards for the Protection of the Environment', in Cassese, A. (ed), *Realizing Utopia: The Future of International Law* (Oxford University Press 2012).

Weiss, E. B. and Jacobson, H. K., Engaging Countries: Strengthening Compliance with International Environmental Accords (MIT Press 1998).

Wolfrum, R., 'Means of Ensuring Compliance with and Enforcement of International Environmental Law' [1998] *Recueil des cours de l'Académie de droit international de La Haye = Collected courses of the Hague Academy of International Law* 9.

Young, O. R., *The Effectiveness of International Environmental Regimes: Causal Connections and Behavioral Mechanisms* (MIT Press 1999).

Young, O. R., 'Effectiveness of International Environmental Regimes: Existing Knowledge, Cutting-Edge Themes, and Research Strategies' (2011) 108 *Proceedings of the National Academy of Sciences* 19853.

Zaelke, D. and others, *Making Law Work: Environmental Compliance & Sustainable Development* (Cameron May 2005).

肖剑鸣, 欧阳光明 and 林芳惠, 比较环境法专论 *Monograph of comparative environmental law* (中国环境科学出版社 2004).

# 16. Principle 12

## *The Environment and Trade*

Margaret A. Young*

**Principle 12**

States should cooperate to promote a supportive and open international economic system that would lead to economic growth and sustainable development in all countries, to better address the problems of environmental degradation. Trade policy measures for environmental purposes should not constitute a means of arbitrary or unjustifiable discrimination or a disguised restriction on international trade. Unilateral actions to deal with environmental challenges outside the jurisdiction of the importing country should be avoided. Environmental measures addressing transboundary or global environmental problems should, as far as possible, be based on an international consensus.



* Associate Professor, Melbourne Law School, University of Melbourne. With thanks to the original conference participants (especially Jorge E. Viñuales and Laurence Boisson de Chazournes), Fabrizio Meliado and Joanne Scott for helpful comments.

## I) Origins and Rationale of the Principle

The idea of a supportive and open international economic system was promoted by the original state parties to the General Agreement on Tariffs and Trade 1947 ('GATT'), alongside an acknowledgement that in certain circumstances, those countries could not be prevented from adopting certain trade measures, including those that related 'to the conservation of exhaustible natural resources' or that were necessary 'to protect human, animal or plant life or health' or 'public morals'.[1] Indeed, unilateral trade measures—such as bans on imports, quotas, tariffs, national laws establishing product-labelling requirements and other policies that formed barriers to trade—were useful enforcement mechanisms for environmental policies. Yet the impact that such trade measures could have on trading partners, particularly developing countries, was acknowledged in the Declaration of the United Nations Conference on the Human Environment, in Stockholm in 1972, which stated that:

> [t]he environmental policies of all States should enhance and not adversely affect the present or future development potential of developing countries, nor should they hamper the attainment of better living conditions for all, and appropriate steps should be taken by States and international organizations with a view to reaching agreement on meeting the possible national and international economic consequences resulting from the application of environmental measures.[2]

The hope was that States would reach consensus, usually within the auspices of international treaties, before adopting environmental measures. This hope was satisfied, for example, in the 1987 Montreal Protocol on Ozone Depleting Substances, where state parties agreed to ban the import of ozone depleting substances from non-parties, and ban their own export of such substances.[3]

The participants to the 1972 Stockholm conference also foreshadowed a concern that trade measures to protect the environment could be a mask for protectionism. In Stockholm's 'Action Plan for the Human Environment', it was recommended that governments ensure '[t]hat all States participating in the Conference agree not to invoke environmental concerns as a pretext for discriminatory trade policies or for reduced access to markets'.[4] Indeed, the idea that developing countries should be compensated from the

[1] GATT art XX provides, *inter alia*, 'Subject to the requirement that such measures are not applied in a manner which would constitute a means of arbitrary or unjustifiable discrimination between countries where the same conditions prevail, or a disguised restriction on international trade, nothing in this Agreement shall be construed to prevent the adoption or enforcement by an [Member] of measures: ...

(a) necessary to protect public morals;
(b) necessary to protect human, animal or plant life or health; ...
(g) relating to the conservation of exhaustible natural resources if such measures are made effective in conjunction with restrictions on domestic production or consumption'.

The preamble to the GATT 1947 also stated that the trade relations between the contracting parties 'should be conducted with a view to raising standards of living, ... developing the full use of the resources of the world and expanding the production and exchange of goods', a sentiment that was substantially revised by the recognition of the need for sustainable development in the Preamble to the World Trade Organization 1994: see section II) 2.1.1 of this chapter and the notes thereto.

[2] Stockholm Declaration, Principle 11.

[3] Montreal Protocol on Substances that Deplete the Ozone Layer, 1522 UNTS 3; 26 ILM 1550 (1987), arts 4, 4A.

[4] Stockholm Conference, Action Plan for the Human Environment, Educational, Informational, Social and Cultural Aspects of Environmental Issues, Recommendation 103(a).

negative effects of trade restrictions was promoted.[5] In addition, it was recommended that 'environmental standards should not be expected to be applied universally by all countries with respect to given industrial processes or products except in those cases where environmental disruption may constitute a concern to other countries'.[6]

The concern that trade measures for environmental purposes could harm the established terms of trade under the GATT was played out in a number of controversial trade disputes.[7] These were heard by GATT panels according to the system of dispute settlement that existed at that time (later to be substantially reformed by the institution of the World Trade Organization in 1994). The most important of these disputes was brought by Mexico against the United States, after the US imposed an embargo on tuna imports from countries whose vessels failed to use fishing techniques to meet the US standards on reducing dolphin mortality. Developing countries purportedly viewed the US position in the dispute as representing a 'new wave of environmental colonialism'.[8] The Panel found, *inter alia*, that the US had failed to demonstrate that the measure was necessary to protect the life and health of dolphins (art XX(b)) because the US had not pursued reasonable alternatives such as 'the negotiation of international cooperative arrangements'.[9] The Panel also asserted that article XX(b) and (g) were not intended to allow for trade measures with extra-jurisdictional effect, a statement that was retracted by a secondary panel relating to the same dispute.[10] The two *US-Tuna* GATT Panel reports were not adopted but the finding against the US seemed to affirm a markedly narrow interpretation of the environmental exceptions in the GATT.[11]

In 1989, when the General Assembly resolved to convene the Rio Conference, it identified as one of the Conference objectives the examination of strategies for action 'to promote a supportive international economic climate conducive to sustained and environmentally sound development'.[12] These would be developed 'bearing in mind that the incorporation of environmental concerns and considerations in development planning and policies should not be used to introduce new forms of conditionality in aid or in development financing and should not serve as a pretext for creating unjustified barriers to trade'.[13]

[5] Stockholm Conference, Action Plan, Recommendation 103 (b).

[6] Stockholm Conference, Action Plan, Recommendation 103 (e).

[7] See *US—Canadian Tuna (United States—Prohibition of Imports of Tuna and Tuna Products from Canada)*, L/5198, adopted 22 February 1982, BISD 29S/91; *US—Superfund, (United States—Taxes on Petroleum and Certain Imported Substances)*, L/6175, adopted 17 June 1987, BISD 34S/136; *Canada—Herring and Salmon (Canada—Measures Affecting Exports of Unprocessed Herring and Salmon)*, L/6268, adopted 22 March 1988, BISD 35S/98; *Thailand Cigarettes (Thailand—Restrictions on Importation of and Internal Taxes on Cigarettes)*, DS10/R, adopted 7 November 1990, BISD 37S/200; *US—Tuna (Mexico) (US—Restrictions on Imports of Tuna)*, DS21/R, 3 September 1991, unadopted, BISD 39S/155; (1991) 30 ILM 1594 *US—Tuna (EEC) (United States—Restrictions on Imports of Tuna)*, DS29/R, 16 June 1994, unadopted, (1994) 33 ILM 839.

[8] Ileana M. Porras, 'The Rio Declaration: A New Basis for International Cooperation' (1992) 1:3 *RECIEL* 245.

[9] *US—Tuna (US—Restrictions on Imports of Tuna (US-Tuna (Mexico))*, DS21/R, 3 September 1991, unadopted, BISD 39S/155; (1991) 30 ILM 1594, 36.

[10] *US—Tuna (EEC) (United States—Restrictions on Imports of Tuna)*, DS29/R, 16 June 1994, unadopted, (1994) 33 ILM 839. See further section II) 2.1.3 (extraterritoriality) of this chapter.

[11] See further section II) 2.1.2 and 2.1.3 of this chapter.

[12] A/RES/44/228 on United Nations Conference on Environment and Development, 22 December 1989, para 15(i).

[13] A/RES/44/228 on United Nations Conference on Environment and Development, 22 December 1989, para 15(i).

In 1990, the General Assembly resolved to request the Secretary General of the United Nations Conference on Trade and Development (UNCTAD), to prepare an analytical study on this subject for the Preparatory Committee on UNCED.[14] This was transmitted to the third session in 1991.[15] At its 1992 meeting in Cartagena, UNCTAD participants noted that the debate on environment and trade issues was intensifying.[16] On the eve of the Rio Conference, UNCTAD participants issued its 'Cartagena Commitment' providing, *inter alia*:

> Unilateral actions to deal with environmental challenges outside the jurisdiction of the importing country should be avoided. Environmental measures addressing transborder or global environmental problems should, as far as possible, be based on an international consensus. Domestic measures targeted to achieve certain environmental objectives may need trade measures to render them effective. Should trade policy measures be found necessary for the enforcement of environmental policies, certain [GATT-related and other] principles and rules should apply.[17]

This formulation was to closely influence the subsequent wording of the controversial penultimate sentence of Principle 12, which provides that '[u]nilateral actions to deal with environmental challenges outside the jurisdiction of the importing country should be avoided'. As is evident from the *travaux préparatoires,* however, Principle 12 failed to accommodate some of the known and emerging sensitivities within the relationship between trade measures and environment protection and was not universally supported.

## II) The Principle as Enshrined in the Rio Declaration

### 1. Preparatory work and context

A series of negotiating sessions of a Preparatory Committee ('PrepCom') preceded the Rio Conference. The second session of the PrepCom established a Working Group on legal and institutional matters. This 'Working Group III' held its first substantive meeting during the Preparatory Committee's third session (PrepCom III) in Geneva from 12 August to 4 September 1991. The Secretariat of UNCED noted that the Working Group would examine possible areas of future development of international environmental law including the 'resolution and prevention of conflicts, including potential conflicts between environmental and economic/trade agreements or instruments.'[18] Working Group III subsequently compiled comments submitted by delegations in a consolidated

[14] General Assembly UN A/RES/45/210 21 December 1990. Note also UNCED's resolution to request UNCTAD to study such trends: Report of the Second Committee on the UNCED, 12 Dec A/45/850.

[15] UNCTAD, A/CONF.151/PC/48 (Noted in PrepIII Report, para 33(e)).

[16] UNCTAD, A New Partnership for Development: The Cartagena Commitment, UN Conference on Trade and Development, 8th Sess (1992), 27 February 1992, para 155.

[17] UNCTAD, A New Partnership for Development: The Cartagena Commitment, UN Conference on Trade and Development, 8th Sess (1992), para 152. See <http://unctad.org/en/Docs/tdviiimisc4_en.pdf>. The principles, which generally follow GATT principles, are: 'the principle of non-discrimination; the principle that the trade measure chosen should be the least trade-restrictive necessary to achieve the objectives; an obligation to ensure transparency in the use of trade measures related to the environment and to provide adequate notification of national regulations; and the need to give consideration to the special conditions and developmental requirements of developing countries as they move towards internationally agreed environmental objectives.'

[18] Note by the Secretariat, 'Survey of Existing Agreements and Instruments, and Criteria for Evaluation, A/CONF.151/PC/77, 16 (para 7(e)) (26 June 1991). I note that the Secretariat's 'Annotated Check-list of Principles on General Rights and Obligations' (A/CONF.151/PC/78, 26 July 1991), did not contact reference to a possible clause relating to trade and the environment.

draft.[19] Under the heading of 'Principle on Environment and World Trade',[20] seven delegations recorded comments, which included concern about the use of unilateral trade measures for environmental purposes (India, Singapore),[21] concern about non-tariff barriers (Republic of Korea),[22] support for attention to the needs of developing countries within a free trade system (China),[23] a broad desire for consistency and cooperation on trade matters (Australia, New Zealand),[24] and even a purported sovereign right to trade (Nigeria/G22).[25] These comments formed part of the background of material which was taken as the basis for discussion at the fourth session of the Preparatory Committee from 2 March to 3 April 1992 (PrepCom IV).

At PrepCom IV, a large number of draft declarations were put forward, most of which referred in some way to the relationship between trade and the environment.[26] A G77 and China proposal for the Rio Declaration[27] included a Principle on Environment and Trade which stated that:

> States shall cooperate to promote an international economic environment supportive of sustainable development. In this connection, the developed countries shall ensure that their actions are conducive to the growth of the world economy in general and the development of the developing countries in particular. Global environmental considerations cannot justify restrictive trade practices or new forms of conditionality.[28]

This statement was subsequently amended by the proponents to note that environmental growth is essential to address environmental degradation, and that multilaterally agreed consensus was necessary for the justification of restrictive trade practices.[29]

The United States' draft declaration's version of the principle[30] called instead for the harmonization of the relevant international regimes:

> Environment and development objectives and policies should be integrated with economic and trade policies, including through appropriate harmonization of the international regimes for international trade and environmental protection.[31]

The differences of views on trade and the environment were too nuanced to suggest a clear North/South divide. For example, Australia claimed '[t]he full incorporation of environmental and social costs in the prices of traded goods and services, coupled with the removal of barriers to trade and of subsidies on production, would provide a significant and fundamental foundation for the achievement of sustainable development in all countries.'[32] Norway, on behalf of itself and Denmark, Iceland and Sweden, stated that:

> Democracy and a well functioning market economy are of fundamental importance for a sustainable development. Markets should reflect full economic accounting of environmental costs and

19 Chairman's Consolidated Draft, A/CONF.151/PC/WG.III/L.8/Rev.l. (30 August 1991).

20 Chairman's Consolidated Draft, 12–13.

21 Chairman's Consolidated Draft, (paras 76, 80).

22 Chairman's Consolidated Draft, (para 77).

23 Chairman's Consolidated Draft, (para 75).

24 Chairman's Consolidated Draft, (paras 74, 78).

25 Chairman's Consolidated Draft, (para 79).

26 A/CONF.151/PC/128, 80 to 111.

27 Introduced by the representative of Pakistan, on behalf of the States Members of the United Nations that are members of the Group of 77, and China, introduced a proposal (A/CONF.151/PC/WG.III/L.20).

28 See A/CONF.151/PC/128, 85.

29 (A/CONF.151/PC/WG.III/L.20/Rev.l), para 14, as reported in A/CONF.151/PC/128, 86.

30 A/CONF.151/PC/WG.III/L.21.

31 As reported in A/CONF.151/PC/128, 94.

32 As reported in A/CONF.151/PC/128, 103.

benefits, and market forces and mechanisms, and other economic instruments should be harnessed to achieve sustainable development goals.[33]

The proposed Principles from PrepComIV were referred to the Rio Conference for further negotiation and finalization. The wording proposed for Principle 12 extracted a section from the relevant passage of the UNCTAD Cartagena Commitment. The Chairman had apparently intended this wording to be a 'place holder' subject to further negotiation, but the small group of seven developing countries and seven industrialized countries that made up the final reviewing group did not have time.[34] PrepCom IV's draft declaration was adopted at Rio without modification. However, the United States issued an interpretative statement for the record. It stated:

The United States understands that, in certain situations, trade measures may provide an effective and appropriate means of addressing environmental concerns, including long-term sustainable forest management concerns and environmental concerns outside national jurisdiction, subject to certain disciplines.[35]

## 2. Scope and dimensions

### *2.1. The four dimensions of Principle 12*

There are four dimensions to Rio Declaration Principle 12, as reflected in each of its four sentences, and the scope for each dimension is different.

#### 2.1.1. Open international economic system to better address degradation

The notion of a 'supportive and open international economic system' has found expression in a wide range of international trade and environmental agreements.[36] Policy makers within developing countries, in particular, have considered that access to foreign markets will provide major opportunities for the development of domestic social and economic stability.[37] Thus, the major founding disciplines of the GATT and WTO—that, subject to exceptions,[38] countries will not differentiate between the imports from other countries (most-favoured nation treatment or 'MFN'),[39] or between imports and domestic products[40]—are generally

[33] As reported in A/CONF.141/PC/128, 109.

[34] Kovar, J. D., 'A Short Guide to the Rio Declaration' (1993) 4 *Colorado Journal of International Environmental Law and Policy* 119, 133.

[35] *UNCED Report* (vol IV) at 21. For further discussion of the US's statement, see section II) 2.1.3 of this chapter.

[36] This commentary focuses on the World Trade Organization (WTO) and its predecessor agreements. However, economic integration agreements and regional trade agreements, such as the European Union, North American Free Trade Agreement (NAFTA), and the African Economic Community, have significant impacts on the relationship between trade and environment: see further Sands, P., Peel, J., Fabra, A., and MacKenzie, R., *Principles of International Environmental Law* (3rd edn, Cambridge University Press 2012), 847–61. The Trans-Pacific Partnership (TPP) currently under negotiation between countries in the Pacific Rim will affect trade relations between a large number of developed and developing countries, including Australia, Brunei, Canada, Chile, Japan, Malaysia, Mexico, New Zealand, Peru, Singapore, Vietnam, and the United States.

[37] See, eg, Stockholm Declaration, Principle 11, extracted in Part I of this chapter.

[38] GATT art XX, XXI. See especially n 1 of this chapter.

[39] See eg GATT art I. (While the focus on this commentary is on goods and the GATT, equivalent disciplines exist for services (GATS)).

[40] GATT art III. Note also GATT art XI, which prohibits the use of quantitative restrictions on the import and export of goods. The primary instruments targeted by art XI are outright trade bans and trade quotas associated with products.

supported.[41] While the legitimate pursuit of social and environmental objectives in trade measures was recognized early in GATT Article XX, the creation of the WTO in 1994—along with its own Committee on Trade and Environment (CTE)—and the recognition of 'sustainable development' in the WTO texts,[42] marked an understanding that the relationship between trade and environmental goals warranted improvement. The quest to enhance the 'mutual supportiveness of trade and environment' has persisted ever since, and is currently being pursued through negotiations that form part of the slow-moving, and perhaps indefinitely stalled, 'Doha Development Agenda'.[43]

The founding GATT disciplines of non-discrimination are augmented by disciplines on 'behind the border' measures such as food safety and labelling regulations. These disciplines underwent substantial renegotiation and development in the 'Uruguay Round' of trade negotiations that led to the establishment of the WTO in 1994, and two new agreements: the Agreement on Technical Barriers to Trade ('TBT Agreement') and the Agreement on the Application of Sanitary and Phytosanitary Agreement ('SPS Agreement'). These agreements seek to ensure that certain domestic regulations—which are ubiquitous in protecting humans, animals, or plants—are not more trade restrictive than necessary. While there are a wide range of legitimate objectives that can justify the use of such measures, especially where measures are based on international standards or proven science,[44] the deep penetration of WTO disciplines into domestic regulatory policy-making has brought renewed challenges to the interface between trade and the environment.

In addition to encouraging non-discrimination and the harmonization of standards in the pursuit of an open international economic system, WTO Members have agreed to constrain their use of subsidies. This issue is particularly complex in the context of environmental policy. On the one hand, subsidies can lead to perverse incentives to exploit finite resources: this has led to the grave situation in global fisheries, for example, where state aid for the purchase and maintenance of vessels has led to the trade-distorting and

[41] On non-discrimination, see section II) 2.1.2 of this chapter.

[42] The 1994 Preamble to the WTO states that trade is to be conducted 'while allowing for the optimal use of the world's resources in accordance with the objective of sustainable development, seeking both to protect and preserve the environment and to enhance the means for doing so in a manner consistent with their respective needs and concerns at different levels of economic development'. As observed by the WTO Appellate Body, the negotiators believed that the 1947 preambular objective of 'full use of the resources of the world' 'was no longer appropriate to the world trading system of the 1990's': *US—Shrimp (United States—Import Prohibition of Certain Shrimp and Shrimp Products)* ('*US Shrimp* case') WTO/DS58/AB, adopted 6 November 1998, para 152.

[43] WTO Ministerial Declaration, WT/MIN(01)/DEC/1, 20 November 2001, para 28 and 31: see further section II) 2.1.4 of this chapter. Note also the ongoing work of the CTE in the context of the effect of environmental measures on market access, especially in relation to developing countries; the relevant provisions of the Agreement on Trade-Related Aspects of Intellectual Property Rights ('TRIPS'); and labelling requirements for environmental purposes. The Plan of Implementation of the World Summit on Sustainable Development ('WSSD') (2002) endorses the continued enhancement of 'mutual supportiveness of trade, environment and development with a view to achieving sustainable development': see para 97.

[44] SPS Agreement, art 5, provides that relevant 'SPS' measures must be based on a risk assessment that takes into account, *inter alia*, available scientific evidence and relevant processes and production methods, and relevant ecological and environmental conditions. TBT Agreement art 2.2 provides that 'technical regulations shall not be more trade-restrictive than necessary to fulfil a legitimate objective, taking account of the risks non-fulfilment would create.' Such legitimate objectives include the protection of human health or safety, animal or plant life or health, or the environment, and the assessment of such risks can take into account 'available scientific and technical information, related processing technology or intended end-uses of products'.

ecologically disastrous market failure of too many boats fishing for fewer and fewer fish. On the other hand, subsidies can be helpful for sustainability, because governments can provide financial aid for research and development, as is especially important for the renewable energy sector and other areas compatible with a 'green economy'. The current framework to assess and 'discipline' subsidies is contained in the Agreement on Subsidies and Countervailing Measures ('SCM Agreement'),[45] and this framework is currently ill-equipped to deal with the complexities of environmental policies. Whilst the SCM Agreement originally provided for a 'green-box' of permitted subsidies, which included subsidies for the adaptation of existing facilities to environmental sustainability, this has lapsed.[46] Members are negotiating to clarify and improve amendments to deal with fisheries subsidies in the WTO Doha Round,[47] and there have also been calls for similar negotiations to reduce harmful fossil fuel subsidies.[48] In the meantime, government intervention to support the renewable energy sector faces an uneasy relationship with subsidies disciplines and has been found to fall foul of other trade rules.[49]

Coexistence between an open international economy and environmental protection seems fraught but possible. But the agreed phrasing of the first sentence of Rio Declaration Principle 12 goes further than promoting economic growth with due regard to the environment. It asserts that support for such growth will allow the problems of environmental degradation to be '*better address[ed]*'. The idea that a growing global economy is good for the environment is heavy with assumptions and beliefs, and has come under specific criticism, especially during the Rio+20 World Summit on Sustainable Development.[50] In considering problems of climate change, for example, experts now agree that an increase in world trade can compromise efforts to address the problem.[51] The effect of 'scale' means that the liberalization and expansion of the production, international transportation, and consumption of goods and services increases greenhouse gas emissions. A counter-argument, however, is that liberalized trade can increase the availability and lower the cost of 'climate-friendly' goods and services.[52]

[45] If the trade interests of WTO Members are adversely affected by other Members' industrial subsidies, they can complain within the WTO dispute settlement system or levy countervailing duties after domestic investigations: SCM Agreement, Part V. Agricultural products are dealt with separately in the Agreement on Agriculture.

[46] SCM Agreement, arts 8, 9. The green-box was adopted on a provisional basis for a period of five years: SCM Agreement, art 31. When it expired on 31 December 1999, a lack of consensus among WTO Members meant that it was not renewed.

[47] WTO Ministerial Declaration, WT/MIN(01)/DEC/1, 20 November 2001, para 28. See further Young, M. A., *Trading Fish, Saving Fish: The Interaction between Regimes in International Law* (Cambridge University Press 2011), 85–133.

[48] Bigdeli, S. Z., 'Will the "Friends of Climate" Emerge in the WTO? The Prospects of Applying the "Fisheries Subsidies" Model to Energy Subsidies' (2008) 1 *Carbon and Climate Law Review* 81.

[49] *Canada—Renewable Energy (Canada—Certain Measures Affecting the Renewable Energy Generation Sector/Canada—Measures Relating to the Feed-In Tariff Program)* ('Canada-Renewables') (WTO/DS412/AB/R), adopted 6 May 2013. The measures challenged by Japan were the requirements for domestic content in the design and construction of electricity generation facilities that utilized solar photovoltaic and windpower technology, which Ontario established as conditions to qualify for guaranteed prices offered under its Feed-In Tariff Programme. The WTO Appellate Body found that the measures were contrary to the Agreement on Trade Related Investment Measures ('TRIMS') and the GATT. See also the current challenge brought by China in *European Union and certain Member States—Certain Measures Affecting the Renewable Energy Generation Sector* (DS452) (request for consultations December 2012).

[50] See response to *The Future We Want* outcome document of the Rio+20 conference by civil society groups, compiled in a letter to the United Nations as 'The Rio+20 We Don't Want' (disseminated online 21 June 2012).

[51] See generally WTO-UNEP, *Trade and Climate Change* (2009), 90–110.

[52] WTO-UNEP, *Trade and Climate Change* (2009), 90–110.

The hope that the 'technique' of liberalized trade can better address problems of environmental degradation underpins the current negotiations on environmental goods and services ('EGS') in the WTO Doha Development Round. Negotiations have attempted to agree on the modalities for 'the reduction or, as appropriate, elimination of tariffs and non-tariff barriers to environmental goods and services'.[53] There is no generally accepted definition of EGS, and uncertainties persist about whether processes and production methods ('PPMs')[54] are relevant to their status. More broadly, the impacts on developing countries of these negotiations are unclear. On the one hand, the increase in access to and use of EGS can help in improving energy efficiency, waste disposal services, and pollution reduction techniques. Enhanced trade in these sectors can also generate economic growth and enable the transfer of skills and technology. Yet on the other hand, the main beneficiaries of the negotiations as they currently stand seem to be transnational corporations essentially from developed countries, given their comparative advantage in the goods and services under discussion. Moreover, liberalization could impact negatively on vulnerable industries in developing countries, in particular small and medium-sized enterprises, as well as state-run management services. The EGS negotiations are a good example of the complexity of the idea of a supportive and open economic system to better address environmental degradation. Indeed, a compulsion for states to freely exchange scientific and technological knowledge—as set out in the Rio Declaration's Principle 9[55]—may be a necessary precondition for the full realization of the goals of the first sentence of Principle 12.

### 2.1.2. Non-discrimination

#### *2.1.2.1. The chapeau*

The second sentence of Principle 12 is a paraphrasing of the introductory paragraph (or 'chapeau') of GATT article XX, which provides that trade measures that are exempt from the general GATT disciplines must still meet the requirement:

> that such measures are not applied in a manner which would constitute a means of arbitrary or unjustifiable discrimination between countries where the same conditions prevail, or a disguised restriction on international trade...

This accords with WTO jurisprudence that emphasizes that to be exempt according to GATT article XX, responding parties would need to show (1) that the design of their trade measures falls within one of the enumerated paragraphs (such as GATT article XX(b) or (g)); and (2) that the application of their trade measures accords with the *chapeau*.[56] While respondents are often successful in demonstrating the former, they have failed to meet the requirements of the chapeau, and the Appellate Body has been exacting in the need for states to be even-handed in the implementation of their schemes.[57]

[53] See WTO Ministerial Declaration, WT/MIN(01)/DEC/1, 20 November 2001, para 31(iii).

[54] On PPMs, see section II) 2.1.2.3 of this chapter.

[55] See the commentary to Principle 9 in this volume.

[56] *US Shrimp* case, especially paras 116–22.

[57] See, eg, *US—Gasoline (United States—Standards for Reformulated and Conventional Gasoline)* WT/DS2/AB, adopted 20 May 1996; *US-Shrimp; Brazil-Tyres (Brazil—Measures Affecting Imports of Retreaded Tyres)* ('*Brazil Tyres* case') WT/DS332/AB, adopted 17 December 2007. *EC—Seal Products (European Communities—Measures Prohibiting the Importation and Marketing of Seal Products)* ('*EC Seal Products* case') WT/DS400, 4011/AB/R, adopted 18 June 2014.

There are two other major issues affecting the scope of Principle 12's second sentence: the identification of the 'like' products that should not suffer discrimination ('likeness'); and whether the way in which a product is made affects its categorization ('PPMs').

*2.1.2.2. Likeness*

To facilitate open and supportive trade, the national-treatment rule[58] requires that imported products be accorded regulatory treatment no less favourable than 'like' domestic products, and that imported products not be subject to internal taxes in excess of those applied to 'like' domestic products. The MFN rule[59] requires that any treatment accorded to a foreign product be offered immediately and unconditionally to the 'like product' from a WTO member. Ascertaining whether the relevant products are 'like' is thus a central task in any dispute relating to trade in goods.

In imposing trade measures for environmental purposes, countries may discriminate between environmentally harmful and environmentally friendly goods and deny that such goods are 'like'. If a complaining (exporting) country fails to establish likeness at the WTO, the measure may be regarded as WTO-consistent even without resort to the exemptions in GATT article XX.[60]

GATT-era and WTO jurisprudence has established general criteria for analysing 'likeness', although the Appellate Body has emphasized that such criteria is neither mandated nor exhaustive.[61] This includes considering evidence about '(i) the properties, nature and quality of the products; (ii) the end-uses of the products; (iii) consumers' tastes and habits...; and (iv) the tariff classification of the products.'[62] In *EC Asbestos*, the Appellate Body drew on these criteria to establish that notwithstanding the same end-uses of two types of building materials—one, produced in Canada, containing asbestos, and one, produced domestically, that did not—the complainant had failed to establish them as 'like', especially given the health risks of the Canadian product and the impact this would have on consumer preferences and physical properties.[63]

Trade measures may seek to differentiate between goods on environmental grounds, given the way that they have been made (see PPM discussion, below), or because consumers' tastes and habits have evolved to differentiate between two sets of products with similar end-uses (such as genetically modified ('GM') and non-GM food). It will be for the complainant to demonstrate 'likeness' in such cases.[64]

---

58 See GATT art III.    59 GATT art I.

60 If two products are found to be 'like', there will be a remaining question as to whether the imported products have been treated in a less favourable manner than domestic products, as happened, for example, in *US-Gasoline*. The burden of proof will then shift to the respondent to demonstrate that the measure could be justified according to art XX.

61 *EC—Asbestos (European Communities—Measures Affecting Asbestos and Asbestos-Containing Products)* ('*EC Asbestos*'), WT/DS135, adopted 5 April 2001, paras 101–2.

62 *EC Asbestos* case, para 101, drawing on, *inter alia*, the Report of the Working Party on *Border Tax Adjustments*.

63 *EC Asbestos* case, paras 133–48. Note also the concurring statement of one of the members of the Appellate Body, who would have found the products were not like even without an analysis of end-uses and consumers' tastes and habits, given the grave health impacts of one of them, and who expressed reservation in adopting a fundamentally 'economic' analysis of 'likeness' in what might be philosophical questions: paras 149–54.

64 In *EC—Biotech (European Communities—Measures Affecting the Approval and Marketing of Biotech Products)* WT/DS 291,292,293/R, adopted 21 November 2006, the panel found that it did not need to consider 'likeness', by making the unprecedented move of considering whether the complainant had made a prima facie case of less favourable treatment.

Rio Declaration Principle 12 does not add anything to the enduring questions about whether goods that are, broadly speaking, 'environmentally-friendly' are 'like' similar goods that are not. Taken in full, however, Rio's instructions to states to intervene to promote sustainable development (by, for example, adopting measures to reduce unsustainable patterns of production and consumption)[65] may lead to the accumulation of evidence of original or unique characteristics of particular products, thereby facilitating justifiable distinctions between environmentally-friendly and non-environmentally friendly products.

### *2.1.2.3. PPMs*

A related question to 'likeness', and one that is very important in environmental matters, is whether the way in which a product is made can render it 'unlike' other products, even if the physical characteristics of the final products are identical (often referred to as 'non-product-related processes and production methods'). A law requiring tuna to be harvested in ways not harmful to dolphins is a PPM; a law prohibiting the sale of fish smaller than a prescribed size is not.[66]

Misunderstanding and uncertainty about the legality of PPM-related trade measures was common in policy circles at the time of the *Tuna Dolphin* dispute.[67] That case implicitly ruled that differential treatment between products based solely on their PPM was GATT-inconsistent. Since that (unadopted) case, the WTO—and its preambular reference to 'sustainable development'—has been institutionalized,[68] and the case law has developed considerably. The reasoning of the Appellate Body in *EC Asbestos*[69] and *US Shrimp*[70] appears to sanction discrimination between products on the basis of their PPMs. However, the design and application of trade measures relating to PPMs must adhere to conditions of inclusivity and transparency in order to maintain a non-discriminatory character.

The implicit allowance of PPMs has also been clarified with respect to the TBT Agreement.[71] In *US-Tuna II*, Mexico challenged US regulations that established conditions for the use of 'dolphin-friendly' labels on tuna products.[72] The conditions varied depending on the area where the tuna was harvested and the type of vessel and fishing

65 Principle 8; see further comparison with other Principles in Part III) of this chapter.

66 See further Charnovitz, S., 'The Law of Environmental "PPMs" in the WTO: Debunking the Myth of Illegality' (2002) 27 *YJIL* 60.

67 See further Part I of this chapter and the notes thereto. For a review of other GATT cases involving PPMs (including, with respect to GATT Art I, *Belgian Family Allowances* and *Spain—Coffee*; together with WTO-era cases (including *Indonesia-Automobiles* and *Canada-Automobiles*), see Charnovitz, 'The Law of Environmental "PPMs" in the WTO' 83–4.

68 While there is no explicit reference to the legality or illegality of non-product related PPM measures in the post-Uruguay Round WTO Agreements, the GATT, SPS, and TBT Agreements all make reference to the legitimate use of measures related to processing and production methods: see further Charnovitz, 'The Law of Environmental "PPMs" in the WTO' 61–2.

69 See section II) 2.1.2.2 of this chapter and the notes thereto.

70 The *US Shrimp* case did not deal with the question of PPM legality in the context of GATT articles I or III, because the measure was an import ban found to be inconsistent with Article XI. See further discussion of the case and 'extra-territoriality', in section II) 2.1.3 of this chapter and the notes thereto.

71 Note that the Panel and the Appellate Body in the *EC Seal Products* case did not find it necessary to rule on whether the European Communities' regime prohibiting the import of seal products lay down PPMs (see esp Panel Report, para 7.111–112; AB Report, para 5.69). The Panel's findings on the TBT Agreement were reversed by the AB: see para 5.70.

72 *US—Tuna II (United States—Measures Concerning the Importation, Marketing and Sale of Tuna and Tuna Products) ('US Tuna II')* WT/DS381/AB, adopted 13 June 2012.

method. While the Appellate Body did make a finding of discrimination, this finding was based on the measure's scope of application (which set stricter labelling conditions for tuna caught in the Eastern Tropical Pacific Ocean),[73] rather than its targeting of PPMs per se. This case also has implications for the idea of measures taken outside of the jurisdiction of an importing country, as is discussed below with respect to the third sentence of Rio Declaration Principle 12.

### 2.1.3. Unilateral measures and extraterritorality

The third sentence of Rio Declaration Principle 12 is its most controversial one. Although it does not go so far as suggesting that unilateral, extra-territorial trade measures are prohibited (which would be contrary to the letter and spirit of the WTO legal texts as well as other international norms),[74] it cautions against the use of such measures. The sentence is said to have been suggested by Mexico and the European Community, whose trade interests were substantially affected by US measures that targeted fishing techniques outside of US jurisdiction and in the high seas and who were complainants in the *Tuna Dolphin* dispute.[75] As noted above, the US responded to Mexico's and the European Community's complaint by arguing that its trade embargo on tuna caught with purse-seine nets was necessary to protect the life and health of dolphins (and there was no alternative measure reasonably available for those dolphins outside the US jurisdiction);[76] it was also said to relate to the conservation of dolphins as an exhaustible natural resource.[77] The Panel held that 'even if Article XX(b) were interpreted to permit extra-jurisdictional protection of life and health', the US measure would not meet the requirement of necessity because it had failed to demonstrate that it had pursued reasonable alternatives such as 'the negotiation of international cooperative arrangements'.[78] The Panel referred to previous GATT panel decisions on article XX(g) and rejected an interpretation that allowed for extra-jurisdictional application;[79] it also found that the conditions of the trade ban were unpredictable for the Mexican authorities and thus not primarily aimed at the conservation of dolphins.[80] This position was subsequently substantially retracted by a second panel,[81] although the general finding of violation was upheld.

When the Rio Declaration was agreed, the US issued an interpretative statement that contradicted the third sentence of Principle 12, and set out the understanding that trade measures could be 'an effective and appropriate means of addressing environmental concerns, including...environmental concerns outside national jurisdiction, subject to

[73] *US Tuna II*, see especially paras 298–9.

[74] See further Young, M.A., 'Trade Measures to Address Environmental Concerns in Faraway Places: Jurisdictional Issues' (2014) 23:3 *RECIEL*: note also that the ILC Articles on State Responsibility recognize the right of a state to resort to unilateral measures as countermeasures under certain circumstances: see 2001 *ILC Articles on the Responsibility of States for Internationally Wrongful Acts*, art 22.

[75] Handl, G., 'Declaration of the United Nations Conference on the Human Environment (Stockholm Declaration), 1972 and the Rio Declaration on Environment and Development 1992' (2012) *United Nations Audiovisual Library of International Law* 7; see <http://www.un.org/law/avl/>.

[76] ie, GATT art XX(b) (see GATT Panel Report, *US-Tuna*, para 3.33-3.39).

[77] ie, GATT art XX(g) (see GATT Panel Report, *US-Tuna*, para 3.40-3.52).

[78] GATT Panel Report, *US-Tuna (Mexico)*, para 5.28.

[79] GATT Panel Report, *US-Tuna (Mexico)*, para 5.32.

[80] GATT Panel Report, *US-Tuna (Mexico)*, para 5.33.

[81] GATT Panel Report, *US-Tuna (EEC)*, para 5.20 ('the Panel could see no valid reason supporting the conclusion that the provisions of Article XX (g) apply only to policies related to the conservation of exhaustible natural resources located within the territory of the contracting party invoking the provision').

certain disciplines'.[82] The sentiment expressed by this statement is consistent with subsequent WTO case law that has supported the notion of extraterritorial trade measures in certain circumstances.

A major trade dispute that had been looming in the years leading up to Rio was adjudicated by the WTO Appellate Body in 1998 in a decision that has been described as a full vindication of the US's position regarding the third sentence of Principle 12.[83] In the early 1990s, a series of domestic measures adopted by the US to prevent the drowning of sea turtles in US shrimp trawling nets were extended to a trade embargo on shrimp products harvested abroad in ways that did not prevent sea turtle mortality.[84] At first the embargo was limited geographically to the wider Caribbean/western Atlantic region, but it was subsequently extended to shrimp caught worldwide. While countries could, in theory, apply to be exempt from the embargo if they adopted comparable regulatory programs to the US, in practice exporting countries had to demonstrate the same regulatory programmes (requiring the adopting of the same fishing techniques as US shrimp trawl vessels). Malaysia, India, Pakistan, and Thailand complained to the WTO that the measures were contrary to the GATT.

The Appellate Body in *US Shrimp* acknowledged that unilateral trade measures to address extraterritorial environmental problems could indeed be a 'common aspect' of measures authorized by article XX of the GATT.[85] To suggest otherwise would be contrary to a correct interpretation of article XX according to established rules of treaty interpretation.[86] The sea turtle species that the US measure was designed to protect occurred in waters over which the US had jurisdiction as well as other waters, given their recurrent migrations. The Appellate Body found there was a sufficient nexus between the endangered marine populations and the US for the purposes of article XX(g).[87]

The question of nexus arises in the context of other provisions in article XX. A pertinent example is article XX(a), which provides that certain trade measures might be justified if they are necessary to protect public morals. The *EC Seal Products* case demonstrates how this may be applied in the context of 'environmental challenges'. In response to Canada and Norway's dispute over the European Union's trade ban on seal products, the Appellate Body upheld the Panel's finding that the unilateral ban falls within the requirements of article XX(a), given that the inhumane nature of overseas seal hunts impacts on the sense of morality of the EU's citizens at home.[88] The link to the territory in *EC Seals* is quite distinct from the nexus required in *US Shrimp*, in that the expression of a non-physical public morality serves to 're-territorialise' the environmental harm.

The question of nexus arose indirectly in the *Brazil Tyres* case, when the Appellate Body ruled on whether Brazil's import ban on retreaded tyres was necessary for health and thus justified under art XX(b), given the heightened disease potential and other problems

[82] For full wording, see the extract in section II) 1. of this chapter.

[83] Handl, 'Declaration of the United Nations Conference on the Human Environment'.

[84] *US Shrimp* case (Panel Report circulated 15 May 1998; Appellate Body Report circulated 12 October 1998), adopted 6 November 1998. For a detailed discussion of the case, including the background international agreements, see Young, *Trading Fish, Saving Fish*, 189–240.

[85] *US Shrimp* case, AB Report, para 121 ('[c]onditioning access to a Member's domestic market on whether exporting Members comply with, or adopt, a policy or policies unilaterally prescribed by the importing Member may, to some degree, be a common aspect of measures falling within the scope of one or another of the exceptions (a) to (j) of Article XX').

[86] *US Shrimp* case, AB Report, para 121.

[87] *US Shrimp* case, AB Report, para 133.

[88] *EC Seal Products* case, Panel Report, paras 7.630–7.631; 7.637–7.639; AB Report, para 5.290. The AB reviewed the jurisdictional question at para 5.173. See further Young, M.A., 'Trade Measures to Address Environmental Concerns in Faraway Places: Jurisdictional Issues' (2014) 23:3 *RECIEL*.

arising from stockpiling of excessive quantities of tyres. Whilst the health issues were territorially bounded, the Appellate Body made broader observations recognizing that:

> certain complex public health or environmental problems may be tackled only with a comprehensive policy comprising a multiplicity of interacting measures... Moreover, the results obtained from certain actions—for instance, measures adopted in order to attenuate global warming and climate change, or certain preventive actions to reduce the incidence of diseases that may manifest themselves only after a certain period of time—can only be evaluated with the benefit of time.[89]

Whilst the design of the unilateral trade measures in *Brazil Tyres*, *EC Seal Products*, and *US Shrimp* met the requirements of art XX(b), art XX(a), and art XX(g) respectively, their application violated the *chapeau* of art XX relating to arbitrary and unjustified discrimination. In *Brazil Tyres*, the trade ban was not applied to countries with whom Brazil had concluded the separate MERCOSUR agreement. In *EC Seal Products*, the EU had designed and applied exceptions to the trade ban that related to Inuit and other indigenous hunting practices and marine resources management, and the Panel and Appellate Body considered these to be unjustified because they were not even-handed (especially regarding beneficiaries in Greenland and Sweden as compared to potential beneficiaries in Canada, Alaska, and Russia).[90] In *US Shrimp*, the US had failed to engage the complainants in serious negotiations to try to solve the problem of sea turtle mortality, and had applied the laws in a rigid and inflexible way.[91] Thus, rather than discouraging unilateral measures, the Appellate Body emphasizes that the regulating state should apply measures in a sufficiently flexible way, with serious attempts at negotiations with other countries. This approach has similarities to approaches of other tribunals.[92] Indeed, the pursuit of international consensus is recognized in the final sentence of Rio Declaration Principle 12.

#### 2.1.4. International consensus

The final sentence of Rio Declaration Principle 12 is not contentious. It is connected to the penultimate sentence, because the Appellate Body has emphasized that unilateral trade measures adopted to address transboundary or global environmental problems should be preceded by bilateral or multilateral negotiations.[93]

In *US Shrimp*, the risk of sea turtles becoming endangered was a transboundary or global problem: given the migratory nature of the species, their risk of mortality from

[89] *Brazil Tyres* case, AB Report, para 151 (citation omitted).

[90] *EC Seal Products* case, Panel Report, paras 7.644–7.651; 8.3; AB Report, para 5.339.

[91] *US Shrimp* case, AB Report, especially paras 163, 177; See also *US Shrimp* case, AB Report, *(21.5) (Recourse to Article 21.5 of the DSU by Malaysia)* circulated 22 October 2001, paras 119–25.

[92] For a related finding in the context of the EU's measures in the aviation sector, see the European Court of Justice's decision in Case C-377/10, *Air Transport Association of America and others v. Secretary of State for Energy and Climate Change* (AG Opinion of 6 Oct. 2011 and Judgment of the Court (Grand Chamber) of 21 Dec. 2011). The Court emphasized the non-discriminatory application of the measures as between aircraft operators established both in the European Union and in third States, as well as the territorial link, given the relevant routes departed from or arrived to the territory of a Member State. For a discussion of territorial extension in EU law in the context of climate change, environment, maritime transport, air transport, and financial services regulation, see Scott, J., 'Extraterritoriality and Territorial Extension in EU Law' (2014) 62 *American Journal of Comparative Law* 87.

[93] See section II) 2.1.3 of this chapter and the notes thereto. Transboundary issues are regarded as distinct as far as the obligation to negotiate is concerned: see, eg, *US-Gambling (United States—Measures Affecting the Cross-Border Supply of Gambling and Betting Services)* WT/DS/285/AB/R, adopted 20 April 2005. The Panel's finding that a failure to consult with Antigua rendered the US's measures as not 'necessary to protect public morals or to maintain public order' was reversed by the Appellate Body: see paras 315–321.

shrimp harvesting techniques could not be addressed simply by the adoption of regulations in US waters. In recognition of this fact, the US policy measures were designed to begin with bilateral and multilateral negotiations on turtle conservation *before* the imposition of any trade embargoes. However, apart from a regional agreement—the Inter-American Agreement Convention for the Protection and Conservation of Sea Turtles, concluded in 1996—the Appellate Body found that no agreements with the broader group of states affected by the embargo were reached 'or seriously attempted'.[94] The Appellate Body emphasized that 'concerted and cooperative efforts on the part of the many countries whose waters are traversed in the course of recurrent sea turtle migrations'[95] was necessary for the protection and conservation of sea turtles. The Appellate Body expressly cited and emphasized the final sentence of Rio Declaration Principle 12 to support the requirement of such efforts, in addition to a number of other international instruments.[96]

It is important to note that Principle 12 encourages international consensus 'as far as possible'. In the second phase of the *US Shrimp* litigation, Malaysia brought proceedings against the US arguing that it had failed to comply with the original ruling.[97] Malaysia alleged that the US had failed to implement the requirement to reach an agreement on sea turtle conservation. The Panel differentiated between a requirement to reach agreement and a duty to negotiate in good faith and found that the latter was the relevant standard against which to judge the US.[98] It found that the measures adopted by the United States were justified under art XX as long as there were 'ongoing serious good faith efforts to reach a multilateral agreement' on turtle conservation.[99] The Appellate Body upheld this decision,[100] and emphasized that negotiations with exporting partners would have to be 'comparable' with existing efforts, 'in the sense that comparable efforts are made, comparable resources are invested, and comparable energies are devoted to securing an international agreement'.[101] To hold otherwise would of course give negotiating parties an unfair trump card.[102] The Appellate Body expressly cited Rio Declaration Principle 12 to make it clear that a multilateral approach was *preferred* rather than required.[103] It is therefore recognized that international consensus is a goal that may not always be realized in the context of trade measures for environmental purposes.

The adoption of multilateral environment agreements (MEAs) which contain specific trade obligations to address transboundary or global environmental issues often provide examples of international consensus, especially when they achieve sufficiently broad support among developing and developed countries. There are about twenty MEAs with specific trade obligations currently in force.[104] Six prominent examples are: the Convention

94 *US Shrimp* case, AB Report, para 167.
95 *US Shrimp* case, para 168.
96 *US Shrimp* case, para 168.
97 *US Shrimp* case, Panel Report, *(21.5)*.
98 *US Shrimp* case, Panel Report, *(21.5)*, paras 5.63, 5.67.
99 *US Shrimp* case, Panel Report, *(21.5)*, para 6.1.
100 *US Shrimp* case, AB Report, *(art 21.5)*, para 153.
101 *US Shrimp* case, AB Report, *(art 21.5)*, para 122.
102 In effect, it would give Malaysia 'a veto over whether the United States could fulfil its WTO obligation': *US Shrimp* case, AB Report, *(art 21.5)*, para 123.
103 *US Shrimp* case, AB Report, *(art 21.5)*, para 124 ('Yet it is one thing to *prefer* a multilateral approach in the application of a measure that is provisionally justified under one of the subparagraphs of Article XX of the GATT 1994; it is another to require the *conclusion* of a multilateral agreement as a condition of avoiding "arbitrary or unjustifiable discrimination" under the chapeau of Article XX. We see, in this case, no such requirement').
104 For a list, see WT/CTE/W/160/Rev.5; TN/TE/S/5/Rev.3 (15 June 2011).

on the International Trade in Endangered Species of Flora and Fauna ('CITES'), the Montreal Protocol on Substances that Deplete the Ozone Layer ('Montreal Protocol'), the Basel Convention on the Control of Transboundary Movements of Hazardous Wastes and their Disposal ('Basel Convention'), the Cartagena Protocol on Biosafety to the Convention on Biological Diversity ('Biosafety Protocol'), the Rotterdam Convention on the Prior Informed Consent Procedure for Certain Hazardous Chemicals and Pesticides in International Trade ('PIC') and the Stockholm Convention on Persistent Organic Pollutants ('POPs').

The use of specific trade obligations in MEAs leads to the question of whether such obligations will always be justified according to GATT art XX and other trade law provisions. However, there has not yet been a case in which a WTO Member has sought to defend its trade policies by explicitly invoking obligations contained in an MEA such as the CITES.[105] A dispute between EU and Chile over the landing of swordfish came close: here, Chile alleged at the International Tribunal for the Law of the Sea ('ITLOS') that Spanish vessels were not complying with relevant conservation and management objectives in the United Nations Convention on the Law of the Sea ('UNCLOS'); the EU alleged at the WTO that Chile's measures were in breach of their WTO commitments. The dispute was settled before it had progressed before either tribunal.[106]

The common view is that MEAs will likely satisfy the WTO rules.[107] Of particular relevance is the principle of 'mutual supportiveness', which does not assume away conflict or seek harmonization, but instead ensures that separate regimes function together and take account of one another, as recognized by a number of international courts and tribunals.[108]

An alternative to judicial settlement of these questions is, of course, renewed agreements between states. As part of the Doha Development Agenda negotiations, WTO Members have agreed to negotiate on 'the relationship between existing WTO rules and specific trade obligations set out in multilateral environmental agreements (MEAs)'.[109] Yet these negotiations are 'limited in scope to the applicability of such existing WTO rules as among parties to the MEA in question'.[110] As such, they have limited benefit,

[105] While CITES was relevant to the *US Shrimp* dispute (in that the listing of sea turtles on CITES assisted in determining its endangered status), the measure at issue did not seek to restrict the trade in endangered species; it was aimed at the trade of shrimp because certain shrimp harvesting techniques were known to drown sea turtles. In *EU Biotech,* the EU invoked a number of MEAs as relevant to the interpretation of WTO agreements, including the Convention on Biological Diversity and the Biosafety Protocol, but was not able to invoke them as applicable law between the disputing parties, because the complainant states were not *all* parties to them: see further Young, M. A., 'The WTO's use of relevant rules of international law: an analysis of the Biotech case' (2007) 56 *ICLQ* 907, 912–13. Other cases that have indirectly drawn upon MEAs include *Brazil Tyres* (where reference was made to the Basel Convention and its Technical Guidelines on the Identification and Management of Used Tyres).

[106] See further Orellana, M., 'The Swordfish Dispute between the EU and Chile at the ITLOS and the WTO' (2002) 71 *Nordic Journal of International Law* 55. See also ITLOS Press Release: <http://www.itlos.org/fileadmin/itlos/documents/press_releases_english/PR.141-E.pdf> (last accessed 30 September 2013).

[107] See, eg, Pauwelyn, J., *Conflict of Norms in Public International Law* (Cambridge University Press 2003), 351.

[108] Boisson de Charzournes, L., and Mbengue, M. M., 'A "Footnote as a Principle" Mutual Supportiveness in an Era of Fragmentation', in Hestermeyer, H. P. et al (eds), *Coexistence, Cooperation and Solidarity—Liber Amicorum Rüdiger Wolfrum* (Martinus Nijhoff 2011), 1615 (citing *Arbitration Regarding the Iron Rhine ('Ijzeren Rijn') Railway* (*Belgium v. The Netherlands*), Permanent Court of Arbitration, Award of 24 May 2005, among others).

[109] WTO Ministerial Declaration, WT/MIN(01)/DEC/1, 20 November 2001, para 31(i).

[110] WTO Ministerial Declaration, WT/MIN(01)/DEC/1, para 31(i).

although they have been very useful in procuring and tabling practical information about the implementation of specific trade obligations for environmental purposes to the special session of the Committee on Trade and Environment.[111]

The Doha Development Agenda includes the related topic of negotiations on 'procedures for regular information exchange between MEA Secretariats and the relevant WTO committees, and the criteria for the granting of observer status'.[112] The United Nations Environment Programme is central to these efforts.[113] This kind of institutionalized interaction between regimes is extremely important not only for the ongoing committee work within the WTO, but for the broader negotiation, implementation and adjudication of environment-related trade matters.[114]

## *2.2. Legal nature*

As discussed above, there are some aspects of Principle 12 that have direct analogues with the GATT. The idea of an open and supportive economic system has legal grounding expressed as disciplines of MFN and non-discrimination within the GATT, the TBT Agreement, the SPS Agreement, and other WTO covered agreements.[115] The aspiration for international consensus for environmental measures has been applied in WTO case law, and a failure to attempt to find consensus may even establish arbitrary discrimination.[116] Yet the statement of the penultimate sentence—which was only a soft-law aspiration and one that did not achieve consensus even at Rio[117]—has not found legal support.

# 3. Normative impact

## *3.1. Instruments adopted at UNCED*

### 3.1.1. Agenda 21

Other instruments passed at UNCED adopted related but slightly different versions of Principle 12. In Agenda 21, a longer version of Principle 12 was adopted in chapter 17 relating to Oceans, Seas and Coastal Areas. This included the fuller language of UNCTAD's Cartagena Commitment (recognizing that trade measures may be necessary for the enforcement of environmental policies, but certain GATT-related and other principles and rules should apply to those measures).[118]

Agenda 21's chapter 2 on International Cooperation called for environment and trade policies to be mutually supportive, and recognized that trade measures have 'been used in certain specific instances, where considered necessary, to enhance the effectiveness of environmental regulations for the protection of the environment', and that '[s]uch regulations should address the root causes of environmental degradation so as not to result in unjustified restrictions on trade.'[119]

[111] See eg Matrix of MEA specific trade measures at WT/CTE/W/160/Rev.5; TN/TE/S/5/Rev.3 (15 June 2011).

[112] WTO Ministerial Declaration, WT/MIN(01)/DEC/1, para 31(ii).

[113] See also WTO Doc TN/TE/S/2/Rev.2 (16 January 2007).

[114] See more generally Young, *Trading Fish, Saving Fish*. See also Young, M. A. (ed), *Regime Interaction in International Law: Facing Fragmentation* (Cambridge University Press 2012).

[115] See sections II) 2.1.1 and 2.1.2 in this chapter.

[116] See section II) 2.1.4 in this chapter.

[117] See section II) 2.1.3 in this chapter.

[118] Agenda 21, para 17.118. Note that the terminology of 'international environmental problems' was used rather than Rio's terminology of 'transboundary or global environmental problems' or the Cartegena Commitments' terminology of 'transborder or global environmental problems'.

[119] Agenda 21, para 2.20. See also para 2.19.

### 3.1.2. The Forest Principles

The Forest Principles adopted at the Rio Conference called for 'open and free international trade in forest products'.[120] In similar sentiments to the controversial penultimate sentence of Principle 12, unilateral trade measures to restrict or ban trade in timber or other forest products 'should be removed or avoided'.[121] The later 'non-legally binding instrument on all types of forests' developed within the United Nations Forum on Forests and adopted by the General Assembly on 17 December 2007 builds expressly on the Rio Declaration but does not make reference to Principle 12.[122]

### 3.1.3. The UNFCCC and border adjustments

The UNFCCC did not refer to the removal or avoidance of unilateral measures. However, article 3.5 provides:

> The Parties should cooperate to promote a supportive and open international economic system that would lead to sustainable economic growth and development in all Parties, particularly developing country Parties, thus enabling them better to address the problems of climate change. Measures taken to combat climate change, including unilateral ones, should not constitute a means of arbitrary or unjustifiable discrimination or a disguised restriction on international trade.

This suggests that unilateral trade measures might be permitted as part of efforts to address climate change, but they should meet the requirements of the WTO GATT art XX, particularly its *chapeau*.

This topic has become extremely sensitive in Conferences of the Parties (COP) to the UNFCCC. At the Cancun COP in December 2010, the prospect of unilateral trade measures imposed on imports by developed countries such as the US and the EU loomed large. Measures such as tax adjustments have been mooted to address the competitiveness and 'carbon leakage' concerns created when trade partners fail to impose comparable greenhouse gas emissions reductions requirements. Yet such 'border carbon adjustments' could shift the burden of reducing greenhouse gas emissions on to developing countries, thus violating the principle of 'common but differentiated responsibilities' enshrined in the UNFCCC (and the Rio Declaration itself—Principle 7).

While countries attempted to negotiate the issue at Cancun (and at the preceding COP in Copenhagen in December 2009), the only decision made merely repeated the language of article 3.5 of the UNFCCC.[123] Adding to the complexity is the Durban Platform for Enhanced Action agreed at the COP 17 in 2011.[124] The suggestion now is that mitigation action will be taken by both developed and developing countries, and the result may well

[120] Non-Legally Binding Authoritative Statement of Principles for a Global Consensus on the Management, Conservation and Sustainable Development of All Types of Forests (1992) A/CONF.151/26 (vol III) ('Forest Principles'), para 13.

[121] Forest Principles, para 14. The US issued an understanding that paralleled its statement on Principle 12: *UNCED Report* (vol IV), at 21.

[122] A/RES/62/98.

[123] The Cancun Agreements: Outcome of the work of the Ad Hoc Working Group on Long-term Cooperative Action under the Convention, Decision 1.CP.16 (FCCC/CP/2010/7/Add.1).

[124] India has continued to make submissions to the Ad Hoc Working Group on the Durban Platform for Enhanced Action calling for avoidance of unilateral measures: see, eg, Indian Ministry for Environment and Forestry, 3 March 2013 at <http://pib.nic.in/newsite/erelease.aspx?relid=93042> (last accessed 20 May 2014). (For its original submission seeking a specific agreement that '[D]eveloped country Parties shall not resort to any form of unilateral measures, including tariff, non-tariff, and other fiscal and non-fiscal border trade measures, against goods and services from developing country Parties on any grounds related to climate change', see FCCC/CP/2011/INF.2/Add.1 (7 October 2011.)

be fewer justifications (on grounds of competitiveness and carbon leakage) for unilateral trade action.

### 3.2. *Other instruments*

As set out in section II) 2.1 above, Principle 12 has impacted upon a wide range of international trade and environmental agreements, including regional and bilateral agreements.[125] The institutionalization of the WTO and its Committee on Trade and Environment ('CTE') in 1994 is perhaps the most important direct development. The WTO Ministerial Declaration on Trade and Environment 1994 established the CTE as the successor to an earlier GATT group, creating as one of its terms of reference:

> to make appropriate recommendations on whether any modifications of the provisions of the multilateral trading system are required, compatible with the open, equitable and non-discriminatory nature of the system, as regards, in particular: ... the avoidance of protectionist trade measures, and the adherence to effective multilateral disciplines to ensure responsiveness of the multilateral trading system to environmental objectives set forth in Agenda 21 and the Rio Declaration, in particular Principle 12.[126]

The Ministerial Declaration also took note of the Rio Declaration and Agenda 21 and stated:

> There should not be, nor need be, any policy contradiction between upholding and safeguarding an open, non-discriminatory and equitable multilateral trading system on the one hand, and acting for the protection of the environment, and the promotion of sustainable development on the other.[127]

The following year the Third Session of the Commission on Sustainable Development (currently in the process of being replaced by the High-level Political Forum on Sustainable Development ('HLPF')),[128] reiterated the sentiments of Principle 12, noting:

> trade provisions in multilateral environmental agreements (MEAs) should be transparent and should not constitute a means of arbitrary or unjustifiable discrimination or a disguised restriction on international trade. In accordance with principle 12 of the Rio Declaration, unilateral actions to deal with environmental challenges outside the jurisdiction of the importing country should be avoided. Environmental measures addressing transboundary or global environmental problems should, as far as possible, be based on international consensus.[129]

In the first report of the CTE in 1996, WTO Members noted Principle 12 of the Rio Declaration and stated:

> The CTE endorses and supports multilateral solutions based on international cooperation and consensus as the best and most effective way for governments to tackle environmental problems of a transboundary or global nature. WTO Agreements and multilateral environmental agreements

[125] The proliferation of regional trade and investment agreements has seen parties' trade obligations on matters that relate to the environment based largely—but not solely—on the exceptions expressed in GATT art XX. See Bartels, L., 'Social Issues in Regional Trade Agreements: Labour, Environment and Human Rights', in Lester, S. and Mercurio, B. (eds), *Bilateral and Regional Trade Agreements: Commentary, Analysis and Case Studies* (Cambridge University Press 2008), 342–66.

[126] Adopted in Marrakesh on 15 April 1994, see <http://www.wto.org/english/tratop_e/envir_e/issu5_e.htm>.

[127] Adopted in Marrakesh on 15 April 1994, see <http://www.wto.org/english/tratop_e/envir_e/issu5_e.htm>.

[128] See <http://www.un.org/News/Press/docs/2013/envdev1377.doc.htm>.

[129] E/CN.17/1995/36—Trade: Third Session of the Commission on Sustainable Development (1995), para 51.

(MEAs) are representative of efforts of the international community to pursue shared goals, and in the development of a mutually supportive relationship between them due respect must be afforded to both.[130]

Later United Nations conferences on sustainable development have continued to uphold Principle 12. In the WSSD Plan of Implementation in 2002, Principle 12 is restated verbatim,[131] amidst other objectives to promote the mutual supportiveness of trade and the environment.[132] In the Rio+20 Conference in 2012, participating states affirmed that:

green economy policies in the context of sustainable development and poverty eradication should:...(f) Strengthen international cooperation, including the provision of financial resources, capacity-building and technology transfer to developing countries;...and (h) Not constitute a means of arbitrary or unjustifiable discrimination or a disguised restriction on international trade, avoid unilateral actions to deal with environmental challenges outside the jurisdiction of the importing country, and ensure that environmental measures addressing trans-boundary or global environmental problems, as far as possible, are based on an international consensus.[133]

In the latter context, the main concern was again green protectionism but also green liberalization, in that developing countries were reluctant to allow their markets to be flooded with 'green products' with which their industries could not yet compete.

Meanwhile a number of international instruments have been developed which profess affinity with the principle of an open international economic system—not by explicit reference to Principle 12, but usually by implicit or explicit regard to the (more nuanced) principles of the World Trade Organization.[134]

In the Food and Agriculture Organization, for example, there has been general agreement that the use of trade measures should follow the principles of non-discrimination.[135] However, for measures to address Illegal, Unreported and Unregulated ('IUU') Fishing, FAO members have agreed that in exceptional circumstances, trade bans should be used to prevent, deter, and eliminate IUU fishing.[136] This support for a PPM-related trade measure to prevent environmental degradation across multiple territories and jurisdictions demonstrates a more open attitude to environment-related trade policies than Principle 12 of the Rio Declaration.

## 4. Jurisprudential relevance

There has been a large amount of case law in the GATT and WTO concerning the relationship between measures to protect the environment and trade disciplines. These cases have formed the background to an understanding of Rio Declaration Principle 12, as

[130] WT/CTE/1, 12 November 1996, para 171. The statement was cited with approval by the Appellate Body in *US Shrimp*: para 168.

[131] Plan of Implementation of the World Summit on Sustainable Development ('WSSD'), para 101.

[132] Plan of Implementation of the World Summit on Sustainable Development, see especially paras 90–9.

[133] *The Future We Want*, Outcome document agreed at 'Rio+20', United Nations Conference on Sustainable Development, Rio de Janeiro, Brazil, 20–22 June 2012 (endorsed by the United Nations General Assembly on 27 July 2012, A/RES/66/288), para 58.

[134] See MEAs mentioned above in section II) 2.1.4 of this chapter, and the notes thereto, n 104 and more broadly the Matrix of MEA specific trade measures.

[135] FAO Code of Conduct for Responsible Fisheries, see especially para 11.2 and 11.3.

[136] International Plan of Action on IUU Fishing, para 66. Note that the language of avoidance of unilateral measures is also reproduced.

discussed in detail in section II of this chapter, and include *EC Seal Products*, *EC-Biotech*, *Brazil Tyres*, *US-Tuna (II)*, and *Canada-Renewables*. However, there have been only two Appellate Body decisions that have referred directly to Principle 12: *US Shrimp* and the follow-up *US Shrimp* compliance report.[137]

In *US-Shrimp*, when discussing the requirements of the *chapeau* of GATT art XX, the Appellate Body reproduced the penultimate and final sentence of Principle 12, emphasizing the final sentence.[138] The Appellate Body used this to emphasize that attempts at serious across the board negotiations were an important part of ensuring unilateral trade measures were not unjustifiable or arbitrary restrictions on trade.[139]

In *US Shrimp (21.5)*, the Appellate Body reproduced the final sentence of Principle 12,[140] in dealing with Malaysia's argument that the US had failed to comply with the earlier ruling because an international agreement on sea turtle conservation had not been reached. The Appellate Body noted the *chapeau* did not require the *conclusion* of a multilateral agreement as a condition of avoiding 'arbitrary and unjustifiable discrimination', but rather that multinational agreements should be reached 'as far as possible'.[141]

## III) Relations with Other Principles

The idea of 'sustainable development' embraced by the Rio Declaration is an aspiration that is broad enough to cover each of the four dimensions of Principle 12. More specifically, Principle 12 has strong links and possible contradictions with Principle 16 (Polluter-Pays), Principle 11 (environmental standards), Principle 8 (patterns of consumption and production), Principle 15 (Precautionary Principle), Principle 7 (cooperation), Principle 4 (integration) and Principle 17 ('EIA').

The 'Polluter-Pays' principle in Principle 16 aims to ensure that international trade and investment is not distorted by displacing costs of pollution away from the source. This sits somewhat uneasily with Principle 11, which asserts that environmental standards applied by some countries may be an unwarranted economic and social cost to other countries. Domestic regulations and standards should thus ensure that the 'true' cost of manufacture is reflected in the goods (even as such costs must accommodate contested political, economic, scientific and social assumptions). There is also arguably an implicit suggestion that governments should avoid subsidizing pollution control—a suggestion that should be read alongside contemporary developments in the WTO Subsidies and Countervailing Duties Agreement ('SCM Agreement'), which originally provided for a 'green-box' of permitted 'environmental' subsidies. Principle 16 also foreshadows current debates about 'border carbon adjustment', where domestic attempts to ensure that the cost of greenhouse gas emissions is adequately reflected in imported goods (through at-the-border duties or fees) may be inconsistent with the GATT.[142]

137 The background of these reports is provided in section II) 2.1.3 of this chapter.

138 *US Shrimp* case, AB Report, para 168.

139 See further, section II) 2.1.4 of this chapter.

140 *US Shrimp* case, AB Report, *(21.5)*, para 124.

141 For discussion, see further section II) 2.1.4 of this chapter.

142 See further section II) 2.1.3 of this chapter. There is an historic link between debates about using pollution control measures as a rationale for national import restrictions: see, eg, GATT Secretariat's rejection of pollution control measures as a rationale for national import restrictions in its report to the Stockholm conference.

The need to reduce unsustainable patterns of production and consumption (Principle 8) arguably underpins Principle 12.[143] The challenge is, of course, how to change such patterns whilst conforming to the WTO rules. Although States may modify consumer behaviour consistently with the WTO rules (through the design and implementation and measures that adhere to the discipline especially as discussed in Part II above), the prospect of trade litigation may have a cooling-effect on such policies.

The Precautionary Principle in Principle 15 comes into tension with Principle 12. WTO disputes have arisen over the adoption by states of measures to prevent the potential but not scientifically proven environmental impacts from a range of imports including hormone treated beef (*EC-Hormones*) and genetically modified foods and food products (*EC-Biotech*). Moreover, while the principle of cooperation in Principle 7 seems to accord with the fourth dimension of Principle 12 relating to the desirability of international consensus in the adoption of environmental measures, the idea of 'common but differentiated responsibilities' gives rise to potential clashes, especially in the context of the adoption by developed countries of unilateral trade measures relating to climate change.[144]

Principle 4, which seeks to integrate environmental protection with the development process,[145] is a related principle that reminds decision makers, such as WTO panelists and the Appellate Body, of the need to accommodate environmental perspectives.[146] Principle 17 on the need for environmental impact assessment ('EIA') for activities that are likely to have a significant adverse impact on the environment foreshadows an increasing recognition of the need to assess environmental impacts of trade agreements. Since NAFTA, EIA has become an important tool to identify whether and how trade, development, and the environment can be mutually supportive. For example, current negotiations for the Trans Pacific Partnership are in Canada subject to initial environmental assessment pursuant to Canada's domestic legislative framework.[147] Such efforts may assist in understanding and mediating the complex and often contradictory social, economic, and environmental objectives of globalized governance.

## IV) Assessment

Principle 12 of the Rio Declaration is a rather clumsy attempt to define the relationship between trade and the environment. It combines hard-law elements from trade agreements such as the GATT as well as soft-law aspirations. Perhaps paradoxically for an outcome of a United Nations conference on environment and development, Principle 12 goes further than WTO disciplines in suggesting that countries should avoid trade measures

[143] This is supported by at least one interpretation of the negotiating proposals that sought the full incorporation of environmental and social costs in the prices of traded goods and services: see, eg, section II) 1 of this chapter, and in particular the views expressed by Australia and Norway (n 32 and n 33).

[144] See section II) 3.1.3 in this chapter and the notes thereto.

[145] Principle 4 (together with Principle 3) is noted by the Appellate Body in the *US Shrimp* case: see para 154.

[146] Compare, for example, the recognition by the Appellate Body in *US-Gasoline* that GATT 'is not to be read in clinical isolation from public international law', 17.

[147] See the 2001 *Framework for the Environmental Assessment of Trade Negotiations* developed in line with the *Cabinet Directive on Environmental Assessment of Policy, Plan and Program Proposals*: reported at <http://www.international.gc.ca/trade-agreements-accords-commerciaux/agr-acc/tpp-ptp/info.aspx?lang=eng> (last accessed 30 September 2013).

dealing with environmental challenges outside their jurisdiction. This suggestion lacks the balance set out in the words of GATT art XX (which recognizes, for example, the necessity of certain trade measures to protect human, animal or plant life or health) and the nuance that has developed through Appellate Body interpretations of relevant terms in cases such as *US Shrimp*, *EC Asbestos*, and *Brazil Tyres*. While the controversy over trade measures for environmental purposes has remained since Rio, some of the overarching attitudes have changed.

As has been demonstrated in this chapter, the sentiments of Principle 12 can be attributed to certain positions taken at Rio and the immediately preceding UNCTAD conference and the coeval GATT trade dispute in *US-Tuna*. Broader concerns about the economic impact of environmental measures—especially for developing countries—were expressed well before, including at the 1972 Stockholm conference. A wariness of 'environmental colonialism' and a perception of a North/South divide accounted for Principle 12's overreach in stating that 'unilateral actions to deal with environmental challenges outside the jurisdiction of the importing country should be avoided'. The idea that GATT article XX was not intended to allow for trade measures with extra-jurisdictional effect was infamously espoused by the first GATT Panel in the *US-Tuna* dispute, but subsequently implicitly retracted by a secondary GATT Panel. Clarification and development of WTO case law has rendered the GATT disputes in *US-Tuna*—tenuous even at that time—of historical interest only. The Appellate Body decision in *US Shrimp* emphasizes that unilateral actions to deal with environmental challenges outside the jurisdiction of the importing country are 'a common aspect' of GATT art XX. Principle 12's discouragement of such actions is thus an overstatement. Yet, consistently with the last sentence of Principle 12, such actions must be implemented in a way that seeks to achieve international consensus through serious negotiations on environmental issues, with due flexibility given to affected trading partners. That such negotiations must be attempted only 'as far as possible' seems to foreshadow the current apparent intransigence of negotiators in forums such as the UNFCCC.

Soon after Principle 12 was agreed, the World Trade Organization came into being, with a modified preamble recognizing the goal of sustainable development and a stronger and more effective dispute settlement body. Similar institutional developments have not occurred in the context of environmental agreements (with the call for a World Environment Court never heeded), and there is a resulting imbalance in the rapid development of trade law jurisprudence as compared to environmental law. When regard is had to how the ethos and biases within international regimes affect decision-making,[148] the normative effects of such an institutional imbalance become apparent.

Also since Principle 12 was developed, a renewed set of trade law disciplines have extended the traditional goal of non-discrimination to promote 'least-trade restrictive' domestic policies. The TBT and SPS Agreement seek to ensure that domestic regulations and product standards do not create obstacles to trade, by aspiring for conformity with international standards or compliance with scientific risk assessments. The resulting expectations for market access—which resonate also with Principle 11's reservation

[148] Howse, R., 'From Politics to Technocracy–and Back Again: The Fate of the Multilateral Trading Regime' (2002) 96 *AJIL* 94; see also Young, *Trading Fish, Saving Fish*.

about environmental standards creating unwarranted economic and social costs to other countries—foreshadows further tensions between the aim of facilitating access to markets and the aim of keeping trade aligned with environmental or social purposes. The increasingly prevalence of bilateral agreements that seek to guarantee investment protections complicate this further—as encapsulated by discussions about 'regulatory trade barriers'. Clear, informed understanding of trade law is essential in this complex legal environment, but there is a danger that a lack of understanding—especially amongst policy makers—could have a 'cooling effect' on legitimate efforts to address environmental problems with trade mechanisms. Moreover, disciplines on subsidies are currently out of step with the twin need to reduce state support for ecologically harmful practices—in fisheries and fossil fuels, to name just two examples—and promote state support for the development of new technologies.

While the sensitivities surrounding 'development' have persisted since Rio, there is a more nuanced attitude to the position of 'developing countries'. For example, in *Brazil Tyres*, it was a 'developing country' that was the respondent imposing trade restrictions for environmental purposes, while a 'developed' country, the EU, made good its challenge on the basis that the measure had been applied in a discriminatory way. Moreover, developing countries have demonstrated that their national objectives are more diverse than simple 'industrialization at all costs': witness, for example, the growth in economic opportunities promised by 'eco-tourism'. Yet to claim that economic opportunities await all who engage in liberalized trade—even within a hoped-for 'low carbon economy'—is to ignore the historical evidence of those who have been socially, environmentally, and economically disadvantaged by a rapidly opening international economy. The challenge remains to build fairness and equity into trade relations, and with the stalling of the Doha Development Agenda—and the inability to add new agenda items such as energy reform—this remains difficult. The economic growth caused by a supportive and open international economic system has been important for many people and many countries, but Principle 12's hope that this would allow the problems of environmental degradation to be better addressed seems overly optimistic.

## V) Select Bibliography

Bartels, L., 'Social Issues in Regional Trade Agreements: Labour, Environment and Human Rights', in Lester, S. and Mercurio, B. (eds), *Bilateral and Regional Trade Agreements: Commentary, Analysis and Case Studies* (Cambridge University Press 2008), 342–66.

Bigdeli, S. Z., 'Will the "Friends of Climate" Emerge in the WTO? The Prospects of Applying the "Fisheries Subsidies" Model to Energy Subsidies' (2008) 1 *Carbon and Climate Law Review* 81.

Boisson de Charzournes, L. and Mbengue, M. M., 'A "Footnote as a Principle". Mutual Supportiveness in an Era of Fragmentation', in Hestermeyer, H. et al (eds), *Coexistence, Cooperation and Solidarity—Liber Amicorum Rüdiger Wolfrum* (Leiden: Martinus Nijhoff 2011), 1615.

Charnovitz, S., 'The Law of Environmental "PPMs" in the WTO: Debunking the Myth of Illegality' (2002) 27 *Yale Journal of International Law* 60.

Charnovitz, S., 'The WTO's Environmental Progress' (2007) 10 *Journal of International Economic Law* 685.

Howse, R., 'From Politics to Technocracy–and Back Again: The Fate of the Multilateral Trading Regime' (2002) 96 *AJIL* 94.

Howse, R. and Trebilcock, M. J., 'The Fair Trade-Free Trade Debate: Trade, Labor, and the Environment' (1996) 16 *International Review of Law and Economics* 61.

International Institute for Sustainable Development/United Nations Environment Programme, *Environment and Trade: A Handbook* (2nd edn, 2005).

Kovar, J. D., 'A Short Guide to the Rio Declaration' (1993) 4 *Colorado Journal of International Environmental Law and Policy* 119.

Orellana, M., 'The Swordfish Dispute between the EU and Chile at the ITLOS and the WTO' (2002) 71 *Nordic Journal of International Law* 55.

Pauwelyn, J., *Conflict of Norms in Public International Law* (Cambridge University Press 2003).

Pauwelyn, J., 'Recent Books on Trade and Environment: GATT Phantoms Still Haunt the WTO' (2004) 15 *EJIL* 575.

Porras, I. M., 'The Rio Declaration: A New Basis for International Cooperation' (1992) 1 *Review of European Community and International Environmental Law* 245.

Sands, P., Peel, J., Fabra, A., and MacKenzie, R., *Principles of International Environmental Law* (3rd edn, Cambridge University Press 2012), 799.

World Trade Organization/United Nations Environment Programme, *Trade and Climate Change* (2009).

World Trade Organization, Matrix of MEA specific trade measures, WT/CTE/W/160/Rev.5; TN/TE/S/5/Rev.3 (15 June 2011).

Young, M. A., 'Trade Measures to Address Environmental Concerns in Faraway Places: Jurisdictional Issues' (2014) 23 *RECIEL* 3.

Young, M. A., *Trading Fish, Saving Fish: The Interaction between Regimes in International Law* (Cambridge University Press 2011).

Young, M. A. (ed), *Regime Interaction in International Law: Facing Fragmentation* (Cambridge University Press 2012).

# 17. Principle 13

## *Liability and Compensation*

Malgosia Fitzmaurice*

**Principle 13**

States shall develop national law regarding liability and compensation for the victims of pollution and other environmental damage. States shall also cooperate in an expeditious and more determined manner to develop further international law regarding liability and compensation for adverse effects of environmental damage caused by activities within their jurisdiction or control to areas beyond their jurisdiction.



## I) Origins and Rationale of the Principle

The confines of this chapter will only allow for a brief introduction of a general framework of State responsibility and liability for environmental damage.[1]

* Professor of Public International Law, Queen Mary, University of London, and the Nippon Foundation Professor of Marine Environmental Protection Law at the IMO International Maritime Law Institute in Malta.

[1] See generally Articles of the International Law Commission for Internationally Wrongful Acts, *Report of the International Law Commission of Its Fifty-Third Session, 56 UN.GAOR Supp. (No.10), at 43.* UN Doc

It may be said that Principle 21 of the 1972 Stockholm Declaration on Human Environment and Principle 2 of the Rio Declaration on Environment and Development laid down obligations of States, a violation of which results in State responsibility for transboundary environmental harm. Although forming part of soft-law instruments, these Principles gained the status of norms of customary international law and also are included in many treaties, such as article 194(2) of the 1982 United Nations Convention on the Law of the Sea.[2] The 1941 *Trail Smelter Arbitration* confirms the above principles.[3] Another case that is frequently relied on is the 1949 *Corfu Channel* case, which, however, relates generally to the prohibition of knowingly using territory for acts contrary to rights of other States.[4] The origins of State liability may also be traced to the doctrine of abuse of rights elaborated by Alexandre Kiss.[5] He envisaged the applicability of this doctrine to transboundary law pollution.[6]

One of the difficulties relating to liability for environmental damage is the lack of a uniform definition of what constitutes environmental damage.[7] Until very recently early liability conventions have not provided legal grounds for claiming 'pure' environmental damage. They were restricted to personal injury or loss of damage to property. Conventions which were adopted after 1990 expressly provide for such liability.[8] As has been noted, the problem with defining 'environmental damage' is twofold. First there is the lack of uniformity in the definition and the scope of the notion of the 'environment'. There is a broad approach, favoured by the International Law Commission ('ILC'), which

A/56 (2001) ('ILC Articles on State Responsibility'). See Crawford, J., *The International Law Commission's Articles on State Responsibility, Introduction: Text and Commentaries* (Cambridge University Press 2002). See also Articles on Prevention of Transboundary Harm from Hazardous Activities. International Law Commission's Report on Its Work, 53rd Session, A/56/10, *Yearbook of International Law Commission*, vol II, Part Two (2001); Draft Principles of Allocation of Loss in the Case of Transboundary Harm Arising out of Hazardous Activities, International Law Commission's Report on Its Work, 58th Session, A/61/10, International Law Commission's Yearbook 2006 ('ILC Principles on the allocation of loss'). See on these issues: Fitzmaurice, M., 'International Responsibility and Liability', in Bodansky, D. et al (eds), *The Oxford Handbook of International Environmental Law* (Oxford University Press 2007), 1011; Kosolapova, E., *Interstate Liability for Climate Change-Related Damage* (Eleven International Publishing 2013), in particular, ch 3.

[2] United Nations Convention on the Law of the Sea, 10 December 1982, 1833 UNTS 397.

[3] 'Under the principles of international law, as well as the law of the United States, no state has the right to use or permit to use of its territory in such a manner as to cause injury by fumes in or to the territory of another properties of person therein, when the case is of serious consequences and the injury is established by clear and convincing evidence', *Trail Smelter Arbitration (United States v. Canada)*, 16 April 1931; 11 March 1941, 2 *United Nations Reports of International Arbitral Awards* 1905 (1941).

[4] *Corfu Channel* case (*United Kingdom v. Albania*), ICJ reports 1949, 4.

[5] Kiss, A., 'Abuse of Rights', in Bernhardt, R. (ed), *Encyclopedia of Public International Law*, vol 1 (North-Holland 1992). Kiss, A., *L'abus de droit en droit international* (Librairie generale de droit et de jurisprudence 1952).

[6] Kiss, A., *Droit international de l'environnement* (Paris: Pedone 1989), 72.

[7] See art 1.6 of the 1969 with a 1992 Protocol International Convention on Civil Liability for Oil Pollution Damage; art 2.c of the 1999 Protocol on Liability and Compensation and Damage resulting from Transboundary Movements of Hazardous Wastes and Their Disposal; art 2.2.d of the 2003 Kiev Protocol on Civil Liability and Compensation for Damages Caused by Transboundary Effects of Industrial Accidents on Transboundary Waters; art 2 of the 2010 Nagoya-Kula Lumpur Supplementary Protocol on Compensation and Redress to the Cartagena Protocol on Biosafety; ILC Principles on the allocation of loss, Principle 2.2, all referred to in Douhan, A., 'Liability for Environmental Damage', in Wolfrum, R. (ed), *Max Planck Encyclopedia of Public International Law* (Oxford University Press 2012).

[8] Douhan, 'Liability for Environmental Damage'.

is not universally accepted.[9] Secondly, in view of the comprehensive character of trans-boundary damage, it is a daunting task to establish which damage is 'environmental' per se.[10]

## II) The Principle as Enshrined in the Rio Declaration

### 1. Preparatory work and context

Principle 13 of the Rio Declaration is one of the least analysed principles in this instrument. The discussion relating to this principle during *travaux préparatoires* to the United Nations Conference on Environment and Development ('UNCED') was limited and not very illuminating. The most interesting aspect of liability and compensation for environmental damage relates to national and international legislation on this subject matter, promulgated prior and post the Rio Summit.

The view was expressed that this principle was intended to strengthen the policy contemplated in Principle 22 of the Stockholm Declaration on the Human Environment.[11] The question of liability for environmental damage had not evolved much since the Stockholm Declaration. In this context, the Rio Declaration was expected to result in a stronger approach to this issue.[12] Indeed, the PrepCom Chairman called for a 'more determined manner' in the development of international law in this area.[13]

During the negotiations, there was some divergence concerning how to delimitate the principle. Principle 13 of the Rio Declaration was initially numbered as Principle 14. The then Principle 13 was, however, closely related to liability as it concerned cost internalization (captured in the Rio Declaration by Principle 16, the 'Polluter-Pays' principle). In addition, the then Principle 14 was more extensive at the time of negotiations and also included settlement of dispute procedures. It was named 'Liability for Damage and Dispute Settlement'.[14] There were several views of States on the centre of gravity of this Principle. Australia was of the view that Principle 14 was a restatement of Principle 21 of the Stockholm Declaration, incorporating the concept of liability and compensation for damage. Australia emphasized the need for universal adherence to and full compliance with relevant international instruments, and the need for the future development of the legal framework relating to the environment. Some of the

[9] This broad approach includes natural resources (biotic and abiotic), and the interaction between the same factors and characteristic aspects of landscape. See ILC Principles on the allocation of loss, Principle 2.b.

[10] See Douhan, 'Liability for Environmental Damage'. According to the ILC Principles on the allocation of loss, 'damage' includes: (iii) loss or damage or impairment of the environment; (iv) the costs of reasonable measures if reinstatement of property, or environment, including natural resources; (v) costs of reasonable response measures, (Principle 2).

[11] 'Declaration of the United Nations Conference on the Human Environment', Stockholm, 16 June 1972, UN Doc A/CONF 48/14/Rev.1, 2 ss ('Stockholm Declaration').

[12] Ling, C. Y., *The Rio Declaration on the Environment and Development: An Assessment* (Third World Network 2012), available at <http://www.twnside.org.sg/title/end/pdf/end12.pdf>.

[13] Ling, *The Rio Declaration on the Environment and Development*, 45.

[14] United Nations Assembly, Preparatory Committee for the United Conference on Environment and Development, Third Session, Geneva, 12 August–4 September 1991, Working Group III, Principles on General Rights and Obligations, Chairman's Consolidated Draft, A/Conf.151/PC/WG/III/L.8/Rev.1 ('Chairman's Consolidated Draft'), paras 108–12, 15.

statements made by States in the context of liability and compensation issues focused on the need for the development of a mechanism on dispute prevention and settlement within the environmental context.[15] The USSR also linked regimes establishing liability and compensation to the victims in national and international law to solving disputes in a peaceful manner.[16] Other States and the (then) EEC stressed the aspect of adequate compensation or other available remedy to be provided to the victims of transboundary environmental interference.[17] Peru specified that liability is objective and that it is an obligation of individuals, employers, institutions and States to make good any damage caused.[18] Some general statements concerned, more broadly, the general spirit of the Rio Declaration and the UNCED itself, such as the one by Canada that: '[a]ll individuals, organisations and States shall pursue and encourage the achievement of the objective of this Earth Charter, in cooperation and in accordance with the means at their disposal and their capabilities'.[19]

During the negotiations, there was also a general divide between developing States (as represented by the Group of 77 and China) and developed States concerning the scope of liability for environmental damage. Initially, Australia, Canada, the US, and the EU objected to the inclusion of this principle as proposed by developing States. Developing States argued that after the Stockholm Declaration there had been no action in the establishing of law in the field of liability for environmental damage.

The addition of national laws in first sentence of Principle 13 (which was not included in the Stockholm Declaration) was proposed by the G77 and China, supported by India after the Bhopal disaster, where the lack of national legislation had been a stumbling block in attaching liability to Union Carbide. This addition is noteworthy because the main line of development of liability regimes since the Rio Declaration has indeed taken place at the domestic or regional level. As noted in a Report of the UN Secretary-General on the implementation of the Rio Declaration,[20] Principle 13 was not one of the most successful examples of the application of the Rio Declaration Principles at the international level. The influence of the Rio Declaration in this regard seemed more noticeable at a national level. The Report submitted several examples of post-Rio enactment of liability legislation. However, it was also observed that national courts frequently analysed environmental liability by reference to general liability rules, for instance, on common law tort actions. The recommendation in this Report was that States should 'effectively cooperate to discourage or prevent the relocation and transfer to other States of any activities and substances that cause severe environmental degradation or are found to be harmful to human health'.[21]

Another proposal of the G77 and China related to the inclusion of economic and human damage in addition to environmental damage, which was a result of destruction during the first Gulf War. The G77 and China argued that such damage had an adverse impact on sustainable development. This proposal was rejected by developed States and

[15] Chairman's Consolidated Draft, statement of Austria, para 109, 15.
[16] Chairman's Consolidated Draft, statement of USSR, para 111, 16.
[17] Chairman's Consolidated Draft, statement of the Netherlands/EEC. para 110, 16.
[18] Chairman's Consolidated Draft, statement of Peru, para 111, 16.
[19] Chairman's Consolidated Draft, statement of Canada, para 109, 15.
[20] Rio Declaration on Environment and Development Application and Implementation, Report of the Secretary-General, Commission on Sustainable Development, Fifth Session, 7–22 April 1997, E/CN/17/1997/8.
[21] Report of the Secretary-General, E/CN/17/1997/8 para 76, 17.

the expression 'adverse effects of environmental damage' was eventually used. However, it has been argued that this formulation can be interpreted as including more than environmental damage.[22]

As is clear from the above-presented views of States there was no uniform approach to the questions of liability for environmental damage at the time of the preparatory work for the Rio Declaration. States expressed vague and general ideas regarding the system of liability. The common theme appeared to be that liability for environmental damage had to be regulated on both national and international levels and that victims were entitled to compensation. One should not forget that at the time of negotiations of the Rio Declaration, there were already in place international regimes resulting from oil pollution and nuclear activities. However, there were few national regimes. Therefore, it is likely that Principle 13 of the Rio Declaration encouraged States to develop national liability regimes and further international ones. The broad formulation of Principle 13 left open to States the adoption of specific rules governing liability regimes.

## 2. Scope and dimensions

### *2.1. Legal nature*

It is unclear whether the wording of Principle 13 states an obligation both to adopt domestic legislation and to cooperate to develop international liability regimes. Although the word 'shall' is used in both cases, in the view of the present author it seems unlikely that Principle 13 contains mandatory obligations and that obligations therein constitute a part and parcel of customary international law.

There were few developed liability regimes at the time (essentially the regimes on liability for oil pollution damage and nuclear damage). Therefore there was no practice of States and the divergent views of States expressed during the preparatory works to the Rio Declaration on Principle 13, clearly indicate the lack of requisite *opinio juris*.

Therefore the more plausible view is that the legal nature of Principle 13 (despite its mandatory language) is that of a policy statement to be spelled out through treaties and domestic law.

### *2.2. The dimensions of liability for environmental damage*

The wording of Principle 13 indicates the different approaches to liability for environmental damage offered to States and legislators: (i) State versus operator liability; (ii) Responsibility versus strict liability; (iii) International versus domestic regimes; (iv) General (tort or State responsibility) versus specifically environmental regimes.

The classification used in Principle 13 will be followed in the discussion of various liability regimes in the present chapter, that is, international regimes and domestic regimes. Although domestic regimes are mentioned first in the wording of the principle, we will discuss them after a survey of international regimes. This is because the international dimension of Principle 13 was already called for in Principle 22 of the Stockholm Declaration and it is, in many ways, an extension of Principle 2 of the Rio Declaration.

[22] Ling, *The Rio Declaration on the Environment and Development*, 44–5.

## 3. Normative impact

### *3.1. International regimes: Treaty practice*

#### 3.1.1. State responsibility for environmental damage

The law of State responsibility is based on the distinction between two types of rules: primary rules, which establish obligations of States, and secondary rules, which relate to breaches of primary rules and define consequences of such breaches. There are, however, cases of environmental damage which arise from lawful activities; these are covered by the rules of State liability. This distinction is based on a difference between liability *ex delicto* (based on a wrongful act) and *sine delicto* (deleterious acts resulting from lawful activities).[23] The International Law Commission ('ILC') struggled with this difference, in particular in relation to liability emanating from hazardous activities, such as nuclear power plants. These considerations prompted the ILC to begin work in 1978 on Articles on Liability for Injurious Consequences of Acts Not Prohibited by International Law.[24] This approach was, however, almost uniformly criticized as 'fundamentally misconceived'. The key complaint of the critics was that in the law of State responsibility the issue is not whether the relevant activity as such is unlawful but whether the home State fulfils its due diligence duty to avoid causing the transboundary harm.[25] Following the criticism of the project the ILC decided to divide the liability topic into a part on prevention of transboundary activities and the part on liability. The first part of the project resulted in the 2001 Articles on Prevention of Transboundary Harm from Hazardous Activities and the 2006 Principles of Allocation of Loss in the Case of Transboundary Harm Arising out of Hazardous Activities. This section focuses only on responsibility for an internationally wrongful act.

The Draft Articles on State Responsibility ('ASR') adopted by the International Law Commission are based on 'triple function' for the wrongful act: preventive function, ie, persuasion directed at States not to engage in conduct which could lead to an internationally wrongful act; corrective function, ie enforcement of primary international obligations; compensatory or reparative function, ie restoring of the *status quo ante* or compensation for damages caused by an internationally wrongful act.[26] The ASR adopted, in Article 2, a definition of a wrongful act under international law: an act or omission must be attributable to a State under international law and must constitute a breach of an international obligation. Such a wrongful act entails a responsibility of the State (Article 1). Chapter 5 Part 1 identifies circumstances precluding wrongfulness. These circumstances include the following: *force majeure*; distress; necessity; compliance with peremptory norms; self-defence; consent of a State against which an otherwise wrongful act has been committed; and the fact that the wrongful act constituted a countermeasure in response to a prior breach of international law (Articles 20–27). Part 2 of the Articles deals with the 'content

[23] Lefeber, R., *Transboundary Environmental Interference and the Origin of State Responsibility* (Kluwer Law International 1996), 147; Kiss, A. and Shelton, D., 'Strict Liability in International Environmental Law', in Nnidiaye, T. M. and Wolfrum, R. (eds), *The Law of the Sea, Environmental Law and Settlement of Disputes, Liber Amicorum Judge Thomas Mensah* (Martinus Nijhoff Publishers 2007), 1131.

[24] Brunnée, J., 'On Sense and Sensibility: Reflections on International Liability Regime' (2004) 53 *ICLQ* 351.

[25] Boyle, A., 'State Responsibility and Liability for Injurious Consequences on Acts Not Prohibited by International Law: A Necessary Distinction?' (1990) 39 *ICLQ* 1.

[26] Kosolapova, *Interstate Liability for Climate Change-Related Damage*, 37.

of the international responsibility of States' which broadly refers to the issue of remedies. These remedies are defined in general terms as reparation for injury, which can be accomplished in a number of ways, including restitution, compensation, and satisfaction. The final Part 3 deals with implementation of the international responsibility of States. It includes rules on the 'invocation' of responsibility (Articles 42 and 48). Under the regime of Article 42 an 'injured' State may always invoke the responsibility for breach of international law. Article 48 provides for circumstances when responsibility may be invoked by others than the injured State. Further, this Part fleshes out the concept of countermeasures (by which are meant measures taken by a State to induce a State which committed a wrongful act to comply with its international obligations, Article 49).

The rules of State responsibility for internationally wrongful act have played a relatively modest role in environmental law, due to several reasons including: (i) that they do not cover the liability of private actors, who are largely responsible for environmental damage;[27] (ii) that they leave unclear the extent to which States are responsible in relation to the environment towards the community of States generally (*erga omnes*) or towards the group of States based on a multilateral treaties ('MEAs') regime (*erga omnes partes*); (iii) that the content of fundamental primary rules relating to the environment, such as the precautionary principle, sustainable development, is still a subject of discussions and is not set;[28] and (iv) that the reparation of environmental damage entails several difficulties.

With respect to the latter point, the core of the rules on State responsibility is to remedy the consequences of a wrongful act, which broadly speaking involves cessation of the wrongful conduct and full reparation, which may take the forms of restitution, reparation and satisfaction (Article 34).[29] Two main forms of reparation-restitution and compensation raise specific kind of difficulties in relation to the environment. Article 35 on restitution focuses on the restoration of the *status quo ante*.[30] Without doubt this is a preferable form of reparation. However, in the environmental context harm is sometimes irreversible, and hence, restitution impossible. In some cases, restitution may be possible but would entail unreasonable burdens. As a result restitution is not always the best option and may have to be complemented by compensation to ensure full reparation. It is generally agreed that compensation is due only for established 'financially accessible damage', including environmental harm falling into this category, which was how the United nations Compensation Commission ('UNCC') assessed Iraq's liability for environmental damage and the depletion of natural resources. As the law stands at present, compensation

[27] It may be said, however, that State has the responsibility under international law to regulate and control the activities of private actors in the territory under its jurisdiction and control: Lefeber, *Transboundary Environmental Interference and the Origin of State Responsibility*, 56. See also the same approach expressed in *Responsibilities and Obligations of States with Respect to Activities in the Area*, Advisory Opinion of the Seabed Disputes Chamber, and International Tribunal for the Law of the Sea, (2011) *ITLOS Rep* 10.

[28] The recent case law had filled some gaps in understanding of certain aspects of these fundamental concepts but still a marked lack of uniformity in their comprehension and implementation remains. See eg *Pulp Mills on the River Uruguay (Argentina v. Uruguay)*, Judgment, ICJ Reports 2010, 14 which clarified certain aspects of environmental impact assessment and sustainable development. See also *Responsibilities and Obligations of States with Respect to Activities in the Area*, (note 29) which clarified certain issues concerning *erga omnes* obligations (*actio popularis*) in relation to environmental matters; the precautionary principle and the due diligence.

[29] ILC Articles on State Responsibility, art 34.

[30] Crawford, *The International Law Commission's Articles on State Responsibility*, 295.

will include clean-up costs and property devaluation. The ILC acknowledged, however, that actual damage would often extend to such environmental values as biodiversity, amenity, so-called 'non–use values', which although real and compensable are difficult to quantify.[31]

Another issue which renders the reparation regime of State responsibility not entirely suitable for the redress of environmental damage is the inherently bilateral system of international law and the classical rule which links claim for reparation to direct injury. Some of the concepts such as common concern of mankind, relating to climate change and biodiversity presuppose interest of the whole community of States in effect being coterminous with obligations with *erga omnes* and *erga omnes partes* legal character of which is not entirely clear. Article 48 of the ASR which allows the *locus standi* for a State which is not directly injured (on behalf of all community of States) is progressive development of international law and, for the time being, has no practical application. The only truly multilateral claim regimes in international environmental law are non-compliance procedures.

### 3.1.2. State liability for environmental damage

As it was explained above the main feature distinguishing responsibility from liability is that the latter is not based on the commission of an internationally wrongful act. Such an approach has been seen as a possible alternative to the due diligence-based approach arising from the combination of the general rules on State responsibility and the duty of prevention of environmental harm. An approach based on strict and absolute liability (strict liability understood as providing greater range of exculpatory factors than absolute) is not free from misconceptions.[32] Moreover, in practice, this approach has almost never been followed. The main illustration of a strict liability regime imposed on States is the 1972 Convention on International Liability for Damage Caused by Space Objects,[33] and it only gave rise to one claim by Canada following the crash of a Soviet satellite with a nuclear reactor (Cosmo 954 claim) on the Canadian territory. On the basis of this Convention, Canada claimed compensation of USD 6 million. However, the claim was settled by *ex grata* payment of 3 million dollars by the USSR to Canada, without admitting liability. Therefore this case has no precedential value. The 1993 Council of Europe Lugano Convention for Damage Resulting for Activities Dangerous to the Environment is yet another example of a failed attempt to impose a State strict liability regime within an environmental context.[34] It harmonizes laws on environmental damage but due to several factors, such as incorporation of unlimited liability and the existence of sectoral liability regimes, it will probably never enter into force.[35]

The 2006 Draft Principles on Allocation of Loss in Case of Transboundary Harm Arising out of Hazardous Activities refer in its Preamble explicitly to Principles 13 and 16 (polluter-pays principle) of the Rio Declaration and the Articles on Prevention

[31] Crawford, 223.

[32] Goldie, L.E.F., 'Concepts of Strict and Absolute Liability and Ranking Liability in Terms of relative Exposure to Risk' (1985) 16 *Netherlands Yearbook of International Law* 175.

[33] 1972 Convention on International Liability for Damage Caused by Space Objects, <http://www.oosa.unvienna.org/pdf/publications/st_space_61E.pdf>.

[34] Council of Europe Lugano Convention on for the Damage Resulting for Activities Dangerous to the Environment, Council of Europe Treaty Series, No 150, (1993) 32 ILM. For its entry into force the Lugano Convention requires only 3 ratifications but no State has ratified it so far.

[35] See generally on the Lugano Convention: Bergkamp, L., *Liability and the Environment* (Kluwer Law International 2001), 29–33.

of Transboundary Harm from Hazardous Activities. Principle 3 identifies the purposes of these Draft Principles: (i) to ensure prompt and adequate compensation to victims of transboundary damage and (ii) to preserve and protect the environment in the event of transboundary damage, especially with respect to mitigation of damage to the environment and its reservation or reinstatement.[36] However, the liability regime broadly outlined in the Draft Principles is addressed to economic operators and not to the State (except when the State is the economic operator). The obligations imposed on States by the Draft Principles concern the implementation of such a regime and, if breached (provided they have a legal basis such as a treaty or—potentially—a custom), they trigger the responsibility (not the liability) of the State for internationally wrongful act. Such obligations relate to the area of response measures, such as obtaining from the operator the necessary information and prompt notification to all affected or likely to be affected States (Principle 5(a)). The State of origin of the damage (with the appropriate involvement of the operator) has the duty to ensure that the appropriate response measures are adopted, and it should rely on the best available technology (Principle 5(b)). The State of origin, as appropriate, should also consult with and seek cooperation of States affected or likely to be affected to mitigate the effects of transboundary damage and if possible eliminate them (Principle 5(c)). States affected or likely to be affected by transboundary damage shall take all possible measures to mitigate and if possible eliminate effects of such damage (Principle 5(d)). According to Principle 5(e) the States concerned should, where appropriate, seek the assistance of competent international organizations or other States on mutually acceptable terms. In addition, the Draft Principles also encourage States to make all efforts to conclude specific international agreements relating to particular categories of hazardous activities, with provisions on compensation, response measures, and international and domestic remedies (Principle 7).

### 3.1.3. Multilateral environmental agreements and civil liability regimes

#### *3.1.3.1. Overview*

Attempts to set up general civil liability regimes under multilateral environmental agreements ('MEAs') were seen as one way to overcome the problems inherent in the paradigm of State responsibility and liability for environmental damage. At present there are quite a few such regimes. This section will be devoted to the Basel Protocol on Liability and Compensation to the 1989 Basel Convention on Transboundary Movement of Hazardous Wastes and Their Disposal, and the 2010 Nagoya-Kuala Lumpur Supplementary Protocol on Liability and Redress to the Cartagena Protocol on Biosafety.

#### *3.1.3.2. The Basel Liability Protocol*

The drafting of the Basel Liability Protocol[37] was a drawn-out process which took six years to complete. The Protocol's aim is to set up 'a compensation regime for liability and for adequate and prompt compensation for damage' deriving from transboundary movement of hazardous wastes and their disposal (article 1). It is based on the principle

[36] It may be said that the basis for the obligation to ensure prompt and adequate compensation can be found in the *Trail Smelter Arbitration* and the *Corfu Channel* case. as well in the Principles 21 and 2 of the Stockholm and Rio Declarations respectively. See also Kosolapova, *Interstate Liability for Climate Change-Related Damage*, 47.

[37] The Basel Protocol on Liability and Compensation was adopted at the Fifth Conference of Parties ('COP-5') on 10 December 1999. The Protocol shall enter into force on the ninetieth day after the date of deposit of the twentieth instrument of ratification, acceptance, formal confirmation, approval or accession. The total number of ratifications as of April 2013 is 11. See also Silva Soares, G. F. and Vieira

of prompt, effective, and adequate compensation, similar to Principle 3 of 2006 Articles. Article 6 imposes a duty to notify other States concerned of the proposed transboundary movement of hazardous wastes. Due to the fact that the process of exporting such wastes is very complicated, there may be many different parties liable. However, the Protocol identifies as the party usually liable the actual exporter who is strictly liable, albeit only to a certain limit (article 12 and Annex B). The Protocol also imposes time limits on making claims of ten years from the date of the incident and five years from the date when the claimant knew, or reasonably ought to have known, of the damage (article 13). The definition of damage includes: loss of life or personal injury; loss or damage to property; loss of income deriving from an economic interest in use of impaired environment; and costs of certain measures to prevent, minimize, or mitigate damage or to effect environmental cleanup (article 2). One of the contentious issues during negotiations was the problem of supplementary payment in the event of damage to the environment exceeding the liability limits set by the Protocol. Article 15 (1) provides that in such an event any supplementary measures must be covered by existing mechanisms. It is understood that such a mechanism is provided by the Technical Co-operation Trust Fund, set up under the Basel Convention and supplied by voluntary contributions. Developing countries, however, were in favour of a separate fund. The Basel Protocol provides the possibility of liability based on fault in cases of damage caused by non-compliance with the requirements of the Basel Convention or through intentional or negligent conduct (article 5). This Protocol demonstrates the complexity of designing the civil liability regimes and of the issues to be reconciled. The Protocol had to take into account the economic interest of the industry (including insurance concerns relating to waste transfer) and concerns of transit and recipient countries as to the risk involved in movements of such materials and securing proper compensation. It also had to reconcile the interests of developed and developing States. It is not expected that this Protocol will ever enter into force.

#### *3.1.3.3. The Nagoya-Kuala Lumpur Supplementary Protocol*

Regarding the Nagoya-Kuala Lumpur Supplementary Protocol,[38] its objective is to 'contribute to the conservation and sustainable use of biological diversity, taking into account risks to human health, by providing international rules and procedures in the field of liability and redress relating to living modified organisms'. This Protocol applies to 'damage resulting from living modified organisms which find their origin in a transboundary movement' (article 3.1). The living modified organisms referred to are those: 'intended for direct use as food or feed, or for processing'; 'destined for contained use'; and 'intended for intentional introduction into the environment' (article 3.1). In addition, the Protocol

Vargas, E., 'The Basel Liability Protocol on Liability and Compensation for Damage Resulting from Transboundary Movements of Hazardous Wastes and Their Disposal' (2001) 12 *YbIEL* 69.

[38] Nagoya-Kuala Lumpur Supplementary Protocol to the Cartagena Protocol on Biosafety was adopted by the Conference of the Parties on 15 October. The Protocol will enter into force on the ninetieth day after the date of deposit of the 40th instrument of ratification, acceptance, approval or accession (art 18). (not in force). Text of the Protocol at <http://bch.cbd.int/protocol/NKL_text.shtml>. See Lefeber, R., 'The Legal Significance of the Nagoya-Kuala Lumpur Supplementary Protocol: The result of Paradigm Evolution', Amsterdam Law School Research Paper No 2012-87 <http://papers.ssrn.com/sol3/papers.cfm?abstract_id=2151282> 10; Telesetsky, A., 'The 2010 Nagoya–Kuala Lumpur Supplementary Protocol: A New Treaty Assigning Transboundary Liability and Redress for Biosafety Damage Caused by Genetically Modified Organisms', *ASIL Insights*, 10 January 2011, <http://www.asil.org/insights>. See in depth: Shibata, A. (ed),

covers damage arising from 'unintentional transboundary movements' (article 3.3) or from 'illegal transboundary movements' (article 3.3). The coverage is limited to damage arising 'within the limits of the national jurisdiction of Parties' (article 3.5) and only to the extent it results from a transboundary movement that started after the Protocol entered into force for the party where the damage occurs (article 3.4).

The Protocol also includes a provision on response measures according to which State parties undertake to require the appropriate operator or operators, in case of damage, to notify the relevant authorities, evaluate the damage, and take response measures (article 5.1). More generally, article 12 requires States parties to adopt a civil liability system in their domestic law addressing the type of damage covered by the Protocol. As other international civil liability systems, the Protocol sets some (albeit minimal) parameters guiding the domestic legislative process. Parties must address, *inter alia*, the following elements: damage; standard of liability, including strict or fault-based liability; channelling of liability, where appropriate; the right to bring claims (article 12.3).

The Parties to the Supplementary Protocol did not agree to harmonization in respect of many issues but left it to the discretion of the Parties whether and how to regulate the issues in domestic law,[39] such as: the identification of an operator (article 2, c); the right to of the operator to invoke exemptions (article 6); the time limitation of liability (article 7); financial limitation of liability (article 8); and the establishment and maintenance of financial security by the operator (article 10).[40] As Lefeber explains, States cannot easily exercise the jurisdiction over natural and legal persons in another State. The legal issues regarding the transboundary damage caused by private actors require private sector involvement. Representatives of the private sector participated in the negotiations for the Supplementary Protocol, but also developed a proposal for self-regulation, which evolved into a contractual mechanism, a 'Compact', addressing damage to biological diversity caused by the release of living modified organisms.[41]

### 3.1.4. Traditional civil liability regimes established by treaty

#### *3.1.4.1. Overview*

Civil liability regimes are, it may be said, classical liability regimes, many of which (see below) were already in existence before the articulation of Principle 13 of the Rio Declaration. There is no doubt that the existence of these regimes influenced to a certain degree the formulation of Principle 13. However, it is rather implausible that this Principle had a major influence on the further development of these liability regimes, which evolved rather through the necessity of their expansion due to growth of maritime transportation.

#### *3.1.4.2. Liability and compensation for oil pollution from ships*

3.1.4.2.1. The legal framework: The original civil liability regimes were conceived as a result of the Torrey Canyon incident in 1967. [42] Pollution from ships in general constitutes

*International Liability Regime for Biodiversity Damage: The Nagoya-Kuala Lumpur Supplementary Protocol* (Routledge Research in International Environmental Law 2014).

[39] Lefeber, 'The Legal Significance of the Nagoya-Kuala Lumpur Supplementary Protocol'.

[40] Lefeber, 'The Legal Significance of the Nagoya-Kuala Lumpur Supplementary Protocol'.

[41] Lefeber, 'The Legal Significance of the Nagoya-Kuala Lumpur Supplementary Protocol', 15.

[42] On this topic see eg a very useful study: 'Liability and Compensation for Ship-Source Pollution: An Overview of the International Legal Framework for Oil Pollution Damage from Tankers', *Studies*

only about 15% of all pollution of the marine environment due to effective international legal regulation of this pollution.[43] The liability conventions were drafted under the auspices of the International Maritime Organisation ('IMO'). The first Convention which regulated liability for oil pollution was the 1969 Convention on Civil Liability for Oil Pollution Damage (1969 CLC, entered into force in 1975).[44] The 1969 CLC established a first tier of compensation for oil spills from ships that carry oil as a cargo. The 1971 International Convention of the Establishment of the International Fund for Compensation for Oil Pollution Damage (the 1971 Fund Convention, entered into force in 1978)[45] established the International Oil Pollution Compensation Fund (the 1971 'IOPC Fund') to provide a second tier of compensation in respect to damage in excess of liability under the 1969 CLC, but also limited to an overall monetary cap per incident.[46] The current system is based on two new Conventions adopted in 1992, namely the Convention for Oil Pollution Damage ('1992 CLC', entered into force in 1996)[47] and the 1992 International Convention for the Establishment of an International Fund for Compensation for Oil Pollution Damage (the '1992 Fund Convention').[48] The 1992 CLC is a consolidated version of the 1969 CLC (as amended by the 1992 Protocol to amend the 1969 CLC). The 1992 Protocol provides that both instruments are to be read and interpreted together as a single instrument (article 1). Similarly, the 1992 Fund Convention is a consolidated version of the 1971 Fund Convention as amended by the 1992 Protocol to Amend the Fund Convention, and according to article 27 both instruments are to be read and interpreted together as one single instrument.[49] The 1971 Fund Convention ceased to exist in 2002. However the 1969 CLC still exists and some States are still Parties to this Convention (which co-exists with 1992 CLC). Therefore after 2002 the second tier of compensation is only provided by the 1992 Fund.[50]

*in Transport Law and Policy*—2012 No 1, United Nations Conference on Trade and Development, UNCTAD/DTL/TLB/ 011/4, available at: <http://unctad.org/en/PublicationsLibrary/dtltlb20114_en.pdf>; see also Oosterveen, W., 'Some Recent Developments Regarding Liability for Damage Resulting from Oil Pollution-from the Perspective of and EU Member State', *Environmental Law Review* 223; Wang, Hui, *Civil Liability for Marine Oil Pollution damage: A Comparative Study of the International, US and Chinese Compensation Regime* (Wouters Kluwer, Law and Business 2011); Farahani, M. M., 'Liability and Compensation Regime for Oil Pollution Damage under International Conventions', master thesis, University of Lund: <http://lup.lub.lu.se/luur/download?func=downloadFile&recordOId=1974126&fileOId=1977590>.

[43] There are several conventions which regulate the pollution from ships: MARPOL which covers all sources of pollution from ships; the 1969 International Convention Relation to the Intervention on the High Seas in cases of Oil Pollution Casualties; the 1974 Convention for the safety of Life at Sea ('SOLAS'); the 1990 International Convention on Oil Pollution Preparedness, Response and Cooperation ('ORPC').

[44] 1969 Convention on Civil Liability for Oil Pollution ('1969 CLC'), available at <http://treaties.un.org/doc/Publication/UNTS/Volume%20973/volume-973-I-14097-English.pdf>.

[45] 1971 International Convention of the Establishment of the International Fund for Compensation for Oil Pollution Damage, available at <http://www.admiraltylawguide.com/conven/oilpolfund1971.html>.

[46] UNCTAD, 9–10. Mention also must be made of two (not in force since 1997) private schemes: TOVLAP (Tankers Owners Voluntary Agreement Concerning Liability for Oil Pollution) and CRISTAL (Contract Regarding and Interim Supplement to Tanker Liability for Oil Pollution).

[47] Convention for Oil Pollution Damage (1992 CLC, available at: <http://www.iopcfunds.org/uploads/tx_iopcpublications/Text_of_Conventions_e.pdf>.

[48] 1992 International Convention for the Establishment of an International Fund for Compensation for Oil Pollution Damage (the 1992 Fund Convention), available at: <http://www.iopcfunds.org/uploads/tx_iopcpublications/Text_of_Conventions_e.pdf>.

[49] UNCTAD, 10. [50] UNCTAD, 11.

The Erika incident in 2000 resulted in amendments to the 1992 Protocol which further increased compensation levels by 50%. The amendments are binding on all States parties to the 1992 CLC and the 1992 Fund Convention. Higher limits of compensation are available to the Parties to these Conventions regarding oil pollution incidents occurring after 2003. After the Prestige incident an optional third tier of compensation was established by way of the 2003 Supplementary IOPC Fund Protocol to the 1992 IOPC Fund (entered into force in 2005),[51] up to an aggregate maximum amount of 750 million Special Drawing Rights ('SDR', a basket currency[52]) per incident (approximately US $ 1157.2 million). The maximum liability of the shipowner depends on the tonnage of the ship. Under the 1969 CLC, the shipowner is entitled to limit its liability in respect to one incident to an aggregate maximum of SDR 14 million. The overall aggregate compensation per incident under the 1992 CLC and 1992 Fund Convention is SDR 203 million (irrespective of the ship size). The overall amount of compensation per incident depending on ship size under the 1992 CLC is limited to a maximum of SDR 89.77 million.[53]

The territorial scope of the CLC 1969 is rather narrow and covers only a State's territory and territorial sea. The 1992 CLC extended this scope encompassing also the exclusive economic zone ('EEZ') of States. Both treaties cover pollution damage caused by persistent oil escaping or discharged by a tanker carrying oil in bulk as its cargo. The term pollution damage is defined as loss or damage caused outside the ship by contamination resulting from the escape or discharge of oil from the ship, along with impairment of the environment and the costs of preventive measures (article 1(6) of 1992 CLC; article 1(2) of Fund Convention; article 1(6) of the Supplementary Fund Convention).[54] Both instruments lay out a strict liability regime.[55] As in most such regimes, the liable entity, ie the registered shipowner, benefits from a monetary cap the amount of which depends on the ship's tonnage.[56] In addition, the shipowner also benefits from some liability exemptions, in cases of war or natural disaster, or when the casualty has been entirely caused by the intentional act of a third party, or when public authorities have been negligent in maintaining lights or other navigational aids. The shipowner may also plead contributory negligence from the claimant as a defence.[57] The shipowner may not avail itself of the applicable cap if it has acted with some level of fault. Under the 1969 CLC such will be the case if the claimant establishes that the incident was the result of 'actual fault or privity', ie knowledge of the shipowner. Similarly, under the 1992 CLC, the limitation of liability will not be available if the pollution damage resulted from an 'intentional act or omission' or when the shipowner acted 'recklessly with knowledge that such damage would probably result'. Finally, both conventions provide for mandatory insurance in order to ensure that the reparation of loss is not defeated by the insolvency of the liable entity.[58]

The 1992 IOPC Fund provides a second tier of compensation in some specific cases: when no liability for pollution damage results from the 1992 CLC; or when the shipowner

[51] 2003 Supplementary IOPC Fund Protocol to the 1992 IOPC Fund, available at: <http://www.iopcfunds.org/uploads/tx_iopcpublications/Text_of_Conventions_e.pdf>.

[52] A SDR is the unit of currency of the International Monetary Fund, approximately equal to 1.5 US dollars.

[53] 2003 Supplementary IOPC Fund Protocol to the 1992 IOPC Fund, 12.

[54] UNCTAD, 'Liability and Compensation for Ship-Source Pollution', 14.

[55] UNCTAD, 'Liability and Compensation for Ship-Source Pollution', 10.

[56] UNCTAD, 'Liability and Compensation for Ship-Source Pollution', 15.

[57] UNCTAD, 'Liability and Compensation for Ship-Source Pollution', 15.

[58] UNCTAD, 'Liability and Compensation for Ship-Source Pollution', 15–16.

cannot compensate in full and insurance falls short of the amounts due; or when the damage goes beyond the liability limitation of the shipowner under the 1992 CLC.[59] However, there are also some exceptions to compensation by the IOPC Fund, such as cases of pollution that occurred in States that are not parties to the 1992 IOPC Fund, or when the pollution damage resulted from war or, still, when the claimant has failed to establish that the damage resulted from an incident that involved a covered ship. The IOPC Fund may also plead contributory negligence to limit compensation.[60]

The 2003 Supplementary Fund Protocol provides a third tier of compensation that comes into play when the 1992 CLC and 1992 IOPC Fund provide insufficient coverage. The 2003 Supplementary Protocol is only open to States parties to the previous two treaties. The Supplementary IOPC Fund established by the Protocol provides compensation for pollution damage occurring in a State party and only to the extend that the claims have been recognized by the 1992 IOPC Fund but exceed the relevant compensation limit ('established claims').[61]

Finally, two industry initiatives, the 2006 Small Tankers Oil Pollution Indemnification Agreement ('STOPIA') and the Tanker Oil Pollution Indemnification Agreement ('TOPIA'), must also be mentioned. These two schemes have been established by the shipping industry to compensate for the imbalance introduced by the 2003 Supplementary IOPC Fund. The two Agreements provide a mechanism for the IOPC Fund to reallocate liability to the relevant industries. Thus, they do not operate at the level of individual victims of oil pollution damage.[62]

3.1.4.2.2. Jurisprudential applications: Cases relating to liability for oil pollution are notoriously complex. One such example concerns the grounding of the tanker *Erika*. Erika, a Maltese registered tanker broke down off the coast of Brittany (France) resulting in substantial harm to the coast of Brittany, including various enterprises and communities and environmental damage. Its cargo belonged to a Panama branch of the French company 'Total International Ltd' ('TOTAL SA'). The case involved both criminal and civil claims. It was decided in the first instance by the Tribunal de Grande Instance in Paris, which rendered a judgment in 2008. An appeal followed this decision.[63]

The judgment of first instance discussed all individuals involved in this case: Mr Savarese (Tevere Shipping), the owner of the tanker; Mr Pollara (who executed work on Erika, commissioned by the owner); RINA— a classification society (according to an expert, who examined Erika, it did not conform to the standards imposed by RINA and should not have been accredited); and finally, the French oil company TOTAL SA, the owner of the cargo. The Court found that all parties contributed to the Erika disaster. It decided that these various parties and entities committed acts that led to criminal liability based on Act Nr 83-583 of 1983, a statute which attached criminal liability for pollution following an accident at sea resulting from fault.[64]

[59] UNCTAD, 'Liability and Compensation for Ship-Source Pollution', 16.

[60] UNCTAD, 'Liability and Compensation for Ship-Source Pollution', 16.

[61] UNCTAD, 'Liability and Compensation for Ship-Source Pollution', 17.

[62] UNCTAD, 'Liability and Compensation for Ship-Source Pollution', 18–19.

[63] Faure, M., 'Criminal Liability for Oil Pollution Damage: An Economic Analysis', in Faure, M., Lixin, H., and Hongjun, S. (eds), *Maritime Pollution Liability and Public Policy—China, Europe, and the US* (Kluwer Law International 2010), 183.

[64] Faure, 'Criminal Liability for Oil Pollution Damage', 183–4.

In 2010 the Court of Appeal confirmed the criminal liability of the four parties for the offence of causing pollution. The Court of Appeal also confirmed civil liability imposed on the parties except for TOTAL SA.[65] This case is noteworthy because the grounding of a vessel was decided under criminal law. Other unusual features were the presence among the accused parties of the classification society RINA and the analysis of the interactions between French and European law and international conventions.[66] The Court held that there is no conflict between the French law on environmental pollution and the International Convention for the Prevention of Pollution from Ships ('MARPOL'). It also noted that the definition of oil pollution under MARPOL is so wide that the sinking of a tanker due to earlier negligence or omissions can be assessed as wrongdoing. In addition, the Court established that the 1992 Civil Liability Convention for Oil Pollution ('CLC') provides coverage for civil liability. Applying this framework, the Court concluded *inter alia* that while the owner of the tanker may benefit from civil compensation based on the CLC, it is not protected for its wrongdoing under criminal law. Regarding the operator and the classification company, they are not covered by the terms of the CLC and cannot rely on its channelling system. As for the shipper, TOTAL SA, it was guilty of criminal wrongdoing but, on a civil level, it can benefit from the CLC's channelling system.[67] All four parties were thus found guilty of 'environmental crime', but on different grounds and with different consequences. On this basis, the Court assessed the applicable fines. The total amounted to 200 million Euros. However, the Court also held that TOTAL SA was exempt from civil liability under the terms of the CLC, while considering that it had already paid compensation on a voluntary basis for a total amount of 170 million Euros.[68]

The decision was challenged before the Court of Cassation on the grounds *inter alia* that France had no jurisdiction to prosecute criminally oil spills occurring beyond its territorial sea, in its exclusive economic zone, and that TOTAL SA could not benefit from the channelling in the event of gross negligence. In 2012 the Court of Cassation rendered its judgment partially annulling and reforming the decision of the Court of Appeal.[69] The Court of Cassation rejected the argument that France had no jurisdiction and admitted the challenge against the exemption of civil liability of TOTAL SA, on the grounds that the 'channelling' protections stemming from CLC were not applicable in the event of gross negligence or recklessness.

Another example of the complexity of such cases is the *Prestige* case.[70] The Bahamas-registered tanker Prestige ran aground off the coast of Spain. Approximately 63,272 tonnes of heavy fuel oil were spilled. The spill resulted in damage to fisheries, aquaculture, tourism, and business in Spain and France. Extensive clean-up and preventive measures were conducted in Spain, France, and Portugal. The shipowner's British insurer and the 1992 Fund established offices to handle claims in both Spain and France.

[65] See <http://www.iopcfunds.org/news-events/detail/item/82/>.

[66] Mink, E., '*Erika* Process: French Appeal Court Pronounced Judgment' July 10 (3) *Mainbrace 16*, available at <http://www.blankrome.com/index.cfm?contentID=37&itemID=2271>.

[67] Mink, '*Erika* Process: French Appeal Court Pronounced Judgment'.

[68] Mink, '*Erika* Process: French Appeal Court Pronounced Judgment'.

[69] Cour de Cassation, arrêt n° 3439 du 25 septembre 2012 (10-82.938) de la Chambre criminelle. The decision is available at: <http://www.courdecassation.fr/IMG/Crim_arret3439_20120925.pdf>.

[70] The following account is based on the Note of the Secretariat of the IOPC Funds, 'Prestige', 13 September 2011, available at: <http://www.documentservices.iopcfunds.org>.

Legal proceedings were initiated in these two countries as well as in the United States by Spain against the American Bureau of Shipping ('ABS'), the classification society that had certified the Prestige. In July 2010 the Criminal Court in Corcubión, in charge of investigating the cause of the incident, concluded that four persons should stand trial for criminal and civil liability, namely the master, the Chief Officer, the Chief Engineer of the Prestige, and the Spanish civil servant who refused to allow the ship into a place of refuge in Spain. The Court also found that the insurer and the 1992 Fund were directly as well as jointly and severally liable for the damages arising from the incident. Vicarious liability was imposed on the shipowner, the management company, and the Spanish State. At the time of writing, the legal proceedings in Spain were still ongoing. It must also be noted that, since 2003, Spain brought claims of more than USD 1 billion in civil suits against ABS before US Courts alleging that ABS was 'reckless' in certifying the ship seaworthy for its final voyage. However, these claims were dismissed in 2012 by a US Court of Appeals.[71]

### *3.1.4.3. Liability for nuclear damage*

The main difficulty relating to civil liability regimes regarding nuclear damage stems from the fact that since the early 1960s there have been two co-existing liability regimes. The first originated under the Organisation for Economic Co-operation and Development ('OECD'), which includes the 1960 Convention on Third Party Liability in the Field of Nuclear Energy (Paris Convention, entered into force in 1968) and the 1963 Brussels Supplementary Convention (entered into force in 1974).[72] The second was developed under the auspices of the International Atomic Energy Agency ('IAEA'), and includes the 1963 Convention on Civil Liability for Nuclear Damage (the Vienna Convention, entered into force in 1997).[73] The key difference between these two regimes was participation: the regime set up under the Vienna Convention was directed at global, worldwide participation, whilst the regime under the OECD was aimed at the participation mostly of the OECD members. The Chernobyl accident in 1986 was the reason that the IAEA initiated work on all aspects of nuclear liability in order to improve the basic Conventions and structure a comprehensive liability regime, and in 1988, following the cooperation by

[71] 'We conclude that we need not resolve the question whether a classification society may be held liable in tort to a third party such as Spain for reckless conduct in connection with the classification of vessels. Rather, we assume *arguendo* for purposes of this appeal that Defendants did owe the claimed duty to Spain. In our view, Spain has nonetheless failed to adduce sufficient evidence to create a genuine dispute of material fact as to whether Defendants recklessly breached that duty such that their actions constituted a proximate cause of the wreck of the Prestige', cited in 'ABS Cleared in "Prestige" Liability Suit' *gCaptain*, 29 August 2019, available at <http://gcaptain.com/cleared-prestige-charges/>.

[72] The Paris Convention and 1964 and 1982 Additional Protocols have 17 Contracting Parties; the 1964 Additional Protocol 1963 Brussels Supplementary Convention to the Paris Convention was amended by three Protocols successively adopted in 1964, 1982, and 2004. For the list of all Parties to the Paris Convention and Signatories see: <http://www.oecd-nea.org/law/paris-convention-ratification.html>. The Brussels Supplementary Convention has 11 Parties. For the list of Parties and Signatories see: <http://www.oecd-nea.org/law/brussels-convention-ratification.html>.

[73] For text of all Conventions see: <http://www.iaea.org/Publications/Documents/Conventions/liability.html>. There are 39 Parties to the Vienna Convention. See the list of the Parties and Signatories: <http://www.iaea.org/Publications/Documents/Conventions/liability_status.pdf>. There are 11 Parties to the Protocol to Amend the Vienna Convention on Civil Liability for Nuclear Damage: <http://www.iaea.org/Publications/Documents/Conventions/protamend_status.pdf>.

the IAEA and OECD/NEA, the Joint Protocol Relating to the Application of the Vienna Convention and the Paris Convention was adopted (see below).[74]

The Vienna Convention was amended by the 1997 Protocol to Amend the Vienna Convention on Civil Liability for Nuclear Damage and the 1997 Convention on Supplementary Compensation for Nuclear Damage (entered into force 2003). The Paris Convention was amended several times by Protocols adopted in 1964, 1982, (entered into force in 1988 and in 1991 respectively) and 2004 (not yet in force). Contracting parties to the OECD Paris (and Brussels) Conventions signed Amending Protocols which brought the Paris Convention more into line with the IAEA Conventions amended or adopted in 1997.[75] In 1988 a Joint Protocol Relating to the Application of the Vienna Convention and the Paris Convention (Joint Protocol) was adopted (entered into force in 1992).[76] The Joint Protocol established a link between both Conventions, combining them into one expanded liability regime. The parties to the Joint Protocol are treated as though they are the Parties to both Conventions and choice of rule of law is provided to determine which of two Conventions should apply to the exclusion of the other in respect of the same incident.

The main principles of these Conventions have been summarized as follows: strict liability of the nuclear operator; exclusive liability of the operator of a nuclear installation; compensation without discrimination based on nationality, domicile, or residence; mandatory financial coverage of the operator's liability; exclusive jurisdiction (only courts of the State in which the nuclear accident occurs have jurisdiction); limitation of liability in amount and in time.[77] Strict liability means that it is not based on fault, presence of which (or of negligence) does not have to be proved by the Claimant.[78] In order to ensure that sufficient funds will be available mandatory insurance coverage has to be obtained by the operator (the amounts are set by domestic law).[79]

The liability cap set by the Paris Convention was SDR 15 million but the Brussels Supplementary Convention subsequently increased the cap to SDR 300 million, including contributions both from the installation State, of up to SDR 175 million, and from other States parties to the Convention collectively based on their installed nuclear capacity, for the balance.[80] The 1963 Brussels Supplementary Convention is based on a three-tiered system of compensation. The first tier of compensation is derived from the nuclear operator's liability under the Paris Convention. The second tier is provided by the State where the accident occurs, which must cover the difference between the level of operator's liability (set by domestic law) and SDR 70 million.

74 World Nuclear Association, available at <http://www.world-nuclear.org/info/Safety-and-Security/Safety-of-Plants/Liability-for-Nuclear-Damage/#.UdL-LvJrhbA>.

75 Text of the OECD Convention available at <http://www.oecd-nea.org/law/paris-convention.html>. See also <http://www.world-nuclear.org/info/Safety-and-Security/Safety-of-Plants/Liability-for-Nuclear-Damage/#.UX-m0PJfKIA>.

76 Joint Protocol Relating to the Application of the Vienna Convention and the Paris Convention (Joint Protocol) was adopted (entered into force in 1992). Available at <http://www.iaea.org/Publications/Documents/Infcircs/Others/inf402.shtml>.

77 See World Nuclear Association, 'Liability for Nuclear Damage'. Available at: <http://www.world-nuclear.org/info/Safety-and-Security/Safety-of-Plants/Liability-for-Nuclear-Damage/#.UYDVFPJfKIB>. The following presentation is based on this document.

78 World Nuclear Association, 'Liability for Nuclear Damage'.

79 World Nuclear Association, 'Liability for Nuclear Damage'.

80 World Nuclear Association, 'Liability for Nuclear Damage'.

The third tier is based on contributions from all States parties to the Convention and brings an additional amount of up to SDR 50 million, for a total of SDR 120 million. This amount, set in 1963, has since then been increased. Indeed, the second tier was subsequently raised to the difference between the amount for which the operator is liable under domestic law and SDR 175 million, whereas the third tier was increased to SDR 125 million, for a total of SDR 300 million available for compensation.[81] Regarding the system of the IAEA Vienna Convention, as last amended in 1997, the cap applicable to the liability of the operator reaches SDR 300 million. The definition of nuclear damage encompasses environmental damage and preventive measures. The amended system also extends the geographical reach of the Convention, as well as the period within which a claim for loss of life or personal injury may be brought.[82]

The 1988 Joint Protocol sought to harmonize the situation of victims subject to one of the two systems by considering States parties to the Protocol as being parties to both conventions.[83] Further attempts at harmonizing and extending both systems were made in 2004 with the signature of amending protocols to the Paris Convention. These amendments, which are not yet in force, aim to bring the system of the Paris Convention more in line with that of the amended IAEA Vienna Convention as well as to expand the protection accorded to victims in case of nuclear accident. The need for such expansion was tragically recalled by the 2011 Fukushima accident. Half of the nuclear reactors of the World are indeed outside of both the Paris or the Vienna systems.[84]

In conclusion it may be said that despite some similarities, the regime for compensation for nuclear liability damage differs from that of oil pollution as it also includes certain residual State involvement, whilst the liability regime for oil pollution is based entirely on civil (private) schemes. Moreover, whereas oil pollution regimes have so far been quite effective, nuclear liability regimes are a source of contention between States and appear not to offer a sufficient cover.

## 3.2. *Domestic regimes: Selected case studies*

### 3.2.1. Overview

This Section will deal with environmentally-specific liability regimes which can be distinguished from other regimes through which environmental damage can also be redressed, such as, for example, common law torts. In the law of torts, negligence is the main concept on which the protection of victims against personal injury, damage to property, and economic loss is based.[85] All kinds of negligence include three fundamental features: the defendant should be bound by the duty of care; he must be in breach of this duty of care; the breach of that duty must result in damage to the plaintiff.[86] In English law, torts of nuisance may be actionable in private and public law. Most cases of public nuisance are deemed to be crime. Private nuisance is defined as an interference with the use or enjoyment of any land in which a person has a proprietary interest. Private nuisance is only actionable if it emanates from the defendant's land.[87]

81 World Nuclear Association, 'Liability for Nuclear Damage'.
82 World Nuclear Association, 'Liability for Nuclear Damage'.
83 World Nuclear Association, 'Liability for Nuclear Damage'.
84 World Nuclear Association, 'Liability for Nuclear Damage'.
85 Farahani, 'Liability and Compensation Regime for Oil Pollution Damage', 9.
86 Farahani, 'Liability and Compensation Regime for Oil Pollution Damage', 9.
87 Farahani, 'Liability and Compensation Regime for Oil Pollution Damage', 10.

### 3.2.2. The EU Environmental Liability Directive

#### *3.2.2.1. The legal framework*

The EU Liability Directive[88] is based on the 'polluter-pays principle' (article 1). The Directive covers environmental damage and other damage as defined by article 1.[89]

Damage is defined as a measureable adverse change in natural resource or measurable impairment of natural service which may occur directly or indirectly. Environmental damage covers the following:

(a) damage to protected species and natural habitats that have significant adverse effects on reaching or maintaining the favourable conservation status of such habitats or species. This definition covers species and habitats mentioned in Directives 79/409 and 92/43. Member States can include other species or habitats in the protection;
(b) water damage. This relates to any damage that significantly affects the ecological, chemical and/or quantitative status and/or ecological potential 'as defined in Directive 2000/60/EC of the water concerned';
(c) land damage. This is any land contamination that creates a significant risk of human health being adversely affected as a result of the direct or indirect introduction, in, or under land, of substances, preparations, organisms, or microorganisms.

According to article III, the Directive refers to environmental damage where it is caused by activities listed in Annex III.[90] The Directive adopts a wide definition of environmental damage. Article 5 covers indeed situations where environmental damage has not yet occurred but there is an imminent threat of such damage. For activities listed in Annex III, responsibility for environmental damage is structured as a strict liability system (applicable to 'environmental damage caused by any occupational activities listed in Annex III, and to any imminent threat of such damage occurring by reasons of any of those activities', article 3.1 a). The strict liability scheme covers damage to EU protected natural habitats and species, waters covered by the Water Framework Directive, and soil pollution, if the damage exceeds the applicable thresholds.[91] However, the Directive also includes fault and negligence-based liability of an operator in relation to damage to protected species and natural habitats caused by any occupational activities other than those listed in Annex III, and to any imminent threat of such damage occurring by reason of any of those activities (article 31.b).[92] It applies to any occupational activity. Occupational activity is defined in

[88] Directive 2004/35/CE of the European Parliament and of the Council of 21 April 2004 on Environmental Liability with Regard to the Prevention and Remedying of Environmental Damage, L 143/56 EN *OJEU* 30.4.2004EUR lex, available at <http://eur-lex.europa.eu/LexUriServ/LexUriServ.do?uri=CELEX:32004L0035:EN:NOT>. See Wolfrum, R., Langenfeld, C., and Minnerop, P., *Environmental Liability in International Law: Towards a Coherent Conception* (Erich Schmidt Verlag 2005); Bergkamp, L. and Goldsmith, B. J. (eds), *The EU Environmental Liability Directive: A Commentary* (Oxford University Press 2013); Betlem. G. and Brans E. (eds), *Environmental Liability and the EU: The 2004 Directive compared with US Member State Law* (Cameron & May 2006); van den Brock, G., 'Environmental Liability and nature Protection Areas. Will the EU Liability Directive Actually Lead to the Restoration of Damage Resources?' (2009) 5 *Utrecht Law Review* 117.

[89] Krämer, L., 'Directive 2004/35/EC on Environmental Liability', in Betlem and Brans, *Environmental Liability and the EU*, 29.

[90] The Annex lists activities covered by several Directives or Regulations.

[91] Krämer, 'Directive 2004/35/EC on Environmental Liability', 32.

[92] 'damage to protected species and natural habitats caused by any occupational activities other than those listed in Annex III, and to any imminent threat of such damage occurring by reason of any of those activities, whenever the operator has been at fault or negligent'.

article 2.7 as 'any activity carried out in the course of economic activity, as a business or an undertaking, irrespectively of its private or public, profit or non-profit character'.

Liability is bestowed on the operator (article 6.1).[93] 'Operator' is defined in the Directive as any natural or legal person who operates or controls an occupational activity or, when it is provided for in national legislation. The type of liability in the Directive is very complex. In broad brushstrokes it may be said that damage for habitats and species protected under the EU or nature conservation is covered (notwithstanding whether or not it is caused by a dangerous activity) but the type of liability varies depending on the kind of activity that caused damage (strict liability applying to activities covered by the EU legislation, listed in Annex III, which has already been amended several times). Damage to waters covered by the Framework Water Directive and soil pollution can be recovered only if caused by such activities. If damage was caused by an activity not listed in EU legislation, States and other persons must have recourse to their national laws in order to remedy the damage.[94] According to article 6(3):

> competent authority shall require that the remedial measures are taken by the operator. If the operator fails to comply with the obligations laid down in paragraph 1 or 2(b), (c) or (d), cannot be identified or is not required to bear the costs under this Directive, the competent authority may take these measures itself, as a means of last resort.

The Directive's objective is, as well, restoration of damage to natural resources. The Directive's preferred method is restoration of damaged resources rather than monetary value of the affected natural resources (article 7.2, Annex II). The Directive also addresses so-called 'interim losses' which relate to liability for the loss or impairment of natural resources and natural resource services during the restoration (articles 2(13) and Annex II (1 c–d)).[95] The cost for preventive and remedial action shall be borne by the operator (article 8.1).

There are a number of exclusions from the Directive. The Directive does not apply to environmental damage or to an imminent threat of such damage, if it is caused or threatened to be caused by an act of armed conflict, hostilities, or civil war, or by a natural phenomenon of exceptional, inevitable, or irresistible character (article 4.1). Further, the Directive does not cover damage which is covered by: international conventions relating to oil pollution damage; carriage of hazardous and noxious substances by sea; civil liability for damage caused during carriage of dangerous goods by road, rail, or inland ships; and nuclear risks (article 4.2–4.4 and Annexes IV and V). Also excluded from the Directive are national defence, international security, or civil protection activities (article 4.6). However, as has been noted, such civil liability Conventions have more limited scope with regard to preventive and remediation measures, and do not include coverage of interim losses.[96] The Directive also in general does not apply to damage caused by pollution of

[93] The operator has to take 'all practicable steps . . . in order to limit or to prevent further environmental damage and adverse effects on human health or further impairment of services and the necessary remedial measures'. These measures are specified in art 7.

[94] See generally on the Directive: Branes, E., 'Fundamentals of Liability For Environmental Harm under the ELD', in Bergkamp and Goldsmith, *The EU Environmental Liability Directive: A Commentary*, 42–43. See also Bergkamp, L. and van Bergeijk, A., 'Scope of the ELD Regime' in Bergkamp and Goldsmith, 51.

[95] The liable party may also have to cover the costs of assessing damages, administrative, legal and enforcement costs, data collection costs, and monitoring oversight costs. See Bergkamp and Goldsmith, 'The EU Environmental Liability Directive: A Commentary', 39.

[96] Bergkamp and Goldsmith, 'The EU Environmental Liability Directive: A Commentary', 44. Brans, E., 'Fundamentals of Liability for Environmental Harm under the ELD', in Bergkamp and Goldsmith, *The EU Environment Liability Directive*, 44.

a diffuse nature, only when it is possible to establish a causal link between activities of individual operators (article 4.5).

The Directive applies to damage caused by emissions, events, or incidents which took place after the date of the Directive's date of transposal, which is 30 May 2007. It does not apply to damage which was caused after this date, if the damage derived from a specific activity which took place and finished before 15 May 2007. It also has no application if more than 30 years have passed since the emission, event, or incident which resulted in the damage occurred (article 17).

The operator has a defence if the environmental damage was caused by a third party, or resulted from compliance with a compulsory order or instruction deriving from a public authority (article 8.3). A right to request the competent authorities to take action to prevent or remedy environmental damage is bestowed on natural and legal persons who are affected or are likely to be affected by environmental damage. A non-governmental organization promoting environmental protection shall be deemed to have sufficient interest or to have rights capable of being impaired. These persons shall have access to a court or other independent and impartial public body to review the substantial and legality of the decisions, acts, and failures of the competent authority (articles 12 and 13).

The EC Directive does not have the legal character of a civil liability regime; it is 'in essence a public or administrative law regime'.[97] This is due to the fact that such a liability is enforced only by public authorities through duties imposed on the operator to take measures to prevent and/or to remedy environmental damage.[98] According to Annex II the restoration of damage to waters and protected species and natural habitats is effected through primary, complementary, and compensatory remediation measures.[99] An exception to the above-mentioned measures is soil pollution cases. Annex II states that the measures adopted in such a case should:

> ensure, as a minimum, that the relevant contaminants are removed, controlled, contained or diminished so that the contaminated land, taking into account its current use or approved future use at the time of damage, no longer poses significant risk of adversely affecting human health (Annex II. 2).

The EU Environmental Liability Directive has been assessed as an important development in redress of environmental damage. One of the most important features of this Directive is that it is of no importance for its application whether the affected natural resources are owned publicly or privately or un-owned, as the public authorities act as trustees of covered natural resources and the legal status of these resources is irrelevant.

[97] Brans, 'Fundamentals of Liability for Environmental Harm under the ELD', 38.

[98] Brans, 'Fundamentals of Liability for Environmental Harm under the ELD', providing more information on the advantages and disadvantages of this liability regime.

[99] By primary remediation is understood 'any remedial measure which returns the damaged natural resources and/or impaired services to, or towards, the baseline condition' (Annex II). Complimentary remediation is defined as 'any remedial measure taken in relation to natural resources and/or services to compensate for the fact that primary remediation does not result in fully restoring the damaged natural resources and/or services' (Annex II). Compensatory measures are required during the remediation period and they are aimed at compensation during the interim period. This type of compensation may involve additional improvements to protected natural habitats and species or waters at either the damaged site or alternative site (specific equivalency methods are included in Annex II), see also Brans, 'Fundamentals of Liability for Environmental Harm under the ELD', 40.

However, there are certain features of this Directive which many impede application of the regime in specific cases. Such provisions are, for example, the threshold criteria, the damage assessment rules of Annex II, and, depending on how the Directive has been implemented in member States concerned, the available defences.[100] As Brans noted, 'the resulting uncertainty and risks cause member States to be cautious in applying the regime'.[101] Other factors impeding the application of the Directive are the lack of the insurance and the danger of insolvency. Therefore, the Directive although a very important legal instrument, 'is not without its problems'.[102]

### *3.2.2.2. Jurisprudential applications*

There are several recent cases which arose under article 18 of the Liability Directive. Member States must report to the Commission regarding the experience gained in the application of this Directive (including the information articulated in Annex VI). Member States must also report the following issues: (1) the type of environmental damage; (2) classification of legal person(s); (3) whether judicial proceedings were required; (4) the outcome of the remedial activities; (5) the date the proceedings closed; and (6) any additional information and/or data that the member States identify as useful for the purposes of evaluating the Directive's effectiveness.[103] Goldsmith et al refer to a number of cases relating to these obligations. These cases concern Greece, Poland, and the United Kingdom.

In Greece, the Coordination Office for the Directive Implementation ('SYGAPEZ') has received approximately 30 cases for administrative examination under the Greek legislation transposing the Directive. To identify the damage in each instance the governmental authority asked the operators to submit the data (with chemical analysis or other measurements of soil or water characteristics). Additionally, they have been requested to submit detailed reports on the actions undertaken to remedy environmental damage. Approximately five cases have resulted in a proposal for remedial measures, implementation of which is at present monitored by governmental authorities.[104]

In Poland, 83 cases were reported in 2009, which required prevention and/or remediation of environmental damage (13 cases of land and water damage; 3 cases of water damage). In 2010, 65 cases were reported (33 cases of land damage; 18 cases of damage of land and water; 11 cases of protected habitats and species damage; 3 cases of water damage).[105] In the United Kingdom, a public website is maintained by the Department of Environment, Food and Rural Affairs, which provides updated information on the implementation of the Directive, including Incidents Reports. In the 2009 Incidents Report, 4 incidents were reported (3 involving alleged land damage; 1 involving water damage). The 2010 Incident Report concerned 4 alleged cases of land damage; 2 alleged cases of damage to protected species and habitats. In 2011, there were 3 incidents reported of alleged damage to protected areas and habitats.[106]

Goldsmith et al present a detailed example of a UK case concerning the implementation of the Directive, concerning water damage. Due to a failure at a water company pumping

[100] Brans, 'Fundamentals of Liability for Environmental Harm under the ELD', 49.

[101] Brans, 49. [102] Brans, 50.

[103] Goldsmith, B., DeSanti, R. J., and Lockhart-Mummery, E., 'Case-Studies', in Bergkamp and Golsdmith, 250–1.

[104] Goldsmith et al, 'Case Studies', 252. [105] Goldsmith et al, 'Case Studies', 253.

[106] Goldsmith et al, 'Case Studies', 253.

station, a sewage discharge was introduced into a river in July 2009. The discharge led to the reduction of oxygen levels, which further resulted in significant fish kill. A report of the Environmental Agency noted the decrease in the water body's biological quality from 'good' to 'poor' status and that this reduced the water's body ecological quality in a stretch of 3 km from 'good' to 'poor'. Based on these findings the Environmental Agency determined that the incident fell under the Directive's transposing legislation. The water company agreed to restock the river and the parties conducted a damage and remediation evaluation. Subsequently, various options were considered for compensation for significant services losses (such as restocking; habitats improvements; access improvements; and combinations thereof). Habitat equivalency analysis was used to determine the scale of measures required and the remediation option were assessed using the criteria specified in the Directive. The Environmental Agency concluded, having consulted with the fishing community and other stakeholders, to pursue the option of a combination of habitat and access improvements. These measures were completed in 2012.[107]

### 3.2.3. Liability for environmental damage in the United States

#### *3.2.3.1. The CERCLA*

3.2.3.1.1. The legal framework: The 1980 Comprehensive Environmental Response, Compensation and Liability Act ('CERCLA') is a very complex piece of legislation and only a very general discussion of its structure can be provided in this chapter.[108]

Section 104(a) of CERCLA authorizes the President to respond to a release (or substantial threat thereof) of a hazardous substance into the environment, or of a pollutant or contaminant which may present an 'imminent and substantial danger to the public health or welfare'. Such authority has been delegated to the Environmental Protection Agency (EPA) and other federal agencies. Response actions taken under CERCLA may include: clean-up activities involving the containment, removal, or treatment of environmental contamination to prevent potentially harmful exposure; and may also include the temporary or permanent relocation of potentially exposed individuals if so warranted.[109] There are several exclusions from CERCLA, which are regulated by other acts (eg releases of petroleum or of nuclear materials). Section 101(22) also excludes three other types of releases from the CERCLA: (1) a release that would result in exposure solely within the workplace; (2) emissions from the engine exhaust of a motor vehicle, train, aircraft, vessel, or power pumping station; and (3) the 'normal' application of fertilizer.[110]

The system under the CERCLA rests upon the identification by response authorities of priority sites (they must develop a National Priorities List or 'NPL' of federal or

[107] Goldsmith et al, 'Case Studies', 253–4.

[108] This Act was amended several times: 1986 Superfund Amendments and Reauthorisation Act; 1990 Omnibus Budget Reconciliation; 1992 Community Environmental Response Facilitation Act; 1996 National Defence Authorisation Act for Fiscal Year 1997; 1999 Superfund Recycling Equality Act; 2002 Small Business Liability Relief and Brownfields Revitalisation Act. See Bearden, D. M., 'Comprehensive Environmental Response, Compensation, and Liability Act: A Summary of Superfund Clean-up Authorities and Related Provisions of the Act', Congressional Research Service (2012), available at <http://www.fas.org/sgp/crs/misc/R41039.pdf>. The following presentation is based on Bearden's study.

[109] Bearden, 'Comprehensive Environmental Response, Compensation, and Liability Act', 5.

[110] Bearden, 'Comprehensive Environmental Response, Compensation, and Liability Act', 6–7, also noting that Section 104(a)(3) further limits the authority under CERCLA to respond to releases of hazardous substances, pollutants, or contaminants in certain situations.

State sites) and their ranking (through a Hazard Ranking System or 'HRS' which is annually updated by the EPA[111]) as well as on the legal authority provided to such agencies to adopt response actions. The latter consist of either 'removal' or 'remedial' actions (Sections 101(23) 22 and 101(24) 23 of CERCLA respectively). Under Section 104(c)(3), the State where a non-federal NPL site is located shares the costs of remedial actions taken at that site, as a precondition for federal financing of such actions (through the so-called Superfund).[112] Importantly, the CERCLA calls for the general public to be consulted on the type of remedial actions to be adopted at individual sites (this requirement does not apply to removal actions).[113]

Section 107(a) establishes a liability system for the costs associated with response actions, damage to natural resources, or public health assessments, among others.[114] The courts have interpreted the liability arising under Section 107 of CERCLA to be strict, joint and several, and retroactive. There are defences to liability: an act of God; an act of war; an act or omission of a third party with whom the defendant has no contractual relationship, if the defendant exercised due care with respect to the hazardous substance and took precautions against foreseeable acts or omissions of that third party and against the foreseeable consequences of such acts or omissions; or any combination of these three circumstances.[115]

The CERCLA established the Hazardous Substance Superfund Trust Fund to provide financial resources for the federal government to cover the clean-up of contaminated sites where the responsible parties cannot pay or cannot be identified.[116] Finally, if the responsible parties can be identified and are not insolvent, the federal government can use three main mechanisms to enforce cleanup liability: judicial or administrative orders; cost recovery actions; and voluntary settlement agreements.[117] Although the EPA is responsible for enforcing clean-up liability, 1986 amendments to CERCLA authorized citizens to challenge the adequacy of a clean-up action in court.

3.2.3.1.2. Jurisprudential applications: An interesting application of CERCLA is *Pakootas v. Teck Cominco Metals LTD*, which is in many ways an iteration—at the domestic level—of the famous Trail Smelter Arbitration.[118]

Defendant Teck Cominco Metals is a Canadian corporation that owns and operates a lead-zinc smelter in Trail, British Columbia ('Trail Smelter'), close to the Canada-United States border. In the period between 1906 to 1995, the Trail Smelter discharged significant amounts of waste annually into the Canadian portion of the Columbia River. In August 1999, the group of affected minorities requested the US Environmental Protection Agency ('EPA') to study the pollution of the River in Northeastern Washington. The EPA found that the site was seriously contaminated. The plaintiffs, two members of the affected minorities (the Colville Tribes) filed a 'citizen suit' under CERCLA before a US federal court. They requested *inter alia* injunctive relief preventing Teck from continuing to pollute, and penalties for non-compliance.[119] A key contention of the plaintiffs was the extraterritorial application of CERCLA (to a Canadian company situated in Canada).

[111] Bearden, 7. [112] Bearden, 8–9. [113] Bearden,12. [114] Bearden, 13.
[115] See in depth on this issue Bearden, 14–15. [116] Bearden, 20–21. [117] Bearden, 23–29.
[118] 452 F.3d 1066 (9th Cir. 2006). See also in depth analysis of this decision: Zhang, L., '*Pakootas v. Teck Cominco Metals LTD*' *(2007) 3 HELR* 545. The following account is based on Zhang's study.
[119] Zhang, '*Pakootas v. Teck Cominco Metals LTD*' 546–7.

The court reasoned that CERCLA could be applied extraterritorially and found that Teck was potentially liable under CERCLA.[120] Teck filed an appeal but the case subsequently reached a settlement with the EPA. However, the action was not rendered moot because two of the plaintiffs (Pakootas and the State of Washington) were not parties to the settlement agreement.[121] On appeal, a circuit court concluded that CERCLA was not being applied extraterritorially but domestically in the present case and that Teck could be held liable under CERCLA for the environmental pollution. The release or threatened release of hazardous substances from the smelter into the United States was sufficient to establish liability under the CERCLA.[122]

*3.2.3.2. The OPA*

3.2.3.2.1. The legal framework: A short mention must be made of the 1990 Oil Pollution Act ('OPA') which was largely promulgated as a response to the *Exxon Valdez* incident. As noted above, oil pollution is excluded from the scope of the CERCLA. The OPA contains 80 sections, divided into 9 chapters, including comprehensive provisions on liability and compensation as well as prevention and removal. It has a wide scope of damages including natural resource damage. The OPA imposes liability on the 'responsible party', which is defined as a 'person owning, operating or demise chartering a vessel' (therefore the liability is imposed on the shipowner; operator; and demise charterer).[123]

The OPA is based on strict liability (Section 2702) with contributory negligence of the claimant also being taken into account. Section 2703 deals with exceptions from liability, which are: an act of God; and act of war; an act or omission of a third party; or a combination thereof. The damages under the OPA include damages to natural resources, rural or personal property, subsistence use, revenues, profits and earning capacity and public services, and costs of assessing damage. Under certain circumstances pure economic loss is also compensable.[124]

The OPA established the national Oil Spill Liability Trust Fund, which can provide up to USD one billion per spill incident. Section 1002(a) provides that the responsible party for a vessel or facility from which oil is discharged, or which poses a substantial threat of a discharge, is liable for: (1) certain specified damages resulting from the discharged oil; and (2) removal costs incurred in a manner consistent with the National Contingency Plan ('NCP'). Section 1002(d) provides that if a responsible party can establish that the removal costs and damages resulting from an incident were caused solely by an act or omission by a third party, the third party will be held liable for such costs and damages. Section 1004 provides that the liability for tank vessels larger than 3,000 gross tons is increased to USD 1,200 per gross ton or USD 10 million, whichever is greater. Responsible parties at onshore facilities and deep water ports are liable for up to USD 350 million per spill; holders of leases or permits for offshore facilities, except deep water ports, are liable for up to USD 75 dollars million per spill, plus removal costs. The Federal government has the authority to adjust, by regulation, the USD 350 million liability limit established for onshore facilities.

120 Zhang, '*Pakootas v. Teck Cominco Metals LTD*' 548.
121 Zhang, '*Pakootas v. Teck Cominco Metals LTD*' 548.
122 Zhang, '*Pakootas v. Teck Cominco Metals LTD*' 549.
123 Wang, *Civil Liability for Marine Oil Pollution damage*, 208. The following account is based on Hui Wang's study and on the information available on the website of the EPA: <http://www.epa.gov/osweroe1/content/lawsregs/opaover.htm>.
124 Wang, *Civil Liability for Marine Oil Pollution damage*, 210.

Moreover, the OPA requires contingency planning both by government and industry. The National Oil and Hazardous Substances Pollution Contingency Plan ('NCP') has been restructured to follow a three-tiered approach: the Federal government has direct responsibility for all public and private response efforts for certain types of oil spills; Area Committees—composed of federal, state, and local government officials—must develop detailed, location-specific Area Contingency Plans; and owners or operators of vessels and certain facilities that pose a serious threat to the environment are required to prepare their own Facility Response Plans.[125]

The OPA's provisions are very complex as they exist on two levels: federal and state laws. At the federal level the principal statute is the 1990 Oil Pollution Act. However, this Act does not pre-empt the right of individual states to promulgate their won legislation on oil pollution from ships. The US liability regime is two-tiered: the first tier is the liability of the shipping industry (this is strict liability of the shipowner, operator, and bareboat charterer, which may be joint and several). The second tier is the liability of the oil industry. Despite strong initial opposition to the OPA by all industries (including the insurers), they adapted to the requirements. Insurers argued that such liability would not be insurable, due to the restricted capacity of the insurance market, and the oil industry was wary of the possibility of the increased transportation and insurance costs thus leading to an increase in oil prices.[126]

3.2.3.2.2. Jurisprudential applications: In connection with the application of the OPA, one must mention the Deepwater Horizon 2010 oil spill in the Gulf of Mexico. From the legal point of view the BP Oil Spill is a very complex case in which the OPA played a significant role,[127] although many other aspects have been framed through different bodies of law. The OPA, with the Clean Water Act ('CWA') and other environmental law, provides a federal framework for oil spill liability, but explicitly does not pre-empt similar state laws.[128] In this case, BP voluntarily gave funds directly to the states and to a trust fund used to establish the Gulf Coast Claims Facility ('GCCF').[129] BP was sued under both the CWA and the OPA.[130]

### 3.2.4. Liability for environmental damage in the People's Republic of China

#### *3.2.4.1. The Tort Liability Law*

On December 26, 2009, China passed a Tort Liability Law ('TLL'), which came into force in 2010.[131] Article 1 of the General Provisions chapter of the TLL states that in addition to promoting 'social harmony and stability', the purpose of the TLL is to 'prevent and punish tortious conduct'.

[125] Information available on the aforementioned section of the EPA website. See also Wang, *Civil Liability for Marine Oil Pollution damage*, in particular 207–46.

[126] Wang, *Civil Liability for Marine Oil Pollution damage*, 223–4.

[127] On the legal dimension of this case see Osofsky, H. M., 'Multidimensional Governance and the BP Deepwater Horizon Oil Spill' (2011) 63 *Florida Law Review* 1077. Available at <http://scholarship.law.ufl.edu/flr/vol63/iss5/2>.

[128] Osofsky, 'Multidimensional Governance and the BP Deepwater Horizon Oil Spill' 1087.

[129] Osofsky, 1087. [130] Osofsky, 1087.

[131] See O'Meleveny and O'Myers LLP, 'China Adopts Environmental Tort Law' <http://www.omm.com/china-adopts-environmental-tort-law-01-20-2010/>; Kelley, J. E., 'Seeking Justice for Pollution Victims in China: Why China Should Amend the Tort Liability Law to Allow Punitive Damages in Environmental Tort Cases' (2012) 35 *Seattle University Law Review* 527. The following account is based on these two studies.

Chapter 8 of the Tort Liability Law (articles 65–8 of the TLL)[132] relates to specific provisions regarding liability for environmental pollution (ie environmental torts) and codifies special liability and evidentiary rules that are significantly more stringent than prior environmental legislation and court interpretations. Under this new law, a company that pollutes the environment will be strictly liable in tort for damage caused and will bear the burden of proof in respect of causation.[133] China has based TLL on the continental European civil law approach, however, the 'punish' language used therein is a deviation from continental European civil tort law, the purpose of which is to compensate a victim for his/her loss and to prevent future harm, but not to punish the violation.[134] The polluter is strictly liable (article 65) and the defendant bears the burden of proof (article 66). TLL provides for punitive damages only for products liability causes of action that arise under article 47 of the Product Liability chapter. They are not included for environmental damage.[135] China has weak and poorly-enforced environmental laws; therefore TLL, based on strict liability and a burden-shifting approach, 'is an important step in the development of law in China'.[136]

It is argued, however, that in order to make the TLL more effective in relation to environmental liability 'China should amend the TLL to add a punitive damages remedy for environmental pollution torts cases in which the polluter has knowledge that its activities do not meet environmental regulations yet continues to pollute'.[137] The compatibility of the prevention and punishment language in the General Provisions with the environmental tort liability articles should also be addressed.[138] It is also suggested that there is lack of continuity between the stated purpose of the law— to 'prevent and punish'— and the specific guiding statutory language in the Liability for Environmental Pollution Torts chapter. The TLL does not provide a mechanism to punish and deter polluters.[139]

### *3.2.4.2. Oil pollution compensation schemes*

An outline will be given of oil pollution compensation schemes in China.[140] The system is very complex as there are several relevant statutes: the 1999 Marine Environmental Protection Law of the Peoples' Republic of China ('MEPL', the first Act was promulgated in 1982 and amended in 1999); the China Maritime Code; and following the promulgation of MEPL in 1982, the 2009 Regulations on the Prevention and Control of Marine of Pollution from Ships (Regulations 2009, in force from 2010, which superseded the 1983 Regulations Concerning the Prevention of Pollution by Sea Areas by Vessels).

[132] Art 65: 'Where any harm is caused by environmental pollution, the polluter shall assume the tort liability'. Art 66: 'Where any dispute arises over an environmental pollution, the polluter shall assume the burden to prove that it should not be liable or its liability could be mitigated under certain circumstances as provided for by law or to prove that there is no causation between its conduct and the harm'. Art 67: 'Where the environmental pollution is caused by two or more polluters, the seriousness of liability of each polluter shall be determined according to the type of pollutant, volume of emission and other factors'. Art 68: 'Where any harm is caused by environmental pollution for the fault of a third party, the victim may require compensation from either the polluter or the third party. After making compensation, the polluter shall be entitled to be reimbursed by the third party'.

[133] O'Meleveny and O'Myers LLP, 'China Adopts Environmental Tort Law'.

[134] Kelley, 'Seeking Justice for Pollution Victims in China', 529.

[135] Art 47: 'Where a manufacturer or seller knowing any defect of a product continues to manufacture or sell the product and the defect causes a death or any serious damage to the health of another person, the victim shall be entitled to require the corresponding punitive compensation'. Kelley, 530.

[136] Kelley, 541. [137] Kelley, 545. [138] Kelley, 546. [139] Kelley, 547.

[140] See in depth, Wang, *Civil Liability for Marine Oil Pollution damage*, in particular 225–47. The following account is based on Wang's study.

Article 66 of MEPL provides that China shall implement civil liability for marine oil pollution and ensure the establishment of oil pollution insurance and a compensation fund. The compensation for oil pollution is shared by the shipowner and the cargo owner. However, this provision has not yet been in operation as no implementing legislation has been passed by the State Council and no compensation fund set up.[141] According to MEPL's article 90, pollution damage to marine environment should be eliminated by a polluter and also losses should be compensated (these civil law remedies are recognized by China in its tort laws).[142] This article is unclear and it has been interpreted in two ways. One is that the polluter compensates full damage and losses; therefore there is no ceiling to liability. The second interpretation entails that it is only a general principle that the polluter is strictly liable. The specific amount of compensation can be limited if the polluter complies with the conditions of the China Maritime Code for the shipowner, charterer, and operator, to limit his/her liability.[143] Article 90(2) relates to heavy losses from damages to marine ecosystems, marine aquatic resources, and marine nature reserves, suffered by the State. In such cases the relevant State departments will make a compensation demand to the polluter. However, this article only applies to 'heavy losses' and there is no definition of what is considered to be 'heavy'. Further, it only refers to losses suffered by a State and not by private parties. Such vague formulations result in a disadvantaged position for claimants bringing an action on the basis of the MEPL and it does not suffice to provide for satisfactory oil pollution compensation in practice.[144]

The China Maritime Code limits the polluter's liability. An important provision is article 208, which excludes from the scope of the Code claims for oil pollution damage under the 1992 (as amended 2000) CLC, to which China is a party. The Code's limitation of liability does not apply to cases where CLC applies. Shipowners, charterers, and operators can limit their liability under certain conditions specified in the Code (articles 207 and 210, principles of calculation). 2009 Regulations provide for further limitation of liability and also for compulsory insurance. On 2010 the Ministry of Transport promulgated the Implementing Measures on Civil Liability Insurance for Vessel-Source Pollution. Ships navigating Chinese waters must have insurance reflecting possible liability under CLC.[145] There are some issues concerning the application of CLC in China. Due to the lack of specific domestic rules, the application of CLC is not harmonized across regions and, therefore, liability and compensation frequently depends on courts' decisions, which vary.[146] It must also be added that China is not a party to the Fund Convention.

In conclusion it may be said that Chinese statutes do not have clear provisions on liability for oil pollution compensation and the scope of damages compensated. The general principle prevailing in China is that the shipowner is liable for clean-up costs. As for losses incurred by fishermen, there are no specific provisions as to whether and how they are recoverable.[147] Also, the lack of rules defining accurate liability limits add to a rather confused picture of liability for oil pollution in China. The requirement of compulsory financial guarantees was established very recently, which will help to effectively deal with insolvency of the shipowner.[148]

[141] Wang, 228. [142] Wang, 228. [143] Wang, 228. [144] Wang, 228–9.
[145] Wang, 233. [146] Wang, 237–42. [147] Wang, 227. [148] Wang, 242.

The International Oil Pollution Compensation Fund ('IOPC') is only available in the Hong Kong Special Administrative Region ('SAR'). China's reluctance to become a party to IOPC is of economic nature, as one of the largest importers of crude oil in the world would also be one of largest contributors to the IOPC.[149] As of 2012, an additional compensation source is available under the Chinese National Compensation Fund.[150]

## III) Relations with Other Principles

The core considerations of Principle 13 are somewhat at odds with the main approach followed in international environmental law, namely prevention. Reparation, whether it is viewed from the perspective of the polluter (responsibility/liability) or that of the injured party (compensation) only takes place when damage has occurred or, in other words, when it is too late to prevent it. Yet, reparation is important for two core principles of the Rio Declaration, ie the prevention principle (Principle 2) and the polluter-pays principle (Principle 16). These two principles are not only important at an international level but also at a domestic level, as a component of the general exhortation in Principle 11 of the Rio Declaration to enact environmental legislation.

Principle 13 relates to Principle 2 first as a form of extension of the prevention obligation stated in the latter. Principle 13 is an extension in two ways. First, by calling for States to adopt domestic legislation on liability and compensation for environmental damage it seeks to deter polluters or encourage them to prevent such damage. Second, it also encourages States to organize a system of compensation that may facilitate compensation of such damage, even when it takes place in a transboundary context. In the latter regard, the most efficient solution would be an international framework. Yet, Principle 13 recognizes that this is difficult to achieve and its call for domestic legislation must be understood as pointed not only to purely domestic environmental damage but also to damage with an international dimension.

Principle 13 also relates to Principles 11 and 16. It is a specific form of the environmental legislation called for in Principle 11 and it has the specific purpose of identifying the polluter targeted by Principle 16 and assigning consequences to its acts. The polluter-pays principle is indeed the foundation of the overwhelming majority of the liability regimes designed either at the domestic or at the international level. Although the polluter-pays principle may find expression beyond mere liability regimes (eg environmental taxation, efficiency standards, etc), such regimes are a major form of implementing it.

## IV) Assessment

This outline of the problems relating to Principle 13 of the Rio Declaration clearly indicates that after over twenty years there is not much progress in developing a coherent and uniform system of international and national regimes for liability for environmental

[149] Zhu, L. and Li, K. X., 'Compensation for Oil Pollution from Ships in China: A Way Toward International Standards (2013) 44 *Ocean Development and International Law* 90; See also Zhu, L., Dong, B. and Li K. X., 'China's 2012 Regime for Compensation for Vessel Oil Pollution: A Comparative Study' (2013) 44 *Ocean Development and International Law* 270.

[150] Zhu and Li, 'Compensation for Oil Pollution from Ships in China', 91.

damage. There are several obstacles, one of them being the lack of a widely accepted definition of the environment and environmental damage.

State responsibility rules do not offer much help in remedying environmental damage, which in fact is mostly due to activities of individuals and in any case only covers damage by a State resulting from wrongful acts. Civil liability of operators (*sine delicto*) embodied in the parameters suggested to States in the 2006 ILC Principles has not been influential in practice. Liability regimes based on MEAs are not particularly successful either, as illustrated by the still un-ratified Protocol of the Basel Convention. It appears that the most successful approach is the one taken by the regime on oil pollution, entirely based on the involvement of private actors. The nuclear liability regime (with residual State participation) is, instead, largely inadequate. National regimes vary greatly and some like the Chinese are very complex and not yet fully implemented.

It may be said that one of the common features of all liability regimes is that they are based on the polluter-pays principle. In the view of the present author there is still a long way forward before we reach uniform regimes which would be widely accepted by States.

## V) Select Bibliography


Bearden, D. M., 'Comprehensive Environmental Response, Compensation, and Liability Act: A Summary of Superfund Cleanup Authorities and Related Provisions of the Act', *Congressional Research Service* (2012).

Bergkamp, L., *Liability and the Environment* (The Hague: Kluwer Law International 2001).

Bergkamp, L. and Goldsmith, B. J., *EU Environmental Liability Directive: A Commentary* (Oxford University Press 2013).

Betlem, G. and Brans, E. (eds), *Environmental Liability and the EU. The 2004 Directive compared with US Member State Law* (London: Cameron & May 2006).

Boyle, A., 'State Responsibility and Liability for Injurious Consequences on Acts Not Prohibited by International Law: A Necessary Distinction?' (1990) 39 *ICLQ* 1.

Brans, E., 'Fundamentals of Liability for Environmental Harm under the ELD', in Bergkamp, L. and Goldsmith, B., *The EU Environment Liability Directive: A Commentary* (Oxford University Press 2013), 31.

Brunnée, J., 'On Sense and Sensibility: Reflections on International Liability Regime' (2004) 53 *ICLQ* 351.

Crawford, J., *The International Law Commission's Articles on State Responsibility, Introduction: Text and Commentaries* (Cambridge: Cambridge University Press 2002).

Douhan, A., 'Liability for Environmental Damage', in Wolfrum, R. (ed), *Max Planck Encyclopedia of Public International Law* (Oxford: Oxford University Press 2013).

Faure, M. G., Lixin, H., and Hongjun, S. (eds), *Maritime Pollution Liability and Policy: China, Europe and the United States* (The Hague: Kluwer Law International 2010).

Fitzmaurice, M., 'International Responsibility and Liability', in Bodansky, D., Brunee, J., and Hey, E. (eds), *The Oxford Handbook of International Environmental Law* (Oxford: Oxford University Press 2007), 1011.

Goldie, L. E. F., 'Concepts of Strict and Absolute Liability and Ranking Liability in Terms of relative Exposure to Risk' (1985) 16 *Netherlands Yearbook of International Law* 175.

Kelley, J. E., 'Seeking Justice for Pollution Victims in China: Why China Should Amend the Tort Liability Law to Allow Punitive Damages in Environmental Tort Cases' (2012) 35 *Seattle University Law Review* 527.

Kiss, A.-Ch., *L'abus de droit en droit international* (Paris: LGDJ 1952).

Kiss, A.-Ch. and Shelton, D., 'Strict Liability in International Environmental Law', in Nnidiaye, T. M. and Wolfrum, R. (eds) *The Law of the Sea, Environmental Law and Settlement of Disputes, Liber Amicorum Judge Thomas Mensah* (Leiden: Martinus Nijhoff Publishers 2007), 1131.

Kosolapova, E., *Interstate Liability for Climate Change-Related Damage* (The Hague: Eleven International Publishing 2013).

Krämer, L., 'Directive 2004/35/EC on Environmental Liability', in Betlem, G. and Brans, E. (eds), *Environmental Liability and the EU. The 2004 Directive compared with US Member State Law* (London: Cameron & May 2006), 29.

Lefeber, R., *Transboundary Environmental Interference and the Origin of State Responsibility* (The Hague: Kluwer Law International 1996).

Lefeber, R., 'The Real Significance of the Nagoya-Kuala Lumpur Supplementary Protocol. The result of Paradigm Evolution', Amsterdam Law School Research Paper No 2012-87 (2012).

Ling, C.Y., *The Rio Declaration on Environment and Development: An assessment* (Penang: Third World Network 2012).

Shibata, A., *International Liability Regime for Biodiversity Damage: The Nagoya-Kuala Lumpur Supplementary Protocol* (London: Routledge Research in International Environmental Law 2014).

Silva Soares, G. F. and Vieira Vargas, E., 'The Basel Liability Protocol on Liability and Compensation for Damage Resulting from Transboundary Movements of Hazardous Wastes and Their Disposal' (2001) 12 *YbIEL* 69.

Telesetsky, A., 'The 2010 Nagoya–Kuala Lumpur Supplementary Protocol: A New Treaty Assigning Transboundary Liability and Redress for Biosafety Damage Caused by Genetically Modified Organisms', in *ASIL Insights*, 10 January 2011.

United Nations Commission on Trade and Development, 'Liability and Compensation for Ship-Source Pollution: An Overview of the International Legal Framework for Oil Pollution Damage from Tankers', *Studies in Transport Law and Policy* 2012 No 1, UNCTAD/DTL/TLB/011/4.

van den Brock, G. M., 'Environmental Liability and nature Protection Areas. Will the EU Liability Directive Actually Lead to the Restoration of Damage Resources?' (2009) 5 *Utrecht Law Review* 117.

Wang H., *Civil Liability for Marine Oil Pollution damage. A Comparative Study of the International, US and Chinese Compensation Regime*' (Alpen aan den Rijn: Wouters Kluwer 2011).

Wolfrum, R., Langenfeld, C., and Minnerop, P., *Environmental Liability in International Law: Towards a Coherent Conception* (Berlin: Erich Schmidt Verlag 2005).

Zhang, L., 'Pakootas v. Teck Cominco Metals LTD' (2007) 3 *HELR* 545.

Zhu, L. and Li, K. X., 'Compensation for Oil Pollution from Ships in China: A Way Toward International Standards' (2013) 44 *Ocean Development and International Law* 90.

Zhu, L., Dong, B., and Li, K. X, 'China's 2012 Regime for Compensation for Vessel Oil Pollution: A Comparative Study' (2013) 44 *Ocean Development and International Law* 270.

# 18. Principle 14

## *Dangerous Activities and Substances*

Makane M. Mbengue*

**Principle 14**

States should effectively cooperate to discourage or prevent the relocation and transfer to other States of any activities and substances that cause severe environmental degradation or are found to be harmful to human health.



* Associate Professor, Faculty of Law, University of Geneva and Institute of Environmental Sciences (Geneva), Visiting Professor, Sciences Po Paris (School of Law). The author would like to express his gratitude to Susanna Waltman, PhD candidate at the University of Geneva, for her precious help in the preparation of this contribution.

# I) Origins and Rationale of the Principle

## 1. Overview

The transboundary movement of activities and substances that cause environmental degradation or are harmful to health is a continuing problem of modernity. Developing countries are particularly vulnerable to this problem due to reduced labour and operational costs and weaker regulation or enforcement that entice the relocation of hazardous activities and substances to their territories. This includes the exporting of waste for disposal and the dumping of hazardous substances and production activities that industrialized countries find cheaper and easier to dispose of in the less regulated developing world. Principle 14 is of vital importance, as it aims to prevent the dumping of hazardous substances and the relocation of hazardous operations in and to developing (and potentially developed) states.

As will be evidenced below, hazardous substances and activities are not governed by any single international instrument that establishes general principles or rules of general application to all such activities or substances. Principle 14 is the broadest normative enunciation on the matter, and is therefore of particular relevance to the development of the normative framework in this area. International agreements relevant to the discussion of Principle 14 are found in three main areas that create regulatory regimes covering three categories of goods: hazardous wastes, hazardous chemicals, and genetically modified organisms ('GMOs') and other aspects related to biodiversity management.[1] Principle 14 refers broadly to 'activities' and 'substances' that harm the environment and/or human health; it is therefore necessary to consider the issues surrounding the hazardous wastes regime, hazardous chemicals regime, and biodiversity management regime both in terms of the origins of the Principle and for the examination of the scope and impact of the Principle on international instruments.[2] These instruments are in the spirit of Principle 14, as a central theme throughout all three regimes is the protection of the environment and human health through the prevention or regulation of the transboundary movement of dangerous substances or activities. Since there is no general definition under international law as to what constitutes a dangerous or hazardous substance or activity,[3] it is all the more necessary to examine the wide reach of the Principle and the disjointed manner in which it has been implemented.

Due to several publicized incidents in the mid 1980s involving hazardous wastes produced in industrialized countries and dumped in developing countries, international law has focused primarily on the permissibility of international movements and trade in waste and other hazardous substances.[4] In this focus, a particular tension has emerged: the desire of many developing countries, particularly African states, to ban international trade in waste, and the opposition by many industrialized countries, desiring to keep their waste disposal options open.[5] There are significant economic incentives that influence state policies regarding trade in hazardous substances and activities, and the industries and

[1] Langlet, D., *Prior Informed Consent and Hazardous Trade: Regulating Trade in Hazardous Goods at the Intersection of Sovereignty, Free Trade and Environmental Protection* (Kluwer Law International 2009), 4.

[2] See section II) 3 of this chapter.

[3] Sands, P., *Principles of International Environmental Law* (Cambridge University Press 2003), 620.

[4] Sands, *Principles of International Environmental Law*, 690.

[5] Sands, *Principles of International Environmental Law*, 690.

agricultural sectors that produce the substances in question are often of significant economic and therefore political importance regionally.[6] Due to the high costs of disposal of such activities and substances in developed countries with stronger environmental regulation and enforcement, these industries seek to dispose of these substances in the developing world where costs are significantly lower. Moreover, some economic incentives favour the import of these substances and activities even when they pose a significant threat to the environment and/or human health: the import and dismantling of decommissioned ships may create jobs and provide raw materials for other industries; the application of imported hazardous pesticides may be perceived as necessary for the economic viability of certain agriculture or for the fight against disease carrying insects; the import and use of GMOs may boost profits in the agricultural sector or make the cultivation of new areas of land possible, etc.[7] This has created a vicious cycle that has stagnated the implementation of Principle 14, in that the focus has shifted away from the prevention of such transfers or relocation and towards their regulation for environmentally sound management.

Against this background, industrialized states accepted that production of hazardous wastes should be minimized as far as possible, that disposal should take place within the state concerned where consistent with environmentally sound management, and that trade should be reduced and take place only on a basis of prior notification and environmentally sound management; but they refused to accept the outright elimination of transboundary disposal in its entirety.[8] Developing countries asserted that regulation would simply legitimize an unacceptable practice, and consistently advocated for its outright elimination.[9] Tensions further rose due to the continued emergence of substances that are banned from consumption or sale in developed countries into the markets of some developing countries.[10]

Various international legal arrangements arose in the wake of the tension of the 1980s during a two-year period.[11] Most notably, one universal treaty and a regional one, each of which established different rules, emerged to regulate the transboundary movements of hazardous and other wastes: The 1989 Basel Convention on the Control of Transboundary Movements of Hazardous Wastes and their Disposal ('Basel Convention') and the 1991 Bamako Convention on the Ban on the Import into Africa and the Control of Transboundary Movement and Management of Hazardous Wastes within Africa ('Bamako Convention').[12] Principle 14 of the Rio Declaration followed in this wake and directly reflects the tension between the conflicting desires of developing and developed countries. It is necessary to examine these agreements that form the basis of Principle 14 in order to fully inform any understanding of the practical implications of it.

## 2. The Basel Convention

The 1989 Basel Convention was the first attempt at international regulation of international trade in hazardous and other wastes. It establishes rules aimed to regulate trade, not prohibit it, despite the vigorous attempt of African states to secure a trade ban.[13]

[6] Langlet, *Prior Informed Consent and Hazardous Trade*, 11. [7] Langlet, 11.

[8] Birnie, P. and Boyle, A., *International Law and the Environment* (Oxford University Press 2002), 428.

[9] Birnie and Boyle, *International Law and the Environment*, 428.

[10] Sands, *Principles of International Environmental Law*, 630.

[11] Birnie and Boyle, *International Law and the Environment*, 428.

[12] For a discussion of other regional treaties, see Langlet, *Prior Informed Consent and Hazardous Trade*, 91–2.

[13] Langlet, *Prior Informed Consent and Hazardous Trade*, 429.

The Basel Convention also reflects an approach based on what has become known as the 'proximity principle': that wastes should, as far as possible, be disposed of in the state where they were generated.[14] It permits the transboundary movements of waste but sets forth general obligations requiring all parties to ensure that such transboundary movements are reduced to a minimum.:

In particular, article 4 of the Basel Convention sets out general obligations designed to minimize waste generation and its transboundary movement, and to ensure its environmentally sound management.[15] The Basel Convention further sets out detailed conditions for the international regulation of transboundary movements of hazardous and other wastes between parties, based on a system of 'prior informed consent'. Under the regime, the exporting state must notify the states concerned of any transboundary movement and the importing state responds by giving its consent with or without conditions, denying permission, or requiring additional information.[16] No transboundary movement can occur until the exporting state has received the written consent of the importing state and confirmation from that state of the existence of a contract between the exporter and the disposer that specifies the environmentally sound management of the wastes.[17] In addition, transit states can prohibit transit passage.[18] These provisions clearly provided the foundation for Principle 14 of the Rio Declaration and further help inform its scope and dimension, which will be discussed in section II) 2 below. However, they fell short of establishing an outright ban on trade in wastes as advocated by many African states, which led to the establishment of a regional African agreement on the matter.

### 3. The Bamako Convention

Having been unable to secure a trade ban in the Basel Convention, the 1991 Bamako Convention was adopted by African states following its negotiations under the auspices of the Organization of African Unity ('OAU'). The OAU has called the dumping of nuclear and industrial waste a crime against the African people. This view is enshrined in the 1991 Bamako Convention, which establishes a regional regime to prohibit trade in waste. The Bamako Convention follows the Basel Convention to a large extent but with an important deviation: it prohibits trade in hazardous waste by requiring parties to prohibit the import of all hazardous wastes into Africa from non-contracting parties and declare such imports illegal and criminal.[19] In addition, the definition of hazardous waste adopted therein is broader than that of the Basel Convention and there are a number of other subtle differences between the regimes. Nonetheless, these two regimes are the inspiration for Principle 14 of the Rio Declaration and inform its application. Moreover, they

[14] Sands, *Principles of International Environmental Law*, 693.

[15] Basel Convention on the Control of Transboundary Movements of Hazardous Wastes and their Disposal, 22 March 1989, ('Basel Convention') 1673 UNTS 57, art 4(2)(d), (e) and (h). These provisions provide that: parties shall not allow exports to parties that have prohibited by legislation all imports, or where they have reason to believe that the wastes will not be managed in an environmentally sound manner, and they are obliged to cooperate to improve and achieve environmentally sound management of such waste.

[16] Basel Convention, art 6(1), (2) and (3); art 2(13); art 7.

[17] Basel Convention, art 6(1), (2) and (3); art 2(13); art 7.

[18] Basel Convention, art 6(4).

[19] Bamako Convention on the Ban on the Import into Africa and the Control of Transboundary Movement and Management of Hazardous Wastes within Africa, 30 January 1991, ('Bamako Convention') 30 ILM 773, art 4(1). See Sands, *Principles of International Environmental Law*, 697.

demonstrate the tension between developed and developing country positions and the compromise struck in the wording of Principle 14 itself.

In addition, other relevant regimes at the origin of Principle 14 are the 1973 Convention on International Trade in Endangered Species of Wild Fauna and Flora ('CITES') and the 1987 Montreal Protocol on Substances that Deplete the Ozone Layer ('Montreal Protocol'). These regimes form part of the biodiversity management regime and the hazardous chemicals regime as referred to earlier. Both agreements, in addition to regulating trade and transfer of such substances, impose trade restrictions with respect to third parties for the regulated substances. These trade restrictions with respect to non-parties support the effective implementation of the respective regimes and are a further expression of Principle 14. In particular, the CITES prohibits trade in species listed in its Appendix I, regulates trade in species included in Appendix II, and encourages states to bring endangered species in their territory under Appendix III. Further, it only permits transboundary movements to non-parties if the non-party provides comparable documentation that substantially conforms to the requirements of the CITES,[20] thereby supporting the environmentally sound management of endangered species of wild fauna and flora. The Montreal Protocol prohibits trade with non-parties unless the party uses standards equivalent to those established by the Protocol,[21] thereby ensuring the implementation of the regime and the environmentally sound management of trade in substances that deplete the ozone layer.

## II) The Principle as Enshrined in the Rio Declaration

### 1. Preparatory work and context

Due to the conflicting desires of developed and developing states regarding the transboundary movement of hazardous wastes and activities, several variations of Principle 14 were proposed and discussed throughout the preparatory process of the Rio Declaration. The Group of 77 along with China proposed the following formulation:

> Principle 12. International and transboundary movement of hazardous activities and substances:
>
> Measures taken in a specific country to reduce and/or control activities or projects harmful to the environment shall not lead to the displacement and transfer of these activities or projects to another country. Toxic and hazardous substances and wastes, dangerous genetically modified organisms, and radioactive wastes shall be treated at the point of generation. Transboundary treatment or disposal of these substances shall be banned. Measures shall also be taken to halt the international illicit traffic in toxic and hazardous substances and wastes. The countries of origin and entities involved in such activities shall bear the liability for compensation.[22]

Another proposal formulated the Principle in the following manner:

> As the largest part of the current emission of pollutants into the environment, including toxic and hazardous wastes, originates in developed countries, they shall be responsible for combating such

[20] Convention on International Trade in Endangered Species of Wild Fauna and Flora (CITES), 3 March 1973, 993 UNTS 243 art X.

[21] See Montreal Protocol on Substances that Deplete the Ozone Layer, 16 September 1987, ('Montreal Protocol') 1522 UNTS 29, art 4.

[22] Report of the Preparatory Committee for the United Nations Conference on Environment and Development on the Work of its Fourth Session, 1992, A/CONF.151/PC/128.

pollution and ensuring that toxic and hazardous wastes, including dangerous genetically modified organisms and radioactive waste, are disposed of in the proximity of their production.[23]

The following proposal was also formulated and discussed:

Principle 15

Measures taken in a specific country to reduce or control activities and projects harmful to the environment shall not lead to the displacement and transfer of these activities or projects to another country.

Principle 16

All States shall promote agricultural development policies based on the economically rational, efficient and sustainable use of the factors of production and resources, and shall avoid production practices which, in addition to distorting internal and external markets, have environmentally detrimental effects.

The United States, in its proposal for consideration, formulated the Principle as providing that:

environment and development objectives and policies should be integrated with economic and trade policies, including through appropriate harmonization of the international regimes for international trade and environmental protection.[24]

These varying formulations demonstrate the tension between developed and developing countries: in particular, the desire to ban all trade and transboundary movement in hazardous activities and waste by the developing world, and the desire by the developed world to leave their options open in this regard while ensuring environmentally sound management. Further, it is evident that many states would have preferred to enshrine the 'proximity principle'—the principle whereby waste is disposed of in its state of generation. This was not possible to achieve given the position of the US and other industrialized states who preferred a softer formulation of a moral objective rather than a binding legal obligation. In fact, many industrialized states argued against the inclusion of the Principle altogether.[25]

The formulation of Principle 14 as adopted in the Rio Declaration is a direct result of this tension and a compromise between the conflicting views. The Principle as agreed upon is therefore significantly weaker than developing countries would like as it uses persuasive rather than mandatory language ('should' instead of 'shall') and is significantly less detailed than most of the formulations proposed and discussed throughout the preparatory process. The original formulations were stronger and covered a broad range of hazardous wastes, including radioactive wastes and GMOs; although 'substances' can be interpreted to include such materials as they cause environmental degradation or are harmful to human health within the meaning of Principle 14.[26]

[23] Report of the Preparatory Committee for the United Nations Conference on Environment and Development, 1992, A/CONF.151/PC/128.

[24] Report of the Preparatory Committee for the United Nations Conference on Environment and Development, 1992, A/CONF.151/PC/128.

[25] Ling, C. Y., *The Rio Declaration on Environment and Development: An Assessment* (The Third World Network 2011), 47.

[26] Ling, *The Rio Declaration on Environment and Development*, 47.

It is significant that the Preparatory Committee noted 'the need to adopt normative measures to protect the interests of all countries, particularly developing countries, against illegal or unwarranted export of hazardous wastes.'[27] This intention to create normative measures in this regard should inform any interpretation of Principle 14 of the Rio Declaration. The Committee further highlighted:

the wish to communicate to relevant bodies the recommendation to examine the feasibility of establishing an international mechanism to regulate and, as appropriate, prohibit the trade in, or dumping of, hazardous substances, products, processes and technologies that, having been considered harmful for health and environment, have been prohibited or seriously restricted in their country of origin.[28]

## 2. Scope and dimensions

### *2.1. Prior informed consent*

Principle 14 establishes a norm of international cooperation to discourage or prevent the relocation and transference of substances and activities that harm the environment or human health in a context where it is understood that economic incentives favour their relocation or transference to states without adequate protection.[29]

The UN Secretary-General, in his report on the application and implementation of the Rio Declaration therefore observed in relation to Principle 14:

At a minimum, the principle requires prior informed consent of the importing State or State of relocation and imposes a duty on the originating State to ensure that the State to which the hazardous activity or substance is to be transferred has the appropriate capacity to minimize the risks. As a principle of cooperation, it further requires that if a State chooses to ban or restrict the importation of hazardous substances or the translocation of hazardous activities, the ban or restriction should be respected by other States.[30]

In this regard, the principle of 'prior informed consent' ('PIC') has been defined as:

the principle that international shipment of a chemical that is banned or severely restricted in order to protect human health or the environment should not proceed without the agreement, where such agreement exists, or contrary to the decision, of the designated national authority in the importing country.[31]

The PIC procedure was established in the legally binding arrangements for international trade in hazardous wastes in the Basel Convention, the Bamako Convention and numerous other instruments, which will be discussed in sub-section 3 later in this chapter.

It has been observed that Principle 14 is of crucial importance in light of the rapid expansion of agricultural chemical production over the last few years in the Asia-Pacific

[27] Report of the Preparatory Committee for the United Nations Conference on Environment and Development, 1991, Volume I, A/46/48, 39.

[28] Report of the Preparatory Committee for the United Nations Conference on Environment and Development, 1991, Volume I, A/46/48, 42.

[29] Report of the Secretary-General, 'Rio Declaration on Environment and Development: Application and Implementation', 1997, E/CN.17/1997/8.

[30] Report of the Secretary General, 'Rio Declaration on Environment and Development: Application and Implementation' 1997, E/CN.17/1997/8.

[31] Adopted by UNEP Governing Council Decision 14/27 of 27 June 1987, amended by UNEP Governing Council Decision 15/30 of 25 May 1989, para 1 (g); found in Sands, *Principles of International Environmental Law*, 630.

region.[32] Developing countries are going into the business of chemical exports, which is effectively an endorsement of chemical use and the introduction of potentially hazardous industries in the region.[33] Principle 14 is of fundamental importance in this regard as it provides the normative framework for preventing the transfer and relocation of such activities and substances that cause environmental degradation or harm human health, and works in conjunction with other Principles and instruments to reduce their occurrence. Although, as noted above, Principle 14 is not as detailed and specific as desired by developing countries, the terms 'activities' and 'substances' are broad enough to apply to any material or practice that harms the environment and/or human health. It is therefore the guiding principle for many international instruments regulating hazardous wastes, hazardous chemicals, and biosafety management.

However, it should be noted that Principle 14 only addresses the transfer or relocation of substances that cause *severe* environmental degradation or are harmful to human health. Further, the wording of the Principle itself does not reflect any particular degree of precaution, for example, by requiring states to act when a substance or activity 'may cause' or 'is likely to cause' severe degradation.[34] Nonetheless, the need for precaution is generally recognized in Principle 15, and the elaboration of PIC-applying international agreements can be seen as a means by which states 'heed the call' for effective cooperation in Principle 14.[35] It has been further noted in this regard that the general requirement that transboundary shipments of hazardous wastes be minimized may also be considered a regulatory approach founded on precaution, although it is hardly a radical version since the wastes in question are already defined as hazardous.[36]

While the applicable legal arrangements on the matter arose out of concern over high profile incidents involving the dumping of hazardous wastes, developing countries are increasingly vulnerable to the dumping of hazardous industries and technologies.[37] In fact, a survey report released in 1991 by the former UN Centre on Transnational Corporations revealed that the bulk of technologies that exist in industrialized states are hazardous in nature.[38] It therefore follows that the bulk of technology transferred to developing states is also hazardous to the environment and human health.[39] Principle 14 therefore persuades states to invest further in cleaner technologies so that the transference of such hazardous activities can be prevented. This will be returned to in section III) 4 of this chapter in the discussion of the relationship with the principle of sustainable development.

The 'polluter pays' principle and the environmental impact assessment as a national instrument, included in Principles 16 and 17 of the Rio Declaration respectively, are important in order to enforce Principle 14.[40] In this regard, the International Court of Justice (ICJ) has held that:

> in accordance with a practice, which in recent years has gained so much acceptance among States that it may now be considered a requirement under general international law to undertake an environmental impact assessment where there is a risk that the proposed industrial activity may have a significant adverse impact in a transboundary context.[41]

[32] Ling, 47. [33] Ling, 47. [34] Langlet, 61.

[35] Langlet, 61. See section II) 3.2 of this chapter for a discussion of these developments.

[36] Langlet, 209. However, the precautionary approach is expressly referred to in the Cartagena Protocol, which will be discussed in section II) 3.3 of this chapter.

[37] Langlet, 48. [38] Langlet, 48. [39] Langlet, 48.

[40] Ling, 46. See the commentary for these Principles in this volume for further elaboration on their content.

[41] *Pulp Mills on the River Uruguay (Argentina v. Uruguay)*, Judgment, ICJ Reports 2010 (I), 83, para 204.

The ICJ has recently developed this in the context of the right to be free from transboundary harm, which will be discussed in section II) 4 of this chapter.

Agenda 21 is of further interest as it elaborated upon the general objective espoused in Principle 14. Having been adopted at the same time as the Rio Declaration, it further informs the understanding of the Principle. It includes several relevant chapters for Principle 14, particularly Chapter 19 on 'Environmentally Sound Management of Toxic Chemicals, Including Prevention of Illegal International Traffic in Toxic and Dangerous Products'. Chapter 19 proposed six programme areas; of particular relevance here is the prevention of illegal international traffic in toxic and dangerous products. This programme called for the strengthening of international cooperation to prevent illegal transboundary movement of dangerous and toxic products. It does not, however, call for the strengthening of United Nations Environmental Programme ('UNEP') and Organisation for Economic Cooperation and Development ('OECD') non-binding instruments, or for the development of a binding international agreement.[42] It therefore does little to strengthen Principle 14, but does elaborate upon the implementation of the Principle. Chapter 20 of Agenda 21 on hazardous wastes further seeks to eliminate or reduce transboundary movements to a minimum, and implements the 'proximity principle' to ensure that management should, as far as possible, take place in the country of origin.[43] Chapter 20 includes four programme areas: promoting the prevention and minimization of waste; strengthening institutional capacities for management; strengthening international cooperation in management of transboundary movements; and preventing illegal traffic.[44]

### 2.2. *Legal nature*

Principle 14 of the Rio Declaration is ultimately a treaty-based principle, grounded in the Basel and Bamako Conventions most notably, and is an echo of the views and tensions expressed throughout the negotiating process of those agreements. The spirit behind the Principle is further grounded in customary law through the formation of the duty of prevention, no-harm, the obligation to conduct an environmental impact assessment, and sustainable development. This will be further elaborated upon in section III of this chapter. It has been noted that the Rio Declaration includes provisions that were either understood to already reflect customary international law at the time of their adoption or were expected to shape future normative expectations.[45]

Principle 14 is a provision that has shaped normative expectations and continues to do so today. It served to strengthen the moral force behind the objective to the extent that the Basel Convention eventually adopted a ban on trade in all such substances.[46] In addition, the ICJ has recently ruled that the right to be free from transboundary harm is a corollary of the no-harm principle.[47] These developments demonstrate that Principle 14 plays an important role in developing the normative framework in this area of the law.

[42] Agenda 21: Programme of Action for Sustainable Development, UN GAOR, 46th Sess., Agenda Item 21, UN Doc A/Conf.151/26 (1992), paras 19.66 to 19.76; see Sands, *Principles of International Environmental Law*, 672.

[43] Agenda 21: Programme of Action for Sustainable Development, para 20.7(a).

[44] See Sands, 706.

[45] Handl, G., 'Declaration of the United Nations Conference on the Human Environment (Stockholm Declaration), 1972 and the Rio Declaration on Environment and Development, 1992', United Nations Audiovisual Library of International Law, 2012, available at: <http://legal.un.org/avl/pdf/ha/dunche/dunche_e.pdf>.

[46] See section IV) of this chapter.

[47] Order on Request presented by Nicaragua for the indication of provisional measures in the *Construction of a Road in Costa Rica Along the San Juan River (Nicaragua v. Costa Rica)*, 13 December 2013, 6 para 19, see section II) 4 for further discussion.

## 3. Normative impact

### *3.1. Hazardous wastes*

#### 3.1.1. The Basel trade ban

Perhaps the most significant development since the adoption of Principle 14 is the trade ban on hazardous wastes established in the Basel Convention. As discussed above, developing nations argued for a trade ban from the very beginning, but developed countries were unable to agree. The Conference of the Parties ('COP') agreed to Decision II/12 in 1994, however, which immediately banned the export of hazardous wastes from OECD to non-OECD countries for final disposal, and by 1998, banned those wastes intended for recovery and recycling.[48] This amendment was formally incorporated in the Basel Convention in 1995.[49] However, the failure of the US to commit to the Basel Convention has limited its effectiveness in this regard.

#### 3.1.2. Radioactive waste

The 1997 Convention on the Safety of Spent Fuel Management and on the Safety of Radioactive Waste Management regulates radioactive waste management. Article 27 therein deals with the transboundary movement of radioactive wastes and provides that the importing state must be notified and give its consent to such imports.[50] However, notification and consent are not required for transit states, whereas they are required for transit states in the movement of hazardous wastes. This Convention therefore does less to fulfil the spirit of Principle 14 than the Basel Convention currently does.

### *3.2. Hazardous chemicals*

#### 3.2.1. The Rotterdam Convention

Another development that echoes Principle 14 is the 1998 Rotterdam Convention on the Prior Informed Consent Procedure for Certain Hazardous Chemicals and Pesticides in International Trade (the 'Rotterdam Convention'). The objective of the Rotterdam Convention is:

> to promote shared responsibility and co-operative efforts among Parties in the international trade of certain hazardous chemicals in order to protect human health and the environment from potential harm and to contribute to their environmentally sound use, by facilitating information exchange about their characteristics, by providing for a national decision-making process on their import and export and by disseminating these decisions to Parties.[51]

It applies the PIC procedure for chemicals listed in Annex III to the Convention, which is, subject to certain exceptions, applicable to banned or severely restricted chemicals and severely hazardous pesticide formulations.[52]

[48] Krueger, J., *International Trade and the Basel Convention* (The Royal Institute of International Affairs 1999).

[49] Decision II/12 Rept. of 2nd COP, UNEP/CHW.2/30 (1994); Decision III/1, Rept. of 3rd COP, UNEP/CHW.3/35 (1995), inserting new preambular para 7bis, new art 4A, and new Annex VII. Only Russia expressly refused to accept the ban. Found in Birnie and Boyle, *International Law and the Environment*, 448.

[50] The Convention applies a similar PIC procedure as the Basel Convention and others, for a fuller discussion and comparison, see Langlet, *Prior Informed Consent and Hazardous Trade*, 199.

[51] Rotterdam Convention on the Prior Informed Consent Procedure for Certain Hazardous Chemicals and Pesticides in International Trade, 10 September 1998, 2244 UNTS 337, found in Sands, *Principles of International Environmental Law*, 633.

[52] Rotterdam Convention on the Prior Informed Consent Procedure for Certain Hazardous Chemicals and Pesticides in International Trade, ('Rotterdam Convention') 10 September 1998, 2244 UNTS 337,

Although the objective of the Rotterdam Convention is often perceived as being to prohibit trade, its objective is in fact to promote shared responsibility with respect to the regulation of trade in certain chemicals through domestic regulatory measures taken by individual parties, combined with a review by a scientific body and final decisions made by the COP.[53] Consequently, Principle 14 did not influence the area of hazardous chemicals as it did hazardous wastes, since a trade ban was eventually adopted in the latter,[54] but could not be agreed upon in the Rotterdam Convention. Nonetheless, the Rotterdam Convention provides for the environmentally sound management of such hazardous chemicals and is therefore in the spirit of Principle 14 of the Rio Declaration.

### 3.2.2. The Stockholm Convention

The 2001 Stockholm Convention on Persistent Organic Pollutants ('Stockholm Convention') goes further than other international instruments addressing international trade in hazardous wastes, hazardous chemicals, or biodiversity management by directly limiting the production and release of certain chemicals as well as regulating the transboundary movement of those that are not prohibited.[55] It therefore pursues the objective of Principle 14 and goes further to ensuring environmental and health protection.

The Stockholm Convention regulates the production, use, and transboundary movement of hazardous chemicals known as Persistent Organic Pollutants ('POPs'). These chemicals remain intact in the environment for extensive periods, are widely dispersed geographically, accumulate in the fatty tissue of living organisms, and are toxic to wildlife and humans.[56] The Stockholm Convention therefore requires states to prohibit and/or eliminate the production and use of chemicals listed in Annex A to the Convention,[57] and to restrict the use of other harmful chemicals, such as DDT, listed in Annex B.[58]

### 3.2.3. The Minamata Convention

Most recently, the 2013 Minamata Convention on Mercury ('Minamata Convention') follows in the same vein, but provides for a much more strict regime. It too falls short of fully realizing Principle 14 by not banning trade in mercury, but is in the spirit of the Principle along with the other instruments as it establishes a PIC procedure and regulatory framework for the environmentally sound management of mercury, including issues surrounding its transboundary movement.[59] However, the Minamata Convention goes further than other international instruments by providing that parties may not trade in mercury with non-parties unless such non-parties *de facto* implement the substantive

art 3(1), arts 2 (b), (c) and (d). See Langlet, *Prior Informed Consent and Hazardous Trade*, 122–31 for an in-depth analysis of the Rotterdam Convention, including a detailed discussion of the PIC procedure.

[53] Langlet, 144. It is noted therein that 'The President of COP 3 felt prompted to stress that the inclusion of a chemical in Annex III of the Convention does not have the effect of banning or even restricting the use of such chemical. UNEP/FAO/RC/COP.3/26, para 73.'

[54] See section II) 3.1.1 of this chapter.

[55] See Wirth, D.A., 'Hazardous Substances and Activities', in Bodansky, D., Brunnee, J., and Hey, E. (eds), *Oxford Handbook of International Environmental Law* (Oxford University Press 2007), 394, at 403 for further analysis and discussion of the Stockholm Convention.

[56] Sands, 683.

[57] Stockholm Convention on Persistent Organic Pollutants ('Stockholm Convention') 22 May 2001, 40 ILM 532 (2001), art 3(1)(a)(i).

[58] Stockholm Convention, art 3(1)(b).

[59] See art 3 of the Minamata Convention on Mercury ('Minamata Convention') 10 October 2013.

requirements of the regime, thereby ensuring the environmentally sound management of mercury.[60]

The Minamata Convention also goes further than the objective of Principle 14 in some ways as it provides for the phase-out of mercury mining,[61] and prohibits the manufacture, import or export of mercury-added products listed in Part I of Annex A after the phase-out date specified for those products.[62] Article 11 therein is a rather particular provision that implements Principle 14 to a certain extent by providing that, for Parties to the Basel Convention only, mercury waste shall not be transported across international boundaries except for the purpose of environmentally sound disposal, while other parties shall allow transport 'only after taking into account relevant international rules, standards, and guidelines.'[63] Given that the latter only applies to non-parties of the Basel Convention, it is unclear what international rules would be relevant in this context. The Minamata Convention has nonetheless built on Principle 14 by phasing out mercury as a harmful substance altogether.

### *3.3. Genetically modified organisms*

Due to the general understanding that species are becoming extinct and that biodiversity is diminishing at an alarming rate, measures have been taken in response.[64] Regulating the safety aspects of GMOs is highly contentious, especially due to the varying perceptions of the potential risks involved.[65] The regulation of transboundary movement of such substances is necessary to control the exploitation of species and genetic resources or to prevent or control the spread of invasive or alien species and GMOs.[66]

[60] The Minamata Convention, art 3(6) provides that
Each Party shall not allow the export of mercury except:

(a) To a Party that has provided the exporting Party with its written consent, and only for the purpose of:
  (i) A use allowed to the importing Party under this Convention; or
  (ii) Environmentally sound interim storage as set out in Article 10; or
(b) To a non-Party that has provided the exporting Party with its written consent, including certification demonstrating that:
  (i) The non-Party has measures in place to ensure the protection of human health and the environment and to ensure its compliance with the provisions of Articles 10 and 11; and
  (ii) Such mercury will be used only for a use allowed to a Party under this Convention or for environmentally sound interim storage as set out in Article 10.

Article 3(8) further provides that 'Each Party shall not allow the import of mercury from a non-Party to whom it will provide its written consent unless the non-Party has provided certification that the mercury is not from sources identified as not allowed under paragraph 3 or paragraph 5 (b).'

[61] See art, 3(3) and (4). [62] See art 4(1).

[63] Art 11(3)(c). Art 11(3) states that Each Party shall take appropriate measures so that mercury waste is:

(a) Managed in an environmentally sound manner, taking into account the guidelines developed under the Basel Convention and in accordance with requirements that the Conference of the Parties shall adopt in an additional annex in accordance with Article 27. In developing requirements, the Conference of the Parties shall take into account Parties' waste management regulations and programmes;
(b) Only recovered, recycled, reclaimed or directly re-used for a use allowed to a Party under this Convention or for environmentally sound disposal pursuant to paragraph 3 (a);
(c) For Parties to the Basel Convention, not transported across international boundaries except for the purpose of environmentally sound disposal in conformity with this Article and with that Convention. In circumstances where the Basel Convention does not apply to transport across international boundaries, a Party shall allow such transport only after taking into account relevant international rules, standards, and guidelines.

[64] Louka, E., *International Environmental Law: Fairness, Effectiveness, and World Order* (Cambridge University Press 2006).

[65] Langlet, 157. [66] Rayfuse, R., 'Biological Resources', in Bodansky, Brunnee, and Hey, 362 at 384.

The 2000 Cartagena Protocol on Biosafety ('Caratgena Protocol') is a direct response to these risks to biodiversity and responds to the call of Principle 14 in this area by aiming 'to contribute to ensuring an adequate level of protection in the field of the safe transfer, handling and use of living modified organisms, specifically focusing on transboundary movements.'[67] The Cartagena Protocol does so by introducing an advance informed agreement ('AIA') procedure based on a precautionary approach for the transboundary movement of certain living modified organisms ('LMOs').[68] It further provides that transboundary movements between parties and non-parties shall be consistent with the objectives of the Cartagena Protocol, thereby ensuring the effective implementation of the regime and fulfilling the spirit of Principle 14.[69]

### *3.4. Pragmatism and environmentally sound transfers*

The agreements referred to above with provisions that impose trade restrictions on third parties[70] fulfil the objectives of Principle 14 as they ensure such transfers and relocation are done in an environmentally sound manner. They do not implement Principle 14, in that they do not prevent such relocation or transference, but they reflect the reality that such transfers will occur, and should therefore be regulated so that they are conducted in an environmentally sound manner. Trade restrictions with third parties further provide incentives for non-parties to *de facto* implement a treaty regime, which is greatly beneficial to its overall implementation. It is therefore a necessary trade-off: it may be impossible to entirely prevent the relocation and transference of such harmful substances and activities, but regulation can ensure some adherence to environmentally sound practices and can serve as an important incentive for states to implement a treaty regime.

Rules have further been developed since the Rio Declaration to govern the transportation of hazardous goods and substances by rail,[71] sea,[72] and air.[73] Although these rules are not an implementation of Principle 14, in that they do not prevent the relocation and transfer of such substances, they fulfil the spirit of the Principle by ensuring that such transfers are conducted in an environmentally sound manner. This reinforces the objectives of Principle 14.

[67] Cartagena Protocol on Biosafety to the Convention on Biological Diversity, 29 January 2000, ('Cartagena Protocol') 39 ILM 1027 (2000), art 1.

[68] In terms of content and practical effect, the AIA procedure may be equated with the PIC procedure discussed above, with only minor variations, see Langlet, *Prior Informed Consent and Hazardous Trade* at 165 for an in depth comparison of the procedures as applied in the Cartagena Protocol, Rotterdam Convention, and Basel Convention. It is further noted at 182 that whereas the Basel Convention is clear in recognizing a Party's right to ban or otherwise regulate hazardous waste, and the Rotterdam Convention precisely defines each specific substance to be covered by its PIC procedure, the Cartagena Protocol is unique in this context 'by explicitly referring to and regulating the way in which precaution and socio-economic considerations may be taken into account by the Parties when making decisions on import.' For a full comparison of the three regimes see Langlet, 195–213.

[69] Art 24.

[70] See the restrictions imposed by the Minamata Convention and the Cartagena Protocol, as well as by other instruments adopted prior to Principle 14, namely the CITES, the Montreal Protocol, and the Basel Convention (see section I) of this chapter).

[71] Regulations Concerning the International Carriage of Dangerous Goods by Rail (RID), 2013, available at: <http://www.otif.org/fileadmin/user_upload/otif_verlinkte_files/07_veroeff/99_geschuetzt/RID_2013_e/RID_2013_E.pdf]>.

[72] International Maritime Dangerous Goods Code ('IMDG Code'), as amended.

[73] ICAO Technical Instruction for the Safe Transport of Dangerous Goods by Air, DOC 9284-AN/905 (ICAO TI); Convention Concerning the Safe Transport of Dangerous Goods by Air (Annex 18 to the 1994 ICAO Convention).

## 4. Jurisprudential relevance

### *4.1. The International Tribunal for the Law of the Sea*

Principle 14 has never been expressly referred to or raised in international jurisprudence, but the objective of protecting health and the environment from the harm of transboundary movement of hazardous activities and substances has been discussed in several cases.

In particular, it was raised by Ireland in its request for Provisional Measures to the International Tribunal for the Law of the Sea ('ITLOS'), during the *MOX Plant* case. Ireland referred to the risks in the transportation of the MOX fuel from the UK to Japan and highlighted its concern as well as the strong protest by many countries against the shipment of radioactive materials.[74] It further highlighted the expression of the Caribbean Community (CARICOM) Heads of Government against:

> the increasing frequency and volume of the hazardous material being shipped, in spite of the repeated protests by States in and bordering on the Caribbean Sea, and appealed to the Governments of France, Japan and the United Kingdom to desist from such transports through the Caribbean Sea.[75]

Ireland therefore requested that ITLOS order the UK to immediately ensure that there are no movements into or out of its waters of any radioactive substances or materials that are somehow related to the operation of the MOX plant. This action by Ireland and expression by the CARICOM Heads of Government is in direct pursuit of Principle 14.

### *4.2. The International Court of Justice*

More recently, the ICJ has made pronouncements supporting the evolution of Principle 14 into customary law.

In its Order on Provisional Measures in the case concerning the *Construction of a Road in Costa Rica Along the San Juan River* (*Nicaragua v. Costa Rica*), the Court noted that 'the claimed right to be free from transboundary harm is the principal right underpinning Nicaragua's Request and is derived from the right of a State to sovereignty and territorial integrity.'[76] The Court then recalled that the no-harm principle is part of the corpus of international law relating to the environment and considered that 'a correlative right to be free from such transboundary harm is plausible.'[77] The Court considered Nicaragua's claimed right to receive a transboundary environmental assessment from Costa Rica. It recalled its previous finding in the *Pulp Mills on the River Uruguay* and found the rights for which Nicaragua sought protection to be plausible.[78] Given that this is an incidental proceeding to the case, the Court could not prejudge the merits and develop its reasoning in this regard.

It is nonetheless highly significant that the Court has recognized the right to be free from transboundary harm, the objective behind Principle 14, as a correlative right stemming from the no-harm principle. This will be further developed in section III) 1 of this

[74] See paras 33–43 of Ireland's Request for Provisional Measures in the *MOX Plant* case *(Ireland v. United Kingdom)*, ITLOS Case No 10.

[75] *Ireland v. United Kingdom*, para 36.

[76] Order on Request presented by Nicaragua for the indication of provisional measures in the *Construction of a Road in Costa Rica Along the San Juan River (Nicaragua v. Costa Rica)*, 13 December 2013, 6 para 19.

[77] *Nicaragua v. Costa Rica*, 6, para 19.

[78] *Nicaragua v. Costa Rica*, 6, para 19; see *Pulp Mills on the River Uruguay* (*Argentina v. Uruguay*), Judgment, ICJ Reports 2010 (I), 83, para 204.

chapter. It is possible that the Court's judgment on the merits in this case could formalize the objective of Principle 14 as binding customary law if it develops its reasoning in the same manner.

## *4.3. Investment arbitration*

Unfortunately, other tribunals have been less supportive of Principle 14 and the objective espoused therein.[79] In *S.D. Meyers, Inc. v. the Government of Canada*, an American corporation engaged in the treatment of Polychlorinated biphenyl (PCB), an environmentally hazardous chemical compound brought a claim against Canada under the North American Free Trade Agreement (NAFTA) Chapter 11 for Canada's order prohibiting the export of PCB waste. The Tribunal found that:

> Canada's policy was shaped to a very great extent by the desire and intent to protect and promote the market share of enterprises that would carry out the destruction of PCBs in Canada and that were owned by Canadian nationals.[80]

It therefore found in favour of S.D. Meyers and ordered Canada to pay compensation. However, as discussed in section II) 1 above, there is considerable support for the 'proximity' principle, particularly in its implication that waste should be disposed of in its country of origin. As highlighted above, developing countries tried to enshrine this into Principle 14, but it was rejected by the industrialized states. It is nonetheless included in Agenda 21 and a widely recognized principle.

Consequently, even if Canada's order were based on its desire to protect its own industry related to the destruction of PCBs, it would be supported by Principle 14 and Agenda 21. The Tribunal, however, does not refer to either. It briefly discusses the Basel Convention based on Canada's argument that the Convention 'imposed obligations upon Canada to ensure that it had adequate destruction facilities within its borders and to ensure that it reduced the transboundary movement of PCBs to a minimum.'[81] The Tribunal reviewed the Transboundary Agreement between the US and Canada, and found that it emphasized 'the potential benefits of cross-border movement of toxic wastes in achieving economies and better protecting the environment.'[82] It noted the objectives of the Basel Convention, that production of wastes is reduced, that adequate disposal facilities are available, and that transboundary movement is reduced to the minimum consistent with

[79] It should also be noted here that the case of *Metaclad Corporation v. United Mexican States* (ICSID Case No. ARB (AF)/97/1, Award 30 August 2000) concerning the development and operation of a hazardous waste landfill should have taken note of Principle 14 or considered the objective contained therein, as expressed in the numerous international instruments referred to above. It shockingly did not consider the Basel Convention or any other environmental issues surrounding the development and operation of a hazardous waste landfill. However, the case is complicated by the fact that Mexican authorities initially consented to the operation throughout the construction of the operation. Due to this initial consent, that was withdrawn through a complicated process for the Claimant, the Tribunal found that Metaclad was not treated fairly or equitably and that Mexico's actions were tantamount to expropriation. It therefore awarded Metaclad $16,685,000.00. Principle 14 was intended to prevent this very occurrence: the US and other developed countries dumping its hazardous waste into the developing world. It is quite unfortunate that, regardless of whether initial authorization was granted or not, a state cannot rely on its duty to prevent the transfer of hazardous activities and substances (of which a landfill for hazardous wastes is both) as articulated in Principle 14, as a defence in these circumstances.

[80] *S.D. Myers v. Government of Canada*, NAFTA Arbitration under the UNCITRAL Arbitration Rules, Partial Award, 13 November 2000, para 162.

[81] *S.D. Myers v. Government of Canada*, para 186.

[82] *S.D. Myers v. Government of Canada*, para 212.

environmentally sound and efficient management of such wastes. It concluded that the Basel Convention 'acknowledges that the environmentally sound and efficient management of waste is not necessarily accomplished by avoiding cross-border shipments.'[83]

The Tribunal therefore found that since there was no difference in terms of the environmental impact in this case between the destruction of the PCBs in Canada or the US, the measure was in violation of Canada's obligation under NAFTA. It further found that 'where a state can achieve its chosen level of environmental protection through a variety of equally effective and reasonable means, it is obliged to adopt the alternative that is most consistent with open trade.'[84] Principle 14 has therefore not had a great impact in arbitration.

## III) Relations with Other Principles

### 1. Principle 14 and 'no-harm'

The no-harm principle, the principle that states have the responsibility to ensure that activities within their jurisdiction do not damage the environment of other states, has become one of the most fundamental customary law rules relevant to environmental protection.[85] Principle 14 is a corollary and extension of the no-harm principle, since it discourages the spreading of harmful activities and substances. It reinforces the no-harm principle by ensuring that harmful activities are not transferred or relocated. It is an extension of the no-harm principle by ensuring any harmful activities and substances carried out within a state's jurisdiction pursuant to its sovereign right are not transferred or relocated to other states.

It has been noted, however, that there is little to substantiate a claim that the parties to the relevant agreements relied on or intended to make a connection to the broader 'no-harm' principle when elaborating specific agreements pertaining to trade in hazardous substances.[86] While a number of multilateral environmental agreements expressly refer to the principle, it is not referred to in the context of multilateral agreements addressing trade in hazardous substances. It has therefore been asserted that it is not possible to simply expand customary rules on transboundary pollution to cover the export of dangerous goods and technology in addition.[87] Nonetheless, the ICJ seems to have done just that in its recent Order on Provisional Measures.[88] In any case, whether the Parties intended to make a broader connection to the 'no-harm' principle is irrelevant; the fact is Principle 14 is a logical extension and corollary of the no-harm principle, but also an issue in its own right, which is why it is a free-standing Principle and not dealt with in the context of Principle 21 of the Rio Declaration on the 'no-harm' principle.

### 2. Principle 14 and cooperation

As a corollary to the no-harm principle, customary law provides for a duty of cooperation in the control of transboundary pollution and environmental risks.[89] This duty of

[83] *S.D. Myers v. Government of Canada*, para 212.

[84] *S.D. Myers v. Government of Canada*, para 221. For more on this aspect of the case see paras 215–21.

[85] Kummer, K., *International Management of Hazardous Wastes: The Basel Convention and Related Legal Rules* (Oxford University Press 2000), 13.

[86] Langlet, 62.

[87] Langlet, 63.

[88] See section II) 4.2 of this chapter.

[89] Langlet, 17.

cooperation is inherent in Principle 14, and mandatory for any efforts to prevent or regulate transboundary movements of dangerous substances and activities. The obligations of prior notification and consultation with states likely to be affected by a potentially harmful activity are a concrete expression of this duty.[90] Given that this duty is firmly established in customary law, it is on this basis that the duty of prior informed consent is implicit in Principle 14, since the Principle is founded upon the duty to cooperate. These obligations of notification and consultation, inherent in the duty to cooperate, are the foundation of Principle 14.

The duties of cooperation and information are significant in the context of transboundary movements of hazardous wastes. It has been observed in this context that:

> if the state of origin is required by customary law to give prior information to, and enter into consultations with, neighbouring states that are potentially affected by hazardous activities carried out in its own territory, it follows, *a fortiori*, that this duty applies equally to a hazardous activity initiated or authorized within the state of origin but planned to be carried out within the recipient state. The recipient state's right to be notified is essential in that it provides the basis for the exercise of its right to prohibit or control the activities in question. For these reasons, it can justifiably be argued that the duty of prior information and consultation in the case of pollution source transfer is based in customary law.[91]

It is further on this basis that Principle 14 implies the operation of the PIC procedure.

## 3. Principle 14 and the obligation to conduct an environmental impact assessment

It has been noted that an environmental impact assessment is important to enforce Principle 14.[92] It is certainly necessary to understand the impact an activity or substance has on the environment in order to determine if it is harmful and therefore necessary to prevent its relocation or transference. The need for an environmental impact assessment is therefore implicit in Principle 14. The ICJ has recently ruled that Nicaragua's claim to be free from transboundary harm in the context of the construction of a road on its territory by Costa Rica, along with Nicaragua's claimed right to receive a transboundary environmental impact assessment in this regard, are plausible in the context of the indication of provisional measures.[93] As discussed in section II) 4 of this chapter, the Court has confirmed the requirement under general international law to undertake an environmental impact assessment where there is a risk the proposed activity may have significant adverse transboundary effect.[94] This is a necessary practical step in fulfilling the objectives of Principle 14.

## 4. Principle 14 and sustainable development

Principle 14 fully supports the general principle that states should ensure the development and use of their natural resources in a sustainable manner. By discouraging the transference of harmful activities, the Principle encourages investment in sustainable

[90] Langlet, 17. [91] Langlet, 17–18. [92] Ling, 46.

[93] *Nicaragua v. Costa Rica*. See section II) 4 of this chapter.

[94] See *Pulp Mills on the River Uruguay* (*Argentina v. Uruguay*), 83, paras 204–5 for a discussion of the requirement. For a more-in-depth discussion, see the commentary for Principle 17 in this volume.

development as an alternative. It has been noted that the principle of sustainable development requires that environmental protection be treated as integral to the development process and not in isolation from it. Principle 14 further reinforces this principle by requiring investment in clean development and technologies to fulfil the duty to prevent transference of harmful technologies and other activities.

### 5. Principle 14 and prevention

The preventative approach has widespread support in the context of the issue of hazardous waste management in particular.[95] Chapters 20 and 21 of Agenda 21 define the overall objective of any waste-related activities as 'the prevention or minimization of the generation of hazardous wastes, and their management in a way that does not cause harm to human health and the environment'.[96] Given that the preventative principle requires action to be taken at an early stage and, if possible, before damage has actually occurred, Principle 14 is a direct expression of this. Principle 14 seeks to prevent the harm caused by the transfer of hazardous substances and activities. The principle of prevention is therefore inextricably linked to Principle 14.

## IV) Assessment

The absence of global rules governing all hazardous substances and activities is a real problem, especially since they may be easily transportable and do not distinguish in their damaging effects between different environments and people.[97] Of more general concern is the fact that many industrial and other activities that may, over time, pose a threat to the environment or human health are not subject to specific international environmental regulation.[98] Nonetheless, the normative value of the strengthened moral force behind Principle 14 can provide a framework to deal with these issues.

There was increased concern expressed by developing countries in the late 1980s to 1990s over hazardous substances, directed primarily at adopting national and international laws aims to stop 'dumping' of hazardous wastes in their territory. As evidenced above, more recent international efforts have been directed towards the adoption of legally binding rules on regulating trade in hazardous chemicals and biodiversity management in an environmentally sound manner, after the trade ban in hazardous wastes was established under the auspices of the Basel Convention in 1995. Of the regimes that have developed to fulfil the objectives of Principle 14 discussed in section II) 3 of this chapter, only the hazardous wastes regime provides for a trade ban *stricto sensu* as a central element of the regime. The other regimes have therefore fallen short of truly fulfilling Principle 14, although the recent Minamata Convention seems to provide new life to the spirit of the Principle.

These efforts partially fulfil the objective of Principle 14 by ensuring that transfers of hazardous activities and substances are conducted in an environmentally sound manner, but they do not implement the Principle itself since they do not prevent such transfers. Regardless of the use the word 'should' therein, the moral command behind

[95] Kummer, 28. [96] Kummer, 28. [97] Sands, 619. [98] Sands, 620.

Principle 14 is that transfers of hazardous substances and activities should be prevented. Nonetheless, the agreements that regulate such transfers in an environmentally sound manner reflect the same compromise struck in the soft language of the Principle itself. The hazards of such substances and activities and the danger and risks involved in their transboundary movements seem to have been forgotten as the high profile incidents of the 1980s fade from memory. There seems to have been a recognition, which, although present implicitly in the soft language of Principle 14, has been further reinforced with new agreements: transfers of dangerous activities and substances will occur and must therefore be regulated to ensure environmentally sound management. This regulation has centred on prior notification and informed consent. Given that developing countries have now joined in the industrialized party to a greater extent than they had in the late 1980s, it seems the initiative to prevent such transboundary movements has fallen by the wayside.

Moreover, the dumping of hazardous wastes has continued unabashedly in the developing world due to poor enforcement of national legislation. Further, for some developing countries, the economic and political advantages of importing waste or other hazardous activities continue to outweigh environmental and health considerations.[99] The Principle has therefore struggled to reach full implementation. It does, however, hold tremendous normative value for the development of customary law in this area. The Principle and its normative force are available, as evidenced above; it simply needs to be relied on and developed to fulfil its full potential. Significantly, it remains as a benchmark identifying the direction in which international law should progressively evolve in this area. In this process, it must be borne in mind that:

> unlike human laws, the laws of nature are non-negotiable. When our activities subject organisms and ecosystems to certain levels of stress, rivers do get poisonous, individuals do develop cancer, species do become extinct, and land does become uninhabitable. Our motives for the stressful activities are in this sense immaterial.[100]

## V) Select Bibliography

Barrios, P., 'The Rotterdam Convention on Hazardous Chemicals: A Meaningful Step towards Environmental Protection?' (2004) 16 *GIELR* 679.

Bitar, F., *Les mouvements transfrontières de déchets dangereux selon la Convention de Bâle. Etude des régimes de responsabilité* (Paris: Pedone 1997).

Bombier, N., 'The Basel Convention's complete ban on hazardous waste exports: Negotiating the compatibility of trade and the environment' (1997) 7 *Journal of Environmental Law and Practice* 325.

Edvokia, M., 'La Convention de Bâle sur les mouvements transfrontières de déchets dangereux (22 March 1989)' (1989) 93 *Revue générale de droit international public* 899.

Emory, R. W., 'Probing the Protections in the Rotterdam Convention on Prior Informed Consent' (2001) 12 *Colorado Journal of International Environmental Law and Policy* 47.

Grosz, M., *Sustainable Waste Trade under WTO Law* (Leiden: Martinus Nijhoff 2011).

[99] Sustainable Development in the 21st century, 'Review of implementation of Agenda 21 and the Rio Principles', Study prepared by the Stakeholder Forum for a Sustainable Future, January 2012, 45.

[100] Langlet, 12.

Kummer, K., *International Management of Hazardous Wastes: The Basel Convention and Related Legal Rules* (Oxford University Press 2000).

Lallas, P., 'The Stockholm Convention on Persistent Organic Pollutants' (2001) 95 *AJIL* 692.

Lallas, P., 'The Role of Process and Participation in the Development of Effective International Environmental Agreements: A Study of the Global Treaty on Persistent Organic Pollutants' (2002) 19 *UCLA Journal of Environmental Law and Policy* 83.

Langlet, D., *Prior Informed Consent and Hazardous Trade: Regulating Trade in Hazardous Goods at the Intersection of Sovereignty, Free Trade and Environmental Protection* (The Hague: Kluwer Law International 2009).

Ling, C.Y., *The Rio Declaration on Environment and Development: An Assessment* (Penang: Third World Network 2012).

Mbengue, M. M., *Essai sur une théorie du risque en droit international public. L'anticipation du risque environnemental et sanitaire* (Paris: Pedone 2009).

McDorman, T., 'The Rotterdam Convention on the Prior Informed Consent Procedure for Certain Hazardous Chemicals and Pesticides in International Trade: Some Legal Notes' (2004) 13 *Review of European Community and International Environmental Law* 187.

Montjoie, M., *Droit international et gestion des déchets radioactifs* (Paris: LGDJ 2011).

Olsen, M. A., *Analysis of the Stockholm Convention on Persistent Organic Pollutants* (Dobbs Ferry N.Y.: Oceana 2003).

Pallemaerts, M., *Toxics and Transnational Law: International and European Regulation of Toxic Substances as Legal Symbolism* (Oxford: Hart Publishing 2003).

Pasquali, L., *Le régime juridique des mouvements transfrontières de déchets en droit communautaire et en droit international* (Aix-en-Provence: Presses universitaires d'Aix-Marseille 2004).

Redgwell, C., 'Regulating Trade in dangerous Substances: Prior Informed Consent under the 1998 Rotterdam Convention', in Kiss, A. et al (eds), *Economic Globalization and Compliance with International Environmental Agreements* (The Hague: Kluwer 2003), 75.

Selin, H., 'Global Environmental Law and Treaty-Making on Hazardous Substances: The Minamata Convention and Mercury Abatement' (2014) 14 *Global Environmental Politics* 1.

United Nations Department of Social and Economic Affairs, Division for Sustainable Development, *Review of implementation of Agenda 21 and the Rio Principles*, December 2011.

Wirth, D. A., 'Hazardous Substances and Activities', in Bodansky, D., Brunnée, J., and Hey, E. (eds), *The Oxford Handbook of International Environmental Law* (Oxford: Oxford University Press 2007), 394.

# 19. Principle 15

## *Precaution*

Antônio Augusto Cançado Trindade*

**Principle 15**

In order to protect the environment, the precautionary approach shall be widely applied by States according to their capabilities. Where there are threats of serious or irreversible damage, lack of full scientific certainty shall not be used as a reason for postponing cost-effective measures to prevent environmental degradation.



* Judge of the International Court of Justice; Former President of the Inter-American Court of Human Rights; Emeritus Professor of International Law of the University of Brasília, Brazil; Honorary Fellow (Sidney Sussex College), University of Cambridge; Member of the *Curatorium* of the Hague Academy of International Law; Member of the *Institut de Droit International*; President of the Latin American Society of International Law (LASIL).

## I) Origins and Rationale of the Principle

Principle 15 of the Rio de Janeiro Declaration (1992) on the obligation to adopt a precautionary approach[1] comes as a new addition to the principles enshrined earlier on into the Stockholm Declaration on the Human Environment (1972).[2] According to Principle 15 of the Rio Declaration, the absence of scientific uncertainty regarding the existence or extent of a risk should not delay the adoption of measures of environmental protection. Accordingly, anticipated action is justified even though the likelihood of environmental damage occurring remains uncertain.

At the domestic law level, the origins of the precautionary principle can be found in the national legal system of the then Federal Republic of Germany, in the form of the *Vorsorgeprinzip*, which emerged in the early 1970s as national measures were taken on to limit threats to the environment.[3] The application of the principle at the international level started in the mid-1980s. The inclusion of Principle 15 in the Rio Declaration reflects a logical development in the evolution of the concept within international environmental law.

Ten years before the Rio de Janeiro Conference (United Nations Conference on Environment and Development—UNCED, 1992), the rationale of precaution had made its first appearance in an international document, namely, the 1982 World Charter for Nature, which read:

> Activities which are likely to pose a significant risk to nature shall be preceded by an exhaustive examination; their proponents shall demonstrate that expected benefits outweigh potential damage to nature, and where potential adverse effects are not fully understood, the activities should not proceed.[4]

The idea of precaution then spread into the field of the protection of the marine environment. The Preamble to the 1984 Ministerial Declaration of the International Conference on the Protection of the North Sea highlighted the importance of anticipatory action despite scientific uncertainty by providing that States 'must not wait for proof of harmful

[1] Unless otherwise stated this chapter uses indistinctively the term 'principle' and 'approach' to refer to the expression of precaution in international environmental law.

[2] 'Declaration of the United Nations Conference on the Human Environment', Stockholm, 16 June 1972, UN Doc A/CONF 48/14/Rev.1 ('Stockholm Declaration').

[3] See von Moltke, K., 'The Vorsorgeprinzip in West German Environmental Policy', in Royal Commission on Environmental Pollution, Twelfth Report: Best Practicable Environmental Option, 1988, at 57: 'Environmental policy is not fully accomplished by warding off imminent hazards and the elimination of damage which has occurred. Precautionary environmental policy requires furthermore that natural resources are protected and demands on them made with care'.

[4] World Charter for Nature, UNGA Res. 37/7 (XXXVII) (30 October 1980), art 11(b).

effects before taking action'.[5] Three years later, the 1987 Ministerial Declaration of the Second North Sea Conference made an explicit reference to precaution by providing that 'in order to protect the North Sea from possibly damaging effects of the most dangerous substances, a precautionary approach is necessary'.[6]

The precautionary principle was also recommended by the United Nations Environment Programme ('UNEP') Governing Council in 1989 to promote the prevention and elimination of marine pollution.[7] The fact that the precautionary principle began to thrive in the field of marine protection is linked to the fact that damage to oceans and seas is often costly and irremediable. In addition, the emergence of the precautionary principle coincided with the adoption of the 1982 United Nations Convention on the Law of the Sea[8] ('UNCLOS'), that is, at a time of intense interest for the protection of the marine environment and, more generally, for all issues of a maritime nature.

Similarly, the uncertainty surrounding the damage caused by atmospheric pollution also contributed to the emergence of the precautionary principle in international environmental law. Indeed, the first treaty regime that explicitly referred to precaution was the 1985 Vienna Convention for the Protection of the Ozone Layer[9] and further developed by its 1987 Montreal Protocol.[10] Last but not least, the principle was consecrated by the 1990 Bergen Ministerial Declaration on Sustainable Development in the Economic Commission for Europe Region held in advance of UNCED which read:

> In order to achieve sustainable development, policies must be based on the precautionary principle. Environmental measures must anticipate, prevent and attack the causes of environmental degradation. Where there are threats of serious or irreversible damage, lack of full scientific certainty should not be used as a reason for postponing measures to prevent environmental degradation.[11]

The Bergen Declaration was central to the development of precaution into a key legal concept: it affirmed the general applicability of the principle to all fields of international environmental law and provided decision-makers with a first legal definition of precaution. It is this provision that was to be used as a first draft for negotiations over the inclusion of the precautionary principle in the Rio Declaration and thus played a key role in the consecration of the principle in international environmental law.

The emergence of the precautionary principle is the result of two key changes in environmental policy in the 1980s. First, a new attitude towards the existence of risks emerged during the decade.[12] While consciousness about the need to provide a legal framework in

[5] Declaration of the International Conference on the Protection of the North Sea, 1 November 1984, conclusion A.7.

[6] Second International Conference on the Protection of the North Sea, London, 24–5 November 1987, Preamble, para VII.

[7] UNEP Governing Council decision 15/27 (1989).

[8] United Nations Convention on the Law of the Sea, Montego Bay, 10 December 1982, 1833 UNTS 397 ('UNCLOS'), entered into force on 16 November 1994.

[9] Convention for the Protection of the Ozone Layer, Vienna, 22 March 1985, in force 22 September 1988, (1985) 26 ILM 1529, Preamble.

[10] Protocol on Substances that Deplete the Ozone Layer, Montreal, 16 September 1987, in force 1 January 1989, (1987) 26 ILM 154, Preamble.

[11] Report of the Economic Commission for Europe on the Bergen Conference (8–16 May 1990), A/CONF.151/PC/10, annex I, para 7.

[12] *Pulp Mills on the River Uruguay* (*Argentina v. Uruguay*) (Judgment) (2010) ICJ Rep 14, para 101 ('*Pulp Mills* case'), Separate Opinion of Judge Cançado Trindade, para 62.

order to prevent environmental risks grew in the 1960s–1970s, the perception of risks[13] was transformed in the 1980s, with the new awareness that human activities might create new risks for the environment that science could not yet anticipate. The necessity to anticipate risks became increasingly manifest, as man continued to engage in evermore hazardous activities. Adopting a precautionary approach with regard to issues such as CFCs, GMOs, or hormone-disrupting chemicals, became necessary to avoid environmental and health disasters.

Secondly, an increased awareness of the role played by science in framing environmental issues also explains the rise of the precautionary principle. Risk evaluation being at the heart of international environmental law, it is undeniable that '[s]cience is the linchpin around which environmental law is organised'.[14] While the precautionary principle marks an increased awareness that law—national and international—has to welcome science within its realm, it also came with an increased 'awareness of scientific uncertainties surrounding the issue at stake'.[15] As a result, '[t]he growth of scientific knowledge came to be appreciated with the awareness of human fallibility'[16]: as a result, law has to adapt to the inherent limitations brought about by the 'humane ends of knowledge'.[17] In sum, both a transformed attitude towards risks and towards science contributed to the emergence of the precautionary principle in the 1980s and its consecration in the Rio Declaration of 1992.

## II) The Principle as Enshrined in the Rio Declaration

### 1. Preparatory work and context

The precautionary principle was first envisaged by the Preparatory Committee (PrepCom) of the Rio Conference as applicable with regards to the protection of the marine environment—a logical development given the key role played by the principle in this field in the previous decade. PrepCom I thus discussed the '[p]romotion and application of the precautionary approach, as appropriate, and use of incentives and disincentives to promote clean production methods to combat marine pollution'[18] while PrepCom II opened up the application of precaution to waste management[19] and freshwater resources.[20]

PrepCom III saw a great variety of proposals made regarding the 'precautionary principle and prior assessment'.[21] As a result, the proposals concerning precaution were first made in relation to the obligation to carry out an environmental impact assessment, but a

13 For a discussion of risk in international law, see Peel, J., *Science and Risk Regulation in International Law* (Cambridge University Press 2013).

14 de Sadeleer, N., 'The Principle of Prevention and Precaution in International Law: Two Heads of the Same Coin?', in Ong, D. et al (eds), *Research Handbook on International Environmental Law* (Edward Elgar Publishing 2010), 185.

15 *Pulp Mills* case, Separate Opinion of Judge Cançado Trindade, para 62.

16 *Pulp Mills*, Separate Opinion of Judge Cançado Trindade, para 73.

17 *Pulp Mills*, Separate Opinion of Judge Cançado Trindade, para 74.

18 Decision 1/20, in *Report of the Preparatory Committee for the United Nations Conference on Environment and Development,* GA Official Records A/45/46, 35.

19 Decision 2/17, in *Report of the Preparatory Committee for the United Nations Conference on Environment and Development,* GA Official Records A/46/48, 43.

20 Decision 2/20, GA Official Records A/46/48, 48.

21 'Principles on General Rights and Obligations, Chairman's consolidated draft', A/CONF.151/PC/WG.III/L.8/Rev.1, 30 August 1991, paras 48–56.

free-standing precautionary principle—independent from the idea of prior assessment—then appeared preferable.[22] While the need to adopt a precautionary approach was recognized, the transformation of the precautionary logic into a legal obligation remained a challenge. In this respect, attitudes toward scientific uncertainty were worded in different ways. For instance, the Soviet (later Russian) proposal considered that '[a]ny type of economic or other activity whose environmental consequences are unpredictable is inadmissible',[23] while the proposal of the European Economic Community (recalling the Bergen Declaration, discussed earlier) was more moderate. This latter, used as basis for negotiations, read as follows:

> Environmental measures must anticipate, prevent and attack the causes of environmental degradation, and where there are threats of serious or irreversible damage, lack of full scientific certainty should not be used as a reason for postponing measures to prevent environmental degradation. Proposed activities which are likely to have a significant adverse effect on the environment shall not be undertaken without prior assessment of the environmental risks.[24]

PrepCom IV worked on improving the formulation.[25] The reference to a 'precautionary principle' was replaced by the more consensual 'precautionary approach'. Despite the fact that the PrepCom had first envisaged precaution as a principle, negotiators discarded suggestions to promote precaution as a 'principle', and preferred to reach consensus over the term 'approach'. In addition, a reference to State capabilities and the necessity to take cost-effective measures was added to the phrasing of the Bergen Declaration—in line with the focus of the Rio Conference on the linkage between environmental and developmental issues.[26] In sum, the wording of Principle 15 is reflective of the consecration of the precautionary approach within international environmental law and of the Rio concerns for the environment-development nexus.

## 2. Scope and dimensions

### 2.1. *The many faces of precaution*

#### 2.1.1. Justification or obligation?

As a result of the broad formulation provided by Principle 15, the precautionary principle came to be interpreted in different ways. Commentators usually distinguish between several versions of the principle,[27] which require different levels of commitment towards precaution on the part of States. It is undeniable that Principle 15 acts as a reason not to

[22] 'Report of the Preparatory Committee for the United Nations Conference on Environment and Development on the Work of its Fourth Session', A/CONF.151/PC/I28, 12 May 1992, 102.

[23] 'Principles on General Rights and Obligations, Chairman's consolidated draft', para 56 (USSR).

[24] 'Principles on General Rights and Obligations, Chairman's consolidated draft', para 54 (Netherlands/EEC).

[25] 'Report of the Preparatory Committee', A/CONF.151/PC/I28, 102.

[26] See Cançado Trindade, A. A., 'Environment and Development: Formulation and Implementation of the Right to Development as a Human Right', in Cançado Trindade, A. A. (ed), *Derechos Humanos, Desarrollo Sustentable y Medio Ambiente/Human Rights, Sustainable Development and the Environment* (IIHR/IDB 1992), 39; Cançado Trindade, A. A., 'Sustainable Human Development and Conditions of Life as a Matter of Legitimate International Concern: The Legacy of the U.N. World Conferences', *in Japan and International Law—Past, Present and Future* (International Symposium to Mark the Centennial of the Japanese Association of International Law), (Kluwer 1999), 285.

[27] For discussion over different versions, see eg Bodansky, D., 'Deconstructing the Precautionary Principle', in Caron, D. and Scheiber, H. N. (eds), *Bringing New Law to Ocean Waters* (Martinus Nijhoff 2004), 381.

postpone action and to counter claims that regulation should only occur when a real risk is proven. But the precautionary principle has at times moved beyond this approach. It is clear that, given its consecration in international environmental instruments, Principle 15 could also be understood not only as a justification not to postpone action but potentially as an obligation to take action despite the absence of conclusive evidence regarding the harm an activity may cause to the environment. This is how some treaties have spelled out the idea of precaution, sometimes moving from a prevention-based to a precaution-based approach.[28]

### 2.1.2. Precaution and prudence

Principle 15 can be conceptualized as a 'very general rule of conduct of prudence'.[29] The Commission on Sustainable Development considered that '[a]t a general level the principle is understood to mean that States should act carefully and with foresight when taking decisions which concern activities that may have an adverse impact on the environment.'[30] Understanding precaution as a rule of prudence creates a parallel with the obligation of due diligence, requiring States to take all the necessary steps to protect the environment. As observed by the Seabed Chamber of the International Tribunal on the Law of Sea ('ITLOS'),[31] the obligation of due diligence includes an obligation to follow a precautionary approach as it requires States to take into account scientific uncertainty in their decision-making processes. It follows that the obligation of precaution is also implicitly present in broader obligations of environmental protection.

For instance, article 20 of the United Nations Convention on the Law of the Non-Navigational Uses of International Watercourses ('New York UN Watercourse Convention'), which states that '[w]atercourse States shall, individually or jointly, protect and preserve the ecosystems of international watercourses',[32] implies an obligation of due diligence and thus of precaution in its broad sense. The commentary to article 20 of the draft of the International Law Commission ('ILC') that served as the basis for the adoption of the Convention, mentions, in effect, that '[t]he obligation to protect the ecosystems of international watercourses is thus a general application of the principle of precautionary action'.[33] This comment is based on the assumption that the general obligation to protect ecosystems requires the application of the precautionary principle.

[28] The protocol amending the 1972 Dumping Convention turned the latter into a precautionary instrument. Convention on the Prevention of Marine Pollution by Dumping of Wastes and Other Matter, 29 December 1972 ('London Convention'), subsequently modified by the Protocol of 7 November 1996 to the Convention of 1972 on the Prevention of Marine Pollution by Dumping of Wastes and Other Matter, 7 November 1996, 1046 UNTS 120 ('London Protocol').

[29] International Law Commission, 'Draft Articles on Prevention of Transboundary Harm from Hazardous Activities (with Commentaries)' (2001) *Yearbook of the International Law Commission* (vol II, part 2) 148 ('ILC Prevention Articles'), commentary to art 10, para 7, 163.

[30] Commission on Sustainable Development, Report of the Expert Group Meeting on Identification of Principles of International Law for Sustainable Development, Geneva, Switzerland, 26–28 September 1995, paras 71–2.

[31] See *Responsibilities and Obligations of States sponsoring Persons and Entities with respect to Activities in the Area*, Case No. 17, ITLOS (Seabed Dispute Chamber), Advisory Opinion of 1 February 2011 ('Advisory Opinion on the Area'), para 135.

[32] United Nations Convention on the Law of the Non-Navigational Uses of International Watercourses, 21 May 1997, 36 ILM 700 ('New York UN Watercourse Convention'), art 20.

[33] 'Draft Articles on the Law of the Non-navigational Uses of International Watercourses (with Commentaries)' (1994) *Yearbook of the International Law Commission* (vol II, part 2), footnote n°328, 119.

This obligation would also apply to article 192 of UNCLOS, which is very similar to article 20 of the New York UN Watercourse Convention: therefore, the general obligation to protect the marine environment irrespective of the location of harm can be interpreted as including an obligation to follow a precautionary approach. In sum, the precautionary approach, when understood as a broad obligation of prudence, finds an implicit place in provisions regarding the protection of ecosystems and in the obligation of due diligence.

### 2.1.3. Precaution and the burden/standard of proof

Finally, another interpretation of precaution could shift the burden of proof by requiring the proponent of the activity to demonstrate that it will not cause harm to the environment. Traditionally the burden of proof requires that the party opposing an activity prove that it causes or is likely to cause environmental harm. But it has been pondered in expert writing that the precautionary approach requires a reversal of the burden of proof or at least a lowering of the standard of proof in international litigation.[34]

The reason underlying this position is of a practical nature: the necessary information to prove the likelihood of environmental harm is often in the hands of the entity carrying out the harmful activity, not of the other party. But this position has so far not been clearly admitted in the jurisprudence. In the *Pulp Mills on the River Uruguay* case, for example, the International Court of Justice ('ICJ') considered that 'while a precautionary approach may be relevant in the interpretation and application of the treaty agreed between both States it does not follow that it operates as a reversal of the burden of proof.'[35]

Yet, State practice is changing. It has recently been pointed out that this trend 'is beginning to be supported by state practice, even if it still falls short of having sufficient support to allow it to be considered a rule of general application'.[36] Similarly, the International Law Association ('ILA') Report on legal principles relating to climate change highlighted that:

> there is some State practice to indicate that a form of burden shifting may be required by the precautionary principle, in that sense that the mere presumption of irreversible harm may be sufficient to trigger precautionary measures.[37]

Even if the precautionary principle does not bring about a complete reversal of the burden of proof in all cases, it is increasingly understood to bring about a shifting of the burden of proof to those who plan or conduct activities that 'may cause long-term serious or irreversible harm', as stated in the ILA New Delhi Declaration of Principles on Sustainable Development.[38]

[34] See, in particular, Troubworst, A., *Precautionary Right and Duties of States* (Martinus Nijhoff 2006), ch 8; Foster, C., *Science and the Precautionary Principle in International Courts and Tribunals: Expert Evidence, Burden of Proof and Finality* (Cambridge University Press 2011), Part III. And cf, to the same effect (reversal of the burden of proof), *Request for an Examination of the Situation in Accordance with the Court's Judgment of December 1974 in the Nuclear Tests (New Zealand v. France)*, Order of 22 September 1995, ('*second Nuclear Tests* case') (1995) ICJ Rep 288, Dissenting Opinion of Judge Weeramantry, at 342, a view also shared by Judge Palmer, at 412.

[35] *Pulp Mills*, para 164. See also *Whaling in the Antarctic* (*Australia v. Japan*: New Zealand intervening), Counter-memorial of Japan, submitted on 9 March 2012, para 9.34. Lucchini also argues that precaution does not entail a reversal of the burden of the proof, in Lucchini, L., 'Le principe de précaution en droit international de l'environnement: ombres plus que lumières' (1999) 45 *Annuaire français du droit international* 729.

[36] Sands, Ph. and Peel, J., *Principles of International Environmental Law* (3rd edn, Cambridge University Press 2012), 223.

[37] International Law Association, Committee on Legal Principles relating to Climate Change, 'Second Report' (Sofia, 75th session, 2012), 30.

[38] International Law Association, Committee on the Legal Aspects of Sustainable Development, 'New Delhi Declaration of Principles of International Law Relating to Sustainable Development' (New Delhi, 70th session, 2002) ('ILA New Delhi Declaration'), para 4.2 (d).

## 2.2. *Triggering thresholds*

The pervasive references to probability ('may'), time-span ('long-term') or seriousness ('serious' or 'irreversible') to specify the operation of the precautionary principle raise, of course, the difficult question of what the triggering thresholds should be. The wording of Principle 15 of the Rio Declaration differs in this respect from that of Principle 4 of the ILA New Delhi Declaration. Principle 15 hides the probabilistic question behind the obscure expression 'where there are threats', and does not qualify the serious or irreversible character of the damage by the additional specification 'long-term' used by Principle 4. In one case and the other, the ambiguity as to the proper province of the precautionary principle remains.

This difficulty was identified by the Seabed Chamber of the ITLOS in its 2011 Advisory Opinion on the Area, wherein it noted, in effect, that

> while the first sentence of Principle 15 seems to refer in general terms to the 'precautionary approach', the second sentence limits its scope to threats of 'serious or irreversible damage' and to 'cost-effective' measures adopted in order to prevent 'environmental degradation'.[39]

It thus highlighted the fact that the precautionary approach only applies when certain conditions are met. The next question concerns the criteria that trigger the application of the precautionary principle. Four elements are relevant for the implementation of Principle 15.

First, according to Principle 15, the precautionary principle applies only to threats of 'serious or irreversible damage'. This threshold, however, varies significantly, depending on the instrument in question. A treaty may require 'significant' harm,[40] 'reasonable grounds for concern',[41] or completely omit this criteria.[42]

Secondly, the notion of 'uncertainty' at the heart of the principle is not defined, thereby leaving open the question of the level of scientific uncertainty necessary to trigger precaution. Does uncertainty mean insufficient, inconclusive, or imprecise information?[43] Is any scientific evidence required to justify precaution, and if so, how much evidence is necessary? The practice of the Court of Justice of the European Union, under European law, suggests that insufficiency, inconclusiveness, or imprecision may not as such be a bar to the operation of the precautionary principle:

> Where it proves to be impossible to determine with certainty the existence or extent of the alleged risk because of the insufficiency, inconclusiveness or imprecision of the results of studies conducted, but the likelihood of real harm to public health persists should the risk materialise, the precautionary principle justifies the adoption of restrictive measures, provided they are non-discriminatory and objective.[44]

[39] ITLOS, Advisory Opinion on the Area, para 128.

[40] See eg Convention on Biological Diversity, Nairobi, 22 May 1992, in force 29 December 1993, (1992) 31 ILM 822, Preamble.

[41] See eg Convention for the Protection of the Marine Environment of the North-East Atlantic, Paris, 22 September 1992, in force 25 March 1998, (1993) 32 ILM 1068, art 2(2)(a).

[42] See eg Convention on the Ban of Import into Africa and the Control of Transboundary Movement and Management of Hazardous Wastes within Africa, Bamako, 29 January 1991, not yet in force, (1991) 30 ILM 775, art 4(3)(f).

[43] De Sadeleer, 'The Principle of Prevention and Precaution', 186.

[44] Case *Gowan Comércio Internacional e Serviços L$^{da}$ v. Ministero della Salute*, CJEU Case C-77/09, Judgment (22 December 2010), para 76.

Thirdly, economic considerations also play a role in the implementation of the precautionary principle. Principle 15 mentions that precautionary measures need to be 'cost-effective'. The criteria of cost-effectiveness is not always present in the various formulations of the principle. Some exclude this criterion on the ground that the precautionary approach should act in opposition to a cost-benefit analysis. Even when admitted as part of 'risk management' processes, the requirement of cost-effectiveness remains vague and open to interpretation. It appears that cost-effectiveness would include not only economic considerations but also other considerations, 'such as the efficacy of possible options and their acceptability to the public'.[45] Such interpretation—it should not pass unnoticed—empowers decision-makers with the duty to assess cost-effectiveness on the basis of elements difficult to quantify, like public perceptions of risk.

Fourthly, Principle 15 introduces a *caveat* on the requirements of the precautionary approach, which 'shall be applied' by States but only 'according to their capabilities'. It thereby creates a relative obligation of precaution based on the level of development but leaves open the question of the extent to which the level of development can be a justification for inaction.

## 2.3. *Legal nature*

### 2.3.1. Principle or approach?

There is no agreement regarding the nature of Principle 15 in international law. The phrasing of the principle itself is somewhat paradoxical: while enlisted as a 'principle', the wording of the provision speaks of a 'precautionary approach'. Both terms—'principle' and 'approach'—are frequently used to describe the nature of the obligation of precaution in international law. As a result, there is some controversy as to whether the differing denominations of the term have an impact on its legal nature. Both terms are sometimes used interchangeably in the same international document and some commentators have argued that no distinction between the two terms is necessary.[46] They are sometimes even combined to make a 'principle of the precautionary approach'.[47]

Yet, the two terms have distinct implications and the use of one over the other is not without consequences. The distinction between a 'principle' and an 'approach' lies in the normative character of the concept and in its potential role in international law. Taken as a 'principle', precaution leads to the creation of norms of conduct regarding potential harm in a context of scientific uncertainty. 'General principles' of law, set forth under article 38(1)(c) of the ICJ Statute, transcend norms and rules, in informing and conforming these latter, and guiding their intepretation and application.[48] They are 'basic pillars of the international legal system [that] give expression to the idée de droit, and furthermore to the *idée de justice*, reflecting the conscience of the international community'.[49] In this respect, precaution must be understood as reflecting the 'conscience of the international

[45] European Commission, COM(2000) 1 final (2 February 2000), 5.

[46] Birnie, P., Boyle, A., and Redgwell, C., *International Law and the Environment* (3rd edn, Oxford University Press 2009), 116.

[47] International Law Association, 'New Delhi Declaration of Principles of International Law relating to Sustainable Development', New Delhi, 70th session, 2002 ('New Delhi Principles'), s 4.

[48] *Pulp Mills* case, Separate Opinion of Judge Cançado Trindade, paras 5 and 6; and Cançado Trindade, A. A., 'Foundations of International Law: The Role and Importance of Its Basic Principles', in *XXX Curso de Derecho Internacional Organizado por el Comité Jurídico Interamericano*—OEA (2003) 359.

[49] *Pulp Mills* case, Separate Opinion of Judge Cançado Trindade, para 39.

community' regarding the need for environmental protection and its realization of the limitations of human knowledge.

The term 'approach', on the other hand, is less normative in content, leaving room for the States' discretion to undertake precautionary actions at national level. Such a perspective was highlighted by the arbitral tribunal of the *Indus Waters Kishenganga Arbitration* which refused in its Final Award to adopt a precautionary approach, on the basis that it would thus 'assume the role of policymaker in determining the balance between acceptable environmental change and other priorities'.[50] An 'approach' operates more as advice to national governments rather than conforming norms of conduct at international law level. The focus is, thus, rather on promoting a certain degree of 'flexibility'.[51] The fact remains that the distinction between the two terms is difficult to capture.[52] Whilst the term 'precautionary approach' seems to be preferred by US policy-makers, EU institutions refer to a 'precautionary principle'.[53] But, as rightly noted in expert writing, this distinction in the debate over precaution discloses 'different attitudes to risk rather than fundamentally different appreciations of the importance of taking scientific uncertainty into account' in decision-making.[54] In sum, the debate over precaution points to the existence of distinct concepts of risk management without compromising the key role it plays in international law.

### 2.3.2. Legal basis

Like the debate over the nature of Principle 15, the legal basis of the precautionary principle is a matter of much controversy and debate. The principle has undeniably gained considerable weight since its formulation at the Rio de Janeiro Conference. In effect, the precautionary principle has become prevalent in State practice: it has been incorporated in a large number of preambles and operative articles of international agreements and is regularly invoked by parties to international disputes. Overall, it enjoys a prominent place in international environmental law.[55] In addition, the principle has been widely implemented through national legislation and is regularly mentioned in national judicial decisions. Yet, its specific content and grounding remain controversial, as perceptions of the notion of risk and uncertainty vary considerably.

This being so, one must not overlook the fact that the States parties to recent disputes before the ICJ have not questioned the existence or core content of the principle. Such is the case for Uruguay, the defendant in the *Pulp Mills* case, where Argentina referred specifically to the precautionary principle; such is also the case for Japan, the defendant in the case of *Whaling in the Antarctic*, where Australia based its claim largely on the precautionary principle. In both the *Pulp Mills* and the *Whaling in the Antarctic* cases I deemed it fit to dwell upon the relevance of the precautionary principle, in the circumstances of each *cas d'espèce*.[56]

[50] *Indus Waters Kishenganga Arbitration* (*Pakistan v. India*), Permanent Court of Arbitration, Final Award, 20 December 2013, para 112.

[51] Peel, J., 'Precaution: A Matter of Principle, Approach or Process?' 5 (2004) *Melbourne Journal of International Law*, at 491.

[52] Peel, 'Precaution: A Matter of Principle, Approach or Process?', 491.

[53] See eg de Sadeleer, 'The Principle of Prevention and Precaution', 186.

[54] Peel, 500.

[55] Lucchini, 'Le principe de précaution en droit international', 712.

[56] This feature of the two cases is highlighted in the *Pulp Mills* case, Separate Opinion of Judge Cançado Trindade, para 112, and the *Whaling in the Antarctic* case, Separate Opinion of Judge Cançado Trindade, para 64.

Moreover, some domestic judicial decisions lend support to the customary basis of the precautionary principle in international law, with specific reference to Principle 15 of the Rio Declaration. By way of illustration, the Supreme Court of Pakistan has noted, in connection with the normative value of Principle 15, that:

Without framing a law in terms of the international agreement the covenants of such agreement cannot be implemented as a law nor do they bind down any party. This is the legal position of such documents, but the fact remains that they have a persuasive value and command respect. The Rio Declaration is the product of hectic discussion among the leaders of the nations of the world and it was after negotiations between the developed and the developing countries that an almost consensus declaration had been sorted out. Environment is an international problem having no frontiers creating transboundary effects. In this field every nation has to cooperate and contribute and for this reason the Rio Declaration would serve as a great binding force and to create discipline among the nations while dealing with environmental problems.[57]

In a similar vein, in the *Vellore Citizens Welfare Forum* case, the Supreme Court of India has observed that:

we have no hesitation in holding that the Precautionary Principle... [is] part of the environmental law of the country... Even otherwise once these principles are accepted as part of the Customary International Law there would be no difficulty in accepting them as part of the domestic law. It is almost an accepted proposition of law that the rules of Customary International Law which are not contrary to the municipal law shall be deemed to have been incorporated in the domestic law and shall be followed by the courts of law.[58]

Still another indication of the growing support for this principle in domestic case-law can be found in the decision of the Supreme Court of Canada in the *Spraytech* case, where the Court implied that the precautionary principle has a customary law basis in the light of which domestic law had to be interpreted.[59]

It is in this context that one is to understand the remarks made by the Seabed Chamber of the ITLOS in its 2011 Advisory Opinion on the Area:

The Chamber observes that the precautionary approach has been incorporated into a growing number of international treaties and other instruments, many of which reflect the formulation of Principle 15 of the Rio Declaration. In the view of the Chamber, this has initiated a trend towards making this approach part of customary international law.[60]

The Chamber thus recognizes the controversial nature of the principle but, at the same time, it stresses that the customary process in this respect is already in progress. In addition to the above authorities, there is also support for the proposition that the precautionary principle is a regional customary norm in the EU. Indeed, the precautionary principle is enshrined at the very heart of EU law. It has been embodied in article 191 of the Treaty on the Functioning of the European Union[61] and in secondary legislation. In 2000, the

[57] *Ms Shela Zia and others v. WAPDA P.L.D.*, 1994 SC 693, cited in Ramlogan, R., *Sustainable Development: Towards a Judicial Interpretation* (Martinus Nijhoff 2011), 87.

[58] *Vellore Citizens Welfare Forum v. Union of India* (1996) 5 SCC 647, cited in Ramlogan, *Sustainable Development*, 91. See also *A.P. Pollution Control Board v. Nayudu*, 1999 S.O.L. Case No 53, at para 27.

[59] *Canada Ltée (Spraytech, Société d'arrosage) v. Hudson (Town)* [2001] 2 SCR 241, 2001 SCC 40, para 30–2.

[60] Advisory Opinion on the Area, supra n. 31, para 135.

[61] Art 191 of the Treaty on the Functioning of the European Union (formerly Art 174 of the EC Treaty).

European Commission recognized in a communication on the PP that the application of the precautionary principle is a 'key tenet of [Community] policy'.[62]

## 3. Normative impact

### *3.1. Overview*

Principle 15 is a general formulation of precaution applicable to all fields of environmental law.[63] As a result, precaution has thrived in various fields and can be found in a variety of international instruments. The precautionary principle has been incorporated in some sixty multilateral agreements[64]—universal and regional environmental agreements, as well as agreements governing other matters.

### *3.2. Precaution and the marine environment*

The precautionary principle has thrived in its field of origin, that of marine protection. Given that data collected on marine pollution was abundant but difficult to interpret, the precautionary principle emerged as a key concept in this field. While UNCLOS, adopted in 1982, was negotiated before the emergence of the principle and thus does not provide for a precautionary approach, the Fish Stocks Agreement mentions the precautionary approach. Its article 5(c) makes the precautionary approach one of the general principles of the Agreement and article 6 gives very detailed guidelines regarding the 'application of the precautionary approach'.[65]

The 1996 Protocol to the London Dumping Convention also builds on the development of the precautionary principle in international law. By prohibiting the dumping into the sea of any material unless otherwise stated instead of listing materials which cannot be dumped—the approach chosen by the 1972 London Dumping Convention,[66] the aim of the Protocol is to make sure that the dumping of materials for which proof of harm has not be ascertained is illegal. As a result, the Protocol makes the precautionary approach the first of its 'general obligations' listed in article 3.[67]

The precautionary principle is also present in many regional law of the sea treaties, including the 1992 OSPAR Convention,[68] the 1992 Convention on the Protection of the Marine Environment of the Baltic Sea Area,[69] and the 2003 Framework Convention for the Protection

[62] European Commission, COM(2000) 1 final (2 February 2000) para 3.

[63] Confirmed by its multiple references in Agenda 21, 'Annex II to the Report of the United Nations Conference on Environment and Development' (Rio de Janeiro, 3 to 14 June 1992), UN Doc A/CONF.151/2: 'the precautionary approach' is deemed applicable to the marine environment (paras 17.1, 17.5, 17.21, 17.22), climate change (paras 17.97, 17.128), water pollution (para 18.40), hazardous substances and wastes (paras 19.14, 19.48, 19.49, 19.60, 20.32, 22.5).

[64] de Sadeleer, 'The Principle of Prevention and Precaution', 187.

[65] Agreement for the Implementation of the Provisions of the United Nations Convention on the Law of the Sea of 10 December 1982 relating to the Conservation and Management of Straddling Fish Stocks and Highly Migratory Fish Stocks, New York, 4 August 1995, in force 11 December 2001, 2167 UNTS 3. See also annex II to the Agreement.

[66] Convention on the Prevention of Marine Pollution by Dumping of Wastes and Other Matter, London, 29 December 1972, in force 30 August 1975, (1972) 11 ILM 1294.

[67] Protocol to the Convention on the Prevention of Marine Pollution by Dumping of Wastes and Other Matter, London, 7 November 1996, in force 24 March 2006, (1997) 36 ILM 1, Art 3(1).

[68] OSPAR Convention, Art 2(2)(a).

[69] Convention on the Protection of the Marine Environment of the Baltic Sea Area, Helsinki, 9 April 1992, in force 17 January 2000, 35 BNA 0401, ('Baltic Sea Convention'), Art 3(2).

of the Marine Environment of the Caspian Sea.[70] The success of the principle in the field of marine protection is exemplified in a striking manner in the recent Rio+20 document which mentioned the precautionary principle only in the section on oceans and seas.[71]

### *3.3. Precaution and watercourses*

The precautionary principle is also represented in the field of watercourse protection, and can be found in numerous regional conventions, including the 1992 UNECE Convention on the Protection and Use of Transboundary Watercourses and International Lakes,[72] the 1994 Convention on Co-operation for the Protection and Sustainable Use of the River Danube,[73] the 1994 Agreement on the Protection of the Rivers Meuse and Scheldt[74] and the 1998 Convention on the Protection of the Rhine.[75]

Although the New York UN Watercourse Convention does not directly mention precaution, the ILC Draft Articles on Watercourses which served as the basis for negotiations mention in their commentaries the necessity to apply the precautionary principle 'to protect the ecosystems of international watercourses'.[76] As a result, it hints at the existence of an obligation of precaution at the universal level in the field of watercourse protection.

### *3.4. Precaution and the atmosphere*

Concerns over the protection of the atmosphere had also contributed to the emergence of the precautionary principle, which found its way into treaty law via the Vienna Convention and the Montreal Protocol. The precautionary principle was then included also in the 1992 UN Framework Convention on Climate Change.[77] In addition, the Convention on Long-Range Transboundary Air Pollution,[78] adopted before the emergence of precaution, has also been updated via its Protocols that affirm the importance of the precautionary approach.[79]

[70] Framework Convention for the Protection of the Marine Environment of the Caspian Sea, Tehran, 4 November 2003, in force 12 August 2006, 44 ILM 1, art 5.

[71] *The Future We Want*, UNGA Res. 66/288 (27 July 2012), paras 158 and 167.

[72] Convention on the Protection and Use of Transboundary Watercourses and International Lakes, Helsinki, 17 March 1992, in force 6 October 1996, (1992) 31 ILM 1312, art 2(5)(a).

[73] Convention on Co-operation for the Protection and Sustainable Use of the Danube River, Sofia, 29 June 1994, in force 22 October 1998, ECOLEX TRE-001207, art 2(4).

[74] Agreement on the Protection of the Rivers Meuse and Scheldt, Charleville Mézières, 26 April 1994, in force 1 March 1995, (1995) 34 ILM 851, arts 2(a) and 3(2)(a).

[75] Convention on the Protection of the Rhine, Rotterdam, 22 January 1998, in force 12 April 1999, Official Journal of the European Communities L 289 (16 November 2000) 30, art 4.

[76] 'Draft Articles on the Law of the Non-navigational Uses of International Watercourses (with Commentaries)'.

[77] United Nations Framework Convention on Climate Change, New York, 9 May 1992, in force 24 March 1994, 1771 UNTS 107 ('UNFCCC'), art 3 (3).

[78] Convention on Long-Range Transboundary Air Pollution, Geneva, 13 November 1979, in force 16 March 1983, (1979) 18 ILM 1442 ('LRTAP Convention').

[79] The four post-Rio Protocols to the LRTAP Convention reaffirm Principle 15 in their Preambles: Protocol to the 1979 Convention on Long Range Transboundary Air Pollution on Further Reduction of Sulphur Emissions, Oslo, 14 June 1994, in force 5 August 1998, (1998) 33 ILM 1540; Convention on Long Range Transboundary Air Pollution on Persistent Organic Pollutants, Aarhus, 24 June 1998, in force 23 December 2003, (1998) 37 ILM 505; Protocol to the 1979 Convention on Long Range Transboundary Air Pollution to Abate Acidification, Eutrophication and Ground-Level Ozone, Gothenburg, 30 November 1999, in force 17 May 2005, UN Doc EB/AIR/1999.

### 3.5. *Precaution and chemicals*

The precautionary principle is also present in the field of hazardous activities which carry significant risk of environmental damage and for which scientific assessments can be time-consuming and expensive. In this respect, the 2001 Stockholm Convention on Persistent Organic Pollutants set precaution as its objective in the Preamble[80] and in article 1: 'Mindful of the precautionary approach as set forth in Principle 15 of the Rio Declaration on Environment and Development, the objective of this Convention is to protect human health and the environment from persistent organic pollutants'. For its part, the 2003 UNECE Protocol on Pollutant Release also reaffirms Principle 15 twice in its text.[81] However, it is noticeable that the principle has not yet secured a strong place in waste management[82] and is not enshrined in agreements dealing with nuclear energy.

### 3.6. *Precaution and biodiversity*

The necessity to conserve biodiversity despite a lack of data and understanding of the functioning of ecosystems has contributed to the development of the precaution principle in the field of biodiversity. The 1992 Convention on Biological Diversity, adopted at UNCED, affirms precaution in its Preamble: 'where there is a threat of significant reduction or loss of biological diversity, lack of full scientific uncertainty should not be used as a reason for postponing measures to avoid or minimize such a threat'. The principle has also been adopted in several agreements on the conservation of migratory species.[83]

Furthermore, the risk represented by the use of GMOs to the environment and human health has gathered momentum at the international level. As a result, the principle of precaution has been placed at the heart of the 2000 Cartagena Protocol on Biosafety to the Convention on Biological Diversity which reaffirms Principle 15 and authorizes Parties to refuse to import living modified organisms on a precautionary basis.[84] Also relevant in this connection is the 1994 Agreement on the Application of Sanitary and Phytosanitary Measures.[85]

### 3.7. *Precaution and the ILC Prevention Articles*

More generally, although precaution is not explicitly mentioned in the ILC Prevention Articles, the commentaries to the articles do consider that Principle 15 is relevant for the implementation of article 7 on risk assessment and the implementation of article 10(c). Specifically, they list 'the risk of significant harm to the environment and the availability

[80] Convention on Persistent Organic Pollutants, Stockholm, 22 May 2001, in force 17 May 2004, (2001) 40 ILM 532, Preamble.

[81] Protocol on Pollutant Release and Transfer Registers to the Aarhus Convention, Kiev, 21 May 2003, in force 8 October 2009, UN Doc MP/PP/2003/1, Preamble and art 3(4).

[82] It is only present in the Bamako Convention, not yet in force, in art 4(3)(f).

[83] Agreement on the Conservation of the African-Eurasian Migratory Waterbirds, The Hague, 15 August 1996, in force 1 November 1999, <http://www.unep-aewa.org/en/documents/agreement-text>, art 2(2); Agreement on the Conservation of Cetaceans of the Black Sea, Mediterranean Sea and Contiguous Atlantic Areas, Monaco, 24 November 1996, in force 1 June 2001, <http://sedac.ciesin.columbia.edu/entri/texts/cetaceans.conservation.96.html>, art 2(4); Agreement on the Conservation of Albatrosses and Petrels, Canberra, 19 June 2001, in force 1 February 2004, <http://www.acap.aq/index.php/en/acap-agreement>, art 2(3).

[84] Cartagena Protocol on Biosafety to the Convention on Biological Diversity, Montreal, 29 January 2000, in force 11 September 2003, 39 ILM 1027, arts 10(6) and 11(8).

[85] Agreement on the Application of Sanitary and Phytosanitary Measures, 15 April 1994, Marrakesh Agreement establishing the World Trade Organization, Annex I, Legal Instruments—Results of the Uruguay Round, (1994) 33 ILM 1125, art 5(7).

of means of preventing such harm, or minimizing the risk thereof or restoring the environment' as one of factors that States should take into account to achieve an equitable balance of interests with other States which might be affected by transboundary harm. The Prevention Articles thus indirectly include an obligation to follow a precautionary approach when cooperating with other States in order to prevent transboundary damage.

## 4. Jurisprudential developments

### *4.1. Overview*

Given its uncertain normative status, the precautionary principle has given rise to a cautious approach in international jurisprudence. While the principle is regularly invoked before international courts and tribunals, international adjudicatory bodies have broadly remained cautious with regard to explicitly recognizing the normative status of the principle. At the same time, a number of dissenting and separate opinions regularly lament the cautious approach privileged by international courts and tribunals, thereby revealing a lack of consensus regarding the applicability of the precautionary principle.

### *4.2. International Court of Justice*

In contrast with its stance on the prevention principle,[86] the ICJ has been reluctant to give a role to the precautionary principle in its jurisprudence. The precautionary principle was first invoked in front of the Court in the second *Nuclear Tests* case, a few years after its consecration at the Rio Conference.[87] New Zealand relied extensively on the principle,[88] describing it as 'a very widely accepted and operative principle of international law' that shifted the burden of proof to France to prove that the tests would not result in environmental damage.[89] The status of the principle was challenged by France.[90] The ICJ itself did not refer to the precautionary principle in its judgment.

Likewise, while precaution was invoked by Hungary and Slovakia in the *Gabčíkovo-Nagymaros* case, the ICJ did not recognize the precautionary principle as one of customary international environmental law, and declined to declare that the principle could override the obligations of the treaty at issue. Although it recognized that Hungary's concerns for its environment could be considered as an 'essential interest' of the State, the ICJ found that 'the peril claimed by Hungary was to be considered in the long term, and, more importantly, remained uncertain' and refused to apply the precautionary principle to the case.[91]

The attitude of the Court evolved slightly in the *Pulp Mills* case, as it made its first reference to precaution in acknowledging that a precautionary approach might be relevant 'in the interpretation and application' of applicable texts. Yet, the Court considered that the

[86] See Viñuales, J.E., 'The Contribution of the International Court of Justice to the Development of International Environmental Law' (2008) 32 *Fordham International Law Journal* 232.

[87] *Second Nuclear Tests* case, paras 105–8.

[88] As I noted in my Separate Opinion to the *Pulp Mills* case, in the first *Nuclear Tests* case New Zealand had already resorted to arguments revealing 'the importance of the awakening of conscience as to the need to resort to precaution, beyond prevention' (at paras 64–5).

[89] *Second Nuclear Tests* case, para 105, and *Oral Pleadings*, ICJ CR/95/20, New Zealand, at 20–1 and 36–8.

[90] *Oral Pleadings*, ICJ CR/95/20, New Zealand, at 71–2 and 75; France replied that the legal status of the principle was 'uncertain'.

[91] *Gabčíkovo-Nagymaros Project* (Hungary/Slovakia) (1997) ICJ Rep 7, para 56.

precautionary approach does not 'operate as a reversal of the burden of proof',[92] and thus did not apply it to the case.

Last but not least, in the recent *Whaling in the Antarctic* case, the precautionary approach was once more invoked by the parties, each pleading a different interpretation of the norm. Both Parties acknowledged that States have an obligation to follow a precautionary approach and yet differed on the consequences of this obligation. While Australia[93] and New Zealand[94] argued that the precautionary approach required that no whales would be killed to carry out research or that, if necessary, the number of whales taken must be low, Japan contrariwise argued that the precautionary approach required that action be taken in order to alleviate the scientific uncertainty existing regarding whale conservation and exploitation, thus justifying the killing of whales for scientific reasons.[95]

The ICJ did not address the precautionary principle in its Judgment on the *Whaling in the Antarctic* case,[96] though I examined it in my Separate Opinion appended thereto (paras 60–71). And earlier on, in the *Pulp Mills* case, I pondered, in my previous Separate Opinion, that while the Court has 'so far had so much precaution with the precautionary principle..., the fact that the Court has not expressly acknowledged the existence of this general principle of International Environmental Law does not mean that it does not exist.'[97]

## 4.3. *International Tribunal for the Law of the Sea*

The International Tribunal for the Law of the Sea ('ITLOS') has been more open than other tribunals to recognize the role of precaution in international law, a reality primarily explained by the fact that the tribunal is the guardian of UNCLOS, a convention that has made environmental protection one of its pillars. Nevertheless, the tribunal has remained cautious regarding precaution by not relying expressly on the precautionary principle—which is not mentioned in UNCLOS—but by creating an obligation for parties to act with 'prudence and caution'. This expression, which it has embraced regularly,[98] can be deemed to create an obligation to follow a precautionary approach—confirmed by the French translation of the word which directly employs the word 'precaution'.[99]

[92] *Pulp Mills*, para 164.

[93] *Whaling in the Antarctic*, Memorial of Australia, submitted 9 March 2011, where, relying on Principle 15, it put forward the precautionary approach in the face of uncertainty regarding the status of whale stocks and the effect of lethal takes, at para 4.87–4.90.

[94] *Whaling in the Antarctic*, Written Observations of New Zealand, submitted 4 April 2013, where it argued that the precautionary approach 'requires that no whales will be killed unless that is necessary to achieve the objectives of the intended research—non-lethal research alternatives should be given preference. If whales are to be killed, precaution requires that the number taken must be as low as necessary to meet those objectives', at paras 74–5.

[95] *Whaling in the Antarctic*, Counter-memorial of Japan: 'Japan does not dispute that it should act with prudence and caution. A precautionary approach necessarily envisages that steps will be taken to illuminate uncertainties and provide a sounder scientific basis for conservation and sustainable exploitation', at para 9.33.

[96] *Whaling in the Antarctic* (*Australia v. Japan*: New Zealand intervening), Judgment (31 March 2004) (not yet reported).

[97] *Pulp Mills* case, Separate Opinion of Judge Cançado Trindade, paras 67–8.

[98] *Land Reclamation by Singapore in and around the Straits of Johor* (*Malaysia v. Singapore*) (provisional measures), ITLOS No. 12 (8 October 2003), para 99; *MOX Plant*, para 84; *Southern Bluefin Tuna* (*New Zealand v. Japan*; *Australia v. Japan*) (provisional measures) ITLOS Nos 3 and 4 (27 August 1999), para 77.

[99] The expression used in the French translation is 'prudence et précaution'. Lucchini nevertheless makes a distinction between the two and argues that prudence is a general attitude while precaution implies a more pragmatic approach: it is because of prudence that we take precautions—Lucchini, 'Le principe de précaution

In effect, in the *Southern Bluefin Tuna* case, ITLOS recognized that the parties should 'act with prudence and caution to ensure that effective conservation measures are taken to prevent serious harm to the stock of southern Bluefin tuna', that there was 'scientific uncertainty regarding measures to be taken to conserve the stock of southern bluefin tuna'.[100] Similarly, in the *MOX Plant* case, the Tribunal did not directly refer to the principle but ordered the parties to cooperate and enter into consultations to exchange information on possible consequences for the Irish Sea and to devise measures to prevent pollution of the marine environment.[101] In both cases, some judges lamented the fact that the Tribunal did not make a direct reference to precaution.[102]

Recently, ITLOS directly embraced the precautionary principle in its Advisory Opinion on the Area. It confirmed that the inclusion of Principle 15 to the ISBA Nodules and Sulphides Regulations transformed the non-binding statement of Principle 15 into a binding obligation,[103] and observed that:

> the precautionary approach has been incorporated into a growing number of international treaties and other instruments, many of which reflect the formulation of Principle 15 of the Rio Declaration. In the view of the Chamber, this has initiated a trend towards making this approach part of customary international law.[104]

ITLOS thus considered that the precautionary approach is applicable as a result of the ISBA Regulations but also as a principle which is 'an integral part of the general obligation of due diligence'.[105] It provided that the obligation of due diligence:

> applies in situations where scientific evidence concerning the scope and potential negative impact of the activity in question is insufficient but where there are plausible indications of potential risks. A sponsoring State would not meet its obligation of due diligence if it disregarded those risks. Such disregard would amount to a failure to comply with the precautionary approach.[106]

This affirmation strengthens the status of precaution in international law by recognizing that it is on the way towards becoming customary, and also by making clear that an obligation of due diligence necessarily implies an obligation of precaution.

### 4.4. *The WTO dispute settlement body*

As a principle applicable in fields other than international environmental law, the precautionary principle has also been addressed in other contexts. It has been an issue before the WTO Appellate Body, which described the status of the precautionary principle to be 'less than clear'.[107] In the *EC-Hormones* case, for example, while the EU had argued

en droit international', at 717: 'La prudence ne correspond-elle pas à une attitude générale, tandis que la «précaution» impliquerait, quant à elle, une démarche plus pragmatique? La prudence n'est-elle pas la vertu qui conduit à prendre des précautions?'.

[100] *Southern Bluefin Tuna*, para 77. [101] *MOX Plant*, para 89(1).

[102] cf in the *Southern Bluefin Tuna* case, the Separate Opinion of Judge Treves lamenting the fact that the precautionary principle was not explicitly referred to in the Order (para 8), corroborated by the position of Judge ad hoc Shearer in his own Separate Opinion; cf also, to the same effect, in the *MOX Plant* case, the Separate Opinion of Judge ad hoc Szekely (para 22).

[103] ITLOS Advisory Opinion on the Area, para 127.

[104] ITLOS Advisory Opinion on the Area, para 135.

[105] ITLOS Advisory Opinion on the Area, para 131.

[106] ITLOS Advisory Opinion on the Area, para 131.

[107] *European Communities—Measures Concerning Meat and Meat Products (Hormones)—Arbitration under Article 21.3(c) of the Dispute Settlement Understanding, Appellate Body* (29 May 1998) DSR 1998:V, WT/DS26/15 and WT/DS26/15,1833 ('*EC–Hormones*'), paras 123–5.

that the principle was a customary rule of international law, the Appellate Body ruled that 'the precautionary principle has been incorporated and given a specific meaning in article 5.7 of the SPS Agreement',[108] but remained cautious, considering that 'it is unnecessary, and probably imprudent, for the Appellate Body in this appeal to take a position on this important, but abstract, question.'[109] Similarly, in the *EC-Biotech Products* case, the WTO panel noted that the legal status of the precautionary principle was 'unsettled' and 'there has, to date, been no authoritative decision by an international court or tribunal which recognizes the precautionary principle as a principle of general or customary international law'.[110]

### 4.5. *European Court of Human Rights*

Precaution has also been discussed in the domain of human rights protection. For many years, the European Court of Human Rights ('ECtHR') seemed reluctant to accept the precautionary principle. Its position in *Balmer-Schafroth v. Switzerland*, a case concerning the extension of the operating life of a 1971 nuclear power plant, provides a good illustration of this stance.[111] By twelve votes to eight, the ECtHR decided that the applicants, who were people potentially affected by the threat presented by the operation of the nuclear facility, had failed to demonstrate that they were personally exposed to a serious, specific, and imminent danger.

Yet, the seeds of jurisprudential change were already present in this case. In a dissenting opinion by Judge Pettiti, joined by six other judges, the reluctance of the ECtHR was highly criticized; it was stated that

> The Court's assessment of the tenuousness of the connection and of the absence of imminent danger is, in my opinion, unfounded. Does the local population first have to be irradiated before being entitled to exercise a remedy?[112]

More recently, in a case concerning gold mining in Romania using sodium cyanide (a water pollutant), the ECtHR reversed its position on the precautionary principle, recognizing

> the importance of 'the precautionary principle (enshrined for the first time in the Rio Declaration), which was intended to apply in order to ensure a level of high protection of health, the safety of consumers and the environment in all Community activities'.[113]

### 4.6. *European Courts*

At the European level, the European Court of Justice has clearly recognized the normative basis of the precautionary principle as a general principle of EU law. Several decisions can be referred to in this regard.[114] A clear and detailed discussion of the operation of the precautionary principle with reference to the relevant prior jurisprudence appears in

108 *EC–Hormones*, para 120. 109 *EC–Hormones*, para 123.

110 *European Communities—Measures Affecting the Approval and Marketing of Biotech Products*, Panel Report (29 September 2006), WT/DS291/R, WT/DS292/R, WT/DS293/R ('*EC-Biotech Products*'), para 7.88. In taking this view, the panel followed the Appellate Body in *EC–Hormones*, para 124.

111 *Balmer-Schafroth v. Switzerland*, ECtHR Application no 22110/93, Judgment (26 August 1997).

112 *Balmer-Schafroth v. Switzerland*, dissenting opinion of Judge Pettiti, joined by Judges Golcuklu, Walsh, Russo, Valticos, Lopes Rocha, and Jambrek.

113 ECtHR, case *Tatar v. Romania*, ECtHR Application no 67021/01, Judgment (27 January 2009, Final 6 July 2009), para 120 (unofficial translation from the French original).

114 See, eg *Pfizer Animal Health SA v. Council*, CJEC n° T-13/99, paras 114–15.

the recent *Gowan* case. The case pertained to severe restrictions placed by the European Commission on pesticide uses of fenarimol, despite the fact that the Commission's earlier risk assessment had concluded that it caused limited harm. The Court upheld the measure challenged, noting however *inter alia* that

> A correct application of the precautionary principle presupposes, first, identification of the potentially negative consequences for health of the proposed use of the substance at issue, and, secondly, a comprehensive assessment of the risk to health based on the most reliable scientific data available and the most recent results of international research.[115]

Yet, the reception of the precautionary principle in European courts follows the express recognition of this principle in European law and may not necessarily be a good indicator of the fortune of such principle in the larger context of general international law.

### *4.7. Inter-American Court of Human Rights*

The Inter-American Court of Human Rights (IACtHR) has contributed to the subject matter under review within a larger framework, concerning more directly the principle of prevention. In my book of memories of the IACtHR I devote an entire chapter precisely to the *preventive dimension* of the protection of the rights of the human person (chapter XXI) under the American Convention on Human Rights, developed in particular in its pioneering and unparalleled case law on provisional measures of protection, endowed with a conventional basis.[116] International Human Rights Law has indeed contributed to International Environmental Law,[117] more than what is commonly realized.

To evoke but one example, with a bearing on the precautionary principle, in cases of *grave* violations of human rights, revealing a consistent pattern of such violations leaving victims in a state of extreme adversity and vulnerability, if not defencelessness, the IACtHR has proceeded on the basis of presumptions and inferences, and has proceeded to a shifting or reversal of the burden of proof (or at least a lowering of the standard of proof in international litigation), for one particular reason: in those circumstances, the respondent State (rather than the individual applicants) withholds the information and probationary elements concerning the alleged grave violations.[118]

## III) Relations with Other Principles

### 1. Prevention and precaution

The distinction between Principle 2 and Principle 15 of the Rio Declaration is sometimes overlooked, as prevention and precaution are both often at the heart of environmental treaties. As I pondered in my Separate Opinion in the *Pulp Mills* case, they have both

[115] *Gowan Comércio Internacional e Serviços L^da v. Ministero della Salute*, CJEU Case C-77/09, Judgment (22 December 2010), para 75.

[116] Cançado Trindade, A. A., *El Ejercicio de la Función Judicial Internacional—Memorias de la Corte Interamericana de Derechos Humanos*, (3rd edn, Edit. Del Rey 2013), ch XXI, 177–86.

[117] See Cançado Trindade, A. A., 'The Contribution of International Human Rights Law to Environmental Protection, with Special Reference to Global Environmental Change', in Brown Weiss, E. (ed), *Environmental Change and International Law* (United Nations University Press 1992–1993), 244.

[118] For a study on this particular issue, cf Cançado Trindade, A. A., *State Responsibility in Cases of Massacres: Contemporary Advances in International Justice* (Universiteit Utrecht 2011), 1–71.

emerged as a result of the consciousness of the 'pressing need to secure the protection of the environment, given its vulnerability, the risks surrounding everyone, and the harmful consequences of irreparable damages caused to it',[119] and they share the common goal of enhancing environmental protection and 'far from excluding each other, serve their purposes together'.[120] Yet, given their slight overlap,[121] the two principles sometimes tend to be used interchangeably, often assuming that the application of one entails that of the other.

While the 1972 Stockholm Declaration consecrated the prevention principle, and the 1992 Rio Declaration emanating from UNCED reaffirmed the prevention principle while also adding the precautionary approach, some view the ensuing consecration of the precautionary principle as an alternative to prevention, thereby contributing to the growing attention in expert writing devoted to the precautionary principle, perhaps overshadowing the prevention principle. While prevention emerged as a result of a new consciousness regarding environmental damage, precaution developed out of the realization that risks cannot always be predicted.

As a result, '[p]revention envisaged risks, but assumed they were certain. Precaution thus emerged, as an ineluctable principle, to face also uncertain risks, given the uncertainties of life itself, and the intuition of surrounding death.'[122] As noted by J.E. Viñuales, there is a clear-cut difference between 'risk', as an identifiable adverse outcome (the realm of prevention), and 'uncertainty' (the realm of precaution).[123] Both overlap to some extent (eg, more or less likely risk), as many of the uses of precaution are applications of prevention. L. Lucchini grounds the distinction between prevention and precaution on how serious the risk is: while prevention is a general concept that dictates the general actions of States in terms of environmental protection, precaution amounts to a reinforcement of the obligation in light of a potential serious danger that cannot yet be predicted.[124] The former approach considers the two principles to be different concepts while the latter approach sees them as part of a *continuum*. Yet, both conceptualizations focus on a key conceptual difference: prevention frames risks that are certain, while precaution provides a basis for uncertain 'risks'.

[119] *Pulp Mills* case, Separate Opinion of Judge Cançado Trindade, para 52.

[120] *Pulp Mills* case, Separate Opinion of Judge Cançado Trindade, para 98.

[121] *Pulp Mills* case, Separate Opinion of Judge Cançado Trindade, para 61: 'a series of International Environmental Law instruments were to capture the rationale of the principle of prevention and the precautionary principle together'. For instance, the OSPAR Convention directly links preventive measures and scientific uncertainty by stating that preventive measures are to be taken where there are 'reasonable grounds for concern ... even when there is no conclusive evidence of a causal relationship between the inputs and the effects' (art 2(2)(a)). Similarly, the 1992 Baltic Sea Convention provides that preventive measures are to be taken 'when there is reason to assume' that harm might be caused 'even when there is no conclusive evidence of a causal relationship between inputs and their alleged effects' (art 3(2)).

[122] *Pulp Mills* case, Separate Opinion of Judge Cançado Trindade, para 69.

[123] See Viñuales, J. E., 'Legal Techniques for Dealing with Scientific Uncertainty in Environmental Law' (2010) 43 *Vanderbilt Journal of Transnational Law* 437 (as noted by this commentator, the entire insurance industry is based on the distinction between risk and uncertainty).

[124] Lucchini, 'Le principe de précaution en droit international', at 715: 'Elle nous paraît résider dans le degré plus ou moins élevé de la gravité du risque. La prévention a un caractère de généralité. Elle doit dicter, en permanence et pour toutes circonstances, le comportement des acteurs. La précaution, quant à elle, nécessite un renforcement de cette attitude face à un danger plus grave et préoccupant et dont on ne sait pas, compte tenu des connaissances scientifiques du moment, les conséquences qu'il pourrait entraîner s'il venait à se réaliser'.

Given their close ties, prevention and precaution will most likely keep on acting in a temporal continuum, providing a legal framework for a moving society characterized by risks and scientific advances.[125] In the recent case of *Whaling in the Antarctic* (2013), I had the occasion to dwell upon this matter in my Separate Opinion appended to the ICJ's Judgment; I deemed it fit to observe that:

> Even if the Court, in the present Judgment in the *Whaling in the Antarctic* case, has not seen it fit to pronounce on the principle of prevention and the precautionary principle, it is, in my view, significant that the contending parties, Australia and Japan, and the intervenor, New Zealand, have cared to refer to these principles, in general, in their arguments as to whether or not Japan's whaling practices under Special Permits conform to them. Such principles are to inform and conform any programmes under Special Permits within the limited scope of article VIII of the ICRW Convention [International Convention for the Regulation of Whaling]. Furthermore, the principles of prevention and precaution appear interrelated in the present case of *Whaling in the Antarctic.* May I add just one final remark in this respect. Despite the hesitation of the ICJ (and of other international tribunals in general) to pronounce and dwell upon the precautionary principle, expert writing increasingly examines it, drawing attention to its incidence when there is need to take protective measures in face of risks, even in the absence of corresponding scientific proof. The precautionary principle, in turn, draws attention to the time factor, the temporal dimension, which marks a noticeable presence in the interpretation and application of treaties and instruments of international environmental law.[126] In this domain in general, and in respect of the ICRW Convention in particular, there has occurred, with the passing of time, a move towards conservation of living marine resources as a common interest, prevailing over State unilateral action in search of commercial profitability.[127] This move has taken place by the operation of the system of collective guarantee, collective decision-making and collective regulation under the ICRW Convention.[128]

## 2. Precaution and the obligation to carry out an environmental impact assessment

Considered together during the drafting of the 1992 Rio Declaration, the obligation to carry out an environmental impact assessment ('EIA') and the obligation of precaution share a direct link.[129] The close link between precaution and the EIA was recognized early on and was invoked by New Zealand in the *second Nuclear Tests* case.[130] The relationship has also been put forward in the Commentaries to the ILC Prevention Articles which

[125] This was confirmed in the ILA 2014 'Declaration of Principles Relating to Climate Change' (Washington DC, 76th session, 2014) which dealt with prevention and precaution under the same art 7 and provides that 'Where scientific knowledge about damage from climate change improves sufficiently', protective measures shall be taken, not any more in application of the precautionary approach but in application of the duty of prevention (art 7B(3)).

[126] See generally eg Tanaka, Y., 'Reflections on Time Elements in the International Law of the Environment' (2013) 73 *Zeitschrift für ausländisches öffentliches Recht und Völkerrecht* 143–7, 150–6, 165–7, and 170–5.

[127] See Bowman, M., '"Normalizing" the International Convention for the Regulation of Whaling' (2008) 29 *Michigan Journal of International Law* 139, 163, 175–7, and 199.

[128] *Whaling in the Antarctic* case, Separate Opinion of Judge Cançado Trindade, paras 70–1.

[129] *Pulp Mills* case, Separate Opinion of Judge Cançado Trindade, referring to 'the emergence of the precautionary principle brought about the requirement to undertake complete environmental impact assessments' (para 71).

[130] New Zealand argued that the precautionary principle required an EIA 'as a precondition for undertaking the activities, and to demonstrate that there was no risk associated with them', *second Nuclear Tests* case, para 35.

provide that 'the environmental impact assessment... combines the precautionary principle with the principle of preventing environmental damage'.[131]

The relationship between precaution and the EIA illustrates the specific roles played by prevention and precaution in the assessment of risks. Indeed, while the EIA is based on the 'premise that project-related environmental impacts can be predicted'[132]—the assumption on which prevention is also based—in reality it is not always possible to predict the impact of an activity of the environment. As a result, the precautionary approach is justified when scientific understanding is insufficient. The precautionary approach thus recognizes the limitations of the EIA and offers an alternative solution. Furthermore, the approach relies on the EIA to recognize areas when 'information is incomplete but where analysis indicates the risk or possibility of large scale, serious, or irreversible environmental change', thus justifying a precautionary approach and not going ahead with some proposals or finding alternatives.[133]

Both principles are thus strongly interconnected. If, as some commentators argue, precaution should be understood primarily as a 'process' of risk regulation that influences decision-making,[134] then the EIA plays a key role in this process by providing the basis for a comprehensive and objective risk evaluation. In addition, if the precautionary principle implies a reversal of the burden of proof, then the EIA is a central instrument in this matter, as it will provide the State engaged in the potentially risky activity the necessary information to prove its due diligence and its knowledge as to the limited impact of the activity.

Despite the close relationship between the two principles, there is an asymmetry between the two principles as enshrined in the Rio Declaration. Indeed, the similar phrasing between Principle 15 and Principle 17 indicates a strong relationship, but while the precautionary approach is justified where 'there are threats of serious or irreversible damage', the obligation to carry out an EIA is necessary for 'proposed activities that are likely to have a significant adverse impact on the environment'. As a result, under the Rio Declaration, the obligation of precaution arises in cases of 'serious or irreversible damage', while the obligation to carry out an EIA exists in cases of 'significant' damage.

The level of the threshold thus appears to be lower in the case of the EIA than in the case of precaution. In a sense, this asymmetry is explained by the fact that the EIA is essential for the implementation of the prevention principle for which the threshold is commonly one of 'significant' damage, while the application of the precautionary principle would appear to remain exceptional. However, the different variations of the precautionary principle outside of the Rio Declaration that sometimes provide for its application in cases of significant damage blur this asymmetry.

## 3. Precaution and the obligation to notify and consult

The precautionary principle has a dual audience: it is here to address the concerns of other States regarding potential transboundary impacts but it also aims to ease the concerns of populations over the impacts of human activities over their health and environment.

[131] ILC Prevention Articles, Commentary to art 7, para 4, 158.

[132] UNEP, *Environmental Impact Assessment and Strategic Impact Assessment: Towards an Integrated Approach* (UNEP 2004), 53.

[133] UNEP, *Environmental Impact Assessment and Strategic Impact Assessment*, 107.

[134] Peel, 'Precaution: A Matter of Principle, Approach or Process?,' at 204.

As such, the precautionary principle implies an obligation to notify and consult both States and local populations. In a transboundary perspective, precaution requires notification and consultation of States regarding the potential effects of an activity on their territory. This obligation of notification and consultation is part of a more general obligation to cooperate in good faith to implement the principles of the Declaration.[135]

Precaution requires cooperation with other States not only to notify them of potential risks but also to share information and scientific knowledge. In this respect, ITLOS made a strong link between the obligation of precaution and the necessity to exchange information in the *MOX Plant* case, by providing that 'prudence and caution require that Ireland and the United Kingdom cooperate in exchanging information concerning risks or effects of the operation of the MOX plant and in devising ways to deal with them'.[136] In extreme cases where the risk of damage can be particularly serious and widespread or where the risk might affect the global commons, precaution would also entail an obligation of notification and information sharing 'with the international community'.[137]

But the precautionary principle goes beyond Principle 19, which provides for information to potentially affected States and requires taking into account public participation as provided for by Principle 10. It is estimated that '[t]he obligation to notify and share information with the affected populations is one which ensues from the precautionary principle'.[138] As such, the precautionary principle is less focused on inter-State relations than on providing the population with confidence over its health and environment. The idea of 'uncertainty' is one that directly addresses the concerns of the individual and feelings of unease. As a result, precaution is primarily concerned with the safety of the population and thus implies a duty of notification and consultation with the local populations.

## 4. Precaution and sustainable development

The relationship between precaution and sustainable development[139] appears evident in international instruments. Both concepts have emerged at the same time in the 1980s and were both consecrated at UNCED in Rio de Janeiro. Their concurrent rise in the international sphere has played a key role in shaping their interconnectedness. Since its formulation in the Bergen Ministerial Declaration which claimed that '[i]n order to achieve sustainable development, policies must be based on the precautionary principle', the precautionary principle—as a principle of international environmental law—has been directly linked to sustainable development. It is commonly recognized that sustainable development can only be achieved through the application of the precautionary principle.

The work of the ILA on sustainable development has made ample references to the applicability of the precautionary principle in the field of sustainable development.[140] The

[135] Rio Declaration, Principle 27.

[136] *MOX Plant* case (*Ireland v. United Kingdom*) (provisional measures) ITLOS No 10 (3 December 2001), para 84.

[137] *Pulp Mills* case, Separate Opinion of Judge Cançado Trindade, para 71.

[138] *Pulp Mills* case, Separate Opinion of Judge Cançado Trindade, para 156.

[139] cf, generally, Cançado Trindade, A. A., 'The Contribution of Recent World Conferences of the United Nations to the Relations between Sustainable Development and Economic, Social and Cultural Rights', in Prieur, M. and Lambrechts, C. (eds), *Les hommes et l'environnement: Quels droits pour le vingt-et-unième siècle?—Études en hommage à Alexandre Kiss* (Éd. Frison-Roche 1998), 119.

[140] See also the resolution of the Institut de droit international on the 'Environment' (Session of Strasbourg, 1997) which links in its Preamble the 'prevention and precautionary principles' to the 'requirements of the sustainable development of human societies'.

New Delhi Declaration devotes a section to the 'principle of the precautionary approach' and provides the following:

A precautionary approach is central to sustainable development in that it commits States, international organizations and the civil society, particularly the scientific and business communities, to avoid human activity which may cause significant harm to human health, natural resources or ecosystems, including in the light of scientific uncertainty.[141]

The key element that links precaution and sustainable development is their shared temporal dimension. Precaution aims to protect future generations from environmental degradation due to activities having been carried out despite scientific uncertainty. Similarly, sustainable development aims at preserving the Earth for the benefit of future generations. The relationship between precaution and sustainable development is so widespread that it goes unquestioned.[142] Yet, assuming a direct relation between the two concepts challenges the rationale on which they are based: while precaution is based on the idea of prevention in a broad sense, sustainable development relies on the idea of distribution and satisfactory balance between distinct considerations at issue.[143] Consequently, although the relationship between the two principles is a close one, given their shared temporal dimension, they operate on two distinct epistemological bases.

## 5. Precaution and CBDR

Principle 15 links precaution to Principle 7 on common but differentiated responsibilities by referring the application of the precautionary approach 'by States according to their capabilities'. Such a reference parallels the addition made to Principle 2 on the right of States to exploit their resources pursuant to their 'development policies', and consecrates the objective of UNCED to focus on the environment-development nexus. Precaution is thus not an absolute obligation, but depends on the level of development of the countries and the threshold varies depending on the State. This gives developing States more leverage to combine economic development with environmental protection and also takes into consideration their limitations in terms of scientific and technological advances.

In its aforementioned Advisory Opinion on the Area, ITLOS consecrated this approach by stating that

Principle 15 provides that the precautionary approach shall be applied by States 'according to their capabilities'. It follows that the requirements for complying with the obligation to apply the precautionary approach may be stricter for the developed than for the developing sponsoring States.[144]

Therefore, the precautionary principle has to be flexible enough to adapt to different levels of economic and technological development. Its relationship with the

[141] Confirmed by the ILA 2012 Sofia resolution on sustainable development, which includes a reference to precaution: 'The precautionary principle has significant and increasingly precise legal implication, notwithstanding ongoing debate surrounding its formal legal status' (International Law Association, 'Sofia Guiding Statements on the Judicial Elaboration of the 2002 New Delhi Declaration of Principles of International Law Relating to Sustainable Development' (Sofia, 75th session, 2012)).

[142] It has been rightly observed, for instance, that '[t]he close ties between the precautionary principle and the concept of sustainable development represent such an uncontentious issue that they need not be discussed in any more detail at this point', in Troubworst, *Precautionary Rights and Duties*, 35.

[143] Dupuy, P.-M. and Vinuales, J. E., *International Environmental Law: A Modern Introduction* (Cambridge University Press, 2015), ch 3.

[144] ITLOS Advisory Opinion on the Area, para 161.

concept of CBDR transforms the precautionary principle from an absolute to a relative obligation.

## IV) Assessment

The precautionary principle continues to challenge the minds of lawyers and policy-makers. Despite the pervasive references to it since the adoption of the Rio Declaration in 1992 as well as the growing body of legislative and judicial practice, there is still no consensus as to its exact meaning and its legal consequences. Yet, how can one speak of international environmental law today without referring to general principles,[145] amongst which the precautionary principle?

Humankind has come to realize that addressing solely risk is not feasible without incorporating into the picture probable risk or uncertainty. Some measure of uncertainty surrounds the potential consequences of many widespread activities, such as, for example, massive production of genetically modified organisms, or large-scale use of mobile phones, to mention but two examples often arising in jurisprudence. Uncertainty is likely to be dissipated in the next years, turning from probable into actual risk—the proper domain of prevention. Concrete examples include the causes of ozone depletion or climate change, which at the time of their initial regulation at the international level were surrounded by significant uncertainty. The precautionary principle is a key instrument to tackle this grey area that goes from advocacy to legal regime formation. It has also many uses, including in litigation, where a shifting or reversal of the burden of proof could potentially apply.

The reluctance of the ICJ and other jurisdictions to ascribe to the precautionary principle the proper place it deserves may most likely come to be seen, some decades from now, as a conservative—if not reactionary—posture. Much in the same way could one point to the early reluctance of the ECtHR to capture the significance of the more recent practice; another illustration lies in the ECtHR's new preparedness, from the mid-90s onwards—in the same way as the IACtHR from its very start—to acknowledge the ineluctable inter-relationship between due compliance with procedural obligations (such as the duty of investigation of the facts) and the safeguard of the substantive protected rights.

Irrespective of the pace of this jurisprudential transformation, it is remarkable that, in little more than twenty years, the precautionary principle—more specifically, Principle 15 of the Rio de Janeiro Declaration adopted at UNCED in 1992—has exerted such a profound influence on international and domestic law and practice. This is yet another reminder of the strength of the outlook of legal thinking open to the progressive development of international law. As one of the great humanists of the twentieth century, Stefan Zweig, used to say, an ideal which has not yet been fully realized becomes invincible; it is only a matter of time.

## V) Select Bibliography

Bodansky, D., 'Scientific Uncertainty and the Precautionary Principle' (1991) 33 *Environment* 4.

Bodansky, D., 'Deconstructing the Precautionary Principle', in Caron, D. and Scheiber, H. N. (eds), *Bringing New Law to Ocean Waters* (Leiden: Martinus Nijhoff 2004), 381.

145 This is a point I made in my Separate Opinion in the *Pulp Mills* case; cf Separate Opinion of Judge Cançado Trindade, para 113: 'We can hardly speak of International Environmental Law nowadays without those general principles'.

Cançado Trindade, A.A., 'Environment and Development: Formulation and Implementation of the Right to Development as a Human Right', in Cançado Trindade, A. A. (ed), *Derechos Humanos, Desarrollo Sustentable y Medio Ambiente/Human Rights, Sustainable Development and the Environment* (San José of Costa Rica/Brasília: IIHR/IDB 1992), 39.

Cançado Trindade, A.A., *El Ejercicio de la Función Judicial Internacional—Memorias de la Corte Interamericana de Derechos Humanos* (3rd edn, Belo Horizonte/Brazil: Edit Del Rey 2013).

Cançado Trindade, A.A., 'Foundations of International Law: The Role and Importance of Its Basic Principles', *in XXX Curso de Derecho Internacional Organizado por el Comité Jurídico Interamericano*—OEA (2003), 359.

Cançado Trindade, A.A., 'Sustainable Human Development and Conditions of Life as a Matter of Legitimate International Concern: The Legacy of the U.N. World Conferences', in *Japan and International Law—Past, Present and Future* (International Symposium to Mark the Centennial of the Japanese Association of International Law) (The Hague: Kluwer 1999), 285.

Cançado Trindade, A.A., 'The Contribution of Recent World Conferences of the United Nations to the Relations between Sustainable Development and Economic, Social and Cultural Rights', in Prieur, M. and Lambrechts, C. (eds), *Les hommes et l'environnement: Quels droits pour le vingt-et-unième siècle?—Études en hommage à Alexandre Kiss* (Paris: Éd. Frison-Roche 1998), 119.

de Sadeeler, N., *Environmental Principles: from Political Slogans to Legal Rules* (Oxford: Oxford University Press 2002).

Fisher, E., Jones, J., and von Schomberg, R. (eds), *Implementing the Precautionary Principle: Perspectives and Prospects* (Cheltenham: Edward Elgar 2006).

Foster, C. E., *Science and the Precautionary Principle in International Courts and Tribunals: Expert Evidence, Burden of Proof and Finality* (Cambridge University Press 2011).

Freestone, D., 'Caution or Precaution: "A Rose by Any Other Name..."?' (1999) 10 *YbIEL* 25.

Freestone, D. and Hey, E., *The Precautionary Principle and International Law: The Challenge of Implementation* (The Hague: Kluwer 1996).

Hey, E., 'The Precautionary Concept in Environmental Policy and Law: Institutionalizing Caution' (1992) 4 *GIELR* 303.

Lucchini, L., 'Le principe de précaution en droit international de l'environnement: ombres plus que lumières' (1999) 45 *Annuaire français de droit international* 710.

Martin-Bidou, P., 'Le principe de précaution en droit international de l'environnment' (1999) 103 *Revue générale de droit international public* 631.

Mbengue, M., *Essai sur une théorie du risque en droit international public. L'anticipation du risque environnemental et sanitaire* (Paris: Pedone 2009).

Peel, J., *The Precautionary Principle in Practice* (Annandale NSW: The Federation Press 2005).

Peel, J., *Science and Risk Regulation in International Law* (Cambridge University Press 2010).

Scovazzi, T., 'Sul principio precauzionale nel diritto internazionale dell'ambiente' (1992) 75 *Rivista di diritto internazionale* 699.

Tanaka, Y., 'Reflections on Time Elements in the International Law of the Environment' (2013) 73 *Zeitschrift für ausländisches öffentliches Recht und Völkerrecht* 143.

Trouwborst, A., *Evolution and Status of the Precautionary Principle in International Law* (The Hague: Kluwer 2002).

Trouwborst, A., *Precautionary Rights and Duties of States* (Leiden: Nijhoff 2006).

Viñuales, J. E., 'Legal Techniques for Dealing with Scientific Uncertainty in Environmental Law' (2010) 43 *Vanderbilt Journal of Transnational Law* 437.

Wiener, J., 'Precaution', in Bodansky, D., Brunee, J., and Hey, E. (eds), *The Oxford Handbook of International Environmental Law* (Oxford University Press 2007), 597.

# 20. Principle 16

## *The Polluter-Pays Principle*

Priscilla Schwartz*

**Principle 16**

National authorities should endeavour to promote the internalization of environmental costs and the use of economic instruments, taking into account the approach that the polluter should, in principle, bear the cost of pollution, with due regard to the public interest and without distorting international trade and investment.



## I) Origins and Rationale of the Principle

The Polluter-pays principle ('PPP') was borne out of the need to find a global strategy for pollution control that would minimize the regulatory burden on states.[1] The Stockholm

* Senior Lecturer in Law, School of Law and Social Sciences, University of East London, United Kingdom.

[1] This article builds substantially on previous work: Schwartz, P., 'Polluter Pays Principle', in Fitzmaurice, M., Ong, D., and Merkouris, P. (eds), *Research Handbook on International Environmental Law* (Edward Elgar 2010), 243.

Declaration initiated this action, calling on states to take measures against environmental pollution including of the seas, and to cooperate on liability regimes.[2] The quest for a common pollution regulatory policy was achieved through the adoption of Principle 16 of the Rio Declaration.

The OECD had previously applied the PPP since the early 1970s, highlighting the role of the principle in environmental matters as a useful instrument for allocating the costs of pollution prevention and control. It had an objective 'to encourage the rational use of scarce environmental resources and to avoid distortions in international trade and investment'.[3] The *expenses* for carrying out the pollution prevention and control measures that are introduced by public authorities in member countries must be borne by the polluter.[4] The OECD and the Rio PPP are similar save that the former has application only to its members while the latter has a wider application for achieving sustainable development.

This chapter analyses the meaning and legal character of the Rio PPP, bringing out its interaction with other relevant environmental principles. It illustrates how the principle is applied through incentive-based economic instruments in domestic and global pollution regulation. It also discusses the caveat in Principle 16, revealing the challenges in balancing trade, investment and public interest considerations and examines the role of the private sector in harnessing international investment for environmental objectives.

What emerges from the review is that, the concept and scope of 'polluter' and 'environmental costs' has diverged so much that, while the main focus continues to be on 'costs', it is not always the polluter's costs, nor necessarily an endeavour to make the polluter pay.

## II) The Principle as Enshrined in the Rio Declaration

### 1. Preparatory work and context

The inclusion of the PPP within the Rio Declaration was an initiative of developed countries, particularly the United States and European countries. Their aim was to streamline economic approaches to environmental regulation as well as to address the major environmental impacts of Soviet-style planned economies.[5]

The bulk of the discussions regarding Principle 16 took place during the third week of PrepCom IV in the contact group established under the co-chairmanship of Mukul Sanwal (India) and Ole Kristian Holthe (Norway). Whereas the draft of the G77+China[6] did not contain any reference to cost internalization, those tabled by the United States,[7]

[2] Stockholm Declaration of the United Nations Conference on the Human Environment (1972), UN Doc A/Conf.48/14, reprinted in ILM 11, 1416.

[3] Recommendation of the Council Concerning International Economic Aspects of Environmental Policies, C(72)128, (OECD 1972).

[4] Recommendation on the Implementation of the Polluter-pays Principle C(74) 223/Final OECD 1974 (OECD Implementation); The Polluter-Pays Principle: OECD Analyses and Recommendations OCDE/GD(92)81 (OECD Paris 1992), 9.

[5] See Kovar, J., 'A Short Guide to the Rio Declaration' (1993) 4 *Colorado Journal of International Environmental Law and Policy* 119, 135.

[6] 'Rio de Janeiro Charter/Declaration on Environment and Development', UN DocA/CONF.151/PC/WG.III/L.20/Rev.1 ('L.20').

[7] UN Doc A/CONF.151/PC/WG.III/L.21 ('L.21'), Principle 14.

Canada,[8] Australia[9] and the European Community countries[10] all contained a specific principle on this issue. The two most influential formulations were those contained in the US and European drafts. According to Principle 14 of the US draft:

> Polluters should bear the costs of carrying out pollution prevention and control measures introduced by public authorities. These costs should be reflected in the cost of goods and services that cause pollution in production and/or consumption to encourage rational use of scarce environmental resources and to avoid distortion in international trade and investment. Market should reflect full economic accounting of environmental costs and benefits.

Principle 5 of the EC draft was shorter:

> The polluter shall bear the expenses of carrying out the necessary pollution prevention and control measures introduced by public authorities to protect the environment. States shall endeavour to ensure that markets in products, services and natural resources reflect environmental costs.

The essence of the discussion turned on competitiveness concerns, with developing countries expressing reluctance towards the potential straitjacket that environmental cost-internalization measures may place on their products as well as on their room for development policies. Therefore they sought to water down the wording so as to allow for sufficient room for manoeuvre, most notably by bringing the operative level of the principle at the national level and constraining the scope for the principle to impose competitive disadvantages on less environmentally-produced goods.[11] The discussions on Principle 16 are in many ways representative of the clash between developing and developed countries in the run up to Rio, the latter emphasizing environmental concerns (aligned with their higher competitiveness) and the former advocating from development as the foremost goal to be achieved through international cooperation.

The compromise language reached at PrepCom IV was adopted without any changes at the Rio Summit. Despite its frustration with the watering down of the wording, the United States did not appended an interpretative statement to Principle 16, as it did for other principles.

## 2. Scope and dimensions

### 2.1. *The polluter, the obligation and the 'costs'*

#### 2.1.1. Overview

Principle 16 entails some peculiar elements that may raise contestations. National authorities would need to determine who is a *polluter*, the pollution obligation, the *costs* for polluting and the ascription of such cost—whether of pollution directly resulting from the activity or relative. This section ascertains these matters.

[8] 'Earth Charter', UN Doc A/CONF.151/PC/WG.III/L.23 ('L.23'), Principle 8.

[9] 'Structure and outline of the Rio de Janeiro Declaration/Earth Charter and comments on UN DocA/CONF.151/PC/WG.III/L.8/Rev.1', UN Doc A/CONF.151/PC/WG.III/L.24 ('L.24'), Principle 13.

[10] 'Elements for the Earth Charter', UN Doc A/CONF.151/PC/WG.III/L.25 ('L.25'), Principle 5.

[11] Ling, C.Y., *The Rio Declaration on Environment and Development: An assessment* (Penang: Third World Network 2012), 50.

### 2.1.2. The scope of the polluter's obligation

The polluter personality, the types of polluting activity, and the scope of polluter responsibility continues to evolve in the literature, treaties, and state practice. Originally, 'polluter' implied someone engaged in polluting activities through industrial emissions in excess of legally binding stipulated thresholds; or 'who directly or indirectly damages the environment or who creates conditions leading to such damage'.[12] Principle 16 entails no delimiting criteria on the polluter-personality category. There is authority however suggesting that a polluter includes states, corporations, industries, and individuals who engage in a polluting activity, and global practice tends to confirm this;[13] although in practice, the regulatory focus is largely on corporations, including multinational corporations ('MNCs').

Also, the polluting conduct or activity (that may incur a *cost*), extends beyond the responsibility for industrial emissions to uses of natural resources that contribute to environmental deterioration.[14] It is elasticized further by the common but differentiated responsibility ('CBDR') principle, by which developed countries assume a higher emission reduction burden and are required to make financial contributions to the developing countries as incentive to preserve their environmental quality.[15] Producers also assume 'polluter' responsibility for the environmental impact associated with their products including the post-consumer state of the product life cycle. In some cases the responsibility for product waste is shifted upstream to consumers.[16] These dimensions of polluter obligation[17] reflect the complex regulatory dynamics that Principle 16 evokes in promoting environmentally sustainable development.

### 2.1.3. Bearing environmental and pollution prevention costs

Rio Principle 16 gives us some indication of the types of cost (*environmental costs*) and the main methods by which the polluter could satisfy the costs—internalization and use of economic instruments. But the principle is silent on what constitutes '*environmental*' in relation to the *costs* to pay. But we can argue that the identification of '*environmental*' as the costs burden widens the concept of *costs* to include many pollution challenges deriving from modern economic activities and technology, and the variety of methods needed to tackle them. For example, in the context of financial liability for the costs of disposing of waste, the ECJ clarified that Member States may '*choose the form and the methods* to be applied in order to attain that result', including by means of a tax or of a charge *or in any other manner*'.[18] They have a broad discretion, when laying down national rules developing or giving concrete expression to the polluter-pays principle.[19]

[12] Recommendation on the Implementation of the Polluter-pays Principle, OECD Implementation (1974).

[13] Council Recommendation of 3 March 1975 regarding cost allocation and action by public authorities on environmental matters (75/436/EURATOM, ECSC, EEC) para 2—'Polluter' is defined as 'natural or legal persons governed by public or private law who are responsible for pollution...'

[14] This may be for economic or social purposes. See Agenda 21, Report of the UNCED, I (1992) UN Doc A/CONF.151/26/Rev. l, ILM 31, 874, ch 8, 8:28.

[15] Rio Declaration: Principle 7; United Nations Framework Convention on Climate Change ('UNFCCC'), UNFCCC/INFORMAL/84 GE.05-62220 (E) 200705 (United Nations 1992) arts 3(1); 4(2)(a) and (b); Kyoto Protocol to the United Nations Framework Convention on Climate Change, Kyoto, 11 December 1997, 2303 UNTS 148, Annex I.

[16] The assumption is that the polluters will improve the waste profile of their products, decreasing waste and increasing the possibility of reuse and recycling. See the Waste Electrical and Electronic Equipment ('WEEE') Directive 2002/96/EC, 2002): Schwartz, 'Polluter Pays Principle', 257–8.

[17] Categorized as: 'polluter responsibility principle', 'beneficiary-pays principle', 'user pay principle' 'Producer responsibility', 'extended polluter responsibility'; see Schwartz, 'Polluter Pays Principle', 247–8.

[18] *Futura Immobiliare srl Hotel Futura*, Case C-254/08, ('*Futura* case') (2009) OJ C 220/13 paras 47–8.

[19] *Futura* case, paras 52, 55.

Thus the broad formulation of 'environmental costs' can accommodate other costs that may be connected with pollution regulation, environmental protection, and management. The polluter costs-burden could therefore include: the cost of achieving prescribed environmental quality, preventing harm, accidental pollution, or remedying environmental damage; the cost of the clean-up or reinstatement of the environment; the cost of exceptional measures needed to protect human health and the environment and social costs; the remaining external cost of investment on technology, the cost incurred when a ban is placed on polluting activity, indemnity cost, operational costs, loss of profit, costs associated with trade-offs, off-sets and subsidies; and the cost of promoting best practices and best available technology.[20]

## 2.2. *The caveat: trade, investment, and the public interest*

Principle 16 entails a condition that in implementing the principle, States should have due regard to the *public interest* and must not *distort international trade and investment.* Distortion to trade and investment could arise through various forms of 'differentiation' existing in environmental policies, which introduce differential treatment by, for instance, taxing carbon-intensive activities or end products and providing subsidies to carbon-efficient activities or 'climate friendly' technologies.[21] Similarly, the WTO *China—Raw Materials* case[22] illustrates how domestic pollution regulatory policy/measures (eg export/production restrictions on minerals) could be viewed as trade distortive unless, *inter alia*, the WTO member ensures that such measures are domestic, as well as international.[23]

Also, the caveat sought to recognize the variations in the levels of countries' development, their trade and investment capabilities, the capacity to invest or subsidize technology development, or ownership and diffusion, and the nature of business generally. It has acquired more relevance with the *green economy* agenda which aims to motivate and guide policy makers to create the enabling conditions for *increased investments* in a transition to a *green economy.*[24] Thus, the application of economic instruments to address pollution costs amidst the disparity in the wealth of nations is bound to have implications for the 'public interest'—that is, at what cost to the economy?

Moreover, by prohibiting distortions, Principle 16 impresses the need to secure a competitive environment between varying polluter-business types who may seek to

[20] These costs are identified in treaties, statutes, and academic literature; Schwartz, 'Polluter Pays Principle', 248–50.

[21] Viñuales, J. E., *Foreign Investment and the Environment in International Law* (Cambridge University Press 2012), 253–4, 267; (for case examples on this aspect, see 261–70).

[22] See Appellate Body Report, China—Measures Related to the Exportation of Various Raw Materials, WT/DS394/AB/R, WT/DS395/AB/R, WT/DS398/AB/R (Jan. 30, 2012). (Note that at issue was whether an infringement of a provision in China's Accession Protocol could be cured by the domestic policy exceptions under art XX of the GATT discipline). Also see China—Measures Related to the Exportation of Rare Earths, Tungsten, and Molybdenum, DS431 (US), DS432 (EU), DS433 (Japan) (Mar. 13, 2012).

[23] This will avoid the effect of a *de facto* subsidization of consumption by the producing domestic industry and a disadvantage to competing foreign industries; see Matsushita, M., 'A Note on the Appellate Body Report in the Chinese Minerals Export Restrictions Case' (2012) 4(2) *Trade Law & Development* 400, 419–20.

[24] UNEP, Towards a Green Economy: Pathways to Sustainable Development and Poverty Eradication, (2011), 16, available at <htttp://www.unep.org/greeneconomy>; See also UNEP, Report on the Green Economy In The Context Of Sustainable Development And Poverty Eradication in Report of the United Nations Conference on Sustainable Development (Rio de Janeiro, Brazil, 20–22 June 2012) A/CONF.216/16 (Part III); see REN21 Renewables: Global Status Report (Renewable Energy Policy Network 2013).

internalize their environmental costs or use economic instruments through international trade and investment. The application of the EU Aviation Directive to non-EU airlines for example, is driven by the need to protect domestic industry competitiveness from the effects of carbon leakage on market competitiveness resulting from pricing carbon.[25]

Furthermore, in terms of 'public interest' the greenhouse gas ('GHG') tax or the auctions of emission allowances under emission trading schemes ('ETS') for example, has the potential to raise revenues for the government, which it could use to cut on the total costs of programmes.[26] The tax could also be used to address equity issues such as 'avoiding burdensome impacts on particular households and businesses' or to fund clean energy research and development ('R&D') and adaptation programmes.[27] The concern for the public interest and international trade influenced the recent climate proposals, wherein the design for the allocation of emission allowances aimed *inter alia* at public utilities that could use it for the benefit of their consumers.[28]

However, the conditioning of the PPP with trade, investment and the public interest considerations raises some pertinent issues. One area noted is the determination of property rights in GHG ERC in the carbon trading. In the US statutory ETS, only the reduction of GHG emissions in specified activities could count as certified ERC. But in voluntary cap-and-trade markets, firms could have different requirements regarding what activities qualify as carbon credits.[29] The variance breeds disparity between the voluntary and statutory cap-and-trade markets and could lead to a distortion in the international carbon trade, unless a uniform definition of carbon credits is maintained among all traders especially in the US.[30]

Further, the PPP caveat engenders economic efficiency and cost effectiveness issues relating to incentive schemes and technologies, such as the EU ETS and Renewable energy feed in tariffs schemes ('REFiT'). EU law requires emissions reductions to take place in a cost-effective and economically efficient manner subject to the overall cap—the 'lowest-cost abatement'.[31] The EU ETS is applied in combination with the REFiT, a non-market based incentive, creating an overlap in incentive mechanisms. Spassov et al explain that overlapping incentive mechanisms may put different technologies into competition with each other for scarce capital and ignore the competition for

[25] Meltzer J., 'Climate Change & Trade: The EU Aviation Directive & the WTO' (2012) 15(1) *Journal of International Economic Law* 118.

[26] eg by reducing existing distortionary taxes on labour and capital investments; see United States Policy 'Market Mechanisms: Understanding The Options' (Center for Climate change and Energy solutions March 2012) (US Policy), 4; GHG taxes have been used to offset taxes on labour and businesses in Sweden and British Columbia.

[27] US Policy 'Market Mechanisms': Several states in the Regional GHG Initiative in the US dedicate much of the revenue to renewable and energy efficiency investments.

[28] US Policy 'Market Mechanisms', other targets include: businesses that could face international competitive impacts, funding for low-carbon technology R&D, and programmes to ease the transition to a low carbon economy.

[29] A US court likened carbon credits to 'junk bonds, or low-grade investments with a low likelihood of return, but potential for a high yield carbon credits'; Monterubio, J., 'Recognition of Property Rights in Carbon Credits Under California's New Greenhouse Gas Cap-And-Trade Program' (2011) 12 *Sustainable Development Law and Policy* 32.

[30] Monterubio, 'Recognition of Property Rights in Carbon Credits', 32.

[31] Directive 2003/87/EC of the European Parliament and of the Council of 13 October 2003 establishing a scheme for GHG allowance trading within the Community and amending Council Directive 96/61/EC, art 1.

investments.[32] This 'creates an uneven playing field between "capital-intensive" renewable energy technologies and negative-costs forms of abatement'. They point out that additional incentives like REFiT offering higher and more secure returns than EU ETS incentives corners all the investments in the electricity sector, prejudicing the 'lowest-cost abatement' principle.[33]

Another challenge involves the balancing of 'environmental costs' with investment costs, and the public interest, especially where the investment costs may heavily influence decision-making, to leave a disproportionate share of the burden on the public. The application of the REFiT policies in Africa highlight such challenges. In Algeria, the scheme was deemed ineffective because it lacked a 'guaranteed "floor" price' that will provide the investors with the certainty they require.[34] Kenya's policy was more of a barrier than an incentive for the energy-poor communities to invest in.[35] This said, Ghana's REFiT policy provides for a 'green fund' to finance energy-related measures that will 'help distribute the *costs* of the REFIT and ensure they are borne fairly according to energy usage, emissions, or ability to pay'.[36] Perhaps South Africa's policy choice of the Renewable Energy Independent Power Producer Procurement Programme ('REIPPPP') over the REFiT system best illustrates the public interest caveat. The REIPPPP offers the country more control over installed capacity and related costs in relation to the tariff for the electricity produced and the specified cap set by the developer.[37] The programme also considers the public interest concerns in the investment policy design for renewable energy through local content requirements for equipment, material, and services that could benefit its economy.[38]

## 2.3. *Legal nature*

The PPP has a firm legal basis as a principle of law deriving from a variety of legal sources including international and regional treaties, domestic legislation, and as a regional custom particularly in Europe. The legal forms of the PPP circumscribe different types of polluters and the nature of polluter obligation. Some treaties require that the PPP be used as an 'approach' that forms the basis for fulfilling their mandate, or urge members to be 'guided' by the principle, 'take it into account', or 'apply' it in their respective contexts.[39]

[32] Spassov, Y. et al, 'Lowest-cost Abatement in Light of the EU ETS and Renewable Feed-in Tariffs in the Electricity Sector in Bulgaria' (2011) 29 *Journal of Energy & Natural Resources Law* 281, 289–90.

[33] Spassov et.al, 'Lowest-cost Abatement', 290, 301.

[34] ie despite the tariff being in the range of as much as 300% of the average electricity price; Stiftung, H. B., 'Powering Africa through Feed-In Tariffs' (World future Council, Green Peace England, Wales & Northern Ireland 2013), 34.

[35] Stiftung, 'Powering Africa', 40–1; the urban communities consumer bear 70% of the cost of the REFiT tariff (85% for solar), and prices for electricity are rising.

[36] Adopted under the 2011 Renewable Energy Act (Act 832); eg the implementation of a social transfer mechanism, provision of incentives for domestic production, and facilitation of effective grid integration. Stiftung, 'Powering Africa', 93.

[37] The reasons for abandoning the REFiT policy is REFiT's guarantee to buy all renewable electricity, combined with falling prices for solar PV, raised concerns about unchecked growth of expenses and poor value for money. Stiftung, 'Powering Africa', 55–6.

[38] Stiftung, 'Powering Africa', 57. Also, candidate projects are evaluated against an economic development scorecard, linked to the country's Broad-Based Black Economic Empowerment (BBBEE) law which applies to all government tenders.

[39] See: London Protocol to the Convention on the Prevention of Marine Pollution by Dumping of Waste and other Matters, 1996: art 3(2); Rotterdam Convention on the Protection of the Rhine, 1998: art 4; Helsinki Convention on the Protection of the Marine Environment of the Baltic Sea Area, 1992: art 2(5);

Other instruments require regulated entities to pay the costs of meeting national environmental standards demonstrating responsibility for polluting activities or their potential effects.[40] It has also been applied in international liability regimes, which impute responsibility to persons dealing with dangerous substances requiring them to take preventive or remedial action, notably for oil pollution, sea transfer of noxious substances, and hazardous waste disposal.[41]

The PPP is also prominently applied in EC law and policy relating to waste landfills, packaging of wastes, climate change emissions reduction, renewable energy, and civil aviation.[42] The ECJ has applied the principle providing specific guidance on the scope of polluter responsibility in certain activities in the EU Directives.[43] What is also important to recognize is that prior to the Rio Declaration, the PPP informed the market-based types of policies employed by the developed OECD countries to combat atmospheric pollutants, acid rain, water effluent, wetland protection, and to reflect the social costs of using resources.[44] Domestic legislation implementing the cap-and-trade schemes evidences implementation of the PPP. Also, as illustrated in section 3.2, the private sector is addressing pollution and global environmental issues through a variety of ECI mechanisms.

Thus, this international pollution policy and regulatory tool has such wide application in law and practice to become a legitimate legal principle. Its consistent application in the OECD and the EC, in binding treaties, and EC secondary legislation cements its legal status. Similarly the wide practice of carbon trading and investments in renewable energy to address emissions reduction commitments certifies the PPP as a regional custom certainly in the EC, and potentially in many countries.

Helsinki Convention on the Protection and Use of Transboundary Watercourses and International Lakes, 1992: art 2:5(b); Convention on Co-operation for the Protection and Sustainable Use of the Danube River, 1994: art 4:4; Convention on the Protection of the Marine Environment of the North East Atlantic, 1992: art 2:2(b).

40 UNFCCC Kyoto Protocol, 2303 UNTS 148, Annex I.

41 Some examples include: Convention on the Establishment of an International Fund for Compensation for Oil Pollution Damage, 1971 (replaced by Protocol of 1992), (The Fund Convention); International Convention on Liability and Compensation for Damage in Connection with the Carriage of Hazardous and Noxious Substances by Sea, 1996 (HNS Convention); Protocol on Liability and Compensation for Damage Resulting from Transboundary Movement of Hazardous Wastes and their Disposal, 1999.

42 Directive 1999/31/EC on Waste Landfill, 1999: art 10; Directive 94/62/EC on Packaging and Packaging of Wastes, 1994; Directive 2000/60/EC on Water Policy, 2000: art 9; Directive 2009/29/EC of 23 April 2009 amending Directive 2003/87/EC so as to improve and extend the greenhouse gas emission allowance trading scheme of the Community 0J 2009 L 140/63; see Directive 2008/101/EC of the European Parliament and of the Council of 19 November 2008 amending Directive 2003/87/EC so as to include aviation activities in the scheme for greenhouse gas emission allowance trading within the Community, 2009 OJ (L 8/3).

43 Case C-172/08 *Pontina Ambiente Srl v. Regione Lazio* (2010) OJ C 100/2.—ECJ interpreting art 10 of Directive 1999/31; *Futura* case (Interpreting Directive 75/442 and Directive 2006/12 of the European Parliament and of the Council of 5 April 2006 on waste (OJ 2006 L 114, 9)).

44 See United States CERCLA, December 11 1980; The Clean Air (Amendments) Act 1990 (Title I, IV, VI); New Zealand implemented the cap-and-trade through the Climate Change Response (Emissions Trading) Amendment Act 2008, Public Act 2008 No. 85, 25 September 2008; See also art 130(r)(2) and art 174(2) Single European Act (1986); EC Recommendation Regarding Cost Allocation and Action by Public Authorities on Environmental Matters, 1975.

## 3. Normative impact

### *3.1. Regulatory economic approaches to make the polluter pay*

#### 3.1.1. Instruments

Principle 16 promotes environmental costs *internalization* and the use of *economic instruments* to implement and enforce the PPP.[45] Both policy approaches complement each other or could substitute for other policy instruments. The following discussion is intended as a survey of the different regulatory techniques that have been used to express the PPP.

Given the breadth of substantive areas where such techniques operate, the focus will be on negative externalities arising from energy and transportation or, more generally, from emissions-intensive activities. The discussion addresses tour à tour standards and charges, emissions-trading, financial assistance to low-impact industries, or, simply, liability regimes.

#### 3.1.2. Standards and charges

##### *3.1.2.1. Overview*

Under this approach, the regulator uses the traditional or command-and-control regime to set (and directly enforce) the environmental quality targets or the aggregate limits on pollution loading. A 'legal emission ceiling' is placed on a number of specific sources, and an emissions charge is imposed on each unit of pollution or residuals that each actor or each source must generate.[46] The tax (eg emissions tax or a tax on goods or services) then becomes an additional cost burden on the entity for the amount of pollution they emit. To reduce the tax burden, the entity will have to reduce the quantity of emissions it produces by changing its processes or by adopting new technology.[47]

Emission standards and charges can be either for *efficiency*—aiming to produce an efficient outcome by forcing the polluter to compensate completely for all damage caused; or a *cost-effective* charge—to achieve *the lowest possible control cost*.[48] In addition to encouraging firms to adopt pollution control equipment, air pollution emissions charges have been applied as a market-based incentive through the following economic instruments: corporate average fuel economy; fees and rebates; and renewable electricity/energy standards.

[45] Internalization facilitates the inclusion of external effects in economic calculation and corrects misallocations, while assuring the rational management of resources; See Recommendation on the Implementation of the Polluter-pays Principle (OECD 1974), 23. See also Recommendation of the Council on the Use of Economic Instruments in Environmental Policy, C(90)177/Final (OECD, 1991). See also Tietenberg, T.H., 'Economic Instruments For Environmental Regulation' (1990) 6 *Oxford Review of Economic Policy* 17, at 18.

[46] The emissions standards are set by reference to the amount of emission reduction achievable based on specific technological choices. See Stewart, R.B., 'Economic Incentives for Environmental Protection: Opportunities and Obstacles', in Revesz, E. et al (eds), *Environmental Law, The Economy and Sustainable Development* (Cambridge University Press 2000), 171 at 175; also Tietenberg, 'Economic Instruments For Environmental Regulation', 18.

[47] US Policy 'Market Mechanisms', at 2.

[48] see Tietenberg, 'Economic Instruments For Environmental Regulation', 20–1. In Europe and Japan, emission charges apply especially to control water pollution and to raise revenue in order to fund effluent standards activities.

*3.1.2.2. Corporate average fuel economy (CAFE)*

The regulator uses CAFE standards to regulate the fuel economy of new vehicles. The authority sets the fuel economy targets or standard that is based upon each vehicle's footprint. The automaker must meet or exceed the target, otherwise the firm must pay a fine. Companies that exceed their fuel economy requirements can sell credits associated with that additional fuel economy to firms that do not meet the standard in a given year.[49]

*3.1.2.3. Feebates*

Feebates (fees and rebates) instruments aim to influence and change the relative purchase prices of certain goods based on their fuel economy by taxing the less environmentally friendly product. For example, feebates have been used to increase the rate at which consumers would purchase cars equipped with a catalytic converter, especially in Sweden. The fees collected may be used to subsidize fuel-efficient purchases, including of other consumer durables (eg refrigerators, washer-dryers, televisions).[50]

*3.1.2.4. Renewable electricity/energy standards ('RES')*

RES are used to encourage firms to shift away from carbon-intensive production toward the use of cleaner fuels. RES focus on propelling transition to or use of renewable electricity and commercialization of renewable energy technologies. Its instruments tend to require each energy utility within a particular territory to obtain a certain percentage of its delivered electricity from a defined set of clean or renewable sources—wind, hydro, solar, bio, and geothermal energy. Renewable energy incentives are the most effective and specifically targeted stimulus to decarbonize the economy in numerous Member States of the EU.[51]

### 3.1.3. Emissions trading

*3.1.3.1. Cap-and-trade systems*

The emissions trading or 'cap-and-trade' is an economic incentive system aiming to inject more flexibility into the manner in which pollution regulation objectives are met. It allows for a wider range of choices in how polluters satisfy their legal pollution control responsibilities and how to figure out the least expensive way to do it.[52] Under the mechanism, the authority mandates an overall 'cap' on emissions and the regulated entities are left to decide how to reduce their emissions.[53] A company that succeeds in reducing emissions below its requirements can deal with the excess allowance in various ways. For instance, a firm may store its excess allowance as certified emissions reduction credits (ERC) for future use (*emissions banking*). It may trade the ERC to another firm which has been unsuccessful in reducing its own emission within its allowance (*offsets*); or it may actually use it to raise revenue.[54] A firm may also use its ERC to secure a regulatory relief that

[49] US Policy 'Market Mechanisms', 5; see Directive 2009/30/EC of 23 April 2009 amending Directive 98/70/EC as regards the specification of petrol, diesel, and gas-oil, and introducing a mechanism to monitor and reduce greenhouse gas emissions: OJ L 140/88.

[50] US Policy 'Market Mechanisms', 5; Directive 2009/30/EC of 23 April 2009.

[51] See Directive 2009/28/EC of the European Parliament and of the Council of 23 April 2009 on the promotion of the use of energy from renewable sources and amending and subsequently repealing Directives 2001/77/EC and 2003/30/EC OJ EU, L 140/16; in fact, support for renewable energy in the EU does not constitute state aid (see Case C-379/98 *Preussen Elektra, G v. Schhleswag AG* [2001] EU ECJ); also see Spassov et al, 'Lowest-cost Abatement', at 287.

[52] Tietenberg, 'Economic Instruments For Environmental Regulation', 18.

[53] The approach is a quantity-based, as opposed to setting a price on each unit of pollution.

[54] US Policy 'Market Mechanisms', 3; Tietenberg, 'Economic Instruments For Environmental Regulation', 19.

allows modified or expanding sources to remain under the threshold and thereby avoid the need to meet the stringent requirements imposed for new sources (*Netting*).[55]

Thus, in the cap-and-trade system, firms can buy and sell the certified emission allowances through a tradable quota system, or via variable ERC and transferable market permit systems based on their polluting needs.

*3.1.3.2. The Kyoto Protocol*

The Kyoto Protocol to the UNFCCC is an example of economic instrument implementing the PPP. The parties can meet their commitments to reduce GHG emissions either by transferring or purchasing GHG emission reductions from other parties through emissions trading; or increasing their removal by sinks through emissions reduction units between developed countries (joint implementation); or as certified emissions reduction obtained through investments in clean development projects in developing economies ('CDM'), or a combination of these. The EU uses ETS to meet obligations under the Kyoto protocol, and it is the largest multinational GHG ETS, allowing regulated entities to use carbon credits and projects to reduce their global warming GHG emissions.[56] In addition to other incentives, the EU provides for the auctioning and free allocation of CO2 allowances in Phase III of the EU ETS (post-2013).[57] The cap-and-trade has been extended to the aviation sector requiring all airlines to hold permits to cover their CO2 emissions for flights operating in EU airspace.[58]

*3.1.3.3. New market mechanisms for emissions trading ('NMM')*

3.1.3.3.1. Overview: There are proposals for NMM, aiming *inter alia* to improve on the existing CDM to better address pollution responsibility.[59] NMM would go beyond the pure offsetting framework of the CDM, to scale-up GHG emission reductions in sector-wide segments in developing economies. The design options for sectoral carbon market mechanisms ('SCMM') are categorized as 'sectoral trading' and 'sectoral crediting'. Countries could use 'absolute target crediting' to issue credits *ex post*, based on an absolute quantity of GHG emissions; or 'absolute target trading' to allocate allowances *ex ante* to the sector/country.[60] A discussion of PPP instruments proposed under the NMM follows.

3.1.3.3.2. Government crediting system ('GCS'): The GCS aims to attract participation in sectors where installation-level emission accounting entails high transaction costs or to enhance technical capacity to implement an installation-level system in the relevant sector. Accordingly, the CDM host country government will adopt a sectoral crediting threshold that is agreed between it and an international regulatory body.[61]

[55] Note that the ERC is the currency used in emissions trading, while the emissions banking, offset, and netting policies govern how this currency can be stored and spent; see Tietenberg, 19.

[56] Directive 2003/87/EC.

[57] Directive 2009/29/EC, Recital 44; art 10(a)(3) (to the power sector).

[58] See Directive 2008/101/EC; also, the US applies ETS through the Clean Air Act of 1990.

[59] The atmospheric benefit of the CDM is at zero owing to ERC from CDM projects used to offset emissions in developed countries; and most of Africa has so far been bypassed; see ECORYS, Design Options For Sectoral Carbon Market Mechanisms, Climate Action Final Report 2012 CLIMA.B.3/SER/2011/0029 Rotterdam, 2012, 12 ('ECORYS Report'); also see OECD Scaled-up Market Mechanism: What is Needed to Move Forward? (OECD/IEA 2010) ('OECD Market Mechanisms').

[60] OECD Market Mechanisms.

[61] The resulting ERC will accrue to the host country government. See ECORYS Report,12.

3.1.3.3.3. Tradable intensity standard ('TIS'): TIS instruments may be designed for *intensity based trading* or *intensity based crediting*.[62] In the TIS, the crediting threshold is passed on to individual installations, which are issued with international credits *ex post*, after their emission reductions or carbon intensity reduction have been verified to be below their individual threshold.[63] According to the OECD, an intensity baseline makes it difficult to link individual investment to the carbon price signal.[64]

3.1.3.3.4. Installation-based emission trading system ('IB-ETS'): In the IB-ETS, the host country government would adopt a sectoral trading target at the international level against which it is issued with trading units *ex ante*. In order to achieve the trading target, it will set up an installation-level ETS for the sector and ensure that emissions of the host country do not exceed its target, otherwise it will have to buy additional units.[65] Also, subsidies and regulatory policies could be adapted at the installation level so as to encourage the changes needed to outperform the baseline or target.[66]

*3.1.3.4. Carbon capture and storage ('CCS') instruments*

Technology innovation and investment continue to define how polluter cost is born or shared among different participants even if some innovative methods turn the PPP on its head. The CCS instrument is such innovative method for reducing GHG emissions to mitigate climate change and is applicable to a variety of stationary sources of CO2.[67] But CCS only prevents emission of CO2 into the atmosphere but not its production. While CO2 emission is what the polluter ought to pay for under PPP, in the CCS system, the cost is in the pollution prevention and control—the operation and maintenance of the CO2 storage facility, including the cost of all liabilities associated with the mechanism. CCS entails 'first-of-a-kind technology risks' and is costlier relative to other technologies.[68]

Some countries have adopted regulatory instruments providing financial incentives for CCS investments and the long-term liability costs associated with it.[69] They tend to transfer the CO2 storage facility owner/operator responsibility to pay for CO2 pollution to the public. Bailey et al argue that the transfer of liability and frameworks serves as a subsidy that could prevent polluters from bearing the full costs of the pollution they have caused.[70] However the EU has amended its ETS to encourage investment in CCS to reduce CO2 emissions in the

[62] OECD Market Mechanisms, 4–5; IBT—the *ex ante* issuance allocation based on a forecast of output levels and *ex post* adjustments of total allocation; and IBC—*ex post* issuance of credits based on GHG performance per unit of output (tons of product, megawatt-hour, or other indicator of GHG intensity).

[63] ECORYS Report,12. Meeting the crediting threshold must therefore be a binding commitment for each individual installation.

[64] OECD Market Mechanisms 4–5.

[65] ECORYS Report, 12.

[66] Such as from subsidies to performance targets; see OECD Market Mechanisms 4–5.

[67] Report of the Interagency Task Force on Carbon Capture and Storage August 2010 ('CCS Report').

[68] CCS Report, 8.

[69] See eg: Environmental Protection: Storage of CO2 (Termination of Licenses), 2011, S.1 2221/8, 7(2) (UK); Carbon Capture and Sequestration Deployment Act of 2010 S 3589/S 3591 (2010) US; The Department of Energy Carbon Capture and Sequestration Program Amendments Act of 2011 (S. 699); The Australian Offshore Petroleum and Greenhouse Gas Storage Act 2006. See also Directive 2009/31/EC of the European Parliament and of the Council of 23 April 2009 on the geological storage of CO2 and amending Council Directive 85/337/EEC; European Parliament and Council Directives 2000/60/EC, 2001/80/EC, 2004/35/EC, 2006/12/EC, 2008/1/EC, and Regulation (EC) No 1013/2006.

[70] Bailey, P., McCullough, E., and Suter, S., 'Can Governments Ensure Adherence to the Polluter Pays Principle in the Long-Term CCS Liability Context?' (2011) 12 *Sustainable Development Law & Policy* 46, 46–8.

EU.[71] In the US, the Interagency Task Force on CCS observes that a price on carbon is at the fore of barriers for further CCS technological development.[72]

### 3.1.4. Non-market-based instruments

#### *3.1.4.1. Subsidies and Financial assistance*

Governments may provide financial assistance to low-emitting activities or technology as an incentive to motivate a particular environmentally beneficial outcome. These can take the form of tax credit, tax breaks, or other forms of financial assistance. Here, the cost is not borne by the polluter but by the tax-payer. But the OECD argues that tax benefits, subsidies, financial assistance, and other payments to a polluter reinforce other measures designed to achieve appropriate natural resource use and pricing.[73] Similarly, 'aid and payments' are used as a bargaining instrument for buying from the polluter his or her right to pollute, or to auction polluting rights. Incentivized subsidies are popular in countries seeking the deployment of renewable energy technologies.

#### *3.1.4.2. Renewable energy feed in tariffs schemes ('REFiT')*

REFiT policies has been applied in the energy sector of most countries as the preferable financial incentive to encourage uptake of renewable electricity-generating technologies.[74] Many renewable energy technologies have high initial investment costs. The German Renewable Energy Act 2000 ('EEG') for example, provides for investment protection through guaranteed FiT and connection requirements. But while, REFiT remuneration rates are subsidies free, the cost allocation pursuant to the PPP tends to be on the 'consume more and pay more' basis. A similar scheme is being introduced for heat generation—the *renewable heat incentive*.[75]

### 3.1.5. 'Polluter-pays': the liability context

Boyle has rightly argued that 'liability' for loss or damage does remain an important part of most systems of environmental law in addition to regulatory regime, risk avoidance procedures or the criminal penalties.[76] However its role under the Rio PPP is more than subdued. The argument here is not to suggest that victims of pollution and other forms of environmental damage are not entitled to redress by the polluter, but rather to distinguish the focus and scope of the principle.

Rio PPP is a tool for making the polluter pay or to accept some form of responsibility for his or her activities by taking necessary steps to address it regardless of the loss or damage emanating from his activities. It allows for incentives by which a polluter can be assisted or encouraged to become compliant. Also, as opposed to traditional fault based liability,

[71] Council Directive 2009/29/EC, 140; they suggest that the 'industry-funded pooled trust fund' mechanism is the most feasible for making the polluter pay under CCS schemes.

[72] CCS Report, 8.

[73] Council Recommendation on the Use of Economic Instruments in Environmental Policy, C (90)177/ Final (OECD 1991).

[74] REFiT encourages investment in renewable energy generation—from individual homeowners and communities to big companies—by guaranteeing to buy and pay for all the electricity produced. Stiftung, 'Powering Africa', 11; note that the economic rationale in cost-bearing of the PPP is seen in other aspects of market schemes of REFiT such as an export tariff (the sale of surplus energy), or a generation tariff (sale of unused units back to the supplier), Stiftung, 11, 14.

[75] Council Directive 2009/28/EC.

[76] Boyle, A.E., 'Globalising Environmental Liability: The Interplay of National and International Law' (2005) 17(1) *JEL* 3, at 3.

PPP relies on cost internalization and economic instruments for its implementation. It is further distinguished by Principle 13 of the Rio Declaration which directs governments to develop international and national law regarding liability and compensation for victims of pollution and environmental damage.

That said, the PPP could however find application in institutional practices of international non-fault liability and compensation schemes which channel environmental and pollution cost implications of high-risk activities to operators. Under this system states impose non-fault liability on operators to establish and maintain financial security and guarantees to cover compensation claims and establish industry-wide funds at the national level and allocate additional financial resources.[77]

Moreover, the fact that the polluter is not always made to pay for all pollution or environmental damage sustained under an owner/operators legal control under the fault-based liability systems makes the PPP economic instrumentalism invaluable to pollution regulation. For example, environmental contamination from oil spills in the Nigerian Niger Delta remains largely untreated. But a Netherlands district court recently quashed four out of five allegations against the Shell oil company for the oil spills including non-liability for the damage.[78] The court may wish to consider the ruling in the *Raffereine* case which established that for a competent authority to require the operator to clean up the pollution, an EU Member State need only establish a weak causal link between an operator's activities and diffuse pollution.[79] But then Nigeria is not an EU Member State.

## *3.2. International investment and environmental cost-spreading mechanisms*

### 3.2.1. Overview

In addition to the foregoing regulatory or 'top-down' mechanisms, the private sector can be harnessed to address pollution and environmental cost issues through a variety of softer mechanisms, which can be referred to as *environmental cost-spreading investment* ('ECI') mechanisms.[80] This section locates ECI within corporate accountability, socially responsible investment ('SRI') and corporate social responsibility ('CSR') arguments for private sector engagement with the environment, and illustrates the ECI implementation mechanisms. Unlike the myopic focus of the Rio PPP on the public sector (national authorities) for implementation, the ECI includes international and global systems. Thus, this section discusses in many ways what at Rio was not, and perhaps could not be, anticipated.

### 3.2.2. Foreign investment: corporate accountability, SRI, and CSR perspectives

Corporate accountability perspective on investment considers that *the rights* which international investment protection law creates for MNCs must be adequately balanced with

[77] Examples include: oil-transporting shipowners, carriers of dangerous goods, waste transporters, recipient waste disposers, and operators of nuclear plants. See (*supra* note 41) for examples of the relevant treaties.

[78] 'Shell blames the leaks on sabotage and on thieves.' see Harvey, F. and Hirsch, A., 'Shell acquitted of Nigeria pollution charges' (2013), available at <http://www.guardian.co.uk/environment/2013/jan/30/shell-acquitted-nigeria-pollution-charges> (accessed 25 July 2013).

[79] Case C-378/08 *Raffinerie Mediterranee (ERG) SpA and Others v. Ministeriodello Sviluppoeconomico and Others* 9 Mar 2010 (InfoCuria—Case law of the Court of Justice); see Fogleman, V., First Environmental Liability Directive cases from European Court of Justice 2010 available at <http://www.commercialriskeurope.com/cre/190/57/First-Environmental-Liability-Directive-cases-from-European-Court-of-Justice/> (accessed 20 June 2013).

[80] The author uses ECI generally to refer to private sector (corporations/institutional) investment policies and measures that seek to promote or influence (directly or indirectly) sustainable production practices and development of environmental technology for environment protection globally.

corresponding *duties* at the international level to make them accountable for the protection of the environment.[81] The argument is that the dichotomy between guaranteed investment protection rights for MNCs and their environmental obligations at the international level could pose significant problems in investment disputes where investment disciplines are applied to consider the issues.[82] Morgera therefore recommends that standards that international financial institutions ('IFIs') establish, which translate international environmental laws, principles, and objectivities that states have assented to, could be useful for promoting corporate accountability at the international level—they can be applied in practice to the private sector through loan agreements.[83] But Viñuales cautiously observes that the private sector is being assigned an increased role in global environmental strategies that is, to a 'limited extent, mirrored by the growing space left for environmental considerations in investment and free trade agreements'.[84]

The SRI proponents seek to enable 'ethical investors' to overcome the barriers created by the legal nature of financial corporations in order to challenge corporations for irresponsible environmental practices that are overlooked by government officials.[85] Richardson terms financial institutions as the '*unseen polluters*', because they 'capitalise companies and projects that may harm the environment' and profit from such businesses.[86] SRI therefore calls for financial institutions to go beyond the practice of requirements for higher environmental standards as conditions for financing; and rather to consider 'more ethical investment choices or a more enlightened approach to financing that is not predicated on maximising financial returns'.[87] The main financial instruments for private environmental finance are collective investment schemes (private funds),[88] project finance,[89] and market mechanisms. However, the business case for SRI, and the lack of transparency in promulgating SRI codes undermines its potency to alter corporate behaviour, leading to calls for public regulation to steer the financial sector towards sustainability.[90]

[81] Morgera, E., *Corporate Accountability in International Environmental Law* (Oxford University Press 2009), 51–6.

[82] For example investment disciplines were applied (in *Société Arcelor Atlantique et Lorraine et al v. Premier Ministre, Ministre de l'Economie, des Finances et de l'Industrie, Ministre de l'Ecologie et du Développement Durable*, ECJ Case C-127/07, Judgment (16 December 2008)) to consider the question of differentiation, namely: 'whether the ETS Directive can validly cover the steel sector while leaving outside of its scope the chemical and aluminium sectors'; see Viñuales, *Foreign Investment and the Environment*, 261–2.

[83] Morgera, *Corporate Accountability*, 149, 170.

[84] Viñuales, *Foreign Investment and the Environment*, 391.

[85] Corporations raise questions of legal personality, economic purpose, and shareholder primacy interests: Richardson, B. J., 'Can Socially Responsible Investment Provide a means for Environmental Regulation?' (2009) 35(2) *Monash University Law Review* 262, at 262; Richardson. B. J., *Socially Responsible Investment Law: Regulating the Unseen Polluters* (Oxford University Press 2008), 12.

[86] Richardson, 'Can Socially Responsible Investment Provide a means for Environmental Regulation?', 263; Richardson, *Socially Responsible Investment Law*, 281.

[87] Richardson, 'Can Socially Responsible Investment Provide a means for Environmental Regulation?', 262, 265–6.

[88] These are pooled assets managed under a specific legal structure (and risk management), for investment in profitable economic activities: 'private for-profit funds'; not-for-profit funds; public funds; and 'international funds'. See Langer, M. J., 'Key Instruments Of Private Environmental Finance: Funds, Project Finance And Market Mechanisms', in Dupuy, P. and. Viñuales, J. E. (eds), *Harnessing Foreign Investment To Promote Environmental Protection* (Cambridge University Press 2013), 131, at 138; cf Richardson, B. J., 'Financing Sustainability: The New Transnational Governance of Socially Responsible Investment' (2007) 17 *YbIEL* 73.

[89] Contractual agreements that link disbursement of funds to compliance with specific environmental standards.

[90] Richardson, 'Can Socially Responsible Investment Provide a means for Environmental Regulation?', 267, 284.

The CSR perspective aims to address the 'real regulatory difficulty' to control MNCs by the *command* approach, due to the 'multijurisdictional' nature of their activities and complex organizational structure.[91] Zerk argues that *self-regulation* would harness investor and consumer power to promote environmental and social sustainability.[92] Along this trend, the EC 2011–14 CSR strategy states that enterprises can meet CSR, 'by having in place a process to integrate social, environmental, ethical, human rights, and consumer concerns into their business operations and core strategy in close collaboration with their stakeholders'.[93] However, constructions of CSR do not emphasize any particular element, making it susceptible to be portrayed in priorities of some of its elements, and according to the individual business preferences—as an ethical aspiration, a legal regulation, a market tool, or a risk management instrument.[94] Empirical evidence suggests that in most African countries lacking social institutions, CSR practice largely focuses on social objectives, thereby constricting the direction of investment toward environmental costs and related technologies.[95]

### 3.2.3. ECI implementation systems

#### *3.2.3.1. Public-private partnerships and market mechanism*

Public-private partnerships[96] usually seek to create an enabling business environment, promote innovation, competition, and risk-sharing between public and the private sector and ensure international cooperation on these.[97] The world bank, governments, international institutions, CSOs and the private sector, team in various partnerships, and apply this economic rationale: to pursue environmental objectives through low-carbon investments, principally under the Global Environment Facility ('GEF')[98] and the climate investment funds ('CIF') mechanisms.[99]

[91] Zerk, J., *Multinationals and Corporate Social Responsibility: Limitations and Opportunities in International Law* (Cambridge University Press 2006), 36, 45.

[92] Self-regulation means the abrogation of the responsibility to regulate for environmental and social sustainability entirely to the MNCs; self-regulatory schemes include government or industry sponsored codes of conduct, transparency initiatives, 'comply or explain' requirements, incentives, and publication of social and environmental performance; see Zerk, J., *Multinationals and Corporate Social Responsibility*, 36–40.

[93] European Commission Communication: 'A renewed EU strategy 2011–14 for Corporate Social Responsibility', Brussels, 25.10.2011 COM (2011) 681 final ('EC COM on CSR'), available at <http://ec.europa.eu/enterprise/newsroom/cf/_getdocument.cfm?doc_id=7010 > 12 January 2012.

See also ISO 26000 'Guidance on social responsibility' <http://www.iso.org> (accessed 19 December 2012).

[94] Schwartz, P., '"*Corporate Socialising*" and Environmental Sustainability in Africa', Paper Presented at 'Sustainable Companies: We Make it Happen', Conference, University of Oslo, Department of Private Law, 4–5 December 2013, 5; (forthcoming in *European Journal of Corporate Law*, Spring 2014).

[95] Schwartz, '*Corporate Socialising*', 5.

[96] It represents a hybrid of public and private actors involved in the private sector supply of infrastructure assets, services, or products (that is traditionally the domain of the public sector).

[97] Schwartz, P., 'Public Private Partnerships and Government Services in LDCs: Regulatory Paradoxes', in Szyszczak, E. et al (eds), *Developments in Services of General Interest* (TMC Asser Press 2011), 2.

[98] The GEF is a financial organization of partnerships providing grants for projects that address global environmental issues (falling under specified environmental treaties including climate change), and supporting national sustainable development initiatives. See 'Instrument for the Establishment of the Restructured Global Environment Facility' (16 October 2011), available at: <http://www.thegef.org/gef/instrument> accessed 14 December 2013.

[99] The CIF is a partnership of carbon funds and facilities, under the control of the World Bank, that supports carbon credit operations, projects, programmes, and policies in developing countries that facilitate climate change mitigation action through carbon markets; see World Bank, 'Carbon Finance for Sustainable Development' Annual Report (2012), 12–19 (World Bank 2012) available at <http://www.carbonfinance.org/publications> accessed 15 December 2013; also World Bank, 'Carbon Finance for Sustainable

Viñuales identifies four systems by which the GEF leverages investment flows to benefit the global environment.[100] The *indirect engagement* strategy, aims to create environmental markets and conditions where pro-environment firms can thrive, by being able, for example, to take advantage of the outputs of a piece of equipment.[101] The *direct engagement* strategy of funding seeks to induce companies consciousness and induce environmentally friendly conduct of business. The *funding/co-finance* scheme is designed to promote the transition to a green economy by supporting development of clean technologies.[102] The *procurement* policy strategy encourages companies to participate in the procurement of GEF-funded projects.[103] Through these ECI strategies, the GEF has especially pioneered technology and market mechanisms to ensure 'widespread adoption and dissemination of climate-friendly technologies'.[104]

The Prototype Carbon Fund ('PCF') is a component of CIF partnerships—an environmental fund and market mechanism—that funds the Kyoto protocol assets in developing countries through joint implementation ('JI') projects, generated ERs and CDM in order to reduce GHG emissions.[105] Other CIF mechanisms entail diverse investments schemes/projects such as: linking carbon finance to tangible poverty reduction through purchase of ERs from small-scale projects that provide community benefits ('co-benefit approach');[106] purchasing ERs from soil carbon projects in farming communities;[107] using market mechanisms to promote low-carbon growth programmes across various sectors and technologies in areas needing government policy measures to invest.[108] The 'next generation' carbon initiatives (ie post 2012 Kyoto commitment period) seek to extend activities to boost the impact of low-carbon initiatives, from landscapes to energy access for the poor.[109]

### *3.2.3.2. Environmental project financing (EPF)*

IFIs project loan agreements, and direct commercial arrangements involving public investors and private entities creating economic and risk obligations, and environmental conditions supporting the financing, represent ECI evidencing EPF.[110] The IFC

Development' Annual Report (2010) ('World Bank 2010') available at <https://wbcarbonfinance.org/docs/64897_World_Bank_web_lower_Res.pdf> (accessed 15 December 2013).

100 Viñuales, *Foreign Investment and the Environment*, 43–5.

101 Such market conditions applicable to renewable energy firms include creating, *inter alia*, a more equitable energy pricing regime, public availability of information on renewable energy resources, and agreed standards for industrial inputs in countries receiving GEF funds (Viñuales, 43–5).

102 For instance, it has supported more than 50 climate-resilient technologies for energy efficiency, renewable energy, sustainable urban transport, and methane reduction. See 'Behind the Numbers: A Closer Look At GEF Achievements', available at <http://www.thegef.org/gef/pubs/behind_numbers_2012> 6.

103 Viñuales, 44–5.

104 In 21 years, GEF has 'invested directly $11.5 billion and co-financed $57 billion and supported 3,215 projects' in over 165 countries ('Behind the Numbers', 6).

105 World Bank 2010, 24; eg Land Use, Land-use Change, and Forestry ('LULUCF') projects are in the PCF portfolio needing an official CDM verification and CERS.

106 The Community Development Carbon Fund ('CDCF'); World Bank 2010.

107 The Bio Carbon Fund ('Bio CF')—includes afforestation, reforestation, and avoided deforestation activities yielding carbon credits—eg the UN-REDD Programme. See World Bank 2010, 37. Note also the Umbrella Carbon Facility ('UCF').

108 Carbon Partnership Facility ('CPF')—Pertinent areas involve energy generation, distribution/efficiency, and waste management; See World Bank 2010, 75–6.

109 These include the: FCPF, CPF, PMR, Bio CF T3, and the Ci-Dev.; World Bank 2012, 21.

110 EPF involves the allocation of public and private funds in accordance with environmental as well as other 'socially responsible' criteria. Viñuales, *Foreign Investment and the Environment*, 42.

2006 performance standards for pollution prevention and abatement is a pertinent example.[111] Through its 'project approach', the IFC incorporates its standards (specifically Performance Standards 3) into loan agreements with private companies, and contractually bind them to adopting them. It requires companies, for example, to apply pollution prevention and control technologies during the life cycle of the project. The obligation is however qualified by financial feasibility, cost effectiveness, and commercial availability of skills.[112]

A similar system exists for private commercial banks through the equator principles,[113] an SRI code that has multi-jurisdictional and global application to financial markets.[114] The equator principles provide benchmarks for funding international projects, requiring borrowers to meet certain environmental criteria before a project can qualify for investment. The credibility of the principles is bolstered by the IFC Safeguard Policies.[115] However, focus on the 'business case' rationale of SRI and the 'in-house' promulgation of SRI codes has led Richardson to call for public regulation to steer the financial sector towards sustainable development.[116]

## III) Relations with Other Principles

The polluter cost burden under Principle 16 should be borne by persons (natural or legal) who engage in or are connected with polluting activities. From this standpoint the PPP might seem to conflict with other pertinent environmental principles, particularly the principles of prevention and CBDR.

The principle of prevention (or 'no-harm' rule) is expressed in Principle 2 of the Rio declaration and is recognized in international law and custom prohibiting transboundary environmental damage including the duty to take preventive and risk control measures.[117] The ICJ affirmed in the *Pulp Mills* case that the 'no harm' principle is the 'principle of prevention' requiring the state to observe due diligence in its territory. The State is 'obliged to *use all the means at its disposal in order to avoid* [domestic] activities causing significant damage to the environment of another State.'[118] Also, States are presumed to have CBDR

[111] It seeks to promote polluter accountability by requiring the application of international recognized technology and best practices from its client. See IFC Performance Standards on Social and Environmental Sustainability adopted 30 April 2006; available at http://www.ifc.org/sustainability> (accessed 16 December 2013).

[112] Morgera, *Corporate Accountability*, 156.

[113] Equator principles available at <http://www.equator-principles.com> (accessed 16 August 2013); for analysis of the principle, see Richardson, B. J., 'The Equator Principles: The Voluntary Approach to Environmentally Sustainable Finance' (2005) 14 *European Environmental Law Review* 280.

[114] The codes tend to set in place procedures for a more transparent and accountable financial decision making; Richardson, (2009(a))(*supra* note 85) 266;. Other examples include: the UNPRI—available at: <http://www.unpri.org/principles> (accessed 16 August 2013); UNEP Finance Initiative, 'Statement by Financial Institutions on the Environment and Sustainable Development' available at: <htt://www.unepfi.org>; (accessed 16 August 2013).

[115] They particularly target commercial lending in developing countries and emerging economies providing a framework to manage social and environmental impact associated with projects; Richardson, 'Can Socially Responsible Investment Provide a means for Environmental Regulation?', 279.

[116] Richardson, 'Can Socially Responsible Investment Provide a means for Environmental Regulation?', 284.

[117] See *Trail Smelter* case (United States, Canada) 16 April 1938 and 11 March 1941, Vol III, Reports Of International Arbitral Award Spp. 1905–1982 UN, 2006; Birnie, P., Boyle, A., and Redgwell, C., *International Law and the Environment* (3rd edn, Oxford University Press 2009), 143–52.

[118] *Pulp Mills on the River Uruguay* case (*Argentina v. Uruguay*), ICJ Reports 2010, 1, 38, para 101.

by which, the developed countries assuming a higher global environmental cost-burden for past pollution, and 'in view of the pressures their societies place on the global environment and of the technologies and financial resources they command'.[119]

The controversy seems to be that the 'principle of prevention' and the CBDR principle, unlike the PPP, hold the state directly responsible for the pollution caused by a corporation or industry. Also the no-harm rule is limiting in that it defines environmental damage specifically in relation to another state; whereas the PPP covers environmental cost for damage. But it may be difficult to trace such damage to any one state's failure to avoid the polluting activities or to a specific victim. Boyle therefore argues that unless state responsibility is made no more than a residual source of redress for environmental damage, it could undermine the PPP.[120] Similarly while the Rio PPP aims to solve domestic and global pollution problems through a *cost effective* system, the CBDR applies equitable principles to define a polluter based on the concept of historic pollution responsibility, meaning that a developing state could pollute most but pay less.[121]

Notwithstanding the seeming contradictions, the PPP performs a distinct but complimentary function to the principles of prevention and CBDR. Their concurrent application should be encouraged in order to foster procedural coherence. Such an interactive view (on PPP and prevention) is adopted by the ECJ in the *Raffinerie Mediterranee* case. It held, *inter alia*, that a higher level of protection than originally prescribed under Directive 2004/35, could be applied with respect to national measures designed to facilitate urgent preventive action.[122] Countries need this regulatory space in determining the nature, cause, and effect of polluter responsibility. The principles together should guide national authorities on how to efficiently allocate pollution costs and equitably attribute the responsibility. Moreover, the PPP and CBDR work as procedural tools to give effect to the substantive rule of prevention.

## IV) Assessment

The analysis of the variety of make-the-polluter-pay economic approaches demonstrates that the concept and scope of 'environmental costs' and 'polluter' has diverged so much that while the main focus continues to be on 'costs', it is not always the polluter's costs, or an endeavour to make the polluter pay. The trade, investment, and the public interest caveat amplifies the challenges in ensuring a consistent application of the PPP as characterized in Principle 16.

The implementation of this Principle, especially through process and product taxes, effluent charges, or emissions crediting and trading, provides an invaluable revenue stream for governments which should help reduce the total cost of pollution control to society. Costs of complying with the requirements of pollution standards have lowered

[119] Rio Declaration Principle 7: also in the UNFCCC; see generally UNFCCC/CP/1998.MISC.7 available at <http://unfccc.int/resource/docs/cop4/misc07.htm> (accessed 2 July 2013).

[120] Boyle, 'Globalising Environmental Liability', at 8–9.

[121] eg China and India view the EU extension of the cap-and-trade system to the aviation sector as a violation of the CBDR principle: see Meltzer, J., 'Regulating CO2 Emissions from Aviation in the EU' (2012) 16 *ASIL Insight* available at <http://www.asil.org/insights/volume/16/issue/27/regulating-co2-emissions-aviation-eu>.

[122] *Raffinerie Mediterranee*, paras 69–70.

and products are redesigned in order to comply with recycling laws. By the turn of the century, the main concern of the PPP was the disproportionally costly regulatory burden that the technology-based command requirement imposed on profitable industries, seemingly penalizing innovation and investment.[123]

The focus has significantly changed since then. Various PPP implementation methods see technology as the miracle solution to environmental problems and so rely on economic incentives to encourage adaptation to technology and further investment in the development of new technologies. This orientation of the PPP, in combination with the use of evolving market and non-market mechanisms entrenches a culture of property rights. Thus polluter-pays dealings have nurtured a meaning of 'environmental cost' that is different from that envisaged in the Rio Declaration to mean: financial gains or other benefit from the business of pollution at a cost to the environment. By some ingenious calculation we learn that the 'polluter' can 'green' the economy ('green growth') *via* investments (and subsidies) in 'green' technology. We need only recognize the connection between the cost of technology, market competitiveness, productivity (and consumption), and environmental pollution to indict this assumption.

By way of illustration, one of the reasons for abandoning the REFiT policy in South Africa is the fall in the prices of solar PV and 'fears' about an unchecked growth of expenses.[124] Scholars have also questioned the need for the EU to resort to state subsidies or REFiT for bringing 'capital intensive technologies' on stream when there are efficiency options that could account for significant carbon emissions reductions at a lower cost.[125] Even the US ETS programme did not produce the magnitude of cost savings that was anticipated, because the transactions involved the introduction of innovative control technologies.[126] We are also uncertain about the long-term environmental consequences of the CCS technology. Fossil fuel use is still on the rise and we are at the brink of a shale gas revolution. The REN21 reports a decrease in global investment in renewable energy owing *inter alia* to falling technology prices, declining policy support in established markets, higher subsidies to fossil fuels, and ongoing tensions in international trade.[127]

In the opinion of this author, there is need for states to rethink the purpose of the PPP as a philosophy of responsibility and accountability toward the way we perceive our environment and how we use it. At first glance the principle gives the perception that environmental deterioration is inevitably linked with economic activity and that a right to pollute exists as long as the 'environmental cost' is accounted for. But the principle that the polluter-pays must also influence our conduct: to restrain or reduce our capacity to over-produce, over-consume, over-charge, over-invest, over-innovate, over-trade, and over-compete. An interesting development in this connection is the attempt to engage with the private sector in addressing pollution-related and global environmental issues through ECI mechanisms of partnerships, environmental financing, and market mechanisms applying innovative methodologies. The private sector is not only made aware of the

[123] Stewart, 'Economic Incentives for Environmental Protection', 185.

[124] Stiftung, 'Powering Africa', 55–6.

[125] Spassov et al, 'Lowest-cost Abatement', 288; The efficiency options include: fuel-switching; operational efficiency and co-firing coal with biomass; costs to refurbish air heaters to boost boiler efficiency and to upgrade pulverizers and steam turbines.

[126] Tietenberg, 'Economic Instruments For Environmental Regulation', 19.

[127] REN21 Renewables; Note that investments in renewables seemed to have done well in developing countries.

cost of its operations but it is also mobilized to address them (not simply to pay for them) either through public or financier-pressure, or through structures that engage industry in depolluting activities. Changing the behaviour of companies from the inside is, of course, not easy. But it is a welcome step in the direction of moving from a purely burden-sharing version of PPP to a more preventive one.

## V) Select Bibliography


Bailey, P. et al, 'Can Governments Ensure Adherence to the Polluter Pays Principle in the Long-Term CCS Liability Context?' (2011) 12 *Sustainable Development Law and Policy* 46.

ECORYS, *Design Options For Sectoral Carbon Market Mechanisms EC, DG Climate Action Final Report 2012*, CLIMA.B.3/SER/2011/0029, Rotterdam, 31 August 2012.

European Commission, Recommendation Regarding Cost Allocation and Action by Public Authorities on Environmental Matters (EC 1975).

European Commission, 'A renewed EU strategy 2011–14 for Corporate Social Responsibility' Brussels, 25.10.2011 COM (2011) 681.

Fogleman, V., 'First Environmental Liability Directive cases from European Court of Justice' (2010), available at: <http://www.stevens-bolton.com>.

Global Environmental Facility, *Behind the Numbers: A Closer Look at GEF Achievements* (2012).

Langer, M.-J., 'Key Instruments Of Private Environmental Finance: Funds, Project Finance And Market Mechanisms', in Dupuy, P. and Viñuales, J. E. (eds), *Harnessing Foreign Investment To Promote Environmental Protection* (Cambridge University Press 2013), 131.

Meltzer, J., 'Climate Change & Trade: The EU Aviation Directive & the WTO' (2012) 15 *Journal of International Economic Law* 111.

Meltzer, J., 'Regulating CO2 Emissions from Aviation in the EU' (2012) 16 *ASIL Insight*, available at <http://www.asil.org/insights/volume/16/issue/27/regulating-co2-emissions-aviation-eu>.

Monterubio, J., 'Recognition of Property Rights in Carbon Credits Under California's New Greenhouse Gas Cap-And-Trade Program' (2011) 12 *Sustainable Development Law & Policy* 32.

Morgera, E., *Corporate Accountability in International Environmental Law* (Oxford University Press 2009).

Organisation for Economic Cooperation and Development, Recommendation of the Council Concerning International Economic Aspects of Environmental Policies, C(72)128 (OECD 1972).

Organisation for Economic Cooperation and Development, Recommendation on the Implementation of the Polluter-pays Principle, C(74) 223/Final (OECD 1974).

Organisation for Economic Cooperation and Development, Recommendation of the Council on the Use of Economic Instruments in Environmental Policy, C(90)177/Final (OECD 1991).

Organisation for Economic Cooperation and Development, 'The Polluter-Pays Principle' OECD Analyses and Recommendations OCDE/GD(92)81 (OECD 1992).

Organisation for Economic Cooperation and Development, *Scaled-up Market Mechanism: What is Needed to Move Forward?* (OECD/IEA 2010).

Renewable Energy Policy Network, *Renewables: Global Status Report* (Renewable Energy Policy Network 2013).

Report of the Interagency Task Force on Carbon Capture and Storage, August 2010.

Richardson, B. J., 'The Equator Principles: The Voluntary Approach to Environmentally Sustainable Finance' (2005) 14 *European Environmental Law Review* 280.

Richardson, B. J., 'Financing Sustainability: The New Transnational Governance of Socially Responsible Investment' (2007) 17 *YbIEL* 73.

Richardson, B. J., *Socially Responsible Investment Law: Regulating the Unseen Polluters* (Oxford University Press 2008).

Richardson, B. J., 'Can SRI Provide a means for Environmental Regulation?' (2009) 35 *Monash University Law Review* 262.

Schwartz, P., 'Sustainable Energy Infrastructure: Law, Policy and Practice' (2009) 2 *International Journal of Private Law* 135.

Schwartz, P., 'Polluter Pays Principle', in Fitzmaurice, M., Ong, D., and Merkouris P. (eds), *Research Handbook on International Environmental Law* (Cheltenham: Edward Elgar 2010), 243.

Schwartz, P., 'Public Private Partnerships and Government Services in LDCs: Regulatory Paradoxes', in Szyszczak, E. et al (eds), *Developments in Services of General Interest* (The Hague: TMC Asser Press 2011), 197.

Schwartz, P., '"Corporate Socialising" and Environmental Sustainability in Africa', Paper Presented at 'Sustainable Companies: We Make it Happen', Conference, University of Oslo, Department of Private Law, 4–5 December 2013 (forthcoming in *European Journal of Corporate Law*, Spring 2014).

Spassov, Y., et al, 'Lowest-cost Abatement in Light of the EU ETS and Renewable Feed-in Tariffs in the Electricity Sector in Bulgaria' (2011) 29 *Journal of Energy & Natural Resources Law* 281.

Stewart, R. B., 'Economic Incentives for Environmental Protection: Opportunities and Obstacles', in Revesz, E. et al (eds), *Environmental Law, The Economy and Sustainable Development* (Cambridge University Press 2000), 171.

Stiftung, H. B., *Powering Africa through Feed-In Tariffs* (World Future Council/Greenpeace 2013).

Tietenberg, T. H., 'Economic Instruments for Environmental Regulation' (1990) 6 *Oxford Review of Economic Policy* 17.

United Nations Environment Programme, *Towards a Green Economy: Pathways to Sustainable Development and Poverty Eradication* (2011).

Viñuales, J. E., *Foreign Investment and the Environment in International Law* (Cambridge University Press 2012).

Zerk, J., *Multinationals and Corporate Social Responsibility: Limitations and Opportunities in International Law* (Cambridge University Press 2006).

# 21. Principle 17

## *Environmental Impact Assessment*

Neil Craik*

**Principle 17**

Environmental impact assessment, as a national instrument, shall be undertaken for proposed activities that are likely to have a significant adverse impact on the environment and are subject to a decision of a competent national authority.



## I) Origins and Rationale of the Principle

### 1. The NEPA

Predating the Rio Declaration by more than twenty years, environmental impact assessment ('EIA') has its origins in the US federal *National Environmental Policy Act* ('NEPA').[1] As the name suggests, this piece of legislation, enacted in 1970, set out the environmental

* Director and Associate Professor of Law, School of Environment, Enterprise and Development, University of Waterloo, Canada.

[1] 42 USC §§ 4321–4370(f).

objectives that were to inform federal agency decision-making. The policy declaration was drafted in highly abstract, even hortatory terms, but the legislation included a requirement that proposed federal government actions significantly affecting the environment must include a 'detailed statement' describing the environmental impact of the proposed action, as well as alternatives to the proposed action. The responsible agency was also required to consult other appropriate federal and State agencies, as well as the public, and make the detailed statement and any comments publicly available.[2] The idea that animates NEPA, and which is carried through to modern EIA, is that environmental goals are not self-activating, but need to be projected into decision-making processes. Described as an 'action forcing mechanism',[3] EIA was intended to bring environmental considerations to bear on broader policy processes.

The fundamental nature of EIA was established early on by the US courts, which imposed rigorous procedural obligations on agencies, but did not require agencies to adopt the least impactful alternative or to necessarily mitigate identified environmental harms. The obligation was neatly summed up by the US Supreme Court when it noted that NEPA 'merely prohibits uninformed—rather than unwise—agency action'.[4] Because the policy goals that underlie the process are open-ended, they impose 'soft' substantive constraints, requiring public justification in light of shared environmental goals, but not compliance with predetermined standards.

## 2. Expansion

Out of the simple set of requirements described in the preceding section grew the modern system of EIA, which quickly expanded both horizontally to other domestic legal systems and vertically to international instruments and organizations.[5]

EIA should not be thought of as a rigidly defined process that must conform to some predetermined set of requirements. As a technical undertaking, EIAs will adhere to an evolving set of practice methodologies that seek to identify and predict environmental outcomes. Best practices in relation to EIA respond to advances in scientific knowledge on ecological systems (as well as greater appreciation of the limitations of that knowledge). As a legal concept, EIA is best understood as both the study of impacts, but also the accompanying process of notification, consultation, and decision-making. The particulars of both the study requirements and the broader deliberative processes vary from system to system, but retain their unity through common adherence to a basic or generic form consisting of the following key elements: screening (the processes that determine whether an activity will be subject to an EIA); scoping (the processes that define the scope, or terms of reference, of the environmental impact study); impact prediction; agency and public review and consultation; and the final decision regarding the activity itself.[6]

[2] 42 USC § 4332(C).

[3] Lynton Caldwell, Hearings on S. 1075, S. 237 and S. 1752 before Senate Comm., *On Interior and Insular Affairs*, 91 Cong. 1st Sess. 116 (1969).

[4] *Robertson v. Methow Valley Citizens Council* (1989) 490 US 332 at 350–1.

[5] It is estimated that 191 countries have some form of EIA legislation (Richard Morgan, 'Environmental Impact Assessment: the state of the art' (2012) 30 *Impact Assessment and Project Appraisal* 5, 6).

[6] On the generic form of EIA see Holder, J., *Environmental Assessment: The Regulation of Decision Making* (Oxford University Press 2004), ch 1.

As an international instrument, EIA has largely, but not exclusively, been concerned with the assessment of transboundary impacts, whereby the commitment to conduct an EIA is triggered by an activity's potential to cause environmental harm beyond its national jurisdiction. An early draft of the Stockholm Declaration contained a reference to the provision of information where planned activities may potentially harm areas beyond national jurisdiction, but this provision was dropped as a result of concerns from developing countries that such an obligation would constrain the right to develop.[7] Subsequent to the Stockholm Conference, EIA obligations did find their way into a number of UN based soft-law instruments, indicating a growing acceptance of EIA as a norm of international environmental law,[8] although these early instruments do not elaborate upon the precise requirements of the obligation, leaving the details of implementation to individual States.

One exception to this was the 1987 UNEP Goals and Principles of Environmental Impact Assessment, which sought to provide guidance to States in the development of domestic EIA procedures,[9] and to provide guidance respecting reciprocal procedures in relation to activities that may result in transboundary pollution, which included obligations to notify affected States, including the provision of relevant information from the EIA, and a weak obligation of consultation.[10] The UNEP Principles are significant in that they demonstrate the increasing willingness of the international community to define the minimum content of an EIA.[11] They also point to the important link between the duties to notify and consult affected States under conditions of potential transboundary harm and EIA, whereby EIA is contemplated as one of the legal tools by which these distinct international obligations can be implemented. At a minimum, States should ensure that their assessment and consultation practices do not stop at national borders.

UNEP's influence in promoting EIA as a key tool in managing shared environmental resources is also evident in the regional seas programme, where EIA obligations have been included in the regional seas conventions and action plans since 1978.[12] Similarly the United Nations Convention on the Law of the Sea ('UNCLOS'), concluded in 1982, contained a qualified EIA obligation in article 206.[13] The obligation under UNCLOS does not dictate the content of an EIA, but does link it to a duty to notify other States of potentially harmful environmental effects.[14] Of particular importance in the inclusion of EIA obligations in these treaties is that the obligations are not limited to situations where environmental effects impact other State's territory, but include impacts on the global commons.

[7] UN Doc A/Conf/48/4, Annex, Principle 20; discussed in Sands, P. and Peel, J., *Principles of International Environmental Law* (3rd edn, Cambridge University Press 2012), 602.

[8] 'Co-operation between States in the Field of the Environment', UNGA Res. 2995 (XXVII), UN GAOR, 27th Sess., Supp No.30 (1972) at 42; World Charter for Nature, UNGA Res. 37/7, UN GAOR, 37th Sess., UN Doc A/Res/37/7(1982), reprinted in (1983) 22 ILM 455.

[9] UNEP Res. GC14/25, 14th Sess. (1987), endorsed by GA Res. 42/184, UN GAOR, 42nd Sess., UN Doc A/Res/42/184 (1987) ('UNEP EIA Goals and Principles'), Goal 2.

[10] UNEP EIA Goals and Principles, Goal 3.

[11] UNEP EIA Goals and Principles, Principle 4.

[12] Kuwait Regional Convention for Co-operation on the Protection of the Marine Environment from Pollution, Kuwait, 24 April 1978, 1140 UNTS 133, (1978) 17 ILM 511, in force 1 July 1979, art XI; for complete list see Craik, N., *The International Law of Environmental Impact Assessment: Process, Substance and Integration* (Cambridge University Press 2008), 97.

[13] United Nations Convention on the Law of the Sea, December 10, 1982 ('UNCLOS'), (1982) 21 ILM 1261, in force 16 November 1994, art 206.

[14] UNCLOS, art 205.

## 3. The broader context of the Rio negotiation

Three significant developments occurred prior to, or contemporaneously with, the negotiation of the Rio Declaration.

First, in 1985, the European Community enacted a directive on environmental assessment.[15] The EIA Directive, which required that member States enact implementing legislation in line with the EC requirements, provided the principal structural elements of the EIA procedures, including obligations to notify and consult affected States in the likelihood of significant transboundary impacts.[16] This brought the European Community under a common set of EIA commitments in relation to their domestic environment and provided a process to address transboundary impacts.

Second, the members of the UN Economic Commission for Europe (European States, including the USSR and other eastern European States, and the US and Canada) negotiated the Convention on Environmental Impact Assessment in a Transboundary Context ('Espoo Convention'), which was signed in 1991.[17] The Espoo Convention provided a detailed set of procedures that govern notification, the content of EIAs and consultation procedures where transboundary harm was likely to occur from planned activities (defined as harm originating from an activity under one State's jurisdiction and having effects in areas under another State's jurisdiction, but excluding harm to areas beyond national jurisdiction). The Espoo Convention, like previous international EIA commitments, identified EIA as a national procedure, giving States some autonomy in the development of international EIA procedures that conform to their particular domestic requirements. The treaty contains a weak obligation to prevent transboundary harm, but does not include any express obligation to mitigate identified transboundary harms, preferring to leave the determination of acceptable levels of transboundary harm to consultations between parties. One element of the Espoo Convention that is of particular note is that it extended the obligation to consult not only to affected States, but also to the members of the public of the affected State. In essence, the treaty required the State of origin (that is, the State proposing the activity) to extend rights of participation to the public of the affected State that were equivalent to those extended to its own citizens.[18]

Finally, the Madrid Protocol to the Antarctic Treaty on Environmental Protection, which was also concluded in 1991, requires an EIA for all activities that have at least a 'minor or transitory impact'.[19] The protocol contains a detailed annex on EIA, and given the status of the Antarctic as a commons, the Protocol provides for a mechanism, through the Committee on Environmental Protection, by which the Parties to the Protocol may review the assessment and may make recommendations as to whether the activity should proceed.[20]

[15] European Council Directive 85/337 on the Assessment of the Effects of Certain Public and Private Projects on the Environment, [1985] OJ l 175/40. Subsequently amended by EC, Council Directive 97/11, EC, Council Directive 03/35, and EC, Council Directive 09/31 ('EIA Directive').

[16] EIA Directive, art 7.

[17] Convention on Environmental Impact Assessment in a Transboundary Context, 25 February 1991 ('Espoo Convention'), 1989 UNTS 310.

[18] Espoo Convention, art 2(6).

[19] Protocol on Environmental Protection to the Antarctic Treaty, 4 October 1991 ('Antarctic Protocol'), (1991) 30 ILM 1455, art 8(1).

[20] Antarctic Protocol, Annex 1.

In summary, by the time that the Rio Declaration was being negotiated, EIA was becoming an integral part of the domestic environmental regulatory landscape of most developed States and a growing number of developing States. It was also an emerging principle of international law, as recognized by leading publicists.[21] EIA was put forward as both a specific tool to address transboundary pollution issues, but was also understood as a more general principle of sound environmental planning regardless of the location of the impacts. The swift international reception of EIA can be attributed in part to the common sense appeal of requiring proponents to inform themselves of the environmental consequences of their proposed activities, as well as its established role in domestic legal systems. As discussed in this chapter, EIA is consonant with the well established due diligence obligation in relation to transboundary harm, and also provides a uniform manner of implementing the duties to notify and consult.

## II) The Principle as Enshrined in the Rio Declaration

### 1. Preparatory work

As the text of the Rio Declaration was negotiated, EIA was strongly tied to the principles of prevention and precaution, as well as to principles relating to the important role of public participation in environmental protection.[22] The United States presented in the third preparatory meeting a set of very detailed EIA provisions under a proposed principle dedicated to public participation and democracy. The structure of the proposal was very similar in form to NEPA, including a threshold of 'significant impact', a requirement to examine alternatives, to provide information about measures for mitigating harm, rights of participation, including extending rights to members of the public in an affected State, and to issue a final decision that accounts for the EIA and the comments received.[23] Other States, principally but not exclusively developed States, put forward proposals that included less elaborated EIA commitments as part of a proposed principle to take precautionary and preventive measures.[24]

In the fourth preparatory meeting, a number of States put forward draft proposals that referenced EIA, with proposals from the Nordic States and from the European Community containing distinct EIA provisions.[25] The final wording adopted by Working Group III and then by the plenary is very similar to the Nordic and European proposals, but added a further qualifier that EIA is a national instrument, which reflects the prevailing understanding that EIA procedures are going to originate in domestic, not supranational instruments, and allows States to retain greater authority over the structure and form of EIA processes.

[21] See, for example, the International Law Association, 'Legal Aspects of the Conservation of the Environment', *Report of the Sixtieth Conference* (1982) 157 at 174; and Experts Group on Environmental Law of the WCED, *Environmental Protection and Sustainable Development: Legal Principles and Recommendation* (Graham & Trotman/Martinus Nijhoff Publishers 1987).

[22] Kovar, J., 'A Short Guide to the Rio Declaration' (1993) 4 *Colorado Journal of International Environmental Law and Policy* 13.

[23] Preparatory Committee for the United Nations Conference on Environment and Development, Third Session, A/CONF.151/PC/WG.III/L.8/Rev.1, 30 August 1991, paras 125–9.

[24] Preparatory Committee for the United Nations Conference on Environment and Development, Third Session, paras 48 (Australia), 50 (Chile), 54 (Netherlands/EEC), 55 (Italy), 56 (USSR).

[25] Preparatory Committee for the United Nations Conference on Environment and Development, Fourth Session, A/CONF.151/PC/128, 12 May 1992, paras 23 (EEC), 25 (Nordic States).

## 2. Scope and Dimensions

### *2.1. Scope of the obligation*

#### 2.1.1. Type of activity

The wording of Principle 17 requires that EIAs be undertaken for 'proposed activities' that are 'subject to a decision of a competent national authority'. This wording clearly restricts EIAs to planned activities that are under the control of the State of origin. This makes sense in the context of due diligence, which only extends to activities that are foreseen and controllable by the State. Principle 17 does not require States to ensure that planned activities are subject to some prior authorization, although that would seem to be implied by the principle of due diligence.[26] States cannot avoid their duty to conduct EIAs simply by refraining from subjecting potentially harmful activities to prior authorization, but the phrase does allow States a further measure of independence to determine the precise application of EIAs.[27]

In this context, the term 'activity' is limited to project level assessments, as distinct from environmental assessments of policies, plans, and programmes. The latter, which are higher order assessments that seek to ensure that when policy documents are developed they too consider the environmental and social consequences of the policy decision, are usually referred to as strategic environmental assessments ('SEA'). The rationale for SEA is that higher order decisions are likely to influence the choice of activities undertaken and limit the range of alternatives considered, and thus have important environmental consequences that cannot be fully captured at the project level. The importance of assessing impacts at programmatic levels was recognized in NEPA, which included requirements to assess 'legislation and other major Federal actions'.[28] However, since its inception in NEPA and in its implementation in other domestic systems, EIA has focused on project assessment. The Espoo Convention, which also uses the term 'activities', expressly differentiates between project level assessment, which is mandatory, and the assessment of 'policies, plans and programmes', which is permissive.[29]

SEA has become part of European law with the promulgation of a European Community Directive on SEA. The parties to the Espoo Convention also negotiated an SEA Protocol in 2003, although the Protocol was only signed by European States.[30] While these developments show some expansion of the application of traditional EIA in Europe, there is minimal evidence that the international commitment to perform EIA has similarly expanded.[31] The focus on physical undertakings that can cause environmental harm directly is consistent with the interpretation of the harm principle and the duties to notify and consult, which are also limited to activities with direct physical consequences.

The other emerging area of application of EIA is in relation to international investment law. The World Bank has had an elaborate system of EIA in place since 1989 that governs

[26] See eg International Law Commission, 'Commentaries to the Draft Articles on Prevention of Transboundary Harm from Hazardous Activities' ('ILC Draft Articles') in *Report of the International Law Commission, Fifty-Third Session*, UN GAOR, 56th Sess., Supp. No. 10, UN Doc A/56/10 (2001) 377, art 5.

[27] Pallemaerts, M., 'Environmental Law in the Age of Sustainable Development: A critical assessment of the UNCED Process' (1995–1996) 15 *Journal of Law and Commerce* 623.

[28] NEPA, USC 42 § 4331(c).

[29] Espoo Convention, art 2(7).

[30] Protocol on Strategic Environmental Assessment (Kiev) 21 May 2003, in force 11 July 2010, UN Doc ECE/MP.EIA/2003/2.

[31] But see the Convention on Biological Diversity, 5 June 1992, 1760 UNTS 79, art 14(1)(b).

projects financed through World Bank mechanisms.[32] EIA procedures are also embedded in the operational procedures of the Multilateral Investment Guarantee Agency and the International Finance Corporation, as well as the operating procedures of other international development banks.[33] Outside the World Bank Group, the banking industry has adopted a voluntary set of guidelines, the Equator Principles, which require EIA for project lending activities.[34] Taken together, the emerging practice is that where internationally financed projects are likely to have a significant environmental impact, lending States are required to assess the environmental and social impacts of the proposed activity. This extends the reach of the EIA obligation beyond those actors that are directly involved in physical undertakings by including those actors that facilitate the undertakings through financing activities. In addition, foreign investment schemes made without complying with the obligation to conduct a prior EIA may be potentially denied the protection of investment treaties.[35] A related, but distinct, area of assessment is requirements for States to conduct environmental assessments of international trade and international investment treaties. These requirements can be best understood as a species of SEA in that they relate not to the environmental impacts of a single undertaking, but to a broader policy of trade or investment that is likely to have environmental impacts.

### 2.1.2. Threshold

The threshold requirement that triggers the duty to conduct an EIA is the likelihood of 'significant adverse impact on the environment'. The standard of significant harm to trigger EIA obligations is uniformly adopted in both international law and in domestic EIA legislation. Again, there is a strong link to the prevention principle, which can be traced back to the *Trail Smelter Arbitration*'s requirement that international obligations are only triggered by transboundary harm that has 'serious consequence(s)'.[36]

The ILC also adopts 'significance' as the threshold for harm prevention obligations, defining 'significant' as 'something more than 'detectable', but need not be at the level of 'serious' or 'substantial'.[37] While the standard is ambiguous and leaves considerable room for interpretation, it is clearly intended as an objective standard. For example, the Espoo Convention provides for third-party assessments of significance through an independent inquiry procedure,[38] and the issue of whether a significant transboundary impact is likely has been placed before international tribunals for determination.[39] There are instances where unique ecological conditions give rise to a lower threshold. Most notably, the Antarctic Protocol uses a threshold of 'minor or transitory impact'.[40]

A fundamental difficulty with determining whether a proposed activity triggers an EIA is that an environmental assessment of sorts is required to determine whether the threshold has

[32] World Bank, *Operational Policies—Environmental Assessment*, January 1999, OP 4.01.

[33] Multilateral Investment Guarantee Agency, *Performance Standard 1—Assessment and Management of Environmental and Social Risks and Impacts*, October 2013; online: <http://www.miga.org/documents/performance_ standards_env_and_social_sustainability.pdf>; International Finance Corporation, *Environmental and Social Review Procedures Manual*. Online: <http://www.ifc.org/wps/wcm/connect/190d25804886582fb 47ef66a6515bb18/ESRP+Manual.pdf?MOD=AJPERES>.

[34] *The Equator Principles*, Principle 2, June 2013 (version III), online: <http://www.equator-principles.com/>.

[35] See Viñuales J. E., *Foreign Investment and the Environment in International Law* (Cambridge University Press 2012), 96–100, 102–4.

[36] *Trail Smelter* Arbitral Award (*United States v. Canada*), 3 RIAA 1905, at 1965.

[37] ILC Draft Articles, art 2, Comm. 4.

[38] Espoo Convention, art 3(7).

[39] See discussion in section II) 4. of this chapter.

[40] Antarctic Protocol, art 8.

been reached, but a project proponent is only required to conduct such an assessment once the threshold has been demonstrated. This circularity has lead to two principal approaches for determining significance. The first is that the proponent conducts an initial environmental assessment—a form of simplified EIA—for a very broad array of activities, in order to determine whether the activity is likely to result in a significance impact and, as a result, requires a full EIA. The second approach is to identify on an *ex ante* basis those activities that are likely to present a risk of significant transboundary harm and to require an EIA for those activities or classes of activities identified. Both approaches find some expression in both international and domestic EIA systems.[41] Principle 17, however, does not require States to adopt a particular approach to determining whether an EIA is warranted, preferring to leave that determination to State discretion. The requirement, which forms part of the larger obligation of due diligence, is to have a reasoned process for the determination of significance.

### 2.1.3. Geographic scope

As drafted, Principle 17 does not restrict the obligation to perform EIAs to transboundary impacts, leaving open the possibility that States are under an international legal obligation to perform EIAs for potential impacts to the global commons and for impacts that remain entirely domestic in their scope. The most straightforward case is the transboundary one. The legal requirement for a State of origin to conduct an EIA where activities undertaken within its territory are likely to have a significant impact in the territory of another State follows from the harm principle and has been affirmed by the ICJ, most recently and most definitively in the *Pulp Mills* case.[42] The transboundary obligation has been accepted in international, regional, and domestic instruments.

The extension of the duty to conduct EIAs in the event of harm to the global commons is supported by the clear application of the harm principle to 'areas beyond the limits of national jurisdiction' enshrined in Principle 2 of the Rio Declaration. This position is supported through treaty practice by article 206 of UNCLOS that requires EIAs in connection with potential harm to the high seas as a constituent part of the marine environment, and the EIA provisions in the Antarctic Protocol.[43] The International Tribunal for the Law of the Sea has recognized, in the context of its advisory opinion on the *Responsibilities and Obligations of States sponsoring persons and entities with respect to activities in the Area*, the extension of a duty to conduct EIAs to areas beyond national jurisdiction.[44]

The difficulty with the extension of a duty to conduct EIAs to global commons is determining to which States the duty is owed, and as a result, which States have a right to be notified and be consulted. The structure under the Antarctic Protocol is to treat the impacts as a matter of shared concern for all Parties to the treaty and to facilitate notification and consultation through the Committee for Environmental Protection and the Antarctic Treaty Consultative Meeting.[45] Under UNCLOS, the matter of notification is

[41] For the former, see Antarctic Protocol; for the latter see the EIA Directive 85, and the Espoo Convention.

[42] Pulp Mills on the River Uruguay (*Argentina v. Uruguay*) ('*Pulp Mills*'), ICJ 20 April 2010, para 204.

[43] See also Convention on the Prevention of Marine Pollution by Dumping of Wastes and Other Matter, 29 December 1972, as modified by the Protocol of 7 November 1996, 1046 UNTS 12011, art IV and Annex III; and Agreement for the Implementation of the Provisions of the United Nations Convention on the Law of the Sea of 10 December 1982 Relating to the Conservation and Management of Straddling Fish Stocks and Highly Migratory Fish Stocks, 4 August 1995, 2167 UNTS 88, arts 5(d) and 6(3)(d).

[44] ITLOS, Advisory Opinion on the Responsibilities and Obligations of States Sponsoring Persons and Entities With Respect to activities in the Area, 1 February 2011, paras 145, 148.

[45] Antarctic Protocol, Annex 1, Art 3(3)—3(5).

addressed under article 205, which requires that States 'publish' reports prepared under article 206 and provide those reports to 'competent international organizations'.[46] Both are terms are vague, but do indicate a duty owed to the international community at large.[47] As for whether a particular State can demand the production of an EIA or the right to be notified and consulted, on the basis of an activity's potential to harm part of the global commons, some have argued that EIA rights may flow from a broader duty that has an *erga omnes* character.[48] However, a general right of standing to enforce EIA obligations has not been determined with certainty. This uncertainty respecting standing does not serve to derogate from the obligation to assess impacts to the global commons. Rather it points to the necessity of developing specific mechanisms, such as those found under UNCLOS or the Antarctic Protocol, to implement the duty.

There are some indications that the duty to conduct EIAs may extend to activities that have impacts that are confined to the State of origin's territory, but have consequences for issues of common concern. Principle 17 is drafted without differentiation between transboundary and entirely domestic environmental harm, suggesting an intention to have EIA apply to significant harm irrespective of its location. A similar approach is found under UNCLOS, which applies the EIA obligation in relation to the 'marine environment', which includes areas under State jurisdiction. Likewise, the Convention on Biological Diversity includes a qualified obligation to conduct EIAs for proposed projects that are likely to have a significant impact on biological diversity.[49] EIA is also noted as a mechanism that ought to be employed in order to take climate change considerations into account in domestic decision-making processes.[50] Extending international EIA commitments to issues of common concern signals the international community's legal interest in these issues, and qualifies the sovereign right of States to impact such resources without regard for the interests of the international community. State practice in support of the extension of EIA obligations to issues of common concern can be found in the increasing application of domestic EIA processes to issues of biodiversity and climate change.[51] Like global commons issues there will be a need for international institutions, such as treaty bodies, to oversee these obligations, but the absence (or under-development) of such mechanisms does not derogate from the international legal character of obligation.

### 2.1.4. Content of EIA

International law does not prescribe the contents of an EIA. While there are examples of more fully elaborated EIA commitments, such the Espoo Convention and the Antarctic Protocol, international law leaves the determination of the precise requirements of an EIA to the discretion of States.[52] While it has been argued that the specific requirements found in the Espoo Convention and the UNEP EIA Goals and Principles ought to be taken as

[46] UNCLOS, art 205.

[47] See Craik, *The International Law of Environmental Impact Assessment* 145.

[48] This was argued by New Zealand in the *Nuclear Tests* case *(New Zealand v. France)*, ICJ Reports 1974, 457.

[49] Convention on Biological Diversity, 5 June 1992, 1760 UNTS 79, art 14 (qualified by 'as far as possible and as appropriate').

[50] United Nations Framework Convention on Climate Change, 9 May 1992, 31 ILM 849, art 4(1)(f).

[51] See eg Council on Environmental Quality, Draft NEPA Guidance on Consideration of the Effects of Climate Change and Greenhouse Emissions, 18 February 2010; and European Union, Guidance on Integrating Climate Change and Biodiversity into Environmental Impact Assessment, 2013.

[52] *Pulp Mills*, para 205, ILC Draft Articles, art 7, commentary 7.

evidence of growing consensus in international law of the required minimum contents of an EIA, these arguments have not been accepted.[53] Because EIA are so closely tied to internal decision-making processes, the discretion granted to States recognizes EIA processes will be a product of the unique regulatory and political conditions within each State. If international law were to prescribe too narrowly the specific requirements of EIA, States may be required to significantly alter their domestic EIA processes and how those processes integrate into the broad structure of decision-making within the State.

The minimum requirements of an EIA will, however, need to satisfy the requirements of due diligence. Thus, an assessment will need to clearly identify likely environmental harms, predict their potential impacts and assess the significance of those impacts. The results of the EIA must be made available to affected States and must form the basis of consultations. The specific approaches for matters such as determining the scope of an EIA will be left to State discretion. Similarly, the requirement to assess alternatives, which is a common but not universal feature of EIA systems, is not an international legal requirement. Two aspects of EIA that are central to due diligence and ought to be considered as mandatory under international law are cumulative impact assessment and post-project monitoring. Cumulative impact assessment is identified as an important component of EIA in the UNEP EIA Goals and Principles and in the Antarctic Protocol.[54] But more significantly, the harm principle does not differentiate between forms of harm, and assessing the combined impacts of multiple sources ought be viewed as a reasonable preventative measure. Requiring cumulative impact assessment also guards against project proponents seeking to divide larger projects into smaller and individually less impactful activities in order to avoid triggering international obligations. The ongoing monitoring of environmental impacts from a project once built is a distinct obligation that flows from due diligence, but is often implemented as part of an EIA process and is contained in both domestic and international EIA requirements, including the Espoo Convention and the Madrid Protocol, and was affirmed as a requirement in the *Pulp Mills* case.[55] Cumulative impact assessment and post-project monitoring may not be required in every circumstance, but where conditions warrant their inclusion, States cannot unilaterally ignore these elements of EIA.

### 2.1.5. Participation

Participation in connection with EIA occurs at both State and individual levels. The obligation in relation to other States, which is influenced by distinct obligations to notify and consult, requires that potentially affected States be given notice and the opportunity for meaningful cooperation. International law does not dictate when notification must occur or the precise content of the notification, but at a minimum the notification must be sufficiently in advance of the final decision to allow for consultation and have enough detail to allow States to make reasonably informed decisions about their interests.[56] Does this require that the affected State be notified prior to the start of the EIA process and be invited to participate in the development of the EIA study itself? Certainly as a matter of sound practice, the earlier the better. Public participation in the screening, scoping, and study stages of environmental assessment is integrated into many domestic EIA processes

[53] *Pulp Mills*, para 205.
[54] UNEP EIA Goals and Principles, Principle 4(e); Antarctic Protocol, Annex I, art 3(2)(f).
[55] *Pulp Mills*, para 205.
[56] *Pulp Mills*, paras 112–18; see also Espoo Convention, art 3(1).

and forms part of the process under the Espoo Convention. However, the obligations of notice and consultation relate to the activity itself, not the EIA. The approach of the ILC in this regard is to require notification once the EIA has revealed the likelihood of significant transboundary harm.[57] The EIA provides the content of the notification; although the ILC limits the obligation to providing 'the available technical and other relevant information on which the assessment is based'.[58] Insofar as this approach requires the State of origin to provide the background data to the affected State for their review, this appears sound. However, there is no reason that the EIA as a whole should not be transmitted. Indeed, part of the underlying rationale of EIA is to ensure transparency, which requires that those affected by decisions understand and can critically review the documents upon which the decision is based.[59]

The requirement to provide opportunities for public participation also extends to the members of the public of the affected State. For example, article 2(6) of the Espoo Convention provides that the State of origin shall provide opportunities of participation to the public of the affected State that are equivalent to the opportunities available to the public in the State of origin. The right of public participation in the context of EIA has also been recognized in the Convention on Biological Diversity, the Convention on the Law of the Non-Navigational Uses of International Watercourses, and the Convention on Access to Information, Public Participation and Access to Justice in Environmental Matters.[60] The obligation is consistent with Principle 10 and is also influenced by the principle of non-discrimination, which provides that States shall not discriminate against persons on the basis of nationality or residence in relation to access to legal and administrative procedures of the State of origin that address environmental harm.[61] In essence, the State of origin shall treat the public of the affected State no differently than its own citizens and residents. The duty of a State of origin to afford rights of public consultation to the public of an affected State was found not to be required by international law in the *Pulp Mills* case, but in light of the increasing recognition of individual rights in relation to the environment in international law, the conclusion is open to question and should be restricted to the particular scheme governing the parties to that dispute.[62]

### 2.1.6. Final decision

The relationship between the final approval of an activity and the EIA varies considerably among EIA systems, and will be largely determined by domestic requirements. However, international law does impose some constraints on this element of the EIA process. The UNEP EIA Goals and Principles require that any final decision on an activity subject to an EIA shall be in writing and shall provide reasons.[63] The Espoo Convention goes further and requires that the final decision take 'due account' of the EIA report and any

[57] ILC Draft Articles, Principle 8. [58] ILC Draft Articles, Principle 8(1).

[59] Aarhus Convention Compliance Committee case concerning Romania, ACCC/C2005/15; ECE/MP.PP/2008/5/Add.7, 16 April 2008, at para 30.

[60] Convention on Biological Diversity, art 14(1)(a); United Nations Convention on the Law of the Non-Navigational Uses of International Watercourses, 21 May 1997, 36 ILM 700 (not yet in force), art 16; Convention on Access to Information, Public Participation and Access to Justice in Environmental Matters, 25 June 1998, 2161 UNTS 447 ('Aarhus Convention'), art 6.

[61] ILC Draft Articles, arts 13 and 15.

[62] See Boyle, A., 'Developments in the International Law of Environmental Impact Assessments and their Relation to the Espoo Convention' (2011) 20(3) *RECIEL* 227, at 231.

[63] UNEP Goals and Principles, Principle 9.

comments received on the report by affected persons and States.[64] This approach is again consistent with the broader trend to transparency in domestic and international environmental law.[65] The right to reasons is a fundamental element of domestic administrative law and concepts of procedural justice. In the absence of reasons, the affected State has little basis by which to assess whether the State of origin has discharged its obligation to consult in good faith.

## *2.2. Legal nature*

Principle 17 is firmly established as a customary rule of international law. Its status as a customary rule has been recognized by the ICJ in the *Pulp Mills* case and ILC, as well as by expert publicists in international law.[66] The evidence in support of State practice is wide-ranging and extensive. Typically cited in this regard are the numerous instances of EIA obligations that appear in various international treaties and soft-law documents, the practice of other international organizations, such the World Bank, and other regional development banks, and the International Sea Bed Authority, as well as the adoption of EIA procedures by treaty bodies in their internal decision-making procedures. Domestic State practice provides further evidence of the rule. Of particular relevance here are instances of States applying their domestic EIA processes to transboundary impacts and their willingness to engage other States and affected members of the public in domestic EIA processes. Also relevant to State practice is that States have raised EIA obligations in inter-State disputes, but more significantly, responding States have not disputed the presence of EIA obligation, but have disputed either the need for an EIA in the instance at hand or have argued that an EIA has been conducted in accordance with international law.

The customary status of the obligations is further supported by the strong link of EIA obligations to other customary rules of international environmental law; namely the no-harm principle and the duty to notify and consult. The reasoning of the ICJ in the *Pulp Mills* case is instructive in this regard:

> In this sense, the obligation to protect and preserve, under Article 41 *(a)* of the Statute, has to be interpreted in accordance with a practice, which in recent years has gained so much acceptance among States that it may now be considered a requirement under general international law to undertake an environmental impact assessment where there is a risk that the proposed industrial activity may have a significant adverse impact in a transboundary context, in particular, on a shared resource. Moreover, due diligence, and the duty of vigilance and prevention which it implies, would not be considered to have been exercised, if a party planning works liable to affect the régime of the river or the quality of its waters did not undertake an environmental impact assessment on the potential effects of such works.[67]

Effectively, the court argues that EIA is an integral part of a State's due diligence. Due diligence requires that a State inform itself of the environmental consequences of its planned activities. EIA is recognized as the accepted manner by which States discharge that obligation. Similarly, States are under an obligation to inform affected States and affected persons in those States of significant adverse environmental consequences and

[64] Espoo Convention, art 6. [65] Aarhus Convention, art 6(7), (8).

[66] Birnie, P., Boyle, A., and Redgwell, C., *International Law and the Environment* (3rd edn, Oxford University Press 2009), 164–75; Sands and Peel, *Principles of International Environmental Law*, 602.

[67] *Pulp Mills*, para 204.

EIA is recognized as the accepted means by which those duties are implemented. As these customary rules apply to transboundary harm affecting both other States' territory and global commons, the scope of the customary EIA rule is similarly circumscribed.

## 3. Normative impact

As is apparent from the preceding discussion, EIA obligations are ubiquitous in international legal instruments. In terms of the evolution of the obligations, there has been a tendency for international instruments to follow the existence and characteristics of domestic EIA systems. The more elaborated instruments, such as the Espoo Convention and the Antarctic Protocol, which impose minimum EIA standards, have arisen between States with well-developed domestic EIA systems. European Community members have the most extensive set of international commitments under the Espoo Convention and the SEA Protocol, as well as highly defined EIA obligations under European based regional seas conventions, which reflects the highly developed EIA systems that are required under EC instruments and individual domestic requirements.

These more elaborated EIA regimes also point to the regional development of EIA in international instruments. The reciprocity of international EIA commitments is most salient for States in close proximity to each other, since States are not likely to seek out transboundary obligations from States that have little or no direct environmental impact on their territory. Thus we see more detailed rules in areas and between States where there is a higher likelihood of transboundary impacts, such as within Europe, in the polar regions, and within various shared resource regimes, such as regional seas conventions and shared watercourse agreements. The truly global EIA commitments, such as those contained in the CBD and UNCLOS, are not structured to provide minimum procedural requirements. Instead, they indicate applicability of EIA to those particular environmental issues, be it biological diversity or the marine environment. The unique characteristics of these environmental issues often require the development of new assessment methodologies. In this regard, international instruments have played an important role in the broader development of EIA processes through the development of non-binding implementation guidelines that address the specific challenges of applying EIA to certain kinds of environmental problems, such as biological diversity, or in ecosystems that may have unique ecological sensitivities, such as in the polar regions.[68]

As for the role that EIA obligations are playing within these instruments, they can, perhaps, be best understood as a tool for implementing the no-harm principle. As a consequence, the inclusion of EIA obligations in international treaties is tied to the underlying goal of harm prevention within particular regimes. For example, the obligation to assess under article 206 of UNCLOS is tied to the more general obligations to protect and preserve the marine environment.[69] Likewise, the Espoo Convention contains a qualified duty to prevent transboundary harm, as does the Madrid Protocol (in relation to the

[68] 'Guidelines for Incorporating Biodiversity-Related Issues into Environmental Impact Assessment Legislation and/or Processes and in Strategic Environmental Assessment', Report of the 6th Meeting of the Conference of the Parties to the Convention on Biological Diversity, UN Doc UNEP/CBD/COP/6/7, Annex; and 1997 Guidelines for EIA in the Arctic, adopted by the Arctic Council in the 1997 Alta Declaration on the Protection of the Arctic Environmental Protection Strategy, online at <http://arctic-council.org/filearchive/The%20Alta%20Declaration.pdf>.

[69] UNCLOS, art 194.

Antarctic environment) and the CBD (in relation to biological diversity). Understood in this light, it is not surprising that EIA obligations are not found in regimes that have a high degree of substantive specificity, such as the Convention for the Protection of the Ozone Layer, or the Convention on Long-Range Transboundary Air Pollution. In those treaties, the standards of acceptable harm are defined *ex ante* in the form of emission standards. This is quite different from instances of marine pollution, where there are few agreed upon substantive standards. In these circumstances, the EIA plays a crucial role in requiring the concerned States to deliberate over the acceptable level of harm that accords with the broader principle of harm prevention. While abstract standards may be quite difficult to arrive at internationally, the structure of EIA commitments provides the opportunity to consider the level of acceptable impact in relation to a very specific proposal.

## 4. Jurisprudential relevance

EIA obligations have been the subject of a significant number of inter-State disputes before international tribunals. The most significant of these cases is the *Pulp Mills* case (*Argentina v. Uruguay*). This case involved a dispute over Uruguay's decision to site two pulp mills on the River Uruguay, a shared watercourse with Argentina. The pulp mills were subject to an EIA process, but Argentina disputed the adequacy of the EIA itself and Uruguay's compliance with related obligations to notify Argentina and engage in good faith negotiations. There was a bilateral treaty in place, the Statute of the River Uruguay, governing the shared use of the watercourse, but the treaty (concluded in 1975) did not contain an EIA obligation. As discussed above, the ICJ held that the proposed activity did pose a likelihood of significant environmental harm, and under those circumstances, a customary obligation to conduct an EIA was owed. However, on the facts, Uruguay had discharged its obligation to conduct an EIA, the specific contents of which it had the right to determine. The court went on to hold that the obligation to assess transboundary harm continued once the plant began its operations. This latter obligation could be discharged through post-project monitoring provisions that are connected to the EIA process, but the manner of implementation is again left to the source State's discretion.

The decision in the *Pulp Mills* case was presaged by a number of earlier cases that were not decided on their merits, but contained separate opinions that acknowledged the emerging customary status of the international obligation to conduct an EIA.[70] Subsequent to the *Pulp Mills* case, the ITLOS, in its *Advisory Opinion on the activities in the Area*, affirmed the rule's customary status and extended the application of the obligation to areas beyond national jurisdiction. The tribunal relied specifically on the reasoning in paragraph 204 of the *Pulp Mills* case, which linked the EIA obligation to a State's duty of due diligence, noting that the ICJ's reference to 'shared resources' could be extended to resources that are 'the common heritage of mankind'.[71]

One particular aspect of the *Pulp Mills* case that has important implications for the future adjudication of EIA disputes is the ICJ's determination of the remedy that flowed from Uruguay's breach of its obligation to notify and engage in good faith negotiations

[70] Notably, the Request for an Examination of the Situation in Accordance with the Court's Judgment in the *Nuclear Tests* case (*New Zealand v. France*), ICJ Reports 1995, 288; see also Judge Weeramentry's separate opinion in the *Gabčíkovo-Nagymaros Dam* case (*Hungary v. Slovakia*), ICJ Reports 1997, 7.

[71] ITLOS, Advisory Opinion on Activities in the Area, para 148.

with Argentina under the terms of the Statute of the River Uruguay. Argentina sought the dismantling of the mill in question, which had been constructed by Uruguay by the time the matter was adjudicated. The basis of this request was that the breach of the procedural obligations was an internationally unlawful act and, on the basis of restitution, Argentina should be placed in the same position it would have been had the beach not occurred. In rejecting Argentina's request, the ICJ draws a distinction between procedural and substantive obligations, noting that while Uruguay breached procedural obligations, there were no substantive breaches. As Uruguay was not under any affirmative obligation to cease construction of the mill once the disagreement reached an impasse, the court maintained that the remedy sought would be inappropriate.[72]

Interestingly, while the ICJ characterizes notice and consultation obligations as procedural, and further recognizes the functional connection between notice and assessment, it characterizes the EIA obligation as a constituent part of due diligence and therefore, substantive. On that basis, the failure to conduct an adequate EIA could result in restitution, even in the absence of actual harm to the environment. On the other hand, one might expect that the remedy would be limited to preventing actual harm to the affected State, and thus might treat EIA, as a procedural obligation, which is how it is commonly understood. On that understanding, restitution would not flow. Neither scenario is satisfactory. On the former, it ought to be borne in mind that an EIA does not guarantee an absence of harm, but rather is part of a reasonable set of steps to prevent harm. Requiring the undoing of an activity in the absence of significant harm actually goes further than international law requires. On the latter, to allow States to ignore their EIA obligations would appear to undermine the duty of prevention.

Judges Al-Khasawneh and Simma point to this difficulty in their separate reasons:

26. A final observation: in matters related to the use of shared natural resources and the possibility of transboundary harm, the most notable feature that one observes is the extreme elasticity and generality of the substantive principles involved. Permanent sovereignty over natural resources, equitable and rational utilization of these resources, the duty not to cause significant or appreciable harm, the principle of sustainable development, etc., all reflect this generality. The problem is further compounded by the fact that these principles are frequently, where there is a dispute, in a state of tension with each other. Clearly in such situations, respect for procedural obligations assumes considerable importance and comes to the forefront as being an essential indicator of whether, in a concrete case, substantive obligations were or were not breached. Thus, the conclusion whereby non-compliance with the pertinent procedural obligations has eventually had no effect on compliance with the substantive obligations is a proposition that cannot be easily accepted. For example, had there been compliance with the steps laid down in Articles 7 to 12 of the 1975 Statute, this could have led to the choice of a more suitable site for the pulp mills. Conversely, in the absence of such compliance, the situation that obtained was obviously no different from a *fait accompli*.

27. The Court does recognize a functional link between procedural and substantive obligations laid down by the 1975 Statute (see Judgment, paragraph 79). However, the Court does not give full weight to this interdependence, neither when assessing whether a breach of Article 41 of the 1975 Statute has occurred nor in determining the appropriate remedies for the breach of Articles 7 to 12 thereof. According to the Court, as long as compliance with substantive obligations has been assured (or at least lack of it not proved), the breach of procedural obligations would not matter

[72] *Pulp Mills*, para 275.

very much and hence a declaration to that effect constitutes appropriate satisfaction; this is not the proper way to pay due regard to the interrelation of procedure and substance.[73]

The more nuanced approach suggested by Judges Al-Khasawneh and Simma suggest that any remedy for the failure to conduct an adequate EIA cannot be determined with reference to a process/substance divide. Rather, international courts will have to consider what the affected State actually lost as a result of the breach. This necessarily involves some counterfactual analysis, but more accurately reflects the deliberative nature of EIA. It is also salient to recognize that EIA processes in these circumstances are not simply a means to a substantive end, but are an integral part of the democratic objectives that underlie EIA. Indeed, as Judges Al-Khasawneh and Simma note, the substantive obligations, in this case the avoidance of harm, are contingent upon, and determined through, adherence to procedural requirements.

These circumstances also point to the importance that provisional measures will play in ensuring compliance with EIA requirements. In the *Pulp Mills* case, Argentina was not granted provisional measures that would require Uruguay to suspend its work on the mill, principally on the basis that it could not show the potential for harm that could not be remedied upon a hearing on the merits. Although in hindsight it is apparent that the procedural breaches could not in fact be remedied. However, provisional measures were granted in the Singapore *Land Reclamation* case, in which Singapore maintained that the activities it was undertaking in the Strait of Johor did not trigger an international obligation to conduct an EIA under article 206 of UNCLOS; the court ordered that the parties engage in cooperative efforts that included an expert review of the impacts and consultation.[74] An important difference between these cases is that in the *Pulp Mills* case, an EIA had been undertaken, while in the Singapore Land Reclamation case no EIA had been undertaken at the time of the provisional measures hearing.

## III) Relations with Other Principles

### 1. Principle 2—Prevention

EIA is inextricably linked to Principle 2 of the Rio Declaration. This link, which is expressly acknowledged by the ICJ in the *Pulp Mills* case, is crucial to understanding the nature of EIA, and in particular, the relationship between EIA's procedural obligations and the substantive obligation to prevent harm. As noted, EIA has become the chief mechanism by which States may discharge their due diligence obligations in relation to planned activities. It is the means by which States inform themselves of the environmental consequences of the actions and by which they examine measures to prevent significant harm.

The more complicated question is whether the substantive obligation to prevent harm finds expression in EIA obligations. In other words, does the international EIA obligation, unlike its domestic counterpart, require that States refrain from, or mitigate, harmful activities? At the poles, the answer is fairly straightforward. In some instances, where significant transboundary harm is clearly not likely, then the no-harm principle is not

[73] *Pulp Mills*, Joint Dissenting Opinion of Judges Al-Khasawneh and Simma, paras 26, 27.

[74] Land Reclamation by Singapore in and Around the Straits of Johor (*Malaysia v. Singapore*), Provisional Measures, 8 October 2003, (ITLOS).

engaged, and the source State may proceed with the proposed activity. In cases where significant transboundary harm is present, the no-harm principle requires States take measures to prevent the predicted harm. The current focus on harm prevention, as opposed to liability for actual harm caused, means that States are not required to suffer harm in order to access remedies in international law, since it is a breach of international law to proceed with an activity where future harm to another State or to the global commons is likely. The prior obligation of EIA prevents States from remaining ignorant of foreseeable harm, and as such, States can be enjoined from proceeding with risky activities where they have failed to examine those risks through an EIA.

The hard case, and the circumstance that is most likely to arise, is where States disagree over the likelihood for significant harm. It is in these cases that the two elements of Principle 2, the sovereign right for a State to develop its resources and the sovereign right of a State to be free from significant transboundary harm, come into tension. This tension cannot be resolved with reference to the standard of 'significant harm', despite its objective nature, given the 'extreme elasticity and generality' (to use Al-Khasawneh and Simma's phrase) of the standard. As a result, the harm principle turns back to process in the form of good faith consultation. EIA again plays an important role in structuring these consultations, as the assessment of the project, potential mitigation approaches, and alternatives provides the factual basis of the assessment, and, through the requirements for transparency, public participation and reasoned final decisions. International tribunals have not opted to resolve these disputes by substituting their own views on whether an activity presents a likelihood of significant harm for those of the source State.[75] Instead, international decision-makers are more apt to ensure that the EIA has been carried out in accordance with international requirements and the results of the EIA and the consultation have been taken into account.

## 2. Principle 19—Notice and consultation

EIA systems implement the requirements for notice and consultation contained in Principle 19 and the two Principles ought to be read together.[76] Notice and consultation are an integral part of EIA, and in that sense Principles 17 and 19 overlap, but the obligations in Principle 19 will also apply to contexts outside the scope of EIA. Both are triggered by the threshold requirement of 'significant adverse impact/effect', and both apply to activities. Principle 19 is limited to transboundary harm, while Principle 17 is not. This tells us two things. First, the limitation of notice and consultation to transboundary impacts reflects the practical and theoretical uncertainty of providing notice in instances of harm to the global commons. Second, the difference in wording affirms the broader application of the EIA obligation to harm in areas beyond national jurisdiction (and its general applicability to domestic environmental harm). In those instances, such as the high seas and the Antarctic, notice and consultation are governed by treaty specific requirements.

The other potentially meaningful difference between the two Principles is that Principle 17 is triggered where significant harm is 'likely', while Principle 19 contains a

[75] For example, in the *Gabčíkovo-Nagymaros Dam* case, the court ordered the Parties to engage in further negotiations based on principles (such as sustainable development) identified by the court; see also Boyle, 'Developments in the International Law of Environmental Impact Assessments', 230.

[76] Kovar, 'A Short Guide to the Rio Declaration'.

lower evidentiary requirement of activities that 'may' cause significant adverse effects. EIA obligations in treaty form have not used consistent wording in this regard, with some using 'likely' (Espoo) and others using 'may' (UNCLOS). The precautionary principle would push the evidentiary requirement towards the lower threshold, but it may not be helpful to try to reduce the standard of proof to a single term, rather the threshold will be determined by a combination of the magnitude of the harm, the probability of its occurrence and the level of scientific uncertainty in determining both.

The structure of the notice and consultation obligations is consonant with the broader turn to process under the no-harm principle. The right to be consulted does not include the right to prior consent, but requires the parties engage one another with 'a genuine intention to achieve a positive result'.[77] EIA requirements provide greater certainty with respect to the information that ought to be supplied to the affected State and the procedures that the States must follow in carrying these duties. The requirement for a final decision under the EIA process attaches some finality to the consultation process and the accompanying reasons provide a basis upon which an affected State can determine whether its views were accounted for; a key element of good faith.

### 3. Principle 10—Public participation

Principle 10, which emphasizes the commitment of States to provide the public with information respecting environmental risks and to provide opportunities for participation in decision-making processes, supports the extension of participatory rights in EIA to the public of the affected State. Both Principle 10 and Principle 17 are drafted in terms that are not restricted to environmental activities that have impacts beyond a State's territory. The wording of Principle 10 does not, for example, differentiate between the obligations owed to one's own citizens and the citizens in other States, rather the obligation to engage the public is owed to citizens regardless of their geographic location. In this regard, EIA is one mechanism that implements the obligation to engage the public by affording rights of notice and consultation to any member of the affected public.

## IV) Assessment

Assessing the effectiveness of EIA has been a constant challenge over its forty-year history. At the heart of this challenge is the procedural nature of EIA, which requires detailed and systematic consideration of the environmental consequences of planned activities, but stops short of preventing harmful activities. In the domestic context, the logic concedes that other values and other priorities may subvert environmental goals. EIA seeks to ensure that those trade-offs are made in an informed, consultative, and transparent manner. The international legal requirements for EIA can be understood in similar, but perhaps not identical terms. A decision to trade off environmental values in favour of economic goals may be a valid exercise of the sovereign right to develop a State's own natural resources, but where the exercise of that right affects other States, that trade-off cannot be determined solely by the State of origin. In this regard, EIA ought to be understood

[77] *North Sea Continental Shelf* case ICJ Reports 1984, 292 at 209 (describing the duty to negotiate in good faith).

as a tool as equally concerned with maintaining the legitimacy of decisions, as it is with achieving environmentally benign outcomes.

Empirical assessments have tentatively concluded that EIA does in fact make a positive contribution to the environmental performance of planned activities.[78] These outcomes arise on a project basis through improved predictions of outcomes, identification of mitigation measures and improved project design. In addition, EIA has been found to contribute to the broader process of norm internalization, whereby decision-makers come to view environmental values as an important agency goal.[79] In the international context, participation in EIA processes provides States with an opportunity to apply what are often very abstract environmental principles to concrete proposals, which affords an opportunity for States to consider how their interests are affected by the application of international environmental norms to domestic decisions. Because States are obligated to apply EIA to international environmental issues, domestic EIA processes become sites of implementation of international norms, be they norms respecting transboundary impacts, biodiversity, marine pollution, or climate change.

Assessing the extent to which EIA contributes to the legitimacy of decisions that implicate the interests of more than one State is more speculative. Certainly, the theory that underlies EIA is that decisions that are made in an information rich, consultative and transparent environment will produce outcomes that are more likely to be accepted by those impacted by the decision. Legitimacy will be affected by both adherence to right process, and to adherence to shared environmental values. Returning then to the comments of Judges Al-Khasawneh and Simma, the interrelationship of process and substance has a democratic dimension that ought to be seen as central, not peripheral to Principle 17. The absence of substantive specificity requires that impacted States be fully informed of those impacts and consulted in good faith because EIA processes provide a necessary alternative to State consent.

## V) Select Bibliography


Boggs, J., 'Procedural v. Substantive in NEPA Law: Cutting the Gordian Knot' (1993) 15 *Environmental Professional* 25.

Boyle, A., 'Developments in the International Law of Environmental Impact Assessments and their Relation to the Espoo Convention' (2011) 20 *Review of European Community and International Environmental Law* 227.

Council on Environmental Quality (US), The National Environmental Policy Act: A Study of its Effectiveness After Twenty-five Years (CEQ 1997).

Craik, N., *The International Law of Environmental Impact Assessment: Process, Substance and Integration* (Cambridge University Press 2008).

Experts Group on Environmental Law of the WCED, *Environmental Protection and Sustainable Development: Legal Principles and Recommendation* (London: Graham & Trotman/Martinus Nijhoff Publishers 1987).


[78] Sadler, B., *Environmental Assessment in a Changing World: Final Report of the Study of the Effectiveness of Environmental Assessment* (Canadian Environmental Assessment Agency 1996); Council on Environmental Quality (US), *The National Environmental Policy Act: A Study of its Effectiveness After Twenty-five Years* (CEQ 1997).

[79] Taylor, S., *Making Bureaucracies Think: The Environmental Impact Statement Strategy of Administrative Reform* (Stanford University Press 1984); Boggs, J., 'Procedural v. Substantive in NEPA Law: Cutting the Gordian Knot' (1993) 15 *Environmental Professional* 25.

Holder, J., *Environmental Assessment: The Regulation of Decision Making* (Oxford University Press 2004).

Knox, J., 'The Myth and Reality of Transboundary Environmental Impact Assessment' (2002) 96 *AJIL* 291.

Kovar, J., 'A Short Guide to the Rio Declaration' (1993) 4 *Colorado Journal of International Environmental Law and Policy* 13.

Morgan, R., 'Environmental Impact Assessment: the state of the art' (2012) 30 *Impact Assessment and Project Appraisal* 5.

Robinson, N. A., 'EIA Abroad: The Comparative and Transnational Experience', in Hildebrand, S. G. and Cannon, J. B. (eds), *Environmental Analysis: The NEPA Experience* (Boca Raton: Lewis 1993), 679.

Sadler, B., *Environmental Assessment in a Changing World: Final Report of the Study of the Effectiveness of Environmental Assessment* (Canadian Environmental Assessment Agency 1996).

Taylor, S., *Making Bureaucracies Think: The Environmental Impact Statement Strategy of Administrative Reform* (Stanford University Press 1984).

Viñuales J. E., *Foreign Investment and the Environment in International Law* (Cambridge University Press 2012).

Wood, C., *Environmental Impact Assessment: A Comparative Review* (2nd edn, Essex: Pearson Education 2003).

# 22. Principle 18

## *Notification and Assistance in Case of Emergency*

Phoebe Okowa*

**Principle 18**

States shall immediately notify other States of any natural disasters or other emergencies that are likely to produce sudden harmful effects on the environment of those States. Every effort shall be made by the international community to help States so afflicted.



* Professor of Public international Law at Queen Mary, University of London.

## I) Origins and Rationale of the Principle

Even the most sceptical would concede that the dangers posed by natural disasters to human life and the environment have dramatically increased in the last decades and in ways that could hardly be envisaged at the time of the Rio Declaration in 1992. Indeed, the two decades since the Rio Declaration have witnessed some of the most visible changes in the global temperatures, a fact which many believe accounts for the increase in the number of natural disasters in the same period.[1]

There has been much renewed impetus on how to prevent or mitigate the devastation caused by these disasters, how to better improve information about the likelihood of their occurrence, and how to harness new technology to mitigate damage caused given that their occurrence is in most cases unavoidable. Interest at the legal and policy level has been particularly pronounced in the wake of the Indian Ocean Tsunami in 2004, the earthquake in Haiti in 2010, and in Japan in 2011; the latter as is now well known had a devastating impact on the country's nuclear infrastructure, and contaminated its environment as well as food supply chain.[2] The most recent natural disaster of major significance is the devastation resulting from the earthquake in the Philippines in 2013.[3] All these events have profoundly tested the resilience of national governments and brought to the fore the whole question of international co-operation in the wake of these disasters and how best to secure it.[4] The devastation in all these cases had serious implications not just for human life and the economies of the communities affected but also long-term environmental consequences.

The first part of this article is explanatory. It evaluates the content of the notification obligation in the event of disasters in light of state practice both before and since Principle 18 of Rio Declaration was adopted. The *lex lata* content of this part of Principle 18 has never been in doubt.[5]

The second part of Principle 18 of the Declaration was couched in *lex ferenda* terms. It exhorts the 'international community' to provide assistance to States affected by natural disasters but does not, on the face of it, impose a mandatory, legally justiciable obligation. In form, it is essentially an obligation of solidarity, exhorting the community of States to act in the public interest. Like other communitarian obligations,

[1] International Federation of Red Cross and Red Crescent Societies ('IFRC'), World Disasters Report, 2009, Focus on Early Warning and Early Action, available at <http://www.ifrc.org/en/publications-and reports/world-disasters-report/wdr>. UN Office for International Strategy for Disaster Risk Reduction ('UNISDR'), Global Assessment Report on Risk Reduction 2013, available at <http://www.unisdr.org/we/inform/publications/33013>; See Sir Kenneth Keith, 'Natural Disasters and International Law: A preliminary Note' Institut de Droit International, Tokyo, September 2003.

[2] See WHO Health-Risk Assessment from the Nuclear Accident after the 2011 Great East Japan Earthquake and Tsunami, ISBN 9789241505130; Final Report of the International Mission to Support the Remediation of Large Contaminated area off-site of the Fukushima Daiichi Nuclear Power Plant (NPP) Document NE/NEFW/2011 Vienna Atomic Energy Agency, 2011, available at <http://reliefweb.int/sites/reliefweb.int/files/resources/Full_Report_2895.pdf>.

[3] Philippines Typhoon, *Disasters Emergency Committee*, available at <http//www.dec.org.uk/facts-and-figures>.

[4] In 2006 at its fifty-eighth session, the International Law Commission included the topic 'protection of persons in the event of disasters' in its long-term programme of work (see *Official Records of the General Assembly, Sixty-first Session, Supplement No. (A/6/10)*, para 257). The topic was moved the following year to the ordinary work programme of the ILC. See also Hyogo Declaration, A/CONF.206/6, available at <http://www.unisdr.org/we/inform/publications/1037>.

[5] Okowa, P., *State Responsibility for Transboundary Air Pollution in International Law* (Oxford University Press 2000), 167.

which are increasingly part of the corpus of international law, questions arise about their binding character. In this context, two questions are explored: first, the extent to which under contemporary international law States can be said to be under a duty to offer assistance to other States in the event of natural disasters; second, whether the affected State is under an obligation, if any, to accept offers of assistance.

Central to the debate about assistance duties is the entrenched deference to state sovereignty in much of international law and whether these should in some cases be qualified, where such deference stands in the way of meaningful action to protect the environment or human suffering.[6] Moreover, if the duty to provide assistance is a binding legal obligation, and its theoretical basis remains problematic since much of binding international law consists of obligations adopted *jus inter gentes*, voluntarily assumed by States and for clearly recognizable benefits. The law in general does not obligate states to assume a duty when there is no benefit. As is well known the appropriate limits on sovereignty have been a central feature of the debate in the area of humanitarian intervention in the law of armed conflict,[7] but similar questions have been raised especially following the catastrophic floods in Myanmar, when the Burmese government refused to accept offers of assistance in the face of appalling human suffering after the Cyclone Nargis.[8] The *lex specialis* treaties in the field of nuclear and industrial accidents[9] of course create a binding framework governing the offer and acceptance of assistance. In reality these too are a nod to state sovereignty since the assistance can only be effected with the territorial state's consent and must be terminated if the latter withdraws its consent.

The discussion in this chapter is confined to the notification and assistance duties within the context of environmental harm and attendant obligations. The wider implications of assistance duties in human rights and humanitarian law have been extensively considered elsewhere and strictly speaking fall outside the remit of this project.[10] Here they are mentioned only in passing and to the extent that they are relevant to assess the existence of broad general principles beyond the *lex specialis.*

## II) The Principle as Enshrined in the Rio Declaration

### 1. Preparatory work

The adoption of Principle 18 at PrepComm IV did not raise much controversy. The core content of the principle was well established in international law in other contexts.[11] Moreover,

[6] Keith, K., 'Natural Disasters and International Law', 10.

[7] See Wheeler, N., *Saving Strangers: Humanitarian Intervention in International Society* (Oxford University Press 2000).

[8] See Statement by M. Bernard Kouchner, Minister of Foreign and European Affairs, published in *Le Monde*, Paris, 20 May 2008.

[9] Convention on Assistance in the Case of a Nuclear Accident or Radiological Emergency, 18th November 1986, INFCIRC/336 ('Convention on assistance on nuclear accidents'); Convention on the Transboundary Effects of Industrial Accidents, 17 March 1992, 2105 UNTS 457 ('Convention on Industrial Accidents').

[10] See eg Inter-agency Standing Committee, *Operational Guidelines on Human Rights and Natural Disasters* (Washington DC: Brookings-Bern Project on Internal Displacement 2006). See more generally Kalshoven, F. (ed), *Assisting the Victims of Armed Conflict and Other Disasters: Papers delivered at the International Conference on Humanitarian Assistance in Armed Conflict, the Hague, 22–24th June 1989* (Dordrecht 1989); Hardcastle, R. J. and Chua, A. T. L., 'Humanitarian Assistance: Towards a right of Access to Victims of Natural Disasters' (1998) 325 *International Review of the Red Cross* 35.

[11] See section II) 2.1.4 of this chapter.

the obligation of notification had been strongly reaffirmed after the Chernobyl catastrophe not only by G7 countries but also by other countries affected, particularly in Europe.[12] Principle 18 extended the obligation beyond industrial accidents to cases of natural disasters and emergencies.

Principle 9, second paragraph, of the draft tabled by the European Community, provided the main basis of the provision according to which 'States shall immediately notify other States of any emergency situation that might produce sudden harmful effects on the environment of those other States'.[13] The compromise consisted in combining the wording of this principle with that of Principle 17 of the revised draft submitted by the G77+China, according to which: '[a]all efforts shall be made by the international community to help States afflicted by natural disasters'.[14]

The formulation of Principle 18 agreed at PrepComm IV was adopted without any changes at the Rio Summit. As it will be discussed in this chapter, the two components of Principle 18 as adopted reflect fundamentally different views of international law, and their normative implications have also largely evolved in different ways.

## 2. Scope and dimensions

### *2.1. The duty to notify*

#### 2.1.1. The trigger: natural disasters and emergencies

Although explicit reference is made to natural disasters, the inclusion of other emergencies in Principle 18 has generally been understood to extend the scope of the provision to man-made disasters as well.[15]

In the subsequent literature, it has been accepted that natural disasters include earthquakes, volcanic eruptions, windstorms, torrential rains, floods, droughts, fires, famine, and epidemics.[16] Similarly man-made disasters are not a closed category but extend to industrial accidents including chemical or nuclear accidents. The 2011 earthquake in Japan triggered a tsunami and a nuclear accident, underlining the interconnectedness between natural and man-made disasters, and the futility of treating them as different phenomena for

[12] See Tokyo Summit of the Group of Seven Major Industrial Nations Consisting of Canada, France, Italy, Japan, FRG, UK, and USA (1986) 25 ILM 1005.

[13] 'Elements for the Earth Charter', UN Doc A/CONF.151/PC/WG.III/L.25 ('L.25'), Principle 9, para 2.

[14] 'Rio de Janeiro Charter/Declaration on Environment and Development', UN Doc A/CONF.151/PC/WG.III/L.20/Rev.1 ('L.20'), Principle 17.

[15] Report of the United Nations Conference on Environment and Development, Rio de Janeiro, 3–14 June 1992, Vol I, Resolutions Adopted by the Conference (United Nations Publication, Sales No E93.I.8), Resolution 1, annex I, Principle 18. See also Convention on Early Notification of a Nuclear Accident, 18 November 1986, INFCIRC/335, available at <https://www.iaea.org/Publications/Documents/Infcircs/Others/infcirc335.shtml>; Convention on Industrial Accidents; Convention on the Protection and Use of Transboundary Watercourses and International Lakes, Helsinki 17 March 1992, available at <http://www.unece.org/fileadm/DAM/en/water/pdf/watercon.pdf>. ('UNECE Watercourses Convention'); International Law Commission, Draft Articles on Prevention of Transboundary Harm with commentaries, *Yearbook of the International Law Commission 2001* Vol II (part 2) ('ILC Prevention Articles'), commentary ad art 17, para 3.

[16] In 2004 the United Nations International Strategy for Disaster Reduction ('ISDR') defined a disaster as 'a potentially damaging physical event, phenomenon or human activity that may cause the loss of life or injury, property damage, social and economic disruption, and environmental degradation. Hazards can include latent conditions that may represent future threats and can have different origins: natural (geological, hydrometeorelogical, and biological) or induced by human processes (environmental degradation and

the purpose of legal regulation. The draft Articles provisionally adopted by the ILC define natural disaster as:

a calamitous event or series of events resulting in widespread loss of life, great human suffering or distress, or large-scale material or environmental damage, thereby seriously disrupting the functioning of society.[17]

The resolution adopted by the *Institut de Droit International* in Bruges also adopts a definition that includes both natural disasters and man-made accidents.[18]

Almost all instruments import an element of gravity in their definition of disaster, thus expressly excluding those calamities whose overall impact is far from catastrophic, however serious. In the ILC's definition, the disaster in question must be calamitous, widespread, great, and large scale. And seriously disruptive of the functioning of society. Although the decision whether a particular activity has significant transboundary impact and therefore warrants notification is left to the discretion of the affected state, almost all instruments require an element of gravity.[19] There is a presumption of gravity if the activity in question is intrinsically hazardous, or if it is located in close proximity to a frontier or an area of significant ecological importance.[20] Many of these disasters directly implicate international law and its institutions since they seldom affect just one state. It is estimated that the Tsunami of 2004 killed approximately 240,000 people in 12 States.[21]

### 2.1.2. Content of the duty: disaster phase

#### *2.1.2.1. The duty*

The first part of Principle 18 proclaims a mandatory duty to notify parties of a disaster that has occurred. That this obligation is unquestionably binding as a matter of *lex lata* has considerable support in state and treaty practice both before and since the Rio Declaration, as will be discussed in sections II) 2.2. and II) 3 of this chapter. However, the scope of this duty raises a number of interrelated questions, specifically, who must notify? When should the notification take place? And what should be the content of the information forming the basis of the notification?

#### *2.1.2.2. Who must notify?*

On the face of it, the notification duty envisaged in the first part of Principle 18 is borne by the State where the natural disaster or emergency occurs, and is a self-judging provision. Such a State is accorded a broad margin of appreciation with respect to both the seriousness of the disaster or other emergency, and the need to notify other States. There is no

technological hazards) ('Living with Risk: A Global Review of Disaster Reduction Initiatives', <http://www.unisdr.org/files/657_lwr1.pdf>, 16). See also the definition of natural disaster adopted by the *Institut de Droit International*, 'Humanitarian Assistance', M. Budislav Vukas Rapporteur, Bruges 2003, available at: <http://www.idi-iiil.org/idiE/resolutionsE/2003-bru-03-en.PDF> ('IDI Resolution'), I(2).

17 Protection of Persons in the Event of Natural Disasters, ILC Report of the 61st session, A/CN.4/L.758, available at <http://WWW.ifrc.org/FedNet/Resources_and_Services/IDRL/ILC%20docs/ILC%20-%>, art 3.

18 IDI Resolution, I(2).

19 See: art 14 of the 1992 Convention on Biological Diversity, UNTS, Vol 1760, 79; art 17 of the Cartagena Protocol on Bio-safety to the Convention on Biological Diversity, UNTS, Vol 2226, 208.

20 Convention on Industrial Accidents, Annex III.

21 Protection of Persons in the Event of Disasters, Memorandum prepared by the Secretariat, UN Doc A/CN.4/590 ('ILC Memorandum'), 8.

suggestion that the decision of the territorial State as to the seriousness of the emergency is to be subjected to independent review, although some treaty instruments require that the decision be guided by generally agreed scientific criteria.[22] The priority accorded to the territorial State may be seen as a sensible safeguard against unwarranted interference in the sovereign powers of governments in relation to matters occurring on their territory.[23]

However, the language employed in the Rio Declaration admits of the possibility that the obligation to notify may extend to all other States that become aware of an emergency situation warranting notification. It states in the relevant part that 'States shall immediately notify other States of any natural disasters or other emergencies that are likely to produce sudden harmful effects on the environment of other states.'

In a number of treaty instruments, the obligation to notify extends beyond the territorial State to other States that become aware of an impending disaster.[24] The ILC in its *Draft Articles on Prevention of Harm from Hazardous Activities* gave examples of situations where weather forecasting systems indicated that a disaster was imminent as an example of a situation where the duty to notify was not just confined to the territorial State but would extend to all States in possession of the information on the likelihood of a disaster.[25]

### *2.1.2.3. 'Immediately'*

According to Principle 18, the duty bearer(s) must notify 'immediately'. Other instruments use different terms but they all converge in that notification must be made without delay.[26] For instance the ASEAN Agreement on Disaster Management and Emergency Response specifies that the notification must be made 'promptly',[27] while the 1992 Industrial Accidents Convention specifies that the notification must be made 'without delay'.[28]

The rationale of this requirement is simple; the potentially affected States (and, as the case may be, the other addressees of the notification) must be given sufficient time to respond to the emergency. Second, prompt action is of the essence in these emergencies, and delay is likely to render any intervention futile.

[22] See arts 10 and 11 of the Industrial Accidents Convention, and art 14 of the ECE Watercourses Convention.

[23] Art 3(1) of the ASEAN Agreement on Disaster Management and Emergency Response, 25 July 2005 ('ASEAN Agreement'), provides that 'The Sovereignty, territorial integrity and national unity of the Parties shall be respected, in accordance with the Charter of the United Nations and the Treaty of Amity and Co-operation in Southeast Asia, in the implementation of this agreement. In this context, each party shall have the primary responsibility to respond to disasters occurring within its territory and external assistance or offers of assistance shall only be provided upon the request or with the consent of the affected party'; the text of the Agreement is available at: <https://www.ifrc.org/Docs/idrl/N112EN.pdf> (accessed on 10 April 2014).

[24] For example art 198 of the United Nations Convention on the Law of the Sea, 10 December 1982, 1833 UNTS 397 ('UNCLOS') requires notification 'when a state becomes aware of cases in which the marine environment is in imminent danger of being damaged or has been damaged by pollution'. An obligation on any State party who becomes aware of a serious threat is also imposed on parties to the 1976 Convention on the Protection of the Rhine against Pollution from Chlorides, December 3, 1976, art 2 (1), reprinted in (1977) 16 ILM 265, art 11; for other examples see ILC Memorandum, 39.

[25] See Commentary to Article 17 of the draft Articles on prevention of transboundary harm from hazardous activities ((2001) *Yearbook of the International Law Commission, Vol II, part II*), para 98.

[26] See UNCLOS, art 198; Convention on the Law of the Non-Navigational Uses of International Watercourses 1997, art 28(2), available at <legal.un.org/ilc/texts/instruments/English/conventions/8_3_1997.pdf>; Convention on Industrial Accidents, art 10(2).

[27] ASEAN Agreement, art 4.

[28] Convention on Industrial Accidents, art 10(2).

### *2.1.2.4. Information*

The territorial State may be placed under a duty to respond to specific requests for information from third States. A provision to this effect can be found in the 2005 ASEAN Agreement on Disaster Management and Emergency Response, which provides for a duty to respond to requests for information if requested by a third State which has become aware of an impending disaster.[29]

Do third States have any further power to question the assessment of the territorial State as to the seriousness of the incident? None of the treaties referred to provide for oversight or independent means of verifying the information provided by the territorial State. However, it could be argued that as a logical application of the precautionary principle, a State that is concerned about the imminence of harm, may provide evidence to that effect, and expect the territorial State to respond to its concerns.

At the very least, if a further request of information is not satisfied, that may provide an additional basis to question the *bona fides* of the territorial State or the accuracy of its assessment of the situation and, specifically, for third States to notify their concerns to potentially affected States. This appears to be the only realistic response in the absence of an organized framework of oversight or review of the judgment of the territorial state.

### *2.1.2.5. Who must be notified?*

The wording of Principle 18 refers to States at risk of being affected as the addressees of the notification. However, in some cases, there is a further duty to extend notification to appropriate UN and non-governmental organizations that are in a position to provide relief assistance.[30]

In addition, it has indeed been suggested that State obligations in the human rights field, specifically to protect life and to provide access to food, also implicitly placed States under a duty to notify their own populations and those of third States of natural disasters which may put their lives and livelihood at risk; and crucially to prevent foreseeable life-threatening disasters.[31] In this context, an increasing feature of the emerging normative regimes is the requirement that information be shared directly with the public likely to be affected. For instance article 9(1) of the Convention on the Transboundary Effects of Industrial Accidents requires State parties to provide the population in the areas capable of being affected by an industrial accident with information about the dangers they face from the hazardous nature of the activity. Moreover, this treaty goes further and requires State parties:

> to give the public in the areas capable of being affected an opportunity to participate in the relevant procedures with the aim of making known its views and concerns on prevention and preparedness measures.

29 ASEAN Agreement, art 4(b).

30 The Convention on Early Notification of a Nuclear Accident requires, at art 2(a), such notification to be extended also to the International Atomic Agency,. See also the International Convention on Oil Pollution Preparedness, Response and Cooperation, art 5(2), available at <www.ifrc.org/docs/idrl/1245EN.pdf>, which requires the notification to be extended to the International Maritime Organisation; and the European Commission, under art 2 (1) of the EURATOM treaty, available at <http://europa.eu/eu-law/decision-making/treaties/pdf/consolidated_version_of_the_treaty_establishing_the_european_atomic_energy_community/consolidated_version_of_the_treaty_establishing_the_european_atomic_energy_community_en.pdf>.

31 Fifth Report of the Special Rapporteur on Protection of Persons in the Event of Natural Disasters, UNGA, 9th April 2012, A/CN.4/652, available at <daccess-dds-ny.un.org/UNDOC/GEN/N12/287/13/PDF/N1228713.pdf?>; See also IDI Resolution, Preamble.

Public participation in designing contingency plans in the pre-disaster phase as well as at the emergency management stage reflects the increased sensitivity to public participation in environmental decision-making as a discrete right but also as the most effective way of designing workable preventative regimes.[32] Other treaties also address the issues of confidentiality that may arise from such activities by permitting disclosure restrictions on grounds of national security.[33]

The right of disaster relief personnel to effective communication and the obligation on the territorial State to facilitate such communication is also increasingly provided for in treaty instruments, and some of the more recent treaties require the States parties to them to establish a dedicated emergency operations system. The most advanced systems are found in some regional instruments regulating disaster emergency response. These include the Caribbean Disaster Emergency Response Agency[34] and within the European Union, the matter is effectively dealt with in a council decision of 23 October 2001, which mandates the Commission to establish and manage a reliable emergency communication and information system.[35]

### 2.1.3. Prevention and management: pre and post-disaster phases

Principle 18 incorporates a narrowly circumscribed time element: the obligation is to notify regarding disasters that have just occurred. There is no express mention in the text of an obligation to put in place mechanisms that would prevent the disaster in the first place or limit its effects.

However, in the subsequent practice of States, it is now broadly accepted that the obligation is not confined to notification and assistance in dealing with the emergency that has arisen but that States must take certain preliminary steps to prevent the occurrence of such emergencies in the first place and to mitigate their effects. The duties to adopt preventive and mitigation strategies are seen as inherent in the due diligence obligation of States (prevention principle) and the precautionary principle, which were also recognized as free standing principles at the Rio conference and are considered elsewhere in this volume. After an extensive study of State practice, the memorandum prepared by the UN Secretariat for the ILC in support of its work on *Protection of persons in the event of disaster* observed that:

> issues of disaster prevention, mitigation and preparedness are crucial to disaster relief, and provisions on such issues are now regularly found alongside the traditional provisions on disaster response. Disaster risk reduction activities serve both to build resilience to hazards and to ensure the development efforts do not increase vulnerability to those hazards. At the legal level, this involves developing and implementing a legal framework which facilitates, inter alia, undertaking risk assessments, developing public awareness campaigns, implementing technical and physical risk mitigation programmes and promoting the sharing of information and knowledge.[36]

[32] See Convention on Access to Information, Public Participation in Decision-Making and Access to Justice in Environmental Matters, 25 June 1998, 2161 UNTS 447.

[33] See Convention on assistance on nuclear accidents, art 6; See also UNECE Watercourse Convention, art 8.

[34] See Agreement Establishing the Caribbean Disaster Emergency Response Agency, available at <http://www.ifrc.org/docs/idrl/N740EN.pdf>.

[35] See European Union, Council decision 2001/792/EC of 23rd October 2001 establishing a Community mechanism to facilitate reinforced cooperation in civil protection assistance interventions (Official Journal of the European Communities, Vol 44, and No L297, 15 November 2001, 7), art 4 (b), available at <http://eur-lex.europa.eu/legal-content/EN/TXT/?uri=CELEX:32001D0792>.

[36] ILC Memorandum, 2.

In other words a meaningful response regime requires the establishment of preliminary preventive steps in advance of the disaster. Such steps may involve a pre-disaster evaluation of risk, consensus gathering on what information systems are to be put in place, and what precisely should be communicated to the States potentially affected to allow for mitigation strategies to be developed and synchronized. Given that prevention is a due diligence obligation, the preventive strategies to be adopted must be commensurate with the State's technical and economic capacity.[37]

### 2.1.4. Legal nature of the duty to notify

The duty to warn States of the dangers to which they have become exposed as a result of emergency situations was endorsed by the ICJ as far back as 1949 in the *Corfu Channel* case. In that case the Court referred to the obligation of Albania to warn shipping in general of the dangers to which they were exposed in Albania's territorial waters. Although the statement was made in the context of the right of States to unimpeded transit through international straits, it is clear that the Court perceived the principle as one of general application. The Court observed that:

> The obligations incumbent upon Albanian authorities consisted in notifying, for the benefit of shipping in general, the existence of a minefield in Albanian territorial waters and in warning the approaching British warships of the imminent danger to which the minefield exposed them. Such obligations are based not on the Hague Convention of 1907, No. VIII which is applicable in time of war, but on certain general and well recognised principles: namely elementary considerations of humanity even more exacting in peace than in war... and every state's obligation not to allow its territory to be used for acts contrary to the rights of others.[38]

In fact, Albania neither notified the existence of the minefield nor warned the British warships of the danger they were approaching. It is significant that Albania did not contest the proposition that if it knew of the danger, then it was under a duty to warn other States of its existence.[39] Importance may also be attached to the fact that the Court based the obligation of Albania to warn other States on 'elementary considerations of humanity', a fact that may be taken to indicate that the obligation was not specific to mines in maritime waters. In the *Nicaragua* case, the Court referred to its judgment in the *Corfu Channel* case and reaffirmed the duty of States to warn others of the dangers to which they had become exposed.[40]

Another important precedent is the reaction of States to the Soviet Union's failure to issue a warning in the aftermath of the Chernobyl nuclear accident. This is perhaps the clearest evidence to date that in the view of the States affected, the Soviet Union was under a duty to warn them of the dangers to which they had become exposed. The G7, meeting in Tokyo soon after the disaster, stressed the obligation of the Soviet Union to issue a warning and supply information relating to the accident that had taken place on its territory. Since there was no treaty imposing such a duty on the Soviet Union, it can be inferred that the G7

[37] ILC Prevention Articles, commentary ad art 3, para 17; See also General Assembly Resolution 46/182.

[38] *Corfu Channel (United Kingdom of Great Britain and Northern Ireland v. Albania),* judgment of 9th April 1949, ICJ Reports 1949, 22–3.

[39] *Corfu Channel* case, 22.

[40] *Military and Paramilitary Activities in and Against Nicaragua (Nicaragua v. United States of America),* Merits, Judgment, ICJ Reports 1986, 14 ('*Nicaragua* case'), para 215.

States were of the view that such notification was required under the existing principles of customary law. The G7 statement noted *inter alia* that:

Each country, furthermore, is responsible for prompt provision of detailed and complete information on nuclear emergencies and accidents, in particular those with transboundary consequences. Each of our countries accepts that responsibility and we urge the government of the Soviet Union, which did not do so in the case of the Chernobyl, to provide urgently such information, as our and other countries have requested.[41]

As a direct result of the Chernobyl accident, a multilateral *Treaty on Early Notification in case of Nuclear Accident* was adopted, which has been ratified by most States that possess nuclear reactors.[42] Although the conclusion of a treaty may in fact indicate that the subject matter under consideration is not regulated by general international law, the better view is that it sought to dispel any doubts about the existence of such a duty, an important clarification in a Cold War context. This view is consistent with the aforementioned decisions of the ICJ, the unanimous position taken by codification bodies,[43] including in the run up to UNCED,[44] and by subsequent treaty practice.[45]

## *2.2. Assistance in case of disaster*

### 2.2.1. A duty of assistance?

The second part of Principle 18 states that '[e]very effort shall be made by the international community to help States so afflicted'. The history, preamble, scheme and structure of the Declaration clearly indicate that this statement was not intended to create immediately binding obligations on States where these were not already supported by State practice.[46] Rather it was intended to act as a catalyst for more detailed subsequent regulation. Unfortunately more than two decades after Rio the precise implications of this provision remain undefined and its consequences hortatory and symbolic as a matter of general international law. However, at the regional level some attempts are being made to operationalize this obligation by creating specific mechanisms for its realization.[47] Indeed the imposition of obligations on mere bystanders is in almost all legal systems and international law is no exception.

At the heart of the provision is a tension between pluralist and solidarist conceptions of international law.[48] Pluralists have long argued that the international order depends on different national conceptions of what is right and it is for each State to decide on how best to protect and secure the rights of its population. Solidarist approaches firmly believe that individuals have rights, which must be enforced by the collective action of States

[41] Tokyo Economic Summit Conference Statement on the Soviet Nuclear Reactor Accident at Chernobyl, 5 May 1986, para 2.

[42] Convention on Early Notification.

[43] ILC Prevention Articles, art 17.

[44] See section II) 1 of this chapter.

[45] See section II) 3 of this chapter.

[46] See Kiss, A., 'The Rio Declaration on the Environment and Development', in Campiglio, L. et al (eds), *The Environment After Rio: International Law and Economics* (London: Graham and Trotman/M. Nijhoff 1994), 55; Sand, P. H., 'UNCED and the Development of International Environmental Law' 8 *Journal of Natural Resources and Environmental Law* 209, 216–17.

[47] For a critical commentary on the development of the law in this field see Asian-African Legal Consultative Committee, Intersessional meeting of Legal Experts to Discuss Matters Relating to International Law Commission, New Delhi 10th April 2012; <http://www.aalco.int>. See Treaty on the Functioning of the European Union ('TFEU'), Consolidated Texts of the EU Treaties as Amended by the Treaty of Lisbon, art 196. Available at <http://www.gov.uk/government/uploads/attachment_data/file/2288>.

[48] See eg Kingsbury, B., *International Law as Inter-Public Law*, 181. Available at <http://www.iilj.org/aboutus/documents/internationallawasInter-PublicLaw.pdf>; Cullet, Ph., *Differential Treatment in International law: Towards a Paradigm of Inter-State Relations* (1999) *EJIL* 1.

even in the face of protests by their own governments. Increasingly solidarity approaches have extended their reach to include the right to act to protect human rights even against the wishes of national governments. For pluralists any attempt to deliver humanitarian assistance threatens the international system of public order by undermining a State's monopoly of power in relation to matters on its territory.

The UN and regional institutions have endorsed solidarity as the basis of assistance obligations, although the implications of this stance remain uncertain.[49] For instance, the UN Secretary-General observed that:

> the belief in dignity and value of human beings as expressed in the preamble of the Charter of the United Nations is and must be the prime motive for the international community to give humanitarian assistance. The concept of international solidarity so often evoked following major emergencies and understood as a feeling of responsibility towards people in distress equally has its roots in the ethical principles of the Charter. Solidarity in this sense is not charity.[50]

The early jurists of international law acknowledged that States may be under a duty to act in defence of strangers but they characterized this duty as an 'imperfect obligation' in the sense that States were only bound by their conscience. For these jurists, failure to comply with the duty did not warrant punishment.[51]

There are also systemic difficulties in viewing assistance as an affirmative duty, not least because it is difficult to visualize what consequences should attach to non-compliance. How could a legally binding duty of assistance be enforced? Is it only binding on those who have the means but fail to respond to the natural disaster or is it a duty binding on all States? There are also related questions of how to evaluate State capacity to assist and whether a failure to do so is something that can meaningfully be subjected to international oversight?[52] These and other difficulties undermine attempts at recognizing a customary character to the duty of assistance, as discussed in section II) 2.2.3 of this chapter.

### 2.2.2. Duties of the territorial State (in this context the 'affected State')

The practice since Rio places an explicit obligation on the State where the disaster or emergency takes place (the 'affected State') to facilitate assistance by removing domestic legislative and other barriers that may impede the delivery of assistance.

[49] See for instance ASEAN Agreement, art 3(5): 'The parties shall, in the spirit of solidarity and partnership and in accordance with their respective needs, capabilities and situations strengthen co-operation and co-ordination to achieve the objectives of this agreement.'

[50] 'New International Humanitarian Order: Humanitarian Assistance to Victims of Natural Disasters and Similar Emergency Situations', Report of the Secretary-General, UN Doc A/45/587 para 5. See also Hyogo Declaration, January 2005, UN Doc A/CONF.206/6, preamble.

[51] See Pufendorf, S., *The Law of Nature and Nations*, Kennett, B. (trans), Clark, (Law book Exchange 2005), I VII.7; de Vattel, E., *The Law of Nations*, Kapossy, B. and Whatmore, R. (eds), (Liberty Fund 2008), 11.1.3.262. More recently Lea Brilmayer and Isaiah Yemane Tesfalidet have questioned whether international law could impose universal duties on state strangers in the absence of a pre-existing legal duty, See 'Third State Obligations and the Enforcement of International Law' (2011) 44 *New York Journal of International Law and Politics*, especially 40; available at <jilpblog.files.wordpress.com/2011/12/brimlayer.pdf>.

[52] In November last year it was widely reported that China, the world's largest economy, pledged to give only two million dollars to help the Philippines deal with the aftermath of the Typhoon Halyan. The sum was seen as derisory and significantly less than the pledge made by the furniture store Ikea! The sum was increased by a small amount in the face of mounting international criticism. See the guardian.com, 14 November 2013.

A recent statement in this sense can be found in articles 10, 11, 13, and 14 of the ILC's ongoing draft on the Protection of persons in the event of disaster, according to which:

Article 10

Duty of the affected State to seek assistance
To the extent that a disaster exceeds its national response capacity, the affected State has the duty to seek assistance from among other States, the United Nations, other competent intergovernmental organizations and relevant non-governmental organizations, as appropriate.

Article 11

Consent of the affected State to external assistance

1. The provision of external assistance requires the consent of the affected State.
2. Consent to external assistance shall not be withheld arbitrarily.

...

Article 13

Conditions on the provision of external assistance
The affected State may place conditions on the provision of external assistance. Such conditions shall be in accordance with the present draft articles, applicable rules of international law, and the national law of the affected State. Conditions shall take into account the identified needs of the persons affected by disasters and the quality of the assistance. When formulating conditions, the affected State shall indicate the scope and type of assistance sought.

Article 14

Facilitation of external assistance

1. The affected State shall take the necessary measures, within its national law, to facilitate the prompt and effective provision of external assistance, regarding in particular
   (a) Civilian and military relief personnel in fields such as privileges and immunities, visa and entry requirements, work permits, and freedom of movement and
   (b) Goods and equipment, in the fields such as customs requirements and tariffs, taxation, transport and disposal thereof
2. The affected State shall ensure that its relevant legislation and regulations are readily accessible to facilitate compliance with national law.[53]

Clearly the affected State does not have an unqualified right to consent or not to external assistance. It can subject such consent to conditions. However, the language suggests the discretion of the State in giving such consent is not without limits. In particular it is expected that it will take into account obligations under human rights instruments. It is also expected to put in place legislative and other institutional structures, well in advance, if it is to be in a position to receive assistance when emergencies arise.

### 2.2.3. Legal nature of the duty of assistance

One important question is whether in the period since the Rio Declaration States have taken any concrete steps to concretize this hortatory obligation and crucially whether there is now an explicit obligation to provide assistance.

[53] Protection of persons in the event of disasters. Texts and titles of draft articles 10 and 11 provisionally adopted by the Drafting Committee on 19 July 2011, 20 July 2011, A/CN.4/L.794; Protection of persons in the event of disasters. Texts and titles of draft articles 5bis, 12, 13, 14, and 15, provisionally adopted by the Drafting Committee from 5 to 11 July 2012, 12 July 2012, UN Doc A/CN.4/L.812. See also IDI Resolution, VII(3) and VIII.

There are those who argue that even in the absence of justiciable language, commitments made publicly on the international plane are intended to be acted on and that these agreements entail a strong moral expectation that States should implement them.[54] More recently Benvenisti has argued, with reference to analogous situations, that States are trustees of humanity and may be under a duty to act in the interest of human dignity even in the absence of a treaty commitment and even when it is not in their rational self-interest to do so.[55]

Others see decisions to act in these instances as driven primarily by rational self interest—States on the whole do not want to be seen as free riders or unreliable partners.[56] It may for instance be in the self-interest of a State to render assistance so as to stem the overflow of refugees fleeing the disaster to its own territory. Moreover to be seen as morally indifferent to an international catastrophe, has conceivably long term reputational damage for States. The rendering of assistance may also act as a catalyst for long-term cooperation in other areas where the participation of the affected state is crucial.

In its resolution adopted at Bruges in 2003 the *Institut de Droit International* boldly proclaimed the existence of a right to humanitarian assistance by victims in the event of a disaster. It stated the following:

1. Leaving the victims of disaster without humanitarian assistance constitutes a threat to human life and an offence to human dignity and therefore a violation of fundamental human rights.
2. The victims of disaster are entitled to request and receive humanitarian assistance. Assistance may be sought on behalf of the victims, by the members of the group, by local and regional authorities, the government of the affected State and national or international organisations.[57]

However it is significant that only the affected State (characterized as 'the territorial entity where humanitarian assistance is needed') is placed under an explicit duty to provide assistance, as a result of its effective control over the relevant portion of territory.[58] In relation to third States and international organizations, the resolution provides that they have a right to offer humanitarian assistance without such offering being considered as interference in internal affairs.[59] They are further encouraged to do to so but the language of the resolution in this respect is qualified by expressions such as 'should', 'to the extent possible' and only when 'such assistance would [not] result in seriously jeopardizing their own economic, social, or political conditions. It is in any case significant that it does not impose an unequivocally binding duty'.[60] Inter-governmental organizations are exhorted to provide assistance having regard to their own mandates.[61]

[54] See for example Christine Bell who makes this general point but specifically in the context of peace agreements, *On the Law of Peace: Peace Agreements and the Lex Pacifictoria* (Oxford University Press 2008).

[55] Benvenisti, E., 'Sovereigns as Trustees of Humanity: On the Accountability of States to Foreign Stakeholders' (2013) 107 *AJIL* 295.

[56] See Hurrell, A. and Kingsbury, B., *The International Politics of the Environment* (Oxford University Press 1992), 23–4.

[57] IDI Resolution, II.1-2, <http://www.idi-iil.org/idiE/resolutionsE/2003-bru-03-en.pdf>.

[58] IDI Resolution, III.1-3.

[59] IDI Resolution, IV.

[60] IDI Resolution, V.1.

[61] IDI Resolution, V.2.

The International Law Commission considered the normative character of assistance in the context of its project on the responsibility of persons in the event of national disasters and concluded that the obligation remains essentially discretionary.[62] Suggestions had been made that the increased recognition of a responsibility of States to protect populations whose lives are in danger should extend to those affected by national disasters. However, the suggestion did not garner support either with individual members of the Commission or State representatives in the Sixth committee of the United Nations. These delegations argued that responsibility to protect should be confined to situations of genocide, ethnic cleansing, and crimes against humanity as identified in the report of the High Level Panel of the United Nations.[63] In his extensive survey of State practice in this area, the Special Rapporteur of the ILC on the protection of persons in the event of disaster, Eduardo Valencia Ospina, concluded that the enforceable content of international law did not impose any duties on third States to provide assistance. He also rejected the suggestion that the so-called 'responsibility to protect' had any scope for application outside the specific area of humanitarian law where its applicability was first mooted.[64]

## 3. Normative impact

### 3.1. *Overview*

The specificities of the two components of Principle 18 analysed in the foregoing sections explain why their normative impact has fundamentally differed. This is because unlike other principles of the Rio Declaration, Principle 18 presupposes a fundamentally different logic underpinning the operation of international law, especially the idea that obligations may be imposed for the collective good and even in the absence of a tangible benefit for the addressee of the duty. Therefore, it is no surprise that whereas the first component (the duty to notify) has been widely taken up and expanded in international instruments, the second (duty of assistance) has had very limited impact.

### 3.2. *The duty to notify in Some Selected Instruments*

#### 3.2.1. The 1992 UNECE Convention on Industrial Accidents

The notification obligation finds expression in modern form in article 10(2) of the 1992 Industrial Accidents Convention. According to this provision:

> In the event of an industrial accident, or imminent threat thereof, which causes or is capable of causing transboundary effects, the Party of origin shall ensure that affected Parties are, without delay, notified at appropriate levels through the industrial accident notification systems.[65]

[62] Valencia-Ospina, E., Second Report on the Protection of Persons in the Event of Disasters, May 2009, A/CN.4/615, part III, 16–25.

[63] Valencia-Ospina, E., Fifth Report on the Protection of Persons in the Event of Natural Disasters, para 16, UN Doc/CAN.4/652 April 2012; but see Wong, J., "Reconstructing the Responsibility to Protect in the Wake of Cyclones and Separatism' (2009) 84 (2) *Tulane Law Review* 219. The idea of obligation to provide assistance was explicitly rejected by members of the Asia/African Legal Consultative committee who spoke on the topic at the New Delhi meeting in 2012, see <http://www.aalco.int/UNGA%202012.pdf> especially para 91 and p 62.

[64] Valencia-Ospina, E., Special Rapporteur, ILC, Preliminary Report on the Protection of Persons in the Event of Disasters, 5 May 2008, UN Doc A/CN.4/598 para 35.

[65] See Boyle, A. and Harrison, J., 'Environmental Accidents', in Wolfrum, R., *Max Planck Encyclopedia of Public International Law* (Oxford University Press 2008), online version at <opil.ouplaw.com/view/10.1093/law: epil/9780199231690/law-9780199231690>.

The provision further specifies, by reference to an annex (Annex IX), the matters to be contained in the notification. These include:

(a) the type and magnitude of the industrial accident, the hazardous substances involved (if known), and the severity of possible effects;
(b) the time of occurrence and the exact location of the accident;
(c) such other available information as necessary for an efficient response to an industrial accident.[66]

The parties are also required to immediately activate pre-agreed contingency measures and to keep these under constant review.

Advance preparedness also forms a core element of the Convention.[67] Article 8(3) encourages parties to cooperate before, during, and after an industrial accident. It explicitly enjoins the parties to:

> take appropriate measures to establish and maintain adequate emergency preparedness to respond to industrial accidents. The parties shall ensure that preparedness measures are taken to mitigate transboundary effects of industrial accidents, on site duties being undertaken by operators... (3) Each state party shall ensure for hazardous activities the preparation and implementation of off-site contingency plans covering measures to be taken within its territory to prevent and minimize transboundary effects...where appropriate, joint off-site contingency plans shall be drawn up in order to facilitate the adoption of adequate response measures.[68]

### 3.2.2. The 1998 Tampere Convention

An important multilateral instrument in this area is the Tampere Convention on the Provision of Telecommunication Resources for Disaster Mitigation and Relief Operations,[69] concluded under the aegis of the International Telecommunications Union ('ITU').

This treaty envisages cooperation between States in adopting disaster mitigation strategies. Its essential focus is on sharing and facilitating communication systems in emergency situations. Its declared objective, as stated in the preamble, is to create a framework for cooperation and coordination through use of reliable telecommunications systems. In particular, it seeks to predict the likelihood of disaster and to facilitate disaster mitigation and relief operations. These are defined as measures designed to prevent, predict, prepare for, respond to, monitor, and/or mitigate the impact of disasters.[70]

The Convention operates as a framework instrument. It anticipates the conclusion of model agreements at the multilateral or bilateral level, tailored to the particular circumstances of the region or the targeted hazard. However, it also contains within it a number of substantive provisions on telecommunication assistance. For instance, under article 4, each State party has the right to request telecommunication assistance from any other State party, for the purpose of mitigation and relief in disaster situations. It also

[66] Convention on Industrial Accidents, Annex IX, para 2.
[67] Convention on Industrial Accidents, arts 2 and 8.
[68] Convention on Industrial Accidents, art 8(3).
[69] Tampere Convention on the Provision of Telecommunication Resources for Disaster Mitigation and Relief Operations, 18 June 1998, 2296 UNTS 5. A treaty with broadly similar provisions has been adopted by the Association of Caribbean States, see Agreement Establishing the Caribbean Disaster Emergency Response Agency.
[70] Tampere Convention, art 3.

removes a number of regulatory barriers traditionally encountered in relief operations. For instance, under article 5, it requires States parties to grant immunity from arrest, detention, and legal process to humanitarian organizations taking part in relief operations. It also requires states to waive taxes that would normally be charged to bring equipment into the country and to expedite licensing procedures.

Although significant in terms of its vision, the Tampere Convention is by no means a universal agreement and as of May 2013 had only 47 ratifications. It nevertheless contains within it, a viable framework for disaster relief, by encouraging the parties to pursue a common set of objectives and standards in communication in times of disaster. Its strength lies in its flexibility, in removing regulatory barriers, although the modest ratifications illustrates the general reluctance of states to assume obligations which are not obviously in their self-interest.[71]

### 3.2.3. The 2001 European framework

Since 2001 the European Union has also put in place a regulatory framework of cooperation to govern the relations between the Union and its member States in cases of major emergencies.

The relevant council decision set great store on the importance of developing preventative strategies against natural, technological, and environmental disasters.[72] A wide range of measures are anticipated and these include training, identifying in advance intervention teams, as well as establishing a monitoring capability and an emergency communication and information system. A financial support mechanism is established with the specific objective of supplementing the efforts of member states in protecting their populations from natural and man-made disasters. These regional efforts are further supplemented by action at the sub-regional level.

### 3.2.4. The 2005 ASEAN Agreement

Another significant instrument is the ASEAN Agreement on Disaster Management and Emergency Response.[73]

This instrument contains a comprehensive disaster management approach and requires the parties to identify potential sources of risk by undertaking risk assessment and to take precautionary measures with a view to preventing, monitoring, and mitigating disasters. A further obligation on the parties is to mainstream disaster risk reduction efforts by incorporating them into sustainable development policies. Furthermore, the parties are required to develop comprehensive risk reduction strategies including early warning systems. Advance preparedness for accidents includes providing adequate information to parties capable of being affected by accidents. Under the Convention, those likely to be affected must be given the opportunity to participate in relevant procedures for accident prevention and preparedness, as well as the contingency plans in the event of an accident. An institutional framework for the coordination and management of the disaster is also established.[74]

[71] The majority of ratifying States are relatively poor nations that have recently been devastated by natural disasters.

[72] Council decision 2001/792/EC, Preamble, recital 4.

[73] ASEAN Agreement on Disaster Management and Emergency Response, 25 July 2005.

[74] The treaty establishes the ASEAN Coordinating centre for humanitarian Assistance. See ASEAN Agreement, arts 5(3) 4, 8(4), 5(6), and 9(2) 3 as well as art 20.

### 3.2.5. The Hyogo process

At the institutional and policy level, significant progress was made after the General Assembly proclaimed the decade 1990–99 as the International Decade of Disaster Reduction.[75] In 1994, a World Conference on Natural Disaster Reduction was organized, and a set of principles on natural disaster reduction were adopted at Yokohama, Japan.[76] A subsequent conference on disaster reduction held at Kobe, Japan, in 2005, focused on building a culture of disaster prevention and resilience as a continuum, requiring action from the local through to the international level. A major result of this conference was the adoption of the Hyogo Framework for Action 2005–2015 ('HFA'), which is a detailed plan of action aimed at building resilience to disasters.[77] A 'Mid-Term Review' of progress in the achievement of resilience was conducted in 2010–11 and the HFA was found to have played a decisive role in improving resilience.[78]

The responses envisaged in the instruments vary depending on the geographical, economic, and social circumstances of the particular community. Significantly, like obligations in other areas of international environmental law, it is expected that strategies and measures will reflect the technical and economic capacity of participating States. The Hyogo Declaration proclaims that:

> In view of the particular vulnerabilities and the insufficient capacities of least developed countries to respond to and recover from disasters, support is needed by the least developed countries as a matter of priority, in executing substantive programmes and relevant institutional mechanisms for the implementation of the framework of action, including financial and technical assistance for and capacity building in disaster risk reduction as an effective and sustainable means to prevent and respond to disasters . . . disasters in Africa pose a major obstacle to the African continents efforts to achieve sustainable development, especially in view of the regions insufficient capacities to predict, monitor, deal with and mitigate disasters . . . financial and technical assistance is needed to strengthen the capacities of African countries, including observation and early warning systems, assessments, prevention, preparedness, response and recovery.[79]

The Declaration goes on to encourage States to adopt effective bilateral and multilateral systems of financial and technical assistance programmes. Other factors to be taken into account in the overall scheme of preparedness include programmes specifically directed at the vulnerability of small island nations to disaster.[80]

These initiatives attempt to move the emphasis away from the management of disaster and place increased emphasis on building the resilience of communities in reducing the occurrence of disasters and in the event that they occur, mitigating their effects by reducing vulnerability to those hazards. The measures called for here include appropriate legal and institutional processes such as risk assessments, public awareness campaigns, setting

[75] UN General Assembly Resolution 44/236 of 22 December 1989.

[76] Report of the World conference on Natural Disaster Reduction (Yokohama, 23–27 May 1994), A/CONF.172/9, 27 September 1994.

[77] See Report of the World conference on Natural Disaster Reduction.

[78] See Hyogo Framework for Action 2005–2015 mid-term review (2010/2011), available at: <http://www.unisdr.org>.

[79] Hyogo Framework for Action 2005–2015: Building the Resilience of Nations and Communities to Disasters, paras 26 and 27, United Nations World Conference on Disaster Reduction, Kobe, Japan, 18–22 January 2005, A/CONF.206/6.

[80] Hyogo Framework for Action 2005–2015, para 32 and discussion on 31–4 of the Report of the World conference on Natural Disaster Reduction.

up programmes of technical support, as well as the development of physical infrastructure to mitigate the effects of disasters.

#### 3.2.6. The ILC work on Protection of persons in the event of disaster

The Protection of persons in the event of disaster was introduced in the long-term programme of work of the ILC in 2006, largely as a result of the strong impression left by the 2004 tsunami that severely affected India and Thailand. It was subsequently introduced in the ILC's normal programme of work in 2007 and a Special Rapporteur, Eduardo Valencia-Ospina from Colombia, was appointed.[81] Since then, the codification work has moved remarkably fast, with some sixteen draft articles adopted at the time this chapter was written.

The draft articles provisionally adopted so far expressly see notification in the event of disasters as a continuum that incorporates pre-risk assessment and the taking of measures to prevent and mitigate the effects of the disaster in its aftermath. Draft Article 16 incorporates a duty to reduce the risk of disasters and provides that:

1. Each State shall reduce the risk of disasters by taking the necessary and appropriate measures, including through legislation and regulations, to prevent, mitigate and prepare for disasters.
2. Disaster risk reduction measures include the conduct of risk assessments, the collection and dissemination of risk and past loss information, and the installation and operation of early warning systems.[82]

### *3.3. The duty of assistance*

#### 3.3.1. Imperfect obligations

The duty of assistance loosely articulated in Principle 8 of the Rio Declaration failed to permeate binding instruments in the decades since the Rio Summit. In some of the multilateral treaties such as the 1992 Industrial Accidents Convention, the 1998 Tampere Convention, or the 2000 Convention on Civil Defence Assistance, the language of obligation is employed but they are arguably imperfect obligations since States are left with a wide discretion in choosing the moment, form and extent of compliance.

By way of illustration, article 12(1) ('Mutual assistance') of the 1992 Industrial Accidents Convention provides that:

> If a Party needs assistance in the event of an industrial accident, it may ask for assistance from other parties, indicating the scope and type of assistance required. A party to whom a request for assistance is directed shall promptly decide and inform the requesting Party whether it is in a position to render the assistance required and indicate the scope and terms of the assistance that might be rendered.

In a similar vein, the 1992 UNECE Convention on Watercourses emphasizes that such assistance shall only be provided on request and following mutually agreed procedures.[83]

Yet the response to the Indian tsunami, the Haitian earthquake or the Japanese earthquake/tsunami conveys a strong expectation that States should provide assistance. The popular condemnation of the Japanese and Chinese governments for the derisory sums contributed in the

[81] *Official Records of the General Assembly, Sixty-second Session, Supplement No. 10* (A/62/10), para 375.
[82] Protection of Persons in the Event of Disasters, Report of the ILC to the UN 6th Committee A.68/10.
[83] UNECE Watercourses Convention, art 15(1).

aftermath of the floods in the Philippines further suggests that the pressure to comply with the duty of assistance is significant. In most cases, States will comply not because of a sense of legal obligation but either as a moral duty or because it is in their self-interest to provide assistance. Failure to respond to a disaster could create general regional instability through displacement of populations and the inevitable loss of trade and investment opportunities. It has also been suggested that although no instrument explicitly creates such a right, it may be a logical consequence of the human rights obligations imposed on states including the right to life.

### 3.3.2. Assistance and sovereignty

Rather than strengthening the duty of third States or of the international community (presumably through international organizations) to provide assistance, international law has maintained strict checks on the provision of such assistance.

In the Draft Articles on Protection of persons in the event of disaster, the ILC Special Rapporteur stressed the centrality of State sovereignty as an overriding principle in the provision of emergency assistance. Under draft article 9, it is the affected State that by virtue of its sovereignty has the duty to ensure protection of persons and, under draft article 11; the provision of external assistance in its territory requires this State's consent. The Institut de Droit International reached a similar conclusion. The articles adopted at the Bruges session recognize the sovereignty of the affected State and its prerogative to withhold consent to the provision of assistance.[84]

Yet this overriding and unqualified deference to state sovereignty may in practice act as an impediment to the expeditious delivery of assistance. It was by reference to sovereignty that the Myanmar authorities strictly controlled the delivery of relief aid in the face of an unfolding humanitarian catastrophe. However, the majority of States roundly rejected the suggestion that the UN Security Council should forcibly deliver aid. Even in a closely integrated community of States such as the European Union, priority is given to national sovereignty in matters of assistance protection. In a significant provision, article 196(2) of the Treaty on the Functioning of the European Union (TFEU), the consent principle is upheld.[85] There is thus a clear consensus that assistance is impermissible without the consent of the affected State.

The underlying rationale is to prevent the assistance process from being manipulated for political purposes. Yet we live in an age where uncontrolled State power has in most cases proved to be most destructive of their own environment and the livelihoods of their populations. Some reserve power to override abuse of sovereignty on the face of it seems desirable. Moreover, the human rights and environmental obligations at the heart of assistance obligations are not bilateral duties; they are owed to the international community as well and appropriate methods of safeguarding them cannot be within the unilateral discretion of affected governments.

## III) Relations with Other Principles

Principle 18 entertains close relationships with two main principles, namely Principle 2 (prevention) and Principle 19 (notification and consultation regarding activities with

[84] IDI Resolution.

[85] Hatzigeorgopoulus, M., 'The EU's Mutual Assistance and Solidarity Clauses' (2012) 61 *European Security Review* 1.

transboundary effects). It also interacts with at least two other principles, namely Principle 15 (Precaution) and Principle 10 (Public participation).

Both Principle 18 and 19 stem, in fact, from the same template principle (Principle 9) of the draft tabled by the European Community.[86] The main initial difference between the two is the phase at which each principle operates. Principle 19 is mainly a prevention and cooperation principle focusing on activities, whereas Principle 18 is mainly a response and mitigation principle focusing on disaster and emergencies. That said, as discussed in this chapter, in practice, it is difficult to clearly separate efforts towards response and mitigation from those aimed at prevention. This separation is particularly difficult in connection with 'other emergencies' arising from activities such as industrial processes. It is perhaps less so when it comes to 'natural disasters'. In both cases, prior cooperation to improve resilience makes these two principles aspects of a broader obligation of environmental cooperation in a transboundary context.

As such, both Principle 18 and 19 are an extension, much in the same way as Principle 17 on the conduct of an environmental impact assessment, of the prevention principle stated in Principle 2 of the Rio Declaration. Principle 2 echoes both the 1941 decision of the tribunal in the *Trail Smelter* arbitration[87] and Principle 21 of the Stockholm Declaration.[88] The notification is intended to make it possible for those States likely to be affected by natural disasters to trigger response and mitigation strategies and, to that extent, it is a practical application of the due diligence duty imposed on States by customary international law.

Notification may also be a practical consequence of the application of the precautionary principle, particularly when there is uncertainty as to whether a 'natural disaster' or 'other emergency' may have an impact on another State.[89] In such cases, notification as a precautionary measure seems nevertheless warranted and the consequences for failure to comply with the duty of notification for the State applies equally here.

Finally, the growing importance of public participation in environmental matters, enshrined in Principle 10 of the Rio Declaration, may also require that the public be not only made aware of the 'natural disaster' or the 'other emergency' that can potentially affect them, but also that they are actively involved in the elaboration of preventive, response, and management measures addressing the catastrophe.

[86] See L.25, Principle 9 (the first paragraph of which became Principle 19 of the Rio Declaration, whereas the second become Principle 18).

[87] *Trail Smelter* case (*United States, Canada*) RIAA, 16 April 1938 and 11 March 1941, Vol III, 1905–1982.

[88] Report from the United Nations Conference on the Human Environment held in Stockholm, 1972, available at <http://www.unep.org/documents/default.asp?documentid=7&articleid=503>.

[89] In its *Advisory Opinion on the Responsibilities and Obligations of States Sponsoring Persons and Entities with Respect to Activities in the Area*, the ITLOS Seabed disputes Chamber observed that the precautionary approach has been incorporated into a growing number of international treaties. The precautionary approach is specifically intended to provide guidance in the development and application of international environmental law where there is scientific uncertainty. The core of this approach is reflected in Principle 15 of the Rio Declaration—and other instruments many of which reflect the formulation of Principle 15 of the Rio Declaration. In the view of the Chamber, this has initiated a trend towards making this approach part of customary law. The precautionary approach should guide state action in the face of threats to the environment. Similarly in the *Pulp Mills* case, the Court recognized the importance in interpreting rules of international law in light of the precautionary approach.

## IV) Assessment

This chapter has attempted to isolate the more important provisions in treaties and soft-law instruments regarding response, mitigation, and also preventive action regarding disasters. This is necessary because there is, to date, no general comprehensive multilateral treaty on this question. As a result, the content and operation of the obligation on notification and assistance has to be assessed by reference to a variety of sparse legal materials. In relation to the duty of notification they clearly reflect the existence of customary law duty to notify other states of impending emergencies.

The absence of a comprehensive treaty is not due to lack of effort. There were concerted attempts during the period of the League of Nations, resulting in a multilateral treaty, the 1927 International Relief Union.[90] However, by all accounts, this was hardly an effective instrument for the short period that it was in existence.[91] The content of the obligation has continued to be developed in discrete bilateral treaties dealing with the issues in specific sectors.[92] The diverse nature of the disasters and emergencies that may arise, as well as the related geological and geomorphological factors, suggest that this is not a matter that can be effectively regulated in one universal instrument.

Moreover the underpinnings of the two duties combined within Principle 18 are, as noted in this chapter, fundamentally at odds with each other. The provision of assistance, included on the initiative of developing countries was itself contradictory with the great emphasis on sovereignty that the latter advocated for in all principles as well as at UNCED at large. Under such circumstances, despite the significant influence of other areas of international law such as humanitarian law and human rights, the limited recognition of a duty of assistance is hardly surprising.

## V) Select Bibliography

Benvenisti, E., 'Sovereigns as Trustees of Humanity: On the Accountability of States to Foreign Stakeholders, (2013) 107 *AJIL* 295.

Boyle, A. and Harrison, J., 'Environmental Accidents', in *Max Planck Encyclopedia of Public International Law* (Oxford University Press 2008).

Brilmayer, L. and Tesfalidet, I. Y., 'Third State Obligations and the Enforcement of International Law' (2011) 44 *New York University Journal of International Law and Politics* 1.

Cullet, Ph., 'Differential Treatment in International law: Towards a Paradigm of Inter-State Relations' (1999) 10 *EJIL* 549.

De Guttry, A., Gestri, M., Venturini, G. (eds), International Disaster Response Law (The Hague: TMC Asser Press 2012).

Hardcastle, R. J. and Chua, A. T. L., 'Humanitarian Assistance: Towards a right of Access to Victims of Natural Disasters' (1998) 38 *International Review of the Red Cross* 589.

[90] Convention Establishing an International Relief Union, LNTS, Vol 135, P. 247. It entered into force in 1932 having received 30 ratifications.

[91] Its key objective as contained in the preamble was 'to render aid to each other in disasters, to encourage international relief by a methodical coordination of available resources, and to further the progress of international law in this field'. The text of the Convention establishing an International Relief Union, 1927 is available at <http://treaties.un.org/pages/LONViewDetails.aspx?sc=LON&id=564&lang=en>.

[92] Convention on Assistance in the Case of a Nuclear Accident or Radiological Emergency; Convention on Early Notification of a Nuclear Accident.

Inter-agency Standing Committee, *Operational Guidelines on Human Rights and Natural Disasters* (Washington DC: Brookings-Bern Project on Internal Displacement 2006).

International Law Commission, Protection of Persons in the Event of Disasters, Memorandum prepared by the Secretariat, UN Doc A/CN.4/590.

Kalshoven, F. (ed), Assisting the Victims of Armed Conflict and Other Disasters (The Hague: Martinus Nijhoff 1989).

Keith, K., 'Natural Disasters and International Law: A preliminary Note', Institut de Droit International, Tokyo, September 2003.

Okowa, P., *State Responsibility for Transboundary Air Pollution in International Law* (Oxford University Press 2000).

Wheeler, N., *Saving Strangers: Humanitarian Intervention in International Society* (Oxford University Press 2000).

Wong, J., 'Reconstructing the Responsibility to Protect in the Wake of Cyclones and Separatism' (2009) 84 *Tulane Law Review* 219.

# 23. Principle 19

## *Notification and Consultation on Activities with Transboundary Impact*

Laurence Boisson de Chazournes* and Komlan Sangbana**

**Principle 19**

States shall provide prior and timely notification and relevant information to potentially affected States on activities that may have a significant adverse transboundary environmental effect and shall consult with those States at an early stage and in good faith.



## I) Origins and Rationale of the Principle

Not expressly mentioned in the Stockholm Declaration on the Human Environment of 1972, the principle to notify and to consult appears as a significant component of the Rio Declaration.[1] The principle provides that States which plan to carry out or permit activities that may cause a significant adverse transboundary environmental effect to another

* Professor of International Law and International Organization at the Faculty of Law of the University of Geneva.

** Research and Teaching Assistant at the Faculty of Law of the University of Geneva.

[1] 'Declaration of the United Nations Conference on the Human Environment', Stockholm, 16 June 1972, UN Doc A/CONF 48/14/Rev.1 ('Stockholm Declaration').

State shall give timely notification of such planned activities to such other States and enter into consultation with them in good faith.

The basic rationale underlying the principle to notify and to consult is to prevent the commission of unlawful transboundary interferences and to prevent other States from being confronted with *faits accomplis*.[2] Thus the principle appears as a mechanism to avoid disputes by creating the conditions for cooperation.[3]

In this regard, the principle to notify and to consult is understood as a specific application of the general principle of cooperation.[4] It specifies the content of one of the facets of the principle and facilitates the implementation of other obligations relating to the principle of cooperation, such as the obligation not to cause significant harm to the environment of other States (Principle 2), which is in many ways the backbone of the Rio Declaration.

## II) The Principle as Enshrined in the Rio Declaration

### 1. Preparatory work and context

The codification of the principle within the Rio Declaration appears mainly as the culmination of a long process of its recognition as a principle of international law that is critically important in the environmental area. Before the Rio Declaration, a number of treaties and judicial decisions as well as the works of the *Institut de Droit International* and the International Law Association have dealt with the duty to notify and to consult.[5]

This practice seems to justify why the inclusion of this principle in draft negotiated at PrepCom IV and eventually adopted at the Rio Summit did not raise significant controversies. The first proposal of the principle, included in Principle 9 of the draft tabled by the EC countries, entailed widely accepted aspects including notification in emergency situations and notification for planned activities:

> States shall provide prior and timely notification and relevant information to *other concerned States* on activities that may have a significant international or transboundary effect and shall consult with those other States at an early stage and in good faith.

[2] Munro, R. and Lammers, J. G., *Environmental Protection and Sustainable Development: Legal Principles and Recommendations* (Graham and Trotman 1987), 99.

[3] McCaffrey, S. C., *The Law of International Watercourses* (Oxford University Press 2007), 473; Boisson de Chazournes, L. and Tignino, M., 'Droit international et eau douce', in *Jurisclasseur, Environnement et developpement durable* (LexisNexis 2013) 1, at 14.

[4] See Delbrück, J., 'The International Obligation to Cooperate—An Empty Shell or a Hard Law Principle of International Law? A Critical Look at a Much Debated Paradigm of Modern International Law', in Hestermeyer, H. et al (eds), *Coexistence, Cooperation and Solidarity: Liber Amicorum Rüdiger Wolfrum* (Nijhoff 2012), 3–16; Francioni, F. and Neuhold, H., 'International Cooperation for the Protection of the Environment: The Procedural Dimension', in Lang, W., Neuhold, H., and Zemanek, K. (eds), *Environmental Protection and International Law* (Graham and Trotman, 1991), 203–26; Boyle, A., 'The principle of co-operation: the environment', in Warbick, C. and Lowe, V. (eds), *The United Nations and the Principles of International Law, Essays in Memory of Michael Akehurst* (Routledge 1994), 120.

[5] Concerning the international practice dealing with the duty to notify and to consult, see, Munro and Lammers, *Environmental Protection*, 99 and 104; Kiss, A. and Beurier, J-P., *Droit international de l'environnement* (Pedone 2010), 149–50; Okowa, P., 'Procedural Obligations in International Environmental Agreements' (1997) 67 *BYIL* 275; Farrajota, M. M., 'Notification and Consultation in the Law Applicable to International Watercourses', in Boisson de Chazournes, L. and Salman, S. M. A. (eds), *Water Resources and International Law* (Academy of International Law and Martinus Nijhoff Publishers 2005), 281.

States shall immediately notify other States of any emergency situation that might produce sudden harmful effects on the environment of those other States.[6]

The second paragraph of this draft principle became Principle 18 and the first paragraph became, almost with no changes, Principle 19.

The two differences with the text proposed by European countries were the replacement of the reference to 'other concerned States' with 'potentially affected States' which is broader in scope and that of the expression 'significant international or transboundary effect' with 'significant adverse transboundary effect', which stresses the transboundary focus on the notification obligation, particularly if compared with the prevention obligation of Principle 2 that applies also to harm to the global commons.

No changes were introduced at the Rio Summit to the formulation agreed at PrepCom IV.

## 2. Scope and dimensions

### 2.1. *Characterization of the trigger effect*

The trigger condition for implementation of the duty of notification and consultation as enshrined in Principle 19 of the Rio Declaration is the existence of activities that have significant adverse transboundary environmental effect.[7] What kind of 'activities' and 'transboundary adverse effect' are concerned?

It appears from State and treaty practice that identification of relevant activities and the form of injuries do not lend themselves to a single formula. Sometimes it is the nature of the resources being used that is taken as the point of departure.[8] For example, article 12 of the 1997 UN Watercourses Convention requires notification for 'planned measures which may have a significant adverse effect upon other watercourse States'. In this case, the shared river represents the point of departure. In the 1979 Convention on Long-Range Transboundary Air Pollution, the protection of airspace represents this point of departure. Article 3 of the Convention provides that:

The Contracting Parties, within the framework of the present Convention, shall by means of exchanges of information, consultation, research and monitoring, develop without undue delay policies and strategies which shall serve as a means of combating the discharge of air pollutants…

In other cases it is the potential scale or probability of harm to which the activity gives rise that may determine the reference to notification.[9] In this regard, notification and consultation concern all activities that may have a significant adverse transboundary environmental effect.[10] The 1980 Memorandum of Intent between the United States and Canada concerning Transboundary Air Pollution specifies that notification is required not only for individual projects, but also for proposed changes of policy, regulations, or practices which may cause transboundary air pollution.[11] Considering the changing nature of technology and knowledge about the effects of activities, the International Law Commission (ILC)

[6] See 'Elements for the Earth Charter', UN Doc A/CONF.151/PC/WG.III/L.25 ('L.25'), Principle 9 (italics added).

[7] Munro and Lammers, *Environmental Protection*, 9, 104–5; McCaffrey, *The Law of International Watercourses*, 473; Boisson de Chazournes and Tignino, 'Droit international et eau douce', 14,

[8] Okowa, 'Procedural Obligations', 291.

[9] Okowa, 'Procedural Obligations', 291.

[10] Kiss and Beurier, *Droit international de l'environnement*, 150, para 266.

[11] Point 3 (a) 1980 Memorandum of Intent between the Government of the United States of America and the Government of Canada Concerning Transboundary Air Pollution, The Marine Mammal Commission Compendium Bilateral/Canada, volume(s) 1–3, 2796–801.

in its Draft Article on the prevention of Transboundary Harm from Hazardous Activities preferred to not draw a definitive list of activities that would necessitate a notification requirement.[12] For its part, the 1991 Espoo Convention on Environmental Impact Assessment in a Transboundary Context lists activities that require notification in its Appendix I. It includes, among other things, oil refineries, coal gasification plants, thermal power stations, large diameter oil and gas pipelines, trading ports, waste disposal installations for incineration, chemical treatment or landfills of toxic and dangerous wastes, offshore hydrocarbon production, and major storage facilities for petroleum, petrochemical and chemical products. At the initiative of any such party, concerned states can enter into discussions on whether other proposed activities, not listed in Appendix I, are likely to cause a significant adverse transboundary impact and should be treated as if they were listed (article 2 (5)).

International law does not define in a strict manner the gravity threshold that requires notification implementation. Very often, practice requires that the transboundary harm must present some level of gravity. The ILC makes reference to the notion of 'significant transboundary harm'.[13] However, this term remains ambiguous. The commentaries of the Draft Articles on the Prevention of Transboundary Harm from Hazardous Activities describe the term 'significant' as something more than 'detectable' but which need not rise to the level of 'serious' or 'substantial'.[14] Finally, it is for States to assess what constitutes a significant adverse transboundary effect but 'the harm must lead to a real detrimental effect on matters such as, for example, human health, industry property, environment, or agriculture.'[15]

Article 1 of the 1992 UNECE Water Convention provides that: 'such effects on the environment include effects on human health and safety, flora, fauna, soil, air, water, climate, landscape and historical monuments, or other physical structures, or the interaction among these factors; they also include effects on the cultural heritage or socio-economic conditions resulting from alterations to those factors'. Practice can provide guidance on criteria to be taken into account in determining significant adverse impact. For example, Appendix III of the 1991 Espoo Convention on Environmental Impact Assessment in a Transboundary Context provides the following criteria: a) size of the activity; b) proximity to areas of specialized environmental sensitivity or importance location; and c) activities with particularly complex and potentially adverse effects.

## *2.2. The conditions of implementation of the principle*

### 2.2.1. The initiative of notification

According to Principle 19 of the Rio Declaration, it is the responsibility of the State which plans the measures to inform the concerned States, even though the project is owned or

[12] See commentary article 1 of the 2001 Draft articles on the prevention of Transboundary Harm from Hazardous Activities, ILC Yearbook, 2001, vol II, part II, 149–50, paras 3 and 4.

[13] See the 1997 UN Watercourses Convention, UNGA Res. 51/229 (art 12); 2001 Draft articles on the prevention of Transboundary Harm from Hazardous Activities, ILC Yearbook, 2001, vol II, part II ('ILC Prevention articles'), art 8. See also the 1991 Convention on Environmental Impact Assessment in a Transboundary Context, Espoo, ('Espoo Convention') 25 Feb. 1991, 1989 UNTS. 310 (art 3); '2003 Revised African Convention on the Conservation of Nature and Natural Resources', in Boisson de Chazournes, L., Desgagné, R., Mbengue, M. M., and Romano. C. (eds), *Protection internationale de l'environnement*, (Nouvelle éd. remise à jour et augmentée, Pedone 2005), 187 (art 16 (c)).

[14] See ILC Prevention articles, commentary ad art 2, p 152, para 4.

[15] See ILC Prevention articles, commentary ad art 2, p 152, para 4.

placed under the responsibility of a private person.[16] The ICJ stressed this point in the *Pulp Mills* case. In rejecting Uruguay's argument in this case that the Administrative Commission on the Uruguay River ('CARU') had been made aware by private entities, the Court considered that:

> the information on the plans for the mills which reached CARU via the companies concerned or from other non-governmental sources cannot substitute for the obligation to inform laid down in Article 7, first paragraph, of the 1975 Statute, which is borne by the party planning to construct the works referred to in that provision.[17]

To avoid inertia within the planning State, practice recognizes that the implementation of notification is not only dependent upon the appreciation of the planning State. The potentially affected State has a right to require notification if it considers that there is a risk of transboundary effect. This is what emerged in the *Lake Lanoux* case. In this case, facing the refusal of France to inform the Spanish authorities on the derivation of the Carol River (on the basis that the projected works would cause no significant prejudice beyond France's own borders), the Tribunal considered that:

> In any event, the possibility of prejudicing the course or the volume of the water mentioned in Article 11 cannot in any case be left exclusively to the discretion of the State which proposes to execute those works or to grant new concessions; the assertion of the French Government that the projected works can cause no prejudice to the Spanish riparian owners is, despite what has been said in argument... not sufficient to relieve that Government from any of the obligations contained in Article 11... A State which is liable to suffer repercussions from work undertaken by a neighbouring State is the sole judge of its interests...[18]

In the absence of a general standard of appreciation, this right appears as an assurance for the potentially affected State.

The notification is generally addressed to the State that may be affected. In this regard, it is traditionally considered that the implementation of notification and consultation duties is designed to take place in a bilateral inter-state context.[19] The growing implication of international organizations can also be observed. Recent practice shows that organizations can be used as intermediaries to notify all States parties concerned of planned measures. This has generally been the case when a multiplicity of States is involved, which is true of some river basins. Article 24 of the 2002 Water Charter of the Senegal River provides for example that: '*Pour les projets susceptibles d'avoir des effets significatifs, il est fait obligation, avant leur exécution, de les notifier aux États parties, par l'intermédiaire du Haut-Commissariat.*' A similar provision can be found in article 20 of the 2008 Water Charter of the River Niger Basin.[20] In the marine area, the 1995 Convention for the Protection of the Marine Environment and the Coastal Region of the Mediterranean designates the

[16] Boisson de Chazournes and Tignino, 'Droit international et eau douce', 14,

[17] *Pulp Mills on the River Uruguay (Argentina v. Uruguay)*, Judgment, ICJ Reports 2010, 14, para 110.

[18] *Lake Lanoux Arbitration* case, ILR (1957), 314, para 21.

[19] *Lake Lanoux Arbitration* case, 15; see also Okowa, 'Procedural Obligations', 290.

[20] 'Before a State Party implements or permits the implementation on its territory of measures that may have significant adverse effects upon other Basin States, it shall provide the latter with timely notification through the Executive Secretariat'. See also 1975 Statute of the River Uruguay, Salto, 26 Feb. 1975, 1295 UNTS 340 (art 7); 1994 Danube River Protection Convention (art 11), available online at: <http://www.icpdr.org/main/icpdr/danube-river-protection-convention> (accessed 24 April 2014); 1995 Agreement on the cooperation for the sustainable development of the Mekong River Basin, Chiang Rai, 5 April 1995, (1995) 34 ILM 864 (arts 5 and 26); 2010 Agreement on the Nile River Basin Cooperative Framework (art 8), available online at <http://www.internationalwaterlaw.org/documents/africa.html> (accessed 24 April 2014).

United Nations Environment Programme to carry out administrative functions which include notification (article 17).[21] Notification to those institutions can be an obligation for the concerned States.

This is what emerged in the *Pulp Mills* case concerning the interpretation of article 7 of the 1975 Uruguay River Statute, which requires that a State which is initiating a planned activity inform the Administrative Commission on the Uruguay River ('CARU'). Rejecting Uruguay's argument, the Court observed firstly that:

> Since CARU serves as a framework for consultation between the parties, particularly in the case of the planned works..., neither of them may depart from that framework unilaterally, as they see fit, and put other channels of communication in its place. By creating CARU and investing it with all the resources necessary for its operation, the parties have sought to provide the best possible guarantees of stability, continuity and effectiveness for their desire to co-operate in ensuring 'the optimum and rational utilization of the River Uruguay'.[22]

Secondly, the Court added: '[t]hat is why CARU plays a central role in the 1975 Statute and cannot be reduced to merely an optional mechanism available to the parties which each may use or not, as it pleases...'[23]

This argument justifies why the Court considers that '*the obligation of the State initiating the planned activity to inform CARU constitutes the first stage in the procedural mechanism.*'[24]

### 2.2.2. Content and time of the notification

#### *2.2.2.1. Content*

Similarly to provisions in other instruments, Principle 19 of the Rio Declaration does not give a precise definition of the content of notification. However considering that the scope of the notification is to allow the potentially affected State to study and evaluate the possible effect of the planned measures,[25] the content appears to be characterized by the elements that permit an informed determination about the effect of a planned project. In this regard, the practice requires adequate information to assess the effect of a project or a plan.[26]

For example, Article 3 (2) of the 1991 Espoo Convention on Environmental Impact Assessment in a Transboundary Context provides that:

> This notification shall contain, inter alia: (a) Information on the proposed activity, including any available information on its possible transboundary impact; (b) The nature of the possible decision; and (c) An indication of a reasonable time within which a response under paragraph 3 of this Article is required, taking into account the nature of the proposed activity.

Likewise paragraph 3 of the World Bank Procedure (BP) 7.50 relating to projects on international waterways provides that:

> The notification contains, to the extent available, sufficient technical specifications, information, and other data (Project/Program Details) to enable the other riparians to determine as accurately

[21] Art 17: 'The Contracting Parties designate the United Nations Environment Programme as responsible for carrying out the following secretariat functions... ii) To submit to the Contracting Parties notifications, reports and other information received...'.

[22] *Pulp Mills*, para 90. [23] *Pulp Mills*, para 91. [24] *Pulp Mills*, para 94.

[25] *Pulp Mills*, para 113.

[26] 1979 Convention on Long-Range Transboundary Air Pollution, Geneva, 13 Nov. 1979, (1979) 18 ILM 1442 (art 8); Espoo Convention, art 3; 1997 UN Watercourses Convention, art 12; ILC Prevention articles, art 8(1).

as possible whether the proposed project has potential for causing appreciable harm through water deprivation or pollution or otherwise....[27]

In this context, the requirement to produce an environmental impact assessment among the elements of notification has gained attention in practice. The environmental impact assessment is perceived as a vehicle for providing relevant information and data.[28] For example, article 12 of the 1997 UN Watercourses Convention provides that:

notification shall be accompanied by available technical data and information, including the results of any environmental impact assessment, in order to enable the notified States to evaluate the possible effects of the planned measures.

Article 24 of the Water Charter of the Senegal River meanwhile envisages more systematization in this area: 'The notification must be done in good time and be accompanied by all the technical data necessary to its evaluation, in particular the impact studies.'

Similarly, the International Court of Justice in its judgment in the *Pulp Mills* case pointed out '*the need for a full environmental impact assessment in order to assess any significant damage which be caused by a plan.*'[29] In this regard, the Court considered that environmental impact assessment is a customary law obligation.[30]

Various instruments specify the context of undertaking an environmental impact assessment. Article 4 of the 1991 Espoo Convention on Environmental Impact Assessment in a Transboundary Context provides that the environmental impact assessment of a State party should contain, at a minimum, the information described in Appendix II to the Convention. Appendix II lists nine items, as follows:

(a) A description of the proposed activity and its purpose; (b) A description, where appropriate, of reasonable alternatives (for example, locational or technological) to the proposed activity and also the no-action alternative; (c) A description of the environment likely to be significantly affected by the proposed activity and its alternatives; (d) A description of the potential environmental impact of the proposed activity and its alternatives and an estimation of its significance; (e) A description of mitigation measures to keep adverse environmental impact to a minimum; (f) An explicit indication of predictive methods and underlying assumptions as well as the relevant environmental data used; (g) An identification of gaps in knowledge and uncertainties encountered in compiling the required information; (h) Where appropriate, an outline for monitoring and management programmes and any plans for post-project analysis; and (i) A non-technical summary including a visual presentation as appropriate (maps, graphs, etc.).[31]

[27] See Salman, S. M. A. and Boisson de Chazournes, L., *Enhancing Cooperation and managing conflict—Proceeding of a World Bank Seminar*, World Bank Technical Paper n°414 (1998) 197–9.

[28] See McCaffrey, *The Law of International Watercourses*, 475; Farrajota, 'Notification and Consultation', 315–19.

[29] *Pulp Mills*, para 116.

[30] '... In this sense, the obligation to protect and preserve, under Article 41 (a) of the Statute, has to be interpreted in accordance with a practice, which in recent years has gained so much acceptance among States that it may now be considered a requirement under general international law to undertake an environmental impact assessment where there is a risk that the proposed industrial activity may have a significant adverse impact in a transboundary context, in particular, on a shared resource', *Pulp Mills*, para 204.

[31] Similar provisions are included in the 1997 Draft North American Transboundary Environmental Impact Assessment Agreement, available online at: <http://www.cec.org/> (accessed 24 April 2014), and the 2005 Transboundary environmental assessment guidelines for shared ecosystems in East Africa, available online at: <http://www.eac.int/environment/> (accessed 24 April 2014).

*2.2.2.2. Time*

Generally, to ensure that the notification is not to be deprived of practical significance, practice requires a timeliness condition. Principle 19 of the Rio Declaration requires prior and timely notification. Early notification avoids the risk of additional costs of redesign to the planning States.

Treaty practice lacks preciseness. Provisions use vague terms like 'timely' or 'early as possible'; sometimes they do not contain provisions relating the time when notification must be provided. However the ILC has given some indication on this matter. It defined the term 'timely' as 'intended to require notification sufficiently early in the planning stages to permit meaningful consultations and negotiations ... if such prove necessary.'[32] In this regard, the appreciation of the timeliness of the notification is made in reference of its objective. Notification should happen at such point in time as is required relative to the intended objective of notification.[33] The International Court of Justice confirmed this in considering that: '[n]otification must take place before the State concerned decides on the environment viability of the plan taking due account of the environmental impact assessment submitted to it.'[34]

### 2.2.3. Consultation and negotiation

*2.2.3.1. Consultation and negotiation process*

In accordance with Principe 19 of the Rio Declaration, consultation appears as the process that ensues if the potential affected State does not agree with the planned measures. The purpose of consultations is for the parties to find acceptable solutions regarding measures to be adopted in order to prevent significant transboundary harm, or at any event to minimize the risk thereof.[35] In case of failure of consultation, the parties will enter into negotiation to find a solution to their dispute.[36] Whereas Principle 19 of the Rio Declaration provides a rather clear understanding of the link between notification and consultation, such a link is not clearly established in practice. The two processes have usually been addressed separately. For example, the final report of the expert group on the environment, which appears as one of working papers of the Rio conference, had made reference to them in two different principles: Principle 16 concerning the duty to give prior notice, and Principle 17 concerning the duty to consult. The formulation of Principle 19 highlights the interdependence between consultation and notification. Notification appears as the first stage of the consultation process on planned measures.[37]

In practice, the requirement of consultation and negotiation may conduct to equitable (or acceptable[38]) solutions between parties. To achieve this equitable solution, the parties must enter into consultations in good faith. The principle of good faith is an integral part of any requirement of consultations and negotiations.[39] It falls on the State which foresees

[32] Draft articles on the law of the non-navigational uses of international watercourses and commentaries, 1994, vol II, part II, 89, commentary ad art 12, para 4.

[33] Leb, C., *Cooperation in the Law of Transboundary Water Resources* (Cambridge University Press 2013), 132.

[34] *Pulp Mills*, para 120.

[35] Munro and Lammers, *Environmental Protection*, 104–5.

[36] UN Watercourse Convention, art 22.1.

[37] Leb, *Cooperation in the Law of Transboundary Water Resources*, 137.

[38] Term used in the ILC Prevention articles, art 9.1,

[39] ILC Prevention articles, commentary ad art 9, para 3.

a project or a plan to take into account legitimate interests of others. This is what emerges from the *Lake Lanoux* case. The Tribunal considered that consultation:

> cannot be confined to purely formal requirements, such as taking note of complaints, protests or representations made by the downstream State.... According to the rules of good faith, the upstream State is under the obligation to take into consideration the various interests involved, to seek to give them every satisfaction compatible with the pursuit of its own interests, and to show that in this regard it is genuinely concerned to reconcile the interests of the other riparian State with its own.[40]

This view was also pointed out by the International Court of Justice in the *Pulp Mills* case on the River Uruguay. The Court observed that:

> as long as the procedural mechanism for co-operation between the parties to prevent significant damage to one of them is taking its course, the State initiating the planned activity is obliged not to authorize such work and, a fortiori, not to carry it out.[41]

And it adds:

> there would be no point to the co-operation mechanism... if the party initiating the planned activity were to authorize or implement it without waiting for that mechanism to be brought to a conclusion. Indeed, if that were the case, the negotiations between the parties would no longer have any purpose.[42]

#### 2.2.3.2. *Consultation and prior consent*

First of all, the obligation to consultation does not imply an obligation to reach an agreement. This view is largely reflected in practice. In the *Lake Lanoux* case, the Tribunal considered that: 'it places an essential restriction on the sovereignty of a State, and such restriction could only be admitted if there were clear and convincing evidence.'[43] In this regard, the Tribunal considered that the prior consent requirement agreement can only exist by virtue of treaty.[44] This is case for the 2002 Water Charter of the Senegal River which provides that:

> En tout état de cause, aucun projet susceptible de modifier d'une manière sensible les caractéristiques du régime du Fleuve, ses conditions de navigabilité, d'exploitation industrielle, l'état sanitaire des eaux, les caractéristiques biologiques de sa faune ou de sa flore, son plan d'eau, ne peut être exécuté sans avoir été au préalable approuvé par les États contractants.[45]

A similar provision can be found in the 1975 Statute of the River Uruguay (arts 7–13) and the 1995 Agreement on the cooperation for the sustainable development of the Mekong River Basin (arts 5 and 26).

In case of failure to reach agreement, international law permits the State to resort to diplomatic or judicial methods of dispute settlement. Article 87 of the 1973 Treaty concerning the Rio de la Plata and article 60 of the 1975 Statute of the River Uruguay provide for the submission of this issue to the International Court of Justice when the States do not reach agreement on the planned projects.

[40] *Lake Lanoux*, para 22. [41] *Pulp Mills*, para 144. [42] *Pulp Mills*, para 147.
[43] *Lake Lanoux*, para 22. [44] *Lake Lanoux*, para 22.
[45] The Water Charter of the Senegal River, 18 May 2002, art 24 available online at: <http://lafrique.free.fr/traites/omvs_200205.pdf> (accessed 24 April 2014); see also art 4, 1972 Convention Relating To the Statute of the Senegal River, Nouakchott, 11 March 1972, LEX-FAOC016004, available online at <http://faolex.fao.org/docs/texts/mul16004.doc> (accessed 24 April 2014).

Concerning the obligation of 'no construction' incumbent on the State which plans the project, international practice limits to the period of consultation and negotiation. For example, article 17 paragraph 3 of the 1997 UN Watercourses Convention provides that:

> During the course of the consultations and negotiations, the notifying State shall, if so requested by the notified State at the time it makes the communication, refrain from implementing or permitting the implementation of the planned measures for a period of six months unless otherwise agreed.[46]

In the *Pulp Mills* case, Argentina attempted to extend this to the period between the end of negotiation and final resolution of the case by the ICJ.[47] The ICJ rejected this argument:

> The Court observes that the 'no construction obligation', said to be borne by Uruguay between the end of the negotiation period and the decision of the Court, is not expressly laid down by the 1975 Statute and does not follow from its provisions. Article 9 only provides for such an obligation during the performance of the procedure laid down in Articles 7 to 12 of the Statute.
>
> Furthermore, in the event of disagreement between the parties on the planned activity persisting at the end of the negotiation period, the Statute does not provide for the Court, to which the matter would be submitted by the State concerned, according to Argentina, to decide whether or not to authorize the activity in question. The Court points out that, while the 1975 Statute gives it jurisdiction to settle any dispute concerning its interpretation or application, it does not however confer on it the role of deciding in the last resort whether or not to authorize the planned activities. Consequently, the State initiating the plan may, at the end of the negotiation period, proceed with construction at its own risk.[48]

### *2.3. Legal nature*

The obligation to notify and to consult is now considered as a norm of customary international law.[49] The ILC went as far as to consider that:

> The obligation to notify other States of the risk of significant harm to which they are exposed is reflected in the Corfu Channel case, where ICJ characterized the duty to warn as based on 'elementary considerations of humanity.'[50]

As to its content, the obligation to notify and to consult appears to be a specific obligation of performance—*obligation de faire*—stipulating that the State must inform and consult the potential affected States before implementing an activity which might have significant adverse transboundary effects. The obligation provides a standard of behaviour in the conduct of hazardous activities in general. As discussed next, the obligation has been stated in a large number of treaties. The latter in some occasions have specified the content of the obligation.

[46] See also UN Watercourses Convention, art 18.3 concerning the Procedures in the absence of notification.

[47] *Pulp Mills on the River Uruguay (Argentina v. Uruguay)*, Counter-memorial of Uruguay, 29 January 2009, 180–183, available on the website of the ICJ: <http:www.icj-cij.org>.

[48] *Pulp Mills*, para 154.

[49] However, a handful of States have questioned this assertion, see eg the position of the Turkish delegation, Summary report of the 21th session of the Working group of the Whole on the Elaboration of a Framework Convention on the Law of the Non-Navigational Uses of International Watercourses, 1996, SR. 21, n°18, Doc NU, A/C.6/51/SR.21.

[50] ILC Prevention articles, commentary ad art 8, para 3.

## 3. Normative impact

### *3.1. Reception in treaties*

The principle of notification and consultation is vastly enshrined in the context of transboundary watercourses; however, its implementation extends to other areas such as nuclear power installations and the protection of air, weather modification, or marine space. Among the international instruments relating to international watercourses that addressed the issue of prior notice, reference should be made to the 1964 Niamey Agreement concerning the River Niger Commission and the Navigation and Transport on the River Niger, which provides:

> In order to achieve maximum co-operation in connection with the matters mentioned in Article 4 of the Act of Niamey, the riparian States undertake to inform the Commission . . . at the earliest stage, of all studies and works upon which they propose to embark. They undertake further to abstain from carrying out . . . any works likely to pollute the waters, or any modification likely to affect biological characteristics of its fauna and flora, without adequate notice to, and prior consultation with, the commission.[51]

A recent example of the inclusion of the principle in a treaty concluded in the African region is the 2002 Water Charter of the Senegal River (article 10).[52] Others include the 2008 Water Charter of the Niger Basin (articles 20–3)[53] and the Code of Conduct for the sustainable and equitable management of shared water resources of the Volta Basin (articles 21–2).[54]

In Asia, one can refer to 1960 Indus Waters Treaty concluded between India and Pakistan (article 7 (2))[55] and the 1995 Agreement on the cooperation for the sustainable development of the Mekong River Basin (article 5).[56]

In Europe, reference may be made to treaties such as the 1964 Agreement between Poland and the USSR concerning the Use of Water Resources in Frontier Waters (article 6),[57] and the 1980 Agreement between Norway and Finland concerning a Norwegian Finnish Commission for Frontier Watercourses (article 1).[58] The principle was also adopted by the 1994 Danube River Protection Convention (article 11)[59] and the 2008 Draft Agreement on cooperation on conservation and sustainable development of the Dniester River basin (article 18).[60]

In the American region, reference may be made to the 1909 Boundary Waters Treaty between Canada and the United States (articles 3 and 4),[61] the 1978 Great Lakes Water Quality Agreement (article 10 (2)),[62] the 1971 Act of Santiago between Argentina and

[51] Art 12 of the Agreement concerning the River Niger Commission and the Navigation and Transport on the River Niger, Niamey, 25 Nov. 1964, 587 UNTS 8507 (1964).

[52] Available online at: <http://lafrique.free.fr/traites/omvs_200205.pdf> (accessed 24 April 2014).

[53] Available online at <http://www.abn.ne/> (accessed 24 April 2014).

[54] In Garane, A., *Le cadre juridique international du bassin de la Volta* (IUCN 2009), 219.

[55] Karachi, 19 Sept. 1960, Legislative Texts, Treaty No 98,300.

[56] Chiang Rai, 5 April 1995, Ch. II, (1995) 34 ILM 864.

[57] Warsaw, 17 July 1964, 552 UNTS 175 (1964).

[58] In Overenskomster med fremmede Stater 1981, 236.

[59] Available online at: <http://www.icpdr.org/main/icpdr/danube-river-protection-convention> (accessed 24 April 2014).

[60] Available online at <http://dniester.org/materials/dnestr2/> (accessed 24 April 2014).

[61] Washington, 11 Jan. 1909, 36 Stat. 2448.

[62] Ottawa, 22 novembre 1978, UNTS 1153 (1978).

Chile concerning Hydrologic Basins (article 5),[63] and the 1971 Buenos Aires Declaration between Argentina and Uruguay on Water Resources (article 3).[64]

More generally reference may be made to article 6 of the 1992 United Nations Economic Commission for Europe Convention on the Protection and Use of Transboundary Watercourses and International Lakes[65] which requires the parties to provide for exchange of information, as early as possible, on issues covered under its provisions. Article 10 of the Convention calls for consultations on the basis of reciprocity and good faith. Similar provisions can be found in the 1997 United Nations Convention on the Law of the Non-Navigational Uses of International Watercourses (UN Watercourses Convention),[66] and the 2008 Draft Articles on the Law of Transboundary Aquifers (article 15)[67] require timely and prior notification and consultation for planned measures. Furthermore, the 1997 UN Watercourses includes detailed requirement on the duties arising from notification and consultation (articles 11–19).

Notification and consultation requirements are also required in areas such as long-distance air pollution (eg the 1979 ECE Convention on Long-Range Transboundary Air Pollution (articles 5 and 8 (b))),[68] weather modification (eg the 1975 Agreement between Canada and the United States on the Exchange of Information on Weather Modification Activities (articles 2, 5)),[69] and marine pollution (eg the 1974 Paris Convention for the Prevention of Pollution from Land Basel Sources (article 9)).[70]

In the area of nature conservation and biodiversity protection reference may be made to the 1968 African Convention on the Conservation of Nature and Natural Resources (article 5 (2)),[71] the 1974 Nordic Environmental Protection Convention (articles 5, 11),[72] the 1985 ASEAN Agreement on the Conservation of Nature and Natural Resources (articles 19 (2) (d, e) and 20 (3) (b, c))[73] and the 2001 Draft Articles on the Prevention of Transboundary Harm from Hazardous Activities (articles 8 and 9).[74]

### *3.2. Codification institutions*

The Institute of International Law and the International Law Association have both contributed to the development of the principle of notification and consultation. The first instrument of the Institute of International Law which makes reference to the principle is the 1961 Salzburg Resolution on the use of International Non-Maritime Waters (Except for Navigation) which requires prior notification if the works or utilization of the waters might produce serious effects on the use of those waters by other States (article 5). Articles 6 to 8 state that: 'in the event that an objection is made, States should enter into negotiations in order to reach an agreement within a reasonable period of time; and during negotiations States should, in accordance with the principle of good faith, abstain from

[63] UN Doc A/CN.4/274; text reproduced in *ILC Yearbook*, 1974, vol II, part II, 324.
[64] Text reproduced in *ILC Yearbook*, 1974, vol II, part II, 324.
[65] Helsinki, 17 Mar. 1992, 31 (1992) ILM 1312.
[66] UNGA Res. 51/229.
[67] UNGA Res. A/63/439.
[68] Geneva, 13 Nov. 1979, 18 (1979) ILM 1442.
[69] Washington, 26 March 1975, (1975) 14 ILM 589.
[70] Paris, 4 June 1974, (1974) 1514 UNTS 119.
[71] Algiers, 15 Sept. 1968, (1968) 1001 UNTS 3.
[72] Stockholm, 19 Feb. 1974, (1974) 13 ILM 511.
[73] Kuala Lumpur, 9 Jul. 1985, (1985) 15 EPL 64.
[74] In *ILC Yearbook*, 2001, vol II, part II, 146.

implementing the works or utilization of the waters or from taking any other measure that could aggravate the situation'. The principle was also included in the 1979 Institute Athens Resolution on Pollution of Rivers and Lakes and International Law (article 7 (1) (d)) adopted in Athens.

The International Law Association, for its part, included rules on notification and consultation in several of its resolutions: the 1966 ILA Helsinki Rules on the Uses of the Waters of International Rivers (article 29); the 1980 ILA Belgrade Articles on the Regulation of the Flow of Water of International Watercourses (article 7 (1)); the 1982 ILA Montreal Rules on Water Pollution in an International Drainage Basin (article 5 (b)); and the 1982 ILA Montreal Rules of International Law applicable to Transfrontier Pollution (article 5 (1)). Recently, the Berlin Rules on Water Resources also make reference to the duty to notify and to consult (articles 57 and 58).[75]

## 4. Jurisprudential relevance

Notification and consultation have retained great attention in the context of two contentious cases. The first is the *Lake Lanoux* case, which opposed Spain and France. It dealt with the diversion of the waters of Lake Lanoux, situated in the Eastern Pyrenees in France, into the Ariège River, which was flowing into Spain. The diverted waters were to be completely returned to the River Carol by means of a tunnel connecting the rivers Ariège and Carol above the outlet to the Puigcerda Canal. Fearing that the French works would adversely affect Spanish rights and interests, Spain claimed that under the treaty of Bayonne of May 26, 1866, that these works could only be undertaken with its consent. The tribunal made a number of important statements concerning the content and the extent of the principle of notification and consultation. The Tribunal considered that France had to give prior notice of works that could change the course or the volume of watercourses flowing into Spain.[76] The Tribunal concluded that the French scheme was in compliance with the obligations of article XI of the Additional Act to the Treaty of Bayonne.[77]

The second case is the *Pulp Mills on the River Uruguay* which opposed Argentina to Uruguay. The case dealt with the construction of a pulp mill along the left bank of the river. Due to the harm that the project could cause to the river, Argentina argued that Uruguay should have initiated the procedure of consultation set out in articles 7 to 12 of the 1975 Statute of the River Uruguay. Thus, it claimed that Uruguay breached the above mentioned obligations under the 1975 Statute by giving authorization for the construction of the pulp mill without having fully exhausted the notification and consultation process provided for in articles 7 to 12. In its analysis, the International Court of Justice (ICJ) emphasized that the obligation to notify:

> is intended to create the conditions for successful co-operation between the parties, enabling them to assess the plan's impact on the river on the basis of the fullest possible information and, if necessary, to negotiate the adjustments needed to avoid the potential damage that it might cause.[78]

[75] For the contribution of the ILA, see generally, Bourne, C. B., 'The International Law Association's Contribution to International Water Resources Law' 36 *Natural Resources Journal* 155.

[76] *Lake Lanoux*, para 21. [77] *Lake Lanoux*, para 21–4.

[78] *Pulp Mills*, para 113; see also McCaffrey, *The Law of International Watercourses*; Boisson de Chazournes and Tignino, 'Droit international et eau douce'.

The Court concluded that Uruguay had the obligation to inform Argentina, through the Administrative Commission of the Uruguay River (CARU), when it prepared itself to issue the initial environmental authorization for the pulp mill. As it did not do so, Uruguay was in breach of its obligation to inform, notify, and negotiate under the 1975 Statute.[79]

## III) Relations with Other Principles

Regarding its scope and profile, the principle to notify and to consult is linked with the other principles of the Rio Declaration. Firstly, the principle contributes to the realization of the general principle of prevention (Principle 2). Considering that the ultimate purpose of the principle to notify and to consult is to protect other States from potential transboundary damage, the principle materializes the diligence expected from a State in protecting the environment. Thus the principle is closely linked with the principles which contribute to this materialization.

Secondly, this link can also be established with the principles of cooperation (Principles 18 and 27) and the principle of environmental impact assessment (Principle 17). The principle to notify and to consult appears as a specific application of the former, before an emergency arises (by contrast with Principle 18) and in a transboundary context (by contrast with Principle 27). Principle 17 is, as Principle 19, a modality of the realization of Principle 2 on prevention. More specifically, Principle 17 may be seen as a technique for implementing Principle 19 or, at least, to inform the cooperation called for by the latter.

The interconnection between these different principles reflects the integrated character of the Rio Declaration, which requires a holistic view of its principles in the protection of environment.[80]

## IV) Assessment

The basic rationale underlying the obligation to notify and consult is to prevent adverse transboundary effects on other States. Thus the principle appears as a mechanism to avoid disputes by creating the conditions for cooperation through notification and consultation.

A remaining challenge is to clarify more precisely its content. This will reduce the margin of appreciation of States with respect to its initiation and to the modalities of its implementation. Ensuring its respect is crucial for a sound protection of the environment. The ICJ has noted in this regard that:

> The Court considers that the procedural obligations of informing, notifying and negotiating constitute an appropriate means... These obligations are all the more vital when a shared resource is at issue, as in the case of the River Uruguay, which can only be protected through close and continuous co-operation between the riparian States.[81]

[79] *Pulp Mills*, paras 120–2.

[80] Boisson de Chazournes, L, Desgagné, R. Mbengue, M. M., Romano. C. (eds), *Protection internationale de l'environnement*, (Nouvelle éd. remise à jour et augmentée, Pedone 2005), 7–10.

[81] *Pulp Mills*, para 81.

## V) Select Bibliography

Boisson de Chazournes, L., Desgagné, R., Mbengue, M. M., and Romano. C. (eds), *Protection internationale de l'environnement* (Paris: Pedone 2005).

Boisson de Chazournes, L. and Tignino, M., 'Droit international et eau douce', in *Jurisclasseur, Environnement et developpement durable* (Paris: LexisNexis 2013), 1.

Bourne, C. B., 'The International Law Association's Contribution to International Water Resources Law' (1996) 36 *Natural Resources Journal* 155.

Boyle, A., 'The principle of co-operation: the environment', in Warbick, C. and Lowe, V. (eds), *The United Nations and the Principles of International Law, Essays in Memory of Michael Akehurst* (London: Routledge 1994), 120.

Delbrück, J., 'The International Obligation to Cooperate—An Empty Shell or a Hard Law Principle of International Law? A Critical Look at a Much Debated Paradigm of Modern International Law', in Hestermeyer, H. et al (eds), *Coexistence, Cooperation and Solidarity: Liber Amicorum Rüdiger Wolfrum* (Leiden: Nijhoff 2012), 3.

Farrajota, M. M., 'Notification and Consultation in the law applicable to international Watercourses' in Boisson de Chazournes, L. and Salman, S. M. A. (eds), *Water Resources and International Law* (The Hague: Academy of International Law/Martinus Nijhoff Publishers 2005), 281.

Francioni, F. and Neuhold, I., 'International Cooperation for the Protection of the Environment: The Procedural Dimension', in Lang, W., Neuhold, H., and Zemanek, K. (eds), *Environmental Protection and International Law* (London: Graham and Trotman 1991), 203.

Kiss, A. and Beurier, J.-P., *Droit international de l'environnement* (Paris: Pedone 2010).

Leb, C., *Cooperation in the Law of Transboundary Water Resources* (Cambridge University Press 2013).

McCaffrey, S. C., *The Law of International Watercourses* (Oxford University Press 2007).

Munro, R. and Lammers, J. G., *Environmental Protection and Sustainable Development: Legal Principles and Recommendations* (London: Graham and Trotman 1987).

Okowa, P., 'Procedural Obligations in International Environmental Agreements' (1997) 67 *BYIL* 275.

Salman, S. M. A. and Boisson de Chazournes, L., *Enhancing Cooperation and managing conflict—Proceeding of a World Bank Seminar*, World Bank Technical Paper n°414 (1998).

# 24. Principle 20

## *The Role of Women*

Claire Mahon*

**Principle 20**

Women have a vital role in environmental management and development. Their full participation is therefore essential to achieve sustainable development.



## I) Origins and Rationale of the Principle

Although the connection between the role of women in relation to the environment and development was discussed prior to 1992, it had not been previously recognized in an international instrument. Women make up approximately half of the world's population and whilst the role of women is evolving, their lives still vary greatly from those of men. The majority of people living in poverty are women and children and throughout the world women do not have access to the same opportunities as men. Women play a distinct role from men with respect to the environment as many of their daily domestic tasks require them to utilize natural resources. By doing so, they contribute to the management, protection, and use of the environment and have developed intimate knowledge and

* Claire Mahon is a Geneva-based international lawyer. She was a Research Fellow at the Geneva Academy of International Humanitarian Law and Human Rights, where she was joint Coordinator of the Project on Economic, Social and Cultural Rights. The author wishes to thank Shamistha Selvaratnam for her invaluable research and assistance in preparation of this chapter.

expertise from their experiences about how to manage the environment.[1] Further, women have valuable knowledge about natural resources as they are often the most affected by environmental degradation due to the high-level of interaction they have with the environment and their dependence on it to meet their daily needs.

In the years leading up to the Earth Summit, there was some discussion in international fora about the role of women; for example, in 1985, the link between women, the environment, and development was considered at the United Nation's Third World Conference on Women in Nairobi. In this instance, although no formal international instrument on the issue was adopted, women's participation in national and international ecosystem management was emphasized in the Nairobi Forward-looking Strategies for the Advancement of Women.[2] Meanwhile, at the Non-Governmental Organisations' Forum held in parallel to the Nairobi World Conference in 1985, an action plan was developed that focused on strengthening female leadership with respect to environmental management and educating women about environmental issues. Further, in 1987, the Report of the Brundtland Commission also mentioned the crucial role of women with respect to population growth, food security, education, and health.[3] These historical developments paved the way for the Rio Declaration, which was the first international instrument to recognize the vital role of women in achieving sustainable development.

The role of women in environmental management was not mentioned in the 1972 Stockholm Declaration and was not referenced in the General Assembly Resolution 44/228, which called upon UNCED to 'promote the further development of international environmental law'.[4] However, the Resolution did call for the examination of the 'feasibility of elaborating general rights and obligations of States... in the field of the environment' which allowed for the incorporation of Principle 20 into the Rio Declaration, thereby recognizing that women must be provided the opportunity to participate in decision-making so that policies take into account gender equality enabling sustainable development.

## II) The Principle as Enshrined in the Rio Declaration

### 1. Preparatory work and context

The first mention of the role of women was in the opening address by Maurice Strong, the Secretary-General of the UNCED, at the first PrepCom, where he referred to the contributions of important constituencies including women. However, the role of women was not on the agenda to be considered by Working Groups I or II. It was not until Working Group III was created during PrepCom II, which had a mandate allowing for the consideration of the rights and obligations of other stakeholders including women in development, that the role of women was discussed as a principle to be incorporated into the Rio Declaration.

[1] Oslo, 10 December 2004, Prof. Dr. Wangari Maathai, speech accepting the Nobel Peace Prize.
[2] *The Nairobi Forward-Looking Strategies for the Advancement of Women*, New York 1986.
[3] World Commission on Environment and Development, Our Common Future.
[4] General Assembly Resolution 44/228, 22 Dec, 1989.

Decision 3/5 was adopted in PrepCom III and focused on women in the environment and development, recognizing that a gender dimension is important in order to protect and enhance the environment. Specifically, it was decided that 'women should be recognized as active and equal participants' in ecosystem management and control of environmental degradation.

A G77 draft was submitted at PrepCom III which listed possible suggestions proposed by states for inclusion in the Declaration. With respect to the role of women, there were submissions by Australia, New Zealand, Norway, and Zimbabwe. Australia's submission focused on the right of women to 'full and active participation at all levels of activity relating to environment and development'. New Zealand stated that women should be accorded 'full partnership in all fields... including environment and development'. Norway submitted that the Rio Declaration should make reference to the 'role of women in the development process' and Zimbabwe submitted that States should act to ensure the 'incorporation of women's perspectives, aspirations, needs, concerns and participation at all levels... relating to the promotion of sustainable development'.[5]

At PrepCom IV the actual drafting of the Declaration text began. A G77 negotiating text was submitted and used as a basis for negotiations and discussion regarding the principles to be included in the Declaration. The initial wording of Principle 20 was:

> The role of women in all activities should reflect their central importance. Issues of special concern to women must be integrated into all aspects of environmental and developmental activities.[6]

The final text was narrowed down during PrepCom IV.[7] Significantly, Principle 20 was the first principle to be agreed upon. The role of women's groups, led by the former US Congresswoman Bella Abzug, played a significant role in this outcome. Throughout the world, women advocated for the recognition of their role in the environment. Most notably, before the PrepComs for UNCED met, two meetings were held which considered the importance of women's participation in environmental management in order to allow for sustainable development. The Global Assembly on Women and the Environment: Partners in Life, convened by SWAG,[8] issued the document 'Women's Perspectives: Recommendations of the Global Assembly for a Sustainable Future'. This document included findings and recommendations on women's points of view concerning environmental issues such as energy, water, and waste. WEDO organized the World Women's Congress for a Healthy Planet where the document 'Women's Action Agenda 21' was presented and the full and equal participation of women with respect to environmental issues was proposed. These documents, along with proposals submitted to be included in the debate at UNCED from different regions, which included information on the main environmental problems and their effects on women, were the basis for integrating gender equality issues into the official programme of UNCED and subsequently into the Rio Declaration.

[5] A-CONF.151-PC-WG.III-L.8-Rev.1 (1991), 6.
[6] A-CONF.151-PC-128, 91.
[7] A-CONF.151-PC-WG.III-L.33-Rev.1 (1992), 5.
[8] Senior Women's Advisory Group on Sustainable Development (SWAG) established by the United Nations Environment Programme (UNEP) in 1984 to (explore/study) the links between the role of women and the damage done to the environment in the course of development.

## 2. Scope and dimensions

### *2.1. The components of the principle*

#### 2.1.1. Women's role in 'environmental management'

The roles that men and women play in society are social constructions which have evolved over time with their origins in biological sex. Although the roles of men and women are varied due to socioeconomic, cultural, ethnic, and religious factors, men are traditionally the economic providers for their families and have little interaction with the environment around them. Women, on the other hand, are considered to be the primary caretakers of their families and carry out domestic tasks including food production, collecting water, gathering firewood for fuel, tending to their farms, and caring for and educating their children. Women are users, producers, and managers of natural resources and therefore have greater daily interaction with the environment as their everyday decisions involve the use of land, water, and energy.

Women have specific knowledge and experience in relation to the environment as a result of the material practices they perform on a daily basis and therefore, they play an essential role in the management and preservation of the earth's natural resources. However, women often lack decision-making power over natural resources making them vulnerable to environmental degradation. In developing countries women represent almost half of the global agricultural workforce, but are often denied the same access as men to agricultural resources and training. This restricts their ability to produce food for their families and use sustainable agricultural methods. As a result, women's productivity, agricultural output, and ability to contribute to economic growth is detrimentally affected. Principle 20 recognizes that by allowing women to fully participate in the management of environmental resources, their productivity and agricultural output can be increased, which has the potential to contribute to economic growth and sustainable development.

Furthermore, women are often the primary users of water in domestic consumption, agriculture, health, and sanitation. They play a central role in the management, allocation, and safeguarding of this resource. However, water deprivation is a serious concern as many countries lack a safe supply of water. This exposes women to numerous challenges as a result of using unsafe water, such as health risks. Allowing women to equally participate in the decision-making process is essential to take advantage of women's unique knowledge and experience with scarce resources such as water. This will ensure that services meet the different capacities of men and women and therefore enable the achievement of sustainable development.

#### 2.1.2. Women's role in development

Women play an essential role in economic development, social development, and environmental protection and ensuring their full participation in these three areas is critical to attaining sustainable development. Women constitute half of the world's human capital, however, their limited education and training affects their ability to contribute to economic growth and development. Women's domestic work is often unpaid and they lack access to resources and opportunities which would increase their productivity. By providing greater education to women, it not only increases their labour force participation and earning power, but also impacts the well-being of their families. It lowers infant and child mortality rates and reduces fertility which slows population growth. It also has the potential to reduce poverty and increase the likelihood that their children will receive an education. Thus, women have the ability to positively impact not only economic growth but also social development. This highlights the vital role women play in achieving sustainable development.

Women also have an important role in decision-making and policymaking with regard to development, as they are often directly affected by such decisions. Women's lack of involvement in decision-making stems from their low labour force participation and historical stereotypes. Traditionally, men have held positions of power preventing women from having a role in governance. However, Principle 20 emphasizes the importance of providing women with the opportunity to fully participate in policy development. This will ensure that policies are representative of the needs of society, therefore enabling development. Women offer differing perspectives on issues and have different priorities to those of men including issues related to marginalized and vulnerable groups and allowing them to actively participate in decision-making will not only benefit women but society as a whole and therefore assist in development.

#### 2.1.3. Women's full participation

Principle 20 calls for the 'full participation' of women in order for sustainable development to be achieved. Whilst participation refers to the engagement of women in the environmental, social, and economic aspects of development, 'full participation' with respect to gender is a much broader concept. 'Full participation' refers to the need for women to be able to engage in, contribute to, and benefit from sustainable development. It recognizes that it is essential for women to be given the opportunity to participate in environmental management to the same extent as men. Therefore, women should be given the ability to participate using their knowledge, skills, and experience so that sustainable development can be achieved through environmental management and development.

### *2.2. Legal nature*

Principle 20 contains no obligatory language but rather is a broad statement of recognition, containing no obligation or even goals or intentions on the part of those states making the declaration. Whereas other principles in the Rio Declaration utilize language such as 'states should' and 'states shall', Principle 20 is merely a policy statement. It contains insufficient content as to measures that need to be taken to give effect to the principle. However, there is a legal basis for the weakly-worded recognition of the importance of women's role, namely the treaty-based law that underlies Principle 20. This includes the right to freedom from discrimination[9] in the ICCPR, as well as the obligations contained in the Convention on the Elimination of Discrimination against Women ('CEDAW')[10] that aim to eradicate discrimination against women. Therefore, although Principle 20 does not on first blush appear mandatory, it is grounded in the well-established principles of international human rights law.

## 3. Normative impact

Principle 20 in the Rio Declaration was the first international instrument to explicitly recognize the need for the empowerment of women and the need for them to effectively

9 International Covenant on Civil and Political Rights, 16 December 1966, 999 UNTS 171, art 26.

10 Convention on the Elimination of All Forms of Discrimination Against Women, opened for signature 18 December 1979, 1249 UNTS 455 (entered into force 3 September 1981).

participate in environmental, economic and social processes as a condition for sustainable development. The inclusion of this provision led to the subsequent consideration and inclusion of women's role in relation to the environment in international environmental instruments, international gender-related conferences, and regional human rights instruments.

Principle 20 reaffirms the existing language used in the CEDAW. CEDAW utilizes the idea of participatory rights, which emphasize the need for measures to ensure that women have the opportunity to participate in all aspects of life. The Protocol to the African Charter on Human and People's Rights on the Rights of Women (2003),[11] which was influenced by the Rio Declaration, also utilizes participatory language. It recognizes the need for greater participation from women in managing and preserving the environment and that women should participate at all levels of decision-making and in the creation of development policies.

Principle 20 of the Rio Declaration contributed to the creation of international environmental instruments which have specific references to gender and the environment. The preamble of the Convention on Biological Diversity recognizes the 'vital role' of women in the conservation and sustainable use of biological diversity and affirms the need for the 'full participation of women' in policy-making and implementation.[12] Further, the preamble to the Convention to Combat Desertification stresses the 'important role' of women in regions affected by desertification and the importance of ensuring the 'full participation' of both men and women in programmes to combat desertification.[13]

International gender-related conferences following UNCED also considered the role of women with respect to the environment. In the outcome document of the International Conference on Population and Development held in Cairo in 1994, it was recognized that there is a need to empower women, improve their status, and ensure their 'full participation' as essential to achieving sustainable development.[14] At the Platform for Action of the Fourth World Conference on Women in Beijing in 1995, specific reference was made to the 'essential role' women have in developing sustainable and ecologically sound consumption, production patterns, and approaches to natural resource management.[15]

The UN Millennium Declaration reaffirmed the Rio Principles but did not make reference to the role of women in its section on 'protecting our common environment'.[16] Gender equality is, however, one of the values identified in the first section of the Declaration and 'gender equality and the empowerment of women' is also stressed as an effective way 'to combat poverty, hunger and disease and to stimulate development that is truly sustainable'.[17]

[11] Protocol to the African Charter on Human and Peoples' Rights on the Rights of Women in Africa, adopted by the 2nd Ordinary Session of the Assembly of the Union, Maputo, CAB/LEG/66.6 (13 September 2000).

[12] Convention on Biological Diversity, June 5, 1992, 1760 UNTS 79.

[13] Convention to Combat Desertification, 17 June 1994.

[14] 'Programme of Action', *Report of the International Conference on Population and Development* (A/CONF.171/13) 1994, New York.

[15] *Report of the Fourth World Conference on Women* (A/CONF.177/20) 1995, New York.

[16] UNGA Resolution 55/2 'United Nations Millennium Declaration' (2000), para 22.

[17] 'United Nations Millennium Declaration' (2000), para 20.

The outcome document of the Rio 2012 Summit, *The Future We Want*, makes reference to 'gender equality and women's empowerment' several times. In paragraph 45 of the section devoted to 'Engaging major groups and other stakeholders' the following is stated:

> We underscore that women have a vital role to play in achieving sustainable development. We recognize the leadership role of women and we resolve to promote gender equality and women's empowerment and to ensure their full and effective participation in sustainable development policies, programmes and decision-making at all levels.[18]

The outcome document subsequently devotes an entire section to 'Gender equality and women's empowerment',[19] the first paragraph of which reaffirms 'women's vital role and full and equal participation and leadership in all areas of sustainable development' and calls for accelerating the implementation of CEDAW, Agenda 21, the Beijing Declaration and the Millennium Declaration.

## III) Relations with Other Principles

### 1. Women and indigenous peoples as vulnerable/marginalized groups?

The marginalization of women and indigenous people is entrenched in tradition, history, and culture. Both historically and in recent times, women and indigenous persons have been the victims of human rights violations and as a result, they require special protection to ensure the equal and effective enjoyment of their human rights. Women are considered to be a vulnerable and marginalized group, especially in developing countries, as they have been and are still discriminated against on the basis of their gender, which has resulted in gender inequality in society such that women have often not been given the opportunity to actively participate in environmental management and development. Indigenous people, like women, are also considered to be a vulnerable group as they have been subject to colonization and racial discrimination. Principle 22 on the rights of indigenous people is similar to Principle 20 in that it seeks to protect the rights of a group of people who have been marginalized and therefore require separate protection to ensure their effective participation in environmental management and development.

### 2. Connection with Principle 10

Principle 10 is an important principle to be considered alongside Principle 20. Principle 10 focuses on participatory rights and like Principle 20, it calls for the participation of people in environmental management and development. However, Principle 10 is a much broader principle than Principle 20. It focuses on the participation of 'all concerned citizens' and articulates that each person should have 'appropriate access to information' concerning the environment and the 'opportunity to participate in decision-making processes'. It also contains obligatory language stating that 'States shall' facilitate and encourage participation and provides accountability by State parties.

Comparatively, Principle 20 is weakly formulated, calling for the participation of women without directly providing obligations on States or any accountability to States for

[18] *The Future We Want*, 11 September 2012, UN Doc A/Res/66/288, para 45.

[19] *The Future We Want*, paras 236–44.

failing to uphold the principle. However, as both principles refer to participatory rights, they can effectively be read together. The reference to 'active participation' in Principle 20 can be read as including the need for women to be given the opportunity to participate in decision-making, and being given access to relevant information by public authorities when required.

## IV) Assessment

The introduction of Principle 20 in the Rio Declaration marked a breakthrough in international law for women. The recognition of the importance of women's contribution to environmental management and development increased awareness of gender inequality. It has had a follow-on effect, resulting in the incorporation of gender issues in other international instruments and documents. It has also contributed to the movement towards the full realization of equal rights and opportunities for women. It is clear that the Rio Declaration increased the potential for women to participate in and benefit from sustainable development through the provision of greater opportunities and improved access to resources.

Although Principle 20 has resulted in progress in some areas with respect to gender equality, the ability of women to contribute to SD has not yet been fully realized.[20] There still remain great social and economic disparities between men and women and gender inequality remains entrenched in social attitudes. Although the role of women is evolving, women are still marginalized in many different aspects of life. Whilst some governments have made taken steps to advance women's self-sufficiency, in other states, women's rights have regressed. Despite the recognition of the vital role of women by the international community, it has not necessarily resulted in meaningful action in practice. Further, as the Rio Declaration is not legally binding on States and is considered to be 'soft law', it lacks enforcement mechanisms, States are not obliged to take steps to ensure that the objective of the principle is met and can instead avoid implementing measures that comply with the principle.

The Rio+20 Conference marked the 20th anniversary of the UNCED and the introduction of the Rio Declaration. This was an opportunity to consider the principles contained the Rio Declaration and to build upon them in setting a global environmental agenda for the next 20 years. At Rio+20, the commitment of the international community to gender equality was reaffirmed and it was acknowledged that women's full participation in environmental management and development is yet to be achieved. The outcome document of Rio+20, *The Future We Want*,[21] promotes women's empowerment and gender equality, not only in a separate section, but throughout the document in relation to decision-making, employment, health, maternal mortality, education, and food security, and nutrition. This demonstrates the importance of empowering women so they can participate in all aspects of life.

Whilst there was some progression in recognizing the rights of women at the Rio+20 Conference, an opportunity was missed to make actual progress for women's rights in not

[20] Rio+20: UN Conference on Sustainable Development, 20–22 June, 2012, *The Future We Want*, para 237.

[21] Resolution 66/288, UN Doc A/66/L.56 (Jul. 24, 2012) (outcome document adopted at Rio+20), available at <http://www.uncsd2012.org/content/documents/727The%20Future%C20We%C20Want%C2019%C20June%1 230pm.pdf>.

only environmental management but also in sustainable development. States committed themselves to promoting equal access of women and girls to 'education, basic services, economic opportunities, and health-care services'[22] and empowering women to be able to participate in sustainable development. However, they failed to deal with some critical aspects of sustainable development including failing to recognize that sexual and reproductive rights are critical to the attainment of sustainable development. Thus, the consensus amongst women's groups and advocates is that the outcome document of Rio+20 lacks any 'real progress and commitments for addressing pressing and critical sustainable development needs'.[23]

## V) Select Bibliography

International Women's Health Coalition (IWHC), Realizing Sexual and Reproductive Justice (RESURJ), Development Alternatives with Women for a New Era (DAWN), and the Youth Coalition for Sexual and Reproductive Rights (YCSRR), Analysis Paper on the Rio+20 Process and Outcome Document (2011), available at <http://www.dawnnet.org/advocacy-cso.php?id=254>.

Rico, M., 'Gender, the Environment, and the Sustainability of Development' (1998) 25 *United Nations Economic Commission for Latin America and the Caribbean*. 2LC/L.1144 October 1998, available at <http://www.cepal.org/publicaciones/xml/6/4706/lcl1144i.pdf>.

Warth, L. and Koparanova, M., 'Empowering Women for Sustainable Development', *United Nations Economic Commission for Europe*, UNECE Discussion Paper No 2012.1, Geneva 2012.

Women in Europe for a Common Future, 'Report: Activities, commitments and results at Rio+20 achieved by members of Women's Major Group and WECF in the run up to Rio and from 13–22 of June 2012' (2012).

Women's Major Group, 'Rio+20 Position Statement—Summary' (2011).

[22] Rio+20: UN Conference on Sustainable Development, 20–22 June, 2012, *The Future We Want*, para 240.

[23] IWHC, RESURJ, DAWN and YCSRR Analysis of Rio+20.

# 25. Principle 21

## *The Role of the Youth*

Magnus Jesko Langer*

**Principle 21**

The creativity, ideals and courage of the youth of the world should be mobilized to forge a global partnership in order to achieve sustainable development and ensure a better future for all.



## I) Origins and Rationale of the Principle

Without the inclusion of young people in the complexities of environmental governance, the entire international environmental law-making process would, to a large extent, be devoid of its compass. The insertion of the text of Principle 21 into the Rio Declaration was by no means a foregone conclusion, and in spite of the soft and ambiguous formulation of Principle 21, the mention of 'youth' in the web of principles contained in the Declaration is not only a significant victory for the many devoted young people involved in the Rio process, but even more importantly, a milestone in the new articulation of an environmental law inscribed in a transtemporal dimension.

Like some other principles of the Rio Declaration, Principle 21 is a prime example of a true soft law provision.[1] However, the first impression of international lawyers when

* Associate, Lévy Kaufmann-Kohler, Attorneys-at-Law, Geneva; PhD Candidate in International Law at the Graduate Institute, Geneva.

[1] On the concept of soft law in international environmental law, see Dupuy, P.-M., 'Soft Law and the International Law of the Environment' (1990–1991) 12 *Michigan Journal of International Law* 420.

reading Principle 21, which is that it lacks normativity, is misleading in at least three respects. First, on the epistemological level, were it not for the sake of our present youth and all future generations, the corpus of international environmental law could well remain within the confines of its classic framework, and thus determined by its bilateral and reparatory nature. Arguably, the real revolution brought about by UNCED lies in its holistic and transtemporal approach to global environmental governance, epitomized in the concepts of sustainable development, intergenerational equity, and ultimately youth mobilization so as to 'ensure a better future for all'.

Second, Principle 21 entertains a constructive relationship with most, if not all other principles of the Declaration. On the one hand, seeking active participation and input from youth is expected to increase the overall effectiveness in attaining the objectives enshrined in the Declaration. On the other hand, some provisions of the Declaration, mostly those with a future-oriented outlook, build upon the understanding that youth, on a global scale, will receive the necessary information and education in environmental matters so as to influence our future behaviours in line with the overarching objective of sustainable development.

Third, and notwithstanding its soft formulation, Principle 21 constitutes more than just a political formulation of good intentions. Indeed, Principle 21 provides interesting insights into the diverse facets of the international law-making process. For instance, a host of institutional arrangements have mushroomed in the aftermath of Rio 1992, notably through international organizations or at international conferences, so as to include youth movements in decision-making processes. Youth advocacy may nowadays eventually lead to real outcomes in terms of the drafting of environmental norms and maybe even more so in securing their implementation. On another level, the spirit of Principle 21 percolates gradually into the legislative landscape of many States, notably through the adoption of legislative or other measures providing for the inclusion of environmental education and training into the curricula of schools and universities.

## II) The Principle as Enshrined in the Rio Declaration

### 1. Preparatory work and context

The inclusion of Principle 21 in the Rio Declaration is essentially the result of three loosely-related developments. First, on the more general level, the UN had already been fostering youth participation in UN matters for several decades. Since the mid-1960s, the UN repeatedly called on its member States to include youth as members of national delegations in the UN process (at large, although at that time with a particular focus on peace and development).[2] Second, the intergenerational approach which came to dominate the

[2] See, for instance: Res. 2037 (XX) of 7 December 1965 *Declaration on the Promotion among Youth of the Ideals of Peace, Mutual Respect and Understanding between Peoples*; Res. 2447 (XXIII) of 19 December 1968 *Education of youth in the respect for human rights and fundamental freedoms*; Res. 2497 (XXIV) of 28 October 1969 *Youth, its education in the respect for human rights and fundamental freedoms, its problems and needs, and participation in international development*; Res. 2499 (XXIV) of 31 October 1969 *Celebration of the twenty-fifth anniversary of the United Nations*; Res. 2633 (XXV) of 11 November 1970 *Youth, its education in the respect of human rights and fundamental freedoms, its problems and needs, and its participation in national development*; Res. 31/130 of 16 December 1976 *Role of youth*; Res. 33/7 of 3 November 1978 *International Youth Year*; Res. 34/151 of 17 December 1979 *International Youth Year: Participation, Development, Peace*; A/RES/40/14 of 18 November 1985 *International Youth Year: Participation, Development, Peace*; A/RES/43/196 of 20 December 1988 *United Nations Conference on Environment and Development*; A/RES/44/228 of

Rio process made inclusion of youth as distinctive participants in the process almost inevitable. Finally, and maybe more directly, through their activism and self-mobilization, various youth organizations or young individuals feeling a certain 'sense of urgency' benefited from the momentum achieved in the build-up of UNCED and made their voice clear and present.[3] In any event, the pathos in the wording of Principle 21 suggests that this provision was not the result of a detailed and meticulous drafting process.

Pursuant to Res. 43/196, the General Assembly of the UN decided in Res. 44/228 of 22 December 1989 to convene UNCED.[4] This resolution also marks the entry point for participation of various stakeholders in PrepCom, providing for 'participation of observers, in accordance with the established practice of the General Assembly'.[5] This, together with the invitation extended to NGOs with consultative status at ECOSOC to contribute to the conference,[6] technically allowed youth organizations or representatives to actively take part in the process, albeit in various capacities. National and international associations of the youth movement were able to participate, if they qualified as NGOs, and some States such as Sweden pioneered in including young persons in their delegations.[7]

In the build-up to UNCED, several youth organizations held special events to discuss programmes of action.[8] For instance, following a Global Seminar Series in 1988 on environmental matters, a World Theme Conference was held in August 1990 in Tokyo leading to the adoption of the 'Youth Action Guide'.[9] A 'World Youth Preparatory Forum for UNCED' (Youth'92) was organized in March 1992 in San José, Costa Rica, leading to the adoption of the World Youth Statement for UNCED.[10]

With regard to the PrepCom proceedings, the role of 'youth' was not discussed at all during the first two sessions.[11] At PrepCom III, three decisions on the involvement of

22 December 1989 *United Nations Conference on Environment and Development.* For further youth resolutions, refer to: <http://undesadspd.org/Youth/ResourcesandPublications/Youthresolutions.aspx> (all websites referred to in this chapter have been last accessed on 28 December 2013).

[3] Woods, Z., 'Young People and Sustainable Development', in: Dodds, F. (ed), *The Way Forward: Beyond Agenda 21* (Earthscan 1997), 158.

[4] A/RES/44/228 of 22 December 1989, operative Part I, para 1.

[5] A/RES/44/228 of 22 December 1989, operative Part II, para 1.

[6] A/RES/44/228 of 22 December 1989, operative Part II, para 12 in combination with para 11.

[7] In fact, next to representatives of 172 governments, 2400 representatives of NGOs, including youth organizations, had finally registered for participation in the Rio Conference; see <http://www.un.org/geninfo/bp/enviro.html>. During the four meetings of the PrepCom, some governmental delegations even pioneered a movement to include NGO-representatives as members, led by the Canadian delegation. See Dawkins, K., *Sharing Rights and Responsibilities for the Environment: Assessing Potential Roles for Non-Governmental Organizations in International Decision-Making* (MIT 1991), 48.

[8] MacDonald, M., *Agendas for Sustainability: Environment and Development in the Twenty-First Century* (Routledge/SEI 1998), 10. See also Alpizar, L., 'Youth Participation in the UNCED Process', in: IISD, *Youth Source Book on Sustainable Development*, available at: <http://www.iisd.org/youth/ysbk086.htm>.

[9] See AIESEC, *Youth Action Guide on Sustainable Development: A Guide for Young People and Others interested in Environment and Development Initiatives*, AIESEC World Theme Conference, Tokyo, Japan, 22–26 August 1990 (AIESEC International 1990).

[10] Youth 92, *World Youth Statement and Plan of Action on Environment and Development*, San José, Costa Rica, 22–29 March 1992.

[11] Following a meeting on organizational matters in New York from 5–16 March 1990 (PrepCom I a), the first meeting on substantive matters was held from 6–31 August 1990 in Nairobi (PrepCom I b); the second meeting took place in Geneva from 18 March to 5 April 1991 (PrepCom II), as did the third meeting from 12 August to 4 September 1991 (PrepCom III); the fourth meeting took place in New York from 3 March to 3 April 1992 ('PrepCom IV'). For the matters dealt with during these meetings, see Halpern, S., *The United Nations Conference on Environment and Development: Process and Documentation* (United Nations 1992), available at: <http://www.ciesin.org/docs/008-585/unced-ch1.html>.

civil society were adopted: one on 'Women in environment and development', another on 'Youth in environment', and the third on 'Indigenous people and local communities'.[12] Having recalled 'the vital role that youth can and should play in the protection of the environment and the promotion of economic and social development', the Committee decided to include in Decision 3/6 'the promotion of the effective participation of youth in the field of environment and development' as a 'global goal' both in the Rio Declaration and in the Agenda 21.[13]

During that session, and on the basis of proposals submitted by (groups of) States to the Working Group III ('WG III') dealing with 'cross-sectoral' issues,[14] the Chairman of WG III submitted a consolidated draft on 'principles on general rights and obligations',[15] Principle 3 of which covered the rights of individuals and of groups.[16] At this stage of the deliberations and in spite of the fact that WG III had adopted Decision 3/6, none of the proposals submitted by (groups of) States included a reference to 'youth'.[17]

At PrepCom IV, WG III further considered the question of 'principles on general rights and obligations' on the basis of proposals submitted by (groups of) States.[18] Pakistan, on behalf of the Group of 77 and China, introduced a draft decision entitled 'Rio de Janeiro Charter/Declaration on Environment and Development' which reflected several amendments to the text originally introduced.[19] While both the 'role of women' and the concerns 'of indigenous cultures and local communities' were included, the role of youth was not mentioned.[20] It was only on 2 April 1992, the penultimate day of PrepCom IV, that the chairman of the PrepCom introduced a text entitled 'Principles on General Rights and Obligations—Rio Declaration on Environment and Development' containing for the first time Principle 21 in its actual wording.[21] This text eventually became the final draft Principle 21 without any substantive discussion on its content.[22]

[12] PrepCom III, 15, 16, paras 56–8; the relevant decisions 3/5, 3/6 and 3/7 are reproduced on 40–1.

[13] PrepCom III, 41, Decision 3/6. At the same time, the Committee asked the Secretariat to present to the fourth session of the Committee 'concrete recommendations and specific actions needed in each of the sectoral and cross-sectoral areas of Agenda 21 to ensure the effective participation of youth towards the integration of environment and development'.

[14] During its first substantive session, PrepCom decided to establish a Working Group III dealing with 'legal, institutional, and all related matters', including 'cross-sectoral issues'. See PrepCom I b, 8 and 28. Cross-sectoral matters included, *inter alia*, poverty, sustainability, health, and education; under the heading 'sustainability' also the issues relating to women, youth, and indigenous people were subsumed. See PrepCom III, 15, para 50 *seq.*

[15] WG III consolidated draft on 'principles on general rights and obligations', A/CONF.151/PC/WG.III/L.8/Rev.1.

[16] WG III consolidated draft, 6 *seq.*

[17] WG III consolidated draft, proposals of Australia, 6, para 13; Denmark, para 17; Holy See, para 18; New Zealand, 7, para 22; Norway, para 24; Jamaica, 8, para 32; Zimbabwe, para 35. In this context, Malta submitted a proposal to appoint a 'guardian' of future generations who would make submissions on behalf of these generations, 8, para 33. The full text of the Maltese proposal is reproduced in Doc A/CONF.151/PC/WG.III/L.8/Rev.1/Add.2 of 21 February 1992. This proposal was, however, not pursued further.

[18] See PrepCom IV, Annex IV, Report of Working Group III, 82–113.

[19] See PrepCom IV, 86, para 15.

[20] See PrepCom IV, 91, Principle 20 (role of women) and Principle 21 (productive activities of indigenous cultures and local communities).

[21] Doc A/CONF.151/PC/WG.III/L.33/Rev. 1. On 2 April 1992, this text was transmitted by WG III to the plenary of PrepCom. See PrepCom IV, 113, para 9. It was then introduced for consideration and decision by the Conference as Doc A/CONF.151/5 'Rio Declaration on Environment and Development'.

[22] UNCED Report, vol I, 3.

Regarding the inclusion of Principle 21, Alpizar claims that it was the influence of youth organizations that led to this result,[23] and Chee notes that the 'three most visible and active lobby groups, in addition to NGOs, were women, youth, and indigenous peoples' groups'. She therefore assumes that their influence 'was largely the reason for the specific inclusion of these three principles'—ie Principles 20 (women), 21 (youth), and 22 (indigenous peoples)—in the final draft.[24] It appears that after different (groups of) States had introduced proposals without any reference to youth, youth representatives managed to influence consultations within WG III.[25] For instance, youth representatives were allowed on several occasions to take the floor already during the plenary and working group meetings of PrepCom IV.[26] In addition, the UNCED Secretariat under its Secretary-General, Maurice Strong, supported the idea to promote the involvement of youth in sustainable development, as Maurice Strong also underlined during his opening statement to the Conference on 3 June 1992.[27]

## 2. Scope and dimensions

### *2.1. Legal nature*

Notwithstanding the political declarations adopted by the UN General Assembly since the 1960s calling on member States to foster youth participation in decision-making processes, the idea that youth has a crucial role to play in environmental governance is one of the *new* advances achieved by UNCED. Principle 21 is neither a legal principle nor a rule of international law imposing clear-cut obligations on States. In this sense, Principle 21 is a prime example of a soft law provision, enshrined in a soft instrument, and with a soft content.

And yet, the normative incidence of Principle 21 is at least twofold. On the one hand, Principle 21 is a crucial building block of the concept of sustainable development.

[23] Alpizar, L., 'Youth Participation in Global Decision-Making Processes—The official UNCED Preparatory Process', in: IISD, *Youth Source Book on Sustainable Development*, available at: <http://www.iisd.org/youth/ysbk088.htm>. Alpizar adds that 'the text developed by the UNCED Secretariat with no real consultation with the youth sector, was far from fulfilling youth expectations'. For a summary of PrepCom proceedings with regard to the strengthening of the role of major groups, see also ESB, vol 1, No 27, 20 April 1992, 6: 'In the section on youth, Canada took the lead in proposing amendments'. As mentioned earlier in note 7, Canada was the first country to include NGO representatives in its delegation.

[24] Chee, Y. L., *The Rio Declaration on Environment and Development: An Assessment* (Third World Network 2012), 53.

[25] The participation of youth organizations in the Conference itself gave, however, rise to some incidents. As mentioned by Alpizar 'the internal television system mysteriously "broke down"', when the Kenyan youth delegate, Ms Wagaki Mwangi, on behalf of the youth organizations represented during the conference, addressed the 13th plenary session of the conference on 11 June 1992. Due to this breakdown, the statement was audible only in the plenary room, but not outside, as was the case with the statements of other delegates. As Alpizar insinuates, this breakdown was organized on purpose, since Wagaki Mwangi's statement was highly critical of the UNCED process. Alpizar mentions too that security forces broke up a youth press conference following the speech and that the conference passes of some youth delegates were withdrawn. See Alpizar, L., 'Youth participation in Global Decision-Making Processes—The Earth Summit, Rio Centro', in: IISD, *Youth Source Book on Sustainable Development*, available at: <http:www.iisd.org/youth/ysbk099.htm>.

[26] See eg ESB vol 1 No 17, 24 March 1992, 1; ESB vol 1 No 19, 26 March 1992, 2.

[27] 'No constituencies are more important in all countries than women, youth and children... The views, concerns and the interests of our youth and children must be respected and they must be provided with expanding opportunities to participate in the decisions which will shape the future that is so largely theirs'. See Statement by Maurice Strong, reproduced in: UNCED Report, vol II at 50.

Awareness raising, education, and mobilization of youth are indeed the guarantors that future decision-makers and constituencies will comprehend the complexities of sustainable development. On the other hand, Principle 21 has developed a normative dynamic of its own, notably in terms of influencing institutional practices of international organizations and in terms of initiating educational reforms within States.

Finally, young people and youth organizations can legitimately rely on Principle 21 to increasingly claim their entitlement to participate in environmental decision-making processes at local, national, regional, and international levels.

## *2.2. Youth as a 'Major Group'*

Agenda 21, the programme of action for implementing the Rio Declaration, formulates objectives and defines activities involving 'all social groups', in the 'implementation of the objectives, policies and mechanisms agreed to by the Conference in all programme areas of Agenda 21'.[28] Section 3 of Agenda 21 deals with strengthening the role of so-called 'major groups'.[29] Chapter 23 of Agenda 21 extends any policy, definition, or rule regarding NGO access to and participation in the implementation of Agenda 21 to all major groups, its main tenet being that broad public participation is 'essential to achieving sustainable development'.[30] 'Youth and children' form one such major group, and are dealt with in more detail in chapter 25 of Agenda 21.[31]

While Agenda 21 refers to both youth and children, Principle 21 only mentions youth. During the Plenary at PrepCom, the Swedish delegation launched an initiative to include in chapter 25 of the Agenda 21 a new programme area referring to children, in addition to the programme area 'Advancing the role of youth', as originally drafted.[32] This resulted in the inclusion of a new section entitled 'Children in sustainable development'.

It may thus come as a surprise that Principle 21, contrary to Agenda 21, only mentions 'youth' and not also 'children'. There is no established definition of 'youth'. For statistical purposes, the UN has defined 'youth' since 1985 to include persons aged between 15 and 24 years,[33] whereas the UN Convention on the Right of the Child defines 'children'

[28] See Agenda 21 in Report of the UN Conference on Environment and Development, 9. For the *travaux préparatoires* of Agenda 21, see Halpern, *Preparations for the UNCED*, 2–3. In contrast to the Rio Declaration, the most controversial parts of the final text of the Agenda 21 were negotiated during the Conference itself. See also ESB, vol 1, no 27, 1.

[29] Agenda 21, ch 23, para 1. As enumerated in chapters 24 to 32, 'major groups' are the following nine groups: women, children and youth, indigenous people, non-governmental organizations, local authorities, trade unions, business and industry, scientific and technological community, and farmers. This early recognition of 'major groups' as representatives of social groups during the preparations for the conference was a major breakthrough for the standing of NGOs in international negotiations. See further, Kaasa, S. M., *The Commission on Sustainable Development: A Study of Institutional Design, Distribution of Capabilities and Entrepreneurial Leadership* (Fridtjof Nansen Institute 2005), 43, available at: <www.fni.no/doc&pdf/FNI-R0505.pdf>.

[30] Agenda 21, ch 23, para 1.

[31] For more information on the Major Group for Children and Youth ('MGCY'), see <http://www.uncsd childrenyouth.org/index.html>.

[32] ESB, vol 1, No 19, 2.

[33] See eg E/CN.9/2012/4, Report of the Secretary-General *Adolescents and youth*, 3, para 2: 'A chronological definition of who is young, as opposed to who is a child or who is an adult, varies with each nation and each culture. However, the United Nations, for statistical purposes, defines persons between the ages of 15 and 24 as youth without prejudice to other definitions by Member states'. All General Assembly resolutions mentioned in note 2 to this chapter only refer to 'youth'.

as every human being below the age of 18 years.[34] Other institutions define youth as those persons aged between 10 and 24. Therefore, there is a partial overlap between both categories, which might lead some observers to conclude, albeit erroneously, that children (under the age of 15, for instance) are not included in Principle 21. In 2011, the Major Group for Children & Youth ('MGCY') in the Commission on Sustainable Development finally resolved all uncertainty by determining the age of 30 as its upper age limit.[35]

The omission of children may be explained by the fact that Principle 21 is worded in terms of youth participation in the various decision-making processes dealing with sustainable development. In this sense, the omission may be irrelevant to the extent that children (under the age of 15) arguably do not yet possess the necessary tools to frame their interests in terms of policy proposals, for instance, at international conferences. Nonetheless, Principle 21 is not limited to the aspect of participation in decision-making, but extends also to awareness raising, education, and training. It would therefore be unreasonable to exclude children from the scope of Principle 21, simply because children 'will inherit the responsibility of looking after the Earth', as aptly formulated in Agenda 21.[36]

## 2.3. *Youth mobilization as set out in Agenda 21*

Principle 21 postulates that the international community should 'mobilize' youth in order to increase the likelihood of achieving sustainable development.[37] Youth mobilization is best understood as a two-way street. On the one hand, the international community is to involve youth by providing incentives, information, resources, facilities, platforms, and networking possibilities so as to foster youth awareness. But this implies on the other hand, that the international community is to be receptive and sensitive to the 'creativity, ideals and courage',[38] which young people potentially contribute to the general debate on means of achieving sustainable development.

Chapter 25 of Agenda 21 deals with the involvement of youth and children in sustainable development. Because youth represent such an important part of the world's population, Agenda 21 acknowledges that the involvement of youth in environmental

[34] Convention on the Rights of the Child, 20 November 1989, 1577 UNTS 3, art 1. On the various definitions of youth within the UN system, see: <http://www.un.org/esa/socdev/documents/youth/fact-sheets/youth-definition.pdf>.

[35] CSD Major Group for Children and Youth, Processes and Procedures Document, April 2011, point 3.0, available at: <http://uncsdchildrenyouth.org/pdfs/MGCY-Processes-and-Procedures_ADOPTED_April2011.pdf>.

[36] Agenda 21, ch 25, para 12. See also A/RES/S-27/2 of 22 October 2002, *A World Fit for Children*, para 7, point 9, where it is said that '[c]hildren and adolescents are resourceful citizens capable of helping to build a better future for all. We must respect their right to express themselves and to participate in all matters affecting them, in accordance with their age and maturity'.

[37] See the critical comments of the Stakeholder Forum, 186 and again 190: 'A significant challenge to implementing this Principle is the ambiguity in the text regarding the mobilization of the youth. It does not define *who* can play a role in mobilizing the youth nor does it outline *how* the youth ought to be mobilized in order to fulfill the desired objective. Furthermore, the "global partnership" is not expressly defined: it begs the question "who" is a part of the partnership?'.

[38] This wording resembles the one employed in General Assembly Res. 2037 (XX) of 7 December 1965, preambular para 8, which stated that 'the *energies, enthusiasm and creative abilities* of the young should be devoted to the material and spiritual advancement of all peoples' (emphasis added).

governance 'is critical to the long-term success of Agenda 21'.[39] A series of measures is proposed to States to involve youth, in particular:

- consulting with youth and involving them in decision-making processes with regard to the environment at the local, national, and regional levels;
- dialoguing on environment plans and programmes and development issues;
- considering recommendations by youth for inclusion in policy measures;
- ensuring access of youth to education;
- developing and implementing strategies for alternative employment;
- establish joint task forces to develop educational and awareness programmes;
- involving youth in international meetings by including their representatives in Government delegations.[40]

Accordingly, States are to engage at all relevant levels in a dialogue with youth and facilitate access to information.[41] They are also called upon to increase youth access to education, reduce youth unemployment, and combat human rights abuses against youth.[42] Finally, States are invited to support youth representation in all UN processes.[43]

For their part, international organizations are urged to review their respective youth programmes and to disseminate relevant information to youth organizations.[44] In this respect, UNEP, UNDP, and UNESCO play a key role in the implementation of Principle 21.[45]

### 2.4. *Participation in environmental decision-making processes*

The preamble of the Rio Declaration refers to the creation of a 'global partnership' so as to involve all relevant stakeholders in sustainable development. According to Principle 21 such a 'global partnership' can only become reality if youth is adequately included in this process. Thus, the main objective underlying Principle 21 is to foster youth participation in decision-making processes at all relevant levels. As to the realization of this 'global partnership', international organizations, and in particular the UN and its various agencies, are playing the central role in securing that all relevant stakeholders, including youth, are incorporated in the process.[46]

After UNCED, the UN progressively developed new avenues for youth participation. These efforts include the development of general policy instruments designed to address youth mobilization in matters of environmental governance, increased access to international conferences dealing with environmental matters, use of new technologies to communicate and circulate information relating to sustainability issues, and the organization of workshops or youth forums.

The Commission on Sustainable Development ('CSD'), set up to 'monitor progress in the implementation of Agenda 21',[47] provided a platform for the major groups to participate in its work and contribute to the deliberations.[48] During its first session from 14 to 25 June 1993, the CSD decided that any NGO accredited to participate at PrepCom of UNCED

[39] Agenda 21, ch 25, para 1. [40] Agenda 21, ch 25, para 9. [41] Agenda 21, ch 25, para 4.
[42] Agenda 21, ch 25, paras 5–6 and 8. [43] Agenda 21, ch 25, para 7.
[44] Agenda 21, ch 25, para 10. [45] See eg Agenda 21, ch 36, para 4(b) and ch 38, para 25(f).
[46] On the concept of global partnership, refer to A/RES/64/223 of 21 December 2009.
[47] A/RES/47/191 of 22 December 1992, para 3(a). The establishment of the CSD was recommended in Agenda 21, ch 38, paras 11–15.
[48] A/RES/47/191 of 22 December 1992, para 7(b). See also Report of the Secretary-General on Rules of Procedure of the CSD, 4–8, paras 14–20.

would also be accredited to the CSD.[49] The CSD also invited governments to report periodically on environment and development issues affecting, *inter alia*, youth.[50] The role of the major groups was enhanced in 1997 by the introduction of multi-stakeholder dialogues, thus promoting the dialogue between Governments and the major groups in intergovernmental decision-making processes.[51] It has been observed that this development constituted a 'giant step towards the formalization of the major groups' roles as active contributors to sustainable development assigned to them by Agenda 21'.[52] Furthermore, under the coordination of the UN Non-governmental Liaison Service, a CSD Major Group for Children and Youth was formed, its mission being to 'ensure that the interests of children and youth are taken into account in the planning and decision making processes, and that youth in particular participate meaningfully in the CSD-processes'.[53]

On 14 December 1995, the General Assembly adopted the World Programme of Action for Youth ('WPAY'),[54] listing environment and education as two of the ten priority areas.[55] Stating that UNCED had recognized that 'the involvement of youth in environment and development decision making is critical to the implementation of policies of sustainable development', the General Assembly concluded that young people should be increasingly involved in designing and implementing appropriate environmental policies.[56] Referring to WPAY, the General Assembly again emphasized in 2009 the importance of strengthening participation of young people 'as important actors in the protection, preservation, and improvement of the environment at the local, national, and international levels, as envisioned in Agenda 21'.[57]

Following up on WPAY, the UN Secretariat, through its Department of Economic and Social Affairs ('DESA'), together with other UN agencies, set up the 'United Nations Inter-Agency Network on Youth Development' ('IANYD') which meanwhile has grown to 40 members.[58] The Network aims at increasing the effectiveness of UN work related to

[49] This decision was taken on the basis of ECOSOC decision E/1993/215, 12 February 1993. See, Report of the Commission on Sustainable Development on its First Session (New York, 14–25 June 1993), E/1993/25/Add.1, 30 June 1993, para 18. Interested NGOs were given the floor as of the first session. See also Kaasa, *The Commission on Sustainable Development*, 43.

[50] E/CN.17/1993/L.3/Rev.1, 22 June 1993, para 7(m).

[51] DESA, Background information on Major Groups participation in the CSD, available at: <http://sustainabledevelopment.un.org/index.php?menu=1540>.

[52] See CSD Multi-Stakeholder Dialogues, Background Paper No 4, 11.

[53] See UN CSD Youth Caucus: Major Group for Children and Youth Processes and Procedures, April 2011; available at: <http://www.un-ngls.org/IMG/pdf/MGCY_Processes_and_Procedures_ADOPTED_April2011_1_.pdf>.

[54] A/RES/50/81 of 14 December 1995, Annex, *World Programme of Action for Youth to the Year 2000 and Beyond.*

[55] *World Programme of Action for Youth to the Year 2000 and Beyond*, Part IV, A. Education, paras 21–32; E. Environment, paras 64–72, and Part V, Means of implementation at the national, regional and international levels, through data collection and dissemination of information; Research and policy studies; Planning and coordination; Technical cooperation, training and advisory services, and Outreach and partnership among specialized constituencies.

[56] *World Programme of Action for Youth to the Year 2000 and Beyond*, para 70.

[57] A/RES/64/130, *Policies and programmes involving youth*, 18 December 2009, para 5(b). See also: A/RES/58/133, *Policies and programmes involving youth*, 22 December 2003.

[58] IANYD was set up during a Meeting of the UN Heads of Youth Programs at the UNESCO headquarter in Paris on 18 and 19 February 2010, see: <http://www.unesco.org/new/en/social-and-human-sciences/themes/youth/international-year-of-youth/inter-agency-cooperation/>. In environmental matters the following UN agencies or entities are members: The Secretariats of the CBD, UNFCCC, UNCCD, UNDP, UNEP, UN Habitat; and the following regional commissions: ECLAC, ESCAP, ECA, ESCWA, and ECE.

youth development by strengthening the cooperation between the entities concerned.[59] In the framework of the WPAY, the Network reviews the progress on the implementation of UN resolutions and supports youth involvement and participation in UN activities.[60]

Although the outcome documents of the Johannesburg World Summit on Sustainable Development ('WSSD') do not specifically refer to youth mobilization,[61] youth participation in the preparatory process of WSSD, notably as members of national delegations, was noted with appreciation by youth representatives.[62] Nonetheless, youth delegates also highlighted that efforts to increase youth participation in decision-making processes in general were still insufficient.[63]

The outcome document of Rio+20 entitled *The Future We Want* emphasizes the crucial importance of broad public participation and access to information, in particular by the major groups identified in Agenda 21.[64] With specific focus on youth, the document underscores the vital link between the concept of sustainable development, the intergenerational approach, and the role of youth.[65]

For its part, UNEP started to involve young people on the occasion of the International Youth Year in 1985. After UNCED, UNEP expanded its activities continuously to mobilize youth. In 2003, the UNEP Governing Council endorsed the first strategy of cooperation with youth under the title 'Tunza Youth Strategy'.[66] The programme activities include, in particular, awareness building, participation of youth in decision-making, promoting environmental education and information exchange, all to be implemented at the interregional, regional, and national levels. According to UNEP, Tunza generated a network of over 30,000 children and youth organizations allowing UNEP to reach out to millions of young people worldwide.[67] Tunza International Children and Youth Conferences also offer opportunities for adopting declarations like the 2011 Bandung Declaration in preparation for the Rio+20 Conference.[68] In 2013, the Tunza International Youth Conference

[59] Quoting a statement by the Secretary-General that, with one exception, 'no joint work plan has, to date, been adopted by the various inter-agency mechanisms', the organization 'YouthPolicy' has voiced doubts as to the usefulness of the network. YouthPolicy, 'The UN and youth—a cacophony of inconsistent action', 6 August 2012, available at: <http://www.youthpolicy.org/blog/2012/08/un-youth-cacophony>; referring to the Report of the Secretary-General, *Implementation of the World Programme of Action for Youth: United Nations System Coordination and Collaboration Related to Youth*, A/66/61-E/2011/3, 22 November 2010, 13, para 62.

[60] UN Inter-Agency Network on Youth Development, see <http://social.un.org/youthyear/unianyd.html>.

[61] However, the Johannesburg Declaration underscores the continued importance of the major groups and vows to strengthen cooperation with them in accordance with Agenda 21, the Millennium Development Goals and the WSSD Plan of Implementation. See A/CONF.199/20, Annex *Johannesburg Declaration on Sustainable Development*, paras 26 and 30.

[62] See eg A/CONF.199/PC/2, 26, para 11. See also the 'Dialogue paper by youth', E/CN.17/2002/PC.2/6/Add.2, 12 December 2001.

[63] A/CONF.199/PC/2, 27, para 16(t).

[64] A/RES/66/288 of 27 July 2012, para 43.

[65] 'We stress the importance of the active participation of young people in decision-making processes, as the issues we are addressing have a deep impact on present and future generations and as the contribution of children and youth is vital to the achievement of sustainable development. We also recognize the need to promote intergenerational dialogue and solidarity by recognizing their views', A/RES/66/288 of 27 July 2012, para 50.

[66] Tunza, in the Eastern African language Kiswahili, means 'to treat with care or affection'. For the first Tunza Youth Strategy 2003–2009, see UNEP/GC.23/3/Add.1/Rev.1 of 19 December 2002. For the second Tunza Youth Strategy 2009–2014, see UNEP/GC.25/10 of 28 October 2008.

[67] UNEP/GC.25/10 of 28 October 2008, *Final review of the long-term strategy on the engagement and involvement of young people in environmental issues*, Report by the Executive Director, 3, para 5.

[68] The UNEP Tunza International Children and Youth Conference 2011 took place in Bandung, Indonesia, from 27 September to 1 October 2011 and adopted the Bandung Declaration on The Voice of Children and Youth for Rio+20; see: <http://www.unep.bayer.com/de/Bandung-Declaration-2011.pdfx>.

in Nairobi led to the launching of 'Tunza Acting for a Better World: GEO-5 for Youth', a publication engaging youth in environmental issues. UNEP also provides a platform for the Tunza Youth Advisory Council to participate in UNEP's decision-making process by permitting the review of the decisions adopted on the occasion of the UNEP Governing Council/Global Ministerial Environmental Forum ('GC/GMEF').

Also, other UN organizations participated in the process of engaging youth for sustainable development. For instance, the Food and Agriculture Organization ('FAO') maintains a Youth Portal containing information on many environmental themes, publishes youth guides on environmental topics such as climate change, or organizes mini projects engaging young people on the ground such as tree planting excursions. For its part, UNDP implements the GEF Small Grants Programme ('SGP') by putting special emphasis on youth and children. Thus, it provides grants to youth projects in climate change mitigation and adaptation. Other grants are provided for the organization of workshops, signature campaigns, or cultural events such as environmental fairs. UNICEF organized a Children's Climate Forum in the advent of UNFCCC COP15 in Copenhagen in 2009.[69] UNICEF also developed Classroom Education Programmes and sponsors other workshops seeking to raise awareness in school classrooms.

## 2.5. *Environmental education and awareness raising*

Mobilization of youth through participation in decision-making processes is the explicit idea underpinning Principle 21. But effective mobilization presupposes the existence of a more profound dimension constituted of the triptych of awareness raising, education, and training. It is puzzling that the Rio Declaration does not contain a single reference to education, let alone environmental education,[70] while Agenda 21 repeatedly highlights its importance in the context of sustainable development.[71] This omission is all the more astonishing since the 1972 Stockholm Declaration expressly referred to education as a core element of environmental governance and that important milestones were reached in the wake of UNCHE. Principle 19 of the Stockholm Declaration reads as follows:

> Education in environmental matters, for the younger generation as well as adults, giving due consideration to the underprivileged, is essential in order to broaden the basis for an enlightened opinion and responsible conduct by individuals, enterprises and communities in protecting and improving the environment in its full human dimension.[72]

[69] In 1993, UNICEF already decided to incorporate a 'primary environmental care ('PEC') perspective' into its assistance programmes. See in this regard, UNICEF Decision 1993/14, para 1(a); as well as E/ICEF/1993/L.2 and E/CN.17/1993/8, 18, paras 61–2. See also: UNICEF Decision 1992/31 entitled 'Children, Environment and Development'.

[70] For an early definition of environmental education, see Stapp, W. B. et al, 'The Concept of Environmental Education' (1969) 1 *The Journal of Environmental Education* 30–1.

[71] See, for instance, Agenda 21, ch 6, para 18 (human health); ch 11, para 3(b) and (f) (combating deforestation); ch 12, para 14(b) (desertification); ch 14, para 17(c) (agriculture and rural development); ch 17, para 15 (ocean management).

[72] Declaration of the United Nations Conference on the Human Environment, Stockholm, 1972, Principle 19. See also, Recommendation 96 of the UNCHE Action Plan, Report of the United Nations Conference on the Human Environment, Stockholm, June 1972. The need for environmental education was already identified in the Founex Report on Development and Environment (1971), para 3.11. See further the youth statement that was presented to the plenary of the UN Conference on Human Environment on 12 June 1972: Statement on the 'Human Environment' of international youth organizations in consultative status with the United Nations, para 5, reproduced in Angel, W. D. (ed), *The International Law of Youth Rights. Source Documents and Commentary* (Martinus Nijhoff Publishers 1995), 619.

Following the Stockholm conference, various efforts were undertaken to promote formal, non-formal, and informal education in environmental matters. For instance, in 1975, UNESCO and UNEP launched an 'International Environmental Education Programme',[73] followed by the adoption of the Belgrade Charter on Environmental Education,[74] and, in 1977, by the organization of the Intergovernmental Conference on Environmental Education in Tbilisi.[75] In 1982, the World Charter for Nature again highlighted the need to promote 'ecological education'.[76]

These developments gradually produced some results at the regional level,[77] but the decisive breakthrough was reached at the universal level through the adoption of the Convention on the Rights of the Child ('CRC') in 1989, article 29(1)(e) of which provides that the education of the child shall be directed to the 'development of respect for the natural environment'.[78] Then in 1990, the 'World Conference on Education for

[73] UNESCO also launched in 1976 the environmental education newsletter 'CONNECT'. See further Blackburn, A. M., 'Steps Along the Path: the UNESCO/UNEP International Environmental Education Program' (1983) 3 *The Environmentalist* 269.

[74] The Belgrade Charter: A Framework for Environmental Education, 22 October 1975, available at: <http://unesdoc.unesco.org/images/0001/000177/017772eb.pdf>. The Belgrade Charter delves into the objectives of environmental education (awareness, knowledge, attitude, skills, evaluation ability, and participation) and outlines the guiding principles of environmental education programmes, emphasizing the importance of holistic and interdisciplinary approaches. See further Filho, W. L. et al, *A Sourcebook for Environmental Education: A Practical Review based on the Belgrade Charter* (Parthenon Publ. Group 1996).

[75] See the Final Report of the Intergovernmental Conference on Environmental Education, organized by UNESCO in cooperation with UNEP, Tbilisi (USSR) 14–26 October 1977, Doc ED/MD/49, April 1978; see in particular Recommendation No 1. Another UNESCO–UNEP Congress on Environmental Education and Training was organized from 17–21 August 1987 in Moscow, which adopted the International Strategy for Action in the field of Environmental Education and Training for the 1990s, available at: <http://unesdoc.unesco.org/images0008/000805/080583eo.pdf>. For more information on the historical background, see Centre for Ecological Sciences of the Indian Institute of Science, 'Environment Education for Ecosystem Conservation', available at: <http://www.ces.iisc.ernet.in/energy/water/paper/environment_education/environment.htm>. See further, Gough, A., 'A Long, Winding (and Rocky) Road to Environmental Education for Sustainability in 2006' (2006) 22 *Australian Journal of Environmental Education* 72.

[76] World Charter for Nature, A/RES/37/7, 28 October 1982, para 15.

[77] See, for instance, the Bern Convention on the Conservation of European Wildlife and Natural Habitats, 19 September 1979, 1284 UNTS 209, Art 3(3). See also the efforts of the Council of Europe: Resolution (71)14 of the Committee of Ministers to Member States on Introduction of Principles of Nature Conservation into Education, June 1971; Recommendation No R(81)9 of the Committee of Ministers to Member States on Environmental Education, 26 May 1981; and Recommendation 937(1982) of the Parliamentary Assembly on the Role of Education in Protection of the Environment in Europe, 29 January 1982. See also the Resolution of the Council of the Ministers of Education on Environmental Education, adopted in the framework of the European Communities on 24 May 1988.

[78] Convention on the Rights of the Child, 20 November 1989, 1577 UNTS 3, art 29(1)(e). Canada proposed to include this provision, see UN Doc E/CN.4/1985/64, para 88. In its General Comment No 1 of 2001, the Committee on the Rights of the Child indicated that 'for the development of respect for the natural environment, education must link issues of environment and sustainable development with socio-economic, sociocultural and demographic issues. Similarly, respect for the natural environment should be learnt by children at home, in school and within the community, encompass both national and international problems, and actively involve children in local, regional or global environmental projects'; Committee on the Rights of the Child, General Comment No 1 (2001), art 29(1): The Aims of Education, CRC/GC/2001/1, 17 April 2001, para 13. See further Detrick, S., *A Commentary on the United Nations Convention on the Rights of the Child* (Martinus Nijhoff 1999), 516. In 1999, the Committee on Economic, Social and Cultural Rights took note of these normative developments and indicated that the environmental dimension is an element which is 'implicit' and must be reflected in 'a contemporary interpretation of article 13(1)' of the 1966 International Covenant on Economic, Social and Cultural Rights. See CESCR, General Comment No 13 'The Right to Education', E/C.12/1999/10, 8 December 1999, para 5.

All' held in Jomtien, Thailand, again acknowledged the link between education and environmental protection.[79]

Even if the Rio Declaration does not explicitly refer to environmental education, the UN and its agencies have relied upon Agenda 21 in their efforts to promote changes in educational systems at all levels, so as to integrate the problematic of sustainable development in all educational curricula. Chapter 36 of Agenda 21 outlines three programme areas for environmental education:

(1) reorienting education towards sustainable development (36.3);
(2) increasing public awareness (36.8);
(3) promoting training (36.12).

One of the goals of Agenda 21 was that, within the following three years, governments should have prepared or updated strategies aimed at mainstreaming environment and development 'as a cross-cutting issue into education at all levels'. The inter-disciplinary approach is therefore to be integrated in the curricula of all educational institutions, in particular at the secondary and the tertiary levels. International organizations too are called upon to review their educational programmes and to coordinate their efforts under the umbrella of the UNESCO/UNEP International Environmental Education Programme.

Acting pursuant to Agenda 21, the Commission on Sustainable Development designed in 1996 an international work programme on education, public awareness and training.[80] In 2001, UNEP and UNESCO launched the YouthXchange ('YXC') Initiative aimed at educating youth on sustainable consumption and lifestyles.[81] At the 2002 WSSD, the theme of environmental education was anew at the forefront of discussions. UNESCO Director-General Koïchiro Matsuura declared in Johannesburg that 'education—in all its forms and at all levels—is not only an end in itself but is also one of the most powerful instruments we have for bringing about the changes required to achieve sustainable development'.[82] The Plan of Implementation of the WSSD indicates that 'education is critical for promoting sustainable development', and that therefore the necessary resources need to be mobilized to help States to promote primary, secondary, and tertiary education, and in particular to integrate sustainable development at all levels in the educational systems.[83]

[79] The preamble of the *World Declaration on Education for All* reads as follows: '*Understanding* that education can help ensure a safer, healthier, more prosperous and environmentally sound world, while simultaneously contributing to social, economic, and cultural progress, tolerance, and international cooperation'. See the background document for the World Conference on Education for All, 5–9 March 1990, Inter-Agency Commission (UNDP, UNESCO, UNICEF, World Bank), *Meeting Basic Learning Needs: A Vision for the 1990s*, New York, 1990, 156, available at: <http://unesdoc.unesco.org/images/0009/000975/097552e.pdf>. The Framework for Action to Meet Basic Learning Needs—Guidelines for Implementing the World Declaration on Education for All of 9 March 1990 is available at: <http://unesdoc.unesco.org/images/0008/000862/086293eb.pdf>.

[80] *Official Records of the Economic and Social Council, 1996, Supplement No. 8* (E/1996/28), ch I, C, Decision 4/11. See also *Implementation of the work programme on education, public awareness and training. Report of the Secretary-General*, E/CN.17/2000/8, 7 February 2000.

[81] Refer to: <http://www.youthxchange.net/main/home.asp>. See also the Report of the Secretary-General, *Implementation of the World Programme of Action for Youth*, A/66/61-E/2011/3, 22 November 2010, para 29.

[82] UNESCO Media Services, 2 September 2002, available at: <http://portal.unesco.org/en/ev.php-URL_ID=5734&URL_DO=DO_TOPIC&URL_SECTION=201.html>.

[83] A/CONF.199/20, Resolution 2 of 4 September 2002, *Plan of Implementation of the World Summit on Sustainable Development*, paras 116–24.

Following WSSD, the General Assembly acknowledged that 'education is an indispensable element for achieving sustainable development' and proclaimed the United Nations Decade of Education for Sustainable Development ('DESD') for the years 2005–2014.[84] Under the slogan 'Educating for the Future', UNESCO took the lead in the organization of DESD by fostering the promotion of basic education, the reorientation and updating of educational programmes, and providing practical training related thereto.[85]

At the 2009 UNESCO Conference on Education for Sustainable Development the participants adopted the 'Bonn Declaration' containing a call for action at the policy level (eg reorient education and training systems, mobilization of resources, strengthening enabling mechanisms) and the practical level (eg use of integrated and systemic approaches in formal, non-formal and informal education, support teacher education and training, develop partnerships, involve youth in the design of ESD, foster research networks).[86]

An interesting initiative launched by UNEP in 2010 is the 'Global Universities Partnership on Environment and Sustainability' ('GUPES').[87] Its overall objective is 'the integration of environment and sustainability concerns into teaching, research, community engagement, the management of universities . . . as well as to enhance student engagement and participation in sustainability activities both within and beyond universities'.[88] As such, GUPES provides a strategic platform to universities interested in mainstreaming environment and sustainability concerns in their curricula, and keen on sharing their experiences amongst one another.

At Rio+20, the central role of youth 'as custodians of the future' was again emphasized. The outcome document adopted at Rio+20, *The Future We Want*, underlines the need to promote education for sustainable development beyond DESD 2005–2014.[89]

These various efforts have produced results at the regional and national levels. At the regional level, mention can be made of the UNECE Strategy for Education for Sustainable Development.[90] The aim of the Strategy is to encourage UNECE member States to develop and incorporate education for sustainable development 'into their formal education systems, in all relevant subjects, and in non-formal and informal education'.[91] The Strategy aims at improving basic education and training, reorienting education towards sustainable development, increasing public awareness of the problems of sustainable

[84] A/RES/57/254 of 20 December 2002, *United Nations Decade of Education for Sustainable Development*. See further A/RES/58/219 of 23 December 2003 and A/RES/59/237 of 22 December 2004, operative para 1. On DESD, see UNESCO Doc ED/2005/PEQ/ESD/3, *UN Decade of Education for Sustainable Development 2005–2014. The DESD at a Glance* (Paris 2005).

[85] UNESCO, *UNESCO and Sustainable Development* (Paris 2005). See also eg the contribution of the Council of Europe to DESD: Mayer, M. and Tschapka, J., (eds), *Engaging Youth in Sustainable Development. Learning and Teaching Sustainable Development in Lower Secondary Schools* (Council of Europe 2008).

[86] Bonn Declaration, UNESCO World Conference on Education for Sustainable Development, 31 March–2 April 2009, Bonn, Germany, available at: <http://www.esd-world-conference-2009.org>.

[87] GUPES builds on the experience of 'Mainstreaming Environment and Sustainability in African Universities (MESA)', 'Mainstreaming Environment and Sustainability in the Caribbean Universities (MESCA)' and the 'Asia-Pacific Regional University Consortium (RUC)'.

[88] See <http://www.unep.org/training/programmes/gupes.asp>.

[89] A/RES/66/288, *The Future We Want*, 27 July 2012, para 230.

[90] The Strategy document indicates that '[e]ducation, in addition to being a human right, is a prerequisite for achieving sustainable development and an essential tool for good governance, informed decision-making and the promotion of democracy. Therefore, education for sustainable development can help translate our vision into reality'. UNECE Strategy for Education for Sustainable Development, adopted at the High-level meeting of Environment and Education Ministries, Vilnius, CEP/AC.13/2005/3/Rev.1, 23 March 2005, 1.

[91] UNECE Strategy for Education for Sustainable Development, para 6.

development, facilitating access to information, and participation in decision-making.[92] The strategy relies on the partnership between governments, NGOs and the private sector, NGOs being able to act as mediators between governments and the general public.[93]

At the national level, plans and strategies for environmental education are unsurprisingly developed in furtherance of the goals formulated at the international level. Many examples could be cited at this juncture.[94] For instance, the National Environmental Education Action Plan for Sustainable Development in Jamaica (1998–2010).[95] This Action Plan 'seeks to make Jamaicans aware, committed and action-oriented on environmental and sustainable development issues' and comprises the following five programme areas: teacher professional development, curriculum development and implementation, national public awareness, community learning, and resources and practices.[96]

[92] UNECE Strategy for Education for Sustainable Development, paras 12 and 16. See in this context the UNECE Convention on Access to Information, Public Participation in Decision-making and Access to Justice in Environmental Matters, Aarhus, 25 June 1998, 2161 UNTS 447.

[93] UNECE Strategy, para 36.

[94] Brazil, Colombia and Guatemala, for instance, adopted National Environmental Education Policies in 1999, 2002 and 2004 respectively, see: <http://www.guninetwork.org/resources/he-articles/higher-education-environment-and-sustainability>. For achievements in the Southern African Development Community, see: <http://www.sadc-reep.org.za/uploads/documents/general.pdf>. Australia adopted a National Action Plan on Environmental Education for a Sustainable Future, available at: <http://www.environment.gov.au/education/publications/nap/pubs/nap.pdf>; and established a National Environmental Education Council. The United States of America already adopted in 1990 the National Environmental Education Act, Public Law 101-619, 16 November 1990, 20 USC 5501; see also the National Environmental Education Training Program aimed at training environmental educators, available at: <http://www2.epa.gov/education/national-environmental-education-training-program>. In Canada, education is decentralized, and several provinces adopted action plans, such as the Sustainable Development Action Plan of the Commission Scolaire de Montréal or the Education for Sustainability Action Plan adopted by the Manitoba Department of Education, Citizenship and Youth. The United Kingdom adopted an Education Reform Act in 1988, and in 1990 set up a National Curriculum Council ('NCC') which established environmental education as a cross-curricular theme. On UK policies, see UK National Commission for UNESCO, *Education for Sustainable Development in the UK in 2010*, September 2010, available at: <http://www.unesco.org.uk/uploads/UNESCO_educationforsustainabledev_2010_web.pdf>. In Germany, environmental education has been on the parliament's agenda since 2000, and led to the adoption of a National Action Plan in 2004. See Deutscher Bundestag, 'Bildung für eine nachhaltige Entwicklung', Drucksache 14/3319, 10. Juni 2000, available at: <http://dip21.bundestag.de/dip21/btd/14/033/1403319.pdf>; and Deutscher Bundestag, 'Aktionsplan zur UN-Weltdekade Bildung für nachhaltige Entwicklung', Drucksache 15/3472, 30. Juni 2004, available at: <http://www.bne-portal.de/fileadmin/unesco/de/Downloads/Dekade-Projekte/Beschluss_2520Bundestag_25202004.File.pdf?linklisted=5039>. In France, the government integrated sustainability issues into the educational curricula of its schools, through the adoption of Circulaire n° 2004-110 of 8 July 2004, *Généralisation d'une éducation à l'environnement pour un développement durable (EEDD)*, available at: <http://www.education.gouv.fr/bo/2004/28/MENE0400752C.htm>. See also: Circulaire n° 2011-186 of 24 October 2011, *Troisième phase de généralisation*, available at: <http://www.education.gouv.fr/pid25535/bulletin_officiel.html?cid_bo=58234>. Art 8 of the French Environmental Charter enshrines the foundational importance of environmental education. In Italy, environmental education became part of school curricula through Legge 30 diciembre 2008, n. 210, *Gazzetta Ufficiale* n. 2, 3 gennaio 2009, art 7bis. In 2006, the European Union revised its 2001 EU Sustainable Development Strategy by including as the cross-cutting policy theme environmental education and training, see Council of the European Union, Review of the EU Sustainable Development Strategy, Brussels, 9 June 2006, paras 14–17; Commission of the European Communities, Mainstreaming Sustainable Development into EU Policies: 2009 Review of the European Union Strategy for Sustainable Development, COM (2009) 400 final, Brussels, 24 July 2009. Other EU Directives also incorporate provisions dealing with environmental education, such as art 22(c) of Council Directive 92/43/EEC of 21 May 1992 on the Conservation of Natural Habitats and of Wild Fauna and Flora, OJ L 206, 22 July 1992, 7.

[95] This plan is part of the Environmental Action Programme agreed between the Government of Jamaica and the Canadian International Development Agency (CIDA) in 1996, available at: <http://www.nepa.gov.jm.Symposia_03/Policies/NEPAPSD.pdf>.

[96] National Environmental Education Action Plan for Sustainable Development in Jamaica, ch IV, 38.

In Switzerland, the Federal Environmental Office published in November 2010 a strategy for education and training for the years 2011 and onward.[97] The objective of this strategy is to include aspects of environmental education in the curricula at all levels of education in Switzerland and furthermore to include a training component in all legislation concerned with the protection of the environment in order to ensure that all those who are called upon to implement this legislation are properly trained.

## 3. Normative impact

A number of conventions adopted in the wake of UNCED offer good examples of how young people can be involved as partners in the implementation of sustainable development. Under the UNFCCC,[98] several UN agencies have set up an inter-agency cooperation on climate change and sustainable development aiming at involving youth in their activities. Youth involvement in the UNFCCC process initially started during COP 5 in Bonn.[99] So-called 'Conferences of Youth' have regularly been organized since COP 11/CMP 1, providing youth with a platform for information exchange and political advocacy. In October 2008, the UNFCCC Secretariat inaugurated the 'United Nations Joint Framework Initiative on Children, Youth, and Climate Change'.[100] In 2009, youth NGOs, so-called YOUNGOs, were granted by the Secretariat first a provisional and then a permanent 'constituency status'.[101] Since then, youth representatives have 'contributed to the deliberations at the meetings of the COP/CMP through plenary interventions, web-only submissions to the COP/CMP, submissions to the subsidiary bodies and direct lobbying with delegates'.[102] Through an 'Intergenerational Inquiry', youth delegates are also regularly invited to provide their insights on the role and importance of youth in the UNFCCC process.

Under the Convention on Biological Diversity ('CBD'), stakeholders can participate in the work of the Conference of the Parties.[103] In order to better structure the participation of youth representatives, as of 2008, and with increasing support by the Secretariat

[97] OFEV, Stratégie 'Éducation et formation OFEV' pour les années 2011 et suivantes, available at: <http://www.bafu.admin.ch/umweltbildung/11092/index.html?lang=fr>. See its implementation programme for the year 2013: OFEV, Programme de l'éducation à l'environnement (EE) pour 2013, available at: <http://www.bafu.admin.ch/umweltbildung/11092/index.html?lang=fr>. See also: Fachkonferenz Umweltbildung, *Umweltbildung. Position der Fachkonferenz Umweltbildung*, 9. November 2010.

[98] United Nations Framework Convention on Climate Change, 9 May 1992, 1771 UNTS 107.

[99] See <http://unfccc.int/cc_inet/cc_inet/youth_portal/items/6578.php>.

[100] See the Report of the Secretary-General, *Implementation of the World Programme of Action for Youth*, 6, paras 25–7; UNFCCC note on *United Nations Joint Framework Initiative on Children, Youth and Climate Change*, <http://unfccc.int/cc_inet/cc_inet/youth_portal/items/6519.php>. Members of this Initiative are: UNFCCC, FAO, UNICEF, CBD, UNCCD, DESA, UNDP, UNESCO, UNEP, UNHABITAT, UNITAR, NGLS, UNFPA, UN Programme on Youth, UNV, and the World Bank; see: UN Joint Framework Initiative, *Youth in action on climate change; inspirations from around the world*, May 2013, 86, 87; available at <http://unfccc.int/cc_inet/cc_inet/youth_portal>. On the various regional or national youth initiatives related to climate change, refer to: *Growing Together in a Changing Climate. The United Nations, Young People, and Climate Change* (Halmstad 2009).

[101] Constituencies are functional groups representing 'certain stakeholder groups within the negotiations' with an observer status, including the right to speaking slots during plenary sessions. See YOUNGO Earns Full Constituency Status, available at: <https://sites.google.com/site/unfcccyoungo/youngo-earns-full-constituency-status>. See also UN System Engagement with NGOs, Civil Society, the Private Sector, and other actors. A Compendium (2005), 228.

[102] See UN Joint Framework Initiative, *Youth Participation in the UNFCCC Negotiation Process. The United Nations, Young People, and Climate Change* (2010), 12.

[103] Convention on Biological Diversity, 5 June 1992, 1760 UNTS 79, art 23, para 5.

of the CBD, a Global Youth Biodiversity Network ('GYBN') has been set up.[104] GYBN's mission includes, *inter alia*, to 'raise global awareness among young people of the values of biodiversity' and to coordinate youth participation in the negotiations under the CBD.[105] The CBD Secretariat has nominated two staff members as 'Youth Focal Points' and expressly recognizes GYBN's function as the international coordination platform for youth participation.[106]

As regards environmental education, several multilateral environmental treaties contain provisions on the promotion of education and training. For instance, the UNFCCC, the CBD, and the UNCCD[107] include articles obliging the parties to these conventions to promote and facilitate the implementation of up to six elements—education, training, public awareness, public participation, public access to information, and international cooperation—by, *inter alia*, adapting school and university curricula, developing training materials, organizing relevant training events, facilitating public access to information and by pursuing a dialogue with the relevant stakeholders.[108]

The secretariats of these conventions support such activities through their cooperation programmes at the interregional, regional, and national levels. For instance, the 18th Conference of the Parties of the UNFCCC recently adopted the eight-year 'Doha work programme on Article 6 of the Convention',[109] which, while remaining guided by a 'country-driven approach',[110] calls upon the Parties to promote education focused on climate change[111] and to foster 'the participation of all stakeholders in the implementation of Article 6 of the Convention', in particular to 'enhance the active participation of youth, women, civil society organizations and the media'.[112] Parties are also invited to seek input and public participation in the formulation and implementation of efforts to address climate change, and encourage the involvement and participation of representatives of all stakeholders and major groups in the climate change negotiation process.[113]

[104] 'The long road to the establishment of GYBN', available at: <http://www.gybn.net/HistoryofGYBN.aspx>. The founding of GYBN was supported financially by the German Federal Agency for Nature Conservation.

[105] The Global Youth Biodiversity Network Statute, I. Vision, Mission and Objectives, and III. Youth Participation at the CDB, available at: <http://www.gybn.net/Portals/0/GYBN%20Statute.pdf>.

[106] Refer to the CBD site at <http://www.cbd.int/youth/doc/cop-11-youth-related-activities-en.pdf>.

[107] United Nations Convention to Combat Desertification in those Countries Experiencing Serious Drought and/or Desertification, Particularly Africa, 14 October 1994, 1954 UNTS 3.

[108] See UNFCCC, arts 4(1)(i) and 6; CBD, art 13; UNCCD, art 19. See further: Ramsar Convention Resolutions VI.19 and VII.9; Aarhus Convention on Access to Information, Public Participation in Decision-Making and Access to Justice in Environmental Matters, 25 June 1998, 2161 UNTS 447, art 3(3); Protocol on Water and Health to the 1992 Convention on the Protection and Use of Transboundary Watercourses and International Lakes, 17 June 1999, 2331 UNTS 202, art 9(1); Cartagena Protocol on Biosafety to the Convention on Biological Diversity, 29 January 2000, 2226 UNTS 208, art 23(1); Stockholm Convention on Persistent Organic Pollutants, 22 May 2001, 2256 UNTS 119, art 10(1)(c).

[109] FCCC/CP/2012/8/Add.2, Report of the COP on its 18th session, held in Doha from 26 November to 8 December 2012, Decision 15/CP.18, Annex: Doha work programme on Article 6 of the Convention.

[110] Doha work programme, para 14(a). It thus confirms the approach adopted in the Framework for Action to meet Basic Learning Needs, para 16: 'Progress in meeting the basic learning needs of all will depend ultimately on the actions taken within individual countries. While regional and international cooperation and financial assistance can support and facilitate such actions, government authorities, communities and their several in-country partners are the key agents'.

[111] Doha work programme, para 16 and 22(f)–(h).

[112] Doha work programme, para 22 (k).

[113] Doha work programme, para 22 (i). Also NGOs are 'invited to enhance the active participation of youth, women, civil society organizations and the media in climate change activities'. See, Doha work programme, para 26.

## 4. Reception in international jurisprudence

Unsurprisingly, no international court or tribunal has specifically referred to Principle 21. The *Minors Oposa* case, although a case of domestic litigation in the Philippines, attracted the most international attention in recent years, most notably because young persons successfully vindicated their standing and right to seek environmental justice for future, unborn generations.[114]

In the field of environmental education, some discrete successes can be recorded within human rights bodies and courts. While not expressly referring to environmental education, the Inter-American Court of Human Rights ('IACtHR') has expanded on the right to education in its advisory opinion on the *Legal Status and Human Rights of the Child.*[115] In *Juvenile Re-education Institute v. Paraguay*, the IACtHR held that the obligation to provide adequate education programmes (albeit in the re-education centre) follows from a proper interpretation of article 4 of the Inter-American Convention on Human Rights (right to life), read in conjunction with the Convention on the Rights of the Child and article 13 of the Protocol of San Salvador.[116] By doing so, the IACtHR followed the integrationist approach already adopted by the UN Committee on Economic, Social and Cultural Rights in its General Comment No. 13, in which the Committee held that Article 13 of the 1966 Covenant on Economic, Social and Cultural Rights must be interpreted in light of the recent normative developments, *inter alia*, in the field of environmental education.[117]

The European Committee of Social Rights, ruling on the conformity with the European Social Charter, clarified that populations exposed to heightened environmental risks need to receive appropriate environmental education. In *Marangopoulos v. Greece*, the Committee was confronted with a collective complaint of persons living in a lignite mining area.[118] While Greece relied on various figures and surveys showing that it organizes environmental health education courses in primary and secondary schools, the Committee found as a general matter that Greece's environmental health education programmes revealed several shortcomings. More specifically, the Committee held that the Greek authorities failed to provide sufficient environmental health education to the persons exposed to the risks of the lignite mine in question. In this context, the Committee held that, although Greece had a certain margin of discretion to determine its educational

[114] *Minors Oposa v. Secretary of the Department of Environmental and Natural Resources*, Supreme Court of the Philippines, 30 July 1993, (1994) 33 ILM 173. On 15 February 2011, the Supreme Court of the Philippines upheld a claim by young plaintiffs against the Metropolitan Manila Development Authority that this Authority clean up, rehabilitate and preserve the Manila Bay. *Metropolitan Manila Development Authority et al. v. Concerned Residents of Manila Bay*, Supreme Court of the Philippines, G.R. Nos. 171947-48, 15 February 2011. In the United States, young people all over the country have initiated the so-called Atmospheric Trust Litigation in 2011, seeking to expand the public trust doctrine to the protection of the atmosphere. For further information, see: <http://www.ourchildrenstrust.org/Legal>; Wood, M.C., *Nature's Trust. Environmental Law for a New Ecological Age* (Cambridge University Press 2014), 227–9.

[115] ICtHR, *Legal Status and Human Rights of the Child*, Advisory Opinion OC-17/2002 of 28 August 2002, paras 83–6.

[116] ICtHR, *Case of the 'Juvenile Re-education Institute' v. Paraguay*, Preliminary Objections, Merits, Reparations and Costs, Judgment of 2 September 2004, para 172.

[117] See note 78.

[118] *Marangopoulos Foundation for Human Rights (MFHR) v. Greece*, ECSR, Complaint No. 30/2005, Decision on the Merits, 6 December 2006.

policies, it failed in that particular case to 'strike a reasonable balance between the interests of persons living in the lignite mining areas and the general interest'.[119]

Member States of the Council of Europe also submit national reports to the Committee providing information on their level of commitment to environmental education. For instance, the Czech Republic informed the Committee that environmental education is a 'long-term priority and forms part of the cross-disciplinary topics on school curricula', and that in this context it established a post of coordinator in Czech schools to coordinate environmental activities.[120] The Committee also periodically requires member States to specify whether they have introduced environmental education in primary and secondary education, while highlighting the cases where States fail to do so or fail to provide the relevant information.[121]

## III) Relations with Other Principles

A systematic analysis of Principle 21 in the light of the other provisions of the Rio Declaration further underpins the importance of Principle 21 in the general articulation of the concept of sustainable development.

The preamble of the Rio Declaration alludes to the goal of establishing a 'new and equitable global partnership'. Within the corpus of the Rio Declaration, mention of such a global partnership is only found in Principles 7 and 21, the first calling on States to cooperate in a spirit of global partnership, the second indicating that youth must be integrated in the process if such a global partnership is to become reality.

The role of youth is to be put in the larger perspective adopted by Principle 1. Indeed, youth share with women (Principle 20) and indigenous people (Principle 22) the commonality of forming part of so-called 'vulnerable' groups of civil society, needing particular attention and protection in the context of sustainable development. As Principle 1 aptly indicates, human beings are at the centre of concerns for sustainable development, and hence the interests of vulnerable populations, in particular children and youth, are to be adequately taken into consideration. Principle 21 also shares with Principles 20 and 22 the fact that it focuses on one of the three major groups expressly mentioned in the Rio Declaration. Whereas Principle 10 calls on the international community to foster participation of civil society at large, Principle 21 indicates that youth have a particularly important role to play in this participatory process.

On a more substantial note, Principle 21 is closely intertwined with Principle 3 to the extent that young people need to be mobilized in a continuous process in order to ensure a better future for present and future generations. Furthermore, adequate environmental education of young people is in the long run the best course of action if one is to 'reduce and eliminate unsustainable patterns of production and consumption' in line with Principle 8.

Finally, mention should also be made of the constructive role that Principle 21 plays in the implementation and normative development of the substantive principles of the Rio Declaration, in particular with respect to the principles whose normative statuses are not yet clearly determined. Thus, asserting their role on the basis of Principle 21, youth have

[119] *Marangopoulos Foundation for Human Rights*, para 221.
[120] ECSR, Conclusions XIX-2 (2009) (Czech Republic), January 2010.
[121] ECSR, Conclusions XIX-2 (2009) (Latvia), January 2010, 9.

not only secured their entitlement to participate at international conferences, but increasingly propose normative developments of the principles enshrined in the Rio Declaration. For instance, the Major Group for Children and Youth argued in the negotiations leading up to Rio+20 for the development of institutional arrangements in order to achieve the 'full and effective implementation of the precautionary principle'.[122]

## IV) Assessment

The two fundamental dimensions of Principle 21, youth participation and environmental education, are closely intertwined. UNCED marks the starting point for access of youth to decision-making processes at the international and national levels. Particularly at the international level, youth mobilization has been successful to a large extent. Although youth representatives still lament lack of inclusion of youth in national delegations of some countries, the overall development has brought about fruitful results. Youth representatives work on the basis of the Rio Declaration to develop new concepts or programmes that they then propose to decision-makers. For instance, the Major Group for Children and Youth submitted at Rio+20 comments on the proposed outcome document, and submitted interesting proposals such as the creation of an Ombudsperson for Future Generations at the national level under the coordination of a new Office of the UN High Commission for Future Generations. The document also calls, *inter alia*, for the establishment of a World Environment Court, an Intergovernmental Panel on Sustainable Development, a UN Council on Sustainable Development, and a Global Commons Trust for the management of the global commons.[123]

International efforts on the front of environmental education and awareness raising are increasingly gaining momentum. Although Principle 21 does not explicitly refer to environmental education, international organizations have proceeded on the basis of Agenda 21 to include this crucial dimension in the problematic of youth mobilization. In this sense, international organizations have been instrumental in helping States to mainstream sustainable development in the curricula of educational institutions at all levels. At the 7th World Environmental Education Congress held in Marrakesh in June 2013, UNEP Executive Director, Achim Steiner, argued that '[e]nvironmental education is about knowledge and empowerment. The knowledge and power to understand, the knowledge and power to make connections'.[124] It remains to be seen whether these efforts will ultimately succeed in bringing about the desired changes in terms of lifestyles, consumption patterns, and awareness of the environmental challenges faced by decision-makers.

For an international lawyer, Principle 21 is a good example of a normative proposition, which, although not legally binding, can influence the political, and eventually the legal

[122] Major Group for Children and Youth, Contribution to the Outcome Document of Rio+20, under B, available at: <http://www.uncsd2012.org/content/documents/260Major%20Group%20of%20Children%20and%20Youth_Contributions%20to%20Rio%2020_FINAL.pdf>.

[123] Major Group for Children and Youth, Contribution to the Outcome Document of Rio+20.

[124] UNEP Executive Director Emphasizes Environmental Education as Key Driver of Knowledge and Empowerment, UNEP News Centre, 12 June 2013, available at: <http://www.unep.org/NEWSCENTRE/default.aspx?DocumentId=2718&ArticleId=9541>. On the Congress, see UNEP/DEPI/EETU/WEEC7/Summary, 7th World Environmental Education Congress—Summary, Marrakesh, Morocco, 9–14 June 2013, available at: <http://www.unep.org/training/docs/WEEC_7_Congress_summary.pdf>.

environment at the international and national levels. The key to this positive outcome of developments taking place since the mid-1960s, and crystallized through the adoption of the Rio Declaration and Agenda 21, is to be found in the pro-active attitude of the UN system in general, and the standing bodies of multilateral environmental treaties such as UNFCCC or CBD. Technical cooperation offered by these institutions at the national level, related in particular to education and training of youth, while encouraging States to involve youth in constant dialogues on environmental issues, has created a climate in which the involvement of youth is nowadays accepted as good policy.

## V) Select Bibliography

Alpizar, L., 'Youth Participation in the UNCED Process', in: IISD, *Youth Source Book on Sustainable Development*, available at: <http://www.iisd.org/youth/ysbk086.htm>.

Alpizar, L., 'Youth Participation in Global Decision-Making Processes—The official UNCED Preparatory Process', in: IISD, *Youth Source Book on Sustainable Development*, available at: <http://www.iisd.org/youth/ysbk088.htm>.

Angel, W. D. (ed), The International Law of Youth Rights. Source Documents and Commentary (Martinus Nijhoff Publishers 1995), 597 *et seq.*

Detrick, S., A Commentary on the United Nations Convention on the Rights of the Child (Martinus Nijhoff Publishers 1999), 505–30.

Filho, W. L. et al, A Sourcebook for Environmental Education: A Practical Review based on the Belgrade Charter (Parthenon Publ. Group 1996).

Gough, A., 'A Long, Winding (and Rocky) Road to Environmental Education for Sustainability in 2006' (2006) 22 *Australian Journal of Environmental Education* 71.

Halpern, S., *The United Nations Conference on Environment and Development: Process and Documentation* (United Nations 1992).

IISD, *Youth Source Book on Sustainable Development*, available at: <http://www.iisd.org/youth/ysbk086.htm>.

Kaasa, S. M., *The Commission on Sustainable Development. A Study of Institutional Design, Distribution of Capabilities and Entrepreneurial Leadership* (Fridtjof Nansen Institute 2005).

Stapp, W. B. et al, 'The Concept of Environmental Education' (1969) 1 *The Journal of Environmental Education* 33.

Woods, Z., 'Young People and Sustainable Development', in: Dodds, F. (ed), *The Way Forward: Beyond Agenda 21* (Earthscan 1997), 158.

# 26. Principle 22

## *Indigenous People and Sustainable Development*

Dinah Shelton*

**Principle 22**

Indigenous people and their communities and other local communities have a vital role in environmental management and development because of their knowledge and traditional practices. States should recognize and duly support their identity, culture and interests and enable their effective participation in the achievement of sustainable development.



## I) Origins and Rationale of the Principle

The 1987 UN report *Our Common Future* first highlighted the particular situation of indigenous peoples in the context of environment and development, providing a

* Manatt/Ahn Professor of International Law Emeritus at the George Washington University Law School. From 2010–2014 Dinah Shelton was a member of the Inter-American Commission on Human Rights, where she served as the rapporteur on the rights of indigenous peoples. All comments herein are personal and should not be attributed to either institution with which she is affiliated.

preview of the approach of Rio Principle 22. The report pointed out that indigenous peoples are:

> found in North America, in Australia, in the Amazon Basin, in Central America, in the forests and hills of Asia, in the deserts of North Africa, and elsewhere.... The isolation of many such people has meant the preservation of a traditional way of life in close harmony with the natural environment. Their very survival has depended on their ecological awareness and adaptation. But their isolation has also meant that few of them have shared in national economic and social development; this may be reflected in their poor health, nutrition, and education.[1]

In fact, many indigenous peoples would assert that the 'development' problems referred to are the product of contact and invasion from the outside, not from isolation and preservation of traditional economic resources and social structures.

There are more than 200 million indigenous peoples in the world. Most of them live in highly vulnerable ecosystems: the Arctic and tundra, tropical and boreal forests, riverine and coastal zones, and mountains and semiarid rangelands. Once hardly accessible, these territories used and occupied by indigenous peoples have become a major source of hydroelectric power, minerals, hardwoods, and pasture lands. Many regions of indigenous habitation are being threatened or lost as a result of climate change. The invasions of and changes to indigenous lands have brought disease, exploitation, loss of language and culture, and, in too many instances, extinction of groups as distinct entities.

Indigenous peoples generally are highly integrated into the ecosystems which they inhabit, maintaining a closely interdependent relationship with the environment, of which they consider themselves stewards. Their intimate knowledge of the surrounding environment enables them to maintain a self-sufficient lifestyle over the long term, but it also has the effect of making preservation and sustained use of their territories critical to their survival. Indigenous peoples are thus uniquely vulnerable to environmental harm because of the cultural and religious links they maintain with their ancestral territories. Threats and encroachments on their territories directly jeopardize the preservation of their cultures and ways of life.

The remaining indigenous peoples in voluntary isolation as well as those peoples in initial contact face additional pressures because the process of establishing contact generally involves irrevocably altering their relationship with the environment and modifying, often radically, their ways of life and cultural practices. In addition, they often suffer human rights violations at the hands of those who seek to exploit the natural resources in their territories. The aggression against them and the degradation of their environment is rarely prosecuted or punished. Both the groups in isolation and those in first contact are, in most cases, at high risk of extinction.

Indigenous peoples were not mentioned in the 1972 Stockholm Declaration[2] or Plan of Action.[3] Nor was there reference to indigenous peoples in General Assembly Resolution 44/228 of December 22, 1989 that called for and described the objectives of UNCED. The grand objective was to 'elaborate strategies and measures to halt and reverse the environmental degradation of the planet', responsibility for which was squarely placed on the

[1] World Commission on Environment and Development, Our Common Future, 114.

[2] 'Declaration of the United Nations Conference on the Human Environment', Stockholm, 16 June 1972, UN Doc A/CONF 48/14/Rev.1, 2 ss ('Stockholm Declaration').

[3] 'Action Plan for the Human Environment', 16 June 1972, UN Doc A/CONF 48/14, 10–62.

industrialized countries. For the developing world, Part I, paragraph 5 of the resolution affirmed 'that the promotion of economic growth in developing countries is essential to address problems of environmental degradation.' Indeed, the necessity of reconciling environmental protection and economic and social development was at the heart of the call for UNCED, and had already been set forth in the report *Our Common Future.*

Yet, well before UNCED, the United Nations declared 1993 as the International Year of the World's Indigenous People.[4] Other organizations were also taking up this matter: UNESCO designated a special focal point for indigenous peoples and the International Labour Organization set up a programme for indigenous peoples, following its adoption of ILO Convention No. 169 on the rights of indigenous and tribal peoples in 1989. Indigenous peoples themselves were increasingly active in the effort to draft a UN declaration on the rights of indigenous peoples. Given the close connection between many indigenous communities and their lands and resources, as well as the location of UNCED in Brazil—a country with a large indigenous population—it was inevitable that the concerns of indigenous peoples would be raised at UNCED.

## II) The Principle as Enshrined in the Rio Declaration

### 1. Preparatory work and context

With more than 1500 non-governmental organizations accredited to UNCED, the role of major groups and non-state actors could hardly be ignored. Indeed, the movement for environmental protection that led to the first UN Conference on the Human Environment, held in Stockholm in 1972, in large part resulted from grass roots efforts of civil society.

The first mention of a role for indigenous peoples came in the opening address of the Secretary-General of the Conference, Maurice Strong, at the first PrepCom, held in Nairobi on 6 August 1990.[5] In this speech outlining the goals and procedures of the conference, Strong referred to the contributions of important constituencies, including indigenous peoples, who would help shape the outcome. He argued for the broadest possible participation of non-governmental groups, drawing on the experience of an early meeting in which such groups were included as full partners in the preparatory process.

PrepCom III adopted decision 3/7 on involvement of indigenous peoples in programmes for sustainable development, as a result of which the secretariat of the conference prepared a background document.[6] Unlike the actual text of Principle 22 and Agenda 21, Chapter 26, both of which view indigenous people as useful to protecting ecosystems, the secretariat's document examines the issue of environmental soundness and sustainable development from the perspective of ensuring the well-being of indigenous peoples.[7] Yet, it avoids any discussion of indigenous land and resource rights, calling only for empowering indigenous peoples and protecting their 'habitats', as well as recognizing and promoting their values, traditional knowledge, and resource management practices as contributions to environmentally sound and sustainable development.

4 General Assembly Resolution 45/164, 18 December 1990.

5 Report of the Secretary-General of the Conference, Addendum, A/Conf.151/PC/5/Add.1, 6 August 1990.

6 A/CONF.151/PC/100/Add.13, Strengthening the Role of Major Groups.

7 Strengthening the Role of Major Groups, para 35.

Also important in raising awareness of the concerns of indigenous peoples was the World Conference of Indigenous Peoples, which took place in Rio de Janeiro just before UNCED. They shared their experiences and emphasized their traditional knowledge and presence in the most important vulnerable ecosystems. On the first day of UNCED, Maurice Strong counselled the conference to 'hear and heed their voices, learn from their experience and respect their right to live in their own lands in accordance with their traditions, values and cultures.' By this point, Principle 22 had already been drafted without any reference to the rights of indigenous peoples. The text was approved at PrepCom IV, held in New York in April 1992. The draft Declaration was the only text without brackets sent to UNCED.

Indigenous representatives present during the PrepComs did not seek a separate chapter or principle on indigenous peoples, instead seeking to have the issues and perspectives of the indigenous peoples reflected in all the principles and chapters. When these concerns found little reception among the official delegates, the indigenous representatives present shifted their efforts to strengthening Principle 22 and Chapter 26 of Agenda 21. The ability to achieve inclusion of indigenous peoples as one of the major groups was due to lobbying efforts by indigenous peoples, NGOs and some advocates from governments. The result was significant in giving new impetus to efforts to include environmental issues as well as land and resource rights in the then on-going work to conclude the UN Declaration on the Rights of Indigenous Peoples, albeit it took another fifteen years before the Declaration was adopted.

## 2. Scope and dimensions

### 2.1. *Indigenous 'people' and sustainable development*

Principle 22 does not recognize indigenous peoples, omitting the final 's' that acknowledges the collective identity and rights of such groups. It also looks at the role of indigenous peoples through an instrumental lens, foreseeing the contributions such groups can make to achieve sustainable development, because of their unique knowledge and traditional practices that have maintained ecosystems over millennia.

Principle 22 is thus not rights-based and ignores both historical injustices and the insistent demands of indigenous peoples for recognition of their land rights and right to self-determination. Principle 22 instead takes a utilitarian approach to supporting their identity and 'vital role' in environmental management. The text only recommends ('should') that states recognize indigenous identity, cultures, and interests and enable their participation in the achievement of sustainable development.

In this respect, the article is considerably weaker than Principle 10 with its insistence that states shall provide public information, participation, and redress in respect to environmental matters.

### 2.2. *Legal nature*

As noted above, Principle 10 on the rights of information, participation and consultation has been cited far more frequently than Principle 22,[8] which with its weak formulation has been largely superseded by the 2007 UN Declaration on the Rights of Indigenous Peoples

[8] See the chapter by J. Ebbesson in this volume.

('UNDRIP')[9] and jurisprudence on indigenous land rights in the Inter-American and African regional human rights bodies.[10]

Nonetheless, together with article 8j of the Convention on Biological Diversity,[11] Principle 22 influenced the text of the Nagoya Protocol on access to and benefit-sharing from genetic resources[12] and a number of other instruments (section II) 3 of this chapter). This said, none of these texts satisfy indigenous concerns, and they have created some suspicion about other international environmental programmes, such as UN-REDD.[13]

## 3. Normative impact

### 3.1. *Overview*

Prior to UNCED, indigenous peoples had already succeeded in establishing specific forums within the United Nations in which they could press issues of concern to them. Implementation of Principle 22 and Agenda 21[14] became a subject of review in 1996 at the fourteenth session of the UN Working Group on Indigenous Populations. It was clear that efforts had to continue in order to achieve what became the UNDRIP.

### 3.2. *Agenda 21*

Agenda 21 builds on Principle 22 and the related principles concerned with major groups, becoming the first UN document to identify roles and responsibilities for stakeholders. The nine chapters on 'Major Groups' undoubtedly had an impact on the implementation and monitoring of Agenda 21.

Chapter 26 is entitled 'Recognizing and Strengthening the Role of Indigenous People and their Communities.' Again, the term chosen is 'people' and not 'peoples'—a way to avoid any discussion of collective rights to ancestral lands or self-determination, which Chapter 26 studiously and deliberately avoids. Instead, the chapter merely recognizes that indigenous communities have 'an historical relationship with their lands.' The text then calls for 'recognition that the lands of indigenous people and their communities should be protected from activities that are environmentally unsound or that the indigenous people concerned consider to be socially and cultural inappropriate.'

This somewhat paternalistic formulation falls well short of the rights recognized previously in ILO Convention No. 169[15] and subsequently affirmed in the UNDRIP. Even the call for participation in the formulation of policies, laws and programmes related to resource management and other development processes that may affect indigenous

[9] United Nations Declaration on the Rights of Indigenous Peoples, GA Res. 61/295, Annex, UN Doc A/RES/61/295 (13 Sept. 2007) ('UNDRIP').

[10] See section II) 4 of this chapter.

[11] Convention on Biological Diversity, 5 June 1992, 1760 UNTS 142, 31 ILM 822 ('CBD').

[12] Nagoya Protocol on Access to Genetic Resources and the Fair and Equitable Sharing of Benefits Arising from their Utilization to the Convention on Biological Diversity, 29 Oct. 2010, UN Doc UNEP/CBD/COP/DEC/X/. ('Nagoya ABS Protocol').

[13] Barnsley, I., UNU-IAS Guide Reducing Emissions from Deforestation and Forest Degradation in Developing Countries ('REDD'): A Guide for Indigenous Peoples 18–21 (2009), available at <http://www.unutki.org/news.php?news_id=50&doc_id=106>.

[14] Report of the United Nations Conference on Environment and Development, A/CONF.151/26/Rev.l (vol l), Resolution 1, Annex 2: Agenda 21 ('Agenda 21').

[15] ILO, *Convention Concerning Indigenous and Tribal Peoples in Independent Countries* (ILO Doc 169), adopted 27 June 1989, entered into force 5 September 1991, 28 ILM 1382, ('ILO Convention No. 169'), (1989) 28 ILM 1382.

communities, is limited to 'where appropriate.' The one mention of rights is the statement that indigenous people and communities are entitled to non-discriminatory enjoyment of 'the full measure' of human rights and fundamental freedoms.

### *3.3. Multilateral environmental agreements*

Despite its shortcomings, Principle 22 has been echoed in other instruments, mainly in the field of environmental protection.

The 1992 Convention on Biological Diversity, which calls on states to take effective national action to halt the destruction of species, habitats, and ecosystems,[16] also mandates, in articles 8(j), 10(c) and related provisions, consideration of indigenous communities in terms of sharing the benefits derived from the utilization of traditional knowledge.[17]

The CBD Conference of Parties adopted the Nagoya Protocol on Access to Genetic Resources and the Fair and Equitable Sharing of Benefits Arising from their Utilization to the Convention on Biological Diversity,[18] which is mainly designed to ensure indigenous peoples and local communities adequate participation in and the sharing of benefits resulting from the use of genetic resources and traditional knowledge about them.[19]

The parties to the UN Framework Convention on Climate Change have also addressed the potential vulnerability of indigenous peoples in the face of climate change.[20]

Principle 22 is also reflected in some regional environmental instruments, such as the African Convention on the Conservation of Nature and Natural Resources.[21]

### *3.4. Global human rights treaties*

In international law, recognition of the rights of indigenous peoples has expanded considerably in recent years, despite the fact that most early human rights treaties are individualistic in approach and do not mention indigenous peoples.

The International Covenant on Civil and Political Rights ('ICCPR')[22] and the International Covenant on Economic, Social and Cultural Rights ('ICESCR')[23]

[16] See Anton, D. K. and Shelton, D. L., *Environmental Protection and Human Rights* (Cambridge University Press 2011), 98.

[17] CBD, arts 8(j), 10(c), and related provisions.

[18] Rep. of the Seventh Conference of Parties to the Convention on Biological Diversity (Kuala Lumpur, Malaysia), Decision VII/16 UNEP/CBD/COP/7/21, paras 253–79 (13 Apr. 2004), available at <http://www.cbd.int/doc/meetings/cop/cop-07/official/cop-07-21-part1-en.pdf>; Fitzmaurice, M., 'Dilemma of Traditional Knowledge: Indigenous Peoples and Traditional Knowledge' (2008) 10 *Int'l Comm. L Rev* 255, 262–4.

[19] Nagoya ABS Protocol, arts 5–12.

[20] Barnsley, UNU-IAS Guide Reducing Emissions from Deforestation and Forest Degradation in Developing Countries: A Guide for Indigenous Peoples 18–21 (2009); Report of the 16th Sess. of the Conference of Parties to the UN Framework Convention on Climate, Decision 1/CP.16, paras 7, 12, 72, 87, Appendix 1(c), 1(d), UN Doc FCCC/CP/2010/7/Add.11 (15 Mar. 2011), available at <http://unfccc.int/resource/docs/2010/cop16/eng/07a01.pdf#page=12>; SBSTA, Report of the Subsidiary Body for Scientific and Technological Advice on its thirty-fourth session, held in Bonn from 6–16 June, Annex I para 1, UN Doc FCCC/SBSTA/2011/2 (3 Aug. 2011) (Framework Convention on Climate Change subsidiary body report), available at <http://unfccc.int/resource/docs/2011/sbsta/eng/02.pdf>; Report of the Conference of the Parties on its seventeenth session, held in Durban from 28 November–11 December 2011: Addendum: Part Two: Action taken by the Conference of the Parties at its seventeenth session. Decision 6/CP.17, para 4, UN Doc FCCC/CP/2011/9/Add.2 (15 Mar. 2012), available at <http://unfccc.int/resource/docs/2011/cop17/eng/09a02.pdf#page=16>.

[21] African Convention on the Conservation of Nature and Natural Resources, 15 September 1968, 1001 UNTS 3 (revised on 11 July 2003).

[22] See International Covenant on Civil and Political Rights, art 23, opened for signature 16 Dec. 1966, S. Treaty Doc 95-20 (1978), 999 UNTS 171 ('ICCPR').

[23] International Covenant on Economic, Social and Cultural Rights, 16 Dec. 1966, 993 UNTS 3 (1967) ('ICESCR').

guarantee collective or group rights only in respect to the family as 'the natural and fundamental group unit of society',[24] in respect to colonial peoples,[25] and perhaps for victims of the most extreme violations of the human rights of a particular group.[26] For other peoples, article 27 of the ICCPR guarantees individual members of the group the right to enjoy their 'own culture, to profess and to practice their own religion, or to use their own language,'[27] but the group as such is not protected. The right of 'peoples' to self-determination cannot provide the basis of a communication before the Human Rights Committee.[28]

The claims of indigenous peoples to resources, territory, and governmental powers are not explicitly set forth in any of the general human rights treaties.[29] In a 2000 report on the rights of indigenous peoples, the Inter-American Commission found the law deficient, concluding that an:

> approach to the rights of indigenous peoples via the concepts of 'minorities' or 'prohibition on discrimination,' while the only mechanism in some cases, is incomplete and reductionist, and therefore inadequate...as it fails to recognize the nature and complexity of indigenous peoples.[30]

The right to self-determination set out in article 1 of both International Covenants on human rights has been expanded through interpretive efforts. The explicit guarantees have also been read to contain other implicit rights. The Committee on the Elimination of Racial Discrimination, for example, has interpreted the right to collective property in article 5 of the Convention for the Elimination of All Forms of Racial Discrimination to encompass a procedure of free, prior, and informed consultation and consent in cases where major development or investment plans have a profound impact on indigenous communal property.[31] Other general comments and recommendations of treaty bodies

[24] See ICESCR at art 10 (providing that the greatest protection should be afforded to the family unit, as it is the 'fundamental group unit of society.'); ICCPR, art 23(1) ('The family is the natural and fundamental group unit of society and is entitled to protection by society and the State').

[25] Common art 1 of the ICCPR and the ICESCR states that: '[a]ll peoples have the right of self-determination. By virtue of that right they freely determine their political status and freely pursue their economic, social and cultural development.' The collective right to self-determination set forth in common art 1 of the UN Covenants is generally viewed as applicable only to colonial peoples, but see Cassese, A., *Self-Determination Of Peoples: A Legal Reappraisal* (Cambridge University Press 1995), 55–7 (asserting that under art 1, indigenous people have the right to self determination which includes claims to resources, territory, and power).

[26] See the extensive discussion of secession and self-determination in *Reference re Secession of Quebec*, [1998] 2 SCR 217 and *Gunme v. Cameroons*, Comm. 266/2003 Afr. Comm'n HPR, EX.CL/529(XV), 45th Ordinary Session, 13–27 May 2009, Annex 4.

[27] See ICCPR, art 27 (providing that minority groups shall not be impeded from practicing their religion, speaking their native language or taking part in the enjoyment of their culture).

[28] See *Bernard Ominayak and the Lubicon Band v. Canada*, HRC Communication No. 167/1984 (26 March 1990), para 13.3.

[29] See Lenzerini, F., 'Sovereignty Revisited: International Law and Parallel Sovereignty of Indigenous Peoples' (2006) 42 *Texas International Law Journal* 155, 163–4 (noting that indigenous peoples often insist that they should be recognized as a state because of their claims to certain resources, territory, and power).

[30] Inter-American Commission on Human Rights, The Human Rights Situation of the Indigenous People in the Americas, 20 October 2000, Doc 62, OEA/Ser.L/V/II.108, at Introduction.

[31] International Convention on the Elimination of All Forms of Racial Discrimination, 21 Dec. 1965, 660 UNTS 195 (entered into force 4 Jan. 1969); Committee on the Elimination of Racial Discrimination ('CERD'), Report of the Committee on the Elimination of Racial Discrimination: Annex V-General Recommendation XXIII, at 4(d), UN Doc Supp. No. 18 (A/52/18) (26 Sept. 1997); CERD, Consideration of reports submitted by States parties under art 9 of the Convention: Guatemala (concluding observations), para 11, UN Doc CERD/C/GTM/CO/12-13 (19 May 2010). See also the views of Human Rights Committee, on the basis of art 27 of the International Covenant on Civil and Political Rights, on the interdependence between

are particularly relevant and important in safeguarding the rights of indigenous peoples in isolation and first contact.[32]

## *3.5. The ILO Convention No. 169*

Recent specialized legal instruments, concluded largely as a result of litigation and lobbying efforts by indigenous peoples themselves, have advanced the recognition of indigenous rights.

ILO Convention No. 169,[33] negotiated with the intent of replacing ILO Convention No. 107, progressed in referring to 'indigenous peoples' rather than 'indigenous populations'[34] and recognizes the communal land rights of indigenous communities,[35] including natural resource rights.[36]

The Convention is particularly important because it recognizes specific rights in the areas of consultation (art 6), participation (art 7), lands and territories (arts 13–19) and health care (art 25). It also specifies States' obligations in terms of guaranteeing the rights recognized in the Convention (art 2), respecting the cultures and ways of life of indigenous peoples (art 5) and adopting appropriate special measures for safeguarding indigenous people and institutions.

## *3.6. The UNDRIP*

The UN Declaration on the Rights of Indigenous Peoples[37] approved by consensus on 13 September 2007, declares that 'indigenous peoples have the right of self-determination' and states that 'by virtue of that right they freely determine their political status and freely pursue their economic, social and cultural development.'[38] The Declaration guarantees

the cultural rights of indigenous peoples and other rights such as the rights to self-determination, territory, and natural resources, culture and religious practices.

[32] *Indigenous Peoples and United Nations Human Rights Bodies: A Compilation of UN Treaty Body Jurisprudence and the Recommendations of the Human Rights Council* 2–3 (Fergus MacKay, ed, 2011). Relevant general comments include: the Human Rights Committee's general comment No. 23 on the rights of minorities (art 27 of the Covenant) and general comment No. 27 on freedom of movement (art 12 of the Covenant); general recommendation No. XXIII of the Committee on the Elimination of Racial Discrimination, which concerns the rights of indigenous peoples; and general comment No. 14 of the Committee on Economic, Social and Cultural Rights on the right to the highest attainable standard of health (art 12 of the International Covenant on Economic, Social and Cultural Rights). For comments on state reports, see eg: CERD, Consideration of reports submitted by States parties under art 9 of the Convention: Concluding observations of the Committee on the Elimination of Racial Discrimination: Finland, para 14, UN Doc CERD/C/FIN/CO/19 (13 Mar. 2009); CCPR Human Rights Comm., Consideration of reports submitted by States parties under art 40 of the Convention: Concluding observations: Chile, para 9, UN Doc CCPR/C/CHL/CO/5 (18 May 2007); CCPR Human Rights Comm., Consideration of reports submitted by States parties under art 40 of the Convention: Concluding observations: Panama, at 21, UN Doc CCPR/C/PAN/CO/3 (17 Apr. 2008); CCPR Human Rights Comm., Consideration of reports submitted by States parties under art 40 of the Convention: Concluding observations: Nicaragua, para 21, UN Doc CCPR/C/NIC/CO/3, (12 Dec. 2008); Comm. on Economic, Social and Cultural Rights, Consideration of reports submitted by States parties under arts 16 and 17 of the Covenant: Concluding observations: Ecuador, paras 12, 35, UN Doc E/C.12/1/Add.100 (7 June 2004); Comm. on Economic, Social and Cultural Rights, Consideration of reports submitted by States parties under arts 16 and 17 of the Covenant: Concluding observations: Colombia, paras 9–11, UN Doc E/C.12/COL/CO/5 (21 May 2010); Comm. on Economic, Social and Cultural Rights, Consideration of reports submitted by States parties under arts 16 and 17 of the Covenant: Concluding observations: Peru, para 23, UN Doc E/C.12/PER/CO/2-4 (30 May 2012).

[33] ILO Convention No. 169. [34] ILO Convention No. 169, art 1.

[35] ILO Convention No. 169, art 13. [36] ILO Convention No. 169, art 15.

[37] UNDRIP. [38] UNDRIP, art 3.

the rights of indigenous peoples to 'live in freedom...as distinct peoples' (art 7), and requires States to establish effective mechanisms to prevent and redress '[a]ny action which has the aim or effect of depriving them of their integrity as distinct peoples, or of their cultural values or ethnic identities', and '[a]ny form of forced assimilation or integration' of indigenous peoples (art 8.2).

These rights apply to all indigenous peoples, including indigenous peoples in isolation. Indeed, virtually all the rights the Declaration enumerates are important for such peoples: the right to autonomy and self-government (art 4), the right to maintain their own institutions (art 5), the right to preserve their traditions and customs (art 11), the right to practice, develop and teach their traditions and customs (art 12), the right to transmit their cultures and beliefs to future generations (art 13), the right to participation (arts 18, 27, 30, and 31), the right to consultation and to free, prior and informed consent (art 19), the right to maintain their traditional medicines and health practices (art 24) and rights over their lands, territories and resources (arts 25–32).

Also relevant are the obligations it establishes for States and for United Nations bodies and specialized agencies (arts 38 and 42) to facilitate the exercise of the rights set out in the Declaration. While the Declaration was not adopted as a legally binding instrument, its content represents an international consensus on the rights ascribed to indigenous peoples and it provides a touchstone for global and regional human rights bodies examining indigenous issues.[39]

### 3.7. *The Rio Summit 2012*

At the conclusion of the Rio+20 Conference in 2012, the outcome document, *The Future We Want*, explicitly called for action in support of indigenous peoples, such as the eradication of poverty in light of the disproportionate impact globalization has had on destitute populations.[40] The Rio+20 Conference also called for indigenous communities to achieve representation in government and be key participants in political processes.[41]

The UNCED texts may have paved the way for some of the advances in recognition of indigenous rights, but all the texts together have not halted land and resource degradation on indigenous territories. Not all states implement prior consultation or participation of indigenous groups in decisions over development projects. Practices continue to displace indigenous peoples for roads, logging, mining, and hydroelectric projects designed without their participation or recognition of their rights to their lands and self-determination.

[39] The Inter-American Court of Human Rights ('ICtHR'), in *Saramaka People v. Suriname*, uses the UNDRIP, along with ILO Convention No. 169, as the framework for establishing the legal grounds for the judgment, in effect recognizing the Declaration's value as a source of law in the inter-American system, particularly in relation to the issue of free, prior and informed consent. See Case of the *Saramaka People v. Suriname*, Preliminary Objections, Merits, Reparations, and Costs, Judgment, ICtHR (ser. C) No. 172 (28 Nov. 2007).

[40] Rio+20: UN Conference on Sustainable Development, 20–22 June 2012, *The Future We Want*, paras 43, 49, 58(j), Res. 66/288, UN Doc A/66/L.56 (24 Jul. 2012) (outcome document adopted at Rio+20), available at <http://www.uncsd2012.org/content/documents/727The%20Future%C20We%C20Want%C2019%C20June%1230pm.pdf>.

[41] *The Future We Want*, paras 71, 109, 131.

## 4. Jurisprudential relevance

### *4.1. The Inter-American context*

At the regional level, Inter-American human rights bodies have developed a unique jurisprudence that gives prominence to the collective[42] and individual land and resource rights of indigenous peoples,[43] and a host of procedural rights linked to the substance of land ownership and possession. This body of jurisprudence has been developed around the right to property, defined in cultural and religious as well as economic terms.[44] Other rights repeatedly applied in indigenous cases include the rights to participate in government and to have judicial protection of other rights,[45] as guaranteed by the American Declaration on the Rights and Duties of Man (American Declaration),[46] and the American Convention on Human Rights (American Convention).[47] One of the earliest cases bringing the Commission's attention to the plight of the indigenous people was *Yanomami v. Brazil*, Case 7615 (Brazil), *1984–1985 Annual Report of the Inter-American Commission on Human Rights* 24, OEA/Ser.L/V/II.66, doc 10, rev.1 (1985). The petition alleged that the government violated the American Declaration of the Rights and Duties of Man by constructing a highway through Yanomami territory and authorizing exploitation of the territory's resources. These actions led to the influx of nonindigenous, who brought contagious diseases that remained untreated because of a lack of medical care. The Commission found that the government had violated the Yanomami's rights to life,

[42] See: Case of the *Yakye Axa Indigenous Community v. Paraguay*, Merits, Reparations, and Costs, Judgment, ICtHR (ser. C) no. 125, paras 95–6 (17 June 2005); *Sawhoyamaxa Indigenous Community v. Paraguay*, Merits, Reparations, and Costs, Judgment, ICtHR (ser. C) no. 146, para 117 (29 March 2006); *Saramaka People v. Suriname*, paras 92–3; Case of the *Xákmok, Kásek Indigenous Community v. Paraguay*, Merits, Reparations, and Costs, Judgment, ICtHR (ser. C) no. 214, para 157 (24 Aug. 2010); *Pueblo Indígena Kichwa de Sarayaku v. Ecuador*, Merits, and Reparations, Judgment, ICtHR (ser. C) no. 245, paras 160–4, 201 (27 June 2012).

[43] See Tramontana, E., 'The Contribution of the Inter-American Human Rights Bodies to Evolving International Law on Indigenous Rights over Lands and Natural Resources' (2010) *17 International Journal of Minority & Group Rights* 241; Barelli, M., 'The Interplay between Global and Regional Human Rights Systems in the Construction of the Indigenous Rights Regime' (2010) 32 *Human Rights Quarterly* 951; Baluarte, D. C., 'Balancing Indigenous Rights and a State's Right to Develop in Latin America: The Inter-American Rights Regime and ILO Convention 169' (2004) 4 *Sustainable Development Law and Policy* 9, 10; Tramontana, E., 'The Contribution of the Inter-American Human Rights Bodies to Evolving International Law on Indigenous Rights over Lands and Natural Resources' (2010) 17 *International Journal of Minority & Group Rights* 241, 242.

[44] See: *Mayagna (Sumo) Awas Tingni Community v. Nicaragua*, Preliminary Objections, Judgment, ICtHR (ser. C) no. 66 (1 Feb. 2000); *Moiwana Community v. Suriname,* Preliminary Objections, Merits, Reparations and Costs, Judgment, ICtHR (ser. C) no 124 (15 June 2005); *Yakye Axa Indigenous Community v. Paraguay*, Merits, Reparations and Costs, Judgment, ICtHR (ser. C) no. 125 (17 June 2005); *Yatama v. Nicaragua*, Preliminary Objections, Merits, Reparations and Costs, Judgment, ICtHR (ser. C) no. 127 (23 June 2005); *Saramaka People v. Suriname*, Preliminary Objections, Merits, Reparations, and Costs, Judgment, ICtHR (ser. C) no. 172 (28 Nov. 2007); *Xákmok Kásek Indigenous Community v. Paraguay*, Merits, Reparations and Costs, Judgment, ICtHR (ser. C) no. 214 (24 Aug. 2010); *Pueblo Indígena Kichwa de Sarayaku v. Ecuador*, Merits, and Reparations, Judgment, ICtHR (ser. C) no. 245 (27 June 2012).

[45] Page, A., 'Indigenous Peoples' Free Prior and Informed Consent in the Inter-American Human Rights System' (2004) 4 *Sustainable Development Law and Policy* 16, 16.

[46] American Declaration of the Rights and Duties of Man, OAS Res. XXX, *reprinted in* Basic Documents Pertaining to Human Rights in the Inter-American System, OAS/Ser.L/V/I.4 Rev. 9 (2003); (1949) 43 *AJIL* Supp. 133, ('American Declaration'). The American Declaration is utilized as a source of international legal obligations for member States of the Organization of American States ('OAS') by both the Commission and the Court. *Basic Document Pertaining to Human Rights in the Inter-American System: Introduction*, Inter-Am. Commission on Human Rights, <http://www.cidh.oas.org/basicos/english/Basic1.%20Intro.htm>.

[47] American Convention on Human Rights, 22 Nov. 1969, in force 18 July 1978, OAS T.S. No, 36, 444 UNTS 123.

liberty, and personal security guaranteed by article 1 of the Declaration, as well as the right of residence and movement (art 8) and the right to the preservation of health and well-being (art 11). Subsequently, the Commission issued a country report on human rights in Ecuador[48] that expanded on the duties of the state toward indigenous peoples, especially in the context of development projects. The Commission placed its emphasis on the procedural rights of information, participation, and redress. Later cases have added substantive protections.

For its part, the Inter-American Court has recognized the importance of rights to land and territory of all indigenous peoples: 'The relation of an indigenous community with its land must be recognized and understood as the fundamental basis of its culture, spiritual life, integrity and economic survival. For such peoples their communal nexus with the ancestral territory is not merely a matter of possession and production, but rather consists in material and spiritual elements that must be fully integrated and enjoyed by the community, so that it may preserve its cultural legacy and pass it on to the future generation.'[49] International instruments and jurisprudence have devoted considerable attention to the rights to information, participation, and redress in the context of extractive industries and other economic activities potentially destructive of land and territory.

The Court explained in considerable detail the property guarantees afforded indigenous peoples in its 2007 judgment in *Saramaka People v. Suriname.*[50] Like the prior cases, this one concerned land and resource claims stemming from concessions granted by the State for the exploration and extraction of natural resources. The Court concluded that resources related to agricultural, hunting, and fishing activities are protected as subsistence activities, but it also considered the impact on subsistence resources of other activities. The Court attempted to strike a balance. It noted that clean water is essential to the subsistence activity of fishing and that water quality is likely to be impacted by extraction of resources not traditionally used or essential for the survival of the Saramaka. In fact, all extractive activities are likely to affect the use and enjoyment of other resources necessary to the people. However, the Court held that the protection of the right to property is not absolute and cannot be read to preclude all concessions for exploration and extraction in the Saramaka territory. Article 21 itself provides for the limitation of property rights under certain circumstances but even where the State complies with the conditions set forth in the Article, the Court will assess and give crucial weight to the question of 'whether the restriction amounts to a denial of the [indigenous and tribal peoples] traditions and customs in a way that endangers the very survival of the group and its members'.[51]

The Court set forth three safeguards it deemed essential: (1) the State must ensure the effective participation of the members of the Saramaka people, in conformity with their customs and traditions, regarding any development, investment, exploration, or extraction plan within Saramaka territory; (2) the State must guarantee that the Saramakas will receive a reasonable benefit from any such plan within their territory; and (3) the State must ensure that no concession will be issued within Saramaka territory unless and until independent and technically capable entities, with the State's supervision, perform a prior

[48] Report on the Situation of Human Rights in Ecuador, OEA/Ser.L/V/II.96, Doc 10 rev.1, 24 Apr. 1997.

[49] *Case of the Moiwana Community (Suriname)* (2005), ICtHR (Ser. C) no. 124, para 131.

[50] *Saramaka People v. Suriname.*

[51] *Saramaka People v. Suriname*, para 128.

environmental and social impact assessment. It is notable that these requirements parallel the Bonn Guidelines on Access and Equitable Benefit-Sharing, adopted pursuant to the Convention on Biological Diversity, although the Court does not cite them directly. The Court viewed benefit-sharing as inherent to the right of compensation recognized under article 21(2) of the Convention.[52] This right to compensation extends to any deprivation of the regular use and enjoyment of property.

The first duty requires the State both to compile and to disseminate information and entails constant good faith consultations, through culturally appropriate procedures and with the objective of reaching an agreement. Applying its tests, the Court found that the concessions granted by the State failed to comply with the necessary safeguards, violating the right to property of the Saramaka people. The Court ordered: demarcation of Saramaka lands within a specified time frame and abstention from use of the territory until demarcation (unless the Saramaka give prior consent); review of all concessions already granted; environmental impact assessments ('EIAs') to be undertaken prior to any new concessions; and adoption of measures necessary to ensure consultation with the Saramakas and effective redress for them. The Court awarded compensation for the resources already removed as well as USD 600,000 for the environmental damage and destruction of resources that had occurred, to be paid into a community development fund created and established by Suriname for the benefit of the Saramaka.

### 4.2. *The African context*

Like the United Nations Covenants, but unlike other regional human rights treaties, the African Charter on Human and Peoples' Rights contains a right of self-determination. In 2009, the African Commission on Human and Peoples Rights faced a conflict between purported environmental protection measures and the rights of indigenous peoples in Kenya: *Centre for Minority Rights Development (Kenya) and Minority Rights Group International on behalf of Endorois Welfare Council v. Kenya*, Afr. Comm'n HPR, Case 276/2003 (4 Feb. 2010).

The complaint on behalf of the Endorois Community alleged that the government of Kenya forcibly removed the Endorois from their ancestral lands without proper prior consultations or adequate and effective compensation when the government created the Lake Hannington Game Reserve in 1973, and re-gazetted the Lake Bogoria Game Reserve in 1978. After domestic litigation failed to provide redress in 2000, parts of the Endorois' ancestral land was allegedly demarcated and sold by the state to third parties. In 2002, concessions for ruby mining on Endorois traditional land were granted to a private company. The petitioners further alleged that the process of evicting them from their traditional land severed their spiritual, cultural, and economic ties to the land. Endorois sought restitution of their land, with legal title and clear demarcation and compensation to the community for all their losses.

On the merits, the African Commission was 'not convinced that removing the Endorois from their ancestral land was a lawful action in pursuit of economic development or ecological protection' (para 173). The African Commission concluded that the

[52] Art 21(2) provides that '[n]o one shall be deprived of his property except upon payment of just compensation, for reasons of public utility or social interest, and in the cases and according to the forms established by law.'

Endorois property rights were encroached upon, in particular by the expropriation and the effective denial of ownership of their land. In terms of consultation, the Commission found that the threshold is especially stringent in favour of indigenous peoples, as it also requires that *consent* be accorded. Failure to observe the obligations to consult and to seek consent—or to compensate—ultimately results in a violation of the right to property (para 226). The failure to guarantee effective participation was also held to violate the Endorois right to development. The African Commission noted that its own standards state that a Government must consult with respect to indigenous peoples especially when dealing with sensitive issues such as land.[53]

## III) Relations with Other Principles

The impact of Rio Principle 10 on the development of international law on indigenous peoples is incontestable. The UN Declaration on the Rights of Indigenous Peoples, as well as World Bank safeguards policies, and other legal instruments, place heavy emphasis on the duty of the State to engage in prior informed consultations with and allow the participation of indigenous peoples in any decisions that would affect them or their lands and resources. Indigenous peoples themselves are increasingly demanding the full implementation of these obligations by governmental authorities. Human rights bodies insist that the duty to engage in prior consultations and participation cannot be delegated to non-state actors and is encompassed with the right to property as well as the right to political participation and right to information.[54]

Indigenous peoples also have paid particular attention to Principle 8 which acknowledges that unsustainable patterns of production and consumption should be reduced to achieve sustainable development. As one commentator noted, 'indigenous peoples have questioned this kind of development since colonization.'[55] The absence of any reference to mining in the UNCED documents has been a source of particular criticism, because extractive industries have been the source of most displacement, environmental degradation, and loss of land for indigenous peoples.

The 'almost unmitigated disaster'[56] of Rio on the issue of forests must also be considered, given the concentration of indigenous peoples in the tropical and temperate forests of the world. Developed and developing countries split irretrievably over the issue, resulting in a weak, non-binding declaration of forest principles that fails to constrain exploitation of resources, including on indigenous lands. NGOs present at Rio condemned it immediately as a 'Chain-Saw Charter'.

[53] Report of the African Commission's Working Group of Experts on Indigenous Populations/Communities (Twenty-eighth session, 2003). See also ILO Convention 169 which states: 'Consultations carried out in application of this Convention shall be undertaken, in good faith and in a form appropriate to the circumstances, with the objective of achieving agreement or consent to the proposed measures.'

[54] See eg: *Saramaka People v. Suriname*; Comm. 276/03, *Centre for Minority Rights Development (Kenya) and Minority Rights Group (on behalf of Endorois Welfare Council) v. Kenya*, African Commission (4 Feb. 2010). Both of these cases concerned tribal communities who were assimilated to indigenous peoples for purposes of the legal analysis.

[55] Tauli-Corpus, V., 'The Implementation of Agenda 21 and Indigenous Peoples', in Alyanak, L. and Cruz, A. (eds), *Implementing Agenda 21: NGO Experiences from Around the World* (UNCTAD/NGLS/83, 1997), 17.

[56] Johnson, S. P., 'Introduction: Did We Really Save the Earth at Rio?', in *The Earth Summit* (London: Graham & Trotman/Martinus Nijhoff 1993), 5.

## IV) Assessment

UNCED marked a breakthrough for indigenous peoples in some respects, strengthened by the subsequent Johannesburg Summit that acknowledged the collective aspect by adding an 's' to people. It is also obvious that Rio started a process that gave the indigenous leaders an opportunity to pursue their policies for representing their peoples and consequently recognition of participation in processes globally. Still, their participation is hampered by a general lack of resources, and they are far from reaching their targets.

Targeted initiatives and international support structures for indigenous peoples have been established since UNCED, including the UN Declaration on the Rights of Indigenous Peoples. Implementation on the national level has been uneven, and although improvements are visible in some places, some states do not even acknowledge the existence of indigenous peoples within their countries. Indigenous peoples remain marginalized and experience more poverty and health problems than the rest of the population across many regions. Traditional knowledge and ancestral lands lack legal protection.

Indigenous people are recognized as formal stakeholders in a plethora of multilateral processes. Constituency and major group status has been secured in many fora; to some extent, the latter half of the principle has been implemented in the formal processes. However, in practice the voices of indigenous people are too easily ignored and overruled, and without full capacity building, the intricate processes can be alien—resulting in marginalization and a lack of representation that does little to integrate these important perspectives into the mainstream. The rights of indigenous populations have been increasingly recognized over the past 20 years. However despite multiple examples of the principle being incorporated into legislation, indigenous groups are still marginalized and there remains a large implementation gap, with the rights of these groups still frequently ignored despite the significant progress.

## V) Select Bibliography

Anaya, J., *Indigenous Peoples in International Law* (2nd edn, Oxford University Press 2004).

Anaya, J. and Williams, Jr, R. A., 'The Protection of Indigenous Peoples' Rights Over Lands and Natural Resources Under the Inter-American Human Rights System' (2001) 14 *Harvard Human Rights Law Journal* 33.

Anton, D. K. and Shelton, D., *Environmental Protection and Human Rights* (Cambridge University Press 2011).

Francioni, F. and Scheinin, M. (eds), Cultural Human Rights (Leiden: Martinus Nijhoff 2008).

Hitchcock, R. K., 'International Human Rights, the Environment, and Indigenous Peoples' (1994) 1 *Colorado Journal of International Environmental Law and Policy* 1.

Ibarra, M., *Traditional Practices in Respect of the Sustainable and Environmentally Sound Self-Development of Indigenous People*, UN Doc E/CN.4/Sub.2/1992/31/Add.1 (1 May 1992).

Inter-American Commission on Human Rights, *Indigenous and Tribal Peoples' Rights over Their Ancestral Lands and Natural Resources: Norms and Jurisprudence of the Inter-American Human Rights System*, OEA/Ser.L/V/II. Doc 56/09, 30 December 2009.

Shelton, D., 'What happened in Rio to human rights?' (1992) 3 *YbIEL* 75.
Shutkin, W. A., 'International Human Rights Law and the Earth: The Protection of Indigenous Peoples and the Environment' (1991) 31 *Virginia Journal of International Law* 479.
Thornberry, P., *Indigenous Peoples and Human Rights* (Manchester University Press 2002).
Wiessner, S., 'Rights and Status of Indigenous Peoples: A Global Comparative and International Legal Analysis' (1999) 12 *Harvard Human Rights Law Journal* 57.

# 27. Principle 23

## *The Environment of Oppressed Peoples*

Mara Tignino*

**Principle 23**

The environment and natural resources of people under oppression, domination and occupation shall be protected.



## I) Origins and Rationale of the Principle

Principle 23 clearly exemplifies the distinctiveness of the Rio Declaration. With principle 23, the Declaration became the first universal legal instrument to emphasize the rights of oppressed groups in relation to both the use of natural resources and the protection of the environment. Neither the Final Report of the World Commission on Environment and Development ('WCED')—better known as the Brundtland Commission,[1] and considered the most significant precursor of the Rio Conference, nor the 'Legal Principles for Environmental Protection and Sustainable Development' prepared by the WCED's experts

* Senior Researcher and Coordinator, Platform for International Water Law, Faculty of Law, University of Geneva.

[1] See *Environmental Protection and Sustainable Development, Expert Group on Environmental Law of the World Commission on Environment and Development* (Graham & Trotman, Martinus Nijhoff Publishers 1986).

in 1987,[2] directly addressed the need to protect the environmental and natural resource rights of oppressed peoples.

Nonetheless, the need to protect the environmental rights of oppressed people does find precedent in international environmental law materials dating back as far as the 1972 Stockholm Conference on the Human Environment. Although the resulting Stockholm Declaration did not contain language matching the exact expression of Principle 23, there are close parallels in both documents. In particular, Principle 1 of the Stockholm Declaration not only affirms that environmental protection is required to permit a life of dignity and well-being for present and future generations, but also places that principle in direct conflict with apartheid, colonial, and other forms of oppression, and foreign domination.[3] Furthermore, both the 1977 Mar del Plata Declaration of the United Nations Water Conference and the 1982 World Charter for Nature contain references to the protection of natural resources during armed conflicts—and in occupied territories specifically.[4]

## II) The Principle as Enshrined in the Rio Declaration

### 1. Preparatory work and context

In the aftermath of the decolonization process, those responsible for originally drafting Principle 23 wanted to remind governments of the painful legacy of colonialism and restore cooperative sustainable development. In addition, there was the need to protect rights over natural resources in occupied territories, and emphasize the obligations constraining the conduct of the occupying power in those territories.[5]

Against this background, Principle 23 ultimately represented a compromise. In the run-up to the Rio Conference, the G77 group and China proposed the inclusion of a draft of Principle 23 which, together with the protection of the natural resources for oppressed people, would have expressed commitment to the elimination of policies perpetuating racial discrimination, along with an end to foreign occupation or colonial domination. Like Principle 1 of the Stockholm Declaration, early drafts were intended to stress that the elimination of these policies and situations was a necessary condition of environmental sustainability. Other delegations, however, rejected this broader proposal. No doubt, much of the opposition was rooted in concerns about the principle's potential links to the Israeli occupation of the Palestinian Territories.[6] At the close of the negotiations, Principle 23 was therefore limited to expressing the particular need to protect the environmental

[2] *Environmental Protection and Sustainable Development, Expert Group on Environmental Law.*

[3] Principle 1 of the Stockholm Declaration. On the Stockholm Declaration, see generally Sohn, L. B., 'The Stockholm Declaration on the Human Environment' (1973) 14(3) *HILJ* 423.

[4] The resolution on 'Water policies in occupied territories' was adopted at the Mar del Plata Declaration of the United Nations Water Conference in 1976. Report of the United Nations Water Conference, Resolution X, E/CONF/70/29, Mar del Plata, 14–25 March 1977, 80. See the preamble (c) and Principle 5 of the World Charter for Nature. UN General Assembly Resolution on the World Charter for Nature, New York, 28 October 1982.

[5] See Ling, C. Y., *The Rio Declaration on Environment and Development: An Assessment* (Third World Network 2012).

[6] Ling, *The Rio Declaration*, 53–4.

and resource rights of people under oppression, domination or occupation—without speaking to the legitimacy of the underlying policies.

## 2. Scope and dimensions

### *2.1. The two dimensions of the principle*

#### 2.1.1. Overview

Like most of the Rio Declaration, Principle 23 lies at the crossroads of different areas of international law (ie environmental law, human rights law, and the laws of war), and it is best understood in the context of the Declaration's other principles. Both Principle 2 of the Rio Declaration and Principle 21 of the Stockholm Declaration affirm states' sovereign right to exploit their natural resources pursuant to their own environmental (and for Rio also developmental) policies. Principle 23 is among the small number of principles placing limits on, and providing guidance on the exercise of, those overarching rights. The immediately preceding principle, Principle 22, recognizes the vital role played by indigenous people in sustainable development (and environmental management in particular) as a result of their traditional knowledge and practices, while reiterating states' responsibility to protect the interests of those communities. Principle 24, on the other hand, urges maintained respect for international environmental law even during times of armed conflict, and speaks of a further obligation on states to continue developing the international law governing environmental protection during armed conflicts.

In some sense providing a bridge between the two adjacent principles, Principle 23 emphasizes the broader set of environmental and resource rights of people subject to various forms of state domination or foreign occupation. Given its connections, Principle 23 has two distinct but related aspects, which might be respectively called the 'permanent sovereignty' and 'environmental protection' dimensions.

The first dimension addresses the natural resource rights of peoples in general. The result of advocacy by a group of countries which included the Arab States, this principle was intended to ensure that peoples living under foreign occupation would enjoy the benefits arising from the exploitation of natural resources within their territories, and to defend their sovereignty over those resources from illegal exploitation or wanton destruction.[7]

The second is concerned with regulating and protecting against the particular environmental risks faced by dominated people. In some cases, this aspect constitutes a narrow and detailed application of the obligation on states, affirmed in both Principle 21 of the Stockholm Declaration and Principle 2 of the Rio Declaration, not to cause significant transboundary environmental harms. But because it can also be concerned with a dominated population within a single state, this aspect of Principle 23 goes beyond the regulation of border-crossing environmental impacts.

What a consideration of related treaty, custom, and case law demonstrates, however, is that separating these two dimensions in practice is not always easy. In many cases, failure to respect natural resource rights will create environmental harms and in others, harming the environment will threaten the viability and usefulness of natural resources. In most

[7] See Schrijver, N., *Sovereignty over Natural Resources: Balancing Rights and Duties* (Cambridge University Press 2008), 232.

cases, it is easier to think in terms of the underlying human interests protected rather than whether the rights protected are environmental or resource rights.

### 2.1.2. 'Permanent Sovereignty' and the rights of oppressed people

Though it only speaks to people 'living under oppression, domination or occupation', Principle 23 is rooted in the principle of permanent sovereignty of (all) peoples over their natural resources. The principle of permanent sovereignty over natural resources found its first expression in the United Nations during the early 1950s.[8] During the 1960s, the decolonization and human rights movements both supported the rights of peoples to reclaim control over their natural resources. The decolonization agenda refocused concerns about sovereignty, aiming to ensure that peoples that had faced colonial exploitation could benefit from the exploitation of the resources found within their territories.

The Declaration on Permanent Sovereignty over Natural Resources (Resolution 1803) of 1962 is considered a landmark for the recognition of this principle. While it spoke to the 'national development' and 'the well-being of the people of the State concerned' it nonetheless implicitly recognized '[t]he right of peoples and nations to permanent sovereignty over their natural wealth and resources.'[9]

Since then, numerous additional UN resolutions, and each of the ICESCR and the ICCPR of 1966[10] have recognized a principle of permanent sovereignty of peoples over their natural resources. According to these texts, a people's sovereignty over their natural resources is a pillar of the right of self-determination.[11] As stressed by the Human Rights Committee, the capacity of peoples to fully benefit from the natural resources they possess also entails corresponding obligations on states.[12]

In 1972, General Assembly resolution 3005 affirmed 'the principle of the sovereignty of the population of the occupied territories over their national wealth and resources'.[13] The following sessions saw the General Assembly adopt a series of resolutions concerned specifically with the permanent sovereignty over natural resources of the peoples in territories occupied by Israel.[14] In addition to the resolutions expressly referring to permanent sovereignty, a large number of other resolutions condemned, *inter alia*, the illegal exploitation of the natural wealth and resources of the occupied territories.[15]

Although no Security Council resolutions have expressly referred to permanent sovereignty over natural resources, Resolution 465 adopted in 1980 is pertinent. In the resolution, the Security Council requested that a commission established the previous year examine the situation relating to settlements in the occupied Arab territories, including

[8] See Resolution 1314 (VI) of 12 December 1958. See Schwebel, S., 'The Story of the United Nations Declaration on Permanent Sovereignty over Natural Resources', in Schwebel, S., *Justice in International Law: Selected Writings* (Cambridge University Press 1994), 401–15.

[9] Resolution 1803 (XVII), 14 December 1962, para 1.

[10] Art 1.2 common to both Covenants read: 'All peoples may, for their own ends, freely dispose of their natural wealth and resources without prejudice to any obligations arising out of international economic co-operation, based upon the principle of mutual benefit, and international law. In no case may a people be deprived of its own means of subsistence'.

[11] Abi-Saab, G., 'Permanent Sovereignty over Natural and Economic Activities', in Bedjaoui, M. (ed), *International Law: Achievements and Prospects* (Nijhoff 1991), 597.

[12] General Comment No 12, art 1 (Right to Self-Determination), HRI/GEN/1/Rev.9 (vol I), para 5.

[13] Resolution 3005 (XXVII), 15 December 1972, para 4.

[14] See eg Resolutions 3175 (XXVIII), 17 December 1973; 3336 (XXIX) (17 December 1974); 3516 (XXX), (15 December 1976); 37/135 (17 December 1982).

[15] See eg Resolutions 3092 (XXVIII) B (7 December 1973); 37/88 C (10 December 1982).

Jerusalem, and in particular 'investigate the reported serious depletion of natural resources, particularly the water resources, with a view to ensuring the protection of those important natural resources of the territories under occupation'.

In at least two instances, the International Court of Justice ('ICJ') has also touched on matters related to questions over permanent sovereignty over natural resources. They first arose in the context of proceedings instituted by Nauru against Australia in 1989 over the rehabilitation of certain Nauruan phosphate lands mined prior to the Nauru's independence. The application instituting proceedings claimed Australia had breached several international obligations, including an obligation to respect the Nauruan people's permanent sovereignty over their natural wealth and resources. While the court concluded that it had jurisdiction to entertain the application,[16] the parties reached a friendly settlement in 1993 and the case was therefore removed from the court's docket.[17]

Second, the East Timor case between Australia and Portugal arose from a treaty signed in 1989 between Indonesia and Australia—the Timor Gap Treaty[18]—for the purpose of jointly exploring and exploiting the hydrocarbon resources of an area of East Timor's continental shelf lying between East Timor and Australia (the Timor Gap). Portugal, in its capacity as continuing Administering Power,[19] brought an action against Australia alleging *inter alia* a breach both of its own right as Administering Power and the rights of the East Timorese people—namely self-determination and permanent sovereignty over natural resources. The court held that it could not entertain the case, because any determination as to the legality of Australia's conduct would require a prior determination regarding the conduct of a third party not before the court, namely Indonesia. Two dissenting opinions, however, addressed the principle of permanent sovereignty over natural resources, embracing the principle as an important right of contemporary international law with erga omnes character.[20]

### 2.1.3. The law of belligerent occupation and the rights of occupied peoples

One area in which the rights and obligations governing the management and use of natural resources of dominated, oppressed, or occupied people are well understood is the law of belligerent occupation, which regulates the conduct of occupying powers in territories belonging to enemy states during war time.

The body of law regarding occupation should be interpreted in light of the principle of permanent sovereignty over natural resources.[21] In its decision of 2005 regarding the *Armed Activities on the Territory of the Congo*, the International Court of Justice recognized the importance of the principle of permanent sovereignty over natural resources in occupied territories.[22] According to the opinion of Judge Koroma, the right of peoples and

[16] *Certain Phosphates Lands in Nauru (Nauru v. Australia), Preliminary Objections*, Judgment, ICJ Reports 1992, 240.

[17] Australia-Republic of Nauru: Settlement of the case in the International Court of Justice concerning certain phosphate lands in Nauru, (1993) 32 ILM 1471.

[18] Australia/Indonesia Treaty on the Zone of Cooperation in an Area between the Indonesian Province of East Timor and Northern Australia of 11 December 1989, (1990), 29 ILM 469.

[19] See eg General Assembly Resolution 3485 (XXX), 12 December 1975; and Security Council Resolution 384 (1975), 22 December 1975.

[20] See Dissenting opinion, Judge Weeramantry, ICJ Reports 1995, 197–9; Dissenting opinion, Judge Skubizewski, ICJ Reports 1995, 276.

[21] See Tignino, M., *L'eau et la guerre: éléments pour un régime juridique*, Académie de droit international humanitaire et de droits humains de Genève (Bruylant 2011).

[22] *Armed Activities on the Territory of Congo (Democratic Republic of Congo v. Uganda)*, Judgment, ICJ Reports 2005, para 244.

States to permanent sovereignty remain in effect at all times, including during armed conflict and during occupation.[23] Control over natural resources is an attribute of sovereignty which the occupant, as mere controller of the territory, does not possess.

Until the end of the occupation, the occupying power is under an obligation not to interfere with the exercise of permanent sovereignty vested in the local population.[24] Under the Hague Regulations, the occupant 'shall be regarded only as administrator and usufructuary' of the natural resources and 'must safeguard the capital'.[25] Full unrestricted exercise of the right to freely use, control, and dispose of natural resources should be restored only once control over the occupied territories has reverted to the States or peoples concerned.

The rights of an occupying power to use natural resources are thus transitory in time and proscribed in extent. The primary principle on which the law of occupation rests is that the occupant does not acquire any sovereignty over territory; it merely exercises *de facto* authority.[26] In other words, occupation does not result in the acquisition or transfer of sovereignty. The authority of an occupant is both transitory, and accompanied by an overriding obligation to respect the existing laws of the occupied territory.[27]

In exercising its authority, an occupying power must balance two competing goals: fulfilment of its military needs, and respect for the interests of the inhabitants. While military necessity may in some instances supersede, it should never result in total disregard for the interests and needs of the resident population.[28] For this reason, the occupant must not exercise its authority solely in furtherance of its own interests. In no case is it permitted to exploit the natural resources of the territory under its control for the benefit of its own civilian population. This prohibition has clear examples in international practice. In the 1956 *De Bataafsche Petroleum v. War Damage Commission* decision, the Singapore Court of Appeal condemned the seizure of oil in Malaysia by Japanese armed forces, which 'was forwarded to various destinations ... to meet not only military demands but also the civilian requirements' of Japan.[29] In addition, the 1976 Memorandum of the United States on the opening of new oil fields by Israel in the Sinai Peninsula and the Gulf of Suez stated

[23] Declaration of Judge Koroma, ICJ Reports 2005, para 11.

[24] See Implications under International Law of the United Nations Resolutions on Permanent Sovereignty over Natural Resources on the Occupied Palestinian and other Arab Territories and on the Obligations of Israel concerning its Conduct in these Territories (prepared by Sloan Blain), 21 June 1983, ONU Doc A/38/265, E/1983/85.

[25] Art 55 of the 1907 Hague Regulations provides: 'The occupying State shall be regarded only as administrator and usufructuary of public buildings, real estate, forests, and agricultural estates belonging to the hostile State, and situated in the occupied country. It must safeguard the capital of these properties, and administer them in accordance with the rules of usufruct'. See Scobbie, I., 'Natural Resources under Belligerent Occupation: Mutation through Permanent Sovereignty', in Bowen, S. (ed), *Human Rights, Self-Determination and Political Change in the Occupied Palestinian Territories* (Nijhoff 1997), 221.

[26] Art 42 of The Hague Regulations of 1907. This provision affirms: 'Territory is considered occupied when it is actually placed under the authority of the hostile army. The occupation extends only to the territory where such authority has been established and can be exercised'. See Von Glahn, G., *The Occupation of Enemy Territory: A Commentary on the Law and Practice of Belligerent Occupation* (University of Minnesota Press 1957), 28–9.

[27] Art 43 of the Hague Regulations of 1907 establishes the duty to preserve 'public order and safety', while 'respecting, unless absolutely prevented, the laws in force in the country'.

[28] See Glahn, G., 'Taxation under Belligerent Occupation', in Playfair, E. (ed), *International Law and the Administration of Occupied Territories* (Clarendon Press 1992), 207.

[29] *De Bataafsche Petroleum v. War Damage Commission* (1956) 22 *Malayan Law Journal* 155, reproduced in Sassoli, M. and Bouvier, A., *How Does Law Protect in War? Cases, Documents and Teaching Materials on Contemporary Practice in International Humanitarian Law* (ICRC 2003), vol II, 1072.

that giving unrestricted access to natural resources in occupied territory 'would constitute an incentive to territorial occupation by a country... and a disincentive to withdrawal'.[30]

In order to safeguard or protect natural resources, an occupant also has the obligation not to wantonly dissipate or destroy those resources. Article 53 of the Fourth Geneva Convention prohibits the occupant from destroying either state or private property other than for reasons of military necessity.[31] The boundary where a renewable resource becomes non-renewable represents the absolute limit for a belligerent occupation.[32] For example, in the case of groundwater resources, the occupant must respect their rate of replenishment.

The law of belligerent occupation theoretically applies only to populations of occupied states in wartime, but the underlying principle tends to support a restrictive interpretation of the occupant's power to exploit and dispose of natural resources in territory under occupation, even if the occupant has reservations about the 'statehood' of its enemy. While it cannot be suggested that such limitations on the exercise of a *de facto* governing authority are limited in the same way over dominated or oppressed peoples in general, the combination of strict limits and the goal of balancing the priorities of the governing authority with the people's underlying rights provides a useful analogue with other cases.

## 2.2. *Legal nature*

The principle of permanent sovereignty over natural resources represents a norm of international customary law.[33] Looting and illegal exploitation of natural resources is prohibited both in times of peace and armed conflict.[34] Numerous resolutions adopted by the United Nations General Assembly and the Security Council have stressed the importance of this principle during wars and in occupied territories. Some of them have also affirmed a right to compensation for the illegal exploitation of natural resources. For example, in the case of the Palestinian people, the General Assembly noted the right 'to claim restitution as a result of any exploitation, damage, loss or depletion or endangerment of their natural resources resulting from illegal measures'.[35] The legal nature of environmental rights of oppressed people should be defined. Essential natural resources indispensable for life are protected by customary norms such as equitable use, no-harm principle as well as procedural rights such as exchange of information and consultation. The risks of damage to natural resources must be prevented during the conduct of hostilities. Indeed, the precautionary principle has to be taken into account during the operations of war.[36] The lack of scientific certainty does not impede a party to follow due diligence requirements for safeguarding the environment.

[30] US State Department, Memorandum of Law on Israel's Rights to Develop New Oil Fields in Sinai and the Gulf of Suez, (1984) 23 ILM 746.

[31] Art 53 provides: 'Any destruction by the Occupying Power of real or personal property belonging individually or collectively to private persons, or to the State, or to other public authorities, or to social or cooperative organizations, is prohibited, except where such destruction is rendered absolutely necessary by military operations'. Convention (IV) relative to the Protection of Civilian Persons in Time of War, 12 August 1949.

[32] Scobbie, 'Natural Resources and Belligerent Occupation', 281.

[33] *Armed Activities on the Territory of Congo (Democratic Republic of Congo v. Uganda)*, Judgment, ICJ Reports 2005, para 244.

[34] Declaration of Judge Koroma, ICJ Reports 2005, para 11.

[35] A/RES/65/179, para 3.

[36] Rule 44 of the study of the International Committee of the Red Cross (ICRC) on customary international humanitarian law reads as follows: 'Lack of scientific certainty as to the effects on the environment of certain military operations does not absolve a party to the conflict from taking such precautions'. Henckaerts, J.-M. and Doswald-Beck, L. (eds), *Customary International Humanitarian Law*, vol 1: Rules (Cambridge University Press 2005), 147.

## 3. Normative impact

### *3.1. Indigenous 'property' and the rights of dominated people*

While both the law of belligerent occupation and the decolonization movement for national sovereignty dealt with control over the environment and natural resources through the lens of underlying national sovereignty, international human rights law also made it an issue of peoples' rights in general. As touched on above, the common article 1 of the two International Covenants of 1966 held that *all peoples* should be able to freely dispose of their natural wealth and resources, and barred activities that would deprive a people of its means of subsistence. The African Charter on Human and People's Rights of 1981, in addition to a right to property[37] also protects the rights of peoples to freely dispose of their wealth and natural resources.[38] In 2012, the African Commission on Human and Peoples' Rights recalled the importance of the article 21 of the African Charter stating that 'in accordance with the Rio Declaration and African Charter principle of State sovereignty over natural resources, the State has the main responsibility for ensuring natural resources stewardship *with*, and *for the interest of*, the population and must fulfill its mission in conformity with international human rights law and standards'.[39]

These rights have been applied to the benefit of indigenous populations in the jurisprudence of not only the African human rights systems, but also in the Inter-American system under the protection of the right to property found in article 21 of the American Convention on Human Rights. Neither system has hesitated to grant collective rights protection to indigenous groups.[40] These provisions require respect for a people's right to use natural resources, even where they lack formal legal title to the land.[41]

### *3.2. Inter-American human rights system*

The environment in which people live provides the natural resources indispensable for an adequate standard of living and a dignified life. In its *Mayagna (Sumo) Community of Awas Tingni v. Nicaragua* decision, the Inter-American Court of Human Rights, in interpreting the protection of 'property' in article 21 of the Convention in a way that transcended the right of possession under state property law alone, instead linked property rights to the survival of indigenous peoples as peoples and as individuals. This aspect of a people's right to dispose of their natural resources is based on the special relationship that indigenous peoples have with their territory, and on the need to protect that connection in order to safeguard both their physical and cultural survival.[42] As put by the court in the landmark

[37] Art 14 of the African Charter includes indigenous property rights, particularly to their ancestral lands.

[38] Art 21 of the African Charter states the right to free disposition of natural resources. It affirms: '1. All peoples shall freely dispose of their wealth and natural resources. This right shall be exercised in the exclusive interest of the people. In no case shall a people be deprived of it. 2. In case of spoliation the dispossessed people shall have the right to the lawful recovery of its property as well as to an adequate compensation'.

[39] Resolution on a Human Rights' Based Approach to Natural Resources Governance, 51st Ordinary Session of the African Commission on Human and Peoples' Rights, 18 April–2 May 2012.

[40] See Inter-American Court of Human Rights, *The Mayagna (Sumo) Awas Tingni Community v. Nicaragua*, Judgment of 31 August 2001, paras 140 (B), 149, 151; African Commission on Human and People's Rights, Decision 155/96, *The Social and Economic Rights Action Centre and the Centre for Economic and Social Rights v. Nigeria, 2002*, para 63.

[41] Communication 276/03: *Centre for Minority Rights Development (Kenya) and Minority Rights Group (on behalf of Endorois Welfare Council)/Kenya*, 11–25 November 2009, paras 120–4.

[42] See Inter-American Court of Human Rights, *Indigenous Community Sawhoyamaxa v. Paraguay*, 26 March 2007, para 118; *Indigenous Community Yakye Axa v. Paraguay*, 17 June 2005, para 137.

*Awas Tingni* case, 'the close ties of indigenous people with the land must be recognized and understood as the fundamental basis of their cultures, their spiritual life, their integrity, and their economic survival.'[43] As such, the court made clear that these land rights are held by the community in their collective capacity.[44]

The court has since made clear that such a right to land should include the natural resources contained in the territories. In the words of the court in the *Saramaka* case against Suriname, indigenous people's land rights would be rendered meaningless 'if not connected to the natural resources that lie on and within the land'.[45] In its *Kakmok Kasek Indigenous Community v. Paraguay* decision, the Inter-American Court stressed the connection between indigenous people's use of natural resources and their particular cultural identity.[46]

There is a great deal of controversy over whether the land rights of indigenous peoples constitute a form of 'sovereignty'. What is clear in the jurisprudence of the American human rights system is that the rights to land and resources for indigenous peoples constitutes a significant constraint on the state's right to administer land and resources belonging to indigenous people. In a case concerning the American Declaration of the Rights and Duties of Man, the Inter-American Commission held that indigenous property rights required free, prior, and informed consent before the exploitation of any natural resources contained on an indigenous territory, and that allowing concessions for the exploitation of timber and oil on the ancestral lands of the local Maya community without consultation constituted a clear violation of those rights.[47]

### 3.3. *African human rights system*

A similar set of concerns and relationship have been emphasized in the African human rights system. The African Commission on Human and People's Rights (the African Commission) has repeatedly used both article 21, and other provisions of the African Convention, to recognize and protect indigenous peoples' natural resource rights.

Relying heavily on the jurisprudence of the Inter-American human rights system, the African Commission has interpreted both article 14's protection of property and article 21's right to dispose of wealth and resources so as to provide strong protection for indigenous peoples rights to resources on their traditional lands—even when the resources in question are not connected to survival or traditional practices.[48] Moreover, in *Centre for Minority Rights Development v. Kenya*, the African Commission linked the land and water rights with respect for the Convention's protections for freedom of religion and the right to development.[49] In addition, access to information and public participation are means for exercising the right to use natural resources. In this case the

[43] *The Mayagna (Sumo) Awas Tingni Community v. Nicaragua*, para 149.

[44] *The Mayagna (Sumo) Awas Tingni Community v. Nicaragua*, paras 142–53.

[45] Inter-American Court of Human Rights, *Saramaka People v. Suriname*, Judgment of 28 November 2007, para 122.

[46] *Kakmok Kasek Indigenous Community v. Paraguay*, Judgment of 24 August 2010, para 174.

[47] Inter-American Commission on Human Rights, *Maya Indigenous Community of the Toledo District v. Belize*, 2004, paras 117, 143.

[48] *Centre for Minority Rights Development (Kenya) and Minority Rights Group International on behalf of Endorois Welfare Council v. Kenya*, 4 February 2010, para 267.

[49] *Centre for Minority Rights Development (Kenya) and Minority Rights Group International on behalf of Endorois Welfare Council v. Kenya*, 4 February 2010, para 173.

African Commission found Kenya in violation of article 21 of the African Charter for failing to properly consult with the concerned indigenous community, and not having obtained their consent.[50]

The duty to consult placed on the state implies that the land and resource rights vested in indigenous groups are not absolute. Indeed, the African Commission has been clear that, so long as appropriate consultations take place, restrictions on these rights can be justified if they are in the 'general interest of the community.'[51] However, there are strict limits on the state's power to grant concessions against indigenous resources rights. Much in line with the structure of the article 21, and its analogue in article 1 of the human rights Conventions of 1966, no restrictions or violations can be allowed when they would put the subsistence—ie the survival—of the indigenous people in question. The landmark decision of the African Commission on Human and Peoples' Rights in the *Social and Economic Rights Action Centre for Economic and Social Rights v. Nigeria* dealt with just this issue. In the *Action Centre* case, the Commission found that the government's complicity and participation in the destruction and contamination (eg water, soil, and crops) and destruction of food sources as a result of oil company activities had violated article 21 of the African Charter by both destroying the Ogoniland and 'devastatingly affecting' the well-being of the Ogoni people.[52]

Although it may still be uncertain how the right to use natural resources and human rights may be interpreted in various environmental contexts, these cases demonstrate an increasing trend by victims of environmental damage to invoke human rights principles when seeking protection and redress, and a trend among human rights tribunals to apply these doctrines, especially in situations in which the resources in question are essential for subsistence.[53] It remains to be seen, however, whether a general context of 'people facing oppression' can be used to give Principle 23 coherent and consistent substance.

## III) Relations with Other Principles

As briefly noted in Section II) 2.1.1 of this chapter, Principle 23 is at a crossroads of different (and diverse) principles of the Rio Declaration. Between the recognition of the vital role of indigenous peoples (Principle 22), although without clearly stating their rights over their resources, and the broad recognition to protect the environment during armed conflict (Principle 24), Principle 23 adds a necessary link, that between peoples under domination and their environment and resources, in peace or at war.

At the same time, Principle 23 places a significant limitation on the exercise of sovereignty over natural resources (Principle 2), namely that such exercise must not encroach on the environment of oppressed, dominated, or occupied peoples or, as applicable,

[50] *Centre for Minority Rights Development (Kenya) and Minority Rights Group International on behalf of Endorois Welfare Council v. Kenya*, 4 February 2010, paras 266–8.

[51] *Centre for Minority Rights Development (Kenya) and Minority Rights Group International on behalf of Endorois Welfare Council v. Kenya*, 4 February 2010, para 267.

[52] *Social and Economic Rights Action Center for Economic and Social Rights v. Nigeria*, Communication 15/96 (2001), paras 55–8.

[53] See Anton, D. K. and Shelton, D. (eds), *Environmental Protection and Human Rights* (Cambridge University Press 2011).

on that people's own permanent sovereignty over their resources. The Principle refers both to the 'environment' and to the 'natural resources' of peoples under domination or occupation. It thus entails not only a preservation approach to the 'environment' but also a more economic view of the environment as 'natural resources', dating back to the 1960s.

The protection of the environment and natural resources of peoples can be seen as a more specific application—formulated in collective rights terms—of the broader affirmation, in Principle 1 of the Declaration, of the entitlement of individuals to a satisfactory environment. From this perspective, Principle 23 reserves some room for (collective) human rights within the Rio Declaration, as Principles 22 and 1 do.

## IV) Assessment

The rule established in the Rio Declaration on the protection of the environment and natural resources in situations of occupation or foreign domination has not found explicit application in international jurisprudence. Principle 23 has never been expressly mentioned in the judgments of international courts. Yet the above analysis suggests that general principles of human rights law, rulings on indigenous peoples' rights, and the law of belligerent occupation can each contribute to a lucid elaboration of the meaning of Principle 23 in light of current international law.

Though the presentation above suggests a strict separation between the respective rights of oppressed, dominated, and occupied peoples, a shared pattern of placing limits on powerful actors can be discerned. In the case of occupation, gaining control over natural resources can be a strategic tool to extend control over territory and strengthen its political, economic, and military powers. Nevertheless, international law delimits the powers and duties of an occupant in relation to natural resources. Both the law of belligerent occupation and the principle of permanent sovereignty emphasize the right of peoples of occupied states to obtain compensation for damage inflicted by the occupying state.[54] In the same vein, indigenous peoples have a right to redress for loss of access to land and use of resources, via restitution, or other compensation.[55] In this context, it should be recalled that the legal framework for internationally-funded development projects also increasingly includes protection for the rights of indigenous people over natural resources. In cases of displacement of indigenous peoples, for example, the World Bank recognizes a right to compensation.[56] International practice can play a crucial function to ensure legal security and protection to vulnerable groups living in occupied territories or States where practices of oppression or domination exist.

[54] The right to compensation in the case of a breach of the obligations of an occupant is states in many UN resolutions. See eg Resolution 51/160, UN GAOR 51e session (16 December 1996); Resolution 52/207, UN GAOR 52e session (18 December 1997); Resolution 67/229, UN GAOR 67e session (21 December 2012);

[55] See arts 10 and 28 of the *United Nations Declaration on the Rights of Indigenous Peoples*, Resolution 61/295, UN GAOR 61e session (13 September 2007).

[56] The World Bank's Operational Directive 4.10 states that: 'Particular attention should be given to the rights of indigenous peoples to use and develop the lands that they occupy, to be protected against illegal intruders, and to have access to natural resources (such as forests, wildlife, and water) vital to their subsistence and reproduction'. World Bank Operational Directive 4.10, Annex A, Social Assessment, July 2005, para 2 (e).

## V) Select Bibliography

Abi-Saab, G., 'Permanent Sovereignty over Natural Resources and Economic Activities', in Bedjaoui, M. (ed), *International Law: Achievements and Prospects* (Paris: Pedone 1991), 597.

Jérémie, G., 'The Right to Freely Dispose of Natural Resources: Utopia or Forgotten Right?' (2013) 31 *Netherlands Quarterly of Human Rights* 314.

Schrijver, N., *Sovereignty over Natural Resources: Balancing Rights and Duties* (Cambridge University Press 2008).

Schwebel, S., 'The Story of the United Nations Declaration on Permanent Sovereignty over Natural Resources', in Schwebel, S., *Justice in International Law: Selected Writings* (Cambridge University Press 1994), 401.

Scobbie, I., 'Natural Resources under Belligerent Occupation: Mutation through Permanent Sovereignty', in Bowen, S. (ed), *Human Rights, Self-Determination and Political Change in the Occupied Palestinan Territories* (Leiden: Martinus Nijhoff 1997), 221.

Tignino, M., *L'eau et la guerre: éléments pour un régime juridique* (Brussels: Bruylant 2011).

# 28. Principle 24

## *The Environment in Armed Conflict*

Marie-Louise Tougas*

**Principle 24**

Warfare is inherently destructive of sustainable development. States shall therefore respect international law providing protection for the environment in times of armed conflict and cooperate in its further development, as necessary.



## I) Origins and Rationale of the Principle

Although the laws of war always contained rules that may provide some protection to the natural environment, one had to wait until the last third of the twentieth century to see the adoption of specific treaty dispositions providing for the protection of the environment in times of armed conflict. At the end of the 1960s, with the Vietnam War and the

* Legal Adviser, International Committee of the Red Cross (ICRC). The views expressed in this article are those of the author and do not necessarily reflect those of the ICRC.

massive use of defoliant in the daily news on one side and the growing general concern for the protection of the environment and the continuous fear of a nuclear war on the other, the need to address specifically the consequences of warfare on the natural environment became more pressing.

The principle that rules protecting the environment should continue to apply during armed conflict and be taken into account during military operations is rooted in various international declarations, resolutions, and non-binding documents. The Stockholm Declaration, adopted by the United Nations Conference on Human Environment, held in June 1972, was the first general international document to address the protection of the environment and the management of natural resources and to contain a reference to the protection of the environment in relation to armed conflict.[1] The World Charter for Nature, adopted 10 years later, establishes as a general principle that: 'Nature shall be secured against degradation caused by warfare or other hostile activities'.[2]

One of the first notable introductions of a mainly non-anthropocentric concern into international humanitarian law related issues is probably the Resolution 2306, adopted by the United Nations General Assembly in December 1969 which:

> Declares as contrary to the generally recognized rules of international law, as embodied in the Protocol for the Prohibition of the Use in War of Asphyxiating, Poisonous or Other Gases, and Bacteriological Methods of Warfare, signed at Geneva on 17 June 1925, the use in international armed conflicts of:
>
> (a) Any chemical agents of warfare—chemical substances, whether gaseous, liquid or solid—which might be employed because of their direct toxic effects on man, animals or plants;
> (b) Any biological agents of warfare-living organisms, whatever their nature, or infective material derived from them—which are intended to cause disease or death in man, animals or plants, and which depend for their effects on their ability to multiply in the person, animal or plant attacked.[3]

The first international treaty specifically addressing the protection of the natural environment and restricting means of warfare for reasons related to their effects on the natural environment was the Convention on the Prohibition of military or any other hostile use of environmental modification techniques ('ENMOD') adopted at the end of 1976.[4] Although concerns for human welfare are central to the purpose of ENMOD, the need to ensure a certain level of protection to the natural environment is also present. Indeed, the preamble of that treaty directly refers to the Stockholm Declaration.

The next year, in 1977, the First Additional Protocol to the Geneva Conventions of 12 August 1949 relating to the Protection of Victims of International Armed Conflicts (Additional Protocol I)[5] introduced the growing concerns for the protection of the environment into a general international humanitarian law treaty and established specific provisions limiting methods and means of warfare that can be used by the parties to the conflict based on their impacts on the natural environment.

[1] Declaration of the United Nations Conference on the Human Environment, (Stockholm Declaration), 6 June 1972, Principle 26.

[2] UN General Assembly, Resolution A/RES/37/7, 28 October 1982, para 5.

[3] UNGA RES/2306 (A) *Question of chemical and bacteriological (biological) weapon*, 1836th plenary meeting, 16 December 1969.

[4] GA Res. 72, 31st sess., Supp. No. 39, at 36, UN Doc A/31/39 (1977), entered into force 5 October 1978.

[5] 1125 UNTS 3, entered into force 7 December 1978 ('Additional Protocol I').

Twenty years after the Stockholm Declaration, and with the 1990–1991 Gulf War and the burning of Kuwaiti oil wells still vivid in participants' minds, the Rio Declaration on Environment and Development ('Rio Declaration') adopted in June 1992 by the United Nations Conference on Environment and Development reflected this evolution and established as a general principle that:

> Warfare is inherently destructive of sustainable development. States shall therefore respect international law providing protection for the environment in times of armed conflict and cooperate in its further development, as necessary.[6]

## II) The Principle as Enshrined in the Rio Declaration

### 1. Preparatory work and context

The resolution adopted by the United Nations General Assembly in December 1989 convening the Rio Conference contained a reference to the protection of the environment during armed conflict, but it was limited to the issue of remnants of war[7].

The general divide between developing countries which wanted a more substantial and detailed text and industrialized ones favouring a short text that would not go further than the content of the Stockholm Declaration was reflected in the debates on the protection of the environment and warfare. On this issue, the divide could be perceived between those in favour of a strong paragraph denouncing nuclear weapons and other weapons of mass destruction—mainly the Group of 77[8] and USSR[9]; those conceiving the issue in relation with peace and international security—mainly Scandinavian countries[10]—and those preferring not to address the issue of the protection of the environment and warfare (Canada,[11] United States, and Japan). For instance, the reference to weapons of mass destruction was criticized by some delegations, among which the United States was of the opinion that a disarmament conference would be a more appropriate forum to discuss this issue than a conference on environment and development.

It is interesting to mention that none of the proposals submitted by industrialized countries, especially Canada, United States, and Japan, contained a reference to the protection of the natural environment in time of armed conflict.[12] Their position was clearly reflected

[6] 3 to 14 June 1992, Rio de Janeiro, UN Doc A/CONF.151/26 (vol I), Principle 24.

[7] The preamble of the resolution recognized that '*the environmental impact of material remnants of war and the need for further international co-operation for their removal*', United Nations Conference on Environment and Development", Resolution 44/228, UN Doc A/RES/44/228, 22 December 1989.

[8] See eg 'Principles on General Rights and obligations. Draft proposal submitted by Ghana on behalf of the States Members of the United Nations that are members of the Group 77.' UN Doc A/CONF.151/PC/WG.III/L.6, 21 August 1991.

[9] See eg 'Preparations for the United Nations Conference on Environment and Development on the Basis of General Assembly Resolution 44/228 and Taking into Account other Relevant General Assembly Resolutions. Proposal submitted by the Union of Soviet Socialist Republics', UN Doc A/CONF.151/PC/CRP.8, 13 August 1990, para 4.

[10] See UN Doc A/CONF.151/PC/WG.III/L.27.

[11] See eg 'Principles on General Rights and Obligations. Letter dated 15 August 1991 from Head of the delegation of Canada to the Preparatory Committee for the United Nations Conference on Environment and Development at its third session addressed to the Secretary-General of the United Nations Conference on Environment and Development', UN Doc A/CONF.151/PC/WG.III/L.5, 16 August 1991.

[12] See 'Principles on the General Rights and Obligations. Earth Charter. Proposal submitted by Canada.' UN Doc A/CONF.151/PC/WG.III/L.23, 4 March 1992, 'Principles on the General Rights and Obligations.

in proposed amendments and alternative wordings submitted during the discussions. For instance, Australia, Canada, New-Zealand[13], and the United States proposed to delete '[t]he use of such weapons is a crime against humanity and the environment'. The United States proposed the following alternative text: 'A commitment to peace and security for all States and people is fundamental to the achievement of sustainable development'.[14]

The involvement of NGOs that were also active in the preparatory work to the Conference[15], including work on the elaboration of the Rio Declaration, is worth mentioning. On the issue of the protection of the environment and armed conflict, the group 'NGO working group on Militarism and the Environment' was actively trying to foster support for the proposal submitted by the Group of 77 through various means including the distribution of a petition among the delegates to express support for the proposal.[16] Finally, on the last day of the preparatory conference, a text for the Rio Declaration was adopted. Principle 24, as the rest of the Rio Declaration, was sent without pending amendments or alternative text, and was not modified during the Rio Conference.

At the Rio Conference, various declarations addressing the issue of the protection of the environment in times of armed conflicts were made. For instance, Mr Maurice Strong, Secretary-General of the Conference, stated that:

> War and preparation for war are a major source of environmental damage which must be subjected to greater accountability and control. This should include stronger legal instruments with clear provisions for enforcement which provide effective deterrence against future environmental aggressors.[17]

Sweden declared that: 'War is the opposite to sustainable development. States should develop further the international law for the protection of the environment in case of warfare'.[18] Saudi Arabia also addressed the issue in its declaration:

> The dimension of the threats to the environment inherent in armed conflicts call for sustained efforts and untiring endeavours of the international community to protect the environment, rescue marine life, reconstruct and rehabilitate the environment. It calls for a serious review of the provisions of international law applicable to armed conflicts with a view to preventing the recurrence of international crimes against the environment similar to those experienced in the Gulf region.[19]

The ICRC also made a declaration to recall the harmful impact of armed conflict on the environment and the importance of respecting existing rules of international humanitarian law.

Proposal submitted by the United States of America.' A/CONF.151/PC/WG.III/L.21, 4 March 1992, and 'Principles on the General Rights and Obligations. Rights and Obligations. Proposal submitted by Japan.' UN Doc A/CONF.151/PC/WG.III/L.22, 4 March 1992.

[13] These three countries as well as the CEE would have preferred the complete suppression of the paragraph.

[14] See UN Doc A/CONF.151/PC/WG.III/L.34, 1st April 1992, at 19.

[15] Indeed, more than 450 NGOs asked accreditations to follow the work of the preparatory commission and about 15 States, including Sweden and Canada, included NGO representatives in their delegations.

[16] Also worth mentioning is the proposition contained in the Draft Covenant on Environmental Conservation and Sustainable Use of Natural Resources prepared by the International Union for Conservation of Nature ('IUCN') and transmitted by the delegation of Iceland.

[17] As quoted in: ICRC internal report, June 1992, on file with the author.

[18] ICRC internal report, June 1992, on file with the author.

[19] ICRC internal report, June 1992, on file with the author.

## 2. Scope and dimensions

### *2.1. Dimensions*

The wording of Principle 24 is the result of a compromise and therefore its scope and dimensions reflect a balance between delegations in favour of the affirmation of a strong principle and a condemnation of nuclear weapons and those who would have preferred that the issue not be dealt with in the Declaration. More limited in its scope and general in its content than many proposals presented during preparatory work, Principle 24 is nonetheless significant.

The first sentence reflects the need expressed by some delegations to shift the focus from weapons issues and to turn it to the main focus of the conference, that is, sustainable development. It can be seen as a stronger version of the proposal made by the delegation of the United States that: 'A commitment to peace and security for all States and people is fundamental to the achievement of sustainable development'.[20] However, it remains a general affirmation reminding States that armed conflicts are an obstacle to sustainable development and has probably limited real normative dimension.

The second sentence calls on States to respect international law providing for the protection of the environment in times of armed conflict and to cooperate in its further development as necessary. Although formulated in a general manner, the reference to international law is important. 'International law' should not be read restrictively and encompasses all relevant rules of international law providing protection for the environment and applicable in times of armed conflict, especially ENMOD and Additional Protocol I.

The call on States to cooperate to further develop international law in this respect is interesting. After the Gulf War and the extensive damage to the environment caused during this conflict, many people, including State officials, thought that the existing specific dispositions, namely those contained in Additional Protocol I,[21] were insufficient and some were of the opinion that a specific treaty would be needed. Different expert meetings on the issue of international law and the protection of the environment in times of armed conflict were organized in 1991–1993 on ways of improving respect and implementation of existing rules as well as the possibility of developing new ones.[22] The issue was also discussed during the 46th and the 47th sessions of the General Assembly of the United Nations[23]. However, there was no consensus among States on this issue.

[20] See UN Doc A/CONF.151/PC/WG.III/L.34, 1 April 1992, at 19.

[21] It should be noted that at the time of the Gulf War, only Kuwait was party to Additional Protocol I, neither the United States nor Iraq was. Iraq ratified this protocol in 2010.

[22] eg, the *London Conference on a 'Fifth Geneva Convention on the Protection of the Environment in Time of Armed Conflict'* of 3 June 1991 organized by the Centre for Defence Study of the University of London and the *Ottawa Conference on 'The use of the Environment as a Tool of Convention Warfare'* of 10–12 July 1991 co-organized by the Canadian Ministry of External Affairs and Trade and the United Nations. The International Committee of the Red Cross, in response of the request formulated in the United Nations General Assembly's decision 46/417 of 9 December 1991 concluded its deliberations on item 140 of its agenda ('Exploitation of the environment as a weapon in times of armed conflict and the taking of practical measures to prevent such exploitation'), also convened two experts meetings on the protection of the environment in time of armed conflict on 27–29 April 1992 and 25–27 January 1993. See, 'Report submitted by A. Bouvier, ICRC, to the 47th session of the United Nations General Assembly', online at: <http://www.icrc.org/eng/resources/documents/statement/5cjknj.htm>.

[23] The UN General Assembly adopted a resolution on the Protection of the environment in times of armed conflict at its 47th session. GA Res. 47/37, 47 UN GAOR Supp. (No. 49) at 290, UN Doc A/47/49 (1992).

For instance, various States, including members of the European Community, Australia, Canada, Iran, New Zealand, Switzerland, and the United States were of the opinion that existing rules of international law were adequate, but that compliance needed to be strengthened. Others, including Argentina, China, Jordan, and Sweden considered that the Gulf War illustrated the need to strengthen existing rules and to develop new ones.[24] The possible need to further develop international law in this respect is thus acknowledged by Principle 24.

## *2.2. Legal nature*

Principle 24 of the Rio Declaration calls on States to respect international law providing protection to the environment in times of armed conflict. The wording does not directly refer to any specific body of international law, such as international humanitarian law, international environmental law, or international human rights law and its content should be regarded as encompassing all relevant rules of international law and not restricted to any specific one. Its content should also be interpreted in the light of the normative developments in this respect.

The status of the principle enshrined in Principle 24 of the Rio Declaration must be assessed by reference to other bases where it is also expressed as well as to their aggregate meaning as evidence of a customary norm. One feature to be noted at the outset is that the Rio Declaration, with its Principle 24, was unanimously adopted at the Rio Conference. Significantly, the United States did not append an interpretive statement to this principle, as it did to others, including Principle 23. There was therefore no objection to the proposition that the environment must be protected in armed conflict in accordance with international law. Such reference raises the more specific norms that may provide for such protection, which will be discussed in section II) 3 of this chapter.

Regarding the authority of the referral itself, the most notable acknowledgment of Principle 24 is found in the *Advisory Opinion on the Legality of Nuclear Weapons* by the International Court of Justice ('ICJ'):

> Respect for the environment is one of the elements that go to assessing whether an action is in conformity with the principles of necessity and proportionality. This approach is supported, indeed, by the terms of Principle 24 of the Rio Declaration...[25]

Additional support for this proposition is found in the ICRC's *Customary Law Study* under customary rule 44, which also mentions Principle 2 of the Rio Declaration.[26] In 1994, the ICRC also elaborated, in consultation with international experts, *Guidelines for military manuals on the protection of the environment in times of armed conflict*.[27] The guidelines were submitted to the United Nations in the context of the UN Decade of International

[24] See, Statement of Mr Kotliar, Director of the Codification Division of the United Nations, made at the 'ICRC Meeting of Experts on the Protection of the Environment in time of Armed Conflict', Geneva, 27–29 April 1992. Reproduced in ICRC, 'Report of the Meeting of Experts on the Protection of the Environment in time of Armed Conflict', Geneva, September 1992.

[25] *Legality of the Threat or Use of Nuclear Weapons*, 8 July 1996, ICJ, Advisory Opinion, ICJ Reports 1996, para 30. ('ICJ, Advisory Opinion, *Legality of the Threat or Use of Nuclear Weapons*').

[26] See commentary to Rule 44, Henckaerts, J.-M. and Doswald-Beck, L., *Customary International Humanitarian Law* (vols I and II), ICRC (Cambridge University Press 2005) ('ICRC Customary Law Study').

[27] ICRC, *Guidelines for military manuals and instructions on the protection of the environment in times of armed conflict*, 1993, online: <http://www.icrc.org/eng/resources/documents/misc/57jn38.htm>.

Law. During its 49th session, the General Assembly invited States to 'give due consideration to the possibility of incorporating them into their military manuals and other instructions addressed to their military personnel'.[28]

Further support for the need to mainstream environmental protection within the law applicable to armed conflict *lato sensu* (whether the law of armed conflict or other bodies of law) was given by the Parliamentary Assembly of the Council of Europe, which in 2011 adopted a resolution on armed conflicts and the environment.[29] Finally, in the outcome document of the Rio 2012 Summit, the principles of the Rio Declaration and Agenda 21 were reaffirmed.[30]

## 3. Normative impact

### *3.1. The work of the International Law Commission*

#### 3.1.1. Effects of armed conflict on treaties

In recalling that 'States shall therefore respect international law providing protection for the environment in times of armed conflict', Principle 24 builds on the fundamental and general principle of international law *pacta sunt servanda*. The principle that '[e]very treaty in force is binding upon the parties to it and must be performed by them in good faith'[31] is at the centre of the international legal system. This principle also applies to all kinds of agreements, but as the doctrine is divided on its applicability to customary law, the principle *consuetudo est servanda* is also sometimes referred to assert the binding nature of customary international law.[32]

The outbreak of an armed conflict does not necessarily affect in itself the application of international agreements providing rules protecting the environment.[33] According to the International Law Commission ('ILC'), the subject matter of treaties relating to the protection of the environment carries the presumption that they continue to apply, in whole or in part, during armed conflict.[34] However, this issue should be asserted on a case by case basis[35] but the general principle that any international obligations binding upon States and applicable in times of armed conflict should be respected is recalled in Principle 24.

[28] UN Doc A/RES/49/50, 17 February 1995, para 11.

[29] Council of Europe, Parliamentary Assembly, Resolution 1851 (2011), Armed conflicts and the environment, adopted by Standing Committee, acting on behalf of the Assembly, 25 November 2011.

[30] See United Nations Conference on Sustainable Development, *The Future We Want*, Outcome of the Conference, UN Doc A/Conf.216/L.1, 19 June 2012, at para 16.

[31] Art 26, Vienna Convention on the Law of Treaties, 1969, 1155 UNTS 331, entered into force 27 January 1980 ('VCLT').

[32] See Treves, T., 'Customary International Law', *Max Plank Encyclopedia of Public International Law* (Oxford University Press 2006).

[33] See eg art 3, *Draft articles on the effects of armed conflicts on treaties*, adopted by the International Law Commission in 2011, in ILC, 'Effects of armed conflicts on treaties. Titles and texts of the draft articles on the effects of armed conflicts on treaties adopted by the Drafting Committee on second reading', UN Doc A/CN.4/L.777, 11 May 2011 [ILC, *Draft articles on the effects of armed conflicts on treaties*]. This is in line with the Resolution on the Effects of Armed Conflicts on Treaties adopted by the Institut de Droit International in 1985 and with the *Règlement concernant les effets de la guerre sur les traités*, adopted by the same institute in 1912.

[34] Arts 6 and 7, ILC, *Draft articles on the effects of armed conflicts on treaties*.

[35] Although the outbreak of an armed conflict may, in certain cases, be considered as a *fundamental change of circumstance* in the sense of art 62 of the VCLT. See also art 73 VCLT.

#### 3.1.2. The protection of the environment 'in relation to' armed conflict

The ILC has also started work on the protection of the environment 'in relation to' armed conflict and, although this development is very recent, the Special Rapporteur appointed on this topic, Marie Jacobsson from Sweden, has decided to give its mandate a broad scope, analysing not only environmental protection 'during' or 'within' armed conflict but also 'before' and 'after' conflict.[36] This extension may encompass questions such as the production of certain weapons or post-conflict environmental assessments.

### *3.2. International humanitarian law*

#### 3.2.1. Overview

International humanitarian law ('IHL') as the body of law specifically designed to address situations of armed conflict is naturally the first one to mention. IHL is a set of rules, established by treaties or custom, which are specifically intended to solve humanitarian problems directly arising from international or non-international armed conflicts and which, for humanitarian reasons, limit the right of parties to a conflict to use the methods and means of warfare of their choice or protect persons and property that are, or may be, affected by conflict. In other words, IHL is composed of the two following types of rules: rules which limit the right of the parties to use means and methods of war and rules which protect the persons who are not or are no longer participating in the hostilities as well as certain goods, in particular civilian ones, in times of armed conflict. Rules of IHL are thus the result of a careful balance between humanitarian concerns and military requirements. During non-international armed conflict, IHL is equally binding on governmental armed forces and on non-state armed groups.

When it comes to the protection of the environment, articles 35 (3) and 55 of Additional Protocol I or the ENMOD Convention[37] leap to mind; however, many rules of IHL provide protection to the natural environment. They will be briefly outlined in this section.

#### 3.2.2. Principles of international humanitarian law

Under IHL, a distinction shall always be made between military objectives and combatants on one side and civilians and civilian objects on the other. Only the former can be directly attacked and the latter shall be protected against direct attacks. Natural environment generally falls under the definition of civilian objects and is thus protected by the general rules of IHL: the prohibition of direct attacks against civilian objects, the prohibition of indiscriminate attacks, the principle of proportionality, and the obligation to take precautions in attack. These rules are of a customary nature and applicable both in international and non-international armed conflicts.[38] Their specific application to the natural environment is also recognized as a rule of customary law.[39] Furthermore, the general rule

[36] See International Law Commission, 'Report on the work of its sixty-fifth session', UN Doc A/68/10, at ch IX ('ILC, Report on the work of its sixty-fifth session').

[37] This Convention, which has a role in disarmament efforts, prohibits the Contracting Parties from engaging in 'military or any other hostile use of environmental modification techniques having widespread, long-lasting or severe effects as the means of destruction, damage or injury to any other State Party'. These techniques are 'any technique for changing—through the deliberate manipulation of natural processes—the dynamics, composition or structure of the Earth, including its biota, lithosphere, hydrosphere and atmosphere, or of outer space'.

[38] See Rules 7, 11, 14, and 15, ICRC Customary Law Study.

[39] See Rules 43, ICRC Customary Law Study. See also ICJ, Advisory Opinion, *Legality of the Threat or Use of Nuclear Weapons*, para 30: 'Respect for the environment is one of the elements that go to assessing whether an action is in conformity with the principles of necessity and proportionality'.

that: 'Methods and means of warfare must be employed with due regard to the protection and preservation of the natural environment' is also recognized as a customary one.[40]

This protection will only cease if elements of the natural environment can be considered as a military objective, that is, if 'by their nature, purpose or use, these elements make an effective contribution to military action and if their total or partial destruction, in the circumstances ruling at the time, offers a distinct and substantial military advantage.'[41] For instance, if they are used by a party to the conflict as a means to hide from the enemy, elements of the environment will become a military objective. This will also be the case for the natural environment located in areas where armed forces are settled, or surrounding military bases. Therefore, when it is not a military objective, 'destruction of any part of the natural environment is prohibited, unless required by military necessity'[42]—or unless it can be considered as a legally acceptable collateral damage in accordance with the principle of proportionality.[43]

In regard to the protection of the natural environment, the respect of IHL obligations entails a duty to ascertain the consequences for the natural environment of means and methods of warfare at the combatants' disposal in order to avoid or minimize their effects. Potential threat on biodiversity of a specific area is one of the elements that could be taken into consideration, especially if the area is a protected one, such as a national reserve.[44]

### 3.2.3. Specific environmental provisions

IHL also contains specific rules providing protection to the natural environment: articles 35 (3) and 55 of Additional Protocol I. Articles 35 (3) and 55 (1) prohibit high-level damage to the natural environment. It is absolutely prohibited to cause *widespread, long-term and severe* damage to the natural environment. The prohibition applies even when the natural environment is targeted as a military objective. It establishes an 'absolute ceiling of permissible destruction'.[45] In such a case, it is irrelevant to inquire whether the

[40] See Rule 44, ICRC Customary Law Study. See also San Remo Manual on International Law Applicable to Armed Conflicts at Sea ('San Remo Manual'), art 44: 'Methods and means of warfare should be employed with due regard for the natural environment taking into account the relevant rules of international law. Damage to or destruction of the natural environment not justified by military necessity and carried out wantonly is prohibited'; and *The Commander's Handbook on the Law of Naval Operations* of the United States (2007), s 8.4, which provides that:

> It is not unlawful to cause collateral damage to the natural environment during an attack upon a legitimate military objective. However, the commander has an affirmative obligation to avoid unnecessary damage to the environment to the extent that it is practicable to do so consistent with mission accomplishment. To that end, and as far as military requirements permit, methods or means of warfare should be employed with due regard to the protection and preservation of the natural environment.

For additional States practice in this respect, see Practice related to customary rule 44, in ICRC Customary International Humanitarian Law database, online: <http://www.icrc.org/customary-ihl/eng/docs/v2_rul_rule44>.

[41] Art 52 (2) Additional Protocol I.

[42] Rule 43, ICRC Customary Law Study.

[43] Arts 51 (5) b) and 57 2) iii), Additional Protocol I, and Rule 14, ICRC Customary Law Study.

[44] For instance, in 1999 a UNEP/UNCHS Balkans Task Force (BTF) was set up with the mission of asserting the environmental consequences of the conflict in the Balkans. Part of their task was to assess the damage caused to the biodiversity in protected areas of the former Federal Republic of Yugoslavia. The mission could not come to the conclusion that biodiversity would be significantly affected in the long term. However, the report confessed that: 'this issue was not rigorously assessed by this technical mission nor would it have been possible in the short term', UNEP/UNCHS Balkans Task Force (BTF), *Assessment of the Damage to Biodiversity in Protected Areas of the Federal Republic of Yugoslavia*, Technical Mission 7–10 September 1999, Report of October 1999, at 20.

[45] See US Army's Operational law handbook, 2012, 326, available online: <http://www.loc.gov/rr/frd/Military_Law/pdf/operational-law-handbook_2012.pdf>.

damage could be justified by military necessity or whether collateral or incidental damage is excessive.[46] This prohibition is of a customary nature during international armed conflict[47] and is arguably also applicable during non-international armed conflict.[48]

The three conditions of articles 35 (3) and 55 (1) of Additional Protocol I are cumulative.[49] The rule therefore sets a high threshold. For instance, the *Committee Established to Review the NATO Bombing Campaign Against the Federal Republic of Yugoslavia* came to the conclusion that the damage to the natural environment caused by the NATO bombing campaign in Kosovo did not reach the threshold of *widespread, long-term and severe*.[50] However, the fact that an act of warfare is not prohibited under article 35 (3) does not mean it is permitted under IHL. All the rules of IHL protecting the natural environment, directly or indirectly, have to be kept in mind and respected. Indeed, the aforementioned committee suggested that: 'these effects [on the environment] are best considered from the underlying principles of the law of armed conflict such as necessity and proportionality'.[51]

Since the adoption of Additional Protocol I, the high threshold posed by articles 35 (3) and 55 (1) and the significance of each of the three criteria have sparked off numerous debates.[52] Indeed, these terms are not defined in Additional Protocol I, contrary to the ENMOD Convention.[53] Although it is true that the threshold of these articles is high and was intended to be so by the drafters of the Protocol, one should be careful not to unduly restrict their scope of application. For instance, in respect to the temporal criteria of articles 53 (3) and 55 (1), acts of warfare causing short-term damage to the natural environment, such as artillery bombardment, were not intended to be prohibited by the article.[54] However, according to the Biotope Group, an unofficial working group formed to considered further the text of article 55 (then 48 bis), it was 'impossible to say with certainty what period of time might be involved and for this reason, no time is specified in the Article.'[55] The absence of a specific time in the article was not the object of discussion and there seems to have been no proposition by delegations to include one. Therefore, although

[46] However, it must be noted that under international criminal law, the criteria are different and the damage has to be intentional and to be clearly excessive in relation to the concrete and direct overall military advantage anticipated; see art 8 (2) b) iv) of the Rome Statute which introduces a proportionality test in the appreciation of the *widespread, long-term and severe damage to the natural environment* criterion, which does not exist under IHL.

[47] A constant objection of the United Kingdom, the United States, and France to the application of this rule to nuclear weapons must however be noted: see Commentary to Rule 45, ICRC Customary Law Study.

[48] Commentary to Rule 45, ICRC Customary Law Study.

[49] In some treaties, the conditions are alternative. This is the case of the ENMOD Convention and of the revised version of the *African Convention on the Conservation of Nature and Natural Resources* of 2003, not yet into force, see art XV.

[50] *Final Report to the Prosecutor by the Committee Established to Review the NATO Bombing Campaign Against the Federal Republic of Yugoslavia* (2000), para 17.

[51] *Final Report to the Prosecutor*, para 15.

[52] The ENMOD also uses the terms severe, long-term, and widespread but in the case of this Convention the criteria are alternative and not cumulative. For instance, in its report on the protection of the environment during armed conflict, UNEP found that arts 35 (3) and 51 (1) of Additional Protocol I '*do not effectively protect the environment during armed conflict due to the stringent and impressive threshold required to demonstrate damage*'. See United Nations Environment Programme, *Protecting the Environment during Armed Conflict: An Inventory and Analysis of International Law* (UNEP 2009), 4. ('UNEP 2009 Report').

[53] See Annex to the Convention, Understanding Regarding the Convention, Convention on the Prohibition of Military or Any Other Hostile Use of Environmental Modification Techniques, 10 December 1976.

[54] 'Report of the Chairman of the Group "Biotope"', 11 March 1975 (CDDH/III/GT/35), ('Biotope Report') in Levie, H. S., *Protection of War Victims: Protocol 1 to the 1949 Geneva Conventions*, vol III, 267.

[55] See Levie, H. S., *Protection of War Victims: Protocol 1 to the 1949 Geneva Conventions*, vol III, 267.

this term has been generally interpreted as a matter of decades[56] or 'perhaps for ten years or more',[57] one should be careful in restricting its meaning to a minimum of a decade. Unfortunately, no mention of discussion on the meaning of the terms 'widespread' or 'severe' in the records of the negotiating history of the 1977 Additional Protocols to the Geneva Conventions were found.

As for the debate on the question of whether the rules of Additional Protocol I are intended to protect the natural environment as such or only in its relation to health and survival of the population, it seems that both views were expressed among delegates. The general understanding was that what is now article 35 (3) would protect the natural environment as such, as article 55 would protect the natural environment in so far as its purpose is the survival or health of the civilian population. However, the reading of the *travaux préparatoires* shows that such a division would be artificial. For instance, according to the report of the Biotope Group:

> In Article 48 bis [Article 55], the first sentence enjoining the taking of care lays down a general norm, which is then particularized in the second sentence. Care must be taken to protect the natural environment against the sort of harm specified even if the health or the survival of the population is not prejudiced. An instance would be environmental harm which is widespread, long-term and severe but in an unpopulated area.[58]

### 3.2.4. The impact of environmental principles on international humanitarian law

Other general principles of international environmental law remain applicable in time of armed conflict. For instance, the principles of prevention and precaution, as they are known in international environmental law, found an echo in IHL. Indeed, Rule 44 of the ICRC Customary Law Study states that, *inter alia*, 'Lack of scientific certainty as to the effects on the environment of certain military operations does not absolve a party to the conflict from taking such precautions.' Furthermore, as recognized by the International Court of Justice:

> [t]he existence of the general obligation of States to ensure that activities within their jurisdiction and control respect the environment of other States or of areas beyond national control is now part of the corpus of international law relating to the environment.[59]

The prevention and precautionary principles must be taken into account in interpreting IHL concepts in an environmental light. In this context, reference to Principle 24 bridges the distance between pure environmental principles and general humanitarian law principles. The interpretation of what is known as the *Martens Clause* is an area of particular relevance in this context. It is a customary rule of IHL applicable both in international and non-international armed conflicts that:

> in cases not covered by international agreements, civilians and combatants remain under the protection and authority of the principles of international law derived from established custom, from the principles of humanity and from the dictates of public conscience.[60]

[56] See Sandoz, Y., Swinarski, C., and Zimmermann, B. (eds), *Commentary on the Additional Protocols of 8 June 1977 to the Geneva Conventions of 12 August 1949* (ICRC/Martinus Nijhoff Publishers 1987), commentary on art 35, para 1452.

[57] Biotope Report, 267.

[58] 'Report to the Third Committee on the Work of the Working Group', Committee III, 3 April 1975 (CDDH/III/275; XV, 357), in Levie, *Protection of War Victims*, vol III, 270.

[59] ICJ, Advisory Opinion, *Legality of the Threat or Use of Nuclear Weapons*, para 29.

[60] See art 1 (2) Additional Protocols I, Preamble Additional Protocol II, 1125 UNTS 609, entered into force 7 December 1978, and Preamble Hague Convention No IV, Convention (IV) respecting the Laws and

The dictates of public conscience are in constant evolution and are nowadays generally interpreted as including environmental concerns.[61] According to the ICJ, the Martens Clause 'has proved to be an effective means of addressing the rapid evolution of military technology'.[62]

### 3.3. *International criminal law*

In 1998, the Rome Statute of the International Criminal Court ('Rome Statute') includes the war crime of:

> intentionally directing attacks in the knowledge that such an attack will cause widespread, long-term and severe damage to the natural environment which would be clearly excessive in relation to the concrete and direct overall military advantage anticipated.[63]

So far, there has been no prosecution under this article.

The war crime of pillage is well established under international law[64] and may also be used to prosecute damages caused to the environment. The prohibition of pillage extends to the appropriation of all types of property, whether they belong to private persons, to communities or to a State. Natural resources are property and are protected against pillage. For instance, the systematic extraction of oil stocks[65] or the unlawful exploitation of natural resources such as gold or diamonds[66] has been recognized as pillage.

### 3.4. *International human rights law*

International Human Rights Law is also applicable in time of armed conflict.[67] Different human rights enshrined in various treaties provide a protection to the environment either directly or indirectly. For instance, the International Covenant on Economic, Social and Cultural Rights provides for a right to 'the enjoyment of the

Customs of War on Land and its annex: Regulations concerning the Laws and Customs of War on Land, 36 Stat. 2277, 1 Bevans 631, 205 Consol. T.S. 277, 3 Martens Nouveau Recueil (ser. 3) 461, entered into force 26 January 1910 ('Hague Convention IV and Regulations'). ICJ, Advisory Opinion, *Legality of the Threat or Use of Nuclear Weapons*, paras 78 and 84.

[61] See eg ICJ, Advisory Opinion, *Legality of the Threat or Use of Nuclear Weapons*, 'Dissenting opinion of Judge Shahabudeen', 153, at 184:

> In effect, the Martens Clause provided authority for treating the principles of humanity and the dictates of public conscience as principles of international law, leaving the precise content of the standard implied by these principles of international law to be ascertained in the light of changing conditions, inclusive of changes in the means and methods of warfare and the outlook and tolerance levels of the international community. The principles would remain constant, but their practical effect would vary from time to time: they could justify a method of warfare in one age and prohibit it in another.

[62] ICJ, Advisory Opinion, *Legality of the Threat or Use of Nuclear Weapons*, para 78.

[63] Art 8 (2) (b) (iv), Rome Statute.

[64] See eg arts 8(2)(b)(xiii) and 8(2)(b)(xvi), Rome Statute.

[65] See *Singapore Court of Appeal, N.V. de Bataafsche Petroleum Maatschappij and Others v. The War Damage Commission* (*Singapore Oil Stocks* case), (1956) 23 ILR 810.

[66] Case Concerning Armed Activities on the Territory of the Congo (*Democratic Republic of the Congo v. Uganda*), Judgment of 19 December 2005, ICJ Reports 2005, para 250 ('ICJ, *DRC v. Uganda 2005*'). Also, the United Nations War Crimes Commission accused ten German administrators of Polish forest during German occupation (1939–1944) of pillage for their involvement in the 'wholesale cutting of Polish timber to an extent far in excess of what was necessary to preserve the timber resources of the country' in History of the United nations War Crimes Commission and the Development of the Laws of War, compiled by the United Nations War Crimes Commission, London, 1948, at 496.

[67] See, *inter alia*, ICJ, *Advisory Opinion, Legality of the Threat or Use of Nuclear Weapons*, para 25; ICJ, *Legal Consequences of the Construction of a Wall in the Occupied Palestinian Territory*, ICJ, 9 July 2004, Advisory Opinion, ICJ Reports 2004, para 106; ICJ, *DRC v. Uganda 2005*, para 216.

highest attainable standard of physical and mental health' through, *inter alia*, the 'improvement of all aspects of environmental and industrial hygiene'.[68] As for the African Charter on Human and Peoples' Rights, it ensures the right to 'a general satisfactory environment favourable to their development.'[69] Environmental concerns have also been addressed through various human rights including the right to life[70] and the right to privacy and family life[71].

### *3.5. Environmental law treaties*

Environmental law treaties can be taken into account in asserting the legal basis of Principle 24. As mentioned, the outbreak of an armed conflict does not necessarily affect in itself the application of international agreements providing rules protecting the environment. Treaties such as the UN Convention on the Law of the Sea, the International Convention for the Prevention of Pollution of the Sea by Oil, the International Convention for the Prevention of Pollution from Ships and the Convention on Wetlands of International Importance as Waterfowl Habitat (Ramsar Convention) should be given particular consideration. The UNESCO World Heritage Convention, under which a property can be put on the 'List of World Heritage in Danger' at the outbreak or when there is a threat of an armed conflict, is also of particular interest. Regional conventions such as the Barcelona Convention, the Cartagena Convention, and especially the African Convention on the Conservation of Nature and Natural Resources (Revised version 2003)[72] should also be kept in mind[73].

Rules of international environment law will therefore apply simultaneously with IHL and international human rights during armed conflict, unless the agreement explicitly states that it, or part of it, does not apply during armed conflict or is incompatible with IHL. States will remain bound by multilateral environmental agreements during a non-international armed conflict[74]and towards third States during international armed conflict.[75] However, it should be noted that multilateral environment agreements are not binding on non-state armed groups, unlike the rules of IHL.

[68] Art 12, International Covenant on Economic, Social and Cultural Rights, GA Res. 2200A (XXI), 21 UNGAOR Supp. (No. 16) at 49, UN Doc A/6316 (1966), 993 UNTS 3, entered into force 3 January 1976; See also art 11, European Social Charter(Revised), Council of Europe, 3 May 1996, ETS 163; art 11, Additional Protocol to the Inter-American Convention on Human Rights, 'Protocol of San Salvador', OAS Treaty Series No 69 (1988), entered into force 16 November 1999; art 24(2)(c), Convention on the Rights of the Child, GA Res. 44/25, annex, 44 UN GAOR Supp. (No. 49) at 167, UN Doc A/44/49 (1989), entered into force 2 September 1990; arts 4 (1), 7, and 20 (3) (b), Convention Concerning Indigenous and Tribal Peoples in Independent Countries, ILO, C169, 27 June 1989, C169.

[69] Art 24, African Charter on Human and Peoples' Rights, adopted 27 June 1981, OAU Doc CAB/LEG/67/3 rev. 5, (1982) 21 ILM 58, entered into force 21 October 1986.

[70] See eg *Oneryildiz v. Turkey*, ECtHR (2004), Reports of Judgments and Decisions 2004-XII, Inter-American Commission on Human Rights, Report on the situation of human rights in Ecuador, OEA/Ser.L/V/II.96, Doc 10 rev. 1, 24 April 1997, at chapter VIII and Communication No. 67/1980, *EHP v. Canada*, 2 Selected Decisions of the Human Rights Committee (1990).

[71] See eg *Lopez-Ostra v. Spain*, ECtHR (1994), Series A, No. 303C.

[72] Not yet in force.

[73] For a list of potentially relevant environmental law treaties, see UNEP 2009 Report, note 52, ch 4. See also 'Report of the International Law Commission', sixty-third session (23 April–3 June and 4 July–12 August 2011), UN Doc A/66/10, at Annex E.

[74] However, a situation of non-international armed conflict could be raised as a circumstance precluding the responsibility of a State, as a situation of force majeure or of state of necessity for instance. See arts 31–3, Draft Articles on International Responsibility of State for Internationally wrongful acts, in ILC, *Yearbook of the International Law Commission*, 2001, vol II, part II, UN Doc A/CN.4/Ser.A/1973/Add.1.

[75] See 'Protection of the Environment in times of armed conflict', Report of the Secretary-General, UN Doc A/47/328, at para 11, and 'Report of the Secretary-General on the Protection of the Environment in times of armed conflict', UN Doc A/48/269, at para 24.

### 4. Jurisprudential relevance

Due to the limited number of international cases involving damage to the environment before international tribunals since the adoption of the Rio Declaration, reception of Principle 24 in international jurisprudence has been limited. The most notable reference to Principle 24 in international jurisprudence is, as mentioned in section II) 2.2. of this chapter, by the International Court of Justice in its *Advisory Opinion on the legality of the use of Nuclear Weapons*. In this opinion, the Court affirms that:

> Respect for the environment is one of the elements that go to assessing whether an action is in conformity with the principles of necessity and proportionality. This approach is supported, indeed, by the terms of Principle 24 of the Rio Declaration...[76]

Damages to the environment as a result of violations of IHL have been addressed by other international bodies, but the Rio Declaration was not cited. For instance, following the 1998–2000 armed conflict between Eritrea and Ethiopia, the former sought more than $1 billion in compensation for environmental damages caused by Eritrean armed forces before the Claims Commission established by agreement between the two parties. Ethiopia claimed that the destruction of gum Arabic, resin plants, trees and seedlings, and the loss of wild animals was the result of IHL violations (or alternatively violations of *jus ad bellum*) by the Eritreans. The Commission however dismissed this claim because the allegations and evidence 'fall well below the standard of widespread and long-lasting environmental damage required for liability under international humanitarian law'.[77] Claims for environmental damages and depletion of natural resources caused by Iraq during the 1990–1991 Gulf War have also been dealt with by the United Nations Compensation Commission established by the UN Security Council, although in that case Iraq's liability was based on violation of article 2(4) of the UN Charter and not on particular violations of IHL.[78]

## III) Relations with Other Principles

Principle 15 of the Rio Declaration recalls that in order to ensure protection of the environment, States shall apply a precautionary approach. This principle should be kept in mind in relation to warfare issues, in particular when it comes to development, acquisition, or adoption of a new weapon, means, or method of warfare. Indeed, the following is considered as a customary rule of IHL:

> Methods and means of warfare must be employed with due regard to the protection and preservation of the natural environment. In the conduct of military operations, all feasible precautions must be taken to avoid, and in any event to minimize, incidental damage to the environment. Lack of scientific certainty as to the effects on the environment of certain military operations does not absolve a party to the conflict from taking such precautions.[79]

Furthermore, article 36 of Additional Protocol I requires States parties to determine whether the employment of new weapons, means, and methods of warfare would, in

[76] ICJ, *Advisory Opinion, Legality of the Threat or Use of Nuclear Weapons*, para 30.

[77] Central Front Ethiopia's Claim 2, Partial Award, Between Federal Democratic republic of Ethiopia and State of Eritrea, 28 April 2004, Hans van Houtte President, par. 100, accessible online: <http://www.pca-cpa.org/showpage.asp?pag_id=1151>.

[78] UN SC/RES/687. See also UNEP 2009 Report, 27–8.

[79] Rule 44, ICRC Customary Law Study.

some or all circumstances, be prohibited by any applicable rules of IHL. In the conduct of their review, and to be able to assess whether a weapon contravenes a rule of IHL, States will have to considered different factors, including health and environment related ones.[80] Article 36 does not specify how this review is to be carried out, but environmental impact assessments, as foreseen in Principle 17, should be either part of the review or considered during the process undertaken by the national authority in charge. Indeed, to determine whether a weapon or a means or method of warfare is consistent with the rules of IHL which provide for protection to the environment, scientific data on their effects on the environment are necessary.

Principle 23 is another principle that has to be read in conjunction with Principle 24. Indeed, IHL is applicable to situations of occupation. The rules of belligerent occupation govern the management and exploitation of natural resources in an occupied territory. For instance, under the Hague Regulation, the Occupying Power shall be regarded only as administrator and usufructuary of the natural resources and is not allowed to exploit such resources in a manner that would undermine its capital.[81] Furthermore, the Occupying Power has a positive duty to prevent looting, plundering, and exploitation of natural resources in the occupied territory not only by its agents but also by private individuals and entities, including business entities.[82]

Finally, the first sentence of Principle 24, affirming that warfare is inherently destructive of sustainable development, finds an echo in Principle 25, which affirms that peace, development, and environmental protection are interdependent and indivisible.

## IV) Assessment

In conclusion, Principle 24 of the Rio Declaration did not change existing rules of international law protecting the environment in times of armed conflict, but it marked important progress in this field. Indeed, it affirms concerns shared by the international community about adverse impacts of armed conflicts on the environment and recalls the importance to respect international law in that matter. Its call on States for further cooperation, which should be read in conjunction with paragraph 39.6 (a) of Agenda 21, has led to various initiatives, including the ICRC Guidelines for military manuals.

Since 1992, much progress in this area has been achieved. In addition to the ICRC Guidelines, one can mention the recognition of the importance of taking the protection of the environment into account during the conduct of hostilities by the ICJ, the development of customary international law, in particular in the field of IHL, the work undertaken by UNEP and the numerous impact assessments it has published.

However, a lot remains to be done, in particular in the context of non-international armed conflicts and in developing better comprehension of the interplay between the different fields of law in this area. In this respect, the work of the ILC on the protection of environment in relation to armed conflict is welcome. The Special Rapporteur, Marie Jacobsson, divided her work into three different periods: before, during and after armed

[80] On measures to implement art 36 of API, see ICRC, 'A Guide to the legal review of new weapons, means and methods of warfare' (2006).

[81] Art 55, Hague Convention IV and Regulations, and Rule 51 b), ICRC Customary Law Study.

[82] ICJ, *DRC v. Uganda 2005*, paras 245–9.

conflict.[83] Each period will be addressed in a specific report. This structure has the potential to provide for a better understanding of the broader legal framework relevant to the protection of the environment in relation to warfare activities and of the interplay between the different bodies of law applicable, in particular IHL, international human rights law, and international environmental law.

## V) Select Bibliography

Al-Duaij, N., *Environmental Law of Armed Conflict* (New York: Transnational Publishers 2004).

Austin, J. E. and Bruch, C. E. (eds), The Environmental Consequences of War (Cambridge: Cambridge University Press 2000).

Bothe, M., Bruch, C., Diamond, J., and Jensen, D., 'International law protecting the environment during armed conflict: gaps and opportunities' (2010) 92 *International Review of the Red Cross* 879.

Droege, C., 'Elective affinities? Human rights and humanitarian law' (2008) 90 *International Review of the Red Cross* 871.

Droege, C. and Tougas, M,-L., 'The Protection of the Natural Environment in Armed Conflict—Existing Rules and Need for Further Legal Protection' (2013) 82 *Nordic Journal of International Law* 21.

Guillard, D., *Les armes de guerre et l'environnement naturel* (Paris: L'Harmattan 2006).

Henckaerts, J.-M. and Constantin, D., 'Protection of the Environment', in Clapham, A. and Gaeta, P. (eds), *The Oxford Handbook on International Humanitarian Law* (Oxford University Press 2014), ch 19.

Hulme, K., *War Torn Environment: Interpreting the Legal Threshold* (Leiden: Martinus Nijhoff Publishers 2004).

Hulme, K., 'Taking care to protect the environment against damage: a meaningless obligation?' (2010) 92 *International Review of the Red Cross* 879.

Koppe, E., The Use of Nuclear Weapons and the Protection of the Environment during International Armed Conflict (Oxford: Hart Publishing 2008).

Lawrence, J. C. and Heller, K. J., 'The Limits of Article 8 (2) (b) (iv) of the Rome Statute, The First Ecocentric Environmental War Crime' (2007) 20 *GIELR* 61.

Mollard-Bannelier, K., *La protection de l'environnement en temps de conflit armé* (Paris: Pedone 2001).

Plant, G., *Environmental Protection and the Law of War. A 'Fifth Geneva' Convention on the Protection of the Environment in Time of Armed Conflict?* (New York and London: Belhaven Press 1992).

Rayfuse, R. (ed), *War and the Environment: International Law and the Protection of the Environment in Relation to Armed Conflict* (2013) 82(1) *Nordic Journal of International Law* (Special Issue).

Sjöstedt, B., 'The Role of Multilateral Environmental Agreements in Armed Conflict: "Green-keeping" in Virunga Park. Applying the UNESCO World Heritage Convention in the Armed Conflict of the Democratic Republic of the Congo' (2013) 82 *Nordic Journal of International Law* 129.

Tignino, M., *L'eau et la guerre. Elements pour un régime juridique* (Bruxelles: Bruylant 2011).

Desgagné, R., 'The Prevention of Environmental Damage in time of Armed Conflict: Proportionality and Precautionary Measures' (2000) *Yearbook of International Humanitarian Law* 109.

Wyatt, J., 'Law-making at the intersection of international environmental, humanitarian and criminal law: the issue of damage to the environment in international armed conflict' (2010) 92 *International Review of the Red Cross* 593.

[83] ILC, 'Report on the work of its sixty-fifth session'.

# 29. Principle 25

## *Peace, Development and Environmental Protection*

Annyssa Bellal* and Gilles Giacca**

**Principle 25**

Peace, development and environmental protection are interdependent and indivisible.



## I) Origins and Rationale of the Principle

### 1. Origins

A good starting point to elaborate the origins of Principle 25 of the Rio Declaration is the Stockholm Declaration of 1972, which paved the way to the process leading to the Earth Summit of 1992. The relationship between peace, development, and environmental protection does not appear per se in the principles adopted in Stockholm, but is mentioned in paragraph 6 of the first part of the Declaration, which proclaims that:

> [t]o defend and improve the human environment for present and future generations has become an imperative goal for mankind—a goal to be pursued together with, and in harmony with, the established and fundamental goals of peace and of world-wide economic and social development.


* PhD Graduate Institute of International and Development Studies, Legal Advisor at Geneva Call.

** PhD Graduate Institute of International and Development Studies, Legal Adviser within the Arms Unit of the ICRC's Legal Division.

In subsequent documents, there was some reference to the relationships between peace (or absence of peace, ie conflicts) and environment on the one hand, and development on the other, but not necessarily linking the *three* notions together.[1]

Later on, the 1987 Final Report of the World Commission on Environment and Development ('WCED'), also known as the Brundtland Report, addressed more precisely the links between peace and sustainable development:

> Among the dangers facing the environment, the possibility of nuclear war, or military conflict of a lesser scale involving weapons of mass destruction, is undoubtedly the gravest. Certain aspects of the issues of peace and security bear directly upon the concept of sustainable development. Indeed, they are central to it.[2]

The report also recognized that environmental stress, such as erosion or desertification, was a source of conflicts and that environmental degradation could create environmental refugees, which in turn has the potential to sustain or create more conflict situations.[3] In addition, conflict was recognized as a cause of unsustainable development, particularly because of the arms competition, inasmuch as such competition:

> pre-empt human resources and wealth that could be used to combat the collapse of environmental support systems, the poverty, and the underdevelopment that in combination contribute so much to contemporary political insecurity.[4]

Finally, the Report also underlined the impact of nuclear weapons (as well as other weapons of mass destruction such as biological ones) on development and the environment:

> the likely consequences of nuclear war make other threats, to the environment pale into insignificance... In addition to the destructive effects of blasts and heat, immensely magnified by these weapons, they introduce a new lethal agent—ionizing radiation—that extends lethal effects over both space and time.[5]

The Moscow Declaration adopted at the 1990 Global Forum on Environment and Development for Human Survival pursued this line of reasoning and referred to peace as a condition of an environmentally sound development:

> World peace, the full and equal participation of women and men, fairness, the elimination of poverty and a determination to protect our children from preventable disease and death, are essential conditions for sustainable, environmentally sound development in our interdependent world.

However, one should note that, whereas all of these documents hinged on the relationship between peace, environment, and/or development, none of them used precisely the terms

[1] The Preamble of the World Charter for Nature of 1982 states that: '*Competition for scarce resources creates conflicts, whereas the conservation of nature and natural resources contributes to justice and the maintenance of peace and cannot be achieved until mankind learns to live in peace and to forsake war and armaments*'. The preamble of the 1986 UN Declaration on the right to Development considers that '*international peace and security are essential elements for the realization of the right to development*'. Art 7 of the same declaration proclaims that '*All States should promote the establishment, maintenance and strengthening of international peace and security and, to that end, should do their utmost to achieve general and complete disarmament under effective international control as well as to ensure that the resources released by effective disarmament measures are used for comprehensive development, in particular that of the developing countries.*'

[2] UN Report of the World Commission on Environment and Development, Our Common Future, ch 11, para 1.

[3] Our Common Future, ch 11, paras 5 and 6.

[4] Our Common Future, ch 11, para 16.

[5] Our Common Future, ch 11, para 18.

'interdependent and indivisible' as in Principle 25 of the Rio Declaration to refer to the links between these different notions.[6]

## 2. Meaning and rationale

### *2.1. The notion/meaning of peace*

It is important to state at the outset that the concept of 'peace' laid down in this principle is at best imprecise.[7] It can be linked to friendly relations, equal rights, self-determination or to the absence of violence. There are a number of principles under international law that are directly pertinent, such as the principles of non-intervention in the field of collective security and *ius ad bellum*, or peaceful settlement of disputes. Although the respect for human rights in general may be of some relevance to the principle, the Rio Declaration did not adopt a human rights approach. However, in the context of the Rio Declaration and the end of the Cold War, the concept of peace sought to integrate broader conditions of social development, although its contours remain difficult to delineate. The UN Security Council's 1992 statement can provide a useful illustration of this broad conception of peace and security:

> The absence of war and military conflicts among States does not in itself ensure international peace and security. The non-military sources of instability in the economic, social, humanitarian and ecological fields have become threats to peace and security. The United Nations membership as a whole, working through the appropriate bodies, needs to give the highest priority to the solution of these matters.[8]

It seems evident that a comprehensive understanding of the structural causes of conflict and the circumstances that give rise to instability are necessary. Poverty, discrimination and gender inequality, environmental degradation, social and economic marginalization and inequity, and armed conflict interact in complex and potent ways. In effect, a number of elements can be identified that can negatively affect development, such as a high rate of population growth, the lack of economic growth, foreign debt, armed conflicts, structural adjustment programmes, increases in food and oil prices, inflationary pressures, or natural disasters hampering the economy of a nation.

### *2.2. The concepts of interdependency and indivisibility*

A simple textual interpretation of Principle 25 generates a number of remarks as to its meaning and rationale. Unlike most principles of the Rio Declaration, Principle 25 is not couched in mandatory language. Its wording is not sufficiently specific to suit the category

[6] After the adoption of the Rio Declaration, some documents used this wording, albeit from a human rights point of view. In the Draft Declaration of Principles on Human Rights and the Environment of 1994, Principle 1 proclaims that: '*Human rights, an ecologically sound environment, sustainable development and peace are interdependent and indivisible*'. Similar wording was also used in the 1995 Copenhagen Declaration adopted at the World Summit for Social Development: '*We are deeply convinced that economic development, social development, and environmental protection are interdependent and mutually reinforcing components of sustainable development, which is the framework for our efforts to achieve a higher quality of life for all people (Principle 6)*'. Finally, article 4 of the Draft International Covenant on Environment and Development of 1995 stipulates in article 4 that '*Peace, development, environmental protection and respect for human rights and fundamental freedoms are interdependent.*'

[7] See eg Galtung, J., 'Violence, Peace, and Peace Research' (1969) 6 *JPR* 167.

[8] See for example UN Security Council's 1992 statement: UNSC Presidential Note (31 January 1992) UN Doc S/23500, 3.

of rules. It can rather be understood as a principle with a relatively high degree of generality and abstraction.

The reference to the interdependency and indivisibility of peace, development, and environmental protection seeks to promote equality among them. The principle calls for the international community to treat them on the same footing and with the same emphasis, stressing that these concepts cannot be considered in isolation from each other. They are complementary and they witness a wider and more inclusive understanding of interests and values to be protected and fulfilled by the international community.

Of both formulations, the term 'interdependent' is relatively straightforward. To say that peace, development, and environmental protection are interdependent despite their distinctiveness as particular endeavours means that the realization of any of them requires the realization of the others. It means that they are brought into a situation of mutual relationship and dependency. Certain aspects relating to peace and environmental protection bear directly upon the concept of sustainable development. Environmental threats or underdevelopment can be both a cause and an effect of political tension and armed conflict. Generally, experts agree that conflict can slow down economic growth and development in a variety of ways.[9]

The concept of indivisibility for its part is more difficult to determine. Its literal meaning—unable to be divided or separated—carries a rather strong meaning. Since peace, development, and environmental protection are indivisible, the full realization of one without the realization of the other is simply impossible. This would require effective coordinated national and international policies in those areas.

It seems intuitive that meeting the basic needs of poor communities will eliminate many of the situations leading to armed conflicts. In addition, it is unequivocally true that armed conflicts destroy natural resources, infrastructure, and human lives, which inevitably impact the development of any given society. The 'interdependence' of peace and development, as expressed in Principle 25, also signifies that maintaining or establishing peace in certain regions is closely related to addressing pressing challenges of sustainable development. For instance, the dispute over water rights represents one of the principal causes of conflicts in different parts of the world.[10] On the other hand, experiences of sustainable development in the area of management of supply of water have also led to the creation of allocation mechanisms, thus replacing pre-existing or latent conflicts by democratic process.[11]

Overall, the nature of Principle 25 reflects more of a process of coordination and integration. It might be understood as a guide for the integration of peace, development, and environmental protection. In other words, it may require States to take peace and environmental considerations into account in the process of development decision-making. This may strive to provide new directions in which international law, as well as international

[9] Collier, P. and Hoeffler, A., 'On economic causes of civil war' (1998) 50 (4) *Oxford Economic Papers* 563.

[10] Telesetsky, A., 'Resource Conflicts over Arable Land in Food Insecure States: Creating an United Nations Ombudsman Institution to Review Foreign Agricultural Land Leases' (2011) 3 *Goettingen Journal of International Law* 283; or Magsig, B.-O., 'Overcoming State-Centrism in International Water Law: "Regional Common Concern" as the Normative Foundation of Water Security' (2011) *3 Goettingen Journal of International Law 317.*

[11] International Symposium, 'Sustainable Development: Implications for World Peace', Tom Slick Conference, University of Texas, <http://www.utexas.edu/courses/sustdevt/conceptual.html>. See also for the challenges, Kraus, K. and Jütersonke, O., 'Peace, Security and Development in Post-Conflict Environments', <http://www.prio.no>, 2005.

public policy goals in those fields should be progressively developed to contribute to major coherence.

However, the principle is abstractly formulated and lacks practical reference to the circumstances in which the interrelationship between the concepts may be applied. In this context, international cooperation may represent an important aspect of what the principle of coordination and integration involves, which will be discussed further below. This begs, nonetheless, the question of the kind of actions required of States for the purpose of Principle 25, beyond mere rhetoric. Although this close interrelationship seems beyond dispute, how can diverse and complex challenges in areas such as development, peace, and environmental protection be meaningfully linked to each other and placed under a single framework? This process of coordination and integration might reveal more of a procedural obligation to take into account this relationship, which is instrumental in the achievement of an objective—the realization of sustainable development.

## II) The Principle as Enshrined in the Rio Declaration

### 1. Preparatory work and context

In all fairness, there is not much information to be found in the *travaux préparatoires* to better understand what States had in mind when drafting Principle 25. The first draft of the principle seems to have been submitted by Pakistan on behalf of the Group of 77 and China during the fourth Preparatory Committee ('PrepCom') in 1992. The formulation proposed then was slightly different from the existing Principle, in the sense that a second sentence was also added. The then principle '24' read thus as follows:

> Peace, development and environmental protection are indivisible. Any international regime cannot be considered equitable and just if it ignores the disparities in standards of living between nations and is insensitive to the development needs of the majority of the people of the world.[12]

As one can note, the accent in this proposal seems to be put on development issues. This is understandable since the Group 77 and China represented, during the negotiations, the views of 'the South' wishing to see development concerns balanced with environmental ones, which were defended by the more industrialized countries of the North.[13]

The United States also proposed a similar principle during the same PrepCom. Principle 10 of the US proposal proclaimed that 'A commitment to peace and security for all States and people is fundamental to the achievement of sustainable development.'[14] Here also, the accent seems to be put on the issue of development and no mention is made to the link between peace and environment (perhaps because it was meant to be implied in the term 'sustainable' development).

[12] Report of the Preparatory Committee for the United Nations Conference on Environment and Development on the work of its fourth Session, New York, 2 March–3 April 1992, A/CONF.151/PC/128, 92.

[13] Ling, C. Y., 'The Rio Declaration on Environment and Development: An Assessment', in *Environment and Development*, Series 12, published by the Third World Network, 2012, available at <http://www.twnside.org.sg/title/end/pdf/end12.pdf> (accessed 24 January 2014).

[14] Report of the Preparatory Committee for the United Nations Conference on Environment and Development on the work of its fourth Session, 95.

The next reference to this principle can be found in the proposal of the government of Australia, which made the following comments with regard to a proposed article 10 entitled 'Peace and security':

- Preferred location/association: preambular statement or free-standing principle.
- Preferred text: should note the interrelationship between environment, peace and security.
- Other possible elements: recognition of the Charter of the United Nations and the basic principles of international law for the peaceful resolution of disputes.[15]

The Australian comments are a case in point. They show that Principle 25 was meant to be relatively generic in its meaning and purpose, hence the idea to have it rather as a preambular statement or freestanding principle. The link with the notion of peaceful resolution of disputes is also mentioned here. In the Rio Declaration, peaceful resolution of disputes indeed follows Principle 25. Principle 26 provides that states are to resolve all of their environmental disputes peacefully, by appropriate means, in accordance with the Charter of the United Nations. Principle 26 is designed to play a role in avoiding international tension and conflict arising from disputes concerning natural resources, transboundary environmental damage, or damage to global commons.

In the final text, as adopted during the Earth Summit, the G77 and Chinese proposal was preferred but without the second sentence. The final draft of Principle 25 simply declares that 'Peace, development and environmental protection are interdependent and indivisible'. It is not clear why this was so and no further explanation can be found in the *travaux préparatoires*.

During the Conference, States made no interpretative statements regarding Principle 25. Mention of the interdependence of peace, development, and environment were, however, made in some of the statements delivered at the conference by high-level officials. For instance, the President of Brazil noted that 'there will be no healthy environment or equitable development if we are not able to build a true and permanent peace among nations'.[16]

The then Prime Minister of Denmark and former Chairman of the World Commission on Environment and Development, Gro Harlem Brundtland, also declared that 'a sharp reduction in the arms race and the expected peace dividend can be used to finance today most urgent forms of collective security—environmental security'.[17]

Although those statements by high-level state officials do not constitute legal means of interpretation of Principle 25, they are useful to understand its general meaning. In particular, among the ideas expressed, the notions of 'environmental security' and the impact of disarmament on development seem to be two angles of analysis allowing us to assess the scope and aims of Principle 25, which will be taken up below.

## 2. Scope and dimensions

### 2.1. *Peace and environment/environmental security*

The relationship between peace and environment is often portrayed in terms of the 'scarcity of natural resources leading to conflicts' dichotomy. Other research, however, has tried

[15] Report of the Preparatory Committee on the work of its fourth Session, 104.

[16] Report of the United Nations Conference on Environment and Development, Rio de Janeiro, 3–14 June 1992, vol II, Proceedings, A/CONF.161/26/Rev.1 (vol II), 65.

[17] Report of the United Nations Conference on Environment and Development, A/CONF.161/26/Rev.1 (vol II), 55.

to look at the relationship from the other end, by arguing that environmental cooperation also leads to peacemaking. For example, the UNEP 2004 Report on 'Understanding Environment, Conflict and Cooperation', showed how sustainable environment management could become a tool for conflict prevention by bringing parties together to work on environmental issues in ways that build confidence and reduce political tensions.[18]

The concept of 'environmental security' is particularly helpful to understand the scope and aim of Principle 25, even though the notion was developed prior to the Rio Declaration.[19] There is no agreed definition of the notion,[20] but it has been described as 'the current and future availability (determined by the factors—supply, accessibility and management) of life supporting ecosystem services and goods for human needs and natural processes which contribute to poverty alleviation and conflict deterrence'.[21] In this definition, one can note that environmental security is linked both to the notion of peace (conflict deterrence) and development (reducing poverty alleviation).

The notion of environmental security stems from the idea that traditional security concerns, framed in terms of threats to national security (such as terrorism) are not able to address new threats such as environmental stress. One of the early warnings on the consequences that environmental crises could have on national as well as international security, was voiced by the journalist Robert Kaplan in his article 'The Coming Anarchy', published in *The Atlantic* in 1994:

> It is time to understand the Environment for what it is: the national-security issue of the early twenty-first century. The political and strategic impact of surging populations, spreading disease, deforestation and soil erosion, water depletion, air pollution, and, possibly, rising sea levels in critical, overcrowded regions . . . development that will prompt mass migrations, and in turn, incite group conflicts.[22]

Environmental security is a multifaceted concept. It touches upon issues such as resource scarcity (including water security),[23] food security, climate change, warfare, marine pollution, marine biological resources, as well as biosafety and genetically modified organisms.[24] From an international law point of view, the recent ICJ decision on the case of the *Maritime Dispute* opposing *Peru v. Chile* on fisheries and maritime boundaries issues is a good illustration of the implementation of the notion of environmental security.[25]

[18] See Adelphi Research, Wilton Park and Woodrow Wilson International Centre for Scholars, 'Environment, Development and Sustainable Peace: Finding Paths to environmental peacemaking', available at <http://www.wiltonpark.org.uk> (accessed on 24 January 2014).

[19] See eg Brown, L., 'Redefining National Security', *Worldwatch Paper*, n°14, 1977; Myers, N., 'The Environmental Dimension to Security Issues', (1986) 6 *The Environmentalist* 251–7.

[20] See Barnett, J., 'Environmental Security and Peace' (2007) 3 (1) *Journal of Human Security* 4–16.

[21] Hecker, J. H., 'Peace and sustainable development through environmental security', *Institute for Environmental Security*, January 2011, 12, available at <http://www.envirosecurity.org> (accessed on 24 January 2014). Another definition refers to the notion of environmental security 'as a condition in which a nation or region, through sound governance, capable management, and sustainable utilisation of its natural resources and environment, takes effective steps toward creating social, economic, and political stability and ensuring the welfare of its population', Foundation for Environmental Security and Sustainability, <http://www.fess-global.org/about.cfm> (accessed in January 2014).

[22] Kaplan, R., 'The Coming Anarchy', *The Atlantic*, 1994.

[23] See on that issue Wouters, P., Vinogradov, S. and Magsis, B., 'Water Security, Hydrosolidarity, and International Law: A River Runs Through it' (2008) 19(1) *YbIEL* 97–134.

[24] On these issues, see Hulme, K., 'Environmental Security: Implications for International Law' (2008) 19(1) *YbIEL* 3–26.

[25] ICJ, Maritime Dispute (*Peru v. Chile*), Judgment of 27 January 2014.

As such, Principle 25, by reaffirming the links between peace, environment, and development is another expression of the concept of environmental security. One could even argue that the many policy initiatives put in place to address the issue of environmental security, are also a way to implement Principle 25 of the Rio Declaration.[26]

Since the early 1990s, the practice of the UN Security Council ('SC') has expanded in the area of conflict prevention, although the conceptual linkage between peace and environment is missing in the UN Charter.[27] More specifically, the High Level Panel on Threats, Challenges and Change took a broad approach to the interpretation of SC's role, stating that '[t]he Security Council is fully empowered under Chapter VII of the Charter of the United Nations to address the full range of security threats with which States are concerned'.[28] However, in the area of environment issues, such as climate change, the SC has not addressed those issues under the framework of Chapter VII action[29] and the question remains controversial.[30] The potential link between environmental questions and conflict was considered more of a development issue rather than a security threat.[31] The SC noted that in

> matters relating to the maintenance of international peace and security under its consideration, conflict analysis and contextual information on, inter alia, possible security implications of climate change is important, when such issues are drivers of conflict, represent a challenge to the implementation of Council mandates or endanger the process of consolidation of peace.[32]

The UN Secretary-General also addressed the link between environmental concerns, peace, and development. He remarked that 'our experiences tell us that environmental stress due to lack of water may lead to conflict and would be greater in poor nations'.[33] It is, indeed, a fact that poverty increases vulnerability to environmental crises.[34]

## *2.2. Peace, development, and disarmament*

The link between peace, development, and disarmament has been frequently examined. To a certain extent, one could even argue that this relationship was already recognized

[26] See for example the Institute for environmental security, <http://www.envirosecurity.org/>; the Institute for environmental diplomacy and security, <http://www.uvm.edu/ieds/> or The environment and security initiative, <http://www.envsec.org/index.php?lang=en>.

[27] True-Frost, C., 'The Security Council and Norm Consumption' (2007) 40 *NYU J Intl L & Pol* 115, 138–74.

[28] See UNGA 'Report of the High Level Panel on Threats, Challenges and Change' (2 December 2004) UN Doc A/59/565. See also 'Security Council holds first-ever debate in impact of climate change on peace, security, hearing over 50 speakers', UN Press release, <http://www.un.org/News/Press/docs/2007/sc9000.doc.htm>.

[29] Scott, S. V., 'Climate Change and Peak Oil as Threats to International Peace and Security: Is It Time for the Security Council to Legislate?' (2008) 9 *Melbourne Journal of International Law* 495.

[30] According to the UN Secretary-General, 'The facts are clear: climate change is real; it is accelerating in a dangerous manner; and it not only exacerbates threats to international peace and security, it is a threat to international peace and security.' *Remarks to the Security Council on the Impact of Climate Change on International Peace and Security*, 20 July 2011. UNSC Presidential Statement (20 July 2011) UN Doc S/PRST/2011/15 and the discussion in UNSC Verbatim Records (20 July 2011) UN Doc S/PV.6587.

[31] UNSC Verbatim Records (20 July 2011) UN Doc S/PV.6587.

[32] UNSC Presidential Statement (20 July 2011) UN Doc S/PRST/2011/15.

[33] Ban Ki-moon, Address by the UN Secretary-General to the Session: 'Time is running Out on Water' of the Davos World Economic Forum, January 2008, Davos, Switzerland, available at <http://www.un.org/News/Press/docs/2008/sgsm11388.doc.htm>.

[34] See eg on that issue, Pielke, Jr, R. A., Rubiera, J., Landsea, C., Fernandez, M. L., and Klein, R., 'Hurricane Vulnerability in Latin America and The Caribbean: Normalized Damage and Loss Potentials', available at <http://secure.nameservers.com/ambergriscaye.com/hurricane/resource-1827-200321.pdf>.

in the UN Charter, in particular in article 26 and article 55. The principle of 'the least diversion of the world's human and economic resources' in article 26 introduces an economic rationale. The objective of this concept is to preserve resources at *both* national and global levels for the purposes of development.[35] For instance, the reduction in military expenditures could serve as a means to give effect to the aspirations of the UN Charter.[36] Such an interpretation is supported by the evolution of a new conception of peace and security that encompasses both human rights and development as the constitutive elements.[37]

Indeed, outside the purview of article 26 of the UN Charter, this goal has increasingly gained some weight of its own and has been associated with different concepts such as the 'peace dividend', 'positive peace', the 'right to development', or 'human security'.[38] The notion has developed beyond the realm of article 26, and has been referred to or reformulated in many UN resolutions and statements of international conferences. The inclusion of the link between military spending and development in the 1986 Declaration on the Right to Development is a good example. It stipulates that

> All States should promote the establishment, maintenance and strengthening of international peace and security and, to that end, should do their utmost to achieve general and complete disarmament under effective international control, as well as to ensure that the resources released by effective disarmament measures are used for comprehensive development, in particular that of the developing countries.[39]

The General Assembly resolution establishing the UN Register of Conventional Arms to increase the transparency in armaments stated in 1991

> its determination to prevent the excessive and destabilizing accumulation of arms, including conventional arms, in order to promote stability and strengthen regional or international peace and security, taking into account the legitimate security needs of States and the principle of undiminished security at the lowest possible level of armaments.[40]

In 2008, Costa Rica convened a meeting of the UN Security Council to discuss article 26 of the Charter. The modest outcome of this initiative produced a Presidential Statement, where the Security Council, stressing its concern at increasing global military expenditures, 'urge[d] all States to devote as many resources as possible to economic and

[35] This goal has to be understood in the context of art 26 where the standard, which is binding on the Security Council, should be taken into account when making plans for the regulation of armaments to achieve the least diversion of resources. The President of Costa Rica describes 'the least diversion of resources' as finding alternatives to excessive military spending that do not damage security, one of these alternatives being the strengthening of multilateralism. (Oscar Arias Sanchez, President of Costa Rica, and President of the UN Security Council, 19 November 2008).

[36] 'Declaration on the strengthening of international security', UN General Assembly Resolution 2734 (XXV), paras 19, 20.

[37] See 'Declaration on the strengthening of international security'. See also *Report of the International Conference on the Relationship between Disarmament and Development*, UN Doc A/CONF.130/39, New York, 24 August–11 September 1987, Final document, point 31.

[38] The 2003 Commission on Human Security (p 135) called for an internationally accepted common reporting framework on military spending. See Commission on Human Security, *Human Security Now. Final Report* (2003), Chapter 8, p 135.

[39] Art 7 of the UN Declaration on the Right to Development, UN Doc A/RES/41/128, 4 December 1986.

[40] The UN Register of Conventional Arms is a voluntary arrangement established after the 1990–1 Iraq-Kuwait War by the Secretary-General on 1 January 1992, under General Assembly Resolution 46/36 L of 9 December 1991, entitled 'Transparency in Armaments'.

social development, in particular in the fight against poverty and the achievement of the Millennium Development Goals.'[41]

For its part, article 55 of the UN Charter states that the promotion of higher standards of living, full employment, and conditions of economic and social progress and development create the conditions of stability and well-being which are necessary for peaceful and friendly relations among nations.

A number of approaches have been developed to study the impact of violence on socio-economic development. Among them, one notable example is the study of the 'Global Burden of Armed Violence' in the framework of Geneva Declaration on Armed Violence and Development,[42] or research conducted in the context of the 2011 World Bank's *World Development Report*.[43] But these efforts also tend to establish the contours of cost factors of armed violence and relate to the general phenomenon of violence, where the issue of military spending, including for arms acquisitions, forms but one aspect of the spectrum of issues.[44] Another recent iteration of the principle is in the UN Programme of Action on Small Arms and Light Weapons, which similarly notes that the 'excessive accumulation and uncontrolled spread' of small arms and light weapons has 'a wide range of humanitarian and socio-economic consequences and pose a serious threat to peace, reconciliation, safety, security, stability and sustainable development.'[45]

The relationship between disarmament and development is controversial, despite the frequency of its incantation in international discourse. Some States do not see any automatic link between the two. Thus, for example, in 2002 in its explanation of the vote against UN General Assembly resolution 57/65, the United States of America (USA) stated: 'We continue to believe that disarmament and development are two distinct issues that do not lend themselves to being linked.'[46] To give another example: today's

[41] Statement by the President of the Security Council, UN Doc S/PRST/2008/43, 19 November 2008. Costa Rica convened this debate in order to examine what was contained in article 26 of the UN Charter stressing that the 'time had come to recognize the link between the waste of resources devoted to arms and the need for resources for development.' It further presented the 'Costa Rica Consensus', an initiative to create mechanisms to forgive debts, and provide international financial resources, for developing countries that spend more on environmental protection, education, health care, and housing for its citizens, and less on weapons and soldiers. Based on article 26, this initiative seeks ultimately to reward developing countries that divert fewer of its economic and human resources to the purchase of arms.

[42] See in addition to the general publication *Global Burden of Armed Violence 2011* and *Global Burden of Armed Violence 2008* available at <http://www.genevadeclaration.org>; Geneva Declaration on Armed Violence and Development, *Armed Violence Prevention and Reduction: A Challenge for Achieving the Millennium Development Goals*, Background Paper (June 2008); and *More Violence, Less Development Examining the Relationship Between Armed Violence and MDG Achievement*, September 2010.

[43] World Bank, *World Development Report 2011: Conflict, Security, and Development*, World Bank Publications 2011, 412.

[44] For example, there is a substantial literature on the impact of armed violence on economic factors—direct impact on issues such as GDP growth, on the composition of a country's economy, foreign investments, and on spending. See Collier, P. and Hoeffler, A., 'On economic causes of civil war', (1998) 50 (4) *Oxford Economic Papers* 563–73. It must, though, be noted that arms acquisitions and military spending are not interchangeable even though they are closely related. In general, the notion of military spending is considered a broader category than arms acquisition as it encompasses personnel, operations, other procurement, and maintenance, in addition to the purchase of arms.

[45] UN, *Programme of Action to Prevent, Combat and Eradicate the Illicit Trade in Small Arms and Light Weapons in All Its Aspects*, 2001, UN Doc A/CONF.192/15, Section I, para 2.

[46] It also reiterated that the USA did not consider itself bound by the Final Document of the 1987 International Conference, cited in Report of the Secretary-General, *The Relationship Between Disarmament*

most important development agenda, the Millennium Development Goals ('MDGs'), contains no reference to disarmament.[47] Similarly, the 2002 Monterrey Consensus on Development Financing, which is a major reference point for mobilizing resources to fund poverty reduction and development (eg the MDGs), omits completely any reference to the possibility of accruing resources through a reduction of arms expenditure. The absence of this debate in the 2005 UN Summit's Outcome Document further supports the preliminary conclusion that the linking of development and disarmament remains tentative.

Indeed, although socio-economic considerations are occasionally taken into account, at least in theory, when considering military spending, save for article 26 of the UN Charter the basis for this does not emanate from international legal instruments. In truth, the concept as it has been enunciated thus far is too vague to generate concrete standards.

## III) Relations with Other Principles

Principle 25 intersects with a number of other Rio Declaration principles, providing an instrumental role for provisions of the Rio Declaration that aim to promote peaceful and friendly relations among states. Thus, Principle 25 belongs to the category of principles of the Rio Declaration which seek to promote and operationalize international cooperation and peace, such as Principle 9 on transfer of technology and Principle 12 calling for the establishment of an open and supportive international economic system, as well as Principle 26 on the peaceful resolution of environmental disputes.

One perhaps better understands the rationale of Principle 25 by looking at Principle 24. Principle 24 of the Rio Declaration states that 'Warfare is inherently destructive of sustainable development. States shall therefore respect international law providing protection for the environment in times of armed conflict and cooperate in its further development, as necessary.'

Both principles address similar issues. Warfare, or the absence of peace, has an impact on sustainable development and environment. Principle 24 however contains a clear injunction to States about the respect of international law regarding the environment in armed conflict situations. In that sense, Principle 24 has a much more straightforward and legal approach than Principle 25. Indeed, Principle 25 is much broader and general in this sense. It does not refer to *expressis verbis* to international law. It could be best described as *statement of principle*, in the most literal sense of the expression.

## IV) Assessment

The inclusion of Principle 25 was not controversial in the preparation and adoption of the Rio Declaration and there is little evidence that Principle 25 has had subsequently

*and Development in the Current International Context*, New York (2004), available at <http://www.un.org/disarmament/HomePage/ODAPublications/DisarmamentStudySeries/PDF/DSS_31.pdf>.

47 Note, however, the UN Secretary-General's Report on Promoting Development through the Reduction and Prevention of Armed Violence, which also refers to 'the negative impact of armed violence on the prospects for achieving the Millennium Development Goals, and the tremendous human and economic costs associated with armed violence.' 'Report on Promoting Development through the Reduction and Prevention of Armed Violence', UN Doc A/64/228, para 42.

a significant influence upon other international instruments. Moreover, the principle has not been referred to in decisions of domestic or international courts and tribunals.

As referred to previously, it should be noted that the Rio Declaration did not adopt a human rights approach. The absence of references to human rights can be explained by a number of factors. First, development and human rights evolved separately from their inception. For mainstream development, human rights issues were widely perceived as self-contained and even irrelevant for a long period of time. Second, the dominant development approach to human rights incorporates only a selected number of elements from human rights discourse, largely focusing on certain civil and political rights rather than socio-economic rights.[48] This is not the right place to explore in detail problems on the relationship between human rights and development, but there has been, so far, limited explicit integration of human rights concerns in development, as attested in the Rio Declaration process. However, it is fair to say that since the 1990s the concept of development has expanded to include as well human rights, good governance, democracy, and social dimensions. The human dimension of development is often associated with human rights discourse, and has brought the focus of development on the individual as an ultimate beneficiary. This undoubtedly resonates with Principle 1 of the Rio Declaration that the ultimate beneficiary is and remains the 'human being' rather than 'the environment'.[49]

Questions remain as to the potential operationalization of Principle 25. As noted above, the principle seeks to incorporate development, peace, and environmental protection in an interdisciplinary fashion. It calls for the international community to treat them in an equal manner, in the process of development decision-making. The principle espouses mostly broad policy goals and objectives rather than detailed normative positions, which may be found in a number of documents and instruments discussed above. However, global awareness on the linkages between peace, development, and environmental protection increased dramatically, as did international law. It certainly represents an attempt at forging a basic common outlook on how to address the challenge of preserving peace.

## V) Select Bibliography


Adelphi Research, Wilton Park and Woodrow Wilson International Centre for Scholars, 'Environment, Development and Sustainable Peace: Finding Paths to environmental peacemaking', available at <http://www.wiltonpark.org.uk>.

Barnett, J., 'Environmental security and Peace' (2007) 3(1) *Journal of Human Security* 4.

Brown, L., 'Redefining National Security' (1977) *Worldwatch Paper*, n°14.

Collier, P. and Hoeffler, A., 'On Economic Causes of Civil Qar' (1998) 50(4) *Oxford Economic Papers* 563.

De Feyter, K., *Human Rights: Social Justice in the Age of the Market* (London: Zed Books 2005).

Galtung, J., 'Violence, Peace, and Peace Research' (1969) 6 *JPR* 167.


48 de Feyter, K., *Human Rights: Social Justice in the Age of the Market* (Zed Books 2005), 218.

49 See the chapter by F. Francioni in this commentary.

Giacca, G. and Karimova, T., 'The Implications of Economic and Social Rights for Arms Acquisitions', in Casey-Maslen, S. (ed), *Weapons under International Human Rights Law* (Cambridge University Press 2014).

Hulme, K., 'Environmental Security: Implications for International Law' (2008) 19 (1) *YbIEL* 3.

Hyde Hecker, J., 'Peace and Sustainable development through environmental security', *Institute for Environmental Security*, January 2011, 12, available at <http://www.envirosecurity.org>.

Kaplan, R., 'The Coming Anarchy', *The Atlantic*, 1 February 1994.

Kraus, K. and Oliver Jütersonke, O., 'Peace, Security and Development in Post-Conflict Environments' (2005) 36(4) *Security Dialogue* 447, available at <http://www.prio.no>.

Ling, C. Y., 'The Rio Declaration on Environment and Development: An Assessment' in *Environment and Development*, Series 12, published by the Third World Network, 2012, available at <http://www.twnside.org.sg/title/end/pdf/end12.pdf>.

Magsig, B. 'Overcoming State-Centrism in International Water Law: "Regional Common Concern" as the Normative Foundation of Water Security' (2011) 3 (1) *GoJiL* 317.

Myers, N., 'The Environmental Dimension to Security Issues' (1986) 6 *The Environmentalist* 251.

Penny, C. K., 'Greening the Security Council: Climate Change as an Emerging "Threat to International Peace and Security"'(2007) 7 *Intl Env Agreements* 35.

Pielke, R. A., Rubiera, J., Landsea, C., Fernandez, M., and Klein, R., 'Hurricane Vulnerability in Latin America and The Caribbean: Normalized Damage and Loss Potentials' (2003) 4 *Natural Hazards Review* 101, available at <http://secure.nameservers.com/ambergriscaye.com/hurricane/resource-1827-200321.pdf>.

Scott, S. V., 'Climate Change and Peak Oil as Threats to International Peace and Security: Is It Time for the Security Council to Legislate?' (2008) 9 *Melb J Intl L* 495.

Simma, B. et al (eds), *The Charter of the United Nations—A Commentary* (Oxford University Press 2012).

True-Frost, C., 'The Security Council and Norm Consumption' (2007) 40 *NYU J Intl L & Pol* 115, 138–174.

Wouters, P., Vinogradov, S., and Magsis, B., 'Water Security, Hydrosolidarity, and International Law: A River Runs Through it' (2008) 19(1) *YbIEL* 97.

# 30. Principle 26

## *International Environmental Dispute Settlement*

Tim Stephens*

**Principle 26**

States shall resolve all their environmental disputes peacefully and by appropriate means in accordance with the Charter of the United Nations.



## I) Origins and Rationale of the Principle

Principle 26 of the *United Nations Declaration on Environment and Development*[1] ('Rio Declaration') provides that states are to resolve all of their environmental disputes peacefully, by appropriate means, in accordance with the Charter of the United

* Associate Professor and Associate Dean (Postgraduate Coursework), Faculty of Law, University of Sydney. Sincere thanks are extended to Eloise Scotford and Jorge E. Viñuales for their helpful comments on a draft of this Chapter.

[1] UN Doc A/CONF.151/26 (vol I) (1992); (1992) 31 ILM 874.

Nations. The obligation upon states to resolve disputes peacefully is a foundation stone of international law in the United Nations era. Article 2(3) of the Charter requires all members to 'settle their international disputes by peaceful means in such a manner that international peace and security, and justice, are not endangered.' It is an obligation that accompanies and complements the *jus cogens* prohibition on the use of force expressed in article 2(4) of the Charter. Article 33 of the Charter further elaborates upon the article 2(3) obligation, providing that '[t]he parties to any dispute, the continuance of which is likely to endanger the maintenance of international peace and security, shall, first of all, seek a solution by negotiation, enquiry, mediation, conciliation, arbitration, judicial settlement, resort to regional agencies or arrangements, or other peaceful means of their own choice.'

## II) The Principle as Enshrined in the Rio Declaration

### 1. Preparatory work and context

#### *1.1. The origins of Principle 26*

Preparations for the United Nations Conference on Environment and Development ('UNCED') and Agenda 21 and the Rio Declaration were formally initiated by United Nations General Assembly Resolution 44/228, adopted in December 1989.[2] The Resolution set out the objectives for UNCED to prevent 'the continuing deterioration of the state of the environment and the serious degradation of the global life-support systems...that...could disrupt the global ecological balance, jeopardize the life-sustaining qualities of the earth and lead to an ecological catastrophe'. The final of 23 identified objectives of UNCED in Resolution 44/228 to address 'environmental issues in the developmental context' related to dispute settlement, and requested that UNCED:

> assess the capacity of the United Nations system to assist in the prevention and settlement of disputes in the environmental sphere and to recommend measures in this field, while respecting existing bilateral and international agreements that provide for the settlement of such disputes.

The response to this request in the documentary outcomes of UNCED can be seen in Principle 26 of the Rio Declaration and Chapter 39 of Agenda 21. Whereas Principle 26 of the Rio Declaration is confined to stating the general obligation upon states to resolve their environmental disputes peacefully, Chapter 39 of Agenda 21 is more programmatic in its treatment of dispute settlement issues. This is consistent with the intention that Agenda 21 be a detailed action plan for achieving sustainable development. Agenda 21 provides, relevantly, that:

> 39.10. In the area of avoidance and settlement of disputes, States should further study and consider methods to broaden and make more effective the range of techniques available at present, taking into account, among others, relevant experience under existing international agreements, instruments or institutions and, where appropriate, their implementing mechanisms such as modalities for dispute avoidance and settlement. This may include mechanisms and procedures for the exchange of data and information, notification and consultation regarding situations that might lead to disputes with other States in the

[2] UN Doc UNGA Res 44/228 (1989).

field of sustainable development and for effective peaceful means of dispute settlement in accordance with the Charter of the United Nations, including, where appropriate, recourse to the International Court of Justice, and their inclusion in treaties relating to sustainable development.

### *1.2. The work of the preparatory committee*

The preparatory work for UNCED was advanced in several phases. Following the adoption of Resolution 44/228 the UNCED Preparatory Committee ('PrepCom') and the UNCED Secretariat were established, and initial drafts of UNCED decisions and other materials (including background papers) were produced. PrepCom comprised around 175 national delegations that participated in UNCED, and carried out its work across four sessions in Nairobi in August 1991 (PrepCom I), in Geneva in March 1991 (PrepCom II) and in August (PrepCom III) and finally in March 1992, at the United Nations Headquarters in New York (PrepCom IV).

Within the PrepCom, Working Group III (WG-III) on legal and institutional issues was tasked with developing an instrument, charter, statement, or declaration in response to the request in Resolution 44/228 'to promote the further development of international law, taking into account the Declaration of the United Nations Conference on the Human Environment.' There was no principle in the *Declaration of the United Nations Conference on the Human Environment* ('Stockholm Declaration')[3] upon which PrepCom could draw for the purposes of devising Principle 26. However, the PrepCom did have the benefit of considerable background work by the World Commission on Environment and Development, chaired by Gro Brundtland. The Brundtland Commission made recommendations for a comprehensive 'Earth Charter' that would include, among substantive environmental protection obligations, detailed provisions concerning dispute settlement.[4] The Chairman of UNCED, Maurice Strong, had also called for the Conference to produce a binding 'Earth Charter',[5] however this idea was rejected in favour of a shorter, non-binding, instrument that was formulated and agreed upon relatively quickly towards the end of the PrepCom process.

The first substantive meeting of WG-III was held during PrepCom III, and the drafting of the Rio Declaration took place at the final PrepCom meeting, PrepCom IV.[6] Various proposals were put before WG-III, including a set of previously agreed principles compiled by the UNCED Secretariat,[7] and drafts by a number of delegations including from Argentina, Australia, Canada, the European Community, Japan, the Nordic countries (Denmark, Iceland, Norway, and Sweden), the United States, the Group of 77 ('G77') and China.[8] The negotiators were provided with a background paper prepared by Prafullachandra Bhagwati, the former Chief Justice of India, on existing provisions and mechanisms for dispute resolution.[9] The Bhagwati paper was part of a survey of existing

[3] UN Doc A/CONF.48/14/Rev. 1 (1973), (1972) 11 ILM 1416.

[4] World Commission on Environment and Development, *Our Common Future* (Oxford University Press 1987), 395.

[5] Kovar, J. D., 'A Short Guide to the Rio Declaration' (1993) 4 *Colorado Journal of International Environmental Law and Policy* 119, at 119.

[6] Kovar, 'A Short Guide to the Rio Declaration', 120.

[7] UN Doc A/CONF.151/PC/78 (1991).

[8] Kovar, 'A Short Guide to the Rio Declaration', 121–2.

[9] Reproduced in Robinson, N. A. (ed), *Agenda 21 and The UNCED Proceedings* (Oceana Publications 1992) vol III, 1519.

international environmental instruments undertaken in preparation of UNCED, pursuant to decisions taken at PrepCom III.

The initial process for drafting the Rio Declaration was fraught, with a disagreement emerging between developed countries and the G77, which sought to have their proposal used as the negotiating text.[10] While Principle 26 was one of the least controversial provisions of the Rio Declaration, Kovar notes that there was some disagreement over the content of Principle 26 during the PrepCom negotiations because of the linkage in the discussion between dispute settlement and questions of liability for environmental harm:[11]

> Principle 26 restates the obligation of all UN member states to resolve their disputes—in this case environmental disputes—in accordance with the Charter of the United Nations. This principle was a disappointment for many Nordic and Central European countries, who sought more specific language regarding methods of dispute resolution. Developing countries, led by Brazil, Pakistan, and India, blocked greater specificity on dispute resolution.

Despite these disagreements, it was possible to reach agreement on Principle 26, and other more controversial provisions in the Rio Declaration. In relation to Principle 26 this appears to be because any connection with liability for environmental loss or damage was severed.

With progress slow in WG-III, the drafting of the Rio Declaration was advanced by a small group of 14 states representing both the North and South (seven developed, and seven developing states) that was chaired by the PrepCom Chairman Tommy Koh.[12] Koh took an important leadership role, proposing the text of key aspects of the Rio Declaration, and the final instrument was presented as the Chairman's text for discussion and adoption at UNCED.[13] The draft Rio Declaration was subsequently adopted at UNCED without amendment.

### *1.3. A specific role for the International Court of Justice?*

The topic of dispute settlement did not figure prominently in discussions at UNCED concerning the Rio Declaration and Agenda 21. However, there was a notable contribution from the President of the ICJ, Sir Robert Jennings, who prepared a statement for UNCED that was read by the Registrar of the Court on Sir Robert's behalf.[14] Sir Robert acknowledged that '[t]he dangers to the environment are global and therefore international in character',[15] and '[t]hat new international law for the protection of the environment needs urgently to be developed cannot be a matter of doubt.'[16] However, Sir Robert expressed some doubt as to whether there was a need for a new specialized international court for the environment. He observed that 'there is . . . sometimes a tendency to suppose that a new and particular branch of international law might be better served by a new and particular tribunal of specialists or "experts" '[17] but argued that 'a court applying general international law is the right forum for the development of environmental law'.[18] Pointing to the role of the ICJ, Sir Robert noted that one of the reasons a generalist court

[10] Kovar, 'A Short Guide to the Rio Declaration', 122. [11] Kovar, 139. [12] Kovar, 139.
[13] UN Doc A/CONF.151/5 (1992).
[14] (1991–1992) 46 *International Court of Justice Yearbook*, 212.
[15] 46 *International Court of Justice Yearbook, 212.*
[16] 46 *International Court of Justice Yearbook*, 213.
[17] 46 *International Court of Justice Yearbook*, 215.
[18] 46 *International Court of Justice Yearbook*, 216.

should be preferred is that it is in a better position to reconcile 'great differences between the interests and the point of view of the developed and the developing nations'.[19] Sir Robert also observed that the function of international courts such as the ICJ extends beyond the resolution of disputes as the ICJ has 'a vital role in the development and elaboration of general law.'[20]

## 2. Scope and dimensions

### *2.1. The three elements of Principle 26*

#### 2.1.1. Overview

There are three main elements of Principle 26. The first is the restatement of the obligation contained in article 2(3) of the Charter of the United Nations that states resolve their disputes peacefully. The second is that Principle 26 extends this general obligation to apply to 'environmental disputes'. Third, Principle 26 requires states to utilize 'appropriate means' in resolving their environmental disputes. The following discussion considers each of these elements in turn.

#### 2.1.2. Obligation to resolve 'all of their' disputes peacefully

Principle 26 stipulates that states 'shall' resolve 'all of their environmental disputes peacefully' in accordance with the Charter of the United Nations. This differs from the formulation in article 2(3) of the Charter in the inclusion of the word 'all'. This suggests that Principle 26 requires states to take a proactive approach in settling their environmental disputes, rather than allowing them to persist. Article 2(3) of the Charter, by contrast, carries no suggestion that states must settle their disputes, but only that if and when they do so, that the process occurs peacefully.[21] Under the Charter, states are free to leave their disputes unsettled, and there are many examples of unresolved disputes, particularly concerning territorial and maritime boundaries, stretching across many years or decades.

The requirement in Principle 26 that states resolve *all* of their environmental disputes indicates that the failure to do so carries implications not only for the states themselves, but for the natural environment itself. The failure to resolve an environmental dispute means not only that the controversy itself is not settled, but also that the underlying cause of the dispute may not be addressed. Where, for instance, an environmental dispute stems from the pollution of an international watercourse, in meeting the objectives of the Rio Declaration as a whole it is important that the source of the dispute, the pollution problem itself, is addressed. Another reason for compelling the resolution of environmental disputes is the increasing realization that environmental and natural resource disputes may be a significant source of inter-state tension and even armed conflict.[22] However, it must be noted that the obligation in Principle 26 is to resolve disputes, rather than providing remedy or sanction in respect of unlawful environmental harm. It is Principle 13 which

[19] 46 *International Court of Justice Yearbook*, 218.

[20] 46 *International Court of Justice Yearbook*, 214.

[21] Bilder, R. B., 'An Overview of International Dispute Settlement' (1986) 1 *Emory Journal of International Dispute Resolution* 1, at 7.

[22] United Nations Department of Economic and Social Affairs, Division for Sustainable Development, *Sustainable Development in the 21st Century: Review of Implementation of Agenda 21 and the Rio Principles* (2011) 223.

requires states to develop national and international legal frameworks for liability for environmental harm.

This element of Principle 26, impelling states to overcome their differences on environmental issues peacefully, raises broader questions as to *why* environmental, or any other international, disputes should be resolved. Historically, the obligation to resolve disputes peacefully emerged as the complement to the prohibition on the use of force. Its primary purpose has been to resolve disagreements between states in service to the overriding aim, expressed in the United Nations Charter's foremost goal, 'to save succeeding generations from the scourge of war'.[23] With the development of an increasingly detailed body of international law, including on environmental questions, the international community has looked beyond this baseline objective of maintaining peace, to additional important functions that dispute settlement can serve. These include the development of international environmental law through the production of a body of jurisprudence on environmental questions, and acting as a mechanism for ensuring that states comply with their environmental obligations. Compliance is a particularly important objective in the context of environmental disputes, because often they involve not only a competing set of 'private' interests between two (or more) states, but also the 'public' interest of the international community in safeguarding the natural environment. This means that a dispute settlement system that is designed to prevent and resolve disputes per se, in the interests of promoting greater international harmony, is not necessarily appropriate for protecting the environment. Considering the objectives of the Rio Declaration as a whole it is certainly arguable that Principle 26 is concerned not only to remove friction between states over environmental issues, but to encourage states to use dispute settlement mechanisms so that states in default of their environmental protection obligations are held to account.

### 2.1.3. 'Environmental disputes'

In the *Mavrommatis Palestine Concessions* case, the Permanent Court of International Justice provided a definition of a dispute at international law that has been widely cited and endorsed: 'A dispute is a disagreement on a point of law or fact, a conflict of legal views or of interests between two persons.'[24] Or, as Merrills puts it, '[a] dispute may be defined as a specific disagreement concerning a matter of fact, law or policy in which a claim or assertion of one party is met with refusal, counter-claim or denial by another.'[25]

These definitions are sufficiently broad to capture virtually any disagreement between states. In some contexts it is necessary to define a dispute more narrowly for the purposes of determining the jurisdiction of an international court or tribunal (or other body) that is asked to resolve a dispute arising from a particular treaty.[26] Principle 26 of the Rio Declaration is not confined in this way, and applies to 'all . . . environmental disputes'. In general terms, an environmental dispute may be defined as any legal or factual disagreement between states which involves one or more questions of environmental protection or

[23] Stephens, T., *International Courts and Environmental Protection* (Cambridge University Press 2009), 71.

[24] 1924 PCIJ Ser A No 2, 11.

[25] Merrills, J. G., *International Dispute Settlement* (5th edn, Cambridge University Press 2011), 1.

[26] Note, for instance, in the context of the United Nations Convention on the Law of the Sea, 10 December 1982, 1833 UNTS 397 that the Part XV dispute settlement system normally applies only to disputes 'concerning the interpretation or application of this Convention' (art 279).

natural resource use or management.[27] Such a definition is preferable to one which refers to disputes that *only* involve environmental treaties or environmental issues, as in practice it is impossible to identify a purely environmental treaty or environmental dispute in international law.

The difficulties encountered in defining an 'environmental dispute' in a clear and uncontested way has been the subject of significant commentary.[28] A practical example of the implications of this definitional debate appears in the context of the establishment by the ICJ of a Chamber for Environmental Matters in 1993. One of the explanations advanced to explain why the ICJ Chamber for Environmental Matters was never used, and was abandoned in 2006, is that there can be no 'pure' inter-state environmental dispute, as an apparently environmental controversy also engages general questions of international law such as the law of state responsibility.[29] This has been reflected in the practice of states in bringing matters before the ICJ. Rather than utilizing the ICJ's Chamber for Environmental Matters, states have preferred that environmental disputes are resolved by the ICJ in plenary. Hence the recent *Pulp Mills*,[30] *Whaling in the Antarctic*,[31] and *Marshall Islands Nuclear Disarmament*[32] cases were brought to the Court *en banc*. There has been a similar experience in the International Tribunal for the Law of the Sea ('ITLOS'). ITLOS followed the ICJ in establishing a Chamber for Marine Environmental Disputes, however that Chamber has never been utilized. This is despite the fact that virtually all of the matters brought to ITLOS have involved environmental and natural resource questions.

### 2.1.4. 'Appropriate means'

The third key element of Principle 26 is its requirement that environmental disputes be settled by 'appropriate means'. There has been considerable discussion concerning what process or mechanism constitutes the most 'appropriate means' for addressing disputes that have environmental dimensions.

#### *2.1.4.1. External vs internal means of settlement*

Dispute settlement mechanisms engaged in addressing international environmental disputes may be separated into two main categories.[33] First, there are internal mechanisms that are created by environmental regimes to deal with disputes arising under those regimes. For instance, ITLOS has jurisdiction over disputes concerning many of the environmental and fisheries management obligations contained in the 1982 United Nations Convention on the Law of the Sea ('UNCLOS').[34] Second, there are mechanisms external to environmental treaties that can be used to deal with disputes arising under the treaty. The ICJ is a prime example of an external process, as it may be conferred general

[27] Bilder, R., 'Settlement of Disputes in the Field of International Law of the Environment' (1975-I) 144 *Recueil des Cours* 153; Boyle, A. and Harrison, J., 'Judicial Settlement of International Environmental Disputes: Current Problems' (2013) 4 *Journal of International Dispute Settlement* 245, 250.

[28] See, eg Boyle, A., 'The *Gabčíkovo-Nagymaros* Case: New Law in Old Bottles' (1997) 8 *YbIEL* 13.

[29] Fitzmaurice, M., 'The International Court of Justice and Environmental Disputes', in French, D., Saul, M., and White, N. (eds), *International Law and Dispute Settlement* (Hart Publishing 2010), 17, at 54–5.

[30] ICJ Reports 2010, 14. [31] ICJ Reports 2014.

[32] Applications by Marshall Islands against China, North Korea, France, India, Israel, Pakistan, Russia, the United Kingdom, and the United States of 25 April 2014. Available at <http://www.icj-cij.org>.

[33] Romano, C. P. R., 'International Dispute Settlement', in Bodansky, D., Brunnee, J., and Hey, E. (eds), *The Oxford Handbook of International Environmental Law* (Oxford University Press 2007), 1036–56.

[34] 10 December 1982, 1833 UNTS 397. See Rothwell, D. and Stephens, T., *The International Law of the Sea* (Hart Publishing 2010), ch 18.

subject-matter jurisdiction over disputes arising out of treaties and customary international law in any field of international law. In contemporary practice in environmental dispute settlement, there has been increasing use made of both internal mechanisms, such as compliance procedures, and external mechanisms, such as the ICJ. And in both contexts there have been significant developments in improving their capacity to resolve environmental matters.

#### *2.1.4.2. The role of international adjudication*

Environmental disputes have a tendency to be 'polycentric' (implicating multiple issues, and involving contests between multiple state and non-state actors) rather than 'unicentric' (involving confined legal disputes arising between only a select number of states and non-state actors).[35] On this basis, some commentators have argued that many environmental disputes are not susceptible to resolution through the traditional, bilateral, means of inter-state dispute settlement.[36]

State practice in the period before, and immediately after, the adoption of the Rio Declaration provided some support for this argument. Few environmental disputes were brought before international courts or arbitral tribunals throughout most of the twentieth century. However, there has been a marked shift in practice in the late twentieth and early twenty-first centuries, with much more frequent use being made of dispute settlement bodies to address environmental and other disputes.[37] This practice also suggests that the promise of Principle 26 of the Rio Declaration is being fulfilled, with states now more willing to seek the resolution of their environmental disputes than there were prior to UNCED.

The dockets of the ICJ, ITLOS, the Permanent Court of Arbitration ('PCA'), human rights courts and complaints procedures, and the World Trade Organization's ('WTO') Dispute Settlement Understanding, have all included a significant number of environment disputes. Environmental issues have also been raised in a significant (and increasing) number of investment disputes, with 24 such disputes with environmental components giving rise to arbitral proceedings, and a host of important decisions on the interface between environmental protection and investment obligations.[38] This growth in international environmental litigation has allowed a number of important environmental disputes to be settled, has contributed to the development of rules and principles of international environmental law, including several key Rio Declaration principles, and has also led to greater levels of compliance by states with their environmental obligations.

[35] Fuller, L. L., 'The Forms and Limits of Adjudication' (1978) 92 *Harvard Law Review* 353, 401.

[36] Fuller, 'The Forms and Limits of Adjudication', 401. See also, Brown Weiss, E., 'Understanding Compliance with International Environmental Agreements: The Baker's Dozen Myths' (1999) 32 *University of Richmond Law Review* 1555.

[37] Lowe, V., 'The Function of Litigation in International Society' (2012) 61 *ICLQ* 209. But see Kingsbury, B., 'International Courts: Uneven Judicialisation in Global Order', in Crawford, J. and Koskenniemi, M. (eds), *The Cambridge Companion to International Law* (Cambridge University Press 2012), 203, at 212, who lists a number of environmental issues, including land, forests, water, and air as not subject to 'dense' judicialisation.

[38] Viñuales, J. E., *Foreign Investment and the Environment in International Law* (Cambridge University Press 2012), 18. See also Miles, K., *The Origins of International Investment Law: Empire, Environment and the Safeguarding of Capital* (Cambridge University Press 2013).

*2.1.4.3. Relaxation of standing rules*

One of the most striking, and recent, developments in international environmental dispute settlement which has assisted in fulfilling the objective of Principle 26 is the relaxation in rights of standing in relation to multilateral environmental agreements. Standing is the requirement that a state seeking to enforce a legal right have a legal interest in enforcing the obligation.[39] The ICJ has recognized the existence of collective obligations owed to all states (obligations *erga omnes*) or to all parties to a treaty (obligations *erga omnes partes*).[40] Multilateral environmental agreements addressing components of the global commons—the oceans, atmosphere, and biodiversity—are classic examples of treaties establishing such collective obligations. However, there has been a disjuncture between international law's recognition of the need to protect common environmental interests, and the system for enforcing collective norms.[41]

It is only very recently that the ICJ and ITLOS have both clarified the circumstances in which obligations *erga omnes partes* can be invoked by any states parties to an environmental treaty, even when they themselves have not sustained a direct injury. The invocation of state responsibility in such situations is envisaged in article 48 of the International Law Commission's Articles on State Responsibility, but this provision has generally been regarded as *de lege ferenda*. In a recent, non-environmental, case the ICJ accepted that any state party to certain multilateral treaties could invoke the violation of the treaty by another party. *Questions relating to the Obligation to Prosecute or Extradite (Belgium v. Senegal)*,[42] concerned whether Senegal had fulfilled its obligations under the *1984 Convention Against Torture*[43] given its failure to prosecute Hissène Habré, the former President of the Republic of Chad, or to extradite him to a jurisdiction where he would face criminal proceedings for torture. The ICJ concluded that the *Convention Against Torture* established obligations *erga omnes partes* that any party could seek to enforce against another, reasoning that '[t]he common interest in compliance with the relevant obligations under the Convention against Torture implies the entitlement of each State party to the Convention to make a claim concerning the cessation of an alleged breach by another State party'.[44]

A similar conclusion was reached in the Advisory Opinion of the ITLOS Seabed Disputes Chamber in *Responsibilities and Obligations of States Sponsoring Persons and Entities with Respect to Activities in the Area* ('*Deep Seabed Advisory Opinion*').[45] The *Deep Seabed Advisory Opinion* arose from a request from the Council of the International

39 Tams, C. J., *Enforcing Obligations Erga Omnes in International Law* (Cambridge University Press 2005), at 26; *South West Africa Cases* (*Ethiopia v. Liberia; Liberia v. South Africa*) (Judgment) ICJ Reports 1966, 6, at 219 (*South West Africa*); *Barcelona Traction, Light and Power Company, Limited* (Preliminary Objections) (Judgment) ICJ Reports 1964, 6, at 35–6.

40 *Barcelona Traction, Light and Power Company, Limited*, ICJ Reports 1970, 32, at paras 33–4.

41 Rosenne, S., 'Some Reflections Erga Omnes', in Anghie, A. and Sturgess, G. (eds), *Legal Visions of the 21st Century: Essays in Honour of Judge Christopher Weeramantry* (Martinus Nijhoff Publishers 1998), 509, 519.

42 *Questions relating to the Obligation to Prosecute or Extradite* (*Belgium v. Senegal*), ICJ Reports 2012.

43 10 December 1984, entered into force 26 June 1987, 1465 UNTS 85.

44 *Questions relating to the Obligation to Prosecute or Extradite*, para 69.

45 *Responsibilities and Obligations of States Sponsoring Persons and Entities with Respect to Activities in the Area*, Advisory Opinion of the Seabed Disputes Chamber of the International Tribunal for the Law of the Sea, 1 February 2011, ('*Deep Seabed Advisory Opinion*') available at: <http://www.itlos.org>.

Seabed Authority ('ISBA') for an advisory opinion concerning the responsibilities and obligations of States sponsoring persons and entities engaging in activities in the deep seabed, the 'Area'. The Seabed Disputes Chamber's advisory opinion addressed several questions posed to it by the ISBA Council, including what enforcement action could be taken where there was damage to the marine environment beyond areas of national jurisdiction. The Chamber noted that UNCLOS did not explicitly allow the ISBA to make a claim for 'damage to the Area and its resources constituting the common heritage of mankind, and damage to the marine environment.'[46] However, the Chamber concluded that this entitlement was 'implicit' in article 137(2) of UNCLOS which provides that ISBA must act 'on behalf' of humankind. The Chamber went further, concluding that:

> Each State Party may also be entitled to claim compensation in light of the *erga omnes* character of the obligations relating to the preservation of the environment of the high seas and in the Area. In support of this view, reference may be made to article 48 of the ILC Articles on State Responsibility.[47]

In reaching this conclusion, the Chamber became the first international judicial body to endorse article 48 of the Articles on State Responsibility. This means that in principle an *actio popularis* is now possible, at least as respect to damage to the marine environment of the seabed beyond national jurisdiction. The Chamber also accepted that a claim could be brought for environmental damage even when this did not involve particular injury to the complaining state.

A further development in standing to advance compliance with environmental treaties would be to open international courts beyond states to international organizations. In this respect Elihu Lauterpacht argued thirty years ago in his landmark work on international litigation that:

> the international community should certainly contemplate the day when the enforcement of obligations under, say, conventions for the prevention of aerial pollution, or the protection of the ozone layer, will take the form of proceedings initiated before the ICJ at the instance of the United Nations Environment Programme or some other agency[48]

### 2.1.4.4. *Compliance procedures*

Rights of standing have not expanded so significantly as to allow United Nations agencies or other international organizations to instigate proceedings in external forums for environmental dispute settlement such as the ICJ. But allowing standing to international organizations to enforce environmental protection obligations has become a feature of dispute settlement systems in the form of 'compliance procedures' established internally within a range of environmental treaties.

A distinctive characteristic of contemporary international environmental dispute settlement is the development and use of sophisticated internal mechanisms of settlement. These procedures have been specifically tailored to deal with disputes arising from environmental regimes (although they have application beyond the environmental context). Compliance procedures have been established under many multilateral environmental regimes, beginning with the 1987 Montreal Protocol on Substances

[46] *Deep Seabed Advisory Opinion*, para 179. [47] *Deep Seabed Advisory Opinion*, para 180.

[48] Lauterpacht, E., *Aspects of the Administration of International Justice* (Cambridge University Press 1991), 63–4.

that Deplete the Ozone Layer.[49] Compliance procedures are unique in several respects. First, they are focused on improving compliance with an environmental regime, rather than upon legal questions of breach and state responsibility. Second, they provide a basis for a form of *actio popularis*. Many can be activated by any state party to a regime, and in some cases by institutions of the regime itself, whereas traditional dispute settlement can normally be invoked only by a state that has suffered identifiable injury as a result of a breach of an international legal obligation which is owed to that state.

Compliance procedures have emerged to supplement rather than replace existing dispute settlement processes. This means that the landscape of international environmental dispute settlement is now complex, with disputes able to be resolved in a wide array of mechanisms, and with both state and non-state actors having the capacity in some regimes to pursue dispute settlement options.[50] Many of these developments would have been inconceivable at the time Principle 26 of the Rio Declaration was being negotiated.

### 2.2. *Legal nature*

Principle 26 restates in the international environmental context the obligation under article 2(3) of the Charter of the United Nations for states to resolve disputes peacefully. Article 2(3) creates a legally binding obligation, and 'can by no means be considered a mere recommendatory provision, compliance with which would be within the discretion of States.'[51] This has been confirmed by the International Court of Justice in a case with significant environmental and resource management dimensions: the *Fisheries Jurisdiction* (*Spain v. Canada*) case.[52]

It follows that Principle 26 also sets out a legally binding obligation upon states to resolve their international environmental disputes, and incorporates the core elements of article 2(3) of the Charter of the United Nations: that states seek to the best of their abilities to resolve their disputes (with no obligation to reach a specific outcome),[53] that states use one or several of the means of settlement set out in article 33 (or any other peaceful means of their choosing).[54]

As has been noted, Principle 26 includes the requirement that states resolve their environmental disputes by 'appropriate means'. This formulation is not part of article 2(3) of the Charter of the United Nations, which qualifies 'peaceful means' by the requirement that the method chosen does not endanger international peace and security, and justice. This raises the question whether Principle 26 seeks to extend the article 2(3) obligation by mandating the use by states of the environmentally appropriate dispute settlement systems. Given the wide-ranging discussion among commentators, and the diverse practice of states in utilizing various forums for environmental dispute settlement, it is not possible to identify, in a definitive manner, those mechanisms of dispute settlement that are appropriate or not-appropriate for the purposes of Principle 26. Hence the core legal

[49] 16 September 1987, 1522 UNTS 29.

[50] An example is the range of disputes that may arise out of the operation of the Kyoto Protocol: Brown, C., 'The Settlement of Disputes Arising in Flexibility Mechanism Transactions under the Kyoto Protocol' (2005) 21 *Arbitration International* 361.

[51] Simma, B. (ed), *The Charter of the United Nations: A Commentary*, vol I (2nd edn, Oxford University Press 2002), 106.

[52] ICJ Reports 1998, 432, at 456.

[53] Simma, *The Charter of the United Nations*, vol I, 106.

[54] Simma, *The Charter of the United Nations*, vol I, 106.

requirement of Principle 26, as for article 2(3) of the Charter, is the obligation of conduct to seek a resolution of disputes according to peaceful means.

## 3. Normative impact

There is little evidence that Principle 26 has had a significant impact upon other international instruments, including environmental agreements concluded post 1992. This is to be expected, given that Principle 26 is a restatement of a well-accepted international law obligation to resolve disputes peacefully, rather than an innovative principle that seeks to encourage states to address their environmental disputes in the most appropriate and effective manner possible, or even to prevent them altogether.

Most environmental treaties that pre- and post-date the Rio Declaration contain a provision similar to Principle 26 that requires states to resolve their disputes peacefully, and allows them a choice of those means referred to in article 33 of the Charter of the United Nations in doing so.[55]

## 4. Jurisprudential relevance

### *4.1. Overview*

It does not appear that Principle 26 of the Rio Declaration has been referred to expressly by any international or domestic court or tribunal. Principle 26 of the Rio Declaration should not be confused with Principle 26 of the Stockholm Declaration which stipulates that 'man and his environment must be spared the effects of nuclear weapons', a principle that was invoked before the ICJ in the *Nuclear Tests* case[56] and the *Nuclear Weapons Advisory Opinion*.[57]

### *4.2. The development of inter-State environmental dispute settlement*

#### 4.2.1. Means of environmental dispute settlement

While Principle 26 has not been referred to, since 1992 there have been very noteworthy developments in using existing and developing new mechanisms and forums for international environmental dispute settlement.

The traditional dispute settlement methods are listed in article 33 of the United Nations Charter, and these are negotiation, enquiry, mediation, conciliation, arbitration, and resort to regional agencies or arrangements. Most of these have been utilized to greater or lesser extent in international environmental dispute resolution. In this regard there is quite a degree of diversity among environmental regimes. A number of environmental treaties make no provision for dispute settlement at all,[58] many simply repeat the formulation in article 33 and state that the parties are free to choose a procedure of their liking,[59] while relatively few provide for compulsory settlement via conciliation,[60] arbitration or judicial settlement.[61]

[55] Stephens, *International Courts and Environmental Protection*, 24.

[56] *Nuclear Tests* (*Australia v. France*) (interim measures) ICJ Reports 1973, 99, *(merits)* ICJ Reports 1974, 253; (*New Zealand v. France*) (interim measures) ICJ Reports 1973, 135, (merits) ICJ Reports 1974, 457.

[57] ICJ Reports, 226.

[58] International Convention for the Regulation of Whaling, 2 December 1946, 161 UNTS 72.

[59] eg Convention for the Conservation of Southern Bluefin Tuna, 10 May 1993, 1819 UNTS 359.

[60] eg Convention on Biological Diversity, 5 June 1992, 1760 UNTS 143.

[61] eg UNCLOS.

### 4.2.2. Negotiation

As with international dispute settlement generally, negotiation has proven to be the most commonly used method for resolving disputes. It is less usual for states to turn from negotiation, which involves only the parties to a dispute, to other forms of dispute settlement involving a third party such as mediation, conciliation, arbitration, and judicial settlement.

Negotiation can take place at any stage in the emergence or resolution of a dispute. It is of particular value as both a dispute avoidance and dispute settlement technique. Both general international law and specific environmental treaties establish obligations for states to consult with neighbouring states before approving activities in their territory or under their jurisdiction that may have transboundary impacts. This was seen in the *Lake Lanoux* case in which an arbitral tribunal held that France was under an obligation to consult with Spain in relation to a hydroelectricity project that affected the flow of water from French to Spanish territory.[62] A more recent example is found in the *Pulp Mills* case where the ICJ emphasized the importance of states providing advance notification of planned works that could have transboundary impacts, to enable negotiations and consultations to eliminate or minimize environmental risks.[63] The case primarily concerned the scope and operation of a bilateral river treaty, the *1975 Statute of the River Uruguay*.[64]

### 4.2.3. Mediation and conciliation

Mediation is a process of dispute settlement in which a third party becomes involved and has a role in brokering a settlement between the disputants. Although it is very widely referred to in environmental treaties as a dispute settlement option, it does not appear to have been used in practice at all. Conciliation differs from mediation in that it not only involves a third party, but one which takes a more active role and who delivers a non-binding report. Several environmental treaties make reference to conciliation as a dispute settlement option. A well-known example is the 1992 Convention on Biological Diversity[65] which New Zealand considered utilizing when France resumed nuclear testing in the South Pacific in the 1990s.[66]

### 4.2.4. Commissions of inquiry and fact finding

Commissions of inquiry, and fact-finding processes, are closely related to conciliation. These involve the use of individuals or a small panel to conduct an independent investigation of factual issues underlying a dispute. Generally the main goal of commissions of inquiry or fact-finding bodies is to arrive at an independent assessment of the facts that narrows the dispute between the parties. A prominent example of the use of such a process of inquiry is the 1997 UN Convention on the Non-Navigational Uses of International Watercourses.[67] That process is compulsory, in that it may be invoked by any party to a dispute under the Convention unless the parties have agreed to an alternative procedure or have declared their acceptance of judicial settlement by the ICJ or arbitration by an arbitral tribunal.[68]

[62] *Lake Lanoux* case (*France/Spain*) (1957) 12 RIAA 285.

[63] *Pulp Mills on the River Uruguay* (*Argentina v. Uruguay*), Judgment of 20 April 2010, <http://www.icj-cij.org>, at para 115.

[64] 26 February 1975, 1295 UNTS 340.

[65] Art 27(2).

[66] Stephens, *International Courts and Environmental Protection*, 75.

[67] 21 May 1997, (1997) 36 ILM 700.

[68] 21 May 1997, (1997) 36 ILM 700, art 33(3).

### 4.2.5. Arbitration and judicial settlement

Negotiation, mediation, conciliation, and inquiry are all diplomatic means of dispute settlement, and can involve the consideration of a range of factors relevant to a dispute, including legal questions. Arbitration and judicial settlement are by contrast legal forms of dispute settlement in which rules of international law supply the controlling criteria, at least ostensibly, for resolving the dispute. Arbitration and judicial settlement are not only legal processes, but also directed at producing a legally significant outcome in the form of a decision that is binding on the parties to the dispute, and which may contribute to the development of international law.

Arbitration and judicial settlement are, in most respects, identical in contemporary international law. Historically, arbitration was political in character, but with the establishment of the PCA over a century ago, it became a predominantly legal process. The main difference now relates to the institutional basis of arbitration and judicial settlement, with the latter characterized by the use of a standing court of tribunal. There are also some other important differences, the most significant being that the arbitration process is closely controlled by the parties. In an arbitration, the parties can determine the composition of the arbitral panel, rules of procedure, and the applicable law. Because arbitration is within party control, it may not be as suited as adjudication before a permanent international court in addressing questions of a public interest character, which environmental disputes often raise.[69]

Relatively few multilateral environmental treaties rely upon arbitration or judicial settlement as the primary means of resolving disputes arising from them. Several environmental regimes, including the 1985 Vienna Convention for the Protection of the Ozone Layer[70] allow for compulsory and binding adjudication where the parties have opted in to the procedure, and several others such as the 1980 Convention for the Physical Protection of Nuclear Material[71] provide for compulsory and binding adjudication unless the parties have opted out. However the usual approach is to present adjudication as one option among many from which the parties may choose when seeking to resolve their dispute.[72] The notable exception is UNCLOS, which establishes a mechanism for compulsory and binding adjudication of most disputes concerning the interpretation and application of the Convention, including its environmental protection obligations.

Nonetheless, as with other areas of international law, international environmental law has felt the influence of the process of 'judicialisation' under which there has been a turn to more formal, legal processes of dispute settlement, in particular international courts and tribunals. This is seen most clearly in the proliferation of international courts and tribunals, most of which were established in the second half of the twentieth century. There are now a large number of courts and tribunals that have some jurisdictional capacity to address environmental issues, from well-established courts such as the ICJ that have general jurisdiction, through to more recently established bodies such as the WTO dispute settlement system, regional institutions such as the European Court of Justice, and human rights courts and complaints procedures that have more specialized subject-matter jurisdiction, but which are increasingly called upon to address environmental disputes.[73]

[69] Stephens, *International Courts and Environmental Protection*, 36.

[70] 22 March 1985, 1513 UNTS 324.

[71] 3 March 1980, 1456 UNTS 124.

[72] Stephens, *International Courts and Environmental Protection*, 25.

[73] Stephens, *International Courts and Environmental Protection*, ch 2.

A negative side-effect of judicialisation of environmental dispute settlement is that conflicts are increasingly arising from the operation of multiple dispute settlement fora. Because international environmental law disputes may be brought before any number of diverse processes the concern has been expressed that this may lead to 'fragmentation'.[74] This is because it may result in environmental disputes being resolved in forums that do not have an environmental specialization, leading potentially to decisions that favour the values underlying the particular regime which the dispute settlement procedure serves. There is also a related concern that the multiplicity of dispute settlement options will produce practical problems of forum shopping.

These concerns have been especially strongly felt in the context of the relationship between international trade law and international environmental law.[75] This is because the WTO dispute settlement system is broad-ranging and compulsory, and can be utilized when states take measures that have an effect upon international trade, including where they have an environmental purpose. However WTO jurisprudence to date suggests that the Appellate Body has been aware of the possibility of fragmentation, and has avoided open conflict between trade and environmental norms.[76]

The concerns that international environmental law may be fragmented by a proliferation of courts and tribunals also applies in other areas such as human rights, where there also exists a well-developed system of dispute settlement. Complainants will tend to use whatever forums are available, even if they are not ideally suited to the dispute at hand, as seen in the use of the Human Rights Committee and similar regional bodies by complainants bringing what are really environmental claims. As in the trade context, this will not necessarily undermine the objective of Principle 26 of the Rio Declaration that environmental disputes be resolved by 'appropriate means'. This is because there exist well-established principles in international law for reconciling norms that can come into tension or conflict. The International Commission study group on fragmentation, chaired by Martti Koskenniemi, noted in this respect that the Vienna Convention on the Law of Treaties[77] provides detailed rules of interpretation designed specifically to minimize such conflict.[78]

Missing from the patchwork of jurisdictions with a capacity to address environmental disputes is a dedicated international court for the environment. A proposal for such a court was formulated in the lead up to UNCED,[79] but the proposal gained no support in the work of the PrepCom or at UNCED itself. As has been noted, in an address to UNCED the President of the ICJ, Sir Robert Jennings, contended that environmental

[74] See Stephens, T., 'Multiple International Courts and the "Fragmentation" of International Environmental Law' (2006) 25 *Australian Yearbook of International Law* 22.

[75] Eckersley, R., 'The Big Chill: The WTO and Multilateral Environmental Agreements' (2004) 4 *Global Environmental Politics* 24.

[76] Stephens, *International Courts and Environmental Protection*, 340–1.

[77] 23 May 1969, 1155 UNTS 331.

[78] Fragmentation of International Law: Difficulties Arising from the Diversification and Expansion of International Law: Report of the Study Group of the International Law Commission, Finalised by Chairman M. Koskenniemi, UN Doc A/CN.4/L.682

[79] See Postgilione, A., 'A More Efficient International Law on the Environment and Setting Up an International Court for the Environment Within the United Nations' (1990) 20 *Environmental Law* 321 and Postiglione, A., *The Global Environmental Crisis: The Need for an International Court of the Environment* (Giunti 1996). See also Pedersen, O. W., 'An International Environmental Court and International Legalism' (2012) 24 *JEL* 547.

disputes were best handled by existing institutions. Since the conclusion of UNCED there have been no indications of any significant support by states for the establishment of an international court for the environment.[80]

## III) Relations with Other Principles

Principle 26 intersects with a number of other Rio Declaration principles, providing a supporting role for provisions of the Rio Declaration that aim to promote peaceful international relations, that seek to prevent environment harm, and that are directed at holding states responsible for transboundary environmental damage, or damage to global commons.

Principle 26 is one of a number of the Rio Declaration principles that 'seek to promote international cooperation and peace.'[81] These include Principle 9, dealing with technology transfer, Principle 12, calling for a fairer international economic system, and Principle 25, on the important linkages between peace, development and environmental protection. These intersections highlight the role that Principle 26 is designed to play in avoiding international tension and conflict arising from disputes concerning natural resources and environmental services.

Several Rio Declaration principles emphasize the need for environmental damage to be prevented and there are linkages between these principles and Principle 26. Principle 14 speaks of the need to 'prevent the relocation and transfer to other States' of activities or substances that may cause environmental degradation or damage human health. And Principle 15 expresses the precautionary principle; that states should not seek to rely on scientific uncertainty about potential environmental harm to postpone measures to protect the environment. Duties of prevention and precaution recognize that international environmental law should be oriented to avoiding unnecessary environmental harm, rather than seeking to remediate such damage after the event (which is often impossible or impractical). Traditional mechanisms of dispute settlement such as international courts and tribunals are normally reactive institutions (with the important exception of provisional or interim measures that can be issued to prevent environmental harm.[82]) By contrast, compliance measures have been developed specifically to identify potential breaches of environmental treaties before they occur, or become serious, and to assist states meet their environmental commitments before there is environmental harm.

There is also a close relationship between Principle 26 and provisions of the Rio Declaration concerned with state responsibility and liability for environmental harm. One way that these provisions can be given practical effect is by providing avenues for dispute settlement. Hence Principle 2, which provides that states are entitled to exploit their own resources and a responsibility to ensure that their activities do not damage the environment of other states, can be operationalized if states are able to instigate proceedings in

80 Boyle and Harrison, 'Judicial Settlement of International Environmental Disputes', 275.

81 Porras, I., 'The Rio Declaration: A New Basis for International Cooperation', in Sands, P. (ed), *Greening International Law* (Earthscan 1993), 20, at 21.

82 See, eg art 290 of the UNCLOS which allows for the making of interim orders by either an agreed court or, failing agreement, by ITLOS in order 'to preserve the respective rights of the parties to the dispute or to prevent serious harm to the marine environment, pending the final decision.' Art 290 makes clear that the provisional measures jurisdiction of ITLOS has a strong environmental objective.

an international court or other forum in response to transboundary environmental law. Similarly, it is implicit in Principle 13, which calls for 'further international law regarding liability and compensation for adverse effects of environmental damage caused by activities within their jurisdiction or control to areas beyond their jurisdiction', that states develop both substantive rules of liability and accompanying mechanisms for resolving disputes concerning liability for environmental harm. A system of liability that can be actively engaged by any state serves both a corrective function and also a deterrent one in providing an incentive to States and non-State actors to take measures to protect the environment.

## IV) Assessment

Given the venerable Charter and customary law obligation upon states to resolve disputes through peaceful means, the inclusion of Principle 26 was greeted with relatively little controversy in the preparation and adoption of the Rio Declaration. Moreover, unlike several Rio Declaration principles, Principle 26 has not subsequently generated significant discussion or disagreement, and has not been referred to in decisions of domestic or international courts and tribunals. Nor was Principle 26 referred to in the documentary outcomes of the United Nations Conference on Sustainable Development ('Rio+20').[83] Moreover, because it applies only to inter-state disputes, on the plane of international law, it also differs from other Rio Declaration principles (such as precautionary and the polluter-pays principles) that are able to influence or interact with domestic law and legal processes.[84]

For all of these reasons, Principle 26 might therefore appear as a 'motherhood statement', adding relatively little to existing international legal obligations concerning dispute settlement. However, Principle 26 does carry significance in several key respects, as has been seen in this commentary.

First, Principle 26 uses the term 'environmental disputes' rather than more general phrasing (such as 'disputes involving environmental issues'). This recognizes that many inter-state disputes relating to environmental protection are distinctive and need to be approached differently from other categories of dispute. There are several reasons for this, including because environmental disputes often relate to matters of collective, global, concern.[85]

Second, Principle 26 requires that states utilize 'appropriate means' for resolving their environmental disputes. This emphasizes the desirability of having environmental

[83] There is no mention made of Principle 26 of the Rio Declaration or the topic of environmental dispute settlement in the *Report of the United Nations Conference on Sustainable Development*, UN Doc A/CONF.216/16 (2012) or the outcome document *The Future We Want*, adopted at the Conference and subsequently endorsed by the United Nations General Assembly in Resolution 66/288, UN Doc A/RES/66/288 (2012).

[84] For accounts of this process see, in particular, chapters in this volume concerning principles directed to domestic environmental law reform, such as Principle 10 (environmental issues are best handled with citizen participation). See further Scotford, E., *Environmental Principles and the Evolution of Environmental Law* (Hart Publishing 2014) and de Sadeleer, N., *Environmental Principles: From Political Slogans To Legal Rules* (Oxford University Press 2002).

[85] Brunnée, J., 'Common Areas, Common Heritage, and Common Concern' in Bodansky, D., Brunnée, J., and Hey, E. (eds), *The Oxford Handbook of International Environmental Law* (Oxford University Press 2007), 550, at 555–6.

disputes addressed by processes and institutions that are appropriately designed to deal with environmental issues. In this context there have been significant developments since the Rio Declaration was adopted, as seen most clearly in the development of 'compliance procedures' under a host of multilateral environmental agreements. Also notable has been the judicialization of international environmental dispute settlement, with the ICJ and other courts now routinely adjudicating environmental matters.

## V) Select Bibliography

Bilder, R., 'Settlement of Disputes in the Field of International Law of the Environment' (1975-I) 144 *RCADI* 153.

Boyle, A. and Harrison, J., 'Judicial Settlement of International Environmental Disputes: Current Problems' (2013) 4 *Journal of International Dispute Settlement* 245.

Pedersen, O. W., 'An International Environmental Court and International Legalism' (2012) 24 *JEL* 547.

Romano, C. P. R., 'International Dispute Settlement', in Bodansky, D., Brunnee, J., and Hey, E. (eds), *The Oxford Handbook of International Environmental Law* (Oxford University Press 2007), 1036.

Romano, C. P. R., *The Peaceful Settlement of International Environmental Disputes: A Pragmatic Approach* (Kluwer 2000).

Stephens, T., *International Courts and Environmental Protection* (Cambridge University Press 2009).

# 31. Principle 27

## *Cooperation in a Spirit of Global Partnership*

Peter H. Sand*

**Principle 27**

States and people shall cooperate in good faith and in a spirit of partnership in the fulfillment of the principles embodied in this Declaration and in the further development of international law in the field of sustainable development.



## I) Origins and Rationale of the Principle

Cooperation in good faith in relations between States has long been recognized as a general principle of international law, affirmed in numerous treaties, in the jurisprudence of international courts and tribunals, and in the codification work of the International Law Commission.[1] In the case of multilateral environmental agreements in particular, the

* Lecturer in International Environmental Law, University of Munich. Comments by Sander Chan and Jorge E. Viñuales on an earlier draft of this chapter are gratefully acknowledged.

[1] eg, see the sources listed by Kotzur, M., 'Good Faith (*Bona fides*)', in Wolfrum, R. (ed), *Max Planck Encyclopedia of Public International Law*, vol IV (Oxford University Press 2012), 508; art 4 of the 2001 ILC Draft Articles on Prevention of Transboundary Harm from Hazardous Activities, *Report of the International Law Commission on its fifty-third session*, UN Doc A/56/10 (2001), 396. See also O'Connor, J. F., *Good Faith in International Law* (Dartmouth 1991); White, G., 'The Principle of Good Faith', in Lowe, A. V. (ed), *The United Nations and the Principles of International Law: Essays in Memory of Michel Akehurst* (Routledge 1994), 230; Kolb, R., *La bonne foi en droit international public: Contribution à l'étude des principes généraux de droit* (Presses Universitaires de France 2000); and Delbrück, J. (ed), *International Law of Cooperation and State Sovereignty* (Duncker and Humblot 2002).

cooperation principle also serves an additional function, as driving force for the progressive development and dynamic evolution of treaty law,[2] in the form of supplementary instruments and norms adopted by conferences of the parties.[3] With regard to the global partnership concept, Principle 27 does not seem to add anything new to the formulations found in the preamble and in Principles 7 and 21 of the Declaration, or in the corresponding sections of Agenda 21 for that matter.[4]

At first glance, therefore, Principle 27 of the Rio Declaration would appear merely to reiterate past practice, and language already contained in other parts of the Rio documents. Closer analysis in light of the *travaux préparatoires* shows, however, that—unlike all other Rio Principles—Principle 27 is not a further normative postulate, but an authentic operational directive for future implementation of the Rio Declaration as a whole.[5]

## II) The Principle as Enshrined in the Rio Declaration

### 1. Preparatory work and context

The position of Principle 27 as the concluding sentence of the Rio Declaration conveys a prominence which this principle never really had in the overall drafting context. It certainly was not one of the six pivotal principles that emerged from the North-South compromise text hammered out by the chairman of the UNCED Preparatory Commission ('PrepCom'), Tommy Koh, in the dramatic New York night sessions of 1 and 2 April 1992;[6] nor was it among the four principles subsequently 'black-listed' in the US State Department's interpretative statement after the adoption of the Declaration by the Rio Conference on 14 June 1992.[7] In fact, previous versions or parts of Principle 27 had been shifted around in various earlier drafts considered by PrepCom Working Group III, in more or less fortuitous combination with other components of the Declaration—alternatively in what is now Principle 18 (notification of emergencies),[8] or in Principle 7 (common but differentiated responsibilities).[9]

[2] Wolfrum, R., 'Co-operation, International Law of', in Wolfrum, *Max Planck Encyclopedia of Public International Law*, vol II, 783, at 789.

[3] See Gehring, T., 'Treaty-Making and Treaty Evolution', in Bodansky, D., Brunnée, J., and Hey, E. (eds), *Oxford Handbook of International Environmental Law* (Oxford University Press 2007), 467; and Wiersema, A., 'The New International Law-Makers? Conferences of the Parties to Multilateral Environmental Agreements' (2009) 31 *Michigan Journal of International Law* 231.

[4] In particular, *Agenda 21* ss 27.5 and 27.10.b (non-governmental organizations), 30.7 and 30.23 (business and industry), and 31.4 (scientific and technological community). See also text in II) 2.2 of this chapter, and Chap 4 by Francioni ('Preamble'), Chap 11, Cullet, and Chap 25, Langer, in this volume.

[5] See the drafting history of the principle, at n 36 of this chapter.

[6] See Koh, T. T.-B., 'UNCED Leadership: A Personal Perspective', in Spector, B. I., Sjösted, G., and Zartman, I. W. (eds), *Negotiating International Regimes: Lessons from the United Nations Conference on Environment and Development (UNCED)* (Graham and Trotman 1994), 165, at 168. On the uneasy balance of the three key 'Northern' Principles (10, 15, 16) against three 'Southern' ones (3, 5, 7), see Sand, P. H., 'UNCED and the Development of International Environmental Law' (1992) 3 *YbIEL* 3, 8; and Porras, I. M., 'The Rio Declaration: A New Basis for International Cooperation' (1992) 1 *RECIEL* 245.

[7] While joining consensus on the Declaration, the US delegation expressed reservations on Principles 3, 7, 12, and 23. See UN Doc A/CONF.151/26, vol II (1993), para 16; and Kovar, J. D., 'A Short Guide to the Rio Declaration' (1993) 4 *Colorado Journal of International Environmental Law and Policy* 119, 122.

[8] Proposal by the Netherlands (on behalf of the European Community/EC), as draft principle 7 paras 63–4, UN Doc A/CONF.151/PC/WG.III/L.8/Rev.1 (30 August 1991); and proposal by the US, as draft principle 7, UN Doc A/CONF.151/PC/WG.III/L.21 (4 March 1992).

[9] Proposal by Australia, as location for draft Principles 2 and 7, UN Doc A/CONF.151/PC/WG.III/L.24 (5 March 1992); and Chairman's proposal, as draft Principle 7 para 1, UN Doc A/CONF.151/PC/

Ultimately, most of the wording initially suggested by the EC delegation, from August 1991 onwards,[10] ended up as the last part of a consolidated draft by the Group of 77 ('G77') in March 1992,[11] which after lengthy inconclusive negotiations served as the basis for Koh's text.[12]

Yet, for all its fortuity,[13] Principle 27 did contribute innovative concepts to international law and governance, by explicit formulation as well as by implicit new approaches.

## 2. Scope and dimensions

### 2.1. *International law of sustainable development*

The G77 's major original contribution to Principle 27 was the addition of a call for 'the further development of international law in the field of sustainable development'[14]—ostensibly in response to the mandate of UNCED as formulated by UN General Assembly Resolution 44/228 of 22 December 1989, 'to promote the further development of international *environmental* law'.[15] Last-minute salvage attempts (by Austria and New Zealand) to re-insert a reference to environmental protection in the draft were unsuccessful. Moreover, PrepCom Working Group III also agreed on consequential amendments in draft chapter 39 of Agenda 21 ('International Legal Instruments and Mechanisms'):[16] The terms 'international environmental law' were thus changed to 'international law in the field of the environment' throughout—prompting the Brazilian delegate to comment, only half tongue-in-cheek: 'That will keep you lawyers busy well into the twenty-first century'.[17]

Even though Principle 27 suggests that 'international sustainable development law' already existed before,[18] the Rio Declaration's call for its progressive 'further development' has been welcomed by scholars as 'a profound renewal of international environmental law',[19] some even proposing that the International Law Commission ('ILC') 'will need to be given direction, as it will require the evolution of international law for sustainable development as a whole and not only for environmental concerns'.[20] It spawned,

WG.III/L.33 (31 March 1992). This is where part of the language from Principle 27 remained in the final text.

10 Proposal by the Netherlands, UN Doc A/CONF.151/PC/WG.III/L.8/Rev.1; and proposal by the USA, UN Doc A/CONF.151/PC/WG.III/L.21.

11 UN Doc A/CONF.151/PC/WG.III/L.20/Rev.1 (19 March 1992).

12 Chairman's re-draft, UN Doc A/CONF.151/PC/WG.III/L.33/Rev.1 (2 April 1992); see Chasek, P., 'The Story of the UNCED Process', in Spector et al, *Negotiating International Regimes*, 45, at 56.

13 Some commentators on the Rio Declaration even omit Principle 27 altogether; eg see Panjabi, R. K. L., 'From Stockholm to Rio: A Comparison of the Declaratory Principles of International Environment Law' (1993) 21 *Denver Journal of International Law & Policy* 215, 287.

14 Initially 'to develop international law needed for the achievement of sustainable development'; see the Chairman's proposal, UN Doc A/CONF.151/PC/WG.III/L.33, Principle 26.

15 See Sand, P. H., 'International Law on the Agenda of the United Nations Conference on Environment and Development: Towards Global Environmental Security?' (1991) 60 *Nordic Journal of International Law* 5, 6.

16 Similar 'editorial' amendments were made in Agenda 21, ch 8, part B ('Providing an Effective Legal and Regulatory Framework'); eg, see the reference to 'sustainable development law' in s 8.19.

17 Sand, 'UNCED and the Development of International Environmental Law', 17.

18 Sands, P. J. and Peel, J., *Principles of International Environmental Law* (3rd edn, Cambridge University Press 2012), 212.

19 Kiss, A. C. and Doumbé-Billé, S., 'La Conférence des Nations Unies sur l'environnement et le développement' (1992) 38 *Annuaire français de droit international* 823, 841.

20 Sanwal, M., 'Sustainable Development, the Rio Declaration, and Multilateral Cooperation' (1993) 4 *Colorado Journal of International Environmental Law and Policy* 49, 59 n 37 (economist Mukul Sanwal co-chaired the drafting group of PrepCom Working Group III).

*inter alia*, the establishment of a specialized committee of the International Law Association ('ILA'),[21] the foundation of new academic institutions,[22] several specialized law journals,[23] and a sizable amount of literature.[24]

Other observers were sceptical, suggesting that 'all international law could be seen as being for sustainable development, rather than having the legal community struggle to define a new, separate or overarching branch' of sustainable development law;[25] while some even expressed alarm at the risk of international environmental law 'being reduced to a mere appendage of international development law, and subordinated to economic rationality',[26] viewing Principle 27 as 'a challenge to the legitimacy, perhaps even to the very existence of international environmental law as an autonomous body of rules of international law'.[27]

In retrospect though, the 'change of paradigm' so anticipated (whether feared or hoped for)[28] does not seem to have occurred. Following the report of an expert meeting on identification of principles of international law for sustainable development in 1995,[29] the UN Commission on Sustainable Development decided to request a study by UNEP of 'the concept, requirements and implications of sustainable development and international law'. In light of the study,[30] the UNEP Governing Council's 1997 Nairobi Declaration then affirmed its commitment to further the development of 'its [sic] international environmental law aiming at sustainable development',[31] virtually reducing the dichotomy to lexical semantics. As one commentator had already put it in 1995, 'future developments

[21] Established in 1992 as 'Committee on Legal Aspects of Sustainable Development', the Committee changed its name in 2003 to 'Committee for International Law on Sustainable Development', dissolved in 2012 by ILA Resolution No. 7/2012, and reconstituted in November 2012 as 'Committee on the Role of International Law in Sustainable Natural Resource Management for Development'. See Schrijver, N. J. (ed), *Final Report on International Law on Sustainable Development* to the 75th ILA Conference in Sofia (ILA 2012).

[22] eg, the Centre for International Sustainable Development Law (McGill University, Montreal); and the Law of Sustainable International Development Graduate Program (University of Washington School of Law, Seattle).

[23] eg, the *International Journal of Sustainable Development Law and Policy* (McGill University), the *Sustainable Development Law Journal* (University of South Dakota School of Law), *Sustainable Development Law and Policy* (American University Washington College of Law), and the *Journal of Sustainable Development Law and Policy* (Afe Babalola University, Nigeria).

[24] eg, see Futrell, J. W., 'The Transition to Sustainable Development Law' (2003) 21 *Pace Env'l L Rev* 179; Cordonier-Segger, M. C. and Khalfan, A. (eds), *Sustainable Development Law: Principles, Practices and Prospects* (Oxford University Press 2004); French, D., *International Law and Policy of Sustainable Development* (Juris Publishing 2005); and Schrijver, N. J., 'Development: The Neglected Dimension in the Post-Rio International Law of Sustainable Development', in Bugge, H. C. and Voigt, C. (eds), *Sustainable Development in International and National Law* (Europa Law Publishing 2008), 223–50, at 237 ('international law of sustainable development under construction').

[25] Mann, H., 'Comment', in Lang, W. (ed), *Sustainable Development and International Law* (Graham and Trotman 1995), 67–72, at 72.

[26] Pallemaerts, M., 'International Environmental Law from Stockholm to Rio: Back to the Future?' (1992) 1 *RECIEL* 254, 264.

[27] Pallemaerts, M., 'International Environmental Law in the Age of Sustainable Development: A Critical Assessment of the UNCED Process' (1995) 15 *Journal of Law and Commerce* 623, 674.

[28] Pallemaerts, 'International Environmental Law in the Age of Sustainable Development', 673.

[29] Report of the Expert Group Meeting on Identification of Principles of International Law for Sustainable Development (Geneva, 26–28 September 1995), Background Paper 3 for the Fourth Session of the Commission on Sustainable Development, UN Doc E/CN.17/1996/17/Add.1 (1996).

[30] Final Report of the Expert Group Workshop on International Law Aiming at Sustainable Development, UN Doc UNEP/IEL/WS/3/2 (4 October 1996).

[31] UNEP Governing Council Decision 19/1 (1997) of 7 February 1997, Annex.

may well demonstrate that the apparent tension between the existing international law of the environment on the one hand and the Rio Declaration's allusions to a new international law of sustainable development on the other is illusory'.[32]

## *2.2. Cooperation between States and people: Public-private partnership*

Another innovative element in Principle 27 was potentially more significant for the evolution of international law and governance. The 1972 Stockholm Declaration,[33] role model for the Rio Declaration in many respects, had relegated the question of implementation to the preamble,[34] an option also favoured by the Chairman of Rio PrepCom Working Group III (former Czech Environment Minister Bedřich Moldan) in an unsuccessful early draft.[35] By contrast, however, the Working Group chose to define the shared responsibility for 'fulfilment of the principles' in the operative part of the Rio Declaration,[36] specifying it in Principle 27 as a duty of cooperation between 'States and people'.

Identification of the addressees of that duty varied in the course of the *travaux préparatoires*, from 'States, organizations and individuals';[37] 'States, transnational corporations, institutions and NGOs';[38] 'States, individuals and social groups';[39] to 'all people';[40] or 'all States and peoples'.[41] The term 'peoples' was eventually changed to 'people' in Koh's compromise text;[42] from the beginning, though, it was understood as a reference to civil society as a whole, rather than to 'peoples' as distinct communities in a Rawlsian sense.[43] Along the same lines, the preamble of the Declaration calls for 'the creation of new levels of cooperation among States, key sectors of societies and people'.[44]

[32] Wirth, D. A., 'The Rio Declaration on Environment and Development: Two Steps Forward and One Back?' (1995) 29 *Georgia Law Review* 599, 649; but see the Report of the ILA Committee on International Law on Sustainable Development to the 73rd ILA Conference (Rio de Janeiro 2008), at 7 (perceiving continued 'creative tension').

[33] Declaration of the United Nations Conference on the Human Environment (Stockholm, 16 June 1972), UN Doc A/CONF/48/14/Rev.1 (1972), 11 ILM 1416 ('Stockholm Declaration').

[34] Stockholm Declaration, para 7 ('to achieve this environmental goal...the Conference calls upon Governments and peoples to exert common efforts for the preservation and improvement of the human environment for the benefit of all the people and for their posterity'); see Sohn, L. B., 'The Stockholm Declaration on the Human Environment' (1973) 14 *HILJ* 423, at 451.

[35] Draft reference text sent to all delegations by diplomatic note No. 5557/91-SE from the Permanent Mission of Czechoslovakia (19 December 1991). On this ill-timed abortive proposal, see Koh, 'UNCED Leadership: A Personal Perspective', 168; and Chasek, P., *Earth Negotiations: Analyzing Thirty Years of Environmental Diplomacy* (United Nations University Press 2001), 163.

[36] The original term 'implementation' was changed to 'fulfilment' in the Chairman's re-draft of 2 April 1992, UN Doc A/CONF.151/PC/WG.III/L.33/Rev.1; the purpose of the change clearly was to avoid even a semblance of binding force. Curiously, the final French version kept the original term as '*application*'.

[37] Proposal by the Netherlands/EC, draft Principle 7 para 63.

[38] Proposal by Peru, UN Doc A/CONF.151/PC/WG.III/L.8/Rev.1 (30 August 1991), draft Principle 7 para 66.

[39] Proposal by the Chairman of Working Group III, Draft reference text sent to all delegations by diplomatic note No. 5557/91-SE from the Permanent Mission of Czechoslovakia (19 December 1991), preambular para (c).

[40] Proposal by the USA, draft Principle 7.

[41] Proposal by Portugal/EC, UN Doc A/CONF.151/PC/WG.III/L.25 (6 March 1992), draft Principle 13.

[42] Chairman's re-draft of 2 April 1992. Note, however, that the final French text (as in the preamble) kept the plural version 'peuples'.

[43] See Rawls, J., *The Law of Peoples* (Harvard University Press 1999), 23.

[44] See the chapter on the preamble by Francioni in this volume.

The new prominence so accorded to the participation of civil society is generally acknowledged to be part of a genuine paradigm change, aptly termed 'participatory revolution',[45] that can be attributed at least in part to the Rio Conference.[46] The new social partnership between States and people postulated in Principle 27 and the preamble was further articulated in the preamble and chapters 8 and 23 of Agenda 21.[47] The fact that it also determines, through Principle 27, the modus of implementation of the Rio Declaration is structurally significant, as confirmed by post-Rio practice.

The operational implementation of the principle took the form of a multitude of 'public-private partnership' programmes and projects developed after Rio between governments, NGOs and business groups, starting out under the auspices of the UN Commission on Sustainable Development ('CSD'), streamlined since 2000 by the UN 'Global Compact' programme (with a focus on business stakeholders),[48] and included as 'type II outcomes' in the plan of implementation of the 2002 World Summit on Sustainable Development ('WSSD') at Johannesburg.[49] Several of the partnership projects specifically focused on implementation of the Rio Declaration,[50] including the 'Partnership for Principle 10 (PP10)', a network of seven governments, four international organizations and twenty non-governmental bodies led by the World Resources Institute ('WRI'), cooperating to promote public participation in environmental decision-making;[51] and the 'Partnership for International Law on Sustainable Development' led by the

[45] Raustiala, K., 'The "Participatory Revolution" in International Environmental Law' (1997) 21 *Harvard Env'l L Rev* 537. On the fundamental role of social participation in this context, see also Viñuales, J. E., 'The Rise and Fall of Sustainable Development' (2013) 22 *RECIEL* 3, 8.

[46] Kiss, A. C., 'The Rio Declaration on Environment and Development', in Campiglio, L. et al (eds), *The Environment after Rio: International Law and Economics* (Graham and Trotman 1994), 55, at 64.

[47] Report of the United Nations Conference on Environment and Development, UN Doc A/CONF.151/26/Rev.1 (1993), vol I, 12 (paras 1.1–1.3), 95 (para 8.2) and 373 (para 23.4).

[48] Website <http://www.unglobalcompact.org>. See Ruggie, J. G., 'The Theory and Practice of Learning Networks: Corporate Social Responsibility and the Global Compact' (2002) 5 *Journal of Corporate Citizenship* 27; Deva, S., 'Global Compact: A Critique of the UN's Public-Private Partnership for Promoting Corporate Citizenship' (2006) 34 *Syarcuse Journal of International Law & Commerce* 107; Utting, P. and Zammit, A., 'United Nations-Business Partnerships: Good Intentions and Contradictory Agendas' (2009) 90 *Journal of Business Ethics* 39; Bull, B. and McNeill, D., 'From Business UNusual to Business as Usual: The Future Legitimacy of Public-Private Partnerships with Multilateral Organizations', in Bexell, M. and Mörth, U. (eds), *Democracy and Public-Private Partnerships in Global Governance* (Palgrave Macmillan 2010), 103–21, at 108–11; and Khan, R., 'Global Compact', in Wolfrum, *Max Planck Encyclopedia of Public International Law*, vol IV, 482–5.

[49] Report of the World Summit on Sustainable Development, UN Doc A/CONF.199/20 (2002); see Sand, P. H., 'Environmental Summitry and International Law' (2002) 13 *YbIEL* 21, 27–8; Witte, J. M., Streck. C., and Benner, T. (eds), *Progress or Peril? Partnerships and Networks in Global Environmental Governance: The Post-Johannesburg Agenda* (Global Public Policy Institute 2003); Andonova, L. B. and Levy, M. A., 'Franchising Global Governance: Making Sense of the Johannesburg Type II Partnerships' (2004) 11 *Yearbook of International Cooperation, Environment and Development* 19; Joyner, C. C., 'Rethinking International Environmental Regimes: What Role for Partnership Coalitions?' (2005) 1 *Journal of International Law & International Relations* 89; Beisheim, M., Campe, S., and Schäferhoff, M., 'Global Governance through Public-Private Partnerships', in Enderlein, H., Wälti, S., and Zürn, M. (eds), *Handbook on Multi-Level Governance* (Edward Elgar 2010), 370–82; Mert, A., *Environmental Governance through Transnational Partnerships* (Edward Elgar, forthcoming 2014); and Ralston, H. A., *Subnational Partnerships for Sustainable Development: Transatlantic Cooperation between the United States and Germany* (Edward Elgar 2014).

[50] See Bruch, C. and Pendergrass, J., 'Type II Partnerships, International Law, and the Commons' (2003) 15 *Georgetown Int'l Env'l L. Rev.* 855.

[51] PP10 ceased operating as an institution in 2010, but its activities are continued by the World Resources Institute's 'Access Initiative' ('TAI'), linking more than 150 civil society groups in over 40 countries; see Foti, J. et al, *Voice and Choice: Opening the Door to Environmental Democracy* (World Resources Institute 2008).

Centre for International Sustainable Development Law ('CISDL'), in cooperation with the ILA and the International Development Law Organization ('IDLO').[52] After the abolition of the CSD in the wake of the Rio+20 Conference, coordination of the programme continues under the auspices of the new High-level Political Forum on Sustainable Development.[53]

Although general criteria and guidelines for type-II partnerships were laid down in 2004,[54] the more than 340 UN-registered public-private networks for sustainable development do not correspond to any particular legal form, but show a wide variety of organizational patterns, in some instances including normative (transnational private law and/or 'soft law') functions.[55] Reviewing the overall performance of post-Rio partnership operations, however, several recent assessments paint a rather mixed picture, concluding that they 'fall short of the high expectations that they were to fulfil';[56] and that 'weaknesses in the overall normative framework, partnership governance, monitoring, evaluation, and follow-up have sapped a significant part of the momentum created by the developments of the last two decades'.[57]

## 2.3. *A vision unfulfilled? Global trusteeship*

In the eyes of the Secretary-General of UNCED, Maurice F. Strong, the Rio Conference did not meet expectations in two major areas: One was his proposal of an 'Earth Charter', which fell victim to the diplomatic North-South compromise in the final New York PrepCom sessions.[58] His valiant efforts to resurrect the Charter after Rio, as a civil society initiative,[59] regrettably failed to garner broad intergovernmental endorsement.

Maurice Strong's other disappointment was the lack of political support for the concept of global *environmental trusteeship*, an idea which he had first promoted in 1971 as part of the UN Secretariat's outline for what was to become the Stockholm Declaration,[60]

52 For background see Cordonier-Segger, M. C., 'Significant Developments in Sustainable Development Law and Governance: A Proposal' (2004) 28 *UN Natural Resources Forum* 61.

53 UN General Assembly Resolution on 'Format and organizational aspects of the high-level political forum on sustainable development', adopted on 9 July 2013, UN Doc A/67/L.72 (27 June 2013).

54 Approved by UN General Assembly Resolution 58/129 (19 February 2004).

55 Abbott, K. W., 'Public Private Partnerships', in Wolfrum, R. (ed), *Max Planck Encyclopedia of Public International Law*, vol VIII, 582, at 583 and 585, citing the example of the *Global Reporting Initiative* ('GRI') between UNEP, the UN Global Compact, the Organisation for Economic Cooperation and Development ('OECD'), the International Organization for Standardization ('ISO') and the multi-stakeholder NGO Coalition for Environmentally Responsible Economies ('CERES').

56 Biermann, F., Chan, S., Mert, A., and Pattberg, P., 'The Overall Effects of Partnerships for Sustainable Development: More Smoke than Fire?', in Pattberg, P., Biermann, F., Chan, S., and Mert, A. (eds), *Public-Private Partnerships for Sustainable Development: Emergence, Influence and Legitimacy* (Edward Elgar 2012), 69–87, at 85; and Pattberg et al, 'Conclusions', in Pattberg et al, *Public-Private Partnerships*, 239, 246.

57 Abbott, 'Public Private Partnerships', at 586–7.

58 See Koh, 'UNCED Leadership: A Personal Perspective', 168; Kovar, 'A Short Guide to the Rio Declaration', 119; and Strong, M. F., *Where on Earth are We Going?* (Texere 2001), ch 19. Whereas early PrepCom drafts (see notes 8, 38, 41) had used the alternative titles 'Earth Charter/Rio de Janeiro Declaration on Environment and Development', the G77 proposal of 19 March 1992 (UN Doc A/CONF.151/PC/WG.III/L.20/Rev.1) was titled 'Rio de Janeiro Charter/Declaration on Environment and Development', consolidated as 'Rio Declaration on Environment and Development' on 2 April 1991.

59 Initiated in 1994 by the NGO Earth Council (chaired by Maurice Strong), later joined by Green Cross International (chaired by Mikhail Gorbachev), and launched after worldwide consultations in 2000; text at <http://www.earthcharterinaction.org>. The Charter declares the protection of Earth's vitality, diversity and beauty 'a sacred trust'. See Bosselmann, K. and Engel, J. R. (eds), *The Earth Charter: A Framework for Global Governance* (KIT Publications 2010).

60 Background note by the UN Secretary-General, UN Doc A/CONF.48/PC/WG.1/CRP.4 (1971), 13.

expressly referring to 'the duty of all nations to carefully husband their natural resources and to hold *in trust* for present and future generations the air, water, lands, and communities of plants and animals on which all life depends'.[61] Although the proposal was incorporated in the initial draft prepared at the first session of the Preparatory Committee,[62] the 'trust' language was not retained in the final text of Stockholm Principle 2 as adopted in 1972,[63] apparently because the word was considered untranslatable into French.[64] Unperturbed, Strong reverted to the concept in 1988, proposing a new mandate for the UN Trusteeship Council 'as the organ within which the nations of the world exercise their trusteeship for the integrity of the planetary system on which our security and survival depends, as well as for the global commons'.[65] The idea was taken up by then Maltese Foreign Minister Guido de Marco, in his closing statement as president of the 45th UN General Assembly in 1991;[66] however, a related proposal by Malta to Working Group III of the Rio PrepCom was not adopted,[67] and the Rio Declaration contains no explicit reference to the concept of environmental trusteeship.

Nevertheless, in July 1997 UN Secretary-General Kofi Annan proposed, as part of his report on UN governance reform,[68] that the Trusteeship Council:

> be reconstituted as the forum through which Member States exercise their collective trusteeship for the integrity of the global environment and common areas such as the oceans, atmosphere and outer space. At the same time, it should serve to link the United Nations and civil society in

[61] Emphasis added; for drafting history see Sohn, 'The Stockholm Declaration on the Human Environment', 456–7.

[62] UN Doc A/CONF.48/PC.12 (1971), Annex I, 3.

[63] Stockholm Declaration; see Maggio, G. F., 'Inter/Intra-Generational Equity: Current Applications under International Law for Promoting the Sustainable Development of Natural Resources' (1997) 4 *Buffalo Environmental Law Journal* 161, 203.

[64] The same terminological problem arose during the simultaneous drafting of the UNESCO World Heritage Convention (1037 UNTS 151, originally 'World Heritage *Trust* Convention') in 1971–2; see Batisse, M. and Bolla, G., 'L'invention du "patrimoine mondial"', in *UNESCO Action as Seen by Protagonists and Witnesses: History Paper No 2* (Association of Former UNESCO Staff Members 2003), 17; and Redgwell, C., 'Protecting Natural Heritage and its Transmission to Future Generations', in Yussuf A. A. (ed), *Standard-Setting in UNESCO, Vol 1: Normative Action in Education, Science and Culture* (UNESCO/Nijhoff 2007), 267–88, at 268/n 9. Half a century earlier, Woodrow Wilson's famous invocation of the 'sacred trust of civilization' in art 22 of the League of Nations Covenant had been (mis)translated as '*mission sacrée*' in the French text (later repeated in art 73 of the UN Charter).

[65] Presidential address to the World Federation of United Nations Associations (Halifax: WFUNA 1988); Strong, M. F., 'The United Nations in an Interdependent World' (1989) 1 *International Affairs* 11, 20; see Palmer, G., 'New Ways to Make International Environmental Law' (1992) 86 *AJIL* 259, 279.

[66] UN Doc A/45/PV.82 (1991), 21. See Borg, S., 'The Trusteeship Council as a Keeper of the Global Commons for Future Generations, and the Role of Diplomacy in Implementing Effective Environment Protection', in Attard, D. J. (ed), *Colloquium on the Legal Protection of the Environment Beyond the Limits of National Jurisdiction* (Mediterranean Academy of Diplomatic Studies 1992); Willson, C. L., 'Changing the Charter: The United Nations Prepares for the Twenty-First Century' (1996) 90 *AJIL* 115, 122; and De Marco, G., 'A Renewed Trusteeship Council: Guardian of Future Generations', in *Proceedings of Pacem in Maribus XXVII* (International Ocean Institute 1999).

[67] See Kindall, M. P. A., 'UNCED and the Evolution of Principles of Environmental Law' (1991) 25:1 *John Marshall Law Review* 19, 27. For sceptical reactions see Szasz, P. C., 'Restructuring the International Organizational Framework', in Brown Weiss, E. (ed), *Environmental Change and International Law: New Challenges and Dimensions* (United Nations University Press 1992), 340–84, at 362; see also Redgwell, C., 'Reforming the United Nations Trusteeship Council', in Chambers, W. B. and Green, J. F. (eds), *Reforming International Environmental Governance: From Institutional Limits to Innovative Reforms* (United Nations University Press 2005), 178–203, at 187 and 190.

[68] Renewing the United Nations: A Programme for Reform, UN Doc A/51/950 (14 July 1997), para 85 (Maurice Strong served as Kofi Annan's Executive Coordinator for UN Reform at the time).

addressing these areas of global concern, which require the active contribution of public, private and voluntary sectors.

The Annan Report was followed by a note on *A New Concept of Trusteeship*,[69] regrettably entrusting the matter to a proverbial UN committee—the 'Task Force on Environment and Human Settlements' chaired by the Executive Director of UNEP. The task force report to the General Assembly in 1998 refrained from making any recommendations on the trusteeship issue,[70] and the buck was passed to an 'Open-ended Intergovernmental Group of Ministers on International Environmental Governance' launched by the UNEP Governing Council, which referred the matter to expert consultations, held in Cambridge in May 2001. The experts, in their wisdom, concluded that 'it would be very difficult to undertake measures that would affect the main organs established by the United Nations Charter, like the ECOSOC and the Trusteeship Council'.[71] As a result, the topic never even reached the agenda of the 2002 and 2005 World Summits,[72] and was eventually mooted by UN General Assembly Resolution 60/1 of 16 September 2005 ('World Summit Outcome'), which wound up the defunct UN Trusteeship Council for good.

Yet, regardless of its unfortunate linkage to abortive attempts at UN reform, the idea of global environmental trusteeship remains valid as an innovative approach to redefine the relationship between states and 'people' under Principle 27. As I shall try to demonstrate in the remarks which follow, the characteristic triangular pattern of public trusteeship—with the international community as creator ('settlor') of the trust, sovereign states as trustees (or else as 'guardians' or 'custodians'),[73] and civil society ('people', present and future) as beneficiaries[74]—is indeed the most plausible legal construct for effective implementation of the Rio Declaration.

[69] Note by the Secretary-General on United Nations Reform Measures and Proposals: A New Concept of Trusteeship, UN Doc A/52/849 (31 March 1998).

[70] Report of the Secretary-General to the General Assembly: Environment and Human Settlements, UN Doc A/53/463 (6 October 1998), Annex, para 20. See Redgwell, 'Reforming the United Nations Trusteeship Council', at 189; Agarwal, A., Narain, S., and Sharma, A. (eds), *Green Politics: Global Environmental Negotiations* 1 (Centre for Science and Environment 1999), at 365; and Desai, B. H., 'Revitalizing International Environmental Institutions: The UN Task Force Report and Beyond' (2001) 40 *Indian Journal of International Law* 455, 486.

[71] Estrada Oyuela, E. (ed), Expert Consultations on International Environmental Governance: Chairman's Summary, UNEP IEG Working Document (29 May 2001), 1.

[72] See Sand, 'Environmental Summitry and International Law', 12.

[73] Pound, R., *An Introduction to the Philosophy of Law* (rev edn, Yale University Press 1954), 111, aptly defined the role of states in the management of common natural resources as 'a sort of guardianship for social purposes'. See also eg Iwama, T., 'Emerging Principles and Rules for the Prevention and Mitigation of Environmental Harm', in Brown Weiss, *Environmental Change and International Law*, 107–23, at 115 (states as 'guardians or custodians of the international community'); Wolfrum, R., *Die Internationalisierung staatsfreier Räume* (Springer 1984), at 657 ('custodian as a kind of *Treuhänder*'); and Birnie, P., Boyle, A. and Redgwell, C., *International Law and the Environment* (3rd edn, Oxford University Press 2009), 84 ('states to exercise a fiduciary or trusteeship role in the protection of the environment, other species, and future generations').

[74] The preamble of the Rio Declaration explicitly reaffirms the Stockholm Declaration, the preamble of which in turn uses the terms 'for the benefit of all the people and for their posterity' (para 7).

## *2.4. Legal nature*

The origins of public trusteeship over environmental resources can be traced back to Roman law, and to a famous maxim in the *Corpus Iuris Civilis* of Emperor Justinian I. (533 AD), based in turn on the earlier writings of a learned jurist, Aelius Marcianus (c. 220 AD): 'So surely by the law of nature, the atmosphere, watercourses, the sea and hence the seashores, are common to all'.[75]

From the 18th century onwards, English courts interpreted this text as not only excluding private property rights in tidelands and navigable waters, but also as conferring fiduciary (trusteeship) rights and duties on the sovereign so as to ensure public access for the benefit of 'the people'. US courts in the 19th century took the British Crown's trusteeship title to seashore areas as having been transmitted to the American colonies upon statehood, thereby designating the state governments as the 'public trustees' to ensure beneficial uses of navigable territorial and internal waters as well as subjacent lands. Subsequent US jurisprudence gradually extended the scope of public trusteeship to a broader range of natural/environmental resources, including living resources (fisheries, forests, and wildlife).[76]

The 'public trust doctrine' ('PTD') has also been codified in state legislative and constitutional provisions, starting with the 1970 Michigan Environmental Protection Act.[77] The idea of a state's fiduciary rights over certain natural resources has since been taken up by a number of courts and legislatures outside the United States, including a series of decisions by the Indian Supreme Court,[78] environmental legislation in South Africa,[79] and the Constitution of Uganda.[80]

At this point, however, it is important to dispel some myths and misunderstandings about the nature of public trusteeship in the context of comparative environmental law. To begin with, the public trust over natural resources is a concept that belongs to the field of *public law* (including constitutional and administrative law and institutions), and should not be confused with classic legal analogues in the field of private property law—such as the Anglo-Saxon common law of private trusts, and corresponding contractual institutions in continental Europe (*fiducie, Treuhand*). Since most contemporary civil law systems have no direct equivalent of the trust in either private or public law, references to trusteeship thus

[75] *Et quidem naturali iure omnium communia sunt illa: aër, aqua profluens, et mare, et per hoc litora maris*; Institutes II.1.1 (*de rerum divisione*), and Digest I.8.2.1 (referring to vol 3 of the Institutes of Marcianus). The evolution of the environmental 'public trust doctrine' in comparative and international law is summarized, with detailed source references, in Sand, P. H., *The Rise of Public Trusteeship in International Environmental Law*, GlobalTrust Working Paper Series 03/2013 (Tel Aviv University: Buchmann Faculty of Law 2013).

[76] For a recent overview, see Blumm, M. C. and Wood, M. C. (eds), *The Public Trust Doctrine in Environmental and Natural Resources Law* (Carolina Academic Press 2013).

[77] Public Act No. 127 of 27 July 1970; see the seminal study by Sax, J. L., 'The Public Trust Doctrine in Natural Resources Law: Effective Judicial Intervention' (1970) 68 *Michigan Law Review* 471.

[78] *Mehta v. Kamal Nath et al* (1996), [1997] 1 SSC 388; see Razzaque, J., 'Application of Public Trust doctrine in Indian Environmental Cases' (2001) 13 *JEL* 221.

[79] National Environmental Management Act (NEMA) No. 107 of 1998, art 2(4)(o); see Van der Schyff, E., 'Steward Doctrines of Public Trust: Has the Eagle of Public Trust Landed on South African Soil?' (2013) 130 *South African Law Journal* 369 (citing a 2006 High Court decision interpreting section 24 of the 1996 Constitution).

[80] Constitution of Uganda (1995), art 237(2); see Blumm, M. C. and Guthrie, R. D., 'Internationalizing the Public Trust Doctrine: Natural Law and Constitutional and Statutory Approaches to Fulfilling the Saxion Vision' (2012) 45 *University of California at Davis Law Review* 741 (citing a 2005 High Court decision applying the article).

tend to be either mistranslated,[81] or else discarded as 'inappropriate private-law analogies' by lawyers outside the common-law family.[82]

On the other hand, there are some striking similarities to the concept of *domaine public* in French public/administrative law, which has been identified as a parallel to the Anglo-American public trust,[83] investing the state with custodianship (*droit de garde*, rather than ownership)[84] over inalienable natural resources such as the seashore, which must remain accessible for everybody. The approach also compares to the German constitutional concept of social restrictions on property rights (*Sozialpflichtigkeit*),[85] facilitated by 'fiduciary' rights of action for non-governmental organizations.[86] In Italy, state authorities designated as trustees for the community interest may take judicial recourse for damage to the nation's environmental resources;[87] in Sweden, the Nature Conservation Board has since 1964 served as public trustee for protected natural areas.[88] A further parallel is the charitable *habûs* or *waqf* in Islamic legal systems, where nature conservation is one of the legitimate purposes for establishing a charity.[89]

These examples drawing on comparative analysis may not suffice to elevate the public trust doctrine to a mutually recognized general principle of law.[90] There have been a number of initiatives, however, to extrapolate environmental trusteeship to the international level, especially in the context of the debate on intergenerational equity.[91] Transnational application of the PTD has thus been advocated in the literature for the Antarctic; for the Amazon rainforest; for all genetic resources, or for designated endangered species, protected areas

[81] See Section II) 2.3 of this chapter and the notes thereto.

[82] Bothe, M., 'Whose Environment? Concepts of Commonality in International Environmental Law', in Winter, G. (ed), *Multilevel Governance of Global Environmental Change: Perspectives from Science, Sociology and the Law* (Cambridge University Press 2006), 539, at 551 and 558.

[83] Kiss, A. C., 'La notion de patrimoine commun de l'humanité' (1982) 175 *RCADI* 99, at 131.

[84] Lagrange, M., 'L'évolution du droit de la domanialité publique' (1974) 90 *Revue du droit public et de la science politique en France et à l'étranger* 1, at 19. The definition comes close to Roscoe Pound's concept of guardianship for social purposes (Pound, *An Introduction to the Philosophy of Law*).

[85] Kube, H., 'Private Property in Natural Resources and the Public Weal in German Law: Latent Similarities to the Public Trust Doctrine' (1997) 37 *Natural Resources Journal* 857; see also Dagan, H., 'The Social Responsibility of Ownership' (2007) 92 *Cornell Law Review* 1255.

[86] Gassner, E., *Treuhandklage zugunsten von Natur und Landschaft: Eine rechtsdogmatische Untersuchung zur Verbandsklage* (Erich Schmidt Verlag 1994), 40–8.

[87] Bianchi, A., 'Harm to the Environment in Italian Practice: The Interaction of International Law and Domestic Law', in Wetterstein, P. (ed), *Harm to the Environment: The Right to Compensation and the Assessment of Damages* (Clarendon Press 1997), 103–29, at 105.

[88] Hillmo, T. and Lohm, U., 'Nature's Ombudsmen: The Evolution of Environmental Representation in Sweden' (1997) 3 *Environment and History* 19.

[89] Khalfoune, T., 'Le *habous*, le domaine public et le trust' (2005) 57 *Revue internationale de droit comparé* 441, at 467; and Bagader, A. A. et al, *Environmental Protection in Islam*, Environmental Policy and Law Paper No. 20/Rev. (2nd edn, IUCN 1994), 27. A historical example cited by Baslar, K., *The Concept of the Common Heritage of Mankind in International Law* (Kluwer Law International 1998), 66–7/n 150, is a public *waqf* in the 17th century Ottoman Empire, dedicated to the protection of wild storks and the facilitation of their intercontinental migration—not unlike the use of charitable title acquisition to preserve strategic natural areas, initiated by the 'land trust movement' in 19th century Britain and America; see Fairfax, S. K. and Guenzler, D. (eds), *Conservation Trusts* (University Press of Kansas 2001), and Sands, T. (ed), *Wildlife in Trust: A Hundred Years of Nature Conservation* (Elliott and Thompson 2012).

[90] As suggested, somewhat optimistically, by Blumm and Guthrie, 'Internationalizing the Public Trust Doctrine', at 750.

[91] See Brown Weiss, E. B., *In Fairness to Future Generations: International Law, Common Patrimony, and Intergenerational Equity* (Transnational Publishers 1989); Redgwell, C., *Intergenerational Trusts and Environmental Protection* (Manchester University Press 1999); and Shelton, D., 'Intergenerational Equity',

or biological resources; for shared water resources; for regional seas; for all ocean resources; for the atmosphere; for the global commons; and for the entire global environment.[92] The common thread and indeed the logical rationale of these proposals is the recognition of an external accountability of states as 'trustees of humanity' for complying with certain minimal normative and procedural 'other-regarding' obligations in managing the Earth's natural resources under their sovereign control.[93]

## 3. Normative impact

### 3.1. *The World Heritage Convention*

There is only scant evidence of public trust approaches in post-Rio treaty law. The example most frequently cited in this context is the practice evolving under the Convention on the World Natural and Cultural Heritage since the 1990s.[94] Not withstanding the lack of explicit trusteeship language in the original treaty text,[95] the 'operational guidelines' for implementation of the Convention subsequently developed by the UNESCO World Heritage Committee ('WHC') may well qualify as the first instance of transnational public trusteeship:

(a) world heritage sites are dedicated [as *corpus* of the trust] through nomination by a host state and acceptance of the nomination by the WHC representing the community of all member states [as collective trustor/settlor];
(b) the host state of a site [as trustee] incurs fiduciary duties to protect and conserve the site so dedicated for the benefit of present and future generations of 'all the peoples of the world' [as beneficiaries], and to report to the trustor [and the co-trustees] through the WHC on the conservation status of the site (so-called 'active monitoring'); and
(c) the beneficiaries, represented by civil society organizations, may invoke the terms of the trust to hold the host/trustee state accountable for non-compliance with the terms of the trust, either through their national courts,[96] or through the WHC by requesting the down-listing of a site as 'world heritage in danger', or eventual de-listing (based on external 'reactive monitoring').[97] In view of its wide media attention in particular, the WHC down-listing/de-listing practice thus evolved into an effective participatory instrument to induce compliance with the trusteeship regime.

in Wolfrum, R. and Kojima, C. (eds), *Solidarity: A Structural Principle of International Law* (Springer 2010), 123–62.

[92] For bibliographical references see Sand, *The Rise of Public Trusteeship in International Environmental Law*, 14–15/nn 65–73; and Wood, M. C., *Nature's Trust: Environmental Law for a New Ecological Age* (Cambridge University Press 2013). But see also the more sceptical assessment by Cho, H. S., *The Public Trust Doctrine and Global Commons*, J.S.D. dissertation (University of California at Berkeley, 1995), who considers the doctrine 'politically unacceptable to the international community' (at 332, 337).

[93] Benvenisti, E., 'Sovereigns as Trustees of Humanity: On the Accountability of States to Foreign Stakeholders' (2013) 107 *AJIL* 295, at 322; see also Keohane, R. O., 'Global Governance and Democratic Accountability', in Held, D. and Koenig-Archibugi, M. (eds), *Taming Globalization: Frontiers of Governance* (Polity Press 2003), 130–59.

[94] Kiss, A. C. and Shelton, D., *Guide to International Environmental Law* (Nijhoff 2007), 16; Benvenisti, 'Sovereigns as Trustees of Humanity, 329.

[95] On the reasons, see note 64 in this chapter.

[96] eg, see the world heritage cases brought by NGOs in Australian courts, reviewed in Boer, B. and Wiffen, G., *Heritage Law in Australia* (Oxford University Press 2006).

[97] See sections 169–74 of the *Operational Guidelines for the Implementation of the World Heritage Convention*, UNESCO Doc WHC.12/01 (July 2012); and Battini, S., 'The Procedural Side of Legal Globalization: The Case of the World Heritage Convention' (2011) 9 *International Journal of Constitutional Law* 340.

### 3.2. *The Treaty on Plant Genetic Resources*

Another, more recent example is the International Treaty on Plant Genetic Resources for Food and Agriculture ('ITPGR'), adopted under FAO auspices in 2001,[98] consolidating a *de facto* trusteeship regime for twelve major international *ex situ* plant germplasm collections under the auspices of the Consultative Committee on Agricultural Research ('CGIAR'):[99]

(a) the germplasm material listed in Annex I of the treaty (including wild predecessors of 35 cultivated food crop genera and 29 forage species) is designated as the *corpus* of the trust, pursuant to a model 'in-trust agreement' (ITA) under which the host states and institutions [as trustees] agree to 'hold the designated germplasm in trust for the benefit of the international community, in particular the developing countries';[100]
(b) transnational access under this multilateral system is governed by a standardized materials transfer agreement (SMTA, adopted in 2006), which also addresses benefit-sharing issues—in somewhat uneasy coexistence with the Convention on Biological Diversity and its 2010 Nagoya Protocol on Access to Genetic Resources and the Fair and Equitable Sharing of Benefits Arising from their Utilization (ABS);[101] and
(c) compliance with the treaty is monitored and controlled by a Compliance Committee (established in 2006) reporting to the ITPGR Governing Body under procedures adopted in 2011.[102] However, there is little or no procedural opportunity so far for the actual participation of civil society, currently represented predominantly by business stakeholders in the regime.[103]

[98] 3 November 2001, 2400 UNTS 303; see Moore, G. and Tymowski, W., *Explanatory Guide to the International Treaty on Plant Genetic Resources for Food and Agriculture*, Environmental Policy and Law Paper No. 57 (IUCN 2005); and Halewood, M. et al (eds), *Crop Genetic Resources as a Global Commons: Challenges in International Law and Governance* (Routledge 2012).

[99] ITPGR, art 15.1; see Moore, G. and Frison, E., 'International Research Centres: The Consultative Committee on International Agricultural Research and the International Treaty', in Frison, C., López, F., and Esquinas-Alcázar, J. T. (eds), *Plant Genetic Resources and Food Security: Stakeholder Perspectives on the International Treaty on Plant Genetic Resources for Food and Agriculture* (Earthscan 2011), 149–62. See also Siebeck, W. E. and Barton, J. H., 'The Implications of Applying the Legal Concept of Trust to Germplasm Collections at CGIAR Research Centers' (1992) 8 *Diversity* 29.

[100] ITA, art 3; on the evolution of these agreements (starting in pre-treaty practice since 1994), see Gotor, E. et al, 'The Perceived Impact of the In-Trust Agreements on CGIAR Germplasm Availability: An Assessment of Bioversity International's Institutional Activities' (2010) 38 *World Development* 1486.

[101] 5 June 1992, 1760 UNTS 79, and UN Doc UNEP/CBD/COP/DEC/X/1 (29 October 2010, not yet in force); see Moore, G. and Williams, K. A., 'Legal Issues in Plant Germplasm Collecting', in Guarino L., Ramanatha Rao, V., and Reid, R. (eds), *Collecting Plant Diversity: Technical Guidelines* (Bioversity International 2011); and Chiarolla, C., Louafi, S., and Schloen, M., 'An Analysis of the Relationship between the Nagoya Protocol and Instruments related to Genetic Resources for Food and Agriculture and Farmers' Rights', in Morgera, E., Buck, M., and Tsioumani, E. (eds), *The Nagoya Protocol on Access and Benefit-Sharing in Perspective: Implications for International Law and Implementation Challenges* (Nijhoff Brill 2012), 83–122.

[102] ITPGR Governing Body Resolution 2/2011 on Procedures and Operational Mechanisms to Promote Compliance and Address Issues of Non-Compliance (Bali, 18 March 2011); see the summary report in 9:550 *Earth Negotiations Bulletin* (21 March 2011), 4.

[103] On the checkered history of NGO involvement in ITPGR, see Mooney, P., 'International Non-Governmental Organizations: The Hundred-Year (or so) Seed War—Seeds, Sovereignty and Civil Society—A Historical Perspective on the Evolution of "The Law of the Seed"', in Frison et al, *Plant Genetic Resources and Food Security*, 135–48, at 145.

## 4. Jurisprudential relevance

Historically, attempts at applying the public trust doctrine to the conservation of living natural resources in international adjudicatory proceedings date back to the 1893 *Pacific Fur Seal Arbitration.*[104] In that instance, the US had claimed a right to protect the seal population in the Bering Sea, acting as '*trustee for the benefit of mankind*'.[105] The US government thus argued by analogy that 'the coffee of central America and Arabia is not the exclusive property of those two nations; the tea of China, the rubber of South America, are not the exclusive property of those nations where it is grown; they are, so far as not needed by the nations which enjoy the possession, the common property of mankind; and if nations which have custody of them withdraw them, they are failing in their trust, and other nations have a right to interfere and secure their share'.[106] However, the US reasoning was not accepted by the arbitral tribunal at the time.[107]

Still prior to the Rio Conference, the Court of Justice of the European Communities declared all member states '*trustees of the common interest*' with regard to the conservation of marine resources;[108] and in its interpretation of the 1979 Bird Conservation Directive, considered wild birds 'a case where *the management of the common heritage is entrusted to the member states* in their respective territories'.[109] And in a much-quoted separate opinion in the post-Rio Danube Dam case before the International Court of Justice, Judge Weeramantry referred to a '*principle of trusteeship for earth resources*'.[110] Yet, these occasional (and largely *obiter*) pronouncements hardly qualify as evidence of international judicial reception of the PTD,[111] and are more appropriately characterized as metaphoric invocations of an ethical postulate.

# III) Relations with Other Principles

Critics of the Rio Declaration point out a subtle but essential difference—or even 'regression'—vis-à-vis the Stockholm Declaration, discernible both in the Preamble and in Principle 1; viz, a failure to translate the environmental obligations of states into corresponding fundamental human rights.[112] While the causes of that failure are sometimes ascribed to the omnipresent North-South divide (with the South allegedly prioritizing the right to development over environmental rights),[113] the *travaux préparatoires* show

[104] 'Bering Sea Fur Seals Fisheries Arbitration' (Great Britain/United States, 15 August 1893); Moore, J. B. (ed), *History and Digest of the International Arbitrations to which the United States has been a Party* (US Government Printing Office 1898), vol 1, 755.

[105] Moore, *History and Digest of the International Arbitrations*, 814.

[106] Moore, *History and Digest of the International Arbitrations*, 853 (oral argument by Carter, J. C., on behalf of the US).

[107] See Romano, C. P., *The Peaceful Settlement of International Environmental Disputes: A Pragmatic Approach* (Kluwer Law International 2000), 140–2.

[108] Case C-804/79 (*European Commission v. UK*), [1981] 1 ECR, 1045, para 30; and Case C-325/85 (*Ireland v. European Commission*), [1987] 3 ECR, 5041, para 15.

[109] Case C-339/87 (*European Commission v. Netherlands*), [1990] 1 ECR, 851, at 885 [emphasis added].

[110] Case concerning the Gabčíkovo-Nagymaros project (Hungary/Slovakia), ICJ Reports 1997, 7; 37 ILM 204, at 213.

[111] Notwithstanding well-established *national* case law, eg in the United States, India, South Africa, and Uganda, as reviewed in a comparative perspective in the studies cited in notes 75–80 in this chapter.

[112] See the chapter on the preamble by Francioni in this commentary.

[113] See the chapter on Principle 1 by Francioni in this commentary.

that support from the North for a 'rights-based approach' was not altogether unanimous. While the US delegation favoured a non-binding general statement of democratic human rights,[114] it also sought initially to restrict NGO standing in administrative and judicial proceedings—in the context of Principle 10—to 'groups and organizations with a recognized legal interest';[115] and it subsequently tried to avoid any formulation that might be interpreted as introducing new 'actionable' environmental rights in national or international law, both during the Rio negotiations and in the post-Rio drafting process for the 1998 Aarhus Convention and its implementing protocol.[116] In the end, though, attempts at restricting the procedural legitimation of environmental 'entitlements' of individuals and major social groups turned out to be unsuccessful, as demonstrated by the progressive recent jurisprudence of international human rights courts in environment-related cases.[117]

In this context, the stated objective of Rio Principle 27—to guide the 'fulfilment' (ie, implementation) of the Declaration by cooperation between states and civil society—takes on special significance. On the one hand, it suggests a direct link to the procedural means specified in Principle 10: public access to environmental information; citizen participation in environmental decision-making; and non-discriminatory access to judicial and administrative proceedings.[118] Along the same lines, the public trust doctrine empowers the trust's beneficiaries ('people', ie individuals and NGOs) to take judicial action, by way of 'citizen suits' to enforce the terms of the trust against the trustees (states and governmental authorities), so as to hold them accountable for their fiduciary management of environmental resources.[119] In a trusteeship perspective, therefore, Rio Principles 10 and 27 are indeed closely related and mutually supportive. Evidence of this special relationship abounds. For instance, the environmental 'right to know' (free public access to government-held environmental information, as postulated in Principle 10) is well on its way to becoming a recognized (actionable) human right, not withstanding

[114] Draft principle 3 of the US proposal (4 March 1992), UN Doc A/CONF.151/PC/WG.III/L.21.

[115] Draft principle 15, para 131 (USA), in UN Doc A/CONF.151/PC/WG.III/L.8/Rev.1 (30 August 1991).

[116] The Aarhus Convention on Access to Information, Public Participation in Decision-Making and Access to Justice in Environmental Matters (25 June 1998, 2161 UNTS 447, ratified by 46 states) was never submitted for ratification to the US Senate; and in November 2001, the US delegation withdrew from negotiations for the subsequent Kiev Protocol on Pollutant Release and Transfer Registers (PRTRs, 21 May 2003, UN Doc ECE/MP.PP/2003/1, ratified by 38 states). When the 3rd World Conservation Congress of the International Union for Conservation of Nature ('IUCN') at Bangkok in November 2004 unanimously adopted a recommendation for the implementation of Rio Principle 10, the US delegation alone abstained, upon instructions from the State Department; see Res. REC/WCC3.081, *World Conservation Congress: Resolutions and Recommendations* (2005), at 95–6.

[117] On the European Court of Human Rights' progressively broader interpretation of art 10 of the European Human Rights Convention (4 November 1950, 213 UNTS 221) in this regard, see Miller, C., 'The European Convention on Human Rights: Another Weapon in the Environmentalist's Armoury' (1999) 11 *JEL* 170, 171; and Pedersen, O. W., 'The Ties That Bind: The Environment, the European Convention on Human Rights, and the Rule of Law' (2010) *European Public Law* 571. On the Inter-American Court of Human Rights' interpretation of (identical) art 13 of the American Convention on Human Rights (22 November 1969, 1144 UNTS 17, 955), see Lixinsky, L. 'Treaty Interpretation by the Inter-American Court of Human Rights: Expansionism at the Service of the Unity of International Law' (2010) 21 *EJIL* 585, 595. See also the first report of the UN Human Rights Council's independent expert on the relationship between human rights and the environment, UN Doc A/HRC/22/43 (24 December 2012); and Boyle, A., 'Human Rights and the Environment: Where Next?' (2012) 23 *EJIL* 613, 615.

[118] See the chapter by Ebbesson in this volume; and notes 45–46 in this chapter.

[119] See Sax, 'The Public Trust Doctrine in Natural Resources Law'; and Blumm and Guthrie, 'Internationalizing the Public Trust Doctrine'.

a contemporary backlash of governmental secrecy in the wake of new security threats after the tragic events of 11 September 2001.[120] By the same token, Principle 27 engages the fiduciary accountability of states inherent in the participatory rights of major social groups (women, youth, indigenous and local communities) under Principles 20–22.[121]

## IV) Assessment

Principle 27, though quite inconspicuous in the overall framework of the Rio Declaration, introduced several innovative concepts in international law and governance, with a focus on the cooperative relationship between states and civil society. Its call for 'global partnership' inspired a wide range of public-private partnership projects and networks for sustainable development, a number of which continue to operate under UN auspices. While the proposal of an 'international sustainable development law' fell short of ushering in the paradigm change anticipated by some, Maurice Strong's (yet unfulfilled) 'public trusteeship' vision may ultimately have a lasting impact on the evolution of international environmental law.

## V) Select Bibliography

Benvenisti, E., 'Sovereigns as Trustees of Humanity: On the Accountability of States to Foreign Stakeholders' (2013) 107 *AJIL* 295.

Koh, T. T.-B., 'UNCED Leadership: A Personal Perspective', in Spector, B. I., Sjösted, G., and Zartman, I. W. (eds), *Negotiating International Regimes: Lessons from the United Nations Conference on Environment and Development* (UNCED) (Graham and Trotman 1994).

Pallemaerts, M., 'International Environmental Law in the Age of Sustainable Development: A Critical Assessment of the UNCED Process' (1995) 15 *J L & Commerce* 623.

Pattberg, P., Biermann, F., Chan, S. and Mert, A. (eds), *Public-Private Partnerships for Sustainable Development: Emergence, Influence and Legitimacy* (Edward Elgar 2012).

Sand, P. H., 'UNCED and the Development of International Environmental Law' (1992) 3 *YbIEL* 3.

Wirth, D. A., 'The Rio Declaration on Environment and Development: Two Steps Forward and One Back?' (1995) 29 *Georgia Law Review* 599.

Wood, M. C., *Nature's Trust: Environmental Law for a New Ecological Age* (Cambridge University Press 2013).

[120] See Sand, P. H., 'The Right to Know: Freedom of Environmental Information in Comparative and International Law' (2011) *Tulane Journal of International & Comparative Law* 203, 221.

[121] See the chapters by Mahon, Langer, and Shelton in this volume; see also, eg Westra, L., *Environmental Justice and the Rights of Indigenous Peoples: International and Domestic Legal Perspectives* (Earthscan 2008), 219.

# APPENDIX

# The Rio Declaration on Environment and Development

United Nations
**General Assembly**

**A/CONF.151/26 (Vol. I)**

Distr. GENERAL
12 August 1992
ORIGINAL: ENGLISH

REPORT OF THE UNITED NATIONS CONFERENCE ON ENVIRONMENT AND DEVELOPMENT*

(RIO DE JANEIRO, 3–14 JUNE 1992)

ANNEX I

RIO DECLARATION ON ENVIRONMENT AND DEVELOPMENT

The United Nations Conference on Environment and Development,

Having met at Rio de Janeiro from 3 to 14 June 1992,

Reaffirming the Declaration of the United Nations Conference on the Human Environment, adopted at Stockholm on 16 June 1972, and seeking to build upon it,

With the goal of establishing a new and equitable global partnership through the creation of new levels of cooperation among States, key sectors of societies and people,

Working towards international agreements which respect the interests of all and protect the integrity of the global environmental and developmental system,

Recognizing the integral and interdependent nature of the Earth, our home,

Proclaims that:

**Principle 1**

Human beings are at the centre of concerns for sustainable development. They are entitled to a healthy and productive life in harmony with nature.

**Principle 2**

States have, in accordance with the Charter of the United Nations and the principles of international law, the sovereign right to exploit their own resources pursuant to their own environmental and developmental policies, and the responsibility to ensure that activities within their jurisdiction or control do not cause damage to the environment of other States or of areas beyond the limits of national jurisdiction.

**Principle 3**

The right to development must be fulfilled so as to equitably meet developmental and environmental needs of present and future generations.

**Principle 4**

In order to achieve sustainable development, environmental protection shall constitute an integral part of the development process and cannot be considered in isolation from it.

* *This document has been posted online by the United Nations Department of Economic and Social Affairs (DESA). Reproduction and dissemination of the document—in electronic and/or printed format—is encouraged, provided acknowledgement is made of the role of the United Nations in making it available.*

**Principle 5**

All States and all people shall cooperate in the essential task of eradicating poverty as an indispensable requirement for sustainable development, in order to decrease the disparities in standards of living and better meet the needs of the majority of the people of the world.

**Principle 6**

The special situation and needs of developing countries, particularly the least developed and those most environmentally vulnerable, shall be given special priority. International actions in the field of environment and development should also address the interests and needs of all countries.

**Principle 7**

States shall cooperate in a spirit of global partnership to conserve, protect and restore the health and integrity of the Earth's ecosystem. In view of the different contributions to global environmental degradation, States have common but differentiated responsibilities.

The developed countries acknowledge the responsibility that they bear in the international pursuit of sustainable development in view of the pressures their societies place on the global environment and of the technologies and financial resources they command.

**Principle 8**

To achieve sustainable development and a higher quality of life for all people, States should reduce and eliminate unsustainable patterns of production and consumption and promote appropriate demographic policies.

**Principle 9**

States should cooperate to strengthen endogenous capacity-building for sustainable development by improving scientific understanding through exchanges of scientific and technological knowledge, and by enhancing the development, adaptation, diffusion and transfer of technologies, including new and innovative technologies.

**Principle 10**

Environmental issues are best handled with the participation of all concerned citizens, at the relevant level. At the national level, each individual shall have appropriate access to information concerning the environment that is held by public authorities, including information on hazardous materials and activities in their communities, and the opportunity to participate in decision-making processes. States shall facilitate and encourage public awareness and participation by making information widely available. Effective access to judicial and administrative proceedings, including redress and remedy, shall be provided.

**Principle 11**

States shall enact effective environmental legislation. Environmental standards, management objectives and priorities should reflect the environmental and developmental context to which they apply. Standards applied by some countries may be inappropriate and of unwarranted economic and social cost to other countries, in particular developing countries.

**Principle 12**

States should cooperate to promote a supportive and open international economic system that would lead to economic growth and sustainable development in all countries, to better address the problems of environmental degradation. Trade policy measures for environmental purposes should not constitute a means of arbitrary or unjustifiable discrimination or a disguised restriction on international trade. Unilateral actions to deal with environmental challenges outside the jurisdiction of the importing country should be avoided. Environmental measures addressing transboundary or global environmental problems should, as far as possible, be based on an international consensus.

**Principle 13**

States shall develop national law regarding liability and compensation for the victims of pollution and other environmental damage. States shall also cooperate in an expeditious and more determined manner to develop further international law regarding liability and compensation for adverse effects of environmental damage caused by activities within their jurisdiction or control to areas beyond their jurisdiction.

**Principle 14**

States should effectively cooperate to discourage or prevent the relocation and transfer to other States of any activities and substances that cause severe environmental degradation or are found to be harmful to human health.

**Principle 15**

In order to protect the environment, the precautionary approach shall be widely applied by States according to their capabilities. Where there are threats of serious or irreversible damage, lack of full scientific certainty shall not be used as a reason for postponing cost-effective measures to prevent environmental degradation.

**Principle 16**

National authorities should endeavour to promote the internalization of environmental costs and the use of economic instruments, taking into account the approach that the polluter should, in principle, bear the cost of pollution, with due regard to the public interest and without distorting international trade and investment.

**Principle 17**

Environmental impact assessment, as a national instrument, shall be undertaken for proposed activities that are likely to have a significant adverse impact on the environment and are subject to a decision of a competent national authority.

**Principle 18**

States shall immediately notify other States of any natural disasters or other emergencies that are likely to produce sudden harmful effects on the environment of those States. Every effort shall be made by the international community to help States so afflicted.

**Principle 19**

States shall provide prior and timely notification and relevant information to potentially affected States on activities that may have a significant adverse transboundary environmental effect and shall consult with those States at an early stage and in good faith.

**Principle 20**

Women have a vital role in environmental management and development. Their full participation is therefore essential to achieve sustainable development.

**Principle 21**

The creativity, ideals and courage of the youth of the world should be mobilized to forge a global partnership in order to achieve sustainable development and ensure a better future for all.

**Principle 22**

Indigenous people and their communities and other local communities have a vital role in environmental management and development because of their knowledge and traditional practices. States should recognize and duly support their identity, culture and interests and enable their effective participation in the achievement of sustainable development.

**Principle 23**

The environment and natural resources of people under oppression, domination and occupation shall be protected.

**Principle 24**

Warfare is inherently destructive of sustainable development. States shall therefore respect international law providing protection for the environment in times of armed conflict and cooperate in its further development, as necessary.

**Principle 25**

Peace, development and environmental protection are interdependent and indivisible.

**Principle 26**

States shall resolve all their environmental disputes peacefully and by appropriate means in accordance with the Charter of the United Nations.

**Principle 27**

States and people shall cooperate in good faith and in a spirit of partnership in the fulfilment of the principles embodied in this Declaration and in the further development of international law in the field of sustainable development.

*****

Source: Report of the United Nations Conference on the Human Environment, Stockholm, 5–16 June 1972 (United Nations publication, Sales No. E.73.II.A.14 and corrigendum), chap. I.

*Date last updated: by DESA/DSD*

# *Index*

Note: statutory instruments are only listed in the index when mentioned at length. All other references can be found in the instruments list.